SpringBoard®
English
Language Arts

TEACHER EDITION   ENGLISH III

About The College Board

The College Board is a mission-driven not-for-profit organization that connects students to college success and opportunity. Founded in 1900, the College Board was created to expand access to higher education. Today, the membership association is made up of over 6,000 of the world's leading educational institutions and is dedicated to promoting excellence and equity in education. Each year, the College Board helps more than seven million students prepare for a successful transition to college through programs and services in college readiness and college success—including the SAT® and the Advanced Placement Program®. The organization also serves the education community through research and advocacy on behalf of students, educators, and schools. For further information, visit collegeboard.org.

ISBN: 978-1-4573-1290-8

1 2 3 4 5 6 7 8   20 21 22 23 24 25 26

Printed in the United States of America

Acknowledgements

The College Board gratefully acknowledges the outstanding work of the classroom teachers who have been integral to the development of this program. The end product is testimony to their expertise, understanding of student learning needs, and dedication to rigorous and accessible English Language Arts instruction.

Lance Balla
Everett School District
Everett, Washington

Carisa Barnes
San Diego Unified School District San Diego, California

Leia Bell
Hillsborough County Public Schools Tampa, Florida

Alysa Broussard
Lafayette Parish School System
Lafayette, Louisiana

Robert J. Caughey
San Dieguito Union High School District San Diego, California

Susie Challancin
Bellevue School District 405
Bellevue, Washington

Doug Cole
Cherry Creek School District
Greenwood Village, Colorado

Cari Davis
Rio Rancho Public School District
Rio Rancho, New Mexico

Paul De Maret
Poudre School District
Fort Collins, Colorado

Sylvia Ellison
Hillsborough County Public Schools
Hillsborough, Florida

Karen Fullam
Hillsborough County Public Schools
Tampa, Florida

Michael Gragert
Plano Independent School District
Plano, Texas

Nancy Gray
Brevard County Schools
Viera, Florida

Charise Hallberg
Bellevue School District 405
Bellevue, Washington

T.J. Hanify
Bellevue School District 405
Bellevue, Washington

Jessi Hupper
Peninsula School District
Gig Harbor, Washington

Nimat Jones
ICEF Public Schools, Los Angeles, California

Karen Kampschmidt
Fort Thomas Independent School District
Fort Thomas, Kentucky

Karen Kennedy
Peninsula School District
Peninsula, Washington

LeAnn Klepzig
Bradley County Schools
Cleveland, Tennessee

Susie Lowry
Volusia County School District Deland, Florida

Michelle Lewis
Spokane Public School Spokane, Washington

John Marshall
Mead School District
Mead, Washington

Cassandra Mattison
Hillsborough County Public Schools Tampa, Florida

Glenn Morgan
San Diego Unified School District San Diego, California

John Murray
Garland Independent School District Sachse, Texas

Kristen J. Ohaver
Charlotte-Mecklenburg Schools Charlotte, North Carolina

Amanda Olinger
Harrisburg School District
Harrisburg, South Dakota

Julie Pennabaker
Quakertown Community School District Quakertown, Pennsylvania

Bryan Sandala
School District of Palm Beach County West Palm Beach, Florida

Angela Seiler
Rio Rancho Public School District Rio Rancho, New Mexico

Amanda Shackelford
Lafayette Parish School System
Lafayette, Louisiana

Kimberlyn Slagle
Lafayette Parish School System
Lafayette, Louisiana

Sarah Smith Arceneaux
Lafayette Parish School System
Lafayette, Louisiana

Holly Talley
Hillsborough County Public Schools Ruskin, Florida

Derek Thomas
Hillsborough County Public Schools Tampa, Florida

Maria Torres-Crosby
Hillsborough County Public Schools Tampa, Florida

Susan Van Doren
South Lake Tahoe, California

JoEllen Victoreen
San Jose Unified School District San Jose, California

Rebecca Wenrich
Peninsula School District
Gig Harbor, Washington

Research and Planning Advisors

We also wish to thank the members of our SpringBoard Advisory Council and the many educators who gave generously of their time and their ideas as we conducted research for both the print and online programs. Your suggestions and reactions to ideas helped immeasurably as we created this edition. We gratefully acknowledge the teachers and administrators in the following districts.

ABC Unified School District
Cerritos, California

Allen Independent School District
Allen, Texas

Bellevue, School District 405
Bellevue, Washington

Burnet Consolidated Independent School District
Burnet, Texas

Community Unit School District 308
Oswego, Illinois

Fresno Unified School District
Fresno, California

Frisco Independent School District
Frisco, Texas

Garland Independent School District
Garland, Texas

Grapevine-Colleyville Independent School District
Grapevine, Texas

Hamilton County Schools
Chattanooga, Tennessee

Hesperia Unified School District
Hesperia, California

Hillsborough County Public Schools
Tampa, Florida

ICEF Public Schools
Los Angeles, California
IDEA Public Schools
Weslaco, Texas

Irving Independent School District
Irving, Texas

Keller Independent School District
Keller, Texas

KIPP Houston
Houston, Texas

Lafayette Parish Schools
Lafayette Parish, Louisiana

Los Angeles Unified School District
Los Angeles, California

Lubbock Independent School District
Lubbock, Texas

Mansfield Independent School District
Mansfield, Texas

Midland Independent School District
Midland, Texas

Milwaukee Public Schools
Milwaukee, Wisconsin

New Haven School District
New Haven, Connecticut

Ogden School District
Ogden, Utah

Rio Rancho Public Schools
Rio Rancho, New Mexico

San José Unified School District
San José, California

Scottsdale Unified School District
Scottsdale, Arizona

Spokane Public Schools
Spokane, Washington

Tacoma Public Schools
Tacoma, Washington

SpringBoard English Language Arts

Lori O'Dea
Executive Director
Content Development

Natasha Vasavada
Executive Director,
Pre-AP & SpringBoard

Doug Waugh
VP, SpringBoard & Pre-AP
Programs

Sarah Balistreri
Senior Director
ELA Content Development

Florencia Duran Wald
Senior Director
ELA Content Development

Julie Manley
Senior Director
Professional Learning

Joely Negedly
Senior Director
Pre-AP Humanities

Jessica Brockman
Product Manager
English Language Arts

Suzie Doss
Director
SpringBoard Implementation

Jennifer Duva
Director
English Language Arts

Spencer Gonçalves
Director
Digital Content Development

Rebecca Grudzina
Senior Editor
English Language Arts

Georgia Scurletis
Senior Instructional Writer
Pre-AP English Language Arts

Abigail Johnson
Editor
English Language Arts

Casseia Lewis
Assistant Editor
English Language Arts

Natalie Hansford
Editorial Assistant
English Language Arts

Table of Contents

CONTENTS

CONTENTS

CONTENTS

Resources

Texts not included in these materials.

Introduction to SpringBoard English Language Arts

About SpringBoard ELA

SpringBoard is a different kind of instructional program for grades 6–12. Developed by teachers for teachers, SpringBoard offers core instructional materials in print and digital form that are aligned to College and Career Readiness Standards, Advanced Placement (AP) coursework, and the SAT Suite of Assessments. The program features student materials, teacher resources, and formative and summative assessments, as well as professional learning for teachers and administrators. SpringBoard was built around a simple belief: if you give teachers the best materials, engaging methods, and ongoing professional support, then student success will surely follow.

Instructional Materials

SpringBoard English Language Arts supplies a Student Edition and Teacher Edition, in print and digital form, for each grade level. You can customize the basic curriculum with materials including Language Workshop, Close Reading Workshop, and Writing Workshop.

Design that Begins with the End in Mind

- Based on the Understanding by Design model, SpringBoard teaches students the skills and knowledge that matter most to meet AP and college and career readiness standards.
- Teachers and students start each unit by unpacking the assessment so that students know where they're heading and why the skills they're developing matter.
- Teachers and students receive clear, standards-aligned learning targets when they begin each activity.

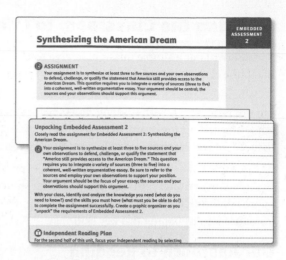

The Practice of Reading Closely

- SpringBoard puts a special focus on close reading, giving students strategies and structure for developing this key skill.
- Students encounter compelling texts—fiction, nonfiction, poetry, drama, visuals, and film.

A Living System of Learning

- SpringBoard puts students in charge of how they learn to create a more dynamic classroom experience.
- With a flexible design and rich library of tools and resources, SpringBoard helps educators personalize instruction to meet student needs.

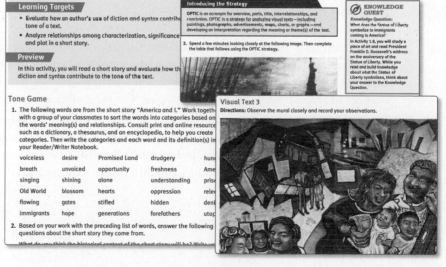

Bringing the Classroom to Life

SpringBoard has a simple mission: to give teachers and districts the exact kind of support they want to bring more life to the classroom—and greater success to students.

When you enter a SpringBoard classroom you don't hear a teacher talking in the front of the room. You hear a buzz of excitement, with students working together and taking charge of how they learn. That's what the teachers who designed SpringBoard wanted for their classrooms, so they created a curriculum and materials that are focused on real classroom needs, encouraging teacher and student involvement.

SpringBoard helps teachers translate the expectations of state standards into engaging daily lessons. We believe that reading, writing, speaking, and listening should all be learned together. You'll see examples of our integrated approach throughout our materials. And we put a special focus on close reading, giving students strategies and structure for developing this key skill.

Our Approach to Reading

In SpringBoard ELA, we move right into compelling texts—fiction, nonfiction, poetry, drama, visuals, and film—and give teachers the tools, supports, and pedagogical approaches that will help students engage with the content.

The Practice of Reading Closely

Texts take center stage in the SpringBoard ELA classroom, where students will prepare for close, critical reading of a wide range of materials. With teacher guidance, high school students develop the habits of close reading that will serve them for a lifetime.

- **As You Read:** Students prepare for the first reading of a text with guidance about which elements to notice and annotate, questions to ask before and during reading, and genre characteristics to pay attention to.

- **First Reading:** Students read and annotate. They begin to comprehend the text and uncover meaning as they read individually, in pairs, in groups, or together as a class.

- **Making Observations:** Students pause during or right after the first reading to observe the small details within a text in order to arrive at a deeper understanding of the whole.

- **Returning to the Text:** Students continue to deepen their understanding of the text by responding to a series of text-dependent questions. They use text evidence, speak with new vocabulary words, reflect on their classmates' ideas, and make connections among texts, ideas, and experiences.

- **Working from the Text:** Students use the text as a source as they move from reading and analysis to productive work, including academic discussion and writing.

Reading Independently

SpringBoard students practice good reading habits in class so that they can read challenging texts in other classes and on their own. Independent reading is an integral part of every SpringBoard English Language Arts unit. At the beginning of each grade, students learn how to make a plan for independent reading. **Independent Reading Lists** in each unit give students a jump-start on selecting texts by offering a list of suggested titles, including a number of Spanish-language titles, that connect to the themes, genres, and concepts of the SpringBoard unit.

While students work their way through each unit, they respond to **Independent Reading Links** that prompt them to make connections between the reading they're doing on their own and the skills and knowledge they're developing in class. Twice per unit, **Independent Reading Checkpoints** give students a chance to reflect on and synthesize their independent reading in an informal writing assignment or discussion.

Reading to Build Knowledge

SpringBoard units are designed thematically so that students can delve deeply into the overarching topics, themes and ideas. Each unit begins with essential questions that relate to the ideas and texts within the unit. Students return to these questions throughout the unit, each time refining their responses as their understanding increases and they are able to cite new evidence that supports their points of view. Students also have the opportunity to conduct both on-the-spot and extended research, asking and answering questions, evaluating multiple sources, and synthesizing information.

Twice a unit, students engage in a **Knowledge Quest**, which involves reading a collection of texts curated around a topic, theme, or idea, and completing some text-dependent tasks. On these quests, students build their knowledge of the topics as well as related vocabulary. Each Knowledge Quest begins with a Knowledge Question and supporting questions that focus student learning. After students read the final text in a set, they have the opportunity to return to the Knowledge Question and demonstrate their growing understanding of the topic by responding to a writing-to-sources prompt or engaging in an academic discussion.

At the end of a Knowledge Quest, students are encouraged to continue building their knowledge of the topic by going to **Zinc Reading Labs** and searching for and reading related texts. Zinc Reading Labs offers a variety of informational and literary texts that you can assign and that students can self-select. Vocabulary sets for each text provide additional practice opportunities that can be assigned for classwork or homework.

Students' independent reading can also enhance their understanding of the topics being covered in class if they are interested. SpringBoard's **Independent Reading Lists** include suggested books that relate to the topics and themes from each unit. By choosing those books students can see a different side of the topic, learn new words, and discover other topics they might want to explore more deeply.

Through engagement with a wide range of content-rich informational and literary texts, and work on an array of tasks that let them demonstrate their increasing understanding, SpringBoard supports students to build knowledge of topics, themes, and ideas.

Reading to Gain Perspectives

Gaining Perspectives features use a text as a jumping off point for examining an issue or concern relevant to students. Students are asked to consider the perspectives of others and to empathize with others who have different points of view. They are asked think about social and ethical norms and to recognize the family, school, and community resources available to them. When relevant, Gaining Perspectives features include standards-aligned tasks that require students to make social studies and/or health education connections. Each Gaining Perspectives feature concludes with a writing task, in which students summarize the classroom discussion in their Reader/Writer Notebooks.

Understanding Text Complexity

Understanding text complexity is a key part of advancing students' knowledge and skills through reading. Students should read texts that are appropriately challenging—not so challenging that students get frustrated and give up, but not so easy that students get bored and stagnate. For each prose text in SpringBoard English Language Arts, teachers will see text complexity guidance:

 TEXT COMPLEXITY

Overall: Complex
Lexile: 1000L
Qualitative: Moderate Difficulty
Task: Challenging (Evaluate)

Discerning the complexity of a text involves examining the text in a few different ways:

- A **Lexile** score indicates the complexity as measured by an algorithm that analyzes text characteristics including sentence length and word frequency.

- Expert teachers assigned a **qualitative rating** of High, Moderate, or Low Difficulty by considering qualities including the text's implicit and explicit meanings, the author's use of language to achieve a purpose, the organizational patterns and structure of the text, the sophistication of vocabulary, and cognitive and knowledge demands of each text.

- **Task** requirements are designated as High, Moderate, or Low based on the cognitive demands of the task associated with the text. Anderson and Krathwohl's taxonomy was used for this analysis, and verbs such as evaluate, analyze, and understand are included as descriptors. (Reader variables such as motivation and background must be determined at the classroom level.)

- After analyzing each text based on these factors, teachers assigned an **overall rating** of Accessible, Complex, or Very Complex, with Complex representing on-grade-level texts.

Our Approach to Writing

SpringBoard English Language Arts provides a scaffolded approach to writing in all the major modes, emphasizing argumentative, informational, and narrative. Students write often, and they learn to become critical reviewers of their own and their peers' work through frequent opportunities for revision and editing. They learn to plan with purpose, audience, topic, and context in mind; develop drafts with engaging ideas, examples, facts and commentary; revise for clarity, development, organization, style, and diction; and edit using the conventions of the English language.

The Craft of Writing

As students read texts by skilled authors, they observe the many choices those authors make. They tune in to the ways authors purposefully use words, sentences, and structures to convey meaning. After analyzing and critiquing others' work, students learn to apply their understanding of author's craft to their own written products. A few SpringBoard features help them do just that:

- **Writing prompts** scaffold to the Embedded Assessments and give students practice with writing texts in multiple genres, including personal narratives, argumentative essays, editorials, letters, myths, research papers, and more. Writing to Sources writing prompts drive students back to texts they have read or viewed to mine for evidence.

- **Focus on the Sentence** tasks help students process content while also practicing the craft of writing powerful sentences.

- **Grammar & Usage** features highlight interesting grammar or usage concepts that appear in a text, both to improve students' reading comprehension and to help them attend to these concepts as they craft their own texts.

- **Language & Writer's Craft** features address topics in writing such as style, word choice, and sentence construction.

- **Language Checkpoints** offer in-depth practice with standard English conventions and usage and guide students to revise sample sentences as well as their own work.

Modes of Writing

SpringBoard provides multiple opportunities for authentic, task-based writing and writing to sources. Direct instruction in writing in different modes --narrative, argumentative, and informational --is a primary focus of each unit of instruction, and students learn to consider task, audience, and purpose in structuring and organizing their writing.

- Guided writing instruction focuses on analysis and argument, but also allows students opportunities to develop creative writing skills.
- Instruction emphasizes the writing process with modeling the incorporation of details, reasons, and textual evidence to support ideas.
- Structured opportunities require short and extended student research in order to practice evaluating sources, gathering relevant evidence, and citing and reporting findings accurately.
- A wide range of research-based strategies are embedded within the instructional activities that take students through the writing process and encourage best practices.
- Mode-specific writing workshops, formative writing prompts, and performance-based Embedded Assessments with Scoring Guides provide regular practice.

Writing with a Focus on the Sentence

SpringBoard English Language Arts leverages sentence writing strategies that were developed by The Writing Revolution. These evidence-based strategies are part of the Hochman Method, the Writing Revolution's system for teaching writing across all content areas and grades that builds from the foundation of sentences to help students master techniques for writing powerful paragraphs and full-length compositions. The Writing Revolution emphasizes the importance of embedding writing and grammar instruction into content. That's why SpringBoard's Focus on the Sentence tasks integrate sentence-level writing into the curriculum. These tasks not only help students learn and practice important grammar concepts and sentence forms, but they also provide a chance for students to process and demonstrate understanding of texts, images, class discussions, and other content.

Our Approach to Vocabulary

Vocabulary is threaded throughout each unit and developed over the course of the SpringBoard English Language Arts year. Students are given ample opportunities to read and hear new words, explore their meanings, origins, and connotations, and use them in written and oral responses.

- Important academic and literary terms that students need to actively participate in the ELA classroom are called out in the student book.
- Challenging vocabulary terms found in reading passages are glossed at the point of use.
- Periodic Word Connections boxes guide students through the process of exploring a word with multiple meanings and nuances, an interesting etymology, a telling root or affix, a helpful Spanish cognate, a relationship to another word, or a connection to another content area.

Zinc Reading Labs

Zinc Reading Labs combines the best features of a typical vocabulary program with those of a typical reading program and makes reading and learning new words a game. Zinc offers a variety of nonfiction and fiction texts that teachers can assign (and students can choose from) based on individual needs and interest. Each article has a corresponding vocabulary set that pre-teaches challenging words through spaced repetition, ensuring students genuinely learn and internalize the vocabulary. Additional vocabulary games focus on SAT/ACT power words and foundational words for English language learners. All of the tests are auto-graded and teachers can use the detailed reports to plan for differentiation.

SpringBoard and Pre-AP

Shared Instructional Vision

SpringBoard and Pre-AP's shared instructional vision and principles are evident in every SpringBoard activity. We place a deliberate focus on learning that sets students on a pathway to AP and college readiness, enabling students to slow down and spend time tackling excellent texts and meaningful tasks. The following principles are central to SpringBoard and are shared across every Pre-AP course, resulting in a powerful multiplier effect for students' skills across disciplines.

Close Observation and Analysis
... to notice and consider

When reading, SpringBoard students are guided to pause to make observations and notice details in the text before being asked to analyze or explain. Only after they have noticed and enjoyed elements of the text do they then return to the text for deeper analysis and inferential thinking. This close reading sequence supports students in interacting and engaging with the text in increasingly meaningful ways.

Evidence-Based Writing
... with a focus on the sentence

SpringBoard offers varied and frequent writing opportunities, with specific attention to developing complex and precise sentences as the building block to sophisticated paragraph and essay length writing. Instead of being isolated from reading, sentence-level grammar and writing exercises are integrated into the curriculum to enhance students' comprehension and ability to compose a variety of texts.

Higher-Order Questioning
... to spark productive lingering

Each unit opens with essential questions that relate to the topics, themes, and texts within that unit. Students return to these questions throughout the unit and refine their answers as new evidence emerges. SpringBoard also encourages students to craft their own questions, and to dig deeply into the texts they read. After each passage, students evaluate the meaning of the text and examine the choices that the author made when writing it.

Academic Conversations
... to support peer-to-peer dialogue

SpringBoard classrooms are places where students engage in collaborative learning. Students participate in discussion groups, writing groups, debates, Socratic seminars and literature circles. These activities create an environment where students develop the ability to share, compare, critique, debate, and build on others' ideas to advance their learning.

Pre-AP Course Connections

SpringBoard's English I and English II courses have been designed with their counterpart official Pre-AP courses in mind. Students using the SpringBoard program in English I and II will be strategically prepared for the Pre-AP system of formative assessments, thereby setting them on a natural pathway toward AP success.

SpringBoard and PSAT/SAT

We want students to be rewarded for the hard work they do in their English Language Arts courses, including when they sit down to take important assessments. Therefore, SpringBoard English Language Arts focuses on the same essential knowledge and skills that are the center of the Evidence-Based Reading and Writing sections of the SAT Suite of Assessments. To make our alignment transparent, we conducted a research study, the results of which showed strong to exemplary alignment between SpringBoard ELA and the corresponding SAT Suite tests. This means that SpringBoard ELA students are getting ready for the SAT, PSAT/NMSQT, PSAT™ 10, and PSAT™ 8/9 in the classroom every day. SAT Connections are called out in the teacher edition to show targeted opportunities for students to practice skills that will serve them well on the SAT.

Teacher Edition Features

Planning the Unit

We believe that purposeful planning leads to powerful learning experiences. That's why each unit starts with support for lesson planning, guidance on differentiation, and information about unit resources. The Planning the Unit provides the following information:

- Descriptions of the context and instructional sequence of the unit to help teachers see how each activity scaffolds toward the Embedded Assessments

- A list of notable AP and SAT connections in the unit

- A cognate directory that provides the Spanish cognates for unit vocabulary terms

- Unit Resources at a Glance chart outlining resources like assessments, English language development supports, foundational language skills supports, and more

- Resources to support independent reading, including a list of suggested texts

- Detailed Instructional Pathways to help teachers thoughtfully plan the best way to approach the unit in response to students' learning needs

Instructional Pathways

SpringBoard is designed to allow teachers to personalize instruction to meet student needs. Teachers can find information in the Planning the Unit to help them build a customized pathway through each unit that delivers the support and practice students need most.

- **English Language Arts Pathway:** student-centered activities that gradually develop the skills and knowledge needed for the Embedded Assessments and are aligned to grade-level standards

- **Language Development Pathway:** linguistically accommodated activities that advance students' English language proficiency through vocabulary support, leveled texts that build background knowledge, guided close reading, sentence frames for academic discussions, and foundational language skills support

- **Flexible Pathways:** flexible activities from SpringBoard's Close Reading Workshop, Writing Workshop, or Flexible Novel Units that enable teachers to extend, support, or customize instruction

Instructional Guidance

Plan-Teach-Assess-Adapt

In the teacher edition, every activity is organized into four phases: Plan, Teach, Assess, and Adapt. Plan contains information about pacing and materials. Teach guides the class through the main steps of the activity with thoughtful suggestions for how to conduct close readings, how to group students, and when to check for understanding. Assess calls out opportunities to measure student progress. Adapt suggests ways to adjust an activity in response to students' needs.

Teacher to Teacher

Additional suggestions are sprinkled through activities in Teacher to Teacher features. These boxes give practical classroom tips, recommend additional resources to enhance and support the activity, and suggest ways to differentiate and extend instruction.

Differentiation

A rich library of tools, resources, and supports lets teachers adapt their instruction for all students, including those who need extra support, those who are still learning English, and those who are ready to go further.

Leveled Differentiated Instruction

Throughout the activities in the SpringBoard program, teachers will find Leveled Differentiated Instruction features that offer suggestions for scaffolding the challenging tasks of the activity. The suggestions provide the tools that learners at various levels of language proficiency need to successfully participate in class. Teachers will discover that the scaffolding suggestions model techniques that they can adapt to other tasks in other activities.

The differentiation spans six levels. The first four levels map to the proficiency level descriptors defined by WIDA:

Beginning Beginning represents the initial stage of language acquisition.

Bridging Bridging represents the advanced high stage of proficiency, where students need little support to understand grade-appropriate English.

Developing Developing represents the intermediate stage of proficiency, where students understand simple, high-frequency spoken English used routinely.

Support Support scaffolds learning for students who may not be English language learners but still need support with reading and producing grade-level academic language.

Expanding Expanding represents the advanced stage of proficiency, where students understand grade-appropriate English with support.

Extend Extend suggests ways to stretch students who are ready for a challenge.

As students become more proficient in English, teachers can select flexibly from the leveled scaffolding options provided to find the one that will enable the student to complete the task successfully while remaining appropriately challenged. The ultimate goal is to build students' capacity so they can perform tasks with increasing independence.

Instructional Supports for Differentiation

Among the resources available to SpringBoard teachers is a collection of graphic organizers and English language development strategies that can help scaffold instruction in boundless and creative ways. One effective way to support English language learners and students who are struggling with a task is to give them a graphic organizer that helps spark ideas, activate metacognition, organize thoughts, or frame academic discussion. The resources section of this book includes dozens of graphic organizers designed to do just that. In addition, the final part of the SpringBoard Learning Strategies section includes strategies and techniques teachers can use to boost students' ability and confidence with using academic language. Like all other strategies, they can be used flexibly, and teachers can experiment to see which strategies work best with a given set of students, and then weave them throughout instruction.

Language Workshop

Research supports the notion that all students, including those who are still developing English language skills, should have the opportunity to read complex and engaging texts appropriate for their grade level. That's why SpringBoard offers Language Workshops alongside each English Language Arts course. Language Workshops map directly to each ELA unit and include robust differentiation options that can be used flexibly depending on learners' needs. Supports include vocabulary previews and practice, accessible texts that help students build background knowledge, scaffolded close reading and discussion of an anchor text that's shared with ELA, and more. Because Language Workshops are so closely integrated with ELA, they build a bridge to help English language learners and other students progress smoothly toward proficiency with grade level skills.

Assessment for Learning

With SpringBoard English Language Arts, teachers have frequent opportunities to monitor student progress over the course of the year. Assessment for learning is the philosophical basis of assessment opportunities in SpringBoard, and we make assessment and evaluation transparent and explicit so students and teachers can focus on the key skills and knowledge to be learned.

Integrated Assessments

Each unit of SpringBoard English Language Arts is built from **Embedded Assessments** that drive the instructional pathway and give students and teachers a clear destination so they can "begin with the end in mind." These come with scoring support for teachers including scoring guides and student examples. Along the way, there are many opportunities built into daily lessons for teachers to make sure their students are on track:

- **Making Observations** questions help teachers quickly gauge students' initial understanding of key details in a text.

- **Returning to the Text** includes text-dependent questions aligned to College and Career Readiness Standards that guide students to develop and demonstrate their comprehension and analysis of a text.

- **Check Your Understanding** tasks occur at key moments in the instructional sequence when it is appropriate for students to demonstrate learning before moving on to subsequent work.

- **Focus on the Sentence** provides a quick but worthwhile opportunity for teachers to assess students' understanding of key concepts or comprehension of texts, films, discussions, or visuals.

- **Graphic organizers** throughout the student edition prompt students to map out ideas, evidence, and analysis based on the materials they're studying.

- **Writing prompts** provide useful evidence of how students are progressing toward the Embedded Assessment task. Sometimes, the responses to writing prompts can be used as early drafts that students later develop and revise for the Embedded Assessment.

- **Reflection** questions follow each Embedded Assessment and provide opportunities for students to take ownership of their learning by identifying strategies that worked for them.

Activity Quizzes on SpringBoard Digital

Activity Quizzes are quick, multiple choice assessments that assess students' learning of the knowledge and skills practiced in SpringBoard activities. Teachers can select which quizzes to assign over the span of a unit to monitor student understanding and make instructional adjustments based on results. These assessments are available on SpringBoard Digital.

Unit Assessments on SpringBoard Digital

Unit Assessments are aligned to the standards in each half unit of SpringBoard English Language Arts. Each assessment includes multiple choice and open-response questions, modeled on the types of questions students will encounter on assessments including the SAT. These assessments are available on SpringBoard Digital.

Workshops

Language Workshop

SpringBoard Language Workshop is a part of the SpringBoard program that is dedicated to building academic language proficiency in all students, including English language learners. The Language Workshop delivers grade-level English Language Arts content and tasks through the lens of developing students' academic language skills. Every activity in every workshop gives students an opportunity to listen, speak, read, and write at a level that can grow with them as they become more proficient in English.

- Each Language Workshop corresponds to one half of an ELA unit.
- Language Workshops have the same Embedded Assessments as ELA, only they are modified to be collaborative.
- Every Language Workshop activity has explicit guidance about where it is most appropriate in the sequence of ELA instruction.
- Familiar teacher edition features streamline the planning process.
- Spanish language translations of two complete activities per workshop allow Spanish-speaking students to build on their primary language literacy by reading and discussing complex, grade-appropriate texts.

Close Reading Workshop

SpringBoard English Language Arts addresses the skill of reading with deliberate attention to purpose, audience, language, and tone with activities in every unit that guide students through the steps of close reading. We also offer Close Reading Workshops, which can be used with the SpringBoard program as extra support or on their own.

The workshops offer a variety of high-quality texts, including fiction, nonfiction, and visual texts. The selected passages are appropriate for multiple close readings, and they increase in complexity from grade to grade.

Each workshop includes three texts that students read multiple times. After every reading, students use various close reading strategies, such as marking the text or SOAPSTone, to understand the content. These strategies include individual and collaborative approaches, and they support different student abilities and learning styles.

The workshops end with an assessment, which teachers can assign as an individual, small-group, or whole-class activity. The assessments always require synthesis of the three texts from the workshop, but responses may take the form of an essay, a debate, a discussion, or a multimedia presentation.

Writing Workshop

Beyond the writing instruction included in every English Language Arts unit, SpringBoard also offers stand-alone workshops—10 per grade level—for a deep dive into this skill. The Writing Workshop provides students with direct instruction of the writing process and practice writing in modes including narrative, argumentative, and informational, as well as creative modes like poetry and script writing. Each workshop includes four activities structured to gradually move students from class writing exercises to writing independently.

During the workshop, students are guided through planning, drafting, revising and editing, researching (if applicable), and other steps. All writing workshops are accompanied by a Scoring Guide that outlines the performance expectations for each writing mode and provides an evaluation tool for the learning targets identified at each grade level.

Additional ELA Tools and Supports

SpringBoard Digital

SpringBoard puts students in charge of what they learn and gives teachers the flexibility and support they need. SpringBoard Digital is an interactive program that provides always-available online content that's accessible from any device—desktop computer, laptop, tablet, or interactive whiteboard. The student edition allows users to interact with the text, respond to prompts, take assessments, and engage with a suite of tools, all in the digital space. Teachers get access to a correlations viewer that embeds correlations at point of use, a lesson planner, progress reports, grading, messaging, and more.

Zinc Reading Labs

All SpringBoard users have access to Zinc Reading Labs, where teachers and students can find a huge library of reading material chosen specifically to align with the SpringBoard curriculum.

Zinc offers students:

- Fresh and engaging nonfiction and fiction content for independent reading.

- Interactive games, quizzes, and tasks that build skills and confidence.

- Freedom of choice: Zinc's massive and ever-growing library means that all students should find texts they want to read.

Zinc offers teachers:

- Alignment to SpringBoard unit themes: Teachers browse by unit to find companion articles to the texts they're using in class and can even select vocabulary sets that are aligned to unit texts.

- Standards alignment: Quiz questions are aligned with standards so teachers can easily target specific skills.

- Detailed reporting based on results of Zinc's auto-graded quizzes.

Turnitin Revision Assistant

When students develop drafts of an available Embedded Assessment through SpringBoard Digital, they can use a tool called Turnitin Revision Assistant. This online tool gives instant feedback to students as they write so they can polish their drafts and practice their revision skills. The feedback model Revision Assistant uses is based on scoring by SpringBoard teachers, and it's trained to assess the same rubric areas that they assess.

Revision Assistant offers students:

- A template to help them create an outline.

- Actionable, instant feedback in specific areas such as structure, use of language, and ideas.

- Identification of strengths and weakness in their writing.

Teachers can access students' improved drafts and see the feedback, which lets them:

- Gain insight to student progress over time.

- Use feedback in student writing conferences.

- Identify trends in student writing to inform instruction.

SpringBoard Works

Research-based

SpringBoard is a research-based, classroom-tested curriculum created by teachers for teachers. As classroom practitioners, SpringBoard's creators understand the central role that research plays in designing effective English Language Arts instruction. They also have the hands-on experience to know what works in the classroom. Incorporating research from the field with practical experience, SpringBoard makes learning goals clear and scaffolds instruction so students master those goals.

SpringBoard uses the widely respected Wiggins and McTighe "Understanding by Design" model. The program "back maps" from a defined set of essential skills and knowledge that is shown to propel students on their path to college and career. Each SpringBoard unit begins by unpacking the Embedded Assessment, and there are multiple formative assessments throughout each unit to measure progress toward that goal. This instructional design allows students and teachers to see the connections between the work they're doing in everyday activities and the larger instructional goals of the unit and the school year.

SpringBoard's lesson design also takes into account the work of the American Institutes for Research in its focus on students moving through multiple levels of cognitive engagement: progressing fluidly from comprehension and understanding, to analysis, and ultimately to synthesis and the creation of new content. Each lesson is designed to allow for the type of facilitation and flexibility referenced by Charlotte Danielson in her work on teacher instruction. We have also integrated the research of Marzano and Pickering by building students' background knowledge in the area of academic vocabulary development. Finally, SpringBoard is directly informed by Robyn Jackson's work on rigorous instruction. As Jackson suggests, our content requires students to be "active, not passive," and our units feature activities that stress "implicit meaning, ambiguity, layers, and complexity."

Making an Impact

Statewide and nationwide studies demonstrate that SpringBoard is generating positive results. One measure of that success: SpringBoard has been shown to improve both engagement in the classroom and readiness for college. One nationwide study, comparing SpringBoard and non-SpringBoard schools, showed a considerable increase in the number of students enrolled in AP Exams and courses, as well as increased SAT performance.

SpringBoard helps more students succeed:

- High schools using SpringBoard showed a 48% increase in students taking AP Exams in English— and an even greater increase among black and Hispanic students.

- SpringBoard schools saw a 4–8% increase in AP and PSAT/NMSQT performance and saw SAT scores rise 26 points on average.

- High schools using SpringBoard for three to five years had substantially more students taking AP courses.

- SpringBoard has been shown to improve AP scores, particularly among black and Hispanic students.

A Letter to the Teacher

Dear Teacher,

We at SpringBoard are always learning from teachers like you, asking for your ideas and mining your best practices to create a program that puts students at the center of instruction. As a result, the SpringBoard classroom is one in which students can practice reading closely, writing effectively, thinking critically, working collaboratively, and speaking confidently with a teacher who is prepared to guide, support, and challenge them.

We know that the dedicated teachers who use this program come to it with a variety of experiences that they can—and should—bring to the classroom. We celebrate the amazing work that is being done in high schools around the country, and hope that all teachers who use SpringBoard can make it their own. To that end, let us share some thoughts with you.

We believe in starting each unit by showing students the Embedded Assessment assignment. By asking students to identify the skills and knowledge they will need for the task, we give them ownership of their learning. Students should be able to see how every class period develops these important skills and builds their knowledge.

We believe that learning how to learn is as important as learning the content of an English Language Arts and Reading course. A solid foundation in close reading and writing will serve students in every content area in every grade—and in every future career. SpringBoard includes a range of reading and writing strategies, and you are encouraged to choose those that work well with your students.

We believe that instruction needs to be differentiated, but common assessments are a necessary tool to drive that differentiation. The results of a common assessment will let you plan instruction based on what you see in your students' work, and might foster rich discussions in your professional learning communities and district meetings.

Finally, we hope you will take the time to become part of the larger SpringBoard community of teachers, all of whom are focused on preparing all students for college and career success. Let yourself be inspired and challenged during professional development, find support through our online community, and share your ideas with us. The SpringBoard family welcomes you.

Sincerely,
The SpringBoard Team

Planning the Unit

Context

This unit introduces the American Dream as the thematic focus of the year by asking students to examine their own preconceived notions and exposing students to the historical and literary foundations of that dream. Students will take a stance on what it means to be an American and read contemporary and historical texts across multiple genres that ask them to challenge and revisit their understanding. They then synthesize information from these texts to write an essay about who has access to the American Dream. By considering the American Dream in its historical context, being exposed to multiple viewpoints, working with seminal historical documents, and reflecting on and adjusting their own position, students will move towards an insightful understanding of the American Dream.

Suggested Texts and Materials

You will need the following materials for this unit:

- Activity 1.8: You may choose to play audio recordings of speeches that students will study in this unit, including Roosevelt's speech on the 50th Anniversary of the Statue of Liberty. Look for these at websites such as history.com or americanrhetoric.com.

- Activity 1.14: Students will be conducting research on an iconic American image of historical significance. You may want to generate a digital scrapbook of images to help students select an appropriate topic.

- Activity 1.16: You may choose to have students listen to an audio version of the Declaration of Independence (optional).

- Activity 1.19: Provide students with images or short videos related to Ellis Island (optional).

Instructional Sequence

The first half of the unit establishes students' understanding of the American Dream and asks students to examine the definition of key terms such as *freedom* and *patriotism*. Once students have created a working definition of the American Dream, they will use a variety of strategies with multiple genres (visual text, poetry, essay, historical document, and short story) to clarify their understanding and refine their analytical skills. Students will apply this knowledge, along with an understanding of primary and secondary sources, to write a definition essay in Embedded Assessment 1.

In the second half of the unit, students will continue to read contemporary and historical texts across several genres while developing their argumentative writing skills. Students will synthesize the viewpoints of multiple writers, poets, and even their peers, to create a coherent argument about the American Dream in Embedded Assessment 2.

AP® CONNECTIONS

In this unit, students will focus on refining these important skills and knowledge areas for AP/College Readiness:

- Developing a deep understanding of rhetoric and how an author presents an argument through a variety of literary and stylistic elements (Activities 1.6, 1.13, 1.17, 1.19)

- Applying the elements of a strong argument including the hook, claim, support, concessions/refutations, and call to action (Activities 1.16, 1.17, 1.18)

- Extending knowledge of the writing types, or modes, to include definition and synthesis (Activities 1.6, 1.15)

- Focusing deliberate attention on the craft of sentence-level writing (Activities 1.7, 1.8, 1.18)

SAT® CONNECTIONS

In this unit, students will practice many important skills that will help them succeed on the SAT and other college readiness exams, including:

- Recognizing and correcting problems in modifier placement (e.g., misplaced or dangling modifiers) (LC 1.8)

- Explaining how an author builds an argument to persuade an audience (Activity 1.17)

Unpacked Embedded Assessments

Embedded Assessment 1: Writing a Definition Essay	Embedded Assessment 2: Synthesizing the American Dream
Skills and Knowledge:	**Skills and Knowledge:**
• Use the writing process to produce a polished and engaging multiparagraph definition essay on what it means to be an American.	• Synthesize sources to defend, challenge, or qualify a claim.
• Synthesize different perspectives from a variety of texts as well as personal experience.	• Write an essay using the elements of an argument.
• Construct a clear, focused thesis statement that expresses complex elements of an original definition.	• Analyze a variety of sources and genres in order to gather relevant evidence.
• Support the thesis with a variety of definition strategies and quoted, paraphrased, and summarized evidence.	• Voice a clear opinion on the American Dream that demonstrates an understanding of the nuances and complexities of the topic.
• Sequence ideas to build a clear and convincing definition, using meaningful transitions to link ideas and create coherence.	• Draft a position statement and use appropriate textual support that relates to the central idea.
• Use specific, varied diction and a variety of sentence patterns.	• Sequence ideas to present a convincing argument with a logical conclusion.
	• Use varied diction, transitions, and sentence openings in writing.

Cognate Directory

Encouraging students to notice the connections between their primary language and English can help them develop academic vocabulary more quickly. If your class includes Spanish speakers, consider adding the following cognates to the classroom Word Wall. For English Language Learners whose primary language is not Spanish, consider using an online translator or dictionary to support comprehension of vocabulary terms.

Unit 1 Vocabulary Terms with Spanish Cognates

Academic Vocabulary		Literary Terms	
English	**Spanish**	**English**	**Spanish**
defend	defender	diction	dicción
plagiarism	plagio	imagery	imaginería
qualify	calificar	syntax	sintaxis
rhetoric	retórica	tone	tono

Activity Features at a Glance

The activities in every ELA unit reflect the interconnected nature of reading, writing, listening, speaking, and thinking. The Activity Features at a Glance chart highlights the types of tasks or supports that students and teachers will encounter in each activity.

 Writing and Revision

 Grammar and Language

 Listening, Speaking, and Discussion

 Independent Reading

 Vocabulary Development

 ELL Support

 Knowledge Quest

 Gaining Perspectives

ELA Activity	Activity Features
1.1	✏️ 🗣️ 📖 ELL
1.2	✏️ 🗣️ ELL
1.3	✏️ G 🗣️ 📖 V ELL
1.4	✏️ G 🗣️ V
1.5	🗣️
1.6	✏️ 🗣️ V ELL
1.7	🗣️ 🌱
1.8	✏️ G 🗣️ V 🧭
LC 1.8	✏️ G 🗣️
1.9	✏️ 🗣️ 📖
1.10	✏️
1.11	✏️ 🗣️ 📖 ELL
1.12	G 🗣️

ELA Activity	Activity Features
1.13	🗣️
1.14	✏️ 🗣️ 📖
1.15	✏️ 🗣️ 📖
1.16	✏️ 🗣️ 📖 V ELL 🌱
1.17	✏️ 🗣️ ELL
1.18	🗣️ V ELL
1.19	✏️ 🗣️ V 🧭
1.20	📖
1.21	✏️ 🗣️ 📖
1.22	✏️ G 🗣️ V ELL
1.23	✏️ G 🗣️ 📖
1.24	✏️ 🗣️ 📖 V ELL

Unit Resources at a Glance

Formative Assessment Opportunities	Digital Assessments	Family Connections
Text-dependent questions Writing prompts Check Your Understanding tasks Focus on the Sentence tasks Language Checkpoint exercises Language & Writer's Craft practice	Activity Quizzes 1.2–1.24 Unit Assessment Part 1 Unit Assessment Part 2 **SBD**	Suggestions for Independent Reading Family Letters (English and Spanish) Student Reports **SBD**
English Language Development	**Foundational Skills**	**Independent Reading**
Leveled Differentiated Instruction Graphic Organizers ELD Strategies Language Workshop 1A Language Workshop 1B	Foundational Skills Screening Assessment Observational Look-fors Foundational Skills Workshop	My Independent Reading List Independent Reading Links Independent Reading Checkpoints Independent Reading Log Reader/Writer Notebook Suggestions for Independent Reading

ⓘ Suggestions for Independent Reading

This list, divided into the categories of **Literature** and **Nonfiction/Informational Text**, comprises titles related to the themes and content of the unit. For their independent reading, students can select from this wide array of titles, which have been chosen based on complexity and interest. Spanish-language titles are included for those students who can read with greater independence or at a higher grade level in Spanish than in English, since building on their first language literacy can bolster their acquisition of English. Titles on this list have been suggested by teachers and school librarians, but you should be sure to preview texts to assess their appropriateness for your specific students and setting. You can also encourage students to do their own research and select titles that intrigue them.

Unit 1: The American Dream

Literature		
Author	**Title**	**Lexile**
Avi	*Nothing but the Truth*	N/A
Azuela, Mariano	*Los de abajo*	810L
Beatty, Patrica	*Lupita Mañana*	760L
Erdrich, Louise	*Love Medicine*	780L
Flores-Scott, Patrick	*American Road Trip*	HL550L
Gansworth, Eric	*If I Ever Get Out of Here*	N/A
Hamil, Pete	*Snow in August*	N/A
Jen, Gish	*Who's Irish?*	840L
Kadohata, Cynthia	*Kira-Kira*	740L
Ryan, Pam Muñoz	*Esperanza Rising*	750L
Ryan, Pam Muñoz	*Esperanza renace*	740L

Restrepo, Bettina	*Illegal*	540L
Smith, Betty	*A Tree Grows in Brooklyn*	810L
Steinbeck, John	*Of Mice and Men*	630L
Taylor, Mildred D.	*Roll of Thunder Hear My Cry*	920L
Wells, Ken	*Meely LeBauve*	N/A

Nonfiction/Informational

Author	Title	Lexile
Benson, Kathleen and James Haskins	*Space Challenger: The Story of Guion Bluford*	980L
Bissinger, H.G.	*Friday Night Lights: A Town, a Team, and a Dream*	1220L
Brown, Daniel James	*Boys in the Boat*	1260L
Dillard, Annie	*An American Childhood*	1040L
Doherty, Craig A. and Katherine M.	*Building America: Statue of Liberty*	1160L
Ebrahim, Zak	*The Terrorist's Son: A Story of Choice*	N/A
Ehrenreich, Barbara	*Nickel and Dimed*	1340L
Finkel, Michael	*The Stranger in the Woods: The Extraordinary Story of the Last True Hermit*	N/A
Gladwell, Malcolm	*Outliers: The Story of Success*	1080L
Guerrero, Diane	*In the Country We Love: My Family Divided*	HL780L
Guerrero, Diane	*En el país que amamos: Mi familia dividida*	
Haley, Alex and Malcolm X	*Autobiography of Malcolm X: As Told to Alex Haley*	1120L
Hillenbrand, Laura	*Seabiscuit: An American Legend*	990L
Hillenbrand, Laura	*Unbroken*	1010L
Jemison, Mae	*Find Where the Wind*	960L
Junger, Sebastian	*The Perfect Storm: A True Story of Men Against the Sea*	1140L
Kurlanksky, Mark	*Frozen in Time*	1220L
Levitt, Steven	*Freakonomics*	N/A
Maclean, Normal	*A River Runs Through It*	1160L
McBride, James	*The Color of Water: A Black Man's Tribute to His White Mother*	1240L
McBride, James	*Kill 'Em and Leave: Searching for James Brown and the American Soul*	N/A
Nasar, Sylvia	*A Beautiful Mind*	N/A
Ngai, Mae	*The Lucky Ones: One Family and the Extraordinary Invention of Chinese America*	N/A
Peralta, Dan-el Padilla	*Undocumented: A Dominican Boy's Odyssey from a Homeless Shelter to the Ivy League*	930L
Saedi, Sara	*Americanized: Rebel Without a Greencard*	N/A
Sheinkin, Steve	*Undefeated: Jim Thorpe and the Carlisle Indian School Football Team*	980L
Vance, Ashlee	*Elon Musk*	1200L
Wolff, Tobias	*This Boy's Life*	N/A

Unit 1 Instructional Pathways

Instructional Pathways

Teachers can build customized pathways through this unit by making purposeful choices about which resources to use based on students' learning needs. The charts below outline a few possible pathways to show how teachers might integrate digital assessments, Language Workshops, Close Reading Workshops, and Writing Workshops into instruction. Additional planning resources—including detailed standards correlations—are available on SpringBoard Digital.

English Language Arts Unit 1: The American Dream		
Activity	**SBD Digital Assessments**	**Pacing**
Activity 1.1: Previewing the Unit	N/A	1
Activity 1.2: Analyzing Visual Texts	Activity Quiz 1.2	1
Activity 1.3: An American Story	Activity Quiz 1.3	2
Activity 1.4: Writing a Literary Analysis and Revising for Sentence Fluency	Activity Quiz 1.4	1
Activity 1.5: Questioning the Text	Activity Quiz 1.5	3
Activity 1.6: Writing an Analysis of an Extended Definition	Activity Quiz 1.6	2
Activity 1.7: What Is Freedom?	Activity Quiz 1.7	2
Activity 1.8: America's Promise	Activity Quiz 1.8	2
LC 1.8: Language Checkpoint: Placing Modifiers (optional)	Activity Quiz LC 1.8	1
Activity 1.9: Defining an American	Activity Quiz 1.9	2
Activity 1.10: Whitman's America	Activity Quiz 1.10	1
Activity 1.11: America's Voices	Activity Quiz 1.11	2
Activity 1.12: A Hyphenated American	Activity Quiz 1.12	2
Activity 1.13: Drafting Your Definition Essay	Activity Quiz 1.13	1
Activity 1.14: Revising and Editing	Activity Quiz 1.14	1
Embedded Assessment 1: Writing a Definition Essay	**Unit Assessment Part 1**	2 | 1
Activity 1.15: Unpacking Embedded Assessment 2	Activity Quiz 1.15	1
Activity 1.16: The Structure of an Argument	Activity Quiz 1.16	2
Activity 1.17: Annotating an Argumentative Text	Activity Quiz 1.17	1
Activity 1.18: A Call to Action	Activity Quiz 1.18	3
Activity 1.19: Coming to America	Activity Quiz 1.19	2
Activity 1.20: The Sonnet and the American Dream	Activity Quiz 1.20	1

Activity	SBD Digital Assessments	Pacing	
Activity 1.21: Money and the American Dream	Activity Quiz 1.21	2	
Activity 1.22: Working Toward the Dream	Activity Quiz 1.22	1	
Activity 1.23: The Road to Success	Activity Quiz 1.23	2	
Activity 1.24: American Dream: Real or Imagined	Activity Quiz 1.24	2	
Embedded Assessment 2: Synthesizing the American Dream	Unit Assessment Part 2	3	1
	Total 50-minute Class Periods:	45–48	

Language Development Pathway

Consider using some or all of the Language Workshop and Foundational Skills Workshop activities with English Language Learners or with any student who would benefit from extra support with academic English. More detailed guidance about the timing and purpose of each Language Workshop and Foundational Skills Workshop activity can be found in the Language Workshop teacher edition.

Language Workshop 1A and 1B		
Activity or Workshop		**Pacing**
Activity 1.1: Previewing the Unit		1
Activity 1.2: Analyzing Visual Texts		1
Language Workshop 1A.1: Genre Focus		1
Language Workshop 1A.2: Building Knowledge		1
Language Workshop 1A.3: Academic Vocabulary		1
Language Workshop 1A.4: Vocabulary Preview and Practice		1
Activity 1.3: An American Story	**Language Workshop 1A.5:** Close Reading of an Anchor Text*	1
	OR **Language Workshop 1A.6:** Academic Collaboration*	2 / 1
Activity 1.4: Writing a Literary Analysis and Revising for Sentence Fluency		1
Activity 1.5: Questioning the Text		3
Language Workshop 1A.7: Language Checkpoint		1
Activity 1.6: Writing an Analysis of an Extended Definition		2
Activity 1.7: What Is Freedom?		2
Activity 1.8: America's Promise		2
LC 1.8: Language Checkpoint: Placing Modifiers		1
Activity 1.9: Defining an American		2
Activity 1.10: Whitman's America		1
Activity 1.11: America's Voices		2
Activity 1.12: A Hyphenated American		2
Activity 1.13: Drafting Your Definition Essay		1

Activity or Workshop			Pacing	
Activity 1.14: Revising and Editing			1	
Embedded Assessment 1: Writing a Definition Essay	OR	**Collaborative Embedded Assessment:** Writing a Definition Essay	2	4
Activity 1.15: Unpacking Embedded Assessment 2			1	
Language Workshop 1B.1: Genre Focus			1	
Language Workshop 1B.2: Building Knowledge			1	
Language Workshop 1B.3: Academic Vocabulary			1	
Language Workshop 1B.4: Vocabulary Preview and Practice			1	
Activity 1.16: The Structure of an Argument	OR	**Language Workshop 1B.5:** Close Reading of an Anchor Text*	2	1
		Language Workshop 1B.6: Academic Collaboration*		1
Activity 1.17: Annotating an Argumentative Text			1	
Activity 1.18: A Call to Action			3	
Activity 1.19: Coming to America			2	
Activity 1.20: The Sonnet and the American Dream			1	
Activity 1.21: Money and the American Dream			2	
Activity 1.22: Working Toward the Dream			1	
Activity 1.23: The Road to Success			2	
Language Workshop 1B.7: Language Checkpoint			1	
Activity 1.24: American Dream: Real or Imagined			2	
Embedded Assessment 2: Synthesizing the American Dream	OR	**Collaborative Embedded Assessment:** Synthesizing the American Dream	3	4
		Total 50-minute Class Periods:	45–59	

* These activities are available in Spanish.

Foundational Skills Workshop

The Foundational Skills Workshop offers instructional and practice materials for providing small-group instruction to students who are still developing foundational reading skills.

Activity	Pacing
Activity 1: Practicing Letter-Sound Relationships	15 min.
Activity 2: Recognizing Words by Sight	10 min.
Activity 3: Words with Inconsistent but Common Spellings	
Activity 4: Irregularly Spelled Words	
Activity 5: Common Prefixes	
Activity 6: Common Suffixes	35–40 min. per activity
Activity 7: Using Roots and Affixes to Read Multisyllabic Words	
Activity 8: Reading Multisyllabic Words	
Activity 9: Reading Informational Text with Purpose and Understanding	
Activity 10: Reading Poetry with Fluency	

Flexible Pathways

Teachers may build a flexible pathway that focuses on developing students' close reading and writing skills with the Close Reading and Writing Workshops. Each workshop addresses a specific set of standards and includes multiple assessment opportunities to allow students to demonstrate the knowledge and skills that are the focus of that workshop.

Close Reading Workshops

Workshop	Genre Focus	Assessment Opportunities	Pacing
Close Reading Workshop 1: Informational/Literary Nonfiction Texts	Essay Photograph Speech	Writing Prompt Debate/Discussion Multimedia Presentation	8
Close Reading Workshop 2: Close Reading of Argumentative Nonfiction Texts	Legal Documents Cartoons	Writing Prompt Debate/Discussion Multimedia Presentation	8

Writing Workshops

Workshop	Genre Focus	Assessment Opportunities	Pacing
Writing Workshop 1: The Writing Process	n/a	Writing as a Class Independent Writing	5
Writing Workshop 2: Argumentative Writing	Argument	Writing as a Class Writing with a Peer Independent Writing	6
Writing Workshop 3: Explanatory Writing: Definition	Explanatory Essay	Writing as a Class Writing with a Peer Independent Writing	6

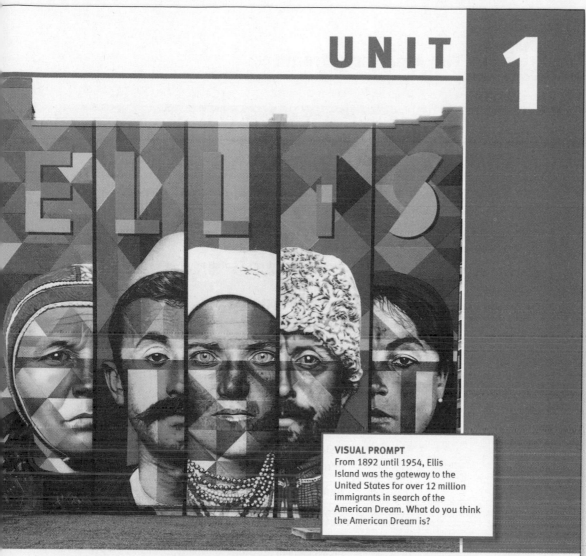

VISUAL PROMPT
From 1892 until 1954, Ellis Island was the gateway to the United States for over 12 million immigrants in search of the American Dream. What do you think the American Dream is?

UNIT 1

THE AMERICAN DREAM

A merica! From the other end of the earth from where I came, America was a land of living hope, woven of dreams, aflame with longing and desire.

—from "America and I" by Anzia Yezierska

Leveled Differentiated Instruction Directory

For guidance on differentiating tasks for English language learners at various levels of language proficiency, refer to the Leveled Differentiated Instruction suggestions in these activities:

1.1 Support students at an early stage of English language development by giving them the option of reading a text in their home language.

1.2 Provide students at an early stage of English language development with a **Conclusion Builder** graphic organizer to help them analyze visual texts.

1.3 Help students identify key ideas and details in an extended text by using a **Notes for Reading Independently** graphic organizer.

UNIT 1

Read aloud the unit title, "The American Dream," and the quotation. Ask students: What is the "American Dream"? What does it involve? Is the American Dream "one size fits all," or does every American have his or her own dream? Then ask students to write at least one question they have about the unit and have them share their questions with a partner.

Have students look at the photograph and respond to the visual prompt. You may want to have students **think-pair-share** to write a short response.

UNIT 1

CONTENTS

Have students skim/scan the activities and texts in this unit. Have them note any texts they have heard about but never read and any activities that sound particularly interesting.

GOALS

Have students read the goals for the unit and mark any words that are unfamiliar. Have students add these words to the classroom Word Wall along with definitions.

You may also want to post these goals in a visible place in the classroom for the duration of this unit, allowing you and students to revisit the goals easily and gauge progress throughout the unit.

VOCABULARY DEVELOPMENT

Adding to vocabulary knowledge is essential for reading fluency. Students will encounter new vocabulary in this course in multiple ways:

• Academic Vocabulary
• Literary Terms
• Vocabulary in Context (terms glossed in text selections)
• Word Connections
• Oral discussions

Encourage students to use new vocabulary expressively in class discussions and in writing. Have them keep a **Reader/Writer Notebook** in which they record new words, their meanings, and their pronunciations.

See the Resources section for examples of graphic organizers suitable for word study. Having students use word-study graphic organizers will greatly enhance their understanding of new words and their connection to unit concepts and to the broader use of advanced vocabulary.

Have students review the list of academic and literary terms and sort them in a QHT chart. Revisit the chart periodically to see how students' understanding progresses throughout the unit.

UNIT 1

The American Dream

VOCABULARY

ACADEMIC
challenge
defend
plagiarism
qualify
rhetoric
rhetorical devices

LITERARY
diction
imagery
syntax
tone

Leveled Differentiated Instruction Directory (continued)

1.6 To prepare for writing rhetorical analysis paragraphs, let students develop their ideas in a small group discussion using a **Round Table Discussion** graphic organizer.

1.11 Support students in completing the **Venn Diagram for Writing a Comparison** graphic organizer, focusing on how the word *sing* is represented in each text.

1.16 Provide students with an **Idea and Argument Evaluator** graphic organizer to support them in identifying the main ideas of a challenging text.

1.17 Pair students and provide them with the **Conversation for Quickwrite** graphic organizer to collaboratively brainstorm key words and phrases to use in their response.

CONTENTS

My Independent Reading List

Leveled Differentiated Instruction Directory (continued)

1.18 Boost students' comprehension of the text and provide a clear model for pronunciation and intonation by having them read along as they listen to a passage.

1.22 Pair students and provide them with the **Persuasive/Argument Writing Map** graphic organizer to complete together as a prewriting support.

1.24 Allow partners to script their speaking points prior to presenting. Provide students with sentence stems and multiple opportunities to rehearse before their presentation.

UNIT 1

LANGUAGE DEVELOPMENT

Several recurring SpringBoard features focus on building students' knowledge of grammar and usage concepts. Language & Writer's Craft features guide students to examine a writer's use of a language concept in context before incorporating the concept into their own writing. Grammar & Usage features briefly highlight and explain an interesting grammar or usage concept that appears in a text, both to improve students' reading comprehension and to increase their understanding of the concept. Periodic Language Checkpoints offer in-depth practice with standard English conventions and usage and guide students to revise sample sentences as well as their own work.

INDEPENDENT READING

In this half of the unit, while reading texts focused on the American Dream, students will have the opportunity to independently read other texts that explore the concept. Student choice is paramount. The Planning the Unit section of the Teacher's Edition and the Resources section of the Student Edition contain reading lists to help you and your students find the right books.

Independent Reading Links in the unit periodically prompt students to reflect on the reading they are doing outside of class and to make connections to the texts, themes, and ideas addressed in the unit.

KNOWLEDGE QUEST

Within the unit, students will engage in two Knowledge Quests. They will read collections of texts about the Statue of Liberty and the immigrant experience, building their understanding of the topics and related vocabulary. Each Knowledge Quest begins with a knowledge question and supporting questions that focus student learning. After students read the final text in a set, they will have the opportunity to return to the Knowledge Question and express their growing understanding of the topic by responding to a writing-to-sources prompt or engaging in an academic discussion.

UNIT 1

CONTENTS

📖 My Independent
    Reading List

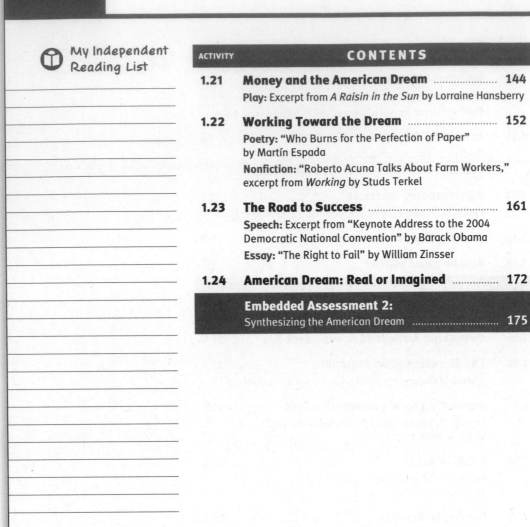

Previewing the Unit

Learning Targets

- Preview the big ideas for the unit.
- Create a plan for reading independently.

Preview

In this activity, you will explore the big ideas and tasks of the unit to come and make plans for your own independent reading.

About the Unit

In this unit, you will read a variety of texts and be asked to think about ideas and concepts that are "American." For the first embedded assessment, you will define what it means to be an American. Some words, concepts, and ideas are too complex for a simple definition and require a multi-paragraph essay to define. Definitions also provide a writer the opportunity to clear up misconceptions about a concept or idea. You will learn to define a word or concept using four definition strategies: by example, by classification, by function, and by negation.

Essential Questions

Based on your current thinking, how would you answer these questions?

1. What does it mean to be an American?

2. What is the "American Dream"?

3. Does America still provide access to the "American Dream"?

Unpacking Embedded Assessment 1

Closely read the assignment for Embedded Assessment 1: Writing a Definition Essay.

Your assignment is to write a multi-paragraph essay that defines your interpretation of what it means to be an American. This essay should use the strategies of definition and different perspectives from the unit to help you develop a complex and thoughtful definition. If possible, incorporate an iconic image in your essay.

Find the Scoring Guide and work with your class to paraphrase the expectations for the assignment. Create a graphic organizer to use as a visual reminder of the required skills and concepts. Copy the graphic organizer into your Reader/Writer Notebook and revisit it after each activity to check your progress.

Learning Strategies

Paraphrasing
Previewing
Skimming/Scanning
Think-Pair-Share

My Notes

College and Career Readiness Standards

Focus Standards:

RI.11-12.10 By the end of grade 11, read and comprehend literary nonfiction in the grades 11–CCR text complexity band proficiently, with scaffolding as needed at the high end of the range.

RL.11-12.10 By the end of grade 11, read and comprehend literature, including stories, dramas, and poems, in the grades 11–CCR text complexity band proficiently, with scaffolding as needed at the high end of the range.

L.11-12.6 Acquire and use accurately general academic and domain-specific words and phrases, sufficient for reading, writing, speaking, and listening at the college and career readiness level; demonstrate independence in gathering vocabulary knowledge when considering a word or phrase important to comprehension or expression.

ACTIVITY 1.1

PLAN

Materials: books for independent reading or access to a library
Suggested Pacing: 1 50-minute class period

TEACH

1 Read aloud the Learning Targets, Preview, and About the Unit sections with students and ask them to jot down any questions they have about the unit.

2 Students should provide answers to the Essential Questions and briefly discuss them with a partner. Explain that throughout the unit, they will revisit the Essential Questions to see how their responses have changed.

3 Read aloud the assignment for the first Embedded Assessment. Have students **mark the text** and **think-pair-share** the skills and knowledge they will need for success.

4 Unpack the Embedded Assessment assignment with students. Post the unpacking graphic during the unit so students can make connections between each activity and requirements for the assessment. Consider using one of these approaches:

- Create a web on poster paper and list the skills and knowledge.
- Use the EA 1 Scoring Guide and list the skills and knowledge under the matching criteria.

5 This activity begins the yearlong effort to encourage and facilitate independent reading. You may want to prepare by previewing the titles found in the Planning the Unit pages. Decide which books you think would be most suitable for your students and use them as recommendations. To begin, **activate prior knowledge** by asking students about their successful experiences with reading in school and for pleasure.

6 To help students select appropriate materials to read, guide them in **previewing** their selected texts by analyzing the visuals and text on both covers.

LEVELED DIFFERENTIATED INSTRUCTION

Beginning Consider giving students who are at an early stage of English language development the option of reading a text in their home language. These students can build on native language literacy as they begin to develop academic English.

7 Students should independently read the start of the text, considering readability and interest. To help students determine whether a book is "just right," ask them if the vocabulary and writing style allow them to understand the text and if the narrative elements (setting, characters, dialogue) make them want to read further.

8 Group students to conduct a book pass. Provide them with oral instructions on how to pass their books around the group to preview texts selected by their peers. Guide them to ask pertinent questions that will help them clarify meaning and to respond appropriately to your instructions.

9 Guide students to make a final choice and create their Independent Reading Plan.

➤ TEACHER TO TEACHER

To build oral fluency, students could provide a quick book talk about their selected texts. Students should bring their texts and Reader/Writer Notebooks to the group so they can record their notes about each book.

ASSESS

Review students' Reader/Writer Notebooks for evidence of previewing and rating each text. Look for reasonable reading goals.

ADAPT

If students need additional help choosing a book, use their notes from the book pass to help them choose a highly rated text that suits their reading level.

📎 Planning Independent Reading

To enhance this unit's focus, look for nonfiction essays, memoirs, autobiographies, or biographies that that will help you understand how others define the American Dream. Consider how these readings connect to what you read in the unit and to your own perspectives. Choose exceptional readings to recommend to and discuss with your peers. To help you choose the right book, use the following questions as a guide.

1. What have you enjoyed reading in the past? What is your favorite book or favorite type of book? Who is your favorite author?

2. When you select a potential book, preview it. What do you notice about the front cover design? What type of visual is shown? What types of fonts and colors are used? What information is on the back cover? Are there awards or brags that tell you about the book?

3. Read the first few pages. Are they interesting? How does the author try to hook you to keep reading? What can you tell about the characters and setting so far? Are there any connections that you can make to personal experiences, ideas in other texts, or society? Does this seem too hard, too easy, or just right?

Reading Discussion Groups

Listen carefully as your teacher guides you through a book pass and group discussion. Practice previewing each book by looking at the covers and reading the first few pages.

1. In your Reader/Writer Notebook, record each book's title and author, something from your previewing that stands out to you, and your rating of the book.

2. After previewing each book and thinking about the goals of this unit, do you want to continue reading the book you brought to the group or choose something else?

3. Create an Independent Reading Plan to help you set personal reading goals. Keep this plan in your Reader/Writer Notebook.

   I have chosen to read _____

   by (author) _____

   because (reason from previewing) _____

   _____

   I will set aside time to read at (time, place) _____

   I should finish this text by (date) _____

4. Record your daily reading pace in your Independent Reading Log. Write a brief daily report in your log responding to what you have read. Include in your report questions, connections, or predictions about what you have read.

5. Respond to the Independent Reading Links you encounter throughout the unit.

Analyzing Visual Texts

Learning Targets
- Use details in a series of visual texts to make inferences about the creators' perspectives on the American Dream.
- Reflect on and adjust responses based on research.
- Describe personal connections to visual texts.

Preview
In this activity, you will read a series of visual texts to observe the details they contain and use your observations to make inferences about the creators' perspective on the American Dream.

The American Dream
On July 4, 1776, the founders of the United States signed the Declaration of Independence. Early in that document, we find the sentence "We hold these truths to be self-evident, that all men are created equal, that they are endowed by their Creator with certain unalienable Rights, that among these are Life, Liberty and the pursuit of Happiness." Those last words in particular are a direct statement of the American Dream—the idea that people have the right to live in ways that makes them happy.

Think for a moment about your own potential. What kinds of things interest you? What pursuits bring you happiness? What kinds of accomplishments do you find worthwhile? Imagine the life you want to live and think about ways to build that life. That is your American Dream.

Quickwrite: After spending a few minutes considering the preceding questions, use the following lines to describe your perspective on the American Dream.

Learning Strategies
Making Inferences
Note-taking

My Notes

College and Career Readiness Standards

Focus Standards:

RL11-12.1 Cite strong and thorough textual evidence to support analysis of what the text says explicitly as well as inferences drawn from the text, including determining where the text leaves matters uncertain.

W.11-12.9 Draw evidence from literary or informational texts to support analysis, reflection, and research.

SL.11-12.1 Initiate and participate effectively in a range of collaborative discussions (one-on-one, in groups, and teacher-led) with diverse partners on *grades 11–12 topics, texts, and issues*, building on others' ideas and expressing their own clearly and persuasively.

Additional Standards Addressed:

W.11-12.7, W.11-12.10

ACTIVITY 1.2

PLAN

Suggested Pacing: 1 50-minute class period.

TEACH

1 Read the Learning Targets and Preview with your students. Remind students that an inference is an idea or conclusion that is drawn from evidence and reasoning. By using what they already know and details from each of the visual texts, students will make inferences about the creator's perspective on the American Dream.

2 Begin by guiding students through the section titled "The American Dream." Explain that as they work through the activity, they will continue to think about what the idea of the American Dream means to them.

LEVELED DIFFERENTIATED INSTRUCTION

Beginning To support students who are at an early stage of English language development, consider providing them with a **Conclusion Builder** graphic organizer for each of the three visual texts analyzed in this activity. Guide students in writing class observations in the Evidence boxes and conclusions/interpretations in the box at the bottom of the organizer.

3 **FIRST READ:** Conduct a shared examination of the lithograph "Welcome to All!" Begin by drawing students' attention to the figure of Uncle Sam and the sign over his head. Point out the artist's evocation of the Biblical story of Noah and the ark. Ask students to consider what analogy the creator of the lithograph is using. Encourage them to point out details in the illustration that support the analogy. Assist students in noting the approaching storm and other details. Highlight the text of the sign next to the entrance ramp and discuss what it (and the central analogy) implies about the artist's perspective on the American Dream.

1.2

Visual Text 1

Directions: Observe the illustration closely and record your observations.

This color lithograph by J. Keppler titled "Welcome to All!" was originally published in *Puck* magazine in 1880. *Puck* magazine was a weekly humor magazine in the United States in circulation from 1871 to 1918.

What details do you observe in this illustration?

_____

_____

What details in this illustration could be significant clues about how the creator perceives the American Dream?

_____

_____

_____

Scaffolding the Text-Dependent Questions

1. **The people depicted in both "Welcome to All!" and "World's Highest Standard of Living" are standing in lines. Use details from the visual texts to make inferences about how their experiences are different.** Merriam-Webster defines the term *standard of living* as "the necessities, comforts, and luxuries enjoyed by an individual or group." Where are the people in the illustration headed, and why? In which country do the people in the photograph live? Where in each image is the higher standard of living depicted? How does that standard of living seem to compare to that of the people in the lines in both the lithograph and the photograph? What are the people in each of these two images holding in their hands? RI.11-12.1

ACTIVITY 1.2 continued

Visual Text 2

Directions: Observe the photograph closely and record your observations.

This photograph titled, "World's Highest Standard of Living," was taken by photographer Margaret Bourke-White and was featured in *Life* magazine's February 1937 issue.

What details do you observe in this visual text?

_____

_____

What details in this visual could be significant clues about how the creator perceives the American Dream?

_____

_____

4 Bring students' attention to the next visual text. Explain that the photograph was featured in *Life* magazine during the depression. **Activate prior knowledge** by asking students what they know about the Great Depression and how this image portrays American life during that era. Help students to notice the juxtaposition of narratives depicted in the photograph. Students may assume that the line of people in the photograph are waiting in an unemployment line, but they are actually waiting in line at a relief station in the aftermath of the Ohio River flood, which devastated the city of Louisville, Kentucky.

Scaffolding the Text-Dependent Questions

2. What can you infer through the juxtaposition the artist creates in Visual Text 2? What message does it send to the viewer? What is the attitude of the white family? Where are they headed? What is the attitude of the African-Americans in line? What might they be waiting for? RI.11-12.1

5 Conduct a shared examination of the mural "Stepping into the American Dream." Ask students about the significance of the piggy bank, currency, and house. Point out to students that the security of home ownership is a large part of many people's idea of the American Dream. Ask them to consider who is "stepping into" the American Dream here and how the artist portrays it.

1.2

Visual Text 3

Directions: Observe the mural closely and record your observations.

Xavier Cortada's painted his 96" x 96" mural "Stepping into the American Dream" for the White House Conference on Minority Home Ownership in 2002.

What details do you observe in this mural?

_____

_____

What details in this mural could be significant clues about how the creator perceives the American Dream?

_____

_____

Scaffolding the Text-Dependent Questions

3. Look closely at the mural "Stepping into the American Dream." Describe the expressions on the people's faces. Name some of the objects in the mural. Based on these details, what do you think the title means? Compare the action described in the title with what the people in the image are doing. Why did the artist choose families as his subjects? What inanimate objects appear in the mural, and what do those objects represent? How does the title of the mural connect to its literal and symbolic content? RI.11-12.1

Returning to the Images

- Return to the visual texts as you respond to the following questions. Use evidence from the texts to support your responses.
- Write any additional questions you have about the visual texts in your Reader/Writer Notebook.

1. The people depicted in both "Welcome to All!" and "World's Highest Standard of Living" are standing in lines. Use details from the visual texts to make inferences about how their experiences are different.

The people standing in line in the illustration are awaiting entrance into the United States,

a place that promises "free education, free land, free speech," whereas the people in the

photograph already live in the United States. They are holding baskets and buckets, and based

on these details, they may be in line for food or supplies, signaling that their experiences may

not be living up to the promises of the illustration.

2. What can you infer through the juxtaposition the artist creates in Visual Text 2? What message does it send to the viewer?

The artist creates a juxtaposition between the image of the white family smiling and driving

a car into hills that proclaim, "there's no way like the American way," and a line of African-

Americans waiting below. The message is that white Americans have access to the American

Dream, while African-Americans must wait for it.

3. Look closely at the mural "Stepping into the American Dream." Describe the expressions on the people's faces. Name some of the objects in the mural. Based on these details, what do you think the title means?

The mural depicts various people smiling. There are objects such as a key, a piggy bank,

a door, houses, and a pen and possible contract. Based on these details, the title must mean

that owning a home is part of the American Dream.

ACTIVITY 1.2 continued

6 **RETURNING TO THE IMAGES:** Guide students to return to the visual texts and respond to the text-dependent questions. Invite them to work in pairs to reexamine the images and answer the questions. Remind them to use details from the images in their responses.

7 Move from pair to pair and listen in as the students answer the text-dependent questions. If they have difficulty, scaffold the questions by rephrasing them or breaking them into smaller parts. See the Scaffolding the Text-Dependent Questions boxes for suggestions.

8 Introduce the On the Spot Research task by setting some guidelines for conducting research during class. You can provide students with specific websites for them to use, or you can help them come up with useful search terms based on the visual texts' captions. Students should spend no more than 10 minutes researching the text's creator or the context in which it was created. As they learn new information, have them take notes in the My Notes column. Once students have completed their research, they should reflect on their previous responses and adjust them as needed based on the new information they found.

 TEACHER TO TEACHER

The sentence frame in the On the Spot Research section provides a good opportunity to review agreement in the phrase "a *detail* that reveals." Point out that the singular noun *detail* calls for the singular form of the verb that ends in "s" (a *detail* that *reveals*); however, if students write sentences using the plural *details*, the plural form of the verb drops the "s" (*details* that *reveal*).

9 After students have completed their sentences, divide them into small groups to complete the Collaborative Discussion prompt.

10 Give students an opportunity to create a visual text for Check Your Understanding that represents their current perspective on the American Dream.

ASSESS

As students are completing the Check Your Understanding task, check in with groups and listen to their explanations of their visual texts. Make sure that they are discussing details in their image and how those details connect to their perspectives.

ADAPT

If students need support coming up with ideas for their visual text, have them create a brainstorming web while they take part in a collaborative discussion.

1.2

On the Spot Research

Choose one of the visual texts to reexamine. Do some research about the creator or the context in which the text was created and use that information to reflect on your previous response and adjust it as needed. Decide which of the text's details are particularly revealing about the creator's perspective on the American Dream. Write three sentences that connect those details to the information you learned.

You can use the following sentence frame to help you write each of your sentences:

The_____ is a detail that reveals _____.

_____

_____

4. **Collaborative Discussion:** In a small group, share the information you learned about the visual text you chose to reexamine. Then expand the conversation to discuss how the text is similar to or different from your own perception of the American Dream. Are there details in the text that are opposed to or supportive of your ideas? What personal connections can you make?

☑ Check Your Understanding

Create a visual text that reflects your current perception of the American Dream using the art supplies provided by your teacher. You will present your visual text to a small group. Use the On the Spot Research sentence frame to help you express how the details in the visual text support your ideas about the American Dream.

An American Story

Learning Targets

- Evaluate how an author's use of diction and syntax contributes to the tone of a text.
- Analyze relationships among characterization, significance of setting, and plot in a short story.

Preview

In this activity, you will read a short story and evaluate how the author's diction and syntax contribute to the tone of the text.

Learning Strategies

Discussion Groups
Marking the Text
Predicting
Think-Pair-Share

My Notes

Tone Game

1. The following words are from the short story "America and I." Work together with a group of your classmates to sort the words into categories based on the words' meaning(s) and relationships. Consult print and online resources, such as a dictionary, a thesaurus, and an encyclopedia, to help you create categories. Then write the categories and each word and its definition(s) in your Reader/Writer Notebook.

voiceless	desire	Promised Land	drudgery	hunger
breath	unvoiced	opportunity	freshness	America
singing	shining	alone	understanding	prison
Old World	blossom	hearts	oppression	release
flowing	gates	stifled	hidden	denied
immigrants	hope	generations	forefathers	utopia

2. Based on your work with the preceding list of words, answer the following questions about the short story they come from.

What do you think the historical context of the short story will be? Write your answer and explain which words support your response.

I think the story will probably be set sometime during the late 1800s to early 1900s. This was a period of high immigration from the Old World to America. People from Europe saw America as a Promised Land of opportunity and came with the hope of escaping the oppression and drudgery of their homelands.

3. What do you think the tone of the short story is most likely to be?

I think the tone will probably vary throughout the story. In some parts, it will be optimistic and happy, using words like *singing*, *shining*, *hope*, and *opportunity*. In others, it will be pessimistic and sad, using words like *voiceless*, *stifled*, *drudgery*, *oppression*, and *denied*.

LITERARY

VOCABULARY

Tone is a writer's or speaker's attitude toward a subject, character, or audience. A writer's diction and syntax contribute to the tone of their work. Diction is the writer's choice or words and syntax is the arrangement of words and the order of grammatical elements in a sentence; the way in which words are put together to make meaningful elements, such as phrases, clauses, and sentences.

College and Career Readiness Standards

Focus Standards:

RL.11-12.4 Determine the meaning of words and phrases as they are used in the text, including figurative and connotative meanings; analyze the impact of specific word choices on meaning and tone, including words with multiple meanings or language that is particularly fresh, engaging, or beautiful.

L.11-12.3 Apply knowledge of language to understand how language functions in different contexts, to make effective choices for meaning or style, and to comprehend more fully when reading or listening.

Additional Standards Addressed:

RL.11-12.1, RL.11-12.3, RL.11-12.5, L.11-12.4a, L.11-12.4c, W.11-12.3, W.11-12.3a, W.11-12.3b, W.11-12.3c, W 11-12.3d, W.11-12.3e

PLAN

Materials: print and online reference resources (dictionary, thesaurus, encyclopedia), projector
Suggested Pacing: 2 50-minute class periods

TEACH

1 Read the Learning Targets and Preview with your students. Remind them that they should focus their reading of the story with the Essential Questions in mind.

2 Highlight the Vocabulary box. Read its text aloud. Discuss the contents and clarify as needed to reinforce student understanding of definitions of the words *tone, diction,* and *syntax.*

3 Read aloud the instructions for the Tone Game. List any terms students are unclear about on the board. Then ask students to look up what is still unclear and write brief definitions in their Reader/Writer Notebooks.

4 Demonstrate that the Tone Game is a way to analyze the relationship between diction (writer's choice of words) and tone. Write the word *voiceless* on the board and ask students how they think an author probably feels about something described as voiceless. Tell them that a thesaurus indicates that synonyms of *voiceless* include *ignored* and *helpless.* Then ask students what adjective could name the connotation of all of these words. Write the word *sad* on the board above *voiceless* and tell students that *sad* is your first Tone Game classification. Then consult a dictionary for the definition of *voiceless* (without the means to be heard) and write that definition next to the word on the board. Instruct students to work in groups to duplicate your procedure and format with the other Tone Game words in their Reader/Writer Notebooks. Visit with groups and supervise their progress.

5 When the class has completed the Tone Game, guide students through student steps 2 and 3. Encourage them to note the specific Tone Game words that support their **predictions** about historical context and tone.

6 Examine some of responses to the Check Your Understanding task to ensure that students are composing appropriate, text-based statements.

7 Conduct a shared reading of the Opening Writing Prompt. Before having students complete the activity, conduct a **close read** of the excerpt from "America and I." Read the text aloud, pausing to focus on:

- The text "beating, beating out their hearts at their gates for a breath of understanding" in the excerpt's first paragraph. Note that the writer's word choice (diction) evokes basic processes of life (heartbeats, breathing) and that the arrangement (syntax) of the words presents the desire of immigrants to enter America as a longing similar to the desire for life itself.

- The diction used to describe America and Russia in the second and third paragraphs. In the second, the writer uses the phrase "from the other end of the earth" (a metaphorical expression, since Earth has no literal "ends") to convey the idea of a great distance from where she began to where she is going. Her subsequent choice of words to describe America, a "land of living hope, woven of dreams, aflame with longing and desire," adds a subtle tonal element to the description of distance; not only is her new home physically far away, it is distant in terms of the nature of the life she is accustomed to. The hopeful, almost magical tone evoked in describing America is accentuated even further by her comparison between America and Russia in the third paragraph. There she describes her native land as a place of "airless oppression," "darkness," and "prison-bars," contrasting that hopeless tone with a description of America as a "Promised Land" providing "wings for my stifled spirit," "sunlight," and "freedom" that she compares to "strings of a beautiful violin."

- The diction and syntax in the fourth paragraph, which revisits the approach of the first in its comparison of basic life processes (youth, strength, pregnancy) with the hope and enthusiasm she feels as she begins a life in a new and unknown home.

1.3

☑ Check Your Understanding

Make a prediction about the story based on what you have inferred from the words that come from it. Use the following sentence frame to help you write your prediction. Include vocbulary from the text in your response.

I predict that the short story will be about _____ because _____.

> ### 📝 Opening Writing Prompt
>
> Listen as your teacher reads aloud the excerpt from "America and I." Then respond to the following question in a quickwrite. Later you will discuss your response in a class discussion.
>
> Based on the **diction** and **syntax** in the excerpt, what is the author's tone toward America and the American Dream? What details about word choice and syntax support your answer?

As one of the dumb, voiceless ones I speak. One of the millions of immigrants beating, beating out their hearts at your gates for a breath of understanding.

Ach! America! From the other end of the earth from where I came, America was a land of living hope, woven of dreams, aflame with longing and desire.

Choked for ages in the airless oppression of Russia, the Promised Land rose up—wings for my stifled spirit—sunlight burning through my darkness—freedom singing to me in my prison—deathless songs tuning prison-bars into strings of a beautiful violin.

I arrived in America. My young, strong body, my heart and soul pregnant with the unlived lives of generations clamoring for expression.

What my mother and father and their mother and father never had a chance to give out in Russia, I would give out in America. The hidden sap of centuries would find release; colors that never saw light—songs that died unvoiced—romance that never had a chance to blossom in the black life of the Old World.

In the golden land of flowing opportunity I was to find my work that was denied me in the sterile village of my forefathers. Here I was to be free from the dead drudgery for bread that held me down in Russia. For the first time in America, I'd cease to be a slave of the belly. I'd be a creator, a giver, a human being! My work would be the living job of fullest self-expression.

But from my high visions, my golden hopes, I had to put my feet down on earth. I had to have food and shelter. I had to have the money to pay for it.

I was in America, among the Americans, but not of them. No speech, no common language, no way to win a smile of understanding from them, only my young, strong body and my untried faith. Only my eager, empty hands, and my full heart shining from my eyes!

As You Read

- As you read, pause after each chunk and summarize what you just read. Ask question to make sure that you are comprehending what you are reading.
- Circle unknown words and phrases. Try to determine the meaning of the words by using context clues, word parts, or a dictionary.

About the Author

Anzia Yezierska (mid-1880s–1970) was a Jewish-American writer who emigrated from Poland with her family as a child. Her writing first appeared in the early 1920s in general interest magazines. Yezierska's realism and emotional openness, combined with her frequent use of first-person narration, are so convincing that many readers mistakenly believe all of her stories to be literally autobiographical. "America and I" first appeared in a 1923 collection of short stories called *Children of Loneliness*. Like much of Yezierska's work, it explores the changes and challenges immigrants face as they assimilate into the United States.

Short Story

America and I

by **Anzia Yezierska**

Chunk 1

1   As one of the dumb, voiceless ones I speak. One of the millions of immigrants beating, beating out their hearts at your gates for a breath of understanding.

2   Ach! America! From the other end of the earth from where I came, America was a land of living hope, woven of dreams, aflame with longing and desire.

3   Choked for ages in the airless oppression of Russia, the Promised Land rose up—wings for my stifled spirit—sunlight burning through my darkness—freedom singing to me in my prison—deathless songs tuning prison-bars into strings of a beautiful violin.

4   I arrived in America. My young, strong body, my heart and soul pregnant with the unlived lives of generations clamoring for expression.

5   What my mother and father and their mother and father never had a chance to give out in Russia, I would give out in America. The hidden **sap** of centuries would find release; colors that never saw light—songs that died unvoiced—romance that never had a chance to blossom in the black life of the Old World.

My Notes

sap: energy, vitality

8 Pause after the fourth paragraph to ensure students understand the tone of the text to that point. Read the remainder of the excerpt and have them complete the writing prompt.

9 As students work, monitor their progress to make certain they are engaged with the text. Assist them as needed in noting and interpreting how the author uses diction and syntax to create a specific tone.

10 Have students read the As You Read and About the Author sections. Prompt them to consider whether the predictions they made earlier about the story still seem likely to be correct.

TEACHER TO TEACHER

Anzia Yezierska's "America and I" is quite long. Pre-read the text and determine whether to chunk it as indicated or break the text into smaller sections. While it is important for students to build reading stamina, the length of the passage might increase the complexity for some students.

11 FIRST READ: Conduct a shared reading of "America and I." Pause after paragraph 8 to reconsider the tone of this first section. Do a quick recap of examples of how the author's diction and syntax have contributed to the tone of the story to this point.

1.3

△ **TEXT COMPLEXITY**

Overall: Accessible
Lexile: 790L
Qualitative: Moderate Difficulty
Task: Moderate (Analyze)

12 As students are reading, monitor their progress. Be sure they are engaged with the text, summarizing each chunk after reading and **marking the text** for unknown words and phrases.

13 Tell students to pause at the end of paragraph 11. Review the Grammar & Usage feature. Make sure students understand the use of quotation marks to suggest irony or sarcasm.

14 Tell students to pause at the end of paragraph 14 and have them explain what the narrator means by the statement "My great chance to learn to be a civilized being, to become an American by living with them." Prompt students to speculate how adopting this attitude helped her diminish her concern about her wages.

My Notes

GRAMMAR & USAGE

Quotation Marks for Effect
Writers sometimes place quotation marks around a word to suggest irony or sarcasm. Yezierska does this with the word American in paragraph 11. By using quotation marks, she implies that her new employers are not really American. Overuse of ironic quotation marks, however, makes them lose their effect.

Study the author's uses of quotation marks around American and Americans in paragraphs 39 and 40. What new tone do these words in quotations help to express?

sterile: unable to grow or develop
drudgery: dull, boring work

6 In the golden land of flowing opportunity I was to find my work that was denied me in the **sterile** village of my forefathers. Here I was to be free from the dead **drudgery** for bread that held me down in Russia. For the first time in America, I'd cease to be a slave of the belly. I'd be a creator, a giver, a human being! My work would be the living job of fullest self-expression.

7 But from my high visions, my golden hopes, I had to put my feet down on earth. I had to have food and shelter. I had to have the money to pay for it.

8 I was in America, among the Americans, but not of them. No speech, no common language, no way to win a smile of understanding from them, only my young, strong body and my untried faith. Only my eager, empty hands, and my full heart shining from my eyes!

Chunk 2

9 God from the world! Here I was with so much richness in me, but my mind was not wanted without the language. And my body, unskilled, untrained, was not even wanted in the factory. Only one of two chances was left open to me: the kitchen, or minding babies.

10 My first job was as a servant in an Americanized family. Once, long ago, they came from the same village from where I came. But they were so well-dressed, so well-fed, so successful in America, that they were ashamed to remember their mother tongue.

11 "What were to be my wages?" I ventured timidly, as I looked up to the well-fed, well-dressed "American" man and woman.

12 They looked at me with a sudden coldness. What have I said to draw away from me their warmth? Was it so low for me to talk of wages? I shrank back into myself like a low-down bargainer. Maybe they're so high up in well-being they can't any more understand my low thoughts for money.

13 From his rich height the man preached down to me that I must not be so grabbing for wages. Only just landed from the ship and already thinking about money when I should be thankful to associate with "Americans." The woman, out of her smooth, smiling fatness assured me that this was my chance for a summer vacation in the country with her two lovely children.

14 My great chance to learn to be a civilized being, to become an American by living with them.

15 So, made to feel that I was in the hands of American friends, invited to share with them their home, their plenty, their happiness, I pushed out from my head the worry for wages. Here was my first chance to begin my life in the sunshine, after my long darkness. My laugh was all over my face as I said to them: "I'll trust myself to you. What I'm worth you'll give me." And I entered their house like a child by the hand.

16 The best of me I gave them. Their house cares were my house cares. I got up early. I worked till late. All that my soul hungered to give I put into the passion with which I scrubbed floors, scoured pots, and washed clothes.

Scaffolding the Text-Dependent Questions

4. Reread paragraphs 1–6 and summarize how the narrator feels about leaving Russia and immigrating to the United States. How does she expect her life to be better in America? Use text evidence to support your response. How does the narrator describe Russia? How does she describe America? What were her employment opportunities in Russia? What kind of work does she expect to find in America? RL.11-12.1.1

15 Tell students to pause after paragraph 27 and predict what the narrator will do next.

I was so grateful to mingle with the American people, to hear the music of the American language, that I never knew tiredness.

17 There was such a freshness in my brains and such a willingness in my heart I could go on and on—not only with the work of the house, but work with my head—learning new words from the children, the grocer, the butcher, the iceman. I was not even afraid to ask for words from the policeman on the street. And every new word made me see new American things with American eyes. I felt like a Columbus, finding new worlds through every new word.

18 But words alone were only for the inside of me. The outside of me still branded me for a steerage immigrant. I had to have clothes to forget myself that I'm a stranger yet. And so I had to have money to buy these clothes.

19 The month was up. I was so happy! Now I'd have money. *My own, earned* money. Money to buy a new shirt on my back—shoes on my feet. Maybe yet an American dress and hat!

20 Ach! How high rose my dreams! How plainly I saw all that I would do with my visionary wages shining like a light over my head!

21 In my imagination I already walked in my new American clothes. How beautiful I looked as I saw myself like a picture before my eyes! I saw how I would throw away my immigrant rags tied up in my immigrant shawl. With money to buy—free money in my hands—I'd show them that I could look like an American in a day.

22 Like a prisoner in his last night in prison, counting the seconds that will free him from his chains, I trembled breathlessly for the minute I'd get the wages in my hand.

23 Before dawn I rose.

24 I shined up the house like a jewel-box.

25 I prepared breakfast and waited with my heart in my mouth for my lady and gentleman to rise. At last I heard them stirring. My eyes were jumping out of my head to them when I saw them coming in and seating themselves by the table.

26 Like a hungry cat rubbing up to its boss for meat, so I edged and simpered around them as I passed them the food. Without my will, like a beggar, my hand reached out to them.

27 The breakfast was over. And no word yet from my wages.

28 "*Gottuniu!*" I thought to myself. "Maybe they're so busy with their own things, they forgot it's the day for my wages. Could they who have everything know what I was to do with my first American dollars? How could they, soaking in plenty, how could they feel the longing and the fierce hunger in me, pressing up through each visionary dollar? How could they know the gnawing ache of my **avid** fingers for the feel of my own, earned dollars? *My* dollars that I could spend like a free person. *My* dollars that would make me feel with everybody alike!"

My Notes

avid: very eager, desirous

Scaffolding the Text-Dependent Questions

5. Summarize the way in which the narrator builds suspense about her wages in paragraphs 19–33. Reread paragraph 19–33. What is her mood when she first thinks about being paid? What does she think she will do with the money? How does her mood change as the time she expects to be paid draws near? RL.11-12.3, RL.11-12.5

16 **Vocabulary Development:**
Pause after paragraph 42. Highlight the Word Connections box. Tell students that learning the etymology and history of a word can enrich knowledge of its meaning. Select a few compelling words from the text, such as *ghetto*, and ask students about the author's possible intent for using them. Elicit other words that the author could have used.

My Notes

29 Lunch came. Lunch passed.

30 Oi-i weh! Not a word yet about my money.

31 It was near dinner. And not a word yet about my wages.

32 I began to set the table. But my head—it swam away from me. I broke a glass. The silver dropped from my nervous fingers. I couldn't stand it any longer. I dropped everything and rushed over to my American lady and gentleman.

33 "Oi weh! The money—my money—my wages!" I cried breathlessly.

34 Four cold eyes turned on me.

35 "Wages? Money?" The four eyes turned into hard stone as they looked me up and down. "Haven't you a comfortable bed to sleep, and three good meals a day? You're only a month here. Just came to America. And you already think about money. Wait till you're worth any money. What use are you without knowing English? You should be glad we keep you here. It's like a vacation for you. Other girls pay money yet to be in the country."

36 It went black for my eyes. I was so choked no words came to my lips. Even the tears went dry in my throat.

Chunk 3

37 I left. Not a dollar for all my work.

38 For a long, long time my heart ached and ached like a sore wound. If murderers would have robbed me and killed me it wouldn't have hurt me so much. I couldn't think through my pain. The minute I'd see before me how they looked at me, the words they said to me—then everything began to bleed in me. And I was helpless.

39 For a long, long time the thought of ever working in an "American" family made me tremble with fear, like the fear of wild wolves. No—never again would I trust myself to an "American" family, no matter how fine their language and how sweet their smile.

WORD CONNECTIONS

Etymology
In modern history, the word *ghetto* refers to crowded urban areas of minority groups. In seventeenth-century Italy, the ghetto was the part of a city in which Jews were required to live. The word's origin is uncertain, but it may come from the Yiddish word *get*, meaning "deed of separation." A similar Italian word, *borghetto*, means "a small section of town."

40 It was blotted out in me all trust in friendship from "Americans." But the life in me still burned to live. The hope in me still craved to hope. In darkness, in dirt, in hunger and want, but only to live on!

41 There had been no end to my day—working for the "American" family.

42 Now rejecting false friendships from higher-ups in America, I turned back to the Ghetto. I worked on a hard bench with my own kind on either side of me. I knew before I began what my wages were to be. I knew what my hours were to be. And I knew the feeling of the end of the day.

43 From the outside my second job seemed worse than the first. It was in a sweatshop of a Delancey Street basement, kept up by an old, wrinkled woman that looked like a black witch of greed. My work was sewing on buttons. While the morning was still dark, I walked into a dark basement. And darkness met me when I turned out of the basement.

Scaffolding the Text-Dependent Questions

6. How has the author been affected by her experience working for an American family? What decision does the experience lead her to make in paragraph 42?
Reread paragraph 42. What opinion does she form about "Americans"? What does she believe they have to offer her? Where does she end up finding work? How does she feel about her new job? RL.11-12.1

44 Day after day, week after week, all the contact I got with America was handling dead buttons. The money I earned was hardly enough to pay for bread and rent. I didn't have a room to myself. I didn't even have a bed. I slept on a mattress on the floor in a rat-hole of a room occupied by a dozen other immigrants. I was always hungry—oh, so hungry! The scant meals I could afford only sharpened my appetite for real food. But I felt myself better off than working in the "American" family where I had three good meals a day and a bed to myself. With all the hunger and darkness of the sweat-shop, I had at least the evening to myself. And all night was mine. When all were asleep, I used to creep up on the roof of the tenement and talk out my heart in silence to the stars in the sky.

45 "Who am I? What am I? What do I want with my life? Where is America? Is there an America? What is this wilderness in which I'm lost?"

46 I'd hurl my questions and then think and think. And I could not tear it out of me, the feeling that America must be somewhere, somehow—only I couldn't find it—*my America*, where I would work for love and not for a living. I was like a thing following blindly after something far off in the dark!

47 "*Oi weh*." I'd stretch out my hand up in the air. "My head is s 23 o lost in America. What's the use of all my working if I'm not in it? Dead buttons is not me."

48 Then the busy season started in the shop. The mounds of buttons grew and grew. The long day stretched out longer. I had to begin with the buttons earlier and stay with them till later in the night. The old witch turned into a huge greedy maw for wanting more and more buttons.

49 For a glass of tea, for a slice of herring over black bread, she would buy us up to stay another and another hour, till there seemed no end to her demands. One day, the light of self-assertion broke into my cellar darkness. "I don't want the tea. I don't want your herring," I said with terrible boldness "I only want to go home. I only want the evening to myself!"

50 "You fresh mouth, you!" cried the old witch. "You learned already too much in America. I want no clock-watchers in my shop. Out you go!"

Chunk 4

51 I was driven out to cold and hunger. I could no longer pay for my mattress on the floor. I no longer could buy the bite in my mouth. I walked the streets. I knew what it is to be alone in a strange city, among strangers.

52 But I laughed through my tears. So I learned too much already in America because I wanted the whole evening to myself? Well America has yet to teach me still more: how to get not only the whole evening to myself, but a whole day a week like the American workers.

53 That sweat-shop was a bitter memory but a good school. It fitted me for a regular factory. I could walk in boldly and say I could work at something, even if it was only sewing on buttons.

My Notes

INDEPENDENT READING LINK

Read and Respond

For many authors in this unit, the American Dream is found in daily life and work. Select a moment in your independent reading that reflects this idea. Write how the American Dream is reflected in small details.

---

17 Make sure students attend to the Independent Reading Link. Direct them to select a detail that connects the American Dream with everyday life and write it in their Reader/Writer Notebooks. To assess their independent reading, set a date to check for this assignment in students' notebooks.

18 Tell students to pause after paragraph 69. Have them consider and discuss the first Making Observations question.

1.3

My Notes

54 Gradually, I became a trained worker. I worked in a light, airy factory, only eight hours a day. My boss was no longer a sweater and a blood-squeezer. The first freshness of the morning was mine. And the whole evening was mine. All day Sunday was mine.

55 Now I had better food to eat. I slept on a better bed. Now, I even looked dressed up like the American-born. But inside of me I knew that I was not yet an American. I choked with longing when I met an American-born, and I could say nothing.

56 Something cried dumb in me. I couldn't help it. I didn't know what it was I wanted. I only knew I wanted. I wanted. Like the hunger in the heart that never gets food.

57 An English class for foreigners started in our factory. The teacher had such a good, friendly face, her eyes looked so understanding, as if she could see right into my heart. So I went to her one day for an advice:

58 "I don't know what is with me the matter," I began. "I have no rest in me. I never yet done what I want."

59 "What is it you want to do, child?" she asked me.

60 "I want to do something with my head, my feelings. All day long, only with my hands I work."

61 "First you must learn English." She patted me as if I was not yet grown up. "Put your mind on that, and then we'll see."

62 So for a time I learned the language. I could almost begin to think with English words in my head. But in my heart the emptiness still hurt. I burned to give, to give something, to do something, to be something. The dead work with my hands was killing me. My work left only hard stones on my heart.

63 Again I went to our factory teacher and cried out to her: "I know already to read and write the English language, but I can't put it into words what I want. What is it in me so different that can't come out?"

64 She smiled at me down from her calmness as if I were a little bit out of my head.

65 "What *do you want* to do?"

66 "I feel. I see. I hear. And I want to think it out. But I'm like dumb in me. I only know I'm different—different from everybody."

67 She looked at me close and said nothing for a minute. "You ought to join one of the social clubs of the Women's Association," she advised.

68 "What's the Women's Association?" I implored greedily.

69 "A group of American women who are trying to help the working-girl find herself. They have a special department for immigrant girls like you."

Chunk 5

My Notes

70 I joined the Women's Association. On my first evening there they announced a lecture: "The Happy Worker and His Work," by the Welfare director of the United Mills Corporation.

71 "Is there such a thing as a happy worker at his work?" I wondered. Happiness is only by working at what you love. And what poor girl can ever find it to work at what she loves? My old dreams about my America rushed through my mind. Once I thought that in America everybody works for love. Nobody has to worry for a living. Maybe this welfare man came to show me the *real* America that till now I sought in vain.

72 With a lot of polite words the head lady of the Women's Association introduced a higher-up that looked like the king of kings of business. Never before in my life did I ever see a man with such a sureness in his step, such power in his face, such friendly positiveness in his eye as when he smiled upon us.

73 "Efficiency is the new religion of business," he began. "In big business houses, even in up-to-date factories, they no longer take the first comer and give him any job that happens to stand empty. Efficiency begins at the employment office. Experts are hired for the one purpose, to find out how best to fit the worker to his work. It's economy for the boss to make the worker happy." And then he talked a lot more on efficiency in educated language that was over my head.

74 I didn't know exactly what it meant—efficiency—but if it was to make the worker happy at his work, then that's what I had been looking for since I came to America. I only felt from watching him that he was happy by his job. And as I looked on the clean, well-dressed, successful one, who wasn't ashamed to say he rose from an office-boy, it made me feel that I, too, could lift myself up for a person.

75 He finished his lecture, telling us about the Vocational Guidance Center that the Women's Association started.

76 The very next evening I was at the Vocational Guidance Center. There I found a young, college-looking woman. Smartness and health shining from her eyes! She, too, looked as if she knew her way in America. I could tell at the first glance: here is a person that is happy by what she does.

77 "I feel you'll understand me," I said right away.

78 She leaned over with pleasure in her face: "I hope I can."

79 "I'm different."

80 She gave me a quick, puzzled look from the corner of her eyes. "What are you doing now?"

81 "I'm the quickest shirtwaist hand on the floor. But my heart wastes away by such work. I think and think, and my thoughts can't come out."

> shirtwaist: a tailored blouse worn by women

Scaffolding the Text-Dependent Questions

7. What theme or central idea is suggested by the author's response in paragraph 71 to the factory lecture "The Happy Worker and His Work"? Does it prove to be true for her? Reread paragraph 71. Think about the conclusion she draws from the lecture. How does she pursue the happiness spoken about in that lecture? RL.11-12.1.1

19 Have students pause after paragraph 94 and discuss the second Making Observations question.

1.3

My Notes

82 "Why don't you think out your thoughts in shirtwaists? You could learn to be a designer. Earn more money."

83 "I don't want to look on waists. If my hands are sick from waists, how could my head learn to put beauty into them?"

84 "But you must earn your living at what you know, and rise slowly from job to job."

85 I looked at her office sign: "Vocational Guidance." "What's your vocational guidance?" I asked. "How to rise from job to job—how to earn more money?"

86 The smile went out from her eyes. But she tried to be kind yet. "What *do* you want?" she asked, with a sigh of last patience.

87 "I want America to want me."

88 She fell back in her chair, thunderstruck with my boldness. But yet, in a low voice of educated self-control, she tried to reason with me:

89 "You have to *show* that you have something special for America before America has need of you."

90 "But I never had a chance to find out what's in me, because I always had to work for a living. Only, I feel it's efficiency for America to find out what's in me so different, so I could give it out by my work."

91 Her eyes half closed as they bored through me. Her mouth opened to speak, but no words came from her lips. So I flamed up with all that was choking in me like a house on fire:

92 "America gives free bread and rent to criminals in prison. They got grand houses with sunshine, fresh air, doctors and teachers, even for the crazy ones. Why don't they have free boarding-schools for immigrants—strong people—willing people? Here you see us burning up with something different, and America turns her head away from us."

93 Her brows lifted and dropped down. She shrugged her shoulders away from me with the look of pity we give to cripples and hopeless lunatics. "America is no Utopia. First you must become efficient in earning a living before you can indulge in your poetic dreams."

Chunk 6

94 I went away from the vocational guidance office with all the air out of my lungs. All the light out of my eyes. My feet dragged after me like dead wood.

95 Till now there had always lingered a rosy veil of hope over my emptiness, a hope that a miracle would happen. I would open up my eyes some day and suddenly find the America of my dreams. As a young girl hungry for love sees always before her eyes the picture of lover's arms around her, so I saw always in my heart the vision of Utopian America.

Scaffolding the Text-Dependent Questions

8. How do the narrator's exposure and reaction to American history in paragraphs 99–105 change her outlook toward her new country? Reread paragraph 100 to the end of the text. What does the author learn from her reading? What connection does she make between her own experiences and those of the Pilgrims? What does she realize? RL.11-12.1

My Notes

96 But now I felt that the America of my dreams never was and never could be. Reality had hit me on the head as with a club. I felt that the America that I sought was nothing but a shadow—an echo—a **chimera** of lunatics and crazy immigrants.

97 Stripped of all illusion, I looked about me. The long desert of wasting days of drudgery stared me in the face. The drudgery that I had lived through, and the endless drudgery still ahead of me rose over me like a withering wilderness of sand. In vain were all my cryings, in vain were all frantic efforts of my spirit to find the living waters of understanding for my perishing lips. Sand, sand was everywhere. With every seeking, every reaching out I only lost myself deeper and deeper in a vast sea of sand.

98 I knew now the American language. And I knew now, if I talked to the Americans from morning till night, they could not understand what the Russian soul of me wanted. They could not understand *me* any more than if I talked to them in Chinese. Between my soul and the American soul were worlds of difference that no words could bridge over. What was that difference? What made the Americans so far apart from me?

99 I began to read the American history. I found from the first pages that America started with a band of Courageous Pilgrims. They had left their native country as I had left mine. They had crossed an unknown ocean and landed in an unknown country, as I.

100 But the great difference between the first Pilgrims and me was that they expected to make America, build America, create their own world of liberty. I wanted to find it ready made.

101 I read on. I delved deeper down into the American history. I saw how the Pilgrim Fathers came to a rocky desert country, surrounded by Indian savages on all sides. But undaunted, they pressed on—through danger—through famine, pestilence, and want—they pressed on. They did not ask the Indians for sympathy, for understanding. They made no demands on anybody, but on their own **indomitable** spirit of persistence.

102 And I—I was forever begging a crumb of sympathy, a gleam of understanding from strangers who could not understand.

103 I, when I encountered a few savage Indian scalpers, like the old witch of the sweat-shop, like my "Americanized" countryman, who cheated me of my wages—I, when I found myself on the lonely, untrodden path through which all seekers of the new world must pass, I lost heart and said: "There is no America!"

104 Then came a light—a great revelation! I saw America—a big idea—a deathless hope—a world still in the making. I saw that it was the glory of America that it was not yet finished. And I, the last comer, had her share to give, small or great, to the making of America, like those Pilgrims who came in the *Mayflower*.

WORD CONNECTIONS

Roots and Affixes
The word **persistence** comes from the Latin prefix *per*, meaning "through, completely"; the root *sist*, meaning "to stand"; and the suffix *-ence*, meaning "the quality of." *Persistence* is therefore "the quality of standing or lasting completely."

chimera: illusion
indomitable: incapable of defeat

ACTIVITY 1.3 continued

20 Vocabulary Development: Pause after paragraph 102. Refer to the Word Connections box. Remind students that knowing the meanings of roots and affixes can help them figure out an unknown word. Then ask them to think of other words that share the prefix *per-*, the root *sist*, or the suffix *-ence*, as in *persistence*. As an extension, have students complete the **Roots and Affixes Brainstorm** graphic organizer.

21 After they have finished the first reading of the text, have students answer the third Making Observations question. Guide the class in a discussion of whether their predictions from earlier in the activity proved correct and how specifically their predictions were or were not accurate. Check students' general comprehension of the text based on their observations, asking follow-up questions as needed.

LEVELED DIFFERENTIATED INSTRUCTION

In this activity, students may need support reading an extended text.

Developing Have students complete a **Notes for Reading Independently** graphic organizer. Model completing the boxes based on their observations and discussions of the text. This support will ensure that students understand the basic plot and structure of the text before moving deeper into the text during the second reading.

Expanding Allow students to work in pairs to complete the **Notes for Reading Independently** graphic organizer. Have students summarize each aspect of the narrative before creating a summary for the entire passage.

Bridging Ask students to complete the **Notes for Reading Independently** graphic organizer independently. Then have partners share their organizers to strengthen their understanding of the information they placed in the six boxes of the organizer.

Support Allow students to work in small groups to complete the **Notes for Reading Independently** graphic organizer. Have groups compare their notes with another group by summarizing the passage and filling in anything they may have missed.

1.3

My Notes

105 Fired up by this revealing light, I began to build a bridge of understanding between the American-born and myself. Since their life was shut out from such as me, I began to open up my life and the lives of my people to them. And life draws life. In only writing about the Ghetto I found America.

106 Great chances have come to me. But in my heart is always a deep sadness. I feel like a man who is sitting down to a secret table of plenty, while his near ones and dear ones are perishing before his eyes. My very joy in doing the work I love hurts me like secret guilt, because all about me I see so many with my longings, my burning eagerness, to do and to be, wasting their days in drudgery they hate, merely to buy bread and pay rent. And America is losing all that richness of the soul.

107 The Americans of tomorrow, the America that is every day nearer coming to be, will be too wise, too open-hearted, too friendly-handed, to let the least lastcomer at their gates knock in vain with his gifts unwanted.

In the late 1800s and early 1900s, young women worked in the textile industry in unsafe conditions for sometimes more than 80 hours a week. This photograph was taken in January 1917 of 15-year-old Bessie Blitch sewing curtains on a sewing machine at Boutwell, Fairclough & Gold in Boston, Massachusetts.

Making Observations
- What have we learned about the narrator so far?
- What emotions do you feel as you read the narrator's experiences?
- Were your predictions about the story correct?

Returning to the Text

• Return to the story as you respond to the following questions. Use text evidence to support your responses.

• Write any additional questions you have about the text in your Reader/Writer Notebook.

4. Reread paragraphs 1–6 and summarize how the narrator feels about leaving Russia and immigrating to the United States. How does she expect her life to be better in America? Use text evidence to support your response.

The narrator feels that there is a wealth of opportunity for her in the United States as

compared to in Russia. She says, "In the golden land of flowing opportunity I was to find my

work that was denied to me in the sterile village of my forefathers." She is excited to find work

that will be self-fulfilling.

5. Summarize the way in which the narrator builds suspense about her wages in paragraphs 19–33.

The narrator builds suspense by creating a mood of increasing anticipation. She anticipates

the joy she will feel at being paid and at buying American clothes, imagining that it will make

her more American. She describes how her anticipation makes her work especially hard and

attentively. She also describes her building excitement as the day goes on and time for her

payment seems to grow near.

6. How has the author been affected by her experience working for an American family? What decision does the experience lead her to make in paragraph 42?

She now believes that "Americans," even though they share her home country, have only

"false friendship" (paragraph 42) to offer her. The first part of Chunk 3 relates how she reacts

to this belief by avoiding direct contact with them. Instead, she finds work in the Ghetto,

sewing buttons onto clothes for very low wages. She prefers to work on "a hard bench with my

own kind" because she knows what her wages and hours are to be and when her workday will

end.

7. What theme or central idea is suggested by the author's response in paragraph 71 to the factory lecture "The Happy Worker and His Work"? Does it prove to be true for her?

She concludes that "happiness is only by working at what you love." Though she wonders

if a poor girl can achieve happiness this way, in the paragraphs that follow, the author does

pursue happiness through hard work.

Extend Pair students who have completed their graphic organizers and ask them to "teach" one another what the passage is about by pointing to key quotes they noted and what they can infer about the message of the piece.

22 RETURNING TO THE TEXT: Guide students to return to the text to respond to the text-dependent questions. Have students work in pairs or small groups to reread the text and respond to the questions. Remind them to use text evidence in their responses.

23 Move from group to group and listen in as students answer the text-dependent questions. If they have difficulty, scaffold the questions by rephrasing them or breaking them into smaller parts. See the Scaffolding the Text-Dependent Questions boxes for suggestions.

24 Read aloud the instructions for the section Appreciating the Author's Craft. Invite students to meet in pairs after they have written responses to the numbered student steps 9–12. Partners can review each other's work and ask and answer questions to ensure complete responses. Visit with student pairs to monitor progress.

8. How do the narrator's exposure and reaction to American history in paragraphs 99–105 change her outlook toward her new country?

By examining the stories of the Pilgrims, she realizes that they had to work hard to build lives

in America. She concludes that she should not expect to simply have the American Dream

handed to her any more than the Pilgrims did.

Appreciating the Author's Craft

Now that you have completed a second reading of the text, return to it again to underline words, phrases, and sentences that show the tone of the text. Answer the following questions based on your annotations.

9. Name five examples of images or diction that evoke the American Dream in the first three paragraphs of "America and I."

Examples include "living hope," "woven of dreams," "aflame with longing and desire,"

"Promised Land," "wings for my stifled spirit," "sunlight burning through my darkness,"

"freedom singing to me in my prison," and "deathless songs tuning prison-bars into strings of

a beautiful violin."

10. Cite two or three examples of the narrator's use of some form of the word *America* in paragraphs 10–13. What idea does each use communicate?

Examples include the following: "My first job was as a servant in an Americanized

family"(paragraph 10), which suggests that people from other countries can become

American; the use of "American" and "Americans" (in quotes) in paragraphs 11 and 13

communicates the idea that immigrants are not exactly the same as native-born Americans.

11. Describe the tone created by the syntax of this sentence in paragraph 53: "That sweat-shop was a bitter memory but a good school." What does the narrator mean by this sentence?

The narrator chose words that create a contrast in tone between how she feels about the

actual sweat-shop experience (which was unpleasant) and what her working there taught her

(how to do repetitive work for long periods). She calls the place a "school" to emphasize that

she learned something there, even though it was not a literal school.

12. Describe how the tone of Yezierska's writing differs between the first five paragraphs of Chunk 1 and the first five paragraphs of Chunk 6. Include examples of the author's word choice and syntax.

The tone of the first five paragraphs of Chunk 1 is light and optimistic, with words and phrases

such as "living hope," "young, strong body," "release," "colors," and "romance." The tone of

the first five paragraphs of Chunk 6 is dark and pessimistic, with words and phrases such as

"all the air out of my lungs," "[a]ll the light out of my eyes," "never was and never could be,"

"chimera," "lunatics," and "drudgery."

☑ **Check Your Understanding**

Explain how the author's diction and syntax in the final paragraph convey her hope for America.

📝 **Writing Prompt: Literary**

Think about the experience of the narrator you read about in "America and I" and how she describes a difficult experience in her life. Write a three- to five-paragraph narrative about a difficult moment from your own life. Be sure to:

- Develop the events using well-chosen details and a well-structured sequence of events with a clear problem that is solved.
- Use narrative techniques, such as dialogue, description, or reflection, to develop the events. The events should build toward a particular tone and outcome.
- Use precise sensory details and figurative language to convey a vivid picture of the events, settings, and characters.
- Include a conclusion that reflects on what is experienced, observed, or resolved over the course of the narrative.

ACTIVITY 1.3 continued

25 Based on their responses to the text-dependent questions, students should complete the Check Your Understanding.

ASSESS

Review students' responses to the Check Your Understanding task. Students should clearly connect the syntax and diction of the final paragraph to the hopeful tone it conveys. Look specifically for references to diction and syntax denoting the future ("tomorrow," "will be") and positivity ("open-hearted," "friendly-handed").

ADAPT

If students need additional help understanding how an author's syntax and diction contribute to the tone of a text, have them choose a sentence or paragraph from "America and I" that they find particularly impactful. Invite them to play the Tone Game with each significant word in the excerpt to articulate its tone and to explain how word choice and sentence construction create that tone.

📝 **WRITING PROMPT: LITERARY**

The following standards are addressed in the writing prompt:
- W.11-12.3, W.11-12.3a
- W.11-12.3b, W.11-12.3c
- W.11-12.3d
- W.11-12.3e

ACTIVITY 1.4

PLAN

Suggested Pacing: 1 50-minute class period

TEACH

 TEACHER TO TEACHER

The writing exercise in this activity is a good opportunity to review with students what constitutes a good thesis. Remind students that a thesis is a one- or two-sentence statement that presents an essay's topic along with a debatable position on that topic.

1 Read aloud the Learning Targets and Preview. Review and illustrate as necessary the definition of *syntax* (the way words are combined to form phrases and sentences). Tell students they will be paying particular attention to fluency within and between sentences as they revisit the short story "America and I."

2 Read aloud the instructions at the beginning of the Planning to Write section. Then have students read and annotate the Writing Prompt. Divide them into small groups to share their annotations and generate a thesis statement and list of relevant details.

 **WRITING PROMPT: LITERARY ANALYSIS**

The following standards are addressed in the writing prompt:

- W.11-12.5
- W.11-12.9
- W.11-12.9
- W.11-12.4

Writing a Literary Analysis and Revising for Sentence Fluency

Learning Strategies

Drafting
Paraphrasing
Self-Editing/Peer Editing
Summarizing

Learning Targets

- Use summarized, paraphrased, or directly quoted text evidence along with original commentary to develop a draft of a literary analysis in a timed writing situation.
- Analyze an author's syntax to help you revise drafts to improve fluency both within and between sentences.

Preview

In this activity, after completing a timed writing prompt, you will reexamine Anzia Yezierska's syntax in "America and I" to learn more about fluency both within and between sentences and revise your own writing to demonstrate what you have learned.

My Notes

Planning to Write

1. Read and annotate the following writing prompt. In small groups, share your annotations. Work together to create a thesis statement and decide which details you noted are most relevant in supporting your thesis.

> **Writing Prompt: Literary Analysis**
>
> **Timed Prompt:** The tone of "America and I" changes and develops over the course of the narrative as Anzia Yezierska has new experiences. Draft an essay evaluating how Yezierska's use of diction and syntax affects the evolution of tone in the narrative. Be sure to:
>
> - Include a clear thesis that states how the tone changes over the course of the narrative and evaluates the author's use of diction and syntax to create those changes.
> - Support your evaluation by citing specific examples and details from the story, including the author's use of diction syntax, and add original commentary.
> - Use summaries, paraphrases, and direct quotations, as appropriate, to support your thesis and introduce and punctuate all quotations correctly.
> - Include clear transitions as you describe changes in tone over time and a clear and strong conclusion.

College and Career Readiness Standards

Focus Standards:

W.11-12.5 Develop and strengthen writing as needed by planning, revising, editing, rewriting, or trying a new approach, focusing on addressing what is most significant for a specific purpose and audience.

RL.11-12.4 Determine the meaning of words and phrases as they are used in the text, including figurative and connotative meanings; analyze the impact of specific word choices on meaning and tone, including words with multiple meanings or language that is particularly fresh, engaging, or beautiful.

Additional Standards Addressed:

W.11-12.1, W.11-12.4, W.11-12.5, W.11-12.9, L.11-12.1

My Notes

LANGUAGE & WRITER'S CRAFT:
Using Text Evidence in Your Writing

There are three correct ways to use someone else's words in your own writing: quoting, paraphrasing, and summarizing.

Quoting is using a text's exact words.

Example: Toward the end of Yezierska's story, the narrator states, "But the great difference between the first Pilgrims and me was that they expected to make America, build America, create their own world of liberty. I wanted to find it ready made."

Paraphrasing is restating a text's ideas in your own words. A paraphrase is usually slightly shorter than the original text.

Example: Yezierska's narrator tells herself that, like the Pilgrims, she must assert herself and create her own path to success.

Summarizing is similar to paraphrasing, but it includes only a text's main point.

Example: Yezierska's narrator realizes that she must work for her own success.

Always use text evidence in a way that preserves its original meaning and the order of its events or points. It is also important to make certain that your source is clearly cited; otherwise you are guilty of plagiarism, or claiming the work of others as your own.

PRACTICE Write three separate sentences quoting, paraphrasing and summarizing the story excerpt.

> "Now I had better food to eat. I slept on a better bed. Now, I even looked dressed up like the American-born. But inside of me I knew that I was not yet an American."

Quote: Yezierska's narrator realizes that although her life is better and she "even looked dressed up like the American-born," she is "not yet an American."

Paraphrase: Yezierska's narrator believes that although she lives and looks more like an American, she herself is not yet there.

Summary: Yezierska's narrator believes that she is not yet an American.

Drafting

2. Use what you learned about the three ways to incorporate text evidence in your writing and the planning work you completed in groups to write a draft response to the writing prompt.

ACADEMIC
By citing text evidence, you avoid the mistake of plagiarism, which is using or imitating another person's words or ideas without giving proper credit. Whether intentional or accidental, plagiarism is not ethical and must be avoided in all writing.

VOCABULARY

ACTIVITY 1.4 continued

3 Vocabulary Development: Review the meaning of the term *plagiarism* with students. Have them work in pairs to define the term in their own words and think of both examples and non-examples.

4 Use the Language & Writer's Craft section to discuss with students how writers use quoting, paraphrasing, and summarizing to avoid plagiarism. Guide them through the Practice on the use of these three methods.

5 Read aloud the instructions in the Drafting section. Then give students time to complete the writing prompt.

6 Read aloud the Analyzing Sentences for Fluency section, including the example texts. On the board, compare sentences from the two paragraphs to model text "before and after" it has been revised for fluency.

TEACHER TO TEACHER

This activity is essential to students' recognizing what makes writing fluent and how fluency can affect readers. For additional practice in recognizing fluent writing (and as a preview to the work students will complete for student step 3), you might provide small groups with a print or online newspaper or magazine. Students can skim the contents to identify a brief excerpt and discuss what makes it fluent as well as how that fluency affects them as readers. Visit groups to answer questions and guide their progress.

7 Read aloud the Revising for Sentence Fluency section, making certain students understand each of the areas being examined. Have students return to Chunk 1 of "America and I." Analyze that text as a class using the narrative analysis chart, which is adapted from "SOS: Sentence Opening Sheet" in *Stack the Deck* by Robert B. Cahill and Herbert J. Hrebic (Chicago Writing Program, 1994). Its purpose is to focus a writer on syntactical content and sentence variety.

Analyzing Sentences for Fluency

This advice for writing with **fluency** comes from Steve Peha, an award-winning writer of young adult nonfiction: "When we write, we write in sentences. Beginning with a capital letter, we wind our way over words and phrases until we've expressed a complete thought, and then we mark the endpoint with a period, question mark, or exclamation mark."

Readers read the same way. They follow the shape of each sentence from beginning to end trying to understand the single complete thought the writer is expressing. In order for readers to do that, your writing needs to flow smoothly from word to word, phrase to phrase, and sentence to sentence. **Sentence fluency** refers to the flow between words in a sentence and between sentences in a text. Fluent writing reads smoothly, with an easy movement between words, sentences, paragraphs, and ideas. Notice the ways the two following paragraphs vary.

Example Text:

Sometimes a musical act gives something new to the world. The Beatles were from Liverpool, England. They formed in 1957 and lasted about 13 years until their breakup in 1970. There were four of them. Their name was a pun using the musical term "beat." A lot of their music was traditional, but some of it was experimental. They were hugely popular while they were together. They are still very famous and popular today.

Text Revised for Fluency:

Sometimes something special comes along at the right time and creates an influence that's felt everywhere. In 1957, four young men from Liverpool, England, formed a local band. By the time they broke up in 1970, they'd become a household word. Their name was a play on words, blending the musical term "beat" with the image of a funny little bug. Their music was amazingly varied. Some of it sounded Elizabethan; other tunes seemed to have come from the distant future. Today, their work remains among the most famous and influential ever created. As you read this, someone, somewhere, is listening (and probably singing along) to the Beatles.

Revising for Sentence Fluency

When revising sentences for fluency, examine them for:

Word choice: Sometimes complicated words are necessary, but in general it is better to express an idea in simpler, more straightforward language. Clear, plain diction makes ideas more accessible to the reader.

- **Instead of:** Yezierska's narrator came to America anticipating an enhancement in the fabric of her existence.
- **Try:** Yezierska's narrator came to America hoping for a better life.

Appropriate length and variety of sentences: Using very long sentences, especially in a short text, creates the risk of boring or confusing the reader. It is often a good idea to divide long sentences into shorter ones. Keep in mind, though, that using *too many* short sentences will make your writing choppy and irritating to read. Fluency includes a variety of sentence lengths while avoiding sentences that are so long they become dull or lose their point altogether.

- **Instead of:** Yezierska's narrator had a fear of how she would be regarded as an immigrant by those who had assimilated into the culture of America, leading her to dream of going out with her first wages and replacing her "immigrant rags" with a wardrobe worthy of one who had fully adopted the American lifestyle.
- **Try:** Yezierska's narrator disliked her "immigrant rags." She feared being looked down upon because of how she dressed. Once she was paid, she would buy new clothes. She hoped that doing so would make her look truly American.

ACTIVITY 1.4 continued

8 Have students read student step 3. Explain that they will first number each sentence in the section they read. Those sentence numbers from the short story will be the ones used to reference the numbers on the chart.

Redundancy: Sometimes writers repeat themselves in an effort to make a point. This is almost always unnecessary and an obstacle to fluency. Deleting redundant language improves fluency without changing meaning.

- **Instead of:** Yezierska's narrator was a novice when it came to housekeeping, a beginner who lacked experience.
- **Try:** Yezierska's narrator lacked experience in housekeeping.

Self-reference: It Is seldom necessary to point out that a text is expressing its writer's point of view. Phrases like "I think" or "in my opinion" are usually distractions that can be safely omitted.

- **Instead of:** It's obvious to me that Yezierska's narrator had much to learn about being American.
- **Try:** Yezierska's narrator had much to learn about being American.

Voice: Sometimes writers rely too strongly on passive voice. While it might be appropriate in specific instances, its repeated use creates unnecessary wordiness and detracts from a text's fluency.

- **Instead of:** Buttons were sewed on for little pay by Yezierska's narrator.
- **Try:** Yezierska's narrator sewed on buttons for little pay.

Flow between sentences: A fluent text is more than a series of smoothly composed sentences. Those sentences as a whole must "flow" in a clear, logical order. Writers revise how their thoughts are presented in order to establish that order. Good writing requires a coherent text structure, which can be chronological, sequential, cause-and-effect, order of importance, or compare-and-contrast depending on which is best for presenting the idea.

- **Instead of:** Yezierska's narrator eventually worked out her own vision of the "American Dream." Her worst job was sewing on buttons for a factory. She came from Russia to find a better life. At first, she worked for a family who came from Russia for only room and board. It took her a while to understand what was required of her in her new home. She had been poor and unemployed in her native land.
- **Try:** Yezierska's narrator had come from Russia to find a better life. She had been poor and unemployed in her native land. Her first job was working for a Russian family for room and board. From there, she went to a terrible job sewing on buttons at a factory. It took a while for her to understand what would be required of her in her new home. Eventually, she worked out her own vision of the "American Dream."

3. Analyzing sentences for fluency when reading can help you improve your writing. Practice looking for fluency by analyzing a portion of the narrative you just read. Complete the following chart as your teacher directs.

9 To help determine whether the author uses a variety of sentence openings, direct students to write down in the second column the first four to six words from each sentence they read.

10 As students reread the story to analyze sentence structure, ask them to note how the author achieves fluency within and between sentences.

11 Finally, counting the number of words in each sentence will help students make connections between variations in sentence length and the effect of sentence length on a text's overall fluency.

12 When the chart has been completed, examine it as a class. Discuss how having students use the chart could help them analyze and improve their own writing. Then have students complete the Check Your Understanding.

ASSESS

Review students' responses to the Check Your Understanding task. Note whether they have revised sentences from their Timed Prompt as instructed (by changing their beginnings, length, and structure).

ADAPT

If students need additional help revising sentences for fluency, invite them to exchange their Timed Writing exercises with a partner. Assist them as needed in suggesting revisions to their partner's work, consulting the Revising for Sentence Fluency section and pointing out instructions that are relevant to the text they are examining. Then have them explain to each other the revisions they proposed. Invite students to work together to further improve sentence fluency in their Timed Writing exercises.

To extend students' ability to analyze sentences for fluency within and between paragraphs, have them identify a piece of fiction or nonfiction writing they admire and discuss with a partner how the author avoided issues noted in the Revising for Sentence Fluency section.

1.4

Sentence Number	Sentence Beginning (First Four to Six Words)	Structure of Sentence (Simple, Compound, Complex, Compound/Complex, Fragment, etc.)	Words in Sentence
1	As one of the dumb, voiceless	complex	9

4. Afterward, reflect on what the chart tells you about the fluency of this particular text. What might using this chart teach you about your own writing?

☑ Check Your Understanding

After completing the table and reviewing the various ways to improve fluency, review your Timed Writing with a partner. Analyze your sentences, looking specifically at their flow and ease of understanding. Select a few sentences and revise them by changing their beginnings, length, and structure.

Questioning the Text

Learning Targets

- Use the strategy questioning the text, before, during, and after reading.
- Generate questions about a text to deepen understanding and gain information.

Preview

In this activity, you will generate levels of questions before, during, and after reading the essay "The Two Clashing Meanings of 'Free Speech'" by Teresa M. Bejan to deepen your understanding and to gain information about the freedom of speech guaranteed by the First Amendment and how it is being interpreted or misinterpreted on some college campuses today.

Introducing the Strategy

Questioning the Text

A strategy for thinking actively and interpretively about your reading is to ask questions before, during, and after reading. As you read any text, you can ask questions that aid your understanding with different levels of ideas. Questioning helps you experience a text in depth, gain information, and monitor your understanding.

Level 1, Literal: Literal questions can be answered by referring to the text or consulting references.

> **Example:** In Anzia Yezierska's "America and I," what was the narrator's first job in her new country?

Level 2, Interpretive: Interpretive questions call for inferences because the answers cannot be found directly in the text, but textual evidence points to and supports the answers.

> **Example:** By the end of the story, how does the narrator's view of the "American Dream" align with the commonly held conception of that idea?

Level 3, Universal: Universal questions go beyond the text. What are the larger issues or ideas raised by the text?

> **Example:** What do people everywhere require to be happy?

1. Write two questions about the text you are about to read.

As You Read

- Jot down any questions you have about the essay as you read.
- Circle unknown words and phrases. Try to determine the meaning of the words by using context clues, word parts, or a dictionary.

Learning Strategies

Questioning the Text

My Notes

ACTIVITY 1.5

PLAN

Suggested Pacing: 3 50-minute class periods

TEACH

1 Read the Learning Targets and Preview with students.

✦ TEACHER TO TEACHER

The topic of this activity's essay provides a good opportunity to preview the text of the First Amendment to the United States Constitution, which will be further discussed in Activity 1.7 of this unit. The text of the First Amendment reads:

"Congress shall make no law respecting an establishment of religion, or prohibiting the free exercise thereof; or abridging the freedom of speech, or of the press; or the right of the people peaceably to assemble, and to petition the Government for a redress of grievances."

2 Introduce students to the **Questioning the Text** strategy by reading the Introducing the Strategy feature. Unpack the three levels of questions—literal, interpretive, and universal—and explain that students are about to read an essay about interaction between free speech, the First Amendment, and societal attitudes.

3 Read the examples of the three levels of questions.

4 Instruct students to use the sample questions as a guide to write two questions about the text they are about to read.

5 Read aloud the As You Read section.

College and Career Readiness Standards

Focus Standards:

RI.11-12.1 Cite strong and thorough textual evidence to support analysis of what the text says explicitly as well as inferences drawn from the text, including determining where the text leaves matters uncertain.

RI.11-12.2 Determine two or more central ideas of a text and analyze their development over the course of the text, including how they interact and build on one another to provide a complex analysis; provide an objective summary of the text.

Additional Standards Addressed:
RI.11-12.4, RI.11-12.1, RI.11-12.6

6 Read aloud the About the Author Section. Ask students what they expect from the passage based on what they now know about the author.

7 **FIRST READ:** Conduct a shared reading of "The Two Clashing Meanings of 'Free Speech.'" Pause after paragraph 2 to ensure that students understand the concepts of *isegoria* and *parrhesia*. Tell them that understanding the two terms is key to understanding the essay. Have volunteers read aloud the two sentences that explain the two terms. Then give these examples and invite students to classify each as *isegoria* or *parrhesia* and explain why:

- Reading a prepared statement at a town council meeting (*isegoria*)
- Writing a letter to the editor supporting a curfew for minors (*parrhesia*)
- Retweeting a review of a controversial film or musical release (*parrhesia*)
- Arguing a case before the Supreme Court (*isegoria*)

If time permits, invite volunteers to come up with their own examples of each type of "free speech." Point out that the forum in which each of these examples occurs is instrumental in determining which type it is and that this will be elaborated upon later in the article.

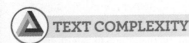

TEXT COMPLEXITY

Overall: Complex
Lexile: 1300L
Qualitative: Difficult
Task: Moderate (Analyze)

8 As students read, monitor their progress. Be sure they are engaged with the text. Remind them to note questions as they occur as well as circle unknown words and phrases and try to determine their meanings by examining context clues and word parts or by referring to a print or online dictionary.

My Notes

About the Author

Teresa M. Bejan (b. 1984) received her PhD in political philosophy from Yale University in 2013 and is an associate professor of political theory at Oxford University in England. Her writing focuses on present-day issues while drawing upon the work of Enlightenment thinkers such as John Locke and Thomas Hobbes. Her essay "The Two Clashing Meanings of 'Free Speech'" appeared in *The Atlantic* on December 2, 2017.

Essay

The Two Clashing Meanings of "Free Speech"

Today's campus controversies reflect a battle between two distinct conceptions of the term—what the Greeks called *isegoria* **and** *parrhesia*.

by **Teresa M. Bejan**

1   Little distinguishes democracy in America more sharply from Europe than the primacy—and **permissiveness**—of our commitment to free speech. Yet ongoing controversies at American universities suggest that free speech is becoming a partisan issue. While conservative students defend the importance of inviting controversial speakers to campus and giving offense, many self-identified liberals are engaged in increasingly disruptive, even violent, efforts to shut them down. Free speech for some, they argue, serves only to silence and exclude others. Denying hateful or historically "privileged" voices a platform is thus necessary to make *equality* effective, so that the **marginalized** and vulnerable can finally speak up—and be heard.

2   The reason that appeals to the First Amendment cannot decide these campus controversies is because there is a more fundamental conflict between two, very different concepts of free speech at stake. The conflict between what the ancient Greeks called *isegoria*, on the one hand, and *parrhesia*, on the other, is as old as democracy itself. Today, both terms are often translated as "freedom of speech," but their meanings were and are importantly distinct. In ancient Athens, *isegoria* described the equal right of citizens to participate in public debate in the democratic assembly; *parrhesia*, the license to say what one pleased, how and when one pleased, and to whom.

3   When it comes to private universities, businesses, or social media, the would-be censors are our fellow-citizens, not the state. Private entities like Facebook or Twitter, not to mention Yale or Middlebury, have broad rights to

> **permissiveness:** tolerance
> **marginalized:** those kept in a powerless position within society

Scaffolding the Text-Dependent Questions

2. What controversy does the author describe in the first paragraph of the essay? Reread the first paragraph. Which two groups are involved in the controversy described? What democratic principle frames the controversy? Which group feels that exceptions should be made to this principle, and why? RI.11-12.2

3. Reread the second paragraph of the article and summarize the author's thesis. How do conservatives and liberals approach the concept of "free speech"? What do those conceptions have in common? How do they differ? RI.11-12.2

regulate and exclude the speech of their members. Likewise, online mobs are made up of outraged individuals exercising their own right to speak freely. To invoke the First Amendment in such cases is not a knock-down argument, it's a non sequitur.

4   John Stuart Mill argued that the chief threat to free speech in democracies was not the state, but the "social tyranny" of one's fellow citizens. And yet today, the civil libertarians who style themselves as Mill's inheritors have for the most part failed to refute, or even address, the arguments about free speech and equality that their opponents are making.

5   The two ancient concepts of free speech came to shape our modern liberal democratic notions in fascinating and forgotten ways. But more importantly, understanding that there is not one, but *two* concepts of freedom of speech, and that these are often in tension if not outright conflict, helps explain the frustrating shape of contemporary debates, both in the U.S. and in Europe—and why it so often feels as though we are talking past each other when it comes to the things that matter most.

6   Of the two ancient concepts of free speech, *isegoria* is the older. The term dates back to the fifth century BCE, although historians disagree as to when the democratic practice of permitting any citizen who wanted to address the assembly actually began. Despite the common translation "freedom of speech," the Greek literally means something more like "equal speech in public." The verb *agoreuein*, from which it derives, shares a root with the word *agora* or marketplace—that is, a public place where people, including philosophers like Socrates, would gather together and talk.

7   In the democracy of Athens, this idea of addressing an informal gathering in the *agora* carried over into the more formal setting of the *ekklesia* or political assembly. The herald would ask, "Who will address the assemblymen?" and then the volunteer would ascend the *bema*, or speaker's platform. In theory, *isegoria* meant that any Athenian citizen in good standing had the right to participate in debate and try to persuade his fellow citizens. In practice, the number of participants was fairly small, limited to the practiced rhetoricians and elder statesmen seated near the front. (Disqualifying offenses included prostitution and taking bribes.)

8   Although Athens was not the only democracy in the ancient world, from the beginning the Athenian principle of *isegoria* was seen as something special. The historian Herodotus even described the form of government at Athens not as *demokratia*, but as *isegoria* itself. According to the fourth-century orator and patriot Demosthenes, the Athenian constitution was based on speeches (*politeia en logois*) and its citizens had chosen *isegoria* as a way of life. But for its critics, this was a bug, as well as a feature. One critic, the so-called 'Old Oligarch,' complained that even slaves and foreigners enjoyed *isegoria* at Athens, hence one could not beat them as one might elsewhere.

Harvard University students chant slogans as they protest a scheduled speaking appearance of author Charles Murray on the campus of Harvard University, Wednesday, Sept. 6, 2017, in Cambridge, Mass. Murray, who co-wrote a book discussing racial differences in intelligence, touched off a boisterous protest earlier in 2017 at Vermont's Middlebury College.

My Notes

_____

9 Tell students to pause at the end of paragraph 4. Ask them if they've learned anything new about freedom of speech and, if so, what.

10 Have students pause at the end of paragraph 7. Ask them to explain why speech in the forum described here is *isegoria* and not *parrhesia*.

Scaffolding the Text-Dependent Questions

4. Notice the author's use of the word *non sequitur* in the third paragraph. *Non sequitur* is a foreign word that is now frequently used in English. What does the term *non sequitur* mean in the third paragraph? What point does the author make by using it? Reread the third paragraph and examine the term *non sequitur* in context. Note that the author contrasts the term with a "knock-down argument." If a *non sequitur* is a term for something that is *not* a "knock-down argument," then what *is* it a term for? And how does the author apply it to an explanation of free speech in private forums? RI.11-12.4

5. How does the author's reference to John Stuart Mill in the fourth paragraph support the idea expressed in the third paragraph? Reread the third and fourth paragraphs. Who does Mill believe is the biggest threat to free speech? Is free speech protected in private forums? Why or why not? RI.11-12.1

11 Tell students to pause at the end of paragraph 10 as a way to respond to the third question ("What questions did you have while reading this text?") in Making Observations. Ask them what questions have they jotted down so far about what they have read. Write these sample questions on the board and invite volunteers to contribute their own:

- Literal: What type of free speech was more valued in Ancient Greece?
- Interpretive: Which type of free speech would be an offensive political statement?
- Universal: Is true free speech both free and equal?

My Notes

paradigmatic: model example

9 Critics like the Old Oligarch may have been exaggerating for comic effect, but they also had a point: as its etymology suggests, *isegoria* was fundamentally about equality, not freedom. As such, it would become the hallmark of Athenian democracy, which distinguished itself from the other Greek city-states not because it excluded slaves and women from citizenship (as did every society in the history of humankind until quite recently), but rather because it included the poor. Athens even took positive steps to render this equality of public speech effective by introducing pay for the poorest citizens to attend the assembly and to serve as jurors in the courts.

10 As a form of free speech then, *isegoria* was essentially political. Its competitor, *parrhesia*, was more expansive. Here again, the common English translation "freedom of speech" can be deceptive. The Greek means something like "all saying" and comes closer to the idea of speaking freely or "frankly." *Parrhesia* thus implied openness, honesty, and the courage to tell the truth, even when it meant causing offense. The practitioner of *parrhesia* (or *parrhesiastes*) was, quite literally, a "say-it-all."

11 *Parrhesia* could have a political aspect. Demosthenes and other orators stressed the duty of those exercising *isegoria* in the assembly to speak their minds. But the concept applied more often outside of the *ekklesia* in more and less informal settings. In the theater, *parrhesiastic* playwrights like Aristophanes offended all and sundry by skewering their fellow citizens, including Socrates, by name. But the **paradigmatic** *parrhesiastes* in the ancient world were the Philosophers, self-styled "lovers of wisdom" like Socrates himself who would confront their fellow citizens in the *agora* and tell them whatever hard truths they least liked to hear. Among these was Diogenes the Cynic, who famously lived in a barrel […] and told Alexander the Great to get out of his light—all, so he said, to reveal the truth to his fellow Greeks about the arbitrariness of their customs.

12 The danger intrinsic in parrhesia's offensiveness to the powers-that-be—be they monarchs like Alexander or the democratic majority—fascinated Michel Foucault, who made it the subject of a series of lectures at Berkeley (home of the original campus Free Speech Movement) in the 1980s. Foucault noticed that the practice of *parrhesia* necessarily entailed an asymmetry of power, hence a "contract" between the audience (whether one or many), who pledged to tolerate any offense, and the speaker, who agreed to tell them the truth and risk the consequences.

13 If *isegoria* was fundamentally about equality, then, *parrhesia* was about liberty in the sense of license—not a right, but rather an unstable privilege enjoyed at the pleasure of the powerful. In Athenian democracy, that usually meant the majority of one's fellow citizens, who were known to shout down or even drag speakers they disliked (including Plato's brother, Glaucon) off the *bema*. This ancient version of "no-platforming" speakers who offended popular sensibilities could have deadly consequences—as the trial and death of Socrates, Plato's friend and teacher attests.

Scaffolding the Text-Dependent Questions

6. According to the author, what common translation do the words *isegoria* and *parrhesia* share, and why is that translation inadequate when discussing democratic ideas of free speech? Reread paragraph 10. What three-word phrase is used as a translation of both words? Is the phrase an accurate translation of both words? What is different between the two? RI.11-12.4

7. Of the two types of free speech described by the author, which is protected by the government and which is subject to the will of the people? Explain. Reread paragraphs 11–13. Which word pertains to political speech? Which is protected by the First Amendment? Which word pertains to everyday speech? Does the government protect that speech? If not, who does? RI.11-12.4

14 Noting the lack of success that Plato's loved ones enjoyed with both *isegoria* and *parrhesia* during his lifetime may help explain why the father of Western philosophy didn't set great store by either concept in his works. Plato no doubt would have noticed that, despite their differences, *neither* concept relied upon the most famous and distinctively Greek understanding of speech as *logos*—that is, reason or logical argument. Plato's student, Aristotle, would identify *logos* as the capacity that made human beings essentially political animals in the first place. And yet neither *isegoria* nor *parrhesia* identified the reasoned speech and arguments of *logos* as uniquely deserving of equal liberty or license. Which seems to have been Plato's point—how was it that a democratic city that prided itself on free speech, in all of its forms, put to death the one Athenian ruled by *logos* for speaking it? [...]

***

15 Debates about free speech on American campuses today suggest that the rival concepts of *isegoria* and *parrhesia* are alive and well. When student protesters claim that they are silencing certain voices—via no-platforming, social pressure, or outright censorship—in the name of free speech itself, it may be tempting to dismiss them as insincere, or at best confused. As witnessed at an event at Kenyon College in September, when confronted with such arguments the response from gray-bearded free-speech fundamentalists like myself is to continue to preach to the converted about the First Amendment, but with an undercurrent of solidaristic despair about "kids these days" and their failure to understand the fundamentals of liberal democracy.

16 No wonder the "kids" are unpersuaded. While trigger warnings, safe spaces, and no-platforming grab headlines, poll after poll suggests that a more subtle, shift in mores is afoot. To a generation convinced that hateful speech is itself a form of violence or "silencing," pleading the First Amendment is to miss the point. Most of these students do not see themselves as standing against free speech at all. What they care about is the *equal right* to speech, and equal access to a public forum in which the historically marginalized and excluded can be heard and count equally with the privileged. This is a claim to *isegoria*, and once one recognizes it as such, much else becomes clear—including the contrasting appeal to *parrhesia* by their opponents, who sometimes seem determined to reduce "free speech" to a license to offend.

17 Recognizing the ancient ideas at work in these modern arguments puts those of us committed to America's *parrhesiastic* tradition of speaking truth to power in a better position to defend it. It suggests that to defeat the modern proponents of *isegoria*—and remind the modern *parrhesiastes* what they are fighting for—one must go beyond the First Amendment to the other, orienting principle of American democracy behind it, namely equality. After all, the genius of the First Amendment lies in bringing *isegoria* and *parrhesia* together, by securing the equal right and liberty of citizens not simply to "exercise their reason" but to speak their minds. It does so because the alternative is to allow the powers-that-happen-to-be to grant that liberty as a license to some individuals while denying it to others.

My Notes

12 Have students pause at the end of paragraph 14 and discuss the fault Plato found in both *isegoria* and *parrhesia*. What particular incident prompted him to form that conclusion?

13 Have students pause at the end of paragraph 18. Invite a volunteer to identify and **paraphrase** the essay's conclusion statement. Ask students to state the author's opinion on the degree of limitation that should be applied to both *isegoria* or *parrhesia*.

14 After reading the text for the first time, guide the class in a discussion by asking the Making Observations questions. Write the following questions on the board as examples of after-reading questions, invite students to add their own, and discuss each:

- Literal: Why does the author feel it is unsafe to keep people from "speaking their minds"?
- Interpretive: Which type of free speech does the author feel it is more important to protect?
- Universal: Is free speech a natural right, whether protected by law or not?

1.5

My Notes

18 In contexts where the Constitution does not apply, like a private university, this opposition to **arbitrariness** is a matter of culture, not law, but it is no less pressing and important for that. As the evangelicals, protesters, and provocateurs who founded America's *parrhesiastic* tradition knew well: When the rights of all become the privilege of a few, neither liberty nor equality can last.

Making Observations
- What ideas in the text capture your attention?
- What about freedom of speech do you know now that you didn't before?
- What questions did you have while reading this text?

> **arbitrariness:** not being based on any principle, plan, or system

Scaffolding the Text-Dependent Questions

8. What does the author believe is the best approach toward free speech in the private sector? Cite evidence from the text to support your answer. Reread paragraphs 15–18. Does the author believe that a democracy's government is solely responsible for protecting its free speech? To what degree, if any, should that government protect free speech within the public sector? To what degree does she think private-sector speech should be protected, by whom, and why? Where in her essay does she state this? RI.11-12.1

Returning to the Text

- Return to the essay as you respond to the following questions. Use text evidence to support your responses.
- Write any additional questions you have about the text in your Reader/Writer Notebook.

2. What controversy does the author describe in the first paragraph of the essay?

   The author describes challenges to America's commitment to free speech by those who feel
   that traditionally privileged speech should be denied a platform in order to put traditionally
   marginalized points of view on an equal footing.

3. Reread the second paragraph of the article and summarize the author's thesis.

   Controversies between conservatives and liberals about free speech issues are difficult
   to settle, and the reason for this is a conflict between two opposing concepts of free speech.

4. Notice the author's use of the word *non* sequitur in the third paragraph. *Non sequitur* is a foreign word that is now frequently used in English. What does the term *non sequitur* mean in the third paragraph? What point does the author make by using it?

   A *non sequitur* is a conclusion that is not supported by its argument. She is saying that
   evoking the First Amendment to defend free speech in private forums is not a valid
   argument.

5. How does the author's reference to John Stuart Mill in the fourth paragraph support the idea expressed in the third paragraph?

   Mill's contention is that the biggest threat to free speech in our country comes from fellow
   citizens. The third paragraph makes this same point when it states that "free speech" is not a
   governmentally protected right in private forums.

6. According to the author, what common translation do the words *isegoria* and *parrhesia* share, and why is that translation inadequate when discussing democratic ideas of free speech?

   Both words are commonly translated "freedom of speech." The translation is inadequate
   because, although both terms do name a type of free speech, they do not name the *same*
   type.

15 **RETURNING TO THE TEXT:**
Guide students to return to the text to respond to the text-dependent questions. Invite them to work in small groups to reread the text and answer the questions. Remind them to use text evidence in their responses.

16 Move from group to group and listen in as students answer the text-dependent questions. If they have difficulty, scaffold the questions by rephrasing them or breaking them into smaller parts. See the Scaffolding the Text-Dependent Questions boxes for suggestions.

17 After reviewing student responses to the Returning to the Text questions, have students work in groups to complete the Working from the Text step.

18 Instruct students to write a one- or two-paragraph statement defining and explaining the difference between *isegoria* and *parrhesia*. Their statements should include a description of which type of free speech is protected by our First Amendment, which type is managed by society, and their opinions on the relative importance of each.

19 Give students time to respond to the Check Your Understanding task. As needed, review with them the distinction between literal, interpretive, and universal questions.

ASSESS

Review students' responses to the Check Your Understanding task. As a way to gauge their understanding, compare the questions they wrote earlier for teacher step 14 with their responses to the task assignment. Note whether they have clearly defined and differentiated the two kinds of free speech addressed in Bejan's essay.

ADAPT

If students need additional help in writing their questions for the Check Your Understanding task, have them work with partners to review the examples for literal, interpretive, and universal levels of questions from the Introducing the Strategy section. Visit with pairs and, as needed, point out additional question examples presented in teacher step 14.

To extend students' ability to develop questions about texts, encourage them to find a news article that addresses a situation related to freedom of speech. Have them read the article and craft a literal, interpretive, and universal question they have about the article, including any relationship between the article's view of freedom of speech and the meaning of the Greek words *isegoria* and *parrhesia*.

---

7. Of the two types of free speech described by the author, which is protected by the government and which is subject to the will of the people? Explain.

Isegoria pertains to political speech and is fundamentally protected by government through the First Amendment. *Parrhesia*, on the other hand, refers more to everyday speech among citizens, which enjoys less government protection and is more subject to the standards of society.

8. What does the author believe is the best approach toward free speech in the private sector? Cite evidence from the text to support your answer.

The author believes that *parrhesia* in the private sector should be defended as strongly as *isegoria* is by the government. In the last paragraph, she states that, "When the [free speech] rights of all become the privilege of a few, neither liberty nor equality can last." She makes it clear that this applies to social suppression of speech as much as it does governmental suppression.

Working from the Text

9. Work with your group to come up with questions to ask about the text that would help a reader deepen his or her understanding and gain information about the freedom of speech guaranteed by the First Amendment and how it is being interpreted or misinterpreted on some college campuses today. Write your questions in the space. Then return to the text to find evidence that would support their answers. If the text does not answer your questions, conduct an informal research project to find the answers. Remember to use text evidence in your answers by quoting, paraphrasing, or summarizing in ways that avoid plagiarism and gives credit to your sources.

☑ Check Your Understanding

With the essay in mind, write three questions about freedom of speech: one literal, one interpretive, and one universal.

Writing an Analysis of an Extended Definition

Learning Targets
- Explain how an author uses definition strategies to support his or her definition of a concept.
- Write a rhetorical analysis.

Preview

In this activity, you will revisit "The Two Clashing Meanings of 'Free Speech'" to write a rhetorical analysis that explains how Teresa M. Bejan uses definition strategies to support her definition of free speech.

Characteristics of a Definition Essay: Definition Strategies

Some complex terms and concepts are best understood through extended definitions. For Embedded Assessment 1, you will write an extended definition in the form of an essay to share your personal understanding of what it means to be an American. To write this definition, you will need to use your knowledge of rhetoric and rhetorical devices to develop your ideas in ways that reach your audience, fit your purpose, and effectively communicate your message. Remember that rhetoric is the art of effective speaking and writing and rhetorical devices are techniques that writers and speakers use to convey meaning, persuade the audience, or evoke emotion. Rhetorical devices that are used to define complex concepts are called definition strategies. Read the following descriptions and examples of the definition strategies.

Classification: a rhetorical device that separates what is being defined into separate groups or classes. It is used to list smaller facets of a larger idea.

> **Example:** Most words have both denotative and connotative meanings.

Negation: a rhetorical device that negates, or excludes, something that is not part of a definition. It helps describe that definition by stating a limitation to its meaning.

> **Example:** Freedom doesn't mean being able to do whatever you like.

Exemplification: a rhetorical device that uses examples to add weight to a concept. The use of examples evokes images that help the reader connect to the idea being defined.

> **Example:** Classification, negation, and exemplification are examples of rhetorical device.

Function: a rhetorical device that explains facets of a definition in terms of their purpose.

> **Example:** Nouns are words that are used to name things, and verbs are words that are used to name actions.

Learning Strategies
Marking the Text
Rereading

ACADEMIC
Rhetoric is the art of speaking or writing effectively. Effective speakers or writer's often use **rhetorical devices** to convey meaning, to persuade the audience, or to evoke an emotion. Some rhetorical devices include allusion, anecdote, classification, function, metaphor, etc.

VOCABULARY

My Notes
_____
_____
_____
_____
_____
_____
_____
_____
_____
_____
_____
_____
_____
_____
_____
_____
_____
_____
_____
_____

College and Career Readiness Standards

Focus Standards:

RI.11-12.1 Cite strong and thorough textual evidence to support analysis of what the text says explicitly as well as inferences drawn from the text, including determining where the text leaves matters uncertain.

RI.11-12.2 Determine two or more central ideas of a text and analyze their development over the course of the text, including how they interact and build on one another to provide a complex analysis; provide an objective summary of the text.

Additional Standards Addressed:

RI.11-12.4, RI.11-12.1, RI.11-12.6, W.11-12.1, W.11-12.1a

ACTIVITY 1.6

PLAN

Suggested Pacing: 2 50-minute class periods

TEACH

1 Read the Learning Targets and Preview with students. Explain that this activity will expose them to a broader use of the word *definition* than they might be accustomed to.

★ TEACHER TO TEACHER

Consider asking students to define *definition*. Use their ideas as a starting point to clarify what a definition essay is. Elicit from students that a definition essay, like a dictionary definition, is an attempt to convey the meaning of a word, term, or concept. However, a definition essay is typically used for in-depth descriptions of things with more complex meanings and is frequently used to explain the writer's point of view of an abstract term, such as *success* or *love*. Mention that definition essays make use of many rhetorical devices, in particular definition strategies.

2 **Vocabulary Development:** Review the meaning of the Academic Vocabulary *rhetoric* and *rhetorical devices* with students. Have them work in pairs to define these terms in their own words and think of both examples and non-examples.

3 Guide students through the Characteristic of an Essay: Definition Strategies introduction.

4 Have volunteers read aloud the four definition strategies. To help clarify the information, write the following additional examples on the board and invite students to identify the definition strategy employed in each:

- Dogs and cats are the most popular domestic house pets. (classification)
- A racoon is not a species of rodent. (negation)
- Butterflies, ants, and spiders are types of insect. (exemplification)
- A hammer is a tool used in construction. (function)

5 For the Working from the Text exercise, have students work in pairs to answer the first three questions. Move from group to group and listen in as they work. If they have difficulty, scaffold the questions by rephrasing them or breaking them into smaller parts. Consult the Scaffolding the Text-Dependent Questions text if needed.

1.6

Working from the Text

As Bejan did in her essay, you will need to weave these definition strategies into your essay in ways that support your thesis. Return to Bejan's essay in the previous activity to answer the following text-dependent questions to analyze the effects of rhetorical devices, specifically definition strategies, on the way the text is read and understood.

1. In paragraph 1, Bejan says, "Free speech for some, they argue, serves only to silence and exclude others. Denying hateful or historically 'privileged' voices a platform is thus necessary to make equality effective, so that the marginalized and vulnerable can finally speak up—and be heard." What rhetorical device is being used? How does its use affect the way the text is read and understood?

   This is an example of function, and it helps the reader understand the rationale behind certain activists' insistence on suppressing certain speech.

2. How does Bejan use classification in paragraph 2 to support her thesis?

   Bejan says, "The conflict between what the ancient Greeks called *isegoria*, on the one hand, and *parrhesia*, on the other, is as old as democracy itself," classifying the thinking about the concept of free speech into two categories. This illustrates the fundamental issue at hand when it comes to arguments about freedom of speech on college campuses.

3. Quote the sentence in which Bejan employs a rhetorical device in paragraph 3, name the device, and explain how it influences the reader's understanding of the text.

   The text is "Private entities like Facebook or Twitter, not to mention Yale or Middlebury, have broad rights to regulate and exclude the speech of their members." It is an example of exemplification, and it helps the reader understand what is meant by the *parrhesia* type of free speech.

Scaffolding the Text-Dependent Questions

1. **In paragraph 1, Bejan says, "Free speech for some, they argue, serves only to silence and exclude others. Denying hateful or historically 'privileged' voices a platform is thus necessary to make equality effective, so that the marginalized and vulnerable can finally speak up—and be heard." What rhetorical device is being used? How does its use affect the way the text is read and understood?** Reread paragraph 1 in Bejan's essay. Remember that a rhetorical device is a technique used to convey meaning, persuade the audience, or evoke emotion. Where in the paragraph does Bejan do that? Which of the four types of definition strategy does she employ? RI.11-12.4, RI.11-12.6

1.6

4. Continue to reread the essay and underline and label additional instances that you can find of the rhetorical devices classification (c), exemplification (e), negation (n), and function (f). Then sort, list, and label the excerpts in the table and note the effect of each device on the way the text is read and understood.

Type of Rhetorical Device	Text from "The Two Clashing Meanings..." by Teresa M Bejan	Effect
function (f)	"The two ancient concepts of free speech came to shape our modern liberal democratic notions in fascinating and forgotten ways...helps explain the frustrating shape of contemporary debates..."	thesis statement
classification (c)	"As a form of free speech then, *isegoria* was essentially political. It's competitor, *parrhesia*, was more expansive."	classifies the two meanings of free speech
exemplification (e)	"But the paradigmatic *parrhesiastes* in the ancient world were the Philosophers, self-styled 'lovers of wisdom' like Socrates..."	provides examples of people who practiced *parrhesia*
negation (n)	"And yet neither *isegoria* nor *parrhesia* identified the reasoned speech and arguments of *logos* as uniquely deserving of equal liberty or license."	states a limitation to the meanings of both concepts of free speech

Scaffolding the Text-Dependent Questions

2. How does Bejan use classification in paragraph 2 to support her thesis? Reread paragraph 2 and revisit the description of the classification definition strategy. What text in the paragraph uses that strategy to sort two or more concepts that support her thesis? RI.11-12.1

3. Quote the sentence in which Bejan employs a rhetorical device in paragraph 3, name the device, and explain how it influences the reader's understanding of the text. Reread paragraph 3 in Bejan's essay and compare the text with the four types of definition strategy. Look in particular for the word *like* or *as* and remember what those words often signify. RI.11-12.4, RI.11-12.6

6 When students have completed their work, help pairs get started in filling out the table for student step 4. Begin by revisiting the first sentence of paragraph 5 from Bejan's essay. Have students copy that sentence into the center box of the table's first row. Assist them in identifying the sentence as an example of a "function (f)" rhetorical device and identify its effect as a "thesis statement."

7 Give pairs time to complete their tables. Accept any suitable examples from Bejan's text.

8 Invite the pairs to compare and critique each other's tables. Then have them create a set of observation statements as directed in student step 6. Write the following text on the board to illustrate the correct form of an observation statement:

Bejan uses the classification rhetorical device to distinguish between the two meanings of free speech. This is effective because understanding this distinction is vital for comprehending her essay.

9 Direct students to write a topic sentence for a rhetorical analysis paragraph as directed in student step 7. Make certain they understand that the topic sentence is for a paragraph, not an essay.

10 Give students time to respond to the Writing Prompt. Remind them of the definitions of *rhetoric* and *rhetorical devices* in the Academic Vocabulary box.

5. Compare your completed table another pair's table. Discuss and resolve any discrepancies between your tables and revise your table to reflect your unified thinking.

6. Use your enhanced table as a guide for a set of observation statements upon which you will base your analysis. Construct your statements in this format:

Bejan uses the _____ rhetorical device to _____. The effect is

_____.

Write your observation statements on the following lines. You may use scratch paper for any additional writing space you need.

Bejan uses the classification rhetorical device to distinguish between two types of free speech. The effect is to provide a sharp and necessary distinction between the two.

Bejan uses the exemplification rhetorical device to give examples of private entities that are not bound by First Amendment restrictions. The effect is to let the reader connect the concept Bejan is presenting with real-world examples.

Bejan uses the negation rhetorical device to cite John Stuart Mill's observation that society is a bigger threat to free speech than the government. The effect is to introduce a point that proves to be central later in Bejan's essay.

Bejan uses the function rhetorical device to assert that denying certain voices a platform is necessary to ensure equality. The effect is to appeal to emotion rather than to logic (and, to Bejan's credit, she discounts the argument elsewhere in her essay).

7. Use your research and notes to write a topic sentence for a rhetorical analysis paragraph. The sentence should contain a claim pertaining to how the author uses a particular rhetorical device in her essay. You can use this sentence frame to help you construct your topic sentence:

Bejan uses the rhetorical device (classification/exemplification/function/negation) in order

to _____.

Writing Prompt: Rhetorical Analysis

Write a paragraph that analyzes the author's use of a rhetorical device (classification, exemplification, function, or negation). Be sure to:

- Include a topic sentence that states the rhetorical device.
- Provide textual evidence for support.
- Describe the effect the author achieves with the use of that rhetorical device.

WRITING PROMPT: RHETORICAL ANALYSIS

The following standards are addressed in the writing prompt:
- W.11-12.1a
- W.11-12.1
- W.11-12.1

LEVELED DIFFERENTIATED INSTRUCTION

Some students may benefit from developing their ideas about Bejan's rhetorical devices in a small group discussion before writing their rhetorical analysis paragraphs.

Developing Help students organize their observations by using the **Round Table Discussion** graphic organizer to revisit their answers in the Working from the Text section. Have them draw from those answers to write examples of topic sentences, text containing rhetorical devices, and ideas about the effects of those devices.

Expanding Have groups skim Bejan's text, sharing observations about her use of rhetorical devices and the effects of that use and taking notes in a **Round Table Discussion** graphic organizer.

Extend Have student pairs share their completed responses. For which types of rhetorical device did they have similar examples, and for which ones did they have different responses? How did their appraisals of the effects of the rhetorical devices differ?

ASSESS

In reviewing students' rhetorical analysis paragraphs, look for an accurate understanding of the rhetorical device chosen and a thoughtful explanation of the effect the author achieves with its use.

ADAPT

If students need additional help responding to the Writing Prompt, they can revisit the table they completed for student step 4. Instruct them to compare their table with the essay and look for further examples of the types of rhetorical devices they noted on the table.

ACTIVITY 1.7

PLAN

Suggested Pacing: 2 50-minute class periods

TEACH

1 Review the Learning Targets and Preview with students. Explain that the class is about to examine documents that are part of the foundation of the idea of the American Dream.

2 Introduce students to the idea of metacognition and **metacognitive markers** by reading out loud the text contained in the Introducing the Strategy box.

3 Read the As You Read bullets with students. Ask them what they already know about the United States Constitution. Then proceed by asking a volunteer to read the About the Document section aloud.

 TEACHER TO TEACHER

The text of the Preamble has a high lexile, but the concepts it outlines are ones that students should be able to grasp. As needed, help students understand its meaning by reading and discussing phrases separately to construct an overall understanding. Consider starting a shared Google document in which students list unfamiliar and difficult words and supply their own definitions based on context and experience.

Learning Strategies

Brainstorming
Metacognitive Markers

My Notes

Learning Targets

- Read historical documents to analyze the author's purpose, audience, and message.
- Evaluate the use of text structure to achieve the author's purpose.
- Participate collaboratively in a mock Constitutional Convention.

Preview

In this activity, you will read the Preamble to the Constitution and the Bill of Rights to analyze the framers' purpose, audience, and message and evaluate the use of text structure to achieve their purpose.

Introducing the Strategy

Metacognitive Markers

Metacognition refers to the thinking you do about your own learning. Using metacognitive markers involves marking the text with symbols to reflect the thinking you are doing as you read. After reading, you can scan the text and use your metacognitive markers to quickly find evidence when you are talking or writing about a text. Here are the markers:

?   Use a question mark for questions you have about the text.

!   Use an exclamation point for a reaction to what you are reading.

*   Use an asterisk for a comment about the text.

_   Use an underline to identify a key idea or detail in the text.

As You Read

- Use metacognitive markers as you read.
- Circle unknown words and phrases. Try to determine the meaning of the words by using context clues, word parts, or a dictionary.

About the Document

The Preamble to the Constitution of the United States was a part of the original document that was ratified on June 1, 1788. Almost immediately after that ratification, Congress approved 12 proposed amendments called the Bill of Rights and sent them to the individual states for ratification. Nine states approved 10 of the amendments within six months. The endorsement of 11 states was necessary before anything could take effect, however. Vermont and Virginia finally accepted the 10 amendments in 1791, and the Bill of Rights became part of the Constitution that same year.

College and Career Readiness Standards

Focus Standards:

RI.11-12.9 Analyze seventeenth-, eighteenth-, and nineteenth-century foundational U.S. documents of historical and literary significance for their themes, purposes, and rhetorical features.

RI.11-12.5 Analyze and evaluate the effectiveness of the structure an author uses in his or her exposition or argument, including whether the structure makes points clear, convincing, and engaging.

Additional Standards Addressed:

L.11-12.4a, SL.11-12.1b

1.7

Historical Document

The Preamble to the Constitution of the United States

We the People of the United States, in Order to form a more perfect Union, establish Justice, insure domestic Tranquility, provide for the common defence, promote the general Welfare, and secure the Blessings of Liberty to ourselves and our Posterity, do ordain and establish this Constitution for the United States of America.

Historical Document

The Bill of Rights: A Transcription

Note: The following text is a transcription of the first ten amendments to the Constitution in their original form. These amendments were ratified December 15, 1791, and form what is known as the "Bill of Rights."

Amendment I

Congress shall make no law respecting an establishment of religion, or prohibiting the free exercise thereof; or **abridging** the freedom of speech, or of the press; or the right of the people peaceably to assemble, and to petition the Government for a **redress** of grievances.

Amendment II

A well regulated Militia, being necessary to the security of a free State, the right of the people to keep and bear Arms, shall not be infringed.

Amendment III

No Soldier shall, in time of peace be quartered in any house, without the consent of the Owner, nor in time of war, but in a manner to be prescribed by law.

Amendment IV

The right of the people to be secure in their persons, houses, papers, and effects, against unreasonable searches and seizures, shall not be violated, and no Warrants shall issue, but upon probable cause, supported by Oath or affirmation, and particularly describing the place to be searched, and the persons or things to be seized.

Amendment V

No person shall be held to answer for a capital, or otherwise infamous crime, unless on a presentment or indictment of a Grand Jury, except in cases arising in the land or naval forces, or in the Militia, when in actual service in time of War or public danger; nor shall any person be subject for the same offence to be twice put in jeopardy of life or limb; nor shall be compelled in any criminal case to be a witness against himself, nor be deprived of life, liberty, or property, without due process of law; nor shall private property be taken for public use, without just compensation.

My Notes

abridging: shortening, curtailing

redress: remedy, correction

ACTIVITY 1.7 continued

4 **FIRST READ:** Conduct a shared reading of "The Preamble to the Constitution of the United States" and "The Bill of Rights: A Transcription."

 TEXT COMPLEXITY

Overall: Complex
Lexile: 1930L
Qualitative: Moderate Difficulty
Task: Moderate (Analyze)

 TEXT COMPLEXITY

Overall: Very Complex
Lexile: 1480L
Qualitative: Moderate Difficulty
Task: Moderate (Analyze)

5 Pause after the Preamble to ensure that students understand that it is an introduction to our Constitution. Point out that, as such, it comes at the very beginning of the Constitution, while the Bill of Rights they are about to read is made up of amendments placed at the end of the Constitution. Also clarify that the Constitution itself is not part of this activity. Explain that the note at the beginning of the Bill of Rights is not a part of the document itself.

6 As students read, monitor their progress. Be sure they are engaged with the text, using **metacognitive markers** appropriately.

7 Tell students to pause after Amendment I and explain the freedoms it guarantees. Ask them whose actions are restricted by this amendment. Prompt students to understand that these freedoms might seem to be plainly stated, but they have been subject to nearly 200 years of debate and interpretation.

Scaffolding the Text-Dependent Questions

1. For whom did those who ratified the U.S. Constitution claim to speak, and on what authority did they make that claim? Reread the first sentence of the Preamble. How do the authors identify themselves? What positions of authority did those authors actually hold? RI.11-12.1

2. What is a word that accurately describes the government's proper relationship to religion, the press, and public assembly according to Amendment I of the Bill of Rights? Reread the First Amendment of the Constitution. How does it explain governmental authority over religion, the press, and public assembly? What is a word that describes that relationship? L.11-12.4a

8 Tell students to pause after Amendment IX and have them **paraphrase** it in a way that it might be stated today.

My Notes

Amendment VI

In all criminal prosecutions, the accused shall enjoy the right to a speedy and public trial, by an impartial jury of the State and district wherein the crime shall have been committed, which district shall have been previously ascertained by law, and to be informed of the nature and cause of the accusation; to be confronted with the witnesses against him; to have **compulsory** process for obtaining witnesses in his favor, and to have the Assistance of Counsel for his defence.

Amendment VII

In Suits at common law, where the value in controversy shall exceed twenty dollars, the right of trial by jury shall be preserved, and no fact tried by a jury, shall be otherwise re-examined in any Court of the United States, than according to the rules of the common law.

Amendment VIII

Excessive bail shall not be required, nor excessive fines imposed, nor cruel and unusual punishments inflicted.

Amendment IX

The **enumeration** in the Constitution, of certain rights, shall not be construed to deny or disparage others retained by the people.

Amendment X

The powers not delegated to the United States by the Constitution, nor prohibited by it to the States, are reserved to the States respectively, or to the people.

Created by Howard Chandler Christy in 1940, this oil on canvas painting titled "The Signing of the Constitution of the United States in 1787" depicts the Constitutional Convention at Independence Hall in Philadelphia on September 17, 1787. Do you recognize any of the historical figures in the image?

compulsory: required by law
enumeration: complete and ordered listing

Scaffolding the Text-Dependent Questions

3. Who does Amendment VI guarantee must participate in a trial on behalf of the person being tried? Reread the text of the Sixth Amendment. Who is specifically named? RI.11-12.1

4. Why do you think the framers of the Constitution felt they had to include Amendment VIII in the Bill of Rights? Reread the text of the Eighth Amendment. What kinds of unfair treatment were people who were arrested but not convicted in danger of? RI.11-12.1

5. Explain how Amendments IX and X affirm the rights of states and individual citizens. Reread Amendments IX and X. What kinds of rights and powers do those amendments name? What do the amendments state about those kinds of rights and powers? Which rights are reserved to states, and which are reserved for citizens? RI.11-12.1

Making Observations

- What catches your attention about the amendments?
- Which amendments have you heard of before?

Returning to the Text

- Return to the historical documents as you respond to the following questions. Use text evidence to support your responses.
- Write any additional questions you have about the text in your Reader/Writer Notebook.

1. For whom did those who ratified the U.S. Constitution claim to speak, and on what authority did they make that claim?

   As stated in the first sentence of the Preamble, those who ratified the Constitution claimed

   to speak for "the People of the United States." They made the claim based on the fact

   that they were members of Congress, placed in their position through their election by their

   states' voters.

2. What is a word that accurately describes the government's proper relationship to religion, the press, and public assembly according to Amendment I of the Bill of Rights?

   Correct answers include: neutrality, detachment, impartiality.

3. Who does Amendment VI guarantee must participate in a trial on behalf of the person being tried?

   Any witnesses that can be found in the accused's favor, and a lawyer.

4. Why do you think the framers of the Constitution felt they had to include Amendment VIII in the Bill of Rights?

   They wanted to make absolutely sure that people who were arrested did not suffer from

   excessive fines or unfair punishment.

ACTIVITY 1.7 continued

9 After reading the text for the first time, guide the class in a discussion by asking the Making Observations questions. Check students' general comprehension of the documents based on their observations and ask follow-up questions as needed.

10 **RETURNING TO THE TEXT:** Guide students to return to the text and respond to the text-dependent questions. Invite them to work independently to reread the text and answer the questions. Remind them to use text evidence in their responses.

11 Move among the students and examine their answers to the text-dependent questions. If they have difficulty, scaffold the questions by rephrasing them or breaking them into smaller parts. See the Scaffolding the Text-Dependent Questions boxes for suggestions.

12 Use the introductory text to the Author's Purpose section to guide students toward completion of the graphic organizer. Point out that they will be discerning not only the authors' purpose but their audience and message. Add that each amendment has a message of its own, although those messages are linked by their connection to the authors' purpose.

13 Have students complete the Focus on the Sentence task. Work as a class to create the first sentence using the phrase *the Constitution*. As students complete the task, make sure they are correctly constructing sentences with information from the text as well as using correct punctuation. If they are having difficulty creating the sentences, give them access to print or digital media that can help them research the meanings contained in the Preamble.

14 Have students complete the Gaining Perspectives discussion. As students are discussing, be prepared with a list of amendments and their descriptions not mentioned in the activity that they can refer to. Allow pairs to conduct further research if necessary.

⭐ TEACHER TO TEACHER

The next exercise in this activity will be a mock Constitutional Convention. Consider showing students a timeline of the original Constitutional Convention or reading a short article about the event to set the mood for the activity.

15 Read the introduction to the Governing Your Island section as a class and call upon individual students to read and explain each guiding question. Discuss each question as necessary to ensure a common understanding of the nature of each issue to be discussed.

1.7

5. Explain how Amendments IX and X affirm the rights of states and individual citizens.

Amendments IX and X address non-enumerated rights and undelegated powers, affirming that citizens have rights other than those listed and that any power not specifically given to the federal government is reserved to states and citizens.

Author's Purpose

Remember that an author's purpose is the reason that an author or group of authors writes about a specific topic. Nearly all texts are written to either inform, entertain, or explain something to an audience.

Reread the About the Document section at the beginning of this activity, along with the historical documents that follow. Like any text, the Preamble and Bill of Rights can be analyzed in terms of author's purpose, audience, and message. To discern that information, examine the text while applying what you know about the early history of our country. Ask yourself:

- Why did the founders of the United States write and ratify a constitution?
- For whom was the information in the Constitution intended?
- What is the message of each of the Constitution's first 10 amendments?

6. With a partner, complete the following graphic organizer.

The Constitution's Preamble and Bill of Rights	
Author's Purpose: To inform the reader of the inalienable rights of American citizens	
Audience: The U.S. government, the American people, and anyone interested in learning which individual rights the U.S. government preserve and defend.	

Amendment	Message Within the Text
Amendment I	Citizens have the rights to worship, publish, assemble, and protest as they please.
Amendment II	Citizens have the right to bear arms.
Amendment III	Citizens in peacetime do not have to feed or shelter soldiers.
Amendment IV	Government agents cannot search private property without a warrant.
Amendment V	Citizens accused of a crime have the right to due process.
Amendment VI	Citizens accused of a crime have the right to a fair and speedy trial.
Amendment VII	Citizens accused of a crime have the right to a jury trial.
Amendment VIII	Citizens shall not face excessive bail or fines or cruel or unusual punishment.
Amendment IX	Citizens have rights not specifically cited in the Constitution.
Amendment X	Powers not granted to the federal government are reserved to the states and the people.

7. How does the presentation of the Bill of Rights as a list support the author's purpose?

It presents the amendments in a clear, concise way that communicates their content to

the reader.

☑ Focus on the Sentence

Turn the following fragments into complete sentences, using what you know about the Constitution. Use correct punctuation and capitalization.

the Constitution

The Constitution was written to inform readers of the inalienable rights of American citizens.

founders wanted

The founders wanted to establish the government of the United States.

guaranteeing basic rights

The Bill of Rights lists the first ten amendments to the Constitution, guaranteeing basic rights.

Gaining Perspectives

With the creation of the Preamble and the Bill of Rights, citizens of the United States were given certain rights and liberties. The founding fathers were wise enough to know that they could not predict what rights and liberties would need defining as the country grew. Therefore, they created amendments. Adding an amendment to the Constitution is a lengthy process that underscores the importance of the right being added. With a partner, think about the amendments you know of that have not been mentioned in this activity and discuss how these amendments expanded civil rights and liberties. When you are done, present the ideas you discussed with another pair.

Governing Your Island

8. Imagine that on a school trip sailing to a small and remote island, you and all of your classmates become stranded without the ability to communicate with the outside world and with little hope of being rescued in the foreseeable future. The island that you are stranded on can provide the basic necessities of food, water, and shelter, but you must work together to survive. Working in small groups, brainstorm a list of recommendations to consider when developing a new government following these guiding questions:

   - How will you make sure that everyone works toward common goals?
   - How will you make sure that everyone has the opportunity to speak and be heard?
   - How will you make sure that everyone will take part in protecting the island?
   - How will you make sure that resources are used fairly among the people?
   - How will you ensure that all people are free to do what they want as long as others are not hurt?
   - How will you make sure that your rules and laws are protected for future generations?

9. Per directions from your teacher, work with your classmates to participate in a mock Constitutional Convention. Work as a group to establish roles, set goals, and create deadlines.

ACTIVITY 1.7 continued

16 Divide the class into small groups to hold the mock constitutional convention and then follow this suggested procedure:

- A chairperson, a secretary, and a recorder will be selected by a vote of the group. The chairperson manages the convention, maintains order, and allows each member of the group to speak. The secretary takes notes. The recorder writes down the group's decisions.
- Have students consider each guiding question, with each person suggesting a rule to address that particular issue. The secretary will note the question and all suggestions. After a discussion in which every suggestion is fairly considered, students should vote to decide which will become articles of the island's constitution. The recorder will write down the vote results and, in the process, construct a six-item constitution.
- After the activity, the recorder for each group will read that group's constitution to the class. The class will suggest possible amendments.
- Each group will reconvene to debate and vote on suggested amendments. Amendments that pass will be added to the end of the island constitution.

ASSESS

Review student groups' responses to the Governing Your Island section. Make sure that each group has fairly selected a chairperson, a secretary, and a recorder. Check their constitutions to ensure that each question has been adequately and realistically addressed.

ADAPT

If groups need additional help in writing their constitutions, supervise their **brainstorming** and discussion processes. Review the rules with students and guide them through the writing process as needed.

ACTIVITY 1.8

PLAN

Materials: audio recording of Roosevelt's speech
Suggested Pacing: 2 50-minute class periods

TEACH

1 Read the Learning Targets and Preview with students.

2 Ask students to respond to the quickwrite. Record their responses on the board and point out the close connection between the idea of America's promise and that of the American Dream.

Learning Strategies

Marking the Text
OPTIC
Previewing
Think-Pair-Share
SOAPSTone

My Notes

Learning Targets

- Synthesize information presented in two primary sources: an illustration and a speech to create a new understanding about America's promise to new immigrants.
- Cite evidence from multiple texts to define a concept.
- Integrate ideas from multiple texts to build knowledge and vocabulary about what the Statue of Liberty symbolizes.

Preview

In this activity, you will look at an illustration and read a speech that both describe the immigrant experience in the United States of America.

1. **Quickwrite:** Based on what you already know about immigration, how would you define America's promise to immigrants entering the United States?

College and Career Readiness Standards

Focus Standards:

RI.11-12.2 Determine two or more central ideas of a text and analyze their development over the course of the text, including how they interact and build on one another to provide a complex analysis; provide an objective summary of the text.

RI.11-12.1 ite strong and thorough textual evidence to support analysis of what the text says explicitly as well as inferences drawn from the text, including determining where the text leaves matters uncertain.

RI.11-12.7 Integrate and evaluate multiple sources of information presented in different media or formats (e.g., visually, quantitatively) as well as in words in order to address a question or solve a problem.

Additional Standards Addressed:

W.11-12a, W.11-12b, W.11-12c, W.11-12d, W.11-12.8

Introducing the Strategy

OPTIC is an acronym for overview, parts, title, interrelationships, and conclusion. OPTIC is a strategy for analyzing visual texts—including paintings, photographs, advertisements, maps, charts, or graphs—and developing an interpretation regarding the meaning or theme(s) of the text.

2. Spend a few minutes looking closely at the following image. Then complete the table that follows using the OPTIC strategy.

This image was originally printed on July 2, 1887, in *Frank Leslie's Illustrated Newspaper* and is titled "New York—Welcome to the land of freedom—An ocean steamer passing the Statue of Liberty: Scene on the steerage deck / from a sketch by a staff artist."

KNOWLEDGE QUEST

Knowledge Question:
What does the Statue of Liberty symbolize to immigrants coming to America?

In Activity 1.8, you will study a piece of art and read President Franklin D. Roosevelt's address on the anniversary of the Statue of Liberty. While you read and build knowledge about what the Statue of Liberty symbolizes, think about your answer to the Knowledge Question.

My Notes

---

3 Discuss the Knowledge Question. Have students work in small groups to discuss the symbolism of the Statue of Liberty.

4 Introduce students to the OPTIC strategy and apply it to the illustration of the immigrants passing the Statue of Liberty. Model for them how the strategy approaches thinking about a visual source and its caption.

5 Assist students in applying the OPTIC strategy to the illustration. Give them the following guiding questions to support their analysis:

- Why might the date of the source be significant?
- Where is the scene depicted in the illustration taking place?
- What do you see in the illustration?
- What information is contained in the caption?
- What feelings or thoughts do you think people might have looking at the Statue of Liberty for the first time as new arrivals to this country?

6 Once students have completed their graphic organizers, have one or two volunteers share them with the class.

7 Invite students to use the information in their graphic organizers to complete the Focus on the Sentence exercise.

8 Go over the As You Read section with students, making sure they understand what they should be paying attention to and annotating during their first reading of Roosevelt's speech.

O (Overview): Write notes on what the visual appears to be about.	This illustration appears to be of immigrants in the late 1800s arriving in New York Harbor.
P (Parts): Zoom in on the parts of the visual and describe any elements or details that seem important.	Important details include the Statue of Liberty, the continent behind it, and boat passengers (immigrants) looking and pointing at the land.
T (Title): Highlight the words of the title of the visual (if one is available).	The image was originally printed on July 2, 1887 in *Frank Leslie's Illustrated Newspaper* and is titled "New York—Welcome to the land of freedom—An ocean steamer passing the Statue of Liberty: Scene on the steerage deck / from a sketch by a staff artist."
I (Interrelationships): Use the title as the theory and the parts of the visual as clues to detect and specify how the elements of the graphic are related.	The title suggests that the people on the boat are newcomers. The phrase "Welcome to the land of freedom" and the image of the Statue of Liberty suggest that they are arriving in America for the first time. They are dressed like European peasants, which suggests they have little material wealth.
C (Conclusion); Draw a conclusion about the visual as a whole. What does the visual mean? Summarize the message of the visual in one or two sentences.	The illustration shows European immigrants arriving in New York. They have been drawn by the promise of a new and better life.

☑ Focus on the Sentence

Use your OPTIC analysis of the illustration to answer the questions that follow. Then use what you know about ordering clauses to expand the kernel sentence into an informative caption.

Kernel: An ocean steamer carries immigrants

When? On July 2, 1887

Where? Past the Statue of Liberty

Why? So they can begin new lives in America

Expanded Sentence: On July 2, 1887, an ocean steamer carries immigrants past the Statue of Liberty on their way to new lives in America.

As You Read

- Underline phrases that help you create mental images about America.
- Highlight phrases that describe the immigrants Roosevelt is referring to.
- Circle unknown words and phrases. Try to determine the meaning of the words by using context clues, word parts, or a dictionary.

About the Author

Franklin Delano Roosevelt (1882–1945) was president of the United States from 1933 to 1945. FDR, as he is commonly called, replaced one-term president Herbert Hoover, who had become very unpopular due to his inadequate response to the Great Depression. Roosevelt made the economy his top priority, pushing through a set of economic reforms called the "New Deal." The economy improved somewhat, but the Depression did not end until the United States joined World War II in 1941. The following excerpt is from a speech FDR gave commemorating the fiftieth anniversary of the Statue of Liberty.

Speech

Address on the Occasion of the Fiftieth Anniversary of the Statue of Liberty,

October 28, 1936

by President Franklin D. Roosevelt

1   " … It is the memory of all these eager seeking millions that makes this one of America's places of great romance. Looking down this great harbor I like to think of the countless numbers of inbound vessels that have made this port. I like to think of the men and women who, with the break of dawn off Sandy Hook, have **strained** their eyes to the west for a first glimpse of the New World.

2   They came to us—most of them—in **steerage**. But they, in their humble quarters, saw things in these strange horizons which were denied to the eyes of those few who traveled in greater luxury.

3   They came to us speaking many tongues—but a single language, the universal language of human aspiration.

4   How well their hopes were justified is proved by the record of what they achieved. They not only found freedom in the New World, but by their effort and **devotion**, they made the New World's freedom safer, richer, more far-reaching, more capable of growth.

5   Within this present generation, that stream from abroad has largely stopped. We have within our shores today the materials out of which we shall continue to build an even better home for liberty.

6   We take satisfaction in the thought that those who have left their native land to join us may still **retain** here their **affection** for some things left behind—old customs, old language, old friends. Looking to the future, they wisely choose that their children shall live in the new language and in the new

 KNOWLEDGE QUEST

What does the Statue of Liberty symbolize to immigrants coming to America?

GRAMMAR & USAGE

Placement of Modifiers

Writers are careful to place phrases as near as possible to the words they modify, especially when they are writing complex sentences with multiple-word modifiers. In this sentence from Roosevelt's speech, it's clear that the underlined phrase modifies *I*: "<u>Looking down this great harbor</u> I like to think of the countless numbers of inbound vessels that have made this port." Roosevelt is looking down into the harbor.

Look for other descriptive phrases in the speech and make sure you understand what is being modified in each case.

strained: used intense effort
steerage: section of a ship for low-fare passengers
devotion: loyalty, strong attachment
retain: continue to have
affection: fondness, liking

ACTIVITY 1.8 continued

9 Have students read the About the Author section, circling any unfamiliar words they encounter. Model ways to determine the meanings of these words, whether through the use of context clues, word parts, or dictionaries.

10 Review the Grammar & Usage feature with students. Read aloud the text and follow its directions to help acquaint or reacquaint students with the importance of modifier placement.

11 FIRST READ: Conduct a small-group reading of "Address on the Occasion of the Fiftieth Anniversary of the Statue of Liberty, October 28, 1936" by President Franklin D. Roosevelt. Pause after paragraph 5 to help students understand that Roosevelt begins his speech by describing a period that had recently ended at the time of his speech.

TEXT COMPLEXITY

Overall: Complex
Lexile: 1260L
Qualitative: Moderate Difficulty
Task: Moderate (Analyze)

12 As students are reading, monitor their progress. Be sure they are engaged with the text and annotating words and phrases that describe America and the immigrants Roosevelt is referring to. Evaluate whether the small-group reading mode is effective.

Scaffolding the Text-Dependent Questions

1. **In paragraph 3, what does Roosevelt mean by** *universal* **when he refers to "the universal language of human aspiration"?** How can language be universal? What common aspirations do people share? RI.11-12.4

2. **Summarize Roosevelt's description of the Statue of Liberty's significance in the first five** paragraphs of his speech. **What has prompted his oratory on this occasion?** Look for repeated words and phrases in paragraphs 1–5. What does Roosevelt "like to think of"? What images does he evoke? What do they suggest about his opinion of the Statue of Liberty's significance? RI.11-12.1

13 Tell students to pause at the end of paragraph 7. Prompt them to share the images that come to mind as they read.

14 **Vocabulary Development:** At the end of paragraph 12, highlight the Words Connections box. Select a few compelling words from the text, such as *melting pot*, and ask students about the author's possible intent for using them. Elicit other words that the author could have used.

15 Tell students to pause at the end of paragraph 13 and describe connections between Roosevelt's speech and the image of arriving immigrants and the Statue of Liberty they analyzed earlier in the activity.

16 After reading the text for the first time, guide the class in a discussion by asking the Knowledge Quest questions. Evaluate students' comprehension of the text based on their observations and ask follow-up questions or prompt them to reread sections of the speech if needed. Continue your discussion of the Statue of Liberty. Ask students about their impressions of the landmark after reading Roosevelt's speech.

1.8

WORD CONNECTIONS

Content Connections
Historically, the term **melting pot** referred to the viewpoint that the immigrants who came to the United States from many countries and cultures would combine, or melt, into one American people and culture.

The term can be traced back to 1782, but a 1908 play called *The Melting Pot* popularized it. The playwright, Israel Zangwill, was a Jewish immigrant from Great Britain.

destiny: an experience in the future

customs of this new people. And those children more and more realize their common **destiny** in America. That is true whether their forebears came past this place eight generations ago or only one.

7 The realization that we are all bound together by hope of a common future rather than by reverence for a common past has helped us to build upon this continent a unity unapproached in any similar area or population in the whole world. For all our millions of square miles, for all our millions of people, there is a unity in language and speech, in law and in economics, in education and in general purpose, which nowhere finds its match.

8 It was the hope of those who gave us this Statue and the hope of the American people in receiving it that the Goddess of Liberty and the Goddess of Peace were the same.

9 The grandfather of my old friend the French Ambassador and those who helped him make this gift possible, were citizens of a great sister Republic established on the principle of the democratic form of government. Citizens of all democracies unite in their desire for peace. Grover Cleveland recognized that unity of purpose on this spot fifty years ago.

10 He suggested that liberty enlightening the world would extend her rays from these shores to every other Nation.

11 Today that symbolism should be broadened. To the message of liberty which America sends to all the world must be added her message of peace.

12 Even in times as troubled and uncertain as these, I still hold to the faith that a better civilization than any we have known is in store for America and by our example, perhaps, for the world. Here destiny seems to have taken a long look. Into this continental reservoir there has been poured untold and untapped wealth of human resources. Out of that reservoir, out of the melting pot, the rich promise which the New World held out to those who came to it from many lands is finding fulfillment.

13 The richness of the promise has not run out. If we keep the faith for our day as those who came before us kept the faith for theirs, then you and I can smile with confidence into the future. It is fitting therefore, that this should be a service of rededication, rededication to the liberty and the peace which this statue symbolizes.

⊘ Knowledge Quest
- What emotions did you feel reading this speech?
- What details about Roosevelt's speech stand out to you?

Scaffolding the Text-Dependent Questions

3. Reread paragraph 7. What does Roosevelt believe binds Americans together? What does he cite as evidence for that assertion? Scan paragraph 7 for the words *together, common, millions,* and *unity*. What commonalities does Roosevelt see among the millions of Americans? What hope do they share?
RI.11-12.1

4. In paragraph 11, how does Roosevelt describe the Statue of Liberty's symbolism?

Reread paragraphs 2, 3, and 4. What does Roosevelt feel was symbolized by the Statue of Liberty in its earliest days? What does he say in paragraph 5 became different over time? What does he say about the Statue in paragraph 8? What conclusion does he draw in paragraph 11 as to how the Statue's symbolism has changed?
RI.11-12.4

Returning to the Text

- Return to the speech as you respond to the following questions. Use text evidence to support your responses.
- Write any additional questions you have about the text in your Reader/Writer Notebook.

1. **KQ** In paragraph 3, what does Roosevelt mean by *universal* when he refers to "the universal language of human aspiration"?

   Here Roosevelt discusses the fact that although people arrive in America speaking many

   different languages, they share a common or universal aspiration about the promise of

   freedom that transcends individual languages. By *universal*, he means that it is an aspiration

   understood and shared by many.

2. Summarize Roosevelt's description of the Statue of Liberty's significance in the first five paragraphs of his speech. What has prompted his oratory on this occasion?

   He describes the statue as a symbol of freedom for immigrants who spoke "the language of

   aspiration" in years past. He goes on to say that the statue remains significant even though

   immigration has dwindled because it represents the "materials" out of which "an even better

   home for liberty" can be built. His oratory is prompted by the 50th anniversary of the Statue of

   Liberty.

3. Reread paragraph 7. What does Roosevelt believe binds Americans together? What does he cite as evidence for that assertion?

   Roosevelt asserts that Americans are bound together by the hope of a common future. He

   cites a national unity of language, law, economics, and general purpose that he proclaims is

   unparalleled.

4. In paragraph 11, how does Roosevelt describe the Statue of Liberty's symbolism?

   He says that it has broadened, expanding from representing only liberty to representing both

   liberty and peace.

5. What imagery does Roosevelt use in paragraph 12 of his speech? What does it mean?

   Roosevelt uses the image of a "continental reservoir" to evoke the idea of an untapped

   supply of human talent and ability that is available to help America become freer and more

   prosperous. He uses the term synonymously with "melting pot," an image evoking the idea

   that people from around the world with a variety of talents and abilities are pooling their

   strengths to contribute to a strong America.

17 RETURNING TO THE TEXT: Guide students to return to the text to respond to the text-dependent questions. Have students work in pairs or small groups to reread the text and respond to the questions. Remind them to use evidence in their responses.

18 Move from group to group and listen in as students answer the text-dependent questions. If they have difficulty, scaffold the questions by rephrasing them or breaking them into smaller parts. See the Scaffolding the Text-Dependent Questions boxes for suggestions.

Scaffolding the Text-Dependent Questions

5. What imagery does Roosevelt use in paragraph 12 of his speech? What does it mean? Reread paragraph 12. How does Roosevelt describe the current national situation? What forces does he believe will change that situation for the better? What images does he evoke to describe those forces? How are those images related? RI.11-12.4

6. What comparison does Roosevelt make as he concludes his speech? What is his point in doing so? Examine what Roosevelt says about faith in paragraphs 12 and 13. How does he describe the faith of past, present, and future Americans? What does he conclude from his analysis of that description? RI.11-12.1

7. How does Roosevelt's speech convey what the Statue of Liberty symbolizes? What message is he trying to send? Why does he believe the Statue of Liberty is an important symbol? RI.11-12.1

19 Guide students to return to the Knowledge Quest question they discussed before reading. Ask students how their response to this question has changed or been deepened after viewing the artwork and reading Roosevelt's speech. Then arrange students in small groups to read the instructions for the Knowledge Quest activity. Ask volunteers for examples of discussion rules and role-play applying them with one group. Then model posing and responding to questions and ideas. Circulate to help facilitate collegial discussions.

20 Encourage students to continue building knowledge on this topic as suggested in the Independent Reading Link.

6. What comparison does Roosevelt make as he concludes his speech? What is his point in doing so?

He compares the faith of past Americans—immigrants in particular—with the faith of those in the present. His point is that if the faith that has gotten the nation this far can be maintained, a future of liberty and peace is in store.

7. **KQ** How does Roosevelt's speech convey what the Statue of Liberty symbolizes?

Roosevelt's speech conveys a message of resilience, hope, and common aspirations that drive immigrants to come to America for the promise of liberty and equality. He believes that that Statue of Liberty is an important symbol of hope for immigrants and that they are united as new Americans by this hope.

 INDEPENDENT READING LINK

Read and Discuss

You can continue to build your knowledge about what the Statue of Liberty symbolizes by reading other articles at ZINC Reading Labs. Search for keywords such as *American Dream* or *American symbols*.

ZINC

Knowledge Quest

Think about the Statue of Liberty. With a small group, discuss what the Statue of Liberty symbolizes to immigrants coming to America. Does the Statue of Liberty symbolize the same things for someone born in the United States? Be sure to:

- Set rules with your classmates to facilitate a collegial discussion of the topic.
- Ask and respond to questions to broaden the discussion, connect ideas, and draw others in to the conversation.
- Respond thoughtfully to the various perspectives that classmates offer and summarize points of agreement and disagreement.

1.8

Working from the Text

Introducing the Strategy

SOAPSTone stands for Speaker, Occasion, Audience, Purpose, Subject, and Tone. It is a reading and writing tool for analyzing the relationship among a writer, his or her purpose, and the target audience of the text. SOAPSTone guides you in asking questions to analyze a text or to plan for writing a composition.

- **Speaker:** The speaker is the voice that tells the story.
- **Occasion:** The occasion is the time and place of the story; it is the context that prompted the writing.
- **Audience:** The audience is the person or persons to whom the piece is directed.
- **Purpose:** The purpose is the reason behind the text or what the writer wants the audience to think as a result of reading the text.
- **Subject:** The subject is the focus of the text.
- **Tone:** Tone is the speaker's attitude toward the subject.

8. Complete a SOAPSTone graphic organizer to analyze President Franklin D. Roosevelt's speech given to celebrate the 50th anniversary of the Statue of Liberty.

☑ Focus on the Sentence

Use your SOAPSTone analysis of Roosevelt's speech to compose fragments that name each part of that analysis. Then combine those fragments into a one- or two-sentence summary of the speech.

Speaker: President Franklin D. Roosevelt

Occasion: October 28, 1936—the 50th anniversary of the Statue of Liberty

Audience: a crowd of citizens and radio listeners

Purpose: To rededicate the Statue of Liberty

Subject: the history and significance of the statue

Tone: inspirational and optimistic

Summary: On October 28, 1936, President Franklin D. Roosevelt gave an inspirational and optimistic address to a crowd of citizens and a radio audience. He rededicated the Statue of Liberty on the occasion of its 50th anniversary, citing its history and significance.

ACTIVITY 1.8 continued

21 Form student pairs and ask them to work through the Working from the Text activity by using the **SOAPSTone** strategy. Read aloud the text in the Introducing the Strategy box, clarifying the information as needed. Have student pairs use the strategy to create graphic organizers analyzing President Roosevelt's speech. Then have them use those organizers to complete the Focus on the Sentence activity individually.

22 Read aloud the instructions for the Synthesizing Information section and have students complete the four sentences in the section using their notes from their OPTIC and SOAPSTone analyses.

23 Give students time to respond to the Writing Prompt. Consider allowing them to work in pairs to develop their essays.

ASSESS

In reviewing students' informational essays, look for a meaningful use of definition strategies that support a definition of America's promise. Essays should draw explicitly upon the illustration and speech text and indicate an adequate understanding and thoughtful application of the strategies.

ADAPT

If students need additional help responding to the Writing Prompt, have them revisit their analysis of the illustration and what can be inferred from it as pertains to the hopes of the incoming immigrants. Then have them **skim** Roosevelt's speech and reread and examine in particular its final two paragraphs to consider his views on the promise of America. If necessary, remind them what they learned about text fluency and definition strategies earlier in this unit.

To extend the ability to employ the writing requirements of the Writing Prompt, invite students to work in small groups as editing boards to review the essays and make editing suggestions about the definition, supporting relevant details, and potential transitions that could be included between points and the concluding statement of their essays.

Synthesizing Information

Review the notes you made using your OPTIC and SOAPSTone analyses of the illustration and speech. Consider how the image and speech both present a view of America's promise. Then synthesize the information from both sources, using and combining ideas from each one, to complete the following sentences.

9. In both the speech and the illustration, immigration is presented as

   a positive factor in building and preserving a prosperous way of life for both citizens and

   newcomers.

10. In the speech and the illustration, the Statue of Liberty symbolizes a promise to new Americans of

    an opportunity to be part of a system in which they can better their own lives while making the

    United States a stronger, freer society.

11. The illustration connects to Roosevelt's reference to a "melting pot" by

    providing an image of the immigrants who were part of that "melting pot".

12. Roosevelt's references to the "Goddess of Liberty" and the "Goddess of Peace" are relevant to the illustration because

    they are names he uses for the Statue of Liberty, which overlooks the immigrants in the

    illustration.

> **Writing Prompt: Informational**
>
> Write a short essay that draws on details in both the illustration and the speech to create a definition of America's promise. Use definition strategies that will help you support your thesis. Be sure to:
>
> - Begin with a clear thesis that defines the promise of America.
> - Use the most significant and relevant details from the illustration and the speech to support your thesis on what that promise means.
> - Include rhetorical strategies that help support your definition.
> - Include transitions between points and a concluding statement that ties together your essay.

 WRITING PROMPT: INFORMATIONAL

The following standards are addressed in the writing prompt:
- W.11-12.2a
- W.11-12.2a, W.11-12.8
- W.11-12.2d
- W.11-12.2c

Learning Targets

- Place phrases and clauses correctly in sentences.
- Recognize and correct misplaced and dangling modifiers.

Preview

In this activity, you will learn about how to place phrases and clauses correctly in sentences and correct misplaced and dangling modifiers in your writing.

Placing Modifiers Correctly

Part of being an effective writer is placing modifiers so that your meaning is clear and knowing how to revise misplaced and dangling modifiers.

A **modifier** is a word, phrase, or clause that makes the meaning of another word or word group more specific. For example, the boldfaced words and word groups in the following phrases are all modifiers:

> an **immense** statue
>
> the statue **in New York Harbor**
>
> a statue **that symbolizes freedom**

Modifiers should be placed near the word or word group they modify. A **misplaced modifier** can create confusion or accidental humor.

Modifier placement is particularly important in speeches, when the audience is listening and can't reread to figure out the speaker's meaning. For example, in the speech "Address on the Occasion of the Fiftieth Anniversary of the Statue of Liberty," President Franklin D. Roosevelt says this.

> We have **within our shores** today the materials out of which we shall continue to build an even better home for liberty.

Notice that Roosevelt places the modifying adverb phrase *within our shores* and the adverb *today* directly after the verb *have*.

1. Read the following sentences and underline the misplaced modifiers. Then rewrite the sentence, placing the modifier correctly. The first one has been done for you.

   a. Franklin Delano Roosevelt was the 32nd president of the United States, who was a fifth <u>cousin of President Theodore Roosevelt</u>.

   Franklin Delano Roosevelt, who was a fifth cousin of President Theodore Roosevelt, was the 32nd president of the United States.

College and Career Readiness Standards

Focus Standards:

W.11-12.5 Develop and strengthen writing as needed by planning, revising, editing, rewriting, or trying a new approach, focusing on addressing what is most significant for a specific purpose and audience.

PLAN

Materials: definition essays drafted by students in Activity 1.8
Suggested Pacing: 1 50-minute class period

TEACH

1 Introduce the topic of placing and using modifiers correctly by writing this sentence on the board: *When they are misplaced, readers may have trouble understanding the intended meaning of modifiers.*

2 Ask students what is confusing or humorous about the sentence. Underline the clause *When they are misplaced.* Elicit from students or explain that this clause seems to modify *readers* rather than *modifiers.* Show them that the sentence can be improved by moving the modifying clause to directly follow *modifiers.*

3 Briefly review with students the definition of *modifier* and the examples of modifying words, phrases, and clauses.

4 Have students silently read the instruction preceding student step 1.

5 Ask a student to read aloud the original sentence in student step 1a. Then have another student read aloud the sentence's corrected version. Make sure students understand the difference between the two versions.

6 Allow students to complete student steps 1b, 1c, and 1d. If time permits, have them **think-pair-share** their answers.

7 Have students complete student step 2. Review answers with students.

8 Have students silently read the Correcting Dangling Modifiers section and then complete student step 3. Review answers with students.

 TEACHER TO TEACHER

Students often have more difficulty with identifying and correcting dangling modifiers than with identifying and correcting misplaced ones. If necessary, explain that if students have trouble revising a sentence with dangling modifiers, it may be because information is missing from the sentence. Also point out that a sentence may need substantial revision if it has a dangling modifier, while a sentence with a misplaced modifier usually needs only a simple word rearrangement.

SAT® CONNECTIONS

This activity provides practice with this important SAT skill: recognizing and correcting misplaced and dangling modifiers.

LC 1.8

b. We read about First Lady Eleanor Roosevelt's work championing human rights <u>during our social studies class</u>.

> During our social studies class, we read about First Lady Eleanor Roosevelt's work championing human rights.

c. I wonder how immigrants on ships in New York Harbor <u>passing the Statue of Liberty felt when they saw the statue</u>.

> I wonder how immigrants on ships passing the Statue of Liberty in New York Harbor felt when they saw the statue.

d. "The New Colossus," a famous poem, is inscribed on a plaque inside the base of the statue <u>by Emma Lazarus</u>.

> "The New Colossus," a famous poem by Emma Lazarus, is inscribed on a plaque inside the base of the statue.

2. Revisit each of the sentences you just revised. Pick two and describe what the original sentence literally meant.

> Possible answers: Original sentence 'b' suggests that First Lady Eleanor Roosevelt did her human rights work during the speaker's social studies class. Original sentence 'c' suggests that the ships, not the immigrants, were the ones that had feelings. Original sentence 'd' suggests that Emma Lazarus created the statue, not the poem.

Correcting Dangling Modifiers

A modifier that does not clearly modify any word or word group in a sentence is a **dangling modifier**. While you usually can correct a misplaced modifier by rearranging the sentence, in the case of a dangling modifier, you may need to add or replace words to clarify your meaning.

Dangling: After reading the speech, a discussion took place.

In this example, the phrase does not clearly modify anything in the sentence. After all, the discussion did not read the speech.

Revised: After reading the speech, we discussed it.

Now, the phrase modifies *we*.

Dangling: Holding her torch for more than 120 years now, we marvel at the sculptor's achievement.

The phrase seems to modify *we*, but that doesn't make sense.

Revised: The statue has been holding her torch for more than 120 years now, and we marvel at the sculptor's achievement.

Adding words to the modifier and following the comma with and has clarified the sentence's meaning.

3. Read the following sentences and underline the dangling modifiers. Then rewrite each sentence to make it clear.

a. <u>Listening to the speech</u>, eyes filled with tears, and hearts filled with hope.

Listening to the speech, the crowd sat with eyes filled with tears and hearts filled with hope.

b. <u>Studying the statue</u>, it was surprising to learn that it was engineered by Gustave Eiffel, who also designed the Eiffel Tower.

While studying the statue, I was surprised to learn that it was designed by Gustave Eiffel, who also designed the Eiffel Tower.

c. Weary from the long voyage, the boat pulled into the harbor.

Weary from the long voyage, the passengers watched the boat pull into the harbor.

9 Move to the Revising section and remind students that checking for correct use and placement of modifiers is an important step when revising their writing. Have them read the paragraph and revise it to correct misplaced and dangling modifiers. Review answers with students, eliciting and discussing students' different revision choices.

10 Make sure that students' markup shows that they understand how to place modifiers so that they are used clearly and sensibly.

11 Have students return to their Definition Essay from Activity 1.8 to check for correct use and placement of modifiers.

ASSESS

Look for responses to the Check Your Understanding task that show that students understand how to use modifiers clearly. Additionally, look for Editor's Checklist responses that include questions such as the following: *Does this modifier tell more about something named in the sentence? Is this modifier in the right place? (Is it near the word I want to make more specific? Does it add meaning to the sentence in the way I intended?)*

ADAPT

If students need additional practice, provide or have students write sentences that include humorously misplaced and dangling modifiers. If you provide the sentences, have students work in pairs to correct the sentences. If students write the sentences, have them pair up after they have finished writing. Ask students to trade sentences with their partners and correct the sentences as needed.

Revising

Read the paragraph from a student's essay about the Statue of Liberty. Work with a partner to check whether modifiers are placed correctly and whether each clearly modifies a word or word group. Underline any mistakes you notice and rewrite the paragraph, correcting the mistakes. Not all sentences include errors.

[1] Wanting to honor the abolition of slavery and to celebrate liberty, the statue was first envisioned in 1865 by Edouard de Laboulaye. [2] His friend, the sculptor Frederic Bartholdi, helped make Laboulaye's vision a reality. [3] French citizens and U.S. citizens donated to help pay for the immense sculpture who loved the idea of commemorating the friendship between their countries. [4] Taking years to complete the work, the statue would eventually stand over 151 feet high. [5] Like a beacon of hope, we appreciate how immigrants must have felt as they crossed New York Harbor.

[1] Wanting to honor the abolition of slavery and to celebrate liberty, Edouard de Laboulaye first envisioned the statue in 1865. [2] His friend, the sculptor Frederic Bartholdi, helped make Laboulaye's vision a reality. [3] French citizens and U.S. citizens who loved the idea of commemorating the friendship between their countries donated to help pay for the immense sculpture. [4] Taking years to complete the work, the sculptor and builders eventually finished the statue, which stands over 151 feet high. [5] We appreciate how immigrants must have felt as they crossed New York Harbor and saw that statue, standing like a beacon of hope.

☑ Check Your Understanding

Imagine you are editing a classmate's writing and you notice these sentences:

Astonished, our studies showed that the 225-ton statue was built in France. The pieces were packed into hundreds of boxes to be assembled by workers delivered by ship.

In your own words, write an explanation so that your classmate understands the mistakes and how to correct them. Then add a question to your Editor's Checklist to remind yourself to check for correct use and placement of modifiers.

The word *astonished* is a dangling modifier because it does not modify anything in the sentence; the studies cannot be astonished. The first sentence should be revised so that *astonished* modifies another word or word group. Also, the workers are not *delivered by ship*, so the second sentence should be revised to show that the boxes were *delivered by ship*.

Practice

Return to the essay you wrote in Activity 1.3 and check it for correct use and placement of modifiers. Work with a partner to follow these steps:

a. Underline any modifying words, phrases, and clauses.

b. Check for correct placement and use of modifiers.

c. Rewrite sentences to correct any misplaced or dangling modifiers.

Defining an American

Learning Targets

- Analyze how authors use definition strategies to support their thesis.
- Summarize text clearly and accurately.
- Use brainstorming and collaboration to plan a definition essay.

Preview

In this activity, you will read a letter that explores what it meant to be American when the country was newly formed.

Beginning a Definition

What does it mean to be an American? What makes Americans unique? What characteristics or traits do Americans share? With a partner, review the texts and images you have read in this unit to create a vocabulary tree in your Reader/Writer Notebook. Use your tree to keep track of the multiple aspects of a definition of an American. As you continue through the first part of this unit, add details and examples to your tree.

As You Read

- Underline words and phrases you could add to your vocabulary tree.
- After reading each paragraph, jot down what you think the key idea is based on the details in the margin.
- Circle unknown words and phrases. Try to determine the meaning of the words by using context clues, word parts, or a dictionary.

About the Author

J. Hector St. John de Crèvecoeur (1735–1813) was born in France about 40 years before the American Revolution. He lived in New York during the Revolution and was jailed by the British for his support of colonial independence. Upon his release, he returned to France and wrote the highly successful *Letters from an American Farmer,* a work of fiction that he eventually expanded into a three-volume set. His writing is noted for its charm and optimism, and he is credited with coining the term *melting pot* as a description of American culture.

Learning Strategies

Brainstorming
Summarizing

My Notes

_____
_____
_____
_____
_____
_____
_____
_____
_____
_____
_____
_____
_____
_____
_____
_____
_____
_____
_____
_____
_____
_____
_____
_____
_____
_____
_____
_____
_____
_____
_____
_____
_____

PLAN

Materials: 11 x 17" or larger paper for each student or access to computers
Suggested Pacing: 2 50-minute class periods

TEACH

1 Read the Learning Targets and Preview with students.

2 Read aloud the Beginning a Definition section. Have students reflect on the questions with a partner in a **think-pair-share.** Then instruct students to create a vocabulary word tree with details and images that they associate with the word *American.* Have students share their entries with the class and add to the word tree as appropriate.

★ TEACHER TO TEACHER

Make sure to have students use a large enough piece of paper for this initial brainstorm. They will be asked to review and to add to their thinking throughout the rest of the unit. To help students begin brainstorming, you might construct a list of the texts read so far and how these texts presented what it is to be an American.

3 Have students consider the As You Read section. Make sure they understand what they should pay attention to what and how they should annotate during their first reading of the letter.

4 Read aloud the About the Author section. Prompt students to speculate as to why it was a foreign-born writer who coined the term *melting pot* to describe America.

College and Career Readiness Standards

Focus Standards:

RI.11-12.1 Cite strong and thorough textual evidence to support analysis of what the text says explicitly as well as inferences drawn from the text, including determining where the text leaves matters uncertain.

RI.11-12.2 Determine two or more central ideas of a text and analyze their development over the course of the text, including how they interact and build on one another to provide a complex analysis; provide an objective summary of the text.

Additional Standards Addressed:

L.11-12.4a, L.11-12.4c

5 **FIRST READ:** Conduct a shared reading of "What Is an American?" Pause after paragraph 1 to discuss how the author contrasts America with French-owned Canada.

TEXT COMPLEXITY

Overall: Very Complex
Lexile: 980L
Qualitative: High Difficulty
Task: Moderate (Analyze)

6 As you continue to read the letter from de Crèvecoeur, instruct students to diffuse words, phrases, or concepts that they do not understand. If diffusing is a new strategy for students, direct them to the strategies list in the back of the Student Edition and model the strategy after reading a few sentences of the letter.

1.9

My Notes

Letter

What Is an American?

from *Letters from an American Farmer (1781)*

by J. Hector St. John de Crèvecoeur

1   In this great American asylum, the poor of Europe have by some means met together, and in consequence of various causes; to what purpose, should they ask one another, what countrymen they are? Alas, two thirds of them had no country. Can a wretch who wanders about, who works and starves, whose life is a continual scene of sore affliction or pinching **penury**; can that man call England or any other kingdom his country? A country that had no bread for him, whose fields **procured** him no harvest, who met with nothing but the frowns of the rich, the severity of the laws, with jails and punishments; who owned not a single foot of the extensive surface of this planet? No! Urged by a variety of **motives**, here they came. Every thing has tended to regenerate them; new laws, a new mode of living, a new social system; here they are become men: in Europe they were as so many useless plants, wanting vegetative mould, and refreshing showers; they withered, and were mowed down by want, hunger, and war: but now, by the power of transplantation, like all other plants, they have taken root and flourished! Formerly they were not numbered in any civil list of their country, except in those of the poor; here they rank as citizens. By what invisible power has this surprising **metamorphosis** been performed? By that of the laws, and that of their industry. The laws, the indulgent laws, protect them as they arrive, stamping on them the symbol of adoption; they receive ample rewards for their labours; these accumulated rewards procure them lands; those lands confer on them the title of freemen; and to that title every benefit is affixed which men can possibly require. This is the great operation daily performed by our laws. From whence proceed these laws? From our government. Whence that government? It is derived from the original genius and strong desire of the people ratified and confirmed by government. This

penury: extreme poverty
procured: gained
motives: reasons
metamorphosis: change

Scaffolding the Text-Dependent Questions

1. In paragraph 1, what opinion does the author express about a poor "countryman's" place in Europe versus his place in America? Reread paragraph 1. How does the author portray the life of a poor Englishman? How does the author portray the life of a poor American? What relationship does the author say that a poor American has to his government? RI.11-12.1

2. Use print or digital resources to determine possible meanings of the word *asylum.* **List those meanings and then use context clues to determine which meaning applies to the word in the first sentence of paragraph 1.** Use a print or digital resource to find possible meanings of *asylum.* Which of those meanings fits the context of the first sentence of paragraph 1? L.11-12.4c is the great chain which links us all, this is the picture which every **province** exhibits, Nova Scotia excepted. There the crown has done all; either there were no people who had genius, or it was not much attended to: the consequence is, that the province is very thinly inhabited indeed; the power of the crown, in conjunction with the musketos, has prevented men from settling there. Yet some part of it flourished once, and it contained a mild harmless set of people. But for the fault of a few leaders the whole were banished. The greatest political error the crown ever committed in America, was to cut off men from a country which wanted nothing but men!

2 What attachment can a poor European **emigrant** have for a country where he had nothing? The knowledge of the language, the love of a few kindred as poor as himself, were the only cords that tied him: his country is now that which gives him land, bread, protection, and consequence: Ubi panis ibi patria,1 is the motto of all emigrants. What then is the American, this new man? He is either an European, or the descendant of an European; hence that strange mixture of blood, which you will find in no other country. I could point out to you a man, whose grandfather was an Englishman, whose wife was Dutch, whose son married a French woman, and whose present four sons have now four wives of different nations. He is an American, who, leaving behind him all his ancient prejudices and manners, receives new ones from the new mode of life he has embraced, the new government he obeys, and the new rank he holds. He becomes an American by being received in the broad lap of our great Alma Mater.

3 Here individuals of all nations are melted into a new race of men, whose labours and posterity will one day cause great change in the world. Americans are the western pilgrims, who are carrying along with them that great mass of arts, sciences, vigour, and industry, which began long since in the East; they will finish the great circle. The Americans were once scattered all over Europe; here they are incorporated into one of the finest systems of population which has ever appeared, and which will hereafter become distinct by the power of the different climates they inhabit. The American ought, therefore, to love this country much better than that wherein either he or his forefathers were born. Here the rewards of his industry follow with equal steps the progress of his labour; his labour is founded on the basis of nature, self-interest, can it want a stronger allurement? Wives and children, who before in vain demanded of him a morsel of bread, now, fat and frolicsome, gladly help their father to clear those fields whence exuberant crops are to arise to feed and to clothe them all; without any part being claimed, either by a **despotic** prince, a rich **abbot**, or a mighty lord. Here religion demands but little of him; a small voluntary salary to the minister, and gratitude to God; can he refuse these? The American is a new man, who acts upon new principles; he must therefore entertain new ideas, and form new opinions. From involuntary idleness, servile dependence, penury, and useless labour, he has passed to toils of a very different nature, rewarded by ample **subsistence**. This is an American.

1 Where there is bread there is my country.

My Notes

province: part of a country
emigrant: a person leaving his homeland
despotic: authoritarian, oppressive
abbot: head of a monastery
subsistence: livelihood, earnings

ACTIVITY 1.9 continued

7 Point to the rhetorical question at the beginning of paragraph 2. Remind students that authors pose rhetorical questions for effect rather than to obtain an answer. Then read the question aloud and have students state its intended answer. Ask them how they can tell.

8 Tell students to pause after paragraph 3. Ask them to explain in their own words what de Crèvecoeur feels defines an American.

9 After reading the text for the first time, guide the class in a discussion by asking the Making Observations questions. Check students' general comprehension of the text based on their observations, asking follow-up questions if needed.

Scaffolding the Text-Dependent Questions

3. **What does the word *kindred* mean in paragraph 2? What point is the author making with its use?** Locate the word *kindred* in paragraph 2. Look for words in the same sentence and nearby that can help you determine the word's meaning. What smaller word inside *kindred* provides a clue? L.11-12.4a

4. **Summarize the author's main point in paragraph 2.** Reread paragraph 2. What does the author have to say about the national identity of Americans? What example does he give of the new American man? RI.11-12.1

10 RETURNING TO THE TEXT:
Guide students to return to the text to respond to the text-dependent questions. Invite them to work in small groups to reread the text and answer the questions. Remind them to use text evidence in their responses.

11 Move from group to group and listen in as students answer the text-dependent questions. If they have difficulty, scaffold the questions by rephrasing them or breaking them into smaller parts. See the Scaffolding the Text-Dependent Questions boxes for suggestions.

1.9

Making Observations
- What images come to mind as your read this text?
- What details about an American stayed with you after reading the text?

Returning to the Text
- Return to the letter as you respond to the following questions. Use text evidence to support your responses.
- Write any additional questions you have about the text in your Reader/Writer Notebook.

1. In paragraph 1, what opinion does the author express about a poor "countryman's" place in Europe versus his place in America?

   He portrays the life of a poor European as so miserable that the person would have no cause to consider England or any other nation his country. In contrast, a poor countryman in America is protected, rather than harmed, by the laws. He is given the opportunity to work and paid for his efforts. He is part of the government that rules him.

2. Use print or digital resources to determine possible meanings of the word *asylum*. List those meanings and then use context clues to determine which meaning applies to the word in the first sentence of paragraph 1.

   Possible meanings include "a place of retreat and security; a shelter," "protection and security," "political protection," "a caregiving institution." As used in the first sentence of paragraph 1, the word *asylum* means "a place of retreat and security; a shelter."

3. What does the word *kindred* mean in paragraph 2? What point is the author making with its use?

   As used in paragraph 2, the word *kindred* means "family." The author is pointing out that the poor in Europe have little chance of advancement through the help of a family member because their family members are likely to be as poor as they are.

4. Summarize the author's main point in paragraph 2.

   In paragraph 2, the author explains that America provides a sense of national identity unlike that found anywhere else.

Scaffolding the Text-Dependent Questions

5. What are some attributes that define the "new race of men" as the author describes them in paragraph 3? Reread paragraph 3. Use a print or digital resource to find possible meanings of *race*. Which of those meanings fits the context of the first sentence of paragraph 3? What words does the author use to list and describe the attributes (qualities or characteristics) of this "new race"? L.11-12.4a

6. In paragraph 3, how does the author compare the life of a father before and after moving his wife and children to America? Reread paragraph 3. What is the life of a father like before moving his family to America? What is the life of a father like after moving his family to America? RI.11-12.1

5. What are some attributes that define the "new race of men" as the author describes them in paragraph 3?

The author describes them as proficient in arts and sciences, energetic, adaptable, and

industrious.

6. In paragraph 3, how does the author compare the life of a father before and after moving his wife and children to America?

The author describes fathers in Europe as being unable to feed their starving wives and

children. In America, on the other hand, fathers and their families are well fed and

well clothed, and none of what they earn is taken away by the greedy rich.

12 Instruct students to complete the graphic organizer in the Analyzing the Characteristics and Structural Elements of a Definition Essay section. Revisit the definition of *thesis* and help students find an example of each definition strategy in the text. As needed, guide them toward the indicated paragraphs for examples of the exemplification, negation, function, and classification strategies:

- Exemplification: paragraph 2 ("What then is the American...")
- Negation: paragraph 3 ("...without any part being claimed...")
- Function: paragraph 3 ("Americans are the western pilgrims...")
- Classification: paragraph 2 ("He is either an European...")

1.9

Analyzing the Characteristics and Structural Elements of a Definition Essay

7. With a partner, use the chart to record specific evidence of the thesis, definition strategies, and conclusion from de Crèvecoeur's text. Discuss how each contributes to your understanding of de Crèvecoeur's definition of an American.

Characteristic of Definition Essay	Examples from "What Is an American?" by J. Hector St. John de Crèvecoeur
Thesis	"He is an American, who, leaving behind him all his ancient prejudices and manners, receives new ones from the new mode of life he has embraced, the new government he obeys, and the new rank he holds."
Exemplification	"What then is the American, this new man? He is either an European, or the descendant of an European; hence that strange mixture of blood, which you will find in no other country. I could point out to you a man, whose grandfather was an Englishman, whose wife was Dutch, whose son married a French woman, and whose present four sons have now four wives of different nations."
Negation	"... without any part being claimed, either by a despotic prince, a rich abbot, or a mighty lord."
Function	Americans ... are carrying along with them that great mass of arts, sciences, vigour, and industry, which began long since in the East; they will finish the great circle."
Classification	"He is either an European, or the descendant of an European; hence that strange mixture of blood, which you will find in no other country."
Conclusion	"The American is a new man, who acts upon new principles; he must therefore entertain new ideas, and form new opinions."

Writing Prompt: Informational

Write a short summary of de Crèvecoeur's definition of an American using details from his letter to support your summary. Be sure to:

- Include a clear statement of de Crèvecoeur's main idea.
- Provide an objective summary of his thinking, following his organization but stating his points in your own words.
- Include at least one quote with original commentary. Punctuate the quote correctly.

📦 **INDEPENDENT READING LINK**

Read and Research

In this unit and perhaps in your independent reading, you discovered how the idea and experience of the American Dream changed lives. Extend what you learned by researching the subject of your independent reading to find out what happened later in his or her life. Did the author or subject's view of the American Dream change? If so, how? Share your findings with a partner.

ACTIVITY 1.9 continued

13 Give students time to respond to the Writing Prompt. Consider allowing them to work in pairs to develop their summaries.

14 Draw students' attention to the Independent Reading Link. Direct them to write a description in their Reader/Writer Notebook of how the experience of the American Dream changed a life. When the writing is complete, have each student share what he or she has written with a classmate. To assess their independent reading, set a date to check for the description in students' notebooks.

ASSESS

Review students' writing to determine that they were able to draft an objective summary that identifies the main idea of the text, summarizes its key points in the students' own words, and includes at least one correctly punctuated quote with original commentary.

ADAPT

If students need additional help writing a summary, have them collaborate with peers using the **Round Table Writing** strategy. They should work in groups, passing their summary to the next person, writing feedback on the summary they have been passed, and then shifting the summary they have to the next person. This process repeats until all members of the group have provided feedback on one another's writing. When the students are passed their own writing again, they should discuss the feedback they have received and revise their writing as appropriate.

To extend students' ability to write clear and accurate summaries, challenge them to summarize the short story "America and I."

 WRITING PROMPT: INFORMATIONAL

The following standards are addressed in the writing prompt:
- W.11-12.2a
- W.11-12.8
- W.11-12.2a, W.11-12.8

ACTIVITY 1.10

PLAN

Suggested Pacing: 1 50-minute class period

TEACH

1 Read aloud the Learning Targets and Preview. Tell students that in this activity they will examine two poems by the same author that are related in theme and topic.

2 Review the As You Read section with students. Read the titles of the two poems and ask students to predict their common theme.

 TEACHER TO TEACHER

This activity includes two poems depicting Whitman's view on America. You may choose to assign groups and have students work together to answer the Returning to the Text questions or use the first poem as a model and then allow students to work independently on the second poem and answer the Returning to the Text questions. Either way, it is critical to follow the close reading sequence and to give students the opportunity to read their assigned text at least twice.

3 Have students read the About the Author section describing Walt Whitman. Ask them what his life as a young man might have been like based on what they read. Invite them to consider how his poetic style might have been influenced by his work experience.

Learning Strategies

Close Reading
Marking the Text

My Notes

Learning Targets

- Analyze how an author's use of language in poetry shapes reader perceptions.
- Compare similar ideas as explored in different poems.

Preview

In this activity, you will read two poems by celebrated American poet Walt Whitman and write an analytical response that compares them.

As You Read

- Create an image in your mind of the sights, smells, or sounds that the poet describes.
- Circle unknown works and phrase. Try to determine the meaning of the words by using context clues or a dictionary.

About the Writer

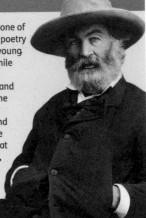

Walt Whitman (1819–1892) is now considered one of America's greatest poets, but his untraditional poetry was not well received during his lifetime. As a young man, he worked as a printer and a journalist while writing free verse poetry. His collection of poems Leaves of Grass first came out in 1855, and he revised and added to it several times over the years. Whitman's work disregards traditional poetic conventions, largely ignoring scheme and meter in favor of common speech patterns. The result is a uniquely American style of poetry that is frequently similar to prose. In the first poem, Whitman describes the various "carols," or songs, of American laborers. It is an early celebration of the country's working class and our nation's cultural diversity.

College and Career Readiness Standards

Focus Standards:

RL.11-12.1 Cite strong and thorough textual evidence to support analysis of what the text says explicitly as well as inferences drawn from the text, including determining where the text leaves matters uncertain.

RL.11-12.9 Demonstrate knowledge of eighteenth-, nineteenth- and early-twentieth-century foundational works of American literature, including how two or more texts from the same period treat similar themes or topics.

Additional Standards Addressed:
RL.11-12.3, RL.11-12.4

Poetry

America

by **Walt Whitman**

My Notes

Center of equal daughters, equal sons,

All, all alike endear'd, grown, ungrown, young or old,

Strong, ample, fair, enduring, capable, rich

Perennial with the Earth, with Freedom, Law and Love,

A grand, sane, towering, seated Mother,

Chair'd in the adamant of Time.

Making Observations

- What emotions does this poem make you feel?
- What details or images do you find striking?

Poetry

I Hear America Singing

by **Walt Whitman**

I hear America singing, the varied carols I hear,

Those of mechanics, each one singing his as it should be **blithe** and strong,

The carpenter singing his as he measures his plank or beam,

The **mason** singing his as he makes ready for work, or leaves off work,

5   The boatman singing what belongs to him in his boat, the deckhand singing on the steamboat deck, The shoemaker singing as he sits on his bench, the hatter singing as he stands,

The woodcutter's song, the plowboy's on his way in the morning, or at noon intermission or at sundown,

The delicious singing of the mother, or of the young wife at work, or of the girl sewing or washing, Each singing what belongs to him or her and to none else,

10 The day what belongs to the day—at night the party of young fellows, robust, friendly, Singing with open mouths their strong melodious songs.

---

perennial: lasting or existing for a long or apparently infinite time
blithe: happy, carefree
mason: a person who builds with brick or stone

ACTIVITY 1.10 continued

4 Conduct a shared reading of Walt Whitman's "America." Pause after the second line and have students consider why Whitman used the word *endear'd* the way he did. Ask: *What words and images stand out to you in the poem? How do you think Whitman wanted to make his reader feel when reading the poem out loud?*

5 As students are reading, monitor their progress. Be sure they are engaged with the text.

6 Tell students to pause after line 5 and discuss the use of the imagery of "Mother." Ask: *What is Whitman saying about America versus the world?*

7 After reading the text for the first time, guide the class in a discussion by asking the Making Observations questions. Check students' general comprehension of the text based on their observations.

8 Conduct a shared reading of Walt Whitman's "I Hear America Singing." Pause after the first line and have students consider Whitman's choice of the word *carols*. Discuss how the connotation of that word differs from that of its synonym *songs*.

Scaffolding the Text-Dependent Questions

1. Describe the tone created by Whitman. What words does he use to contribute to the tone he creates? How does Whitman feel about America? What words does he use to convey emotions? How does he describe America? RL.11-12.1

2. How does the use of commas impact the images Whitman creates? Where do the commas force the reader to pause? How do they guide

the reader to reflect on Whitman's words? RL.11-12.3

3. What is Whitman's message about America? Support you answer with words and phrases from the poem. What does Whitman appreciate about America? How does he want the reader to feel about it? RL.11-12.1

9 As students are reading, monitor their progress. Be sure they are engaged with the text. Remind them to mentally evoke the poem's sights, smells, and sounds as they read.

10 Have a volunteer read aloud lines 5 through 8. Point out that even though Whitman didn't use a traditional rhyme scheme in this poem, he created a sense of music, in part by strategically repeating words in close proximity to one another. As an example, have students find the words *boat*, *deck*, and *sing* within these lines.

11 Tell students to pause after line 9. Ask them to name the quality of the "singers" that is being stressed in this line. Discuss how this quality relates to the image of a chorus that Whitman evokes throughout the poem.

12 After reading the text for the first time, guide the class in a discussion by asking the Making Observation questions. Check students' general comprehension of the text based on their observations, asking follow-up questions if needed.

1.10

Making Observations
- What references to music do you notice?
- What details or images do you find striking?

Returning to the Text
- Return to the poems as you respond to the following questions. Use evidence from the poems to support your responses.
- Write any additional questions you have about the photographs in your Reader/Writer Notebook.

"America"

1. Describe the tone created by Whitman. What words does he use to contribute to the tone he creates?

   Whitman is very proud of America. He sees it as the center of the world and wants to create a triumphant tone for the reader. He lists the characteristics of America as "Strong, ample, fair, enduring, capable, rich," allowing the reader to bring his or her personal interpretation as to how America embodies these characteristics.

2. How does the use of commas impact the images Whitman creates?

   The commas create pauses in the reading of the poem and allow the reader to see each characteristic he is listing as unique and important in the making of America's greatness.

3. What is Whitman's message about America? Support you answer with words and phrases from the poem.

   Whitman wants the reader to appreciate all the great things about America that he sees. His message is that America is a country to be proud of because of the equality that other countries do not share. He uses words and phrases such as "center of equal daughters, equal sons" to emphasize this message.

"I Hear America Singing"

4. Describe the central image Whitman uses to evoke the people of America throughout the poem.

   He portrays the people of America as a large chorus, with each individual singing the song of his or her own occupation.

Scaffolding the Text-Dependent Questions

4. Describe the central image Whitman uses to evoke the people of America throughout the poem. Scan the poem for words that identify different kinds of workers and work. Focus on the verbs in the poem. What do they tell you about how the poet feels about his subject? RL.11-12.1

5. What is unique about the characters in line 8 of Whitman's poem? Examine which characters are depicted in that line. Compare them to every other character depicted in the poem. RL.11-12.1

6. What is Whitman's message about America in this poem? Support you answer with words and phrases from the poem. What kinds of workers are singing in the poem? What does Whitman want the reader to infer about the kinds of workers that make up America? RL.11-12.1

5. What is unique about the characters in line 8 of Whitman's poem?

They are the only female characters (mother, wife at work, young girl washing or sewing)

named in the poem, which uses virtually all of its other lines to celebrate masculine

professions such as mechanic, carpenter, mason, boatman, etc.

6. What is Whitman's message about America in this poem? Support you answer with words and phrases from the poem.

The only workers Whitman has singing in his America are laborers and blue collar workers.

There is no mention of priests or government officials or bankers. Whitman is saying that

America is built on the songs of the laborers and that it is the working class that make America

so strong and proud.

☑ Check Your Understanding

Consider the messages in both poems. What is Whitman saying about being American in the 19th century? How to the poems treat this message similarly and differently? How does Whitman's 19th-century America compare with America today?

Writing Prompt: Literary

Think about what you think it means to be American today. Write a short essay on an experience or observation that led you to this personal definition. In your writing, be sure to:

- Develop the events described using well-chosen details and a well-structured sequence.
- Use narrative techniques, such as dialogue, description, or reflection, to develop the events. The events should build toward a particular tone and outcome.
- Use precise sensory details and figurative language to convey a vivid picture of the events, settings, and characters.
- Include a conclusion that follows from and reflects on what is experienced, observed, or resolved over the course of the narrative.

WRITING PROMPT: LITERARY

The following standards are addressed in the writing prompt:
- W.11-12.3, W.11-12.3a
- W.11-12.1b, W.11-12.3c
- W.11-12.3d
- W.11-12.3e

ACTIVITY 1.10 continued

13 **RETURNING TO THE TEXT:** Guide students to return to the poems to respond to the text-dependent questions. Remind them to use evidence in their responses.

14 Move from group to group and listen in as students answer the text-dependent questions. If they have difficulty, scaffold the questions by rephrasing them or break them into smaller parts. See the Scaffolding of the Text-Dependent Questions boxes for suggestions.

15 Have students complete the Check Your Understanding section. For the Writing Prompt, consider allowing students to work in pairs as they develop their essays.

ASSESS

Review students' answers (in writing or discussion) to the Check Your Understanding exercise. Answers will likely state that both poems have an optimistic and proud view of America. Whitman is saying that the America of the 19th century is built on the hard work of the laboring class and this is allowing people to prosper and achieve an equality that the world should admire. Answers will also likely vary on how Whitman's 19th-century America compares with America today.

ADAPT

If students need more support writing their responses to the Check Your Understanding task, supply a sentence frame, such as: *Whitman is proud of America because* _____.

PLAN

Suggested Pacing: 2 50-minute class periods

TEACH

1 Read aloud the Learning Targets and Preview. Tell students that in this activity they will examine two poems that are related in theme but express different perspectives.

2 Review the As You Read section with students. Read the titles of the two poems and ask students to predict their common theme. Remind them that text that evokes a sensory experience (one related to sight, sound, smell, touch, or taste) is called *imagery*.

 TEACHER TO TEACHER

This activity includes two poems, each depicting a unique experience of what it means to be an American. You may choose to assign groups of students a single poem and have them **jigsaw** after the first read to have students work together to answer the Returning to the Text questions or have the entire class read each poem depending on the amount of time you can devote to this activity. Either way, it is critical to follow the **close reading** sequence and give students the opportunity to read their assigned texts at least twice. The following guidance leads you through an entire class read of all three poems.

3 Have students read the About the Author section describing Langston Hughes. Invite students to share what they know about the Harlem Renaissance and the rhythm of jazz and blues music.

Learning Strategies

Close Reading
Marking the Text

INDEPENDENT READING LINK

Read and Connect

Select a person in your independent reading who identifies an important symbol that keeps the American Dream alive. Compare this symbol to a symbol selected by an author of a reading in this unit. In your Reader/Writer Notebook, note similarities and differences.

My Notes

Learning Targets

- Analyze how an author's use of language in poetry shapes reader perceptions.
- Compare similar ideas as explored in different poems.

Preview

In this activity, you will read two poems by celebrated American writers and write a response that compares them.

As You Read

- While you read each poem, create an image in your mind of the sights, smells, or sounds that the poet describes.
- Circle unknown words and phrases. Try to determine the meaning of the words by using context clues, word parts, or a dictionary.

About the Author

Langston Hughes (1902–1967) began his writing career early. By eighth grade, he was named the class poet. He regularly wrote verse for his high school magazine. Hughes entered Columbia University in 1921 and discovered the arts scene in Harlem. He became a prominent figure in the Harlem Renaissance. His poetry, plays, and stories frequently focus on the African American experience, particularly on the struggles and feelings of people in a segregated society. His poetry was especially informed by the jazz and blues rhythms of African American music.

Poetry

I, Too

by **Langston Hughes**

I, too, sing America.

I am the darker brother.

They send me to eat in the kitchen

When company comes,

College and Career Readiness Standards

Focus Standards:

RL.11-12.1 Cite strong and thorough textual evidence to support analysis of what the text says explicitly as well as inferences drawn from the text, including determining where the text leaves matters uncertain.

RL.11-12.4 Determine the meaning of words and phrases as they are used in the text, including figurative and connotative meanings; analyze the impact of specific word choices on meaning and tone, including words with multiple meanings or language that is particularly fresh, engaging, or beautiful. (Include Shakespeare as well as other authors.)

Additional Standards Addressed:
W.11-12.2a, W.11-12.2b, W.11-12.2c

5   But I laugh,
    And eat well,
    And grow strong.
    Tomorrow,
    I'll be at the table

10 When company
    comes.
    Nobody'll dare
    Say to me,
    "Eat in the kitchen,"
    Then.

15 Besides,
    They'll see how
    beautiful I am
    And be ashamed—
    I, too, am America.

My Notes

Making Observations
* Who is speaking in the poem?
* What emotions are named in the poem?

About the Author

Julia Alvarez was born in 1950 in New York City but spent her early youth in the Dominican Republic. When she was 10, her family returned to the United States and settled in Brooklyn, New York. In 1991, she published her first novel, the critically acclaimed best seller *How the García Girls Lost Their Accents*. Since then, she has written fiction for adults, young adults, and children along with essays and poetry. Much of her work explores the theme of being caught between two cultures.

ACTIVITY 1.11 continued

TEACHER TO TEACHER

During the Harlem Renaissance—named after New York City's Harlem district—a creative African American culture developed and flourished in U.S. cities with large African American populations, influencing the arts throughout the United States and beyond. It started about 100 years ago and lasted some 20 years. Black poets (such as Hughes), dramatists, writers, and visual artists shared their unique perspectives with the world; black singers, dancers, and other performers gained an international audience; black musicians popularized and jazz. Jazz, which incorporates African, African - American, and European - American musical traditions, is recognized as a truly American musical genre. You may want to share some jazz music of the period with students to complement the Hughes poem.

4 Conduct a shared reading of Langston Hughes's "I, Too." Focus for a moment on the title and have students note its connection to the titles and contents of the Whitman poems they read in the previous activity.

5 As students are reading, monitor their progress. Be sure they are engaged with the text. Remind them to mentally evoke the poem's sights, smells, and sounds as they read. Encourage students to pay attention to the poem's rhythm.

6 Tell students to pause after line 17. Who does Hughes expect will "be ashamed," and why?

Scaffolding the Text-Dependent Questions

1. What effect does the word *too* in the first line of the Hughes poem have on the poem's voice? What does the word *too* mean? To what other poem does that first line refer? How does Hughes's first line connect his poem to the other one? RL11.12.4

2. What effect do the short lines in Hughes's poem have on its rhythm, as compared to the long lines in Whitman's poem? Read the poem aloud to hear again its rhythm. How would you describe that rhythm? How does it compare to the rhythm of Whitman's poem? RL11.12.4

3. What change does the speaker hint at in lines 8–10? How will life be different for the speaker after "Tomorrow"? Reread the beginning of the poem. How is the speaker treated when company comes? Reread lines 8–10. What does the speaker imagine will change "tomorrow"? RL11.12.4

7 After reading "I, Too" for the first time, guide the class in a discussion by asking the Making Observations questions. Check students' general comprehension of the text based on their observations, asking follow-up questions if needed.

8 Have students read the About the Author section describing Julia Alvarez. Based on her experience and the previous poems, what expectations or predictions do students have for this poem?

9 Conduct a shared reading of Julia Alvarez's "I, Too, Sing América." Note in particular the spelling of *América* in the poem's title. Discuss how it both references and comments upon the title of Whitman's poem. You also may want to say aloud the Spanish spelling with an accent on the second syllable (or ask a volunteer to do so) to help students appreciate how the word is recognizable but pronounced somewhat differently in Spanish than in English.

10 As students are reading, monitor their progress. Be sure they are engaged with the text. Remind them to mentally evoke the poem's sights, smells, and sounds as they read.

11 Tell students to pause after line 8. Discuss what Alvarez means when she writes, "I know it's been said before / but not in this voice" and then follows that statement with words that reflect her own heritage.

1.11

My Notes

Poetry

I, Too, Sing América

by **Julia Alvarez**

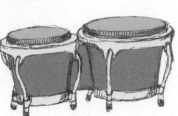

I know it's been said before

but not in this voice

of the plátano[1]

and the mango,

5 marimba y bongó,[2]

not in this sancocho

of inglés

con español.[3]

Ay sí,[4]

10 it's my turn

to oh say

what I see,

I'm going to sing America!

with all América

15 inside me:

from the soles

of Tierra del Fuego[5]

to the thin waist

of Chiriquí[6]

20 up the spine of the Mississippi

through the heartland

of the Yanquis[7]

to the great plain face of Canada —

all of us

---

[1] *plátano*: a plantain, starchier and less sweet than a banana and often cooked before eating
[2] *marimba y bongo*: The marimba and the bongo are musical instruments often heard in Latin American music.
[3] *sancocho* of *inglés con español*: a mixture (*sancocho* = "stew") of English with Spanish
[4] *Ay si*: "Oh, yes!"
[5] *Tierra del Fuego*: an archipelago at the very southern tip of South America.
[6] *Chiriquí*: a province in Panama
[7] *Yanquis*: white Americans ("Yankees")

Scaffolding the Text-Dependent Questions

4. Who is the intended audience for Julia Alvarez's "I, Too, Sing América"? Locate both Spanish and English words throughout the poem, starting in lines 1–3. What subculture is celebrated throughout Alvarez's poem? What language do people of that subculture speak? What separates them from the majority people of the nation? RL11.12.1

5. In lines 16–27, what imagery does Alvarez use to reference the history and heritage of those who live in "América"? What is that imagery's purpose? Explain. Reread lines 16–27. What sort of figure is being described? What is that figure doing? What do the figure's actions represent? RL11.12.4

25 singing America,

    the whole hemispheric

    familia[8]

    belting our canción,[9]

    singing our brown skin

30 into that white

    and red and blue song —

    the big song

    that sings

    all America,

35 el canto

    que cuenta

    con toda América:[10]

    un new song![11]

    Ya llegó el momento,[12]

40 our moment

    under the sun—

    ese sol[13] that shines

    on everyone.

    So, hit it maestro!

45 give us that Latin beat,

    ¡Uno-dos-tres![14]

    One-two-three!

    Ay sí,

    (y bilingually):[15]

50 Yo también soy América[16]

    I, too, am America.

My Notes

---

[8] *familia:* family
[9] *canción:* song
[10] *el canto que cuenta con toda América:* the singing that includes all of America
[11] *un* new song!: a new song!
[12] *Ya llegó el momento:* The time has come.
[13] *ese sol:* that sun
[14] *¡Uno-dos-tres!:* one, two, three!
[15] *(y bilingually):* (and in two languages)
[16] *Yo también soy América:* I, too, am America.

12 After reading the text for the first time, guide the class in a discussion by asking the Making Observations questions. Check students' general comprehension of the text based on their observations, asking follow-up questions if needed.

13 Based on the observations you made during the first readings, you may want to adjust the reading mode. For example, you may decide to model intonation for the second reading using **Echo Reading**, or you may group students differently.

Scaffolding the Text-Dependent Questions

6. What effect is created by the bilingual content of Alvarez's poem? Reread lines 44–51. Which two languages are used in the poem? What tone is created by Alvarez alternating their use? What statement about America can be inferred from Alvarez's alternating use of the two languages? RL.11-12.1, RL11-12.4

14 **RETURNING TO THE TEXT:** Guide students to return to the poems to respond to the text-dependent questions. Invite them to work in small groups to reread the text and answer the questions. Remind them to use text evidence in their responses.

15 Move from group to group and listen in as students answer the text-dependent questions. If they have difficulty, scaffold the questions by rephrasing them or breaking them into smaller parts. See the Scaffolding the Text-Dependent Questions boxes for suggestions.

1.11

Making Observations
- What images come to your mind as you read the poem?
- What do you notice about the mixture of Spanish and English in the poem?

Returning to the Text
- Return to the poems as you respond to the following questions. Use text evidence to support your responses.
- Write any additional questions you have about the texts in your Reader/Writer Notebook.

Hughes

1. What effect does the word *too* in the first line of the Hughes poem have on the poem's voice?

   The word connects Hughes to white Americans. Hughes is trying to unite the various races in

   America by creating a common experience for all.

2. What effect do the short lines in Hughes's poem have on its rhythm, as compared to the long lines in Whitman's poem?

   The short lines in Hughes's poem make it sound more concise, tougher, and less effusive

   and romantic than Whitman's poem. Hughes's song sounds like a terse answer to Whitman's.

3. What change does the speaker hint at in lines 8–10? How will life be different for the speaker after "Tomorrow"?

   At the beginning of the poem, the speaker is sent to the kitchen to eat when company comes,

   but after "Tomorrow," the speaker will eat at the table and "Nobody'll dare / Say to me, / 'Eat

   in the kitchen.'" The speaker will be accepted and admired.

Alvarez

4. Who is the intended audience for Julia Alvarez's "I, Too, Sing América"?

It is speaking to Americans who may not picture Hispanics as an equal part of America. It is

also intended to remind Spanish-speaking Americans that they, too, are part of American

culture.

5. In lines 16–27, what imagery does Alvarez use to reference the history and heritage of those who live in "América"? What is that imagery's purpose? Explain.

She creates the image of a dancer of Hispanic heritage, whose feet ("soles") are the southern

tip of South America, whose waist is the thin isthmus that connects North and South

America, whose torso is the United States, and whose face is Canada. With this imagery, she

connects the history of her people to every part of the Americas in a striking and celebratory

manner.

6. What effect is created by the bilingual content of Alvarez's poem?

She uses Spanish and English interchangeably, which places them on the same level culturally

as American languages. By extension, she is affirming the equality of Hispanic Americans to

white Americans.

16 After students have read and analyzed the poems, have them work individually to fill out the chart in the Working from the Text activity. Guide them in filling out the first row of the chart. If necessary, model examples of language that informs the perception of the reader from the remaining two poems.

17 Have students complete the Check Your Understanding section. Then, for the Writing Prompt, consider allowing students to work in pairs as they develop their essays.

Working from the Text

7. The two poems in this activity and Walt Whitman's "I Hear America Singing" from Activity 1.10 all reflect a unique experience of what it means to be an American. Use the chart to record examples of the language each author uses to inform readers of their experience, as well as the tone the author uses.

Title	Description of Experience	Tone	Evidence
"I Hear America Singing"	communicates his proud, full inclusion in the American experience	joyful, celebratory tone	"Singing with open mouths their strong, melodious songs."
"I, Too"	communicates how he has been excluded from much of the American experience yet hopes to be included soon	proud, assertive tone	"Tomorrow, I'll be at the table."
"I, Too, Sing América"	communicates her readiness to include—and celebrate—herself and her rich heritage in the "song" of America	playful, joyful tone	"So, hit it maestro!"

8. Reread Whitman's poems from Activity 1.10. How might Whitman's poems have inspired Alvarez's and Hughes's works? Cite similar words or phrases that connect the central ideas of all three poets.

1.11

☑ Check Your Understanding

Consider what the speakers in "I Hear American Singing," "I, Too" and "I, Too, Sing América" want us to know about the American Dream. Write a sentence stating what their visions have in common. Write another sentence or two stating how the vision of each is unique.

> ### ✍ Writing to Sources: Informational Text
>
> Write a short essay comparing and contrasting how the three poems "I Hear America Singing," "I, Too" and "I, Too, Sing América" use the image of singing. Think about both the denotative and connotative meanings of the word *sing*. In your writing, be sure to:
>
> - Begin with a clear thesis that states your position about what the three poems mean by the word *sing*.
> - Include examples of diction and imagery from both texts to support each claim you make about similarities and differences in meaning.
> - Include clear transitions between points and a concluding statement that reinforces your thesis.

WRITING TO SOURCES: INFORMATIONAL TEXT

The following standards are addressed in the writing prompt:
- W.11-12.2a
- W.11-12.2b
- W.11-12.2c

ACTIVITY 1.11 continued

LEVELED DIFFERENTIATED INSTRUCTION

Students may need support responding to the Writing Prompt.

Beginning Support students in completing a modified **Venn Diagram for Writing a Comparison**, focusing on how the word *sing* is represented in each text.

Developing Allow partners to generate examples of diction and imagery present in each text and to write collaboratively.

Support Prior to writing, generate a class list of possible thesis statements to the prompt. Ask partners to explain their thesis choices and the reason for their choices.

Extend Ask students to extend their responses by explaining which poem most effectively uses diction and imagery to convey its meaning.

ASSESS

Review students' answers to the Check Your Understanding task. Answers will likely state that all three speakers ultimately embrace a similar, optimistic idea of the American Dream. At the same time, they should reflect an understanding that the America in Whitman's poem is still a future vision for the speaker in Hughes's poem. Answers will also likely reflect an understanding that Alvarez sees "América" as a mixture of world cultures to be nurtured and celebrated.

ADAPT

If students need additional help responding to the Check Your Understanding task, invite them to reread the About the Author sections and then write a sentence about each author that reflects on how people of that author's heritage have, in general, experienced American life. Then have them reread the poems with those insights in mind.

ACTIVITY 1.12

PLAN

Suggested Pacing: 2 50-minute class periods

TEACH

1 Read the Learning Targets and Preview with students. Survey the class to determine who already has a working knowledge of the concept of "hyphenated American."

2 Have students read the As You Read and About the Author sections. Invite them to predict the subject and tone of the essay they are about to read.

TEACHER TO TEACHER

Although the author was born five years after the end of World War II, her childhood was still shaped by that conflict. Consider preparing a brief explanation of what led to the internment of American citizens of Japanese ancestry in the 1940s and why the American government apologized and gave the internees financial compensation in 1988.

Learning Strategies

Marking the Text
Summarizing/Paraphrasing

My Notes

Learning Targets

- Support the analysis of a text with appropriate evidence.
- Analyze and evaluate the effectiveness of the structure of an informational text.

Preview

In this activity, you will read an essay about being a "hyphenated American."

As You Read

- Underline details that vividly indicate the author's feelings about her Japanese heritage.
- Draw a dotted line under details that vividly indicate the author's feelings about her American reality.
- Circle unknown words and phrases. Try to determine the meaning of the words by using context clues, word parts, or a dictionary.

About the Author

Kesaya E. Noda (b. 1950) was born in California and grew up in New Hampshire as the grandchild of Japanese immigrants. Her first book, *The Yamato Colony*, describes the history of the California farming community in which her parents grew up, married, and gave birth to her. (*Yamato* is an ancient word for "Japanese.") That community was founded in 1910 by a group of people of Japanese ancestry. When Japanese-Americans were sent to internment camps 30 years later during World War II, the residents of Yamato had to hire people to manage their land until they were released. The aftermath of these experiences colored Noda's early childhood. Her essay "Growing Up Asian in America" first appeared in the 1989 collection *Making Waves: An Anthology of Writings by and About Asian American Women*. In this excerpt, she touches on how both cultures have shaped her beliefs and character.

College and Career Readiness Standards

Focus Standards:

RI.11-12.1 Cite strong and thorough textual evidence to support analysis of what the text says explicitly as well as inferences drawn from the text, including determining where the text leaves matters uncertain.

RI.11-12.2 Determine two or more central ideas of a text and analyze their development over the course of the text, including how they interact and build on one another to provide a complex analysis; provide an objective summary of the text.

RI.11-12.3 Analyze a complex set of ideas or sequence of events and explain how specific individuals, ideas, or events interact and develop over the course of the text

Additional Standards Addressed:

RI.11-12.4

Essay

My Notes

Growing Up Asian in America

by **Kesaya E. Noda**

1   Sometimes when I was growing up, my identity seemed to hurtle toward me and paste itself right to my face. I felt that way, encountering the stereotypes of my race **perpetuated** by non-Japanese people (primarily white) who may or may not have had contact with other Japanese in America. "You don't like cheese, do you?" someone would ask. "I know your people don't like cheese." Sometimes questions came making allusions to history. That was another aspect of the identity. Events that had happened quite apart from the me who stood silent in that moment connected my face with an incomprehensible past. "Your parents were in California? Were they in those camps during the war?" And sometimes there were phrases or nicknames: "Lotus Blossom." I was sometimes addressed or referred to as racially Japanese, sometimes as Japanese-American, and sometimes as an Asian woman. Confusions and distortions abounded.

2   How is one to know and define oneself? From the inside—within a context that is self-defined, from a grounding in a community and a connection with culture and history that are comfortably accepted? Or from the outside—in terms of messages received from the media and people who are often ignorant? Even as an adult I can still see two sides of my face and past. I can see from the inside out, in freedom. And I can see from the outside in, driven by the old voices of childhood and lost in anger and fear.

I AM RACIALLY JAPANESE

3   A voice from my childhood says: "You are other. You are less than. You are unalterably alien." This voice has its own history. We have indeed been seen as other and alien since the early years of our arrival in the United States. The very first immigrants were welcomed and sought as laborers to replace the dwindling numbers of Chinese, whose influx had been cut off by the Chinese Exclusion Act of 1882. The Japanese fell natural heir to the same anti-Asian prejudice that had arisen against the Chinese. As soon as they began striking for better wages, they were no longer welcomed.

4   I can see myself today as a person historically defined by law and custom as being forever alien. Being neither "free white," nor "African," our people in California were deemed "aliens, ineligible for citizenship," no matter how long they intended to stay here. Aliens ineligible for citizenship were prohibited from owning, buying, or leasing land. They did not and could not belong here. The voice in me remembers that I am always a *Japanese*-American in the eyes of many. A third-generation German-American is an American. A third-generation Japanese-American is a Japanese-American. Being Japanese means being a danger to the country during the war and knowing how to use chopsticks. I wear this history on my face.

GRAMMAR & USAGE

Hyphens
Writers often use **hyphens** to join two or more words into a single adjective or concept called a **compound adjective**. Hyphens in a compound adjective help readers see that two or more words are being linked together to function as one adjective: *third-generation*, *90-year-old*. Hyphens also allow writers to combine the meanings of two or more words to create a new word that conveys a specific concept or idea. These words are usually used as nouns or adjectives and often include proper nouns: *Japanese-American*, *anti-Asian*. What different meanings does the author bring to the hyphenated word *Japanese-American*?

perpetuated: continued, sustained

Scaffolding the Text-Dependent Questions

1. **In paragraphs 3 and 4, the author uses the word** *alien* **to describe how she feels other people view her and how she has come to view herself. Consult a print or online dictionary to examine the possible meanings of that word. How might the word convey the author's discomfort with herself?** Find the various definitions of *alien* in a print or online dictionary. Examine each definition and then reread paragraphs 3 and 4. What does the word *alien* mean in this context? What connotations does the word have when applied to people? How might people feel when called an *alien*? L.11-12.4c, RL.11-12.1

ACTIVITY 1.12 continued

3 **FIRST READ:** Conduct a shared reading of "Growing Up Asian in America."

TEXT COMPLEXITY

Overall: Accessible
Lexile: 890L
Qualitative: Moderate Difficulty
Task: Moderate (Analyze)

4 As students are reading, monitor their progress. Make sure they are engaged with the text, annotating details that reveal the author's feelings, and circling unknown words and phrases.

5 Pause after paragraph 4. Highlight the Grammar & Usage box about hyphenation and review its contents with students. Have students identify and explain uses of hyphenation in the first part of the essay.

6 Tell students to pause at the end of paragraph 8 and have them explain what she means by the statement "I am Japanese." Prompt students to compare that statement to that section's heading. Given the content of that section, do they think the heading and sentence express the same or different sentiments?

1.12

My Notes

5   I move to the other side. I see a different light and claim a different context. My race is a line that stretches across ocean and time to link me to the shrine where my grandmother was raised. Two high, white banners lift in the wind at the top of the stone steps leading to the shrine. It is time for the summer festival. Black characters are written against the sky as boldly as the clouds, as lightly as kites, as sharply as the big black crows I used to see above the fields in New Hampshire. At festival time there is liquor and food, ritual, discipline, and abandonment. There is music and drunkenness and **invocation**. There is hope. Another season has come. Another season has gone.

6   I am racially Japanese. I have a certain claim to this crazy place where the prayers **intoned** by a neighboring Shinto[1] priest (standing in for my grandmother's nephew who is sick) are drowned out by the rehearsals for the pop singing contest in which most of the villagers will compete later that night. The village elders, the priest, and I stand respectfully upon the immaculate, shining wooden floor of the outer shrine, bowing our heads before the hidden powers. During the patchy intervals when I can hear him, I notice the priest has a stutter. His voice flutters up to my ears only occasionally because two men and a woman are singing gustily into a microphone in the compound, testing the sound system. A pre-recorded tape of guitars, **samisens**, and drums accompanies them. Rock music and Shinto prayers. That night, to loud applause and cheers, a young man is given the award for the most netsuretsu—passionate, burning—rendition of a song. We roar our approval of the reward. Never mind that his voice had wandered and slid, now slightly above, now slightly below the given line of the melody. Netsuretsu. Netsuretsu.

7   In the morning, my grandmother's sister kneels at the foot of the stone stairs to offer her morning prayers. She is too crippled to climb the stairs, so each morning she kneels here upon the path. She shuts her eyes for a few seconds, her motions as matter of fact as when she washes rice. I linger longer than she does, so reluctant to leave, savoring the connection I feel with my grandmother in America, the past, and the power that lives and shines in the morning sun.

8   Our family has served this shrine for generations. The family's need to protect this claim to identity and place outweighs any individual claim to any individual hope. I am Japanese.

I AM A JAPANESE-AMERICAN

9   "Weak." I hear the voice from my childhood years. "Passive," I hear. Our parents and grandparents were the ones who were put into those camps. They went without resistance; they offered cooperation as proof of loyalty to America. "Victim," I hear. And, "Silent."

10   Our parents are painted as hard workers who were socially uncomfortable and had difficulty expressing even the smallest opinion. Clean, quiet, motivated, and determined to match the American way; that is us, and that is the story of our time here.

invocation: calling upon spirits
intoned: uttered in a singing voice
samisens: a guitar-like Japanese musical instrument

[1] traditional religion of Japan

Scaffolding the Text-Dependent Questions

2. In paragraph 4, what inference can you make about the author's feelings when she states, "A third-generation Japanese-American is a Japanese-American"? Read paragraph 4 and try to imagine the author's tone of voice. Notice that she mentions how the Japanese were treated unfairly and continue to retain their hyphenated status longer than white immigrants, like Germans. How does this make her feel? RL.11-12.1

3. How do the essay's two headings relate to the author's purpose? Reread the headings. What does the first heading state? What does the second heading state? How do they connect with the title of the essay? RL.11-12.3

11 "Why did you go into those camps," I raged at my parents, frightened by my own inner silence and timidity. "Why didn't you do anything to resist? Why didn't you name it the injustice it was?" Couldn't our parents even think? Couldn't they? Why were we so passive?

12 I shift my vision and my stance. I am in California. My uncle is in the midst of the sweet potato harvest. He is pressed, trying to get the harvesting crews onto the field as quickly as possible, worried about the flow of equipment and people. His big pickup is pulled off to the side, motor running, door ajar. I see two tractors in the yard in front of an old shed; the flat bed harvesting platform on which the workers will stand has already been brought over from the other field. It's early morning. The workers stand loosely grouped and at ease, but my uncle looks as **harried** and tense as a police officer trying to unsnarl a New York City traffic jam. Driving toward the shed, I pull my car off the road to make way for an approaching tractor. The front wheels of the car sink luxuriously into the soft, white sand by the roadside and the car slides to a dreamy halt, tail still on the road. I try to move forward. I try to move back. The front bites contentedly into the sand, the back lifts itself at a jaunty angle. My uncle sees me and storms down the road, running. He is shouting before he is even near me.

13 "What the matter with you," he screams. "What the hell are you doing?" In his frenzy, he grabs his hat off his head and slashes it through the air across his knee. He is beside himself. "You've blocked the whole roadway. How am I supposed to get my tractors out of here? Can't you use your head? You've cut off the whole roadway, and we've got to get out of here."

14 I stand on the road before him helplessly thinking, "No, I don't know how to drive in sand. I've never driven in sand."

15 "I'm sorry, uncle," I say, burying a smile beneath a look of sincere apology. I notice my deep amusement and my affection for him with great curiosity. I am usually devastated by anger. Not this time.

16 During the several years that follow I learn about the people and the place, and much more about what has happened in this California village where my parents grew up. The issei, our grandparents, made this settlement in the desert. Their first crops were eaten by rabbits and ravaged by insects. The land was so barren that men walking from house to house sometimes got lost. Women came here too. They bore children in 114 degree heat, then carried the babies with them into the fields to nurse when they reached the end of each row of grapes or other truck farm crops.

17 I had had no idea what it meant to buy this kind of land and make it grow green. Or how, when the war came, there was no space at all for the subtlety of being who we were—Japanese-Americans. Either/or was the way. I hadn't understood that people were literally afraid for their lives then, that their money had been frozen in banks; that there was a five-mile travel limit; that when the early evening curfew came and they were inside their houses, some of them watched helplessly as people they knew went into their barns to

My Notes

harried: anxious, worried

7 Pause after paragraph 11. Ask students on whom the author first blames her tendency toward passivity. What set of circumstances seems to her to be the original cause of it?

8 Pause after paragraph 15. Ask students what they think might be causing the author amusement, particularly since she is in a situation that would normally make her angry.

9 After reading the text for the first time, guide the class in a discussion by asking the Making Observations questions. Check students' general comprehension of the text based on their observations, asking follow-up questions if needed.

10 Based on observations you made during the first reading, you may want to adjust your reading mode. For example, you may decide for the second reading to read aloud certain complex passages, or you may group students differently.

1.12

My Notes

steal their belongings. The police were patrolling the road, interested only in violators of curfew. There was no help for them in the face of thievery. I had not been able to imagine before what it must have felt like to be an American—to know absolutely that one is an American—and yet to have almost everyone else deny it. Not only deny it, but challenge that identity with machine guns and troops of white American soldiers. In those circumstances it was difficult to say, "I'm a Japanese-American." "American" had to do.

18 But now I can say that I am a Japanese-American. It means I have a place here in this country, too. I have a place here on the East Coast, where our neighbor is so much a part of our family that my mother never passes her house at night without glancing at the lights to see if she is home and safe; where my parents have hauled hundreds of pounds of rocks from fields and arduously planted Christmas trees and blueberries, lilacs, asparagus, and crab apples; where my father still dreams of **angling** a stream to a new bed so that he can dig a pond in the field and fill it with water and fish. "The neighbors already came for their Christmas tree?" he asks in December. "Did they like it? Did they like it?"

19 I have a place on the West Coast where my relatives still farm, where I heard the stories of feuds and backbiting, and where I saw that people survived and flourished because fundamentally they trusted and relied upon one another. A death in the family is not just a death in a family; it is a death in the community. I saw people help each other with money, materials, labor, attention, and time. I saw men gather once a year, without fail, to clean the grounds of a ninety-year-old woman who had helped the community before, during, and after the war. I saw her remembering them with birthday cards sent to each of their children.

20 I come from a people with a long memory and a distinctive grace. We live our thanks. And we are Americans. Japanese-Americans. ...

Making Observations
- Whom do we meet in the essay?
- What emotions do you feel while reading the essay?

angling: turn in a different direction

Scaffolding the Text-Dependent Questions

4. By the end of the essay, the author "can say that I am Japanese-American." What change has brought this decision about? Reread paragraph 18, in which the author makes this statement. Notice that this paragraph includes fond images of her family life in the United States. Why do you think these aspects of everyday life help her understand who she is? RL.11-12.1

5. Each section of this essay is based upon a different central idea. What is the central idea of each? Skim the first section. What does the first section say about being Asian in America? Skim the second section. What does the second section say about the author's Japanese heritage? Skim the third section. What does the third section say about culture perceptions of Japanese-Americans? RL.11-12.2

Returning to the Text

- Return to the essay as you respond to the following questions. Use text evidence to support your responses.
- Write any additional questions you have about the text in your Reader/Writer Notebook.

1. In paragraphs 3 and 4, the author uses the word *alien* to describe how she feels other people view her and how she has come to view herself. Consult a print or online dictionary to examine the possible meanings of that word. How might the word convey the author's discomfort with herself?

The word *alien* means "of a foreign origin." It can refer to someone who is from another country or who is simply strange and unfamiliar. It often has a connotation of being undesirable or unacceptable.

2. In paragraph 4, what inference can you make about the author's feelings when she states, "A third-generation Japanese-American is a Japanese-American"?

She feels that she is considered less American than people of Caucasian ancestry, even though she was born and raised in America. She underscores this feeling when she states, "A third generation German-American is an American."

3. How do the essay's two headings relate to the author's purpose?

The first heading reads "I Am Racially Japanese." The second heading reads "I Am a Japanese American." Both underscore the author's purpose, which is to explain what "growing up Asian in America" is like.

4. By the end of the essay, the author "can say that I am Japanese-American." What change has brought this decision about?

In paragraph 17, the author explains that she has come to realize that the reluctance to embrace the Japanese part of her heritage is part of a different time. In the past, that heritage was seen as suspect. Today it is something to be embraced.

ACTIVITY 1.12 continued

11 RETURNING TO THE TEXT: Guide students to return to the text to respond to the text-dependent questions. Invite them to work in small groups to reread the text and answer the questions. Remind them to use text evidence in their responses.

12 Move from group to group and listen in as students answer the text-dependent questions. If they have difficulty, scaffold the questions by rephrasing them or breaking them into smaller parts. See the Scaffolding the Text-Dependent Questions boxes for suggestions.

13 Form students into pairs and ask them to work collaboratively to complete the Working from the Text section. Begin by asking them to determine the author's purpose. Discuss the aspects of the text that led them to their conclusion.

14 Call attention to the text structure chart in student step 7 of the Working from the Text section. Model the completion of the "First Part" box and have them copy what you write on their own charts. Point out that the first part has no subtitle and that it serves as an introduction to the topic the author will be exploring.

15 Have students complete the text structure chart. When they are finished, discuss their responses.

5. Each section of this essay is based upon a different central idea. What is the central idea of each?

The first section is based upon the confusions and distortion of being an Asian in America,

where members of other racial groups are more numerous. The second section is based upon

the idea that the author's heritage is Japanese and will always be, no matter where she lives.

The third section is based upon the idea that perceptions of what a Japanese-American is have

changed and that both backgrounds can be embraced and celebrated.

Working from the Text

6. What is the author's purpose in this essay?

The author's purpose is to inform the reader about the complexities of growing up Japanese in

the United States.

7. With a partner, review and discuss the text structure of "Growing Up Asian in America." Outline that text structure, noting subtitles and providing a brief summary of each part's content.

> **First Part:**
> The first part of the text has no subtitle. It is an introduction to the topic the author will be exploring: her racial and national identity as an Asian American.
>
> **Second Part:**
> The second part of the text is subtitled "I Am Racially Japanese." In it, the author ponders her place in America and sees herself as overwhelmed by her heritage.
>
> **Third Part:**
> The third part of the text is subtitled "I Am a Japanese-American." In it, the author becomes more aware of the uniqueness of her ancestry. She concludes her narrative with a quiet pride in both her Japanese heritage and her Americanness.

8. What type of text structure (chronological, sequential, cause-and-effect, order of importance, or compare-and-contrast) does Noda use to structure her essay? How does the division of the text into three parts serve the author's purpose?

She structures her essay sequentially, with frequent flashbacks to childhood thoughts and experiences. She divides her essay into three parts because it is a clear way to represent the three distinct stages in the growth of her self-awareness.

9. Describe the process the author undergoes as the story progresses.

She goes from confusion about herself through a sort of shame about and reluctance to accept her origin to a balanced understanding and embracing of her heritage as both Japanese and American.

10. How did the author's environment play a role in how she viewed herself and her race?

Her fellow Americans (mostly white) exposed her to erroneous ideas about Asians, Asian culture, and Asian history (particularly the internment of Japanese-Americans during World War II). They also, as time progressed, helped her see herself as just as American as any other citizen.

11. Discuss as a group the different aspects of being American. Then write a definition of the term *American*. You may wish to consult your vocabulary tree from Activity 1.9 to help you compose your definition. Include details from the essay to support your definition.

Answers will vary. Accept any answer that indicates comprehension of the material covered in this unit.

☑ Check Your Understanding

In a few sentences, explain how the text structure of "Growing Up Asian in America" supports understanding of the information it presents.

The author's purpose is to convey the experience of being a present-day Japanese-American. The structure presents the information by first stating the issues involved, then presenting the difficulties inherent in overcoming those issues, and then portraying an acceptable, positive resolution. This arrangement of text presents the essay's information in a clear, positive way.

ACTIVITY 1.12 continued

16 Complete student steps 8–11 as a class, having volunteers share information from their text structure charts and vocabulary trees as appropriate.

17 Have students complete the Check Your Understanding task in writing or as a class discussion.

ASSESS

Responses to the Check Your Understanding activity should demonstrate the understanding that Noda's conclusion describes how she blends all the facets of her identity. As you check students' work, make sure they have cited appropriate evidence and details to support their analyses.

ADAPT

If students need additional help identifying the structure of an essay or explaining how the parts work together to create meaning, consider directing them to a narrative podcast, such as an episode of *This American Life*, *StoryCorps*, or *The Moth Podcast*. Episodes are widely available online and include concise, structured personal narratives. Search the archives for stories relating to immigration or the American Dream.

To extend an understanding of headings as an organizational tool to create a clear structure, have students work with partners to look through later units and identify other texts with headings. Ask pairs to discuss what the texts with headings have in common and how the headings help readers preview what they will learn when they read the full texts. Visit among pairs to gauge their understanding.

ACTIVITY 1.13

ACTIVITY 1.13

PLAN

Suggested Pacing: 1 50-minute class period

TEACH

1 Read the Learning Targets and Preview with students, making certain that they understand that this activity will lead them through the planning and drafting stages of the first Embedded Assessment.

 TEACHER TO TEACHER

This is a good opportunity to revisit the definitions of an essay's purpose, message, and audience as well as the idea of formal and informal tone.

2 Remind students that the purpose of their essay will be to inform, the message will be their statement of what it means to be an American, and their audience will be their peers. Facilitate a discussion of how the purpose, message, and audience will guide the content of their essay. Questions to be considered include:

• Should the tone be formal or informal?
• What content would interest the audience, and what would not?
• What information will students include to lend credibility to their points of view?
• What rhetorical strategies will they likely use, and why?

3 Moderate a class discussion based on student steps 1 and 2 in the Planning Your Definition Essay section. Have the class **brainstorm** words and concepts based on the students' vocabulary trees from Activity 1.9. Instruct individual students to jot down new ideas that emerge from the session in the chart within student step 3. Then give students time to examine what they have written and determine which ideas might help shape their definition.

4 Have students come up with a tentative definition of what it means to be American. Remind them that it can be modified or discarded as the planning process continues.

ACTIVITY 1.13 Drafting Your Definition Essay

Learning Strategies

Brainstorming
Drafting

My Notes

Learning Targets

• Synthesize information from a variety of text types.
• Plan a piece of writing appropriate for a purpose and audience by generating ideas using brainstorming, discussion, and a graphic organizer.
• Develop drafts into a focused, structured, and coherent piece of writing.

Preview

In this activity, you will plan and develop a draft of your definition essay.

Planning Your Definition Essay

1. Return to your vocabulary tree where you began to record the multiple aspects of a definition of an American and refine or add to any of your ideas as needed.

2. **Collaborative Discussion:** Turn and talk to your neighbors about each other's vocabulary trees. What details and examples do you have in common? What new ideas have been generated from the conversation that you could include in your essay?

3. How would you define the concept of an American? Think about the definition strategies you have learned—negation, function, exemplification, and classification—that will help you prove or support your thesis or definition of what it means to be an American. Use the following graphic organizer to record your responses. Remember to keep in mind your purpose and audience as you plan your essay.

The Definition of an American	
Rhetorical Strategies for Defining a Concept	**Supporting Evidence, Pertinent Examples, Commentary, and Summary**
Negation (What is not an American?)	An American is not defined by his or her race or ethnicity.
Function (What does an American do?)	An American supports our nation's founding principles.
Exemplification (Who are some examples of Americans?)	The black woman who makes a living on Wall Street and the newly naturalized Muslim teen who delivers sandwiches are equally American.
Classification (What are types of Americans?)	Americans can be rich or poor; black, brown, or white; male or female; gay or straight.

College and Career Readiness Standards

Focus Standards:

W.11-12.4 Produce clear and coherent writing in which the development, organization, and style are appropriate to task, purpose, and audience.

W.11-12.5 Develop and strengthen writing as needed by planning, revising, editing, rewriting, or trying a new approach, focusing on addressing what is most significant for a specific purpose and audience.

W.11-12.9 Draw evidence from literary or informational texts to support analysis, reflection, and research.

Developing Your Definition Essay

Use the following outline to help you develop your essay defining the word American. As you execute your essay-writing process, remember to focus on your topic, your purpose (to inform), and your audience (your teacher and fellow students).

Part One: Introductory Paragraph

Begin with a dictionary definition of the word *American*. This will give your reader a familiar focus from which you can proceed. Follow the definition with your thesis statement, which should present your own definition broken down according to the rhetorical device or devices you have chosen to use (classification, exemplification, negation, function). Keep your thesis as short as you can while still maintaining completeness. You will elaborate on the individual pieces of your definition in your body paragraphs.

Introductory Paragraph:

_____

_____

_____

_____

_____

Part Two: Body Paragraphs

For this activity, restrict your number of body paragraphs to three or four at the very most. Each body paragraph will explore a piece of your definition as you broke it down in your introduction. State each piece in a topic sentence that begins a paragraph. This is the place for details and commentary that support your definition. As you compose your individual body paragraphs, remember that you are free to make further use of any rhetorical device that helps place your information in a useful context.

Body Paragraphs:

_____

_____

_____

_____

_____

_____

_____

_____

_____

_____

ACTIVITY 1.13 continued

5 Coach students through the process of developing a tentative thesis on what it means to be an American. Remind them that the first step, selecting a topic (what it means to be an American), has already been done. Take students through further steps in the process, instructing them to:

- Choose the best ideas from their vocabulary tree, Reader/Writer Notebook, and brainstorming session.
- Narrow those ideas into a one- or two-sentence statement that both names the topic and expresses their interpretation of it.

6 Write these sample thesis statements on the board:

- Americans have the opportunity to be whomever and whatever they want to be.
- To be an American means to respect different people, ideas, and beliefs.
- An American is someone who believes in and enjoys freedom of speech and religion.

7 Read aloud student step 3 and review of the Planning Your Definition Essay section. Have students review the texts they have read so far in the unit and the analysis they have done of those texts. Invite them to revise their charts as they synthesize text evidence with their insights as to what it means to be an American. Tell them to create a tentative thesis on that topic. Give them time to experiment with ways to define their ideas by using different rhetorical strategies and their entries in the chart.

8 Instruct students to individually fill out their "The Definition of an American" graphic organizers. Remind them that their thesis should determine their choice of rhetorical strategies, and not vice-versa.

9 Have volunteers share information from their charts with the class. Solicit constructive criticism on how well they have constructed an example of each rhetorical strategy.

10 Read aloud the first paragraph of the Developing Your Definition Essay section.

11 Direct students to the Part One section. Have them write their introductory paragraph according to the instructions. Point out that one way to begin is with a dictionary definition of the word *American* followed by their own (their thesis).

12 Direct students to the Part Two section. Have them read and follow the instructions for composing their body paragraphs.

13 Now direct students attention to Part Three. Have them follow the instructions for composing their conclusion paragraph.

ASSESS

Review students' vocabulary tree, brainstorming session results, and definition strategy chart. Compare those to the written responses in the Developing Your Definition Essay section of this activity. Taken together, they should indicate a clear process of development from idea to rough draft.

ADAPT

If students need additional help with developing support for their definitions of what it means to be American, have them work in pairs to revisit their ideas and their definition strategies. Have each partner critique the other's strategies in terms of how well they do or do not support the thesis.

1.13

Part Three: Conclusion Paragraph

Your final paragraph should be mostly a simple summary of the main points of your essay (without directly repeating your introduction or topic sentences). If you find yourself inserting new information, examine your body paragraphs. If the information is relevant, it should fit into one of your body topics. If not, either revisit your definition or discard the information.

Avoid an overly dramatic or forced final sentence. At the same time, your conclusion should leave your reader with a sense that you have fully explained your definition. No vague ideas or unanswered questions should remain in the reader's mind when he or she is done with your text.

Conclusion Paragraph:

_____

_____

_____

_____

_____

Revising and Editing

Learning Targets

- Revise drafts to improve clarity, development, organization, style, diction, and sentence fluency both within and between sentences.
- Edit drafts to demonstrate a command of standard English convention using a style guide.
- Publish written work for appropriate audiences.

Preview

In this activity, you will revise and edit your definition essay in preparation for publication.

Revising and Editing Your Essay

Once you have completed the first draft of your essay, you may be tempted to consider your work finished. Good writers rarely assume that their first effort is the best they can do. They subject their text to a two-part process called revision and editing (sometimes many, many times over).

- **Revision** is the process of taking a second look at your ideas. Reread the text as though someone else has written it. With an eye on clarity, development, style, diction, and fluency, ask yourself: *What would make these ideas clearer and more convincing?* Sometimes it's a matter of rewording them; other times changing the order of the text, adding a supporting detail, or choosing a more powerful word will create improvement. If a sentence feels like it was grafted in from another essay, it's best to either rewrite it or remove it. As you revise, be sure to look closely at the rhetorical devices you use in your analysis.

1. Reexamine the first draft of your essay. Use what you have learned about the revision process to improve the clarity and fluency of your text. Describe what you revised and why.

_____

_____

_____

_____

- **Editing** is a look at the "nuts and bolts" of your text. It is where you correct misspelled words, fix punctuation errors, and resolve any problems with sentence structure. This is a process for which a style guide often comes in handy. A style guide is a collection of rules for writing. Popular style guides for general writing include *The Elements of Style, The Associated Press Stylebook,* and *The Chicago Manual of Style.* Other good style guides exist for writing in specific fields (science, medical, etc.).

2. Edit your first draft, using an online or print style guide. Describe your edits.

_____

_____

_____

_____

My Notes

_____

College and Career Readiness Standards

Focus Standards:

W.11-12.5 Develop and strengthen writing as needed by planning, revising, editing, rewriting, or trying a new approach, focusing on addressing what is most significant for a specific purpose and audience.

L.11-12.1 Demonstrate command of the conventions of standard English grammar and usage when writing or speaking.

W.11-12.6 Use technology, including the Internet, to produce, publish, and update individual or shared writing products in response to ongoing feedback, including new arguments or information.

ACTIVITY 1.14

PLAN

Materials: projections or printouts of sample texts
Suggested Pacing: 1 50-minute class period

TEACH

1 Read aloud the Learning Targets and Preview. Remind students that they will be continuing to work on the rough drafts of their Embedded Assessment that they composed in the previous activity.

2 Guide students through the introductory paragraph of the Revising and Editing Your Essay section. Be sure they understand that **revising** and **editing** are two related but separate processes.

3 Read aloud the bulleted Revision paragraph. Revisit the following terms and their definitions:

- **Clarity:** the quality of being easily understood
- **Development:** the process of including useful details to support main ideas
- **Style:** the effect that results from a writer's word choices and text construction
- **Diction:** the words and phrases a writer uses to make a text interesting and informative
- **Fluency:** smoothness and logical order between words, sentences, and paragraphs

4 Divide students into pairs or groups. Project the text or distribute it as a handout. Tell students that it is an excerpt from an essay about plastic surgery that they will use as a guide when performing the revision process.

Plastic surgery can be bad. It can be expensive. It has at times proven to be an amalgam of poorly-thought-through processes, techniques, and methods that ultimately resolves neither the physical or emotional issues that prompted it in the first place. It can be painful. It can be expensive, like I said. It can be disappointing.

Coach students through a revision of this text. Point out that well-written essay text avoids:

- general and unsupported statements
- wordiness and lack of conciseness
- imprecise terms such as *good, bad, many,* and *few*
- self-reference
- addressing more than one subtopic in each body paragraph

5 When students have completed their revisions, discuss their work as a class. Work together to construct an effective revision of the text.

6 Instruct students to perform step 1 individually, revising their first draft and explaining their revisions on the lines provided.

7 Read aloud the Editing section. Show students a print or online example of a style guide. Distribute the following text as a handout and use it to model the process of editing with a style guide.

Another problimatic thing about plastic surgery is it's cost. According to Doctor Jonathan Richman in his groundbreaking essay: Looking Young Is More Expensive Than You Think—"More than half of all plastic surgery patients expect to undergo a single procedure. Unfortunately, many discover that reaching their goal entails several more trips to the surgeon than they anticipated." It is also not unusual for patience to undergo surgery, only to discover that their insurance will reimburse the procedure only partially—or not at all.

8 Instruct students to perform student step 2 individually, editing their draft using a print or online style guide and describing their edits on the lines provided.

9 Give students time to respond to the Peer Revising and Editing section. Consider having students repeat the process as time permits.

10 Have a student read aloud the Setting a Purpose for Viewing. Allow students to discuss the iconic images they associate with America.

It's best to treat revision and editing as two separate processes. That lets you focus exclusively on several equally important areas. Because revision deals with the "big picture"—clarity and development of your ideas—it's important to revise first and then edit, as you may add, delete, or rewrite sentences in the revising stage.

Peer Revising and Editing

After you have revised and edited your first draft, it is often a good idea to get feedback from another writer. Choose a partner or have your teacher choose one for you. Swap your definition essays with each other and politely critique (evaluate and analyze) them. Point out the strengths you notice in your partner's essay and suggest changes that might improve the essay if they seem appropriate. Review any concerns or suggestions from your partner and consider how you can use that feedback to make your own essay better.

You might consider repeating this process until your text reads just the way you'd like it to. At that point, it's time to publish your work, or distribute it to your audience.

Setting a Purpose for Viewing

Some images have become a part of the story of the United States. Photographs from an event or of a person often capture some of the essence of what it is to be an American. What makes some images more iconic than the rest is the impact they have on the person viewing the image. There is a point at which an image has a strong enough impact that it becomes a part of our national story and collective memory.

Robert Hariman and John Louis Lucaites define the term *iconic image* in their article "Performing Civic Identity: The Iconic Photograph of the Flag Raising on Iwo Jima": "Iconic photographs are widely recognized as representations of significant historical events, activate strong emotional response, and are reproduced across a range of media, genres, or topics."

American Marines raising flag on Mount Suribachi, Iwo Jima, 1945, taken by Joe Rosenthal on February 23, 1945.

Working from the Text

3. Explain the strong emotional response that this image activates. What makes it an iconic American image?

4. Revisit your vocabulary tree and add details to your working definition of what it means to be an American.

Research Review

Review your familiarity with primary and secondary sources. For the essay you will write for Embedded Assessment 1, explaining your definition is central; the sources should support your explanation.

Primary sources are original documents containing firsthand information about a subject (e.g., letters or diaries). A secondary source is a discussion or commentary about primary sources, offering an interpretation about information gathered from a primary source (e.g., history books or encyclopedias).

To help ensure that you use substantial, accurate, and timely sources to support your position, it is important to consider each source's validity, reliability, and relevancy.

Validity: Does the information appear to be accurate and well documented? Is there a bibliography or list of sources? Does the information appear to be free from bias, or does it present only a single position?

Reliability: Are the author's name and qualifications clearly identified? Is the information from a respected institution (e.g., a university)? If it is an online resource, is the site listed as .gov, .edu, or .org rather than .com?

Relevance: Is the information closely related to your topic? Does it offer support with facts or other information you can quote to support your position?

Researching Iconic American Images

Research and find your own idea of an iconic American image. You will submit an image for your classroom's Gallery of America and provide an explanation of your choice to share with your fellow students.

5. As you think about what iconic American image you will add to the classroom gallery, revisit your vocabulary tree and the images you highlighted in the poem. With a partner, brainstorm a list of significant events that you can remember from history, news, or life.

As you research your iconic American image, keep in mind the three elements of significant images:

• The image is widely recognized as representative of a significant historical event.
• The image evokes strong emotional response.
• The image has been reproduced across a range of media, genres, or topics.

Selecting a Topic

6. Select one or two items on your list and expand your thinking with some notes on what you already know about the topic. Consider these questions as you think about your topics: How is this topic historically relevant for most Americans? What key words are associated with this topic?

Select one topic as the subject of your gallery submission and begin your research.

ACTIVITY 1.14 continued

11 Study the image as a class. Read the caption and direct students complete the Working from the Text section. Consider using the **OPTIC** strategy to analyze the photograph.

12 Engage students in a class discussion about the Research Review section and their short research project, clarifying requirements and answering any questions students may have about the expectations of the assignment.

13 Have students read the Researching Iconic American Images section. Specifically, make sure that students understand the term *iconic* and the three elements of iconic images: (1) They represent significant historical events, (2) they activate a strong emotional response, and (3) they are reproduced across a range of media, genres, or topics. Use the Iwo Jima image as a **visual prompt** to discuss the three elements.

14 Have students pair up and **brainstorm** significant events and images in American history. Once students have completed their initial thinking, ask them to **think-pair-share**. Partners should decide if the possible image represents a historically significant event and activates a strong emotional response.

15 Have students read the Selecting a Topic and Researching Your Image sections. Begin the research project with students by providing access to the Internet, to print media, and to history books. Review the key ideas of primary sources, secondary sources, validity, and reliability.

16 Once students have found their iconic images, they need to prepare to present their images to the class in the **gallery walk**. Students should print out their images and create a placards to place under the images to provide the patrons with key details about the image. Encourage students to model their placard after the examples provided for each image in the activity. Provide a little distance between the images so that students will be able to stand next to their images during the gallery walk.

17 Have students read the Presenting Your Image section and prepare for the gallery walk by practicing their brief presentation with a partner.

18 For the gallery walk, split the class in half. One half will present their iconic images while the other half walks around and listens to the presentations. Monitor presentations to gauge the depth of student understanding.

19 Be sure students respond to the Check Your Understanding task.

20 Have students attend to the Independent Reading Checkpoint. Direct them to write a statement in their Reader/Writer notebooks that summarizes their impressions of how the authors or subjects of their chosen readings have experienced the American Dream. Set a date to check for the summary statement in students' notebooks.

ASSESS

Review students drafts after they have completed the peer revising and editing process. Note whether their completed work indicates an understanding of the related but separate processes of revision and editing.

Review the choices and explanations students gave for the Check Your Understanding task. Students' explanations should show a grasp of the criteria that make an image iconic.

ADAPT

If students need additional help in executing the revising and editing processes, assign them to a **quickwrite** activity that summarizes what they know about revising and editing. As needed, guide students through a revision and edit of their summary. Guide them in the use of a style guide if necessary.

For help researching iconic images, select small groups of students to pursue this assignment as a group project.

To extend the assignment, have students use presentation software, an online slideshow, or another medium to present the images.

Researching Your Image

7. Pictures are everywhere: on the Internet, in print media, and in history books. Internet image searches can be refined to locate black-and-white images, color images, fine art, and so on. Where will you find the most useful information? Use the ideas and the key words that you generated to guide your review of reliable sources. Print a copy of your iconic image and create a plaque with a description, title, and photographic credit.

   Your image:

   When it was created:

   Why it is iconic:

   Why you chose it:

Presenting Your Image

After all images and descriptions have been added to the Gallery of America, prepare a brief presentation of your image for your peers. This presentation should introduce the image, provide some background knowledge, and explain the significance of the image and why you chose it.

In pairs, go through the exhibit, listening to each presenter's brief explanation of his or her iconic image. After you have seen and heard all of the presentations, add additional thoughts and details to your vocabulary tree for defining the term *American*.

☑ Check Your Understanding

Review the presentations that you have seen and select two images you would add to the permanent exhibit of iconic American images. Write your choices and the reasons for your selection on a feedback card.

> **⏱ Independent Reading Checkpoint**
> Review the text or texts you have read independently so far in this unit and the different viewpoints expressed. Then write a statement that summarizes your impressions of how the authors or subjects experienced the American Dream.

Writing a Definition Essay

ASSIGNMENT

Your assignment is to write a multi-paragraph essay that defines your interpretation of what it means to be an American. This essay should use the strategies of definition and different perspectives from the unit to help you develop a complex and thoughtful definition. If possible, incorporate an iconic image into your essay.

Planning and Prewriting	■ What prewriting strategy will help you define what it means to be an American (free writing, webbing, graphic organizer)? ■ What pieces of writing from this unit did you connect strongly with? How can they help to add depth and dimension to your definition? ■ How can you share your ideas with a peer to help you select the strongest material to include in your draft?
Drafting	■ How will you take the complex elements of your definition and work them into a clear, focused thesis statement? ■ How can you sequence your ideas so that they work together to build a clear and convincing definition? ■ What strategies of definition work well with your selected evidence and ideas?
Evaluating and Revising	■ Does your essay have coherence? Does it present ideas that tie together and flow smoothly, making the essay easy to follow for the reader? ■ Does your essay have specific, varied diction and a variety of sentence patterns? ■ Where can you add or revise transitions so that one idea smoothly leads to another? ■ How can you use the Scoring Guide as a tool to evaluate your draft or to seek out feedback from others?
Editing and Publishing	■ How will you check your writing for grammatical and technical accuracy? ■ What sort of outside resources can help you to check your draft (e.g., a format guide, a dictionary)? ■ What is an effective way to use the last read-through of your essay to make final adjustments (e.g., read it out loud or have a peer read it to you)?

Reflection

After completing this Embedded Assessment, think about how you went about accomplishing this assignment and respond to the following:

- In what ways did the process of defining what it means to be an American cause you to rethink or reevaluate your own ideas?
- Did the material that you read in this unit have a role in this? Why or why not?

College and Career Readiness Standards

Focus Standards:

W.11-12.2 Write informative/explanatory texts to examine and convey complex ideas, concepts, and information clearly and accurately through the effective selection, organization, and analysis of content.

W.11-12.2b Develop the topic thoroughly by selecting the most significant and relevant facts, extended definitions, concrete details, quotations, or other information and examples appropriate to the audience's knowledge of the topic.

Additional Standards Addressed:

L.11-12.1, L.11-12.2, L.11-12.2b

Suggested Pacing: 2 50-minute class periods

1 Planning and Prewriting: As students respond to the prewriting questions, monitor their use of brainstorming strategies, notes and activity answers, and their vocabulary trees. These will become the basis of their textual evidence to support their definitions. You may want to allow them to work together during this stage of the writing process.

2 Students can use the four focus questions in the graphic organizer in Activity 1.13 for each definition strategy to help them rework their initial definitions of what it means to be an American. They should try to define the concept by function, classification, example, and negation. Remind students to use specific examples from their sources as well as their own personal experiences to answer the four focus questions.

3 Drafting: In order to respond to the prompt in Embedded Assessment 1, students must first clearly articulate what functional definition of the word *American* they will be working with. Taking into account all of the questions, ask students to choose the definition they will be working with or create a new definition considering their responses. Have them write their definition and discuss their ideas in small groups.

4 Evaluating and Revising: Consider using writing groups to help students examine and apply the Scoring Guide's "Use of Language" criteria to their drafts.

5 Editing and Publishing: Be sure students have access to computers so they can edit and publish their essays in the most polished form possible.

6 You might want your students to turn in their brainstorming, notes, and drafts along with their final essay and use these items as part of a process grade.

7 Reflection: Have students respond to the questions and add them to the folder they are using for their portfolios.

8 Be sure students use this opportunity to move their unit work from the Working Folder into a Portfolio of work that represents important stages in developing an understanding of what it is to be an American. Once you return their definition essays, you might have students staple together all their process work from the unit.

SCORING GUIDE

When you score this Embedded Assessment, you may wish to make copies or download and print copies of the Scoring Guide from SpringBoard Digital so you can have a copy to mark for each student's work.

Scoring Criteria	Exemplary	Proficient	Emerging	Incomplete
Ideas	The essay • asserts a focused, clearly stated thesis • develops and supports the thesis thoroughly with relevant, significant, and substantial facts and quotations • synthesizes information on multiple, relevant perspectives	The essay • asserts a clear thesis • develops and supports the thesis with relevant facts and quotations • incorporates information on various perspectives	The essay • presents an unfocused or limited thesis • attempts to develop and support the thesis with weak evidence that may not be appropriate • inconsistently incorporates information on various perspectives	The essay • asserts a weak thesis • contains facts, quotations, or other information that may not develop or support the topic • contains insufficient information on various perspectives
Structure	The essay • organizes complex ideas so that new elements build to create a unified whole • creates an effective and engaging introduction and conclusion that articulate the significance of the topic • uses a variety of definition strategies with skill and purpose • uses a variety of meaningful transitions	The essay • organizes ideas so that each new element builds on that which preceded it to create cohesion • presents a clear and focused introduction and conclusion • uses a variety of definition strategies effectively • uses transitions to connect the larger ideas of the essay	The essay • creates limited cohesion with inconsistent connections among the elements • contains an underdeveloped or unfocused introduction and/or conclusion • attempts to use definition strategies with limited success • inconsistently uses transitions to connect ideas	The essay • demonstrates limited cohesion; expected elements may be missing • lacks an introduction and/or conclusion • uses few or no definition strategies • presents limited use of transitions
Use of Language	The essay • chooses precise diction and a variety of sentence types and structures to enhance the reader's understanding • demonstrates superior command of conventions • integrates and cites textual evidence smoothly	The essay • uses diction and a variety of sentence types or structures that appropriately manage the topic • demonstrates a command of conventions so that minor errors do not interfere with meaning • integrates and cites textual evidence correctly	The essay • uses diction that is inconsistent and provides little variety in sentence structure • attempts to follow conventions, but errors in usage may cause some confusion • uses textual evidence without smooth or correct integration	The essay • uses diction that is inappropriate at times; shows little or no variety in sentence structure • contains errors in grammar, punctuation, capitalization, or spelling that interfere with meaning • contains little or no integrated textual evidence

Unpacking Embedded Assessment 2

Learning Targets

- Reflect on concepts, essential questions, and vocabulary.
- Identify and analyze the knowledge and skills needed to complete Embedded Assessment 2 successfully.
- Compose a reaction statement that takes a specific position.

Preview

In this activity, you will explore the ideas and tasks involved in Embedded Assessment 2.

Learning Strategies

Close Reading
Graphic Organizer
Quickwrite

Making Connections

An important task of every critical thinker is to be able to read and understand the thinking of others. More importantly, as a critical thinker you must be able to gather together many ideas and sort through them to find what you can use and what you can discard in formulating your own thinking. This act of synthesis, or combining, often entails the creative act of constructing your own definitions. Synthesizing your own thoughts, your reading, and your research will lead to your own personal understanding of a complex idea such as the "American Dream."

Essential Questions

You have constructed a personal definition of an American. Now write about your understanding of Essential Question 2: What is the American Dream?

Unpacking Embedded Assessment 2

Closely read the assignment for Embedded Assessment 2: Synthesizing the American Dream.

Your assignment is to synthesize at least three to five sources and your own observations to defend, challenge, or qualify the statement that "America still provides access to the American Dream." This question requires you to integrate a variety of sources (three to five) into a coherent, well-written argumentative essay. Be sure to refer to the sources and employ your own observations to support your position. Your argument should be the focus of your essay; the sources and your observations should support this argument.

With your class, identify and analyze the knowledge you need (what do you need to know?) and the skills you must have (what must you be able to do?) to complete the assignment successfully. Create a graphic organizer as you "unpack" the requirements of Embedded Assessment 2.

🕮 Independent Reading Plan

For the second half of this unit, focus your independent reading by selecting texts that reflect either the immigrant experience or growing up in America. Consider how your reading connects to your personal definition of the American Dream. Note examples that will help you support your ideas in your argumentative essay.

My Notes

College and Career Readiness Standards

Focus Standards:

SL.11-12.1 Initiate and participate effectively in a range of collaborative discussions (one-on-one, in groups, and teacher-led) with diverse partners on grades 11–12 topics, texts, and issues, building on others' ideas and expressing their own clearly and persuasively.

SL.11-12.1b Work with peers to promote civil, democratic discussions and decision-making, set clear goals and deadlines, and establish individual roles as needed.

ACTIVITY 1.15

PLAN

Materials: 11 × 17 inch or larger paper for each student or access to digital drawing software
Suggested Pacing: 1 50-minute class period

TEACH

1 Introduce the Learning Targets and read the Preview aloud.

2 Read the Making Connections section with students. Make sure they understand that in this part of the unit, they will continue the process of reading and synthesizing information from texts but will move from informational to argumentative writing.

3 Take a few minutes to ask students to respond to Essential Question 2 and then ask them to review their initial response and evaluate how their understanding has grown so far.

4 Guide students to revisit the academic and literary vocabulary for the unit, reviewing their understanding of these unit concepts.

5 As students do a **close read** of the assignment in Unpacking Embedded Assessment 2, be sure to consult the Scoring Guide for more detailed expectations.

6 Work with students to unpack the elements of the Embedded Assessment and create a class "unpacking" **graphic organizer** that can be posted in the room so students understand and prepare for the targeted learning.

7 In the second half of the unit, students will have the opportunity to read texts in addition to the classroom reading. Texts about the immigrant experience or growing up in America are recommended, but student choice is paramount. Review the Independent Reading Plan as a class.

8 As part of an introduction to the idea of the American Dream, students should complete the survey to **activate prior knowledge** and preview the ideas that permeate the texts and assignments within the unit. After students have completed the survey, direct them to share their responses in pairs. Then conduct a **whole-class discussion** and focus on the Essential Question.

9 Ask students to **quickwrite** a reflection on their reactions to their responses and the discussion. Students will be asked to revisit this activity as they proceed through the unit.

ASSESS

Have students write an exit slip describing at least two things they will need to learn in order to complete the Embedded Assessment successfully.

ADAPT

If students need help with the quickwrite activity, have them use the **Conversation for Quickwrite** graphic organizer.

Survey

As you read each of the following statements, use a scale from 1 to 10 and decide to what extent these ideas are prevalent today. If the idea presented in the statement is something you are exposed to on a regular basis, rate it a 10. If you do not see evidence of the statement at all, rate it a 1 (and remember there are plenty of numbers in between).

_____ 1. Education is the foundation of a free society.

_____ 2. Individuals' rights are superior to the needs of society.

_____ 3. All religious beliefs are protected.

_____ 4. Our government was created to guarantee freedoms.

_____ 5. Education is important primarily to get a job.

_____ 6. Community provides strength and support to individuals.

_____ 7. Human beings are basically good and getting better.

_____ 8. Individual liberties must always be controlled by government authority.

_____ 9. Self-reliance and independence are important to a good life.

_____ 10. Science and progress are closely related.

_____ 11. The American Dream means making lots of money.

_____ 12. Hard work equals success.

_____ 13. Everyone can achieve the American Dream.

_____ 14. The American Dream includes freedom from want.

_____ 15. Sacrifice is part of achieving success and prosperity.

Quickwrite: Reflect on your ratings. Share your responses with a partner or a small group. You might choose to share your responses with the whole class. After discussing, select one statement that you and your partners think is an important part of the American Dream. Defend your position and explain the rationale for your thinking.

The Structure of an Argument

Learning Targets
- Analyze the characteristics and structural elements of argumentative texts.
- Evaluate the effectiveness of an argument.
- Analyze how English usage has changed since the 18th century.

Preview
In this activity, you will read the Declaration of Independence and analyze its effectiveness as a piece of argumentative writing.

Learning Strategies
Graphic Organizer
Marking the Text
Quickwrite

Vocabulary of the Declaration of Independence

1. When reading a text from a specific historical period, you will see unfamiliar words that may no longer be used in modern English or had a different meaning when the text was originally written. The Declaration of Independence can be a difficult text to comprehend as it contains both difficult words and unfamiliar words. Familiarize yourself with some of these difficult words by using the definitions in the sidebars of the text to help you complete the sentences.

abdicated	arbitrary	consanguinity	despotism	magnanimity
perfidy	redress	rectitude	unalienable	usurpations

a. The king ruled the land with absolute ___despotism___ that no one could question.

b. Robert became king through ___usurpations___, not through legitimate inheritance.

c. The queen's subjects were in awe of her ___magnanimity___.

d. The harsh punishment for the crime seemed ___arbitrary___ since others received a lighter sentence.

e. The king ___abdicated___ his position as ruler when he failed to send the troops to protect the gates.

f. The shop owner offered a refund as ___redress___ to customers who bought the faulty merchandise.

g. The crooked queen was guilty of ___perfidy___ when she refused to obey the treaty.

h. Life, liberty, and the pursuit of happiness are ___unalienable___ rights in the United States.

i. The ___consanguinity___ of the distant cousins was well known thanks to family records that were kept.

j. Because of her ___rectitude___, I am certain she is innocent

My Notes

College and Career Readiness Standards

Focus Standards:

RI.11-12.8 Delineate and evaluate the reasoning in seminal U.S. texts, including the application of constitutional principles and use of legal reasoning and the premises, purposes, and arguments in works of public advocacy.

RI.11-12.9 Analyze seventeenth-, eighteenth-, and nineteenth-century foundational U.S. documents of historical and literary significance for their themes, purposes, and rhetorical features.

RI.11-12.5 Analyze and evaluate the effectiveness of the structure an author uses in his or her exposition or argument, including whether the structure makes points clear, convincing, and engaging.

Additional Standards Addressed:

RI.11-12.1, RI.11-12.4

ACTIVITY 1.16

PLAN
Materials: audio version of the Declaration of Independence
Suggested Pacing: 2 50-minute class periods

TEACH

1 Read aloud the Learning Targets for the activity. Define and clarify terms as needed.

2 Read the Preview with students. Help them understand that they will be examining a seminal document of American history. They will focus primarily on the document's structure as an argument, but a deeper study of the document's language is also encouraged.

3 Have students complete the Vocabulary of the Declaration of Independence section.

4 Ask students to find a partner and together read the Characteristics and Structural Elements of an Argument section, discussing each element to ensure understanding. Then invite students to share any questions they have on the elements in a brief class discussion.

Characteristics and Structural Elements of an Argument

Read through the explanations of the structural elements of arguments with a partner. Discuss each element to ensure you know its purpose and characteristics so you can recognize and use these elements.

Hook

- The hook grabs the reader's attention and interest.
- It establishes a connection between the writer and a specific, identifiable audience, using information about that audience (its concerns, characteristics, and background knowledge) to do so.
- The hook can be but is not limited to an anecdote, an image, a definition, or a quotation.

Arguable Thesis

- The thesis clearly states the writer's **claim** by telling readers what the writer wishes to argue.
- It concisely states the claim in a well-conceived complex sentence.
- It usually comes in the opening paragraph of the text.

Concessions, Refutations, and Rebuttals

- Concessions are used to recognize counterclaims made by the other side.
- Concessions acknowledge counterclaims fairly and thoroughly.
- Refutations are when a writer argues at length against the opposing viewpoint by proving that his or her claim has more validity.
- Rebuttals are when the writer grants that the other side has some validity and then explains why his or her argument is better.
- All three of these techniques build credibility by discussing strengths and limitations with fairness and objectivity.
- Concessions, refutations, and rebuttals are strongest when they anticipate the concerns, characteristics, background knowledge, and position(s) of the audience.

Support

- Support presents facts to convince the audience of the writer's claim.
- It sets out the reasoning behind the writer's argument.
- It provides supporting evidence of the writer's claim (data, quotes, anecdotes, etc.).
- It blends together logical and emotional appeals and takes into account the kinds of appeals that will have the most impact on the audience.

Convincing Conclusion

- A convincing conclusion restates the main claim of the thesis and provides readers with a call to action.
- A convincing conclusion makes a final new appeal to values.
- A convincing conclusion tries not to repeat information but sums up the argument with a few final facts and appeals.
- The **call to action** is a plea to readers to take a specific action that furthers the cause of the argument being made. It gives readers an action item that they can carry out after the writer has convinced them to support the cause.

As You Read

- Underline strong words and phrases that could appeal to a reader's emotions.
- Circle unknown words and phrases. Try to determine the meaning of the words by using context clues, word parts, or a dictionary.

My Notes

About the Document

The Declaration of Independence, written primarily by Thomas Jefferson, was adopted by the Continental Congress on July 4, 1776. It announced to King George III of Great Britain that the 13 British colonies in North America had decided to become an independent nation. The colonies had been at war with Great Britain for over a year, fighting for their rights under the British Empire. By the summer of 1776, however, the colonists had decided that reconciliation would be impossible and that they needed to be entirely independent from Great Britain. Today, the declaration is considered a foundational document of the United States because it outlines the beliefs of the people who gave birth to the idea of America.

Historical Document

The Declaration of Independence

Chunk 1

1   When in the Course of human events, it becomes necessary for one people to dissolve the political bands which have connected them with another, and to assume among the powers of the earth, the separate and equal station to which the Laws of Nature and of Nature's God entitle them, a decent respect to the opinions of mankind requires that they should declare the causes which **impel** them to the separation.

2   We hold these truths to be self-evident, that all men are created equal, that they are endowed by their Creator with certain **unalienable** Rights, that among these are Life, Liberty and the pursuit of Happiness.—That to secure these rights, Governments are instituted among Men, deriving their just powers from the consent of the governed,—That whenever any Form of Government becomes destructive of these ends, it is the Right of the People to alter or to abolish it, and to institute new Government, laying its foundation on such principles and organizing its powers in such form, as to them shall seem most likely to effect their Safety and Happiness. Prudence, indeed, will dictate that Governments long established should not be changed for light and transient causes; and accordingly all experience hath shewn, that mankind are more disposed to suffer, while evils are sufferable, than to right themselves by

impel: to drive forward, force
unalienable: unable to be taken away

5 Read the As You Read section with students, making sure they understand what they should pay attention to during their first reading of the document.

6 Have students read the About the Document section, encouraging them to circle unfamiliar words and phrases as they read. Model ways to determine the meaning of these words and phrases through context clues, word parts, or dictionaries.

7 FIRST READ: Have small groups read the Declaration of Independence. Ask groups to pause after reading Chunk 1. Have students discuss what the author is saying when he writes, "But when a long train of abuses and usurpations, pursuing invariably the same Object evinces a design to reduce them under absolute Despotism, it is their right, it is their duty, to throw off such Government, and to provide new Guards for their future security." Ask students to restate the sentence in more straightforward language.

 TEXT COMPLEXITY

Overall: Very Complex
Lexile: 1480L
Qualitative: High Difficulty
Task: Moderate (Analyze)

8 As students are reading, monitor their progress. Be sure they are engaged with the text and are underlining strong words and phrases that could appeal to readers' emotions.

TEACHER TO TEACHER

Consider pausing after each chunk to discuss questions students may have. The long and often complex sentences and vocabulary can be challenging for students. Pausing to digest each section will also help students see how the argument builds upon each previous section. For example, pause after Chunk 2 and discuss how each paragraph starts with *He* and lists a specific grievance. Pause after Chunk 3 and point out how each paragraph lists how the colonists have been subjected to a "jurisdiction foreign to our constitution." Pause after Chunk 4 and ask students to restate what the author means when he writes, "In every state of the Oppressions, We have Petitioned for Redress in the most humble terms."

LEVELED DIFFERENTIATED INSTRUCTION

In this activity, students may need support identifying the main ideas of a challenging text.

Developing Allow students to work in small groups to read the text. Provide partners with the **Idea and Argument Evaluator** graphic organizer to support them in identifying the main ideas of the text.

Expanding Allow students to work in pairs to read the text, alternating readers for each paragraph. Have them paraphrase each paragraph as they read. Have a dictionary readily available.

Bridging As students read the text, have them summarize each chunk in the margins. Then have partners compare their summaries to add to their understanding.

Support Assign students one of the 28 injuries and usurpations of the king of Great Britain listed in the Declaration. Have students create a visual representation of their assigned section to share with the class.

My Notes

usurpations: acts of wrongfully taking over a right or power that belongs to someone else

despotism: a political system where the ruler holds absolute power

---

abolishing the forms to which they are accustomed. But when a long train of abuses and usurpations, pursuing invariably the same Object evinces a design to reduce them under absolute Despotism, it is their right, it is their duty, to throw off such Government, and to provide new Guards for their future security. Such has been the patient sufferance of these Colonies; and such is now the necessity which constrains them to alter their former Systems of Government. The history of the present King of Great Britain is a history of repeated injuries and usurpations, all having in direct object the establishment of an absolute Tyranny over these States. To prove this, let Facts be submitted to a candid world.

Chunk 2

3   He has refused his Assent to Laws, the most wholesome and necessary for the public good.

4   He has forbidden his Governors to pass Laws of immediate and pressing importance, unless suspended in their operation till his Assent should be obtained; and when so suspended, he has utterly neglected to attend to them.

5   He has refused to pass other Laws for the accommodation of large districts of people, unless those people would relinquish the right of Representation in the Legislature, a right inestimable to them and formidable to tyrants only.

6   He has called together legislative bodies at places unusual, uncomfortable, and distant from the depository of their public Records, for the sole purpose of fatiguing them into compliance with his measures.

7   He has dissolved Representative Houses repeatedly, for opposing with manly firmness his invasions on the rights of the people.

8   He has refused for a long time, after such dissolutions, to cause others to be elected; whereby the Legislative powers, incapable of Annihilation, have returned to the People at large for their exercise; the State remaining in the mean time exposed to all the dangers of invasion from without, and convulsions within.

9   He has endeavoured to prevent the population of these States; for that purpose obstructing the Laws for Naturalization of Foreigners; refusing to pass others to encourage their migrations hither, and raising the conditions of new Appropriations of Lands.

10   He has obstructed the Administration of Justice, by refusing his Assent to Laws for establishing Judiciary powers.

11   He has made Judges dependent on his Will alone, for the tenure of their offices, and the amount and payment of their salaries.

12   He has erected a multitude of New Offices, and sent hither swarms of Officers to harrass our people, and eat out their substance.

Scaffolding the Text-Dependent Questions

2. According to the text, what five truths are held to be "self-evident"? Review paragraph 2 in Chunk 1. What five phrases finish the sentence that begins, "We hold these truths to be self-evident ..."? RI.11-12.1

5. In paragraph 2, why does the author include the line "To prove this, let the Facts be submitted to a candid world"? Scan Chunk 2 to find the line. What facts does the author want to submit? Why does the author want these facts to be known? What will the facts prove? RI.11-12.4

4. What does the word *assent* mean based on how it is used in paragraph 3? Locate *assent* in paragraph 3. What synonym could be used in place of *assent* in the first sentence in Chunk 2 without changing the authors' meaning? How does the context help you determine the word's meaning here? RI.11-12.4

13 He has kept among us, in times of peace, Standing Armies without the Consent of our legislatures.

14 He has affected to render the Military independent of and superior to the Civil power.

15 He has combined with others to subject us to a jurisdiction foreign to our constitution, and unacknowledged by our laws; giving his Assent to their Acts of pretended Legislation:

Chunk 3

16 For Quartering large bodies of armed troops among us:

17 For protecting them, by a mock Trial, from punishment for any Murders which they should commit on the Inhabitants of these States:

18 For cutting off our Trade with all parts of the world:

19 For imposing Taxes on us without our Consent:

20 For depriving us in many cases, of the benefits of Trial by Jury:

21 For transporting us beyond Seas to be tried for pretended offences

22 For abolishing the free System of English Laws in a neighbouring Province, establishing therein an Arbitrary government, and enlarging its Boundaries so as to render it at once an example and fit instrument for introducing the same absolute rule into these Colonies:

23 For taking away our Charters, abolishing our most valuable Laws, and altering fundamentally the Forms of our Governments:

24 For suspending our own Legislatures and declaring themselves invested with power to legislate for us in all cases whatsoever. Chunk 4

25 He has abdicated Government here, by declaring us out of his Protection and waging War against us.

26 He has plundered our seas, ravaged our Coasts, burnt our towns, and destroyed the lives of our people.

27 He is at this time transporting large Armies of foreign Mercenaries to compleat the works of death, desolation and tyranny, already begun with circumstances of Cruelty & perfidy scarcely paralleled in the most barbarous ages, and totally unworthy the Head of a civilized nation.

28 He has constrained our fellow Citizens taken Captive on the high Seas to bear Arms against their Country, to become the executioners of their friends and Brethren, or to fall themselves by their Hands.

29 He has excited domestic insurrections amongst us, and has endeavoured to bring on the inhabitants of our frontiers, the merciless Indian Savages, whose known rule of warfare, is an undistinguished destruction of all ages, sexes and conditions.

WORD CONNECTIONS

Roots and Affixes
The word jurisdiction contains two Latin roots. The first is *jur-*, which means "right, law." The second is *dic-* or *dict-*, which means "to say." The suffix *-ion* means "act of." What then does *jurisdiction* mean?

My Notes

arbitrary: based on unpredictable decisions rather than law
abdicated: failed to fulfill a responsibility or duty
perfidy: deceitfulness, treachery

ACTIVITY 1.16 continued

9 **Vocabulary Development:** Direct students to the Word Connections box and use the example to explain how they can determine meaning of unfamiliar words by using the word parts. Then ask them to think of other words that share the root *jur* or *dict* or the suffix *-ion*, as in *jurisdiction*. As an extension, have students complete the **Roots and Affixes Brainstorm** graphic organizer.

Scaffolding the Text-Dependent Questions

5. What function do the grievances against the king listed in Chunks 2–4 serve in the argument? What do the authors of the Declaration expect the king to do about the grievances? Why do they bother to itemize them? RI.11-12.6

6. What rhetorical appeals does this foundational U.S. document make in paragraph 29? What effect do they have on the audience? Does this paragraph appeal to the audience's reason, emotions, or both? What specific words in the document help make these appeals? RI.11-12.6

10 After reading the text for the first time, guide the class in a discussion by asking the Making Observations questions. Check students' general comprehension of the text based on their observations, asking follow-up questions if needed.

1.16

My Notes

_____
_____
_____
_____
_____
_____
_____
_____
_____
_____
_____
_____

redress: the correction of wrong, compensation
magnanimity: the condition of being high-minded, noble
consanguinity: having the same origin or ancestry
rectitude: morally correct behavior or thinking

30 In every stage of these Oppressions We have Petitioned for Redress in the most humble terms: Our repeated Petitions have been answered only by repeated injury. A Prince whose character is thus marked by every act which may define a Tyrant, is unfit to be the ruler of a free people.

Chunk 5

31 Nor have We been wanting in attentions to our British brethren. We have warned them from time to time of attempts by their legislature to extend an unwarrantable jurisdiction over us. We have reminded them of the circumstances of our emigration and settlement here. We have appealed to their native justice and magnanimity, and we have conjured them by the ties of our common kindred to disavow these usurpations, which would inevitably interrupt our connections and correspondence. They too have been deaf to the voice of justice and of consanguinity. We must, therefore, acquiesce in the necessity, which denounces our Separation, and hold them, as we hold the rest of mankind, Enemies in War, in Peace Friends.

32 We, therefore, the Representatives of the United States of America, in General Congress, Assembled, appealing to the Supreme Judge of the world for the rectitude of our intentions, do, in the Name, and by Authority of the good People of these Colonies, solemnly publish and declare, That these United Colonies are, and of Right ought to be Free and Independent States; that they are Absolved from all Allegiance to the British Crown, and that all political connection between them and the State of Great Britain, is and ought to be totally dissolved; and that as Free and Independent States, they have full Power to levy War, conclude Peace, contract Alliances, establish Commerce, and to do all other Acts and Things which Independent States may of right do. And for the support of this Declaration, with a firm reliance on the protection of divine Providence, we mutually pledge to each other our Lives, our Fortunes and our sacred Honor.

Making Observations
- What emotions did you feel while reading this text?
- Which "injuries and usurpations" stand out most to you?

Scaffolding the Text-Dependent Questions

7. How does the author's use of the term _unwarrantable jurisdiction_ in paragraph 31 affect the reader's perception of the English's treatment of the Americans? Find the sentence in paragraph 31 that contains the term _unwarrantable jurisdiction_. _Unwarrantable_ means "not authorized." What connotation does the word _unwarrantable_ have? What does it mean if someone is not authorized to have jurisdiction? RI.11-12.4

8. What effect does the authors' use of enumeration have on their argument? Remember that _enumeration_ is listing a number of things one by one. What does the author list in this document? Why does the author list all of those things? RI.11-12.6

Returning to the Text

- Return to the historical document as you respond to the following questions. Use text evidence to support your responses.
- Write any additional questions you have about the text in your Reader/Writer Notebook.

2. According to the text, what five truths are held to be "self-evident"?

The five truths are (1) all men are created equal; (2) they are endowed with unalienable rights; (3) these rights include life, liberty, and the pursuit of happiness; (4) the government protects these rights; and (5) if government fails to do so, it is the right of the people to create a new government.

3. In paragraph 2, why does the author include the line "To prove this, let the Facts be submitted to a candid world"?

The author includes this line to introduce the evidence that supports his claim. Also, by calling the list "Facts," he suggests that the list of grievances are factual and unbiased.

4. What does the word *assent* mean, based on how it is used in paragraph 3?

The word *assent* means "agreement." The king has not agreed upon things the colonists wanted.

5. What function do the grievances against the king listed in Chunks 2–4 serve in the argument?

The grievances serve as evidence of the claim that the colonies have strong reasons to declare their independence. According to the text, the king has abused his power, has taken unjust measures against the colonists, and is essentially waging war against his own subjects.

6. What rhetorical appeals does this foundational U.S. document make in paragraph 29? What effect do they have on the audience?

Paragraph 29 appeals to the audience's pathos and logos, as it delineates all the actions the colonists have taken in the recent past to set things right with the British government. These steps include warning their "British brethren" for extending "unwarrantable jurisdiction over us" and appealing "to their native justice and magnanimity" by reminding them of "the ties of our common kindred."

11 **RETURNING TO THE TEXT:** Guide students to return to the text to answer the text-dependent comprehension questions. You may choose to have students reread and work on the questions in pairs.

12 Move among the pairs and listen in as students answer the text-dependent questions. If they have difficulty, scaffold the questions by rephrasing them or breaking them into smaller parts. See the Scaffolding the Text-Dependent Questions boxes for suggestions.

13 Allow students time to work with a partner to discuss the questions in the Gaining Perspectives feature. Encourage pairs to engage in a mock debate, taking the sides of both King George and the founding fathers. After pairs summarize their discussion, ask volunteers to share their ideas and role-play the founding fathers discussing their ideas about government and their problems with King George.

1.16

7. How does the author's use of the term *unwarrantable jurisdiction* in paragraph 31 affect the reader's perception of the English's treatment of the Americans?

The Latin root *jur-* means "right." The author is saying that the English do not have the right to rule the Americans. This affects the perception of the readers by trying to persuade them to think the English are doing something wrong by ruling the Americans.

8. What effect does the authors' use of enumeration have on their argument?

By providing a long list of adverse effects of English rule, the author makes it seem as if declaring independence from English rule is not only justified but the only solution since there are so many injustices and since previous attempts at compromise were met with "repeated injury." The length of the list also emphasizes the suffering of the colonists and helps strengthen the argument.

🌱 Gaining Perspectives

The Declaration of Independence is considered one of the foundational documents of the United States. In it, the founding fathers laid out the wrongs King George inflicted on his colonial subjects and also created a new way for a government to function. With a partner, discuss the reasons why the colonies wanted to form their own nation as well as the following questions:

- What would it have been like to be a creator and signer of the Declaration of Independence?
- What risks were these men taking?
- What do you think the creators would say of our modern application of the principles of American democracy?

When you are done, summarize your discussion in your Reader/Writer Notebook.

Working from the Text

9. Reread the text with a partner and note the characteristics and structural elements of argumentation in the following graphic organizer.

Characteristics and Structural Elements of an Argument	Details from the Declaration of Independence
Audience	"Such has been the patient sufferance of these Colonies; and such is now the necessity which constrains them to alter their former Systems of Government. The history of the present King of Great Britain is a history of repeated injuries and usurpations, all having in direct object the establishment of an absolute Tyranny over these States. To prove this, let Facts be submitted to a candid world."
The Hook	"The unanimous Declaration of the thirteen United States of America" "It is their right, it is their duty, to throw off such Government, and to provide new Guards for their future security."
The Claim	"… That whenever any Form of Government becomes destructive of these ends, it is the Right of the People to alter or to abolish it, and to institute new Government, laying its foundation on such principles and organizing its powers in such form, as to them shall seem most likely to effect their Safety and Happiness."
Concessions and Refutations	"a decent respect to the opinions of mankind requires that they should declare the causes which impel them to the separation." "Prudence, indeed, will dictate that Governments long established should not be changed for light and transient causes; and accordingly all experience hath shewn, that mankind are more disposed to suffer, while evils are sufferable, than to right themselves by abolishing the forms to which they are accustomed." "Nor have We been wanting in attentions to our British brethren. We have warned them from time to time of attempts by their legislature to extend an unwarrantable jurisdiction over us."
Support	"The history of the present King of Great Britain is a history of repeated injuries and usurpations, all having in direct object the establishment of an absolute Tyranny over these States. To prove this, let Facts be submitted to a candid world." Twenty six numbered reasons follow.
Call to Action	"We, therefore, the Representatives of the United States of America, in General Congress, Assembled, appealing to the Supreme Judge of the world for the rectitude of our intentions, do, in the Name, and by Authority of the good People of these Colonies, solemnly publish and declare, That these United Colonies are, and of Right ought to be Free and Independent States; that they are Absolved from all Allegiance to the British Crown …"

ACTIVITY 1.16 continued

14 Have students revisit the text with a partner and complete the Working from the Text section. Review with students the examples of each of the characteristics/structural elements.

15 Have students work with a partner to complete the student step 10 Discussion Prompt activity.

16 Discuss the Check Your Understanding task. Define *diction* as "the speaker's or writer's choice of words." Explain that diction can be formal, informal, poetic, plain, and so on. Look at paragraph 26 as an example. The framers of the Declaration chose strong—even violent—verbs to express their fury and outrage at the king's actions: "He has plundered our seas, ravaged our Coasts, burnt our towns, and destroyed the lives of our people." Discuss how language changes over time. Then have students complete the task.

17 Read the Writing Prompt assignment aloud to students. Note how the assignment asks them to connect the Declaration of Independence, Preamble, and Bill of Rights to their definition of the American Dream. Encourage students to use a graphic organizer to organize their thoughts, beginning with a thesis that expresses their definition and makes the connection. Then have students search for specific quotes from the texts to support their thesis. If they are having trouble finding supporting quotations, suggest that they revise their thesis based on the evidence they are finding.

18 Draw students' attention to the Independent Reading Link activity. Allow them time to **think-pair-share** their answers to the questions.

ASSESS

Review the modern "translations" students wrote of sentences from the Declaration in the Check Your Understanding task. Make sure that the modern versions maintain the same meanings as the original sentences. Ensure that students understand that the writing prompt is an opportunity for them to connect this foundational document of American political life to the social, cultural, economic, and spiritual hopes and expectations embodied in the American Dream. Review student work with an eye to the elements of quality informational writing.

ADAPT

If students need additional help understanding the content of the document before writing about it, have them complete a **SOAPSTone** analysis.

During the discussion, emphasize a sense of the spirit and purpose of the document, since in many ways it captures the foundational ideas embodied in the American Dream.

To extend students' understanding and appreciation of the Declaration of Independence, consider asking students to write their own "declaration of independence" from something in their own lives. They should be sure to use the five key elements of argument to guide their thinking and writing and express their argument using modern language.

INDEPENDENT READING LINK

Read and Discuss

Meet with a partner or small group to discuss the independent reading you have completed so far. How do your readings challenge or support your definition of the American Dream? Do the subjects or narrators in your readings believe the American Dream is worth fighting for or no longer exists?

---

10. **Discussion Prompt:** In what ways did declaring independence protect the unalienable rights of the people of the United States? With a partner, create a list of ways unalienable rights will be protected.

☑ Check Your Understanding

Choose a sentence from the document that struck you as particularly important or strong. Rewrite the sentence using modern English. Briefly note whether the new version carries the same weight and meaning.

> **Writing to Sources: Informational Text**
>
> What is the modern American Dream? How do the foundational documents of American life still support the American Dream today? Write an explanatory essay in which you explain how you think the ideas in this document, as well as those in the Preamble to the Constitution of the United States and the Bill of Rights, contribute to the idea of the American Dream. Be sure to:
>
> - Introduce your thesis that clearly defines the American Dream and how the foundational documents support the modern evolution of that dream. Explain how the foundational documents are still relevant today.
> - Use significant elements from the founding documents as support of your ideas. Maintain a formal and objective tone while using appropriate vocabulary to develop the body of your essay.
> - Vary your transitions from your points and support to create a cohesive essay.

WRITING TO SOURCES: INFORMATIONAL TEXT

The following standards are addressed in the writing prompt:

- W.11-12.2, W.11-12.2a
- W.11-12.2b, W.11-12.2d, W.11-12.2e
- W.11-12.2c

Annotating an Argumentative Text

Learning Targets

- Recognize and analyze characteristics and structural elements of an argument.
- Defend or challenge the author's claims using relevant text evidence and appeals to logic and emotion.

Preview

In this activity, you will read an article to evaluate the author's argument.

About the Author

David Wallechinsky (b. 1948) is a historian and author. In 1975, he published *The People's Almanac*, a collection of facts and general interest articles on a wide range of subjects. While informative, it was written as a book that people could read for pleasure. Wallechinsky was a founding member of the International Society of Olympic Historians (ISOH) and is founder and editor-in-chief of AllGov.com, a website that provides news updates about departments and agencies of the federal government. His personal library contains about 35,000 volumes.

As You Read

- Put a star next to the author's main arguments.
- Underline key evidence that supports those arguments.
- Use the margin to ask questions that clarify your understanding or challenge the author's position or evidence.

Learning Strategies

Marking the Text
Paraphrasing
Quickwrite

My Notes

College and Career Readiness Standards

Focus Standards:

RI.11-12.5 Analyze and evaluate the effectiveness of the structure an author uses in his or her exposition or argument, including whether the structure makes points clear, convincing, and engaging.

RI.11-12.6 Determine an author's point of view or purpose in a text in which the rhetoric is particularly effective, analyzing how style and

content contribute to the power, persuasiveness or beauty of the text.

RI.11-12.1 Cite strong and thorough textual evidence to support analysis of what the text says explicitly as well as inferences drawn from the text, including determining where the text leaves matters uncertain.

Additional Standards Addressed:

W.11-12.4, W11-12.1, W.11-12.1c

ACTIVITY 1.17

PLAN

Suggested Pacing: 1 50-minute class period

TEACH

1 Read aloud the Learning Targets and Preview for the activity. Clarify terms as needed.

2 Have a volunteer read the About the Author section aloud.

3 Review the As You Read section and the following concepts as needed to remind students of the aspects of the author's argument they should be looking for: claim and evidence.

4 **FIRST READ:** Conduct a read aloud of paragraph 1 from "Is the American Dream Still Possible?" Pause and help students put a star next to the author's main argument. Then have students continue reading the rest of the text as a paired reading.

 TEXT COMPLEXITY

Overall: Complex
Lexile: 990L
Qualitative: Moderate Difficulty
Task: Moderate (Analyze)

5 As students are reading, monitor their progress. Be sure they are engaged with the text. Be sure they are underlining the key evidence that supports writer's arguments and are asking questions that help clarify their understanding.

6 Circulate among students as they work. As needed, remind them to star the author's main arguments, underline key evidence, and write questions in the margin. To help them question the text, ask whether they agree with what the author is saying or if his evidence is convincing.

7 Pause after paragraph 5 and discuss how the author describes the data he used to define *middle class* for this report.

1.17

My Notes

Article

Is the American Dream Still Possible?

by **David Wallechinsky**, *Parade*, October 2014

1   To be "middle class" in America once meant living well and having financial security. But today that comfortable and contented lifestyle is harder to achieve and maintain. PARADE commissioned Mark Clements Research Inc. to survey Americans nationwide about their finances and outlook for the future. Contributing Editor David Wallechinsky—author of recent articles on where your tax dollars go and on pork-barrel spending—interprets the results.

2   The traditional American Dream is based on the belief that hardworking citizens can better their lives, pay their monthly bills without worry, give their children a start to an even better life and still save enough to live comfortably after they retire. But many average Americans are struggling—squeezed by rising costs, declining wages, credit-card debt and diminished benefits, with little left over to save for retirement. (See the following statistics.)

3   Does the dream survive? Do most Americans still believe they can forge better lives for themselves?

4   PARADE surveyed more than 2,200 Americans, of whom fully 84% described themselves as belonging to the middle class, regardless of where they live (living costs are higher in some regions) or the size of their household.

5   For this report, we focused on U.S. households earning between $30,000 and $99,000 a year. Most of those surveyed describe themselves as married and having a family. More than 64% say they are employed full-time or part-time. Most say they are in reasonably good health and have a satisfying religious or spiritual life. They own a home and at least two cars, and they are able to take vacations. By international standards, they live a life of prosperity.

6   Yet behind this prosperity is a growing unease. Half of the employed respondents say that they've experienced either increased health-care costs or a cut in health benefits over the last three years, and 39% have had cuts in their overtime, raises or bonuses. Almost two-thirds say they live from paycheck to paycheck, and 47% say that no matter how hard they work, they cannot get ahead. More than a third worry about job loss.

7   Richard Oden of Conyers, Ga.—married, with five children—worked in the beer industry for 23 years. Last year, he developed pneumonia and required major surgery. When he was unable to return to work by a given date, he says, his company terminated him at age 54—even though he had a perfect attendance record and no performance problems.

Scaffolding the Text-Dependent Questions

1. Why does the author spend time in the opening paragraphs detailing the extent of the study? How does this affect the perception of his readers? Reread paragraphs 1–5 and think about what the author's purpose is for writing this text. What claim is he trying to make? What kinds of information must he provide so that audiences will take his claim seriously? RI.11-12.1

2. Who is the author's target audience? Support your answer with evidence from the text. Reread paragraphs 4–5. What specific "class" does the author mention? Reread paragraphs 5–6. What details does he give about people who are in this "class"? Would people in this "class" be interested in this topic? Why? RI.11-12.1

My Notes

8 To help support his family, Oden had to dip into his 401(k) fund, paying a penalty for premature withdrawal. "This was very stressful," he says. "Everything had gone up—except wages."

9 Oden has since started his own business, a "leadership and personal development" consulting firm. His wife, Josett, works as a representative in the health-care field. "I do believe I will recover financially," Oden says, "and that I will realize a decent retirement. But the traditional American Dream? For most Americans, it's still a dream—a pipe dream."

10 Having drawn on his own retirement fund, Oden knows that saving can be a big problem. In the survey, nearly 83% say that there is not much left to save after they've paid their bills. Statistics from the Commerce Department bear this out: The savings rate for Americans is the lowest it has been in 73 years.

11 Self-reliance and sacrifice. Most of those interviewed display qualities common to American success stories: determination, flexibility, **pragmatism**, willingness to work hard and especially self-reliance. Almost three-quarters of the middle-class respondents surveyed say they take responsibility for their own financial destiny and believe that they will succeed or fail based on their own efforts. Still, many are downsizing their dreams.

12 Shelly Comer, 43, of Dos Palos, Calif., is a divorced mother of three who also takes care of a friend of her oldest child, Michelle. She is going into debt so that Michelle can go to college. Shelly has worked her whole life—as a receptionist, janitor, preschool teacher and activities director at a hospital. Recently, she became a registered nurse and now works the night shift in obstetrics at another hospital. Her annual income is $70,377.

13 Michelle, 19, is a freshman at the University of California at Merced. She says she is concerned about the financial burden her education is placing on her family: "In order to meet our expected family contribution, my mother had to borrow the entire amount of her share." For her part, Michelle earned six small scholarships, two of which are renewable for next year, and took out a federal loan. She also works 16 hours a week in the financial-aid office at the university.

14 Shelly has a retirement plan through the hospital. "But I have nothing saved for me," she says. "I'm putting it all into the kids, so that they can succeed in school. Our parents did everything for us, and I hope to do the same for my kids. I don't count on anyone else to help us get to where we want to go. It's all up to me and my family. And I trust in God to help us."

15 Who is responsible? One of the most intriguing results of the Parade survey is that 89% of the middle class believes that businesses have a social responsibility to their employees and to the community. Yet 81% believe that, in fact, American businesses make decisions based on what is best for their shareholders and investors, not what's best for their employees.

16 Randy Omark, 55, and Cherie Morris, 58, of Stroudsburg, Pa., husband and wife, are former flight attendants for TWA. Cherie took a buyout in the late

pragmatism: a practical approach to thinking about problems

Scaffolding the Text-Dependent Questions

3. What is the author's main claim? What details of the text help to identify the claim? Reread paragraphs 19–22 and think about how the author answers his own question, "Is the dream changing?" What quotations from the interviewees help answer the question? RI.11-12.1

4. Is the author successful at making concessions and directly addressing counterarguments? Explain your answer. Read paragraphs 8–10. What counterargument could be made that Oden is still living the American Dream? How does the author address this potential counterargument? RI.11-12.5

8 Pause after reading paragraph 22. Read the heading "What Can You Do?" Have students predict how the content of this section of the text might differ from the previous paragraphs.

My Notes

1990s—before American Airlines bought TWA in 2001. After the acquisition, Randy was put on "furlough" (as were about 4,000 other former TWA flight attendants) and never rehired. After 26 years with the two airlines, his pension was frozen and then taken over by the government. Now he gets $324 a month in payments.

17 Today, despite having a college education, Randy works for $9 an hour finding community jobs for mentally challenged adults. Cherie works for a greeting-card company for $7.25 an hour.

18 "It used to be that if you stayed with your job, you would be rewarded," says Cherie. "Now there is no guarantee." As for retirement, Randy says, "Eventually, we will just downsize everything, sell our house and move into a smaller one."

19 Is the dream changing? Simone Luevano, 46, and Miguel Gutierrez, 44, run a garage-door installation and repair business in Albuquerque, N.M. While the business grossed $453,000 last year, they took home just $50,000 net to live on. They have a daughter—Marilyn, age 7—who is deaf in one ear and goes to a private school that costs $3600 a year.

20 Simone says that financial stress is part of their lives: "It comes from the 'maybe, could be, should be' nature of our business." When the economy is down, people don't buy a new garage-door system. The cost of gas at the pump is a major factor, she adds: "When the price of gasoline goes down, business goes up."

21 Have they prepared for retirement? Simone laughs, then replies, "The words 'retirement' and ' vacation' are not in our vocabulary. You know that old Tennessee Ernie Ford song: 'I owe my soul to the company store'? We don't think about retirement. They'll have to take me out of here with my high-top tennies on."

22 "The American Dream is a bygone thing," she adds. "It's not the way life is anymore. I used to believe I was responsible for my own destiny. But it's not that simple. Now it's faith and **fortitude**."

What Can You Do?

23 In this (and every) election year, many politicians rev up emotions that keep voters from focusing on the pocketbook and daily-life issues that truly matter. You know what really touches your family and life: The cost of milk, gas and prescription drugs. The quality of schools. The hope that the government will step in fully prepared to keep you safe and secure if a disaster hits your neighborhood.

24 Don't leave decision-making and priority-setting to **zealots** who have an ax to grind—or to the blindly ambitious people who emerge in every generation. For more than 200 years, our system of government has encouraged power to the people. Be an active citizen.

furlough: a period of time when an employee is told not to come to work and is not paid

fortitude: mental strength and courage

zealots: people who are fanatical in pursuing political, religious, or other ideals

Scaffolding the Text-Dependent Questions

5. **Notice the author's choice to change the focus and tone in the final two paragraphs. How do the ideas in those paragraphs affect the thesis and conclusion of the argument?** What has the author argued so far in the essay? What is his call to action? How does it run counter to the claim in his thesis? RI.11-12.3

6. **Does the author successfully prove his claim? Support your answer with text evidence.** Reread the last paragraph. What is the author's claim? How does the author support this claim? Do you think this information adequately supports the claim? RI.11-12.4

Making Observations

- What words does the author use to describe the American Dream?
- What details from the text do you agree or disagree with?
- What questions did you have while reading the text?

Returning to the Text

- Return to the article as you respond to the following questions. Use text evidence to support your responses.
- Write any additional questions you have about the text in your Reader/Writer Notebook.

1. Why does the author spend time in the opening paragraphs detailing the extent of the study? How does this affect the perception of his readers?

By beginning the article with details about the extent and the nature of the study, the author provides evidence up front that his text is factual, reliable, and credible. The author's strategy is an appeal to logos.

2. Who is the author's target audience? Support your answer with evidence from the text.

The author's target audience is any American citizen who is going to vote in the upcoming election. In the call to action, the author directly addresses this audience when he says, "In this (and every) election year, many politicians rev up emotions that keep voters from focusing on the pocketbook and daily-life issues that truly matter." He then goes on the tell readers to "Be an active citizen," which is a call for them to vote.

3. What is the author's main claim? What details of the text help to identify the claim?

The author's main claim is that the traditional American Dream is dying, or at least it is becoming very difficult to achieve, because the cost of living is becoming too expensive for middle-class people. The author gives several examples of people who are working hard and in the past would have been able to achieve the American Dream with what they are doing. He then details how their efforts are not enough to achieve the American Dream today.

9 After reading the text for the first time, guide the class in a discussion by asking the Making Observations questions. Check students' general comprehension of the text based on their observations, asking follow-up questions if needed.

10 RETURNING TO THE TEXT: Guide students to return to the text to answer the text-dependent comprehension questions. Invite students to reread and work on the questions in small groups. Encourage them to use text evidence to support their answers.

11 Move from group to group and listen in as students answer the text-dependent questions. If they have difficulty, scaffold the questions by rephrasing them or breaking them into smaller parts. See the Scaffolding the Text-Dependent Questions boxes for suggestions.

Scaffolding the Text-Dependent Questions

7. How does the author express his purpose in this article? Provide evidence to support your answer. Reread paragraphs 22–24. What is the author's call to action for readers? How does this call to action suggest the author's intended purpose? RI.11-12.6

8. Did the structure of the article lead to the author successfully achieving his purpose, or did it contribute to its failure? Explain your answer. Scan the article and identify text features you find. How does the author provide information to support his claim? Did the quotes from people help or hurt the author in supporting his claim? RI.11-12.6

12 Have students rotate groups and complete the Appreciating the Author's Craft section with new partners. Identify the author's purpose as a group before groups begin the activity.

4. Is the author successful at making concessions and directly addressing counterarguments? Explain your answer.

The author does not make any concessions. He focuses mostly on providing evidence and examples that support his claim. He subtly dances around potential counterarguments by taking examples of people who might seem to be doing well and showing how they are struggling.

5. Notice the author's choice to change the focus and tone in the final two paragraphs. How do the ideas in those paragraphs affect the thesis and conclusion of the argument?

Up to this point in the essay, the author had argued that the American Dream was no longer possible for the middle class. This last part is a call to action that seems to run counter to the claim in the thesis. It gives readers a call to action for how they might still be able to achieve the American Dream.

6. Does the author successfully prove his claim? Support your answer with text evidence.

Answers will vary. Accept any answer that indicates comprehension of the claim and uses text evidence to support whether they think the author successfully proves his claim.

Appreciating the Author's Craft

7. How does the author express his purpose in this article? Provide evidence to support your answer.

The author expresses his purpose of trying to convince middle-class Americans to vote wisely for people who will protect their interests by giving examples of middle-class Americans who are struggling to achieve the American Dream. After giving examples of people who are probably in a similar situation as his readers are, he makes a call to action to the readers to vote for people in the coming election who will protect their interests.

8. Did the structure of the article lead to the author successfully achieving his purpose, or did it contribute to its failure? Explain your answer.

Answers will vary but should give an explanation of how the structure either aided the success or contributed to the failure. The structure of the essay helped the author achieve his purpose. By giving examples of people who are in similar situations to his readers, the author successfully appeals to the readers' emotions. The author then makes a call to action after he has riled up the readers' emotions.

Scaffolding the Text-Dependent Questions

9. **For what purpose did the author include the heading "What Can You Do?" Was its inclusion successful in achieving the purpose?** Reread paragraphs 22–24. What is the call to action? Do you think people would be inspired with this call to action after reading the first 22 paragraphs of the article? Why or why not? RI.11-12.6

10. **In paragraph 17, the author includes the phrase "despite having a college education" to describe Randy. How does the use of this phrase shape the readers' perception of Randy's income?** Find the word *despite* in paragraph 17. What connotations does the word *despite* have? How does including this word affect how you feel about Randy having a college education? RI.11-12.6

9. For what purpose did the author include the heading "What Can You Do?" Was its inclusion successful in achieving the purpose?

The author included the heading to highlight the call to action and to help signal the change in

tone and focus of the article. It was successful in achieving both of these purposes.

10. In paragraph 17, the author includes the phrase "despite having a college education" to describe Randy. How does the use of this phrase shape the readers' perception of Randy's income?

It frames his income as being far lower than expected for someone with a college education.

11. Based on the evidence presented in paragraph 5, what logical fallacy is present, and what is its effect on the way the text is read and understood?

The author seems to be guilty of the logical fallacy of exclusion. The article focuses solely on a

specific group of the middle class and excludes people from other classes.

☑ **Check Your Understanding**

Quickwrite: In the first paragraph of the article, the author begins by defining the American Dream. How does it compare to your definition? How does Wallechinsky's "call to action" show another basic tenet of the American Dream?

Defend or Challenge the Author's Claim

The author gives evidence that supports his claim. Identifying evidence and analyzing how it supports his claim will help you write an analysis of the claim.

12. Begin by restating Wallechinsky's claim. Then use the chart to analyze and explain how the text in the first column supports his claim.

© 2021 College Board. All rights reserved.

Scaffolding the Text-Dependent Questions

11. Based on the evidence presented in paragraph 5, what logical fallacy is present , and what is its effect on the way the text is read and understood?
Reread paragraphs 4–5. What group of people does the article focus on? Does the group include everyone in the United States? What people are not included in this group? RI.11-12.5

ACTIVITY 1.17 continued

13 Reread paragraph 1 of the text. Discuss the author's definition of the American Dream. Then have students complete the **quickwrite** as part of the Check Your Understanding heading.

LEVELED DIFFERENTIATED INSTRUCTION

In this activity, students may need support developing a response to the Quickwrite prompt.

Beginning Pair students and provide each with the **Conversation for Quickwrite** graphic organizer. Allow students to work collaboratively to brainstorm key words and phrases to use in their response. Provide students with sentence starters to answer the prompt.

Developing Pair students and provide each with the **Conversation for Quickwrite** graphic organizer.

Expanding Have student pairs brainstorm examples of compare and contrast transitions to use in their response to the prompt.

Support Refer students back to the definition essay written for Embedded Assessment 1. Have them identify ideas that are both similar to and different from Wallechinsky's definition of the American Dream.

Extend Challenge students to add to their argument response by discussing an additional "call to action" Wallechinsky could have suggested.

14 Read the Defend or Challenge the Author's Claim section. Complete the first row of the Defend or Challenge the Author's Claim graphic organizer as a whole class. Then have groups complete the remaining rows. After students complete the graphic organizer, ask them to compare their answers with those of another group.

Text	Analysis of How Text Relates to Claim
"By international standards, they live a life of prosperity. Yet behind this prosperity is a growing unease. Half of the employed respondents say that they've experienced either increased health-care costs or a cut in health benefits over the last three years, and 39% have had cuts in their overtime, raises or bonuses."	The author tells how Americans are supposedly living a life a prosperity but then gives evidence of how this prosperity is waning.
"Shelly has a retirement plan through the hospital. 'But I have nothing saved for me,' she says. 'I'm putting it all into the kids, so that they can succeed in school.'"	The author tells how Shelly has a retirement plan, but the retirement plan isn't actually being put aside for her to retire.
"Today, despite having a college education, Randy works for $9 an hour finding community jobs for mentally challenged adults."	The author gives an example of a person who is working a job that does not pay at a level appropriate to his background and education. This is an example of how the American Dream has become difficult to achieve.
"While the business grossed $453,000 last year, they took home just $50,000 net to live on. They have a daughter—Marilyn, age 7—who is deaf in one ear and goes to a private school that costs $3600 a year."	This is another example of a middle-class person who seems to be doing well but is actually struggling.

13. Transition words and phrases are important for argumentative writing. As in other writing, transitions help the reader navigate the text. Transitions like *however, still, despite,* and *yet* can signal that the writer is refuting opposing arguments.

In the preceding examples, identify a transition word the author uses and briefly explain how the transition word signals a relationship between ideas.

The author uses *despite* to show that despite Randy having a college education, he works a

low-paying job that is not helping him achieve the American Dream.

_____

_____

14. Write a paragraph that defends or challenges the author's claim that the American Dream is a bygone thing. Use relevant text evidence to support your answer. Be sure to use transitions to help signal purpose and the relationship between ideas in your sentences.

Explain How an Author Builds an Argument

Write an essay that explains how Wallechinsky builds an argument to persuade his readers that the American Dream is a bygone concept. Analyze how Wallechinsky uses evidence, reasoning, and stylistic or persuasive elements to strengthen the logic and persuasiveness of his argument. In your essay, be sure to:

- Identify and write to a specific target audience.
- Write a thesis that identifies Wallechinsky's claim and analyzes how he persuades his readers that his claim is valid.
- Explain what supporting evidence Wallechinsky uses and how counterclaims are addressed. Evaluate the effectiveness of the reasons, evidence, and refutations of counterclaims he provides.
- Consider how Wallechinsky uses reasoning and stylistic or rhetorical appeals.
- Include multiple direct quotations from the text as text evidence, introducing and punctuating them correctly.
- Include transitions between your points and a statement that provides a conclusion.

EXPLAIN HOW AN AUTHOR BUILDS AN ARGUMENT

The following standards are addressed in the writing prompt:

- W.11-12.4
- W.11-12.1
- W.11-12.6

- W.11-12.6
- W.11-12.6
- W.11-12.1c

---

15 Have students identify the transition words and phrases in their Defend or Challenge the Author's Claim activity (student step 13). Then have students write a paragraph that defends or challenges the author's claim (student step 14). Encourage them to use transitions in the paragraph they write.

16 Read aloud the assignment in the Explain How an Author Builds an Argument prompt. Check for student understanding after reading each bullet point. Have students work independently to write their argument essay.

ASSESS

Use student responses to the Check Your Understanding task to be sure they have a working idea of the concept of the American Dream, understand Wallechinsky's definition, and can draw clear comparisons and contrasts between the two.

Review students' work for the writing prompt. Be sure they have attended to the elements of quality argument writing, including a thesis and supporting evidence that includes quotations from the text.

ADAPT

If students need additional help with writing an argument, consider having them write their essays in the form of a script between themselves and Wallechinsky. Pair students and ask them to role-play an exchange between themselves and Wallechinsky, which they can record using a digital device. In constructing this conversation, students should make a claim, use evidence, acknowledge counterclaims, and conclude with a call to action.

SAT® CONNECTIONS

This activity provides practice with the following important SAT skill: explaining how an author builds an argument to persuade an audience. Many resources are available online to support students with this type of writing, including the SAT Essay rubric, sample prompts, and sample essays.

A Call to Action

PLAN

Suggested Pacing: 3 50-minute class periods

TEACH

1 Read the Learning Targets and Preview with students.

2 Vocabulary Development: Draw students' attention to the Literary Vocabulary box. Review the meaning of the term *imagery* with students. Have them work in pairs to define the term in their own words and think of both examples and non-examples.

3 Invite students to work with a partner to read and complete the Drawing Conclusions About Imagery section.

Learning Strategies

Sketching
TP-CASTT

VOCABULARY

LITERARY
Imagery is the descriptive language authors use to create word pictures. Writers create imagery through words and details that appeal to one or more of the five senses.

Learning Targets

- Analyze the context of imagery to draw conclusions about suggested meanings.
- Analyze how authors use paradoxes and calls to action to influence readers.

Preview

In this activity, you will read and analyze a poem in order to understand how an author uses imagery and paradox to convey ideas.

Drawing Conclusions About Imagery

Often in poetry, authors use **imagery** to convey an idea. Based on the context, the idea will have a different interpretation than the literal interpretation of the words. You must analyze the context of the imagery and use that information to draw a conclusion about the concept the author is trying to convey through the imagery. Sometimes, the imagery may have multiple interpretations. The imagery may invoke different feelings in different readers.

For example, the phrase *it's a dog-eat-dog world* creates a specific image that has nuanced meaning, or connotation. The literal interpretation of the words, or denotation, would lead you to believe that dogs are eating dogs. But this phrase is often used to describe a fiercely competitive situation in which people are willing to do anything in order to succeed. Saying "It was a dog-eat-dog world at the cheerleading competition" also creates a more effective image than just saying "The cheerleading competition was fiercely competitive."

1. Discuss with a partner the literal meaning of each of the following underlined phrases. Then discuss a potential nuanced meaning of the imagery based on the context.

It was the end of summer camp, and it was time to go back to school, so we <u>closed the shade on our bright sunshine</u> of summer.

Denotation:

Connotation:

In the world of competitive soccer, <u>the mouse can sometimes outwit the lion</u>.

Denotation:

Connotation:

After being promoted to vice president, Jaina <u>felt trapped by the weight of her success</u>.

Denotation:

Connotation:

College and Career Readiness Standards

Focus Standards:

RL.11-12.4 Determine the meaning of words and phrases as they are used in the text, including figurative and connotative meanings; analyze the impact of specific word choices on meaning and tone, including words with multiple meanings or language that is particularly fresh, engaging, or beautiful. (Include Shakespeare as well as other authors.)

RL.11-12.6 Analyze a case in which grasping a point of view requires distinguishing what is directly stated in a text from what is really meant (e.g., satire, sarcasm, irony, or understatement).

Additional Standards Addressed:

RL.11-12.1, L.11-12.3, L.11.12.5

As You Read

- While you read the poem, create an image in your mind of the sights the author describes.
- Circle unknown words and phrases. Try to determine the meaning of the words by using context clues, word parts, or a dictionary.

Poetry

Let America Be America Again

by **Langston Hughes**

Let America be America again.

Let it be the dream it used to be.

Let it be the pioneer on the plain

Seeking a home where he himself is free.

5 (America never was America to me.)

Let America be the dream the dreamers dreamed—

Let it be that great strong land of love

Where never kings connive nor tyrants scheme

That any man be crushed by one above.

10 (It never was America to me.)

O, let my land be a land where Liberty

Is crowned with no false patriotic wreath,

But opportunity is real, and life is free,

Equality is in the air we breathe.

15 (There's never been equality for me,

Nor freedom in this "homeland of the free.")

Say, who are you that mumbles in the dark?

And who are you that draws your veil across the stars?

I am the poor white, fooled and pushed apart,

20 I am the Negro bearing slavery's scars.

I am the red man driven from the land,

I am the immigrant clutching the hope I seek—

And finding only the same old stupid plan

WORD CONNECTIONS

Content Connections

From the beginning of the poem, Hughes uses words commonly encountered in social studies contexts to forge iconic images of American history: the pioneer, the European kings and tyrants that Americans were trying to escape, the image of Liberty with her patriotic wreath, and the phrase "the homeland of the free." These words form a kind of shorthand, evoking what America is supposed to stand for by referring to common images and concepts. Along with highly connotative words like *opportunity*, *equality*, and *freedom*, these words from history and social studies allow Hughes to evoke the concept of the American Dream before showing the ways in which that dream has not been realized for all people.

My Notes

_____

_____

_____

_____

_____

_____

_____

_____

_____

_____

_____

---

4 Read the As You Read instruction and Word Connections feature aloud. Remind students of strategies they can use to determine the meaning of unknown words.

5 **FIRST READ:** Read aloud "Let America Be America Again." Pause after line 5 and discuss the use of the parentheses in the line. Explain that the parenthetical line serves as an aside that lets readers know the author's contradicting opinion about the lines that were just written. Have students pay attention to how the author continues to use this strategy.

6 As you read, be sure students are engaged with and **marking the text**. Pause to allow for questions, if needed.

LEVELED DIFFERENTIATED INSTRUCTION

Beginning To support students who are at an early stage in their English language development, consider using the passage audio for "Let America Be America Again" available on SpringBoard Digital. Reading along as they listen to the audio can boost students' comprehension of the text. Additionally, the audio performance provides a clear model for pronunciation and intonation.

7 Pause after lines 17 and 18. Ask students why they think these questions are in italics. Discuss potential answers such as to add emphasis to the questions being asked.

8 Pause after line 24 and allow students to respond to the first two Making Observations questions.

Scaffolding the Text-Dependent Questions

2. What do kings and tyrants symbolize in line 8? How is this significant?
Reread line 8. Do common people usually like living under the rule of tyrants? How is not having tyrants related to the idea of freedom? RL.11-12.4

1.18

Jacob Lawrence was one of the most important artists of the 20th century, widely renowned for his modernist depictions of everyday life as well as epic narratives of African American history and historical figures. In this silk-screen print titled "Carpenters," Lawrence celebrates the creative process of the carpenter, an everyday man who makes America great.

My Notes

_____
_____
_____
_____
_____
_____
_____
_____
_____
_____
_____
_____
_____
_____

bondsman: serf or slave
bartered: traded, exchanged

Of dog eat dog, of mighty crush the weak.
25 I am the young man, full of strength and hope,
Tangled in that ancient endless chain
Of profit, power, gain, of grab the land!
Of grab the gold! Of grab the ways of satisfying need!
Of work the men! Of take the pay!
30 Of owning everything for one's own greed!
I am the farmer, bondsman to the soil.
I am the worker sold to the machine.
I am the Negro, servant to you all.
I am the people, humble, hungry, mean—
35 Hungry yet today despite the dream.
Beaten yet today—O, Pioneers!
I am the man who never got ahead,
The poorest worker bartered through the years.
Yet I'm the one who dreamt our basic dream
40 In the Old World while still a serf of kings,
Who dreamt a dream so strong, so brave, so true,
That even yet its mighty daring sings
In every brick and stone, in every furrow turned
That's made America the land it has become.
45 O, I'm the man who sailed those early seas
In search of what I meant to be my home—
For I'm the one who left dark Ireland's shore,
And Poland's plain, and England's grassy lea,
And torn from Black Africa's strand I came
50 To build a "homeland of the free."
The free?
Who said the free? Not me?
Surely not me? The millions on relief today?
The millions shot down when we strike?
55 The millions who have nothing for our pay?
For all the dreams we've dreamed
And all the songs we've sung
And all the hopes we've held

Scaffolding the Text-Dependent Questions

3. Two voices speak in lines 1–18. Who is speaking the words in parentheses (lines 5, 10, 15–16)? How is that voice different from the voice speaking in lines 1–18? What points of view are expressed by the two voices speaking in lines 1–18? Read lines 5, 10, and 15–16 aloud. What words would you use to describe the tone of the speaker who opens the poem? How and why is the tone of the speaker in parentheses different? RL.11-12.1

4. Several times throughout the poem, the speaker ends a pair of lines with the rhyming words *free* and *me*. What is the effect of this pairing and repetition on the reader, and how does it help convey the theme? Reread lines 15–16 and 51–52. Do these lines have a positive or negative tone? How does this tone help convey a theme? RL.11-12.4

And all the flags we've hung,

60 The millions who have nothing for our pay—

Except the dream that's almost dead today.

O, let America be America again—

The land that never has been yet—

And yet must be—the land where *every* man is free.

65 The land that's mine—the poor man's, Indian's, Negro's, ME—

Who made America,

Whose sweat and blood, whose faith and pain,

Whose hand at the foundry, whose plow in the rain,

Must bring back our mighty dream again.

70 Sure, call me any ugly name you choose—

The steel of freedom does not stain.

From those who live like leeches on the people's lives,

We must take back our land again,

America!

75 O, yes,

I say it plain,

America never was America to me,

And yet I swear this oath—

America will be!

80 Out of the rack and ruin of our gangster death,

The rape and rot of graft, and stealth, and lies,

We, the people, must redeem

The land, the mines, the plants, the rivers.

The mountains and the endless plain—

85 All, all the stretch of these great green states—

And make America again!

My Notes

graft: gain by corruption

stealth: secret means

redeem: liberate, rescue, save

Making Observations

- What captures your attention?
- What emotions might someone feel while reading the poem?
- What do you notice about the speakers in the poem?

9 Pause after line 61. Ask students to point out the details the author gives to show why he thinks the dream is almost dead.

10 After reading the text for the first time, guide the class in a discussion by asking the Making Observations questions about the entire poem. Check students' general comprehension of the text based on their observations, asking follow-up questions if needed.

Scaffolding the Text-Dependent Questions

5. What is the author trying to achieve by including the descriptions in lines 65–69? Read line 65. What do the people the author describes in this line have in common? What contributions of these people does he list in lines 66–69? Why would the author group these people together and point out their contributions? RL.11-12.4

6. What idea about America is Hughes trying to convey by including the images of the "steel of freedom" and "leeches on the people's lives" (lines 71–72)? Reread lines 71–72. What are some words you associate with steel? What are some words you associate with leeches? What is the contrast between these words? What might Hughes be saying about America with this contrast? RL.11-12.4

11 RETURNING TO THE TEXT: Guide students to return to the text to answer the text-dependent comprehension questions. Invite students reread and work on the questions in pairs.

12 Move among the pairs and listen in as students answer the text-dependent questions. If they have difficulty, scaffold the questions by rephrasing them or breaking them into smaller parts. See the Scaffolding the Text-Dependent Questions boxes for suggestions.

 TEACHER TO TEACHER

Consider downloading Nikki Giovanni's reading of "Let America Be America Again" at www.pen.org so students can hear the unique cadences of Hughes's lines. Remind students that Langston Hughes also wrote "I, Too."

1.18

Returning to the Text

- Return to the poem as you respond to the following questions. Use text evidence to support your responses.
- Write any additional questions you have about the text in your Reader/Writer Notebook.

2. **What do kings and tyrants symbolize in line 8? How is this significant?**

   Kings and tyrants symbolize oppressive power and rule over the people. Europe had a long history of cruel kings and tyrants, but in America, the idea of an all-powerful individual who can do whatever he or she pleases does not exist. Instead, America represents freedom, a land of opportunity where people can achieve great things without the oppression of a king or tyrant.

3. **Two voices speak in lines 1–18. Who is speaking the words in the parentheses (lines 5, 10, 15–16)? How is that voice different from the voice speaking in lines 1–18? What points of view are expressed by the two voices?**

   These lines are being spoken by someone who disagrees with the positive ideas being expressed in surrounding lines. The surrounding lines are talking about ideas that supposedly make America great. The parenthetical lines express the point of view that America might not be as great as it appears.

4. **Several times throughout the poem, the speaker ends a pair of lines with the rhyming words "free" and "me." What is the effect of this pairing and repetition on the reader, and how does it help convey the theme?**

   Poets pay special attention to the words at the end of each line. Pairing *free* and *me* at line breaks and with rhyme suggests a strong connection between these words—that "me" is "free"—but that is often in direct contradiction of what the lines themselves say ("There's never been equality for me, / Nor freedom in this 'homeland of the free'"). This connection (and contrast with the speaker's reality) is reinforced through the repetition of this pairing throughout in the poem, suggesting that for America to "be America again," he must be free.

5. **What is the author trying to achieve by including the descriptions in lines 65–69?**

   The descriptions name various groups of people who have sacrificed to build America but do not seem to have the same attainable dreams as other Americans. The author is trying to inform readers that several groups of people are experiencing similar hardships.

Scaffolding the Text-Dependent Questions

7. **How does author's choice of language in lines 80–86 shape the reader's perception? How is the author's choice to end the poem this way similar to a call to action?** Reread lines 80–82. What image of America do these lines project? Now reread the final five lines. Paraphrase the challenge that Hughes calls upon Americans to face. Would you say the poem ends on an upbeat or a downbeat note? RL.11-12.4

6. What idea about America is Hughes trying to convey by including the images of the "steel of freedom" and "leeches on the people's lives" (lines 71–72)?

These images suggest that freedom is an idea that cannot be ruined because some bad things

have happened. Even though some people in America have become successful by ruining

other people's freedom, it is still possible for people to take back the land and achieve the

American Dream.

7. How does author's choice of language in lines 80–86 shape the reader's perception? How is the author's choice to end the poem this way similar to a call to action?

The author uses strong language to describe the harsh situations that people will rise from to

make America "America again." The author's purpose in ending the poem this way is to spark

a fire in the readers so they too can rise from a horrible situation to reclaim the idea that great

things can be achieved by anyone in America, which is similar to a call to action.

Paradox

A **paradox** is a literary device in which the author juxtaposes a set of seemingly contradictory concepts. The author does so to reveal a hidden or unexpected truth. A simple example is *less is more*. This is a paradox because it uses two opposite words that contradict one another. An example from literature is the first line of *A Tale of Two Cities* by Charles Dickens: "It was the best of times. It was the worst of times."

8. What is the purpose of the paradox in lines 13–16? Explain whether this paradox is successful in achieving its purpose.

The purpose of the paradox is to point out that America is built on the basic rights of freedom

and equality yet not all citizens have enjoyed these rights. The paradox is successful because

it reminds readers that some people have never enjoyed the freedom and equality others take

for granted.

9. What is the paradox the author uses in lines 25–26? What effect does the paradox have?

The speaker says he is a young man full of strength and hope, but he is tangled in an ancient

endless chain that is preventing him from achieving his goals. This paradox—seemingly

contradictory yet still true—conveys the idea that strong people are trapped and kept from

succeeding by an endless cycle that keeps them down.

☑ Check Your Understanding

For you, what was the most powerful image in the poem? What made it powerful? What point was Hughes trying to make by using the image?

Scaffolding the Text-Dependent Questions

8. What is the purpose of the paradox in lines 13–16? Explain whether this paradox is successful in achieving its purpose. Read lines 13–16. What are the contradictory concepts being juxtaposed? What is the effect of this juxtaposition on the reader? RL.11-12.4

9. What is the paradox the author uses in lines 25–26? What effect does the paradox have? Read lines 25–26. What are the contradictory concepts being juxtaposed? How does the juxtaposition make readers feel? RL.11-12.4

ACTIVITY 1.18 continued

13 Read aloud the opening paragraph of the Paradox section. Have students suggest other examples of paradoxes. Then have students complete the Paradox section with their partners. Review their answers as a class.

14 Complete the Check Your Understanding task and evaluate the choices and explanations students give. Make sure they have strong evidence from the text to support their response. You may wish to use **Discourse Starters** by offering sentence beginnings that employ academic language. For example, "The image evoked..." or "With this imagery, Hughes makes the point that..."

ASSESS

Allow students to share their responses to the Check Your Understanding task. While they are sharing, check that students are providing details from the text to support their opinions of what the most powerful image was.

ADAPT

If students need additional help selecting a powerful image from the poem, provide them with three or four images from the poem. Have them choose their favorite image from the choices. Discuss with students what makes the image powerful. Ask them to identify words they think are powerful, details that appeal to the senses, and emotions that the image evokes. Then allow students to work with a partner to provide evidence as to why the image is powerful.

PLAN

Materials: images and videos related to Ellis Island
Suggested Pacing: 2 50-minute class periods

TEACH

1 Read the Learning Targets and Preview with your students. Help them understand that they will encounter positive and negative images of the past and present nature of America. Stress the idea of contradictions in the American Dream throughout this section.

2 Read aloud the section about making adjustments while reading. Use an analogy to help students understand the concept of monitoring their comprehension and making adjustments when they don't understand something they have read. For example, you could compare reading a complex text to playing a soccer game. Players on a team don't simply pay attention to the ball. They monitor the positions of the other players, they look out for obstacles on the field, they use their knowledge from prior games to improve their play, and they stop at halftime to listen to guidance from their coach before they keep playing. Similarly, strong readers don't simply pay attention to the words on the page. They continuously monitor whether they understand what the text is saying, they look out for obstacles like unfamiliar words, they draw on prior knowledge to help them understand the text, and they take breaks to ask questions of themselves or of their teacher when they need help understanding.

3 Read the As You Read instructions for the activity. Encourage students to use annotations to help them make adjustments while reading.

4 Use the About the Author paragraph to model how to make adjustments when reading. Read the first sentence out loud and then use a **think aloud** to model asking questions of the text. You might ask, "What does it mean to be a storyteller? Does that mean he tells stories for a living?"

Learning Strategies

Brainstorming
Graphic Organizer
Marking the Text
Quickwrite

My Notes

Learning Targets

- Analyze the use of language to explain the impact of a poet's choices on a reader.
- Write responses that compare texts within genres.
- Synthesize information from multiple texts to support a thematic interpretation.
- Integrate ideas from multiple texts to build knowledge and vocabulary about a topic.

Preview

In this activity, you will read three poems and analyze their diverse perspectives on immigration and the attainment of the American Dream.

Making Adjustments While Reading

While reading complex texts, readers sometimes need to pause and make adjustments when their understanding breaks down. When you don't understand something you are reading, try the following adjustments:

- Reread the word, phrase, or sentence you do not understand. Reread out loud to see if hearing the sentence helps you understand it.
- Use your background knowledge to make sense of what you are reading.
- Ask questions about the text. Jot down questions in the My Notes section and return to them later to see if you know the answer after reading more of the text.
- Use annotations, like metacognitive markers, to note the parts of the text where you have questions or comments.

As You Read

- As you read the poems, circle contrasting words and phrases.
- Pause when you do not understand something in the text and try rereading, using background knowledge, asking questions, or annotating to deepen your understanding.
- Circle any unfamiliar words or phrases. Then use context and print or digital dictionary to determine the meanings.

About the Author

Joseph Bruchac (b. 1942) is an award-winning writer and professional storyteller. He grew up in a small town in the foothills of the Adirondack Mountains. As a child of Abenaki Indian ancestry, Bruchac wanted to tell his children the tales of his tribe and others and sought out Native elders to learn more about Native American storytelling. His first book of stories was published in 1975. Bruchac has since written dozens of books for children and adults that seek to promote and preserve Native American stories and culture.

College and Career Readiness Standards

Focus Standards:

RL.11-12.1 Cite strong and thorough textual evidence to support analysis of what the text says explicitly as well as inferences drawn from the text, including determining where the text leaves matters uncertain.

RL.11-12.4 Determine the meaning of words and phrases as they are used in the text,

including figurative and connotative meanings; analyze the impact of specific word choices on meaning and tone, including words with multiple meanings or language that is particularly fresh, engaging, or beautiful.

Additional Standards Addressed:

RL.11-12.5, W.11-12.9, W.11-12.4, W.11-12.5

Poetry

Ellis Island

by **Joseph Bruchac**

Beyond the red brick of Ellis Island
where the two Slovak children
who became my grandparents
waited the long days of quarantine,
5 after leaving the sickness,
the old Empires of Europe,
a Circle Line ship slips easily
on its way to the island
of the tall woman, green
10 as dreams of forests and meadows
waiting for those who'd worked
a thousand years
yet never owned their own.
Like millions of others,
15 I too come to this island,
nine decades the answerer
of dreams.
Yet only part of my blood loves that memory.
Another voice speaks
20 of native lands
within this nation.
Lands invaded
when the earth became owned.
Lands of those who followed
25 the changing Moon,
knowledge of the seasons
in their veins.

 KNOWLEDGE QUEST

Knowledge Question:
What does it mean to be an immigrant in America?
In Activity 1.19, you will read three poems describing immigrants arriving in the United States. While you read and build knowledge about what it means to be an immigrant, think about your answer to the Knowledge Question.

 Knowledge Quest
- What details about the place Ellis Island stand out to you?
- What do you notice about the speaker of the poem's family background?

ACTIVITY 1.19 continued

5 Review the Knowledge Question with students. Remind them to think about their answer to the Knowledge Question as they read and build knowledge about the topic.

6 Follow the **close reading** sequence for each poem before moving on to the next. Students will synthesize the three poems in the Working from the Text section.

7 **FIRST READ:** Ask volunteers to read the poem aloud two or three times. As the poem is read, ask students to **mark the text** by noting contrasting images of the two different sets of people in the poem.

8 After conducting the first read, guide the class in a discussion by asking the Knowledge Quest questions and evaluate students' initial understanding of the poem. Have them pair share their responses to the question in the first bullet point and assess their understanding of lines 1 through 13. Have them pair share their responses to the second bullet point. Ask students the significance of lines 18 through 21.

 TEACHER TO TEACHER

To connect students to Ellis Island and the immigrant experience, show a clip from a film that depicts the experience of immigrants at Ellis Island as an optional activity. Direct students to look for images of immigrants at Ellis Island.

Scaffolding the Text-Dependent Questions

1. In line 4 of the poem, what might the word *quarantine* **mean in the context of the opening lines?** Why might the children have to wait? What would happen if they are sick? RI.11-12.4

2. What image is described in lines 9–10? How does the decision to have the line break after the word *green* **in line 9 affect the imagery?** Reread lines 9–10. What famous statue is in New York Harbor near Ellis Island? How would the text be different if *green* were the first word on line 10? RL.11-12.4

3. How are the first stanza and the second stanza different? What two points of view does the author develop in each stanza? Read lines 17–18. How do these two lines change the tone of the poem? What are the focus and tone of lines 1–16? What is the focus of lines 17–27? RL.11-12.5

9 RETURNING TO THE TEXT:
Guide students to return to the text to answer the text-dependent comprehension questions. Have students reread and work on the questions in a small groups.

10 Move from group to group and listen in as students answer the text-dependent questions. If they have difficulty, scaffold the questions by rephrasing them or breaking them into smaller parts. See the Scaffolding the Text-Dependent Questions boxes for suggestions.

1.19

Returning to the Text

- Return to the poem as you respond to the following questions. Use text evidence to support your responses.
- Write any additional questions you have about the text in your Reader/Writer Notebook.

1. **KQ** In line 4 of the poem, what might the word *quarantine* mean in the context of the opening lines?

    The narrator of the poem describes "two Slovak children who became my grandparents" waiting behind the walls of Ellis Island "after leaving the sickness." Therefore, the word *quarantine* in context means a waiting period to make sure that they are not contagious or a threat to other immigrants and citizens.

2. What image is described in lines 9–10? How does the decision to have the line break after the word *green* in line 9 affect the imagery?

    The author describes the Statue of Liberty. Keeping the word *green* on line 9 helps enforce the image of the Statue of Liberty while also leading into the image of forests and meadows in line 10.

3. How are the first stanza and the second stanza different? What two points of view does the author develop in each stanza?

    The author changes points of view in the two stanzas. In the first stanza, the author takes the point of view of the hopeful immigrant coming to America. The second stanza takes the point of view of the Native American who was displaced by the arriving immigrants.

4. How does the author's choice of the word *invaded* (line 22) help the perception of the reader?

    The word *invaded* paints the immigrants in a different light. It shows the point of view of the Native Americans and helps readers realize that not everyone had positive feeling of hope about the new people settling the land.

5. **KQ** How does the speaker convey what it means to be an immigrant in America?

    The speaker of the poem refers to his grandparents, who were immigrants who came through Ellis Island. His words and imagery convey the difficulty of their experience and how it has affected his own life. The speaker ends the poem by questioning who gets to call themselves a real "native" of America, given that Native Americans lived there long before European immigrants.

Scaffolding the Text-Dependent Questions

4. How does the author's choice of the word *invaded* (line 22) help the perception of the reader? Find the word *invaded*. What lands were invaded? Who was on the lands? Who invaded the lands? What connotation does the word *invaded* have? RL.11-12.4

5. How does the speaker convey what it means to be an immigrant in America? How is his experience similar to or different than his grandparents'? What does he question about who can be called an immigrant? RL.11-12.1

About the Author

David Ignatow was born in Brooklyn, New York, in 1914 to Russian immigrants. His poetry, which is written in straightforward language, often portrays urban life and the lives of the working poor. Ignatow won many prestigious awards for his poetry before he died in 1997.

Poetry

Europe and America

by David Ignatow

My father brought the emigrant bundle
of desperation and worn threads,
that in anxiety as he stumbles
tumble out distractedly;
5 while I am bedded upon soft green money
that grows like grass.
Thus, between my father
who lives on a bed of anguish for his daily bread,
and I who tear money at leisure by the roots,
10 where I lie in sun or shade,
a vast continent of breezes, storms to him,
shadows, darkness to him, small lakes, rough channels
to him, and hills, mountains to him, lie between us.
My father comes of a small hell
15 where bread and man have been kneaded and baked
together.
You have heard the scream as the knife fell;
while I have slept
as guns pounded offshore.

⊘ Knowledge Quest

- What impression do you have of the speaker of the poem's father?
- What contrast do you notice in the poem?

WORD CONNECTIONS

Roots and Affixes
Knowing the meaning of Latin prefixes and roots can show the difference between *immigrant* and *emigrant*. The prefix *im-* means "in or into." The prefix *e-* means "out or from." The root *migr* in both words means "to move from one place to another." So an *emigrant* moves out of a country and becomes an *immigrant* by moving into a new country.

⊘ KNOWLEDGE QUEST

Knowledge Question:
What does it mean to be an immigrant in America?

My Notes

_____
_____
_____
_____
_____
_____
_____
_____
_____
_____
_____
_____
_____
_____
_____
_____
_____

ACTIVITY 1.19 continued

11 Read aloud the About the Author section about David Ignatow as a whole class.

12 Vocabulary Development: Discuss the Word Connections section and remind students of how to use word parts to determine meaning. Then ask them to think of other words that share the prefix *im-* or *e-* or the root *migr*. As an extension, have students complete the **Roots and Affixes Brainstorm** graphic organizer.

13 FIRST READ: Have students read aloud "Europe and America" in groups. Encourage the groups to read the poem two or three times.

14 Have students identify the contrasting images related to weather in lines 10 and 11 ("sun" and "shade" versus "storms").

15 Have students identify the contrast of the positive words used to describe America and the negative words used to describe Europe.

16 After the first read, have the groups answer the Knowledge Quest questions. Check students' general comprehension of the text based on their observations, asking follow-up questions if needed. Return to the Knowledge Question, inviting students to respond to it after having read a second poem related to immigration.

Scaffolding the Text-Dependent Questions

6. In line 1 of the poem, how does the author use the word *bundle* in context? RL.11-12.4

7. What does "while I am bedded upon soft green money" (line 5 of "Europe and America") mean? What does this idea represent? Read line 5. What feelings does something being "soft" evoke? What kind of life is someone presumed to have if the person has money? RL.11-12.4

8. How do the words *bed of anguish* in line 8 shape the perception of the reader? Read line 8. What does *anguish* mean? How does the line make you feel? What would it be like to live on a bed of anguish? How does a "bed of anguish" compare to a bed of "soft green money"? RL.11-12.4

17 RETURNING TO THE TEXT: Guide students to return to the text to answer the text-dependent comprehension questions. Have students reread and work on the questions in their small groups.

18 Move from group to group and listen in as students answer the text-dependent questions. If they have difficulty, scaffold the questions by rephrasing them or breaking them into smaller parts. See the Scaffolding the Text-Dependent Questions boxes for suggestions.

Returning to the Text

- Return to the poem as you respond to the following questions. Use text evidence to support your responses.
- Write any additional questions you have about the text in your Reader/Writer Notebook.

6. **KQ** In line 1 of the poem, how does the author use the word *bundle* in context?

The author uses the word *bundle* in reference to being an emigrant, saying that the bundle contains "desperation and worn threads." In this context, the bundle is both literal and metaphorical, since it refers to both clothing and an emotion. While the term *bundle* is often used literally, here the author hints that immigrants are often dealing with a similar "bundle," or package, of emotions.

7. What does "while I am bedded upon soft green money" (line 5) mean? What does this idea represent?

Being "bedded upon soft green money" is a metaphor for having an easy life. This metaphor juxtaposes the easy life the author has in America with his father's experiences in Europe.

8. How do the words *bed of anguish* in line 8 shape the reader's perception?

These words explain to readers the horror that was his father's life in Europe. *Anguish* has a strong negative connotation, so its use conveys an idea of the pain his father has lived through.

9. How does the poet use imagery to show the differences between life in America and life in Europe? Use text evidence to support your answer.

The author uses positive imagery to create a picture of an easy life in America, such as "I am bedded upon soft green money / that grows like grass." In contrast, he uses dark, negative imagery to portray his father's life in Europe, such as "My father comes of a small hell / where bread and man have been kneaded and baked together" and "You have heard the scream as the knife fell."

10. **KQ** How does the speaker convey what it means to be an immigrant in America?

The speaker of the poem refers to his father, who experienced desperation and poverty as an immigrant in America. Like the previous poem's speaker, he compares his own experience and notes that his experience as an American has gone much more smoothly.

Scaffolding the Text-Dependent Questions

9. How does the poet use imagery to show the differences between life in America and life in Europe? Use text evidence to support your answer. Scan the poem. Which images does the author use to describe life in America? How do those images make you feel? Which images describe his father's life in Europe? How do those images make you feel? What are some differences between the descriptions? RL.11-12.4

10. How does the speaker convey what it means to be an immigrant in America? How is his experience different from his father's? RL.11-12.1

About the Author

Naomi Shihab Nye (b. 1952) was born in St. Louis, Missouri but moved between Jerusalem and San Antonio, Texas, as an adolescent. Her father was a Palestinian refugee, and her mother was an American citizen. She has spoken out against the prejudice that Arab Americans face. Her experiences of living in multiple cultures can be seen in her work. In an interview with the Poetry Foundation, Nye said, "The primary source of poetry has always been local life, random characters met on the streets, our own ancestry sifting down to us through small essential daily tasks."

My Notes

Poetry

My Uncle's Favorite Coffee Shop

by **Naomi Shihab Nye**

Serum of steam rising from the cup,
what comfort to be known personally by Barbara,
her perfect pouring hand and starched ascot,
known as the two easy eggs and the single pancake,
5 without saying.
What pleasure for an immigrant—
anything without saying.

My uncle slid into his booth.
I cannot tell you—how I love this place.
10 He drained the water glass, noisily clinking his ice.
My uncle hailed from an iceless region.
He had definite ideas about water drinking.
I cannot tell you—all the time. But then he'd try.

My uncle wore a white shirt every day of his life.
15 He raised his hand against the roaring ocean
and the television full of lies.

KNOWLEDGE QUEST

Knowledge Question:
What does it mean to be an immigrant in America?

19 Read the About the Author about Naomi Shihab Nye as a whole class. Discuss the similarities and differences between Naomi Shihab Nye, David Ignatow, and Joseph Bruchac.

20 FIRST READ: Have students read aloud "My Uncle's Favorite Coffee Shop" in their groups. Encourage the groups to read the poem two or three times.

21 After reading the second stanza, discuss the contrasts between her uncle and the other people in the coffee shop.

Scaffolding the Text-Dependent Questions

11. In line 11 of the poem, what does the word *hailed* mean in context? What kind of place does the speaker's uncle come from? What is different about it? RL.11-12.4

12. What conclusion can you draw about the meaning of the imagery of the clinking of the ice in lines 10–11? Reread lines 10–11. Why is having ice important to her uncle? Why would

this detail be important for the author to include? What does the detail show? RL.11-12.1

13. How does the use of the word bravado in line 28 shape the perception of the reader about the uncle's choice to move back to the old country? Locate the word bravado. What does it mean? What connotation does the word have? How does this connotation let you know how the speaker feels about the decision? RL.11-12.4

22 After the first read is complete, discuss the Knowledge Quest questions as a whole class. Check students' general comprehension of the text based on their observations, asking follow-up questions if needed. Return to the question, "What does it mean to be an immigrant in America?" Ask students how their responses to that question have been influenced by reading the three poems about the experiences of immigrants.

My Notes

He shook his head back and forth
from one country to the other
and his ticket grew longer.

20 Immigrants had double and nothing all at once.
Immigrants drove the taxis, sold the beer and Cokes.
When he found one note that rang true,
he sang it over and over inside.
Coffee, honey.

25 His eyes roamed the couples at other booths,
their loose banter and casual clothes.
But he never became them.

Uncle who finally left in a bravado moment
after 23 years, to live in the old country forever,

30 to stay and never come back,
maybe it would be peaceful now,
maybe for one minute,
I cannot tell you—how my heart has settled at last.
But he followed us to the sidewalk

35 saying, Take care, Take care,
as if he could not stand to leave us.

I cannot tell—

how we felt
to learn that the week he arrived,

40 he died. Or how it is now,
driving his parched streets,
feeling the booth beneath us as we order,
oh, anything, because if we don't,
nothing will come.

⊘ Knowledge Quest
- What stands out to you about the speaker's uncle?
- What surprises you about the poem?

Scaffolding the Text-Dependent Questions

14. How is the uncle in "My Uncle's Favorite Coffee Shop" portrayed differently than the immigrants portrayed in "Ellis Island"? Reread both poems. Is the uncle happy to be in America? How are his feelings about being in America different than those of the immigrants in "Ellis Island"? RL.11-12.2

15. How does the speaker convey what it means to be an immigrant in America? Why does her uncle go back to his homeland? RL.11-12.1

Returning to the Text

- Return to the poem as you respond to the following questions. Use text evidence to support your responses.
- Write any additional questions you have about the text in your Reader/Writer Notebook.

11. **KQ** In line 11 of the poem, what does the word *hailed* mean in context?

The author uses the word *hailed* in reference to describing where the speaker's uncle comes from: "an iceless region." She hints that the place he comes from has different customs about drinking water and that the place he comes from informs his experience as an immigrant.

12. What conclusion can you draw about the meaning of the imagery of the clinking of the ice in lines 10–11?

The imagery is meant to show how life is different for her uncle in America. He can casually clink his ice in a glass here, but where he was from, they did not have easy access to ice.

13. How does the use of the word *bravado* in line 28 shape the perception of the reader about the uncle's choice to move back to the old country?

This word choice shows that it was a bold move that may not have been well conceived.

14. How is the uncle in "My Uncle's Favorite Coffee Shop" portrayed differently than the immigrants portrayed in "Ellis Island"?

The immigrants in "Ellis Island" are portrayed as people who are happy to be in America. The uncle in "My Uncle's Favorite Coffee Shop" is portrayed as an immigrant who wants to—and eventually does—return to his native country.

ACTIVITY 1.19 continued

23 RETURNING TO THE TEXT: Guide students to return to the text to answer the text-dependent comprehension questions. Have students reread and work on the questions in their small groups.

24 Move from group to group and listen in as students answer the text-dependent questions. If they have difficulty, scaffold the questions by rephrasing them or breaking them into smaller parts. See the Scaffolding the Text-Dependent Questions boxes for suggestions.

 TEACHER TO TEACHER

Once students have read the poems, you might want to ask them to make a text-to-self connection. Are they aware of any dreams, successes, or failures their ancestors had when they were either coming to or growing up in America? Students can think-pair-share with a partner.

25 Return to the Knowledge Question presented to students. Have them work with a partner to reflect on their understanding of the immigrant experience in America from reading the texts. Ask volunteers to share their responses with the class.

26 Encourage students to continue building knowledge on this topic as suggested in the Independent Reading link.

1.19

15. **KQ** How does the speaker convey what it means to be an immigrant in America?

The speaker of the poem refers to her uncle, who hails from "an iceless

region" that has its own customs and that he grew to miss the longer he

stayed in America until he finally returned. She conveys the notion that to

be an immigrant in America is to often feel stuck between two worlds and

homesick for a place that can be hard to return to.

INDEPENDENT READING LINK

You can continue to build your knowledge about this theme by reading related **fiction and poetry** at ZINC Reading Labs. Select the fiction and poetry filters and type keywords such as *immigration* in the **Search all ZINC articles** field.

 ZINC

Knowledge Quest

Use your knowledge about "Ellis Island," "Europe and America," and "My Uncle's Favorite Coffee Shop" to discuss what it means to be an immigrant in America. Be sure to:

• Discuss how the experiences are similar and different by referring to evidence in the texts.
• Take turns speaking, listening, and agreeing or disagreeing respectfully.
• Ask each other to expand on ideas or statements for clarification and to promote discussion.
• Conduct any additional research on the topic as necessary.

1.19

Working from the Text

16. Images often have a powerful connotative effect. Identify the denotation and connotation of key images from the three poems you just read. Discuss the effect that those particular words have on the reader.

Word or Phrase	Denotation	Connotation	Effect on the Reader
Ellis Island "knowledge of the seasons in their veins"	nonsensical in that the denotation implies that blood in the veins is capable of thought	This is a description of someone who has lived off the land and the seasons his or her whole life, so much so that the knowledge of the weather changes is ingrained in the person's blood.	This portrays someone who has an intimate connection with the land. In the context of the land being taken away by immigrants, it makes the reader feel sad for the person.
My Uncle's Favorite Coffee Shop "hand against the roaring ocean"	raising one's hand to an ocean's crashing waves	The uncle is trying to stop something that is inevitable.	The words help set up the uncle as a proud yet stubborn man.
Europe and America "emigrant bundle of desperation"	**emigrant:** one who leaves the country of his or her birth **bundle:** a group of objects held together by tying or wrapping **desperation:** recklessness arising from losing all hope	The father is associated with that which is negative, bringing all his hopelessness to the new world.	The words set up the reader to contrast the father's experience with the son's.

☑ Focus on the Sentence

Turn the following poetic fragments into complete sentences based on a reexamination of the poet's language choices and use of connotation. Add subjects, verbs, punctuation, and capitalization as needed.

bedded upon soft green money

The connotation of the words "bedded upon soft green money" shapes the perception of the readers by "telling them how much easier it is to make money in American than in Europe."

bed of anguish

The connotation of the words "bed of anguish" shapes the perception of the readers by "telling them that people cannot even sleep easy in Europe."

where bread and man have been kneaded and baked together

The connotation of the words "where bread and man have been kneaded and baked together" shape the perception of the readers by "comparing the hard life of Europe to a piece of dough that is beat up and eventually put in an oven."

ACTIVITY 1.19 continued

27 Preview the denotation and connotation chart in the Working from the Text activity. Review the difference between denotation (dictionary definition of a word) and connotation (idea or meaning suggested by or associated with a word or thing).

28 Have students work individually to complete the chart. When they are finished, have them share their answers with their groups.

29 Then have students work individually to complete the Focus on the Sentence section.

30 In preparation for the Writing Prompt, have students create and complete the Comparison and Contrast Venn diagram with their groups. They should consider the conflicts, juxtapositions, or contrasts within each poem. Inform students that this activity will serve as a **prewriting** step for the Writing Prompt.

31 Read aloud the Writing Prompt and have students write a literary analysis based on the prompt.

ASSESS

Review the Venn diagrams students completed as part of the Comparison and Contrast activity. Check to make sure students understood the themes of the poems and how they compared to one another.

Use the bulleted list in the Writing Prompt as a guide in reviewing students' literary analyses.

ADAPT

If students need additional support writing a thesis statement for a literary analysis, you may want to co-construct a thesis that synthesizes the contradictions between the authors' experiences and the American Dream that are presented in the poems. Have students use this thesis to write their essay.

1.19

Comparison and Contrast

Use the following modified Venn diagram to compare and contrast the themes of the three poems. Write any similarities in themes among the three poems in the middle section of the Venn diagram where all three circles overlap. Record differences in the outer areas. You can also record similarities between two poems, but not three, in the overlapping spaces.

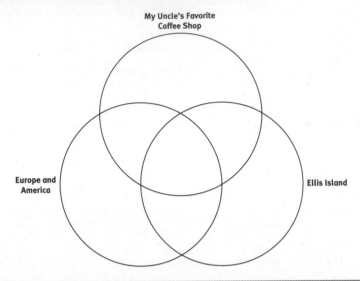

Writing Prompt: Literary Analysis

Consider the three poems you have read, in particular the connections between the speakers and how they present their experiences. Write an essay in which you use the poems to identify and analyze a common theme connecting the speakers' experiences. What contradictions between their experiences and the American Dream do the writers present, and how do they resolve the conflict—if at all? How are those responses to these contradictions similar or different? Be sure to:

- Include a thesis that connects the experiences in all three poems and the speakers' responses to those experiences.
- Provide direct quotations and specific examples from all three poems to support your analysis. Introduce and punctuate all quotations correctly.
- Use a variety of sentence beginnings.

WRITING PROMPT: LITERARY ANALYSIS

The following standards are addressed in the writing prompt:

- W.11-12.4, W.11-12.9
- W.11-12.5
- W.11-12.1

The Sonnet and the American Dream

Learning Targets

- Analyze a poet's message about the American Dream.
- Analyze context to draw conclusions about the meaning of imagery in a sonnet.

Preview

In this activity, you will analyze a poet's message about the American Dream using the TP-CASTT strategy.

Poetic Forms: The Sonnet

A **sonnet** is a 14-line poem. The word *sonnet* comes from the Italian word *sonnetto* meaning "little sound or song." Sonnets typically use a rhythm and rhyme scheme that give them a singsong quality. Sonnets usually focus on a single topic but then have a shift—for example, in plot or tone—in the final lines.

As You Read

- Use the My Notes section to note any mental images the author creates with her language.
- Mark the characteristics of a sonnet that you observe while reading.
- Circle any unfamiliar words or phrases. Then use context and a print or digital dictionary to determine the meanings.

About the Author

Sandra Gilbert (b. 1936) was born in New York City. She has been an author, a professor at the University of California, Davis, and a political activist. She has served as president of the Modern Language Association and has received numerous accolades for her writing. Her poetry is known for its grace and adherence to formal structures. A leading feminist literary critic and coauthor of the classic *The Madwoman in the Attic*, Gilbert infuses her feminist views in much of her writing. She now divides her time between living in Berkeley, California, and Paris, France.

Learning Strategies

Close Reading
Graphic Organizer
Note-taking
TP-CASTT

INDEPENDENT READING LINK

Read and Connect

How is the American Dream portrayed in the book you are reading independently? Compare how the American Dream is shown in your book and the poem. What are the similarities and differences? How has reading about the American Dream changed your thinking about what the American Dream is?

My Notes

College and Career Readiness Standards

Focus Standards:

RL.11-12.5 Analyze how an author's choices concerning how to structure specific parts of a text contribute to its overall structure and meaning as well as its aesthetic impact.

RL.11-12.4 Determine the meaning of words and phrases as they are used in the text, including figurative and connotative meanings; analyze the impact of specific word choices on

meaning and tone, including words with multiple meanings or language that is particularly fresh, engaging, or beautiful.

RL.11-12.1 Cite strong and thorough textual evidence to support analysis of what the text says explicitly as well as inferences drawn from the text, including determining where the text leaves matters uncertain.

ACTIVITY 1.20

PLAN

Materials: Internet access to research the history of the *Ladies' Home Journal*
Suggested Pacing: 1 50-minute class period

TEACH

1 Read the Learning Targets and Preview with students, making sure they understand the goals for this lesson.

2 Read the Poetic Forms: The Sonnet section with students. Write the meanings of the terms *sonnet* and *shift* on the board. Discuss famous sonnets and authors of sonnets to activate any prior knowledge students may have about the form.

3 Read the As You Read section aloud. Remind students of strategies they can use to determine the meaning of unknown words.

4 Have a volunteer read aloud the About the Author section. Have students predict why a leading feminist critic would write a poem about the *Ladies' Home Journal*.

5 Draw students' attention to the Independent Reading Link activity. Invite them to share connections with the book they're reading independently.

6 FIRST READ: Read aloud "Sonnet: The Ladies' Home Journal." Pause after line 4. Have students describe the imagery that the details in the first four lines create.

7 As you read, be sure students are engaged with and marking the text. Pause for questions if needed.

8 Pause after the first stanza. Ask students to describe the tone of the poem so far.

9 After reading line 15, discuss how the tone changed in the second stanza.

10 After reading the poem for the first time, guide the class in a discussion by asking the Making Observations questions. Check students' general comprehension of the text based on their observations, asking follow-up questions if needed.

11 Have partners complete the On the Spot Research. Then have the partners share their findings with another group of partners.

➡ TEACHER TO TEACHER

Consider finding images of covers of the *Ladies' Home Journal* throughout the years. Have students analyze evolution of the magazine through time. Allow students to analyze the life depicted in the photos of the covers to give them an understanding of the context of the sonnet before having them return to the text.

1.20

My Notes

Poetry

Sonnet: The Ladies' Home Journal

by **Sandra Gilbert**

The brilliant stills of food, the cozy
glossy, bygone life—mashed potatoes
posing as whipped cream, a neat mom
conjuring shapes from chaos, trimming the flame—
5 how we ached for all that,
that dance of love in the living room,
those paneled walls, that kitchen golden
as the inside of a seed: how we leaned
on those shiny columns of advice,
10 stroking the thank yous, the firm thighs, the wise
closets full of soap.

But even then
we knew it was lies we loved, the lies
we wore like Dior coats, the clean-cut airtight
15 lies that laid out our lives in black and white.

Making Observations
- What is your initial reaction to the poem?
- What imagery stands out for you?

On the Spot Research
With a partner, research the history of the *Ladies' Home Journal*. Find out the following information:

- In what year was the magazine created?
- What is the historical significance of the magazine?
- How has the magazine influenced women?

Share your findings with another set of partners.

Scaffolding the Text-Dependent Questions

1. In lines 2–3, what conclusion can be drawn about the imagery created by the mashed potatoes posing as whipped cream? Reread lines 2–3. What words describe the mashed potatoes? How would you describe something that looks like one thing, but is actually something else? L.11-12.5

2. Which line of the poem begins the shift? What kind of change happens in the shift? Scan the first stanza. Where does the first stanza end and the second stanza begin? How does the author's tone change after this break? RL.11-12.5

3. What message is the author trying to convey in lines 12–13? Reread lines 12–13. What does the author say about the lies? Why did people love the lies? RL.11-12.1

Returning to the Text

- Return to the poem as you respond to the following questions. Use text evidence to support your responses.
- Write any additional questions you have about the text in your Reader/Writer Notebook.

1. In lines 2–3, what conclusion can be drawn about the imagery created by the mashed potatoes posing as whipped cream?

   This image reveals that things are not what they seem in the pictures in the magazine.

2. Which line of the poem begins the shift? What kind of change happens in the shift?

   The turn is in line 11 and is set up by the stanza break that happens midline. After the shift,

   the poem talks about how magazine readers knew about the lies but loved them anyway.

3. What message is the author trying to convey in lines 12–13?

   Women knew the images in the photos were fake, but they still loved them—just like in real

   life when they bought Dior coats to pretend like their own lives were better than they really

   were.

4. In lines 13–14, why does the author describe the lies as "clean-cut" and "airtight"?

   The lies in real life had to be as perfect as the lies in the magazine. The images of being

   clean-cut and airtight help create a mental picture of perfection. These images also convey the

   contrast between the "clean" magazine images and the messiness of reality.

Introducing the Strategy

TP-CASTT This reading strategy is used to analyze a poetic text by identifying and discussing each element in the acronym Title, Paraphrase, Connotation, Attitude, Shift, Title again, and Theme. The strategy is a guide designed to lead you in an analysis of a literary text. It is most effective if you begin at the top and work your way down the elements. However, you will find that as you study one element, you will naturally begin to explore others. For example, a study of connotation often leads to a discussion of tone and shifts. Revisiting the title often leads to a discussion of the theme.

12 **RETURNING TO THE TEXT:** Guide students to return to the text to answer the text-dependent comprehension questions. Invite students to reread and work on the questions in pairs.

13 Move among the pairs and listen in as students answer the text-dependent questions. If they have difficulty, scaffold the questions by rephrasing them or breaking them into smaller parts. See the Scaffolding the Text-Dependent Questions boxes for suggestions.

14 Read aloud the first paragraph of the Working from the Text section to introduce the **TP-CASTT** strategy. Allow students to ask questions about the strategy.

Scaffolding the Text-Dependent Questions

4. In lines 13–14, why does the author describe the lies as "clean-cut" and "airtight"? Reread lines 13–14. What connotations do the words *clean-cut* and *airtight* have? Is a "clean-cut airtight lie" a believable lie? RL.11-12.4

1.20

Review the rows of the graphic organizer and explain how students will be filling in the right column for each row. Model how to complete the graphic organizer by completing the first three rows of the graphic organizer as a class. Then have students complete the remaining parts of the graphic organizer individually.

Working from the Text

5. Analyze the poem "Sonnet: The Ladies' Home Journal" using the following TP-CASTT graphic organizer.

Title	What does the title mean?	The title is the name of a famous women's magazine.
Paraphrase	Paraphrase parts of the poem.	The pictures in the magazine show perfect scenes of home life, but those scenes are lies. However, people love to dream about the lies.
Connotation	What is the implied meaning of some of the words?	The words *cozy* and *glossy* have a connotation of perfection. The words *clean-cut* and *airtight* also have a connotation of perfection.
Attitude	What is the author's attitude about the subject?	The speaker is fondly reminiscing about a magazine that she loved to read even though the pictures were not realistic.
Shift	What is the shift in tone in the poem?	The shift comes in lines 13–14. The speaker shifts from nostalgic praise of the magazine to admitting knowing about the lies and telling how people loved them.
Title Again	What new meaning does the title offer?	The poem can be seen as a reminiscing journal entry itself.
Theme	What is the theme of the poem?	The American Dream as shown in magazines is a lie and is not achievable for many Americans. But many Americans like to believe the lie is possible.

☑ Check Your Understanding

Based on your analysis of the poem "Sonnet: The Ladies' Home Journal," what does the author think about the American Dream shown in the magazine the *Ladies' Home Journal*?

The author thinks the American Dream shown in the magazine is not real or achievable. People love to lie and pretend like it is achievable, but the reality is that the American Dream as shown in the magazine is fake. Reality is far messier and more chaotic.

ACTIVITY 1.20 continued

16 Have students complete the Check Your Understanding task to show their analysis of the author's opinion of the American Dream shown in the magazine.

ASSESS

Review students' responses to the Check Your Understanding task to ensure that they understand the author's negative opinion about the version of the American Dream shown in the magazine.

ADAPT

If students are struggling to analyze the poem, have them complete the remaining parts of the TP-CASTT graphic organizer in groups. Encourage them to look for details that relate to the American Dream. Ask students to share their findings and discuss their analysis of the sonnet. Have students use this analysis to complete the Check Your Understanding task.

To extend students' ability to analyze poems, provide groups of three students each with three **TP-CASTT** graphic organizers. Have each group member analyze a different one of the three poems in Activity 1.19. Allow time for groups to convene and have each member present his or her completed analysis.

ACTIVITY 1.21

PLAN

Materials: Internet access to research the economic situation of African Americans in Chicago in the 1950s

Suggested Pacing: 2 50-minute class periods

TEACH

1 Read the Learning Targets and Preview with students. Guide students in a discussion of one aspect of the American Dream: money. Explain that Americans often equate success with money. Point out that this activity will ask students to think about their relationship to money as well as American society's relationship to money.

2 Ask students to work in pairs or groups of three to review the quotations about money and **paraphrase** each one. Students should share their responses in groups. Then ask students to choose one quotation with which they agree and one with which they disagree and explain why.

Money and the American Dream

Learning Strategies

Quickwrite
Think-Pair-Share
Visualizing

My Notes

Learning Targets

• Analyze how the economic context and dramatic elements affect the theme and plot of a play.

• Compose a literary analysis of a play and evaluate how the use of language affects readers.

Preview

In this activity, you will analyze quotations about the American Dream. Then you will read, analyze, and write about a drama whose theme centers on the American Dream.

Money and the American Dream

1. Read and review the following quotations about money and in your Reader/Writer Notebook write a brief explanation of each one in your own words. Think of a visual to go with each one.

   a. "The love of money is the root of all evil." (from the Bible)

   b. "Remember that time is money." (Benjamin Franklin)

   c. "Put not your trust in money, but your money in trust." (Oliver Wendell Holmes)

   d. "A good reputation is more valuable than money." (Pubilius Syrus)

   e. "If money be not thy servant, it will be thy master." (Sir Francis Bacon)

   f. "The safest way to double your money is to fold it over twice and put it in your pocket." (Frank McKinney Hubbard)

   g. "Those who believe money can do everything are frequently prepared to do everything for money." (George Savile)

   h. "There's no money in poetry, but then there's no poetry in money, either." (Robert Graves)

   i. "Money cannot buy happiness." (Anonymous)

College and Career Readiness Standards

Focus Standards:

RL.11-12.1 Cite strong and thorough textual evidence to support analysis of what the text says explicitly as well as inferences drawn from the text, including determining where the text leaves matters uncertain.

RL.11-12.3 Analyze the impact of the author's choices regarding how to develop and relate elements of a story or drama (e.g., where a story is set, how the action is ordered, how the characters are introduced and developed).

RL.11-12.10 By the end of grade 11, read and comprehend literature, including stories, dramas, and poems, in the grades 11–CCR text complexity band proficiently, with scaffolding as needed at the high end of the range.

Additional Standards Addressed:

RL.11-12.4, L.11-12.4d

j. "A fool and his money are soon parted." (Benjamin Franklin)

k. "A penny saved is a penny earned." (Benjamin Franklin)

Dramatic Elements

2. Plays are written to be acted out on stage. As a result, they have a unique format when compared with other types of writing. Read through the chart to learn about the elements of dramatic writing.

Dramatic Elements	
Characters	• Characters are listed at the beginning of the play. • Character names will appear before each line to indicate who is speaking. • Some dramas have a character called a narrator who provides additional information to the reader/audience.
Format	• Plays are broken into **acts** and **scenes**. • There are typically five acts in a drama. • Each act is broken into smaller scenes. • The text is largely made of **dialogue** between characters called **lines**.
Stage Directions	• Stage directions appear throughout in parentheses and italic font. • Stage directions explain the setting, give special directions to the speaker/actor, and may provide additional information about where the actor should be on stage. • Stage directions can help establish tone and mood. • Stage directions can help advance the plot, build tension, or aid the timing of the delivery of the lines.
Monologues	• Monologues are long speeches made by a single character in a drama.
Plot	• Like a narrative story, a play has a plot with a **rising action**, **climax**, and **resolution**.

3. With a partner, discuss how drama is different from narrative writing. Create a T-chart in your Reader/Writer notebook describing the characteristics of and differences between both kinds of writing. When you are done, compare your pair's with another pair's chart.

As You Read

• Write down any questions you have about the economic contexts referenced in the play in My Notes.

• Mark the text by putting a star beside the different dramatic elements that you notice as you read.

• Circle any unfamiliar words or phrases. Then use context and print or digital dictionary to determine the meanings.

---

3 As a class, read and discuss the Dramatic Elements section. Be sure that students understand the key vocabulary terms: in bold type. Allow time for students to ask any questions they have about dramatic elements.

4 Read aloud the As You Read section. Encourage students to annotate the dramatic elements in the drama.

5 Read the About the Author section with students.

6 **FIRST READ:** Discuss the three characters in "A Raisin in the Sun." Select two volunteers to read the parts of Mama and Ruth. Have the volunteers read the drama to the class. Pause the reading after line 14 to discuss Mama's opinion of money.

7 As students are reading, monitor their progress. Be sure they are engaged with the text and annotating as directed.

1.21

My Notes

About the Author

Lorraine Hansberry (1930–1965) was born in Chicago, where she grew up in an educated and successful activist family. Her father moved the family into a white neighborhood to challenge discriminatory housing practices. *A Raisin in the Sun* was written with that experience in mind. She later moved to New York City, where she committed to writing full time and where she wrote *A Raisin in the Sun*. The play became a huge success on Broadway and was made into a film. She was the first African American playwright and the youngest American to win a New York Critics' Circle award.

Play

from A Raisin in the Sun

by **Lorraine Hansberry**

Characters:

Walter and Ruth Younger (husband and wife)

Lena Younger (Mama—Walter's mother)

MAMA: What was they fighting about?

RUTH: Now you know as well as I do.

MAMA *(shaking her head)*: Brother still worrying hisself sick about that money?

RUTH: You know he is.

5   MAMA: You had breakfast?

RUTH: Some coffee.

MAMA: Girl, you better start eating and looking after yourself better. You almost thin as Travis.

RUTH: Lena—

MAMA: Un-hunh?

10   RUTH: What are you going to do with it?

MAMA: Now don't you start, child. It's too early in the morning to be talking about money. It ain't Christian.

RUTH: It's just that he got his heart set on that store—

Scaffolding the Text-Dependent Questions

4. In line 3 of the play, how does the stage direction of "shaking her head" help establish Mama's opinions? Locate the line 3 stage direction. Imagine a person shaking his or her head. What does it look like? What feelings is a person expressing by shaking his or her head? RL.11-12.3

8 Pause the reading after line 27 and discuss Ruth's opinion of money. Have students compare it to how Mama views money.

MAMA: You mean that liquor store that Willy Harris want him to invest in?

RUTH: Yes—

15 MAMA: We ain't no business people, Ruth. We just plain working folks.

RUTH: Ain't nobody business people till they go into business. Walter Lee say colored people ain't never going to start getting ahead till they start gambling on some different kinds of things in the world—investments and things.

MAMA: What done got into you, girl? Walter Lee done finally sold you on investing.

RUTH: No. Mama, something is happening between Walter and me. I don't know what it is—but he needs something—something I can't give him any more. He needs this chance, Lena.

MAMA (*frowning deeply*): But liquor, honey—

20 RUTH: Well—like Walter say—I spec people going to always be drinking themselves some liquor.

MAMA: Well—whether they drinks it or not ain't none of my business. But whether I go into business selling it to 'em is, and I don't want that on my ledger this late in life. (*stopping suddenly and studying her daughter-in-law*) Ruth Younger, what's the matter with you today? You look like you could fall over right there.

RUTH: I'm tired.

MAMA: Then you better stay home from work today.

RUTH: I can't stay home. She'd be calling up the agency and screaming at them, "My girl didn't come in today—send me somebody! My girl didn't come in!" Oh, she just have a fit ...

25 MAMA: Well, let her have it. I'll just call her up and say you got the flu—

RUTH (*laughing*): Why the flu?

MAMA: 'Cause it sounds respectable to 'em. Something white people get, too. They know 'bout the flu. Otherwise they think you been cut up or something when you tell 'em you sick.

RUTH: I got to go in. We need the money.

MAMA: Somebody would of thought my children done all but starved to death the way they talk about money here late. Child, we got a great big old check coming tomorrow.

30 RUTH (*sincerely, but also self-righteously*): Now that's your money. It ain't got nothing to do with me. We all feel like that—Walter and Bennie and me—even Travis.

MAMA (*thoughtfully, and suddenly very far away*): Ten thousand dollars—

RUTH: Sure is wonderful.

My Notes

Scaffolding the Text-Dependent Questions

5. In line 21, how does the stage direction of "*stopping suddenly and studying her daughter-in-law*" affect the flow of the plot? Find the stage direction in line 21. Where is the direction in the line? How would this affect how the actor would deliver the line? RL.11-12.5

6. What is the significance of Mama's use of the word *ledger* when she says, "I don't want that [selling alcohol] on my ledger this late in life"? Locate the word *ledger*. What is a ledger? What is it used for? How does the word choice relate to money? RL.11-12.4

7. How do Mama and Ruth view money differently? Support your answer with evidence from the text. Skim the text. How does Mama view money? What lines from the text support this answer? How does Ruth view money? What lines from the text support this answer? RL.11-12.1

9 After reading the text for the first time, guide the class in a discussion by asking the Making Observations questions. Check students' general comprehension of the text based on their observations, asking follow-up questions if needed.

★ TEACHER TO TEACHER

Consider showing a clip of the scene to students so they can see how actors perform the scene. Have students analyze the way the actors read the lines and encourage them to implement that passion into their next reading of the text.

1.21

My Notes

MAMA: Ten thousand dollars.

RUTH: You know what you should do, Miss Lena? You should take yourself a trip somewhere. To Europe or South America or someplace—

35 MAMA (*throwing up her hands at the thought*): Oh, child!

RUTH: I'm serious. Just pack up and leave! Go on away and enjoy yourself some. Forget about the family and have yourself a ball for once in your life—

Making Observations

- What characters are mentioned who do not have speaking lines?
- Which character is most obsessed about money? Why?
- Which character do you most relate to? Why?

Scaffolding the Text-Dependent Questions

8. The author has Mama describe two groups of people as "business people" and "plain working folks." How does her language choice affect the reader's perception of these two groups of people? Scan the scene for where Mama names "business people" and "plain working folks." What connotation does the word *plain* have? How does that connotation express how Mama views working folks in relation to business people? How does the word help tell readers how to feel? RL.11-12.4

9. What message does the author convey about the power of money? Review the text. What problem would having money solve for each character? What do you think will happen to the characters if they do not get the money they think they need? What does that suggest about the real power of money? RL.11-12.1

Returning to the Text

- Return to the play excerpt as you respond to the following questions. Use text evidence to support your responses.
- Write any additional questions you have about the text in your Reader/Writer Notebook.

4. **In line 3 of the play, how does the stage direction of *"shaking her head"* help establish Mama's opinions?**

It shows that she does not think it is right for them to be worried about money. This

establishes her point of view that will recur throughout the scene.

5. **In line 21, how does the stage direction of *"stopping suddenly and studying her daughter-in-law"* affect the flow of the plot?**

Since the stage direction happens in the middle of one of Mama's lines, it adds to the drama

by causing a dramatic pause for emphasis.

6. **What is the significance of Mama's use of the word *ledger* when she says, "I don't want that [selling alcohol] on my ledger this late in life"?**

Ledger is a common bookkeeping term for the book in which people keep track of their money.

It implies that she feels as if someone is keeping a ledger on her life and that she thinks it

would negatively reflect on her life.

7. **How do Mama and Ruth view money differently? Support your answer with evidence from the text.**

Ruth thinks money is important. Ruth spends the scene discussing money and trying to plan

to make more money. Money is not as important to Mama. She says things like "It's too early

in the morning to be talking about money." Being with family is more important to Mama

than money.

ACTIVITY 1.21 continued

10 **RETURNING TO THE TEXT:** Guide students to return to the text to answer the text-dependent comprehension question. Have students reread and work on the questions independently. Then allow time for students to discuss their answers with a partner.

11 Circulate as students answer the text-dependent questions. If they have difficulty, scaffold the questions by rephrasing them or breaking them into smaller parts. See the Scaffolding the Text-Dependent Questions boxes for suggestions.

12 Have students work with the same partner to complete the On the Spot Research part of the Working from the Text section. Have partners discuss their findings with another student pair.

Then have students work individually and answer the question in student step 10.

8. The author has Mama describe two groups of people as "business people" and "plain working folks." How does her language choice affects the reader's perception of these two groups of people?

It establishes for the reader that these are two separate groups of people and the "plain

working folks" are seen as the lower class.

9. What message does the author convey about the power of money?

The message is that money solves a lot of problems. Mama seems carefree about money, but

she is about to get a lot of money. Ruth thinks that since Mama has money coming, she should

be able to escape all of her worries by taking a trip.

On the Spot Research

The play *A Raisin in the Sun* is set in Chicago in the 1950s. With a partner, research the economic situation of African Americans in Chicago in the 1950s. Topics to research include:

- Second Great Migration
- *The Chicago Defender*
- Employment discrimination
- Chicago Housing Authority

Discuss your findings with another pair.

10. What does money mean to Ruth? How does the economic context of the time influence her view of money?

Ruth thinks money is important. Ruth is part of a younger generation who wants and expects

to be able to live better lives. This expectation includes desiring to become business owners,

which is something Ruth does not think is possible for people like them.

☑ **Check Your Understanding**

Look back at the quotes you read at the beginning of this activity. Which quotes relate to characters in the drama? Make a chart in your Reader/Writer Notebook to show your answers.

 Writing Prompt: Literary Analysis

Write a paragraph that analyzes the theme of the American Dream in *A Raisin in the Sun*. Be sure to:

- Analyze the historical and economic context of the setting and how it influences the theme.
- Use examples from the text to support your analysis.
- Use content and academic vocabulary, as appropriate.

INDEPENDENT READING LINK

Read and Connect

Review the time periods in which your independent reading and the unit readings were written. Compare and contrast how views of the American Dream were expressed in different time periods.

13 Have students complete the Check Your Understanding task individually.

14 Provide time for students to complete the Writing Prompt. Remind them to use text evidence to support their brief literary analysis.

15 Draw students' attention to the Independent Reading Link activity. Invite them to share how the American Dream is reflected in the time period in which their book is set.

ASSESS

Review students' selection of quotes (in writing or discussion) from the Check Your Understanding task. Students' charts should demonstrate an understanding of the connection between the quotations and the texts.

Read the students' paragraphs with the bulleted list in the Writing Prompt as a guideline. Be sure they have provided examples from the text to support their analysis of the historical and economic context of the setting and how it influenced the theme.

ADAPT

If students need additional help synthesizing details from the texts as they write about the theme of the American Dream in *A Raisin in the Sun*, work with them In small groups to create an appropriate graphic organizer for gathering examples from the text, possibly in a web with *American Dream* in the center circle. Conduct a **think-aloud** about the prompt, calling on students for help in providing text examples to fill in the graphic organizer as you go. If necessary, model how to show examples from the text in a paragraph of analysis.

To extend students' ability to analyze the theme of the American Dream, have them compare and contrast the treatment of the American Dream by Lorraine Hansberry with another story or poem in this unit.

 WRITING PROMPT: LITERARY ANALYSIS

The following standards are addressed in the writing prompt:

- W.11-12.9a
- W.11-12.9a
- W.11-12.1c

ACTIVITY 1.22

PLAN

Suggested Pacing: 1 50-minute class period

TEACH

1 Read the Learning Targets and Preview with students. Tell them that making connections will help them analyze and understand the themes of texts.

2 Read aloud the Making Connections section. Discuss each example and how it relates to making connections to personal experiences, ideas in other texts, or society.

3 Have students read the As You Read and About the Author sections for "Who Burns for the Perfection of Paper." Remind students that tone is the author's attitude about something.

4 **FIRST READ:** Read aloud "Who Burns for the Perfection of Paper," modeling appropriate pacing. Pause after line 3 to ensure that students know what a legal pad of paper is.

1.22   Working Toward the Dream

Learning Strategies

Graphic Organizer
Marking the Text
Quickwrite
Read Aloud
SOAPSTone
TP-CASTT

Learning Targets

- Analyze multiple texts to identify the development of a recurring idea or theme.
- Synthesize information to make text-to-text connections.

Preview

In this activity, you will read a poem and an essay to expand your thinking about the relationship between work and the American Dream.

My Notes

Making Connections

When analyzing texts, you can increase you understanding by connecting the ideas in texts to something you already know. Make connections to:

- **Personal experiences** by thinking about something similar that happened to you.
  Example: I can relate to how the person is feeling. I know what it feels like to lose a big game because my team lost in the championship game last week.

- **Ideas in other texts** by remembering ideas, concepts, and facts you learned about in texts you have read or the style or structure of those texts.
  Example: I know about the Great Migration because we read about it in our history text book last month.

- Things that are happening or have happened in **society**.
  Example: This text talks about the American Dream being connected to people having jobs and making money. The other day officials announced that a major distribution center would be opening in our town and people were really happy about the number of jobs it would bring. This shows me a real-world example of how jobs are tied to the American Dream.

As You Read

- Underline words and phrases that indicate the narrator's attitude toward his work (tone).
- Make connections to personal experiences, ideas in other texts, or society and record them in the My Notes section.

About the Author

Martín Espada (b. 1957) was born in Brooklyn, New York. He is a former lawyer who is now an English professor at the University of Massachusetts in Amherst. In 2018, he was awarded the Ruth Lilly Prize in Poetry—an award given annually to honor a living U.S. poet whose lifetime achievements warrant extraordinary recognition. In his poetry, Espada writes about the working-class experience, including immigrant struggles in America.

College and Career Readiness Standards

Focus Standards:

RL.11-12.1 Cite strong and thorough textual evidence to support analysis of what the text says explicitly as well as inferences drawn from the text, including determining where the text leaves matters uncertain.

RL.11-12.5 Analyze how an author's choices concerning how to structure specific parts of a text (e.g., the choice of where to begin or end a story, the choice to provide a comedic or tragic resolution) contribute to its overall structure and meaning as well as its aesthetic impact.

Poetry

Who Burns for the Perfection of Paper

by **Martín Espada**

My Notes

At sixteen, I worked after high school hours
at a printing plant
that manufactured legal pads:
Yellow paper
5 stacked seven feet high
and leaning
as I slipped cardboard
between the pages,
then brushed red glue
10 up and down the stack.
No gloves: fingertips required
for the perfection of paper,
smoothing the exact rectangle.
Sluggish by 9 PM, the hands
15 would slide along suddenly sharp paper,
and gather slits thinner than the crevices
of the skin, hidden.
Then the glue would sting,
hands oozing
20 till both palms burned
at the punchclock.
Ten years later, in law school,
I knew that every legal pad
was glued with the sting of hidden cuts,
25 that every open lawbook
was a pair of hands
upturned and burning.

© 2021 College Board. All rights reserved.

College and Career Readiness Standards

W.11-12.1 Write arguments to support claims in an analysis of substantive topics or texts, using valid reasoning and relevant and sufficient evidence.

Additional Standards Addressed:

RL.11-12.3, RL.11-12.4, L.11-12.5, W.11-12.1a, W.11-12.1b, W.11-12.1e, W.11-12.8

⬇ TEACHER TO TEACHER

It is not necessary to do a **TP-CASTT** in groups, but it may support students to work collaboratively to analyze the poem before they synthesize their thinking in the Working from the Text chart.

TP-CASTT

Title: The title is very ambiguous but seems to be about the idea that someone is burning or suffering to make paper perfect.

Paraphrase: The last six lines: *Ten years later, the speaker remembers his teenage experience of working with paper and how much it burned his hands; his open book reminds him visually of a pair of hands upturned and of the pain someone is enduring.*

Connotation: "Perfection of paper" required "fingertips" "burning."

Attitude: A painful memory creates empathy.

Title again: The title relates to the speaker's memory of the long hours and constant injury of a menial job creating perfect pads of paper.

Theme: Empathy comes from allowing oneself to feel painful memories fully.

5 Be sure students are engaged with the text and are annotating details that reveal the author's attitude toward work.

6 Pause after line 21. Ask students how it feels to get glue or a similar substance in a cut. Remind them that understanding this feeling from a personal experience is making a connection.

7 After reading the text for the first time, guide the class in a discussion by asking the Making Observations questions. Check students' general comprehension of the text based on their observations, asking follow-up questions if needed.

8 Have students read the As You Read and About the Author sections for "Roberto Acuna Talks About Farm Workers." Inform students that while this text is written by Studs Terkel, it is an interview transcript with Acuna. The words being spoken and the first-person pronouns are Roberto Acuna's words speaking about his own experiences.

1.22

My Notes

Making Observations
- What words or images stand out for you? How did the descriptions make you feel?
- Would you like to work the job described in the poem? Why or why not?

As You Read
- Underline words and phrases that indicate Acuna's attitude toward his work (tone).
- Make connections to personal experiences, ideas in other texts, or society and record them in My Notes.
- Circle any unfamiliar words or phrases. Then use context and print or digital dictionary to determine the meanings.

About the Author

Studs Terkel (1912–2008) was a legendary radio broadcaster, interviewer, and writer. Born Louis Terkel, he officially adopted the nickname of Studs as a young actor in Chicago. Best known as an oral historian, he interviewed both celebrities and regular people. He turned some of these oral histories into books. He won the Pulitzer Prize for his book *The Good War: An Oral History of World War II*. According to NPR, Terkel said that his books "deal with the lives of ordinary people, not celebrities. What is it like to be a certain kind of person, at a certain circumstance, at a certain time?" His 1974 best seller *Working* chronicles the work life of everyday Americans, from welders and waitresses to farm workers and pharmacists.

Scaffolding the Text-Dependent Questions

1. **What can you infer about the speaker based on the details in lines 1–21?** Reread lines 1–21. Note all the details you learn about the speaker. What kind of worker was the speaker? Which details are particularly revealing? RL.11-12.1

2. **How do the words in lines 14–15 affect the tone of the poem?** Locate descriptive words used in lines 14–15. What connotation do the words *sluggish, suddenly,* and *sharp* have? How do these words show the author's attitude about work? RL.11-12.4

3. **How does the poet's choice to chronologically depict the events of the day affect the meaning of the poem?** Review the poem. Think about how the speaker's age changes from the beginning of the poem to the ending. How does the passage of time change his view of his work in the factory? RL.11-12.5

Nonfiction

Roberto Acuna Talks About Farm Workers
from *Working*

by Studs Terkel

1   I walked out of the fields two years ago. I saw the need to change the California feudal system, to change the lives of farm workers, to make these huge corporations feel they're not not above anybody. I am thirty-four years old and I try to organize for the United Farm Workers of America. …

2   If you're picking lettuce, the thumbnails fall off 'cause they're banged on the box. Your hands get swollen. You can't slow down because the foreman sees you're so many boxes behind and you'd better get on. But people would help each other. If you're feeling bad that day, somebody who's feeling pretty good would help. Any people that are suffering have to stick together, whether they like it or not, whether they be black, brown, or pink. …

3   I began to see how everything was so wrong. When growers can have an intricate watering system to irrigate their crops but they can't have running water inside the houses of workers. Veterinarians tend to the needs of domestic animals but they can't have medical care for the workers. They can have land **subsidies** for the growers but they can't have adequate unemployment compensation for the workers. They treat him like a farm implement. In fact, they treat their implements better and their domestic animals better. They have heat and **insulated** barns for the animals but the workers live in beat-up shacks with no heat at all.

4   Illness in the fields is 120 percent higher than the average rate for industry. It's mostly back trouble, rheumatism, and arthritis, because of the damp weather and the cold. **Stoop labor** is very hard on a person. Tuberculosis is high. And now because of the pesticides, we have many respiratory diseases.

5   The University of California at Davis had

A Mexican field worker on a farm in California packs freshly harvested heads of lettuce for transportation, 1958.

© 2021 College Board. All rights reserved.

GRAMMAR & USAGE

Parallel Structure

Parallel Structure is the repetition of words or phrases that have similar grammatical structures. Such repetition in writing creates rhythm and emphasizes ideas. In the first paragraph, Acuna repeats infinitive phrases—verbs with *to*: "I saw the need to change the California feudal system, to change the lives of farm workers, to make these huge corporations feel they're not above anybody." The overall impact of this repetition is to emphasize his commitment to improving farm workers' lives. Study Acuna's repetition of the verbs *can have* and *can't* in paragraph 3.

WORD CONNECTIONS

Etymology

During the Middle Ages, peasants who worked the land essentially belonged to and were protected by the lord who had been granted the land as part of a feudal system. The origin of **feudal** can be found in Medieval Latin *feudalis* ("land granted"), Old High German *fihu* ("cattle"), and Middle English *feodary* ("one who holds lands in exchange for service"). *Feudal* is not related to *feud*.

subsidies: grants or sums of money

insulated: protected from heat and/or cold

stoop labor: agricultural labor performed in a squatting position

---

Scaffolding the Text-Dependent Questions

4. According to Acuna, how should employers show respect for human farm work and workers? Reread paragraph 3. How does Acuna think the employers treat the workers? What would he like to see changed? RL.11-12.1

5. In paragraph 3, how does Acuna use parallelism? What effect does this parallelism

have? Reread paragraph 3. What word does Acuna use to start many sentences in the paragraph? Who is the "they"? Does Acuna feel like the workers have a good relationship with the employers? L.11-12.5

---

9   FIRST READ: Conduct a shared reading of "Roberto Acuna Talks About Farm Workers." Pause after the first paragraph. Explain that the United Farm Workers of America is a union that formed to help protect the rights of people who work in the fields harvesting crops.

⚠ TEXT COMPLEXITY

Overall: Accessible
Lexile: 760L
Qualitative: Low Difficulty
Task: Moderate (Analyze)

10   Ask a volunteer to read the Grammar & Usage information. Then ask students to find examples of parallel structure in the text and explain how using parallel structure emphasizes ideas.

11   **Vocabulary Development:** Have students review the Word Connections box. Then ask them to explain what is meant by "California feudal system" in paragraph 1. Select a few compelling words, such as *feudal*, from the text and ask students about the author's possible intent for using them. Elicit other words that the author could have used.

12 Pause after paragraph 10. Ask students to name the groups of people mentioned in the paragraph. Discuss who the groups of people are and why they are mentioned in this part of hte text.

1.22

My Notes

denounce: publicly declare to be wrong

government experiments with pesticides and chemicals. They get a bigger crop each year. They haven't any regard as to what safety precautions are needed. In 1964 and '65, an airplane was spraying these chemicals on the fields. Spraying rigs they're called. Flying low, the wheels got tangled in the fence wire. The pilot got up, dusted himself off, and got a drink of water. He died of convulsions. The ambulance attendants got violently sick because of the pesticide he had on his person. A little girl was playing around a sprayer. She stuck her tongue on it. She died instantly.

6   These pesticides affect the farm worker through the lungs. He breathes it in. He gets no compensation. All they do is say he's sick. They don't investigate the cause.

7   There were times when I felt I couldn't take it anymore. It was 105 in the shade and I'd see endless rows of lettuce and I felt my back hurting. … I felt the frustration of not being able to get out of the fields. I was getting ready to jump any foreman who looked at me cross-eyed. But until two years ago, my world was still very small. I would read all these things in the papers about Cesar Chavez and I would denounce him because I still had that thing about becoming a first class patriotic citizen. In Mexicali they would pass out leaflets and I would throw 'em away. I never participated. The grape boycott didn't affect me much because I was in lettuce. It wasn't until Chavez came to Salinas where I was working in the fields, that I saw what a beautiful man he was. I went to this rally, I still intended to stay with the company. But something—I don't know—I was close to the workers. They couldn't speak English and wanted me to be their spokesman in favor of going on strike. I don't know—I just got caught up with it all, the beautiful feeling of solidarity.

8   You'd see the people on the picket lines at four in the morning, at the camp fires, heating up beans and coffee and tortillas. It gave me a sense of belonging. These were my own people and they wanted change. I knew this is what I was looking for. I just didn't know it before.

9   My mom had always wanted me to better myself. I wanted to better myself because of her. Now when the strikes started, I told her I was going to join the union and the whole movement. I told her I was going to work without pay. She said she was proud of me. (His eyes glisten. A long, long pause.) See, I told her I wanted to be with my people. If I were a company man, no one would like me anymore. I had to belong to somebody and this was it right here. She said, "I pushed you in your early years to try to better yourself and get a social position. But I see that's not the answer. I know I'll be proud of you."

10   All kinds of people are farm workers, not just Chicanos. Filipinos started the strike. We have Puerto Ricans and Appalachians too, Arabs, some Japanese, some Chinese. At one time they used us against each other. But now they can't and they're scared, the growers. They can organize conglomerates. Yet when we try organization to better our lives, they are afraid. Suffering people never dreamed it could be different. Cesar Chavez tells them this and they grasp the idea—and this is what scares the growers.

Scaffolding the Text-Dependent Questions

6. What is Studs Terkel's purpose for publishing the words of Acuna? Reread several paragraphs, including paragraph 13. Does Studs Terkel have a similar opinion to Acuna about the treatment of workers? How does using only Acuna's words impact the message? RL.11-12.1

7. In what way do Roberto Acuna and Martin Espada have a similar experience? Explain your answer. Review the Acuna interview. What is Acuna's experience with work? Review Espada's poem. What is Espada's experience with manual labor? Were their job experiences easy or difficult? How are the experiences alike? RL.11-12.3

13 Pause after paragraph 13.
Discuss how Acuna feels about work.

11 Now the machines are coming in. It takes skill to operate them. But anybody can be taught. We feel migrant workers should be given the chance. They got one for grapes. They got one for lettuce. They have cotton machines that took jobs away from thousands of farm workers. The people wind up in the ghettos of the cities, their culture, their families, their unity destroyed.

12 We're trying to **stipulate** it in our contract that the company will not use any machinery without the consent of the farm workers. So we can make sure the people being replaced by the machines will know how to operate the machines.

13 Working in the fields is not in itself a degrading job. It's hard, but if you're given regular hours, better pay, decent housing, unemployment, and medical compensation, pension plans—we have a very relaxed way of living. But growers don't recognize us as persons. That's the worst thing, the way they treat you. Like we have no brains. Now we see they have no brains. They have only a wallet in their head. The more you squeeze it the more they cry out.

Grape pickers carry American flags and National Farm Workers Association banners as they march along a road from Delano to Sacramento to protest their low wages and poor working conditions, 1966.

14 If we had proper compensation we wouldn't have to be working seventeen hours a day and following the crops. We could stay in one area and it would give us roots. Being a migrant, it tears the family apart. You get in debt. You leave the area penniless. The children are the ones hurt the most. They go to school three months in one place and then on to another. No sooner do they make friends, they are uprooted again. Right here, your childhood is taken away. So when they grow up, they're looking for this childhood they have lost.

15 If people could see—in the winter, ice on the fields. We'd be on our knees all day long. We'd build fires and warm up real fast and go back onto the ice. We'd be picking watermelons in 105 degrees all day long. When people have

My Notes

stipulate: demand or specify a condition

Scaffolding the Text-Dependent Questions

8. Why does Acuna want to "take busloads of people out to the fields"? How would their realization be like that of Martin Espada? Reread paragraph 15. What would people see if they went out to the fields? How would this change their opinion about a salad they have for dinner? RL.11-12.1

14 After reading the text for the first time, guide the class in a discussion by asking the Making Observations questions. Check students' general comprehension of the text based on their observations, asking follow-up questions if needed.

15 **RETURNING TO THE TEXT:** Guide students to return to the text to answer the text-dependent comprehension questions. Have students reread and work on them in small groups.

16 Move from group to group and listen in as students answer the text-dependent questions. If they have difficulty, scaffold the questions by rephrasing them or breaking them into smaller parts. See the Scaffolding the Text-Dependent Questions boxes for suggestions.

1.22

melons or cucumber or carrots or lettuce, they don't know how they got on their table and the consequences to the people who picked it. If I had enough money, I would take busloads of people out to the fields and into the labor camps. Then they'd know how that fine salad got on their table.

Making Observations
- Which part of Acuna's story creates the most powerful image for you?
- How does this text make you feel?

Returning to the Text
- Return to the texts as you respond to the following questions. Use text evidence to support your responses.
- Write any additional questions you have about the texts in your Reader/Writer Notebook.

"Who Burns for the Perfection of Paper?"

1. What can you infer about the speaker based on the details in lines 1–21?

   The author was hard-working when he was young because he went to school all day and then worked a tough job after school until at least 9 p.m.

2. How do the words in lines 14–15 affect the tone of the poem?

   These lines change the tone. The reader realizes that the long hours of the tedious job would wear on him. Because he would feel sluggish, the "sudden sharp paper" now became something dangerous that would cause stinging cuts.

3. How does the poet's choice to chronologically depict the events of the day affect the meaning of the poem?

   The chronology of the day helps the reader realize that a job that did not seem too tough at first actually would get very difficult by night. Then the reader realizes this job led to a greater appreciation by the speaker later in life when he would use the same legal pads and knew the hard work it took to make them.

"Roberto Acuna Talks About Farm Workers"

4. According to Acuna, how should employers show respect for human farm work and workers?

Acuna says employers should treat the workers as well as the employers treat the farm

implements and the domestic animals. It would also be respectful if employers gave them

"regular hours, better pay, decent housing, unemployment, and medical compensation,

pension plans."

5. In paragraph 3, how does Acuna use parallelism? What effect does this parallelism have?

Acuna starts several sentences with the word *they* when describing the growers. This helps

to establish for the readers/listeners the "us versus them" problem that exists between the

growers and the migrant workers.

6. What is Studs Terkel's purpose for publishing the words of Acuna?

Terkel's purpose is to make others aware of the issues migrant workers face in the fields. By

letting Acuna tell his story, Terkel hopes to bring awareness to the issues.

Both Texts

7. In what way do Roberto Acuna and Martin Espada have a similar experience? Explain your answer.

They both have worked physical jobs that cause pain and injuries. Acuna describes working

in the fields under terrible conditions, and Espada describes working in a factory assembling

pads of paper where the workers experience cuts in order to glue the cardboard on properly.

8. Why does Acuna want to "take busloads of people out to the fields"? How would their realization be like that of Martin Espada?

Acuna wants to take the people to see the way that people suffer in order to provide for

themselves and their families. This realization would be similar to Espada because Espada

learns how difficult and painful it is to create pads of paper when he has a job putting the pads

of paper together.

17 Guide students to complete the Check Your Understanding task and the Writing Prompt.

LEVELED DIFFERENTIATED INSTRUCTION

To respond to the Writing Prompt, students may need support writing an argument essay.

Developing Pair students and provide them with the **Persuasive/Argument Writing Map** graphic organizer to complete together as a prewriting support. Allow partners to collaborate in responding to the argument prompt.

Support Allow students to work in pairs or groups to brainstorm at least three different audiences to which this essay could be written. Have students discuss the knowledge, concerns, and biases of each group and then select the group to whom they will write.

Extend Encourage students who have written for different audiences to read aloud their argument and evidence to the class. Provide listeners the opportunity to suggest counterclaims to each speaker's argument and allow the speaker to respond with refutations.

ASSESS

Evaluate the sentences that students wrote for the Check Your Understanding task. Verify that they have explained how the jobs described relate to the American Dream.

Read student responses to the Writing Prompt using the bulleted list as a guideline.

ADAPT

To help students plan their essays, have partners use a Venn diagram to list the similarities and differences of what the United States offers immigrants and native-born Americans in terms of opportunities to achieve the American Dream.

1.22

☑ Check Your Understanding

In a few sentences, explain how the jobs described in "Who Burns for the Perfection of Paper?" and "Roberto Acuna Talks About Farm Workers" relate to the American Dream.

☑ Writing Prompt: Argumentative

Write a short essay developing an argument on the difference between an immigrant's and a citizen's sense of opportunity in the United States. Discuss the similarities and differences in what the United States offers immigrants and native-born Americans in terms of opportunities to achieve the American Dream and how both groups view the future. Be sure to:

- Plan effectively by choosing an appropriate audience and thinking about how to write your essay with their knowledge, concerns, and biases in mind.
- Write a thesis statement that clearly states your position.
- Paraphrase, summarize, and use direct quotations from the texts you have read to develop your claim fairly and thoroughly, acknowledging both its strengths and limitations.
- Acknowledge potential counterclaims fairly and provide enough reasons or evidence to convince your audience that those counterclaims are incorrect or that your claim is stronger.
- Provide an effective conclusion.

WRITING PROMPT : ARGUMENTATIVE

The following standards are addressed in the writing prompt:

- W.11-12.1
- W.11-12.1a
- W.11-12.8
- W.11-12.1b
- W.11-12.1e

The Road to Success

Learning Targets

- Analyze the structural elements and characteristics of argumentative texts, including the effects of rhetorical devices.
- Defend or challenge an author's claims using evidence from a text.

Preview

In this activity, you will read and analyze two argumentative texts. Then you will write a narrative essay in which you will imagine that the two authors are having a conversation about the American Dream.

As You Read

- Underline words and phrases that show the author's definitions of the American Dream.
- Highlight words and phrases that indicate how the writer feels about access to the American Dream.
- Circle unknown words and phrases. Try to determine the meaning of the words by using context clues, word parts, or a dictionary.

About the Author

Barack Obama (b. 1961) was the 44th president of the United States and the country's first African American president. He was awarded the Nobel Peace Prize in 2009 for "his extraordinary efforts to strengthen diplomacy and cooperation between peoples." Known as an eloquent orator, Obama has given many famous speeches. In 2004, when Obama was the junior senator from Illinois, his speech at the Democratic National Convention vaulted him to national prominence.

Speech

from Keynote Address to the 2004 Democratic Convention

by Barack Obama

1 On behalf of the great state of Illinois, crossroads of a nation, land of Lincoln, let me express my deep gratitude for the privilege of addressing this convention. Tonight is a particular honor for me because, let's face it, my presence on this stage is pretty unlikely. My father was a foreign student, born and raised in a small village in Kenya. He grew up herding goats, went to school in a tin-roof shack. His father—my grandfather—was a cook, a domestic servant to the British.

Learning Strategies

Discussion Groups
Graphic Organizer
Marking the Text

My Notes

College and Career Readiness Standards

Focus Standards:

SL.11-12.1b Work with peers to promote civil, democratic discussions and decision-making, set clear goals and deadlines, and establish individual roles as needed.

SL.11-12.1c Propel conversations by posing and responding to questions that probe reasoning and evidence; ensure a hearing for a full range of positions on a topic or issue; clarify, verify, or challenge ideas and conclusions; and promote divergent and creative perspectives.

RI.11-12.5 Analyze and evaluate the effectiveness of the structure an author uses in his or her exposition or argument, including whether the structure makes points clear, convincing, and engaging.

PLAN

Suggested Pacing: 2 50-minute class periods

TEACH

1 Read the Learning Targets and Preview with students. Help them understand that they will be analyzing two people's views of the American Dream.

2 Read the As You Read and the About the Author sections. Consider setting the historical context for this text by asking students to do some research about the occasion.

3 FIRST READ: Conduct a guided reading of the excerpt from the "Keynote Address to the 2004 Democratic Convention."

TEXT COMPLEXITY

Overall: Complex
Lexile: 1110L
Qualitative: Moderate Difficulty
Task: Moderate (Analyze)

4 As students are reading, monitor their progress. Be sure they are engaged with the text and annotating words and phrases that define the American Dream.

5 Pause after paragraph 3 to ensure that students understand the references to World War II.

6 After students read the Grammar & Usage box, have them identify other examples of precise language in the speech. In paragraph 3, for example, Obama references the G.I. Bill, a government-sponsored higher education program, and FHA, a type of home mortgage made available by the government. Explain that these are not only precise details drawn from the context of everyday life but also support for Obama's argument that government has a role to play in the realization of the American Dream.

7 Pause after paragraph 6. Ask students to name the parts of the American Dream Obama mentions in the paragraph.

1.23

GRAMMAR & USAGE

Precise Language

Precise language makes use of exact nouns and vivid verbs to create strong images and make writing more understandable. Precise language can also create a specific tone in a piece of writing. In paragraph 3, for example, Obama says his grandfather signed up on a specific day, "the day after Pearl Harbor." Similarly, he says his grandmother worked "on a bomber assembly line." His precise language gives us a clearer picture of events and also helps establish the down-to-earth, populist tone of the speech.

Find other examples of exact nouns and noun phrases in this address. How do they contribute to the tone of the speech?

My Notes

2 But my grandfather had larger dreams for his son. Through hard work and perseverance my father got a scholarship to study in a magical place, America, that shone as a beacon of freedom and opportunity to so many who had come before.

3 While studying here, my father met my mother. She was born in a town on the other side of the world, in Kansas. Her father worked on oil rigs and farms through most of the Depression. The day after Pearl Harbor he signed up for duty, joined Patton's army and marched across Europe. Back home, my grandmother raised a baby and went to work on a bomber assembly line. After the war, they studied on the G.I. Bill, bought a house through FHA, and moved west, all the way to Hawaii, in search of opportunity.

4 And they, too, had big dreams for their daughter, a common dream, born of two continents. My parents shared not only an improbable love; they shared an abiding faith in the possibilities of this nation. They would give me an African name, Barack, or "blessed," believing that in a tolerant America your name is no barrier to success. They imagined me going to the best schools in the land, even though they weren't rich, because in a generous America you don't have to be rich to achieve your potential. They are both passed away now. Yet, I know that, on this night, they look down on me with pride.

5 I stand here today, grateful for the diversity of my heritage, aware that my parents' dreams live on in my two precious daughters. I stand here knowing that my story is part of the larger American story, that I owe a debt to all of those who came before me, and that, in no other country on earth, is my story even possible. Tonight, we gather to affirm the greatness of our nation, not because of the height of our skyscrapers, or the power of our military, or the size of our economy. Our pride is based on a very simple premise, summed up in a declaration made over two hundred years ago, "We hold these truths to be self-evident, that all men are created equal, that they are endowed by their Creator with certain inalienable rights, that among these are life, liberty and the pursuit of happiness."

6 That is the true genius of America, a faith in the simple dreams, the insistence on small miracles; that we can tuck in our children at night and know they are fed and clothed and safe from harm; that we can say what we think, write what we think, without hearing a sudden knock on the door; that we can have an idea and start our own business without paying a bribe; that we can participate in the political process without fear of retribution, and that our votes will be counted—or at least, most of the time.

7 This year, in this election, we are called to reaffirm our values and our commitments, to hold them against a hard reality and see how we are measuring up, to the legacy of our forebearers, and the promise of future generations. And fellow Americans—Democrats, Republicans, Independents—I say to you tonight: we have more work to do. More to do for the workers I met in Galesburg, Illinois, who are losing their union jobs at the Maytag plant that's moving to Mexico, and now they're having to compete with

College and Career Readiness Standards

RI.11-12.6 Determine an author's point of view or purpose in a text in which the rhetoric is particularly effective, analyzing how style and content contribute to the power, persuasiveness or beauty of the text.

W.11-12.9 Draw evidence from literary or informational texts to support analysis, reflection, and research.

RI.11-12.1 Cite strong and thorough textual evidence to support analysis of what the text says explicitly as well as inferences drawn from the text, including determining where the text leaves matters uncertain.

Additional Standards Addressed:
RI.11-12.4, W.11-12.2

My Notes

their own children for jobs that pay seven bucks an hour; more to do for the father I met who was losing his job and choking back tears, wondering how he would pay $4,500 a month for the drugs his son needs without the health benefits he counted on; more to do for the young woman in East St. Louis, and thousands more like her, who have the grades, have the drive, have the will, but doesn't have the money to go to college.

8 Don't get me wrong. The people I meet in small towns and big cities, in diners and office parks, they don't expect government to solve all their problems. They know they have to work hard to get ahead and they want to. Go into the collar counties around Chicago, and people will tell you: They don't want their tax money wasted by a welfare agency or the Pentagon. Go into any inner city neighborhood, and folks will tell you that government alone can't teach kids to learn. They know that parents have to teach, that children can't achieve unless we raise their expectations and turn off the television sets and eradicate the slander that says a black youth with a book is acting white. They know those things. People don't expect government to solve all their problems. But they sense, deep in their bones, that with just a slight change in priorities, we can make sure that every child in America has a decent shot at life, and that the doors of opportunity remain open to all. They know we can do better. And they want that choice. … John Kerry believes in America. And he knows it's not enough for just some of us to prosper. For alongside our famous individualism, there's another ingredient in the American saga, a belief that we are connected as one people. If there's a child on the south side of Chicago who can't read, that matters to me, even if it's not my child. If there's a senior citizen somewhere who can't pay for their prescription drugs and has to choose between medicine and the rent, that makes my life poorer, even if it's not my grandmother. If there's an Arab American family being rounded up without benefit of an attorney or due process, that threatens my civil liberties. It is that fundamental belief—it is that fundamental belief—I am my brother's keeper, I am my sister's keeper—that makes this country work. It's what allows us to pursue our individual dreams, yet still come together as a single American family." "E pluribus unum," out of many, one.

9 Now even as we speak, there are those who are preparing to divide us, the spin masters and negative ad peddlers who embrace the politics of anything goes. Well, I say to them tonight, there's not a liberal America and a conservative America—there's the United States of America. There's not a black America and white America and Latino America and Asian America; there's the United States of America. The **pundits** like to slice-and-dice our country into Red States and Blue States; Red States for Republicans, Blue States for Democrats. But I've got news for them, too. We worship an awesome God in the Blue States, and we don't like federal agents poking around our libraries in the Red States. We coach Little League in the Blue States and, yes, we've got some gay friends in the Red States. There are patriots who opposed the war in Iraq and patriots who supported the war in Iraq. We are one people, all of us pledging allegiance to the stars and stripes, all of us defending the United States of America.

> **pundit:** a critic who makes comments and judgments

8 • Pause after paragraph 8. Discuss how the author feels the phrase *E pluribus unum* is connected to the American Dream.

Scaffolding the Text-Dependent Questions

1. How does Obama use rhetoric in paragraph 6 to advance his point of view? Reread paragraph 6. How does Obama appeal to his audience's ethos—their sense of pride in America? How does this help develop his point of view? RI.11-12.5, RI.11-12.6

2. In paragraph 8, how does Obama address potential counterarguments? Reread paragraph 8. What does Obama say about people's opinion of government? What examples does Obama give of government helping people? RI.11-12.5, RI.11-12.6

3. How does Obama's choice to end the speech by stating a series of beliefs contribute to the speech's overall impact? Reread paragraph 11. What series of beliefs does Obama state there? What effect does this have on you as you read it? How is this rhetoric similar to the Declaration of Independence? RI.11-12.5, RI.11-12.6

9 After reading the text for the first time, guide the class in a discussion by asking the Making Observations questions. Check students' general comprehension of the text based on their observations, asking follow-up questions if needed.

⭐ TEACHER TO TEACHER

Consider showing parts or all of Obama's historic speech, which is available through a search of www.c-span.org. Discuss how Obama uses inflections in his voice as well as hand gestures to support his ideas.

10 Consider using a **guided reading** to identify each of the elements of an argument in Obama's speech. Ask students to **mark the text** and label each element of an argument. Encourage students to discuss and critique each element, using the My Notes space to write ideas.

1.23

My Notes

10 In the end, that's what this election is about. Do we participate in a politics of cynicism or a politics of hope? John Kerry calls on us to hope. John Edwards calls on us to hope. I'm not talking about blind optimism here—the almost willful ignorance that thinks unemployment will go away if we just don't talk about it, or the health care crisis will solve itself if we just ignore it. That's not what I'm talking about. I'm talking about something more substantial. It's the hope of slaves sitting around a fire singing freedom songs; the hope of immigrants setting out for distant shores; the hope of a young naval lieutenant bravely patrolling the Mekong Delta; the hope of a mill worker's son who dares to defy the odds; the hope of a skinny kid with a funny name who believes that America has a place for him, too. Hope in the face of difficulty, hope in the face of uncertainty, the audacity of hope!

11 In the end, that is God's greatest gift to us, the bedrock of this nation; the belief in things not seen; the belief that there are better days ahead. I believe we can give our middle class relief and provide working families with a road to opportunity. I believe we can provide jobs to the jobless, homes to the homeless, and reclaim young people in cities across America from violence and despair. I believe that we have a righteous wind at our backs, and that as we stand on the crossroads of history, we can make the right choices, and meet the challenges that face us. …

Making Observations
- What details in Obama's speech stood out to you?
- What words does Obama use to describe America?

Scaffolding the Text-Dependent Questions

4. What is the main message of Obama's speech? Reread paragraph 11. What is Obama's opinion of the future of America? How does he want people to feel about the future of America? RI.11-12.1

5. In paragraph 9, Obama makes the claim that the United States is not divided. Do you think this claim is correct or incorrect? Defend your answer using text evidence. Reread paragraph 9. What examples does Obama give of people who have differing opinions? Why does Obama give a list of real-life situations that are important to him, even if they are not directly related to him? RI.11-12.5, RI.11-12.6

Returning to the Text

- Return to the speech as you respond to the following questions. Use text evidence to support your responses.
- Write any additional questions you have about the text in your Reader/Writer Notebook.

1. How does Obama use rhetoric in paragraph 6 to advance his point of view?

Obama uses a combination of rhetorical devices. He uses parallelism by repeating "that we can" to reinforce the theme of togetherness and opportunity. He also gives repeated examples to illustrate those points.

2. In paragraph 8, how does Obama address potential counterarguments?

Obama rattles off a list of people from different communities who have concerns about government involvement. He then addresses how those concerns could be fixed with "just a slight change in priorities."

3. How does the Obama's choice to end the speech by stating a series of beliefs contribute to the speech's overall impact?

The series of beliefs leads to an inspirational conclusion that motivates listeners to agree with Obama's point of view that America is a great place despite some of its problems.

4. What is the main message of Obama's speech?

His main message is that, despite its problems, America is a place of great opportunity where people of different beliefs can all have dreams and work to achieve those dreams.

5. In paragraph 9, Obama makes the claim that the United States is not divided. Do you think this claim is correct or incorrect? Defend your answer using text evidence.

Answers will vary and should provide direct support from the text. For example: I think this claim is correct. As Obama states in the paragraph, different kinds of people come together in all different circumstances, and all of those people pledge "allegiance to the stars and stripes."

As You Read

- Underline words and phrases that show the author's definitions of the American Dream.
- Highlight words and phrases that indicate how the writer feels about access to the American Dream.
- Circle unknown words and phrases. Try to determine the meaning of the words by using context clues, word parts, or a dictionary.

ACTIVITY 1.23 continued

11 RETURNING TO THE TEXT: Guide students to return to the text to answer the text-dependent comprehension questions. Have students reread and work on the questions together as a class.

12 If students have difficulty, scaffold the questions by rephrasing them or breaking them into smaller parts. See the Scaffolding the Text-Dependent Questions boxes for suggestions.

13 When students have completed their work with the "2004 Keynote Address," ask them to turn their attention to William Zinsser's "The Right to Fail." Read aloud the As You Read and About the Author sections.

14 FIRST READ: Conduct a read aloud of "The Right to Fail." Pause after paragraph 3. Ask students what the author's opinion is of dropping out.

△ TEXT COMPLEXITY

Overall: Complex
Lexile: 1240L
Qualitative: Moderate Difficulty
Task: Challenging (Evaluate)

15 As students are reading, monitor their progress. Be sure they are engaged with the text and annotating words and phrases that define the American Dream.

1.23

My Notes

About the Author

William Zinsser (1922–2015), American critic and writer, was born in New York and educated at Princeton. He wrote articles for many leading magazines and newspapers and authored 19 books. In perhaps his most famous book, *On Writing Well*, he preached brevity and writing concisely. He was known for his positive attitude and once deadpanned that he was "cursed with optimism."

Essay

The Right to Fail

by William Zinsser

1 I like "dropout" as an addition to the American language because it's brief and it's clear. What I don't like is that we use it almost entirely as a dirty word.

2 We only apply it to people under twenty-one. Yet an adult who spends his days and nights watching mindless TV programs is more of a dropout than an eighteen-year-old who quits college, with its frequently mindless courses, to become, say, a VISTA volunteer. For the young, dropping out is often a way of dropping in.

3 To hold this opinion, however, is little short of treason in America. A boy or girl who leaves college is branded a failure—and the right to fail is one of the few freedoms that this country does not grant its citizens. The American dream is a dream of "getting ahead," painted in strokes of gold wherever we look. Our advertisements and TV commercials are a hymn to material success, our magazine articles a toast to people who made it to the top. Smoke the right cigarette or drive the right car—so the ads imply—and girls will be swooning into your deodorized arms or caressing your expensive **lapels**. Happiness goes to the man who has the sweet smell of achievement. He is our national idol, and everybody else is our national **fink**.

4 I want to put in a word for the fink, especially the teen-age fink, because if we give him time to get through his finkdom—if we release him from the pressure of attaining certain goals by a certain age—he has a good chance of becoming our national idol, a Jefferson or a Thoreau, a Buckminster Fuller or an Adlai Stevenson, a man with a mind of his own. We need **mavericks** and **dissenters** and dreamers far more than we need junior vice presidents, but we paralyze them by insisting that every step be a step up to the next rung of the ladder. Yet in the fluid years of youth, the only way for boys and girls to find their proper road is often to take a hundred side trips, poking out in different directions, faltering, drawing back, and starting again.

5 "But what if we fail?" they ask, whispering the dreadful word across the Generation Gap to their parents, who are back home at the Establishment nursing their "middle-class values" and cultivating their "goal oriented society." The parents whisper back: "Don't!"

lapels: folded flaps of cloth below the collar of a formal jacket or suit coat
fink: a person strongly disliked and viewed with contempt
mavericks: independent individuals who do not conform to the group
dissenters: people who disagree in matters of opinion and belief, rebels

Scaffolding the Text-Dependent Questions

6. **How does the author address a potential counterargument in paragraphs 5–6?** Reread paragraphs 5–6. What question does the author pose in paragraph 5? How does he respond to that question in paragraph 6?
RI.11-12.5, RI.11-12.6

7. **How does the author's mixture of slang, colloquialisms, and pop culture references with his formal tone and language increase the text's effectiveness?** Locate each of these types of language in the text. To what audience does the formal language appeal? To what audience does the informal language appeal? Why would the author want to appeal to those two audiences? RI.11-12.4

6 What they should say is "Don't be afraid to fail!" Failure isn't fatal. Countless people have had a bout with it and come out stronger as a result. Many have even come out famous. History is strewn with **eminent** dropouts, "loners" who followed their own trail, not worrying about its odd twists and turns because they had faith in their own sense of direction. To read their biographies is always exhilarating, not only because they beat the system, but because their system was better than the one that they beat. Luckily, such rebels still turn up often enough to prove that individualism, though badly threatened, is not extinct. Much has been written, for instance, about the fitful scholastic career of Thomas P. F. Hoving, New York's former Parks Commissioner and now director of the Metropolitan Museum of Art. Hoving was a dropout's dropout, entering and leaving schools as if they were motels, often at the request of the management. Still, he must have learned something during those unorthodox years, for he dropped in again at the top of his profession.

7 His case reminds me of another boyhood—that of Holden Caulfield in J. D. Salinger's *The Catcher in the Rye*, the most popular literary hero of the postwar period. There is nothing accidental about the grip that this dropout continues to hold on the affections of an entire American generation. Nobody else, real or invented, has made such an engaging shambles of our "goal-oriented society," so gratified our secret belief that the "phonies" are in power and the good guys up the creek. Whether Holden has also reached the top of his chosen field today is one of those speculations that delight fanciers of good fiction. I speculate that he has. Holden Caulfield, incidentally, is now thirty-six.

8 I'm not urging everyone to go out and fail just for the sheer therapy of it, or to quit college just to coddle some vague discontent. Obviously it's better to succeed than to flop, and in general a long education is more helpful than a short one. (Thanks to my own education, for example, I can tell George Eliot from T. S. Eliot, I can handle the pluperfect tense in French, and I know that Caesar beat the Helvetii because he had enough frumentum.) I only mean that failure isn't bad in itself, or success automatically good.

9 Fred Zinnemann, who has directed some of Hollywood's most honored movies, was asked by a reporter, when *A Man for All Seasons* won every prize, about his previous film, *Behold a Pale Horse*, which was a box-office disaster. "I don't feel any obligation to be successful," Zinneman replied. "Success can be dangerous—you feel you know it all. I've learned a great deal from my failures." A similar point was made by Richard Brooks about his ambitious money loser, *Lord Jim*. Recalling the three years of his life that went into it, talking almost with elation about the troubles that befell his unit in Cambodia, Brooks told me that he learned more about his craft from this considerable failure than from his many earlier hits.

10 It's a point, of course, that applies throughout the arts. Writers, playwrights, painters and composers work in the expectation of periodic defeat, but they wouldn't keep going back into the arena if they thought it was the end of the world. It isn't the end of the world. For an artist—and perhaps for anybody—it is the only way to grow.

My Notes

eminent: successful and respected

© 2021 College Board. All rights reserved.

ACTIVITY 1.23 continued

16 Pause after paragraph 6. Discuss how the phrase "Don't be afraid to fail!" relates to the author's definition of the American Dream.

17 Pause after paragraph 8. Discuss how the author views education in relation to the American Dream.

Scaffolding the Text-Dependent Questions

8. The author places the sentence "Thanks to my own education, for example, I can tell George Eliot from T. S. Eliot, I can handle the pluperfect tense in French, and I know that Caesar beat the Helvetii because he had enough frumentum" in paragraph 8 within parentheses (a *parenthetical* statement). Why does he make this text parenthetical? Reread paragraph 8 without the parenthetical. Then reread the paragraph with the parenthetical. What does the parenthetical add? How is the content of the parenthetical different than the rest of the paragraph? RI.11-12.4

18 After reading the text for the first time, guide the class in a discussion by asking the Making Observations questions. Check students' general comprehension of the text based on their observations, asking follow-up questions if needed.

1.23

My Notes

11 Today's younger generation seems to know that this is true, seems willing to take the risks in life that artists take in art. "Society," needless to say, still has the upper hand—it sets the goals and condemns as a failure everybody who won't play. But the dropouts and the hippies are not as afraid of failure as their parents and grandparents. This could mean, as their elders might say, that they are just plumb lazy, secure in the comforts of an affluent state. It could also mean, however, that they just don't buy the old standards of success and are rapidly writing new ones.

12 Recently it was announced, for instance, that more than two hundred thousand Americans have inquired about service in VISTA (the domestic Peace Corps) and that, according to a Gallup survey, "more than 3 million American college students would serve VISTA in some capacity if given the opportunity." This is hardly the road to riches or to an executive suite. Yet I have met many of these young volunteers, and they are not pining for traditional success. On the contrary, they appear more fulfilled than the average vice-president with a swimming pool.

13 Who is to say, then, if there is any right path to the top, or even to say what the top consists of? Obviously the colleges don't have more than a partial answer—otherwise the young would not be so disaffected with an education that they consider **vapid**. Obviously business does not have the answer—otherwise the young would not be so scornful of its call to be an organization man.

14 The fact is, nobody has the answer, and the dawning awareness of this fact seems to me one of the best things happening in America today. Success and failure are again becoming individual visions, as they were when the country was younger, not rigid categories. Maybe we are learning again to cherish this right of every person to succeed on his own terms and to fail as often as necessary along the way.

Making Observations
- What words does the author use to indicate his feelings?
- What idea captured your attention in this text?

vapid: dull or boring

Scaffolding the Text-Dependent Questions

9. Who is the author's intended audience for this article? Provide details from the text to support your answer. Review the text. To what audience does the formal language appeal? To what audience does the informal language appeal? How does the article appeal to these two audiences? RI.11-12.1

10. Does the author's choice to consider real and fictional examples of "dropouts" have a positive or negative impact on his argument? **Explain your answer using text evidence.** Skim the text for each appearance of the word *dropouts* and review the surrounding text. What examples of dropouts does the author give? Which examples are most effective? Why are those examples effective? RI.11-12.1

Returning to the Text

- Return to the speech as you respond to the following questions. Use text evidence to support your responses.
- Write any additional questions you have about the text in your Reader/Writer Notebook.

6. How does the author address a potential counterargument in paragraph 5–6?

The author poses a question that people might pose as a counterargument. He then goes on to refute the aspects of that counterargument with evidence to prove his claim is the better point of view.

7. How does the author's mixture of slang, colloquialisms, and pop culture references with his formal tone and language increase the text's effectiveness?

It adds to the effectiveness because it illustrates how you don't have to be overly formal or follow the "correct" path to be successful. His argument is successful despite pairing informal words with an otherwise formal structure.

8. The author places the sentence "Thanks to my own education, for example, I can tell George Eliot from T. S. Eliot, I can handle the pluperfect tense in French, and I know that Caesar beat the Helvetii because he had enough frumentum" in paragraph 8 within parentheses (a *parenthetical* statement). Why does he make this text parenthetical?

Parentheses are often used to convey information that may be helpful but is not essential to the text. Here, the author uses the parenthetical to give examples of how his longer education gave him the opportunity to learn things that the common reader does not know. By placing it in parentheses, he suggests, however, that the information is not essential, useful, or important.

9. Who is the author's intended audience for this article? Provide details from the text to support your answer.

The author has two intended audiences. The first is the people who think that there is only one right path to success and people are not allowed to fail along the way. His sentence "To hold this opinion, however, is little short of treason in America" appeals to these readers. The second audience is a younger crowd, whom he encourages to take an unorthodox path if they think that is best for them. He appeals to them with the line "Today's younger generation seems to know that this is true, seems willing to take the risks in life that artists take in art."

19 RETURNING TO THE TEXT: Guide students to return to the text to answer the text-dependent comprehension questions. Have students reread and work on the questions in pairs.

20 Move among pairs and listen in as students answer the text-dependent questions. If they have difficulty, scaffold the questions by rephrasing them or breaking them into smaller parts. See the Scaffolding the Text-Dependent Questions boxes for suggestions.

21 Discuss the new perspectives about the American Dream students learned by reading these pieces. Ask students what parts of the texts complicated, confirmed, or challenged their thinking. Then have students complete the Check Your Understanding independently.

22 Have a volunteer read the instructions for the Working from the Text activity. As a class, discuss the author's claims in each text. Guide students to complete the Author's Claim column of the **graphic organizer**. Then have students return to working with their partner to complete the right column of the graphic organizer.

1.23

10. Does the author's choice to consider real and fictional examples of "dropouts" have a positive or negative impact on his argument? Explain your answer using text evidence.

It positively affects the argument. For example, his inclusion of Holden Caufield is successful

because Caufield's story in *The Catcher in the Rye* is one with which many young people can

relate.

☑ **Check Your Understanding**

How do these pieces complicate, confirm, or challenge what you have learned about the American Dream? Can the American Dream be both failure and success?

Working from the Text

To write a literary analysis that compares two texts, you must first identify the claims that each author makes. Then you must evaluate whether the author is successful at supporting those claims. Complete the graphic organizer.

Passage	Author's Claim	Evaluation of Claim
from "Keynote Address to the 2004 Democratic Convention"	Obama's main claim is that, despite its problems, America is a place of great opportunity where people of different beliefs can all have dreams and work to achieve those dreams.	Yes, he is successful at supporting this claim. He gives numerous examples to support the claim and addresses potential counterarguments.
"The Right to Fail"	Zinsser's claim is that America looks down on people who take unorthodox paths or try something and fail.	Yes, he is successful at supporting this claim. He gives numerous examples of how Americans look down on dropouts and other people who have failed. He gives examples of people who have succeeded by taking unorthodox paths, and he addresses potential counterarguments and refutes them.

11. With a partner, discuss each author's claims. Then discuss if the authors have a similar or opposing viewpoint about the American Dream.

1.23

 Writing Prompt: Literary

Imagine Obama and Zinsser having a conversation about the American Dream. What would that conversation sound like? How would they view and respond to each other's ideas? Working in a small group, think about what ideas each of them would assert, what qualifications they would offer to the other's ideas, which of the other's ideas they would challenge or disagree with, and what responses they could have to defend their own ideas. As a group, plan and write the dialogue they might have. Be sure to:

- Write the dialogue as though it were in a play but without the stage directions.
- Develop each author's ideas based on the texts you have read and represent those ideas fairly and fully.
- Paraphrase or use direct quotations from the texts. If you use direct quotations, make sure they are accurate.

 INDEPENDENT READING LINK

Read and Respond

From your independent reading, select a subject or author who is struggling to achieve what is believed to be the American Dream. Write how this character's dream may be made possible by the work of others or how his or her work may help someone else succeed.

ACTIVITY 1.23 continued

23 Have students complete the Writing Prompt in small groups. Review the prompt to be sure students understand the task. Consider having groups present their completed dialogues to the class.

24 Draw students' attention to the Independent Reading Link and have them complete the activity. Then have students share their responses with a partner.

ASSESS

Review the work students completed in the Check Your Understanding task to ensure that they have evaluated whether the American Dream can include both failure and success.

Review the dialogues completed for the Writing Prompt. Dialogues should show an understanding of both Obama's and Zinsser's arguments and a more nuanced view of the American Dream from the beginning of the unit. The dialogue should effectively use evidence from both texts. Also check that the dialogues were written using proper formatting and conventions of a play.

ADAPT

If groups have a hard time communicating or incorporating the ideas of every member, have them use the Persuasive/Argument Writing Map graphic organizer to be sure everyone contributes. Each student should fill out some part of the graphic organizer for the group.

WRITING PROMPT: LITERARY

The following standards are addressed in the writing prompt:
- W.11-12.3b
- W.11-12.8
- W.11-12.9

ACTIVITY 1.24

PLAN

Suggested Pacing: 2 50-minute class periods

TEACH

1 Read the Learning Targets and Preview with students.

2 **Vocabulary Development:** Review the Academic Vocabulary. Ask students to define the words *defend, challenge,* and *qualify* in their own words. Then have them discuss the connotation of each with a partner.

3 Read the Structured Academic Controversy instruction as a class and begin to share thoughts about access to the American Dream.

4 Divide the class into groups of four and have them form pairs for the initial part of the activity. Assign one pair Side A and the other pair Side B of the question.

5 Review the types of evidence with students. Discuss how to present a fair and balanced argument and how to use a variety of evidence to appeal to an audience.

6 Instruct pairs on student step 1 in the Conducting Research section by reviewing the texts from the unit to provide some background for their position. Once they have done this initial search for support for their position, students will need to assess what other information they will need to address their side of the issue.

7 Students should provide evidence from two or three sources. Have students follow the instructions in student steps 2 and 3, including the completion of the Summary of Your Position table.

8 Each pair should prepare a three- to five-minute presentation that offers a statement about their position and evidence to support their position. Students should work together to identify their three most significant and relevant pieces of evidence.

Learning Strategies

Drafting
Note-taking
Peer Editing
Rereading
Self-Editing
Sharing and Responding

VOCABULARY

ACADEMIC

To defend is to support the statement that has been made. To challenge is to oppose or refute the statement that has been made. To qualify is to consider to what extent the statement is true or untrue (i.e., to what extent you agree or disagree).

My Notes

Learning Targets

- Synthesize multiple sources in order to defend, challenge, or qualify a particular position.
- Collaborate to prepare a formal academic conversation asserting a claim, presenting evidence, and coming to a decision.

Preview

In this activity, you will work with a partner to research and support an argument. Then you and your partner will discuss your position with another pair, reach consensus, and craft a group position statement.

Structured Academic Controversy

In preparation for the writing you will do on Embedded Assessment 2, you will now participate in a small-group discussion model designed to achieve three goals:

- To gain a deeper understanding of an issue
- To find common ground
- To make a decision based on evidence and logic

> **The Issue:** Does the United States still provide access to the American Dream for everyone?

In this activity, you will research and defend one side of the argument:

Side A	Side B
No, the American Dream no longer exists.	**Yes, the American Dream is still a reality.**

Conducting Research

1. With your partner, review the reading and thinking that you have done so far in this unit using the lens of your assigned position. What evidence do you have to support your position fairly and thoroughly? Research and organize evidence to support your side of the argument and write a statement of your position or answer to the question.

Types of Evidence

- Facts and statistics
- Analogy (figurative or literal)
- Personal experience or anecdote
- Illustrative example
- Expert/personal testimony
- Hypothetical case

College and Career Readiness Standards

Focus Standards:

SL.11-12.1 Initiate and participate effectively in a range of collaborative discussions (one-on-one, in groups, and teacher-led) with diverse partners on grades 11–12 topics, texts, and issues, building on others' ideas and expressing their own clearly and persuasively.

SL.11-12.1a Come to discussions prepared, having read and researched material under study; explicitly draw on that preparation by referring to evidence from texts and other research on the topic or issue to stimulate a thoughtful, well-reasoned exchange of ideas.

SL.11-12.1b Work with peers to promote civil, democratic discussions and decision-making, set clear goals and deadlines, and establish individual roles as needed.

2. To present a fair and balanced argument, you also need to research potential counterclaims and evidence that acknowledges their strengths and limitations.

3. To appeal to an audience, a writer and/or speaker uses a variety of evidence to support claims. As you research evidence, consider your audience's knowledge, concerns, values, and possible biases. Use a table like this one to organize your initial research.

Summary of Your Position	
Evidence and Support	**Type of Evidence**

Position Presentation

4. In groups of four, present your position and evidence to the groups with the opposing argument. Be sure to:

   - Take notes while the other argument is being presented and prepare to ask clarifying questions and restate the opponent's position. Evaluate their reasoning and use of evidence.
   - Be fair and thorough in the presentation of your claim and evidence. Respect the norms of formal presentations, giving turns and speaking in a collegial but formal style.

5. Create a graphic organizer for your note-taking during the discussion of the issue. Proceed in the following sequence:

The Side A group presents its argument and evidence, including counterclaims (concessions and refutations).

Notes from the presentation:

Side B restates Side A's argument(s).

Restate the argument:

The Side B group presents its argument and evidence, including counterclaims (concessions and refutations).

Notes from the presentation:

Side A restates Side B's argument(s).

Restate the argument:

ACTIVITY 1.24 continued

9 Guide students to follow student steps 4 and 5. Instruct them to rejoin the members of their group. Have Side A students present their position and evidence. Side B students should listen carefully, take notes, paraphrase the position and evidence, and ask clarifying questions. Remind students to listen and speak respectfully.

10 Once each pair has shared their position, the pairs discard their positions and become a larger group.

LEVELED DIFFERENTIATED INSTRUCTION

In this activity, students may need support presenting ideas to peers.

Developing Allow partners to script their speaking points prior to presenting. Provide students with sentence stems they can use and multiple opportunities to rehearse before their presentation. Partners should also develop *yes/no* and *wh-* questions in preparation for their opponents' presentation.

Expanding Allow partners to script their speaking points prior to presenting. Provide students with multiple opportunities to rehearse before their presentation. Partners should also develop relevant, on-topic questions in preparation for their opponents' presentation.

Support Prior to conducting the group presentations, have student volunteers conduct a mock presentation for the class to model the expectations for the assignment. Have audience members provide positive comments and suggestions for improvement.

Extend Encourage students to prepare visuals for their presentation or create a multimedia presentation to hook the audience and support their main points.

TEACHER TO TEACHER

This activity is intended to prepare students for the research and thinking they must do for the writing of Embedded Assessment 2. We have used the prompt from the Embedded Assessment, but you may want to choose another topic for students to use.

11 Review the Reaching Consensus: Discussion section.

As groups of four, students will participate in a discussion to identify areas where they agree and disagree. Allow groups 15 minutes to discuss each side and to reach a consensus. Remind students to listen and speak respectfully.

12 After reaching a consensus, students will need to construct a thesis that states their position and presents the evidence that supports their position (the Publishing Your Position section).

13 Move to the Getting Ready for the Embedded Assessment section. Review with the class how to defend, challenge, and qualify responses to any prompt. Model generating possible responses to the Embedded Assessment prompt.

14 Put students into groups to complete the Check Your Understanding task.

15 Determine when students should finish their independent reading for the unit and complete the Independent Reading Checkpoint.

ASSESS

Evaluate the lists of texts that students have compiled during the Check Your Understanding activity. Make sure students note whether the texts defend, challenge, or qualify the prompt.

ADAPT

Point out that this is the last activity before Embedded Assessment 2. Have students glance through the Embedded Assessment requirements again. Ask them whether they are prepared and have them note on an exit slip any concepts they are still uncertain about. Review those concepts.

Reaching Consensus: Discussion

6. At this stage of the discussion, each side abandons its position and the group of four begins to work together to build consensus regarding the prompt. Using evidence gathered during their initial conversation, each member of the group should offer purposeful ideas to help move the group toward a consensus. Encourage group members to ask relevant and insightful questions that will help strength the group's position. For example:

   - Who supports this opinion?
   - For what reason do you support this opinion?
   - What position do the facts and statistics support?
   - Why is this position the strongest?
   - What are the counterarguments to this position?

Publishing Your Position

7. Together, craft a position that states the group position and decide what evidence supports the consensus decision on whether the United States still provides access to the American Dream. Post all of the positions on the wall under the categories *Yes* and *No*.

Getting Ready for the Embedded Assessment

8. Begin by reading and discussing the prompt from the Embedded Assessment and then brainstorming three different ways to respond to this type of prompt: by defending, challenging, or qualifying it.

Prompt: Defend, challenge, or qualify the statement "America still provides access to the American Dream."

Response 1 (Defend):

America still provides access to the American Dream to any citizen.

Response 2 (Challenge):

America no longer provides the opportunity and access to the American Dream to all of its citizens.

Response 3 (Qualify):

In some cases, the American Dream is still a reality, but in others, it will always be just a dream.

☑ Check Your Understanding

As a group, review the texts you have read in Unit 1. Create lists of which texts you could use to defend, challenge, or qualify the prompt.

⬡ Independent Reading Checkpoint

After completing your independent readings consider how these texts connect to the question of whether the American Dream is still alive and can be achieved. Synthesize in a short written statement how you think your readings respond to this question. Note which ones best support your stated position.

Synthesizing the American Dream

ASSIGNMENT

Your assignment is to synthesize at least three to five sources and your own observations to defend, challenge, or qualify the statement that America still provides access to the American Dream. This question requires you to integrate a variety of sources (three to five) into a coherent, well-written argumentative essay. Your argument should be central; the sources and your observations should support this argument.

Planning and Prewriting	■ What are the elements of a strong synthesis paper, and how can you use these elements as a sort of "to-do list" for your planning? ■ What texts from this unit provide relevant evidence for your own answer to the essay prompt?
Drafting	■ How will you clearly voice your position on the topic without overlooking the nuances and complexities of the topic? ■ What assumptions or beliefs are either spoken or unspoken in your sources? ■ How do the ideas in your selected sources relate to your position? Do they agree with, disagree with, or offer a sort of qualification to your ideas?
Evaluating and Revising	■ Do you consistently show how each selected quote from your sources relates to your central position? ■ How can you make sure that your syntax is sophisticated and varied, especially the openings of your sentences? ■ Are your ideas sequenced in the best way to guide your reader through your ideas and present a convincing argument? How could reordering some of your ideas improve this?
Editing and Publishing	■ How will you check for grammatical and technical accuracy? ■ What sort of outside resources can help you to check your draft (e.g., a style guide such as MLA, a dictionary)? ■ How will you prepare yourself to present this essay to an audience?

Reflection

After completing this Embedded Assessment, think about how you went about accomplishing this assignment and respond to the following:

- In what ways did your various sources validate your ideas about the American Dream, and in what ways did they add new elements or depth to your thinking?

College and Career Readiness Standards

Focus Standards:

W.11-12.5 Develop and strengthen writing as needed by planning, revising, editing, rewriting, or trying a new approach, focusing on addressing what is most significant for a specific purpose and audience.

W.11-12.8 Gather relevant information from multiple authoritative print and digital sources,

using advanced searches effectively; assess the strengths and limitations of each source in terms of the task, purpose, and audience; integrate information into the text selectively to maintain the flow of ideas, avoiding plagiarism and overreliance on any one source and following a standard format for citation.

EMBEDDED ASSESSMENT 2

Suggested Pacing: 3 50-minute class periods

TEACHER TO TEACHER

As a resource, see "Preparing for the 2007 Synthesis Question: Six Moves toward Success" by David Joliffe (online at College Board AP Central's AP Language and Composition Home Page). You may also want to access Writing Workshop 4 for SpringBoard Senior English, which provides direct instruction in writing a synthesis essay.

1 Planning and Prewriting: Remind students to review the Scoring Guide criteria to ensure that they know the expectations for this assessment.

2 Drafting: Be sure students understand the importance of integrating their own commentary to explain the relevance and significance of the sources they will be using.

3 Evaluating and Revising: You should consider using writing groups or peer evaluators to create a structured approach to evaluating effectiveness and sharing and responding to suggestions for revision. The Scoring Guide "Use of Language" or a Writer's Checklist should be a valuable resource.

4 Editing and Publishing: This can be done in pairs, in small groups, or as a class. Students should use online editing tools.

5 Reflection: Reflections can be collected, placed in a portfolio, or used for a Socratic discussion.

6 At this point, students should begin the process of shifting their work from a Working Folder into a Portfolio that will be a collection of work chosen by the student to represent the depth and extent of his or her learning this semester and year. Therefore, care should be taken to include at least both Embedded Assessments for this unit. It may be that later, after having completed more units, students will choose to omit certain Embedded Assessments, but at this early stage, they are evidence of sustained, polished, complete work.

You may ask students to collect their brainstorming, research notes, and drafts to attach to their final draft so that you and they can have a record of the stages of the writing process.

SCORING GUIDE

You may want to make a copy of the Scoring Guide, attach it to each student's manuscript, and use it to give feedback.

SCORING GUIDE

Scoring Criteria	Exemplary	Proficient	Emerging	Incomplete
Ideas	The essay • effectively synthesizes sources to defend, challenge, or qualify the central claim of the prompt • provides a strong thesis that anticipates audience needs • uses convincing, thorough, and relevant evidence • acknowledges and refutes counterclaims fairly and thoroughly	The essay • adequately synthesizes sources to defend, challenge, or qualify the central claim of the prompt • provides a straight forward thesis that briefly contextualizes the issue • uses support that clearly connects the various source materials to the writer's position	The essay • attempts to synthesize sources but inadequately defends, challenges, or qualifies the central claim of the prompt • provides a thesis that attempts to contextualize the issue • uses support that connects the source material but with lapses in accuracy or completeness	The essay • tries to synthesize sources but does not defend, challenge, or qualify the claim of the prompt • includes a weak thesis or one that is lost in a summary of sources • includes support that paraphrases source material with no commentary or analysis
Structure	The essay • is organized to effectively reinforce the ideas of the argument • moves smoothly with successful use of transitions that enhance coherence • concludes by going beyond the thesis, illuminating how the writers influence the reader	The essay • is organized to support the ideas of the argument • arranges ideas so they are easy to follow, using transitions to move between ideas • includes a conclusion that is logical yet may be somewhat repetitive to the thesis	The essay • follows a simplistic organization with lapses in coherence • arranges ideas in a confusing way and with an inconsistent use of transitions • includes a conclusion that may be logical yet is too close to the original thesis	The essay • shows a lack of organization that detracts from argument, making the ideas difficult to follow • may jump too rapidly between ideas and lack transitions • includes a conclusion that returns directly to the attempted thesis
Use of Language	The essay • demonstrates a mature style that advances the writer's ideas • employs precise diction and skillful use of syntax, with keen attention to varied sentence openings, which helps to create a convincing voice • follows standard writing conventions (including accurate citation of sources)	The essay • demonstrates a style that adequately supports the writer's ideas • uses logical diction and syntax, with some attention to varied sentence openings, creating a suitable voice • largely follows standard writing conventions (including accurate citation of sources); errors do not seriously impede readability	The essay • demonstrates an inconsistent style that minimally supports the writer's idea • unevenly uses diction and syntax to convey a suitable voice, with few varied sentence openings • contains errors in standard writing conventions that may impede readability; some sources are inaccurately cited	The essay • demonstrates a limited style that ineffectively supports the writer's ideas • contains lapses in diction or syntax that may not allow a suitable voice to sustain throughout the essay; sentence openings may be repetitive • contains errors that impede readability; sources may be inaccurately cited

College and Career Readiness Standards

W.11-12.4 Produce clear and coherent writing in which the development, organization, and style are appropriate to task, purpose, and audience.

W.11-12.9 Draw evidence from literary or informational texts to support analysis, reflection, and research.

L.11-12.1 Demonstrate command of the conventions of standard English grammar and usage when writing or speaking.

W.11-12.5 Develop and strengthen writing as needed by planning, revising, editing, rewriting, or trying a new approach, focusing on addressing what is most significant for a specific purpose and audience.

W.11-12.1 Write arguments to support claims in an analysis of substantive topics or texts, using valid reasoning and relevant and sufficient evidence

Planning the Unit

Context

In Unit 2, students continue to explore the American Dream, this time through a lens of persuasive literature. The first part of the unit focuses on Arthur Miller's play *The Crucible*, and students will examine the methods an author can incorporate within a work of fiction to persuade an audience to his or her point of view. Through a close reading of *The Crucible*, students will gain an understanding of the significance of literature in America's social conscience. Students will then move to studying persuasive speeches and investigating how rhetorical appeals and rhetorical devices are used in classic American speeches such as Abraham Lincoln's Gettysburg Address and Franklin D. Roosevelt's First Inaugural Address. The unit highlights America's commitment to freedom of speech by looking closely at the rhetorical tools used by writers and speakers to persuade an audience and to make a statement about American society.

Suggested Texts and Materials

You will need the following materials for this unit:

- Activities 2.2, 2.4–2.7, 2.12–2.14, 2.16: A class set of *The Crucible* by Arthur Miller
- Activities 2.6, 2.12: DVD, *The Crucible*, 1996, directed by Nicholas Hytner (optional)
- Activity 2.14: Clip of "The Witch Scene" from Monty Python and the Holy Grail, 1975, directed by Terry Gilliam and Terry Jones (optional)
- Activities 2.15 and 2.21: SAT Essay scoring rubric found on SpringBoard Digital
- Activity 2.22: Sets of three different colored markers for student groups
- Activity 2.23: Audio recording of Franklin D. Roosevelt's First Inaugural Address
- Activity 2.24: Audio and video recording of Kennedy's Inaugural Address
- Activity 2.25: Copies of speech by Alfred M. Green, included on the last page of this Planning the Unit section
- Activity 2.26: Videos of George W. Bush's 9/11 Address to the Nation and Barack Obama's President-Elect Victory Speech

Instructional Sequence

The first half of the unit begins by establishing historical knowledge of the Salem witch trials through historical documents and accounts. Then students will read Arthur Miller's *The Crucible* as a literary text and as a vehicle of social commentary, drawing connections between the events of the play and the context of the era that Miller wrote it in. Students will also analyze dramatic conventions in the play with an eye to Embedded Assessment 1, which asks them to create a dramatic scene that conveys social commentary.

Students will then participate in activities designed to build a receptive classroom environment for taking a stand on a contemporary issue. Students will work with rhetorical appeals and rhetorical devices as they read speeches by American leaders. Finally, students will apply this knowledge as they create their own persuasive speech about an issue of their choice for Embedded Assessment 2.

AP® CONNECTIONS

In this unit, students will focus on refining these important skills and knowledge areas for AP/College Readiness:

- Analyzing rhetorical devices and techniques used in creating persuasive speeches (Activities 2.13, 2.15, 2.19–2.22)
- Developing stylistic elements, including controlling tone, establishing and maintaining voice, and achieving appropriate emphasis through diction and sentence structure (Activities 2.4, 2.7, 2.15, 2.16, 2.20)
- Analyzing a dramatic work of lasting literary merit in order to arrive at multiple interpretations (Activities 2.6, 2.12)
- Analyzing the social, cultural, political, and historical contexts of a literary text and its contributions to society (Activities 2.2, 2.3, 2.15)
- Focusing deliberate attention on the craft of sentence-level writing (Activities 2.3, 2.5, 2.8, 2.23)

SAT® CONNECTIONS

In this unit, students will practice many important skills that will help them succeed on the SAT and other college readiness exams, including:

- Explaining how an author builds an argument to persuade an audience (Activities 2.15, 2.21, 2.25)
- Recognizing and correcting cases in which unlike terms are compared (LC 2.24)

Unpacked Embedded Assessments

Embedded Assessment 1: Creating and Performing a Dramatic Scene	Embedded Assessment 2: Writing and Presenting a Persuasive Speech
Skills and Knowledge: • Use drama to make a statement about a social conflict or issue. • Work and write collaboratively. • Convey a setting that serves as a backdrop for social commentary. • Compose an original script that demonstrates an understanding of script-writing conventions, theatrical elements, and literary elements. • Write engaging dialogue that maintains a consistent voice and advances a plot. • Make performance choices to convey an interpretation.	**Skills and Knowledge:** • Identify a contemporary issue and compose an argument. • Write for a specific purpose and audience. • Incorporate rhetorical appeals, elements of an argument, and rhetorical devices in an original speech. • Make deliberate choices about syntax in revision. • Use elements of effective physical and vocal delivery. • Write an engaging introduction and a conclusion with a call to action.

Cognate Directory

Encouraging students to notice the connections between their primary language and English can help them develop academic vocabulary more quickly. If your class includes Spanish speakers, consider adding the following cognates to the classroom Word Wall. For English Language Learners whose primary language is not Spanish, consider using an online translator or dictionary to support comprehension of vocabulary terms.

Unit 2 Vocabulary Terms with Spanish Cognates

Academic Vocabulary	
English	**Spanish**
historical context	contexto historico
rhetorical context	contexto retórico
social commentary	comentario social

Literary Terms	
English	**Spanish**
dramatic irony	ironía dramática
motif	motivo
situational irony	ironía situacional
subtext	subtexto
verbal irony	ironía verbal

Activity Features at a Glance

The activities in every ELA unit reflect the interconnected nature of reading, writing, listening, speaking, and thinking. The Activity Features at a Glance chart highlights the types of tasks or supports that students and teachers will encounter in each activity.

Writing and Revision

Grammar and Language

Listening, Speaking, and Discussion

Independent Reading

Vocabulary Development

ELL Support

Knowledge Quest

Gaining Perspectives

ELA Activity	Activity Features	ELA Activity	Activity Features
2.1	Listening, Independent Reading, Vocabulary	2.15	Writing, Grammar, Listening, Vocabulary
2.2	Grammar, Listening, Vocabulary, ELL, Knowledge Quest	2.16	Writing, Listening
2.3	Listening, Vocabulary, ELL	2.17	Listening, Independent Reading
2.4	Listening	2.18	Writing, Listening, Independent Reading
2.5	Listening, Independent Reading, Vocabulary	2.19	Listening, ELL
2.6	Listening, Independent Reading, Vocabulary, ELL	2.20	Listening, Vocabulary, ELL
2.7	Writing	2.21	Writing, Listening, Independent Reading, Vocabulary, ELL
2.8	Writing, Grammar, Listening, Vocabulary, Gaining Perspectives	2.22	Listening, Independent Reading
2.9	Writing, Listening, Independent Reading, ELL	2.23	Listening, Independent Reading, Vocabulary, ELL, Knowledge Quest
2.10	Writing, Listening, ELL	2.24	Writing, Grammar, Listening, ELL, Knowledge Quest
2.11	Listening	LC 2.24	Writing, Grammar, Listening
2.12	Listening	2.25	Writing, Listening
2.13	Writing, Listening, Vocabulary	2.26	Listening, Independent Reading
2.14	Listening, Independent Reading, Vocabulary		

Unit Resources at a Glance

Formative Assessment Opportunities	Digital Assessments	Family Connections
Text-dependent questions Writing prompts Check Your Understanding tasks Focus on the Sentence tasks Language Checkpoint exercises Language & Writer's Craft practice	Activity Quizzes 2.2–2.26 Unit Assessment Part 1 Unit Assessment Part 2 (SBD)	Suggestions for Independent Reading Family Letters (English and Spanish) Student Reports (SBD)
English Language Development	**Foundational Skills**	**Independent Reading**
Leveled Differentiated Instruction Graphic Organizers ELD Strategies Language Workshop 2A Language Workshop 2B	Foundational Skills Screening Assessment Observational Look-fors Foundational Skills Workshop	My Independent Reading List Independent Reading Links Independent Reading Checkpoints Independent Reading Log Reader/Writer Notebook Suggestions for Independent Reading

Reading Plan for *The Crucible*

Text Chunk	Corresponding Activity	Suggested Treatment of Text
Key Lines	2.4 Salem Society: Meet the Characters	Before beginning reading
Act One	2.5 The Beginnings of Characterization	Read **in class** Continue analysis during Activities 2.5–2.7
Act Two	2.11 Rising Action	Read **in class** Continue analysis during Activity 2.12
Act Three	2.13 Courtroom Drama	Read **in class** and for **homework** Continue analysis during Activity 2.14
Act Four	2.16 Integrity Rises to the Top: Writing Dialogue	Read **in class**

⊕ Suggestions for Independent Reading

This list, divided into the categories of **Literature** and **Nonfiction/Informational Text**, comprises titles related to the themes and content of the unit. For their independent reading, students can select from this wide array of titles, which have been chosen based on complexity and interest. Spanish-language titles are included for those students who can read with greater independence or at a higher grade level in Spanish than in English, since building on their first language literacy can bolster their acquisition of English. Titles on this list have been suggested by teachers and school librarians, but you should be sure to preview texts to assess their appropriateness for your specific students and setting. You can also encourage students to do their own research and select titles that intrigue them.

Unit 2: The Power of Persuasion

Literature		
Author	**Title**	**Lexile**
Alcott, Louisa May	*Little Women*	750L
Baldwin, James	*Go Tell It on the Mountain*	970L
Didion, Joan	*Democracy*	1130L
Forbes, Esther	*Johnny Tremain*	840L
Hamid, Moshin	*The Reluctant Fundamentalist*	N/A
Hentoff, Nat	*The Day They Came to Arrest the Book*	890L
Kent, Katherine	*The Heretic's Daughter: A Novel*	N/A
Kingsolver, Barbara	*Animal Dreams*	790L
Lawrence, Jerome and Robert E. Lee	*Inherit the Wind*	850L
Lewis, Sinclair	*It Can't Happen Here*	N/A
Meyers, Anna	*Assassin*	790L
O'Brien, Tim	*The Things They Carried*	880L
Paterson, Katherine	*Lyddle*	860L
Petry, Ann	*Tituba of Salem Village*	840L
Potok, Chiam	*The Promise*	N/A
Rinaldi, Ann	*Or Give Me Death: A Novel of Patrick Henry's Family*	610L
Roth, Philip	*The Human Stain*	N/A
Tan, Amy	*The Joy Luck Club*	930L
Vonnegut, Kurt	*Slaughterhouse Five*	850L

Nonfiction/Informational Text		
Author	**Title**	**Lexile**
Alexander, Michelle	*The New Jim Crow*	1450L
Arbinger Institute	*Anatomy of Peace: Resolving the Heart of Conflict*	N/A
Benoit, Peter	*Salem Witch Trials*	1020L
Bromwich, Jonah Engel	*Memorable Inaugural Speeches: Washington, Lincoln, Jackson, Kennedy and Reagan*	990L
Corey, Shana and R. Gregory Christie	*Es hora de actuar: El gran discurso de John F. Kennedy*	870L
Daley, James (Editor)	*Great Speeches by African Americans*	N/A
Fitzgerald, Stephanie	*McCarthyism: The Red Scare (Snapshots in History)*	N/A
Furedi, Frank	*On Tolerance: A Defense of Moral Independence*	N/A
Garton Ash, Timothy	*Free Speech: Ten Principles for a Connected World*	N/A
Hudak, Heather	*McCarthyism and the Red Scare (Uncovering the Past: Analyzing Primary Sources)*	1070L
Kennedy, Rick	*The First American Evangelical: A Short Life of Cotton Mather*	N/A
Klebold, Sue	*A Mother's Reckoning: Living in the Aftermath of a Tragedy*	N/A
Montefiore, Simon Sebag (Editor)	*Speeches That Changed the World*	N/A
Morcan, James	*Arruinando al Tercer Mundo (Bankrupting the Third World)*	N/A
Neier, Aryeh	*Defending My Enemy: American Nazis, the Skokie Case, and the Risks of Freedom*	N/A
Patterson, Kerry	*Crucial Conversations*	N/A
Safire, William (Editor)	*Lend Me Your Ears: Great Speeches in History*	N/A
Schiff, Stacy	*The Witches: Salem, 1692*	N/A
Stewart, Gail B.	*The Salem Witch Trials*	1260L
Stevenson, Bryan	*Just Mercy*	1130L
Tanaka, Shelley	*A Day That Changed America: Gettysburg*	930L
Wallace, Patricia Ward	*Politics of Conscience: A Biography of Margaret Chase Smith*	1590L
Warburton, Nigel	*Free Speech: A Very Short Introduction*	N/A
Widmer, Ted (Editor)	*American Speeches: Political Oratory from Patrick Henry to Barak Obama*	N/A
Various	*American Sermons: The Pilgrims to Martin Luther King Jr.*	N/A

Unit 2 Instructional Pathways

Instructional Pathways

Teachers can build customized pathways through this unit by making purposeful choices about which resources to use based on students' learning needs. The charts below outline a few possible pathways to show how teachers might integrate digital assessments, Language Workshops, Close Reading Workshops, and Writing Workshops into instruction. Additional planning resources—including detailed standards correlations—are available on SpringBoard Digital.

English Language Arts Unit 2: The Power of Persuasion		
Activity	**SBD Digital Assessments**	**Pacing**
Activity 2.1: Previewing the Unit	N/A	1
Activity 2.2: Preparing to Read *The Crucible*: Setting Context	Activity Quiz 2.2	2
Activity 2.3: The Lessons of Salem	Activity Quiz 2.3	2
Activity 2.4: Salem Society: Meet the Characters	Activity Quiz 2.4	1
Activity 2.5: The Beginnings of Characterization	Activity Quiz 2.5	2
Activity 2.6: Pivotal Scene 1: Considering Interpretations	Activity Quiz 2.6	2
Activity 2.7: Analyzing the Elements of a Script	Activity Quiz 2.7	1
Activity 2.8: Illuminating Hysteria: Characters, Conflict, and Social Commentary	Activity Quiz 2.8	2
Activity 2.9: Conflicts in Salem	Activity Quiz 2.9	2
Activity 2.10: Speaking Like a Puritan	Activity Quiz 2.10	2
Activity 2.11: Rising Action	Activity Quiz 2.11	1
Activity 2.12: Pivotal Scene 2: Proctor and Elizabeth	Activity Quiz 2.12	2
Activity 2.13: Courtroom Drama: Examining Logical Fallacies	Activity Quiz 2.13	2
Activity 2.14: The Role of Irony in Climax	Activity Quiz 2.14	2
Activity 2.15: Speaking Out	Activity Quiz 2.15	3
Activity 2.16: Integrity Rises to the Top: Writing Dialogue	Activity Quiz 2.16	2
Activity 2.17: Contemporary Conflicts	Activity Quiz 2.17	1
Embedded Assessment 1: Creating and Performing a Dramatic Scene	**Unit Assessment Part 1**	2	1

Activity	SBD Digital Assessments	Pacing	
Activity 2.18: Unpacking Embedded Assessment 2	Activity Quiz 2.18	1	
Activity 2.19: Developing Speaking Skills	Activity Quiz 2.19	2	
Activity 2.20: American Rhetoric: Historical Context	Activity Quiz 2.20	1	
Activity 2.21: The Power of Rhetoric	Activity Quiz 2.21	2	
Activity 2.22: The Appeal of Rhetoric	Activity Quiz 2.22	1	
Activity 2.23: Planning the Delivery	Activity Quiz 2.23	1	
Activity 2.24: One Last Stand with Syntax	Activity Quiz 2.24	2	
LC 2.24: Language Checkpoint: Writing Logical Comparisons (optional)	Activity Quiz LC 2.24	1	
Activity 2.25: Explain How an Author Builds an Argument	Activity Quiz 2.25	2	
Activity 2.26: Vocal Delivery	Activity Quiz 2.26	1	
Embedded Assessment 2: Writing and Presenting a Persuasive Speech	Unit Assessment Part 2	2	1

Total 50-minute Class Periods: 47–50

Language Development Pathway

Consider using some or all of the Language Workshop and Foundational Skills Workshop activities with English Language Learners or with any student who would benefit from extra support with academic English. More detailed guidance about the timing and purpose of each Language Workshop and Foundational Skills Workshop activity can be found in the Language Workshop teacher edition.

Language Workshop 2A and 2B

Activity or Workshop		Pacing
Activity 2.1: Previewing the Unit		1
Activity 2.2: Preparing to Read *The Crucible*: Setting Context		2
Activity 2.3: The Lessons of Salem		2
Language Workshop 2A.1: Genre Focus		1
Language Workshop 2A.2: Building Knowledge		1
Language Workshop 2A.3: Academic Vocabulary		1
Activity 2.4: Salem Society: Meet the Characters		1
Language Workshop 2A.4: Vocabulary Preview and Practice		1
Activity 2.5: The Beginnings of Characterization **OR**	Language Workshop 2A.5: Close Reading of an Anchor Text*	2 / 1
	Language Workshop 2A.6: Academic Collaboration*	1
Activity 2.6: Pivotal Scene 1: Considering Interpretations		2
Activity 2.7: Analyzing the Elements of a Script		1
Activity 2.8: Illuminating Hysteria: Characters, Conflict, and Social Commentary		2
Activity 2.9: Conflicts in Salem		2
Activity 2.10: Speaking Like a Puritan		2
Activity 2.11: Rising Action		1
Activity 2.12: Pivotal Scene 2: Proctor and Elizabeth		2
Activity 2.13: Courtroom Drama: Examining Logical Fallacies		2
Activity 2.14: The Role of Irony in Climax		2
Activity 2.15: Speaking Out		3
Language Workshop 2A.7: Language Checkpoint		1
Activity 2.16: Integrity Rises to the Top: Writing Dialogue		2
Activity 2.17: Contemporary Conflicts		1
Embedded Assessment 1: Creating and Performing a Dramatic Scene **OR** Collaborative Embedded Assessment: Writing and Performing a Dramatic Scene		2 / 7

Activity or Workshop		Pacing	
Activity 2.18: Unpacking Embedded Assessment 2		1	
Language Workshop 2B.1: Genre Focus		1	
Language Workshop 2B.2: Building Knowledge		1	
Language Workshop 2B.3: Academic Vocabulary		1	
Activity 2.19: Developing Speaking Skills		2	
Activity 2.20: American Rhetoric: Historical Context		1	
Language Workshop 2B.4: Vocabulary Preview and Practice		1	
Activity 2.21: The Power of Rhetoric	**Language Workshop 2B.5:** Close Reading of an Anchor Text*	2	1
	Language Workshop 2B.6: Academic Collaboration*		1
Activity 2.22: The Appeal of Rhetoric		1	
Activity 2.23: Planning the Delivery		1	
Activity 2.24: One Last Stand with Syntax		2	
LC 2.24: Language Checkpoint: Writing Logical Comparisons (optional)		1	
Activity 2.25: Explain How an Author Builds an Argument		2	
Language Workshop 2B.7: Language Checkpoint		1	
Activity 2.26: Vocal Delivery		1	
Embedded Assessment 2: Writing and Presenting a Persuasive Speech	**Collaborative Embedded Assessment:** Writing a Persuasive Speech	2	7
	Total 50-minute Class Periods:	47–69	

* These activities are available in Spanish.

Foundational Skills Workshop

The Foundational Skills Workshop offers instructional and practice materials for providing small-group instruction to students who are still developing foundational reading skills.

Activity	Pacing
Activity 1: Practicing Letter-Sound Relationships	15 min.
Activity 2: Recognizing Words by Sight	10 min.
Activity 3: Words with Inconsistent but Common Spellings	
Activity 4: Irregularly Spelled Words	
Activity 5: Common Prefixes	
Activity 6: Common Suffixes	35–40 min. per activity
Activity 7: Using Roots and Affixes to Read Multisyllabic Words	
Activity 8: Reading Multisyllabic Words	
Activity 9: Reading Informational Text with Purpose and Understanding	
Activity 10: Reading Poetry with Fluency	

Flexible Pathways

Teachers may build a flexible pathway that focuses on developing students' close reading and writing skills with the Close Reading and Writing Workshops. Each workshop addresses a specific set of standards and includes multiple assessment opportunities to allow students to demonstrate the knowledge and skills that are the focus of that workshop.

Close Reading Workshops

Workshop	Genre Focus	Assessment Opportunities	Pacing
Close Reading Workshop 4: Shakespeare	Drama Visual Text	Writing Prompt Debate/Discussion Multimedia Presentation	8
Close Reading Workshop 5: Informational Texts in Social Studies/History	Legal Documents Cartoons	Writing Prompt Debate/Discussion Multimedia Presentation	8

Writing Workshops

Workshop	Genre Focus	Assessment Opportunities	Pacing
Writing Workshop 9: Script Writing	Drama	Writing as a Class Writing with a Peer Independent Writing	6

Speech by Alfred M. Green
given in Philadelphia in April 1861

Alfred M. Greene delivered the following speech during the first month of the Civil War. African Americans were not yet permitted to join the Union army, but Green felt that they should strive to be admitted to the ranks and prepare to enlist.

1 The time has arrived in the history of the great Republic when we may again give evidence to the world of the bravery and patriotism of a race in whose hearts burns the love of country, of freedom, and of civil and religious toleration. It is these grand principles that enable men, however proscribed, when possessed of true patriotism, to say, "My country, right or wrong, I love thee still!"

2 It is true, the brave deeds of our fathers, sworn and subscribed to by the immortal Washington of the Revolution of 1776, and by Jackson and others in the War of 1812, have failed to bring us into recognition as citizens, enjoying those rights so dearly bought by those noble and patriotic sires.

3 It is true that our injuries in many respects are great; fugitive-slave laws, Dred Scott decisions[1], indictments for treason, and long and dreary months of imprisonment. Th e result of the most unfair rules of judicial investigation has been the pay we have received for our solicitude, sympathy, and aid in the dangers and difficulties of those "days that tried men's souls."

4 Our duty, brethren, is not to cavil over past grievances. Let us not be derelict to duty in the time of need. While we remember the past and regret that our present position in the country is not such as to create within us that burning zeal and enthusiasm for the field of battle which inspires other men in the full enjoyment of every civil and religious emolument, yet let us endeavor to hope for the future and improve the present auspicious moment for creating anew our claims upon the justice and honor of the Republic; and, above all, let not the honor and glory achieved by our fathers be blasted or sullied by a want of true heroism among their sons.

5 Let us, then, take up the sword, trusting in God, who will defend the right, remembering that these are other days than those of yore; that the world today is on the side of freedom and universal political equality; that the war cry of the howling leaders of Secession and treason is: "Let us drive back the advance guard of civil and religious freedom; let us have more slave territory; let us build stronger the tyrant system of slavery in the great American Republic." Remember, too, that your very presence among the troops of the North would inspire your oppressed brethren of the South with zeal for the overthrow of the tyrant system, and confidence in the armies of the living God—the God of truth, justice and equality to all men.

---

[1] The Supreme Court case *Scott v. Sandford* (1857) involved an enslaved man named Dred Scott suing for his freedom on the grounds that he had lived with his slaveholder in multiple northern states where slavery was illegal. The court ruled against Scott stating that slaveholders had the right to freely transport their property, including enslaved people, to any state.

UNIT 2

Read aloud the unit title, "The Power of Persuasion," and the quotation. Address any questions students may have. Then have students begin to think about the power of persuasion by posing the unit's Essential Questions: How can artistic expression advance social commentary? How are the components of rhetoric applied to the creation and delivery of persuasive speeches? Then ask students to write at least one question they have about the unit and have them share their questions with a partner.

Have students look at the photograph and respond to the visual prompt. You may want to have students think-pair-share to write a response.

VISUAL PROMPT
Many of Franklin D. Roosevelt's speeches inspired a nation during difficult times. Why is it important for great leaders to be persuasive speakers?

THE POWER OF PERSUASION

I am certain that my fellow Americans expect that on my induction into the Presidency I will address them with a candor and a decision which the present situation of our people impel. This is preeminently the time to speak the truth, the whole truth, frankly and boldly. Nor need we shrink from honestly facing conditions in our country today. This great Nation will endure as it has endured, will revive and will prosper. So, first of all, let me assert my firm belief that the only thing we have to fear is fear itself ...

—from Franklin D. Roosevelt's First Inaugural Address, March 3, 1933

Leveled Differentiated Instruction Directory

For guidance on differentiating tasks for English language learners at various levels of language proficiency, refer to the Leveled Differentiated Instruction suggestions in these activities:

2.2 Use the **Collaborative Dialogue** graphic organizer to help students express ideas with a partner before writing.

2.3 Use the **Unknown Word Solver** graphic organizer to help determine the meaning of unfamiliar vocabulary.

2.6 Provide extra support for performing a scene using the **Collaborative Dialogue** graphic organizer.

2.9 Support the analysis of conflict and theme using the **Conflict Map** graphic organizer.

2.10 Use questions to guide students to analyze metaphors in *The Crucible*.

UNIT 2

CONTENTS

Have students **skim/scan** the activities and texts in this unit. Have them note any texts they have heard about but never read and any activities that sound particularly interesting.

GOALS

Have students read the goals for the unit and mark any words that are unfamiliar. Have students add these words to the classroom Word Wall along with definitions.

You may also want to post these goals in a visible place in the classroom for the duration of this unit, allowing you and students to revisit the goals easily and gauge progress throughout the unit.

VOCABULARY DEVELOPMENT

Adding to vocabulary knowledge is essential for reading fluency. Students will encounter new vocabulary in this course in multiple ways:

- Academic Vocabulary
- Literary Terms
- Vocabulary in Context (terms glossed in text selections)
- Word Connections
- Oral discussions

Encourage students to use new vocabulary expressively in class discussions and in writing. Have them keep a **Reader/Writer Notebook** in which they record new words, their meanings, and their pronunciations.

See the Resources section for examples of graphic organizers suitable for word study. Having students use word-study graphic organizers will greatly enhance their understanding of new words and their connection to unit concepts and to the broader use of advanced vocabulary.

Have students review the list of academic and literary terms and sort them in a QHT chart. Revisit the chart periodically to see how students' understanding progresses throughout the unit.

UNIT 2

The Power of Persuasion

GOALS

- To interpret texts in consideration of their historical and rhetorical context
- To analyze the characteristics and structural elements of argumentative texts
- To create and present a dramatic scene about a societal issue
- To examine and apply syntactic structures in the written and spoken word
- To write and present an argumentative speech for a specific audience and purpose with appropriate register and effective vocabulary, tone, and voice

VOCABULARY

ACADEMIC
historical context
logical fallacy
rhetorical context
social commentary
vocal delivery

LITERARY
dramatic irony
foil
motif
situational irony
subtext
verbal irony

Leveled Differentiated Instruction Directory (continued)

2.19 Provide students with the **Venn Diagram for Writing a Comparison** graphic organizer to identify similarities and differences between writing and performing a dramatic scene and writing and performing a persuasive speech.

2.20 Differentiate the reading of a complex text with **previewing** and with group or paired reading.

2.21 Use the **Idea and Argument Evaluator** graphic organizer to provide additional support for evaluating an author's claim and reasoning.

2.23 Give students the opportunity to practice their speaking and listening skills using the **Active Listening Feedback** graphic organizer.

2.24 Offer visuals to provide extra support for developing background understanding of John F. Kennedy and the Cold War.

CONTENTS

My Independent Reading List

UNIT 2

LANGUAGE DEVELOPMENT

Several recurring SpringBoard features focus on building students' knowledge of grammar and usage concepts. Language & Writer's Craft features guide students to examine a writer's use of a language concept in context before incorporating the concept into their own writing. Grammar & Usage features briefly highlight and explain an interesting grammar or usage concept that appears in a text, both to improve students' reading comprehension and to increase their understanding of the concept. Periodic Language Checkpoints offer in-depth practice with standard English conventions and usage and guide students to revise sample sentences as well as their own work.

INDEPENDENT READING

In this unit, while exploring the freedom of speech, students will have the opportunity to independently read other texts that explore the concept. Student choice is paramount. The Planning the Unit section of the Teacher's Edition and the Resources section of the Student Edition contain reading lists to help you and your students find the right books.

Independent Reading Links in the unit periodically prompt students to reflect on the reading they are doing outside of class and to make connections to the texts, themes, and ideas addressed in the unit.

KNOWLEDGE QUEST

Within the unit, students will engage in two Knowledge Quests. They will read collections of texts about religion and witchcraft in colonial New England and inaugural speeches by presidents, building their understanding of the topics and related vocabulary. Each Knowledge Quest begins with a knowledge question and supporting questions that focus student learning. After students read the final text in a set, they will have the opportunity to return to the Knowledge Question and express their growing understanding of the topic by responding to a writing-to-sources prompt or engaging in an academic discussion.

UNIT 2

The SpringBoard program been designed so that students interact with the text in meaningful ways, such as note-taking and annotating, to facilitate comprehension and analysis. Have students use Reader/Writer Notebooks actively for vocabulary study, answers to text-dependent questions, predictions and questions about texts, reflections, responding to Independent Reading Links, and so on. The Reader/Writer Notebooks are not listed as part of the materials for each activity, but the expectation is that students will access them frequently.

CONTENTS

My Independent Reading List

Texts not included in these materials.

Previewing the Unit

Learning Targets
- Preview the big ideas for the unit.
- Create a plan for reading independently.

Preview

In this activity, you will explore the big ideas and tasks of the unit and make plans for your independent reading.

About the Unit

Imagine you are a witness to a situation you perceive as being unjust. What is your response? Do you speak out or remain silent? Now, imagine you are an author who has witnessed an unjust situation and you decide to speak out using the most influential forum you know: your writing. Songwriters, poets, dramatists, bloggers—writers and performers of all ages—use **social commentary** to speak out against perceived injustices every day. Using art to advance social commentary has long been a hallmark of artistic expression.

Essential Questions

The following Essential Questions will be the focus of the unit study. Respond to both questions.

1. How can artistic expression advance social commentary?
2. How is rhetoric applied to the creation and delivery of persuasive speeches?

Unpacking Embedded Assessment 1

Closely read the assignment for Embedded Assessment 1: Creating and Performing a Dramatic Scene.

Your assignment is to work with a group to write and perform an original dramatic script in which you make a statement about a conflict that faces society. By doing so, you should be able to demonstrate your understanding of how Arthur Miller spoke out about a contemporary issue (persecution of suspected Communists) while setting his drama in a time period with corresponding events (persecution of suspected witches).

Find the Scoring Guide and work with your class to paraphrase the expectations for the assignment. Create a graphic organizer to use as a visual reminder of the required skills and concepts. Copy the graphic organizer into your Reader/Writer Notebook and revisit it after each activity to check your progress.

Planning Independent Reading

In this unit, you will read literary fiction and nonfiction that explores America's commitment to freedom of speech. Collaborate with peers and discuss the pros and cons of free speech. In what ways is free speech an essential element of democracy? In what ways might free speech be dangerous, at times, for some members of society? Based on this discussion, compile a list of works for independent reading that discuss both sides of the issue.

Learning Strategies
Graphic Organizer
Paraphrase

ACADEMIC
Social commentary is a means of speaking out about issues in a society. It may take the form of rhetoric as well as artistic forms.

VOCABULARY

My Notes

_____

_____

_____

_____

_____

_____

_____

_____

_____

_____

_____

_____

_____

_____

_____

_____

_____

College and Career Readiness Standards

Focus Standards:

RL.11-12.10 By the end of grade 11, read and comprehend literature, including stories, dramas, and poems, in the grades 11–CCR text complexity band proficiently, with scaffolding as needed at the high end of the range.

ACTIVITY 2.1

PLAN

Materials: poster paper
Suggested Pacing: 1 50-minute class period (with Unit Overview and Contents)

TEACH

1 Review the Learning Targets, Preview, and About the Unit with students.

2 **Vocabulary Development:** Ask students to work with a partner to brainstorm words to define the concept of social *commentary*.

3 To access prior knowledge about the concepts of the unit, ask students to respond to the Essential Questions before sharing their answers with a partner.

4 Lead students through a **close reading** of the assignment and Scoring Guide for Embedded Assessment 1. Instruct students to **mark the text** by underlining or highlighting the skills and knowledge necessary to succeed on the Embedded Assessment.

5 Use students' responses to create an unpacking graphic organizer to post in the classroom. Revisit the graphic organizer after each activity to illustrate students' progress.

6 To stimulate discussion that will lead to independent reading selections, have students make lists of how they use free speech in their everyday lives. Ask them to consider how they might use free speech at home, with their friends, and at school. Remind students that the works included in their independent reading lists should discuss both sides of the issue. Give one or two examples.

ASSESS

Review the graphic organizers students have created in Unpacking Embedded Assessment 1 to ensure that they understand the expectations for Embedded Assessment 1.

ADAPT

Help students work on their graphic organizers by putting them in groups to share their paraphrases as well as their understanding of what skills and concepts will be involved in EA 1.

PLAN

Materials: dictionary and thesaurus, either print or online; *The Crucible*; Optional: audio recordings on SpringBoard Digital
Suggested Pacing: 2 50-minute periods

TEACH

1 Read the Learning Targets and Preview with students. Activate students' prior knowledge of primary and secondary sources. Have students volunteer examples of each type of source.

2 Vocabulary Development: Read aloud the definition of the term *historical context* before reading the Researching Historical Context section with students. Consider showing them illustrations of Humpty Dumpty from children's books and images of siege cannons from the English Civil War to support their understanding of historical context.

3 Explain to students that over the next two days, they will conduct research into the historical context of *The Crucible* by Arthur Miller using the primary sources in this activity.

⭐ TEACHER TO TEACHER

You may want to divide the class into four groups and jigsaw the reading of the primary sources. If you choose this approach, have one group read each of the following sources: the sermon, the historical document, the historical account, and the illustration and the legal document. If you choose to do a whole-class reading, use the steps that follow to conduct a guided close reading of the sources.

Preparing to Read *The Crucible*: Setting Context

Learning Strategies
Graphic Organizer
Marking the Text
Note-taking
Questioning the Text

VOCABULARY

ACADEMIC
Historical context refers to political, social, cultural, and economic circumstances or conditions that exist during a certain time and place. When an author sets a fictional work in a specific historical context, he or she must be true to the factual context that informs the significance of time and place.

Learning Targets
- Evaluate textual details to understand key ideas presented in primary source texts.
- Synthesize information from various primary source texts to understand the historical context of a play.
- Integrate ideas from multiple texts to build knowledge and vocabulary about a religion and witchcraft in colonial New England.

Preview
Arthur Miller's play *The Crucible* is set in Puritan New England. In this activity, you will study primary source documents to build your knowledge of the historical context of the play.

Researching Historical Context

When reading a play or novel set in another time or place, researching the historical context of the setting can help you better understand its plot, characters, and themes. Researching the historical context of a piece of literature refers to learning information about aspects like the social, economic, political, and religious conditions of the text's setting. Consider the following nursery rhyme:

> Humpty Dumpty sat on a wall,
>
> Humpty Dumpty had a great fall;
>
> All the king's horses and all the king's men
>
> Couldn't put Humpty together again

If you conducted research into this nursery rhyme's historical context, you would learn that Humpty Dumpty was not the anthropomorphized egg found in most illustrated versions of this text. Instead, Humpty Dumpty was a massive siege cannon that was used by King Charles I's men during the English Civil War that lasted from 1642 to 1651. Humpty Dumpty was strategically positioned at the top of a church tower and for eleven weeks successfully kept the supporters of Parliament from advancing. Eventually, the tower was blown up by the opposition and poor Humpty Dumpty fell into the surrounding marshland and was never recovered. Researching the political aspects of this seemingly simple nursery rhyme unlocks a greater meaning for the reader. In advance of reading *The Crucible* by Arthur Miller, you will read and analyze the various primary sources in this activity to begin to learn more about the historical context of the play.

My Notes

College and Career Readiness Standards

Focus Standards:

RI.11-12.1 Cite strong and thorough textual evidence to support analysis of what the text says explicitly as well as inferences drawn from the text, including determining where the text leaves matters uncertain.

RI.11-12.4 Determine the meaning of words and phrases as they are used in a text, including figurative, connotative, and technical meanings; analyze how an author uses and

refines the meaning of a key term or terms over the course of a text (e.g., how Madison defines faction in Federalist No. 10).

RI.11-12.7 Integrate and evaluate multiple sources of information presented in different media or formats (e.g., visually, quantitatively) as well as in words in order to address a question or solve a problem.

Additional Standards Addressed:

RI.11-12.2, RI.11-12.6

2.2

1. Use this KWL chart to help gain an understanding of *The Crucible*'s historical context. Begin by completing the W column with your teacher's assistance.

What I Know (K) About Puritan New England	What I Want to Know (W) About Puritan New England	What I Have Learned (L) About Puritan New England
Some anticipated responses include: • Puritan New England was inhabited by Puritans who: • came to North American from Britain. • wanted to worship in their own way. • wanted to reform the Church of England. • settled in Salem and Boston. • supported literacy strongly. • were required to read the Bible. • believed in a literal Devil.	Some anticipated responses include: What roles did religion play in the period's government and society? What was Puritan religion like? In what supernatural beings did Puritans believe? Where did Puritan children learn about religion? Why was there a strong belief in witchcraft? Why was witchcraft considered a crime? How were those accused of witchcraft treated?	Some anticipated responses include: Both government and society were structured according to Puritan norms. This is especially implicit in Sources 2, 3, and 5. Puritan religion was strict, fear-ridden, and superstition-riddled (Sources 1, 3, 4, 5). Supernatural beings that Puritans believedw in include God (all sources), witches and sorcerers (Sources 1, 3, 4, 5), and the Devil (Sources 1, 3, 4, 5). Students learned about the Puritan religion everywhere, including school (Source 2).

4 Tell students that before conducting any research it is important to assess what they already know about a topic and to create initial research questions to guide them. Have students complete the K column of the **KWL chart** independently. Have students share their responses.

5 Next, guide students to complete the W column. Remind them to think about the aspects of historical context that they learned: social, economic, political, and religion. Assist them in writing good research questions using the annotations as examples. Tell students that they will return to the chart later in the activity.

6 Before launching into a close reading of each source, review the As You Read instructions with students. Remind them that they are to keep their research questions in mind as they read and underline words and phrases that answer them.

7 Discuss the Knowledge Question. Have students work in small groups to discuss the possible connections between religion and witchcraft in colonial New England.

8 FIRST READ: Conduct a shared reading of "Sinners in the Hands of an Angry God." Pause after paragraph 2 to discuss the imagery Edwards uses and his perception of the nature of the relationship between men, God, and the Devil.

 TEXT COMPLEXITY

Overall: Complex
Lexile: 1360L
Qualitative: High Difficulty
Task: Moderate (Analyze)

9 As students are reading, monitor their progress. Be sure they are engaged with the text and focusing on words and phrases that answer their research questions. This source provides a great deal of insight into the aspect of religion. It provides historical context about the Puritan beliefs about life and the nature of humankind.

10 Tell students to pause at the end of paragraph 3 and ask them what images Edward's words conjure in their minds.

2.2

My Notes

As You Read

- Circle any unknown words or phrases. Try to determine the meaning of the words by using context clues, word parts, or a dictionary.
- Underline any words or phrases that answer the research questions in the Wcolumn of your KWL chart.
- Summarize or paraphrase excerpts from the text (paragraphs, lines, etc.).

About the Author

Jonathan Edwards (1703–1758), the son of a minister, was born in Connecticut Colony and grew up steeped in the Puritan tradition. Ordained as a minister at age 23, he became a prominent leader in the Great Awakening, a movement to reconnect Christians with their faith on a personal level. Although the sermon "Sinners in the Hands of an Angry God" was delivered in 1741, almost 50 years after the Salem witch trials, it reflects the Puritan concepts and ideals of the time.

KNOWLEDGE QUEST

Knowledge Question:

What is the connection between religion and witchcraft in colonial New England? In Activity 2.2, you will read a series of primary documents that provide historical context for *The Crucible*. While you read and build knowledge about its historical context, think about your answer to the Knowledge Question.

dominion: authority
immoderate: excessive
brimstone: sulphur

Sermon

Sinners in the Hands of an Angry God

by **Jonathan Edwards**

1   [Men] deserve to be cast into hell; so that divine justice never stands in the way; it makes no objection against God's using His power at any moment to destroy them. Yea, on the contrary, justice calls aloud for an infinite punishment of their sins.

2   The devil stands ready to fall upon them, and seize them as his own, at what moment God shall permit him. They belong to him; he has their souls in his possession, and under his **dominion**. The Scripture represents them as his goods.

3   The corruption of the heart of man is **immoderate** and boundless in its fury; and while wicked men live here, it is like fire pent up by God's restraints, whereas if it were let loose, it would set on fire the course of nature; as the heart is now a sink of sin, so, if sin was not restrained, it would immediately turn the soul into a fiery oven, or furnace of fire and **brimstone**.

Scaffolding the Text-Dependent Questions

2. In paragraph 1, what does Edwards mean by *divine* when he refers to "divine justice"? What connotation does the word *divine* have? What does it mean to receive justice? RI.11-12.4

3. What support does Edwards provide for his claim that people deserve to go to hell?

Reread paragraph 3. What does Edwards believe is in the "heart of man"? Is the word *corruption* positive or negative? What might happen if this corruption is not restrained? What do Edwards's language and images tell you about his beliefs regarding human nature? RI.11-12.1

4   God has laid Himself under no obligation, by any promise to keep any natural man out of hell one moment. God certainly has made no promises either of eternal life, or of any deliverance or preservation from eternal death, but what are contained in the covenant of grace, the promises that are given in Christ, in whom all the promises are yea and amen.

5   So that, thus it is that natural men are held in the hand of God, over the pit of hell; they have deserved the fiery pit, and are already sentenced to it; and God is dreadfully provoked: His anger is as great towards them as those that are actually suffering the execution of the fierceness of His **wrath** in hell; and they have done nothing in the least to **appease** or abate that anger, neither is God in the least bound by any promise to hold them up for one moment. The devil is waiting for them, hell is gaping for them, the flames gather and flash about them, and would fain lay hold on them, and swallow them up; the fire pent up in their own heart is struggling to break out.

My Notes

⊘ Knowledge Quest
- What images do Edwards's words conjure in your mind?
- What questions do you have after reading the sermon?

Returning to the Text
- Return to the sermon as you respond to the following questions. Use text evidence to support your responses.
- Write any additional questions you have about the text in your Reader/Writer Notebook.

2. **KQ** In paragraph 1, what does Edwards mean by *divine* when he refers to "divine justice"?

Since Edwards is delivering a sermon, his use of the word *divine* likely refers to God's powers, which he mentions in the sentence. Divine justice in this context is the justice meted out by God against people who might be considered sinners, and Edwards points out that God can use his powers for divine justice anytime.

3. What support does Edwards provide for his claim that people deserve to go to hell?

Edwards says, "The corruption of the heart of man Is Immoderate and boundless in its fury ... like fire" and that if not for being held in the hand of God, sin "would immediately turn the soul into a fiery oven, or furnace of fire and brimstone." These statements support his contention that people "deserve to be cast into hell."

wrath: anger
appease: soothe

TEACHER TO TEACHER
You may elect to read the sermon aloud or invite a colleague with a "booming" voice to read to your students. You could also listen to the audio recording available in the e-book on SpringBoard Digital.

11 After reading the text for the first time, guide the class in a discussion by asking the Knowledge Quest questions. Check students' general comprehension of the text based on their observations, asking follow-up questions as needed.

12 RETURNING TO THE TEXT: Guide students to return to the text to respond to the text-dependent questions. Invite them to work in small groups to reread the text and answer the questions. Remind them to use text evidence in their responses.

Scaffolding the Text-Dependent Questions

4. What does Edwards believe can save people from hell? Reread paragraph 4. How does Edwards describe the relationship between people and God? What exception does he mention in the second half of the paragraph? RI.11-12.1

5. Summarize the points that Edwards reemphasizes in the last paragraph of the excerpt. Reread paragraph 5. In what position

is God holding sinful man? What has man done to appease or abate God's anger? RI.11-12.2

6. Based on details in the text, what are some examples of Puritan values and beliefs? What does Edwards say about hell, the devil, divine justice, and sin? What is the path to grace? What do these statements suggest about the values and beliefs or worldview of the Puritans? RI.11-12.1

13 Move from group to group and listen in as students answer the text-dependent questions. If they have difficulty, scaffold the questions by rephrasing them or breaking them into smaller parts. See the Scaffolding the Text-Dependent Questions boxes for suggestions.

2.2

4. What does Edwards believe can save people from hell?

Edwards believes that only Christ can save people from hell. He explicitly states that "God certainly has made no promises either of eternal life, or of any deliverance or preservation from eternal death, but what are contained in the covenant of grace, the promises that are given in Christ, in whom all the promises are yea and amen."

5. Summarize the points that Edwards reemphasizes in the last paragraph of the excerpt.

An angry God holds sinful man over the fires of hell, and God is under no obligation not to hand him over to the devil. Man has angered god, and perhaps deserves to spend an eternity in hell.

6. Based on details in the text, what are some examples of Puritan values and beliefs?

Based on Edwards's descriptions of hell and the devil, these concepts are very real to Puritans. Divine justice "calls aloud for infinite punishment of [people's] sins." God is "dreadfully provoked" at people's sinfulness. "The promises that are given in Christ" are the only path to grace."

7. What is the purpose of Edwards's sermon, and how does he tailor his message to his audience?

Edwards's purpose is to warn people of the dangers of hell and to persuade them to renew their faith and save themselves. His descriptions of the "corruption of the heart of man" that angers God and condemns people to hell and the devil, who "is waiting for them," is an emotional appeal aimed at a Puritan audience who believes in a literal hell and a literal devil.

8. **KQ** How does Edwards's sermon provide historical context about the connection between religion and witchcraft in colonial New England?

Edwards's sermon provides historical context by demonstrating what the prevailing religious beliefs were in colonial New England. Since it was written 50 years after the Salem witch trials, it shows how Puritans conceives of right, wrong, and "divine justice."

Scaffolding the Text-Dependent Questions

7. What is the purpose of Edwards's sermon, and how does he tailor his message to his audience? Is Edwards's purpose to inform, to persuade, or to entertain, and how do you know? How might a Puritan audience have felt as they listened to descriptions of God's anger, hell, and the devil? With these feelings, how might the sermon have caused people to change their thinking or behavior?

8. How does Edwards's sermon provide historical context about the connection between religion and witchcraft in colonial New England? What were the prevailing religious beliefs? What would someone like Edwards think of witchcraft? RI.11-12.1

14 Have students read the About the Document section for *The New England Primer*. Point out that the Bible-based rhymes were meant to build literacy while reinforcing Puritan beliefs in children.

About the Document

For more than 100 years, Puritan children received their first schooling from *The New England Primer*. Because the chief purpose of education in Puritan times was to enable people to read the Bible, it was natural that the alphabet rhymes chanted by the children should be based on Bible stories. *The Primer* is believed to have been in existence by 1688. Several versions have been printed, often with different verses for the letters.

Historical Document

The New England Primer

A	In Adam's Fall, We sinned all.
B	Heaven to find; The Bible Mind.
C	Christ crucify'd For sinners dy'd.
D	The Deluge drown'd The Earth around.
E	Elijah hid, By Ravens fed.
F	The judgment made Felix afraid.

T *Time* cuts down all Both great and small.

U *Uriah's* beauteous Wife Made *David* seek his Life.

W *Whales* in the Sea God's Voice obey.

X *Xerxes* the great did die, And so must you & I.

Y *Youth* forward slips Death soonest nips.

Z *Zaccheus* he Did climb the Tree His Lord to see,

KNOWLEDGE QUEST

Knowledge Question:

What is the connection between religion and witchcraft in colonial New England?

G	As runs the Glass, Our Life doth pass.
H	My Book and Heart Must never part.
J	Job feels the Rod, Yet blesses God.
K	Proud Korah's troop Was swallowed up
L	Lot fled to *Zoar*, Saw fiery Shower On *Sodam* pour.
M	Moses was he Who *Israel's* Host Led thro' the Sea.

N	Noah did view The old world & new.
O	Young Obadias, David, Josias, All were pious.
P	Peter deny'd His Lord and cry'd.
Q	Queen Esther sues And saves the Jews.
R	Young pious Ruth, Left all for Truth.
S	Young Sam'l dear, The Lord did fear.

T	Young Timothy Learnt sin to fly.
V	Vashti for Pride Was set aside.
W	Whales in the Sea, God's Voice obey.
X	Xerxes did die, And so must I.
Y	While youth do chear Death may be near.
Z	Zaccheus he Did climb the Tree Our Lord to see.

15 After reading the primer for the first time, guide the class in a discussion by asking the Knowledge Quest questions. Check students' general comprehension of the document based on their observations, asking follow-up questions as needed.

16 Guide students to the text to respond to the text-dependent question. Invite them to work in small groups to reread the text and answer the question. Remind them to use text evidence in their response.

17 Have students read the About the Author section about Cotton Mather. Ask them what they already know about the Salem witch trials. Discuss their responses briefly, and remind them that they will be examining that historical event in greater detail shortly.

2.2

My Notes

Ø Knowledge Quest
- Which images in the primer catch your attention?
- What religious imagery or words do you notice?

9. The conventions of grammar have changed dramatically since the 17th century, which can make deciphering historical documents challenging. Some of the older conventions to notice in this historical document are the use of noun capitalization and the use of apostrophes to shorten words. It was also common for students to memorize passages, so primers for children included rhyming phrases to make memorization easier. Find two examples each that contain noun capitalization, apostrophe shortening, and rhyming. Then rewrite the lines using modern grammar and phrasing. Think about the reasons behind the changes in grammar conventions over time.

About the Author

Cotton Mather (1663–1728) was born in Boston in the Massachusetts Bay Colony. Following in the footsteps of his father and both of his grandfathers, he became a Puritan minister, and he eventually wrote more than 450 books and pamphlets. He urged caution in the Salem witch trials but largely ended up supporting them and published accounts of the proceedings in Salem.

Historical Account

The Trial of Martha Carrier

by **Cotton Mather**

1 Martha Carrier was indicted for bewitching certain persons, according to the form usual in such cases, pleading not guilty to her **indictment**. There were first brought in a considerable number of the bewitched persons, who not only made the Court sensible of any horrid witchcraft committed upon them, but also **deposed** that it was Martha Carrier, or her shape, that grievously tormented them by biting, pricking, pinching, and choking of them. It was further deposed that while this Carrier was on her examination before the **Magistrates**, the poor people were so tortured that everyone expected their death upon the very spot, but that upon the binding of Carrier they were eased. Moreover, the look of Carrier then laid the **afflicted** people for dead, and her touch, if her eye at the same time were off them, raised them again: which things were also now seen upon her trial. And it was testified that upon the mention of some having their necks twisted almost round, by the shape of this Carrier, she replied, It's no matter though their necks had been twisted quite off.

2 Before the trial of this prisoner, several of her own children had frankly and fully confessed not only that they were witches themselves, but that this their mother had made them so. This confession they made with great shows of repentance, and with much demonstration of truth. They related place, time, occasion; they gave an account of journeys, meetings, and mischiefs by them performed and were very credible in what they said. Nevertheless, this evidence was not produced against the prisoner at the bar, inasmuch as there was other evidence enough to proceed upon.

3 Benjamin Abbot gave his testimony that last March was a twelvemonth, this Carrier was very angry with him, upon laying out some land near her husband's. Her expressions in this anger were that she would stick as close to Abbot as the bark stuck to the tree, and that he should repent of it afore seven years came to an end, so as Doctor Prescot should never cure him. These words were heard by others besides Abbot himself, who also heard her say she would hold his nose as close to the grindstone as ever it was held since his name was Abbot. Presently after this he was taken with a swelling in his foot, and then with a pain in his side, and exceedingly tormented. It bred into a sore, which was **lanced** by Doctor Prescot, and several gallons of **corruption** ran out of it. For six weeks it continued very bad, and then another sore bred in the groin, which was also lanced by Doctor Prescot. Another sore then bred in his groin, which was likewise cut and put him to very great misery. He was brought until

KNOWLEDGE QUEST

Knowledge Question:
What is the connection between religion and witchcraft in colonial New England?

GRAMMAR & USAGE

Sentence Types
A sentence usually begins or ends with the main idea. When the main idea begins a sentence, it is called a cumulative sentence: "Martha Carrier was indicted for bewitching certain persons ..." Here the independent clause, "Martha Carrier was indicted," is followed by details that tell more information about the person and the event. The reader's understanding grows in a cumulative way as he or she combines each new piece of information with previously stated details.

When the main idea comes at the end, a periodic sentence results: "Before the trial of this prisoner, several of her own children had frankly and fully confessed ..." A periodic sentence is usually lengthy and creates a sense of suspense about the main idea.

Find examples of these sentences and think about the effect they have on your understanding of main ideas.

indictment: official accusation of a crime
deposed: testified under oath
magistrates: judges
afflicted: anguished
lanced: cut open
corruption: decay

ACTIVITY 2.2 continued

18 FIRST READ: Begin reading "The Trial of Martha Carrier" as a class. Pause after section 1 to be certain students understand that Cotton Mather's account is sympathetic toward the accusers, not the accused. Have students continue reading independently.

TEXT COMPLEXITY

Overall: Complex
Lexile: 1420L
Qualitative: Moderate Difficulty
Task: Moderate (Analyze)

19 As students read, monitor their progress. Assist them as needed in comprehending the language conventions of the text, and encourage them to use print or online sources to determine the meanings of unknown and undefined words.

20 Tell students to pause at the end of section 3 and ask them what authority is being evoked to add credibility to the accusations against Carrier. Prompt students to understand that Puritans considered the science of medicine and belief in the supernatural to be equally valid.

21 Draw students' attention to the Grammar & Usage feature on sentence types. Have them complete the activity. Students should identify sentence examples. When comparing and contrasting the effects of sentence construction, it may help students to hear the sentences read aloud.

Scaffolding the Text-Dependent Questions

10. 1. In section 1, what does Mather mean by *bewitching* when he refers the charges brought against Martha Carrier? What connotation does the word bewitching have? Why might someone be charged with it in court? RI.11-12.4

11. What are the charges against Martha Carrier? What is the evidence against her? Reread section 1. What is Martha Carrier's alleged crime? How does she plead? What evidence do "bewitched persons" and Carrier's family provide against her? RI.11-12.1

22 Tell students to pause after section 5 and point out how the language Mather uses is intended to make Carrier unsympathetic to the reader.

23 **Vocabulary Development:** Pause after section 6. Highlight the Word Connections box. Tell students that learning the roots and affixes of a word can enrich knowledge of its meaning. Elicit from students other words that use the root *nature*, such as *supernatural*, and discuss how the prefix changes the meaning.

24 After reading the text for the first time, guide the class in a discussion by asking the Knowledge Quest questions. Check students' general comprehension of the text based on their observations, asking follow-up questions as needed.

2.2

The trial of Martha Carrier started on May 31, 1692, when she was transported to the Salem Village Meeting House to face her accusers, many of them young girls. When Martha entered the room, the girls fell to the floor, writhing with cries of agony.

WORD CONNECTIONS

Roots and Affixes

Preternatural is formed from the root *nature*; the suffix *-al*, meaning "of" or "connected to"; and the prefix *preter-*, from the Latin *praeter*, meaning "beyond" or "more than."

Samuel Preston uses *preternatural* to say he lost his cow in a manner that is beyond the explanation of nature.

calamities: great misfortunes or disasters

apprehending: arresting or seizing

variance: difference or disagreement

death's door and so remained until Carrier was taken and carried away by the Constable, from which very day he began to mend and so grew better every day and is well ever since.

Sarah Abbot, his wife, also testified that her husband was not only all this while afflicted in his body, but also that strange, extraordinary, and unaccountable **calamities** befell his cattle, their death being such as they could guess at no natural reason for.

4   Allin Toothaker testified that Richard, the son of Martha Carrier, having some difference with him, pulled him down by the hair of the head. When he rose again, he was going to strike at Richard Carrier, but fell down flat on his back to the ground and had not power to stir hand or foot until he told Carrier he yielded: and then he saw the shape of Martha Carrier go off his breast.

This Toothaker had received a wound in the wars and now testified that Martha Carrier told him he should never be cured. Just afore the **apprehending** of Carrier, he could thrust a knitting needle into his wound, four inches deep; but presently, after her being seized, he was thoroughly healed.

He further testified that when Carrier and he sometimes were at **variance**, she would clap her hands at him, and say he should get nothing by it; whereupon he several times lost his cattle by strange deaths, whereof no natural causes could be given.

5   John Rogger also testified that upon the threatening words of this malicious Carrier, his cattle would be strangely bewitched, as was more particularly then described.

6   Samuel Preston testified that about two years ago, having some difference with Martha Carrier, he lost a cow in a strange preternatural, unusual matter: and about a month after this, the said Carrier, having again some difference with him, she told him he had lately lost a cow and it should not be long before he lost another, which accordingly came to pass: for he had a thriving and well-kept cow, which without any known cause quickly fell down and died.

⊘ Knowledge Quest

- What event does Cotton Mather describe in his account?
- What about Mather's account of the event stands out most to you?

Scaffolding the Text-Dependent Questions

12. What evidence does Cotton Mather include in his account that is not presented at the trial? What does the inclusion of this evidence reveal about Mather's view of Carrier? Reread the beginning of section 2. When does the information presented in this paragraph take place? Why does Mather include evidence that is provided "before the trial" in this account—to persuade, to inform, or to entertain? What other evidence supports this purpose? RI.11-12.1

Returning to the Text

- Return to the account as you respond to the following questions. Use text evidence to support your responses.
- Write any additional questions you have about the text in your Reader/Writer Notebook.

10. **KQ** In section 1, what does Mather mean by *bewitching* when he refers the charges brought against Martha Carrier?

Mather describes Martha Carrier as "bewitching certain persons," inferring that she has used

witchcraft to control other humans or curse them in some way. It has a negative connotation,

since it is an accusation that brought about charges.

11. What are the charges against Martha Carrier? What is the evidence against her?

Martha Carrier is officially charged with "bewitching certain persons," or witchcraft.

Eyewitness testimony is given by "bewitched persons" who testify that Martha, or her

"shape," bites, pricks, pinches, and chokes them. Others accuse Carrier of killing their cows

and causing or preventing the healing of sores and wounds.

12. What evidence does Cotton Mather include in section 2 of his account that is not presented at the trial? What does the inclusion of this evidence reveal about Mather's view of Carrier?

Mather writes that several of Martha Carrier's children, with "much demonstration of truth,"

confessed before the trial that their mother makes them into witches. The information reveals

that Mather views Carrier as guilty of witchcraft.

13. What evidence do Benjamin and Sarah Abbot offer as proof that Martha Carrier is a witch? Would this evidence hold up in a court today? Why or why not?

Benjamin Abbot testifies that after Carrier threatened him, he developed sores that did not

heal until Carrier was arrested. Sarah Abbot testifies that after the threat, their cattle started

dying. This evidence would probably not hold up in a court today because nothing objective

links Carrier's "expressions [of] anger" with the Abbots' misfortunes.

25 **RETURNING TO THE TEXT:** Guide students to return to the text-dependent questions. Invite them to work in small groups to reread the text and answer the questions. Remind them to use text evidence in their responses.

26 Move from group to group and listen in as students answer the text-dependent questions. If they have difficulty, scaffold the questions by rephrasing them or breaking them down into smaller parts. See the Scaffolding the Text-Dependent Questions boxes for suggestions.

Scaffolding the Text-Dependent Questions

13. What evidence do Benjamin and Sarah Abbot offer as proof that Martha Carrier is a witch? Would this evidence hold up in a court today? Why or why not? List the evidence of Martha's witchcraft that Benjamin and Sarah Abbot offer in section 3. How might a remembered conversation be subjective? What is the problem with claiming that when event 1

happens after event 2, it means that event 1 causes event 2? RI.11-12.1

14. Whose trial testimony seems likely to result in a further investigation of someone other than Martha Carrier? Explain. Reread the testimony recounted in section 4. Upon whom does the witness cast suspicion other than Martha? RI.11-12.1

My Notes

14. Whose trial testimony seems likely to result in a further investigation of someone other than Martha Carrier? Explain.

In section 4, The Allin Toothaker's testimony casts suspicion on Richard Carrier, Martha's son. Toothaker describes an instance in which he was fighting with Richard and was knocked and held to the ground by Martha's "shape." This is probably something the authorities would investigate further.

15. What insight can Edwards's ideas in "Sinners in the Hands of an Angry God" provide into the trial of Martha Carrier?

The sermon presents the Puritan notion that the devil is a real and threatening being, anxious to exercise his claim to humans. To people who hold that belief, the idea that some individuals are under the devil's control could easily make sense. It would likewise be easy to blame the devil and those he controls for bad fortune.

16. KQ How does Mather's historical account provide historical context about the connection between religion and witchcraft in colonial New England?

Mather's historical account provides historical context by showing what a witchcraft trial looked like—how the accused was treated in a court of law. Since Mathers was a religious minister, his observations may have been skewed by his beliefs.

Scaffolding the Text-Dependent Questions

15. What insight can Edwards's ideas in "Sinners in the Hands of an Angry God" provide into the trial of Martha Carrier? Review the evidence against Carrier. Which items on the list cause pain or harm? Which have no credible explanation during this time? To what might Edwards ascribe such evil?

Why do women like Carrier become targets of people's fear of the unknown?

16. How does Mather's historical account provide historical context about the connection between religion and witchcraft in colonial New England? How do his religious beliefs influence his account? RI.11-12.1

About the Illustration

Francisco Maria Guazzo was a priest who lived in Italy during the 16th and 17th centuries. The following image is from his *Compendium Maleficarum*, a guide to witch-hunting that Guazzo published in 1608. (A compendium is a collection of information about a specific topic. *Maleficarum* is a Latin word meaning "witch.") In Puritan New England, the book was considered an authoritative reference work. It was routinely consulted by clergy, lawyers, and judges alike as a guide to the detection and prevention of witchcraft.

Illustration

Sorcerer Exchanging Gospels for a
Book of Black Magic

⊘ Knowledge Quest
- Who do you think the figures in the image represent?
- What questions do you have after studying the Image?

⊘ KNOWLEDGE QUEST

Knowledge Question:
What is the connection between religion and witchcraft in colonial New England?

My Notes

_____

_____

_____

_____

_____

_____

_____

_____

_____

_____

_____

_____

_____

_____

_____

_____

_____

_____

_____

_____

_____

ACTIVITY 2.2 continued

27 Have students read the About the Illustration feature about "Sorcerer Exchanging Gospels for a Book of Black Magic."

28 FIRST READ: Conduct a class examination of "Sorcerer Exchanging Gospels for a Book of Black Magic" by asking the Knowledge Quest questions. Check students' general comprehension of the document based on their observations, asking follow-up questions as needed.

29 Have students read the About the Document section for the Deposition of Joseph Hutchinson. Note that the deposition is categorized as a legal document and hold a brief discussion of the part a deposition plays in a legal proceeding (i.e., how it compares to oral trial testimony).

30 FIRST READ: Conduct a shared reading of the Deposition of Joseph Hutchinson. Guide students in a discussion of the document by asking the Knowledge Quest questions. Be sure they are engaged with the text. Check students' general comprehension of the document based on their observations, asking follow-up questions as needed.

2.2

KNOWLEDGE QUEST

Knowledge Question:

What is the connection between religion and witchcraft in colonial New England?

My Notes

About the Document

In Salem in 1692, a frequently ill young girl named Abigail Williams was among the first to exhibit behaviors associated with oppression by witchcraft. She accused several local women of causing her troubles. At one of the seven trials at which she appeared, a local official named Joseph Hutchinson testified against her in favor of the accused. In this deposition, or sworn written testimony, Hutchinson describes to the court conversations he has had with Abigail. The document was entered into evidence at the trial.

Legal Document

The Deposition of Joseph Hutchinson

by **Joseph Hutchinson**

The deposition of Joseph Hutchinson aged 59: year doe testifie as fourth

Abigaill Williams I have heard you spake often of a booke that have bin offred to you. She Said that thare was two Books one wos a short thike book & the other wos a Long booke: I asked her w'h Coler the booke war of: she said the bookes ware as rede as blode I asked her if she had sene the booke opned: shee said that shee had sen it opned many times: I asked her if shee did see any Ritinge in the in the booke: shee said thar wos many lins Riten & at the end of Evary line thar wos a seall: I asked her whoe brought the booke to her: shee towld me that it was the blacke man I asked her whoe the blacke man was: shee towld mee it wos the devell: I asked her if shee wos not afraid to see the devell: Shee said at the first shee was and did goe from him but now shee wos not afraid but Could talke with him as well as shee Could with ~~him~~ mee

Scaffolding the Text-Dependent Questions

17. What does the word *seall* mean in context? What connotation does it have? What might the people in the courtroom think it referred to? RI.11-12.4

18. Summarize the contents of Joseph Hutchinson's deposition accurately and in your own words. Examine the deposition. What does Hutchinson testify that Abigail Williams told him? RI.11-12.2

19. How would someone familiar with the illustration and the book from which it came most likely react to Hutchinson's deposition? Remember the typical worldview of the time and place of the deposition along with the contents of the *Compendium Maleficarum*. What sort of transaction is depicted in that book? RI.11-12.3

Original handwritten deposition of Joesph Hutchinson

📝 Knowledge Quest

- What do you notice about the way the words are spelled in the deposition?
- What is something you noticed about the deposition that someone else may overlook?

Scaffolding the Text-Dependent Questions

20. How does Hutchinson's deposition provide historical context about the connection between religion and witchcraft in colonial New England? What religious references does he make? What does he accuse the girl of? RI.11-12.1

31 RETURNING TO THE TEXT:
Guide students to return to the text to respond to the text-dependent questions. Invite them to work in small groups to reread the text and answer the questions. Remind them to use text evidence in their responses.

32 Move from group to group and listen in as the students answer the text-dependent questions. If they have difficulty, scaffold the questions by rephrasing them or breaking them down into smaller parts. See the Scaffolding the Text-Dependent Questions boxes for suggestions.

2.2

Returning to the Text

- Return to the legal document as you respond to the following questions. Use text evidence to support your restponses.
- Write any additional questions you have about the text in your Reader/Writer Notebook.

17. **KQ** What does the word *seall* mean in context? What connotation does it have?

   Hutchinson uses the word *seall* to refer to a kind of stamp or signature left by the writers of the book being discussed. In this context, *prophesied* means "stamp." The connotation is of something magical or associated with witchcraft.

18. Summarize the contents of Joseph Hutchinson's deposition accurately and in your own words.

   Hutchinson testifies that Abigail Williams told him about two books. She said they were given to her by a black man claiming to be the devil, of whom she was not afraid and who spoke to her often. The books were blood-red in color. She had seen them opened, and every line of writing within them ended with a seal.

19. How would someone familiar with the illustration and the book from which it came most likely react to Hutchinson's deposition?

   He or she would probably assume that Hutchinson's testimony proved that Abigail Williams had indeed gotten her books from the devil, that they were books of black magic, and that she may have traded Gospels or some other sacred object to get them. The *Compendium Maleficarum* illustration "Sorcerer Exchanging Gospels for a Book of Black Magic" would support this assumption.

20. **KQ** How does Hutchinson's deposition provide historical context about the connection between religion and witchcraft in colonial New England?

   Hutchinson's deposition provides historical context by showing how witnesses were called to testify against people accused of witchcraft. Hutchinson used religious references such as the devil in order to imply that witchcraft is influenced by the devil.

2.2

 Knowledge Quest

With a partner, discuss how reading the primary sources helped deepen your understanding of the connection between religion and witchcraft in colonial New England. Be sure to:

- Refer to evidence from the primary sources.
- Take turns speaking, responding, and asking one another follow-up questions.
- Ask clarifying questions.
- Write down notes from your discussion and further questions you have about the topic.

My Notes

Working from the Text

21. Look back at your notes from the five primary sources in this activity. Use what you have learned to complete the L column of the chart. Instead of adding specific details from each source, synthesize the information from multiple sources to write comprehensive and complex notes.

22. Your teacher will sort you into groups and assign each group an aspect of *The Crucible*'s historical context to examine in greater detail. Evaluate the details that you read in each primary source to understand the key ideas about your aspect of setting. After your discussion, individually write a paragraph that briefly explains your aspect of the play's setting.

 INDEPENDENT READING LINK

Read and Discuss

You can continue to build your knowledge about religion and witchcraft by reading other articles at ZINC Reading Labs. Search for keywords such as *persecution* or *religion*.

ZINC

ACTIVITY 2.2 continued

33 Allow students time to work with a partner to complete the Knowledge Quest task. Ask volunteers to share highlights from their discussion. Encourage students to continue building knowledge on this topic as suggested in the Independent Reading link.

LEVELED DIFFERENTIATED INSTRUCTION

Some students may benefit from developing their ideas through discussion before writing their response.

Developing Help students express their ideas by asking and answering questions with a partner about the notes they took on the five primary sources. Have them record ideas using a **Collaborative Dialogue** graphic organizer.

Expanding Have students work with a partner to add relevant ideas and paraphrase key ideas from their notes, working together to synthesize the information. Encourage students to take notes based on the discussion.

Support Provide support for students by modeling how to synthesize information from multiple sources on the board.

Extend Pair students who have completed their charts and ask them to share their responses. For which primary sources did they have similar responses, and for which ones did they have different responses?

34 Ask students to independently complete student step 21 in the Working from the Text section. Assist them in synthesizing the information from multiple sources into comprehensive notes in the L column of their KWL charts.

35 After students have synthesized their notes into their KWL charts, divide the class into four new groups. Assign each group one aspect of the setting: social, economic, political, religion. Once the groups are formed, have them complete student steps 22, 23, and 24.

36 Guide students to return to the Knowledge Quest question they discussed before reading. Ask students how their response to this question has changed or been deepened after reading the primary source documents.

37 Give students time to respond to the Check Your Understanding task.

ASSESS

Review students' responses to the Check Your Understanding task. Check whether their writing accurately describes the historical context of Miller's play, relating the social, economic, political, and religious aspects of Puritan New England.

ADAPT

If students need help writing their Check Your Understanding summaries, have them construct brief outlines or graphic organizers that include thesis statements and labeled sections for Puritan social, economic, political, and religious aspects. Ask students to think about how the Puritan setting supports or reinforces the actions of the people.

---

23. Your teacher will assign you to a new group to discuss your paragraph with other students. Share your insights with theirs to gain an overall understanding of *The Crucible*'s setting.

24. What additional questions do you have about the historical context of *The Crucible*? Write three or four questions that you could use to do additional research about Puritan New England. As you continue to study the context of the play, remember to modify these questions as necessary.

☑ Check Your Understanding

The setting of Arthur Miller's contemporary play *The Crucible* in Puritan New England is key to your understanding of Miller's message. With a partner, summarize what you now know about the historical context of the play. Be sure to:

- Refer to evidence from the primary sources you read.
- Take turns speaking and responding by asking follow-up questions.
- Make clarifying statements.
- Keep a list of questions you still have about the historical context of the play.

The Lessons of Salem

Learning Targets

- Use newly acquired content vocabulary about the Salem witch trials in discussion and writing.
- Evaluate details about the Salem witch trials to understand key ideas.

Preview

In this activity, you will read the article "The Lessons of Salem" by Laura Shapiro and evaluate the details to understand key ideas about the Salem witch trials.

Learning Strategies

Graphic Organizer
Marking the Text
Note-taking
Rereading
Skimming/Scanning

Vocabulary of the Salem Witch Trials

1. To discuss *The Crucible*, you will need to be familiar with vocabulary related to the Salem Witch Trials. In your small groups, conduct informal research and explain each of the terms listed in the chart in the context of the witch trials. Record as much information about the term as possible, including its meaning, part of speech, and different forms of the word. If possible, explain any Greek or Latin roots or other word parts. Then synthesize the information to write a thorough explanation of each term. In the third column, identify other forms each term can take that indicate different meanings or parts of speech.

Salem Witch Trials Vocabulary	Definition/Explanation	Different Forms of the Word
accusation		
acquit		
hysteria		
magistrate		
Puritanism		
spectral evidence		
voodoo		
convulsions		
confess		
prejudice		
theology		

PLAN

Suggested Pacing: 2 50-minute periods

TEACH

1 Read the Learning Targets and Preview with students. Tell them they will read a scholarly, fact-based article about the Salem witch trials.

2 Divide the class into small groups and have them work together to complete the chart in the Vocabulary of the Salem Witch Trials section.

LEVELED DIFFERENTIATED INSTRUCTION

Students may need extra support for the difficult vocabulary in the chart such as *accusation* and *magistrate*. Have them complete the **Unknown Word Solver** graphic organizer for the difficult words from the chart.

Beginning Project or reproduce on the board a dictionary entry for the word *accusation*. Using the entry as a visual aid, explain how it indicates the word's part of speech, definitions, pronunciation, and syllabication. Then guide students to use this information to complete the graphic organizer.

Developing Have students look up the word *accusation* in a print or reliable online dictionary. Guide them as needed in recording part of speech, definitions, pronunciation, and syllabication. Repeat the process with other words on the list until students understand the information.

College and Career Readiness Standards

Focus Standards:

RI.11-12.1 Cite strong and thorough textual evidence to support analysis of what the text says explicitly as well as inferences drawn from the text, including determining where the text leaves matters uncertain.

L.11-12.4 Determine or clarify the meaning of unknown and multiple-meaning words and phrases based on *grades 11–12 reading and content*, choosing flexibly from a range of strategies.

Additional Standards Addressed:
RI.11-12.10

3 FIRST READ: Conduct a close read of "The Lessons of Salem." Pause after paragraph 5 to ensure students understand that the witch trials arose in a settlement that was already in a state of unrest and that suspicions of "voodoo" would be particularly troubling in a Puritan environment.

 TEXT COMPLEXITY

Overall: Complex
Lexile: 1190L
Qualitative: Moderate Difficulty
Task: Moderate (Analyze)

4 As students are reading, monitor their progress. Be sure they are engaged with the text, paying attention to context clues to discern the meanings of the vocabulary words at the beginning of the activity.

5 Discuss the Word Connections feature with students. Have them identify how the word *mind* is used in the text versus how it is typically defined.

2.3

My Notes

WORD CONNECTIONS

Multiple-Meaning Words
In casual usage, the verb **mind** usually means "to object to or dislike something." It can also mean "to worry about something." However, Martha Carrier, as quoted in the first paragraph, uses *mind* to say that the magistrates are listening to and seriously considering the claims of the witnesses against her.

reproach: disgrace

As You Read

- Underline key details about the Salem witch trials.
- Circle the vocabulary words that you studied at the beginning of this activity and make sure that you understand which meanings of the multiple-meaning words make sense based on the context.
- Pause after each chunk, evaluate the details you just read, and write down a key idea in the My Notes section.

Article

The Lessons of Salem

by **Laura Shapiro**

After 300 years, people are still fascinated by the notorious Puritan witch hunts—maybe because history keeps repeating itself.

Chunk 1

1 They came for Martha Carrier at the end of May. There was plenty of evidence against her: Allen Toothaker testified that several of his cattle had suffered "strange deaths" soon after he and Carrier had an argument, and little Phoebe Chandler said that shortly before being stricken with terrible pains, she had heard Carrier's voice telling her she was going to be poisoned. Even Carrier's children spoke against her: they confessed that they, too, were witches and that it was their mother who had converted them to evil. (Their statements were not introduced in court, however—perhaps because two of her sons had to be tied up until they bled from their mouth before they would confess. A small daughter spoke more freely; she told officials that her mother was a black cat.) Most damning of all was the evidence offered by half a dozen adolescent girls, who accused Carrier of tormenting them and who fell into writhing fits as she stood before the magistrate. They shrieked that they had seen the Devil whispering into Carrier's ear. "You see you look upon them and they fall down," said the magistrate. "It is a shameful thing that you should mind these folks that are out of their wits," answered Carrier. "I am wronged." On Aug. 19, 1692, she was hanged on Gallows Hill in Salem Mass., for the crime of witchcraft.

2 Last week marked the 300th anniversary of Carrier's death, an execution carried out during the most notorious summer in Massachusetts history. Between June and September of 1692, 14 women and 5 men were hanged in Salem as witches, and 1 man was tortured to death. Scores more were named as witches and imprisoned. "What will be the issue of these troubles, God only knows," wrote Thomas Brattle, a merchant in nearby Boston who was horrified by the events. "I am afraid that ages will not wear off that **reproach** and those stains which these things will leave behind upon our land."

Scaffolding the Text-Dependent Questions

2. **In paragraphs 1 and 2, what text hints at Shapiro's opinion about Martha Carrier's trial? What is that opinion?** Reread paragraphs 1 and 2. What does the text in parentheses state about some of the testimony? What does the word *confess* mean in this context? How does the author characterize the summer of the witch trials? RI.11-12.1

---

3   He was right: even now the Salem witch trials haunt the imaginations of hundreds of thousands of Americans, tourists and history buffs alike, who visit Salem for a glimpse of our Puritan past at its most chilling. This year Salem is getting more attention than ever: the city is sponsoring an array of programs commemorating the Tercentenary, including dramatizations of the trials and symposiums of the legal and medical aspects of identifying witches in the 17th century. With the participation of such organizations as Amnesty International, the Tercentenary has placed a special emphasis on human rights and the role of the individual conscience in times of terror. In 1692, those who "confessed" to witchcraft were spared; only those who insisted on their innocence were hanged. Earlier this month a memorial to the victims was unveiled and on that occasion the first annual Salem Award, created to honor a significant contribution to social justice, was presented to Gregory Allen Williams of Inglewood, Calif. In the midst of the Los Angeles riots last spring, Williams, who is black, risked his life to save an Asian-American attacked by a mob.

Chunk 2

4   At the heart of the Tercentenary is the awareness that the witch trials represent more than just a creepy moment in history: they stand for the terrible victory of prejudice over reason, and fear over courage—a contest that has been replayed with different actors, again and again since 1692. Modern witch hunts include the roundup of Japanese-Americans during World War II, the pursuit of Communists in the '50s and, according to an increasing number of critics, some of today's outbreaks of community hysteria over **purported** sex abuse in preschools. Experts say that although most child-abuse allegations are valid, the preschool cases are the flimsiest, resting as they do on a mixture of parental terror and children's confusion. Just as in Salem, the evidence in these cases tends to spring from hindsight, fueled by suspicion and revulsion. Whatever the truth may be, it has little chance to surface under such conditions.

5   Like all witch hunts, the troubles of 1692 began in a community that felt torn and besieged. Salem Village, now the town of Danvers, was about eight miles from the seat of local power in Salem Town. A contentious place, chafing to pull free of Salem Town and its taxes, Salem Village had suffered bitter disputes over its first three ministers before settling on a fourth, the Rev. Samuel Parris. During the winter of 1691–92, a few girls, mostly teenagers, started gathering in Parris's kitchen. There they listened to stories, perhaps voodoo tales, told by his Western Indian slave Tituba; they also tried to discern their future husbands by fortunetelling—dropping an egg white into a glass and seeing what shape it took. For girls raised in Puritanism, which demanded lifelong discipline and self-control, these sessions with Tituba represented a rare and risky bit of indulgence in pure fancy. Too risky, perhaps.

My Notes

_____
_____
_____
_____
_____
_____
_____
_____

WORD CONNECTIONS

Word Relationships
Revulsion, *repulsion, aversion,* and *detestation* all refer to a strong feeling of disgust, but each word has its own unique connotation. *Revulsion* might make someone pull away from the object of disgust, while *repulsion* pushes one away. *Aversion* will cause one to avoid the object, and *detestation* involves a strong hatred of the object.

purported: said to be true but not necessarily proven

6 **Vocabulary Development:** Discuss the Word Connections box. Have students clarify the precise meaning for each word using a dictionary. Then have them discuss the connotation of each with a partner.

Scaffolding the Text-Dependent Questions

3. What ironic situation does Shapiro describe in paragraph 3? Reread paragraph 3. What did those accused of witchcraft have to do to save their lives? What happened if they did not do this? What was the moral choice of the two they were given? RI.11-12.4

7 Tell students to pause at the end of paragraph 8 and explain why those who had misgivings about the witch trials largely kept those thoughts and feelings to themselves.

2.3

My Notes

Suddenly one after another of the girls was seized with fits. Their families were bewildered: the girls raved and fell into convulsions; one of them ran around on all fours and barked. Dr. William Griggs was called in and made his diagnosis: the "evil hand" was upon them.

6   Fits identified as satanic possession had broken out among adolescent girls at earlier times in New England. Often their distress was traced to local women who, it was said, had entered into a compact with the Devil and were now recruiting new witches by tormenting the innocent until they succumbed. So the adults in Salem Village began pressing the girls with questions: "Who torments you? Who torments you?" Finally they named three women—Tituba, Sarah Good and Sarah Osborne—all of them easily recognizable as Satan's hand-maidens. Tituba was seen as a shameless pagan, Good was a poor beggar given to muttering angrily as she went from house to house and Osborne was known to have lived with her second husband before they were married. The three were arrested and jailed, but the girls' torments did not cease. On the contrary, fits were spreading like smallpox; dozens more girls and young women went into violent contortions, flailing, kicking and uttering names.

7   And the names! Rebecca Nurse was 71, the pious and beloved matriarch of a large family; she was hanged in July. George Jacobs, an old man whose servant girl was one of the afflicted, thought the whole lot of them were "bitch witches" and said so; he was hanged in August. Susannah Martin was named, but that surprised nobody; people had been calling her a witch for years. Six or seven years earlier, Barnard Peach testified, he had been lying in bed at night when Martin appeared at his window and jumped into his room; she then lay down upon him and prevented him from moving for nearly two hours. Others had similar tales; Martin was hanged in July. Nor was there much doubt about Dorcas Good, who was arrested soon after her mother, Sarah, was jailed. The afflicted girls cried out that Dorcas was biting and pinching them, and although the attacks were invisible to everyone else, the girls had the bite marks to prove it. Dorcas was jailed with the others, and a special set of chains was made for her. She was only 5, and the regular shackles were too big.

8   All along, there were townspeople who had misgivings about what was happening. Several came to the defense of some of the accused citizens, and others testified that they had heard an afflicted girl saying she had made at least one accusation "for sport." But the machinery seemed unstoppable. If a prisoner was released or a jury decided to acquit someone, the girls went into such shrieking torments that the court quickly reversed itself.

9   Spectral evidence: Finally, in October, the governor of Massachusetts stepped in. Too many citizens "of good reputation" had been accused, he wrote, including his own wife. What's more, clergy in both Boston and New York were expressing dismay over the witch trials, especially the reliance on "spectral" evidence, such as the sight of the Devil whispering in Martha Carrier's ear—otherworldly evidence invisible to everyone but the person testifying. The governor ruled out the use of spectral evidence, making it virtually impossible to convict any more of the accused. That fall the witch craze effectively ended, and by spring the last prisoners had been acquitted.

succumbed: stopped trying to resist, yielded

Scaffolding the Text-Dependent Questions

4. What are three possible meanings of the word *possession*? What is its meaning as it is used in paragraph 6? Include definitions from a print or online dictionary in your answer. Use a print or online reference to find three meanings of the word. Examine how it is used in paragraph 6. Which meaning fits that paragraph's context? L.11-12.4

5. Examine the accusations Shapiro describes in paragraph 6. What can be inferred from the similarities of those accusations? What is an "accusation"? Which text in paragraph 6 constitutes accusations? How many separate accusations are there in that paragraph? How are they similar? What do their similarities imply? RI.11-12.1

2.3

Chunk 3

My Notes

10　What really happened in Salem? Scholars have been trying to understand the events of 1692 for three centuries. Even while the witch hunt was in progress, Deodat Lawson, a former minister at Salem Village, made a visit to his old parish and published the equivalent of a quickie paperback describing "the Misterious Assaults from Hell" he had witnessed there. Like everyone else in Salem—in fact, like everyone else in colonial New England—he believed in witches, though he was powerless to understand why or whether they were truly on the loose in Salem.

11　Today many scholars believe it was clinical hysteria that set off the girls in Tituba's kitchen. Fits, convulsions, vocal outbursts, feelings of being pinched and bitten—all of these symptoms have been witnessed and described, most often in young women, for centuries. Sometimes the seizures have been attributed to Satan, other times to God, but ever since Freud weighed in, hysteria has been traced to the unconscious. As Dr. Richard Pohl, of Salem Hospital, told a Tercentenary symposium, hysteria "can mimic all the physical diseases known to man," and occurs when repressed thoughts and emotions burst forth and take over the body. Life could be dreary for girls in 17th century Salem: their place was home and their duty was obedience; many were illiterate, and there were few outlets for youthful imagination except in the grim lessons of Puritan theology. Dabbling in magic in the reverend's own kitchen would have been wonderfully scary, perhaps enough to release psychic demons lurking since childhood.

12　Despite the fact that young girls made the accusations, it was the adults who lodged formal charges against their neighbors and provided most of the testimony. Historians have long believed that local feuds and property disputes were behind many of the accusations, and in "Salem Possessed" (1974), Paul Boyer and Stephen Nissenbaum uncovered patterns of social and civic antagonism that made the community fertile ground for a witch hunt.

Making Observations
- What details in Shapiro's article stand out to you?
- What questions do you have after reading the article?

illiterate: uneducated

Scaffolding the Text-Dependent Questions

6.　How did townspeople with misgivings about the Salem witch trials attempt to put an end to them? How successful were they? Examine paragraph 8. What do the words *acquit* and *accusation* mean in this context? What did the doubtful townspeople know? How did they know it? What actions did they take, and what were the results?

7.　What legal reform by the Massachusetts governor led to an end to the Salem witch trials? Explain. What is the "spectral evidence" mentioned in paragraph 9? How were the outcomes of the trials different without that kind of evidence?

ACTIVITY 2.3 continued

8 Tell the students to pause after paragraph 11 and describe the likely causes of what was interpreted as "satanic possession" in 1600s Salem.

9 After reading the text the first time, guide the class in a discussion by asking the Making Observations questions. Check students' general comprehension of the text based on their observations, asking follow-up questions as needed.

10 **RETURNING TO THE TEXT:**
Guide students to return to the text
to respond to the text-dependent
questions. Invite them to work in
small groups to reread the text
and answer the questions. Remind
them to use text evidence in their
responses.

11 Move from group to group and
listen in as students answer the text-
dependent questions. If they have
difficulty, scaffold the questions by
rephrasing them or breaking them
down into smaller parts. See the
Scaffolding the Text-Dependent
Questions boxes for suggestions.

2.3

Returning to the Text

- Reread the article to answer these text-dependent questions. Use text evidence to support your responses.
- Write any additional questions you have about the text in your Reader/Writer Notebook.

2. In paragraphs 1 and 2, what text hints at Shapiro's opinion about Martha Carrier's trial? What is that opinion?

Shapiro has a low opinion of the trial. Shapiro includes Martha Carrier's statement that she has been accused by "folks that are out of their wits." The author goes on to begin paragraph 2 by characterizing the summer of the witch trials as "the most notorious in Massachusetts history."

3. What ironic situation does Shapiro describe in paragraph 3?

Midway through the paragraph, she explains that "those who 'confessed' to witchcraft were spared; only those who insisted on their innocence were hanged." It is ironic that the accused people who told the truth—the moral action—were put to death while those who said that the false accusations were true—the immoral action—were not executed.

4. What are three possible meanings of the word *possession*? What is its meaning as it is used in paragraph 6? Include definitions from a print or online dictionary in your answer.

Possible meanings include "the state of owning something," "the state of controlling something," and "the state of being controlled by the devil or a demon." Paragraph 6 contains the word in its third sense.

5. Examine the accusations Shapiro describes in paragraph 6. What can be inferred from the similarities of those accusations?

The first three women the afflicted girls named as their "tormentors" were Tituba, who was considered a pagan; Sarah Good, a strange beggar given to muttering; and Sarah Osborne, who was a known fornicator. It can be inferred that all of them were accused at least in part because they were outsiders who were looked down upon by good, practicing Puritans.

Scaffolding the Text-Dependent Questions

8. What does the text of paragraphs 11 and 12 indicate about the purpose, audience, and message of Shapiro's essay? Reread the paragraphs. What is their tone? What do the words *hysteria* and *theology* mean in this context? What is the central point of each of the two paragraphs? What can be inferred from Shapiro's word choice and her references to experts? RI.11-12.6

6. How did townspeople with misgivings about the Salem witch trials attempt to put an end to them? How successful were they?

According to Shapiro, several townspeople with misgivings "came to the defense of some of the accused citizens, and others testified that they had heard an afflicted girl saying she had made at least one accusation 'for sport.'" Their efforts had little effect, however, mostly due to the convincingly frightening behavior of the "afflicted."

7. What legal reform by the Massachusetts governor led to an end to the Salem witch trials? Explain.

The governor ruled out the use of "spectral evidence," which Shapiro explains is "otherworldly evidence invisible to everyone but the person testifying." Without that kind of evidence, it became virtually impossible to convict any more of the accused.

8. What does the text of paragraphs 11 and 12 indicate about the purpose, audience, and message of Shapiro's essay?

The descriptive tone of these paragraphs indicates that the essay's purpose is to inform. Paragraph 11 contains the message that hysteria was the likely cause of the girls' affliction, and paragraph 12 elaborates that adults with their own agendas took advantage of the situation. Shapiro's use of terms like *clinical hysteria* and her references to experts suggest that her audience is educated people.

12 Have students find words and phrases in the article that demonstrate the meaning of the vocabulary words and the key ideas those words support. Have students complete the vocabulary investigation by completing student step 10 with their groups.

2.3

Working from the Text

9. What connections can you make between the article you just read and the primary sources in the previous activity? Use the vocabulary you learned in this activity in your response.

10. Skim Shapiro's article to find a phrase or sentence that contains each vocabulary term on the chart. Then state a key idea of the essay that is supported by that phrase or sentence. You may repeat key ideas.

Vocabulary Term and Context	Key Idea about the Salem Witch Trials
accusation: "Despite the fact that young girls made the accusations, it was the adults who lodged formal charges ..."	The witch trials were engineered by adults.
hysteria: "Today many scholars believe it was clinical hysteria that set off the girls in Tituba's kitchen."	Nobody in Salem was really possessed by Satan.
Puritanism: "For girls raised in Puritanism, which demanded lifelong discipline and self-control ..."	Puritanism itself contributed to the witch hunt hysteria.
spectral evidence: "The governor ruled out the use of spectral evidence ..."	Much of the evidence that convicted "witches" was not rational or valid.
theology: "[T]here were few outlets for youthful imagination except in the grim lessons of Puritan theology."	Puritanism itself contributed to the witch hunt hysteria.

11. In your groups, hold a discussion about the Salem witch trials as they are presented in the article. Try using as many of the vocabulary terms that you learned during your discussion as possible. One member of your group should note each "hit," or each time a group member appropriately uses one of the terms in an oral response. At the end of the discussion, add up the hits to see how well your group did at using acquired content vocabulary in its oral response.

☑ **Focus on the Sentence**

Use the image and the information you have learned so far about the Salem witch trials to answer the questions that follow. Then use what you know about sentence expansion to develop the kernel sentence into an informative caption. Try to include two or three of the content vocabulary terms you learned in this activity in your caption.

Kernel: A young girl has a fit.

When? during a witch trial

Where? in a courtroom in Salem, Massachusetts

Why? because she believes she's being afflicted by witchcraft

Expanded Sentence:

During a witch trial in Salem, Massachusetts, a young girl has a fit because she believes she's being afflicted by witchcraft.

13 Display the image that accompanies the Focus on the Sentence section and tell students that what they have learned so far (including the vocabulary words) provides the information needed to complete the activity. Have students complete the activity individually, answering questions as needed.

ASSESS

Review students' responses to the Focus on the Sentence task. Check to make sure that students are using the newly acquired vocabulary from the activity and that they can express a key idea from the text.

ADAPT

If students need extra support evaluating details from the text to determine key ideas, consider having them use a **Key Ideas and Details** graphic organizer while they read.

PLAN

Materials: *The Crucible*, including "A Note on the Historical Accuracy of This Play" and Act One; index cards with character names and lines, small notebook and pencil or pen for each student
Suggested Pacing: 1 50-minute class period

TEACH

1 Read the Learning Targets and Preview sections with students. Tell them that in this activity, they will begin to learn about the characters in Arthur Miller's *The Crucible*.

2 Have students read the About the Author section on Arthur Miller. Ask students to speculate about what in his life experiences and profession might have helped lead him to write *The Crucible*.

3 Read aloud the first paragraph of the *The Crucible* section. Explain that the last sentence of that paragraph is basically a plan for what students will be doing for the remainder of this unit.

4 Work with the title, as the term *crucible* will probably be unfamiliar. Ask students to guess at its meaning by writing down and defining words that have the same root: *crucify, crucial, crucifix*.

5 Give students the two major definitions of *crucible*: "a container used for melting metals at extremely high heat" and "a severe test of belief." Ask students to predict which definition Miller had in mind for his story. Then invite them to consider the possibility that both definitions might be used in a related manner. Be sure to come back to this word as the play progresses and the conflicts intensify.

Learning Strategies

Drama Game
Note-taking
Predicting
Previewing

Learning Targets

- Analyze a dramatic text to determine appropriate tone and inflection to convey meaning.
- Analyze texts and make inferences based on textual evidence.

Preview

In this activity, you will play drama games as a way of meeting the characters in Arthur Miller's *The Crucible*.

My Notes

About the Author

Arthur Miller (1915–2005) was born in New York to a family of Polish immigrants. He started writing plays in college and went on to win many awards for his writing. His plays *Death of a Salesman*, which won the Pulitzer Prize, and *The Crucible* have found permanent places in American culture. After writing *The Crucible*, Miller was called in front of the House Un-American Activities Committee, where he refused to name other "Communists."

The Crucible

Arthur Miller is a leader among the ranks of writers who use their art to comment on social issues. Miller created *The Crucible* to speak his conscience; he uncovered a setting, developed compelling characters through masterful characterization, created dialogue rich with metaphor and purpose, and structured a plot that transformed ideas into a drama of such persuasive appeal that it continues to speak to audiences all over the world. The most complete way to appreciate a drama of this caliber is to read it, perform it, view it, and, finally, emulate it.

1. Begin by thinking about the title and the meaning of the word *crucible*.

2. Listen closely as the text of the preface is read aloud. What can you infer about why Miller may have felt compelled to begin the play in this manner?

College and Career Readiness Standards

Focus Standards:

RL.11-12.1 Cite strong and thorough textual evidence to support analysis of what the text says explicitly as well as inferences drawn from the text, including determining where the text leaves matters uncertain.

RL.11-12.4 Determine the meaning of words and phrases as they are used in the text, including figurative and connotative meanings; analyze the impact of specific word choices on meaning and tone, including words with multiple meanings or language that is particularly fresh, engaging, or beautiful.

Introducing the Strategy: Drama Games

Drama games are a form of role-playing. Performing a role helps you make meaning of a text and understand it from the viewpoint of both a reader and a performer. Drama games require imagination, teamwork, and rehearsal. They also require a sharing of ideas to help make a text come alive in a visual way.

Drama Game

3. Follow your teacher's instructions to prepare to play the drama game. As needed, ask your teacher or peers clarifying questions to make sure that you understand the task.

Character: Reverend Parris

Line 1: You will confess yourself or I will take you out and whip you to your death, Tituba!

Line 2: How can it be the Devil? Why would he choose my house to strike? We have all manner of licentious people in the village! (to Hale)

Line 3: Rebecca, Rebecca, go to her, we're lost. She suddenly cannot bear to hear the Lord's-

Character: Tituba

Line 1: And I say, "You lie, Devil, you lie!" And then he come one stormy night to me, and he say, "Look! I have white people belong to me. And I look—and there was Goody Good."

Line 2: Mister Reverend, I do believe somebody else be witchin' these children.

Line 3: No, no, don't hang Tituba! I tell him I don't desire to work for him, sir. (to Hale)

Character: Reverend Hale

Line 1: Now let me instruct you. We cannot look to superstition in this. The Devil is precise; the marks of his presence are definite as stone. (to Putnam and Parris)

Line 2: We shall need hard study if it comes to tracking down the Old Boy.

Line 3: Tituba, you must have no fear to tell us who they are, do you understand? We will protect you. The Devil can never overcome a minister. You know that, do you not?

Character: Giles Corey

Line 1: Mr. Hale, I have always wanted to ask a learned man—what signifies the readin' of strange books?

Line 2: A fart on Thomas Putnam, that is what I say to that!

Line 3: I will not give you no name. I mentioned my wife's name once and I'll burn in hell long enough for that. I stand mute.

Character: Rebecca Nurse

Line 1: Goody Ann! You sent a child to conjure up the dead?

Line 2: This will set us all to arguin' again in the society, and we thought to have peace this year.

Line 3: I fear it, I fear it. Let us rather blame ourselves and

Character: John Proctor

Line 1: Can you speak one minute without we land in Hell again? I am sick of Hell.

6 Next, conduct a shared reading of Miller's preface to the book: "A Note on the Historical Accuracy of This Play." Ask students to discuss why Miller might have felt compelled to begin his play with a "commentary" about the people and events of Salem during the time of the trials. In this commentary and in other notes that precede and follow the play, Miller takes great pains to emphasize that although his play is a work of fiction, it is based on actual events. Why do you think he reiterates this point?

7 Introduce the **Drama Games** strategy by explaining that it is just what the name implies: a game based on a dramatic work, in this case Arthur Miller's *The Crucible*. There are enough characters and lines provided in the Drama Game section to accommodate 24 students before duplication becomes necessary. Prepare the cards before class, with each one referencing one character and quoting one line.

8 Explain the rules of the game to the class. Tell them that they will each be receiving an index card with the name of a character from *The Crucible* and a line from the play spoken by that character. They will also be given a notepad and pencil or pen.

9 They will be given time to learn their name and memorize and rehearse their line. When the game begins, they will "assume character" and move about the room as though they are guests at a tea party. As they meet other characters, they are to write down the characters' names and make brief inferences and predictions based on their lines.

10 Give students the opportunity to ask clarifying questions as needed to make sure they understand the instructions. For your EL students, this may be an appropriate time to model the types of questions one may ask to obtain information.

11 Allow enough time for each student to introduce himself or herself to several others. Afterward, students will divide by character into eight discussion groups. These groups will scan Act One of the play and read and discuss the commentary written about that group's character. Like characters should share their lines, exposing each of them to all three lines to support making further inferences and predictions.

12 Give students time to respond to the Check Your Understanding task. Let them interact with one another as necessary to complete the task.

ASSESS

Review students' responses to the Check Your Understanding task. Note whether they made predictions about a character other than their own using text evidence and whether they confirmed or corrected those predictions.

ADAPT

If students need additional help becoming familiar with characters from *The Crucible*, invite them to look at all three quote cards for a single character. Have them make inferences based on the character's three lines and examine information about that character in Act One of the play to find support or correction for their inferences.

Line 2: I come to see what mischief your uncle's brewin' now. Put it out of mind, Abby.

Line 3: Ah, you're wicked yet, aren't y'!

Character: Abigail Williams

Line 1: Can I have a soft word, John?

Line 2: My name is good in the village! I will not have it said my name is soiled! Goody Proctor is a gossiping liar!

Line 3: I danced for the Devil; I saw him; I wrote in his book.

Character: Mr. Putnam

Line 1: ... Mr. Hale. We look to you to come to our house and save our child.

Line 2: Why, we are surely gone wild this year. What anarchy is this? That tract is in my bounds, it's in my bounds, Mr. Proctor.

Line 3: That is a notorious sign of witchcraft afoot, Goody Nurse, a prodigious sign!

4. You will now move around the room as though you are a guest at a tea party. Introduce yourself to your classmates as if you are your assigned character and then give your line. Try to interact with as many classmates as possible. As you meet other characters, note inferences and predictions based on their lines.

5. After the activity, join the others who were assigned your character. Compare information and make inferences about your character based on the quotes you have been given.

☑ Check Your Understanding

Choose a character other than your own, and examine the predictions you made about that character in step 4. Compare your predictions to that character's quotes, and write a few sentences explaining whether the quotes support or contradict your prediction. If necessary, correct your prediction to make it accurate.

The Beginnings of Characterization

Learning Targets

- Make inferences about character motivations by analyzing actions and dialogue.
- Explain how a playwright develops a character in a script.
- Evaluate the author's use of foils to develop a main character.

Preview

In this activity, you will establish a routine for analyzing the development of characters throughout the play.

Motivations

Characters in a work of literature act in ways that advance the plot. As is true of people in real life, fictional characters have reasons for the things they do. Those reasons are called **motivation**.

Sometimes characters react to situations in which they find themselves. Those actions are a result of external motivation. Other times characters act according to their worldviews, values, or personality traits. Those actions are prompted by internal motivation.

Often, as in *The Crucible*, character behaviors and motivations contribute to moral dilemmas. Those dilemmas further motivate characters and move the plot along.

A writer must have a clear understanding of character motivation to make those characters believable. Writers must also clearly present those motivations, either implicitly or explicitly, to make a play or other work believable.

1. Your teacher will assign you a character. Read the commentary sections in Act One that pertain to your character and try to find specific details. Use the Character Note-taking Chart to take notes on your character, writing down words and phrases from the text that describe your character's behaviors and reveal underlying motivations.

2. Use what you already know about the Salem witch trials and your character notes to participate in a class discussion. Complete notes on your chart as different character groups report to the class. Subsequently, as you continue to read the play, add information about characters to your note-taking chart.

Learning Strategies

Graphic Organizer
Note-taking

My Notes

College and Career Readiness Standards

Focus Standards:

RL.11-12.1 Cite strong and thorough textual evidence to support analysis of what the text says explicitly as well as inferences drawn from the text, including determining where the text leaves matters uncertain.

RL.11-12.3 Analyze the impact of the author's choices regarding how to develop and relate elements of a story or drama (e.g., where a story is set, how the action is ordered, how the characters are introduced and developed).

ACTIVITY 2.5

PLAN

Materials: *The Crucible*, Act One; , poster paper
Suggested Pacing: 2 50-minute class periods

TEACH

1 Read the Learning Targets and Preview with students. Tell them that in this activity, they will learn methods for analyzing characters in a play.

2 Read aloud the first four paragraphs of the Motivations section. Make certain students have a clear understanding of the difference between external motivation and internal motivation.

3 Divide the class into the same character groups from the previous activity. Instruct groups to read the commentary sections that pertain to their character and scan Act One. They should use that information to complete that character's row on the Character Note-taking Chart.

 TEACHER TO TEACHER

The words and page numbers are from the Penguin paperback edition (2003) of *The Crucible*.

4 Ask different character groups to report to the class one at a time, starting with John Proctor. As the group reports, create a class to work as a poster-sized graphic organizer with Proctor at the center. Add the details they share to the organizer. Repeat this process with the remaining characters. Keep the organizers visible in the classroom and update them as new details are learned about each character.

5 Once the chart is completed, have students work independently to complete the Focus on the Sentence section. Model completing the sentence frames with one character.

6 Read aloud the information explaining what makes a character a foil, including the definition of the term and the first paragraph of the Character Foils section. To **activate prior knowledge**, allow students to **think-pair-share** about foils encountered in familiar literature and film.

7 Conduct a shared reading of Act One, moving through it rather quickly to familiarize students with the play's plot, characters, and style. Students should pay special attention to the traits of Hale, Proctor, and Corey as they read by **annotating the text.** You might direct students' attention to the following:

- The scene prior to Proctor's first entrance when the girls are alone together and the actual events in the wood are revealed
- Students' perceptions about who is in control in Act One and why
- Possible motivations of Tituba and the girls for lying
- How hysteria is taking root

Character Note-taking Chart

Character	Textual Evidence	Inferences about Character Motivations
Reverend Parris	"villainous," "persecuted" (pp. 3–4)	Motivated by a lack of morality and by paranoia
Tituba	"frightened" (pp. 7–8)	Motivated by fear
Abigail	"dissembling" (pp. 8–9)	Motivated by dishonesty and a need to manipulate
Mr. Putnam	"vindictive," "smirched" (pp. 14–15)	Motivated by anger
John Proctor	"fraud," "sinner" (pp. 20–21)	Motivated by dishonesty and self-seeking
Francis and Rebecca Nurse	respected landowners (pp. 24–26)	Motivated by a desire to keep order
Reverend Hale	"specialist," "intellectual" (p. 34)	Motivated by a desire to find objective truth
Giles Corey	"crank," "nuisance," "innocent," "brave" (p. 38)	Motivated by honesty and an uneducated point of view

☑ Focus on the Sentence

Choose one character from the chart and complete the following sentence frames about that character's actions and motivations using *because*, *but*, and *so*.

...........acts/does/says.........................because.........................

...........acts/does/says........................., but.........................

...........acts/does/says........................., so.........................

Character Foils

A **foil** is a character who is placed in a work to provide a contrast to a more important character. This literary device stresses a main character's traits by giving an example of what the opposite of those traits looks like.

3. Return to Act One to note words and phrases that describe character traits of John Proctor, John Hale, and Giles Corey.

4. John Hale and Giles Corey can be seen as character foils to John Proctor, the main character. This juxtaposition of characters highlights key attributes of the major character. With your class, begin a class poster that lists the similarities and differences in actions and attitudes between Proctor and Hale and between Proctor and Corey. Use the table to make notes about these characters.

Hale	Proctor	Corey

☑ Check Your Understanding

Write a few sentences that analyze how Miller develops Proctor's character in Act One by juxtaposing him against Reverend Hale or Giles Corey.

LITERARY

A foil is a secondary character who is contrasted with the main character to offer insights into facets of the main character.

VOCABULARY

ⓘ **INDEPENDENT READING LINK**

Read and Discuss

Discuss with classmates the types of characters or people you have encountered in your independent reading. Make notes in your Reader/Writer Notebook regarding how these characters or people fit within the setting of the work. What inferences are you able to make about characters and their motivations? What predictions are you able to make regarding these characters, and why?

8 **Vocabulary Development:** Review the meaning of the term *foil* with students. Have them work in pairs to define the term in their own words and think of both examples and non-examples.

9 Complete student step 4 in the Character Foils section. Ask students to share their ideas about Hale, Proctor, and Corey, and create a poster that contrasts Proctor with Hale and Corey. Tell students that you will add to the poster as the play proceeds.

10 Give students time to respond to the Check Your Understanding task. Consider allowing students to work in pairs to develop their character analyses.

11 Make sure to attend to the Independent Reading Link. Direct them to take notes in their Reader/Writer Notebooks stating inferences and predictions about characters they have encountered in their independent reading. To assess their independent reading, set a date to check for those notes in students' notebooks.

ASSESS

Student responses to the Check Your Understanding task should show an ability to connect actions and dialogue to demonstrate character traits that contribute to the theme. Students will need to make these connections in writing their own scene for the Embedded Assessment.

ADAPT

Have students define three main traits each for Proctor, Hale, and Corey, using their notes as a guide. Then have students locate specific examples of how Miller conveys these traits using action and dialogue in Act One. Tell students to write each example next to the trait it exemplifies. Have students use this information in their analysis.

PLAN

Materials: *The Crucible*, Act One; Optional: DVD of *The Crucible* (1996), dir. Nicholas Hytner, DVD player
Suggested Pacing: 2 50-minute class periods

TEACH

1 Read the Learning Targets and Preview with students. Tell them that they will be analyzing a dramatic text in preparation for a presentation of their own.

2 **Vocabulary Development:** Ask students to work with a partner to brainstorm words to define the concept of *subtext*. Be sure students have a clear grasp of subtext before moving into the scene interpretation. You might spend additional time on subtext by posting a line such as "This has been a great day" on the board. Ask students for possible subtexts of that line, which would be conveyed by a character's gestures, movements, facial expressions, and delivery. Some additional possibilities:

"It truly has been awesome." (genuine)

"This was a terrible day." (sarcastic)

"I never expected my day to end up like this." (surprised)

3 Divide students into groups of three and direct them to complete student step 1 in the Drama Study section. Ask pairs to think-pair-share about different ways a director might want to represent the relationship between Abigail and Proctor. Students should imagine the movements, gestures, facial expressions, and delivery between the characters by discussing and even speaking the lines in various ways. Guide them to an understanding that the lines from the play can project very different subtexts depending on how they are presented.

Pivotal Scene 1: Considering Interpretations

Learning Strategies

Graphic Organizer
Note-taking
Rereading

VOCABULARY

LITERARY
Subtext is the underlying meaning in dialogue in a book, movie, play, or film. Not explicitly stated, subtext includes the thoughts of a character that may—or may not—coincide with his or her spoken words.

My Notes

_____

Learning Targets

- Collaborate on preparing a dramatic presentation.
- Evaluate implicit and explicit meanings of a dramatic text as a means of interpreting a scene.
- Analyze the effect of character motivation on the plot of a dramatic work.

Preview

In this activity, you will study lines from *The Crucible* to interpret the relationship between Proctor and Abigail. Then you will examine how that relationship helps shape the moral dilemmas of the play's plot.

Drama Study

1. Imagine that you are the director of a stage version of *The Crucible*. You must decide how you will portray the relationship between Proctor and Abigail. Discuss with a partner the different ways you could enact the following lines from Act One based on the **subtext**, different interpretations you may have of the nature of their relationship:

PROCTOR, *gently pressing her from him, with great sympathy but firmly*: Child—

ABIGAIL, *with a flash of anger*: How do you call me child!

PROCTOR: Abby, I may think of you softly from time to time. But I will cut off my hand before I'll ever reach for you again. Wipe it out of mind. We never touched, Abby.

ABIGAIL: Aye, but we did.

PROCTOR: Aye, but we did not.

ABIGAIL, *with a bitter anger*: Oh, I marvel how such a strong man may let such a sickly wife be—

College and Career Readiness Standards

Focus Standards:

SL.11-12.1 Initiate and participate effectively in a range of collaborative discussions (one-on-one, in groups, and teacher-led) with diverse partners on grades 11–12 topics, texts, and issues, building on others' ideas and expressing their own clearly and persuasively.

RL.11-12.3 Analyze the impact of the author's choices regarding how to develop and relate elements of a story or drama (e.g., where a story is set, how the action is ordered, how the characters are introduced and developed).

W.11-12.9 Draw evidence from literary or informational texts to support analysis, reflection, and research.

2. Following are three possible interpretations of the relationship between Proctor and Abigail. Reread the entire scene in which they are alone for the first time and create gestures, blocking (movements), facial expressions, and vocal delivery to match the different interpretive subtexts suggested. Be sure to identify the specific lines where the stage directions would apply.

Proctor Is in Love with Abigail				
Line	Gestures	Movements (from Stage Directions)	Facial Expressions	Vocal Delivery
Proctor, gently pressing her from him, with great sympathy but firmly: Child –	Obvious gentleness in his hands as he holds her at length; possibly a lengthy holding before he firmly moves her aside	Holding her in a lingering fashion before pushing her gently from him	A serious look that recognizes his own sin, his desire for her, and his need to do the greater good and cut all ties to her	Speaking to her as a father to a child, tenderly, as if trying to win her over as a naïve youth

3. How do the stage directions support the interpretation that Proctor is in love with Abigail and focus your understanding of this scene's staging and blocking choices?

Proctor's "gently pressing her from him, with great sympathy" reveals the desire that he still feels for Abigail, especially his desire to comfort her in her tears, suggesting that she has disclosed secret fears and desires of her own to him in an intimate moment.

Proctor Hates Abigail				
Line	Gestures	Movements	Facial Expressions	Vocal Delivery

ACTIVITY 2.6 continued

4 Assist students in visualizing alternate interpretations of the dramatic text. Help them fill out the first **graphic organizer** in student step 2 ("Proctor Is in Love with Abigail"). Be sure that they are referring to specific theatrical choices (especially about blocking, or actors' movements) tied to specific lines from the scene.

5 Support students in answering the question posed in student step 3. Use their answers to support an understanding of the concept of subtext.

6 Have the student groups complete the second two graphic organizers and respond to the question that follows each.

7 Guide each group in conceiving and performing two alternate interpretations of the scene. Allow time for groups to discuss among themselves what constitutes effective gestures, movements, expressions, and vocal delivery for each interpretation. If time permits, have each group present to the class the interpretation they consider most effective. Afterward, discuss with students which interpretation they believe Arthur Miller most likely had in mind.

LEVELED DIFFERENTIATED INSTRUCTION

In this activity, students may need support performing the assigned scene in front of peers.

Developing Provide students with the **Collaborative Dialogue** graphic organizer and allow time for students to copy the lines of the scene completely into the Speaker 1 (Proctor) and Speaker 2 (Abigail) sections. Allow time for partners to practice reading the parts back and forth until they feel confident and fluent. Applaud students for their performance even if they are unable to add movement or gestures.

Expanding Provide students with the **Collaborative Dialogue** graphic organizer and allow time for students to jot down cues, notes, or other speaking points from the scenes to help them remember their lines while performing. Allow time for partners to practice reading the parts back and forth until they feel confident and fluent. Encourage them to rehearse adding movements and gestures while performing.

Bridging Have students use the **Collaborative Dialogue** graphic organizer to jot down notes to help them remember their lines while performing. Allow them to read from the organizer but encourage them to incorporate gestures, movements, expressions, and vocal delivery to help bring their characters to life.

Extend Encourage students who feel confident enough in their acting abilities to memorize their parts. Prepare to cue students who miss a line while performing and applaud their bravery.

★ **TEACHER TO TEACHER**

A film version of *The Crucible* is available on DVD, or it can be streamed on one of several video streaming sites, such as YouTube, Amazon, Vudu, Google Play, or iTunes. If you wish to incorporate the film, show Scene 1 and then ask **discussion groups** the following questions:

- Which interpretation does the director seem to have in mind? Why?
- Do you see any of your choices in the film version?
- How might you have filmed the scene differently? Why?

4. How do the stage directions support the interpretation that Proctor hates Abigail and focus your understanding of this scene's staging and blocking choices?

Proctor Is Conflicted in His Feelings for Abigail				
Line	Gestures	Movements	Facial Expressions	Vocal Delivery

5. How do the stage directions you have added support the interpretation that Proctor is conflicted in his feelings for Abigail and focus your understanding of this scene's staging and blocking choices?

6. **Perform a Scene:** Now that your group has considered three interpretations of the scene, choose two of these interpretations to enact in a live performance. Take turns acting and observing the acting. When you play the role of actor, be sure to incorporate gestures, movements, expressions, and vocal delivery from your notes. When you play the role of director/audience, provide specific feedback to the performers about their performances. Suggest movements or expressions that you think will make the performances more convincing.

The Crucible by Arthur Miller, directed by Yael Farber, opened at The Old Vic Theatre on March 7, 2014 with Richard Armitage as John Proctor and Samantha Corley as Abigail Williams.

Moral Dilemma

7. In the scene between Proctor and Abigail, Proctor displays evidence of conflicting motivations. What are the conflicting motivations? Cite textual evidence to support your response.

8. When you have completed Act One, analyze how Proctor's behaviors and motivations create a moral dilemma and keep notes in the table about how that dilemma influences the plot and theme of *The Crucible*.

Proctor's Moral Dilemma	Influence on the Plot and Theme

Check Your Understanding

Write a few sentences about the experience of trying out different interpretations. Which interpretation worked best? Why?

INDEPENDENT READING LINK

Read and Respond

In your Reader/Writer Notebook, analyze and interpret an important scene from your independent reading. What movements, gestures, facial expressions, and words contribute to an understanding of the relationships between characters or people? In what ways might these dramatic elements be changed to shift the characters' feelings about one another?

8 Have students consider the content in the Moral Dilemma section. Instruct them to keep notes in the graphic organizer as directed.

9 Give students time to respond to the Check Your Understanding task. Consider allowing them to work within their groups as they write about their interpretations.

10 Make sure students attend to the Independent Reading Link. Direct them to compose an analysis of an important scene from the text they are reading in their Reader/Writer Notebooks. To assess their independent reading, set a date to check for the analysis in students' notebooks.

ASSESS

Review students' sentences about trying out various interpretations of the scene. Make sure that responses clearly indicate which interpretations work best and provide logical reasons and evidence for these choices.

ADAPT

If students need additional help choosing which interpretation works best and why, help them evaluate each interpretation. Do any of the interpretations have gestures, movements, or facial expressions that seemed forced, out of place, or comical? Which interpretation seems most believable?

ACTIVITY 2.7

PLAN

Materials: *The Crucible*, Act One
Suggested Pacing: 1 50-minute class period

TEACH

1 Read the Learning Targets and Preview with students, making sure they understand that they will be examining the features that combine to form a successful script.

2 **Activate prior knowledge** about script writing using the following questions to facilitate a group discussion:

• Why are scripts written?
• How are scripts similar to and different from short stories or novels?
• What are some features of scripts?

3 Form four student groups and assign each group one of the four elements of script writing to analyze. Have students scan the portion of *The Crucible* that they have studied so far (Act One) and **mark the text**.

4 Guide students to create their own **graphic organizers** for **note-taking**. These organizers should contain the focus analysis questions as well as examples from the text. Each student should have his or her own copy of the organizer.

5 Reassign students into **discussion groups** with at least one student per group representing each script-writing element. Have each group complete the **jigsaw** by taking turns sharing notes and insights.

6 After each element has been shared, instruct students to complete the Check Your Understanding task by creating script-writing checklists to guide their writing throughout the rest of the unit.

ASSESS

Review students' responses to the Check Your Understanding task. In reviewing students' script-writing checklists, look for a reasonably complete roster of script elements.

ADAPT

If student groups need help generating a list of script-writing elements, lead students to generate a class script-writing checklist.

Learning Strategies

Graphic Organizer
Note-taking
Skimming/Scanning

My Notes

Learning Targets

• Examine how a scriptwriter uses literary elements, structure, print and graphic features, and language to develop a drama.
• Take notes to construct a checklist of elements for successful script writing.

Preview

In this activity, you will analyze the elements of a dramatic script. You will then construct a script-writing checklist addressing those elements: literary elements, structure, language, and print features.

Elements of a Dramatic Script

1. Embedded Assessment 1 will ask you to write and perform an original dramatic script. It is important that you be familiar with the elements of a script. Now that you have read Act One of *The Crucible*, take a few minutes with a partner to scan the text of *The Crucible* for the characteristics of a script.

2. On your own paper, create a four-square graphic organizer like the one shown. Use the guiding questions in the organizer to help you analyze the text for the elements of a script. For each of the areas, provide a sample from *The Crucible*.

Narrative Elements	Structure
• How do character and motivation influence the plot? • How is conflict introduced? • How does conflict advance the story? • Who speaks the most, and why? • How does the setting influence the characters and their actions?	• How does the writer develop events to create action? • How do dramatic shifts advance the plot and increase knowledge of the characters? • How does the text structure support the author's purpose? • How does the division of the play into acts create certain affects like suspense?
Language	**Print Features**
• How does the writer use diction and syntax in the dialogue to convey a particular time and place? • How does the writer develop mood, tone, and voice through language (syntax and diction)?	• What conventions of script writing are demonstrated by the play? • How do the stage directions contribute to the story? • How do the author's notations enhance understanding of the work?

☑ Check Your Understanding

Generate a script-writing checklist to use when you compose scripts. This checklist should address each element discussed here.

College and Career Readiness Standards

Focus Standards:

RL.11-12.3 Analyze the impact of the author's choices regarding how to develop and relate elements of a story or drama (e.g., where a story is set, how the action is ordered, how the characters are introduced and developed).

W.11-12.9 Draw evidence from literary or informational texts to support analysis, reflection, and research.

Additional Standards Addressed:

W.11-12.5

Illuminating Hysteria: Characters, Conflict, and Social Commentary

Learning Targets
- Evaluate how the motif of hysteria in *The Crucible* advances the plot and sheds light on the theme.
- Create a script for one dramatic scene.

Preview

In this activity, you will evaluate how the motif of hysteria advances *The Crucible*'s plot and illuminates its theme. Then you will write a scene that shows hysteria growing from rumor and unfounded accusations.

Learning Strategies

Graphic Organizer
Note-taking
Rereading
Skimming/Scanning
Summarizing
Word Maps

LITERARY

A **motif** is a recurrent thematic element—such as hysteria, a crucible, or witchcraft—or pattern—such as the Hero's Journey.

VOCABULARY

Motif

1. One **motif** in *The Crucible* is hysteria. The final scene in Act One shows the girls hysterically yelling out the names of people they have seen with the devil. While it is possible that each of the girls is simply lying, it is also possible that they, or at least some of them, are in the grip of hysteria. Eventually, much of the town succumbs to this hysteria. What reasons can you generate for the girls' hysterical behavior? Brainstorm possibilities in the margin and share your ideas with your group.

2. Use the word map to take notes during a class discussion of *hysteria*.

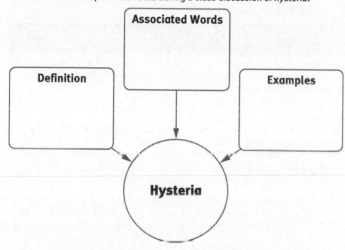

My Notes

3. To help you distinguish *rumor* from *hysteria*, reread the following excerpt from the article "The Lessons of Salem" by Laura Shapiro that you read in Activity 2.3, which provides historical information about hysteria. Mark the text for possible explanations for the girls' behavior. Be prepared to share them in a class discussion.

College and Career Readiness Standards

Focus Standards:

RL.11-12.3 Analyze the impact of the author's choices regarding how to develop and relate elements of a story or drama (e.g., where a story is set, how the action is ordered, how the characters are introduced and developed).

W.11-12.4 Produce clear and coherent writing in which the development, organization, and style are appropriate to task, purpose, and audience.

Additional Standards Addressed:

W.11-12.3a, W.11-12.3b, W.11-12.5

PLAN

Suggested Pacing: 2 50-minute class periods plus homework

TEACH

1 Read the Learning Targets and Preview with students, making sure that they understand that this activity will require them to write a short dramatic script.

2 **Vocabulary Development:** Review the meaning of the term *motif* with students. Have them work in pairs to define the term in their own words. Help students generate examples of a motif from literature, the media, or their personal observations. Be sure they understand that a motif is defined not only as a thematic element but also as a recurrent thematic element.

3 Address with students the information in the first portion of the Motif section. Encourage them to brainstorm possible causes of the girls' hysterical behavior. List their thoughts on the board.

4 Write the word *hysteria* on the board. Draw a circle around it and reproduce the word map from the second portion of the Motif section. Use a print or online source to determine the various possible meanings of the word and identify the definition that relates most effectively to the text. Enter the definition into the word map and then complete the word map with associated words and examples of the concept.

5 Ask students to independently complete student step 3 in the Motif section. Direct them to read and mark to text of the excerpt to distinguish the difference between *rumors* ("accusations that might or might not be factual that tend to spread throughout a community, becoming more embellished along the way") and *hysteria* ("overwhelming emotional reactions, usually of fear, that cause people to behave impulsively or dramatically"). Conduct a class discussion about the terms to ensure students clearly understand the meaning of both.

6 Ask students to independently complete Working from the Text section. Assist them as necessary in completing the graphic organizer.

2.8

Today many scholars believe it was clinical hysteria that set off the girls in Tituba's kitchen. Fits, convulsions, vocal outbursts, feelings of being pinched and bitten—all of these symptoms have been witnessed and described, most often in young women, for centuries. Sometimes the seizures have been attributed to Satan, other times to God, but ever since Freud weighed in, hysteria has been traced to the unconscious. As Dr. Richard Pohl, of Salem Hospital, told a Tercentenary symposium, hysteria "can mimic all the physical diseases known to man," and occurs when repressed thoughts and emotions burst forth and take over the body. Life could be dreary for girls in 17th century Salem: their place was home and their duty was obedience; many were illiterate, and there were few outlets for youthful imagination except in the grim lessons of Puritan theology. Dabbling in magic in the reverend's own kitchen would have been wonderfully scary, perhaps enough to release psychic demons lurking since childhood.

Despite the fact that young girls made the accusations, it was the adults who lodged formal charges against their neighbors and provided most of the testimony. Historians have long believed that local feuds and property disputes were behind many of the accusations, and in *Salem Possessed* (1974), Paul Boyer and Stephen Nissenbaum uncovered patterns of social and civic antagonism that made the community fertile ground for a witch hunt …

Working from the Text

4. Consult your word map and the text of the play to track the growth of hysteria in Act One of *The Crucible*. Chart the growth.

Page Reference	Relevant Text	Part the Text Plays in "Hysteria" Motif
9	ABIGAIL: Uncle, the rumor of witchcraft is all about; I think you'd best go down and deny it yourself.	It sets up the idea that a mass anxiety about witchcraft has taken root.
10	PARRIS: … I saw Tituba waving her arms over the fire when I came on you. Why was she doing that? And I heard a screeching and gibberish comin' from her mouth …	It creates an image of a physical way in which the hysteria might manifest.

5. How do the girls' behaviors contribute to the moral dilemmas that influence *The Crucible*'s theme? What is the nature of those dilemmas, and who faces them the most?

☑ **Focus on the Sentence**

Different types of sentences are used for different purposes. Review these four sentence types.

- A statement tells someone information.
- A question asks others for a response and ends with a question mark.
- An exclamation expresses emotion and typically ends with an exclamation point.
- A command tells another person something to do.
- A command may not have a subject because it is understood that the subject is the person or thing being addressed.

Read these sample sentences about *The Crucible*.

Statement: I read *The Crucible* in 11th grade.

Question: What is the name of John Proctor's wife in *The Crucible*?

Exclamation: This is the best play I have ever seen!

Command: You must read Act Three, so we can discuss the courtroom scene.

Write four different sentences about the hysteria mounting in Salem. Use text evidence in your responses.

Statement: _____

Question: _____

Exclamation: _____

Command: _____

 Gaining Perspectives

In *The Crucible*, the townspeople accuse each other of being witches or of being possessed by the devil based on what they have seen or been told. As you have learned, clinical hysteria can present itself if many physical ways; however, the Puritans did not always investigate people's behavior fully before passing judgment. With a partner, discuss what it would be like to be accused of wrongdoing based on your actions related to a health problem. How could you effectively communicate your health issues to others? What types of communication skills might not be effective and cause people not to believe you? When you are done, summarize your discussion in your Reader/Writer Notebook.

7 Instruct students to read the text that begins the Focus on the Sentence section. Then display the image and caption and have students complete the activity.

8 Have students work in groups to discuss and complete the Gaining Perspectives activity. Then ask a volunteer from each group to share key ideas from the group's discussion.

9 In responding to the writing prompt, suggest that students first identify the rumor in their chosen scenario and then imagine a way in which that rumor fosters hysteria. They can then use that as a guide to their script.

★ TEACHER TO TEACHER

This activity is critical to students' capacity to write and perform a scene for EA 1. It teaches students the necessary skills to develop character and conflict, both of which are critical to a scene that will convey a social message. If students struggle with the prompt, sit with pairs or groups and model how to use a plot diagram to think through the elements of the story and how these elements will work together to present conflicts and resolutions.

ASSESS

Check responses to the writing prompt to assess whether students have a clear understanding of script-writing elements. Then ask several questions about their scenarios and the scripts that emerged from them. Consider having volunteers describe the process by which they developed their scripts.

ADAPT

To increase students' understanding of the link between rumors and hysteria, have them revisit the word map from the Motif section and the graphic organizer from the Working from the Text section. Guide them in replacing the text in the graphic organizer with similar text from their own scenario.

2.8

📝 Writing Prompt: Literary

With a partner or small group, select one of the following scenarios, or create an original scenario. Write a script to illustrate it. In your scene, show how hysteria grows out of rumor and unfounded accusations. Be sure to:

• Include a dramatic scene that illuminates the injustice of hysteria.
• Format your script using the guidelines in your script-writing checklist.
• Use purposeful dialogue and stage directions.

Scenario A: You enter math class one day to find a substitute. Classmates claim the teacher has moved suddenly without telling anyone, but specific details have not yet been provided. Consider the different perspectives students might have based on their perceived knowledge of an adult's character and imagine the rumors and accusations that might begin. How might such a situation create a context for hysteria? What role might justice (or injustice) play in this scenario?

Scenario B: The morning news carries reports of outbreaks of a disease that has affected local teens and young adults. Unusual symptoms have been reported, but there is no conclusive diagnosis from the medical community. What rumors circulate among the students as they attend morning classes? What evidence suggests that these rumors might lead to hysteria? How might students respond to this type of hysteria?

Scenario C: At an all-school assembly, students receive news that the athletic program will be cut due to lack of funding. At first, students speculate over budget cuts at the state level and complain about the injustice of financial restrictions on school programs. Later, rumors of inaccurate bookkeeping within the district begin to circulate. What unfounded accusations might fuel these rumors? How might this scenario become a context for hysteria?

Performers, directed by Wang Xiaoying, stage *The Crucible* in Beijing, China, at the National Center for the Performing Arts on January 11, 2015.

📝 WRITING PROMPT: LITERARY

The following standards are addressed in the writing prompt:
• W.11-12.3a   • W.11-12.3b
• W.11-12.5

Conflicts in Salem

Learning Targets

- Analyze character motivations that cause conflict, moral and otherwise, and advance the plot.
- Analyze the role of conflict in supporting the theme of *The Crucible*.

Preview

In this activity, you will examine how *The Crucible*'s conflicts drive its action and advance one of its themes.

Learning Strategies

Graphic Organizers
Marking the Text
Note-taking
Rereading

Conflicts Driving the Action

1. Even before the accusations of witchcraft start, the people of Salem seem to be in the middle of many different conflicts. The scene just after the commentary about Rebecca illuminates several strained relationships within the community of Salem. What motivates the characters to act as they do?

2. After reading Act One, identify who is fighting with whom as well as the reasons for the conflicts. This will be essential information to know as the community starts tearing itself apart. Reread this scene and mark the text by annotating examples of these conflicts.

Character	Versus	Character	Reasons	Effects on the Plot
Girls	Versus	Adults	Girls have been dabbling in voodoo with Tituba; they are afraid of the adults and sick of being mistreated.	
Proctor	Versus	Abigail	Abigail is angry and infatuated. Proctor refuses to return her affection or even admit his affair with her.	
Parris	Versus	Proctor	Proctor can't stand that Parris is always harping about money during his preaching.	
Giles Corey	Versus	Putnam		
	Versus			
	Versus			

College and Career Readiness Standards

Focus Standards:

RL.11-12.1 Cite strong and thorough textual evidence to support analysis of what the text says explicitly as well as inferences drawn from the text, including determining where the text leaves matters uncertain.

RL.11-12.2 Determine two or more themes or central ideas of a text and analyze their development over the course of the text, including how they interact and build on one another to produce a complex account; provide an objective summary of the text.

Additional Standards Addressed:

RL.11-12.3, RL.11-12.5, W.11-12.2a, W.11-12.2b, W.11-12.2c, W.11-12.2e, W.11-12.2f

---

ACTIVITY 2.9

PLAN

Suggested Pacing: 2 50-minute class periods plus homework

TEACH

1 Read the Learning Targets and Preview with students. Tell them that in this activity they will be analyzing the role of conflict in Arthur Miller's *The Crucible*.

★ TEACHER TO TEACHER

This activity is designed to point out a more practical notion of the cause and continuation of the Salem hysteria. Many of the conflicts deal with the Putnams but also include Parris, Proctor, Giles Corey, the Nurses, and the girls.

2 Read the Conflicts Driving the Action section as a class. Discuss as a class the question at the end of student step 1.

3 Ask students to reread this scene and annotate examples of these conflicts. Have them take notes in the graphic organizer. Guide students to an understanding of how these conflicts represent larger topics, such as personal and social power, moral integrity, social order, and hypocrisy.

LEVELED DIFFERENTIATED INSTRUCTION

In this activity, students may need support understanding the conflict of *The Crucible* and how it ties to a larger theme.

Beginning Have pairs or small groups use the **Conflict Map** graphic organizer to generate ideas for their explanatory essays. Provide sentence frames to help scaffold their discussions of the conflicts in the play, such as: *Abigail is angry because _____. Proctor refuses to _____.*

Developing Direct students to choose the conflict they wish to write about and pair students with similar topics. Have them use the graphic organizer and discussions as prewriting support. Allow them time to connect the conflict to a larger theme.

4 Instruct students to work independently to complete student steps 3 and 4. Remind them that conflict in *The Crucible* is vital to its plot and theme.

5 Ask students to share their thoughts about how the conflicts go beyond the individuals to understand how these conflicts foster tension in Puritan society. Pairs should also think about how all the conflicts are about power. Have them summarize their discussion notes.

6 Give students time to complete the Check Your Understanding task.

7 Allow students time to respond individually to the writing prompt. Writing a paragraph connecting a conflict between characters to a larger theme in the play will help students understand the layers of the multiple plot lines and their connections to Miller's thematic focus.

8 Have students share their drafts with a partner or small writing group. This formative assessment could be added to the student's Portfolio.

9 Make sure students attend to the Independent Reading Link. To assess their independent reading, set a date to check for the conflict analysis in students' notebooks.

ASSESS

Review students' responses to the Check Your Understanding task for the ability to identify what each character in the conflict wants, what stands in the way, and how this conflict connects to a struggle for power in the larger community.

ADAPT

If students need help making connections between a conflict and a broader theme, have them brainstorm conflicts they have heard about in the local and national news during the past week. Compile a master list for the class. Then have students form small groups and choose a conflict from the list.

🔲 **INDEPENDENT READING LINK**

Read and Connect

In your Reader/Writer Notebook, identify and analyze the role of conflict in important scenes in your independent reading. How do character or human motivations lead to conflict? How do these conflicts drive the action and affect the outcome of a scene or of the work? How do these character conflicts compare and contrast with those found in *The Crucible*?

My Notes

_____

_____

_____

_____

_____

_____

_____

_____

_____

_____

_____

_____

_____

_____

_____

_____

_____

_____

3. Choose a conflict from the chart and explain how it advances the plot of *The Crucible*.

4. How does the conflict you chose connect to the theme of the play?

☑ **Check Your Understanding**

Think about how one of these personal conflicts is also a struggle for power in the community. Briefly explain how this conflict mirrors a conflict in your local or national community.

> 📝 **Writing Prompt: Informational**
>
> Select one of the conflicts you listed in the chart earlier in this activity. Write a paragraph analyzing how the conflict between these particular characters connects to a larger theme in the play, such as hysteria, intolerance, power, or reputation. Be sure to:
>
> - Introduce and organize complex ideas by specifically stating how the conflict in the relationship relates to a theme.
> - Write exploratory text that examines the connections between the characters' conflict, the plot, and the larger theme of the work.
> - Use a variety of transitions and sentence structures to link the different sections of your analysis.
> - Maintain a formal style and objective tone to convey your analysis.
> - Provide textual evidence to support your analysis.
> - End with a conclusion that follows logically from your explanation.

✍️ WRITING PROMPT: INFORMATIONAL

The following standards are addressed in the writing prompt:

- W.11-12.2a
- W.11-12.2b
- W.11-12.2c
- W.11-12.2b
- W.11-12.2e
- W.11-12.2f

Speaking Like a Puritan

Learning Targets
- Evaluate how an author's use of language shapes the perception of readers by immersing them in a historical setting.
- Write a scene between two characters emulating their voices.

Preview

In this activity, you will evaluate how Arthur Miller uses both archaic and figurative language to shape the perception of readers—placing them in Puritan New England. Then you will use your evaluation to write a consistently voiced scene between two characters.

Learning Strategies
Diffusing
Graphic Organizer
Note-taking
Skimming/Scanning

Using Language to Create a Historical Setting

In *The Crucible*, Miller uses diction to give his characters voices that are specific to Puritan New England.

1. The following words are among many that Miller chose to use in his quest to create a language that was an "echo" of the language spoken by the Puritans. What impact does this diction have on creating voice?

Act Two Vocabulary	
magistrate	quail (used as a verb)
fraud	lechery
charity	abomination
naught	blasphemy
poppet	vengeance
theology	conjure

2. With a partner or small group, write the definitions of any words you might already know in your Reader/Writer Notebook. Then, as you read Act Two, note where the words occur and how they are used. Use context to help you determine the meanings and consult a dictionary or other resource for confirmation.

3. Another way that Arthur Miller conveys the Puritan setting and mood and central thematic ideas of *The Crucible* is through the use of metaphoric language. Read the following lines and work with your group to determine the meaning behind the metaphors.

My Notes

College and Career Readiness Standards

Focus Standards:

RL.11-12.4 Determine the meaning of words and phrases as they are used in the text, including figurative and connotative meanings; analyze the impact of specific word choices on meaning and tone, including words with multiple meanings or language that is particularly fresh, engaging, or beautiful.

W.11-12.4 Produce clear and coherent writing in which the development, organization, and style are appropriate to task, purpose, and audience.

Additional Standards Addressed:

W.11-12.3a, W.11-12.3b, W.11-12.3d

PLAN

Suggested Pacing: 2 50-minute class periods

TEACH

1 Read the Learning Targets and Preview with students. Tell them that in this activity they will be writing dialogue that emulates Arthur Miller's use of language in *The Crucible*.

2 Point out to students that as they read Act One of *The Crucible*, they were exposed to the challenging language of the play. In the essay "Why I Wrote *The Crucible*," which students will read later in the unit, Miller addresses the language he used. He explains that he saw "a wonderful metaphoric richness" and wanted not just "to imitate the archaic speech but to try to create a new echo of it which would flow freely off American actors' tongues." He is consciously using archaic language and syntax in his play to create this "echo" of the language spoken in these Puritan times.

3 As a class, discuss step 1. Divide students into pairs and have them examine the words in the Act Two Vocabulary chart. As they come across the words in their reading, they are to try to determine their meaning from context and confirm or modify their definitions using a print or online dictionary.

4 As students learn the meanings of the words, reinforce their learning by adding some of them to a *Crucible* Word Wall, creating word sorts by grouping words of the same category and allowing students to draw visual depictions of some of the words as well.

5 Have student pairs complete student step 3. They should use the **graphic organizer** to discover the meanings of the selected metaphors. You might also ask them to write modern metaphors that convey the same meaning as Miller's metaphors.

LEVELED DIFFERENTIATED INSTRUCTION

In this activity, students may need support analyzing the metaphors.

Expanding Direct students to Proctor's metaphor "a funeral marches round your heart." Ask: *What two things are being compared?* (funeral and heart) *Is a funeral literally marching around Elizabeth's heart?* (No, it is figurative language.) *What then is Proctor's meaning?* (Elizabeth is very sad.) Pair students and have them write their own metaphor to describe Mary Warren, Hale, or Abigail.

Bridging Have students work in pairs to review the metaphors in the chart and identify what two things are being compared. For at least two examples, have them answer the question *How does this metaphor add meaning to the description?* Have pairs create a metaphor of their own that describes Mary Warren, Hale, or Abigail.

6 Give students time to complete the Check Your Understanding task. Have students work in pairs or individually to create metaphors or similes to describe the three characters. Share results with the class.

7 Allow students time to respond to the writing prompt. Be sure they refer to their script-writing checklist and perhaps add new elements as they build skills for succeeding on Embedded Assessment 1.

ASSESS

Review the metaphors and similes students created. Assess whether students' comparisons illuminate character traits. Also examine their contemporary diction for evidence of understanding.

ADAPT

Provide students with sentence frames to help them form metaphors, such as: *Mary Warren is a(n) _____ manipulated by _____.*

Metaphor	Meaning of the Words/Phrases and What They Reveal about the Character
Proctor: "a funeral marches round your heart"	
Elizabeth: "the magistrate sits in your heart"	
Proctor: "I will curse her hotter than the oldest cinder in Hell"	
Hale: "Theology is a fortress"	
Francis Nurse: "My wife is the very brick and mortar of the church"	
Proctor: "Vengeance is walking Salem"	

☑ Check Your Understanding

After looking at the metaphoric language Miller's characters speak, try your hand at creating a metaphor or simile to describe Mary Warren, Hale, or Abigail.

Like a puppet on a string, Mary Warren is dangled about by those who have power over her.

John Proctor has a flinty personality that, once struck hard, bursts into flame.

4. Find examples of character speech in the play and examine its diction. Then rephrase that speech using contemporary diction. Compare and note differences between the two.

✏ Writing Prompt: Literary

Write an original scene between two characters from *The Crucible*. In this scene, emulate the language Miller creates to develop or extend a conflict related to one of the themes of the play. Be sure to:

- Include appropriate language that echoes Puritan speech.
- Write stage directions that set the context and guide the actions and vocal delivery of the speakers.
- Provide a clear sense of a central conflict.

✏ WRITING PROMPT: LITERARY

The following standards are addressed in the writing prompt:
- W.11-12.3d
- W.11-12.3b
- W.11-12.3a

Elements of Plot: Rising Action

Learning Targets
- Analyze the impact of minor characters on conflict and plot.
- Analyze how two incidents complicate the conflict and move the plot inevitably to a climax.

Preview
In this activity, you will examine the plot structure of Acts One and Two of *The Crucible* in the framework of Freytag's Pyramid.

Learning Strategies
Diffusing
Graphic Organizer
Rereading

Elements of the Plot

1. Act Two begins one week after the opening act. Once again, the action is set in a domestic context, bringing the conflict into the home of John Proctor, the protagonist. As you read, think about how Miller intensifies the level of personal and social conflict in this act.

2. Review the elements of plot as you read Act Two and think about how Miller uses them.

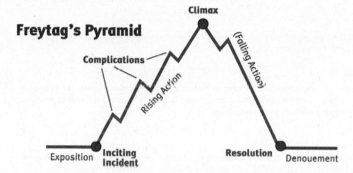

Freytag's Pyramid

Plotting the Conflict

A plot map can guide you as you think about creating a short dramatic scene. Act Two creates complications that set the plot on a path to destruction. Review the elements of effective plotting.

Exposition, or Setup

The beginning of the play must establish a little about the characters, setting, and conflict. This happens through stage directions and dialogue. Early Act One accomplished this for us in *The Crucible*. Locate a sentence or paragraph that functions as exposition in the play.

My Notes

College and Career Readiness Standards

Focus Standards:

RL.11-12.3 Analyze the impact of the author's choices regarding how to develop and relate elements of a story or drama (e.g., where a story is set, how the action is ordered, how the characters are introduced and developed).

RL.11-12.2 Determine two or more themes or central ideas of a text and analyze their development over the course of the text, including how they interact and build on one another to produce a complex account; provide an objective summary of the text.

ACTIVITY 2.11

PLAN

Suggested Pacing: 1 50-minute class period

TEACHER TO TEACHER

Determine how you want students to read Act Two of the play. Since the focus of Embedded Assessment 1 is on creating and performing a scene, you may want students to conduct a shared reading in parts.

TEACH

1 Read the Learning Targets and Preview with students. Make sure they understand that they will examine the plot structure of Acts One and Two of *The Crucible* using a plot map, focusing on the rising action.

2 Read as a class the Elements of the Plot section. Project Freytag's Pyramid or reproduce it on the board. As you explain plot mapping and take students through each of the seven significant points on the pyramid, track your progress on the projected or drawn image.

3 Remind students that as they read Act Two, they should note how important its rising action is to the development of the personal and social consequences of these conflicts:

- Abigail versus Elizabeth
- Abigail versus Proctor
- Proctor versus Elizabeth
- Hale versus Proctor
- Mary Warren versus the Proctors

4 Act Two also brings together minor characters who have been influenced by and who influence the action. Mary Warren, Cheever, and Herrick as well as Giles Corey are all impressed by their new power in the community. As the play continues, ask students to note the reactions of these characters to their new roles in Salem society. Additionally, be sure students add information to their note-taking about Hale and Corey as foils.

5 Discuss with students the role of intensifying conflict in building the plot of a story. Direct students to view the image of plot structure, taking time to note how the events in *The Crucible* fit onto the map.

6 Allow students time to complete the Check Your Understanding task. Consider allowing them to work in groups to write their plot map summaries.

ASSESS

Review students' summaries of the plot elements for the Check Your Understanding task. Make sure students correctly label each example they cite.

ADAPT

If students need help identifying plot elements for a summary, have them practice by summarizing plots of favorite movies or TV episodes. Then lead them to identify the elements of the plot structure for these movies or TV episodes based on the definitions provided in the activity.

Inciting Incident

This is where our protagonist is launched into the action—like it or not. Again, both stage directions and dialogue make this happen. Review Act One of *The Crucible* for this moment in the life of John Proctor.

Rising Action

This is the long hill upward on the way to the climax of the play. Here is where the playwright builds tension by developing characters, deepening their relationships, and complicating the conflicts between them. How do the incidents in Act Two function to build this tension?

Climax

Here is the point of greatest suspense in a play. It doesn't last long, but it culminates all the conflict thus far. It is the moment in which the conflict could go either way. Like the "roller coaster" image, the climax will come close to the end of the play. Be on the lookout for the climax of *The Crucible* as you continue reading Acts Three and Four.

Falling Action

Will our antagonist be defeated? Will our protagonist fulfill his mission? Here's where we get these answers as things move quickly toward the resolution.

Resolution

The resolution of the play occurs when the protagonist solves the main problem or conflict or someone solves it for him or her.

Denouement

Think of denouement as the opposite of the exposition; the author is getting ready to end with a final explanation of any remaining secrets and questions. This section is very difficult to identify, as it is often very closely related to the resolution.

☑ Check Your Understanding

In your Reader/Writer Notebook, briefly summarize each of the elements of the plot structure in *The Crucible*. You may wish to add these elements to a diagram for future reference.

Pivotal Scene 2: Proctor and Elizabeth

Learning Targets
- Visualize different interpretations of a dramatic scene.
- Analyze implicit and explicit aspects of a fictional relationship.
- Engage in a collaborative discussion, responding thoughtfully to diverse perspectives.

Preview
In this activity, you will study lines from *The Crucible* to interpret the relationship between Proctor and Elizabeth. Then you will examine how that relationship helps shape the moral dilemma of the play's plot.

Learning Strategies
Close Reading
Diffusion
Graphic Organizer
Rereading

Drama Study

1. Imagine that you are the director of a stage version of *The Crucible*. How will you portray the relationship between Proctor and Elizabeth? Share your initial reaction to their tense conversation on pages 47–53 and be sure to consider the subtext of the spoken words.

2. Following are four possible scenarios or subtexts that could inform the relationship and interaction between Proctor and Elizabeth. After you have read the scene where they are alone for the first time, describe the gestures, movements, facial expressions, and vocal delivery actors might use at specific places in this scene to communicate the different interpretations. Be sure to identify the specific line where the stage directions might take place.

Proctor Is Cold and Distant				
Line	Gestures	Blocking (Movements)	Facial Expressions	Vocal Delivery

College and Career Readiness Standards

Focus Standards:

RL.11-12.3 Analyze the impact of the author's choices regarding how to develop and relate elements of a story or drama (e.g., where a story is set, how the action is ordered, how the characters are introduced and developed).

RL.11-12.2 Determine two or more themes or central ideas of a text and analyze their development over the course of the text,

including how they interact and build on one another to produce a complex account; provide an objective summary of the text.

SL.11-12.1 Initiate and participate effectively in a range of collaborative discussions (one-on-one, in groups, and teacher-led) with diverse partners on grades 11–12 topics, texts, and issues, building on others' ideas and expressing their own clearly and persuasively.

ACTIVITY 2.12

PLAN

Materials: *The Crucible*, Act Two; index cards with a different interpretation on each (one per discussion group); Optional: DVD of *The Crucible* (1996), dir. Nicholas Hytner, DVD player
Suggested Pacing: 2 50-minute class periods

TEACH

1 Read the Learning Targets and Preview with students, making sure they understand that they will continue to explore the moral dilemma that is building in John Proctor's conscience.

2 After students have read Act Two, ask them to go back to pivotal Scene 2, between Proctor and Elizabeth, at the beginning of Act Two.

3 In this exploration of possible interpretations, assign one interpretation per group. Students are to complete the **graphic organizer** according to their assigned interpretation of the scene when Elizabeth and Proctor are alone for the first time. In addition, students may mark the text. Be sure students consider stage directions and construct a complex sentence stating how the stage directions support the given interpretation.

4 Jigsaw students so that new groups include at least one member from each interpretation group. Students are to share their information and sentence while others complete the graphic organizer.

⭐ TEACHER TO TEACHER

Most print versions of the play include Act Two, Scene 2 in an appendix. A note usually states that, although the scene appeared in the original play, Arthur Miller asked that it be cut from subsequent performances. This scene is between Abigail and Proctor in the woods. It adds a distinctly different tone to the relationship between Proctor and Abigail. Save the reading of this scene until after the reading of the courtroom scene.

TEACHER TO TEACHER

For comparison, you may show students the three-minute scene from *The Crucible* film (Scene 5: 0:36:10–0:39:50). Discussion groups should respond to the following questions:

- Which interpretation of the relationship does the director seem to have in mind? How do you know?

- How does it compare to and contrast with your own interpretation?

- How does the director's interpretive choice about this relationship affect the direction of the conflict?

Have students summarize their discussions and present their summaries to the class.

3. How do the stage directions you have added support the interpretation that Proctor is cold and distant and focus your understanding of this scene's staging and blocking choices?

Elizabeth Is Cold and Distant				
Line	Gestures	Blocking (Movements)	Facial Expressions	Vocal Delivery

4. How do the stage directions you have added support the interpretation that Elizabeth is cold and distant and focus your understanding of this scene's staging and blocking choices?

Proctor and Elizabeth Are in Love				
Line	Gestures	Blocking (Movements)	Facial Expressions	Vocal Delivery

5. How do the stage directions you have added support the interpretation that Proctor and Elizabeth are in love and focus your understanding of this scene's staging and blocking choices?

Select an Interpretation for Yourself				
Line	Gestures	Movements	Facial Expressions	Vocal Delivery

6. How do the stage directions you have added support this interpretation and focus your understanding of this scene's staging and blocking choices?

Richard Armitage as John Proctor and Anna Madeley as Elizabeth Proctor in *The Crucible* directed by Yael Farber in 2014.

5 Have students independently answer the questions in the Moral Dilemma section. Make sure the concept and how it applies to this particular situation are clear to them. Answer questions and discuss the concept and text as necessary.

2.12

Moral Dilemma

Skim or reread pages 47–53. Examine John Proctor's initial reaction to the news of Mary Warren's departure to Salem and how that reaction evolves as he learns more about the situation there.

7. At the scene's beginning, why does Elizabeth believe John should go to Salem?

   She thinks John should tell the court that Abigail had confided to him that she and the other girls were lying about being victims of witchcraft.

8. What is at stake in the Salem court?

   Fourteen people have been accused of witchcraft by Abigail. They have been jailed, will be tried, and may be hanged.

9. Why is John reluctant to talk to the Salem court even though it is obviously the right thing to do?

   Because he and Abigail were alone when she told him. Elizabeth had dismissed Abigail from their household when she learned of Abigail's affair with John. Elizabeth suspects that the affair is still going on, John has no proof that Abigail told him about the lying, and trying to straighten things out now could damage his marriage and create a public scandal.

10. How does the return of Mary Warren intensify John's moral dilemma?

    Mary informs them that the number of accused women has increased to 39 and that Goody Osburn has been condemned to death. Also, Mary herself has become convinced that she is a victim of witchcraft. Mary also relates that Elizabeth has been accused of witchcraft by Abigail, doubtless out of spite. All of this increases the severity of John's dilemma.

11. How does Elizabeth's insistence that John confront Abigail contribute to John's moral dilemma?

It seems likely that John has led Abigail to believe that he has some allegiance to her (and that

that may actually be the case). But now, on top of everything else, John must confront Abigail

and expose the lying girls in order to protect Elizabeth.

☑ **Check Your Understanding**

Write a few sentences about the experience of examining different interpretations. Which interpretation worked best? Why?

6 Give students time to respond to the Check Your Understanding task. Consider allowing students to work in pairs to weigh the various interpretations of the scene being analyzed in this activity.

ASSESS

Review students' responses to the Check Your Understanding task. Note whether they have described the experience of examining different interpretations and whether they have selected a "best" interpretation and explained their choice.

ADAPT

If students need help writing sentences, provide frames, such as: *The interpretation that Proctor (and/ or Elizabeth) is (are) _____ is best because _____. Stage directions such as _____ help to show _____ because _____.*

ACTIVITY 2.13

PLAN

Materials: *The Crucible*, Act Three
Suggested Pacing: 2 50-minute class periods

TEACH

1 Read the Learning Targets and Preview with students. Tell students that they will be examining how Arthur Miller makes deliberate use of logical fallacies in *The Crucible*.

2 **Activate prior knowledge** by having a class discussion of courtroom trials, using the first Setting the Scene question as a springboard. Introducing additional **Visual Cues/Prompts** such as photos found online of courtroom trials may help students who are not familiar with courtroom trials. Photos in which material evidence is being presented are especially helpful.

3 Have students complete student step 2 by thinking back and reviewing their notes to find examples of evidence used in each act to accuse a defendant of witchcraft.

4 For student step 3, divide students into small discussion groups in which they can discuss the role of confession and accusation in the courtroom. Have groups brainstorm reasons why an accused person might or might not confess. Have a spokesperson from each group share that group's answers and write them on the board.

ACTIVITY
2.13

Courtroom Drama: Examining Logical Fallacies

Learning Strategies

Close Reading
Graphic Organizer
Note-taking
Skimming/Scanning

Learning Targets

- Analyze the validity of confession and evidence.
- Identify logical fallacies and examine their effects on the way the text is read and understood.
- Create an original script illuminating a conflict on an ethical issue.

Preview

In this activity, you will analyze the effects of logical fallacies in the way *The Crucible* is read and understood.

My Notes

Setting the Scene

1. Think about a typical courtroom trial. What constitutes evidence in a trial? What role do eyewitness testimonials, confessions, and character witnesses play in determining guilt or innocence? What other types of proof are typically required for a conviction?

2. After a close reading of Act Three, think about the type of evidence that was used to prove someone guilty of witchcraft. List examples from Acts One, Two, and Three of the evidence that was used.

   Act One: girls dancing in the forest; children died in childbirth; attempts to fly; comatose state; hysterical confessions and accusations

   Act Two: poppet; Ten Commandments, not going to church; baptism

   Act Three: invisible bird; accusation; hysteria

3. What is the role of confession and accusation in this courtroom? Considering the consequences, why would someone not confess?

College and Career Readiness Standards

Focus Standards:

RI.11-12.6 Determine an author's point of view or purpose in a text in which the rhetoric is particularly effective, analyzing how style and content contribute to the power, persuasiveness or beauty of the text.

W.11-12.4 Produce clear and coherent writing in which the development, organization, and style are appropriate to task, purpose, and audience.

Additional Standards Addressed:

W.11-12.3a, W.11-12.3c, W.11-12.3d

4. Briefly describe the consequence of Giles Corey's testimony in the courtroom.

Logical Fallacies

Logic is a type of reasoning that applies strict rules to determine whether a statement is valid. A **logical fallacy** is a violation of those rules. Some common logical fallacies are:

- **Ad hominem:** attacking a person instead of his or her arguments. ("You only believe that because you're undereducated.")

- **Bandwagon (appeal to popularity):** accepting a position because most people agree with it. ("Most people don't vote, so there's no point to it.")

- **Circular reasoning:** using an argument's conclusion as an assumption. ("It's alright to yell when you're angry because angry people yell.")

- **False dilemma (either/or):** presenting only two possible conclusions to a complex argument. ("If you love your country, you'll vote against this amendment.")

- **False analogy:** comparing two things that are not similar. ("People who like free samples are just like thieves who like money.")

- **Hasty generalization:** forming a general conclusion based on a few examples. ("I've been bitten by dogs, so I know that dogs usually bite people.")

- **Non sequitur:** a conclusion that does not follow from the evidence. ("Cars should be illegal because moving too fast is bad for people.")

- **Post hoc:** assuming cause and effect simply because one thing followed another. ("She ate a peanut butter sandwich yesterday, so that's what made her sick.")

- **Red herring:** a conclusion that changes the subject. ("I shouldn't have to write this paper because other people have already explored this topic.")

- **Slippery slope:** concluding that accepting something will lead to accepting something else. ("Letting children eat candy bars will lead to widespread obesity among young people.")

- **Stereotyping:** arbitrary statements about groups of people or things. ("French people don't like Americans very much.")

- **Straw man:** misrepresenting an opponent's position and then refuting that misrepresentation. ("While my opponent says she wants to lower income taxes, I support public school teachers, who are paid by our property taxes.")

VOCABULARY

ACADEMIC

Logic is a type of reasoning that applies strict rules to determine whether a statement is valid. A fallacy is a false idea. Therefore, a **logical fallacy** is a violation of those rules; logical fallacies are by definition invalid. An example of a logical fallacy is an *ad hominem* attack, in which the opponent's character, and not the opponent's argument, is debated. Stereotyping and generalizations are also examples of logical fallacies.

ACTIVITY 2.13 continued

5 As a class, complete student step 4 by doing a close read of Giles Corey's testimony and discussing its consequences. Ask students why his tesitmony backfires.

6 **Vocabulary Development:** Review the meaning of the Academic Vocabulary *logical fallacy* with students. Have them work in pairs to define this term in their own words.

7 Read aloud the Logical Fallacies section as a class by having a volunteer read each of the types of fallacy and its example and encourage the volunteer to cite one additional example.

8 Divide students into small groups and have them complete the graphic organizer in the Examining the Evidence section. Then have them share their examples with the class. Track on the board the strongest examples of logical fallacy from dialogue in Act Three.

Examining the Evidence

The dialogue in Act Three of *The Crucible* contains several examples of logical fallacy. Skim the text and find examples to complete the chart.

Character	Dialogue Example	Type of Fallacy	Why?
Parris	"Such a Christian that will not come to church but once in a month!"	ad hominem	Parris is attacking Proctor as a Christian rather than addressing his words.
Giles	"If Jacobs hangs for a witch he forfeit up his property — that's law! And there is none but Putnam with the coin to buy so great a piece. This man is killing his neighbors for their land!"	slippery slope	Giles claims that hanging Jacobs will lead to Putnam accusing others so he can have their land.
Danforth	"[Y]ou are either lying now, or you were lying in the court, and in either case you have committed perjury and you will go to jail for it."	false dilemma (either/or)	Danforth is reducing the possible explanations for a complex situation to one of two possibilities.
Danforth	"No uncorrupted man may fear this court, Mr. Hale."	circular reasoning	Danforth assumes that only guilty men fear the court because the court only convicts the guilty.
Danforth	"All innocent and Christian people are happy for the courts in Salem! These people are gloomy for it."	bandwagon	Danforth assumes that since most approve of the Salem courts, they are correct.

2.13

☑ Check Your Understanding

Choose one logical fallacy from the chart you completed and write a brief explanation of how it affects the way the text is read and understood.

☑ Writing Prompt: Literary

Work with a small group to develop a short scene and then write a script based on one of the following scenarios, or a different scenario. Consider the role that various forms of evidence, including confession, might play in the scene. Write a script for the scene and assign roles. Rehearse the scene and perform it for another group. Be sure to:

- Include dialogue that develops the characters' traits within the setting.
- Write stage directions that set the context and guide the actions and vocal delivery of the speakers.
- Provide a clear sense of a central conflict.

Scenario A: A friend convinced you to donate money to a charity last year. You attended one of its meetings six months ago but did not get actively involved. Last week, you heard that a member of the group blew up an abandoned building in protest. The police arrested that person and want to collect the names of everyone involved in the group to prevent further violence. The police tell you that you have to give them the names of all the people at the meeting you attended. If you do not provide the names, you could be put in jail until you do.

Scenario B: You are an accountant for a large company. Your boss asks you to make some transactions that are possibly illegal. These types of transactions have been going on for some time, and the police are investigating the company and the transactions. You and a coworker are considering becoming whistle-blowers. A whistle-blower is someone with inside information who shares it with authorities. If you become known as a whistle-blower, you could be fired by the company. Other companies might also be wary about hiring you as an accountant. You have been interviewed once by the police, but you have not yet told them all that you know.

Scenario C: The school bus that you ride has been vandalized. The bus driver accuses a student sitting near you. You do not know who vandalized the bus, but you know the student in question was asleep for the entire bus ride. However, you have witnessed the student vandalizing school property in the past. The principal wants to question every student on the bus. If the person responsible is not found, the principal will ban backpacks on the bus route.

WRITING PROMPT: LITERARY

The following standards are addressed in the writing prompt:
- W.11-12.3d
- W.11-12.3a
- W.11-12.3c

ACTIVITY 2.13 continued

9 Give students time to respond to the Check Your Understanding task.

10 For the writing prompt, either assign student groups specific scenarios or allow them to choose their own. Students should consider the subtexts of their scenarios when deciding how to portray the characters. Scripts should show an obvious conflict, present interesting characters, and reflect a social commentary on the topic or idea of evidence and confession.

11 Circulate as students plan and rehearse their scenes to ensure all students are actively participating.

12 Allow each group to rehearse and perform its script. As you view presentations, check that students have a clear understanding of the relationship between confession and evidence.

13 Discuss the scenes presented by the groups. How does one group treat a particular scenario differently than another?

ASSESS

Review student responses for the Check Your Understanding task. Make sure that students have selected a logical fallacy from the chart and explained its use accurately.

Use students' responses to the writing prompt to assess their abilities to portray central conflict based on forms of evidence, including confession.

ADAPT

If students need help analyzing the effect of a logical fallacy on the text, have them revisit the list of fallacies from this activity.

To enhance the writing of the scenes, have groups create maps for the main character:

- What is this character's relationship to the conflict?
- What are this character's traits?
- What evidence might this character have access to?
- What might this character confess to?
- How can you influence this character's testimony through stage directions?

ACTIVITY 2.14

PLAN

Materials: *The Crucible*, Act Three; Optional: DVD or online clip of *Monty Python and the Holy Grail* (1975), DVD player
Suggested Pacing: 2 50-minute class periods plus homework

TEACH

1 Read the Learning Targets and Preview with students, making sure they understand that they will be examining the role of irony in the climax of Arthur Miller's *The Crucible*.

2 **Vocabulary Development:** Tell students that one definition of *irony* is "the use of words to express something other than and especially the opposite of the literal meaning." Read aloud the Literary Vocabulary box. Ask small groups to create a **Venn Diagram** graphic organizer illustrating the differences between the types of irony.

 TEACHER TO TEACHER

Show the brief comic witch scene from *Monty Python and the Holy Grail*. Use the keywords "Monty Python" and "witch scene" to bring up the scene online. After watching the scene, ask students the following questions:

- What types of evidence are accepted by the "judge" in *Monty Python and the Holy Grail*? In *The Crucible*?

- What role does confession play in each scene?

- Identify the irony in each scene.

- How does the director or script writer create irony in the witch scene? How does Miller create irony in the courtroom scene?

Help students recognize the situational irony in these scenes. The situations of these scenes are ironic because the only way to keep from being hanged as a witch is to confess to being a witch.

Point out that irony often comes at a time of great tension for the audience. This is why irony is often found in the climax of the plot.

Learning Strategies

Graphic Organizer
Note-taking
Rereading

 INDEPENDENT READING LINK

Read and Connect

In your Reader/Writer Notebook, construct a graphic organizer similar to the one you completed during this activity to analyze instances of irony in the work you are reading independently. Which types of irony are most prevalent, and what functions do they serve? How does irony move the plot forward, or convey an author's theme or message? What similarities and differences do you notice in how authors use irony?

Learning Targets

- Examine how characters' choices move the conflict toward a climax.
- Evaluate the use of dramatic, verbal, and situational irony to convey a social message.

Preview

In this activity, you will evaluate irony in Act Three of *The Crucible* and how it is used to convey a social message.

Character Choices

One of the key elements of characterization revolves around the choices a character makes. As you reread the scene with Proctor and Elizabeth in the courtroom, answer the following text-dependent questions in your Reader/Writer Notebook to analyze their choices and how these choices move the conflict toward a climax.

1. What secrets do both Proctor and Elizabeth have? What evidence supports your answer?

   Proctor has committed adultery with Abigail, and Elizabeth knows this and
   how important Proctor's integrity is to him.

2. What choices do Proctor and Elizabeth make in this scene? Cite text evidence that demonstrates their choices.

   Proctor confesses to the crime, and Elizabeth chooses to support the lie she
   thinks Proctor will tell.

3. For what reasons do they make their choices? Support your answer with text evidence.

   Proctor's confession reveals Abigail's motives in accusing Elizabeth. Elizabeth
   knows she will not hang; therefore, she lies to protect her husband. She
   wants to show her love of and loyalty to John.

College and Career Readiness Standards

Focus Standards:

RL.11-12.5 Analyze how an author's choices concerning how to structure specific parts of a text (e.g., the choice of where to begin or end a story, the choice to provide a comedic or tragic resolution) contribute to its overall structure and meaning as well as its aesthetic impact.

2.14

4. How does Proctor's choice affect Elizabeth?

Proctor's choice places Elizabeth in a precarious position, as she will also

be asked to testify to his relationship with Abigail and does not know of his

admission.

LITERARY

Dramatic irony occurs when the audience knows more about circumstances or events in a story than the characters within it do. Situational irony occurs when an event contradicts the expectations of the characters or the reader. Verbal irony occurs when a speaker or narrator says one thing while meaning the opposite.

VOCABULARY

Irony

5. Review the definitions of *dramatic*, *situational*, and *verbal* irony. With your group members, create an original graphic organizer on a separate piece of paper that demonstrates the similarities and differences between the different types of irony. Be prepared to explain your creation to the class.

6. Use the graphic organizer to identify and evaluate examples of dramatic, situational, and verbal irony in Act Three of *The Crucible*.

Type of Irony	Text Evidence	Evaluation *How does this example of irony help to convey a social message?*
Dramatic		
Situational		
Verbal		

☑ **Check Your Understanding**

Choose one type of irony illustrated in this scene and explain it.

ACTIVITY 2.14 continued

3 Ask pairs of students to reread the courtroom scene in Act Three, paying attention to the choices of the characters at this climactic scene in the play. Have them use the text-dependent questions to guide their discussion of how the choices Proctor and Elizabeth make move the plot of *The Crucible* toward a climax.

4 Have groups of students complete student steps 5 and 6 in the Irony section. Conduct a class discussion in which you elicit examples of the different types of irony in the scene. Address how Elizabeth's choices are especially ironic and add to the dramatic tension of the play.

5 Give students time to respond to the Check Your Understanding task. Consider allowing them to work in small groups to explain their choice.

ASSESS

Review students' explanations for the Check Your Understanding task. Note whether those explanations correctly identify and explain the type of irony they chose to discuss.

ADAPT

If students need help finding examples of irony to explain, have them answer the following questions:

• How do Proctor and Elizabeth surprise you? What type of irony does this show?

• Do you know more about the situation that Proctor and Elizabeth face than they do? Explain. What type of irony does this show?

• Do any of the characters in the scene say something while meaning something else? Provide an example. What type of irony does this show?

PLAN

Suggested Pacing: 3 50-minute class periods

TEACH

1 Read the Learning Targets and Preview with students. Tell them they will be revisiting the concept of historical context, but this time as it pertains to McCarthyism.

2 Have students work in pairs to address the On the Spot Research section. Allow them no more than 10 minutes to research this topic online. Ask them to share what they learn with their partners and then with the class. Be sure students understand that in 1950 Senator Joseph McCarthy of Wisconsin kicked off a "witch hunt" to ferret out secret Communists who might be working in the U.S. government.

3 Have students read the About the Author section, circling unfamiliar words as they read. Model ways to determine the meanings of these words through the use of context clues, word parts, or print or online references.

Learning Strategies

Marking the Text
Note-taking
Questioning the Text
Rereading

Learning Targets

- Analyze the purpose of a speech and the rhetorical devices used to achieve that purpose.
- Research the historical context in which a literary text was written to understand the social commentary it is presenting.

Preview

In this activity, you will conduct research into McCarthyism to better understand the society Arthur Miller was commenting on.

My Notes

On the Spot Research

- What questions do you have about McCarthyism? Conduct research to extend your knowledge about the historical significance of the Communist "witch hunts" of the early 1950s.
- Reflect on the historical and political significance of the activities of the House Un-American Activities Committee (HUAC) during this period. What evidence from your research helps you gain insight into the plot and theme of *The Crucible*?

As You Read

- Underline or highlight portions of the text in which you find especially powerful use of language.
- Circle unknown words and phrases. Try to determine the meaning of the words by using context clues, word parts, or a dictionary.

About the Author

Margaret Chase Smith (1897–1995) was born in Maine. In 1936 her husband, Clyde, was elected to the U.S. House of Representatives, and Margaret succeeded him after he died in 1940. She went on to be elected multiple times in both the House and the U.S. Senate, the first woman to do so. She was also the first Republican senator to speak out against Senator Joseph McCarthy's anti-Communist campaign.

College and Career Readiness Standards

Focus Standards:

RI.11-12.1 Cite strong and thorough textual evidence to support analysis of what the text says explicitly as well as inferences drawn from the text, including determining where the text leaves matters uncertain.

RI.11-12.4 Determine the meaning of words and phrases as they are used in a text, including figurative, connotative, and technical meanings; analyze how an author uses and refines the meaning of a key term or terms over the course of a text

RI.11-12.5 Analyze and evaluate the effectiveness of the structure an author uses in his or her exposition or argument, including whether the structure makes points clear, convincing, and engaging.

Additional Standards Addressed:

W.11-12.1, RI.11-12.6, W.11-12.1e

2.15

Speech

Declaration of Conscience

by Margaret Chase Smith

This is an excerpt from a speech delivered to the U.S. Senate, June 1, 1950. Smith was protesting the activities of the House on Un-American Activities Committee, which was formed by the U.S. Congress to investigate and identify Americans who were suspected of being Communists.

Mr. President:

1 I would like to speak briefly and simply about a serious national condition. It is a national feeling of fear and frustration that could result in national suicide and the end of everything that we Americans hold dear ...

2 I speak as briefly as possible because too much harm has already been done with irresponsible words of bitterness and selfish political **opportunism**.

3 I speak as briefly as possible because the issue is too great to be obscured by eloquence. I speak simply and briefly in the hope that my words will be taken to heart.

4 I speak as a Republican. I speak as a woman. I speak as a United States senator. I speak as an American.

5 The United States Senate has long enjoyed worldwide respect as the greatest **deliberative** body in the world. But recently that deliberative character has too often been debased to the level of a forum of hate and character assassination sheltered by the shield of congressional immunity. ...

6 I think that it is high time for the United States Senate and its members to do some soul-searching—for us to weigh our consciences—on the manner in which we are performing our duty to the people of America—on the manner in which we are using or abusing our individual powers and privileges.

7 I think that it is high time that we remembered that we have sworn to uphold and defend the Constitution. I think that it is high time that we remembered that the Constitution, as amended, speaks not only of the freedom of speech but also of trial by jury instead of trial by accusation.

8 Whether it be a criminal prosecution in court or a character prosecution in the Senate, there is little practical distinction when the life of a person has been ruined.

9 Those of us who shout the loudest about Americanism in making character assassinations are all too frequently those who, by our own words and acts, ignore some of the basic principles of Americanism:

The right to criticize;

The right to hold unpopular beliefs;

The right to protest;

The right of independent thought.

My Notes

---

opportunism: taking advantage of opportunities for personal gain

deliberative: acting with careful thought

ACTIVITY 2.15 continued

4 **FIRST READ:** Conduct a shared reading of "Declaration of Conscience," beginning with the italicized introduction. Pause after paragraph 4 to ensure that students understand the context of the speech.

 TEXT COMPLEXITY

Overall: Complex
Lexile: 1180L
Qualitative: Moderate Difficulty
Task: Challenging (Evaluate)

5 As students are reading, monitor their progress. Be sure they are engaged with the text, **marking the text** for powerful language Senator Smith uses to condemn the actions of her colleagues. A quick application of the **SOAPSTone** strategy will focus students on the importance of purpose and audience and Smith's rhetorical appeals to them. Ask students to make a statement about Smith's tone. What choices in diction support their interpretations? ("debased," "a forum of hate," "It is high time ...")

6 Tell students to pause at the end of paragraph 9 and have them explain what Smith means by the statement "Those of us who shout the loudest about Americanism in making character assassinations are all too frequently those who, by our own words and acts, ignore some of the basic principles of Americanism." What is the significance of her use of the words *us* and *our*?

Scaffolding the Text-Dependent Questions

1. What does the phrase *obscured by eloquence* mean? What does this phrase reveal about Smith's attitude toward her fellow senators? In paragraphs 1 and 2, what situation have "irresponsible words" created? How does the speaker hope to avoid speaking words that are "irresponsible"? RI.11-12.4

2. Identify and describe the rhetorical device Smith uses in paragraph 4. What effect does it achieve? Is it an example of strong logical

argument? Explain. Reread paragraph 4. What is distinctive about the word choice? What is the name of that kind of word organization? Do her words appeal more to logic or to emotion? RI.11-12.5

3. Explain Smith's use of rhetorical appeal in paragraph 5. What are the guiding beliefs of the U.S. government? In what ways does Smith claim the Senate is acting in accordance with or against these guiding beliefs? RI.11-12.5

7 Tell students to pause after paragraph 13 and speculate as to what Smith's "Declaration of Conscience" will likely contain.

8 After reading the text the first time, guide the class in a discussion by asking the Making Observations questions. Check students' general comprehension of the text based on their observations, asking follow-up questions if needed.

2.15

My Notes

10 The exercise of these rights should not cost one single American citizen his reputation or his right to a livelihood nor should he be in danger of losing his reputation or livelihood merely because he happens to know someone who holds unpopular beliefs. Who of us doesn't? Otherwise none of us could call our souls our own. Otherwise thought control would have set in. ...

11 As an American, I am shocked at the way Republicans and Democrats alike are playing directly into the Communist design of "confuse, divide, and conquer." As an American, I don't want a Democratic Administration "whitewash" or "cover-up" any more than I want a Republican smear or witch hunt.

12 As an American, I condemn a Republican "Fascist" just as much as I condemn a Democrat "Communist." I condemn a Democrat "Fascist" just as much as I condemn a Republican "Communist." They are equally dangerous to you and me and to our country. As an American, I want to see our nation recapture the strength and unity it once had when we fought the enemy instead of ourselves.

13 It is with these thoughts that I have drafted what I call a "Declaration of Conscience."

Making Observations
- What questions do you have about the speech after reading it?
- What emotions do you feel as you read the speech?

Scaffolding the Text-Dependent Questions

4. What is the difference between "trial by jury" and "trial by accusation" (paragraph 7)? Which does Smith believe is a "witch hunt" (paragraph 11)? Explain. Reread paragraphs 7 and 11. The sixth amendment to the Bill of Rights reads in part, "... the accused shall enjoy the right to a speedy and public trial, by an impartial jury of the State." In what ways do the Salem witch trials and the McCarthy hearings support or contradict this amendment? What are possible effects of this support or contradiction? RI.11-12.1

5. What does Smith believe is included among the "free speech" rights of American citizens? Review paragraphs 9 and 10. According to Smith, what are the rights of American citizens? How do the McCarthy hearings threaten these rights? RI.11-12.1

Returning to the Text

- Reread the speech to answer these text-dependent questions. Use text evidence to support your responses.
- Write any additional questions you have about the text in your Reader/Writer Notebook.

1. What does the phrase *obscured by eloquence* mean? What does this phrase reveal about Smith's attitude toward her fellow senators?

   Obscured by eloquence means that fancy words have hidden something. This phrase reveals

   Smith's view that her colleagues' "irresponsible words" have contributed to a "national

   suicide."

2. Identify and describe the rhetorical device Smith uses in paragraph 4. What effect does it achieve? Is it an example of strong logical argument? Explain.

   Paragraph 4 is an example of anaphora, the use of repetition ("I speak as") to emphasize an

   idea or (in this case) for self-affirmation. Its effect is to support her authority to speak credibly

   on her topic. It is powerful and effective, but it is not a strong logical argument. It is arguably

   an example of appeal to authority a fallacy in which an argument is considered valid because

   of who is making it.

3. Explain Smith's use of rhetorical appeal in paragraph 5.

   With the words "The United States Senate has long enjoyed worldwide respect as the greatest

   deliberative body in the world," Smith appeals to her fellow senators' sense of pride. She

   follows with a warning that the Senate's recent actions are threatening that respect by turning

   the Senate into "a forum of hate and character assassination sheltered by the shield of

   congressional immunity."

4. What is the difference between "trial by jury" and "trial by accusation" (paragraph 7)? Which does Smith believe is a "witch hunt" (paragraph 11)? Explain.

   The U.S. Constitution guarantees the right to a trial by jury, which means a chance to be fairly

   judged based on evidence. "Trial by accusation" implies that an accusation of wrongdoing

   alone is enough to assume that a person is guilty. A trial by accusation can be called a "witch

   hunt" because it takes no real evidence to condemn the accused person, as was the case in

   the Salem witch trials.

9 RETURNING TO THE TEXT: Guide students to return to the text to respond to the text-dependent questions. Invite them to work in small groups to reread the text and answer the questions. Remind them to use text evidence in their responses.

10 Move from group to group and listen in as students answer the text-dependent questions. If they have difficulty, scaffold the questions by rephrasing them or breaking them down into smaller parts. See the Scaffolding the Text-Dependent Questions boxes for suggestions.

11 Give students time to respond to the Check Your Understanding task. Consider allowing students to examine Smith's speech in pairs to analyze her diction.

12 Review the As You Read instructions with students.

2.15

5. What does Smith believe is included among the "free speech" rights of American citizens?

In paragraph 9, Smith asserts that free speech includes the rights to criticize, hold unpopular beliefs, protest, and think independently. In paragraph 10, she further asserts that "the exercise of these rights should not cost one single American citizen his reputation or his right to a livelihood nor should he be in danger of losing [those rights] merely because he [knows] someone who holds unpopular beliefs."

☑ Check Your Understanding

What part of Senator Smith's speech do you find most powerful? Explain why and give examples of her diction.

_____

_____

_____

_____

As You Read

- Underline or highlight portions of the text in which you find support for the author's argument.
- Circle unknown words and phrases. Try to determine the meaning of the words by using context clues, word parts, or a dictionary.

2.15

Essay

Why I Wrote The Crucible: An Artist's Answer to Politics

by **Arthur Miller**

October 1996

1   As I watched *The Crucible* taking shape as a movie over much of the past year, the sheer depth of time that it represents for me kept returning to mind. As those powerful actors blossomed on the screen, and the children and the horses, the crowds and the wagons, I thought again about how I came to cook all this up nearly fifty years ago, in an America almost nobody I know seems to remember clearly. In a way, there is a biting irony in this film's having been made by a Hollywood studio, something unimaginable in the fifties. But there they are—Daniel Day-Lewis (John Proctor) scything his sea-bordered field, Joan Allen (Elizabeth) lying pregnant in the frigid jail, Winona Ryder (Abigail) stealing her minister-uncle's money, majestic Paul Scofield (Judge Danforth) and his righteous **empathy** with the Devil-possessed children, and all of them looking as **inevitable** as rain.

2   I remember those years—they formed *The Crucible's* skeleton—but I have lost the dead weight of the fear I had then. Fear doesn't travel well; just as it can warp judgment, its absence can diminish memory's truth. What terrifies one generation is likely to bring only a puzzled smile to the next. I remember how in 1964, only twenty years after the war, Harold Clurman, the director of "Incident at Vichy," showed the cast a film of a Hitler speech, hoping to give them a sense of the Nazi period in which my play took place. They watched as Hitler, facing a vast stadium full of adoring people, went up on his toes in ecstasy, hands clasped under his chin, a sublimely self-gratified grin on his face, his body swiveling rather cutely, and they giggled at his overacting.

3   Likewise, films of Senator Joseph McCarthy are rather unsettling—if you remember the fear he once spread. Buzzing his **truculent** sidewalk brawler's snarl through the hairs in his nose, squinting through his cat's eyes and sneering like a villain, he comes across now as nearly comical, a self-aware performer keeping a straight face as he does his juicy threat-shtick.

empathy: understanding
inevitable: impossible to avoid
truculent: easily annoyed

My Notes

ACTIVITY 2.15 continued

13   **FIRST READ:** Before beginning, go over the As You Read section with students. Conduct a shared reading of "Why I Wrote *The Crucible*: An Artist's Answer to Politics." Pause after paragraph 3 to ensure students understand at which stage of his life Miller wrote the essay.

 TEXT COMPLEXITY

Overall: Complex
Lexile: 1340L
Qualitative: High Difficulty
Task: Moderate (Analyze)

14   As students read, monitor their progress. Be sure they are engaged with the text and annotating words and phrases that they find difficult. Even with the background that students have found and that you have provided, this is a very challenging essay, so encourage students to use metacognitive markers and stop periodically to clarify points in small discussion groups. The note-taking graphic organizer will assist students in grasping the meaning of the text.

15   Evaluate whether the selected reading mode is effective. Based on the observations you make during the first reading, you may want to adjust the reading mode. For example, you may decide for the second reading to read aloud certain complex passages, or you may group students differently.

Scaffolding the Text-Dependent Questions

6. What does the text of paragraph 2 suggest about the purpose of Miller's essay? Reread the paragraph. What observations does Miller make about the nature of memory? RI.11-12.6

16 Vocabulary Development: Discuss the Word Connections features with students. Select a few compelling words from the text, such as *inquisitor*, and ask students about the author's possible intent for using them. Elicit other words that the author could have used.

Senator Joseph McCarthy showing a cropped photo that he claims is evidence of American Communist infiltration at a Senate investigation in 1954.

WORD CONNECTIONS

Content Connections

Between the 12th and 18th centuries, the Catholic Church and Catholic rulers created a number of Inquisitions to fight heresy, or beliefs that did not fit its official theology. The most infamous was the Spanish Inquisition (1478–1834), established by King Ferdinand and Queen Isabella of Spain. Inquisitors notoriously used torture and other harsh methods to question and get confessions from suspected heretics.

conviction: strong belief

opaque: difficult to understand or explain

practitioners: people who regularly perform an activity

discourse: conversation

bid fair: seemed likely

abrogations: cancellation, abolition

4 McCarthy's power to stir fears of creeping Communism was not entirely based on illusion, of course; the paranoid, real or pretended, always secretes its pearl around a grain of fact. From being our wartime ally, the Soviet Union rapidly became an expanding empire. In 1949, Mao Zedong took power in China. Western Europe also seemed ready to become Red—especially Italy, where the Communist Party was the largest outside Russia and was growing. Capitalism, in the opinion of many, myself included, had nothing more to say, its final poisoned bloom having been Italian and German Fascism. McCarthy—brash and ill-mannered but to many authentic and true—boiled it all down to what anyone could understand: we had "lost China" and would soon lose Europe as well, because the State Department—staffed, of course, under Democratic presidents—was full of treasonous pro-Soviet intellectuals. It was as simple as that.

5 If our losing China seemed the equivalent of a flea's losing an elephant, it was still a phrase—and a conviction—that one did not dare to question; to do so was to risk drawing suspicion on oneself. Indeed, the State Department proceeded to hound and fire the officers who knew China, its language, and its opaque culture—a move that suggested the practitioners of sympathetic magic who wring the neck of a doll in order to make a distant enemy's head drop off. There was magic all around; the politics of alien conspiracy soon dominated political discourse and bid fair to wipe out any other issue. How could one deal with such enormities in a play?

6 *The Crucible* was an act of desperation. Much of my desperation branched out, I suppose, from a typical Depression-era trauma—the blow struck on the mind by the rise of European Fascism and the brutal anti-Semitism it had brought to power. But by 1950, when I began to think of writing about the hunt for Reds in America, I was motivated in some great part by the paralysis that had set in among many liberals who, despite their discomfort with the inquisitors' violations of civil rights, were fearful, and with good reason, of being identified as covert Communists if they should protest too strongly.

7 In any play, however trivial, there has to be a still point of moral reference against which to gauge the action. In our lives, in the late nineteen-forties and early nineteen-fifties, no such point existed anymore. The left could not look straight at the Soviet Union's abrogations of human rights. The anti-Communist liberals could not acknowledge the violations of those rights by congressional committees. The far right, meanwhile, was licking up all the cream. The days of "J'accuse1" were gone, for anyone needs to feel right to declare someone else wrong. Gradually, all the old political and moral reality had melted like a Dali watch. Nobody but a fanatic, it seemed, could really say all that he believed.

8　President Truman was among the first to have to deal with the dilemma, and his way of resolving it—of having to trim his sails before the howling gale on the right—turned out to be momentous. At first, he was outraged at the allegation of widespread Communist infiltration of the government and called the charge of "**coddling** Communists" a **red herring** dragged in by the Republicans to bring down the Democrats. But such was the gathering power of raw belief in the great Soviet plot that Truman soon felt it necessary to institute loyalty boards of his own.

9　The Red hunt, led by the House Committee on Un-American Activities and by McCarthy, was becoming the dominating **fixation** of the American psyche. It reached Hollywood when the studios, after first resisting, agreed to submit artists' names to the House Committee for "clearing" before employing them. This unleashed a veritable holy terror among actors, directors, and others, from Party members to those who had had the merest brush with a front organization.

10　The Soviet plot was the hub of a great wheel of causation; the plot justified the crushing of all nuance, all the shadings that a realistic judgment of reality requires. Even worse was the feeling that our sensitivity to this **onslaught** on our liberties was passing from us—indeed, from me. In *Timebends*, my autobiography, I recalled the time I'd written a screenplay ("The Hook") about union corruption on the Brooklyn waterfront. Harry Cohn, the head of Columbia Pictures, did something that would once have been considered unthinkable: he showed my script to the F.B.I. Cohn then asked me to take the gangsters in my script, who were threatening and murdering their opponents, and simply change them to Communists. When I declined to commit this idiocy (Joe Ryan, the head of the longshoremen's union, was soon to go to Sing Sing for racketeering), I got a wire from Cohn saying, "The minute we try to make the script pro-American you pull out." By then—it was 1951—I had come to accept this terribly serious insanity as routine, but there was an element of the marvelous in it which I longed to put on the stage.

11　In those years, our thought processes were becoming so magical, so paranoid, that to imagine writing a play about this environment was like trying to pick one's teeth with a ball of wool: I lacked the tools to illuminate **miasma**. Yet I kept being drawn back to it. I had read about the witchcraft trials in college, but it was not until I read a book published in 1867—a two-volume, thousand-page study by Charles W. Upham, who was then the mayor of Salem—that I knew I had to write about the period. Upham had not only written a broad and thorough investigation of what was even then an almost lost chapter of Salem's past but opened up to me the details of personal relationships among many participants in the tragedy.

12　I visited Salem for the first time on a dismal spring day in 1952; it was a sidetracked town then, with abandoned factories and vacant stores. In the gloomy courthouse there I read the transcript of the witchcraft trials of 1692, as taken down in a primitive shorthand by ministers who were **spelling** each other. But there was one entry in Upham in which the thousands of pieces

My Notes

WORD CONNECTIONS

Word Meanings
The word **marvelous** means miraculous or supernatural. In this use, it has the connotation of improbable or incredible as Miller goes on to associate the word with magic and paranoia.

---

coddling: treating with excessive care
red herring: distraction
fixation: unhealthy focus
onslaught: powerful attack
miasma: thick, unpleasant fog or vapor
spelling: giving a rest, relieving

---

17 Tell students to pause at the end of paragraph 8. How does Miller describe the evolution of Truman's views on the threat of Communism, and what relationship did those views likely have on what was soon to come?

Scaffolding the Text-Dependent Questions

7. How does Miller develop the meaning of the word *magic* in paragraphs 5 and 11? Examine the two paragraphs. In what analogy does Miller first mention magic? What are the next two mentions of magic followed by? How does the close proximity of these terms suggest Miller's meaning of "magic"? RI.11-12.4

8. How does Miller develop the meanings of the terms *alien* and *alienated* in paragraphs

5, 17, and 27? Who are the "aliens" in 1692 Salem and in 1950s America? Reread those three paragraphs. Examine the word *alien* in the context of each. What are some synonyms for *alien*? To whom would the word have been aptly applied in 17th-century Salem and 20th-century America? RI.11-12.4

My Notes

I had come across were jogged into place. It was from a report written by the Reverend Samuel Parris, who was one of the chief instigators of the witch-hunt. "During the examination of Elizabeth Procter, Abigail Williams and Ann Putnam"—the two were "afflicted" teen-age accusers, and Abigail was Parris's niece—"both made offer to strike at said Procter; but when Abigail's hand came near, it opened, whereas it was made up, into a fist before, and came down exceeding lightly as it drew near to said Procter, and at length, with open and extended fingers, touched Procter's hood very lightly. Immediately Abigail cried out her fingers, her fingers, her fingers burned. ..."

13 In this remarkably observed gesture of a troubled young girl, I believed, a play became possible. Elizabeth Proctor had been the orphaned Abigail's mistress, and they had lived together in the same small house until Elizabeth fired the girl. By this time, I was sure, John Proctor had bedded Abigail, who had to be dismissed most likely to appease Elizabeth. There was bad blood between the two women now. That Abigail started, in effect, to condemn Elizabeth to death with her touch, then stopped her hand, then went through with it, was quite suddenly the human center of all this turmoil.

14 All this I understood. I had not approached the witchcraft out of nowhere or from purely social and political considerations. My own marriage of twelve years was teetering and I knew more than I wished to know about where the blame lay. That John Proctor the sinner might overturn his paralyzing personal guilt and become the most **forthright** voice against the madness around him was a reassurance to me, and, I suppose, an inspiration: it demonstrated that a clear moral outcry could still spring even from an **ambiguously** unblemished soul. Moving crabwise across the profusion of evidence, I sensed that I had at last found something of myself in it, and a play began to accumulate around this man.

15 But as the dramatic form became visible, one problem remained unyielding: so many practices of the Salem trials were similar to those employed by the congressional committees that I could easily be accused of **skewing** history for a mere partisan purpose. Inevitably, it was no sooner known that my new play was about Salem than I had to confront the charge that such an analogy was **specious**—that there never were any witches but there certainly are Communists. In the seventeenth century, however, the existence of witches was never questioned by the loftiest minds in Europe and America; and even lawyers of the highest **eminence**, like Sir Edward Coke, a veritable hero of liberty for defending the common law against the king's **arbitrary** power, believed that witches had to be prosecuted mercilessly. Of course, there were no Communists in 1692, but it was literally worth your life to deny witches or their powers, given the exhortation in the Bible, "Thou shalt not suffer a witch to live." There had to be witches in the world or the Bible lied. Indeed, the very structure of evil depended on Lucifer's plotting against God. (And the irony is that klatches of Luciferians exist all over the country today; there may even be more of them now than there are Communists.)

forthright: simple and honest, frank
ambiguously: doubtfully, uncertainly
skewing: changing from facts
specious: false or baseless, fallacious
eminence: rank
arbitrary: unlimited

Scaffolding the Text-Dependent Questions

9. **What key idea does Miller support with his description of liberal reaction to McCarthyism (paragraph 6)?** Reread the paragraph. How does Miller describe that liberal reaction? What emotion does he evoke to explain its cause? RI.11-12.1

10. **In paragraph 11, what difficulty does Miller describe when he writes, "...like trying to pick one's teeth with a ball of wool: I lacked the tools to illuminate miasma"?** Is it easy or difficult to pick one's teeth with a ball of wool? What do a ball of wool and miasma have in common? What do these images suggest about the difficulty of Miller's writing task? RI.11-12.4

18 Tell students to pause after paragraph 18 and explain the "circular" logic Miller relates in their own words.

16 As with most humans, panic sleeps in one unlighted corner of my soul. When I walked at night along the empty, wet streets of Salem in the week that I spent there, I could easily work myself into imagining my terror before a gaggle of young girls flying down the road screaming that somebody's "familiar spirit" was chasing them. This anxiety-laden leap backward over nearly three centuries may have been helped along by a particular Upham footnote. At a certain point, the high court of the province made the fatal decision to admit, for the first time, the use of "spectral evidence" as proof of guilt. Spectral evidence, so aptly named, meant that if I swore that you had sent out your "familiar spirit" to choke, tickle, poison me or my cattle, or to control my thoughts and actions, I could get you hanged unless you confessed to having had contact with the Devil. After all, only the Devil could lend such powers of invisible transport to **confederates**, in his everlasting plot to bring down Christianity.

17 Naturally, the best proof of the sincerity of your confession was your naming others whom you had seen in the Devil's company—an invitation to private vengeance, but made official by the seal of the **theocratic** state. It was as though the court had grown tired of thinking and had invited in the instincts: spectral evidence—that poisoned cloud of paranoid fantasy—made a kind of lunatic sense to them, as it did in plot-ridden 1952, when so often the question was not the acts of an accused but the thoughts and intentions in his alienated mind.

18 The breathtaking circularity of the process had a kind of poetic tightness. Not everybody was accused, after all, so there must be some reason why you were. By denying that there is any reason whatsoever for you to be accused, you are implying, by virtue of a surprisingly small logical leap, that mere chance picked you out, which in turn implies that the Devil might not really be at work in the village, or, God forbid, even exist. Therefore, the investigation itself is either mistaken or a fraud. You would have to be a crypto-Luciferian to say that—not a great idea if you wanted to go back to your farm.

19 The more I read into the Salem panic, the more it touched off corresponding images of common experiences in the fifties: the old friend of a blacklisted person crossing the street to avoid being seen talking to him; the overnight conversions of former leftists into born-again patriots; and so on. Apparently, certain processes are universal. When Gentiles in Hitler's Germany, for example, saw their Jewish neighbors being trucked off, or farmers in Soviet Ukraine saw the Kulaks vanishing before their eyes, the common reaction, even among those unsympathetic to Nazism or Communism, was quite naturally to turn away in fear of being identified with the condemned. As I learned from non-Jewish refugees, however, there was often a despairing pity mixed with "Well, they must have done something." Few of us can easily surrender our belief that society must somehow make sense. The thought that the state has lost its mind and is punishing so many innocent people is **intolerable**. And so the evidence has to be internally denied.

My Notes

WORD CONNECTIONS

Roots and Affixes
The prefix **crypto-** comes from the Greek *kryptos* and means "hidden" or "covered." Miller suggests that only a hidden Satanist would imply that the witch investigations were a fraud. Other related words are *crypt* and *cryptic*.

confederates: allies
theocratic: governed by God or priests
intolerable: unbearable

Scaffolding the Text-Dependent Questions

11. What is "spectral evidence"? To what does Miller compare it in paragraphs 16 and 17? Reread the two paragraphs. The word *spectral* is an adjective form of *specter*, or ghost. The existence of ghosts cannot be objectively proven. How does Miller feel that accusations of McCarthyism rely on something similar to spectral evidence? RI.11-12.1

12. In your own words, summarize the fallacious reasoning that Miller describes in paragraph 18. What is its effect on the way the text is read and understood? Reread paragraph. What is the nature of the "logic" Miller is describing? What effect would it have on people who believe in a literal Devil? RI.11-12.1

My Notes

20 I was also drawn into writing *The Crucible* by the chance it gave me to use a new language—that of seventeenth-century New England. The plain, craggy English was liberating in a strangely sensuous way, with its swings from an almost legalistic precision to a wonderful metaphoric richness. "The Lord doth terrible things amongst us, by lengthening the chain of the roaring lion in an extraordinary manner, so that the Devil is come down in great wrath," Deodat Lawson, one of the great witch-hunting preachers, said in a sermon. Lawson rallied his congregation for what was to be nothing less than a religious war against the Evil One—"Arm, arm, arm!"—and his concealed anti-Christian accomplices.

21 But it was not yet my language, and among other strategies to make it mine I enlisted the help of a former University of Michigan classmate, the Greek-American scholar and poet Kimon Friar (He later translated Kazantzakis.) The problem was not to the **archaic** speech but to try to create a new echo of it which would flow freely off American actors' tongues. As in the film nearly fifty years later, the actors in the first production grabbed the language and ran with it as happily as if it were their customary speech.

22 *The Crucible* took me about a year to write. With its five sets and a cast of twenty-one, it never occurred to me that it would take a brave man to produce it on Broadway, especially given the **prevailing** climate, but Kermit Bloomgarden never faltered. Well before the play opened, a strange tension had begun to build. Only two years earlier, the *Death of a Salesman* touring company had played to a thin crowd in Peoria, Illinois, having been boycotted nearly to death by the American Legion and the Jaycees. Before that, the Catholic War Veterans had prevailed upon the Army not to allow its theatrical groups to perform, first, *All My Sons*, and then any play of mine, in occupied Europe. The Dramatists Guild refused to protest attacks on a new play by Sean O'Casey, a self-declared Communist, which forced its producer to cancel his option. I knew of two suicides by actors depressed by upcoming investigation, and every day seemed to bring news of people exiling themselves to Europe: Charlie Chaplin, the director Joseph Losey, Jules Dassin, the harmonica virtuoso Larry Adler, Donald Ogden Stewart, one of the most sought-after screenwriters in Hollywood, and Sam Wanamaker, who would lead the successful campaign to rebuild the Old Globe Theater on the Thames.

23 On opening night, January 22, 1953, I knew that the atmosphere would be pretty hostile. The coldness of the crowd was not a surprise; Broadway audiences were not famous for loving history lessons, which is what they made of the play. It seems to me entirely appropriate that on the day the play opened, a newspaper headline read "ALL 13 REDS GUILTY"—a story about American Communists who faced prison for "conspiring to teach and advocate the duty and necessity of forcible overthrow of government." Meanwhile, the remoteness of the production was guaranteed by the director, Jed Harris, who insisted that this was a classic requiring the actors to face

> **archaic:** no longer used in ordinary language
> **prevailing:** commonly accepted by most people

Scaffolding the Text-Dependent Questions

13. In paragraph 22, Miller calls Broadway producer Kermit Bloomgarden "brave." Why does it take a "brave man" to produce *The Crucible* for the first time in January 1953? Review the text in Miller's essay that describes the political situation of the time. What was Bloomgarden risking by staging *The Crucible*? RI.11-12.4

front, never each other. The critics were not swept away. "Arthur Miller is a problem playwright in both senses of the word," wrote Walter Kerr of the Herald Tribune, who called the play "a step backward into mechanical **parable**." The Times was not much kinder, saying, "There is too much excitement and not enough emotion in 'The Crucible.'" But the play's future would turn out quite differently.

24 About a year later, a new production, one with younger, less accomplished actors, working in the Martinique Hotel ballroom, played with the **fervor** that the script and the times required, and *The Crucible* became a hit. The play stumbled into history, and today, I am told, it is one of the most heavily demanded trade-fiction paperbacks in this country; the Bantam and Penguin editions have sold more than six million copies. I don't think there has been a week in the past forty-odd years when it hasn't been on a stage somewhere in the world. Nor is the new screen version the first. Jean-Paul Sartre, in his Marxist phase, wrote a French film adaptation that blamed the tragedy on the rich landowners conspiring to persecute the poor. (In truth, most of those who were hanged in Salem were people of substance, and two or three were very large landowners.)

25 It is only a slight exaggeration to say that, especially in Latin America, *The Crucible* starts getting produced wherever a political coup appears imminent, or a dictatorial **regime** has just been overthrown. From Argentina to Chile to Greece, Czechoslovakia, China, and a dozen other places, the play seems to present the same primeval structure of human sacrifice to the furies of fanaticism and paranoia that goes on repeating itself forever as though imbedded in the brain of social man.

26 I am not sure what *The Crucible* is telling people now, but I know that its paranoid center is still pumping out the same darkly attractive warning that it did in the fifties. For some, the play seems to be about the dilemma of relying on the testimony of small children accusing adults of sexual abuse, something I'd not have dreamed of forty years ago. For others, it may simply be a fascination with the outbreak of paranoia that suffuses the play—the blind panic that, in our age, often seems to sit at the dim edges of consciousness. Certainly, its political **implications** are the central issue for many people; the Salem interrogations turn out to be eerily exact models of those yet to come in Stalin's Russia, Pinochet's Chile, Mao's China, and other regimes. (Nien Cheng, the author of "Life and Death in Shanghai," has told me that she could hardly believe that a non-Chinese—someone who had not experienced the Cultural Revolution—had written the play.) But below its concerns with justice the play evokes a lethal brew of illicit sexuality, fear of the supernatural, and political manipulation, a combination not unfamiliar these days. The film, by reaching a broad American audience as no play ever can, may well unearth still other connections to those buried public terrors that Salem first announced on this continent.

My Notes

parable: story that teaches a lesson
fervor: enthusiasm
regime: type of government
implications: suggestions

Scaffolding the Text-Dependent Questions

14. How does Chinese author Nien Cheng's comment about *The Crucible* in paragraph 26 support a key idea of Miller's essay? How does the Chinese Cultural Revolution compare with the Salem witch trials and the McCarthy hearings? What do these similarities across geography and time suggest about human nature? RI.11-12.1

ACTIVITY 2.15 continued

19 After reading the text for the first time, guide the class in a discussion by asking the Making Observations questions. Check students' general comprehension of the text based on their observations, asking follow-up questions if needed.

 TEACHER TO TEACHER

Create a **Cognate Bridge Word Wall** in your classroom and add vocabulary from *The Crucible* and Miller's essay. Cognates help build vocabulary by getting students to recognize patterns in word roots. For example, add *conviction* and the Spanish *convicción*, which both derive from the Latin *convictus*, "to refute."

2.15

My Notes

27 One thing more—something wonderful in the old sense of that word. I recall the weeks I spent reading testimony by the **tome**, **commentaries**, broadsides, confessions, and accusations. And always the **crucial** damning event was the signing of one's name in the Devil's book. This Faustian agreement to hand over one's soul to the dreaded Lord of Darkness was the ultimate insult to God. But what were these new inductees supposed to have done once they'd signed on? Nobody seems even to have thought to ask. But, of course, actions are as irrelevant during cultural and religious wars as they are in nightmares. The thing at issue is buried intentions—the secret allegiances of the alienated heart, always the main threat to the theocratic mind, as well as its **immemorial** quarry.

Making Observations
- What are your first thoughts about the article?
- Which of Miller's observations do you find interesting?
- What images in the essay catch your attention?

tome: large book
commentaries: texts that comment on a topic
crucial: very important
immemorial: beyond time or memory

Scaffolding the Text-Dependent Questions

15. What central idea about cultural and religious wars does Miller express in his final paragraph? Based on this central idea, what inference can be made about the inevitability of witch hunts? What is the difference between actions and intentions? How is it problematic when authorities try to control intentions? What might result from such attempts? RI.11-12.1

Returning to the Text

- Reread the essay to answer these text-dependent questions. Use text evidence to support your responses.
- Write any additional questions you have about the text in your Reader/Writer Notebook.

6. What does the text of paragraph 2 suggest about the purpose of Miller's essay?

   In that paragraph Miller states, "I remember those years—they formed *The Crucible*'s skeleton—but I have lost the dead weight of the fear I had then. Fear doesn't travel well; just as it can warp judgment, its absence can diminish memory's truth." This suggests that one purpose of Miller's writing is to record his memories of that time before more of their emotional content is lost.

7. How does Miller develop the meaning of the word *magic* in paragraphs 5 and 11?

   In paragraph 5, Miller writes that firing people who understood China was like "the practitioners of sympathetic magic who wring the neck of a doll in order to make a distant enemy's head drop off." In paragraph 11, Miller adds a connotation of paranoia to the term *magic*. He expands its meaning to include the illogical thought processes that form the basis of conspiracy theories.

8. How does Miller develop the meanings of the terms *alien* and *alienated* in paragraphs 5, 17, and 27? Who are the "aliens" in 1692 Salem and in 1950s America?

   In paragraph 5, the word *alien* emphasizes a quality of otherness that people fear. In paragraphs 17 and 27, Miller describes the "alienated mind" and the "the alienated heart" of the person suspected or accused of being other. In 1692 Salem, the feared *alien* are "witches" with differing beliefs or morals or sufferers of mental illness; in 1950s America, they are "Communists" who threaten democracy.

9. What key idea does Miller support with his description of liberal reaction to McCarthyism (paragraph 6)?

   When Miller points out the "paralysis that had set in among many liberals who, despite their discomfort with the inquisitors' violations of civil rights, were fearful, and with good reason, of being identified as covert Communists if they should protest too strongly," he supports the key idea that events like the "Red hunt" and the Salem witch trials are complex manifestations of fear.

20 **RETURNING TO THE TEXT:** Guide students to return to the text to respond to the text-dependent questions. Invite them to work in small groups to reread the text and answer the questions. Remind them to use text evidence in their responses.

21 Move from group to group and listen in as students answer the text-dependent questions. If they have difficulty, scaffold the questions by rephrasing them or breaking them down into smaller parts. See the Scaffolding the Text-Dependent Questions boxes for suggestions.

⭐ TEACHER TO TEACHER

If possible, consider showing documentaries about the McCarthy era and Hollywood. Search using keywords such as "Hollywood and McCarthyism," "Joe McCarthy and Edward Murrow," and "understanding McCarthyism."

10. In paragraph 11, what difficulty does Miller describe when he writes, "... like trying to pick one's teeth with a ball of wool: I lacked the tools to illuminate miasma"?

A "ball of wool" and "miasma" are shapeless masses rather than the type of pointed, precise instrument needed for picking teeth. Miller is describing the difficulty of trying to write a play about the Communist scare while the scare is occurring, saying that it is hard to find a focus for such a play in such stressful, confusing circumstances.

11. What is "spectral evidence"? To what does Miller compare it in paragraphs 16 and 17?

"Spectral evidence" is testimony from a Salem accuser that a witch has sent his or her spirit to harass or harm a victim. That mere accusation was sufficient to establish the accused as a witch. Miller compares this to the Red Scare in 1952, with an accused's "thoughts and intentions" being the "familiar spirit," something claimed to be real that cannot be seen or objectively known by the accusers.

12. In your own words, summarize the fallacious reasoning that Miller describes in paragraph. 18 What is its effect on the way the text is read and understood?

The "reasoning" is thus: Not everyone is accused of witchcraft. Therefore, there must be a reason that you were. If you say there isn't, you're claiming that you are targeted by chance. But if the Devil isn't targeting you, maybe he isn't targeting anyone. And if he's not targeting anyone, he may not exist. But since everyone in Puritan New England knew the Devil existed, the accusation must be valid.

13. In paragraph 22, Miller calls Broadway producer Kermit Bloomgarden "brave." Why does it take a "brave man" to produce *The Crucible* for the first time in January 1953?

Miller describes how anti-Communist pressure had been building in the period leading to the play's premiere. Suspected Communists were being investigated by the government, some plays were being closed down, and many actors and writers were moving to Europe. Another of Miller's plays was already being boycotted, and it was brave of Bloomgarden to stage *The Crucible*, given its theme.

22 Direct students to complete the graphic organizer in the Working from the Text section, using notes taken during reading to answer the organizer's six questions.

14. How does Chinese author Nien Cheng's comment about *The Crucible* in paragraph 26 support a key idea of Miller's essay?

Cheng says she "could hardly believe" that someone who did not experience the Chinese

Cultural Revolution had written *The Crucible*. This is because that Cultural Revolution

displayed many of the same characteristics as the Salem witch trials and the McCarthy

hearings. Her comment supports the key idea that the dynamic demonstrated in 1600s Salem

and 1950s America is not unique.

15. What central idea about cultural and religious wars does Miller express in his final paragraph? Based on this central idea, what inference can be made about the inevitability of witch hunts?

Miller says that in "cultural and religious wars" actions are "irrelevant." Instead, the "issue

is buried intentions." The intangibility of this issue suggests that when authorities begin to

police people's thoughts rather than their actions, a witch hunt is probably not far behind.

Working from the Text

16. *The Crucible* premiered in 1953 to critical acclaim and to criticism for its implied social commentary on the activities of the House Un-American Activities Committee. Arthur Miller wrote this essay many years later to explain why he wrote the play. Analyze Miller's and society's responses to McCarthyism as well as Miller's fascination with the witch trials to determine why Miller wrote *The Crucible*. Use your answers to the text-dependent questions and skim the text again to take notes on the following topics.

What are Miller's feelings about McCarthyism?	What was Hollywood's and society's response to McCarthyism?	Why was Miller fascinated by the witch trials?

2.15

What is the connection between witchcraft and communism?	What was the critical and public reaction to *The Crucible* and other Miller plays?	What is the lasting legacy of *The Crucible*?

17. Summarize the main ideas and key themes of *The Crucible*. Think about how the action of this play is a crucible or test for the individuals and the society of Salem.

LANGUAGE & WRITER'S CRAFT: Rhetorical Punctuation

One way to make a point in an argument is to use effective punctuation. Effective punctuation helps a reader understand how to read a sentence, often by using commas to denote a pause, a question mark to show a question, or a period to end a statement. Punctuation can also include apostrophes, colons, and semicolons.

Example: But what were these new inductees supposed to have done once they'd signed on?

Here Miller uses a question mark to pose a rhetorical question. Authors might use a rhetorical question mark in an argument to guide readers to consider a point that is being made.

PRACTICE Decide which of the following sentences are rhetorical questions and punctuate them correctly.

How are we to know what Miller's political beliefs are [ ]

Miller's political beliefs are hard to decipher [ ]

What do Miller's political beliefs have to do with *The Crucible* [ ]

☑ Check Your Understanding

Has Miller's explanation enhanced or limited your interpretation of the play? Briefly explain your answer.

✐ Explain How an Author Builds an Argument

Write an essay in which you explain how the author builds an argument to persuade the audience of the social agenda promoted in a speech or essay. Select one passage as the focus for your essay: Margaret Chase Smith's speech Declaration of Conscience or Arthur Miller's essay "Why I Wrote *The Crucible*: An Artist's Answer to Politics." In your essay, analyze how the author uses three or more of the rhetorical techniques you have studied to strengthen the logic and persuasiveness of the argument. Be sure to:

- Identify the author's claim.
- Label and provide evidence of rhetorical techniques, introducing and punctuating them correctly.
- Analyze the effects of each rhetorical technique.
- Evaluate the overall effectiveness of the passage.
- End with a conclusion that follows logically from your analysis.
- Check to make sure you have correctly used hyphens and other punctuation.

EXPLAIN HOW AN AUTHOR BUILDS AN ARGUMENT

The following standards are addressed in the writing prompt:
- W.11-12.1
- W.11-12.1e
- RI.11-12.6

23 Direct students' attention to the Language & Writer's Craft box on rhetorical punctuation. Read aloud the information and guide students to understand how a rhetorical question is different from a literal question by modeling a few examples on the board. Then have students work independently to complete the Practice section. Go over the correct punctuation as a class.

24 Give students time to respond to the Check Your Understanding task and the Explain How an Author Builds an Argument section. Consider allowing students to discuss Miller's essay before independently writing their reactions to it.

SAT® CONNECTIONS

This activity provides practice with the following important SAT skill: explaining how an author builds an argument to persuade an audience. If students need additional support with this type of writing, direct them to resources available online including the SAT Essay rubric, sample prompts, and sample essays.

ASSESS

Review students' explanations for the Check Your Understanding task. Notice whether students support well-thought-out reasons with evidence and examples from the texts.

Use students' responses to the writing prompt to assess their ability to effectively analyze how an author builds an argument to persuade an audience of a social agenda.

ADAPT

If students need additional help determining whether Miller's explanation enhances or limits their interpretations of the play, have them recall their original interpretations of the play before reading Miller's essay. Then have them ask themselves:

- Does Miller's explanation add valuable insight to my original interpretation of the play? Explain.
- Does Miller's explanation make my original interpretation seem invalid? Explain.

PLAN

Materials: *The Crucible*, Act Four
Suggested Pacing: 2 50-minute class periods plus homework

TEACH

1 Read the Learning Targets and Preview with students. Tell them that in this activity, they will be writing dialogue in preparation for the first Embedded Assessment.

2 Ask students to complete the steps in the Falling Action section. Have them predict the outcome of the play in a quickwrite.

3 Conduct a shared **close reading** of Act Four, directing students to **mark the text** for the following:

• What changes have occurred in the town?
• What is the purpose of a drunk Herrick in the jail scenes?
• What is the tone of that scene?
• How does this act draw a parallel between the Salem witch trials and McCarthyism? Note how Proctor refuses to allow his integrity to be compromised by the power of a corrupt government.

4 Direct students to read the first paragraph in the Analyzing Dialogue section. Stress the possibility that Proctor, Hale, and Corey are representatives of particular points of view in this final act. Divide students into pairs or small groups. Direct them to write adjectives describing each character in the **graphic organizer** in student step 3, and to complete student steps 4 and 5.

5 Have students revisit the posters about Hale, Proctor, and Corey created in Activity 2.5. Add details from this and previous acts to the posters. Discuss with students the question related to character foils in the Check Your Understanding task.

ACTIVITY
2.16 Integrity Rises to the Top: Writing Dialogue

Learning Strategies

Close Reading
Graphic Organizer
Marking the Text
Note-taking
Questioning the Text

Learning Targets
• Analyze the use of dialogue and character interactions in a dramatic text.
• Generate scripted dialogue that reveals character and propels action.

Preview

In this activity, you will study dialogue that reveals character and propels action and then use the insights you have gained to write dialogue.

My Notes

Falling Action

1. **Quickwrite:** With one more act remaining in the play and the tension at its peak, predict the outcome of the play. Use details from the text to support your prediction.

2. As you read the opening section of Act Four (until Elizabeth and Proctor are alone), mark the text for changes that have occurred in the town. Be prepared to share your observations with the class.

Analyzing Dialogue

3. Continue the exploration of foils that you began in Activity 2.5 by tracking the characteristics of Proctor, Hale, and Corey as possible representations of particular points of view in the final pages of Act Four by paying special attention to their dialogue. In the graphic organizer, record adjectives that describe each character.

Hale	Proctor	Corey
proud self-righteous intellectual enthusiastic believer	sinner fraud lecher adulterer honest proud defensive ashamed superior	proud stubborn outspoken courageous

4. Cite a specific example of dialogue from one of the three characters that conveys a point of view. Explain how the dialogue does so.

5. In general, what role does dialogue play in the advancement of *The Crucible*'s plot?

☑ Check Your Understanding
Briefly describe how Hale and Corey function as foils to John Proctor. Which of Proctor's traits are more apparent when comparing him with each of the other men?

College and Career Readiness Standards

Focus Standards:

RL.11-12.5 Analyze how an author's choices concerning how to structure specific parts of a text (e.g., the choice of where to begin or end a story, the choice to provide a comedic or tragic resolution) contribute to its overall structure and meaning as well as its aesthetic impact.

W.11-12.4 Produce clear and coherent writing in which the development, organization, and style are appropriate to task, purpose, and audience.

W.11-12.3b Use narrative techniques, such as dialogue, pacing, description, reflection, and multiple plot lines, to develop experiences, events, and/or characters.

Additional Standards Addressed:

W.11-12.3d

6 Direct students' attention to the Creating a Dialogue section. Explain that their next script-writing task is to write the dialogue that will move the plot forward and reveal characters' relationships. Refer students to the script-writing checklist they created in Activity 2.7.

Creating a Dialogue

The last step in writing a script is to actually write the dialogue. This essential element functions to reveal characters' relationships and to move the action forward. As you look through the three excerpts from the play, review your writer's checklist and add any details that will help you in writing your own script.

Dialogue that reveals characters' relationships:

ACT TWO, SCENE 2

PROCTOR

(*Searching*)

I must speak with you, Abigail. (*She does not move, staring at him.*) Will you sit?

ABIGAIL

How do you come?

PROCTOR

Friendly.

ABIGAIL

(*glancing about*)

I don't like the woods at night. Pray you, stand closer. (*He comes closer to her.*) I knew it must be you. When I heard the pebbles on the window, before I opened up my eyes I knew. (*Sits on log.*) I though you would come a good time sooner.

PROCTOR

I had thought to come many times.

Dialogue that moves the action forward:

ACT THREE

DANFORTH

Your husband—did he indeed turn from you?

ELIZABETH

(*in agony*)

My husband — is a goodly man, sir.

DANFORTH

Then he did not turn from you.

ELIZABETH

(*starting to glance at Proctor*)

He—

DANFORTH

(*reaches out and holds her face, then*)

Look at me! To your own knowledge, has John Proctor ever committed the crime of lechery? (*In a crisis of indecision she cannot speak.*) Answer my question! Is your husband a lecher!

ELIZABETH

(*faintly*)

No, sir.

7 Give students time to respond to the writing prompt. Consider allowing students to work in pairs to revise their scripts from Activity 2.8.

ASSESS

For the Check Your Understanding task, review students' descriptions of how Hale and Corey function as foils to John Proctor. Note how well students understand the concept of a foil. Make sure that they list traits for Proctor that become more apparent when he is compared or contrasted with Hale and Corey.

Use students' responses to the writing prompt to assess their abilities to incorporate monologues in their scenes that effectively convey the inner thoughts of characters and offer social commentary.

ADAPT

If students need additional help describing how Hale and Corey function as foils to John Proctor, have students form pairs. Tell the pairs to combine their list of traits for Proctor, Hale, and Corey. Direct them to identify the traits of Proctor that are opposite from the traits of Hale and Corey. Have them consider whether these differences make Proctor's traits more apparent.

If students have difficulty utilizing believable stage directions for their performances, have them conduct an exercise in which they convey meaning using nonsense syllables. This will force them to rely on inflection, gestures, and facial expressions to convey meaning. Have them incorporate some of the effective stage directions they use in the exercise into their rehearsals using dialogue.

A final type of speaking in a play is a **monologue**, in which a character reveals private thoughts and emotions.

MARY

(*Innocently*)

I never knew it before. I never knew anything before. When she come into the court I say to myself, I must not accuse this woman, for she sleep in ditches, and so very old and poor. ... But then ... then she sit there, denying and denying, and I feel a misty coldness climbin' up my back, and the skin on my skull begin to creep, and I feel a clamp around my neck and I cannot breathe air; and then ... (*Entranced as though it were a miracle*) I hear a voice, a screamin' voice, and it were my voice ... and all at once I remembered everything she done to me! (*Slight pause as Proctor watches Elizabeth pass him, then speaks, being aware of Elizabeth's alarm.*)

Comparing Interpretations

Listen to the audio recording of the monologue from SpringBoard Digital. In your Reader/Writer Notebook, write down your observations as you listen. What words does the actor emphasize? What emotions do you notice? After you listen to the monologue and record your notes, discuss your observations with a small group, comparing how listening to the monologue changed or confirmed your interpretation and why.

> **✎ Writing Prompt: Literary**
>
> With your group, reread the script from Activity 2.7 that shows how hysteria grows out of rumor and unfounded accusations. Working together, revise the script to include a monologue that reveals a character's inner thoughts. Use the monologue to convey your group's social commentary on the scene. Be sure to:
>
> - Include dialogue that moves the action forward and reveals characters' thoughts and emotions.
> - Incorporate varied syntax in the dialogue, keeping in mind that characters need to speak realistically and according to their individual traits (be sure to reference your character notes).
>
> Rehearse the lines and act out the stage directions. Then revise the dialogue and stage directions according to your group's intended effect on the audience. Remember that stage directions are written in the present tense.
>
> When your script is complete, perform the scene for another group in the class. Use the Scoring Guide so the other group can offer feedback on the script. Switch roles and offer suggestions to help the other group improve its script as well.

✎ WRITING PROMPT: LITERARY

The following standards are addressed in the writing prompt:
- W.11-12.3b
- W.11-12.3d

Contemporary Conflicts

Learning Targets

- Brainstorm a variety of contemporary concerns.
- Generate social commentary within a dramatic script.
- Compose a plan for a dramatic script using genre characteristics.

Preview

In this activity, you will work with a group to brainstorm a plan for a dramatic script.

Learning Strategies

Graphic Organizer
Marking the Text
Note-taking
Rereading

Preparing for a Dramatic Scene

1. Before discussing with your group, individually jot notes that answer the following question.

   What personal and community conflicts concern you and your friends? Consider campus, local, national, and global conflicts. You may think in terms of health, families, technology, the environment, and any other area that comes to mind.

2. Gather as a small group. Choose one person to record notes. Say your ideas out loud as the recorder writes them on paper. Together, generate as many ideas as you can.

3. Reread your group's ideas. Choose one conflict from the list to use as a topic for your group's dramatic scene. If you have a hard time agreeing, conduct a silent vote using numbers (three points for your first choice, two points for your second choice, one point for your third choice). Then brainstorm and list possible historical time periods that might provide a good setting for exploring the conflict.

4. In preparing to create and perform the dramatic scene for Embedded Assessment 1, reread this passage from "Why I Wrote *The Crucible*" by Arthur Miller. Mark the text for the universal underlying issues that Miller's play exposed to help you connect personal conflicts with universal conflicts.

   I am not sure what *The Crucible* is telling people now, but I know that its paranoid center is still pumping out the same darkly attractive warning that it did in the fifties. For some, the play seems to be about the dilemma of relying on the testimony of small children accusing adults of sexual abuse, something I'd not have dreamed of forty years ago. For others, it may simply be a fascination with the outbreak of paranoia that suffuses the play—the blind panic that, in our age, often seems to sit at the dim edges of consciousness. Certainly its political implications are the central issue for many people; the Salem interrogations turn out to be eerily exact models of those yet to come in Stalin's Russia, Pinochet's Chile, Mao's China, and other regimes. (Nien Cheng, the author of Life and Death in Shanghai, has told me that she could hardly believe that a non-Chinese— someone who had not experienced the Cultural Revolution—had written the play.) But below its concerns with justice the play evokes a lethal brew of illicit sexuality, fear of the supernatural, and political manipulation, a

My Notes

PLAN

Materials: sticky notes
Suggested Pacing: 1 50-minute class period

TEACH

1 Read the Learning Targets and Preview with students. Tell them that they will be beginning the process that will produce a dramatic script.

2 Guide students through the steps in the Preparing for a Dramatic Scene section. Divide students into discussion groups. Lead them to brainstorm ideas about contemporary issues. Provide each group with a pad of sticky notes. Students are to simultaneously call out and write an issue on a sticky note (calling out is so that all can hear the ideas and get ideas and so that each idea gets written only once). Stop after two minutes.

3 Direct groups to reach a consensus about their top two issues.

4 Ask students to close read the excerpt from Miller's essay in student step 4, marking the text according to the directions.

College and Career Readiness Standards

Focus Standards:

W.11-12.3a Engage and orient the reader by setting out a problem, situation, or observation and its significance, establishing one or multiple point(s) of view, and introducing a narrator and/or characters; create a smooth progression of experiences or events.

W.11-12.4 Produce clear and coherent writing in which the development, organization, and style are appropriate to task, purpose, and audience.

W.11-12.5 Develop and strengthen writing as needed by planning, revising, editing, rewriting, or trying a new approach, focusing on addressing what is most significant for a specific purpose and audience.

5 Use the graphic organizer's three examples to help students see the goal of their dramatic scene. They will consider the underlying issue of the contemporary concerns they have identified and choose a parallel setting for a dramatization that conveys a social message. Insist that students complete the **graphic organizer** for two issues and then determine the one that works best.

6 Guide students in reviewing the Planning and Prewriting steps for Embedded Assessment 1.

7 Write the following Steps for Script Writing on the board. Working collaboratively, students need to complete each step:

- Develop characters
- Identify conflicts
- Outline plot line
- Write stage directions (initial)
- Write dialogue
- Incorporate additional stage directions
- Rehearse/revise/present/reflect

8 Make sure students attend to the Independent Reading Link. Direct them to create an essay in their Reader/Writer Notebooks. To assess their independent reading, set a date to check for their comparison essay in students' notebooks.

ASSESS

Use students' script drafts to assess their abilities to:

- Organize their thoughts about the scene.
- Plan characters, conflicts, plot lines, stage directions, and dialogue.
- Write dramatic scenes using their script-writing checklist as a guide.

ADAPT

If some students have not mastered the skills necessary to write dramatic scenes, tell them to create detailed outlines or storyboards of their scenes. Then have students who have mastered the script-writing elements act as mentors by reviewing the outlines or storyboards and asking questions or making suggestions that will improve the scenes.

---

combination not unfamiliar these days. The film, by reaching a broad American audience as no play ever can, may well unearth still other connections to those buried public terrors that Salem first announced on this continent.

5. Use the graphic organizer to help you organize your thoughts about the scene you will write. The examples provide a model for the three areas you need to identify prior to writing your script.

Contemporary Societal Conflict	Underlying, Universal Conflict	Parallel Historical Setting
Example A: McCarthy trials/political injustice due to paranoia	Political manipulation	Salem witch trials
Example B: The fastest-growing homeless group is families	People have the attitude "It's their own fault"; there is a large stigma attached to receiving charitable help	The Great Depression
Example C: Environmental issues surrounding fuel	Global economic issues; global environmental issues	The time of the invention of the automobile

6. Review the Planning steps in the Embedded Assessment 1 instructions. Use a separate paper to plan your characters, conflicts, plot lines, stage directions, and dialogue.

7. Draft your scene on a separate paper, using *The Crucible* as the model text. Be sure to use the script-writing checklist that you created earlier in the unit.

🔲 Independent Reading Checkpoint

You have read a variety of texts related to social issues, including free speech. Which text did you find most compelling? What made it more compelling than the other texts? Include comparisons of excerpts from different texts that portray similar events or present similar ideas.

Creating and Performing a Dramatic Scene

Materials: student drafts from Activity 2.17; access to computers for word processing (optional)
Suggested pacing: 2 50-minute class periods

 ASSIGNMENT

As a small group, choose a modern social conflict. Then write and perform a dramatic scene set in a different historical time period that makes a statement about the conflict. Your performance should demonstrate your understanding of Arthur Miller's purpose for writing *The Crucible* and how the play's historical setting supports his purpose.

Planning and Prewriting: Take time to plan, write, and rehearse your scene	■ How can you relate your social issue to a personal conflict in a way that is engaging and relevant to the audience?
	■ What historical settings could best convey your group's statement on the social conflict, just as Miller did? How can you find out more information about your scene's historical context?
	■ What roles will each group member play in the performance? How will the number of people in your group affect the characters and plot of your scene?
	■ What is the fairest way to share the responsibilities of the assessment between group members? How can you use a program such as Google Docs to promote collaborative work on the script drafts?
Drafting: Compose a draft of your dramatic script	■ How will you use set design, stage directions, and dialogue to help your audience understand the scene's historical setting?
	■ How will you engage the audience at the beginning of your scene? How can you order the events in your scene so your group's statement is clear to the audience? How do your characters and setting reveal your group's statement?
	■ What role will dialogue, stage directions, and set design play in helping your audience understand the characters, conflict, and plot?
	■ How will you format your text to include dialogue and stage directions?
Revising and Rehearsing: Plan time to revise and rehearse your scene	■ What dramatic props, movement, or sound effects can you use to add to the impact of your writing?
	■ How can you evaluate your performance for vocal delivery, energy of performance, and overall quality?
	■ How can you use the Scoring Guide to help guide your revision?
Editing for Publishing and Performance: Polish the scene and rehearse to deliver a smooth presentation	■ What resources are available to help you edit and finalize your script?
	■ How will you share responsibility to ensure that all the necessary elements of your performance are ready at the assigned time?

TEACHER TO TEACHER

This assignment should be done in groups of no more than four. Keep the number of characters small and the script relatively short.

1 Planning and Prewriting: Students should come to the first group meeting for this assignment with many different ideas. The first job of the group will be to agree on an issue to be addressed. Once they have reached agreement on this, they can proceed.

2 Drafting: Try to make arrangements for students to draft their scene using a collaborative format such as Google Docs so they can mutually participate in the creation of dialogue and plotting of the scene.

3 Revising and Rehearsing: Online file-sharing programs will encourage constant revision and refining and will enhance each group member's ability to create an individualized script.

4 Video recording rehearsals will give students an opportunity to critique their own performances and encourage editing and revision for effect.

5 Editing for Publishing and Performance: A final script can easily be produced based on group contributions. A video of the performances would create a classroom archive of creative work.

6 Reflection: Have students respond to the reflection question after completing the assignment.

Reflection

After completing this Embedded Assessment, reflect on your work for this assignment. Respond to the following:

- What was most challenging about taking your chosen issue and transferring it to another historical context?
- How did that process add new meaning or relevance to your intended message?

College and Career Readiness Standards

Focus Standards:

W.11-12.3a Engage and orient the reader by setting out a problem, situation, or observation and its significance, establishing one or multiple point(s) of view, and introducing a narrator and/or characters; create a smooth progression of experiences or events.

W.11-12.4 Produce clear and coherent writing in which the development, organization, and style are appropriate to task, purpose, and audience.

W.11-12.5 Develop and strengthen writing as needed by planning, revising, editing, rewriting, or trying a new approach, focusing on addressing what is most significant for a specific purpose and audience.

7 Portfolio: Be sure students address the Reflection question as a separate part of the Embedded Assessment assignment so they can include it separately. At this point you may want to ask students to go to their portfolios and find previous unit reflection questions to get a sense of their growth as academic thinkers and producers.

All notes for and drafts of the script should be collected and presented together to show the process students completed in successfully accomplishing the task.

SCORING GUIDE

When you score this Embedded Assessment, you may wish to download and print copies of the Scoring Guide from SpringBoard Digital to have a copy to mark for each student's work.

SCORING GUIDE

Scoring Criteria	Exemplary	Proficient	Emerging	Incomplete
Ideas	The scene • demonstrates a sophisticated understanding of Miller's approach to speaking his conscience about a current event through a drama set in an analogous time period • effectively provides social commentary on the chosen issue • insightfully communicates the intended effect to the audience.	The scene • demonstrates a clear understanding of Miller's approach to speaking his conscience about a current event through a drama set in an analogous time period • serves as social commentary on the chosen issue • plausibly communicates the intended effect to the audience.	The scene • demonstrates a limited understanding of Miller's approach to speaking his conscience about a current event through a drama set in an analogous time period • includes social commentary that may be unclear or confusing • somewhat communicates the intended effect to the audience.	The scene • demonstrates an unclear understanding of Miller's approach to speaking his conscience about a current event through a drama set in an analogous time period • lacks a social commentary • does not successfully communicate the intended effect to the audience.
Structure	The scene • skillfully uses various theatrical elements • strategically uses all elements of vocal delivery • effectively uses elements of visual delivery to create focus and maintain energy for the scene • demonstrates equal sharing of responsibility.	The scene • adequately uses various theatrical elements • knowledgeably uses all elements of vocal delivery • uses elements of visual delivery to create focus and maintain energy for the scene • demonstrates a mostly balanced sharing of responsibility.	The scene • attempts to use various theatrical elements and elements of vocal delivery with limited success • attempts to use elements of visual delivery with limited success • demonstrates an unequal division of responsibilities.	The scene • does not use various theatrical elements • does not use all elements of vocal delivery • does not use elements of visual delivery • demonstrates no division of responsibilities.
Use of Language	The scene • includes written materials that demonstrate a mature style that advances the group's ideas • crafts dialogue that maintains consistent character voice and propels the plot.	The scene • includes written materials that demonstrate a style that adequately supports the group's ideas • includes dialogue that largely maintains character voice and serves the plot.	The scene • includes written materials that demonstrate a limited style that ineffectively supports the group's ideas • includes dialogue that struggles to maintain consistent character voice and/or impedes the plot.	The scene • includes written materials that demonstrate little style and fail to support the group's ideas • includes dialogue that fails to maintain consistent character voice and/or impedes the plot.

College and Career Readiness Standards

SL.11-12.6 Adapt speech to a variety of contexts and tasks, demonstrating a command of formal English when indicated or appropriate.

L.11-12.3 Apply knowledge of language to understand how language functions in different contexts, to make effective choices for meaning or style, and to comprehend more fully when reading or listening.

Unpacking Embedded Assessment 2

Learning Targets
- Reflect on the big ideas for the unit.
- Create a plan for reading independently.

Preview
In this activity, you will explore the big ideas and tasks of the unit and make plans for your independent reading.

Learning Strategies

Brainstorming
Discussion Groups
Graphic Organizer
Marking the Text
Quickwrite

Making Connections
The Crucible is an example of how artistic expression is a significant part of the American ideal of freedom of expression and the freedom to say what we believe. The historic guarantee was a hard-won freedom, and over time our greatest statespeople and politicians have nurtured that freedom through speeches such as Margaret Chase Smith's *Declaration of Conscience*. Public speech, as well as literary work, is still a significant forum for the expression of important ideas and ideals. You will find that your experience creating and presenting an original dramatic scene will prepare you to create and present a speech about an issue of importance.

Essential Questions
Your work with Arthur Miller has given you an idea of how social commentary can be a part of artistic expression. Now, respond to Essential Question 2: How are the components of rhetoric applied to the creation and delivery of effective speeches?

Unpacking Embedded Assessment 2
Closely read the assignment for Embedded Assessment 2: Writing and Presenting a Persuasive Speech.

Your assignment is to write and present an original, persuasive two- to three-minute speech that addresses a contemporary issue. Your speech should include a clear claim, support, counterclaim, and conclusion/call to action. Incorporate rhetorical appeals and devices to strengthen your argument and help you achieve your desired purpose.

Create a graphic organizer that demonstrates your analysis of the assignment. What knowledge must you possess and what skills must you have in order to write and deliver a persuasive speech?

📖 Planning for Independent Reading
For outside reading, you may choose famous speeches and find audio versions for listening. As you listen to each speech, make notes in your Reader/Writer Notebook about the delivery and its effectiveness. Select one speech you find particularly effective and recommend it to classmates, including reasons for your recommendation.

My Notes

PLAN

Materials: poster paper, markers
Suggested Pacing: 1 50-minute class period

TEACH

1 Read aloud the Making Connections section. Write the phrases *artistic expression* and *freedom of expression* on the board and ask volunteers to **brainstorm** definitions, examples, and connections between these phrases. Show their answers as an idea map.

2 Read aloud the Essential Questions section. Lead a class discussion on how social commentary can be artistic expression. Ask volunteers to offer examples of social commentary they've encountered. Then have small groups discuss Essential Question 2. Help students draw connections between the Essential Questions.

3 Help students unpack Embedded Assessment 2. Ask students what a persuasive speech is and have them suggest contemporary examples. Write the terms *claim, support, counterclaim, conclusion/call to action*, and *rhetorical appeals* on the board. Ask volunteers to define the terms.

4 Have students work individually to create a graphic organizer that analyzes the assignment.

5 Have students complete the Planning for Independent Reading task to learn more about effective speeches.

ASSESS

Review students' graphic organizers to ensure that students understand the assignment. They should be able to list the skills and knowledge they will need and understand what makes a speech persuasive.

ADAPT

If students need help creating their graphic organizers, conduct small-group reviews to go over the terms *claim, support, counterclaim, conclusion/call to action*, and *rhetorical appeals*. Guide students to understand how these aspects are a part of persuasive speeches. Model creating a graphic organizer.

College and Career Readiness Standards

Focus Standards:

RL.11-12.10 By the end of grade 11, read and comprehend literature, including stories, dramas, and poems, in the grades 11 -CCR text complexity band proficiently, with scaffolding as needed at the high end of the range.

L.11-12.3 Apply knowledge of language to understand how language functions in different contexts, to make effective choices for meaning or style, and to comprehend more fully when reading or listening.

ACTIVITY 2.19

PLAN

Materials: Venn Diagram for Writing a Comparison graphic organizer, clips of dramatic performances and persuasive speeches
Suggested Pacing: 2 50-minute class periods

TEACH

1 Start the activity by reading aloud the Learning Targets and Preview. Lead an informal discussion by asking students about their experiences giving performances and presentations.

 TEACHER TO TEACHER

To support learning, show students video clips of both dramatic performances and persuasive speeches (YouTube, Ted Talks, DVDs). Ask students to take notes while they watch of the qualities of both dramatic performances and persuasive speeches that feel effective. Then discuss observations as a class.

LEVELED DIFFERENTIATED INSTRUCTION

In this activity, students may need support articulating the similarities and differences between performing a dramatic scene and presenting a persuasive speech.

Beginning Guide students to use the **Venn Diagram for Writing a Comparison** graphic organizer to map out the similarities and differences between writing and performing a dramatic scene and a persuasive speech. Allow these students to use high-frequency words and phrases or their native language to orally express their ideas first.

Developing Allow students to work with a partner to use the **Venn Diagram for Writing a Comparison** graphic organizer to map out the similarities and differences between writing and performing a dramatic scene and a persuasive speech. Have them compare their answers with those of another pair.

Developing Speaking Skills

Learning Strategies

Brainstorming
Discussion Groups
Graphic Organizer
Rehearsal

My Notes

Learning Targets

- Draw connections between giving successful performances and presentations, including awareness of audience and effective delivery of information.
- Collaborate and share ideas with classmates about characteristics of successful oral presentations.

Preview

In this activity, you will reflect on how your experience from writing and performing a scene can be applied to writing and presenting a persuasive speech by considering the roles of the speaker and the audience.

Comparing Performances and Presentations

1. What have you learned from writing and performing a dramatic scene that could be applied to writing and presenting a speech to persuade? How are the two experiences the same and different?

2. In small discussion groups, brainstorm characteristics of speaker and audience during a successful oral presentation. Pass a single sheet of paper and pencil around the table, with each group member writing one characteristic for either speaker or audience. Continue to pass the pencil and paper until your teacher directs you to stop.

Speaker	Audience

3. Choose one group member to stand and share your group's list with the whole class. Each team member should add cumulative list of characteristics in the chart. When your group representative has shared your group's ideas, he or she should sit and remain sitting until all groups' ideas have been shared.

Practice

4. Keep a list of the following oral presentation skills to practice. Model for each other what it looks like to do the following:

- Make eye contact while speaking
- Pause for effect
- Enunciate and speak loudly enough
- Use purposeful gestures
- Communicate ideas effectively

College and Career Readiness Standards

Focus Standards:

SL.11-12.3 Evaluate a speaker's point of view, reasoning, and use of evidence and rhetoric, assessing the stance, premises, links among ideas, word choice, points of emphasis, and tone used.

SL.11-12.4 Present information, findings, and supporting evidence, conveying a clear and distinct perspective, such that listeners can follow the line of reasoning, alternative or opposing perspectives are addressed, and the organization, development, substance, and style are appropriate to purpose, audience, and a range of formal and informal tasks.

SL.11-12.5 Make strategic use of digital media (e.g., textual, graphical, audio, visual, and interactive elements) in presentations to enhance understanding of findings, reasoning, and evidence and to add interest.

5. Work together to turn your list of characteristics of good oral presentations into a brief presentation on effective ways to be either a presenter or a listening audience member. As a group decide if your brief presentation will include:

- Visual elements
- Role-playing
- A multimedia component

Assign each member of your group an element of the presentation to present.

Topic	Tips	Components	Presenter

6. After organizing your presentation and its components, rehearse as a group and give each other feedback on use of eye contact, enunciation, volume, and other presentation skills.

7. Meet with another group and take turns giving your presentations. Fill out the feedback organizer during the other group's presentation and then share your feedback with each other.

Presenter	Did their presentation anticipate the needs of the audience?	How were their eye contact and speaking skills? Were they loud enough? Did they pause for effect?	Did they incorporate any other visual, role-playing, or multimedia components effectively?

☑ Check Your Understanding

As you develop ideas about successful performance and oral presentations, consider these questions: Which performance skills will transfer easily from drama to speech delivery? Which new skills will you need to develop?

College and Career Readiness Standards

SL.11-12.6 Adapt speech to a variety of contexts and tasks, demonstrating a command of formal English when indicated or appropriate.

ACTIVITY 2.19 continued

2 Guide students to get into small **discussion groups** to complete student step 2. When groups have finished, continue to student step 3.

3 Go over with students the oral presentation skills to practice. Choose a volunteer to model each skill with and have students identify which skill is being modeled. Then allow students to practice with each other.

4 Allow groups time to complete student step 5. Make sure students understand the difference between visual elements and multimedia components by having volunteers help brainstorm a few ideas on the board.

5 Allow students time to rehearse their presentations. Remind students to use helpful and encouraging language when providing feedback

6 Have groups get together to share their presentations. Before beginning, go over the feedback organizer with students. After groups finish presenting, come back together as a class to discuss the experience and feedback they received.

7 Have students work independently to complete the Check Your Understanding task and then share their responses with their group.

ASSESS

Use students' presentations to assess their abilities to: -use oral presentation skills and -share respectful and helpful feedback with one another.

ADAPT

If some students have not mastered the skills necessary to make an oral presentation, have them practice each skill in student step 4 when rehearsing. They should rehearse with a peer and create a checklist to confirm that each skill is present. Offer modeling and feedback to help struggling students use each skill correctly.

ACTIVITY 2.20

PLAN

Suggested Pacing: 1 50-minute class period plus homework

TEACH

1 Read the Learning Targets and Preview with students. **Activate prior knowledge** of the Civil War, noting that Lincoln delivered this speech one month before the war offcially ended.

2 **Vocabulary Development:** Review the Academic Vocabulary feature with students. Ask them to work with a partner to brainstorm words to define the concept of *rhetorical context*. Then guide students as they provide examples.

3 Read the Rhetorical Context section with students.

4 Ask a volunteer to read aloud the About the Author and As You Read sections and ask another volunteer to recap how to conduct a **SOAPStone** analysis.

Learning Strategies

Brainstorming
Shared Reading
SOAPSTone

VOCABULARY

ACADEMIC
A **rhetorical context** refers to the subject, purpose, audience, occasion, or situation in which writing occurs. Rhetorical context can help inform the reader of all the other elements that might inform a writer's argument. All these factors work together to influence what the text itself says and how it conveys its message.

Learning Targets

• Analyze the rhetorical context of a seminal U.S. speech.
• Adapt speech for a particular rhetorical context.

Preview

In this activity, you will read a seminal speech given by President Abraham Lincoln and analyze its rhetorical context using the SOAPSTone strategy.

Rhetorical Context

Like historical context, the **rhetorical context** of a speech is an important part of analyzing the ideas and evaluating the reasoning of the speaker. The reading strategy SOAPSTone is a familiar strategy that can help you analyze a speech.

As You Read

• Underline details that you will use during your SOAPSTone analysis.
• Circle unknown words and phrases. Try to determine the meaning of the words by using context clues, word parts, or a dictionary.

My Notes

About the Author

Abraham Lincoln was an American statesman and lawyer who served as the 16th President of the United States from March 1861 until his assassination in April 1865. Lincoln led the United States through the American Civil War. In his First Inaugural Address, President Lincoln had argued at length against secession and urged Americans in both the North and South to remain dedicated to the Union. The tone of his Second Inaugural Address is quite different. As you read the speech, pay attention to Lincoln's use of diction and syntax to create a somber tone that reveals the effects of four years of devastating war on both himself and the American public.

College and Career Readiness Standards

Focus Standards:

RI.11-12.1 Cite strong and thorough textual evidence to support analysis of what the text says explicitly as well as inferences drawn from the text, including determining where the text leaves matters uncertain.

RI.11-12.4 Determine the meaning of words and phrases as they are used in a text, including figurative, connotative, and technical meanings; analyze how an author uses and refines the meaning of a key term or terms over the course of a text

2.20

Speech

Second Inaugural Address of Abraham Lincoln

given **Saturday, March 4, 1865, one month before the end of the Civil War**

Fellow Countrymen:

1 At this second appearing to take the oath of the Presidential office there is less occasion for an extended address than there was at the first. Then a statement somewhat in detail of a course to be pursued seemed fitting and proper. Now, at the expiration of four years, during which public declarations have been constantly called forth on every point and phase of the great contest which still absorbs the attention and engrosses the energies of the nation, little that is new could be presented. The progress of our arms, upon which all else chiefly depends, is as well known to the public as to myself, and it is, I trust, reasonably satisfactory and encouraging to all. With high hope for the future, no prediction in regard to it is ventured.

2 On the occasion corresponding to this four years ago all thoughts were anxiously directed to an impending civil war. All dreaded it, all sought to avert it. While the inaugural address was being delivered from this place, devoted altogether to saving the Union without war, insurgent agents were in the city seeking to destroy it without war—seeking to dissolve the Union and divide effects by negotiation. Both parties deprecated war, but one of them would make war rather than let the nation survive, and the other would accept war rather than let it perish, and the war came.

3 One-eighth of the whole population were colored slaves, not distributed generally over the Union, but localized in the southern part of it. These slaves constituted a peculiar and powerful interest. All knew that this interest was somehow the cause of the war. To strengthen, **perpetuate**, and extend this interest was the object for which the insurgents would rend the Union even by war, while the Government claimed no right to do more than to restrict the territorial enlargement of it. Neither

My Notes

deprecated: criticized

perpetuate: continue indefinitely

ACTIVITY 2.20 continued

5 FIRST READ: Due to the complexity of the passage, consider creating discussion groups. Have the groups read the text using the following format: One student reads a paragraph while the next in line addresses one of the elements of SOAPSTone revealed in that portion of the text. The student who has commented on one portion proceeds to read the next portion while the next student makes a comment and initiates discussion about key ideas. Continue until the entire document has been read.

TEXT COMPLEXITY

Overall: Very Complex
Lexile: 1520L
Qualitative: High Difficulty
Task: Moderate (Analyze)

6 As students are reading, monitor their progress. Circulate among groups during this process to ensure that students are using the strategy and engaging in appropriate conversation about the text. You may need to redirect student focus or take note of questions that you need to address in a whole-class discussion. Note that alliteration, anaphora, and parallel structure are all devices of repetition.

College and Career Readiness Standards

RI.11-12.5 Analyze and evaluate the effectiveness of the structure an author uses in his or her exposition or argument, including whether the structure makes points clear, convincing, and engaging.

RI.11-12.9 Analyze seventeenth-, eighteenth-, and nineteenth-century foundational U.S. documents of historical and literary significance (including the Declaration of Independence, the Preamble to the Constitution, the Bill of Rights, and Lincoln's Second Inaugural Address) for their themes, purposes, and rhetorical features.

Additional Standards Addressed:
W.11-12.1a, W.11-12.1d

LEVELED DIFFERENTIATED
INSTRUCTION

In this activity, students may need support accessing Lincoln's difficult vocabulary and complex sentences.

Developing Before reading, preview the context and important themes in the speech so students will have a familiarity with the material. Also, preface each paragraph by telling students what Lincoln discusses in the text. Check for student understanding after each paragraph by asking: *What are the key ideas in this paragraph?*

Expanding Have students perform a choral reading of the speech with you as you read aloud. Pause after each paragraph to define difficult vocabulary and clarify the meaning of complex sentences. Check for student understanding after each paragraph by asking: *What are the key ideas in this paragraph?*

Bridging Assign students to small groups and have them read the speech aloud to one another. Have them break the text up into paragraphs or half-paragraph chunks to read aloud. After each chunk of text, have students summarize the key ideas covered in the text.

★ TEACHER TO TEACHER

To provide students with a fuller understanding of the historical context of Lincoln's Second Inaugural Address, consider showing documentary clips about this speech. Search YouTube with keywords such as "Lincoln and Second Inaugural Address" and "Lincoln and speeches."

7 After reading the text for the first time, guide the class in a brief discussion by asking the Making Observations questions. Ask students what words or imagery they can recall that helped Lincoln strike the emotional tone he did and allow for a debate about how Lincoln's audience might have reacted.

2.20

My Notes

party expected for the war the magnitude or the duration which it has already attained. Neither anticipated that the cause of the conflict might cease with or even before the conflict itself should cease. Each looked for an easier triumph, and a result less fundamental and astounding. Both read the same Bible and pray to the same God, and each **invokes** His aid against the other. It may seem strange that any men should dare to ask a just God's assistance in wringing their bread from the sweat of other men's faces, but let us judge not, that we be not judged. The prayers of both could not be answered. That of neither has been answered fully. The Almighty has His own purposes. "Woe unto the world because of offenses; for it must needs be that offenses come, but woe to that man by whom the offense cometh." If we shall suppose that American slavery is one of those offenses which, in the providence of God, must needs come, but which, having continued through His appointed time, He now wills to remove, and that He gives to both North and South this terrible war as the woe due to those by whom the offense came, shall we discern therein any departure from those divine **attributes** which the believers in a living God always **ascribe** to Him? Fondly do we hope, fervently do we pray, that this mighty **scourge** of war may speedily pass away. Yet, if God wills that it continue until all the wealth piled by the bondsman's two hundred and fifty years of unrequited toil shall be sunk, and until every drop of blood drawn with the lash shall be paid by another drawn with the sword, as was said three thousand years ago, so still it must be said "the judgments of the Lord are true and righteous altogether."

4 With **malice** toward none, with charity for all, with firmness in the right as God gives us to see the right, let us strive on to finish the work we are in, to bind up the nation's wounds, to care for him who shall have borne the battle and for his widow and his orphan, to do all which may achieve and cherish a just and lasting peace among ourselves and with all nations.

> **Making Observations**
> • What emotional tone does Lincoln strike in his speech?
> • How might Lincoln's audience have reacted given the context?

invokes: calls forth
attributes: qualities
ascribe: think of coming from
scourge: plague or misfortune
malice: desire to cause harm

Scaffolding the Text-Dependent Questions

1. Find one example of anaphora in paragraph 2 and one in paragraph 3. How does this rhetorical strategy contribute to the power of the speech? Review anaphora. Look at the beginning of each clause in paragraph 2. Where do you find a repeated word? What is the effect of this repetition? What is the effect of repetition in paragraph 3? RI.11-12.5

2. What is the effect of Lincoln telling the audience "little that is new could be presented" while giving a speech about the state of the country? How would an audience react to this statement? How would it shape their perception of him as their leader? RI.11-12.4

Returning to the Text

- Return to the speech as you respond to the following questions. Use text evidence to support your responses
- Write any additional questions you have about the text in your Reader/Writer Notebook.

1. Find one example of anaphora in paragraph 2 and one in paragraph 3. How does this rhetorical device contribute to the power of the speech?

   At the beginning of paragraph 2, Lincoln uses anaphora to describe war: "All dreaded it, all sought to avert it." The repetition of *all* gives the clauses similar rhythm and unifies Americans as a singular group: "all." In paragraph 3, Lincoln uses the word *neither* to emphasize two unexpected outcomes of the war. Again, the anaphora serves to unite the two groups as one in their expectations, something Lincoln strives to do for the nation.

2. What is the effect of Lincoln telling the audience "little that is new could be presented" while giving a speech about the state of the country?

   Lincoln telling the audience that they know as much as he does about the state of the country has the effect of demonstrating that he sees the citizens of the country as being active participants in government and that he doesn't aim to hide any information from them. It works to shape the perception of the audience that he is a trustworthy leader who sees them as his equals.

3. Summarize how Lincoln describes the two sides are similar. What rhetorical appeal does he use to warn against laying blame? Why would or wouldn't it be an effective appeal for his audience?

   Lincoln says the two sides are similar because neither expected a long war, the abolition of slavery, or a difficult fight. Both sides have similar religions. Although one side might seem less just, Lincoln makes an ethical appeal using the Bible: "let us judge not, that we not be judged." This appeal would be effective for his audience, who would likely be familiar with the Bible and inclined to relate to its morals, thereby respecting Lincoln for citing it.

4. How might Lincoln's use of language that uses religious reasoning shape his audience's understanding of his call to end the Civil War?

   Lincoln hopes and prays "that this mighty scourge of war may speedily pass away," but he says if "God wills that it continue ... until every drop of blood drawn with the lash shall be paid by another drawn with the sword." By using religious language in his reasoning, he signals to his audience that a power larger than both him and them is ultimately in charge, and therefore they are called upon by a moral duty that is religious in nature.

8 RETURNING TO THE TEXT: During the second reading, students will be returning to the text to answer the text-dependent comprehension questions. Allow students to work in pairs to reared the text and answer the questions. Remind them to use text evidence in their responses.

9 Move among pairs and listen in as students answer the text-dependent questions. If they have difficulty, scaffold the questions by rephrasing them or breaking them down into smaller parts. See the Scaffolding the Text-Dependent Questions boxes for suggestions.

Scaffolding the Text-Dependent Questions

3. Summarize how Lincoln says the two sides are similar. What rhetorical appeal does he use to warn against laying blame? Why would or wouldn't it be an effective appeal for his audience? Paraphrase the sentences that begin with *neither, each,* and *both* in paragraph 3. Why might one side view the other as less just? How do Lincoln's references to the "same God" and the "same Bible" appeal to his audience?

What would his audience think of his reference to the Bible? RI.11-12.2

4. How might Lincoln's use of language that uses religious reasoning shape his audience's understanding of his call to end the Civil War? Reread paragraphs 3 and 4. Which words or phrases would stand out to the audience? What would they think? RI.11-12.1

Throughout the next activities, students will be looking at a variety of rhetorical devices. Encourage students to create and keep a **graphic organizer** to track the definition of each device, examples of the device, and a note on the effect of the device on the speaker's message. This graphic organizer could also be maintained by the entire class in a Word Wall format.

10 Have students get into their groups to review their SOAPSTone annotations. If necessary, lead a Q&A session where students can ask questions about the historical context of the Civil War or allow them time to do secondary research on the topic.

11 Lead a class discussion about what the needs and expectations of Lincoln's audience might have been given the historical context. Then allow groups time to complete student step 7.

5. Who is Abraham Lincoln's intended audience? How does Lincoln anticipate his audience's needs and expectations?

Lincoln's intended audience is the citizens of the country as well as slaves, whose well-being and future are discussed in his speech. He addresses his audience as his "fellow countrymen," signaling the he considers them to be his equals and hopes to have their trust. He anticipates their anxieties and concerns about the state of the country, assumes their knowledge about what has transpired over the previous four years, and seeks to reassure them of their moral duties as a nation.

6. Based on the details you underlined, what specific language does Lincoln use to invoke emotions in his audience?

Lincoln uses powerful and stirring language to invoke emotions in his audience, a country that feels weary of war. He acknowledges that the last time he gave a similar speech, "all thoughts were anxiously directed to an impending civil war." By acknowledging his audience's emotions, he signals that he understands them. Yet Lincoln ends on a stirring emotional note for his audience by providing the imagery of "bind[ing] up the nation's wounds," inciting his audience to remain strong in their convictions to end the war.

Working from the Text

7. Review the SOAPSTone annotations you have made with your group members. As a group, discuss how the historical context of the Civil War is reflected in the speech. Complete the SOAPSTone graphic organizer as a group.

Scaffolding the Text-Dependent Questions

5. Who is Abraham Lincoln's intended audience? How does Lincoln anticipate his audience's needs and expectations? Does he consider slaves to be part of his audience? How does he signal his relationship to his audience as their leader? What might his audience's needs and expectations be given the historical context? RI.11-12.1

6. Based on the details you underlined, what specific language does Lincoln use to invoke emotions in his audience? What emotions do you think his audience would be feeling before the speech? During? After? How does Lincoln acknowledge these emotions? RI.11-12.4

SOAPSTone	Analysis	Textual Support
Speaker What does the listener know about the speaker?	The speaker is the president Abraham Lincoln—his audience would know him because it was his second term.	"At this second appearing to take the oath of the Presidential office there is less occasion for an extended address than there was at the first."
Occasion What are the circumstances surrounding this speech?	The occasion is Lincoln's Second Inaugural Address, after he has taken the office of the president for the second time. The country is currently engaged in a Civil War of the North against the South, with Lincoln and the North fighting to end slavery.	"At this second appearing to take the oath of the Presidential office there is less occasion for an extended address than there was at the first." "On the occasion corresponding to this four years ago all thoughts were anxiously directed to an impending civil war."
Audience Who is the target audience?	Lincoln's immediate audience would have been a large crowd of people listening to his speech in Washington, D.C., but he would be aware that the entire country would soon be able to read his speech in print.	"The progress of our arms, upon which all else chiefly depends, is as well known to the public as to myself, and it is, I trust, reasonably satisfactory and encouraging to all."
Purpose Why did the speaker give this text?	Lincoln's purpose is to prepare his audience for what is to come in the war and what will happen when it ends.	"With malice toward none, with charity for all, with firmness in the right as God gives us to see the right, let us strive on to finish the work we are in, to bind up the nation's wounds, to care for him who shall have borne the battle and for his widow and his orphan, to do all which may achieve and cherish a just and lasting peace among ourselves and with all nations."
Subject What is the topic?	The subject is Lincoln's remarks about the causes of the Civil War.	"Now, at the expiration of four years, during which public declarations have been constantly called forth on every point and phase of the great contest which still absorbs the attention and engrosses the energies of the nation, little that is new could be presented."
Tone What is the author's tone, or attitude?	Lincoln's tone is serious and somber, yet he leaves his speech on an attitude of hope that the country can repair its wounds after the war is over.	"Fondly do we hope, fervently do we pray, that this mighty scourge of war may speedily pass away."

12 Have students work with a partner to complete student step 8 and ask volunteers to read out loud the examples they found in order for the class to hear how the use of parallel structure can be effective when emphasized by the speaker. Students can practice saying the lines different ways to notice the inflections.

13 Give students ample time to apply the elements of SOAPSTone to plan an original speech. This is the speech they will write and deliver for Embedded Assessment 2, so it is crucial that students **brainstorm** a subject that is "up close" to them and that they can support in a two- to three-minute speech.

ASSESS

Review students' plans to ensure they have covered each element of the SOAPSTone strategy successfully. Assess their work for a clear understanding of their roles as speaker, the occasions that inform their speeches, and their audiences, purposes, subjects, and tones.

ADAPT

Show students a recorded example of an effective speech. Have students identify the speaker's audience, purpose, subject, and tone. Also, make sure students understand the role of the speaker and the occasion that informs the speech. Speeches can be found through an Internet search.

2.20

8. The use of parallel structure has a powerful effect on a written and spoken message. Identify the examples of parallelism at work in the speech. Practice reading the paragraph as you believe it would be spoken, using parallel structure to guide your emphasis and inflection.

One of them would <u>make</u> war rather than let the nation *survive*, and the other would <u>accept</u> war rather than let it *perish*.

Fondly do we hope—fervently do we pray

Drawn with the lash—drawn with the sword

As was said—must still be said

🖉 Drafting the Embedded Assessment

Think of an issue close to home where you feel a change is warranted. Brainstorm ideas for a speech that you could give on the topic to the appropriate audience to convey your strongest message. Be sure to:

- Identify your role as speaker in this piece (concerned citizen, student).
- Convey the occasion that informs your writing (the circumstances prompting this piece).
- Identify your audience (whom you are addressing).
- Define your purpose (what you want to accomplish).
- Choose your subject (the topic of your essay).
- Establish your tone (your attitude toward the issue and the opposition).

🖉 DRAFTING THE EMBEDDED ASSESSMENT

The following standards are addressed in the writing prompt:

- W.11-12.1a
- W.11-12.1a
- W.11-12.1a
- W.11-12.1a
- W.11-12.1a
- W.11-12.1d

The Power of Rhetoric

Learning Targets

- Analyze the structure and use of rhetorical devices in an argumentative text.
- Write an analysis of how a speaker builds an argumentative speech.

Preview

In this activity, you will read and analyze a speech for its use of structure and rhetorical devices in order to explain how the author builds his argument.

Learning Strategies

Discussion Groups
Drafting
Marking the Text
Quickwrite
Revisiting Prior Work
Shared Reading

Analyzing an Argument

You have analyzed the rhetorical context of an effective speech. What about the message? Where does it get its power? Powerful writers such as Lincoln use structure and rhetorical devices intentionally; effective argumentation is anything but an accident. And when you add a powerful delivery to strong writing, you move hearts, people, and sometimes whole nations.

As you prepare to read one of the most powerful speeches in our nation's history, a speech pivotal to the colonial revolution against the throne of England, you will be examining two components:

- The structure of an argument
- The use of rhetorical devices

The Structure of an Argument

a. The claim acknowledges the point of the argument.

b. The support uses logical reasoning, relevant evidence, and accurate and credible sources. It also demonstrates an understanding of the topic.

c. The counterclaim acknowledges the opposing point of view and offers reasons and evidence that reject the counterclaim.

d. The concluding statement offers a call to action that asks audience members to change their minds or actions to support the claim.

The Use of Rhetorical Devices

Rhetorical devices are literary devices that a writer uses to enhance the message and/or to create an effect. If the speech is argumentative, the effect should be to persuade for change. In Patrick Henry's speech, be prepared to see devices such as aphorism, allusion, analogy, and rhetorical questions.

As You Read

- Mark elements of the argumentative structure you see in the text.
- Highlight rhetorical devices used by the speaker and note their impact.
- Circle unknown words and phrases. Try to determine the meaning of the words by using context clues, word parts, or a dictionary.

My Notes

College and Career Readiness Standards

Focus Standards:

RI.11-12.1 Cite strong and thorough textual evidence to support analysis of what the text says explicitly as well as inferences drawn from the text, including determining where the text leaves matters uncertain.

RI.11-12.5 Analyze and evaluate the effectiveness of the structure an author uses

in his or her exposition or argument, including whether the structure makes points clear, convincing, and engaging.

Additional Standards Addressed:

RI.11-12.4 , RI.11-12.6, W.11-12.1a, W.11-12.1b, W.11-12.1e

PLAN

Materials: cardstock paper (long, narrow) or sentence strips (one per group), markers; Optional: magazines, newspapers, glue, scissors, Internet access, slide projector
Suggested Pacing: 2 50-minute class periods

TEACH

1 Read the Learning Targets and Preview with students.

2 Read aloud the Analyzing an Argument section. Ask the class to **think-pair-share** the two questions posed in the first paragraph.

3 Ask students what they know about the colonial revolution against the throne of England, and add their answers on the board in a chart. If time allows, allow students to fact check what is listed.

4 Assign **discussion groups** to definitions of important terms related to the structure of argument and rhetorical devices, such as *claim, reasoning, evidence, credible sources, counterclaim, call to action, aphorism, allusion, analogy,* and *rhetorical question.* As you review the structure of an argument using a visual such as a poster that can stay in your classroom throughout the year, assign a key term to each group.

5 Provide each group with cardstock paper or sentence strips and markers. As they approach new terms, students should write the word, a visual, the definition, and an example on the paper. When you have taught both structure and rhetorical devices, ask students to add the important terms to the Word Wall.

6 Ask a volunteer to read aloud the As You Read section and guide students to recall the elements of argumentative structures and rhetorical devices by referring to the work they did in their discussion groups.

7 Allow students time to read the About the Author and About the Speech sections independently. Encourage students to ask any questions they have about the author or the historical context of the speech.

8 **FIRST READ:** Have students conduct a **shared reading** of Patrick Henry's speech, **marking the text** with their comments. Because Henry's language is so rich and the paragraphs are long, you may want to ask students to read smaller portions between discussions.

 TEXT COMPLEXITY

Overall: Complex
Lexile: 980L
Qualitative: High Difficulty
Task: Moderate (Analyze)

9 Ask discussion groups to begin with Henry's biographical information. Comments for this shared reading should focus on argumentative structure (Where do students see the claim, evidence, reasons, counterclaim, call to action?) and on rhetorical devices that strengthen his message and create an effect on the reader/audience.

10 As students find rhetorical devices, be sure they follow up in discussion groups by sharing their favorite examples and noting examples for later reference.

11 **Vocabulary Development:** Discuss the Word Connections feature with students. Select a few compelling words from the text, such as *patriotism*, and ask students about the author's possible intent for using them. Elicit other words that the author could have used.

2.21

My Notes

WORD CONNECTIONS

Etymology
In Latin, *momentum* means "movement." A moment is a particle heavy enough to cause a set of scales to move. Henry calls the question before the House one of "awful moment." He suggests that the way in which the House answers the question will cause movement toward freedom or slavery for the country.

About the Author

Patrick Henry (1736–1799) was born in Virginia. He tried several occupations before becoming a lawyer and then a politician encouraging separation from Great Britain. He served as a delegate from Virginia to the First Session of the Continental Congress in 1774 and became noted as a powerful speaker whose words helped sweep the colonists toward their declaration of independence.

About the Speech

Patrick Henry delivered his most famous speech on March 23, 1775, at the Second Virginia Convention. Henry gave a reasoned and dramatic presentation, building from calm tones to a passionate finale. A deep silence followed Henry's memorable conclusion. After the speech, the delegates voted by a narrow margin to form a Virginia militia to guard against a possible British attack. No record was made of his exact words at the time; this version was assembled in the early 1880s from accounts of several people who attended the convention.

Speech
March 23, 1775

Speech to the Virginia Convention

by **Patrick Henry**

1 Mr. President: No man thinks more highly than I do of the patriotism, as well as abilities, of the very worthy gentlemen who have just addressed the House. But different men often see the same subject in different lights; and, therefore, I hope it will not be thought disrespectful to those gentlemen if, entertaining, as I do, opinions of a character very opposite to theirs, I shall speak forth my sentiments freely and without reserve. This is no time for ceremony. The question before the House is one of awful moment to this country. For my own part, I consider it as nothing less than a question of freedom or slavery; and in proportion to the magnitude of the subject ought to be the freedom of the debate. It is only in this way that we can hope to arrive at truth, and fulfill the great responsibility which we hold to God and our country. Should I keep back my opinions at such a time, through fear of giving offense, I should consider myself guilty of treason towards my country, and of an act of disloyalty toward the Majesty of Heaven, which I revere above all earthly kings.

2 Mr. President, it is natural to man to indulge in the illusions of hope. We are apt to shut our eyes against a painful truth, and listen to the song of that siren[1], till she transforms us into beasts. Is this the part of wise men, engaged in a great and arduous struggle for liberty? Are we disposed to be of the number of those who, having eyes, see not and, having ears, hear not,[2] the things which so nearly concern their **temporal** salvation? For my part, whatever anguish of spirit it may cost, I am willing to know the whole truth; to know the worst, and to provide for it.

3 I have but one lamp by which my feet are guided, and that is the lamp of experience. I know of no way of judging the future but by the past. And judging by the past, I wish to know what there has been in the conduct of the British ministry for the last ten years to justify those hopes with which gentlemen have been pleased to **solace** themselves and the House. Is it that **insidious** smile with which our petition has been lately received? Trust it not, sir; it will prove a snare to your feet. Suffer not yourselves to be betrayed with a kiss. Ask yourselves how this gracious reception of our petition comports with those warlike preparations which cover our waters and darken our land. Are fleets and armies necessary to a work of love and reconciliation? Have we shown ourselves so unwilling to be reconciled that force must be called in to win back our love? Let us not deceive ourselves, sir. These are the implements of war and **subjugation**; the last arguments to which kings resort.

4 I ask gentlemen, sir, what means this **martial** array, if its purpose be not to force us to submission? Can gentlemen assign any other possible motive for it? Has Great Britain any enemy in this quarter of the world, to call for all this accumulation of navies and armies? No sir, she has none. They are meant for us: they can be meant for no other. They are sent over to bind and rivet upon us those chains which the British ministry have been so long forging. And what have we to oppose to them? Shall we try argument? Sir, we have been trying that for the last ten years. Have we anything new to offer upon the subject? Nothing. We have held the subject up in every light of which it is capable; but it has been all in vain. Shall we resort to entreaty and humble supplication? What terms shall we find which have not been already exhausted? Let us not, I beseech you, sir, deceive ourselves. Sir, we have done everything that could be done, to avert the storm which is now coming on. We have petitioned; we have remonstrated; we have supplicated; we have prostrated ourselves before the throne, and have implored its **interposition** to arrest the tyrannical hands of the ministry and Parliament. Our petitions have been **slighted**; our remonstrances have produced additional violence and insult; our supplications have been disregarded; and we have been spurned, with contempt, from the foot of the throne! In vain, after these things, may we indulge the fond hope of peace and reconciliation. *There is no longer any room for hope.* If we wish to be free—if we mean to preserve **inviolate** those inestimable privileges for which

---

[1] "Song of that siren" is an allusion to classical Greek mythology. The Sirens were three dangerous mermaid like creatures who seduced nearby sailors with music, causing the sailors to wreck their ships.

[2] "Having eyes, see not, and having ears, hear not" is an allusion to several passages in the Bible, including Isaiah 6:10, Jeremiah 5:21, and Mark 8:18.

My Notes

temporal: earthly rather than spiritual

solace: comfort

insidious: treacherous

subjugation: act of conquering and subduing

martial: warlike

interposition: intervention

slighted: disrespected

inviolate: pure

Scaffolding the Text-Dependent Questions

1. **The Bible says Judas kisses Jesus before delivering him to his executioners. What is the significance of Henry's use of the allusion "Suffer not yourselves to be betrayed with a kiss" in paragraph 3?** In what ways is the government of Great Britain like Judas? In what ways are the colonists like Jesus? Why might an allusion to the Bible persuade Henry's audience? RI.11-12.6

2. **What central idea does Henry develop in paragraph 3 to strengthen his argument? How is or isn't it effective?** How are British officials treating the colonists' demands on the surface? What actions are British officials taking "behind the scenes"? In what ways are the two sets of actions contradictory? RI.11-12.1

LEVELED DIFFERENTIATED INSTRUCTION

In this activity, students may need support evaluating Patrick Henry's claim and reasoning.

Developing After the first read of the speech, work with students to complete the **Idea and Argument Evaluator** graphic organizer. Have students identify Henry's argument and three ideas from the text that support that argument. Guide them in identifying whether Henry also provided a reason for including this idea. Ask students to discuss whether they feel this argument is persuasive based on evidence from the text.

Expanding After the first read of the speech, divide students into small groups and assign a paragraph from the speech to each group. Have students use the **Idea and Argument Evaluator** graphic organizer to first identify Henry's argument or key idea in the paragraph. Then have students collaborate on identifying the supporting ideas and whether Henry gives a reason for each idea.

Bridging Before students begin the second read of the speech, divide them into groups and assign a paragraph from the speech to each student. Have students work individually to complete the **Idea and Argument Evaluator** graphic organizer for their assigned paragraph.

Support To help visual learners understand Henry's speech, have students form small groups and create poster collages that contain sections for *claim, evidence, reasons,* and *counterclaim.* Students may fill the sections with quotations from the speech as well as images cut from media.

My Notes

we have been so long contending—if we mean not **basely** to abandon the noble struggle in which we have been so long engaged, and which we have pledged ourselves never to abandon until the glorious object of our contest shall be obtained—we must fight!—I repeat it, sir, we must fight! An appeal to arms and to the God of hosts, is all that is left us!

5   They tell us, sir, that we are weak; unable to cope with so formidable an adversary. But when shall we be stronger? Will it be the next week, or the next year? Will it be when we are totally disarmed, and when a British guard shall be stationed in every house? Shall we gather strength by irresolution and inaction? Shall we acquire the means of effectual resistance by lying supinely on our backs, and hugging the delusive phantom of hope, until our enemies shall have bound us hand and foot? Sir, we are not weak if we make a proper use of those means which the God of nature hath placed in our power. The millions of people, armed in the holy cause of liberty, and in such a country as that which we possess, are invincible by any force which our enemy can send against us. Besides, sir, we shall not fight our battles alone. There is a just God who presides over the destinies of nations and who will raise up friends to fight our battles for us. The battle, sir, is not to the strong alone; it is to the vigilant, the active, the brave. Besides, sir, we have no election. If we were base enough to desire it, it is now too late to retire from the contest. There is no retreat but in submission and slavery! Our chains are forged! Their clanking may be heard on the plains of Boston! The war is inevitable—and let it come! I repeat it, sir, let it come.

6   It is in vain, sir, to **extenuate** the matter. Gentlemen may cry, Peace, Peace—but there is no peace. The war is actually begun! The next gale that sweeps from the north will bring to our ears the clash of resounding arms! Our brethren are already in the field! Why stand we here idle? What is it that gentlemen wish? What would they have? Is life so dear, or peace so sweet, as to be purchased at the price of chains and slavery? Forbid it, Almighty God! I know not what course others may take; but as for me, give me liberty, or give me death!

basely: in a lowly way
extenuate: lengthen

Peter F. Rothermel's painting titled "Patrick Henry Before the Virginia House of Burgesses" was created in 1851 and depicts Henry giving his famous speech.

Scaffolding the Text-Dependent Questions

3. In paragraph 4, Henry uses five verbs to describe how the colonists have tried to avoid a confrontation with Britain: *petition, remonstrate, supplicate, prostrate,* **and** *implore*. **How are their meanings related? What is their effect on the readers' perception of Henry's argument? What do all these words emphasize? What effect might they have on his audience's perception of his argument?** RI.11-12.4

4. Which element of the typical structure of an argument does Henry present in paragraph 5? Explain his rhetorical response. What is the claim against Henry's argument? How does he respond to this counterclaim? What rhetorical strategy does he use in his response? RI.11-12.5

2.21

Making Observations

- What is the tone of Henry's speech?
- What argumentative appeals stand out to you as being effective?

Returning to the Text

- Return to the speech as you respond to the following questions. Use text evidence to support your responses.
- Write any additional questions you have about the text in your Reader/Writer Notebook.

5. The Bible says Judas kisses Jesus before delivering him to his executioners. What is the significance of Henry's use of the allusion "Suffer not yourselves to be betrayed with a kiss" in paragraph 3?

Henry uses this allusion to warn that British officials who "smile" insidiously at the colonists'
petitions may be preparing to betray the colonists. His use of this allusion works as an ethical
appeal, elevating the situation by making it biblical.

6. What central idea does Henry develop in paragraph 3 to strengthen his argument? How is or isn't it effective?

Henry argues that past actions shed light on future events. He cites Britain's "warlike preparations
which cover our waters and darken our land" as evidence that it intends to go to war rather than
reconcile with the colonists. The use of this structure is effective because he takes time to draw a
link between the past and the present in order to provide evidence for a call to action.

7. In paragraph 4, Henry uses five verbs to describe how the colonists have tried to avoid a confrontation with Britain: *petition*, *remonstrate*, *supplicate*, *prostrate*, and *implore*. How are their meanings related? What is their effect on the readers' perception of Henry's argument?

Petition, *supplicate*, and *implore* are ways of making a request. *Remonstrate* means "to
express opposition to something." *Prostrate* means "to bow down before." Their effect is to
suggest that the colonists have exhausted all other means to remedy their relationship with
Great Britain.

Scaffolding the Text-Dependent Questions

5. What kinds of appeals does Henry use to convince Virginia to begin to prepare for war with Great Britain? What arguments does Henry use? Which arguments appeal to the colonists' logic, emotion, or sense of right and wrong? RI.11-12.5

---

12 After reading the text for the first time, guide the class in a brief discussion by asking the Making Observations questions. Ask students what they can recall from the speech that helped them form an impression about Henry's tone and to explain why they found certain argumentative appeals to be effective.

13 RETURNING TO THE TEXT: During the second reading, students will be returning to the text to answer the text-dependent comprehension questions. You may choose to have students reread and work on the questions in a variety of ways:

- Independently
- In pairs
- In small groups
- Together as a class

14 Have students answer the text-dependent questions. If they have difficulty, scaffold the questions by rephrasing them or breaking them down into smaller parts. See the Scaffolding the Text-Dependent Questions boxes for suggestions.

15 For student step 6, direct students to revisit their notes on the structure of Henry's speech to help them identify the pattern of the speech. Lead students to discuss the effectiveness of this pattern.

16 For student step 7, have students create an outline of Henry's speech that identifies the speech's order of claim, support, counterclaim, and conclusion/call to action. Lead students to discuss the effectiveness of this sequence.

SAT® CONNECTIONS

This writing prompt on the following page provides practice with the following important SAT skill: explaining how an author builds an argument to persuade an audience. If students need additional support with this type of writing, direct them to resources available online including the SAT Essay rubric, sample prompts, and sample essays.

---

8. Which element of the typical structure of an argument does Henry present in paragraph 5? Explain his rhetorical response.

   In paragraph 5, Henry addresses the counterclaim that "we are weak; unable to cope with so formidable an adversary" as Great Britain. He responds to this counterclaim with the ethical appeal that the colonies are strong because they are united in the holy fight for liberty. God will be with them and will provide "friends to fight our battles."

9. What kinds of appeals does Henry use to convince Virginia to begin to prepare for war with Great Britain?

   Henry uses emotional appeals to fear when he claims that war is inevitable and perhaps has even begun. He rejects claims that the colonies are too weak to fight back and argues logically that the time to prepare is before the British attack. He maintains that the cause of liberty is just and holy and that God will side with the colonists.

Working from the Text

10. Review your notes about the structure of Henry's speech. What pattern do you see?

    The structure of Henry's speech follows a traditional oration pattern of introducing his argument, providing narration (a story about how the country has arrived at this moment) providing proof for his argument, acknowledging refutations, and offering a conclusion with a powerful emotional response. Nearly every paragraph is addressed to the audience directly.

11. With your discussion group, determine the order of claim, support, counterclaim, and conclusion/call to action and create an outline of Henry's speech.

    Claim: We must fight for liberty—diplomacy has failed.
    Support: Great Britain has imposed military occupation on the American colonies and reconciliation attempts have failed.
    Counterclaim: Some say the colonies are not strong enough to take on Great Britain.
    Refutation: We are not weak if we take advantage of the means that God has provided—there are millions of us ready to fight.
    Conclusion/call to action: Other people are already fighting—why shouldn't America fight for its own liberty?

☑ Check Your Understanding

Quickwrite: If you had attended the Virginia Convention for Henry's speech, would you have sided with or against him? Why? What kinds of rhetorical devices did Henry use to persuade his audience?

✍ Explain How an Author Builds an Argument

Write an essay in which you explain how Patrick Henry builds an argument to persuade his audience that the colonies should declare their independence from Great Britain. In your essay, analyze the three most effective rhetorical devices Henry uses to strengthen the logic and persuasiveness of his argument. Your essay should not explain whether you agree with Henry's claims, but rather it should explain how the author builds an argument to persuade his audience. Be sure to:

- Identify Henry's claim.
- Use evidence from the text to show the progression of Henry's argument.
- Explain the effect of each piece of evidence and include transitions to connect your claims, reasoning, and evidence.
- Evaluate the overall effectiveness of Henry's speech.
- Include a conclusion that supports your ideas.

INDEPENDENT READING LINK

Read and Discuss

Using notes from your Reader/Writer Notebook, discuss with classmates a speech you have read independently. How does the author use rhetorical devices to persuade his or her audience? What do you notice about how the author builds his or her argument to a well-reasoned conclusion? Give examples to support your ideas.

✍ EXPLAIN HOW AN AUTHOR BUILDS AN ARGUMENT

The following standards are addressed in the writing prompt:

- W.11-12.1a
- W.11-12.1b
- W.11-12.1b
- W.11-12.1b
- W.11-12.1e

ACTIVITY 2.21 continued

17 Once students have completed the Check Your Understanding task, conduct a silent vote to find out whether students support Henry's position or disagree with it. Tally the votes and record them on the board. Lead students to discuss the results.

18 To help students understand the use of rhetorical devices in persuasive speeches, have them complete the Independent Reading Link.

19 Allow students time to complete the Explain How an Author Builds an Argument essay. Model for students how to create a possible outline for the essay by returning to the annotations they made in the text and consulting the writing they've already done for the text-dependent questions. Guide students to understand that by analyzing, they are doing more than summarizing Henry's argument — they are explaining how the rhetorical devices Henry uses are effective.

ASSESS

Review students' **quickwrites** for the Check Your Understanding task.

Use students' responses to the writing prompt to assess their understanding of the key elements of Henry's speech, including the use of rhetorical devices and the use of progression to build an argument. Also, responses should include an insightful analysis of the effectiveness of Henry's speech.

ADAPT

To reinforce the Check Your Understanding task, have students create lists of reasons for siding with or against Henry. Ask volunteers to share their lists. Create a master list of reasons for the class.

If students need support with identifying the elements of persuasive speeches, have them form pairs. Each student should pick a topic he or she has a strong opinion about. Then he or she should orally attempt to convince a partner that the opinion is correct. The partner should provide feedback concerning why the argument is or is not effective.

PLAN

Materials: 3 different colors of markers (a set of 3 for each group); Optional: audio recorder
Suggested Pacing: 1 50-minute class period

TEACH

1 Read aloud the Learning Targets and Preview. **Activate prior knowledge** by asking students in a group discussion to share what they remember about emotional, ethical, and logical appeals.

2 Direct groups to scan Rhetorical Appeals. As students closely read the descriptions of each appeal, direct discussion groups to sketch an image that captures each type of appeal. Be sure students recognize that ethos is focused on the speaker's credibility, not on the right-or-wrong values associated with the issue.

3 Write the words *pathos*, *ethos*, and *logos* on the board and ask volunteers for an example of what each kind of appeal looks or sounds like. If time permits, give students a topic to debate or discuss in which they must use each kind of rhetorical appeal in their argument, which the rest of the class should then identify.

⭐ TEACHER TO TEACHER

Introduce students to visual arguments and other famous speeches (political speeches, TED Talks) in which they can work to identify the different rhetorical appeals in different mediums. Allow discussion groups to identify the different appeals being used and analyze their effectiveness.

The Appeal of Rhetoric

Learning Strategies

Close Reading
Diffusing
Double-Entry Journal
Drafting
Graphic Organizer
Marking the Text
Outlining
Rereading

Learning Targets

- Analyze the use of rhetorical appeals in an argumentative text.
- Incorporate rhetorical appeals while generating an argument.

Preview

In this activity, you will read and analyze a speech for its rhetorical appeals and create an outline for your own argument that incorporates rhetorical appeals.

My Notes

Rhetorical Appeals

You have analyzed Abraham Lincoln's masterful use of rhetoric in his Second Inaugural Address. Next, you will analyze his use of rhetorical appeals in the Gettysburg Address. Although it is one of the shortest speeches in U.S. history, it is also one of the most recognized. Pay close attention to Lincoln's claim and appeals and what makes his conclusion convincing. Like other great orators, Lincoln swayed his audience by using the **rhetorical appeals** first identified by Aristotle as *pathos*, *ethos*, and *logos*. Writers and speakers choose their appeals based on their intended audience, purpose, and the nature of the argument itself.

Review the types of rhetorical appeals with your group members. Illustrate a representation of each type of appeal in the margin.

Pathos (emotional appeal): This appeal attempts to persuade the reader or listener by appealing to the senses and emotions. Political ads that show politicians kissing babies or shaking hands with the elderly often appeal to the emotions. Also, these appeals usually include statements with vivid sensory details, which are used to awaken the senses and perhaps manipulate the emotions of the audience. In many of Lincoln's speeches, he uses powerful emotional language to achieve his purpose. However, it can be easy for a writer or speaker to wind up using fallacies if he or she relies too heavily on emotional appeals.

Ethos (ethical appeal): This type of appeal attempts to persuade the reader or listener by focusing on the qualifications of the speaker. The speaker's credibility is paramount in an ethical appeal. Ethical appeals focus on the speaker even more than the situation. Examples of ethical appeals in advertising are expert or celebrity endorsements of products. You can increase your credibility, or your "ethos," with your authority, character, sources, fairness, and error-free presentation. Other examples of ethical appeals are a teen's argument that he or she should be allowed to do something because he or she has never been in trouble or because his or her friend is a perfect citizen, and so on. Finally, writers or speakers can enhance their ethos by acknowledging counterarguments or anticipating rebuttals.

Logos (logical appeal): This type of appeal attempts to persuade the reader or listener by leading him or her down the road of logic and causing him or her to come to his or her own conclusion. Logical appeals state the facts and show how the facts are interrelated. If/then statements are examples of logical appeals. Logical appeals are often used in courtroom situations. Compelling logic adds to the ethos of an argument.

College and Career Readiness Standards

Focus Standards:

RI.11-12.1 Cite strong and thorough textual evidence to support analysis of what the text says explicitly as well as inferences drawn from the text, including determining where the text leaves matters uncertain.

RI.11-12.5 Analyze and evaluate the effectiveness of the structure an author uses in his or her exposition or argument, including whether the structure makes points clear, convincing, and engaging.

Additional Standards Addressed:

RI.11-12.4, W.11-12.1b, W.11-12.1c, W.11-12.5, L.11-12.3

2.22

Aristotle tells us that all three appeals are important to persuasive writing. However, he determined that logical appeals are the most persuasive. Emotional appeals often manipulate people's emotions in order to persuade, and ethical appeals rely on qualities that might not pass the truth test. Logical appeals, which present facts and evidence, focus on the truth.

As You Read

- As you read the Gettysburg Address, look for examples of pathos, ethos, and logos. Use different-color highlighters to mark the different appeals.
- Circle unknown words and phrases. Try to determine the meaning of the words by using context clues, word parts, or a dictionary.

About the Speech

On November 19, 1863, President Abraham Lincoln spoke at the dedication of the National Cemetery of Gettysburg in Pennsylvania. Lincoln was not the featured speaker. Noted orator Edward Everett spoke for two hours about the Battle of Gettysburg. Then Lincoln delivered his 272-word speech. Afterward, Everett wrote to Lincoln, "I wish that I could flatter myself that I had come as near to the central idea of the occasion, in two hours, as you did in two minutes."

Speech

The Gettysburg Address

by Abraham Lincoln

1　Four score and seven years ago our fathers brought forth, on this continent, a new nation, **conceived** in liberty, and dedicated to the proposition that all men are created equal. Now we are engaged in a great civil war, testing whether that nation, or any nation so conceived, and so dedicated, can long endure. We are met on a great battlefield of that war. We have come to dedicate a portion, of that field, as a final resting-place for those who here gave their lives, that that nation might live. It is altogether fitting and proper that we should do this. But, in a larger sense, we cannot dedicate, we cannot **consecrate**—we cannot hallow—this ground. The brave men, living and dead, who struggled here have consecrated it far above our poor power to add or detract. The world will little note, nor long remember what we say here, but it can never forget what they did here. It is for us the living, rather, to be dedicated here to the unfinished work which they who fought here

My Notes

conceived: begun
consecrate: dedicate as sacred

Scaffolding the Text-Dependent Questions

1. What is the rhetorical effect of Lincoln opening his speech with "four score and seven years ago"? What type of rhetorical appeal does it represent? What kind of person does he present himself as? How does it help him make a connection with his audience? RI.11-12.4

2. How do Lincoln's different uses of the word *dedicate* affect the tone of the speech? Find the six instances of "dedicate" in Lincoln's speech. In each instance, to what does Lincoln refer? How are the first four instances different from the final two? What effect might that have on listeners? RI.11-12.4

3. What is Lincoln's call to action in The Gettysburg Address? When does he give it in the speech? What does he encourage his listeners to do? How will they do it? RI.11-12.1

ACTIVITY 2.22 continued

4 Read the As You Read section with students. Help them understand the instructions for annotation and model by reading the first sentence aloud and asking if it is an example of pathos, ethos, or logos.

5 Have students read the About the Speech section independently. Ask students to discuss what they think the quote by Everett means and what they can predict about the speech based on it.

6 **FIRST READ:** Provide each discussion group with three colors of highlighters. As they read Lincoln's address, have them highlight the different appeals in different colors. Circulate among groups to clarify the appeals.

◬ TEXT COMPLEXITY

Overall: Very Complex
Lexile: 1490L
Qualitative: High Difficulty
Task: Challenging (Evaluate)

7 As students are reading, monitor their progress. Be sure they are engaged with the text and annotating. Evaluate whether the reading mode is effective.

8 Based on the observations you make during the first reading, you may want to adjust the reading mode. For example, you may decide for the second reading to read aloud certain complex passages, or you may group students differently.

9 To help students better understand rhetorical appeals, have them complete the Independent Reading Link.

10 After reading the text for the first time, guide students in a brief discussion by asking the Making Observations questions. Revisit students' annotations to find the rhetorical appeal they found used the most and discuss its effectiveness.

My Notes

have thus far so nobly advanced. It is rather for us to be here dedicated to the great task remaining before us—that from these honored dead we take increased devotion to that cause for which they gave the last full measure of devotion—that we here highly resolve that these dead shall not have died in vain—that this nation, under God, shall have a new birth of freedom, and that government of the people, by the people, for the people, shall not perish from the earth.

Making Observations
- What is Lincoln's main argument in his speech?
- What rhetorical appeal does Lincoln appear to rely most heavily on?

🎁 INDEPENDENT READING LINK

Read and Connect

In your Reader/Writer Notebook, compare and contrast one of the speeches you have read independently with your analysis of Abraham Lincoln's use of rhetorical appeals. Consider using a Venn diagram. What makes each author's use of rhetorical appeals effective? Note especially any similarities between Lincoln's persuasive argument(s) and those you read independently. What can you learn from these authors about writing a persuasive speech?

Scaffolding the Text-Dependent Questions

4. **Which first-person pronoun is one of the most-repeated words in Lincoln's speech? How would its use affect Lincoln's audience? What can you infer is Lincoln's reasoning for its repeated use?** How would a person in the audience feel hearing it repeated? RI.11-12.4

5. **What inferences can you make about how Lincoln considered the audience and** the situation when choosing his rhetoric? **Cite evidence from the text to support your inference.** What does Lincoln assume about how the audience will view the Battle of Gettysburg? What does Lincoln assume about how the audience views the Civil War? RI.11-12.1

Returning to the Text

- Return to the speech as you respond to the following questions. Use text evidence to support your responses.
- Write any additional questions you have about the text in your Reader/Writer Notebook.

1. What is the rhetorical effect of Lincoln opening his speech with "four score and seven years ago"? What type of rhetorical appeal does it represent?

   The rhetorical effect of Lincoln's opening line is to establish his ethos, or credibility, as someone who understands history and its impact on the present day. Its inclusion helps establish common ground between himself and his audience as members of the same country with the same ideals.

2. How do Lincoln's different uses of the word *dedicate affect* the tone of the speech?

   The first two uses address the nation being "dedicated to the proposition that all men are created equal." The next two uses address the purpose of the gathering: to dedicate the battlefield. In the last two uses, Lincoln asks people to "be dedicated" to the "great task" and the "unfinished work" of those who fought. Expanding the word to encompass people in addition to ideas and things creates emotional impact on the tone of the speech.

3. What is Lincoln's call to action in "The Gettysburg Address?"

   Lincoln's call to action is to spur his audience into continuing the unfinished work of those who died at the Battle of Gettysburg. It is to encourage his listeners to continue fighting for liberty, equality, and justice.

4. Which first-person pronoun is one of the most-repeated words in the speech? How would its use affect Lincoln's audience? What can you infer is Lincoln's reasoning for its repeated use?

   The pronoun *we* is repeated 10 times in the speech, implying that one of Lincoln's purposes for speaking is to unify the country. Its effect on Lincoln's audience would likely be to make them feel as though he is their equal and that they are all in this together   to remember that they hold the same ideals.

5. What inferences can you make about how Lincoln considered the audience and the situation when choosing his rhetoric? Cite evidence from the text to support your inference.

   Lincoln knew his audience was suffering the pain of loss, and he knew that allusions to the Declaration of Independence would ground their pain in the course of American history. He opens the speech with the phrase "our fathers brought forth on this continent a new nation, conceived in liberty, and dedicated to the proposition that all men are created equal."

ACTIVITY 2.22 continued

11 RETURNING TO THE TEXT: During the hghsecond reading, students will be returning to the text to answer the text-dependent comprehension questions. You may choose to have students reread and work on the questions in a variety of ways:

- Independently
- In pairs
- In small groups
- Together as a class

12 Have students answer the text-dependent questions. If they have difficulty, scaffold the questions by rephrasing them or breaking them down into smaller parts. See the Scaffolding the Text-Dependent Questions boxes for suggestions.

13 Allow students time to complete the Check Your Understanding task to show their understanding of the appeals Lincoln uses and to imagine his audience's responses. Have students discuss their answers with a partner.

14 Guide students to return to Lincoln's speech for student step 6. Model how to annotate the speech in order to identify its structure. Ask volunteers to share their answers.

15 Ask volunteers to role-play for the class how to find an annotation that shows pathos, ethos, or logos and work as a class to analyze it together. Then have students work with a partner for student step 7. Ask volunteers to share their findings and analysis.

 TEACHER TO TEACHER

Support learning by using a role-playing game in which students are assigned products to sell to specific groups. Have groups create advertisements that incorporate appeals suitable to the audience. Groups should present their advertisements and explain their persuasive strategies.

2.22

☑ **Check Your Understanding**

What appeals in this speech would likely be most memorable to Lincoln's audience? Which kind of appeal is most prevalent in Lincoln's speech? What effect would it have on the audience?

Working from the Text

6. **What is the structure of Lincoln's speech? How does he work to provide a convincing conclusion?**

   Lincoln structures his speech to first provide an overview of where the country has been and

   the state it is currently in in order to make sure his audience is aware of these points. He

   then acknowledges the sacrifices the soldiers have made, both as their president and from

   the perspective of God and history. Finding this common ground allows him to conclude by

   convincing his fellow countrymen to continue fighting for what they believe in.

7. **With a partner, look through your annotations in the text for pathos, ethos, and logos. Find one example of each and analyze its effectiveness in the organizer.**

	Text Evidence	Analysis
Pathos	"It is rather for us to be here dedicated to the great task remaining before us—that from these honored dead we take increased devotion to that cause for which they gave the last full measure of devotion—that we here highly resolve that these dead shall not have died in vain—that this nation, under God, shall have a new birth of freedom, and that government of the people, by the people, for the people, shall not perish from the earth."	Lincoln uses emotional, stirring language and imagery such as "honored dead," "devotion," and "died in vain" in order to unite his audience behind his plea that they continue fighting.
Ethos	"Four score and seven years ago our fathers brought forth, on this continent, a new nation, conceived in liberty, and dedicated to the proposition that all men are created equal."	Here Lincoln establishes his credibility as the president of the country and someone who understands its history and how it has arrived at this current moment.
Logos	"The world will little note, nor long remember what we say here, but it can never forget what they did here."	Lincoln uses the power of logical deductive reasoning in order to present the case that no matter what he says, the actions of people are what history will remember in the long run.

2.22

📝 Drafting the Embedded Assessment

Revisit your notes from Activity 2.20 for the speech you have begun to plan. With these notes, you have created a rhetorical context for your speech. Now, it is time to outline the structure and incorporate rhetorical devices in the writing of the speech. Remember that an argumentative speech without a well-planned structure, rhetorical devices, and powerful syntax will not achieve its purpose.

The most effective argument uses a combination of all three rhetorical appeals. Choose places to strengthen your argument by appealing to your audience's emotions (pathos), logic (logos), and your own credibility on the topic (ethos). Be sure to:

- Discuss with a partner how you plan to use the appeals of pathos, logos, and ethos in your speech.
- Create an outline that includes the claim, support, counterclaim, concessions and rebuttals, and conclusion/call to action.
- Incorporate two or more rhetorical devices in your speech (metaphor, allusion, rhetorical questions, and imagery). Mark them in your speech.
- Choose a syntactic structure from Patrick Henry's speech to the Virginia Convention to incorporate into your argument. Mark it in your speech and in the margin and note its intended effect.
- Use a variety of rhetorical appeals in your speech. Mark them in your speech.
- Include a concluding statement with a call to action that asks audience members to change their minds or act in support of the claim.
- Practice reciting your speech to a classmate, parent, sibling, or friend. Consider how your delivery can enhance your written words.

 DRAFTING THE EMBEDDED ASSESSMENT

The following standards are addressed in the writing prompt:
- W.11-12.5
- W.11-12.1c
- W.11-12.1b
- L.11-12.3

ACTIVITY 2.22 continued

16 For Drafting the Embedded Assessment, allow student pairs to peer-review and then revise their speech drafts to add or strengthen appeals to pathos, logos, and ethos. Guide students to read the assignment and have pairs use the following questions to give appropriate feedback:

- Which appeal(s) do you hear?
- How does this appeal strengthen the argument?
- How might the syntax be revised to make the appeal even stronger?

ASSESS

Review students' responses to the Check Your Understanding task, making sure they cite evidence from the speech to support their answer.

Use students' responses to the writing prompt to assess their ability to create effective persuasive speeches. They should use efficient outlines, two or more rhetorical appeals, syntactic structures from Henry's speech, and concluding calls to action.

ADAPT

If students need help identifying the effect of Lincoln's rhetorical appeals, have them ask themselves:

- How does the speech make me feel?
- What element of Lincoln's speech most strongly influences me? Why?
- Is this element an appeal that uses pathos, ethos, or logos?

If students have difficulty revising their speeches, tell them to record their speeches and then listen to the recordings. Students should write notes on how to improve their speeches and then implement these notes in their revisions.

PLAN

Materials: audio recording of Franklin D. Roosevelt's First Inaugural Address

Suggested Pacing: 1 50-minute class period

TEACH

1 Read the Learning Targets and Preview with students.

2 Vocabulary Development: Review the meaning of the term *vocal delivery* with students. Have them work in pairs to define the term in their own words. Then ask students what qualities they notice in effective delivery of speeches.

3 Read the As You Read section aloud. Ask students to make a connection between the context and occasion for Lincoln's First Inaugural Address and his Second Inaugural Address. Help them understand the symbols they will be using while annotating and to recall how to look out for diction and syntax.

You may consider using the following symbols to designate elements of delivery, or choose your own.

+ or – volume increase or decrease

^ raised pitch

. . . rate increase

pause

4 Have students read About the Author section independently. Allow students to ask clarifying questions about the historical context of the speech and to summarize the events of the Great Depression, the New Deal, and World War II.

Learning Strategies

Close Reading
Marking the Text
Revisiting Prior Work

VOCABULARY

ACADEMIC

Vocal delivery refers to the way words are expressed onstage through volume, pitch, rate or speed of speech, pauses, pronunciation, and articulation.

Learning Targets

- Identify and evaluate the elements of effective vocal delivery.
- Prepare a text for effective oral delivery.
- Integrate ideas from multiple texts to build knowledge and vocabulary about inaugural addresses.

Preview

In this activity, you will listen to President Franklin D. Roosevelt deliver an inaugural address to an audience worn out by the Great Depression, and you will analyze how you can use elements of his delivery when giving your own speech.

As You Read

- As you listen to an audio recording of Franklin D. Roosevelt's First Inaugural Address, take notes about his style of vocal delivery.
- Circle unknown words and phrases. Try to determine the meaning of the words by using context clues, word parts, or a dictionary.
- Highlight any of Roosevelt's diction that you find impactful and underline instances of varying syntax for effect.

About the Author

President Franklin D. Roosevelt (1882–1945) took office in the United States at the same time as Adolf Hitler did in Germany. Both men led countries caught in economic depressions. Roosevelt, elected in 1932, is known for his New Deal, which sought to help those Americans desperately in need by restoring jobs and supplying basic subsistence. He was the only U.S. president elected for four terms. He led the nation through World War II.

College and Career Readiness Standards

Focus Standards:

RI.11-12.1 Cite strong and thorough textual evidence to support analysis of what the text says explicitly as well as inferences drawn from the text, including determining where the text leaves matters uncertain.

RI.11-12.4 Determine the meaning of words and phrases as they are used in a text, including figurative, connotative, and technical meanings; analyze how an author uses and refines the meaning of a key term or terms over the course of a text

RI.11-12.5 Analyze and evaluate the effectiveness of the structure an author uses in his or her exposition or argument, including whether the structure makes points clear, convincing, and engaging.

Speech

excerpt from the First Inaugural Address of Franklin D. Roosevelt

March 3, 1933

1   I am certain that my fellow Americans expect that on my induction into the Presidency I will address them with a **candor** and a decision which the present situation of our people **impel**. This is preeminently the time to speak the truth, the whole truth, frankly and boldly. Nor need we shrink from honestly facing conditions in our country today. This great Nation will endure as it has endured, will revive and will prosper. So, first of all, let me assert my firm belief that the only thing we have to fear is fear itself—nameless, unreasoning, unjustified terror which paralyzes needed efforts to convert retreat into advance. In every dark hour of our national life a leadership of frankness and vigor has met with that understanding and support of the people themselves which is essential to victory. I am convinced that you will again give that support to leadership in these critical days.

2   In such a spirit on my part and on yours we face our common difficulties. They concern, thank God, only material things. Values have shrunken to fantastic levels; taxes have risen; our ability to pay has fallen; government of all kinds is faced by serious **curtailment** of income; the means of exchange are frozen in the currents of trade; the withered leaves of industrial enterprise lie on every side; farmers find no markets for their produce; the savings of many years in thousands of families are gone.

3   More important, a host of unemployed citizens face the grim problem of existence and an equally great number toil with little return. Only a foolish optimist can deny the dark realities of the moment.

4   Yet our distress comes from no failure of **substance**. We are stricken by no plague of locusts. Compared with the perils which our forefathers conquered because they believed and were not afraid, we have still much to be thankful for. Nature still offers her bounty and human efforts have multiplied it. Plenty is at our doorstep, but a generous use of it **languishes** in the very sight of the supply. Primarily this is because the rulers of the exchange of mankind's goods have failed, through their own stubbornness and their own incompetence, have admitted their failure, and **abdicated**. Practices of the unscrupulous money changers stand indicted in the court of public opinion, rejected by the hearts and minds of men.

KNOWLEDGE QUEST

Knowledge Question:
How can presidents use their inaugural addresses to appeal to he country's citizens? In Activities 2.23 and 2.24, you will read President Roosevelt's and President Kennedy's first presidential addresses. While you read and build knowledge about how speakers can use rhetorical devices to persuade, think about your answer to the Knowledge Question.

My Notes

_____
_____
_____
_____
_____
_____
_____
_____
_____
_____
_____
_____
_____

candor: honesty
impel: feel a strong need for
curtailment: reduction
substance: abundance
languishes: breaks down
abdicated: gave up a position of responsibility

ACTIVITY 2.23 continued

5 Discuss the Knowledge Question. Have students work in small groups to discuss how presidents can use rhetorical appeals in their inaugural addresses to persuade an audience.

6 FIRST READ: Play an audio recording of Franklin D. Roosevelt's First Inaugural Address. You can access it at several online sites. Instruct students to mark the text for volume, pitch, rate, and pauses, using the symbols shown. If you do not have access to audio in your classroom, consider using choral reading and allow time for discussion groups to continue marking the text as they imagine it would be spoken.

 TEXT COMPLEXITY

Overall: Complex
Lexile: 1090L
Qualitative: Moderate Difficulty
Task: Challenging (Evaluate)

7 As students are reading, monitor their progress. Be sure they are engaged with the text and marking the text for volume, pitch, rate, and pauses.

Scaffolding the Text-Dependent Questions

1. In paragraph 1, what does Roosevelt mean by using the word endure in this context? What emotion might this make his audience feel? RI.11-12.4

2. How does the clause "the only thing we have to fear is fear itself" suggest Roosevelt's purpose for speaking? During the Depression, what were people afraid of? With what does Roosevelt replace the items on the list? Why

does he say that fear is dangerous? RI.11-12.4

3. How does Roosevelt use an allusion to the Bible to help people gain perspective on the economic situation? The Biblical plague of locusts was devastating. How does Roosevelt think that the Great Depression compares to or contrasts with the plague of locusts? How does he support his point of view? RI.11-12.1

8 After reading the speech, guide the class in a discussion of the Knowledge Quest questions. Write students' questions on the board in a connected mind map. Be sure students can accurately discuss Roosevelt's vocal delivery by pointing out parts of the speech they annotated while listening.

9 To help students improve their understanding of vocal delivery elements, have them complete the Independent Reading Link.

 TEACHER TO TEACHER

Roosevelt's First Inaugural Address takes on an unusually solemn, religious quality. You may note to students that this is quite different from the buoyant, optimistic, gently paternal tone that he used in campaign speeches.

Roosevelt uses Biblical allusions ("plague of locusts," "money changers") that stir righteous indignation in his listeners. These allusions may be missed by students. Discuss why these allusions would resonate with this audience in the 1930s.

10 **RETURNING TO THE TEXT:** During the second reading, students will be returning to the text to answer the text-dependent comprehension questions. You may choose to have students reread and work on the questions in a variety of ways:

- Independently
- In pairs
- In small groups
- Together as a class

11 Have students answer the text-dependent questions. If they have difficulty, scaffold the questions by rephrasing them or breaking them down into smaller parts. See the Scaffolding the Text-Dependent Questions boxes for suggestions.

2.23

INDEPENDENT READING LINK

Read and Respond
Paste an excerpt from one of the speeches you read independently in your Reader/Writer Notebook. Use colored ink to mark the text for volume increases or decreases (+ or –), raised pitch (^), rate increases (...), and pauses (#). You may want to read passages aloud in various ways before making these decisions. Then reflect in writing on the connections between delivery and message for this text.

My Notes

_____

_____

_____

_____

_____

_____

_____

_____

_____

_____

_____

_____

_____

induce: cause or bring about
evanescent: short-lived

5 True they have tried, but their efforts have been cast in the pattern of an outworn tradition. Faced by failure of credit they have proposed only the lending of more money. Stripped of the lure of profit by which to **induce** our people to follow their false leadership, they have resorted to exhortations, pleading tearfully for restored confidence. They know only the rules of a generation of self-seekers. They have no vision, and when there is no vision the people perish.

6 The money changers have fled from their high seats in the temple of our civilization. We may now restore that temple to the ancient truths. The measure of the restoration lies in the extent to which we apply social values more noble than mere monetary profit.

7 Happiness lies not in the mere possession of money; it lies in the joy of achievement, in the thrill of creative effort. The joy and moral stimulation of work no longer must be forgotten in the mad chase of **evanescent** profits. These dark days will be worth all they cost us if they teach us that our true destiny is not to be ministered unto but to minister to ourselves and to our fellow men.

⊘ Knowledge Quest

- What questions does Roosevelt's speech raise for you?
- What do you think about the effectiveness of Roosevelt's vocal delivery? How is or isn't it memorable?

Returning to the Text

- Return to the speech as you respond to the following questions. Use text evidence to support your responses.
- Write any additional questions you have about the text in your Reader/Writer Notebook.

Scaffolding the Text-Dependent Questions

4. What effect do the phrases "ancient truths" and "temple of our civilization" have on the tone of the speech? Why has money failed to make people happy? What does Roosevelt say is more valuable than money in the pursuit of happiness? What do these phrases link the current moment to? What connections might the audience make? RI.11-12.4

5. Why does Roosevelt use the phrases "not to be ministered unto" and "to minister to ourselves and to our fellow man" in the final sentence? How do they shape the perception of the audience? What does the word *minister* mean? What are the word's connotations? What does Roosevelt understand about his audience that might make him use this word? RI.11-12.4

1. **KQ** In paragraph 1, what does Roosevelt mean by using the word *endure* in this context?

   Roosevelt uses his inaugural address to discuss the history and future of the United States as well as to address its current circumstances. Therefore, in this context, he uses the word *endure* to mean how something can persist and last.

2. How does the clause "the only thing we have to fear is fear itself" suggest Roosevelt's purpose for speaking?

   The phrase is hopeful—it encourages listeners to let go of their fear. This tone suggests that Roosevelt's purpose for this speech, in the heart of the Great Depression, is to calm fear and give people hope.

3. How does Roosevelt use an allusion to the Bible to help people gain perspective on the economic situation?

   Roosevelt refers to the Biblical "plague of locusts," in which the Egyptians lost all their crops to a locust swarm. He makes the point that the situation facing Americans is not as bad as a plague of locusts. The failure is not in the bounty but in the human practice of exchanging goods, something that is more readily remedied than a failure of substance.

4. What effect do the phrases "ancient truths" and "temple of our civilization" have on the tone of the speech?

   Roosevelt expresses the belief that happiness is established through social values: achievement, creativity, work, and ministering to others. His use of the phrases "ancient truths" and "temple of our civilization" links the current moment to the foundation of the past and by extension the notion that happiness is not based on money or materialism.

5. Why does Roosevelt use the phrases "not to be ministered unto" and "to minister to ourselves and to our fellow man" in the final sentence? How do they shape the perception of the audience?

   The word *minister* has a religious connotation, which appeals to people's ethics as well as their emotions. He empowers people who feel powerless with the play on the word when he says that it is the people's destiny not to be helpless but to care for themselves and others.

6. How does Roosevelt's understanding of his audience underscore the purpose of his speech?

   As a first-time president, Roosevelt understands that his audience wishes to hear the truth from him as the new leader of their country. This understanding means that one of the purposes of his speech is to convince them that they have made the right choice in electing him by communicating his understanding of the issues the country faces.

ACTIVITY 2.23 continued

LEVELED DIFFERENTIATED INSTRUCTION

In this activity, students may need to practice their speaking and listening skills before delivering their persuasive speeches.

Developing Pair students and distribute the **Active Listening Feedback** graphic organizer. Have students practice reading their speeches to their partners at least twice, focusing primarily on rate, pausing, and pronunciation.

Expanding Using the **Active Listening Feedback** graphic organizer, have student partners practice volume, rate, pausing, pronunciation, and articulation.

Support Have student partners complete the "Content" section of the **Active Listening Feedback** graphic organizer. Have listeners evaluate whether the speaker used volume, rate, pausing, pronunciation, and articulation confidently and persuasively.

Extend Have students record themselves. Using the Active Listening Feedback graphic organizer, guide them to evaluate their own volume, rate, pausing, pronunciation, and articulation.

Scaffolding the Text-Dependent Questions

6. How does Roosevelt's understanding of his audience underscore the purpose of his speech? What might it mean for his audience that he was a first-time president? What would they need to be convinced of? RI.11-12.5

7. What is the effect of hearing Roosevelt's speech in comparison to reading it? How does he use his voice for emphasis? How might his audience have reacted to it? What would they pay attention to based on his emphasis? RI.11-12.5

8. How does Roosevelt use his inaugural address to appeal to the citizens of the United States? What emotions does he appeal to? RI.11-12.1

12 Have students get in groups to discuss Roosevelt's delivery and the marks they have made while listening. If students have differences in their markings, encourage them to share the reasoning behind their choices. Have them complete student step 8 together.

13 Ask volunteers for examples of diction and syntax they annotated in Roosevelt's speech. Then have students work with a partner for student step 9. Have them discuss their analysis with another pair.

14 Guide students to return to the Knowledge Quest question they discussed before reading. Ask students how their response to this question has changed or been deepened after reading Roosevelt's speech.

7. What is the effect of hearing Roosevelt's speech in comparison to reading it? How does he use his voice for emphasis?

Roosevelt uses his voice to make his speech sound more powerful to the listening audience.

8. **KQ** How does Roosevelt use his inaugural address to appeal to the citizens of the United States?

Roosevelt uses his inaugural address to appeal to the citizens of the United States regarding its current economic circumstances. He appeals to by being honest, "frankly and boldly," in order to urge them to have faith during difficult times. He appeals to their sense of morality, history, and values.

Working from the Text

9. Share with your group the annotations you made about Roosevelt's delivery of the speech. How clear and coherent is Roosevelt's message?

Roosevelt's delivery of his speech is dynamic and confident. He pauses for emphasis and to let an idea sink in for his audience, and he increases his rate of speaking to build urgency. These choices affect the clarity and coherence of his message by showing him as concerned and serious about the state of the country and clearly outlining the steps he plans to take.

10. With a partner, critique one of the paragraphs in Roosevelt's speech for its use of diction and syntax. Bold the words you notice and underline the varying syntax that has an effect. What can you glean about the effect of his use of words and varying sentence structure?

Diction or Syntax	Analysis of Its Effects
In such a spirit on my part and on yours we face our **common difficulties**. They concern, **thank God**, only material things. Values have **shrunken** to **fantastic** levels; taxes have risen; our ability to pay has fallen; government of all kinds is faced by serious curtailment of income; the means of exchange are frozen in the currents of trade; the **withered leaves** of industrial enterprise lie on every side; farmers find no markets for their produce; the savings of many years in thousands of families are gone.	Roosevelt chooses words and phrases that his audience can connect with, such as "common difficulties" and "thank God." This creates a common ground and mutual trust with the audience. He also uses poetic diction such as "withered leaves" to paint an image for dramatic effect. Roosevelt also varies his syntax by following a short and succinct sentence with a long, rhythmic one. His use of listing out the many problems with the economy creates a dramatic effect.

☑ Focus on the Sentence

Using subordinating conjunctions, combine the following sentences from Roosevelt's speech in order to see the effect on their syntax. Read each version aloud with a partner.

The money changers have fled from their high seats in the temple of our civilization. We may now restore that temple to the ancient truths.

Because the money changers have fled from their high seats in the temple of our civilization, we may

now restore that temple to the ancient truths.

This is preeminently the time to speak the truth, the whole truth, frankly and boldly. Nor need we shrink from honestly facing conditions in our country today.

This is preeminently the time to speak the truth, the whole truth, frankly and boldly, and we no

longer need to shrink from honestly facing conditions in our country today.

They know only the rules of a generation of self-seekers. They have no vision, and when there is no vision the people perish.

Because they know only the rules of a generation of self-seekers, they have no vision, and when

there is no vision the people perish.

11. Revisit the persuasive speech you have been writing in the past few activities. Review your rhetorical context (subject, audience, occasion, etc.). What tone do you need to convey to your audience in consideration of your subject and occasion?

12. Quietly read your written speech aloud, noting your vocal delivery elements as you did in Roosevelt's speech. Be sure to consider the following elements of vocal delivery as you plan your presentation with the goal of persuading your audience:

- Eye contact
- Volume
- Pitch
- Rate
- Pauses
- Gestures
- Pronunciation (Do you know how to pronounce every word in your speech?)
- Enunciation (Practice enunciating your words so a person seated in the back of the room would have no trouble hearing your argument.)

ACTIVITY 2.23 continued

15 On the board, ask volunteers to help make a list of possible subordinating conjunctions. Ask a second set of volunteers to use them in a sentence.

16 Have students work with a partner to complete the Focus on the Sentence questions and refer them to the list the class created on the board if they need guidance. Go over answers together as a class.

17 Direct students to confirm the tone they have selected for their persuasive speeches. Ask them to consider how their delivery will convey that tone.

18 Allow students time to practice quietly reading their speeches out loud. Students should mark their speeches for volume, pitch, rate, pauses, and pronunciation. Stress to students the importance of clearly articulating their words during the speeches. Emphasize that an effective speech must be heard, not read. Students will need to experiment with different rates, volumes, pitches, and pauses as they mark the texts.

ASSESS

Use students' responses to the Working from the Text question to assess their abilities to note vocal delivery elements and to incorporate these elements into their speeches. As students rehearse their speeches, make sure that they are accurately pronouncing and effectively articulating the words.

ADAPT

If students have difficulty including vocal delivery elements in their speeches, tell them to record their speeches using the vocal delivery that they have devised thus far. Have students listen to their own recordings. Then have students answer the following:

- What vocal elements are missing from the speech?
- What vocal elements can be improved?

PLAN

Materials: audio recording of Kennedy's Inaugural Address, Internet access, highlighters, poster paper, markers; Optional: video projection equipment, video recorder
Suggested Pacing: 2 50-minute class period

TEACH

1 Read aloud the Learning Targets and Preview for students. Ask volunteers to define the term *syntax*, and ask for examples of how syntax can be used in writing to create a persuasive effect. Write students' examples on the board.

2 **Activate prior knowledge** by asking students what they know about President John F. Kennedy and the historical context of his presidency. Lead a discussion asking students to predict how his Inaugural Address will be similar or different to the other ones they've read in this unit.

3 Have students read the Syntax and Persuasion section independently.

4 Direct students to skim/scan the information about sentence length and sentence structure, stopping to mark the text or illustrate any information that is new or confusing to them. Follow up by asking questions or giving further examples.

5 To give students practice in identifying these sentence types, have them return to drafts of previous writing and annotate their texts for the various sentence types. Remind students that they should use varied sentence structures. Have students evaluate their sentences to determine whether they are using a variety or mostly one type. They should consciously work to improve their sentence variety in future writing and revision.

Learning Strategies

Close Reading
Discussion Groups
Double-Entry Journal
Quickwrite

My Notes

Learning Targets

- Analyze the use of syntax in a historical document.
- Intentionally craft sentences for persuasive effect.
- Integrate ideas from multiple texts to build knowledge and vocabulary about a inaugural speeches.

Preview

In this activity, you will read and analyze John F. Kennedy's Inaugural Address for its use of syntax and persuasion and craft sentences of your own for persuasive effect.

Syntax and Persuasion

Syntax is not a new term for you, but as you grow as a reader and writer, you will encounter increasingly complex sentences. Your ability to decipher meaning in complex syntactic structures and to purposefully use these structures to make meaning in your own texts is critical to your success.

Certain types of sentences or their arrangement affect a passage's overall meaning significantly. Sometimes, authors deliberately choose a variety of syntactical constructions for their sentences; other times, authors consciously repeat certain types of sentences to achieve the desired effect. Syntax can help shape the mood, voice, and tone of a passage.

Sentence Length	Telegraphic	sentences shorter than five words in length
	Short	sentences approximately five words in length
	Medium	sentences approximately 18 words in length
	Long	sentences 30 or more words in length

College and Career Readiness Standards

Focus Standards:

RI.11-12.1 Cite strong and thorough textual evidence to support analysis of what the text says explicitly as well as inferences drawn from the text, including determining where the text leaves matters uncertain.

RI.11-12.4 Determine the meaning of words and phrases as they are used in a text, including figurative, connotative, and technical meanings; analyze how an author uses and refines the meaning of a key term or terms over the course of a text

Sentence Structure	Simple	contains one independent clause	*The goalie waved to his fans.*
	Compound	contains two independent clauses joined by a coordinating conjunction or by a semicolon	*The goalie bowed to his fans, but he gave no autographs.*
	Complex	contains an independent clause and one or more subordinate clauses	*Because the goalie was tired, he went straight to the locker room.*
	Compound-Complex	contains two or more independent clauses and one or more subordinate clauses	*The goalie waved while the fans cheered, but he gave no autographs.*
	Cumulative (or Loose)	makes complete sense if brought to a close before the actual ending	*We reached New York that morning after a turbulent flight and some exciting experiences, tired but exhilarated, full of stories to tell our friends and neighbors.*
	Periodic	makes sense fully only when the end of the sentence is reached	*That morning, after a turbulent flight and some exciting experiences, we reached New York.*
	Balanced	the phrases or clauses balance each other by virtue of their likeness of structure, meaning, or length	*He makes me lie down in green pastures; he leads me beside the still waters.*

6 Read the As You Read section with students. Help them understand what they should annotate.

7 Have students read the About the Author section independently and encourage them to ask any clarifying questions about the context. Remind them that Lincoln and Kennedy gave their addresses nearly a century apart.

As You Read

- Put an exclamation point next to any long sentences.
- Put a star next to any sentence containing repetition.
- Circle unknown words and phrases. Try to determine the meaning of the words by using context clues, word parts, or a dictionary.

About the Author

John F. Kennedy was elected president of the United States in November 1960 and took the oath of office in January 1961. His Inaugural Address has become one of the most famous and most-often-quoted speeches for its rhetoric of both inspiration and challenge.

College and Career Readiness Standards

RI.11-12.5 Analyze and evaluate the effectiveness of the structure an author uses in his or her exposition or argument, including whether the structure makes points clear, convincing, and engaging.

Additional Standards Addressed:

W.11-12.1b, W.11-12.1c, W.11-12.1e, SL.11-12.4

8 FIRST READ: Play a portion of Kennedy's 1961 Inaugural Address on audio or project a video of it (preferable). You may access it at several online sites. As students listen or view, have them highlight especially memorable or powerful syntactic structures.

 TEXT COMPLEXITY

Overall: Very Complex
Lexile: 1430L
Qualitative: High Difficulty
Task: Moderate (Analyze)

9 As students are reading, monitor their progress. Be sure they are engaged with the text and annotating syntactic structures. Evaluate whether the selected reading mode is effective.

LEVELED DIFFERENTIATED INSTRUCTION

Beginning Consider using images or other visuals to support students in comprehending the text "Inaugural Address of John F. Kennedy." Help them to develop background understanding of John F. Kennedy and the Cold War by sharing images of President Kennedy and the effects of the Cold War and asking them to say or write statements about what they observe.

10 Be sure students read the Grammar & Usage feature on antithesis.

 KNOWLEDGE QUEST

Knowledge Question: How can presidents use their inaugural addresses to appeal to he country's citizens?

GRAMMAR & USAGE

Sentence Structure: Antithesis
At times, a speaker may create a kind of parallelism between two opposing ideas to emphasize contrast. When authors juxtapose contrasting ideas in balanced phrases or clauses, they use antithesis. Notice that Kennedy uses antithesis no fewer than three times in the very first sentence of his speech: " ... not a victory of party, but a celebration of freedom—symbolizing an end, as well as a beginning, signifying renewal, as well as change." Each phrase works to emphasize and illuminate its opposing idea.

My Notes

_____
_____
_____
_____
_____
_____
_____
_____

mortal: human
tempered: strengthened through hardship

2.24

Speech

Inaugural Address of John F. Kennedy

January 20, 1961

1 Vice President Johnson, Mr. Speaker, Mr. Chief Justice, President Eisenhower, Vice President Nixon, President Truman, reverend clergy, fellow citizens, we observe today not a victory of party, but a celebration of freedom—symbolizing an end, as well as a beginning—signifying renewal, as well as change. For I have sworn before you and Almighty God the same solemn oath our forebears prescribed nearly a century and three quarters ago.

2 The world is very different now. For man holds in his **mortal** hands the power to abolish all forms of human poverty and all forms of human life. And yet the same revolutionary beliefs for which our forebears fought are still at issue around the globe—the belief that the rights of man come not from the generosity of the state, but from the hand of God.

3 We dare not forget today that we are the heirs of that first revolution. Let the word go forth from this time and place, to friend and foe alike, that the torch has been passed to a new generation of Americans—born in this century, **tempered** by war, disciplined by a hard and bitter peace, proud of our ancient heritage—and unwilling to witness or permit the slow undoing of those human rights to which this Nation has always been committed, and to which we are committed today at home and around the world.

4 Let every nation know, whether it wishes us well or ill, that we shall pay any price, bear any burden, meet any hardship, support any friend, oppose any foe, in order to assure the survival and the success of liberty.

5 This much we pledge—and more.

6 To those old allies whose cultural and spiritual origins we share, we pledge the loyalty of faithful friends. United, there is little we cannot do in a host of cooperative ventures. Divided, there is little we can do—for we dare not meet a powerful challenge at odds and split asunder.

7 To those new states whom we welcome to the ranks of the free, we pledge our word that one form of colonial control shall not have passed away merely to be replaced by a far more iron tyranny. We shall not always expect to find them supporting our view. But we shall always hope to find them strongly supporting their own freedom—and to remember that, in the past, those who foolishly sought power by riding the back of the tiger ended up inside.

8 To those peoples in the huts and villages across the globe struggling to break the bonds of mass misery, we pledge our best efforts to help them help

---

Scaffolding the Text-Dependent Questions

1. In paragraph 2, what does Kennedy mean by using the word *revolutionary* in this context? How might his audience understand this word? RI.11-12.4

2. Use the Grammar & Usage box to recall the definition of *antithesis*. What is the effect of Kennedy's use of antithesis in paragraph 6? How might it also be considered a fallacy? What are the opposing words? What comparison is Kennedy making? RI.11-12.5

My Notes

themselves, for whatever period is required—not because the Communists may be doing it, not because we seek their votes, but because it is right. If a free society cannot help the many who are poor, it cannot save the few who are rich.

9   To our sister republics south of our border, we offer a special pledge—to convert our good words into good deeds—in a new alliance for progress—to assist free men and free governments in casting off the chains of poverty. But this peaceful revolution of hope cannot become the prey of hostile powers. Let all our neighbors know that we shall join with them to oppose aggression or **subversion** anywhere in the Americas. And let every other power know that this Hemisphere intends to remain the master of its own house.

10   To that world assembly of **sovereign** states, the United Nations, our last best hope in an age where the instruments of war have far outpaced the instruments of peace, we renew our pledge of support—to prevent it from becoming merely a forum for **invective**—to strengthen its shield of the new and the weak—and to enlarge the area in which its **writ** may run.

11   Finally, to those nations who would make themselves our adversary, we offer not a pledge but a request: that both sides begin anew the quest for peace, before the dark powers of destruction unleashed by science engulf all humanity in planned or accidental self-destruction.

12   We dare not tempt them with weakness. For only when our arms are sufficient beyond doubt can we be certain beyond doubt that they will never be employed.

13   But neither can two great and powerful groups of nations take comfort from our present course—both sides overburdened by the cost of modern weapons, both rightly alarmed by the steady spread of the deadly atom, yet both racing to alter that uncertain balance of terror that stays the hand of mankind's final war.

14   So let us begin anew—remembering on both sides that civility is not a sign of weakness, and sincerity is always subject to proof. Let us never negotiate out of fear. But let us never fear to negotiate.

15   Let both sides explore what problems unite us instead of **belaboring** those problems which divide us.

16   Let both sides, for the first time, formulate serious and precise proposal for the inspection and control of arms—and bring the absolute power to destroy other nations under the absolute control of all nations.

17   Let both sides seek to invoke the wonders of science instead of its terrors. Together let us explore the stars, conquer the deserts, **eradicate** disease, tap the ocean depths, and encourage the arts and commerce.

18   Let both sides unite to heed in all corners of the earth the command of Isaiah—to "undo the heavy burdens ... and to let the oppressed go free."

---

subversion: weakening or undermining a government
sovereign: self-governing
invective: insults or abuse
writ: written word
belaboring: discussing excessively
eradicate: completely eliminate

Scaffolding the Text-Dependent Questions

3. Which clues in paragraph 11 help you identify the audience to whom Kennedy refers? What message is he sending them? Recall that Kennedy delivers this speech during the Cold War, a period of political and military strain following World War II. Who were the two "sides" of the Cold War? What are "the dark powers of destruction unleashed by science"? Why doesn't Kennedy address Soviet leaders directly? RI.11-12.1

4. In paragraph 16, how does Kennedy use the word *absolute* in different ways to create different effects? What is the effect of the word *absolute* on the word *power*? What is the effect of the word *absolute* on the word *control*? What feelings does each phrase evoke for the listener? RI.11-12.4

11 After reading the text for the first time, guide the class in a discussion by asking the Knowledge Quest questions. Check students' general comprehension of how this speech differs from the other speeches they've read in this unit and ask them to explain why they might feel certain emotions if they were in the audience.

2.24

My Notes

19 And if a **beachhead** of cooperation may push back the jungle of suspicion, let both sides join in creating a new endeavor, not a new balance of power, but a new world of law, where the strong are just and the weak secure and the peace preserved.

20 All this will not be finished in the first 100 days. Nor will it be finished in the first 1,000 days, nor in the life of this Administration, nor even perhaps in our lifetime on this planet. But let us begin.

21 In your hands, my fellow citizens, more than in mine, will rest the final success or failure of our course. Since this country was founded, each generation of Americans has been summoned to give testimony to its national loyalty. The graves of young Americans who answered the call to service surround the globe.

22 Now the trumpet summons us again—not as a call to bear arms, though arms we need; not as a call to battle, though embattled we are—but a call to bear the burden of a long twilight struggle, year in and year out, "rejoicing in hope, patient in tribulation"—a struggle against the common enemies of man: tyranny, poverty, disease, and war itself.

23 Can we forge against these enemies a grand and global alliance, North and South, East and West, that can assure a more fruitful life for all mankind? Will you join in that historic effort?

24 In the long history of the world, only a few generations have been granted the role of defending freedom in its hour of maximum danger. I do not shrink from this responsibility—I welcome it. I do not believe that any of us would exchange places with any other people or any other generation. The energy, the faith, the devotion which we bring to this endeavor will light our country and all who serve it—and the glow from that fire can truly light the world.

25 And so, my fellow Americans: ask not what your country can do for you—ask what you can do for your country.

26 My fellow citizens of the world: ask not what America will do for you, but what together we can do for the freedom of man.

27 Finally, whether you are citizens of America or citizens of the world, ask of us the same high standards of strength and sacrifice which we ask of you. With a good conscience our only sure reward, with history the final judge of our deeds, let us go forth to lead the land we love, asking His blessing and His help, but knowing that here on earth God's work must truly be our own.

beachhead: foothold or staging area for an attack

⊘ Knowledge Quest

- How does this speech differ in tone and topic from the other speeches you've read in this unit?
- What emotions might you feel if you were in the audience for this speech?

Scaffolding the Text-Dependent Questions

5. How does Kennedy's use of repetition in paragraphs 15–18 contribute to the tone of the speech? What idea does the repetition emphasize? How would you describe the tone of the speech? What is Kennedy calling for? RI.11-12.4

6. In paragraph 19, what does Kennedy mean by the clause "a beachhead of cooperation may push back the jungle of suspicion"? What **is the effect of this metaphor?** A metaphor makes a comparison between two items to help readers think in new ways. What do a beachhead and cooperation have in common? What do a jungle and suspicion have in common? How might this metaphor help world leaders think about the relationship between countries? RI.11-12.4

Returning to the Text

- Return to the speech as you respond to the following questions. Use text evidence to support your responses.
- Write any additional questions you have about the text in your Reader/Writer Notebook.

1. **KQ** In paragraph 2, what does Kennedy mean by using the word *revolutionary* in this context?

   Kennedy uses his inaugural address to celebrate a victory and a "celebration of freedom,

   renewal, and change." He calls upon history to show how the world is much different but that

   it has always engaged in dramatic changes that can be described as revolutionary. Therefore,

   the word *revolutionary* links the past and future of the country.

2. Use the Grammar & Usage box to recall the definition of antithesis. What is the effect of Kennedy's use of antithesis in paragraph 6? How might it also be considered a fallacy?

   The opposing first words in parallel sentence structures emphasize the different outcomes

   of being "united" and "divided." Its effect as a rhetorical device is one of making a dramatic

   comparison, but it can also be considered an either/or fallacy—other nations can only be

   united or divided, with no room for nuance.

3. Which clues in paragraph 11 help you identify the audience to whom Kennedy refers? What message is he sending them? Recall that Kennedy delivers this speech during the Cold War, a period of political and military strain following World War II.

   Kennedy addresses "those nations who would make themselves our adversary," so "both

   sides" refers to the United States and an adversary. The Soviet Union was the United States'

   primary nuclear adversary during in the Cold War and was probably the other side to whom

   Kennedy refers, and here he sends a message about the state of their relationship.

4. In paragraph 16, how does Kennedy use the word *absolute* in different ways to create different effects?

   Absolute intensifies the very different words it modifies in each context. The "absolute power

   to destroy" is a terrifying concept, while "absolute control" is safe and comforting.

ACTIVITY 2.24 continued

12 RETURNING TO THE TEXT: During a second reading of the text, chunk the text and assign chunks to **discussion groups**. Assign students the task of creating a note-taking format, writing on the text and in the margins, specifically noting the rhetorical devices they have learned to recognize. Also, students should identify whether Kennedy uses antithesis (Grammar & Usage callout box) within their chunks as they **close read** the speech.

13 Have students answer the text-dependent questions. If they have difficulty, scaffold the questions by rephrasing them or breaking them down into smaller parts. See the Scaffolding the Text-Dependent Questions boxes for suggestions.

Scaffolding the Text-Dependent Questions

7. What is an additional instance of antithesis in Kennedy's speech? What is its effect on voice? What contrasts and distinctions does he aim to call attention to? How are the tone and voice of the speech connected? RI.11-12.5

8. How persuasive is Kennedy's speech? What different appeals does he rely on, and how effective are they? How do they work in combination with each other? How does he establish his ethos? What emotions does he want his audience to feel? How is it memorable? RI.11-12.5

9. How does Kennedy use his inaugural address to appeal to the citizens of the United States? What emotions does he seek to inspire? What argument does he make? RI.11-12.1

5. How does Kennedy's use of repetition in paragraphs 15–18 contribute to the tone of the speech?

Kennedy uses repetition with the opening phrase "let both sides" at the beginning of these paragraphs as a way to underscore and emphasize his ideas, and it contributes to the serious and powerful tone of his speech that calls for "both sides" to find common ground and work together.

6. In paragraph 19, what does Kennedy mean by the clause "a beachhead of cooperation may push back the jungle of suspicion"? What is the effect of this metaphor?

The terms "beachhead of cooperation" and "jungle of suspicion" evoke war imagery. They create the visual imagery of beach next to a thick jungle. As the "jungle of suspicion" is cut back, a clear, safe space emerges. Kennedy expresses the hope that such a safe space might be found in relations with the Soviet Union.

7. What is an additional instance of antithesis in Kennedy's speech? What is its effect on voice?

Kennedy uses antithesis heavily throughout his speech in order to draw contrasts. One example is the line "the belief that the rights of man come not from the generosity of the state, but from the hand of God." This creates a distinction that the state decides what rights people have, when really rights are bestowed by natural, or divine, law, and it creates an emphatic effect on the voice and tone of the speech.

8. How persuasive is Kennedy's speech? What different appeals does he rely on, and how effective are they?

Kennedy's speech is persuasive due to a powerful combination of rhetorical devices such as antithesis and repetition as well as a mix of emotional, logical, and ethical appeals. He establishes ethos by acknowledging that he values unity over partisanship: "We observe today not a victory of party but a celebration of freedom." This is effective because he strives to find common ground with those who may not have voted for him. Kennedy uses logos when he brings up facts about the Cold War in order to propose healing the potential relationship with Russia. Lastly, he establishes pathos by appealing to American patriotism. The combination of these appeals is effective in creating a memorable, balanced, passionate speech.

ACTIVITY 2.24 continued

9. **KQ** How does Kennedy use his inaugural address to appeal to the citizens of the United States?

Kennedy uses his inaugural address to inspire optimism and a sense of

renewal and change. He appeals to their sense of kinship with the rest of the

world and their allies as well as an invitation to explore beginning anew with

adversaries and enemies.

 Knowledge Quest

With a partner, discuss how you think Roosevelt's and Kennedy's audiences may have felt hearing their speeches, given your understanding of the historical contexts. Be sure to:

- Refer to evidence from the speeches.
- Take turns speaking, responding, and asking one another follow-up questions.
- Ask clarifying questions.
- Write down notes and ideas for further research.

 INDEPENDENT READING LINK

Read and Discuss

You can continue to build your knowledge about inaugural speeches by reading other articles at ZINC Reading Labs. Search for keywords such as *inaugural address* or *presidential speech*.

 | ZINC

14 Guide students to return to the Knowledge Quest question they discussed before reading. Ask students how their response to this question has changed or been deepened after both speeches.

15 Allow students time to work with a partner to complete the Closing the Knowledge Quest task. Ask volunteers to share highlights from their discussion.

16 Encourage students to continue building knowledge on this topic as suggested in the Independent Reading Link.

17 Go over student step 10 with students. If necessary, go over the concepts of rhetorical devices and syntax with the class. Ask a volunteer to summarize the task.

18 Play the video of footage of Kennedy's address for the class and allow students to independently fill out the chart with their observations.

19 Guide students to get into groups to share their charts and discuss the questions in student step 10. Ask volunteers to share their observations with the class and lead a discussion around what other students agree or disagree with about those observations.

20 Allow groups time to review their notes and create a poster for student step 11 and 12. Circulate around the room as groups work, helping to troubleshoot, clarify, and re-direct as needed.

21 Have groups present their posters and guide the class in offering constructive feedback and observations.

22 Allow students time to complete the Check Your Understanding task independently in order to demonstrate an understanding of Kennedy's speech and use of rhetorical devices as well as an awareness of their own speeches' structure and devices.

2.24

Working from the Text

10. As a class, watch the video footage of Kennedy's address. Use the chart to keep track of the different aspects and rhetorical devices used in his address, such as repetition, parallel structure, analogy, rhetorical questions, allusions, anaphora, and metaphor. Take note of the rhetorical devices or syntax choices that you find especially effective or memorable. Then discuss your observations as a group. How did Kennedy's delivery of emphasized words, repetition, and syntax affect his message? How do they effect the clarity and coherence of his message?

Use of Rhetorical Devices	Impact of Words or Phrases	Use of Syntax	Effect on Clarity and Coherence

11. Review your notes about syntax as a group. Create a poster that includes the following:
    - A syntactic structure from your chunk of reading (include length, style, and order)
    - An example sentence of this structure from the text
    - Its effect on the audience
    - Your notes on how to vocally deliver it

12. Assign every group member a responsibility and share your syntax discovery with the class. While listening to other groups, consider some syntax styles that you could intentionally incorporate into your original speech.

☑ **Check Your Understanding**

Quickwrite: Compare your speech to Kennedy's. How might you incorporate one of Kennedy's rhetorical devices in your own speech?

📝 **Drafting the Embedded Assessment**

Revise your planned speech again with careful attention to syntax. Refer to your notes on syntactical structure from Kennedy's speech. Consider which styles you can incorporate smoothly into your current draft. Be sure to:

- Read your speech from beginning to end to check for smooth syntax.
- Mark new sentences with notes for vocal delivery.
- Use varied syntax and sentence structure to add to the persuasive impact of your speech and hold audience interest.
- End with a memorable conclusion that uses rhetorical technique.
- Plan and practice inflection, facial expression, and gestures to create an engaging delivery for your audience.

LANGUAGE & WRITER'S CRAFT: Chiasmus

Chiasmus is a type of reverse parallelism in which two clauses are related through a reversal of structure. Consider how a carnival mirror reflects an image of the looker that may be structurally opposite from the original: a small person sees a large image. This type of language reversal helps an author convey a grand and memorable idea to the audience.

Examples:

Let us never negotiate out of fear. But let us never fear to negotiate.

Ask not what your country can do for you—ask what you can do for your country.

PRACTICE Revise your speech to contain at least one example of chiasmus to make a main idea more memorable.

DRAFTING THE EMBEDDED ASSESSMENT

The following standards are addressed in the writing prompt:

- W.11-12.1c
- W.11-12.1b
- W.11-12.1e
- SL.11-12.4

---

23 Direct students to revisit their speeches for final revisions, this time to incorporate syntactic structures. Ask students to highlight their new sentences to show that they have made intentional choices to include rhetorical devices that improve their messages.

24 Read the Language & Writer's Craft information with students. Share other examples of chiasmus to help students understand the device:

- "You forget what you want to remember, and you remember what you want to forget."—Cormac McCarthy, *The Road*
- "I had a teacher I liked who used to say good fiction's job was to comfort the disturbed and disturb the comfortable."—David Foster Wallace, "Interview with Larry McCaffery"

Ask students to indicate which elements each quotation balances.

ASSESS

Review students' quickwrites for the Check Your Understanding task, making sure they understand their chosen rhetorical appeals and how to effectively use them in their speeches.

Use students' responses to the writing prompt to assess their ability to effectively incorporate various syntactical structures into their speeches. Also, determine whether students are using vocal delivery, rhetorical technique, facial expressions, and gestures in effective ways.

ADAPT

If students need help choosing rhetorical appeals, have them review their annotations of Kennedy's speech before starting the quickwrite. Tell them to pick out their favorite rhetorical appeals. Then have them complete the quickwrite using their chosen appeals.

To help students effectively incorporate all the elements of a speech, have them video record their rehearsals of the speeches. Then have them review the recordings. Tell students to note areas that can be improved and incorporate these improvements into their speeches.

LC 2.24

Language Checkpoint: Writing Logical Comparisons

© 2021 College Board. All rights reserved.

PLAN

Suggested Pacing: 1 50-minute class period

TEACH

1 Introduce the topic of making comparisons by writing the following sentence on the board: *Homework in English class is more manageable than math.*

2 Ask students what is being compared in this sentence. Responses may include "Homework in English and math classes" or "English homework and math homework."

3 Circle the words *Homework in English class* and *math*. Elicit from students or explain that the two items being compared in the sentence are not actually similar. While the writer meant homework in math class, the sentence does not make that clear.

4 Read aloud the introduction to Understanding Logical Comparisons. Ask students to read the example sentences. Consider chunking this section in order to make the content clear to students.

5 Allow students a few minutes to discuss student step 1 with a partner. Ask volunteers to share their ideas.

6 In pairs, have students complete student steps 2 and 3. If necessary, ask students to circle the two items being compared.

SAT® CONNECTIONS

This activity provides practice with this important SAT skill: recognizing and correcting cases in which unlike terms are compared.

Learning Targets
- Recognize the structure of a logical comparison.
- Understand what makes a comparison illogical.
- Revise in order to maintain logical comparisons in writing.

Preview

In this activity, you will learn about the structure of logical comparisons and work to revise illogical comparisons.

Understanding Logical Comparisons

Writers frequently use comparisons to help their audience understand their ideas. Comparisons are usually made between two nouns. For example:

> Life on Mars is harder than life on Earth.

Two similar things are being compared—living on Mars and living on Earth. This comparison is logical, and a reader will clearly understand what the writer is trying to say.

Writers make a couple of different mistakes when making comparisons.

Error	Example	Why It Is an Error
Illogical comparison	Life on Mars is harder than Earth.	The things being compared are not actually similar. *Life on Mars* is being compared to *Earth*.
Comparing one specific thing to all things of that type	Earth is better than any planet capable of sustaining life.	The comparison doesn't acknowledge that Earth itself is a planet.

1. Discuss the following questions with a partner:
   - Why might a writer accidentally make an illogical comparison?
   - Why might a reader be able to understand the comparison even though it is illogical?

2. What is the illogical comparison in the following sentence?

   Franklin D. Roosevelt's speech is more revered than **Truman.**

   Roosevelt's speech is being compared to a person, Truman.

College and Career Readiness Standards

Focus Standards:

W.11-12.5 Develop and strengthen writing as needed by planning, revising, editing, rewriting, or trying a new approach, focusing on addressing what is most significant for a specific purpose and audience.

L.11-12.3 Apply knowledge of language to understand how language functions in different contexts, to make effective choices for meaning or style, and to comprehend more fully when reading or listening.

L.11-12.5 Demonstrate understanding of figurative language, word relationships, and nuances in word meanings.

3. Revise the sentence to make the comparison logical.

Franklin D. Roosevelt's speech is more revered than Truman's speech. / Franklin D. Roosevelt's speech is more revered than Truman's.

4. What is the illogical comparison in the following sentence?

Franklin D. Roosevelt is better than **any president**.

Roosevelt is not defined as having been a president himself.

5. Revise the sentence to make the comparison logical.

Franklin D. Roosevelt is better than any other president.

Fixing Illogical Comparisons

Recognizing and fixing illogical comparisons in writing is important to ensure that the meaning is clear to readers. There are a few ways that illogical comparisons can be revised and made logical.

Rewrite a sentence's noun phrases so that each is they are parallel.

Life on Mars is better than **life on Earth**.

Roosevelt's speech was better than **Truman's speech**.

When two phrases are parallel, they have a similar construction that makes clear how the phrases are alike and different. For example, in the preceding sentences, the phrases *life on Mars* and *life on Earth* are parallel, as are the phrases *Roosevelt's speech* and *Truman's speech*

Rewrite the noun phrases so that each uses a possessive noun, or a noun that shows ownership.

Mars's landscape is harsher than **Earth's**.

Roosevelt's speech is better appreciated than **Truman's**.

In the first sentence, both *Mars's* and *Earth's* are possessive, so the sentence implies that both Mars and Earth have landscapes. In the second sentence, both *Roosevelt's* and *Truman's* are possessive, so the sentence implies that both Roosevelt and Truman gave a speech.

---

7 Have students work individually to complete student steps 4 and 5. Circulate and offer support if they struggle with the identification and correction of the comparison errors.

8 Ask a student volunteer to read the section Fixing Illogical Comparisons aloud.

 TEACHER TO TEACHER

The Fixing Illogical Comparisons section contains technical grammar terms, some of which may be new to students. Consider writing some of these terms, such as *noun phrase*, *possessive*, and *determiner*, on the class Word Wall in order to reference them later for practice.

9 Read the instructions for student step 6. Allow students to work in pairs to complete the three. Circulate to spot-check student work. Consider having a student pair that sufficiently completes each of the three parts explain the process for the class, perhaps on the board.

LC 2.24

Add a determiner to the sentence.

Life on Mars is harder than <u>that</u> on **Earth**.

Roosevelt's speeches are more revered than <u>those</u> of **Truman**.

A determiner is a kind of pronoun that shows ownership. The determiner *that* agrees with a singular antecedent, and the determiner *those* agrees with a plural antecedent. In the first sentence, the antecedent of *that* is *life*, which is singular. In the second sentence, the antecedent of *those* is *speeches*, which is plural.

6. Work with a partner to make each of the following comparisons logical.

   a. The audiences in New York were larger than San Francisco.

   The audiences in New York were larger than the audiences in San Francisco. / The audiences in New York were larger than those in San Francisco.

   b. The president's approval ratings were lower than her opponent.

   The president's approval ratings were lower than her opponent's. / The president's approval ratings were lower than those of her opponent.

   c. The United States' swim relay team was faster than the Italians.

   The United States' swim relay team was faster than the Italians' team. /The United States' swim relay team was faster than that of the Italians.

Revising

Read the following paragraph. It includes some illogical comparisons. Mark each illogical comparison, and then rewrite it.

[1] Franklin D. Roosevelt was in office longer than any president. [2] He died while in office, however, and his vice president, Harry S. Truman, took his place. [3] Roosevelt delivered many speeches better known than Truman. [4] Truman's oratory was less vigorous than Roosevelt. [5] Despite these differences, both presidents could command great attention when they spoke. [6] Truman's legacy may never reach the stature of Roosevelt, but he was an important president.

[1] Franklin D. Roosevelt was in office longer than any other president. [3] Roosevelt delivered many speeches that are better known than Truman's. [4] Truman's oratory was less vigorous than Roosevelt's. [6] Truman's legacy may never reach the stature of Roosevelt's, but he was an important president.

☑ Check Your Understanding

What question(s) can you ask yourself whenever you write to be sure that your comparisons are logical? What techniques can you use to make your comparisons logical? Add the question(s) to your Editor's Checklist.

Practice

You have read speeches by Abraham Lincoln, Patrick Henry, John F. Kennedy, and Franklin D. Roosevelt. In a short explanatory text of two or three paragraphs, compare the rhetorical techniques of two of these speakers. After you complete a first draft, underline all the comparisons. Check to make sure the comparisons are logical and revise any that are not.

10 Direct students to the Revising section. Explain that they will read a paragraph that contains several illogical comparisons. They should first mark the text by underlining the errors they find. They should then revise only the sentences requiring correction. Consider having different student volunteers explain the errors and corrections.

11 Direct students to the Check Your Understanding task. Make sure that their Editor's Checklist questions show an awareness of how to check for illogical comparisons.

12 During the Practice section, students may work individually to complete their writing, which can be revisited later in the unit leading up to the Embedded Assessment. Remind them to mark the text appropriately according to the instructions provided.

ASSESS

Responses to the Fixing Illogical Comparisons, Revising, Check Your Understanding, and Practice sections should show that students can consistently make logical comparisons in their writing and recognize when they make comparison errors.

ADAPT

If students need additional practice with writing and revising comparisons, consider opportunities to continue practicing this skill with the John F. Kennedy speech in Activity 2.22. This speech contains rhetorical elements that students can compare to elements in speeches they read earlier in the unit.

PLAN

Materials: speech by Alfred M. Green (see Planning the Unit)

Suggested Pacing: 2 50-minute class periods

TEACH

1 Prior to class, make copies of the speech by Alfred M. Green from Planning the Unit.

2 Explain that this activity will allow students to preview the kind of writing they will do on the SAT: timed argument analysis. Remind students that they have seen many facets of effective arguments in speeches in Unit 2.

3 Distribute copies of the speech by Alfred M. Green. Tell students that they will spend the first class period, 50 minutes, reading the speech, analyzing the speech, and writing an essay.

4 Circulate as students read the prompt silently, read the essay, and respond to the prompt. Do not offer assistance; tell students to do their best and that they will spend the next class period revising their essays and addressing any difficulties they may have. Call time when 50 minutes are up and collect the essays.

SAT® CONNECTIONS

This activity provides practice with the type of writing students will perform on the SAT Essay test: explaining how an author builds an argument to persuade an audience. Responding to this prompt in a timed setting will help students practice using their time efficiently to read an argument, analyze it, and write an essay in response.

Explain How an Author Builds an Argument

Learning Targets

- Read an argument and analyze how the author builds it.
- Write a timed essay that includes an introduction and conclusion, includes relevant and accurate textual evidence, and adheres to standard English conventions.

Preview

In this activity, you will practice writing an analysis of an argument in a timed setting. You will be given a passage to read, analyze, and write about. This activity will take 50 minutes, so be sure to use your time wisely. Read the prompt carefully, annotate the text, and leave yourself time to quickly review what you have written at the end.

Prompt

As you read the passage, consider how Alfred M. Green uses:

- A thesis supported by evidence and examples.
- Evidence, such as facts, to support claims.
- Reasoning to develop ideas and to connect claims and evidence.
- Stylistic or persuasive elements, such as word choice or appeals to emotion, to add power to the ideas expressed.
- Organization of ideas in order to convey a purpose.

Write an essay in which you explain how Alfred M. Green builds an argument to persuade his audience that they, African Americans, should fight for the United States even though they do not yet have equal rights. In your essay, analyze how Green uses one or more of the listed features (or features of your own choice) to strengthen the logic and persuasiveness of his argument. Be sure that your analysis focuses on the most relevant features of the passage and includes details and examples from the text.

Your essay should not explain whether you agree with Green's claims but rather explain how the author builds an argument to persuade his audience.

_____

_____

_____

_____

_____

_____

_____

_____

_____

_____

_____

College and Career Readiness Standards

Focus Standards:

RI.11-12.6 Determine an author's point of view or purpose in a text in which the rhetoric is particularly effective, analyzing how style and content contribute to the power, persuasiveness or beauty of the text.

W.11-12.1 Write arguments to support claims in an analysis of substantive topics or texts, using valid reasoning and relevant and sufficient evidence.

5 On day 2 of the activity, have peer editors or writing groups read and critique each other's essays, referring to the official SAT Essay scoring guide, which can be found in the Teacher Resources section of SpringBoard Digital.

6 Have peer editors follow this process:

- Start with the Reading Scoring Guide.
- Check the essay against scores of 4, 3, 2, and 1 to see where it best fits.
- Assign the essay a score.
- Repeat with the Analysis Scoring Guide and the Writing Scoring Guide.

ASSESS

Have students use the scoring guides and their peers' scores as a basis for revising their essays. Ask them to hand in their drafts, scores, and revised essays. Grade essays based on the effectiveness of the revisions students made.

ADAPT

If possible, meet with students individually to discuss what they learned from the peer editing and how they feel their revisions improved their work. If students had great difficulty with the timed aspect of the writing, offer additional opportunities for timed essay writing over the next few months.

ACTIVITY 2.26

PLAN

Materials: Suggested Texts: George W. Bush's 9/11 Address to the Nation and Barack Obama's President-Elect Victory Speech, Internet access
Suggested Pacing: 1 50-minute class period plus homework

TEACH

1 Read aloud the Learning Targets and Preview with students. Ask volunteers to recall and define the meaning of and difference between diction and syntax.

2 Read aloud the Elements of Speech. **Activate prior knowledge** by having students review and define the list of physical and rhetorical elements. Clarify any confusion and answer any questions students may have.

3 Form **discussion groups** of four students each. Play video of George W. Bush's 9/11 Address to the Nation. It is important to use video and not merely text or audio so that students can observe the physical elements as well as hear the rhetorical elements. You may access the speech at several online sites by searching for "9/11 address to nation."

4 Ask two students from each group to watch for physical elements and the other two students to listen for rhetorical elements. Students should share observations and complete the **graphic organizer** following the speech.

5 Have students switch roles for the second speech: Barack Obama's President-Elect Victory Speech.

▶ TEACHER TO TEACHER

Students can keep the same roles for both speeches, watching for only physical elements or listening only for rhetorical elements. To stress the persuasive power of physical and rhetorical elements, have students encounter one or both of the speeches in three different media: text only, audio only, and video/audio combined.

Learning Strategies

- Debate
- Discussion Groups
- Graphic Organizer
- Note-taking
- Rehearsing
- Revising

Learning Targets

- Analyze a speaker's use of diction and syntax.
- Evaluate clarity and coherence in a speaker's message.

Preview

In this activity, you will watch or listen to two speeches in order to evaluate their delivery and use of language and structure.

My Notes

Elements of Speech

1. Read the following list of physical and rhetorical elements used commonly in effective speeches. As you watch or listen to the speeches, use the chart to take notes on the components that you see or hear. As you watch or listen, consider how the speaker's delivery affects his message.

Physical	Rhetorical	
Volume	Anaphora	Logical appeals
Smooth delivery	Aphorism	Emotional appeals
Gestures	Analogy	Ethical appeals
Speaking Rate	Allusion	Syntax
Movement	Alliteration	Parallelism
Enunciation	Rhetorical questions	Chiasmus
Eye Contact	Diction	Other rhetorical devices

Speech 1:

Physical	Rhetorical

College and Career Readiness Standards

Focus Standards:

SL.11-12.3 Evaluate a speaker's point of view, reasoning, and use of evidence and rhetoric, assessing the stance, premises, links among ideas, word choice, points of emphasis, and tone used.

SL.11-12.6 Adapt speech to a variety of contexts and tasks, demonstrating a command of formal English when indicated or appropriate.

---

6 Conduct a class discussion that compares and contrasts student observations. Be sure students consider how the timing, or rhetorical context, of each speech affects the vocal delivery.

7 Have students get into small groups. Read aloud the instructions for student step 3, and allow groups time to **debate** and create their lists. Ask volunteers to share their insights and experiences during the group debate as well as their lists.

Speech 2:

Physical	Rhetorical

2. Discuss with your classmates the similarities and differences in the vocal delivery of these two speakers. How might their vocal delivery have been affected by the climate of the nation and contemporary issues during their respective terms?

3. In small groups, debate which speaker gave a more persuasive or convincing speech. Use the notes you took earlier in the activity to point to specific physical and rhetorical examples within the speeches to back up your position. After your debate, come up with a list of criteria you decide on as a group about what physical and rhetorical qualities make up a good speech.

Physical	Rhetorical

8 Guide students to revisit the speeches they have been drafting and revising. Refer them to the bullet points in student step 4 to use as a checklist as they go over their speeches and encourage them to annotate for each item to ensure it is there.

9 Allow students time to rehearse the delivery of their speeches and revise them as necessary. Ask them to use the Scoring Guide criteria as they work with partners to practice. Remind students how to give constructive, helpful feedback by role-playing with a volunteer or providing sentence frames on the board.

10 Following rehearsal, ask students to quickwrite a reflection on their performance status at this point for the Check Your Understanding task. Be sure students understand the importance of rehearsal, eye contact, and attire in presentation and that they understand their strengths and areas for improvement by consulting their peer feedback.

11 Have students complete the Independent Reading Checkpoint by answering the questions in a small group. To assess their independent reading, go over their "how-to" lists to ensure that they can name and understand a variety of rhetorical devices and delivery techniques as well as explain their effectiveness.

ASSESS

Review students' assessments of their own performances for the Check Your Understanding task. Compare the accuracy of their assessments with your own assessments.

Use students' "how-to" lists for the Independent Reading Checkpoint to assess what they have learned about physical and rhetorical elements that can be applied to a persuasive speech.

ADAPT

If students need help assessing their performances, have them evaluate video recordings of their performances.

2.26

4. Revisit the speech you have been drafting and revising. By now, you should have a speech with a clear argumentative structure, including the following:

- Rhetorical devices
- Rhetorical appeals
- Intentional, convincing syntax
- Notes about the tone and the way in which it will be delivered

5. Now it is time to practice presenting a clear, persuasive argument to your audience. Rehearse your speech while a peer critiques your speech and delivery based on the physical and rhetorical structures. Revise the speech or delivery style as necessary.

☑ Check Your Understanding

Reflection: How would you assess your performance? List your strengths and areas for improvement.

ⓘ Independent Reading Checkpoint

You have read and listened to a variety of speeches and analyzed how speakers employ rhetorical devices and delivery techniques to effectively persuade audiences. What have you learned about physical and rhetorical elements that you could apply to your own presentation of a persuasive speech? Prepare your answers in the form of a brief "how-to" list for persuasive speakers.

Writing and Presenting a Persuasive Speech

 ASSIGNMENT

Your assignment is to write and present an original, persuasive two- to three-minute speech that addresses a contemporary issue. It should include a clear claim, support, counterclaim, and conclusion/call to action. Incorporate rhetorical appeals and devices to strengthen your argument and to help you achieve your desired purpose.

Planning: Take time to make a plan for writing and rehearsing your speech	■ Out of the various positions that one might take on this issue, which one seems the most promising for a persuasive speech? ■ How have you made careful consideration of your purpose and audience in the planning of your speech? ■ How has your planning allowed you to incorporate the elements of effective physical and vocal delivery?
Drafting: Create a draft of your speech and ask for feedback	■ How can you anticipate and respond to questions or objections that audience members might have before they make them? ■ What outside evidence or quotations can you use to support or reinforce your ideas? ■ Who can you ask to read or listen to your speech to offer suggestions for improvement?
Revising and Rehearsing: Incorporate changes into your speech and practice delivering it	■ How can you use rehearsal of your speech as a way to determine what additional revision is needed? ■ How can you improve the variety of your syntax while crafting sentences that add to your impact on the audience? ■ How can you make sure that your performance includes an appropriate tone of voice and gestures to add to the persuasive effect?
Publishing for Performance: Make final changes and prepare your speech for delivery	■ How will you check your work for grammatical and technical accuracy? ■ Are the rhetorical devices that you have included both effective and apparent to your audience?

Reflection

After completing this Embedded Assessment, think about how you went about accomplishing this assignment, and respond to the following:

- How was writing something meant to be performed in front of an audience different from writing a traditional essay?
- What was the most challenging part about trying to anticipate the reactions of your audience?

College and Career Readiness Standards

Focus Standards:

SL.11-12.3 Evaluate a speaker's point of view, reasoning, and use of evidence and rhetoric, assessing the stance, premises, links among ideas, word choice, points of emphasis, and tone used.

SL.11-12.6 Adapt speech to a variety of contexts and tasks, demonstrating a command of formal English when indicated or appropriate.

EMBEDDED ASSESSMENT 2

Materials: student drafts from Activity 2.24; access to computers for word processing (optional)
Suggested Pacing: 2 50-minute class periods

➤ TEACHER TO TEACHER

Delivering speeches in the classroom is always a challenge. Feel free to adapt the requirements of the Embedded Assessment to meet your needs. You may want to allow students to deliver speeches via video or to smaller groups. The essential elements here are to have students create an effective speech employing rhetorical techniques and devices and then have the opportunity to deliver it.

1 Planning: Students should already have revised drafts completed, but make sure they have completed all the planning and prewriting steps, including having a clear idea of the purpose and audience of the speech.

2 Drafting: If students have used quotations in their speeches, make sure they know how to smoothly integrate them while making it clear in their words or delivery that quoted words and ideas are not their own.

3 Revising and Rehearsing: Make sure students provide constructive and honest—yet tactful—feedback to each other on their ideas and delivery.

4 Video recording rehearsals will give students an opportunity to critique their own performances and encourage editing and revision for effect.

5 Publishing for Performance: Have students review the text of their speeches, using print or online resources to check grammar, usage, and mechanics. This is also a good time to check pronunciation of difficult vocabulary and mark it on their speeches.

6 Reflection: Remind students to respond to the reflection questions and decide whether you want to review their responses.

EMBEDDED ASSESSMENT 2

7 Portfolio: Be sure students address the Reflection question as a separate part of the Embedded Assessment assignment so they can include it separately. At this point you may want to ask students to go to their portfolios and find previous unit reflection questions so that they might get a sense of their growth as academic thinkers and producers.

All notes for and drafts of the speech should be collected and presented together to show the process students completed in successfully accomplishing the task.

SCORING GUIDE

When you score this Embedded Assessment, you may wish to download and print copies of the Scoring Guide from SpringBoard Digital so you can have a copy to mark for each student's work.

SCORING GUIDE

Scoring Criteria	Exemplary	Proficient	Emerging	Incomplete
Ideas	The speech • presents a significant and compelling thesis on a contemporary issue • is clearly developed and supported • presents a convincing argument and adeptly uses a variety of rhetorical appeals.	The speech • presents a clear thesis on a contemporary issue • is sufficiently developed and supported • presents a plausible argument and effectively uses rhetorical appeals.	The speech • presents a thesis • is somewhat developed and weakly supported • attempts to make an argument, but it is not plausible and uses rhetorical appeals ineffectively.	The speech • presents a position that is difficult to distinguish • is insufficiently developed and supported • does not make an argument that is plausible and lacks rhetorical appeals.
Structure	The speech • sequences ideas to aptly reinforce the argument • presents an introduction that intrigues the audience while establishing the topic • concludes with a clear and convincing call to action.	The speech • sequences material to support the argument • presents an introduction that establishes the topic • concludes in a way that provides a finished feeling to the speech, possibly suggesting further action.	The speech • attempts to sequence material with a weak connection to the argument • presents an introduction that weakly established the topic • concludes abruptly or with a proposed action that is inappropriate.	The speech • organizes ideas in a manner that is difficult to follow or jumps too rapidly between ideas • does little to introduce the topic, possibly only stating the subject of the speech • lacks a conclusion or fails to propose action.
Use of Language	The speech • deliberately and effectively uses rhetorical devices for the intended purpose • uses varied syntax in a way that adds to the persuasive impact • demonstrates well placed inflection and gestures that create an engaging delivery style indicative of advance preparation.	The speech • clearly attempts to use rhetorical devices for the intended purpose • varies syntax over the course of the speech • demonstrates some use of inflection and gestures that create an appropriate delivery style indicative of advance preparation.	The speech • attempts to use rhetorical devices, but the result is ineffective for the intended purpose • attempts to vary syntax over the course of the speech with limited success • demonstrates limited use of inflection and gestures, impairing the delivery style.	The speech • does not use rhetorical devices • uses syntax that is largely repetitive and lacks variation • demonstrates minimal use of inflection and gestures.

College and Career Readiness Standards

SL.11-12.1 Initiate and participate effectively in a range of collaborative discussions (one-on-one, in groups, and teacher-led) with diverse partners on grades 11–12 topics, texts, and issues, building on others' ideas and expressing their own clearly and persuasively.

W.11-12.4 Produce clear and coherent writing in which the development, organization, and style are appropriate to task, purpose, and audience.

W.11-12.5 Develop and strengthen writing as needed by planning, revising, editing, rewriting, or trying a new approach, focusing on addressing what is most significant for a specific purpose and audience.

Planning the Unit

Context

Central to any democracy is the way writers use language to influence public opinion. This unit will guide students to discern between arguments that use careful reasoning based on sound evidence and those that rely instead on manipulation, biased language, and fallacious reasoning. In this unit, students will examine both editorial writing and satire as key genres through which writers make statements about issues of the day. Through careful study of how writers use language and evidence, the unit explores the distinction between persuasion and manipulation, and challenges students to construct their own, well-crafted texts.

Suggested Texts and Materials

You will need the following materials for this unit:

- Activities 3.4, 3.6: Class set of two different newspapers (so that students can compare and contrast the papers' coverage of stories as well as their op-ed pages)
- Activity 3.7: Video of 1964 political ad "Peace, Little Girl"
- Activities 3.10, 3.11: Editorial of your choice or students' choice for analysis
- Activity 3.11: Sample letters to the editor
- Activity 3.12: Manipulative cards for matching fallacy terms (see the Resources section)
- Activity 3.13: Sample editorial cartoons and newspaper cartoons to model the characteristic features of editorial cartoons
- Activity 3.16: Various satirical cartoons that show a representative range in tones including playful and silly to biting and dark
- Activity 3.18: Recording or online segment from a television newscast to set up an analysis of a news parody

Instructional Sequence

The unit opens by introducing the thematic issue of the relationship between news media and the free exchange of ideas in a democracy. Students will then explore the distinction between objective and biased reporting before studying editorial texts. Students will analyze how evidence, reasoning, and language all significantly contribute to the presentation of an opinion and whether this presentation is considered effective—and/or ethical—or not. They will apply their understanding in Embedded Assessment 1, where they are asked to collaborate to create an op-ed news project.

In the second half of the unit, students will analyze a variety of satirical pieces, including cartoons, satirical articles, and essays. They will emulate the techniques they identify within these texts and develop an original piece in Embedded Assessment 2, which asks them to create a satirical piece that criticizes an aspect of our society.

AP® CONNECTIONS

In this unit, students will focus on refining these important skills and knowledge areas for AP/College Readiness:

- Addressing and appealing to audiences in a variety of persuasive genres (Activities 3.9, 3.11, 3.13)
- Analyzing how writers effectively use rhetoric, including controlling tone, establishing and maintaining voice, and achieving appropriate emphasis through diction and sentence structure (Activities 3.2, 3.7, 3.8, 3.15, 3.17, 3.18)
- Applying effective rhetorical strategies and techniques in their own writing (Activities 3.9, 3.11, 3.12)
- Focusing deliberate attention on the craft of sentence-level writing (Activities 3.2, 3.5, 3.6)

SAT® CONNECTIONS

In this unit, students will practice many important skills that will help them succeed on the SAT and other college readiness exams, including:

- Explaining how an author builds an argument to persuade an audience (Activity 3.2)
- Recognizing and correcting instances in which a word or phrase is confused with another (LC 3.5)

Unpacked Embedded Assessments

Embedded Assessment 1: Creating an Op-Ed News Project	Embedded Assessment 2: Writing a Satirical Piece
Skills and Knowledge: • Identify and create elements of an op-ed news project. • Research and gather evidence to support focused positions. • Include elements of argumentative writing and rhetorical appeals to persuade an audience. • Use language, visual symbols, and evidence for rhetorical effect. • Evaluate the effectiveness of an author's language and reasoning.	**Skills and Knowledge:** • Use satire and the conventions of satire to express an opinion. • Use diction, syntax, and imagery to develop and manipulate tone for rhetorical effect. • Apply satirical techniques in writing and evaluate their effectiveness. • Differentiate between Horatian and Juvenalian satire. • Tailor a satirical text to a particular audience and context.

Cognate Directory

Encouraging students to notice the connections between their primary language and English can help them develop academic vocabulary more quickly. If your class includes Spanish speakers, consider adding the following cognates to the classroom Word Wall. For English Language Learners whose primary language is not Spanish, consider using an online translator or dictionary to support comprehension of vocabulary terms.

Unit 3 Vocabulary Terms with Spanish Cognates

Academic Terms		Literary Terms	
English	**Spanish**	**English**	**Spanish**
concession	concesión	Horatian satire	sátira de Horacio
credibility	credibilidad	Juvenalian satire	sátira de Juvenal
editorial	editorial	satire	sátira
evidence	evidencia		
reasoning	razonamiento		
refutation	refutación		
secondary audience	audiencia secundaria		

Activity Features at a Glance

The activities in every ELA unit reflect the interconnected nature of reading, writing, listening, speaking, and thinking. The Activity Features at a Glance chart highlights the types of tasks or supports that students and teachers will encounter in each activity.

Writing and Revision | Grammar and Language | Listening, Speaking, and Discussion | Independent Reading | Vocabulary Development | ELL Support | Knowledge Quest | Gaining Perspectives

ELA Activity	Activity Features	ELA Activity	Activity Features
3.1		3.11	
3.2		3.12	
3.3		3.13	
3.4		3.14	
3.5		3.15	
LC 3.5		3.16	
3.6		3.17	
3.7		3.18	
3.8		3.19	
3.9		3.20	
3.10		3.21	

Unit Resources at a Glance

Formative Assessment Opportunities	Digital Assessments	Family Connections
Text-dependent questions Writing prompts Check Your Understanding tasks Focus on the Sentence tasks Language Checkpoint exercises Language & Writer's Craft practice	Activity Quizzes 3.2–3.21 Unit Assessment Part 1 Unit Assessment Part 2 SBD	Suggestions for Independent Reading Family Letters (English and Spanish) Student Reports SBD
English Language Development	**Foundational Skills**	**Independent Reading**
Leveled Differentiated Instruction Graphic Organizers ELD Strategies Language Workshop 3A Language Workshop 3B	Foundational Skills Screening Assessment Observational Look-fors Foundational Skills Workshop	My Independent Reading List Independent Reading Links Independent Reading Checkpoints Independent Reading Log Reader/Writer Notebook Suggestions for Independent Reading

Suggested Media

Publication	Format
BBC News	Television/Website
BBC World Service	Radio/Website
The Christian Science Monitor	Magazine/Website
The Dallas Morning News	Newspaper/Website
Forbes	Magazine/Website
Los Angeles Times	Newspaper/Website
The New York Times	Newspaper/Website
Newsweek	Magazine/Website
Slate	Online Magazine
USA Today	Newspaper/Website
The Wall Street Journal	Newspaper/Website
The Washington Post	Newspaper/Website

ⓣ Suggestions for Independent Reading

This list, divided into the categories of **Literature** and **Nonfiction/Informational Text,** comprises titles related to the themes and content of the unit. For their independent reading, students can select from this wide array of titles, which have been chosen based on complexity and interest. Spanish-language titles are included for those students who can read with greater independence or at a higher grade level in Spanish than in English, since building on their first language literacy can bolster their acquisition of English. Titles on this list have been suggested by teachers and school librarians, but you should be sure to preview texts to assess their appropriateness for your specific students and setting. You can also encourage students to do their own research and select titles that intrigue them.

Unit 3: American Forums: The Marketplace of Ideas

Literature		
Author	Title	Lexile
Anderson, Sherwood	*Winesburg, Ohio*	1050L
Caldwell, Ian	*The Rule of Four*	N/A
Capote, Truman	*In Cold Blood*	1040L
Cather, Willa	*O Pioneers!*	930L
Freeman, Kathie	*Pasos de la gata*	N/A
Heller, Joseph	*Catch-22*	1140L
Miller, Jennifer	*The Year of the Gadfly*	N/A
Pratchett, Terry	*Going Postal*	760L
Sierra i Fabra, Jordi	*El extraordinario ingenio parlante del profesor Palermo*	NA
Stockett, Kathryn	*The Help*	930L
Vonnegut, Kurt	*Breakfast of Champions*	930L
Waugh, Evelyn	*Scoop*	830L
Yep, Lawrence	*Dragonwings*	870L

Nonfiction/Informational Text		
Author	**Title**	**Lexile**
Amar, Akhil Reed	*American's Constitution: A Biography*	1490L
Anderson, Bonnie	*News Flash*	N/A
Craig, Terrance and Mary E. Ludloff	*Privacy and Big Data: The Players, Regulators, and Stakeholders*	N/A
Dakers, Diane	*Information Literacy and Fake News*	1020L
Dentith, Simon	*Parody*	1460L
Donovan, Sandy	*Media: From News Coverage to Political Advertising*	1150L
Edge, Marc	*Greatly Exaggerated: The Myth of the Death of Newspapers*	N/A
Herman, Edwards S. and Noam Chomsky	*Manufacturing Consent: The Political Economy of the Mass Media*	N/A
Kaplan, Fred	*The Singular Mark Twain: A Biography*	N/A
National Children's Book & Literacy Alliance	*Our White House: Looking In, Looking Out*	1110L
Parks, Gordon	*Choice of Weapons*	N/A
Riis, Jacob	*How the Other Half Lives*	N/A
Rudel, Anthony	*Hello Everybody!: The Dawn of American Radio*	N/A
Schlosser, Eric	*Fast Food Nation: The Dark Side of the All-American Meal*	1240L
Sedaris, David	*Me Talk Pretty One Day*	N/A
Sheppard, Alice	*Cartooning for Suffrage*	1430L
Vaidhyanathan, Siva	*Antisocial Media: How Facebook Disconnects Us and Undermines Democracy*	N/A
Various	*Perder es poder (Losing is Power)*	N/A

Unit 3 Instructional Pathways

Instructional Pathways

Teachers can build customized pathways through this unit by making purposeful choices about which resources to use based on students' learning needs. The charts below outline a few possible pathways to show how teachers might integrate digital assessments, Language Workshops, Close Reading Workshops, and Writing Workshops into instruction. Additional planning resources—including detailed standards correlations—are available on SpringBoard Digital.

English Language Arts Unit 3: American Forums: The Marketplace of Ideas		
Activity	**SBD Digital Assessments**	**Pacing**
Activity 3.1: Previewing the Unit	N/A	1
Activity 3.2: Rights and Responsibilities	Activity Quiz 3.2	3
Activity 3.3: The Supreme Court and Free Speech	Activity Quiz 3.3	1
Activity 3.4: Introducing the Media	Activity Quiz 3.4	1
Activity 3.5: The Newspaper Debate	Activity Quiz 3.5	2
LC 3.5: Language Checkpoint: Recognizing Frequently Confused Words (optional)	Activity Quiz LC 3.5	1
Activity 3.6: News or Views: A Closer Look	Activity Quiz 3.6	2
Activity 3.7: The Bias of Rhetoric	Activity Quiz 3.7	2
Activity 3.8: Putting It All Together	Activity Quiz 3.8	2
Activity 3.9: How to Write an Editorial	Activity Quiz 3.9	2
Activity 3.10: Where's Your Proof?	Activity Quiz 3.10	1
Activity 3.11: Reading and Writing a Letter to the Editor	Activity Quiz 3.11	1
Activity 3.12: Fallacies 101	Activity Quiz 3.12	1
Activity 3.13: How to Read and Write an Editorial Cartoon	Activity Quiz 3.13	1
Embedded Assessment 1: Creating an Op-Ed News Project	**Unit Assessment Part 1**	2 / 1

Activity	**SBD** Digital Assessments	Pacing	
Activity 3.14: Previewing Embedded Assessment 2 and Introducing Satire	Activity Quiz 3.14	1	
Activity 3.15: Identifying the Elements of Satire	Activity Quiz 3.15	1	
Activity 3.16: Analyzing Satirical Cartoons	Activity Quiz 3.16	1	
Activity 3.17: The Tone of Satire	Activity Quiz 3.17	1	
Activity 3.18: Writing a Parody	Activity Quiz 3.18	1	
Activity 3.19: Need Some Advice?	Activity Quiz 3.19	1	
Activity 3.20: Twain in Twain	Activity Quiz 3.20	1	
Activity 3.21: The Satirical Critique	Activity Quiz 3.21	2	
Embedded Assessment 2: Writing a Satirical Piece	**Unit Assessment Part 2**	2	1
	Total 50-minute Class Periods:	33–36	

Language Development Pathway

Consider using some or all of the Language Workshop and Foundational Skills Workshop activities with English Language Learners or with any student who would benefit from extra support with academic English. More detailed guidance about the timing and purpose of each Language Workshop and Foundational Skills Workshop activity can be found in the Language Workshop teacher edition.

Language Workshop 3A and 3B

Activity or Workshop		Pacing
Activity 3.1: Previewing the Unit		1
Language Workshop 3A.3: Academic Vocabulary		1
Activity 3.2: Rights and Responsibilities		3
Activity 3.3: The Supreme Court and Free Speech		1
Activity 3.4: Introducing the Media		1
Activity 3.5: The Newspaper Debate		2
LC 3.5: Language Checkpoint: Recognizing Frequently Confused Words (optional)		1
Activity 3.6: News or Views: A Closer Look		2
Activity 3.7: The Bias of Rhetoric		2
Activity 3.8: Putting It All Together		2
Activity 3.9: How to Write an Editorial		2
Activity 3.10: Where's Your Proof?		1
Language Workshop 3A.1: Genre Focus		1
Language Workshop 3A.2: Building Knowledge		1
Language Workshop 3A.4: Vocabulary Preview and Practice		1
Activity 3.11: Reading and Writing a Letter to the Editor	**OR** **Language Workshop 3A.5:** Close Reading of an Anchor Text*	2 / 1
	Language Workshop 3A.6: Academic Collaboration*	1
Language Workshop 3A.7: Language Checkpoint		1
Activity 3.12: Fallacies 101		1
Activity 3.13: How to Read and Write an Editorial Cartoon		1
Embedded Assessment 1: Creating an Op-Ed News Project	**OR** **Collaborative Embedded Assessment:** Creating an Op-Ed News Project	2 / 4

Activity or Workshop		Pacing	
Language Workshop 3B.1: Genre Focus		1	
Language Workshop 3B.3: Academic Vocabulary		1	
Activity 3.14: Previewing Embedded Assessment 2 and Introducing Satire		1	
Activity 3.15: Identifying the Elements of Satire		1	
Activity 3.16: Analyzing Satirical Cartoons		1	
Language Workshop 3B.2: Building Knowledge		1	
Language Workshop 3B.4: Vocabulary Preview and Practice		1	
Activity 3.17: The Tone of Satire	OR	**Language Workshop 3B.5:** Close Reading of an Anchor Text*	1
		Language Workshop 3B.6: Academic Collaboration*	1
Language Workshop 3B.7: Language Checkpoint		1	
Activity 3.18: Writing a Parody		1	
Activity 3.19: Need Some Advice?		1	
Activity 3.20: Twain in Twain		1	
Activity 3.21: The Satirical Critique		2	
Embedded Assessment 2: Writing a Satirical Piece	OR	**Collaborative Embedded Assessment:** Writing a Satirical Piece	2 | 4
		Total 50-minute Class Periods:	33–50

* These activities are available in Spanish.

Foundational Skills Workshop

The Foundational Skills Workshop offers instructional and practice materials for providing small-group instruction to students who are still developing foundational reading skills.

Activity	Pacing
Activity 1: Practicing Letter-Sound Relationships	15 min.
Activity 2: Recognizing Words by Sight	10 min.
Activity 3: Words with Inconsistent but Common Spellings	
Activity 4: Irregularly Spelled Words	
Activity 5: Common Prefixes	
Activity 6: Common Suffixes	35–40 min. per activity
Activity 7: Using Roots and Affixes to Read Multisyllabic Words	
Activity 8: Reading Multisyllabic Words	
Activity 9: Reading Informational Text with Purpose and Understanding	
Activity 10: Reading Poetry with Fluency	

Flexible Pathways

Teachers may build a flexible pathway that focuses on developing students' close reading and writing skills with the Close Reading and Writing Workshops. Each workshop addresses a specific set of standards and includes multiple assessment opportunities to allow students to demonstrate the knowledge and skills that are the focus of that workshop.

Close Reading Workshops

Workshop	Genre Focus	Assessment Opportunities	Pacing
Close Reading Workshop 2: Argumentative Nonfiction Text	Legal Documents Cartoons	Writing Prompt Debate/Discussion Multimedia Presentation	8
Close Reading Workshop 6: Informational Texts in STEM	Informational Texts Graphs	Writing Prompt Debate/Discussion Multimedia Presentation	8

Writing Workshops

Workshop	Genre Focus	Assessment Opportunities	Pacing
Writing Workshop 10: Procedural Texts: Cover Letters	Letters	Writing as a Class Writing with a Peer Independent Writing	6

UNIT 3

VISUAL PROMPT
TV news, news magazines, newspapers, radio, and the Internet give us sometimes vital, and sometimes trivial, facts and opinions, creating a swirling array of often-conflicting information. How do you obtain news and other information?

AMERICAN FORUMS: THE MARKETPLACE OF IDEAS

A self-governing society, by definition, needs to make its own decisions. It cannot do that without hard information, leavened with an open exchange of views.

—George A. Krimsky from "The Role of Media in a Democracy"

Leveled Differentiated Instruction Directory

For guidance on differentiating tasks for English language learners at various levels of language proficiency, refer to the Leveled Differentiated Instruction suggestions in these activities:

3.2 Support students in determining the meanings of unknown words with the **Unknown Word Solver** and **Roots and Affixes Brainstorm** graphic organizers.

3.7 Help student understand the activity's references and terms.

3.8 Support students in explaining the difference between an editorial and a news article with the **Conversation for Quickwrite** graphic organizer.

3.9 Help students generate ideas for writing an editorial using **Opinion Builder** and **Conclusion Builder** graphic organizers.

UNIT 3

Read aloud the unit title, "American Forums: The Marketplace of Ideas," and the quotation. Address any questions students may have. Then have students begin to think about where they get their news and information from. Ask them to scan their news feeds on social media to find out what types of news sources they are exposed to there. What does it mean to be an informed citizen? How do the information sources they choose filter information or guide future choices? As they get closer to voting age, how will they choose information sources to help them make decisions? Then have students look at the photograph and respond to the visual prompt. You may want to have students think-pair-share to write a short response or discuss their responses as a class.

UNIT 3

CONTENTS

Have students **skim/scan** the activities and texts in this unit. Ask them to note any texts they have heard about but never read and any activities that sound particularly interesting.

GOALS

Have students read the goals for the unit and mark any words that are unfamiliar to them. Ask them to add these words to the classroom Word Wall along with definitions.

You may also want to post these goals in a visible place in the classroom for the duration of this unit, allowing you and your students to revisit the goals easily and gauge progress toward achieving goals throughout the unit.

VOCABULARY DEVELOPMENT

Adding to vocabulary knowledge is essential for reading fluency. Students will encounter new vocabulary in this course in multiple ways:

- Academic Vocabulary
- Literary Terms
- Vocabulary in Context (terms glossed in text selections)
- Word Connections
- Oral Discussions

Encourage students to use new vocabulary expressively in class discussions and in their writing. Have them keep a **Reader/Writer Notebook** in which they record new words, their meanings, and their pronunciations.

See the Resources section for examples of graphic organizers suitable for word study. Having students use word-study graphic organizers will greatly enhance their understanding of new words and their connection to unit concepts and to the broader use of advanced and discipline-based terms.

Have students review the list of academic and literary terms and sort them in a **QHT** chart. Revisit the chart periodically to see how students' understanding progresses throughout the unit.

UNIT 3

American Forums: The Marketplace of Ideas

GOALS

- To analyze how writers use evidence, concessions and rebuttals, and rhetorical appeals to advance opinions
- To analyze the effects of rhetorical devices and logical fallacies on a writer's argument
- To compose argumentative and informational texts about a timely and debatable issue using genre characteristics and craft
- To evaluate how writer's use literary devices such as satire and parody to critique aspects of society
- To compose satirical pieces employing techniques of the genre appropriate to purpose, audience, topic, and context

VOCABULARY

ACADEMIC
accuracy
bias
credibility
editorial
evidence
reasoning

LITERARY
concession
Horatian satire
Juvenalian satire
refutation
satire
secondary audience
slanters
target audience

Leveled Differentiated Instruction Directory (continued)

3.11 Support students in dissecting arguments using the **Idea and Argument Evaluator** graphic organizer.

3.15 Guide Spanish-speaking students in using the Spanish/English glossary to look up unfamiliar vocabulary terms and support students in examining how authors use diction to create humor using the **Word Choice Analyzer** graphic organizer.

3.19 Help students understand and write cumulative sentences using the **Idea Connector** graphic organizer.

3.21 Support students in prewriting, drafting, and editing a satirical narrative using the **Conflict Map** and **Peer Editing** graphic organizers.

CONTENTS

🎁 My Independent Reading List

UNIT 3

LANGUAGE DEVELOPMENT

Several recurring SpringBoard features help build students' knowledge of grammar and usage concepts. Language and Writer's Craft features guide students to examine a writer's use of a language concept in context before incorporating the concept into their own writing. Grammar & Usage features briefly highlight and explain an interesting grammar or usage concept that appears in a text, both to improve students' reading comprehension and to increase their understanding of the concept. Periodic Language Checkpoints offer in-depth practice with standard English conventions and usage and ask students to revise sample sentences as well as their own work.

INDEPENDENT READING

In this unit, students will keep track of a news source independently. The Planning the Unit section of the Teacher Edition and the Resources section of the Student Edition contain guidance, Reading Logs, and Reading Lists to help students make reading selections. Independent Reading Links prompt students to actively respond to their reading and record responses in their Reader/Writer Notebooks or Reading Logs. Independent Reading Checkpoints allow for quick check-ins of independent reading prior to each Embedded Assessment.

KNOWLEDGE QUEST

Within the unit, students will engage in two Knowledge Quests. They will read collections of texts about editorials and satire, building their understanding of the topics and related vocabulary. Each Knowledge Quest begins with a Knowledge Question and supporting questions that focus student learning. After students read the final text in a set, they will have the opportunity to return to the Knowledge Question and express their growing understanding of the topic by responding to a writing-to-sources prompt or engaging in an academic discussion.

UNIT 3

CONTENTS

📦 My Independent Reading List

*Texts not included in these materials.

Previewing the Unit

Learning Targets

- Examine the key ideas for the unit.
- Identify and analyze the skills and knowledge necessary for success in completing the Embedded Assessment.

Preview

In this activity, you will explore the big ideas and tasks of the unit and make plans for your independent reading.

Learning Strategies

Close Reading
Graphic Organizer
Marking the Text
Paraphrasing
Summarizing

About the Unit

If you have ever listened to talk radio, watched cable "news" shows, or browsed the Web and social media sites, you may have seen many different versions of the same information. Some news is presented with a biased point of view, and when it comes to the expression of editorial opinions, sources often rely heavily on language and evidence that attempt to persuade through manipulation. So when you come into contact with the news, you should ask what information you are receiving and not receiving, where that information came from, and whether the purveyor of the news might have an agenda. In this unit, you will learn more about how to identify bias and how language is sometimes used as a substitute for logic. Good writers use evidence and reasoning to support their claims; the failure to do so can result in fallacies.

Essential Questions

Based on your current knowledge, respond to the Essential Questions.

1. What is the role of media in our society, and how can we become responsible consumers and producers of information in a digital age?

2. How can writers use satire to bring about change in society?

Unpacking Embedded Assessment 1

Read the assignment for Embedded Assessment 1: Creating an Op-Ed News Project.

Working in groups, your assignment is to plan, develop, write, revise, and present an informational article on a timely and debatable issue of significance to your school community, local community, or national audience. After your group completes its article, you will individually develop a variety of editorial products that reflect your point of view (agreement, alternative, or opposing) on the topic. Be creative with your editorial products and include at least two different pieces, such as cartoons, editorials, letters, posters, photos, and so on.

With your class, read closely and mark the text for the knowledge and skills you must have to successfully complete this project.

My Notes

College and Career Readiness Standards

Focus Standards:

SL.11-12.1c Propel conversations by posing and responding to questions that probe reasoning and evidence; ensure a hearing for a full range of positions on a topic or issue; clarify, verify, or challenge ideas and conclusions; and promote divergent and creative perspectives.

SL.11-12.1d Respond thoughtfully to diverse perspectives; synthesize comments, claims, and evidence made on all sides of an issue; resolve contradictions when possible; and determine what additional information or research is required to deepen the investigation or complete the task.

ACTIVITY 3.1

PLAN

Materials: poster paper
Suggested Pacing: 1 50-minute class period

TEACH

1 Read the Learning Targets and Preview with students. Make sure they understand that they will be examining key ideas and strategies for completing the Embedded Assessment.

2 Read aloud the About the Unit section. You might pause a moment to ask students where they or their households get their news. Ask whether they themselves have a favorite source of news and why it is their favorite.

3 Pair students and ask them to discuss the two Essential Questions and prior knowledge about unit vocabulary terms.

TEACHER TO TEACHER

You might take some time to acquaint students with the idea of satire. Explain to them that *satire* is the use of ridicule and exaggeration to criticize individuals or society. Tell them that satirists often point out the need for change—political, societal, or both. You might cite the websites *The Borowitz Report* and *The Onion*, the television shows *Key and Peele* and *Last Week Tonight with John Oliver*, or the "Weekend Update" segment of *Saturday Night Live* as contemporary examples of satire. (Be sure to consider appropriateness before actually presenting examples from these or other sources to a class.) Ask students to cite their own examples of political satire.

4 Provide students with a clear learning target by asking them to close read the assignment for Embedded Assessment 1. Instruct them to mark the text by underlining or highlighting the places in the text that mention skills or knowledge necessary to succeed on the EA.

5 Have students summarize or **paraphrase** aloud the skills and knowledge they have underlined or highlighted. As you conduct a large-group discussion to unpack the assessment, create a web **graphic organizer** on a sheet of poster paper listing the knowledge and skills as they are mentioned.

6 Revisit the web throughout the unit, reinforcing the purpose of each activity and how each activity allows students to connect to the EA.

7 Make sure that students attend to the Planning Independent Reading section. Introduce them to the newspaper log assignment. Make sure they understand that they will be asked to refer to articles in local, national, or online daily newspapers as they complete the Independent Reading Links in this unit. Encourage them to keep their news articles in portfolios or Internet browser reading lists.

ASSESS

Monitor discussions to ensure that students can identify and understand the skills and knowledge needed for the Embedded Assessment.

ADAPT

Many students may be unfamiliar with the various sections of a newspaper. You may want to give students time to browse several different print and online news sources to see how each source divides and organizes its material and guide them toward their publication choice for Independent Reading.

3.1

My Notes

Planning Independent Reading

During this unit, you will read a local, national, or online newspaper every day. Create a log to keep track of what and when you read and write down the titles of significant articles that you encounter in each section. Don't just read the first page or landing page (if you are reading an online publication); navigate through all the sections. Each day, cut out, scan, copy, or photograph one article that you enjoyed reading. Choose a publication that interests you because you will be spending considerable time with it.

Rights and Responsibility

PLAN

Materials: dictionary (print or online)
Suggested Pacing: 3 50-minute class periods

Learning Targets

- Use print or digital resources to clarify or validate the meaning of words and phrases as they are used in a text.
- Evaluate the opinion of a writer using textual details as support.
- Participate collaboratively in a Socratic Seminar.

Preview

In this activity, you will read the article "The Role of the Media in a Democracy" by George A. Krimsky, examine Krimsky's arguments, and participate in a Socratic Seminar to discuss his ideas about the role of a free press in a democracy.

Learning Strategies

Diffusing
Marking the Text
Metacognitive Markers
Questioning the Text
Rereading

My Notes

TEACH

1 Read the Learning Targets and Preview with students. Make certain they understand that they will be using reference resources to clarify and validate the meanings of words and phrases and analyzing and discussing a historical document and, as a group, an opinion piece.

2 Read aloud the text of the Rights and the American Dream section as a way to review the concept of free speech.

3 Invite a volunteer to read aloud the text of the First Amendment to the United States Constitution. Have students use metacognitive markers to organize their thoughts about the text.

Rights and the American Dream

While the American Dream is central to Americans' shared sense of identity, another defining belief of the American people is in the importance of free speech. As Supreme Court Justice Oliver Wendell Holmes famously observed in 1919, "The best test of truth is the power of the thought to get itself accepted in the competition of the market." Viewed in this way, the expression of contrasting and even conflicting ideas and opinions provides information that is crucial to our ability to make informed decisions about everything from personal beliefs to public policy. Indeed, the ways in which these ideas and voices interact with each other help us to shape, test, and revise our own perspectives on the issues that dominate our lives. This unit, with its focus on the media, begins with an in-depth examination of the constitutional amendment guaranteeing U.S. citizens their freedom of speech.

1. In Unit 1, you read the First Amendment to the United States Constitution as part of your study of the Bill of Rights. Refresh your memory of the First Amendment by rereading the text.

Historical Document

First Amendment to the United States Constitution

Congress shall make no law respecting an establishment of religion, or prohibiting the free exercise thereof; or abridging the freedom of speech, or of the press; or the right of the people peaceably to assemble, and to petition the Government for a redress of grievances.

TEACHER TO TEACHER

You might want to tell students that the idea of a government protecting the civil liberties of citizens arose from the Enlightenment, an 18th-century philosophical movement to which most of our nation's Founders adhered. Other Enlightenment ideas included the belief that all individuals are equal, that governments should be divided into branches, and that leaders should govern in accordance with the will of the people.

College and Career Readiness Standards

Focus Standards:

RI.11-12.1 Cite strong and thorough textual evidence to support analysis of what the text says explicitly as well as inferences drawn from the text, including determining where the text leaves matters uncertain.

RI.11-12.4 Determine the meaning of words and phrases as they are used in a text, including figurative, connotative, and technical meanings; analyze how an author uses and refines the meaning of a key term or terms over the course of a text (e.g., how Madison defines faction in Federalist No. 10).

4 Introduce students to the Vocabulary Study activity. Read student step 2 and clarify as needed what is expected of them. Consider having students complete the chart in pairs or small groups. Remind them that they should try to figure out the meaning of each word or term before consulting a print or online dictionary to clarify and validate understanding.

LEVELED DIFFERENTIATED INSTRUCTION

In this activity, students might need support determining the meaning of unknown words.

Beginning Distribute the **Unknown Word Solver** graphic organizer. Model using the organizer with the word *peaceably: The root is* peace, *which is the opposite of violence, and the suffix* -ably *means "done in a certain way." The word* peaceably *must mean "to do something without violence."* Work through the rest of the terms as a group.

Developing Have small groups work through the list using the **Unknown Word Solver** graphic organizer.

Expanding Distribute the **Roots and Affixes Brainstorm** graphic organizer and allow students to collaborate to dissect the terms.

Bridging Give students copies of the **Roots and Affixes Brainstorm** graphic organizer and encourage them to use this handout while reading Krimsky's text and subsequent texts.

5 Have students complete student step 3. They should paraphrase the amendment using the definitions of the words from the vocabulary list.

6 Make sure they understand the four basic freedoms included in the First Amendment (freedom of religion, freedom of speech, freedom of the press, and freedom of assembly) as they work through student step 4. Discuss their responses as a class and point out that this unit will focus on freedom of speech.

3.2

Vocabulary Study

2. Each of the following terms is taken verbatim from the First Amendment. Read through the list and then underline each word or term where it appears in the text of the First Amendment. Next, define each term. Note that advanced vocabulary often has multiple meanings. Use the context to determine which meaning of the term is correct. Then use a print or digital resource to clarify or validate your understanding of the term and how it is used in the text.

respecting	having anything to do with
establishment	the creation of
prohibiting	preventing, making illegal
free exercise	to do something without fear of reprisal
thereof	having to do with what was previously mentioned
abridge	to curtail, cut short, or curb
the press	news agencies, including newspapers, television, etc.
peaceably	without violence
assemble	to get together in one place as a group
petition	to request or seek
redress	to fix, to make right
grievances	infringements upon one's rights or sensibilities

3. Now transform the text by rewriting the First Amendment, replacing the vocabulary words with their definitions. In some cases, your definition may fit exactly; in others, you may need to rework the phrasing.

   Congress shall make no law that has anything to do with creating or setting up a state-sponsored religion; nor any law that prevents citizens from practicing their faith without fear of reprisal; nor can Congress write laws that curtail, cut short, or in any way curb the freedom of speech or of news outlets to report; or the right of the people to get together for peaceful reasons or seek justice from the Government in the event that one suffers an injustice or other attack on one's rights.

4. The First Amendment includes four basic rights or freedoms. What are they? Which of these will be the focus of this unit?

College and Career Readiness Standards

RI.11-12.6 Determine an author's point of view or purpose in a text in which the rhetoric is particularly effective, analyzing how style and content contribute to the power, persuasiveness, or beauty of the text.

L.11-12.3 Apply knowledge of language to understand how language functions in different contexts, to make effective choices for meaning or style, and to comprehend more fully when reading or listening.

SL.11-12.1 Initiate and participate effectively in a range of collaborative discussions (oneon-one, in groups, and teacher-led) with diverse partners on grades 11–12 topics, texts, and issues, building on others' ideas and expressing their own clearly and persuasively.

Additional Standards Addressed:

RI.11-12.2, RI.11-12.10, W.11-12.2b, W.11-12.4, W.11-12.5

3.2

As You Read

- Use metacognitive markers to monitor your comprehension by noting anything that raises a question for you (?), anything you find surprising (!), and anything that connects to the First Amendment (*).
- Use print or digital resources to clarify your understanding of any unfamiliar terms, including words that have multiple meanings.

About the Author

George Krimsky (1942–2017) worked for 45 years as a journalist, author, lecturer, and media critic. His career began in 1969, when he joined the Associated Press. In 1984, he founded the International Center for Journalists (IFCJ), a group dedicated to supporting innovative and diverse voices in news coverage. He is co-author of the highly regarded *Hold the Press: The Inside Story on Newspapers*, first published in 1995. "The Role of the Media in a Democracy" was written in 1997 and placed on the U.S. Department of State's informational website in 2007.

Informational Text

The Role of the Media in a Democracy

by George A. Krimsky

Chunk 1

1 Volumes have been written about the role of the mass media in a democracy. The danger in all this examination is to submerge the subject under a sludge of platitudes. The issue of whether a free press is the best communications solution in a democracy is much too important at the close of this century and needs to be examined dispassionately.

2 Before addressing the subject, it helps to define the terminology. In the broadest sense, the media embraces the television and film entertainment industries, a vast array of regularly published printed material, and even public relations and advertising. The "press" is supposed to be a serious member of that family, focusing on real life instead of fantasy and serving the widest possible audience. A good generic term for the press in the electronic age is "news media." The emphasis in this definition is on content, not technology or delivery system, because the press—at least in developed

My Notes

platitudes: clichéd statements

ACTIVITY 3.2 continued

7 Have students read the As You Read and About the Author sections, reminding them to use metacognitive markers and clarify the meaning of unfamiliar words as they move through the text. Model determining the meanings of unfamiliar words through the use of context clues, word parts, or a print or online dictionary.

8 **FIRST READ:** Conduct a paired reading of "The Role of the Media in a Democracy." Pause after paragraph 2 to ensure that students understand how the author is defining the terms *media*, *press*, and *news media*. Point out that the last two terms are synonymous and the subject of the article.

⚠ TEXT COMPLEXITY

Overall: Complex
Lexile: 1200L
Qualitative: High Difficulty
Task: Moderate (Analyze)

9 As students are reading, monitor their progress. Be sure they are engaged with the text and annotating unknown words and phrases, raising questions, and making connections to the First Amendment. Evaluate whether the selected reading mode is effective.

Scaffolding the Text-Dependent Questions

5. The word *passion* has at least two meanings. Use print or digital resources, along with your knowledge of context and affixes, to determine the meaning of *dispassionately* in paragraph 1. What word that you know is part of this word? What are the suffixes, and how do they affect the meaning and function of the base word? How does the meaning change when the prefix *dis-* is added? RI.11-12.4

10 Tell students to pause at the end of paragraph 8. Guide them through the Grammar & Usage feature on rhetorical devices, explain the rhetorical question in paragraph 8, and tell students to watch for another rhetorical question as they resume reading.

3.2

My Notes

countries—can be found these days on the Internet, the fax lines, or the airwaves.

3 A self-governing society, by definition, needs to make its own decisions. It cannot do that without hard information, leavened with an open exchange of views. Abraham Lincoln articulated this concept most **succinctly** when he said: "Let the people know the facts, and the country will be safe."

4 Some might regard Lincoln's as a somewhat naive viewpoint, given the complexities and technologies of the 20th century; but the need for public news has been a cornerstone of America's system almost from the start.

5 Thomas Jefferson felt so strongly about the principle of free expression he said something that non-democrats must regard as an absurdity: "If it were left to me to decide whether we should have a government without newspapers or newspapers without a government, I should not hesitate a moment to prefer the latter." The implication of those words is that self-governance is more essential than governance itself. Not so absurd, perhaps, if you had just fought a war against an oppressive government.

Chunk 2

6 In the wake of America's successful revolution, it was decided there should indeed be government, but only if it were accountable to the people. The people, in turn, could only hold the government accountable if they knew what it was doing and could intercede as necessary, using their ballot, for example. This role of public "watchdog" was thus assumed by a citizen press, and as a consequence, the government in the United States has been kept out of the news business. The only government-owned or-controlled media in the United States are those that broadcast overseas, such as the Voice of America. By law, this service is not allowed to broadcast within the country. There is partial government **subsidy** to public television and radio in the United States, but safeguards protect it against political interference.

7 Because the Constitution is the highest law in the land, any attempts by courts, legislators and law enforcement officers to weaken protected liberties, such as free expression, are generally preventable.

8 Fairly simple in theory, but how has all this worked out?

9 Generally speaking, pretty well, although the concept of a free press is challenged and defended every day in one community or another across the land. The American press has always been influential, often powerful and sometimes feared, but it has seldom been loved. As a matter of fact, journalists today rank in the lower echelons of public popularity. They are seen as too powerful on the one hand, and not trustworthy on the other.

10 In its early days, the American press was little more than a pamphleteering industry, owned by or affiliated with competing political interests and engaged in a constant war of propaganda. Trust was not an issue. What caused the press to become an instrument for democratic decision-making was the variety of voices. Somehow, the common truth managed to

GRAMMAR & USAGE

Rhetorical Devices

A rhetorical question is a figure of speech in the form of a question that an author asks to emphasize a point rather than elicit an answer. Rhetorical questions often occur immediately after a comment and suggest the opposite of it—the idea is to make a point more prominent. Authors often use rhetorical questioning as a persuasive device to influence the kind of response they want from an audience.

Notice the question in paragraph 8. The reader is not expected to answer this question but rather to understand that the application of constitutional theory has not proven simple at all.

Find another rhetorical question that the author uses and discuss its effect with a partner.

succinctly: briefly and accurately

subsidy: financial support

Scaffolding the Text-Dependent Questions

6. What details in paragraphs 3–7 support the author's arguments in favor of the First Amendment's "free press" clause? Summarize the first two sentences in paragraph 3. What are the implications of Jefferson's words in paragraph 5? How is a free press a necessary element of holding the government accountable? How have challenges changed the right to a free press? RI.11-12.1

7. How do words and phrases such as "dispassionately" (paragraph 1), "it was decided" (paragraph 6), "accountable" (paragraph 6), and "generally speaking" (paragraph 9) set a tone that contributes to Krimsky's persuasiveness? How do these words and phrases make you feel? Do they help establish a more subjective or objective tone? RI.11-12.4

emerge from under that chaotic pile of information and misinformation. A quest for objectivity was the result.

My Notes

Chunk 3

11 Many critics have questioned whether there is such a thing as "objectivity." Indeed, no human being can be truly objective; we can only *seek* objectivity and **impartiality** in the pursuit of truth. Journalists can try to keep their personal views out of the news, and they employ a number of techniques to do so, such as obtaining and quoting multiple sources and opposing views.

12 The question is whether the truth always serves the public. At times, the truth can do harm. If the truthful report of a small communal conflict in, say, Africa, leads to more civil unrest, is the public really being served? The journalistic purists—often those sitting in comfortable chairs far from conflict—say it is not their job to "play God" in such matters, and that one should not "shoot the messenger for the message."

13 If, however, one takes the rigid view that the truth always needs to be controlled—or Lenin's dictum that truth is **partisan**—the door is wide open for enormous abuse, as history has demonstrated time and again. It is this realization (and fear) that prompted Jefferson to utter that absurdity about the supreme importance of an uncensored press.

14 What Jefferson and the constitutional framers could not have foreseen, however, was how modern market forces would expand and exploit the simple concept of free expression. While media with meager resources in most developing countries are still struggling to keep governments from **suppressing** news that Westerners take for granted, the mass media in America, Britain, Germany and elsewhere are preoccupied with their role as profitable businesses and the task of securing a spot on tomorrow's electronic superhighway. In such an environment, truth in the service of the public seems almost a quaint anachronism.

15 Is the capitalist drive an **inherent** obstacle to good journalism? In one sense, the marketplace can be the ally, rather than the enemy of a strong, free media. For the public to believe what it reads, listens to and sees in the mass media, the "product" must be credible. Otherwise, the public will not buy the product, and the company will lose money. So, profitability and public service can go hand in hand. What a media company does with its money is the key. If it uses a significant portion of its profits to improve its newsgathering and marketing capabilities and eliminate dependence upon others for its survival (e.g. state subsidies, newsprint purchases, or access to printing facilities), the product improves, and the public is served. If it uses its profits primarily to make its owners rich, it might as well be selling toothpaste.

16 The assumption in this argument is that the public overwhelmingly wants to believe its news media, and that it will use this credible information to actively and reasonably conduct its public affairs. Unfortunately, that assumption is not as valid as it was in simpler times. In affluent societies today,

> **impartiality:** lack of support for one side or the other
>
> **partisan:** supports one party over another
>
> **suppressing:** holding down or back
>
> **inherent:** built-in

© 2021 College Board. All rights reserved.

ACTIVITY 3.2 continued

11 Tell students to pause at the end of paragraph 12. Have them identify and discuss the effect of that paragraph's rhetorical question with their partner before continuing.

Scaffolding the Text-Dependent Questions

8. In paragraph 11, how does Krimsky describe journalists' attempts to be objective? How does he himself demonstrate this technique in paragraph 12? Reread paragraphs 11 and 12. How does Krimsky describe journalists' attempts to keep their personal views out of the news? Does the truth serve the small African community in Krimsky's example? Why would some journalists argue that they have the responsibility to report the news regardless of its effect? RI.11-12.6

My Notes

media consumers are seeking more and more entertainment, and the news media's **veracity** (even its **plausibility**) is less important than its capacity to attract an audience.

17 But, you say, look at the new technology that can penetrate any censorship system in the world. Look at the choices people have today. Look at how accessible information is today. Yes, the choices may be larger, but a case can be made they are not deeper—that big money is replacing quality products and services with those of only the most massive appeal. The banquet table may be larger, but if it only contains "junk food," is there really more choice? Declining literacy, for example, is a real problem in the so-called developed world. That's one reason why newspapers are so worried about their future.

Chunk 4

18 Where is the relevance of all this to the emerging democracies around the world? Certainly the American experience, for all its messiness, provides a useful **precedent**, if not always a model.

19 For example, when one talks about an independent media, it is necessary to include financial independence as a prerequisite, in addition to political independence. The American revenue-earning model of heavy reliance on advertising is highly suspect in many former communist countries, but one has to weigh the alternatives. Are government and party subsidies less imprisoning? If journalists are so fearful of contamination by advertiser pressure, they can build internal walls between news and business functions, similar to those American newspapers erected earlier in this century.

20 If they are fearful of political contamination of the information-gathering process, they can build another wall separating the newsroom from the editorial department—another important concept in modern American journalism.

21 The problem in many new democracies is that journalists who once had to toe the single-party line equate independence with opposition. Because they speak out against the government, they say they are independent. But haven't they just traded one **affiliation** for another? There is little room for unvarnished truth in a partisan press.

22 Is objectivity a luxury in societies that have only recently begun to enjoy the freedom to voice their opinions? Listen to a Lithuanian newspaper editor shortly after his country gained its independence: "I want my readers to know what their heads are for." His readers were used to being told not only what to think about, but what to think. Democracy requires the public to make choices and decisions. This editor wanted to prepare citizens for that responsibility with articles that inform but do not pass judgment. His circulation increased.

23 Though nearly 60 percent of the world's nations today are declared democracies—a monumental change from a mere decade ago—most of them have nevertheless instituted press laws that prohibit reporting on a

> **veracity:** truthfulness
> **plausibility:** believability
> **precedent:** prior example
> **affiliation:** close association

Scaffolding the Text-Dependent Questions

9. In Chunk 4, Krimsky specifies two types of independence that a democracy's media must maintain. Name those two types of independence and summarize his suggestions for maintaining them. Examine paragraphs 19 and 20. Why is independence essential to truth-telling? What two solutions does he suggest if journalists are "fearful of ... contamination"? RI.11-12.2

10. Examine the context of the questions "Are government and party subsidies less imprisoning?" (paragraph 19) and "But haven't they just traded one affiliation for another?" (paragraph 21). Why does the author use questions instead of statements to make his point? What is the effect? Reread the two paragraphs. What sort of question does the author use in them? RI.11-12.6

My Notes

whole array of subjects ranging from the internal activity and operations of government to the private lives of leaders. Some of these are well-intentioned efforts to "preserve public stability." But all of them, ALL of them, undermine self-governance.

24 The watchdog role of the free press can often appear as mean-spirited. How do the government and public protect themselves from its excesses? In the United States, it is done in a variety of ways. One, for example, is the use of "ombudsmen." In this case, news organizations employ an in-house critic to hear public complaints and either publish or broadcast their judgments. Another is the creation of citizens' councils which sit to hear public complaints about the press and then issue verdicts, which, although not carrying the force of law, are aired widely.

25 Last, and most effective, is **libel** law. In the United States, a citizen can win a substantial monetary award from a news organization if libel is proven in a court of law. It is much harder for a public official or celebrity than an ordinary citizen to win a libel case against the press, because the courts have ruled that notoriety comes with being in the limelight. In most cases, the complaining **notable** must prove "malice aforethought."

26 There is nothing in the American constitution that says the press must be responsible and accountable. Those requirements were reserved for government. In a free-market democracy, the people—that is the voters and the buying public—ultimately decide as to how their press should act. If at least a **semblance** of truth in the public-service does not remain a motivating force for the mass media of the future, neither free journalism nor true democracy has much hope, in my opinion.

27 The nature and use of new technology is not the essential problem. If true journalists are worried about their future in an age when everyone with a computer can call themselves journalists, then the profession has to demonstrate that it is special, that it offers something of real value and can prove it to the public. There is still a need today—perhaps more than ever—for identifying sense amidst the nonsense, for sifting the important from the trivial, and, yes, for telling the truth. Those goals still constitute the best **mandate** for a free press in a democracy.

28 George Washington's admonition, uttered at the Constitutional Convention, still stands: "Let us raise a standard to which the wise and honest can **repair**."

Making Observations
- Based on your use of metacognitive markers, what connections to the First Amendment do you notice?
- Who are some historical figures Krimsky mentions in his article?

libel: publishing a false statement that hurts someone's reputation
notable: well-known person
semblance: outward appearance
mandate: authorization
repair: go back

12 Tell students to pause at the end of paragraph 24 and state whether they believe the use of ombudsmen and citizens' councils is a good idea. Why or why not?

13 After reading the text for the first time, guide the class in a discussion by asking the Making Observations questions. Check students' general comprehension of the text based on their observations, asking follow-up questions if needed.

Scaffolding the Text-Dependent Questions

11. In paragraph 21, Krimsky suggests that journalists who oppose the government in new democracies **"equate independence with opposition." How does this support his argument for a non-partisan, objective news media?** Revisit the paragraph. Why do reporters think opposition and independence are synonymous? If a journalist wants to report the truth, is he or she able to do so by always opposing or supporting the government? Is either approach objective? Is it useful? RI.11-12.1

14 **RETURNING TO THE TEXT:** Guide students to return to the text to respond to the text-dependent questions. Invite them to work in small groups to reread the text and answer the questions. Remind them to use text evidence in their responses.

15 Move from group to group and listen in as students answer the text-dependent questions. If they have difficulty, scaffold the questions by rephrasing them or breaking them down into smaller parts. See the Scaffolding the Text-Dependent Questions boxes for suggestions.

3.2

Returning to the Text

- Reread the article as you respond to the following questions. Use text evidence to support your responses.
- Write any additional questions you have about the text in your Reader/Writer Notebook.

5. The word *passion* has at least two meanings. Use print or digital resources, along with your knowledge of context and affixes, to determine the meaning of *dispassionately* in paragraph 1.

In this context, the root noun *passion* means "strong feeling." The suffixes *-ate* and *-ly* both mean "having the quality of," and *-ly* converts the word to an adverb. So the word *passionately* means an action that "has the quality of strong feeling." The prefix *dis-* ("not") reverses the meaning of *passionately* to "not having the quality of strong feeling." In other words, it means "without emotion."

6. What details in paragraphs 3–7 support the author's arguments in favor of the First Amendment's "free press" clause?

Krimsky notes that a self-governing society needs "hard information" and "an open exchange of views" to make its own decisions. He quotes Jefferson's sentiment that "newspapers without a government" would be preferable to its opposite. He explains the "watchdog" role of a public press in keeping an eye on the government and holding it accountable.

7. How do words and phrases such as "dispassionately" (paragraph 1), "it was decided" (paragraph 6), "accountable" (paragraph 6), and "generally speaking" (paragraph 9) set a tone that contributes to Krimsky's persuasiveness?

The use of unemotional descriptions and qualifying phrases as well as the passive voice creates an objective and authoritative tone for the text. That tone supports the author's credibility, which makes his arguments about the importance of a free press persuasive.

8. In paragraph 11, how does Krimsky describe journalists' attempts to be objective? How does he himself demonstrate this technique in paragraph 12?

In paragraph 11, Krimsky says journalists "try to keep their personal views out of the news" by "obtaining and quoting multiple sources and opposing views." In paragraph 12, he provides a viewpoint that contradicts most of what has been said so far regarding the question of "whether the truth always serves the public" and does not at that point explicitly refute it.

Scaffolding the Text-Dependent Questions

12. How does the anecdote about the Lithuanian newspaper editor in paragraph 22 support Krimsky's central idea regarding press objectivity? How does it affect the way the text is read and understood? Examine the anecdote in paragraph 22. What does the Lithuanian editor want his readers to know? How does the editor accomplish this goal? How does Krimsky believe that the editor's newspaper benefits as a result? RI.11-12.1

13. Based upon the context of the article's last sentence, what is an *admonition*? Use a print or digital resource to clarify or validate your understanding of this multiple-meaning word. Reread paragraph 28 and look up *admonition*. Examine Washington's words. How does the definition of *admonition* apply to them? Does Washington's admonition apply to those who are framing a government for the newly formed United States of America? RI.11-12.4

9. In Chunk 4, Krimsky specifies two types of independence that a democracy's media must maintain. Name those two types of independence and summarize his suggestions for maintaining them.

Krimsky says the media must be financially and politically independent. To achieve financial independence, he suggests that journalists build "internal walls between news and business functions" that separate advertiser interests from news content. He also suggests that separation between "the newsroom" and the "editorial department" will maintain the political independence of the press.

10. Examine the context of the questions "Are government and party subsidies less imprisoning?" (paragraph 19) and "But haven't they just traded one affiliation for another?" (paragraph 21). Why does the author use questions instead of statements to make his point? What is the effect?

The questions are rhetorical. The author asks to emphasize a point rather than elicit an answer. The first example is a way of stating that government and party subsidies *are* just as imprisoning as advertising revenues. The second is his way of stating that people who reflexively speak out against the government *have* just traded one affiliation for another.

11. In paragraph 21, Krimsky suggests that journalists who oppose the government in new democracies "equate independence with opposition." How does this support his argument for a non-partisan, objective news media?

Krimsky notes that because these journalists "speak out against the government, they say they are independent." He maintains that opposing the government still evidences a lack of objectivity and that there is "little room for unvarnished truth in a partisan press"—in other words, constant opposition to the government is no more a sign of journalistic integrity than constant support of it.

12. How does the anecdote about the Lithuanian newspaper editor in paragraph 22 support Krimsky's central idea regarding press objectivity? How does it affect the way the text is read and understood?

Krimsky uses the anecdote to support a positive point about journalistic objectivity. He relates that the new democracy's newspaper editor wanted to show readers "what their heads are for" by giving them objective information so they could form their own opinions. Krimsky then describes how this objectivity resulted in a more successful press with a higher circulation.

Scaffolding the Text-Dependent Questions

14. Summarize Krimsky's point of view about the importance of a free press within a democracy. Consider the ideas Krimsky explores in the article. Reread paragraphs 27 and 28. What three needs does Krimsky list? Why are these needs important to a democracy? How does a free press serve those needs? RI.11-12.6

16 Use the Focus on the Sentence task to review the uses of conjunctions. Ask students to state the function and meaning of the conjunction in the sample sentence. (*Because* indicates a reason for something.) Then have students construct three additional sentences, guiding them to an understanding that *but* indicates contrast and *so* indicates cause and effect.

3.2

13. Based upon the context of the article's last sentence, what is an *admonition?* Use a print or digital resource to clarify or validate your understanding of this multiple-meaning word.

George Washington utters the following "admonition" at the Constitutional Convention: "Let us raise a standard to which the wise and honest can repair." Within the context of the situation (setting up a government for a new nation), the admonition is a caution or warning, reminding those present that the new government must not fall short of being a model of wisdom and honesty.

14. Summarize Krimsky's point of view about the importance of a free press within a democracy.

Krimsky believes that a free press is important to a democracy. Its purpose is to help people identify "sense amidst the nonsense" and to help them sift "the important from the trivial" as they concentrate on learning "the truth." The press functions to "let the people know the facts," make their own decisions, and hold the government accountable for its actions.

☑ Focus on the Sentence

Examine the arguments and supporting statements Krimsky makes in his article. Write three or four sentences that summarize some of his views using *because*, *but*, or *so* as conjunctions between clauses. You may use the following sentence frame to help you compose your sentences, or you may construct them on your own.

The author states that _____ (because/but/so) _____.

The author states that we should debate the usefulness of a free press because it is a vital issue.

The author states that a democracy needs hard information, so it can make sound decisions.

The author states that the truth is important, but it doesn't always serve the public.

The author states that more news sources aren't an improvement because people can pick and choose the sources that tell them what they want to hear.

LANGUAGE & WRITER'S CRAFT: Diction and Tone

When writers make an argument, they choose between a subjective and an objective tone to convey information. Writers may use a subjective tone if they want to provide an opinion that contains a biased viewpoint, or they might use an objective tone if they want to convey unbiased facts that pertain to the argument. Each choice has its merits and drawbacks—when readers know an argument is subjective, it may feel more personal and contain emotions and judgment. When an argument is objective, it may feel as though the writer's opinions have been removed from the equation to produce a purely fact-based argument. Pay close attention to a writer's diction, or word choice, in order to ascertain whether the tone is subjective or objective. Subjective arguments tend to contain more emotional or opinionated language: "The American press … has seldom been loved." Objective arguments tend to contain more neutral or factual language: "The media embraces the television and film entertainment industries, a vast array of regularly published printed material, and even public relations and advertising."

How do you know which tone to take in crafting an argument? First, consider your audience. A meeting with your teacher about raising a grade might not benefit from subjective emotional language. However, if you provide objective, measurable facts about your performance, the teacher may be more likely to consider your point of view.

PRACTICE Choose one paragraph from "The Role of the Media in a Democracy" and analyze whether the tone is objective or subjective. Which clues from the writer's diction indicate objectivity or subjectivity? Then rewrite the paragraph in the opposing tone, paying close attention to diction.

17 Draw students' attention to the Language & Writer's Craft section. Have a volunteer read the introductory text aloud. Then stress the differences in subjective and objective argument. Write the given examples of opinionated and factual language on the board and have students reword the opinionated example to make it more factual and vice versa for the factual example.

18 Review the Practice exercise on diction and tone. Once students have chosen and rewritten their paragraphs, have them swap with a partner to conduct a quick peer edit.

19 Lead students in analyzing the structure of Krimsky's article by guiding them through an explanation of the first row of the chart.

20 Give students time to complete the remaining sections of the graphic organizer, challenging them to identify and interpret the pertinent parts of the article.

3.2

Working from the Text

15. Skim Krimsky's article to analyze its characteristics and structural elements. List quotes from the text that illustrate those characteristics/elements in the chart and write a short interpretive statement for each.

Characteristic/ Element	Quote	Interpretation
Audience	"The issue of whether a free press is the best communications solution in a democracy is much too important at the close of this century and needs to be examined dispassionately."	The audience for the article is people who live in a democracy.
Thesis	"A self-governing society, by definition, needs to make its own decisions. It cannot do that without hard information, leavened with an open exchange of views."	Citizens in a democracy need access to information and a forum to freely discuss that information and make informed decisions.
Argument	"This role of public 'watchdog' was thus assumed by a citizen press, and as a consequence, the government in the United States has been kept out of the news business."	It is vital that the functions of the press be performed separately from the government.
Counterarguments/ Rebuttals/ Concessions	Counterargument #1: "Many critics have questioned whether there is such a thing as 'objectivity.'" Rebuttal #1: "Journalists can try to keep their personal views out of the news, and they employ a number of techniques to do so, such as obtaining and quoting multiple sources and opposing views."	Counterargument #1: It can be argued that journalists in a free press are no more objective that those in a government-run press. Rebuttal #1: There are methods by which objectivity can be pursued, even if it isn't perfectly obtainable.
Conclusion	"In a free-market democracy, the people— that is the voters and the buying public— ultimately decide as to how their press should act."	In a democracy, the voters and consumers in society determine the quality and integrity of the press.
Call to Action	"If true journalists are worried about their future in an age when everyone with a computer can call themselves journalists, then the profession has to demonstrate that it is special, that it offers something of real value and can prove it to the public."	Journalists themselves must perform their duties in such a way that the public will see the value of a free public press.

Socratic Seminar

You will next participate in a Socratic Seminar. To prepare, review the texts in this activity. Then, in small groups, respond to the pre-seminar questions as they relate to the texts. Discuss the conflicting points of view presented in the article and measure each position against your understanding of the First Amendment. Cite specific details from each text to support your ideas and viewpoints.

Pre-seminar questions:

- How important is a free press to a democratic society? What is the balance between the freedoms guaranteed by the First Amendment and the responsibility of the individual in our society?
- Why is it important that the government is not involved with the media?
- Write one of your own open-ended questions based on the text.

Participation Remember that as you participate in the Socratic Seminar, follow the rules for a collaborative discussion:

- Offer your ideas or judgments that are purposeful in moving the class toward goals.
- Ask relevant and insightful questions.
- Be tolerant of a range of positions and ambiguity in decision making among your peers.
- Evaluate the group's work based on agreed-upon criteria.

> ### Explain How an Author Builds an Argument
>
> Krimsky begins his essay by defining terminology and revisiting some historical and key ideas about the founding of the U.S. government. Write an essay that explains how Krimsky continues to structure his essay to persuade readers of the vital role of free media within a democracy. How effective is this structure in conveying Krimsky's ideas in a convincing way? Be sure to:
>
> - Revise your draft as needed to use diction and precise language that maintain an objective tone as you describe and analyze Krimsky's structure.
> - Employ logical organization as you build an analysis of how Krimsky's ideas progress.
> - Develop your explanation by citing significant and relevant quotations, making sure not to introduce errors of fact or understanding.

EXPLAIN HOW AN AUTHOR BUILDS AN ARGUMENT

The following standards are addressed in the writing prompt:
- W.11-12.2b
- W.11-12.4
- W.11-12.5

ACTIVITY 3.2 continued

21 Read aloud the introductory text to the **Socratic Seminar** section. Instruct students to prepare for a Socratic Seminar by answering the pre-seminar questions and rereading the text.

22 Conduct a brief (10 to 15 minutes) Socratic Seminar using answers to the pre-seminar questions and the unit's Essential Questions to guide the discussion. Be sure students have the text in front of them and that they refer to it often during discussion.

23 Read aloud the text in the Writing Prompt box. Give students time to respond to the prompt. Consider allowing students to work in pairs to analyze Krimsky's article and write their essays.

SAT® CONNECTIONS

This writing prompt provides practice with the following important SAT skill: explaining how an author builds an argument to persuade an audience.

ASSESS

Use students' responses to the writing prompt to assess their ability to identify and analyze the structure of an argument using objective tone, logical organization, and relevant evidence. Ensure that students are analyzing structure rather than agreeing or disagreeing with Krimsky's claims.

ADAPT

If students need additional help responding to the writing prompt, have them review their answers to the text-dependent questions and the work they have done on identifying objective and subjective tone. Guide them in writing in an objective tone, employing logical organization, and citing relevant evidence (including quotations).

ACTIVITY 3.3

PLAN

Suggested Pacing: 1 50-minute class period

TEACH

1 Start the activity by reading aloud the Learning Targets and the Preview. Orient students to the task at hand by reading the As You Read section as a class and give students time to read the About the Document feature independently.

 TEACHER TO TEACHER

You may want to show students coverage of the Supreme Court case that happened during the time it was heard to help students understand the gravity of the case. Provide students with a copy of the First Amendment text so they can understand how the justices were reading and interpreting it.

ACTIVITY
3.3

3.3 The Supreme Court and Free Speech

Learning Strategies

Making Inferences
Note-taking

My Notes

Learning Targets
- Read and evaluate the reasoning of a legal decision.
- Understand central ideas in a text and consider how they might be refuted.

Preview

In this activity, you will read a 1971 Supreme Court ruling and analyze it argument and central ideas.

As You Read
- Highlight details the Supreme Court uses to support its ruling.
- Underline the reasoning the Supreme Court uses in its argument.
- Circle any unknown words or phrases. Try to determine the meaning of the words by using context clues, word parts, or a dictionary.

About the Document

New York Times Co. v. United States was a case brought before the Supreme Court in 1971. The case concerned the First Amendment in regard to whether *The New York Times* and *The Washington Post* should be allowed to publish the Pentagon Papers, which were considered classified government documents. President Nixon had used his executive authority to force *The New York Times* to stop publication of any classified information it may have had, and The New York Times Co. wanted to be able to publish the papers without fear of censorship or punishment. The Supreme Court had to decide whether *The New York Times* was guaranteed the constitutional right of freedom of the press under the First Amendment or whether the government was allowed to halt publication in order to maintain the secrecy of its information. The Supreme Court ultimately ruled that *The New York Times* was protected under the First Amendment and allowed to print the classified information.

College and Career Readiness Standards

Focus Standards:

RI.11-12.1 Cite strong and thorough textual evidence to support analysis of what the text says explicitly as well as inferences drawn from the text, including determining where the text leaves matters uncertain.

RI.11-12.2 Determine two or more central ideas of a text and analyze their development over the course of the text, including how they interact and build on one another to provide a complex analysis; provide an objective summary of the text.

RI.11-12.4 Determine the meaning of words and phrases as they are used in a text, including figurative, connotative, and technical meanings; analyze how an author uses and refines the meaning of a key term or terms over the course of a text.

Legislation

New York Times Co. v. United States, 403 U.S. 713

by U.S. Supreme Court

1   MR. JUSTICE BLACK, with whom MR. JUSTICE DOUGLAS joins, **concurring.**

2   I **adhere** to the view that the Government's case against the Washington Post should have been dismissed, and that the **injunction** against the New York Times should have been vacated without oral argument when the cases were first presented to this Court. I believe that every moment's continuance of the injunctions against these newspapers amounts to a **flagrant**, indefensible, and continuing violation of the First Amendment. Furthermore, after oral argument, I agree completely that we must affirm the judgment of the Court of Appeals for the District of Columbia Circuit and reverse the judgment of the Court of Appeals for the Second Circuit for the reasons stated by my Brothers DOUGLAS and BRENNAN. In my view, it is unfortunate that some of my **Brethren** are apparently willing to hold that the publication of news may sometimes be enjoined. Such a holding would make a shambles of the First Amendment.

3   Our Government was launched in 1789 with the adoption of the Constitution. The Bill of Rights, including the First Amendment, followed in 1791. Now, for the first time in the 182 years since the founding of the Republic, the federal courts are asked to hold that the First Amendment does not mean what it says, but rather means that the Government can halt the publication of current news of vital importance to the people of this country.

4   In seeking injunctions against these newspapers, and in its presentation to the Court, the Executive Branch seems to have forgotten the essential purpose and history of the First Amendment. When the Constitution was adopted, many people strongly opposed it because the document contained no Bill of Rights to safeguard certain basic freedoms. They especially feared that the new powers granted to a central government might be interpreted to permit the government to **curtail** freedom of religion, press, assembly, and speech. In response to an overwhelming public **clamor**, James Madison offered a series of amendments to satisfy citizens that these great liberties would remain safe and beyond the power of government to **abridge.** Madison proposed what later became the First Amendment in three parts, two of which are set out below, and one of which proclaimed: "The people shall not

---

concurring: agreeing

adhere: hold closely

injunction: order

flagrant: offensive

brethren: brothers

curtail: restrict

clamor: protest

abridge: restrict

---

2 Guide students to understand that they may encounter some unfamiliar words as they read the text. Model determining the meanings of unfamiliar words through the use of context clues, word parts, or a print or online dictionary. Hand out copies of the **Unknown Word Solver** graphic organizer for students to use as they read.

3 FIRST READ: Have students conduct small-group readings of the text. Pause after paragraph 1 to ensure that students understand how and why the case made its way to the Supreme Court as well as the justices' initial reactions to hearing it. Be sure students are engaged with the text and marking it.

TEXT COMPLEXITY

Overall: Complex
Lexile: 1360L
Qualitative: Moderate Difficulty
Task: Moderate (Analyze)

4 As students are reading, monitor their progress. Be sure they are engaged with the text and annotating unknown words and phrases, raising questions, and making connections to the First Amendment. Evaluate whether the selected reading mode is effective.

College and Career Readiness Standards

RI.11-12.8 Delineate and evaluate the reasoning in seminal U.S. texts, including the application of constitutional principles and use of legal reasoning (e.g., in U.S. Supreme Court majority opinions and dissents) and the premises, purposes, and arguments in works of public advocacy.

W.11-12.1 Write arguments to support claims in an analysis of substantive topics or texts, using valid reasoning and relevant and sufficient evidence.

Additional Standards Addressed:
RI.11-12.10

5 Ask students to pause after the end of paragraph 3. Come back together as a class to summarize the justices' argument so far and discuss what is or isn't effective about it. Address any questions or uncertainties about the text, helping to clarify main ideas. Then have students return to reading in groups.

6 Tell students to pause after the final paragraph and discuss within their group the effect of words like *bold* and *dangerous* on the tone of the text. Ask volunteers from each group to share their ideas with the class.

My Notes

be deprived or abridged of their right to speak, to write, or to publish their sentiments, and the freedom of the press, as one of the great **bulwarks** of liberty, shall be **inviolable**." (Emphasis added.) The amendments were offered to curtail and restrict the general powers granted to the Executive, Legislative, and Judicial Branches two years before in the original Constitution. The Bill of Rights changed the original Constitution into a new charter under which no branch of government could abridge the people's freedoms of press, speech, religion, and assembly. Yet the Solicitor General argues and some members of the Court appear to agree that the general powers of the Government adopted in the original Constitution should be interpreted to limit and restrict the specific and **emphatic** guarantees of the Bill of Rights adopted later. I can imagine no greater perversion of history. Madison and the other Framers of the First Amendment, able men that they were, wrote in language they earnestly believed could never be misunderstood: "Congress shall make no law . . . abridging the freedom . . . of the press. . . ." Both the history and language of the First Amendment support the view that the press must be left free to publish news, whatever the source, without censorship, injunctions, or prior restraints.

5 In the First Amendment, the Founding Fathers gave the free press the protection it must have to fulfill its essential role in our democracy. The press was to serve the governed, not the governors. The Government's power to censor the press was abolished so that the press would remain forever free to **censure** the Government. The press was protected so that it could bare the secrets of government and inform the people. Only a free and unrestrained press can effectively expose deception in government. And **paramount** among the responsibilities of a free press is the duty to prevent any part of the government from deceiving the people and sending them off to distant lands to die of foreign fevers and foreign shot and shell. In my view, far from deserving condemnation for their courageous reporting, the New York Times, the Washington Post, and other newspapers should be commended for serving the purpose that the Founding Fathers saw so clearly. In revealing the workings of government that led to the Vietnam war, the newspapers nobly did precisely that which the Founders hoped and trusted they would do.

6 The Government's case here is based on premises entirely different from those that guided the Framers of the First Amendment. The Solicitor General has carefully and emphatically stated: "Now, Mr. Justice [BLACK], your construction of . . . [the First Amendment] is well known, and I certainly respect it. You say that no law means no law, and that should be obvious. I can only say, Mr. Justice, that to me it is equally obvious that 'no law' does not mean 'no law,' and I would seek to persuade the Court that that is true. . . . [T]here are other parts of the Constitution that grant powers and responsibilities to the Executive, and . . . the First Amendment was not intended to make it impossible for the Executive to function or to protect the security of the United States."

7 And the Government argues in its brief that, in spite of the First Amendment, "[t]he authority of the Executive Department to protect the

> bulwarks: institutions
> inviolable: not dishonored
> emphatic: forcibly expressed
> censure: disapprove of
> paramount: most important

Scaffolding the Text-Dependent Questions

1. **In paragraph 2, what inferences can be made about how the justices arrived at their decision?** What kind of language do they use? What tone does their language create? RI.11-12.1

2. **In paragraph 3, what premise given by the Government do the justices reject?** On what grounds do they reject the Government's premise?

What does the Government want the court to allow? What do the justices say they are being asked to believe about the First Amendment? RI.11-12.8

3. **In paragraph 4, what do the justices mean by "perversion of history" in context?** What connotation do both of those words have? What is the context of their use? RI.11-12.4

nation against publication of information whose disclosure would endanger the national security stems from two interrelated sources: the constitutional power of the President over the conduct of foreign affairs and his authority as Commander-in-Chief."

8 In other words, we are asked to hold that, despite the First Amendment's emphatic command, the Executive Branch, the Congress, and the Judiciary can make laws enjoining publication of current news and abridging freedom of the press in the name of "national security." The Government does not even attempt to rely on any act of Congress. Instead, it makes the bold and dangerously far-reaching contention that the courts should take it upon themselves to "make" a law abridging freedom of the press in the name of equity, presidential power and national security, even when the representatives of the people in Congress have adhered to the command of the First Amendment and refused to make such a law.

Making Observations
- What tone does the language emphasize?
- What details stand out to you?
- What questions does this text raise for you?

My Notes

7 After reading the text for the first time, guide the class in a discussion by asking the Making Observations questions. Check students' general comprehension of the text based on their observations, asking follow-up questions if needed.

Scaffolding the Text-Dependent Questions

4. What claims do the justices make in paragraph 5? What evidence do they provide for their claim? What do the justices say about the First Amendment and the Founding Fathers? What do they believe the Founding Fathers would hope and trust a free press would do? RI.11-12.8

5. Summarize the arguments the justices make over the course of their ruling. How do they develop their arguments? What is the structure of the argument? Is it effective? RI.11-12.2

3.3

8 **RETURNING TO THE TEXT:** Guide students to return to the text to respond to the text-dependent questions. Invite them to work in small groups to reread the text and answer the questions. Remind them to use text evidence in their responses.

9 Move from group to group and listen in as students answer the text-dependent questions. If they have difficulty, scaffold the questions by rephrasing them or breaking them down into smaller parts. See the Scaffolding the Text-Dependent Questions boxes for suggestions.

Returning to the Text

- Return to the ruling as you respond to the following questions. Use evidence from the text to support your responses.
- Write any additional questions you have about the text in your Reader/Writer Notebook.

1. In paragraph 2, what inferences can be made about how the justices arrived at their decision?

   In paragraph 2, the justices state their disapproval about the case even being brought before the Supreme Court, noting that the cases against *The Washington Post* and *The New York Times* should have been dismissed without oral argument. The justices use strong words such as *indefensible* and *flagrant* to show their frustration.

2. In paragraph 3, what premise given by the Government do the justices reject? On what grounds do they reject the Government's premise?

   They reject the Government's premise that the Government can stop the press from reporting vital news. They reject this on the grounds that the First Amendment means what it says.

3. In paragraph 4, what do the justices mean by "perversion of history" in context?

   The justices refer to the fact that the Solicitor General and some members of the Court side with the Government over the right to censor the press. By referring to this as a "perversion of history," the justices mean that the framers of the First Amendment did not intend for it to be used to censor the press.

4. What claims do the justices make in paragraph 5? What evidence do they provide for their claim?

   The justices claim that only a free press can effectively expose government corruption and that newspapers should be commended for serving the purpose of a free press. They refer to the First Amendment as evidence that the Founding Fathers believed the press was to "serve the governed, not the governors."

5. Summarize the arguments the justices make over the course of their ruling. How do they develop their argument?

   The justices lay out the argument that the case should never have been heard in the first place, as the First Amendment makes it clear that the press's freedom of speech is protected even if the government wants the information to be secret. They develop their argument by referring to the history of the First Amendment as well as rebutting the argument laid forth by the government.

Working from the Text

6. Revisit the annotations you made of the reasoning that the justices use to support their argument. First, identify their reasons and record them in the chart. Then think about possible rebuttals for each using evidence from the text.

Reasons	Possible Rebuttals
The case should have been dismissed.	The government has a right to defend its argument in order to protect sensitive information from getting into the wrong hands.
The First Amendment would be meaningless if the free press can be censored.	The press shouldn't have the same rights as individuals when it comes to free speech.
The Founding Fathers didn't intent for the First Amendment to protect the government.	The Founding Fathers couldn't anticipate what the future of the press or sensitive government information might hold.
Freedom of the press is inherent to the health of a democracy.	The government should have a say in what the press can and can't publish if the publication puts the country at risk.

Check Your Understanding

Quickwrite: How has the Supreme Court ruling on this case affected the freedom of the press since? How might things have turned out differently if the ruling had favored the government?

---

10 Have the student pairs complete the graphic organizer in the Working from the Text section. Begin by reading the instructions and clarifying them as needed. Then lead a discussion to help the class articulate the justices' argument. Guide them to state the justices' thesis in their own words and then give them time to complete the activity. Once pairs are finished, come back together as a class to discuss the reasons and their possible rebuttals.

11 Give students time to respond to the Check Your Understanding task. Consider allowing them to work in pairs to discuss and debate their responses first.

ASSESS

Review students' responses to the Check Your Understanding task. Make sure they used textual support and analysis of the argument to posit how the case affected freedom of the press and predict how things might have turned out differently.

ADAPT

If students need additional help responding to the Quickwrite, help them create a graphic organizer with categories that define freedom of the press, make an observation about the press they read and the information they get from it, and predict how things might be different if the court had ruled in favor of the government.

ACTIVITY 3.4

PLAN

Materials: local newspapers (print or online), poster paper
Suggested Pacing: 1 50-minute class period

TEACH

1 Read the Learning Targets and Preview with students. Make certain they understand that they will be examining the effectiveness of different kinds of news media.

2 Give students time to complete the News Media Survey.

3 As a class, examine the responses of the first four survey questions. Tally the results on the board. Then ask for responses to the fifth question from students who think it is important to be knowledgeable about news and students who do not. Discuss those responses.

Learning Strategies

Discussion Groups
Graphic Organizer
Questioning the Text

My Notes

Learning Targets

- Describe the characteristics of various news sources, including multimodal and digital sources.
- Explain how those characteristics contribute to or detract from their effectiveness.

Preview

In this activity, you will analyze the effectiveness of characteristics of various news sources.

News Media Survey

1. Rank the following news media outlets in the order you would turn to them for information on a major news story. (Use 1 to indicate the outlet you would turn to most often. Write N/A to indicate you would not use that outlet.)

    _____ Newspaper   _____ Radio News
    _____ Local TV News   _____ News Magazines
    _____ Cable News Station   _____ News Podcast
    _____ Word of Mouth   _____ Social Media
    _____ Websites/Internet

2. Rank the following media outlets for accuracy and trustworthiness in how they present information. (Rank the most trustworthy outlet 1.)

    _____ Newspaper   _____ Radio News
    _____ Local TV News   _____ News Magazines
    _____ Cable News Station   _____ News Podcast
    _____ Word of Mouth   _____ Social Media
    _____ Websites/Internet

3. Think back on the past month. About how much time (in hours) did you spend receiving news (not entertainment) from the following media outlets?

    _____ Newspaper   _____ Radio News
    _____ Local TV News   _____ News Magazines
    _____ Cable News Station   _____ News Podcast
    _____ Word of Mouth   _____ Social Media
    _____ Websites/Internet

4. Rank each of the following reasons that you might give for not reading newspapers. (Write 1 next to the reason most appropriate for you. Write N/A if you disagree with the statement.)

    _____ They are boring.
    _____ They take too long to read.

College and Career Readiness Standards

Focus Standards:

RI.11-12.7 Integrate and evaluate multiple sources of information presented in different media or formats (e.g., visually, quantitatively) as well as in words in order to address a question or solve a problem.

SL.11-12.1 Initiate and participate effectively in a range of collaborative discussions (one-on-one, in groups, and teacher-led) with diverse partners on grades 11–12 topics, texts, and issues, building on others' ideas and expressing their own clearly and persuasively.

W.11-12.4 Produce clear and coherent writing in which the development, organization, and style are appropriate to task, purpose, and audience.

_____ They don't have information that applies to me and my life.

_____ They usually focus on scandals, politics, and gossip.

_____ They are often filled with mistakes and lies.

_____ Other:

5. Do you feel that it is important to be knowledgeable about news? Explain.

Exploring News Sources

In today's world, news sources can be divided into two types: **print** and **digital**. Print news sources are defined as any news product that is produced through the traditional printing process—newspapers, magazines, newsletters, and so on. A digital news source transmits digitized news through airwaves, satellite transmissions, or the Internet (or any combination of those media).

Both print and digital news sources are frequently **multimodal**. That means they use two or more communication modes (written language, spoken language, still images, moving images, music, visual effects, sound effects, etc.) to present their content. Presenters of news shape these modes into headlines, images with captions, teasers, quotes, graphics, video images, audio snippets, and so on, in an enormous variety of combinations. Presenters can use these modes in various ways to influence the audience's perception of the content. Thus, two news sources can present the same information but with very different purposes reflected in the format and tone of the presentation.

The form and tone of any particular news presentation are influenced largely by its **target audience**, the group or groups of people for whom the presentation is intended. News presenters also consider their **secondary audience**, those who might also be exposed to the message or have some influence over the target audience.

As guided by your teacher, examine the content of a print and digital news source. Discuss the following questions as a class and write your answers in your Reader/Writer Notebook:

- What is the purpose of the content you are examining?
- Who are the target and secondary audiences for this source?
- What modes are the news presenters using to reach those audiences?
- Why are the news presenters using those particular modes?
- Is their method of presentation effective or ineffective?
- What about their method of presentation makes it effective or ineffective?

6. When you have finished, your teacher will divide the class into small groups. Repeat the activity with your group using a source assigned by your teacher, discussing the questions and presenting your agreed-upon answers to the class when you have finished.

My Notes

LITERARY

A **target audience** is the intended group for which a work is designed to appeal or reach. A **secondary audience** is the group who may also receive the message or may influence the target audience.

VOCABULARY

---

4 Read aloud the first two paragraphs of the Exploring News Sources section. Pause after the second paragraph to ensure that students understand the concept of multimodal news sources. Help them generate examples of news sources that use more than one communication mode.

5 **Vocabulary Development:** As you discuss the third paragraph, review the meaning of the terms *target audience* and *secondary audience* with students. Have them work in pairs to define the terms in their own words. Help students generate examples of a target and secondary audience for various print and digital media.

6 Distribute copies of your local newspaper. They do not need to be current or have the same date, but they should be reasonably complete. Ask students to skim sections of the newspaper and identify the content of each. They might also discuss the amount and type of advertising that appears in various sections. (Point out that advertised items can be a strong clue to a news source's target and secondary audiences.) List the sections and their descriptions on the board. Use the list, descriptions, and the questions in the Exploring News Sources section to frame a class discussion on multimodal news media. Have students take notes and record answers to the questions in their Reader/Writer Notebooks.

7 Divide students into small groups and assign each group a multimodal print or online news source. Have them apply the questions in the Exploring News Sources section to their assigned source. They should note their agreed-upon answers in their Reader/Writer Notebooks. A representative of the group can present the group's answers to the class. You may have groups write their answers on poster paper and create a visual aid.

8 Have the same student groups pick their own sources in accordance with the directions and complete the News Source Analysis Chart section. After all of the groups have completed the graphic organizer, coordinate comparisons of the groups' findings. Afterward, lead a class discussion of those findings, using the questions that follow.

3.4

News Source Analysis Chart

Select two print and two online news sources. Attempt to include sources that address a variety of topic areas, ages, and interest levels. Conduct an analysis of each of your sources using the questions and chart.

Source/items: What is the name of your source, and what are the topics/headlines of two of its news items?

Purpose: What is the news source's purpose in presenting each news item?

Target audience: To whom in particular is each presentation designed to appeal?

Modes and characteristics of source: Are the source's items multimodal? If so, what modes are used? What characteristics or features (headlines, images with captions, teasers, quotes, graphics, video images, audio snippets, etc.) do the news presenters employ?

Effectiveness: Are the choices made by the news presenters effective in achieving the item's purpose and reaching the intended audience? Explain.

Source/Items	Purpose	Target Audience	Modes and Characteristics of Source	Effectiveness
Print Source #1:				
Print Source #2:				
Online Source #1:				
Online Source #2:				

7. Compare your results to those of at least two other groups in your class. What commonalities do you notice among print and online news sources? What differences do you notice? What might explain both the commonalities and the differences?

☑ Check Your Understanding

After discussing similarities and differences in print and online news sources, write a paragraph explaining how a source's coverage of news is shaped to appeal to its target audience. Use a source you have examined in this activity as the framework for your explanation.

9 Give students time to respond to the Check Your Understanding task. Consider allowing them to work in pairs to write their descriptive/explanatory paragraph.

ASSESS

Review students' responses to the Check Your Understanding task. Ensure that students have addressed how a news source's coverage is shaped to appeal to its target audience. Make certain that they have framed their explanation using a source from this activity.

ADAPT

If students need additional help understanding how news coverage is tailored toward a target audience, have them read newspaper coverage from each of the two home cities for a professional sporting competition. How does the city newspaper for each team report the event? How is the coverage different? Why is it different? How does target audience affect coverage?

PLAN

Suggested Pacing: 2 50-minute class periods

TEACH

1 Read the Learning Targets and Preview sections with students.

2 Vocabulary Development: Review the meaning of the term *editorial* with students. Have them work in pairs to define the term in their own words and think of both examples and non-examples. Tell students that they will be examining how claims in an editorial can be conceded and refuted.

3 Have student **discussion groups** analyze the quotations about newspapers. In the space after each quotation, students should work together to **paraphrase** the quotation and state whether they agree with it and why.

Learning Strategies

Discussion Groups
Marking the Text
Paraphrasing
Skimming/Scanning

VOCABULARY

ACADEMIC
An **editorial** is an article in a newspaper or magazine expressing the opinion of its editor or publisher. An editorial is similar to an essay in that it focuses on a specific issue or topic, offers a thesis, and provides reasons and evidence to convince its readers.

Learning Targets

- Analyze how concessions and refutations can be used as responses to an argument.
- Apply strategies of refutation to a set of claims and evidence.
- Integrate ideas from multiple texts to build knowledge and vocabulary about editorials.

Preview

In this activity, you will read and analyze two **editorials**, one that makes a claim about modern media consumption and another that refutes the claim.

Do You Agree?

1. Look over the following quotations about newspapers. In the space after each quote, paraphrase what the author is saying and then state whether you agree and why.

- "Were it left to me to decide whether we should have a government without newspapers, or newspapers without a government, I should not hesitate a moment to prefer the latter." —Thomas Jefferson, 1787

- "The newspapers, especially those in the East, are amazingly superficial and ... a large number of news gatherers are either cynics at heart or are following the orders and the policies of the owners of their papers." —Franklin D. Roosevelt, May 7, 1934

- "For my part I entertain a high idea of the utility of periodical publications; insomuch as I could heartily desire, copies of ... magazines, as well as common Gazettes, might be spread through every city, town, and village in the United States. I consider such vehicles of knowledge more happily calculated than any other to preserve the liberty, stimulate the industry, and ameliorate the morals of a free and enlightened people." —George Washington, 1788

My Notes

College and Career Readiness Standards

Focus Standards:

RI.11-12.1 Cite strong and thorough textual evidence to support analysis of what the text says explicitly as well as inferences drawn from the text, including determining where the text leaves matters uncertain.

RI.11-12.2 Determine two or more central ideas of a text and analyze their development over the course of the text, including how they interact and build on one another to provide a complex analysis; provide an objective summary of the text.

RI.11-12.4 Determine the meaning of words and phrases as they are used in a text, including figurative, connotative, and technical meanings; analyze how an author uses and refines the meaning of a key term or terms over the course of a text (e.g., how Madison defines faction in Federalist No. 10).

- "As people get their opinions so largely from the newspapers they read, the corruption of the schools would not matter so much if the Press were free. But the Press is not free. As it costs at least a quarter of a million of money to establish a daily newspaper in London, the newspapers are owned by rich men. And they depend on the advertisements of other rich men. Editors and journalists who express opinions in print that are opposed to the interests of the rich are dismissed and replaced by subservient ones." —George B. Shaw, Irish playwright, 1949

- "The decline of competing local daily newspaper voices diminishes not only the availability of local and regional news to consumers but also the availability of competing opinions and ideas, not just at local levels but at all levels. Social thinkers, historians, and political analysts have identified such diversity of thought—a marketplace of ideas—as essential to a functioning democracy." —Steven M. Hallock, journalism professor, 2007

My Notes

As You Read

- Highlight details Sunstein uses as **reasoning** and **evidence** to support his argument about modern media consumption.
- Underline any words with British spellings. (The *Financial Times* is a British newspaper.)
- Circle any unknown words or phrases. Try to determine the meaning of the words by using context clues, word parts, or a dictionary.

ACADEMIC

VOCABULARY

Reasoning is the thinking or logic used to make a claim in an argument. **Evidence** is the specific facts, examples, and other details used to support the reasoning. Evaluating an argument requires that you look closely at the writer's or speaker's evidence to determine its validity.

ACTIVITY 3.5 continued

4 Read aloud the Vocabulary box about *reasoning* and *evidence*. Make certain students have a grasp of these two concepts before reading and examining the two editorials.

5 Have students read the As You Read and About the Author sections. Prompt them to make one prediction about the upcoming text based on its title and what they know about the author.

College and Career Readiness Standards

RI.11-12.5 Analyze and evaluate the effectiveness of the structure an author uses in his or her exposition or argument, including whether the structure makes points clear, convincing, and engaging.

RI.11-12.6 Determine an author's point of view or purpose in a text in which the rhetoric is particularly effective, analyzing how style and content contribute to the power, persuasiveness, or beauty of the text.

Additional Standards Addressed:

RI.11-12.10, SL.11.12.1

6 Discuss the Knowledge Question. Have students work in small groups to discuss how editorials make claims.

7 FIRST READ: Conduct an independent reading of "How the Rise of the Daily Me Threatens Democracy." Tell students that the editorial exposes them to an inductive argument that presents evidence from which it draws conclusions in support of a claim. Point out that *The Financial Times* is a British newspaper and tell students to underline any words with British spellings. Ask them to highlight examples of reasoning or evidence and circle unknown words or phrases so they can locate them later and try to determine their meanings.

 TEXT COMPLEXITY

Overall: Complex
Lexile: 1070L
Qualitative: Moderate Difficulty
Task: Moderate (Analyze)

8 Instruct students to pause after paragraph 2. When they have all read that far, ask them questions to ensure that they understand what the author means by the "Daily Me." Tell them that understanding that idea is vital to understanding the editorial.

9 As students are reading, monitor their progress. Be sure they are engaged with the text and annotating unknown words and phrases, identifying Sunstein's reasoning and evidence, and marking examples of British spellings.

3.5

⊘ **KNOWLEDGE QUEST**

Knowledge Question:
How do newspaper editorials make and refute claims? Across Activity 3.5, you will read two editorials that give opinions. While you read and build knowledge about the topic, think about your answer to the Knowledge Question.

My Notes

_____
_____
_____
_____
_____
_____
_____
_____
_____
_____
_____
_____
_____
_____
_____
_____

emergence: rise in popularity
deliberated: thought about or discussed carefully
conformed: held to

About the Author

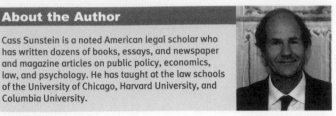

Cass Sunstein is a noted American legal scholar who has written dozens of books, essays, and newspaper and magazine articles on public policy, economics, law, and psychology. He has taught at the law schools of the University of Chicago, Harvard University, and Columbia University.

Editorial

How the Rise of the Daily Me Threatens Democracy

Financial Times, January 10, 2008

by **Cass Sunstein**

1 More than a decade ago the technology specialist, Nicholas Negroponte, prophesied the **emergence** of the Daily Me—a fully personalised newspaper. It would allow you to include topics that interest you and screen out those that bore or annoy you. If you wanted to focus on Iraq and tennis, or exclude Iran and golf, you could do that.

2 Many people now use the internet to create something like a Daily Me. This behaviour is reinforced by the rise of social networking forums, collaborative filtering and viral marketing. For politics, the phenomenon is especially important in campaigns. Candidates in the US presidential race can construct information cocoons in which readers are deluged with material that is, in their eyes, politically correct. Supporters of Hillary Clinton construct a Daily Me that includes her campaign's perspective but offers nothing from Barack Obama, let alone Mitt Romney.

3 What is wrong with the emerging situation? We can find a clue in a small experiment in democracy conducted in Colorado in 2005. About 60 US citizens were put into 10 groups. They **deliberated** on controversial issues, such as whether the US should sign an international treaty to combat global warming and whether states should allow same-sex couples to enter into civil unions. The groups consisted of predominantly either leftwing or rightwing members, with the former drawn from left-of-centre Boulder and the latter from Colorado Springs, which tends to be right of centre. The groups, not mixed, were screened to ensure members **conformed** to stereotypes. (If people in Boulder liked Vice-President Dick Cheney, they were cordially excused.) People were asked to state their opinions anonymously before and after the group discussion.

Scaffolding the Text-Dependent Questions

2. In paragraph 1, what does the word *prophesied* **mean in context? What effect does it have on the tone?** Why would the author choose this word instead of a similar one? What connotations does it have? RI.11-12.4

3. Summarize the "Daily Me" situation Sunstein describes in paragraphs 1 and 2. Examine the paragraphs. What does the author reference in

them? What prediction is made? Does Sunstein think the prediction is valid? RI.11-12.2

4. Summarize the experiment described in paragraphs 3–5. What were its results on the individuals who participated? Examine the paragraphs that describe the experiment. What did the experiment investigate? How was it organized and conducted? What human tendency was demonstrated by its findings? RI.11-12.2

4 In almost every group, people ended up with more extreme positions. The Boulder groups favoured an international treaty to control global warming before discussion; they favoured it far more strongly afterwards. In Colorado Springs, people were neutral on that treaty before discussion; discussion led them to oppose it strongly. Same-sex unions became much more popular in Boulder and less so in Colorado Springs.

5 Aside from increasing extremism, discussion had another effect: it squelched diversity. Before members talked, many groups displayed internal disagreement. These were greatly reduced: discussion widened the rift between Boulder and Colorado Springs.

6 Countless versions of this experiment are carried out online every day. The result is group polarisation, which occurs when like-minded people speak together and end up in a more extreme position in line with their original inclinations.

7 There are three reasons for this. First is the exchange of information. In Colorado Springs, the members offered many justifications for not signing a climate treaty and a lot fewer for doing so. Since people listened to one another, they became more sceptical. The second reason is that when people find their views corroborated, they become more confident and so are more willing to be extreme. The third reason involves social comparison. People who favour a position think of themselves in a certain way and if they are with people who agree with them, they shift a bit to hold on to their preferred self-conception.

8 Group polarisation clearly occurs on the internet. For example, 80 per cent of readers of the leftwing blog Daily Kos are Democrats and fewer than 1 per cent are Republicans. Many popular bloggers link frequently to those who agree with them and to contrary views, if at all, only to ridicule them. To a significant extent, people are learning about supposed facts from narrow niches and like-minded others.

9 This matters for the electoral process. A high degree of self-sorting leads to more confidence, extremism and increased contempt for those with contrary views. We can already see this in the presidential campaign. It will only intensify when the two parties square off. To the extent that Democratic and Republican candidates seem to live in different political universes, group polarisation is playing a large role.

10 Polarisation, of course, long preceded the internet. Yet given people's new power to create echo chambers, the result will be serious obstacles not merely to civility but also to mutual understanding and constructive problem solving. The Daily Me leads inexorably also to the Daily Them. That is a real problem for democracy.

My Notes

⊘ Knowledge Quest

- Where does the writer address you as a reader directly?
- What details in the article most stand out for you?
- What questions do you have after reading the article?

corroborated: strengthened by evidence

inexorably: unstoppably

10 Tell students to pause at the end of paragraph 5. Ask students to make a tentative decision about whether the experiment being described constitutes sound evidence.

11 Tell students to pause after paragraph 8. Ask them to state or guess what the word *polarisation* (*polarization*) means based on the fact that there are two "poles" on opposite sides of the globe.

12 After reading the text for the first time, guide the class in a discussion by asking the Knowledge Quest questions. Check students' general comprehension of the text based on their observations, asking follow-up questions if needed.

Scaffolding the Text-Dependent Questions

5. **What arguable thesis (claim) does Sunstein make, and how does his description of the 2005 experiment in Colorado support that thesis?** Reread paragraphs 6–9. What is group polarization? When and where does it happen? What are the three reasons Sunstein offers for why it happens? Why does it matter? What does Sunstein suggest is wrong with the rise of the "Daily Me"? RI.11-12.1

6. **How does the image of "echo chambers" in paragraph 10 contribute to Sunstein's thesis?** Examine how Sunstein presents the image. If someone is in an echo chamber, whose voice does he or she hear? How do opposing ideas make their way into the chamber? What is the likely effect of the "echo chamber" on an individual's views? RI.11-12.6

13 **RETURNING TO THE TEXT:** Guide students to return to the text to respond to the text-dependent questions. Invite them to work in pairs to reread the text and answer the questions. Remind them to use text evidence in their responses.

14 Move from pair to pair and listen in as students answer the text-dependent questions. If they have difficulty, scaffold the questions by rephrasing them or breaking them down into smaller parts. See the Scaffolding the Text-Dependent Questions boxes for suggestions.

Returning to the Text

- Return to the editorial as you respond to the following questions. Use text evidence to support your responses.
- Write any additional questions you have about the text in your Reader/Writer Notebook.

2. **KQ** In paragraph 1, what does the word *prophesied* mean in context? What effect does it have on the tone?

The author uses the word *prophesied* to refer to the prediction made by a technology specialist about a new kind of newspaper that might emerge in the future. In this context, *prophesied* means *predicted*. The use of this word makes the tone of the editorial mysterious and serious.

3. Summarize the "Daily Me" situation Sunstein describes in paragraphs 1 and 2.

Sunstein references an observation by Nicolas Negroponte, a technology specialist who foresaw the emergence of a fully personalized newspaper (called the "Daily Me") that would give the reader information and opinions only about topics he or she is interested in or supports. Sunstein believes that that vision is becoming a reality through "the rise of social networking forums, collaborative filtering and viral marketing."

4. Summarize the experiment described in paragraphs 3–5. What were its results on the individuals who participated?

Participants in the experiment were interviewed about their opinions on politically controversial issues. They were then divided into groups with shared opinions. Each group discussed its views among its own members. Afterward, individuals were interviewed again and found to hold more extreme versions of the same positions than they had held before the group discussions.

5. What arguable thesis (claim) does Sunstein make, and how does his description of the 2005 experiment in Colorado support that thesis?

Sunstein puts forth the claim that people who filter news and opinions to support their beliefs adopt more extreme positions when exposed only to opinions with which they agree. In describing the Colorado experiment, he points out that while the "Boulder" and "Colorado Springs" groups at first supported or opposed certain positions, their convictions became stronger and less conciliatory after interaction with others who held similar beliefs.

Scaffolding the Text-Dependent Questions

7. What concession does Sunstein make in the article's final paragraph, and how does he address it to support his thesis? Examine paragraph 10. Remember that a *concession* is an admission that your opponent's position has a degree of merit. What does Sunstein believe is correct about his opponent's position, and what does he believe is flawed about it? RI.11-12.5

8. How does the editorial make its claim effectively? What claim does it make? What evidence does it provide? RI.11-12.1

6. How does the image of "echo chambers" in paragraph 10 contribute to Sunstein's thesis?

An "echo chamber" is a room with walls built to cause the repetition of sounds produced within it. Sunstein uses this image as an analogy to describe situations in which people hear only their own views "echoed" back to them; their views are never informed or revised by opposing ideas or viewpoints.

7. What concession does Sunstein make in the article's final paragraph, and how does he address it to support his thesis?

Sunstein concedes that polarization has always existed. At the same time, he reiterates the evidence provided by the Colorado experiment to support his thesis that, in the situation examined in the article, the polarization is intensified and creates "serious obstacles not merely to civility but also to mutual understanding and constructive problem solving" that becomes "a serious problem for democracy."

8. KQ How does the editorial make its claim effectively?

The editorial makes its claim effectively by presenting evidence from which it draws conclusions in support of a claim. Known as an inductive argument, it is effective because it provides evidence first for readers to see and guides them to draw a conclusion based on the evidence.

15 Have student pairs complete the graphic organizer in the Working from the Text section. Begin by reading the instructions and clarifying them as needed. Then lead a discussion to help the class articulate Sunstein's thesis. Instruct them to write the thesis at the top of their graphic organizer and then give them time to complete it.

3.5

Working from the Text

9. Revisit the annotations that you made of the reasons and evidence that Sunstein used to support his arguable thesis (claim). First, identify Sunstein's thesis and then record your annotations in the chart. Lastly, think about possible rebuttals for each using evidence from the text.

Thesis: Personalized news is a problem for American democracy.

Reasons and Evidence	Possible Rebuttals
People who personalize their news are not exposed to every side of an issue. Evidence: 80 percent of Daily Kos readers are Democrats	People are exposed to other sides of issues in the course of their daily lives (TV, news, conversations, etc.).
A study has shown that people who expose themselves only to views they agree with become more extreme in those views. Evidence: a 2000 study in Colorado	Not enough information is given about the study in the article to determine whether its methodology was sound.
The current presidential campaign is creating a high level of extremism and mutual contempt among voters. Evidence: patterns in Internet viewing habits	The "evidence" for this study is subjective and anecdotal.

Refuting an Argument

To refute an existing argument, authors rely on a variety of strategies of **refutation**. These strategies often "attack" different elements of an opponent's position. Some of the most common "attacks" include:

- **Attack on a claim:** Is the writer's claim relevant or arguable?
- **Attack on reasoning:** Does the evidence the writer uses logically support his or her conclusions?
- **Attack on evidence:** Is the evidence timely, accurate, and unbiased? Is there counterevidence?
- **Attack on assumption:** What does the writer assume to be true, and is that assumption accurate? (A writer's assumptions are often unstated.)

As You Read

- Highlight Potter's **concessions** and refutations.
- Circle unknown words and phrases. Try to determine the meaning of the words by using context clues, word parts, or a dictionary.

About the Author

Andrew Potter (b. 1972) is the former editor-in-chief of *The Ottawa Citizen*, a daily newspaper published in Ontario, Canada. He has a PhD in philosophy from the University of Toronto and is an associate professor at McGill University. Andrew coauthored the international bestseller *Nation of Rebels*, which was published in 2004.

My Notes

LITERARY VOCABULARY

A **concession** is an admission in an argument that the opposing side has valid points. A **refutation** is the reasoning used to disprove an opposing point.

ACTIVITY 3.5 continued

16 Cover the material in the Refuting an Argument section, either by reading it aloud or by having volunteers read it. Tell students that they should revisit this section as they examine the next text for refutations and concessions.

17 Read aloud the Literary Vocabulary box about concessions and refutations. Give simple examples of each as needed to make sure students understand the concepts.

Scaffolding the Text-Dependent Questions

10. In paragraph 1, what does the word *circulation* **mean in context? Why is circulation important to the newspaper industry?** What is being circulated? What happens if circulation stops altogether? RI.11-12.4

11. In the editorial's first two paragraphs, how does Potter use imagery and figurative language to present and refute his opponent's argument? Examine paragraphs 1 and 2 for figurative language. What images does Potter

evoke that are obviously not meant literally? What is his purpose in evoking them? How could they be restated literally? RI.11-12.4

12. Which structural element of an argument essay is exemplified by paragraph 4? How does it set the course for the text that follows? Explain. Does the text of paragraph 4 support or refute Potter's thesis? How does Potter address paragraph 4 in the text that follows? RI.11-12.5

18 Review the Knowledge Question with students. Remind them to think about their answer to the Knowledge Question as they read and build knowledge about the topic.

19 FIRST READ: Conduct a small-group reading of "The Newspaper Is Dying – Hooray for Democracy." Pause after paragraph 3 to ensure that students understand that they are reading an editorial with a thesis that disputes that of the first editorial in the activity. Help them locate the concessions and refutations they have come across so far and highlight them. Instruct them to continue doing this as they read the rest of the editorial. Also tell them to circle unknown words and phrases so they can locate them later and try to determine their meanings.

 TEXT COMPLEXITY

Overall: Very Complex
Lexile: 1390L
Qualitative: High Difficulty
Task: Moderate (Analyze)

20 As students are reading, monitor their progress. Be sure they are engaged with the text and circling unknown words and phrases as well as highlighting text that states concessions and refutations. Evaluate whether the selected reading mode is effective.

3.5

🔍 **KNOWLEDGE QUEST**

Knowledge Question: How do newspaper editorials make and refute claims?

My Notes

myriad: huge number of
ideological: beliefs-based

Editorial

The Newspaper Is Dying—Hooray for Democracy

Maclean's, April 7, 2008

by **Andrew Potter**

1   The Newspaper Audience Databank (NADbank) released its readership numbers for 2007 a couple of weeks ago, and for those of us in the industry it was grim reading: almost everywhere you look, circulation, ad revenues and page counts are down, which is why you can now fire a cannon through any given newsroom at midday and not have to worry about committing reportercide.

2   But unless you work in the business, is there any reason to be especially concerned? Each year may put another loop in the newspaper's death spiral, but the overall consumption of news is on the rise, almost entirely thanks to the **myriad** online sources. The Internet is eating the newspaper's lunch, but there's plenty of food on the buffet table.

3   In certain quarters, though, there is growing concern that the demise of the newspaper is a threat to democracy itself. The argument goes something like this: the economic logic of mass circulation meant a newspaper had to try to appeal to as many potential readers as possible. To do so, it brought together in one package a diverse set of voices, presenting each reader with ideas and perspectives that he or she might not otherwise have seen or sought out. This fostered the democratic values of curiosity, enlightenment and toleration, and the worry is that if the newspaper declines, so might democracy.

4   The sharpest version of this argument comes from Cass Sunstein, a law professor at the University of Chicago. In a recent column in the Financial Times, Sunstein fusses about the rise of what he calls the Daily Me, the highly personalized and customized information feeds that will allow you to "include topics that interest you and screen out those that bore or anger you." As Sunstein sees it, the Daily Me is the potential Achilles heel of democracy because of a phenomenon called group polarization: when like-minded people find themselves speaking only with one another, they get into a cycle of **ideological** reinforcement where they end up endorsing positions far more extreme than the ones they started with.

5   Group polarization is everywhere. It helps explain why, for example, humanities departments are so left-wing, why fraternities are so sexist, why journalists drink so much. But, for the most part, it isn't a problem (for

---

Scaffolding the Text-Dependent Questions

13. What claim does Potter make about group polarization in paragraph 5? Does he provide evidence for his idea, and if so, is it convincing? Reread paragraph 5. How does Potter regard Sunstein's position? Does Potter believe that group polarization is a threat to democracy? What evidence does he offer to support his

claim? Does that evidence do so? Why or why not? RI.11-12.1

14. How does the editorial make its claim effectively by refuting the claim made in the first editorial? What does it directly address? What concessions does it make? RI.11-12.1

democracy anyway), since we routinely come into contact with so many people from so many different groups that the tendency toward polarization in one is at least somewhat **tempered** by our encounters with others.

6   Yet Sunstein is worried that group polarization on the Internet will prove far more **pernicious**. Why? Because of the image of the blogosphere as a series of echo chambers, where every viewpoint is repeated and amplified to a hysterical pitch. As our politics moves online, he thinks we'll end up with a public sphere that is partisan and extreme, and as an example, he points out that 80 per cent of readers of the left-wing blog Daily Kos are Democrats, while fewer than one per cent are Republicans. The result, he claims, "will be serious obstacles not merely to civility but also to **mutual** understanding."

7   As upside-down arguments go, this one is ingenious. For decades, **progressive** critics have complained about the anti-democratic influence of the mass media, and that newspapers present a selective and highly biased picture of the world, promoting pseudo-arguments that give the illusion of debate while preserving the status quo. (Remember that the villain in *Manufacturing Consent*, the film about Noam Chomsky, was—wait for it—the New York Times.) And now that the Internet is poised to cast these lumbering dinosaurs of black ink and dead trees into the pit of extinction, we're supposed to say hang on, what about democracy?

8   There's a basic error here, paired with an equally basic misunderstanding of how the marketplace of ideas works. There is no reason at all to be concerned that 80 per cent of Daily Kos readers are Democrats, any more than to worry that 80 per cent of the visitors to McDonald's like hamburgers. Given what each of these outlets is selling, it would be bizarre if it were otherwise. What would be worrisome was if four-fifths of Democrats read only the Daily Kos, but there is absolutely no evidence that is the case.

9   Earlier this month, the Project for Excellence in Journalism, a think tank sponsored by the Pew foundation, released its fifth annual report (at journalism.org) on the state of the news media. For the most part, its analysis of the newspaper business confirmed the trends of declining circulation, revenues and staff. But with respect to public attitudes, the PEJ found that most readers see their newspaper as increasingly biased, and 68 per cent say they prefer to get their news from sources that don't have a point of view. The PEJ also found a substantial disconnect between the issues and events that dominate the news hole (e.g., the Iraq surge, the massacre at Virginia Tech) and what the public wants to see covered—issues such as education, transportation, religion and health. What this suggests, is, aside from some failings of newspapers, that readers go online in search of less bias, not the self-absorption of the Daily Me.

10   Nothing about how people consume media online suggests they are looking for confirmation of preexisting biases. In fact, we have every reason to believe that as people migrate online, it will be to seek out sources of information that they **perceive** to be unbiased, and which give them news they can't get anywhere else. The newspaper may be dying, but our democracy will be healthier for it.

INDEPENDENT READING LINK

Read and Connect
As you read daily from your self-selected news source, do you find yourself creating a kind of "Daily Me" by fully reading only those stories that support your personal interests or beliefs, or do you find yourself reading stories on a variety of topics and with varying viewpoints? Why are you employing this approach? Discuss your ideas with a partner.

My Notes

---

tempered: lessened
pernicious: quietly deadly
mutual: shared
progressive: politically liberal or left-wing
perceive: interpret

Scaffolding the Text-Dependent Questions

15. How do Potter's diction and syntax in paragraphs 4–7 create a tone that reflects his opinion of Sunstein's argument? How does Potter describe Sunstein's concerns in paragraph 4? What do his diction and syntax convey about those concerns? What do Potter's words imply about Sunstein as a person? RI.11-12.6

16. In paragraphs 8 and 9, why is Sunstein concerned that 80 percent of Daily Kos readers are Democrats? In paragraph 8, why does this fact not concern Potter? What evidence does Potter cite in paragraph 9? Return to paragraphs 8 and 9. Why is Sunstein worried that Democrats are learning facts only from like-minded others at the Daily Kos? How does Potter reframe Sunstein's concern? To what does Potter appeal in paragraph 9 to support his point? RI.11-12.1

ACTIVITY 3.5 continued

21 Tell students to pause at the end of paragraph 5 and have them explain what Potter means by this statement: "It helps explain why, for example, humanities departments are so left-wing, why fraternities are so sexist, why journalists drink so much." Prompt students to consider whether Potter is being serious, humorous, or both.

22 Tell students to pause after paragraph 7 and consider what Potter's reference to "progressive critics" implies about his own political worldview.

23 Make sure students attend to the Independent Reading Link. Direct them to write a short statement in their Reader/Writer Notebooks. The statement should address whether their daily independent reading is creating a "Daily Me" and why that is or isn't the case. To assess their independent reading, set a date to check for the statements in students' notebooks.

TEACHER TO TEACHER

This editorial is a good example of counterclaim/concession and refutation. Potter presents the counterclaim in paragraphs 3 and 4, and then after conceding that "polarization is everywhere," he begins his refutation. Potter attacks basic assumptions of Sunstein's thinking as part of his strategy of refutation.

TEACHER TO TEACHER

This passage would be a good place to demonstrate tactful ways to refute a writer's arguments without attacking the writer personally. Ask students:

- How does Potter refute Sunstein's arguments?
- Does Potter attack Sunstein personally?
- Do you think Potter's approach is effective? Explain.

---

24 After reading the text for the first time, guide the class in a discussion by asking the Knowledge Quest questions. Check students' general comprehension of the text based on their observations, asking follow-up questions if needed.

25 RETURNING TO THE TEXT: Guide students to return to the text to respond to the text-dependent questions. Invite them to work together in small groups to reread the text and answer the questions. Remind them to use text evidence in their responses.

26 Move from group to group and listen in as students answer the text-dependent questions. If they have difficulty, scaffold the questions by rephrasing them or breaking them down into smaller parts. See the Scaffolding the Text-Dependent Questions boxes for suggestions.

⊘ Knowledge Quest
- How does the title make you feel?
- What details in the article stand out to you?
- What ideas in the article impress you?

Returning to the Text
- Return to the editorial as you respond to the following questions. Use text evidence to support your responses.
- Write any additional questions you have about the text in your Reader/Writer Notebook.

10. **KQ** In paragraph 1, what does the word *circulation* mean in context? Why is circulation important to the newspaper industry?

The word *circulation* means "the number of copies of news publications that are sold."

Circulation is important to the industry because newspapers need to make money so they can

continue reporting news.

11. In the editorial's first two paragraphs, how does Potter use imagery and figurative language to present and refute his opponent's argument?

In paragraph 1, Potter writes that "you can now fire a cannon through any given newsroom

at midday and not have to worry about committing reportercide." That image is a metaphor

conceding that newspapers have far fewer staff and are on the decline. In paragraph 2, he

metaphorically restates the idea that the rise of the Internet has caused the decline of the

newspaper ("The Internet is eating the newspaper's lunch"), but by stating "there's plenty of

food on the buffet table," he sets up the foundation of his argument: that the decline of the

newspaper and growth of online news sources provide *more* opportunity for people to get

unbiased information, not less.

12. Which structural element of an argument essay is exemplified by paragraph 4? How does it set the course for the text that follows? Explain.

Paragraph 4 is a summary of Sunstein's argument from "How the Rise of the Daily Me

Threatens Democracy." Potter presents that summary as a counterargument to his own

thesis (that democracy is not threatened by the demise of the newspaper). In the paragraphs

that follow paragraph 4, Potter presents arguments and evidence intended to refute that

counterargument.

Scaffolding the Text-Dependent Questions

17. In Potter's conclusion, he claims that "nothing about how people consume media online suggests they are looking for confirmation of preexisting biases." Is his statement convincing? Explain. Examine paragraph 10 and think about the evidence Potter has presented in his editorial. What has he put forth to support his claim? Is it reliable? If so, what makes it sound? If not, what is wrong with it? RI.11-12.1

13. **What claim does Potter make about group polarization in paragraph 5? Does he provide evidence for his idea, and if so, is it convincing?**

Potter claims that group polarization is not a problem in our democracy. As a supporting argument, he presents the observation that we all routinely meet people who hold all sorts of opinions. This is not really evidence, at least not convincingly so, because he has no way of knowing what kinds of people each of us encounters regularly or whether we discuss political issues with them.

14. **KQ How does the editorial make its claim effectively by refuting the claim made in the first editorial?**

The editorial makes its claim effectively by presenting a counterclaim with a concession and refutation in response to the first editorial. This allows the writer to acknowledge what may be correct in the original editorial to show the audience that it is being given fair consideration.

15. **How do Potter's diction and syntax in paragraphs 4–7 create a tone that reflects his opinion of Sunstein's argument?**

Potter's diction (word choice) and syntax (sentence structure) create a tone that is consistently insulting and dismissive. He both trivializes ("fusses") and miscasts ("As upside-down arguments go, this one is ingenious") Sunstein's views. Potter also chooses words and sentences that create a tone of political ridicule, implying that Sunstein is a progressive who is "hysterical" and should not be taken seriously.

16. **In paragraphs 8 and 9, why is Sunstein concerned that 80 percent of Daily Kos readers are Democrats? In paragraph 8, why does this fact not concern Potter? What evidence does Potter cite in paragraph 9?**

Sunstein quotes the statistic that 80 percent of those who read the Daily Kos are Democrats. He is concerned that people are only reading news they agree with. Potter counters that the statistic does not mean that Daily Kos readers don't expose themselves to other viewpoints. Potter also quotes a report claiming that news consumers look not for confirmation of their own views but less overall bias.

27 Guide students to return to the Knowledge Quest question they discussed before reading. Ask students how their response to this question has changed or been deepened after both editorials.

28 Encourage students to continue building knowledge on this topic as suggested in the Independent Reading Link.

3.5

17. In Potter's conclusion, he claims that "nothing about how people consume media online suggests they are looking for confirmation of preexisting biases." Is his statement convincing? Explain.

His statement is not convincing. The only evidence he uses to support it

(a think tank report that states that "68 per cent say they prefer to get their

news from sources that don't have a point of view") is not reliable because

there is no description of how the survey went about determining what

objectively constitutes "bias."

INDEPENDENT READING LINK

Read and Discuss

You can continue to build your knowledge about editorials by reading these and other articles at ZINC Reading Labs. Search for keywords such as *editorial writing* or *opinion piece*.

 ZINC

✐ Knowledge Quest

With a partner, discuss how both of these editorials make claims, refutations, and concessions effectively. Be sure to:

- Refer to evidence from the editorials.
- Take turns speaking, responding, and asking one another follow-up questions.
- Ask clarifying questions.
- Write down notes and ideas about making claims, refutations, and concessions effectively.

3.5

Working from the Text

18. Most of Potter's editorial is dedicated to addressing Sunstein's claims in "How the Rise of the Daily Me Threatens Democracy." Use the chart to list and identify Potter's concessions and refutations in the form of quotations. Revisit the Refuting an Argument section to determine types of refutations (attacks).

Treatment of the Counterargument	Concession or Refutation? (If refutation, include type)
"Group polarization is everywhere."	concession
"We routinely come into contact with so many people from so many different groups that the tendency toward polarization in one is at least somewhat tempered by our encounters with others."	refutation (attack on a claim)
"What would be worrisome was if four-fifths of Democrats read only the Daily Kos, but there is absolutely no evidence that is the case."	refutation (attack on evidence)
"Readers go online in search of less bias, not the self-absorption of the Daily Me."	refutation (attack on assumption)

19. In a deductive argument, the author presents a thesis and then attempts to support it. In an inductive argument, the structure is reversed; evidence is examined, and then a conclusion is reached. Identify the structures of the Sunstein and Potter editorials as deductive or inductive. Cite textual evidence in your answer.

The Sunstein editorial uses deductive argument, although its thesis does not appear until after a fair amount of introductory text. He posits that there are severe problems with the "Daily Me" model of obtaining news, and then he proceeds to support his claim with evidence obtained through research (the "Colorado Springs/Boulder" experiment) and analysis (readership statistics for the Daily Kos). The Potter editorial uses an inductive structure, presenting evidence beginning in paragraph 5 and drawing its actual conclusion ("What this suggests, is, aside from some failings of newspapers, that readers go online in search of less bias, not the self-absorption of the Daily Me") after presenting refutations.

ACTIVITY 3.5 continued

29 Have the student groups complete the exercise in the Working from the Text section. Begin by reading the instructions and clarifying them as needed. Then lead a discussion to help the class fill in the first row of the graphic organizer before giving student groups time to complete the remainder of organizer and address student step 19.

30 Use the Focus on the Sentence task to help students begin sentences with subordinating conjunctions. Model the task by working together as a class to write a sentence beginning with *although*. Then have students complete the exercise independently.

ASSESS

Review students' graphic organizers from student step 18 in the Working from the Text section. Ensure that they have correctly identified each concession and refutation with the type of refutation also identified based on the information in the Refuting an Argument section.

ADAPT

If students need additional help identifying concessions, tell them that a synonym for *concession* is *agreement*. If they need additional help identifying refutations, pair them with students who grasp the concept and have them examine Potter's editorial while consulting the Refuting an Argument section.

To extend students' familiarity with conjunctions, ask them to review one or two informative articles that appeared in this unit or the previous two units and find examples of subordinating conjunctions. Suggest that students work in small groups to share and check their examples.

3.5

☑ Focus on the Sentence

Choose one of the two texts in this activity and write two sentences using text evidence that challenge a claim made by the article. Start the sentences with the subordinating conjunctions that follow.

While it is true that people have always preferred the company of those with whom they agree, I disagree with Sunstein when he says that the result of polarization will be a "serious obstacle not merely to civility but also to mutual understanding and constructive problem solving."

_____

Even though Potter tries to dispute the idea that "the blogosphere is a series of echo chambers" where people do not listen to things they do not want to hear, I disagree with him because of the compelling results of the study that Sunstein cites in his essay.

_____

Language Checkpoint:
Recognizing Frequently Confused Words   LC 3.5

Learning Targets

- Understand the difference between the frequently confused words *effect/affect*, *allusion/illusion*, and *loose/lose*.
- Build an awareness of other words that are frequently confused and use reference materials when necessary.
- Use frequently confused words correctly when writing and editing.

Preview

In this activity, you will differentiate between some similarly spelled and frequently confused words.

Recognizing Frequently Confused Words

Many words in the English language are frequently confused with one another, especially in writing. Even though readers might be able to figure out what is meant, writers' credibility suffers when they use incorrect words. Some commonly confused words include *effect* and *affect*, *allusion* and *illusion*, and *loose* and *lose*.

1. **Quickwrite:** Why might these words be easily confused in writing?

Effect/Affect

The key to keeping *effect* and *affect* straight is to look at how they are being used in the sentence. The word *effect* is usually a noun, and the word *affect* is usually a verb. Look at these examples related to the readings in Activity 3.4.

Aside from increasing extremism, discussion had another **effect**: it squelched diversity.

Here, *effect* is a noun representing a thing; it is not doing any action in the sentence. *Effect* is the correct choice.

Sunstein believes that group polarization will negatively **affect** democracy.

In this case, *will affect* is the verb in the sentence. It is a verb meaning "will influence" or "will change."

2. Add *affect* or *effect* to each sentence.

Reading a newspaper or other news source could definitely ___affect___ your view of politics.

Many teenagers want to have an ___effect___ on the world around them.

Hearing other people's perspectives can ___affect___ your understanding of your own culture.

Blogs are spaces where writers can express their views and have a positive ___effect___ on others.

PLAN

Materials: prepared sentences that misuse frequently confused words
Suggested Pacing: 1 50-minute class period

TEACH

1 Come to this activity prepared with some sentences that incorrectly use frequently confused words. They do not need to be the same words covered in this activity. Consider skimming through social media or the comments section of a website to find sentences with errors.

2 Put the sentences on the board and ask students if they notice anything wrong with the sentences. Work through a revision of the sentences as a group.

3 Review the Learning Targets and Preview with students.

4 Have a volunteer read the Introduction to the Recognizing Frequently Confused Words section. Give students one or two minutes to complete the **quickwrite**.

5 Invite students to share aloud their responses to the Quickwrite. Student responses should indicate that the words sound very similar, and writers might "sound them out" incorrectly.

6 Introduce the first set of words. Provide additional examples if needed.

7 Have students work through student steps 2 and 3 independently. Once they have written their explanations, they should confer with a partner and make sure their answers are correct.

College and Career Readiness Standards

Focus Standards:

L.11-12.3 Apply knowledge of language to understand how language functions in different contexts, to make effective choices for meaning or style, and to comprehend more fully when reading or listening.

L.11-12.4a Use context (e.g., the overall meaning of a sentence, paragraph, or text;

a word's position or function in a sentence) as a clue to the meaning of a word or phrase.

L.11-12.4b Identify and correctly use patterns of word changes that indicate different meanings or parts of speech (e.g., conceive, conception, conceivable).

L.11-12.5b Analyze nuances in the meaning of words with similar denotations.

8 Introduce the words *allusion* and *illusion*. Give students time to explore the meaning of the two words. If they do not immediately recognize the meaning of the allusion (or the allusion itself), give them time to look up the story of Achilles. This is a good opportunity to reinforce use of reference materials. Have students complete student steps 4 and 5 and check their responses with a partner.

SAT® CONNECTIONS

This activity provides practice with this important SAT skill: recognizing frequently confused words.

LC 3.5

3. Write two sentences, one using *affect* and one using *effect*. Then briefly explain how you knew which word to use.

   a. Reading that essay affected the way I think about the situation.
   The effect of reading that essay was immediate.

   b. In the first sentence, the word *affected* is a verb meaning "influenced." In the second sentence, *effect* is a noun meaning "result."

Allusion/Illusion

An allusion is an indirect reference to a person, event, or thing. Authors use allusions to help readers make connections to things they already know or to evoke certain feelings. For example, in "The Newspaper Is Dying—Hooray for Democracy," Potter makes the following allusion:

> As Sunstein sees it, the Daily Me is the potential Achilles heel of democracy because of a phenomenon called group polarization…

4. Briefly describe what Potter is alluding to. (Use one or more reference sources if necessary.) Why do you think he is making this allusion?

Potter is alluding to the Greek myth in which the hero Achilles has one vulnerable spot: his heel. The allusion adds weight to the claim that the Daily Me is something that makes democracy weak.

5. Now read the following sentence.

   > Sunstein's overreaction to expression gives readers the illusion of living in a country where people are forced to accept the same belief system as those around them.

   Use context clues to determine the meaning of the word *illusion*.

   illusion: a deceptive appearance or false belief

6. Use *illusion* or *allusion* to complete each sentence.

Some would say that the idea that democracy is under threat is merely an ___illusion___ .

Potter makes an ___allusion___ to classical myth.

Both authors are going to say the other's perception is an ___illusion___ and their opponent is wrong.

7. Choose one of the sentences and explain to your partner how you knew your answer was correct.

Loose/Lose

8. Use a dictionary to review the definition of the word *loose*, and then write a sentence that uses the word.

The child had a loose tooth.

9. Use a dictionary to review the definition of the word *lose*, and then write a sentence using the word

When did she lose her tooth?

Revising

Read the paragraph and choose the correct word in each sentence.

Voting is a right I'm looking forward to exercising this fall. As a senior in high school, I believe my vote has an [**effect/affect**] on my future. My grandfather, who was my idol, spent hours talking to me about politics when I was a kid. I didn't care much about what he had to say then. I just wanted to be with him, hear his deep voice, watch his bottom teeth pop forward when he got excited, and then see him suck them back in again as he grinned at me. I watched in anticipation as if it were a great [**illusion/allusion**] and not a side [**effect/affect**] of [**loose/lose**] dentures and a crazy sense of humor. He instilled in me a patience to hear out both sides of an issue before jumping to a conclusion and an interest in gathering information before choosing a side. He taught me that even though my candidate may [**loose/lose**], my choosing to use my voice is a victory. So here I am today— finally ready to vote. I am going to [**effect/affect**] my country for the better! I know that my grandfather cannot be with me when I go into the voting booth; however, he would be proud of my choice to stand up for what I believe in.

9 Students should work on student step 6 individually and then pair up to discuss why they chose their answers.

10 Introduce the terms *loose* and *lose*. This part of the activity reinforces the use of reference materials.

11 Students should complete the Revising section independently. Monitor their progress and offer guidance as needed.

12 Guide students to complete the Check Your Understanding and Practice tasks.

ASSESS

Have students share their responses to the Revising section with a partner. If partners' answers differ, guide them to discuss the correct answers. They should remember to look at reference materials for certainty.

Student responses to the Check Your Understanding task should show an awareness of what words they frequently confuse. The **Editor's Checklist** questions should be specific enough to be helpful in future assignments.

ADAPT

If students could benefit from more practice with frequently confused words, search for quizzes online. Many universities have free, easy-to-access quizzes available. Additionally, several websites have lists of frequently confused words for students to add to their Editor's Checklists.

☑ Check Your Understanding

What words do you commonly confuse? What question can you ask yourself about frequently confused words to make sure you've used the correct one? Identify at least three sets of words and write one question for each set. Add the questions to your Editor's Checklist. Add to your checklist as you discover more words that you frequently confuse.

Have I used *affect* as a verb and *effect* as a noun? Have I used *allusion* to mean an indirect reference and *illusion* to mean a false belief? Have I used *lose* as a verb and *loose* as an adjective?

Practice

Write a paragraph that explains which of Potter's arguments in "The Newspaper Is Dying— Hooray for Democracy" are most and least convincing. Include the words *effect, affect, effective,* and *ineffective* in your paragraph. You may refer to your responses to the Returning to the Text questions in Activity 3.5 as you compose your paragraph. Double-check for correct use of *effect, affect, effective,* and *ineffective.*

News or Views: A Closer Look

Learning Targets
- Examine a news story for credibility, bias, and accuracy.
- Research a timely and debatable issue.

Preview
While editorials openly present opinions, newspaper articles may appear objective until carefully examined for evidence that reveals a more subjective agenda. In this activity, you will read a news story and examine it for credibility, bias, and accuracy.

Examining Credibility and Accuracy
Credibility and accuracy are integral to any news story you're reading. A credible news story is one that's trustworthy and believable. *Accurate* means "factually correct."

Always make sure that the writer whose work you are reading is reliable. Some sources do not name their writers. This doesn't necessarily make a story unreliable, but it does mean that the credibility and accuracy of the source itself should be established.

When trying to determine whether a story is credible and accurate, ask questions such as:

- Who exactly wrote this story?
- Have I heard of the story's author or source?
- What kind of expertise or reputation does the author or source have?
- Are there facts in the story that I can verify independently?

If you don't know the answers to these questions, do some investigating. A good search engine can help you determine the credibility of a story's author or source. If the author's name is given, determine whether he or she has a reputation for credible, accurate reporting. Do similar research on the story's website or print source. Establish whether other reliable sources have used work from the author or source of your story. If so, the information is likely credible and accurate.

Examining Bias
We tend to think that news articles are objective, which means they are based on factual information. However, all news reports are to some extent subjective—or based on feelings or opinions—because they represent the reporter's analysis of the information surrounding the story's topic. Close analysis of the text's content, structure, and publication context can reveal subtle indications of bias in terms of how the writer frames the issue.

1. You will be assigned one of the following six types of bias. In your small group, paraphrase the explanation for your assigned type of bias. Next, generate several guiding questions you can use to discern whether your assigned type of bias is present in a given text.

Learning Strategies
Marking the Text
Paraphrasing
Quickwrite
Skimming/Scanning
Think Aloud

My Notes

ACADEMIC / VOCABULARY
Credibility is the quality of being believed or accepted as true, real, or honest.
Accuracy is the freedom from mistake or error.
Bias is a slanted attitude of either preferring or disliking something.

College and Career Readiness Standards
Focus Standards:

RI.11-12.1 Cite strong and thorough textual evidence to support analysis of what the text says explicitly as well as inferences drawn from the text, including determining where the text leaves matters uncertain.

RI.11-12.2 Determine two or more central ideas of a text and analyze their development over the course of the text, including how they interact and build on one another to provide a complex analysis; provide an objective summary of the text.

RI.11-12.5 Analyze and evaluate the effectiveness of the structure an author uses in his or her exposition or argument, including whether the structure makes points clear, convincing, and engaging.

ACTIVITY 3.6

PLAN
Materials: a class set of newspapers and/or access to online news sources
Suggested Pacing: 2 50-minute class periods

TEACH
1 Read the Learning Targets and Preview with students, making sure they understand that they will be exploring the concepts of credibility, bias, and accuracy.

2 Have volunteers read aloud the Examining Credibility and Accuracy section one paragraph at a time. After each paragraph is read, restate its main point. Those points should include:

- Credible = trustworthy and believable
- Accurate = factually correct
- Make sure a source's writer is reliable.
- If the writer is not named, make sure the source is reliable.
- To determine credibility and accuracy, ask questions and do some investigating.

3 **Vocabulary Development:** Using classroom resources and prior knowledge, have students define and identify connections between these terms: *objectivity, subjectivity, propaganda, opinion, perspective, prejudice, point of view, slant,* and *spin*. These words could be part of a class Word Wall.

4 Read aloud the explanatory text at the beginning of the Examining Bias section. Mention that bias is a type of both non-credibility and inaccuracy. Explain that some information is indeed bias-free, but students should always be on the lookout for bias when reading newspapers or news magazines (or watching TV/online news). Take students through the Types of Bias section by reading it aloud aloud or having volunteers do so.

3.6

My Notes

Types of Bias

A. Bias Through Selection and Omission

- An editor can express a bias by choosing to use or not to use a specific news item. For example, the editor might believe that advertisers want younger readers—they spend more money. Therefore, news of specific interest to old people will be ignored.
- Within a given story, details can be ignored or included to give readers or viewers a different opinion about the events reported. If, during a speech, a few people boo, the reaction can be described as "remarks greeted by jeers." Or the people jeering can be dismissed as "a handful of dissidents" or perhaps not even be mentioned.
- Bias through the omission of stories or details is very difficult to detect. Only by comparing news reports from a wide variety of outlets can this form of bias be observed.
- Bias in local news coverage can be found by comparing reports of the same event from different papers.

B. Bias Through Placement

- Readers of papers judge first-page stories to be more significant than those buried in the back. Television and radio newscasts run the most important stories first and leave the less significant to later. Where a story is placed, therefore, influences what a reader or viewer thinks about its importance and suggests the editor's evaluation of its importance.
- For example, a local editor might campaign against handgun ownership by giving prominent space to every shooting with a handgun and gun-related accident in his or her paper.
- Some murders and robberies receive front-page attention, while others receive only a mention on page 20.
- Similarly, where information appears within an article may also reveal evidence of bias. Because most readers only read the first few paragraphs of any given article, burying information at the end may work to suppress a particular point of view or piece of information, while placing it at the beginning emphasizes it. The opposite might be true as well; the end could reveal the writer's closing thought (and thus his or her personal bias) on the issue.

C. Bias by Headline

- Many people read only the headline of a news item. In addition, most people scan nearly all the headlines in a newspaper. As a result, headlines are the most-read part of a paper. They can summarize as well as present carefully hidden biases and prejudices. They can convey excitement where little exists, they can express approval or condemnation, and they can steer public opinion.

D. Bias by Photos, Captions, and Camera Angles

- Some pictures flatter a person; others make the person look unpleasant. A paper can choose photos to influence opinion about, for example, a candidate for election. Television can show film or videotape that praises or condemns. The choice of which visual images to display is extremely important. Newspapers run captions that are also potential sources of bias and opinion.

College and Career Readiness Standards

W.11-12.2a Introduce a topic; organize complex ideas, concepts, and information so that each new element builds on that which precedes it to create a unified whole; include formatting (e.g., headings), graphics (e.g., figures, tables), and multimedia when useful to aiding comprehension.

W.11-12.2b Develop the topic thoroughly by selecting the most significant and relevant facts, extended definitions, concrete details, quotations, or other information and examples appropriate to the audience's knowledge of the topic.

W.11-12.2c of the text, create cohesion, and clarify the relationships among complex ideas and concepts.

E. Bias Through Statistics and Crowd Counts

- To make a disaster seem more spectacular (and therefore worthy of reading), numbers can be inflated. "One hundred injured in train wreck" is more powerful than "Passengers injured in train wreck."

- Crowd counts are notoriously inaccurate and often reflect the opinion of the person doing the counting. A reporter, event sponsor, or police officer might estimate a crowd at several thousand if he or she agrees with the purpose of the assembly—or a much smaller number if he or she is critical of the crowd's purposes or beliefs. News magazines use specific numbers to enhance believability.

F. Bias by Source Control

- To detect bias, always consider where a news item "comes from." Is the information supplied by a reporter, by an eyewitness, by police or fire officials, by executives, by elected or appointed government officials? Each might have a particular bias that is presented in the story.

- Puff pieces are supplied to media outlets by companies or public relations directors—and even sometimes by the government (directly or through press conferences). The term *puff piece* comes from the word *puffery*, which means "overly flattering words about a topic." For example, the Avocado Growers Association might send a press release in the form of a news story telling of a doctor who claims that avocados are healthy and should be eaten by all. A food company might supply recipes for a newspaper's food section that recommends use of its products in the recipes. A country's tourist bureau will supply a glowing story, complete with pictures of a pleasant vacation. Recently, even government agencies have sometimes issued such releases.

- A pseudo-event is some event (demonstration, sit-in, ribbon cutting, speech, ceremony, ground breaking, etc.) that takes place primarily to gain news coverage.

- Similarly, the question of who is quoted in an article can point to bias. Be sure to consider who is quoted, what the quote seems to reveal or imply (negatively or positively) about the position, who is merely paraphrased, and what perspectives are unrepresented or remain silent in the article.

My Notes

Identifying Bias

2. Use the following graphic organizer to keep track of examples of the guiding questions each group developed for identifying bias. Then apply those questions to a sample newspaper article or online news source.

Bias Type	Guiding Questions	Examples
Bias Through Selection and Omission	Have they left out important details that might change our perspective?	
Bias Through Placement	Have they placed information at the end of a page or end of an article to deemphasize it?	

College and Career Readiness Standards

SL.11-12.1 Initiate and participate effectively in a range of collaborative discussions (one-on-one, in groups, and teacher-led) with diverse partners on grades 11–12 topics, texts, and issues, building on others' ideas and expressing their own clearly and persuasively.

Additional Standards Addressed:

RI.11-12.10

5 Divide the class into six groups and assign each a type of bias. Have them work within their groups to **paraphrase** the explanation of their type of bias. Next, each group should generate several guiding questions to discern whether their type of bias is present in a text. Then each group should share its questions so the class can complete the graphic organizer in the Identifying Bias section.

6 As a class, use the completed graphic organizer as a tool to analyze a sample print or online news story.

7 Read the As You Read section with students. Remind them to underline text that answers any of the guiding questions they have generated regarding bias and to circle unknown words and phrases so they can determine their meaning using context clues, word parts or a dictionary.

Bias Type	Guiding Questions	Examples
Bias by Headline	Does the headline express approval or condemnation?	
Bias by Photos, Captions, and Camera Angles	Do pictures show the subject in a flattering/unflattering way?	
Bias Through Statistics and Crowd Counts	Do numbers seem emphasized or downplayed?	
Bias by Source Control	Who gets to speak, and who is only paraphrased?	

As You Read

- Underline any text that answers one of the guiding questions your class generated.
- Circle unknown words and phrases. Try to determine the meaning of the words by using context clues, word parts, or a dictionary.

3.6

Article

Facebook Photos Sting Minnesota High School Students

The Associated Press

The Associated Press

1   EDEN PRAIRIE, Minn. — For 16-year-old Nick Laurent, walking out of Eden Prairie High School yesterday to protest the school's punishment of students seen partying on Facebook pages was about asking administrators to be fair.

2   More than a dozen students joined Laurent after learning of the walkout from fliers the junior handed out the day before. The students said school administrators overreacted to the **perception** that students in the photos were drinking.

3   "It's the loudest thing we could do," said Laurent, who organized the walkout but said he wasn't one of the students in the photos.

4   Laurent tried to make his point by passing out red plastic cups that were similar to those seen in some of the photos. He noted that it was impossible to see what was inside the cups, so administrators couldn't prove that students were drinking.

5   Laurent agreed that athletes and other students who sign a code of conduct to be involved in activities should face consequences if they break the rule against drinking alcohol. But he said the punishments were too harsh.

6   "They don't have (the) support of the students to hand out **arbitrary** punishments and punishments that don't fit the crime," he said.

7   Once the photos on the social-networking Web site came to the attention of administrators, 42 students were interviewed and 13 face some discipline over the pictures, school officials said.

8   School officials haven't said how the students were disciplined, but Minnesota State High School League penalties start with a two-game suspension for the first violation. Laurent and other students said they knew of classmates who were banned from their sports teams for five weeks.

9   Principal Conn McCartan did not return a call seeking comment on the walkout, but students said they expected they'd be punished.

10   In earlier statements, the school's principal said school officials did not seek out the pictures. But he didn't say who gave the school the photos.

My Notes

> perception: impression
> arbitrary: unreasonable

Scaffolding the Text-Dependent Questions

3. **Does the article's focus in paragraphs 1–3 make the article seem more or less objective? Why?** Examine the first three paragraphs. Who or what is focused upon? Does the focus concentrate on a source directly involved with the incidents the school is investigating? How does its inclusion affect the article's overall objectivity? Why? RI.11-12.1

ACTIVITY 3.6 continued

8 **FIRST READ:** Conduct an independent reading of "Facebook Photos Sting Minnesota High School Students." Pause after paragraph 5 and, as a class, summarize the situation being addressed in the article. You might also note the use of the word *sting* in the headline. Tell students that, as used here, the word means "a deception used to catch criminals." Ask students whether the word is accurate in this context or whether it indicates bias. What might that say about the credibility of the source?

▲ TEXT COMPLEXITY

Overall: Complex
Lexile: 1240L
Qualitative: Moderate Difficulty
Task: Challenging (Evaluate)

9 As students are reading, monitor their progress. Be sure they remain engaged with the text.

10 Based on the observations you make during the first reading, you may want to adjust the reading mode. For example, you may decide to group students differently for the second reading.

✦ TEACHER TO TEACHER

As a news story, this article can help students recognize how to use sources effectively, even in research papers. Remind them of these principles in quoting sources:

- Using a combination of quotations, paraphrases, and narration or commentary makes ideas easy to follow. This news story opens with two paragraphs of narration before quoting student Nick Laurent.

- Paraphrases speed the story along and keep the reader focused on the important details. The first time the school principal, Conn McCartan, is mentioned as a source is in paragraph 9. His words are paraphrased in paragraph 10 before being indirectly quoted (from an email to student families, not from a statement made to the reporter) in paragraph 11.

11 Tell students to pause at the end of paragraph 16. Ask them to imagine a scenario where images of the students partying came to the attention of school authorities.

- Who might have taken the pictures?
- What might have been done with the pictures?
- How might the administrators have seen them?

3.6

My Notes

11 "We do not go out looking at student social networking sites. We do however take action when we are given **legitimate** information about school or Minnesota State High School League violations," McCartan said in an e-mail to families of his students.

12 McCartan said interviews with students suggested, however, that the pictures might have been posted on such sites, and warned of the dangers.

13 "These sites are not private places," he wrote. "Their content forms a permanent and public record of conversations and pictures."

14 In an e-mail to parents and guardians, Superintendent Melissa Krull said, "We are not legally at liberty to discuss further details of this investigation."

15 Fourteen-year-old Ali Saley said cutting class for the cause was worth it. She held signs such as, "They walk or we do," in **solidarity** with the students who were punished. A few cars honked in support of the students as they gathered on a footbridge over the road in front of the school.

16 The Eden Prairie High School students who got into trouble ran afoul of a new reality: digital cameras and social networking sites make the entire world a public space.

17 It's becoming increasingly common for schools and potential employers to check social networking sites such as Facebook and MySpace, and to penalize kids or other people for what they find, said William McGeveran, a professor at the University of Minnesota Law School and an expert on data privacy.

18 "Facebook is largely a public space. Users don't always perceive it that way, but that's what it is," McGeveran said.

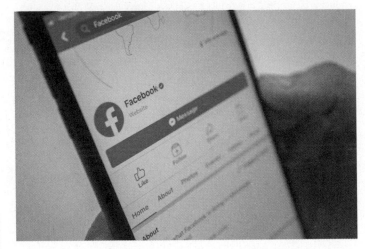

legitimate: real or true
solidarity: togetherness

Scaffolding the Text-Dependent Questions

4. How does the structure of the first half of the article support the writer's central idea that students are being punished unfairly? Which three people are approached in the first half of the article (paragraphs 1–14)? How much authority does each have over the situation being described? How does each of them respond to the reporter's attempts to investigate the situation? What conclusions can be drawn from this? RI.11-12.5

5. Examine the text of the student's sign in paragraph 15 of the article. What are some questions that readers might ask themselves to interpret the meaning of that text? What does the sign mentioned in paragraph 15 say? What questions might the sign's text raise? RI.11-12.1

3.6

19 Even when young people are cautious about what they put on the pages, he said, friends or acquaintances can post pictures of them in questionable situations without their knowing about it.

20 McGeveran cited research by the Pew Internet & American Life Project that suggested most teens were aware of the risks of posting personal information on the Internet. A report issued last month found that most teens restrict access to their posted photos and videos at least some of the time, and that few consistently share them without any restrictions.

21 "But some students are still foolish about what they put on their pages," he said.

22 Eden Prairie High School has about 3,300 students, and Facebook lists about 2,800 members in its network for the school, including more than 500 from the current senior class. A spot check on Jan. 9 showed that some had posted dozens and even hundreds of pictures of themselves and their friends. However, most members used a privacy setting to limit access to their profiles to friends and other authorized people.

23 Schools in Minnesota have limited ability to regulate the conduct of students after hours. When students participate in sports or certain fine-arts activities, however, they must agree in writing to abide by the long-standing rules of the Minnesota State High School League, which prohibit the use of alcohol, tobacco and controlled substances, even over the summer.

24 League spokesman Howard Voigt noted that parents must sign the forms, too, certifying that they understand the rules and penalties. Still, he said, complaints are common.

25 "We run into that all the time here—parents call and accuse us of being too hard on their kid," he said.

26 Voigt said there had been several cases of students' running afoul of league rules because of potential violations posted on social-networking sites.

27 It's not safe for kids to assume what they do in small groups won't be broadcast to the entire world, McGeveran said.

28 "I don't think most of us would have liked to have lived our teen years in an era of ubiquitous camera phones and social networking," he said. "It really changes the perception of what places are private and which ones aren't."

Making Observations
- What details in this article feel important to you?
- What words that the students use catch your attention?
- What questions do you have after reading the article?

My Notes

ubiquitous: ever-present

ACTIVITY 3.6 continued

12 Tell students to pause after paragraph 23. Discuss why administrators are allowed to hold students who participate in some extracurricular activities to a higher standard than other students and whether it's fair to these students to hold them to those standards.

13 After reading the text for the first time, guide the class in a discussion by asking the Making Observations questions. Check students' general comprehension of the text based on their observations, asking follow-up questions if needed.

Scaffolding the Text-Dependent Questions

6. How does the information provided by expert William McGeveran in paragraphs 17–21 and paragraphs 27–28 develop the central idea that social media sites are not private places? How does McGeveran describe Facebook? What research does he cite? What warning does he give near the end of the article? RI.11-12.2

7. What questions might you ask after reading the article to learn more about Eden Prairie High School students' social lives, social media, and private spaces? Skim the article. How does the author describe the social interaction of the high school students? What social activities and social media sources are mentioned? What does this tell you about the students? What questions does it raise for you about how the students interact with each other? RI.11-12.1

14 RETURNING TO THE TEXT: Guide students to return to the text to respond to the text-dependent questions. Invite them to work independently to reread the text and answer the questions. Remind them to use text evidence in their responses.

15 Move among the students and observe as they answer the text-dependent questions. If they have difficulty, scaffold the questions by rephrasing them or breaking them down into smaller parts. See the Scaffolding the Text-Dependent Questions boxes for suggestions.

3.6

Returning to the Text

- Return to the article as you respond to the following questions. Use text evidence to support your responses.
- Write any additional questions you have about the text in your Reader/Writer Notebook.

3. **Does the article's focus in paragraphs 1–3 make the article seem more or less objective? Why?**

Those paragraphs focus on a student named Nick Laurent. Laurent is not personally involved in the incidents the school is investigating. He is at no risk for any disciplinary action due to those incidents and is joining in the walkout because he believes in its cause. Beginning with his story adds balance to the school's side of the issue presented later, thus making the article seem more objective.

4. **How does the structure of the first half of the article support the writer's central idea that students are being punished unfairly?**

The first half of the article is structured in a way to show rising hierarchy—from student to principal to superintendent. The author focuses on Laurent for the first eight paragraphs and then shifts in paragraph 9 to the principal, who was not available for comment, and in paragraph 14 to the superintendent, who says she is not "legally at liberty" to discuss the investigation. This contrasts the openness of the students to the silence of the school administrators and supports the idea that the administrators aren't being fair.

5. **Examine the text of the student's sign in paragraph 15 of the article. What are some questions that readers might ask themselves to interpret the meaning of that text?**

The text of the sign is "They walk or we do." Questions might include: "Who are 'they'?" "Who are 'We'?" "In what sense or senses is the word *walk* intended?" "What is meant by 'we do'?"

6. **How does the information provided by expert William McGeveran in paragraphs 17–21 and paragraphs 27–28 develop the central idea that social media sites are not private places?**

McGeveran reinforces the idea by stating Facebook is "largely a public space." He cites research that most teens are aware of the risks but says a few "are still foolish." At the end of the article, he warns that kids cannot assume that what they do in small groups "won't be broadcast to the entire world."

16 Read aloud student steps 8 and 9 in the Working from the Text section. Have the students return to their groups and collaboratively answer their guiding questions. They should choose spokespeople for their groups to participate in the discussion afterward, with individual students allowed to contribute as they wish.

7. What questions might you ask after reading the article to learn more about Eden Prairie High School students' social lives, social media, and private spaces?

What non-school social activities are common for high school students? What social

networking sites are popular among the students? What advantages do the students see in

using those sites? What roles do the sites play in social interaction? What roles to those sites

play in planning non-school student activities?

Working from the Text

8. In preparation for group work, revisit the annotations that you made while you read.

9. Meet with your group to examine the article for credibility, accuracy, and bias by collaboratively answering the guiding questions you established at the start of this activity. Be prepared to discuss your findings with the rest of the class.

Guiding Question #1: Who exactly wrote this story?

Response #1: No specific reporter's name is given. It is attributed to the Associated Press.

Guiding Question #2: Have I heard of the story's author or source?

Response #2: Yes.

Guiding Question #3: What kind of expertise or reputation does the author or source have?

Response #3: The Associated Press has been rated as unbiased by at least two independent

bias-checking groups: Media Bias/Fact Check and AllSides. Internet research shows no

discernable claims against the credibility or accuracy of the AP.

Guiding Question #4: Are there facts in the story that I can verify independently?

Response #4: Coverage in sources such as ABC News and the *Minneapolis Star Tribune*

squares with the AP report. There are also people named in the article who could be contacted.

17 Make sure students attend to the Independent Reading Link. Direct them to find and share at least two types of bias from their self-selected news source. They should note and explain these examples in their Reader/Writer Notebooks. To assess their independent reading, set a date to check for examples in students' notebooks.

18 Get students started on the Focus on the Sentence activity by reading the directions for the exercise. Make sure that they understand that they are to use the conjunctions *because, so,* and *but* one time each in their three sentences. Consider asking volunteers to read their sentences aloud or write them on the board.

19 Pair students to complete the Examining Sources exercise. Remind them to brainstorm with their partners, select their issue independently, and write an independent answer to the question. You might want to quickly review definitions of the terms bias, credibility, and accuracy before they begin.

20 Give students time to respond to the Writing Prompt. Consider allowing them to work in pairs to compose their informational articles.

ASSESS

Review students' informational articles. Ensure that they have included adequate topic statements, developed the topic as instructed, and used varied transitions and sentence structure to indicate relationships between ideas.

ADAPT

If students need additional help responding to the Writing Prompt, have them pair up to choose and analyze a topic about which to provide information. They should revisit the text and exercises that pertain to developing a topic through the use of quotes, examples, and details. They should also review what has been covered in this activity concerning transition words and sentence constructions.

3.6

🔲 INDEPENDENT READING LINK

Read and Discuss

Review several stories in your self-selected news source. Find examples of at least two types of bias. Share these examples with your peers. Explain how each example exemplifies the bias.

My Notes

☑ Focus on the Sentence

Write three sentences about bias (or lack of bias) in "Facebook Photos Sting Minnesota High School Students." Use the transitional words *because, but,* and *so* one time each in your sentences.

because: Some people might think that the article is biased against the school because it doesn't explain the school's legal obligations.

so: The students named in the article might think it is biased against them, but there is no real indication of that.

but: The report gives both sides of the issue, so I think we can assume it is unbiased.

Examining Sources

With a partner, brainstorm possible topics for a short informational article. They should be timely, debatable, and significant to your school or local community or have national importance. Then, on your own, select an issue from your brainstorm list. Examine relevant informational sources and choose two or three that are appropriately bias-free, credible, and accurate.

Why do you believe your sources are trustworthy?

✍ Writing Prompt: Informational

Use your sources to write a short informational article about your chosen issue. Be sure to:

- Introduce a topic statement that states the issue and your view on its significance.
- Develop the topic by selecting direct quotations, specific examples, and concrete details from source texts.
- Use varied transitions and sentence construction to show the relationships among ideas.

WRITING PROMPT: INFORMATIONAL

The following standards are addressed in the writing prompt:

- W.11-12.2a
- W.11-12.2b
- W.11-12.2c

The Bias of Rhetoric

© 2021 College Board. All rights reserved.

Learning Targets

- Analyze how language can be used to inform and shape the perception of readers or viewers.
- Analyze the effects of rhetorical devices on the way the text is read and understood.

Preview

In this activity, you will analyze an editorial to learn how its author uses language to shape readers' perspective.

Slanting Reader Perception

1. **Quickwrite:** While the previous activity focused on how writers can construct the "truth" of their subject via their choices regarding content and structure, this activity focuses on how language itself can be used to shape the reader's perception of the subject. View the advertisement selected by your instructor. Then in a Quickwrite, identify what elements from the advertisement contribute to its power. Record your response in your Reader/Writer Notebook.

2. Sometimes a writer compensates for a lack of evidence and logical argumentation by using slanted language and emotional appeals that present a prejudiced depiction of a subject. This happens so often that there are names for these various **slanters**. As you read through the following techniques, try to think of examples from the media that fit the descriptions. Determine whether the language in the examples contains figurative, connotative, or technical meanings. (Adapted from Brooke Noel Moore and Richard Parker's *Critical Thinking*, 8th ed., 2007)

Types of Slanters

A. Labeling (Euphemisms and Dysphemisms)

Labeling is the use of a highly connotative word or phrase to name or describe a subject or action, a technique also called using **loaded language** or a **question-begging epithet**. When the connotations are positive (or less negative), the writer is using **euphemism**. For example, car dealers try to sell "pre-owned vehicles" rather than "used cars." In the opposite case, when the connotations are negative, the writer is using **dysphemism**. Consider, for example, the differences between these terms: *freedom fighter, guerrilla, rebel,* and *terrorist. Freedom fighter* is a euphemism, while *terrorist* is a dysphemism.

B. Rhetorical Analogy

Rhetorical analogy is the use of a figurative comparison (sometimes a simile or a metaphor) to convey a positive or negative feeling toward the subject. For example, in the 2008 presidential race, Sarah Palin suggested (via a joke) that she was like a pit bull with lipstick.

C. Rhetorical Definition

Rhetorical definition is the use of emotionally charged language to express or elicit an attitude about something. A classic example is defining capital

Learning Strategies

Discussion Groups
Marking the Text
Note-taking
Paraphrasing
Quickwrite
Rereading
SMELL

LITERARY

Slanters are rhetorical devices used to present the subject in a biased way, either positively or negatively.

My Notes

_____

_____

_____

_____

_____

_____

_____

_____

_____

_____

_____

_____

_____

College and Career Readiness Standards

Focus Standards:

RI.11-12.1 Cite strong and thorough textual evidence to support analysis of what the text says explicitly as well as inferences drawn from the text, including determining where the text leaves matters uncertain.

RI.11-12.4 Determine the meaning of words and phrases as they are used in a text, including figurative, connotative, and technical meanings;

analyze how an author uses and refines the meaning of a key term or terms over the course of a text (e.g., how Madison defines faction in Federalist No. 10).

RI.11-12.6 Determine an author's point of view or purpose in a text in which the rhetoric is particularly effective, analyzing how style and content contribute to the power, persuasiveness, or beauty of the text.

ACTIVITY 3.7

PLAN

Materials: video clip of "Peace, Little Girl" (1964 presidential campaign television spot), Internet access

Suggested Pacing: 2 50-minute class periods

TEACH

1 Read the Learning Targets and Preview with students. Tell them that they will be examining how writers use language (including rhetorical devices) to shape the perceptions of their audience.

2 Open class by showing the 1964 political ad "Peace, Little Girl," which Lyndon B. Johnson used to suggest that electing Barry Goldwater would lead to nuclear war. The video can be readily found online. One source is the LBJ Library and Museum.

3 Explain the context of the ad (the presidential election). Although the ad only aired once, it was very controversial and was run repeatedly on news programs throughout the campaign season. It is believed to have played a major role in Goldwater's defeat. Ask students for their initial reactions to the spot. What images, sounds, or dialogue affected them? Why?

4 Ask students to identify what elements contribute to the power of "Peace, Little Girl." Then ask them to explain why they think this ad was pulled after only one airing.

5 Explain that while the ad presents an extreme example, writers often use inflammatory rhetorical techniques (slanters) in place of logical arguments to manipulate an audience into accepting a position.

6 **Vocabulary Development:** Review the meaning of the term *slanters* with students. Have them work in pairs to define the term in their own words. Help students generate examples of slanters, which can come from literature, the media (as the LBJ ad exemplifies), or their personal experiences.

7 Read aloud the content of the Slanting Reader Perception section. Instruct students to complete the **quickwrite** and read the introductory material to slanters presented in student step 2. Tell them that they will be using the definitions of slanters to analyze the editorial text in this activity and others throughout the unit.

8 Cover the information in the Types of Slanters section. Have volunteers read aloud the text about each type of slanter and write the example of each on the board. Guide the class to provide an extra example or two of each type.

My Notes

punishment as "government-sanctioned murder." A rhetorical definition stacks the deck either for or against the position it implies.

D. Rhetorical Explanation

When an opinion is expressed as if it were fact and is expressed in biased language, it is a rhetorical explanation. For example, you might say someone "didn't have the guts to fight back" when taunted by another person. This paints the person as motivated by cowardice. Or you might say the person "took the high road instead of taking a swing."

E. Innuendo

Innuendo is the use of language to imply that a particular inference is justified, as if saying "go ahead and read between the lines!" In this way, the speaker doesn't have to actually make a claim that can't be supported; instead, the audience is led to make the leap on their own. For example, a presidential candidate might say, "Think carefully about whom you choose; you want a president who will be ready to do the job on day one." The implication is that the opposing candidate is not ready.

F. Downplayers

Downplayers are qualifier words or phrases that make someone or something look less important or significant. Words like *mere* and *only* work this way, as does the use of quotation marks, to suggest a term is ironic or misleading. For example: "She got her 'degree' from a correspondence school." Often these are linked to concessions with connectors such as *nevertheless*, *however*, *still*, or *but*.

G. Hyperbole

Hyperbole is the use of extravagant overstatement that can work to move the audience to accept the basic claim even if they reject the extremes of the word choice. Many of the other slanters can be hyperbolic in how they are worded; the key element is that the statement or claim is extreme. For example, in response to a dress code, a student might say, "This school administration is fascist!"

H. Truth Surrogates

Using a truth surrogate is hinting that proof exists to support a claim without actually citing that proof. For example, ads often say "studies show," and tabloids often say things like "according to an insider" or "there's every reason to believe that ..." If the evidence does exist, the author is doing a poor job of citing it; meanwhile, the author has not actually identified any source—or made any claim—that can be easily disproven or challenged.

I. Ridicule/Sarcasm

Ridicule and sarcasm are uses of language that suggest that the subject is worthy of scorn. The language seeks to evoke a laugh or sarcastically mock the subject.

College and Career Readiness Standards

SL.11-12.1 Initiate and participate effectively in a range of collaborative discussions (one-on-one, in groups, and teacher-led) with diverse partners on grades 11–12 topics, texts, and issues, building on others' ideas and expressing their own clearly and persuasively.

Additional Standards Addressed:

RI.11-12.10

Presenting a Slanter

Your teacher will divide you into small groups. With your group, select a slanter from the list. Then work together to complete the following tasks:

- Compose a paraphrased definition of your slanter.
- Study the list's example(s) of your slanter and brainstorm at least three additional examples.
- Discuss and evaluate each brainstormed example.
- As a group, choose which examples most clearly communicate the meaning of your slanter. Narrow your examples to a single choice.
- Create a brief skit using your chosen example to demonstrate the meaning of your slanter along with one or two questions for your audience about what the slanter is and how it is used to influence an audience.
- Present your skit to the class and invite volunteer classmates to answer your question(s). Be prepared to clarify the nature of your slanter as necessary.
- Allow your classmates to evaluate the effectiveness of your skit at communicating the meaning of your slanter.

☑ Check Your Understanding

Write down the slanter example that you used in your presentation. Then rewrite it in a way that conveys the same information in literal, neutral, or straightforward language.

As You Read

- Highlight any slanters you recognize in the editorial and note what kind of slanter each one is.
- Circle unknown words and phrases. Try to determine the meaning of the words by using context clues, word parts, or a dictionary.

About the Author

Raymond A. Schroth, SJ, is a Jesuit priest, journalist, and Jesuit Community Professor of Humanities at Saint Peter's College. He is the author of six books and an award-winning media critic for the *National Catholic Reporter*. Schroth also holds the position of editor emeritus at *America*.

🔲 INDEPENDENT READING LINK

Read and Discuss

Review several stories in your self-selected news source and find examples of at least two types of slanting. Share these examples with your peers. Explain how each example exemplifies bias. Tell the group whether you think the writer's techniques are effective and explain your reasons.

My Notes

---

9 Break students into nine small **discussion groups** and assign one of the slanters from the Types of Slanters to each group (or allow them to choose their slanter, as long as they are all covered). They are to use their slanter in completing the seven bulleted tasks in the Presenting a Slanter section.

10 Direct students to the Independent Reading Link and have the groups further discuss types of slanting and examples of bias found in students' self-selected new sources.

11 After groups present their skits and obtain feedback, give them time to individually respond to the Check Your Understanding task. Students should turn in their rewritten examples, and those examples should indicate an understanding of slanters.

★ TEACHER TO TEACHER

More political ads can be found on the Internet, including on the Museum of the Moving Image's website The Living Room Candidate. Consider having student pairs choose and analyze an ad. Pairs should each create a **double-entry journal** that lists the slanters in the first column and a description of how the ad uses each slanter in the second column. After pairs complete their analyses, have them share their findings with the class.

12 Direct students to the As You Read section. Remind them to circle unknown words and phrases as they read and try to determine the meanings of the words by using context clues, word parts, or a dictionary. Instruct them to also highlight any slanters they recognize in the text and note what type each one is.

13 **FIRST READ:** Conduct a shared reading of "Abolish High School Football!" Tell students to pause after reading the question in paragraph 1. Have them discuss which answer Schroth is implying to be the correct one and how they know what he means.

TEXT COMPLEXITY

Overall: Very Complex
Lexile: 1570L
Qualitative: Moderate Difficulty
Task: Challenging (Evaluate)

TEACHER TO TEACHER

Rather than have students write out full slanter names, consider assigning letters from the list in this activity to each type (i.e., A = labeling, B = rhetorical analogy, C = rhetorical definition, etc.). It may be helpful to list all types, A–I, with or without definitions or examples, on a handout or on the board for students to reference while they read.

The list (and possible examples) might look like this:

A (labeling): "bulk up" for "get big or fat," "bedazzled heroes"

B (rhetorical analogy): "kings of the corridors"

C (rhetorical definition): "concussion"

D (rhetorical explanation): "They [classes or libraries] were irrelevant."

E (innuendo): Saying "some football players are very bright" reinforces stereotype of football players as not very bright.

F (downplayer): "weird" in quotes (description meant as an understatement); "so-called educational institution"

G (hyperbole): the scenario in which the victim "dies"; "bashing their helmeted heads into one another as thousands cheer"

H (truth surrogate): the author's assertion that high school football players are given special treatment by fellow students, teachers, and parents

I (ridicule): mocks the town that values football too much

3.7

My Notes

Editorial

Abolish High School Football!

NJ.com, September 20, 2007

by **Raymond A. Schroth**

1 Are you sure playing high school football is good for your son?

2 I had doubts long before I read the report in the New York Times (Sept 15) that of the 1.2 million teenagers who play high school football, an estimated 50 percent have suffered at least one concussion, 35 percent two or more. Since 1997, throughout 20 states, 50 boys have died.

3 A concussion is a blow to the head that smashes the brain against the skull. Because their brain tissues are less developed, adolescents are most **vulnerable**. The victim feels "weird," has splotchy vision, falls to the ground, vomits, goes into a coma, dies. If he survives he suffers depression, he can't concentrate, drops out, and/or develops symptoms later in life.

4 Worst of all, the young men overwhelmingly told the reporter that if they thought their heads had been damaged they would never tell the coach, because he might take them out of the game.

5 I've felt high school football did more harm than good since I taught high school in the 1960s, since I began getting an inkling of the damage done young bodies in both high school and college, where linemen are encouraged to "bulk up" to a grotesque 300 pounds in order to do more damage to the enemy—to say nothing of the damage done to their own late adolescent bodies by getting so fat.

6 Football, especially in high school, distorts the goals of the so-called educational institution that sponsors it, turns ordinary boys into bedazzled heroes, tells them they're the kings of the corridors, coddled by teachers afraid to flunk them, as their parents try to live out their glamorous dreams over the broken bodies of their children bashing their helmeted heads into one another as thousands cheer.

7 Buzz Bissinger's 1990 bestselling *Friday Night Lights*, a popular book, film, and TV series, was, in the long run, an **indictment** of the small Texas town with nothing going for it but its high school football team. If the town had a library, churches, a theater, a park—if the school had any classes—we never saw them. They were **irrelevant**.

8 The boys went to high school to play, feeding **delusions** that they would be noticed by a scout who would get them college scholarships and contracts on pro teams.

9 But, you say, if high schools drop football, that will deprive colleges and the pros of their feeder system. Right. It will also deprive colleges of many who have come for only one reason—to play—while their paid tutors ease them through the motions of an education.

> **vulnerable:** easily hurt
> **indictment:** strong criticism
> **irrelevant:** not important
> **delusions:** false beliefs

Scaffolding the Text-Dependent Questions

3. Is Schroth's evidence in paragraph 2 subjective or objective? How can you tell, and what purpose does the evidence serve? Reread paragraph 2. What evidence in the paragraph is measurable? Is the source reliable? Why or why not? What central idea do the statistics support? RI.11-12.6

4. Quote and describe the slanters Schroth uses in paragraph 3. Do they make his editorial more or less convincing? Reread paragraph 3. How does Schroth define a concussion? How is this definition slanted? What is slanted about his description of the effects of concussion? How does his use of slanters affect the reader's trust? RI.11-12.6

10 But, you say, some football players are very bright. Absolutely right. I have taught three in recent years who were the best in the class, straight A's, a delight to have in the room. But they are exceptions to the rule, and few and far between.

11 Without football, how can ambitious athletes thrive? They can play soccer, basketball, baseball, tennis, lacrosse, and squash. They can run, swim, row, sail, wrestle, and bike. They can also read, write for the paper, act, sing, dance, walk, and pray. And when they graduate their brains will be enriched, not bruised.

12 The Times article quotes Kelby Jasmon, a high school student in Springfield, Ill., walking around today with two concussions, who says there is "no chance" he would tell the coach if he gets hit hard and symptoms return. "It's not dangerous to play with a concussion," he says. "You've got to sacrifice for the team. The only way I come out is on a stretcher."

13 If the school officials and his parents read that and leave him on the field, something is very, very wrong.

My Notes

Making Observations
- Based on your highlights, what are some words that describe how the author feels about high school football?
- Which sentence stands out most to you?

© 2021 College Board. All rights reserved.

Scaffolding the Text-Dependent Questions

5. **State examples of ridicule and sarcasm in paragraphs 7 and 9. What effects do they achieve? Do they make Schroth's argument more convincing or less so?** Reread paragraphs 7–9. Whom or what is Schroth mocking in paragraph 7? Which word might be read aloud sarcastically in the second part of paragraph 9? How do these elements affect your support of Schroth's argument? RI.11-12.6

6. **Read and analyze paragraph 10. Is Schroth presenting straightforwardly objective evidence, or does he use a slanter? Explain?** Reread paragraph 10. Remember that *objective* means "unbiased" or "impartial." What does he state about the academic ability of his three examples? How does he regard those examples? What does this imply about his thoughts about the academic ability of athletes in general? RI.11-12.1

ACTIVITY 3.7 continued

14 As students are reading, monitor their progress. Be sure they are engaged with the text, annotating words and phrases that show slanters, and watching for unknown words and phrases.

15 Tell students to pause after paragraph 4. Ask students why the writer labels the concern expressed here the "worst of all" and whether they agree or disagree with that appraisal.

16 Have students stop after reading paragraph 10. Ask a volunteer paraphrase that paragraph and then ask the class to state what the writer's opinion seems to be about the likelihood of a student being good at both academics and athletics.

17 Evaluate whether the selected reading mode is effective. Based on the observations you make during the first reading, you may want to adjust the reading mode. For example, you may decide for the second reading to read aloud certain complex passages, or you may group students differently.

18 After reading the text for the first time, guide the class in a discussion by asking the Making Observations questions. Check students' general comprehension of the text based on their observations, asking follow-up questions if needed.

19 RETURNING TO THE TEXT: Guide students to return to the text to respond to the text-dependent questions. Invite them to work in small groups to reread the text and answer the questions. Remind them to use text evidence in their responses.

20 Move between groups and listen as students answer the text-dependent questions. If they have difficulty, scaffold the questions by rephrasing them or breaking them down into smaller parts. See the Scaffolding the Text-Dependent Questions boxes for suggestions.

LEVELED DIFFERENTIATED INSTRUCTION

In this activity, students might need support in understanding some of the text's references and terms.

Beginning English language learners may lack prior knowledge of *Friday Night Lights*, the role of athletic scouts, and the term *feeder system*. Conducting the second read using **reading roles** will give students an opportunity to pose questions about these references and usages. Assign students who you feel may understand these terms to the role of Clarifier.

Developing Allow students at these levels Internet access to research any of the text's references and terms with which they may be unfamiliar. Pair students as appropriate and guide them as needed in choosing appropriate and useful search terms.

3.7

Returning to the Text

- Return to the editorial as you respond to the following questions. Use text evidence to support your responses.
- Write any additional questions you have about the text in your Reader/Writer Notebook.

3. Is Schroth's evidence in paragraph 2 subjective or objective? How can you tell, and what purpose does the evidence serve?

Schroth's evidence in those paragraphs is objective. It consists mostly of neutral and factual language. He gives statistics about concussions and concussion-related deaths among high school football players. This information spells out some of the dangerous effects of high school football to support Schroth's notion that it should be done away with.

4. Quote and describe the slanters Schroth uses in paragraph 3. Do they make his editorial more or less convincing?

Schroth uses rhetorical definition ("A concussion is a blow to the head that smashes the brain against the skull") and hyperbole ("The victim ... falls to the ground, vomits, goes into a coma, dies. If he survives he suffers depression, he can't concentrate, drops out"). The emotionally charged language and overstatement probably make his editorial less convincing for some people.

5. State examples of ridicule and sarcasm in paragraphs 7 and 9. What effects do they achieve? Do they make Schroth's argument more convincing or less so?

In paragraph 7, Schroth mocks "the small Texas town with nothing going for it but its high school football team." By extension, anyone who sees merit in the town as it is portrayed is likewise being ridiculed. In paragraph 9, "Right" is used sarcastically, implying that the counterclaim it addresses is laughable. Both of these word choices make Schroth's case less objective and convincing.

6. Read and analyze paragraph 10. Is Schroth presenting straightforwardly objective evidence, or does he use a slanter? Explain.

At first glance, it may seem that Schroth is being objective. After all, he does describe three high school players as "best in the class, straight A's." However, he also notes that he met those students over a period of "recent years" and that they are "exceptions to the rule, and few and far between." He is suggesting that few high school football players are also good students.

Scaffolding the Text-Dependent Questions

7. In paragraph 12, what kind of slanter does Schroth cite from *The New York Times* article? How does his use of it impact the effectiveness of his conclusion in paragraph 13? Reread paragraphs 12 and 13. How does the student quoted in paragraph 12 regard his two concussions? What sort of statement is that? What point does Schroth make by using that statement in the following paragraph? RI.11-12.6

7. In paragraph 12, what kind of slanter does Schroth cite from *The New York Times* article? How does his use of it impact the effectiveness of his conclusion in paragraph 13?

Schroth quotes high school football player Kelby Jasmon as downplaying his two concussions,

vowing, "The only way I come out is on a stretcher." Jasmon is using a rhetorical expression

implying that football is more important than his safety. Schroth's use of the quote is an

example of what he is decrying, and it strengthens his conclusion.

Gaining Perspectives

You have heard one person's opinion of why football should be banned in high school. With a partner, imagine you are a principal in a school who has a meeting with a parent regarding the safety of student football players. Compare a variety of online sources to gather information about the possible dangers. Then role-play talking with a parent in the school about your research as you negotiate and work together to reduce the safety and health risks for not only football players but all student-athletes. When you are done, summarize the outcome of the discussion in your Reader/Writer Notebook.

Working from the Text

Introducing the Strategy: SMELL

SMELL is an acronym for sender, message, emotional strategies, logical strategies, and language. This strategy is useful for analyzing persuasive texts by asking five key questions:

- **Sender-receiver relationship**—What is the sender-receiver relationship? Who are the images and language meant to attract? Describe the speaker (or writer) of the text.
- **Message**—What is the message? Summarize the thesis of the text.
- **Emotional Strategies**—What is the desired effect?
- **Logical Strategies**—What logic is being used? How does it (or its absence) affect the message? Consider the logic of images as well as words.
- **Language**—What does the language of the text describe? How does it affect the meaning and effectiveness of the writing? Consider the language of images as well as words.

8. In pairs, use the SMELL strategy to analyze this editorial. You have already done some work in the language section of the strategy.

Sender–Receiver Relationship	To whom is the writer explicitly addressing his argument?	
	How does he seem to feel about that target audience?	
	What values does the sender assume readers share or argue that they should share?	

21 Direct students' attention to the Gaining Perspectives task and read it aloud. Allow pairs access to online sources that can help them gather information. Allow pairs time to practice their role play and write the outcome of their discussion in their Reader/Writer Notebooks and then ask volunteers to share their role play with the class.

22 Review the SMELL reading strategy and then have students use it in pairs to analyze the text using the first graphic organizer. Discuss their findings in a large group discussion and have them complete student step 9.

23 Ask student pairs to choose two specific passages from the essay and revise them to be less slanted using the graphic organizer in student step 10. As time permits, they should discuss the impact the changes have on the article's tone and on its persuasiveness. Then ask each pair to share a particularly effective revision with the whole class.

24 Give students time to respond to the Check Your Understanding task. Consider allowing them to remain in their pairs as they Quickwrite responses to the Essential Question.

ASSESS

Review students' responses to the Check Your Understanding Quickwrite. Be sure they demonstrate a growing awareness of how slanters are used to advance opinions.

ADAPT

If students need additional help understanding how bias helps shape our society's media, have each of them revise a slanted passage to remove bias and then give it to a partner. Partners should read the passages and provide written notes for revision with the goal of eliminating slanters from the passages. Students can then revise again according to that feedback.

3.7

Message	What is a literal summary of the content?	
	What is the article's ultimate thesis regarding the subject?	
Emotional Strategies	What emotional appeals does the writer include?	
	What seems to be his desired effect?	
Logical Strategies	What logical arguments or appeals does the writer include?	
	What is their effect on the readers' perception?	
Language	What specific language/slanters are used in the article to support the message or characterize the opposition?	
	What is their effect on the readers' perception?	

9. Review what you have ascertained about the author's use of language (especially slanted language and rhetorical devices). Write a short paragraph in your Reader/Writer Notebook stating how that language use shapes the perception of the reader.

10. Copy two of the more slanted passages from Schroth's editorial and revise them to be more neutral and less rhetorically manipulative.

Original Passage	Revised Passage
The victim feels "weird," has splotchy vision, falls to the ground, vomits, goes into a coma, dies. If he survives he suffers depression, he can't concentrate, drops out, and/or develops symptoms later in life.	Victims of concussions may feel "weird" and can experience splotchy vision as well as lack of balance or coordination. Long-term effects can include depression and an inability to concentrate. Extreme cases can result in death.

☑ Check Your Understanding

Quickwrite: Respond to the Essential Question: What is the role of media in our society, and how can we become responsible consumers and producers of information in a digital age?

Putting It All Together

Learning Targets

- Examine how the target audience affects a writer's choices in diction, syntax, and tone.
- Evaluate an author's use of print and graphic features to support an argument.

Preview

In this activity, you will read and analyze a Pulitzer Prize–nominated editorial from the *Star Tribune*.

Reading an Editorial

As you read through the following guidelines for reading editorials, paraphrase each of the points by writing a word or two in the margins that will help you to remember the point.

a. Examine the headline, sub-headline, and related cartoon (if it exists). What will this editorial be about? What guesses or assumptions can you make about the author's perspective at this point?

b. Look at the author's name and affiliation, if given. What do you know about the author's background and/or potential bias at this point? Is the author or source credible?

c. Read the first two to three paragraphs very carefully. What issue is the author discussing, and what is his or her stance on this issue?

d. Once you have determined the author's stance on the issue, stop reading for a moment or two. What is the other side to the issue? Who might think differently? What are one or two reasons that you know that might support other side of the author's stance?

e. Continue reading the editorial. What are two of the strongest pieces of evidence that the author uses to support his or her side of the issue? Why are they effective or ineffective?

f. Did the author persuade you? Did the author address or refute the main objections of the opposition? Give an example. What did he or she not address? Why might the author have chosen not to address this element? Do you think the author was fair to the other side? Why or why not?

g. Can you detect any biases? Has the author left out any important details that may have changed your perspective? Has any information been placed at the end of the editorial to deemphasize it? Who is or is not quoted in the editorial?

h. Go back through the editorial and circle slanters and other rhetorical devices. How do these words affect your feelings about the issue? About the author?

i. If the author were standing right next to you now, what would you say to him or her?

Learning Strategies

Graphic Organizer
Quickwrite
Predicting

My Notes

ACTIVITY 3.8

PLAN

Materials: editorials of your choice or students' choices, Internet access
Suggested Pacing: 2 50-minute class periods

TEACH

1 Read the Learning Targets and Preview with students, making sure they understand that they will be examining how writers make choices with their target audience in mind.

2 Read aloud the informational text in the Reading an Editorial section. You may choose to have volunteers read each paragraph aloud. Pause after each paragraph to make certain students understand its content and clarify the text as necessary. Assist them with their **paraphrasing**, modeling as needed how to write their marginal notes.

College and Career Readiness Standards

Focus Standards:

RI.11-12.1 Cite strong and thorough textual evidence to support analysis of what the text says explicitly as well as inferences drawn from the text, including determining where the text leaves matters uncertain.

RI.11-12.3 Analyze a complex set of ideas or sequence of events and explain how specific individuals, ideas, or events interact and develop over the course of the text.

RI.11-12.4 Determine the meaning of words and phrases as they are used in a text, including figurative, connotative, and technical meanings; analyze how an author uses and refines the meaning of a key term or terms over the course of a text (e.g., how Madison defines faction in Federalist No. 10).

3 Read aloud the text of the Print and Graphic Features section. Describe or display examples of each type of feature as needed to ensure students understand the different types discussed.

4 Have students read and write a response to the Making Predictions Based on Text Features task.

5 Read aloud the As You Read section.

6 Have students read the About the Author section. Then reread the first two points in the Reading an Editorial section. Invite students to share their thoughts about the author's credibility, perspective, and potential bias. Encourage them to make notes in the margin.

My Notes

Print and Graphic Features

When reading editorials and other news articles, you might find the following print and graphic features:

- **Text divisions** such as introductions, summaries, sections with headings, footnotes or endnotes, and information about the author.
- **Graphics** that present information in a visual format, such as diagrams, charts, tables, graphs, maps, timelines, and so on. Graphics support the information and ideas presented in the text.
- **Special formatting** such as boldface, italics, numbered or bulleted text, or the use of different typefaces and sizes. For example, in this list, the types of text features are placed in boldface to draw attention to them.

Making Predictions Based on Text Features

1. Before you read, look at the title, section heads, and graphics and predict what the text is about.

As You Read

- As you read, underline examples of information that is represented in a graphic.
- Circle unknown words and phrases. Try to determine the meaning of the words by using context clues, word parts, or a dictionary.

About the Author

Jill Burcum has been a member of the Editorial Board at the *Star Tribune* since 2008. Her series of editorials highlighting the poor conditions of Bureau of Indian Education schools titled "Separate and Unequal" was a 2015 Pulitzer Prize finalist for editorial writing. Burcum started her career as a reporter for the *Rochester Post-Bulletin* after graduating from the University of Washington. She writes on a broad range of topics including health care, water quality, and American Indian issues.

College and Career Readiness Standards

RI.11-12.6 Determine an author's point of view or purpose in a text in which the rhetoric is particularly effective, analyzing how style and content contribute to the power, persuasiveness, or beauty of the text.

RI.11-12.7 Integrate and evaluate multiple sources of information presented in different media or formats (e.g., visually, quantitatively) as well as in words in order to address a question or solve a problem.

SL.11-12.1 Initiate and participate effectively in a range of collaborative discussions (one-on-one, in groups, and teacher-led) with diverse partners on grades 11–12 topics, texts, and issues, building on others' ideas and expressing their own clearly and persuasively.

Additional Standards Addressed:

RI.11-12.10

Editorial

Separate and Unequal: Indian Schools, a Nation's Neglect

by **Jill Burcum from the** *Star Tribune*

Part one of four parts: Better futures aren't built by indifference, but that's how the federal government treats dilapidated tribal schools to which it owes resources. The results are tangible.

1 LEECH LAKE INDIAN RESERVATION, MINN.—"Watch. This is the coolest moment of my day," science teacher Allison Barta says, unlocking the door to her classroom at the Bug-O-Nay-Ge-Shig High School.

2 Inside, a freshwater aquarium takes up much of the back wall, providing the only light in the windowless space. For a moment, the room resembles an environmental science lab. Then Barta flips on the lights.

3 This is what years of federal neglect look like at schools such as Bug-O-Nay-Ge-Shig—part of the 183-school federal Bureau of Indian Education system (BIE).

4 Barta's classroom is housed in a rodent-infested building with a shockingly long list of problems: a roof that caves in under heavy snowfall, a failing heating system that has many students wearing coats and blankets in class as soon as the weather turns and a sewer system that backs up during extreme cold—all adding to the discomforts and indignities of an aging, metal "pole barn" that has to be evacuated when wind gusts top 40 miles per hour.

5 In an era when educators emphasize science, technology, engineering and mathematics as keys to students' future success, Barta's science room has no lab tables and few microscopes, and no storage for hazardous materials needed for basic lessons. The ventilation and electrical systems are **antiquated**.

6 At Bug-O-Nay-Ge-Shig in northern Minnesota—and on reservations across the country—the educational promises this nation made to tribes are being broken. It is a policy of disgraceful **indifference**, leaving generation after generation of American Indian children struggling to build better lives.

7 The decrepit conditions at Bug-O-Nay-Ge-Shig are not unusual in the BIE system, which sprawls over 23 states and 64 reservations. Many of the schools serve some of the nation's poorest and most remote communities. Test scores for the system's 49,079 students lag those of both Indians and non-Indians in

My Notes

Source: NCompass Technologies
Star Tribune

antiquated: outdated
indifference: lack of interest

ACTIVITY 3.8 continued

TEACHER TO TEACHER

Students should be aware that although the writer of this editorial is known, she is still writing as a representative of a publication, and the text may represent the views, and therefore the possible biases, of that publication. Remind them that it is always a good idea to research a writer's news organization to help determine its reputation for credibility and accuracy.

7 FIRST READ: Conduct a shared reading of "Separate and Unequal: Indian Schools, a Nation's Neglect." Pause after the italicized text at the beginning and determine the purpose of that special formatting. Instruct students to underline that example of a graphic feature and to underline other graphic features in the editorial as they read.

TEXT COMPLEXITY

Overall: Accessible
Lexile: 1190L
Qualitative: Moderate Difficulty
Task: Moderate (Analyze)

8 As students are reading, monitor their progress. Be sure they are engaged with the text and annotating examples of graphic features.

My Notes

public schools. Yet the estimated $1.3 billion needed to put all BIE schools into good condition has long failed to materialize.

8 For more than a decade, school officials and leaders of the Leech Lake Band of Ojibwe have tried to convince federal officials that Bug-O-Nay-Ge-Shig needs to be rebuilt. Plans for a project with a price now estimated at $27 million were completed four years ago. Hopes rose across the reservation in August when U.S. Interior Secretary Sally Jewell toured the school. Jewell, whose Department of the Interior is the parent agency for the BIE and the Bureau of Indian Affairs, came just two months after President Obama traveled to North Dakota's Standing Rock Reservation and repeatedly underscored his commitment to tribal relations and education.

9 But at Bug-O-Nay-Ge-Shig, the cold reality for the 100 students is that no date has been set—or likely is close to being set—for replacing the school building. Nor does it appear that improvements will come soon enough to spare another generation from having to endure the 62 other BIE schools rated in poor condition.

10 They are not the only schools in America in disrepair—about 3 percent of public school facilities are in similarly poor condition, according to the National Center on Education Statistics—but a far greater share of BIE schools has been ignored.

11 Funding for replacement schools, improvements and repairs to BIE schools has fallen by 76 percent over the past decade. Despite its rhetoric about various tribal relations initiatives, the Obama administration has ignored the system's fundamental need for safe, functional schools. Even more frustrating, the administration is standing by while BIE learning environments fall drastically behind those of the other federal K-12 system: Department of Defense (DOD) schools serving children of military families and civilian employees.

12 The DOD launched a $5 billion construction surge in 2010 to renovate or replace 134 of its 181 schools by 2021. Seventeen new schools have been completed, 23 are under construction and 37 are in the design phase.

13 In contrast, the Interior Department has requested just $3.2 million in replacement school construction funding for one Indian school in 2015. Funding for new BIE schools over the past four years totaled $39 million—less than the cost of one large DOD elementary school that will open next year in Virginia.

14 The Interior Department also zeroed out its budget requests for BIE school replacement construction in 2013 and 2014—more evidence that the agency and the Obama administration's Office of Management and Budget view the BIE system as nothing more than a place to find savings.

15 No American should begrudge the investment in DOD schools: Our military families deserve the best. But under the watch of Obama, Jewell and Education Secretary Arne Duncan, the BIE system has increasingly and inexcusably become what advocates for Indian schools and U.S. Rep. Betty McCollum, D-Minn., have described as "separate and unequal."

16 On South Dakota's Pine Ridge Indian Reservation, which has four deteriorating BIE schools, former tribal President Cecilia Fire Thunder summed up what many tribal students, educators and leaders are wondering about federal officials: "Why aren't they fighting for us?"

Culture in education

17 The BIE school system enrolls about 10 percent of Indian students nationally—with the remainder generally attending local public schools. But the slender enrollment figures belie the essential role these schools play in Indian education. Because of the remote locations of reservations, BIE schools are the only hope for many students. Indian languages and history also typically play a more central role in BIE school curricula, helping to preserve valued traditions nearly eradicated by decades of misguided U.S. government policies.

18 The culture-at-the-core approach is critical for students like Charles Raisch, 17, who felt out of place at the sports-focused public high school near his home in Deer River, Minn. So Raisch, who hopes to become a car mechanic, transferred to Bug-O-Nay-Ge-Shig, where a school day that includes tanning hides, learning to speak Ojibwe or harvesting wild rice helps him make friends and focus on his regular classwork.

19 The smaller school—named for Chief Hole-In-The-Day—and the focus on Raisch's culture has helped him deal with stress and has made him appreciate his heritage. He now often starts his day by walking into the woods near his home to offer tobacco, a sacred plant, to the Creator. He also likes working with younger kids during cultural activities. On a recent trip to nearby Mud Lake to harvest wild rice, Raisch was one of the older boys helping elementary school students in and out of canoes.

20 Knowing that the younger kids look up to him inspires Raisch to work harder at school. At what is affectionately known as the Bug school, he said, "I feel better and more positive overall."

21 Indian leaders believe a culture-rich education can help combat social ills plaguing their communities, such as high rates of drug and alcohol use, crime and suicide.

22 "By going back to our ceremonies and sweat and purification lodges and moving back to the reservation, many people are finding balance again," Pine Ridge's Fire Thunder said. "Our culture is what grounds us, and this is what is going to save us.

My Notes

GRADUATION RATES

Graduation rates for ethnic groups from 1999 through 2010.

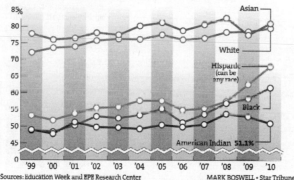

Sources: Education Week and EPE Research Center   MARK BOSWELL • Star Tribune

9 Tell students to pause at the end of paragraph 16. Have them explain the purpose of the editorial's first section and why the writer probably felt it was a good idea to begin with that particular information.

Scaffolding the Text-Dependent Questions

2. **Reread paragraphs 1–16 and summarize the conditions of BIE schools across the United States. How do you feel about the conditions of these schools?** What words and phrases does the author use to make you feel this way? How do the word choices influence your feelings on the topic? RI.11-12.4

3. **Why does Burcum choose to include the personal story of student Charles Raisch in her editorial? What is the intended effect on readers' perceptions of BIE schools?** What does the story illustrate? RI.11-12.6

My Notes

A national disgrace

23 Federal neglect is handicapping learning at BIE schools nationwide, according to a 2014 report commissioned by Jewell and Duncan. But students in the Upper Midwest and the Southwest may be suffering the most.

24 Those two regions have the nation's largest clusters of BIE schools—the legacy of being home to large, influential Indian nations that ceded land and signed treaties with the U.S. government as settlers pushed west in the mid-1800s. The federal government assumed educational obligations as part of this exchange for tribes' ancestral lands. The government's ongoing trust responsibilities are recognized in modern law and unchanged by the advent of tribal casinos. In any case, there aren't enough profitable casinos to fund the BIE system's construction needs.

25 As deplorable as the conditions are at Bug-O-Nay-Ge-Shig, Minnesota is fortunate that it's the only one of the state's four BIE schools currently in poor condition. The others are in Onamia, Cloquet and White Earth.

26 Twenty-eight of Arizona's 54 BIE schools are listed in poor condition, and two—Cove Day School and Little Singer Community School—have been on the BIE's priority replacement list for a decade. BIE officials who oversee the Arizona schools say there's little they can do.

27 "They keep telling us that Congress doesn't have the money," said Deborah Belone, who oversees Cove as well as Red Rock Day School, another school in such disrepair that it needs replacement. In addition to mold, a faulty roof, a failing cooling system, asbestos and an inadequate number of classrooms for a growing student body, Red Rock's dated electrical system is so overloaded that teachers can't use their classroom "smartboards," the modern equivalent of a chalkboard, all at the same time.

CONSTRUCTION FUNDING FALTERS

Replacement school construction funding for schools in the Bureau of Indian Education system has dropped sharply over the past decade. Funding for construction is handled by the deputy assistant secretary for management in the assistant secretary for Indian Affairs department.

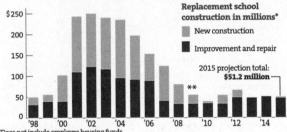

*Does not include employee housing funds.
**2009 figures exclude federal stimulus dollars for school replacement.
Source: Department of the Interior

MARK BOSWELL • Star Tribune

Scaffolding the Text-Dependent Questions

4. What can a reader learn from the bar graph titled "Construction Funding Falters"? What effect is achieved by the inclusion of the graphic feature? How does it support the ideas in the text? RI.11-12.7

10 Tell students to pause after paragraph 28. Invite a volunteer to summarize the relationship between the BIE and Congress as it is being presented by the author.

Schools without books

28 Ten of South Dakota's 22 BIE facilities, and four of North Dakota's 11 schools, are also considered in poor condition, generally meaning that the backlog of needed repairs or renovations is so extensive that it's more economical to put up a new structure.

29 At the Little Wound K-12 school in Kyle, S.D., part of the elementary school still in use was built in 1939. The nurse's office for a school serving about 800 kids is on an auditorium stage; there's no other place for it.

30 The middle school is housed in two structures, one of which is a pole barn that was supposed to be temporary but is now 21 years old. To get to classes in the barn, eighth-graders like Shadow Red Owl, George Killsback and Ryder Tobacco pass through a covered walkway frequented by bats and draped with hanging electrical cables. School officials aren't sure if a nearby portable classroom—which has boarded-up windows, a rotted foundation and an obscenity spray-painted on it—has been condemned yet.

31 But elementary Principal Ardis Iron Cloud doesn't dream of a fancy new facility or high-tech computer labs. She simply wants her students to have access to books. "If you want to raise reading scores," Iron Cloud said, "you have to have a library."

Blaming Congress

32 Asked how the inaction on BIE school construction squares with the Obama administration's commitment to Indian education, Interior Secretary Jewell blamed Congress.

33 "I will not promise what I cannot deliver, and tribal leaders and educators have heard me say this, because I've had conversations with them about the budget atmosphere in which we work in Washington, D.C.," Jewell said. "We have a huge problem on our hands, a problem that is not easily solved. But I want to do what I can administratively, and that means I will continue working with my colleagues in the Cabinet and working with leaders and tribes to see what we can do with the hand that we're dealt right now to begin to make a real difference for Indian children."

34 Jewell's frustration with Congress is fair. Interior belongs to the part of the federal budget hit hard by automatic spending reductions made as part of Washington's 2011 debt ceiling deal. In 2013, these cuts to BIE totaled $58 million.

35 Congress funded BIE school replacement construction at more robust levels during the administration of former President George W. Bush—hitting a high-water mark of $140 million in 2004.

36 Minnesota's Democratic U.S. Sen. Al Franken, who has held field hearings on BIE schools' plight, has publicly urged Jewell to ask for additional funding in fiscal 2016, the budgetary details of which are being worked out right now and are not yet public. Sen. Jon Tester, D-Mont., chairman of the U.S. Senate Committee on Native Affairs, has held hearings on deteriorating schools.

My Notes

11 After reading the text for the first time, guide the class in a discussion by asking the Making Observations questions. Check students' overall general comprehension of the text based on their observations, asking follow-up questions as needed.

12 Make sure students attend to the Independent Reading Link. Direct them to read an editorial from their self-selected news source and to write an analysis of the editorial using the graphic organizer in the Working from the Text section (which is based on the questions in the Reading an Editorial section from earlier in this activity). Have them write their analysis in their Reader/Writer Notebooks. To assess their independent reading, set a date to check for their analyses in their notebooks.

My Notes

That Jewell hasn't been before the committee in 18 months, while her agency is tardy in replies to inquiries from members, has been noticed.

37 Tester's message to Jewell couldn't be clearer: Get going and give us a plan. "The BIE must work with tribes to develop a comprehensive long-term plan to address the education needs of Native students. The **infrastructure** needs at BIE schools are incredibly serious, and it is critical that the BIE's next budget proposal include a plan to address the dismal state of so many BIE schools across Indian Country," he said.

"A better future"

38 Even with a plan, getting funding approved is a daunting challenge, which is why Jewell needs to personally sell it once it's developed. She'll need help from Education Secretary Duncan, whose agency is larger and more influential. The two also need to forcefully advocate for other funding solutions, including one devised by a Minneapolis banker that has already been partly passed by Congress. It would allow tribes to tap into private financing to replace school buildings.

39 If Duncan is serious about addressing educational **disparities**, which has been a focus of his, he can't be absent without leave on the buildings in which some of the nation's most disadvantaged students are trying to learn.

40 It isn't just Indian nations that have placed their trust in Jewell's agency. States that are home to large Indian populations, like Minnesota with its seven reservations and four Indian communities, are depending on BIE schools to educate a new generation of citizens and workers with skills critical for the future.

41 Kids shivering in thin-walled classrooms or studying under leaky roofs year after year aren't getting the education they need or deserve. With the larger community's visible neglect all around them, they receive the wrong message about the value of education.

42 During his June visit to North Dakota, Obama inspired the crowd when he said, "We can break old cycles. We can give our children a better future." Providing BIE students with adequate schools is the place to start.

🔲 INDEPENDENT READING LINK

Read and Connect
Read an editorial from your self-selected news source. Use the Working from the Text questions in this activity to write an analysis of the editorial.

---

infrastructure: system of public works

disparities: fundamentally different qualities

Making Observations

- What print and graphic features did you notice in the text?
- What is one detail from the graphs and map you noticed that someone else might have missed?
- What questions do you have after reading the editorial?

Scaffolding the Text-Dependent Questions

5. What is the claim being made in this editorial, and what evidence is used to support it? How does the evidence support the claim? RI.11-12.1

6. How do the author's examples about individuals contribute to her claim over the course of the text? How does seeing personal stories add to the data and statistics in the article? RI.11-12.3

7. What events does the author describe in order to support her claim? How are the events connected to one another? RI.11-12.3

Returning to the Text

- Return to the editorial as you respond to the following questions. Use text evidence to support your responses.
- Write any additional questions you have about the text in your Reader/Writer Notebook.

2. Reread paragraphs 1–16 and summarize the conditions of BIE schools across the United States. How do you feel about the conditions of these schools? What words and phrases does the author use to make you feel this way?

Sixty-three of the 183 BIE schools have fallen into disrepair, and there is no funding to start

the much needed repairs. The author uses words and phrases such as "rodent-infested

building with a shockingly long list of problems" to make the reader feel concern for the

students and "disgraceful indifference" to influence their feelings toward the government.

3. Why does Burcum choose to include the personal story of student Charles Raisch in her editorial? What is the intended effect on readers perceptions of BIE schools?

Burcum may have included Charles Raisch's story to illustrate for her readers the importance

of the "culture-at-the-core" approach to education at the BIE schools on the lives of American

Indian students.

4. What can a reader learn from the bar graph titled "Construction Funding Falters"? What effect is achieved by the inclusion of the graphic feature?

The bar graph visually represents the decline of funding for the construction of new schools

and the repairs of existing schools.

5. What is the claim being made in this editorial, and what evidence is used to support it?

Burcum claims that BIE schools are being neglected by the federal government. She supports

her claim by reporting on the state of these schools and providing facts about the decline

of funding.

6. How do the author's examples about individuals contribute to her claim over the course of the text?

The author uses examples of individuals such as teacher Allison Barta and student Charles

Raisch to contribute to her claim that Indian schools are separate from and unequal to other

schools in the United States. The individual examples show the effect of these schools on both

teachers and students.

13 RETURNING TO THE TEXT: Guide students to return to the text to respond to the text-dependent questions. Invite them to work in pairs to reread the text and answer the questions. Remind them to use text evidence in their responses.

14 Move from pair to pair and listen in as students answer the text-dependent questions. If they have difficulty, scaffold the questions by rephrasing them or breaking them down into smaller parts. See the Scaffolding the Text-Dependent Questions boxes for suggestions.

15 Lead a class discussion about students' completed Working from the Text graphic organizer and the three bulleted questions that follow it.

16 Have students complete the Check Your Understanding Quickwrite individually.

LEVELED DIFFERENTIATED INSTRUCTION

In this activity, students might need support explaining the difference between an editorial and a news article.

Developing Place students into small groups and have them use the **Conversation for Quickwrite** graphic organizer to identify key words that describe news articles and editorials. Facilitate small-group discussion.

Expanding Distribute the **Conversation for Quickwrite** graphic organizer to student partners. Have students review the articles they have read so far in this unit to identify key words that describe news articles and editorials.

Bridging After students have completed the Quickwrite, ask them why it is important for voters who read the newspaper to understand the difference between an editorial and a news story. Have students add their thoughts to their Quickwrite assignments and invite volunteers to share their ideas.

Support Pair students who have completed their graphic organizers and ask them to share their responses. For what did they have similar responses, and for what did they have different responses?

Extend Ask pairs or groups to prepare a poster or short visual presentation on the difference between editorials and news stories. Encourage the audience to ask clarifying questions.

3.8

7. What events does the author describe in order to support her claim?

The author describes events such as visiting the Bug-O-Nay-Ge-Shig high school and witnessing the neglected classroom. This event supports her claim that the government is not providing Indian schools with the resources they provide other schools. The author also describes the actions that haven't been taken by the government to support her claim.

Working from the Text

8. Use the questions in the Reading an Editorial section to guide your responses to the editorial.

Title: Author:

Issue:

Question	Response
a	
b	
c	
d	
e	

3.8

Question	Response
f	
g	
h	
i	

Using the notes you have generated, be prepared to participate in a class discussion addressing the following questions (as well as any others inspired by the text):

- What does the author seem to assume the audience is feeling about the issue?
- How does the author tailor language and argument to his or her audience?
- Does the author use slanters? If so, what is their effect?

☑ Check Your Understanding

Quickwrite: How is an editorial different from a news story?

> **✏ Writing Prompt: Rhetorical Analysis**
>
> Now independently analyze another editorial of your choice. Then write a text explaining how the writer tailors the language and argument to a target audience. Be sure to:
>
> - Include a clear summary of the argument.
> - Cite specific examples from the text.
> - Comment on the effect the author's language has on the intended audience.

> **✏ WRITING PROMPT: RHETORICAL ANALYSIS**
>
> The following standards are addressed in the writing prompt:
> - W.11-12.2a
> - W.11-12.2b
> - W.11-12.9b

17 Have students respond to the Writing Prompt using a different editorial that you (or they) have located.

TEACHER TO TEACHER

Consider using a site such as pulitzer.org to locate award-winning editorials for student analysis. A good way to find those sites is with the search term "Editorial Writing."

ASSESS

Review students' responses to the Quickwrite. Ensure that students have identified the purpose for each writing type and explained how structure and language fulfill the purpose.

Use students' responses to the Writing Prompt to assess their ability to connect word choice with audience impact.

ADAPT

If students have difficulty understanding how language is used in editorials for a target audience, have them read an editorial about a social problem. Then have students read an informative text on the same issue. How is the language used to describe the same issue different in each piece? How does audience influence the writer's language?

ACTIVITY 3.9

PLAN

Suggested Pacing: 2 50-minute class periods plus homework

TEACH

1 Read the Learning Targets and Preview with students, making sure they understand that they will be writing and revising an editorial of their own in this activity.

2 With students, read the How to Write an Editorial section. Pause after each bulleted paragraph to elicit questions and comments and to clarify the content as needed. Point out that students will be using the SOAPSTone strategy to help them choose their topic and consider their audience.

Learning Strategies

Brainstorming
Drafting
RAFT
Sharing and Responding
SOAPStone

Learning Targets

• Craft an editorial of your own, carefully considering audience and context.

Preview

In this activity, you will draft, write, and revise an editorial about a contemporary issue.

My Notes

How to Write an Editorial

1. You have had the opportunity to read and analyze a couple of editorials. Now you will walk through the steps of writing your own editorial.

Before You Write

• **Brainstorm for topics:** Choose topics in which you have a genuine interest and some prior knowledge. Be sure the topics are issues that are debatable. Do not, for example, argue for school violence because it would be difficult to find anyone in favor of such a thing. Many editorials are written as responses to news articles or other editorials, so be alert for interesting ideas while reading your news sources each day.

• **Research your topic:** Ask opinions, conduct interviews, and locate facts. While editorials are opinion pieces, those opinions must still be supported with evidence.

• **Get both sides:** In addition to having support for your position, be certain that you have information about the other side of the issue. You will need this soon.

• **Consider your audience:** Use SOAPSTone as a prewriting strategy to consider details of your audience. What does your audience currently believe about this issue? Why? How will they respond to you? Why? What can you do to persuade them to change their minds? How will using slanted language affect your credibility and persuasiveness with them?

• **Write a thesis:** Before writing your draft, you must have a clearly stated position on this issue with a strongly worded reason for your position.

• **Write out your topic sentences and/or main ideas:** This preparation will help you organize your thoughts as you draft your editorial.

• **Decide on a structure:** Consider ways of organizing your essay and choose the one that seems most useful. Remember you can change your mind during the writing process if you like.

Writing a Draft

• **Get to the point:** Your first paragraph should immediately bring the reader's attention to the seriousness of the issue. Create a "hook" that will sell the piece to the reader: a current event or imminent danger, for example. You should then provide a concise summary of what you're going to tell the reader and include your thesis statement.

• **Provide context:** Give your readers important background information about the issue. This background should not be common knowledge (e.g., "drugs are dangerous") but should frame the issue and define any key terms that your reader will need to understand in order to consider your argument.

College and Career Readiness Standards

Focus Standard:

W.11-12.1 Write arguments to support claims in an analysis of substantive topics or texts, using valid reasoning and relevant and sufficient evidence.

Additional Standards Addressed:

RI.11-12.1, RI.11-12.2, RI.11-12.4, RI.11-12.5, RI.11-12.6, SL.11-12.1

3.9

- **Make your point:** Give your strongest two or three reasons why the reader should agree with you. Use relevant and appropriate evidence to support your reasons. State the source of your information and be sure that your argument is clear and organized.
- **Address your opposition:** Reasonable people may think differently than you do on the subject. State at least one or two of the most credible reasons why someone might object to your point of view. Then refute their positions by explaining why their assumptions, claims, logic, and/or evidence are wrong.
- **Wrap it up:** Briefly summarize the main points of your argument and think of a powerful way to end your piece. Often this means giving your reader one last thought to consider.

Revising, Editing, and Publishing Your Draft

- **Check your evidence:** As you look back through your draft, consider whether you have included enough evidence to convince someone who thinks differently than you. Also, is that evidence relevant to your position?
- **Check your rhetoric:** Where is your language slanted? What words or phrases could you modify to "tone down" your voice and appeal to more people?
- **Check your grammar and style:** Nothing will make dismissing your ideas easier than misspelled or misused words or phrases. Triple-check your editorial for mistakes. Print or online style guides can be very useful at this stage. Your computer's spell-check feature can be useful, but it won't catch *has* when you meant *had* because it is spelled correctly. Reread your text to make certain that your words are both correctly spelled and the ones you want.
- **Publish your work:** Make your work available to your target audience. You may do it by printing and distributing copies, putting it on a bulletin board, or including it in a class newsletter or website. Ask your teacher which publication method you should use.

Writing Prompt: Argumentative

With a partner, co-write a brief editorial on the subject of the Eden Prairie High School suspensions or another contemporary issue of your choice. Use the steps outlined in the How to Write an Editorial section to guide your writing. Be sure to:

- Introduce and establish the significance of your claim.
- Make use of rhetorical devices, such as appeals to emotion, logic, or ethics, to support your argument.
- Use language and varied sentence structures to establish relationships among reasons and evidence.
- Establish and maintain a formal style and objective tone.

As You Read

- Underline each writer's position and key reasons for his position.
- Circle unknown words and phrases. Try to determine the meaning of the words by using context clues, word parts, or a dictionary.
- Highlight any words or phrases that illustrate the writer's tone.

My Notes

ACTIVITY 3.9 continued

3 Review the Grammar & Usage feature with students. Make sure they understand the concept of diction. Have partners skim the O'Connell editorial for two examples of how diction contributes to the tone of the author's argument.

4 Give students time to respond to the Writing Prompt. Have them work in pairs, with each pair producing one brief editorial.

 WRITING PROMPT: ARGUMENTATIVE

The following standards are addressed in the writing prompt:
- W.11-12.1a
- W.11-12.1b
- W.11-12.1c
- W.11-12.1d

LEVELED DIFFERENTIATED INSTRUCTION

In this activity, students might need support generating ideas for an editorial article.

Beginning Conduct a group discussion of the Eden Prairie High School suspensions, asking students to explain whether they agree or disagree and why. Place students into groups of three based on their opinion. Have students complete the **Opinion Builder** or **Conclusion Builder** graphic organizer as a prewriting activity.

Developing Have partners complete the **Opinion Builder** or **Conclusion Builder** graphic organizer as a prewriting activity for the assignment. Have them use the organizer to brainstorm reasons and evidence for their own opinions and to anticipate and counter opposing arguments.

Expanding Provide students with multiple copies of the **Opinion Builder** and **Conclusion Builder** graphic organizers to use as prewriting support for this activity. Encourage students to keep the extra copies to use in the upcoming personal editorial assignment.

5 To prepare students for reading the first editorial, have them consider the following questions:

- What are the requirements for graduation in your school?
- Should academic graduation requirements be increased for high school students in your district?

6 Review the As You Read section with students. Remind them to highlight words and phrases that indicate the tone of the editorial and to circle unknown words and phrases and try to determine their meanings by using context clues, word parts, or a dictionary.

GRAMMAR & USAGE

Diction

Diction, or the words a writer chooses, plays an important role in establishing tone and credibility. A writer may choose to use formal or informal words, abstract or concrete words, and emotional or clinical words, all to create an overall effect. Notice how O'Connell uses formal diction in his editorial to reflect his position as the state superintendent of schools. He chooses words such as *remediation, rigorous,* and *perform* to establish his credibility on the subject of education.

Find two more examples of the author's diction that reinforce the overall tone of the argument and explain their impact to a partner.

My Notes

_____

_____

_____

_____

_____

_____

_____

_____

rigors: strict requirements

remediation: help

vocational: job-related

socioeconomically: related to money and social status

bound: moving toward

Editorial

Pro and Con: Raising Graduation for High School Students: Time to Raise the Bar in High Schools

by Jack O'Connell

1 The most important challenge we face in public education today is to improve high schools so that all California students graduate prepared to succeed in either college or the workplace. Today, far too many of our 1.7 million high school students are prepared for neither the demands of skilled employment nor the **rigors** of higher education. Employers consistently complain of graduates who lack critical problem-solving and communications skills. More than half of students entering California State University need **remediation** in reading or math. It is clearly time for us to reexamine high school in California, to raise the level of rigor we expect of all of our students and begin preparing every high school student to reach higher expectations.

2 How we meet the challenge of improving high school student achievement will determine the futures of our children and their ability to compete and succeed in the decades to come. Moreover, how we respond to this challenge will significantly affect the economic and social future of our state.

3 Research shows that students who take challenging, college-preparatory courses do better in school, even if they started out with poor test scores and low expectations. Students who take rigorous courses are also less likely to drop out, and they perform better in **vocational** and technical courses.

4 Our high schools today struggle with an achievement gap that leaves African-American, Latino and **socioeconomically** disadvantaged students lagging behind their peers. A failure to provide and expect all students to take demanding academic coursework has also created a high school "reality gap": While more than 80 percent of high school students say they intend to go to college, only about 40 percent actually take the rigorous coursework required for acceptance at a four-year university. The numbers are even lower for African-American graduates (24 percent) and Latinos (22 percent).

5 Many students are not aware that the "minimum requirement" courses they are taking aren't providing the rigorous foundation that will prepare them to fulfill their dreams after high school. In some cases, students are steered away from tough courses or find them overenrolled. The result is thousands of students who must spend significant, unnecessary time and money after high school if they are ever to fulfill their dreams.

6 To reverse this trend, we must make rigorous courses available to all of our students. We must redefine high schools as institutions that provide all students with a strong academic foundation, whether they are **bound** for college or the workplace after graduation.

7 I am proposing a High Performing High Schools Initiative that will raise expectations for our high schools and high school students. It will provide better training and support for high school principals. And it will establish a state "seal of approval" process for high school instructional materials, giving districts guidance in choosing materials that are standards-aligned, and therefore more rigorous than many used in high schools today.

8 It is simply wrong to decide for students as young as age 15 whether or not they are "college material" and capable of challenging courses in high school. Guiding students to an easier academic pathway, even if they show little early motivation or curiosity about possibilities beyond high school, virtually guarantees they won't be prepared with important foundational skills. It limits their opportunities for years to come. Years ago, this was called "tracking." Students facing childhood challenges such as poverty or the need to learn English—the description of fully well over a quarter of California's students today—would be tracked to less-challenging courses and denied opportunities after high school as a result.

9 By advocating for tougher curriculum in high schools, I am not in any way suggesting vocational education programs should be eliminated. In fact, legislation I introduced to improve high school achievement would reward schools that collaborate with businesses or labor unions to expand such successful programs as career partnership academies. These academies have been successful where they have provided rigorous academic instruction geared toward a career pathway.

10 The truth is that we can no longer afford to hold high expectations only for our college-bound students. Today, all of our students need the skills and knowledge contained in the curriculum that was once reserved only for the college-bound. Strong communications skills, knowledge of foreign language and culture, higher-level math and problem-solving skills are needed in technical trades as well as white-collar professions. The job of K-12 education in California must be to ensure that all of our students graduate with the ability to fulfill their potential—whether that takes them to higher education or directly to their career.

My Notes

| aligned: supported |
| virtually: almost completely |

Scaffolding the Text-Dependent Questions

2. Describe O'Connell's diction and the tone it creates. How do his word choice and syntax reflect his position as California State Superintendent of Public Instruction? Skim the article. What tone is created by O'Connell's word choice? What are some examples of specific words that create that tone? What does the tone tell the reader about O'Connell? RI.11-12.4

3. Find an example of a counterargument in O'Connell's editorial. How does he respond to it? Reread paragraph 9. What counterargument is made in the first sentence? What kinds of higher education does he mention other than college? RI.11-12.1

ACTIVITY 3.9 continued

7 **FIRST READ:** Conduct a shared reading of "Pro and Con: Raising Graduation for High School Students: Time to Raise the Bar in High School." Pause after paragraph 1 to ensure that students understand the issue that will be examined in the editorial. Point out that the thesis appears in the last sentence of the paragraph. Have them underline that sentence and instruct them to underline the writer's reasons for that position as they read.

 TEXT COMPLEXITY

Overall: Very Complex
Lexile: 1420L
Qualitative: High Difficulty
Task: Challenging (Evaluate)

8 As students are reading, monitor their progress. Be sure they are engaged with the text and annotating words and phrases as instructed.

TEACHER TO TEACHER

As time permits, lead a discussion about diction and how formal and informal language affects an audience's perception of a writer or speaker. Ask students about times when they observe other formal/informal conventions (e.g., dressing for the prom versus dressing to watch a movie at a friend's house). Formal diction can be inappropriate in some circumstances (Can students think of any?), and informal diction can be inappropriate in others.

9 Tell students to pause at the end of paragraph 5. Have students speculate as to why so many students are unaware of what is needed to enter college and how that situation might be remedied.

10 Tell students to pause after paragraph 9 and describe in their own words the student options that O'Connell is proposing.

11 After reading the text for the first time, guide the class in a discussion by asking the Making Observations questions. Check students' general comprehension of the text based on their observations, asking follow-up questions if needed.

12 RETURNING TO THE TEXT: Guide students to return to the text to respond to the text-dependent questions. Invite them to work as a class to reread the text and answer the questions. Remind them to use text evidence in their responses.

13 Supervise the students as they answer the text-dependent questions. If they have difficulty, scaffold the question by rephrasing it or breaking it down into smaller parts. See the Scaffolding the Text-Dependent Question box for suggestions.

3.9

Making Observations
- What words and phrases does the author enclose in quotation marks?
- Based on the words or phrases you highlighted, what is a detail that feels important to you?

Returning to the Text
- Return to the editorial as you respond to the following questions. Use text evidence to support your responses.
- Write any additional questions you have about the text in your Reader/Writer Notebook.

2. Describe O'Connell's diction and the tone it creates. How do his word choice and syntax reflect his position as California State Superintendent of Public Instruction?

O'Connell chooses words such as *remediation, rigorous,* and *perform* to create a formal, informational tone. This tone establishes his credibility on the subject of education, which befits his expertise, experience, and position.

3. Find an example of a counterargument in O'Connell's editorial. How does he respond to it?

In paragraph 9, O'Connell addresses the counterargument that his support for toughening up high school curricula means that he thinks all students should go to college. His rebuttal points out that he supports career partnership academies, where schools conduct training in collaboration with business and labor unions. He also states in that paragraph that he supports vocational training.

4. What text evidence addresses O'Connell's claim that minorities are disproportionately underserved by the low difficulty level of their academic coursework? Is the evidence objective and valid or subjective and unconvincing? Explain.

In paragraph 4, he points out that only 40 percent of students overall take the level of coursework required for college acceptance. Then he notes that the rate for African Americans and Latinos is about half of that. These statistics are objective evidence that supports his claim.

Scaffolding the Text-Dependent Questions

4. What text evidence addresses O'Connell's claim that minorities are disproportionately underserved by the low difficulty level of their academic coursework? Is the evidence objective and valid or subjective and unconvincing? Explain. Examine paragraph 4. What evidence does O'Connell present in that paragraph? Is it good or bad evidence? Why? RI.11-12.1

Editorial

New Michigan Graduation Requirements Shortchange Many Students

by **Nick Thomas**

1 Imagine waking up in the morning to find the electricity is out, or a pipe has burst or your car won't start. As you look though the Yellow Pages for a technician, do you really care if that person has a working knowledge of matrices, oxidation numbers, and Kepler's laws of planetary motion?

2 Apparently the state of Michigan does. Its new high school graduation requirements will assure that every graduate, regardless of their career choice, will have taken advanced math and science classes.

3 Among the new requirements are one credit each of algebra I, geometry and algebra II and an additional math class in the senior year. Also required is one credit of biology, one credit of physics or chemistry and one additional year of science.

4 This new curriculum may be helpful for a student who plans to go on to college, but it seems excessive for vocational students.

5 Plumbers, mechanics, construction workers, hairdressers and many other positions do not need an advanced math and science background. Math needed for vocational jobs could be learned through an "applied math" class, or on-site learning.

My Notes

ACTIVITY 3.9 continued

14 FIRST READ: Conduct a small-group reading of "New Michigan Graduation Requirements Shortchange Many Students." Tell them to underline text that indicates the writer's position and his reason for that position. They should also highlight words and phrases that indicate the tone of the editorial and circle unknown words and phrases so they can try to determine their meanings by using context clues, word parts, or a dictionary.

TEXT COMPLEXITY

Overall: Complex
Lexile: 1210L
Qualitative: Moderate Difficulty
Task: Challenging (Evaluate)

15 Pause after the first paragraph and invite students to state in their own words the point that Thomas is making. Ask volunteers whether they agree with the point and have them explain why or why not.

16 As students are reading, monitor their progress. Be sure they are engaged with the text and annotating it as directed.

17 Tell students to pause after paragraph 6 and have them explain in their own words the concern that Thomas is expressing.

18 Have students pause after paragraph 7 and explain in their own words the process that Thomas is describing. Prompt them to consider whether his description is realistic, who he fears will be harmed, and how.

19 After reading the text for the first time, guide the class in a discussion by asking the Making Observations questions. Check students' general comprehension of the text based on their observations, asking follow-up questions as needed.

3.9

My Notes

6 I'm concerned that when students are forced to take classes that are unnecessary for their chosen careers, they'll feel discouraged and put little effort into their classes. And if they can't take the classes they want, I'm afraid that more of them will drop out.

Advanced classes becoming basic classes

7 One of my biggest concerns with all students taking advanced classes is that the pace of the courses will slow down. Some students will undoubtedly not try to learn the material, and some will be incapable of learning as fast as others, leaving the teacher compelled to dumb down the class. In effect, advanced classes will become basic classes. This will have no additional benefit for vocational students and will hamper college prep students.

8 There's yet another way college-bound students might suffer from the new requirements. A very gifted English student who lacks ability in math could have their grade point average lowered significantly when required to take advanced math classes. And of course, when applying to college, high school grades are important.

9 A well-rounded education is ideal but can be achieved in many ways, not just through academics. Our economy depends on a variety of jobs. We need carpenters as well as engineers. We need hairdressers as well as doctors, and we need heavy equipment operators as well as lawyers.

10 All jobs are important, and students deserve to pursue their choice of a career without being forced to take unnecessary classes.

Making Observations
- How does the question in the introduction make you feel?
- Where does the author use the first-person point of view?

Scaffolding the Text-Dependent Questions

5. How does Thomas's diction compare with O'Connell's? Which writer's approach do you feel is more engaging and convincing, and why? Skim random paragraphs of this activity's two editorials. Compare examples of O'Connell's diction with examples of Thomas's. Is the diction of each formal and logical or casual and conversational? Which is more effective? RI.11-12.6

6. Locate the subhead Thomas uses in his editorial. Why does he use it, and how does it support his argument? Examine the subhead that precedes paragraph 7. How does it help the reader understand Thomas's argument? How does it communicate the level of importance of the text that follows it? RI.11-12.5

3.9

Returning to the Text

- Return to the editorial as you respond to the following questions. Use text evidence to support your responses.
- Write any additional questions you have about the text in your Reader/Writer Notebook.

5. How does Thomas's diction compare with O'Connell's? Which writer's approach do you feel is more engaging and convincing, and why?

Whereas O'Connell's diction is formal and logical, Thomas's diction is casual and

conversational. Thomas uses common phrases such as "Imagine waking up in the morning" or

"do you really care." This casual style is more accessible to the reader, which makes it more

engaging, and engaging text is more likely to be convincing.

6. Locate the subhead Thomas uses in his editorial. Why does he use it, and how does it support his argument?

Thomas places the subhead "Advanced classes becoming basic classes" before paragraph 7.

The phrase encapsulates the argument that follows, which explains that forcing slower

learners to take advanced classes will result in teachers "dumbing down" the content. This, he

argues, will be a disservice to students who plan to go on to college. Using the subhead also

draws extra attention to the claim, emphasizing the point.

7. Describe a key idea on which O'Connell and Thomas agree.

Both agree that attention needs to be paid to students who do not plan on attending college.

O'Connell wants to pursue a plan that will help students "perform better in vocational and

technical courses." Thomas notes, "Our economy depends on a variety of jobs. We need

carpenters as well as engineers ... hairdressers as well as doctors ... heavy equipment

operators as well as lawyers."

 Gaining Perspectives

You have read two editorials about education. The right to an education and the right to express your opinion are part of the Universal Declaration of Human Rights created by the United Nations. With a partner, research other human rights mentioned in the document. Are these rights protected in the United States? What about other countries around the world? Why is it important to uphold human rights? Summarize you findings and present them to the class.

Scaffolding the Text-Dependent Questions

7. Describe a key idea on which O'Connell and Thomas agree. Skim each editorial for the writer's main points. What does each writer say about students who do not plan to attend college? What alternative courses of action does each support for such students? RI.11-12.2

ACTIVITY 3.9 continued

20 **RETURNING TO THE TEXT:** Guide students to return to the text to respond to the text-dependent questions. Invite them to work in pairs to reread the text and answer the questions. Remind them to use text evidence in their responses.

21 Move from pair to pair and listen in as students answer the text-dependent questions. If they have difficulty, scaffold the questions by rephrasing them or breaking them down into smaller parts. See the Scaffolding the Text-Dependent Question box for suggestions.

22 Guide students to work with a partner to complete the Gaining Perspectives feature. Allow students time and access to research materials on the other human rights mentioned in the Universal Declaration of Human Rights. After pairs finish researching and discussing, ask volunteers to share their findings.

23 Have students work independently to complete the graphic organizer in the Working from the Text section and student step 9. Supervise their work and provide guidance as necessary. If time permits, conduct a brief discussion of the exercises when students are finished.

24 Regroup students into the pairs that worked together on the first writing prompt. Give them time to review their brief editorials. Then have them work alone or together to respond to the second writing prompt, reflecting an alternative perspective to their original editorials.

ASSESS

Check students' responses to the second (argumentative) writing prompt to assess their ability to introduce, establish, and develop a claim, refute a counterclaim, and maintain a formal style and objective tone.

ADAPT

If students need additional help writing editorials, help them identify the opposite viewpoints by working with their partners to brainstorm the most popular reasons against their original claims. Students may conduct brief research, if needed, or consult other students.

3.9

Working from the Text

8. Use the chart to organize the annotations you made while you read each editorial.

Author	Reasons For	Reasons Against	Strongest Statement of Position
Jack O'Connell			
Nick Thomas			
You			
A Person You Know			

9. Use the chart to compare the key ideas the two writers present. In your opinion, which of the two writers made the stronger case? Explain.

> ### 📝 Writing Prompt: Argumentative
> You have co-written a brief editorial, and you have read two editorials with opposing views. Now, compose an editorial that responds to your original editorial. Write from an alternate perspective. Be sure to:
> - Introduce and establish the significance of your claim.
> - Develop the claim and respond to counterclaims with relevant evidence.
> - Establish and maintain a formal style and an objective tone.

✍️ WRITING PROMPT: ARGUMENTATIVE

The following standards are addressed in the writing prompt:
- W.11-12.1a
- W.11-12.1b
- W.11-12.1d

Where's Your Proof?

Learning Targets

- Evaluate the effectiveness of different types of evidence.
- Revise writing to incorporate appropriate evidence.

Preview

In this activity, you will analyze the effectiveness of evidence in this unit's editorials. Then you will revise your own editorial by strengthening the effectiveness of your evidence.

Learning Strategies

Discussion Groups

Rereading

Self-Editing

The Art of Evidence

1. To support the claims they make, authors use a variety of types of evidence. With a partner or small group, revisit one of the editorials you have read in this unit and fill in the chart.

Type of Evidence: What is it used for? What are its limitations? "They X, but they Y."	Example from an Editorial in This Unit	Evaluation: What kind of appeal does it make: logos, ethos, or pathos? Does the evidence logically support the author's claim in this case? Why or why not?
Illustrative Examples (Personal Experience/Anecdotal/Media Example). They add reality to the claim but may not be generalizable.		
Hypothetical Cases. They challenge the reader to consider possible circumstances or outcomes, but there's no reason they will definitely happen.		
Analogies/Comparison. They make the unfamiliar or abstract more accessible, but they need to be more similar than different in order to be persuasive.		
Expert/Testimony. They provide expert support for causal claims, predictions of outcomes, or possible solutions, but they're still just opinions—and the source needs to be checked carefully!		

ACTIVITY 3.10

PLAN

Materials: editorials from the unit or students' drafts
Suggested Pacing: 1 50-minute class period

TEACH

1 Review the Learning Targets and Preview with students. Make sure they know that they will be learning to evaluate evidence and use it to strengthen their writing.

2 Call students' attention to the section called "The Art of Evidence." Point out and review with them the types of evidence listed in the first column of the graphic organizer. Explain when and why these types of evidence are used and their strengths and limitations as tools of persuasion.

3 Divide students into pairs or small groups. Have them select an editorial from among those they have read thus far in this unit and complete student steps 1 and 2. Suggest that they choose an article that uses a wide range of evidence. Encourage them to work closely with their partners as they proceed.

College and Career Readiness Standards

Focus Standards:

RI.11-12.1 Cite strong and thorough textual evidence to support analysis of what the text says explicitly as well as inferences drawn from the text, including determining where the text leaves matters uncertain.

RI.11-12.5 Analyze and evaluate the effectiveness of the structure an author uses

in his or her exposition or argument, including whether the structure makes points clear, convincing, and engaging.

RI.11-12.6 Determine an author's point of view or purpose in a text in which the rhetoric is particularly effective, analyzing how style and content contribute to the power, persuasiveness, or beauty of the text.

4 Guide a discussion of students' work from The Art of Evidence exercises. Have them cite specific examples of each type of evidence from their chosen editorials. Assist them in evaluating how well the evidence they present supports the writer's point. Encourage them to share feedback on one another's results. Discuss why writers who use a variety of evidence are likely more persuasive than writers who rely on only one kind.

5 Give students time to respond to the Check Your Understanding task. Remind them to share their revision with a partner and have that partner identify the type of evidence that has been added. Writers should clearly mark their revisions before turning in their drafts.

ASSESS

Review students' revisions for the Check Your Understanding task. Ensure that students have selected appropriate types of evidence to support their ideas or claims and that they have used suitable transitions to incorporate that evidence into their paragraphs.

ADAPT

If students need additional help revising their paragraphs, have them use **graphic organizers** to separate their paragraphs into central ideas or claims, commentary, and supporting evidence. Help them determine what type of evidence, if any, is being used. Ask them whether the type they are using is the most effective for supporting their central idea or claim. If not, help them determine what other type of evidence might be more effective.

3.10

Type of Evidence: What is it used for? What are its limitations? "They X, but they Y."	Example from an Editorial in This Unit	Evaluation: What kind of appeal does it make: logos, ethos, or pathos? Does the evidence logically support the author's claim in this case? Why or why not?
Statistics/Surveys. They support generalized claims and make strong logical appeals, but they must be reliable and unbiased.		
Causal Relationships. They suggest possible positive or negative outcomes, but there needs to be a clear link between the cause and the effect.		

2. Once you have recorded your observations in the graphic organizer, be prepared to discuss those observations. You will want to make sure to address both the types and effectiveness of each technique the author has used. Make sure you reference specific examples from the text. With a partner, discuss why using a wide variety of evidence might be more persuasive or effective than using only one kind of evidence.

☑ Check Your Understanding

Select one of the editorials you have written in this unit and revise one paragraph in it by adding at least one of the types of evidence from this activity. Share your revision with a partner and ask your partner to identify the type of evidence you used in your writing.

College and Career Readiness Standards

SL.11-12.1 Initiate and participate effectively in a range of collaborative discussions (one-on-one, in groups, and teacher-led) with diverse partners on grades 11–12 topics, texts, and issues, building on others' ideas and expressing their own clearly and persuasively.

Reading and Writing a Letter to the Editor

PLAN

PLAN

Materials: newspaper editorials, letters to the editor written in response to the editorials
Suggested Pacing: 1 50-minute class period

TEACH

1 Read the Learning Targets and Preview with students. Tell them that they will be examining letters to the editor, which are most often a type of editorial.

2 Read aloud the How to Write a Letter to the Editor section or invite volunteers to read individual sections. Pause as needed to ask and answer questions and clarify the content.

Learning Targets

- Evaluate the effectiveness of multiple editorial letters according to specific criteria.
- Write an editorial letter using the criteria for effectiveness.

Preview

In this activity, you will analyze several letters to the editor and then write your own.

Learning Strategies

Drafting
Graphic Organizer
Marking the Text
Sharing and Responding

My Notes

How to Write a Letter to the Editor

Letters that are intended for publication should be drafted carefully. Here are some tips to keep in mind:

- Make one point (or at most two) in your letter. Be sure to identify the topic of your letter. State the point clearly, ideally in the first sentence.
- Make your letter timely. If you are not addressing a specific article, editorial, or letter that recently appeared in the paper you are writing to, try to tie the issue you want to write about to a recent event.
- Familiarize yourself with the coverage and editorial position of the paper to which you are writing. Refute or support specific statements, address relevant facts that are ignored, offer a completely different perspective on the issue, but avoid blanket attacks on the media in general or the newspaper in particular.
- Consider your audience (the newspaper's editors and readers):
  - What does your audience currently believe about the issue? Why?
  - How will they respond to you? Why?
  - What can you do to persuade them to change their minds?
  - How will using slanted language affect your credibility and persuasiveness?
- Check the letter specifications of the newspaper to which you are writing. Length and format requirements vary from paper to paper. (Generally, roughly two short paragraphs are ideal.) You also must include your name, signature, address, and phone number.
- Look at the letters that appear in your paper. Is a certain type of letter usually printed?
- Support your facts. If the topic you address is controversial, consider sending documentation along with your letter. But don't overload the editors with too much information.
- Keep your letter brief. Type and spell-check it. Have a peer edit it.
- When possible, find others in the community to write letters to show concern about the issue. If your letter doesn't get published, perhaps someone else's on the same topic will.
- If your letter has not appeared within a week or two, follow up with a call to the newspaper's editorial department.

College and Career Readiness Standards

Focus Standards:

RI.11-12.5 Analyze and evaluate the effectiveness of the structure an author uses in his or her exposition or argument, including whether the structure makes points clear, convincing, and engaging.

W.11-12.1b Develop claim(s) and counterclaims fairly and thoroughly, supplying the most relevant evidence for each while pointing out the

strengths and limitations of both in a manner that anticipates the audience's knowledge level, concerns, values, and possible biases.

W.11-12.1e Provide a concluding statement or section that follows from and supports the argument presented.

Additional Standards Addressed:

RI.11-12.1, RI.11-12.2, RI.11-12.3, RI.11-12.4, RI.11-12.6

ACTIVITY 3.11 continued

3 Direct students to the As You Read section, instructing them to write down questions as they read and notice how the letter writers use diction to create tone.

4 FIRST READ: Conduct a paired reading of "Letters: The NYC Subway Is Not 'Beyond Repair.'" Instruct students to take turns reading the individual letters aloud. Tell them to jot down any questions that occur to them as they read and to highlight words or phrases that indicate the writer's tone.

 TEXT COMPLEXITY

Overall: Complex
Lexile: 1400L
Qualitative: Moderate Difficulty
Task: Challenging (Create)

5 Monitor students' progress as they read. Be sure they are engaged with the text and annotating words and phrases as directed.

 TEACHER TO TEACHER

Comprehension of "Letters: The NYC Subway Is Not 'Beyond Repair'" relies on several advanced vocabulary words. Prepare a **Cloze Reading** text using the vocabulary words from the essay and read it aloud. Write the words on the board and pause at blanks where a vocabulary word belongs. Students should select the words based on context clues.

3.11

My Notes

As You Read

- Jot down any questions you have about the letters to the editor in the My Notes area.
- Highlight any words or phrases that indicate the writers' tone.

Letters to the Editor

Letters: The NYC Subway Is Not "Beyond Repair"

From **The Atlantic**

June 13, 2018

Last weekend, Peter Wayner advocated for a radical overhaul of the city's current subway system, proposing instead a network of subterranean highways filled with hoverboards, scooters, and autonomous vehicles.

Letter 1

1   After reading "The New York City Subway Is Beyond Repair," I felt compelled to respond to what I see as basic inaccuracies that undermine the piece as a whole. I have a degree in infrastructure engineering and am an engineer-in-training in the field, but the inaccuracies in question are not nearly so arcane as to require such credentials.

2   The respective capacities of free-flowing vehicular lanes and subway transit are well established. Generously, a freeway lane might carry 2,000 vehicles per hour, which—again, generously—might each carry somewhere between one and two travelers, on average. This gives us a high-end estimate of moving 2,000 to 4,000 people per hour in a single direction.

3   An MTA subway track, such as Mr. Wayner effectively proposes to replace with a single lane of traffic, is capable of carrying in excess of 30,000 people per hour. This is not a small difference and makes one wonder whether the author has considered it.

4   This is the simplest critique, as it relies on simple math, but the challenges with Mr. Wayner's proposal are legion. For the geometry alone, there are a number of difficulties with using passenger vehicles rather than trains.

5   Vastly larger stations would be required to accommodate all the spaces for cars picking up and dropping off pedestrians. In order to prevent delays for vehicles not stopping, additional bypass tunnels would need to be excavated at every station. To permit safe operation, much of the signaling equipment that

---

Scaffolding the Text-Dependent Questions

1. Based on paragraph 1 of Patrick Zerr's letter to the editor, what is his purpose for writing? Examine paragraph 1 of the letter. What does Zerr think of Wayner's overall argument? How does he feel about the support Wayner has provided for that argument? RI.11-12.6

2. Summarize the evidence that Zerr provides in paragraphs 3 and 4 to rebut Wayner's proposal. Read the evidence Zerr provides in those two paragraphs. How does he compare the current subway system with Wayner's proposal? How can Zerr's comparison be stated briefly? RI.11-12.2

Mr. Wayner wanted to rip out would instead need to be replaced with much more sophisticated and expensive Intelligent Transportation Systems (ITS) to coordinate a far larger number of vehicles.

6   These are all massive challenges, with huge price tags, that would, again, result in a tremendous decrease in capacity for the system as a whole. It's a pleasant fantasy to believe that innovation and a Silicon Valley mindset are all that's necessary to solve one of America's most intractable infrastructure challenges. The truth, much less attractive, is that it requires massive and consistent funding, collaboration across a range of stakeholders, and time.

Patrick Zerr
North Vancouver, Canada

Letter 2

1   Peter Wayner proposed that we should replace trains in the New York City subway with autonomous cars and hoverboards. He sounds like a modern-day Robert Moses, obsessed with automobiles as a replacement for public transit, proclaiming that cars will be more convenient and efficient for us all. Robert Moses built a system of roads on which only cars and trucks may travel—which are and have always been notoriously congested, especially during the rush hours. Subway riders must tolerate stops at stations they will not get off at because other passengers might be boarding or exiting the train, but automobile passengers must tolerate stops for traffic jams that serve no purpose for anyone.

2   The New York City subway is not broken beyond repair; for all its faults, for all the mismanagement, the subway remains the lifeline of this city. Mr. Wayner suggests that modern technology—autonomous cars, personal transit devices—can replace trains, but it is not as if trains have not benefited from modern technology as well. Computers, artificial intelligence, robotics—all these things are being applied to railroads, improving efficiency and reducing costs for both passenger and freight systems. There is a lot of potential in the subway; unlike most other metro systems that are double-tracked, the New York City system has numerous triple—and quadruple—tracked lines, which are currently used to allow express trains to pass local trains but which could be used to even greater effect with more modern control systems (for example, to allow a super-express service that skips more stops).

3   It is also important to remember that the subway system provides service to neighborhoods that are currently underserved by taxis, and which would almost certainly be underserved by autonomous cars operated by competing, for-profit companies. The most profitable places to serve will be in the city center where there are always people waiting to ride the vehicles; but the people most in need of subway service tend to live far from the city center, and to pick them up the vehicles will be forced to make long and unprofitable trips without passengers, just like subway trains. The reason the government took over the subway and commuter railroads was to maintain a vital but unprofitable service.

My Notes

ACTIVITY 3.11 continued

6 Tell students to pause at the end of paragraph 2 of the second letter and have them explain what part of the argument is represented by the statement "The New York City subway is not broken beyond repair; for all its faults, for all the mismanagement, the subway remains the lifeline of this city. Mr. Wayner suggests that modern technology—autonomous cars, personal transit devices—can replace trains, but it is not as if trains have not benefited from modern technology as well." Ask them to identify the text in that paragraph as a thesis, a concession, or a refutation. Have them explain.

Scaffolding the Text-Dependent Questions

3. How does Zerr conclude his letter? Is it convincing? Skim the text of Zerr's letter and then closely reread its sixth paragraph. What are his last words about his own ideas? What are his last words about Wayner's? Whose ideas seem more strongly supported? Why? RI.11-12.5

4. In the second letter, Kreuter compares Wayner to Robert Moses. What is the effect of this comparison? Reread the first paragraph of the second letter. What does Kreuter find similar about Wayner and Robert Moses? What tone does his comparison set for the letter? RI.11-12.3

5. Summarize Wayner's claim that Kreuter rebuts in paragraph 2. What reasoning and evidence does Kreuter present in his rebuttal? Examine paragraph 2 of the second letter. What claim has Wayner made that Kreuter takes exception to? Why does Kreuter disagree? RI.11-12.2

My Notes

Benjamin Kreuter
Jersey City, N.J.

Several readers responded on Facebook:

Isaac Brumer wrote: For all its problems, the NYC transit system is not "beyond repair." It safely serves millions of people every day, 24/7. How will those people get around while you're ripping out the tracks, repairing the tunnels, then retrofitting them for the transportation system you've dreamed up? And all transportation systems need costly maintenance over time. Does the author believe the new system will be maintenance-free?

Andrea Abarca Coutts wrote: What ever happened to all the flying cars and buses I was promised by movies and TV? Eight year old me definitely thought we'd be hovering around cities by now.

Peter Wayner replies:

1 Mr. Zerr and Mr. Kreuter make the same mistake that many do by assuming that the autonomous vehicles will flow like human-driven cars. Consider as a thought experiment a line of hoverboards a mile long with 10 feet of empty space behind each one. That's 528 people. If they move 15 miles an hour, the tunnel will carry 7,290 people per hour.

2 Hoverboards are slim and we can slice the tunnel into three, four, or maybe five lanes and carry 23,760, 31,680 or 39,600 people per hour. Thinner lanes are a big advantage because a mishap or planned maintenance in one slim lane wouldn't block everything. That speaks to Mr. Brumer's point.

3 Interested readers can repeat the same experiment with two lanes of five-foot-wide autonomous cars spaced 20 feet apart, carrying four passengers and going 30 miles an hour. These can offer airbags and other safety features missing from trains. These are just two hypothetical models that could deliver the same throughput as the one train—when it can follow its official rush hour schedule of approximately sixteen trains per hour.

4 Why can these autonomous vehicles compete with one train that can carry 2,000 people? Local trains need large gaps because the stops take so long. Autonomous vehicles will stop only at their destination, when they zip out of the flow. They can use the large gap.

5 As to Mr. Kreuter's point about the outer boroughs, the competing fleets may still be owned by the city or heavily regulated. We can have both plenty of choices and a differential pricing model with room to help whomever the politicians favor.

6 I agree that we need to sweat many details, but there's plenty of opportunity. The hoverboards might zip over to the next line or carry the passenger to the street. The corridors and roads upstairs are fair game. They could give the handicapped more time to board than the subway at rush hour.

Scaffolding the Text-Dependent Questions

6. What is the rebuttal Isaac Brumer is making in this Facebook post? Reread Brumer's post. What does Brumer believe would happen to public maintenance while Wayner's proposals were being adopted? What does Brumer think about the cost of maintaining Wayner's proposed system? RI.11-12.6

7 There's also plenty of room. The platforms are 600 feet long and Disney loads their rides in much less space.

8 And there's also plenty of budget. We're already being asked to shoulder a $19 billion bill. We can either redesign the signaling and everything else for the last generation or aim for the future.

My Notes

Making Observations

- Based on words and phrases you highlighted in Letters 1 and 2, how does each writer feel about Peter Wayner's proposal?
- Which letter to the editor do you respond to most strongly?

7 Have students pause after paragraph 4 of Peter Wayner's reply and make a statement about what part of an argument the writer is presenting. Have them explain their answers.

8 After reading the text for the first time, guide the class in a discussion by asking the Making Observations questions. Check students' general comprehension of the text based on their comprehensions, asking follow-up questions if needed.

Scaffolding the Text-Dependent Questions

7. Describe the tone Peter Wayner uses to respond to the letters to the editor. Cite examples of diction and syntax in your response. Skim Wayner's response. What tone does he create with his diction? What is noticeable about his syntax? What kinds of words does he use, and how does he address the reader? Does he use any rhetorical devices? If so, why? RI.11-12.4

8. What is Wayner's purpose for including paragraph 6? Reread paragraph 6 of Wayner's response. Think of Wayner's reply as a thesis. What part of a thesis is exemplified by the first sentence of paragraph 6? How does the rest of the paragraph relate to that sentence? RI.11-12.6

9 RETURNING TO THE TEXT: Guide students to return to the text to respond to the text-dependent questions. Invite them to work in small groups to reread the text and answer the questions. Remind them to use text evidence in their responses.

10 Move from group to group and listen in as students answer the text-dependent questions. If they have difficulty, scaffold the questions by rephrasing them or breaking them down into smaller parts. See the Scaffolding the Text-Dependent Questions boxes for suggestions.

Returning to the Text

- Return to the letters as you respond to the following questions. Use text evidence to support your responses.
- Write any additional questions you have about the text in your Reader/Writer Notebook.

1. Based on paragraph 1 of Patrick Zerr's letter to the editor, what is his purpose for writing?

   Zerr's purpose for writing his letter is to address the "basic inaccuracies" that he feels
   undermines Wayner's entire argument.

2. Summarize the evidence that Zerr provides in paragraphs 3 and 4 to rebut Wayner's proposal.

   Zerr uses well-established data of the capacity of free-flowing vehicular lanes and subway
   transit to make a comparison between how many travelers are serviced by the subway versus
   how many would be serviced by Wayner's proposed single lane of traffic.

3. How does Zerr conclude his letter? Is it convincing?

   Zerr concludes his letter by summarizing his previous arguments and rebutting Wayner's
   argument.

4. In the second letter, Kreuter compares Wayner to Robert Moses. What is the effect of this comparison?

   The effect of this comparison is to suggest that, like Moses, Wayner may not have considered
   all the consequences of his idea.

5. Summarize Wayner's claim that Kreuter rebuts in paragraph 2. What reasoning and evidence does Kreuter present in his rebuttal?

   Wayner claims that modern technology can replace trains. However, Kreuter cites all of the
   technological advances that trains have already benefited from.

6. What is the rebuttal Isaac Brumer is making in this Facebook post?

Isaac Brumer rebuts Wayner's proposal by bringing up the people who will be without

public transportation while the new system is being created and by noting the maintenance

costs.

7. Describe the tone Peter Wayner uses to respond to the letters to the editor. Cite examples of diction and syntax in your response.

Wayner uses an instructional tone in his responses. He uses words like *mistake, we,* and

experiment to guide the readers through his thinking as if they were coming to the conclusion

together. He also uses mathematical syntax and rhetorical questions to do this.

8. What is Wayner's purpose for including paragraph 6?

Wayner includes a concession in paragraph 6.

Exploring Additional Letters to the Editor

9. Your teacher will provide an editorial and several letters written in response to the editorial. Fill in the chart for each of the letters to the editor. The last box is for your opinion on the editorial.

Letter Number	Agree or Disagree with Original Editorial?	Reasons/Evidence
1		
2		

ACTIVITY 3.11 continued

11 Focus students' attention on the Exploring Additional Letters to the Editor section. Provide them with copies of an editorial and four responses to it. Number each response and instruct them to reference those numbers as they complete the graphic organizer. Tell them to reserve row 5 for their own response to the editorial (as though they were preparing to write a letter themselves).

LEVELED DIFFERENTIATED INSTRUCTION

In this activity, students may need support articulating the differences between the original editorial and the letters written in response to the editorial.

Beginning Have students work in small groups to use the **Idea and Argument Evaluator** to dissect the editorial and each letter to the editor in response. Have them use the organizer to fill out the chart.

Developing Have students work in pairs to use the **Idea and Argument Evaluator** to dissect the editorial and each letter to the editor in response. Have them use the organizer to fill out the chart.

Support Have students read the editorial and letters to the editor as a group. Guide them to summarize each letter and describe how it agrees or disagrees with the editorial.

Extend Have students write their own letter to the editor in response to the editorial. Have them make sure to provide a clear argument in support of or against it and provide evidence to support their claim.

12 Give students time to respond to the Check Your Understanding task. Consider allowing them to work in pairs or small groups as they respond to the Quickwrite prompt, evaluating which letters are most effective and why.

13 Have students respond to the Writing Prompt. Direct them to use the steps outlined in the How to Write a Letter to the Editor section to guide their writing.

ASSESS

Student responses to the writing prompt should show an ability to logically sequence claims, reasons, and evidence and to address counterclaims.

ADAPT

If students need additional help in writing their letters to the editor, have them pair up with students who have completed the prompt and review the steps outlined in the How to Write a Letter to the Editor section at the beginning of the activity. If applicable, it might be helpful for students to compare what their partner has done with the guidance in the section and revise their own writing accordingly.

3.11

Letter Number	Agree or Disagree with Original Editorial?	Reasons/Evidence
3		
4		
Your Opinion		

☑ Check Your Understanding

Quickwrite: Which of the letters to the editor makes the strongest argument? What makes that argument compelling?

_____

_____

_____

_____

📝 Writing Prompt: Argumentative

Write a letter to the editor in response to one of the editorials you have read in this unit. Use the steps outlined in the How to Write a Letter to the Editor section to guide your writing. Be sure to:

- Utilize an organizational structure that follows the specifications of your local newspaper and logically sequences your claim, reasons, evidence, and response to counterclaims.
- Use a variety of rhetorical techniques, including anecdotes, case studies, or analogies.
- Provide a concluding statement that follows logically from your argument.

✍ WRITING PROMPT: ARGUMENTATIVE

The following standards are addressed in the writing prompt:
- W.11-12.1a
- W.11-12.1b
- W.11-12.1e

Fallacies 101

Learning Targets

- Analyze the effects of logical fallacies on the way a text is read and understood.
- Use logical fallacies and refute the fallacies of others in a debate.

Preview

In this activity, you will analyze news articles to test your knowledge of the logical fallacies that you learned about in Unit 2. As you spot these fallacies, you will determine their likely effect on the reader.

Identifying Fallacies

1. You will be given a set of card manipulatives, some of which will contain the names of specific types of fallacies and others of which will contain the definitions. In your small group, you will need to match the fallacies with their definitions.

2. Next, read through the following informational text and check your answers.

Types of Fallacies

Fallacies are commonplace in advertising, political discourse, and everyday conversations—and they will continue to be as long as they work to persuade.

By learning to recognize them when you see them, you can strip away their power. There are many different ways to categorize fallacies, and many different names for the various types. The following 11 fallacies (adapted from Brooke Noel Moore and Richard Parker's *Critical Thinking*, 8th ed., 2007) are divided into the different types of offense they represent. Learn these, and you'll be ready to see through many of the rhetorical scams that come your way each day.

A. Logical Fallacies: Errors in Reasoning

- **Hasty generalization:** The leap to a generalized conclusion based on only a few instances. For example, on a trip to Paris you meet several rude Parisians, leading you to conclude that French people are rude.

- **Post hoc:** Literally meaning "after this," it's a causal fallacy in which a person assumes one thing caused another simply because it happened prior to the other. For instance, the high school soccer team loses an important game the day after they start wearing new uniforms. The coach blames the loss on the new uniforms.

B. Emotive Fallacies: Replacing Logic with Emotional Manipulation

- **Ad populum:** Literally meaning "appeal to the people"; arguing that something is true because other people think so; refers to a variety of appeals that play on the association of a person or subject with values that are held by members of a target group (think of images of the flag in ads playing on patriotism) or the suggestion that "everybody knows" that something is true (as with bandwagoning).

Learning Strategies

Discussion Groups
Graphic Organizer
Questioning the Text
Quickwrite
Rereading
Self-Editing

My Notes

ACTIVITY 3.12

PLAN

Materials: index cards with fallacy terms and definitions, Internet access
Suggested Pacing: 1 50-minute class period

TEACH

1 Before class, create one set of 22 index cards for each of the student groups that will participate in this activity. Eleven of the cards in each set should contain each of the 11 fallacy names. The other 11 cards should each contain a definition of one of the fallacies. Shuffle each set separately for group work.

2 Read the Learning Targets and Preview with students. Tell them that they will review what they learned in Unit 2 about logical fallacies and that they will use that understanding to analyze news articles for credibility, bias, and accuracy.

3 Read aloud the text of the Identifying Fallacies and Types of Fallacies sections. Ask and answer questions and clarify information as necessary.

4 Divide students into groups and hand out the prepared fallacy index card sets. Have students match the terms with the definitions. When they have completed the matching, have them confirm their choices by consulting the Types of Fallacies section.

College and Career Readiness Standards

Focus Standards:

W.11-12.4 Produce clear and coherent writing in which the development, organization, and style are appropriate to task, purpose, and audience.

W.11-12.5 Develop and strengthen writing as needed by planning, revising, editing, rewriting, or trying a new approach, focusing on addressing what is most significant for a specific purpose and audience.

SL.11-12.1 Initiate and participate effectively in a range of collaborative discussions (one-on-one, in groups, and teacher-led) with diverse partners on grades 11–12 topics, texts, and issues, building on others' ideas and expressing their own clearly and persuasively.

5 Vocabulary Development: Highlight the Word Connections box about foreign words and stress the fact that Latin forms the basis for much of English. Tell students that the area of logic is somewhat unique in that many Latin terms have entered our language while maintaining their original spellings. Then ask students how the example words are similar.

3.12

WORD CONNECTIONS

Foreign Words
Although the study of logic began in Ancient Greece, most terms used today for logical fallacies derive from Latin. Two terms frequently used in the names of logical fallacies are *post* ("after") and *ad* ("for" or "to"). Other words include:

antiquitatem = tradition
baculum = club (weapon)
hoc = this
hominem = person
ignorantium = ignorance
misericordiam = pity
populum = the people
ridiculum = ridicule

Because Latin forms the basis of so much of our own language, you can sometimes guess the English meanings of terms such as *populum, antiqutatem, ignorantium*, and *ridiculum* simply by looking at them closely.

My Notes

_____

_____

_____

_____

_____

_____

_____

_____

_____

_____

_____

_____

_____

_____

- **"Argument" from outrage:** Aristotle said that if you understand what makes a person angry, you can use that anger to persuade him or her to accept a position without critically evaluating it. This fallacy is the backbone of talk radio and of political rhetoric on both extremes of the political spectrum. It often employs loaded language and labels. It also includes scapegoating—blaming a certain group of people or even a single person.

- **Ad misericordiam, or appeal to pity:** If you have ever asked a teacher to give you a better grade or a second chance because things have been tough recently or because you worked so hard, you're guilty of this one! It refers to an attempt to use compassion or pity to replace a logical argument.

- **Ad baculum, or scare tactics:** An appeal to fear in place of logic. If a candidate for office says, "Electing my opponent will open the door for new terrorist attacks," it represents an attempt to scare people into rejecting the person despite providing no evidence to justify the claim.

C. Rhetorical Fallacies: Sidestepping Logic with Language

- **Straw man:** Erecting a distorted or exaggerated representation of a position that is easily refuted. For example, Schroth says, "But, you say, if high schools drop football it will deprive colleges and the pros of their feeder system," an argument that is, of course, a ridiculous attempt to justify high school football—and one that is thus easy to refute.

- **Ad hominem/genetic fallacy:** Literally meaning "to the man," ad hominem refers to attacks against a person himself- or herself rather than the ideas the person presents. This is a dominant feature in political campaigns, where sound-bite 30-second advertisements attack a candidate's character, often with mere innuendo, instead of his or her policy positions. When this extends to criticizing or rejecting a general type of something simply because it belongs to or was generated by that type, it is a genetic fallacy. For example, to say an idea comes from the "media elite" makes it sound like it should be rejected—but who are the media elite?

- **Red herring/smokescreen:** Answering the question by changing the subject. For example, when pulled over for speeding, a person might respond to the officer's question "Why were you speeding?" by saying, "The school no longer offers driver's education classes."

- **Slippery slope:** Half appeal to fear and half a causal fallacy, a person uses a slippery slope when they suggest one action will lead to an inevitable and undesirable outcome. To say legalizing voluntary euthanasia paves the way for forced euthanasia is a slippery slope argument.

- **Either/or (or false dilemma):** This is a conclusion that oversimplifies the argument by suggesting that there are only two possible sides or choices. It is very common in debates of policy, where issues are always complex but are reduced by politicians to simplistic binaries (either/or) for rhetorical purposes.

College and Career Readiness Standards

SL.11-12.3 Evaluate a speaker's point of view, reasoning, and use of evidence and rhetoric, assessing the stance, premises, links among ideas, word choice, points of emphasis, and tone used.

SL.11-12.6 Adapt speech to a variety of contexts and tasks, demonstrating a command of formal English when indicated or appropriate.

ACTIVITY 3.12 continued

6 Read aloud the introduction paragraph of the Analyzing the Effects of Fallacies section and focus students' attention on the graphic organizer in that section. Instruct them to fill out the organizer, modeling the text already in the first row as an example.

Analyzing the Effects of Fallacies

Review the editorials you have read in this unit. In the chart, list some logical fallacies from the editorials, the editorial in which you found each, and the fallacy's possible effect on the reader.

Editorial/Quote	Type of Logical Fallacy	Possible Effect
Potter: "[Sunstein's] worry is that if the newspaper declines, so might democracy."	straw man (nowhere in his editorial does Sunstein assert this) and slippery slope (decline of newspapers does not inevitably mean the decline of democracy)	The reader may be taken in by Potter's refutation of his misstatement of Sunstein's argument. By arguing how important newspapers are to democracy, the slippery slope may seem more likely.
Potter: "For decades, progressive critics have complained about the anti-democratic influence of the mass media."	hasty generalization, ad hominem	The reader may assume all progressives hold the same opinions and that their position as stated by Potter indicates that their views should not be considered on this or any matter.
Schroth: The *Times* article quotes "Kelby Jasmon, a high school student in Springfield, Ill., walking around today with two concussions, who says there is 'no chance' he would tell the coach if he gets hit hard and symptoms return."	hasty generalization	The reader may be led to believe that Jasmon's viewpoint is common. No evidence is presented on how rare the opinion actually is.
O'Connell: "Students who take rigorous courses are also less likely to drop out, and they perform better in vocational and technical courses."	post hoc	The reader may agree with O'Connell's counterintuitive assumption that students who are given harder work are less likely to give up. He presents no evidence for this or any consideration that there might be other factors involved in why the students stay in school and perform better (if his claim is indeed true).

7 Conduct a brainstorming session for current, high-profile, controversial issues and then have the class vote on a favorite for the mock debate described in the Fallacy Face-Off section.

8 Split the class into two or more teams. Give the teams several minutes to come up with a fallacious appeal for each team member. You could have students draw a particular type of fallacy from a pile of their index cards, or you could let them choose their own.

9 Complete the steps as directed in the Fallacy Face-Off section. As individual team members take turns presenting their fallacious appeals to the class, have members of the other teams identify and challenge the fallacy being used by the speakers. Remind students to adapt their speech to the context by using formal language.

10 Have teams discuss the questions in student step 7 among themselves to consolidate their understanding of the power of fallacies and the need to be wary of them in public discourse.

11 Give students time to respond to the Writing Prompt and revise their letters to the editor from Activity 3.11. Have student pairs share their revised letters, clearly marking the text for the added fallacy before turning in the revised draft.

ASSESS

Use students' responses to the Writing Prompt to assess their ability to identify and use fallacies. The skill of identifying fallacies is important because they should be avoided as students prepare their Embedded Assessment.

ADAPT

If students have difficulty choosing a fallacy to use, have them list the central ideas or claims in their original letters. Tell them to ask themselves which fallacy can be used to make each of these ideas or claims false.

3.12

Fallacy Face-Off

3. Now that you have been introduced to the concept of fallacious appeals, take up the challenge to use as many as possible in a **Fallacy Face-Off**. As a class, select a current, high-profile, controversial issue. Feel free to pull this topic from some of your recent newspaper readings. You will use this topic in a **mock debate**.

4. Next, split into teams. Each team member will select or be assigned a fallacious appeal to use regarding the selected topic.

5. When the teams are ready, they will use these fallacious appeals in a mock debate. Each team will take turns presenting their appeals to the class as if presenting at a public rally, televised debate, or other venue of the class's choosing.

6. As other teams present their arguments, you will be responsible for identifying and challenging the nature of the fallacy being used by the speaker. All discourse and interaction will be conducted courteously and respectfully. Be sure to evaluate each speaker's reasoning and use of evidence.

7. After exploring these fallacies in class, discuss the following questions with your team:

   • Why are fallacies so common in our political discourse? Which ones are most common, and why?

   • Why are fallacies so powerful—and so dangerous?

   • Why might you choose to use a fallacy—or rhetorical slanters—in a letter or speech? What would be the pros and cons of doing so?

   • How does the use of fallacies affect the ethos of a writer or speaker?

   • What is the relationship between considering your audience and deciding whether to use fallacious appeals or slanters?

   • How can a speaker or writer's use of fallacies influence an audience's sense of trust in their argument?

> **Writing Prompt: Argumentative**
>
> Review the letter to the editor that you wrote in Activity 3.11 and revise it using at least one of the types of fallacies from this activity. Share your revision with a partner and ask him or her to identify the type of fallacy you used. Be sure to:
>
> • Revise your letter to clearly state your position, if needed.
>
> • Incorporate at least one fallacy into your letter.
>
> • Prepare your letter in final draft, checking that it is grammatically and technically accurate. As needed, consult references to ensure that you are spelling and using words correctly.

WRITING PROMPT: ARGUMENTATIVE

The following standards are addressed in the writing prompt:

• W.11-12.4   • W.11-12.5
• W.11-12.1b

How to Read and Write an Editorial Cartoon

Learning Targets
- Analyze the effectiveness of characteristics of editorial cartoons.
- Apply knowledge from this analysis to create an editorial cartoon.

Preview
In this activity, you will delve into the world of editorial cartoons. Once you have studied the genre and analyzed some examples, you will have an opportunity to create your own cartoon.

As You Read
- Circle unknown words and phrases. Try to determine the meaning of the words by using context clues, word parts, or a dictionary.
- Put a question mark next to anything that raises a question for you.
- Put an exclamation point next to anything that you have a strong response to or surprises you.

Informational Text

An Inside Look at Editorial Cartoons

by **Bill Brennen**

1 A few weeks ago, Joy Utecht, the journalism teacher at Grand Island Senior High, asked if I could visit with some of her students about editorial cartoons.

2 The invitation was exciting because editorial cartoons are one of my favorite subjects. Very few items are as unique to a newspaper as editorial cartoons.

3 A very brief history lesson: Editorial cartoons first appeared in the United States on single-page broadsheets during the colonial times. The first popular cartoon is a snake severed into 13 parts with the names of each colony by each piece. The caption is simple, "Divided we die."

4 Such a theme helped the colonies, with their diverse locations and interests, unite under a common cause.

5 Flash forward to the years in New York City after the Civil War, when Tammany Hall[1] became such a powerful political machine that it nearly sucked the life out of its residents. In addition, William Tweed stole millions from the taxpayers.

---

[1] Tammany Hall was the name given to the Democratic political machine that dominated New York City politics from the 1790s until the 1960s.

Learning Strategies
Brainstorming
Sketching
Skimming/Scanning
Visualizing

My Notes

WORD CONNECTIONS

Etymology
Broadsheets, also called *broadsides*, were originally large pieces of paper printed on one side, often used for announcements. They later evolved into the modern newspaper. Newspapers considered broadsheets are larger and tend to cover serious stories, as opposed to *tabloids*, which are smaller and tend to cover more sensational stories.

College and Career Readiness Standards

Focus Standards:

RI.11-12.1 Cite strong and thorough textual evidence to support analysis of what the text says explicitly as well as inferences drawn from the text, including determining where the text leaves matters uncertain.

W.11-12.5 Develop and strengthen writing as needed by planning, revising, editing, rewriting, or trying a new approach, focusing on addressing what is most significant for a specific purpose and audience.

Additional Standards Addressed:
RI.11-12.10

ACTIVITY 3.13

PLAN
Materials: various one-panel cartoons and editorial cartoons, Internet access
Suggested Pacing: 1 50-minute class period

TEACH

1 Read the Learning Targets and the Preview sections with students.

2 Before class, put together an equal number of comic strips and editorial cartoons. As a warm-up activity, provide one cartoon to each student. Have each student identify it as an editorial cartoon or a comic strip and find a partner who has the other type of illustration. Tell pairs to construct Venn diagrams indicating the similarities and differences between the two types of illustrations, considering subject matter, style, demonstration of humor, and so on. Have the class use their diagrams to contribute to a master list of similarities and differences and arrange those in a master Venn diagram on the board.

 TEACHER TO TEACHER

You might choose to have students find the cartoons themselves. Split them into two groups. Have one group scan newspaper op-ed pages and cut out editorial cartoons. Have the other scan the comics section and cut out single-panel comic strips. (You could assign this as homework for the previous night.)

3 Vocabulary Development: Highlight the Word Connections box. Remind students that learning a word's etymology is often a useful way to remember its meaning. Select a compelling word, such as *caricatures* or *syndicated*, and have students research the word's current meaning and etymology. Invite a volunteer to explain the connection between the word's origins and its current use and meaning.

4 FIRST READ: Conduct a shared reading of "An Inside Look at Editorial Cartoons." Direct students to place a question mark next to text that raises a question for them, place an exclamation point next to text that elicits a strong response, and circle unknown words and phrases and try to determine their meanings by using context clues, word parts, or a dictionary.

 TEXT COMPLEXITY

Overall: Accessible
Lexile: 1050L
Qualitative: Moderate Difficulty
Task: Accessible (Understand)

5 As students are reading, monitor their progress. Be sure they are engaged with the text, annotating it as directed.

6 Tell students to pause at the end of paragraph 7 and state two things that Thomas Nast is remembered for today.

7 Tell students to pause after paragraph 11 and give the word exemplified by "the JFK haircut, the LBJ ears, the Nixon eyebrows, the Carter teeth and the Clinton jaw."

3.13

My Notes

6 Eventually, *The New York Times* and eventually law enforcement officials began investigations of the Tweed Ring, but it was the powerful cartoons of Nast that brought the politicians to their knees. At one point, Nast, who worked for *Harper's Weekly*, turned down a bribe of $500,000 to discontinue his cartoons.

7 Instead, Nast made Tweed the most recognizable face in America. When Tweed tried to flee conviction, he was arrested in Spain, because authorities recognized his face from Nast's cartoons.

8 By the way, Nast deserves partial credit for another icon, one that has stood the test of time. Along with an artist named Clement Moore, Nast drew the first Santa Claus.

9 Photography became a part of American newspapers and magazines as early as the Civil War, but the process was difficult and illustrations remained a part of American newspapers until early into the 20th Century.

10 But the sketches known as editorial cartoons are as popular today as they ever have been. People love the humor, simplicity and caricatures of politicians of the day. Caricatures, I told the students at Senior High, are exaggerations of one's physical features.

11 In recent years, there have been the JFK haircut, the LBJ ears, the Nixon eyebrows, the Carter teeth and the Clinton jaw. Of course, each cartoonist has his or her own style, but it is amazing how they reach out to the same features to identify a politician.

12 A good editorial cartoon must have five basic features.

- It must be simple. ...

- People must understand it. The cartoon must make sense to those who read the particular paper. A school newspaper might run a cartoon about cafeteria food that includes an inside joke and isn't readily understood by the general public. The cartoon would only make sense in the school newspaper.

- The cartoon must be timely. ...

- It must evoke emotion. A good cartoon should make people laugh or make them mad.

- Always, the cartoon must give a point of view. The cartoon may be looking at the truth, but it usually is coming from a specific viewpoint. When we look down at an object, the viewpoint is very different when we look up at the object. Editorial cartoons are the same way.

13 The *Independent* doesn't always agree with the viewpoint of each cartoon in the paper. Most certainly the readers don't always agree with them. But we all should agree that political cartoons are thought provoking. Just like a photograph, a well-illustrated editorial cartoon can be worth a thousand words.

Scaffolding the Text-Dependent Questions

1. What details in paragraphs 5–7 indicate that editorial cartoons can be agents of change? Reread paragraphs 5–7. What information does the author include about the work of Thomas Nast? What was he offered to stop drawing? What effect did his cartoons eventually have on the life and career of William Tweed? RI.11-12.1

14 There probably are about 100 newspapers, give or take a few, that employ full-time cartoonists. Unfortunately, it is a luxury that only metropolitan-sized newspapers can afford. Smaller newspapers subscribe to syndicated features for the right to reprint some of the better cartoons that have been published.

15 The next time you look at an editorial cartoon in the newspaper, try to look at it a new way. Instead of thinking about just whether you agree or disagree with the message, see if the cartoons have the five basic components to it[*sic*]. Then you can determine whether the message is getting through.

Making Observations
- What print features did you notice in the text?
- Based on your question marks and exclamation points, what most surprises or interests you in the text?

My Notes

8 After reading the text for the first time, guide the class in a discussion by asking the Making Observations questions. Check students' general comprehension of the text based on their observations, asking follow-up questions if needed.

Scaffolding the Text-Dependent Questions

2. What are some questions you might research in preparation for an informational report on editorial cartoons? Skim the informational text. After each paragraph, come up with a question that would lead to a better understanding of that section. Which questions would make the best research questions? W.11-12.5

3. What explanation is given in paragraphs 10–12 for why photographs have never replaced editorial cartoons? Reread the three paragraphs. In paragraph 10, what three things do people love about editorial cartoons? In paragraph 12, what should "a good editorial cartoon" evoke in viewers? What can cartoons accomplish that photographs cannot? How can exaggerating an image help communicate a message? RI.11-12.1

9 RETURNING TO THE TEXT: Guide students to return to the text to respond to the text-dependent questions. Invite them to work together as a class to reread the text and answer the questions. Remind them to use text evidence in their responses.

10 Observe and listen as students answer the text-dependent questions. If they have difficulty, scaffold the questions by rephrasing them or breaking them down into smaller parts. See the Scaffolding the Text-Dependent Questions boxes for suggestions.

3.13

Returning to the Text

- Return to the informational text as you respond to the following questions. Use text evidence to support your responses.
- Write any additional questions you have about the text in your Reader/Writer Notebook.

1. What details in paragraphs 5–7 indicate that editorial cartoons can be agents of change?

   Brennen relates how the cartoons of Thomas Nast were instrumental in bringing down William Tweed and the other corrupt, powerful politicians of New York's Tammany Hall, even though these same politicians offered Nast a half-million dollar bribe if he would stop drawing them. When Tweed tried to escape, his face was so familiar from Nast's cartoons that he was recognized in Spain and arrested.

2. What are some questions you might research in preparation for an informational report on editorial cartoons?

   Who are some of the most famous editorial cartoonists? What are some instances in which editorial cartoons have helped bring about social change? How are editorial cartoons interpreted? Are any issues considered off-limits to editorial cartoonists? Have there ever been scandals or lawsuits over editorial cartoons? What methods do editorial cartoonists use to convey their messages?

3. What explanation is given in paragraphs 10–12 for why photographs have never replaced editorial cartoons?

   Unlike photographs, editorial cartoons have "humor, simplicity, and caricatures." They are drawn to show a specific "point of view" and to "make people laugh or make them mad." Photographs show what actually happens; they cannot be manipulated to the extent that cartoons can to include exaggerated features or situations, to create humorous effects, or to provide social commentary.

Reading Editorial Cartoons

4. Because there is so little space for an editorial cartoonist to make his or her point, the cartoonist often uses symbols and allusions as shorthand for the meaning of the cartoon. Examine each of the cartoons your teacher supplies and identify the symbols and allusions. Why might the cartoonist have chosen these symbols or allusions?

5. What is there about editorial cartoons that make them particularly suited to publication in newspapers?

6. Most editorial cartoons present a specific political perspective. Do the cartoons you are examining have an identifiable point of view? Examine and describe the author's use of print and graphic features in expressing his or her perspective.

7. Editorial cartoons are designed to evoke emotion—humor, anger, or outrage, for example. What emotions are evoked in the cartoons you are analyzing?

8. Based on your responses to the other questions here, what does the messages of your assigned cartoons seem to be, and what can you infer about their intended purpose?

Creating Your Own Editorial Cartoons

9. Now that you have had some experience reading and analyzing political cartoons, try to create some of your own.

   - Brainstorm topic ideas by thinking about current events in your school, your hometown, or the world. List a few ideas.
   - Choose one of your ideas and describe a point that you might want to make about that event. Perhaps you agree and want to show your support, or perhaps you would like to ridicule those who might feel differently.
   - What symbols, sayings, pop culture allusions, or other easily recognizable references might be appropriate for this topic?
   - Sketch a very rough draft of what your cartoon might look like.

11 Read through the text of the Reading Editorial Cartoons section with the class. Divide students into pairs and have them analyze the editorial cartoons they were provided at the beginning of the activity. Encourage them to identify symbols and allusions. Ask them to write responses to each of the questions in the section in their Reader/Writer Notebooks.

12 Read aloud the text of the Creating Your Own Editorial Cartoons section. Take students through the bulleted steps. Ask them to write a statement they might want to make about an issue of importance to their school, their hometown, or the world. Then ask them to visualize the issue and sketch their ideas. Remind them that the purpose is not to create great artwork but rather to make a meaningful point on a particular subject.

13 Make sure students attend to the Independent Reading Checkpoint. Direct them to create in their Reader/Writer Notebooks a portfolio of the self-selected articles they have read with commentary after each article as described in the task. To assess their independent reading, set a date to check the portfolios in their notebooks.

ASSESS

Use students' sketches for the Creating Your Own Editorial Cartoons task to determine their ability to illustrate clear points of view on issues, including the use of recognizable symbols and allusions.

ADAPT

If students are having difficulty creating editorial cartoons, have them summarize in writing their topics and their viewpoints on these topics. Encourage them to include the reasoning behind their viewpoints. Then give students guidance on translating their views the reasons into visual images.

3.13

⊕ Independent Reading Checkpoint

Review your self-selected news source. Which articles have you read? Create a portfolio of these articles by printing copies or writing brief summaries. Add commentary after each article, including the writer's claim or topic, a description of rhetorical organization or strategies, and an analysis of effectiveness.

Creating an Op-Ed News Project

Materials: student drafts of informational articles (3.6), editorials (3.9), letters to the editor (3.11 and 3.12), and editorial cartoons (3.13); access to computers for word processing (optional)
Suggested Pacing: 2 50-minute class periods

ASSIGNMENT

Working in groups, your assignment is to plan, develop, write, revise, and present an informational article on a timely and debatable issue of significance to your school community, your local community, or a national audience. After your group completes its article, you will individually develop a variety of editorial products that reflect your point of view (agreement, alternative, or opposing) on the topic. Be creative with your editorial products and include at least two different pieces, such as cartoons, editorials, letters, posters, photos, and so on.

TEACHER TO TEACHER

You may want to keep groups small (three or four students) to make sure each member has a clear role in producing the various editorial projects, perhaps one piece per student.

1 Read the Assignment with students to ensure they understand their task for the Embedded Assessment.

2 **Planning and Prewriting:** Help student groups split up tasks and decide on the formats for their pieces as needed. Remind students that they need a variety of perspectives.

3 **Drafting:** Remind students to review informational and persuasive models from this unit. Ask them to carefully select rhetorical elements, balancing the need for persuasiveness and appeal while responsibly avoiding emotional manipulation.

4 **Evaluating and Revising:** As part of revising, have groups review the work of another group and comment on how effectively they have constructed their arguments. Peers could comment on the technical correctness, timeliness, relevance, and persuasive use of language and reasoning.

5 **Checking and Editing for Publication:** Have students consider submitting this project for publication through a class or school newspaper or website. Emphasize the importance of grammatical and technical accuracy in real-world publishing. If you prefer, you can expand the scope of the presentation aspect from the layout of an actual newspaper op-ed section to include features of an online editorial (wikis, blogs, etc.).

Planning and Prewriting: Take time to plan all the texts that you will include.	■ How can you build a list of potential issues that are both interesting to your group and debatable and timely? ■ What format will your opinion pieces take (e.g., editorials by newspaper staff, letters to the editor, editorial cartoon)? ■ How will you split the various tasks and roles among your group members so that everyone is doing a fair amount of work?
Drafting: Decide how you will incorporate support and organize texts.	■ How will you gather evidence to support your positions? ■ How can you use models of argumentative writing from this unit to help you add rhetorical elements that will appeal to your audience? ■ What sort of organizational patterns do the kinds of pieces you are writing tend to follow? How can you emulate these so that your pieces read like a real informational or editorial publication?
Evaluating and Revising: Create opportunities to review and revise.	■ What sort of strategies can you use to provide feedback to each other on the quality of your pieces (e.g., SMELL, SOAPSTone)? ■ What kinds of feedback from peers and the Scoring Guide can help guide your revision? ■ How will you ensure that your product as a whole represents multiple perspectives on your topic?
Checking and Editing for Publication: Be sure your work is the best it can be.	■ How can you use examples of either print or online newspapers to create a realistic layout for your articles? ■ How will you check your own or each other's work for grammatical and technical accuracy? What references will you consult?

Reflection

After completing this Embedded Assessment, think about how you went about accomplishing the assignment, and respond to the following:

- How do newspapers affect public opinion or public perception?
- Which of the rhetorical techniques that your group used do you think were the most effective in appealing to your audience? Why?

College and Career Readiness Standards

Focus Standards:

W.11-12.1a Introduce precise, knowledgeable claim(s), establish the significance of the claim(s), distinguish the claim(s) from alternate or opposing claims, and create an organization that logically sequences claim(s), counterclaims, reasons, and evidence.

W.11-12.1b Develop claim(s) and counterclaims fairly and thoroughly, supplying the most relevant evidence for each while pointing out the strengths and limitations of both in a manner that anticipates the audience's knowledge level, concerns, values, and possible biases.

W.11-12.1c Use words, phrases, and clauses as well as varied syntax to link the major sections of the text, create cohesion, and clarify the relationships between claim(s) and reasons, between reasons and evidence, and between claim(s) and counterclaims.

6 **Reflection:** Have students respond to the Reflection questions. Be sure they address the Reflection questions as a separate part of the Embedded Assessment assignment so they can include that response separately.

7 **Portfolios:** At this point you may want to ask students to go to their portfolios and find previous unit reflection questions so that they can get a sense of their growth as academic thinkers and producers.

All notes for and drafts of the editorial products should be collected and presented together to show the process students completed in successfully accomplishing the tasks.

SCORING GUIDE

When you score this Embedded Assessment, you may wish to download and print copies of the Scoring Guide from SpringBoard Digital to have a copy to mark for each student's work.

SCORING GUIDE

Scoring Criteria	Exemplary	Proficient	Emerging	Incomplete
Ideas	The project • explicitly represents multiple and varied editorial perspectives • is extremely persuasive throughout every piece, demonstrating a thorough understanding of persuasive techniques • provides evidence of thorough and original research throughout; each piece demonstrates appropriate and ample evidence to support the thesis.	The project • represents various perspectives that are implied throughout the work as a whole • demonstrates a clear intention to persuade in most pieces, showing an adequate understanding of persuasive techniques • demonstrates that research has been conducted to support the positions; the majority of pieces demonstrate sufficient evidence supporting the thesis.	The project • represents a limited range of perspectives • demonstrates an intention to persuade in a few of the pieces; some of the pieces may be descriptive or expository rather than persuasive • demonstrates that some research has been conducted to support the positions with lapses in completeness to adequately support the thesis.	The project • lacks a range of perspectives • offers pieces that may be descriptive or expository rather than persuasive • does not demonstrate adequate research; the majority of the pieces demonstrate insufficient evidence to adequately support the thesis and/or opinions remain unsupported.
Structure	The project • is organized exceptionally, so that ideas move smoothly and comfortably • accurately follows the organizational pattern of the article type, whether informational or editorial.	The project • is organized in a way that is clear and easy to follow • largely follows the organizational pattern of the article type, whether informational or editorial.	The project • is unevenly organized with lapses in coherence • attempts to follow the organizational pattern of the article type, whether informational or editorial, with some lapses.	The project • is difficult to follow and may jump too rapidly between ideas • struggles to follow the organizational pattern of the article type, whether informational or editorial.
Use of Language	The project • demonstrates purposeful use of rhetoric designed to appeal to the target audience(s) • contains few or no errors in grammar or conventions.	The project • demonstrates functional use of rhetoric but may not directly appeal to the target audience • may include minor errors in grammar and conventions that do not interfere with understanding.	The project • attempts to use rhetoric with limited appeal to the target audience • includes some errors in grammar and conventions that interfere with the meaning.	The project • inconsistently demonstrates rhetoric • includes many errors in grammar and conventions that seriously interfere with the meaning.

College and Career Readiness Standards

W.11-12.1e Provide a concluding statement or section that follows from and supports the argument presented.

W.11-12.4 Produce clear and coherent writing in which the development, organization, and style are appropriate to task, purpose, and audience.

W.11-12.5 Develop and strengthen writing as needed by planning, revising, editing, rewriting, or trying a new approach, focusing on addressing what is most significant for a specific purpose and audience.

W.11-12.10 Write routinely over extended time frames (time for research, reflection, and revision) and shorter time frames (a single sitting or a day or two) for a range of tasks, purposes, and audiences.

Previewing Embedded Assessment 2 and Introducing Satire

Learning Targets
- Reflect on concepts, Essential Questions, and vocabulary.
- Identify and analyze the knowledge and skills needed to complete Embedded Assessment 2 successfully.
- Generate examples of satirical writing.

Preview
In this activity, you will review the Essential Questions, preview the assignments for Independent Reading and Embedded Assessment 2, and learn about the literary genre of satire.

Making Connections
The op-ed page is an important forum for the exchange of ideas in our society, but the conversation does not stop there. Not everyone who contributes to the conversation means exactly what they say. Satire may be the tool of choice for some writers (and cartoonists) who prefer to use irony and a range of tones to make statements about the issues of the day. If you have ever enjoyed watching late-night comedy shows, you know how effective—and how much fun—this approach can be when it comes to changing perception of the subjects being lampooned. Immersing yourself in the art of satire, you will explore how writers use a range of genres and techniques to present their messages in indirect ways. In this way, satirists can make powerful contributions to the marketplace of ideas.

Essential Questions
Based on your study of the first part of the unit, review and revise your answers to the Essential Questions.

1. What is the role of media in our society, and how can we become responsible consumers and producers of information in a digital age?

2. How can writers use satire to bring about change in society?

Unpacking Embedded Assessment 2
Closely read the assignment for Embedded Assessment 2: Writing a Satirical Piece.

You have been studying how opinions are expressed and perceived in a democratic society through a variety of rhetorical formats including satire. Your assignment is to develop a satirical piece critiquing some aspect of our society.

In your own words, summarize what you will need to know to complete this assessment successfully. With your class, create a graphic organizer to represent the skills and knowledge you will need to complete the tasks identified in the Embedded Assessment.

Learning Strategies
Close Reading
Graphic Organizer
Marking the Text

My Notes

College and Career Readiness Standards

Focus Standards:

SL.11-12.1b Work with peers to promote civil, democratic discussions and decision making, set clear goals and deadlines, and establish individual roles as needed.

SL.11-12.5 Make strategic use of digital media (e.g., textual, graphical, audio, visual, and interactive elements) in presentations to enhance understanding of findings, reasoning, and evidence and to add interest.

L.11-12.6 Acquire and use accurately general academic and domain-specific words and phrases, sufficient for reading, writing, speaking, and listening at the college and career readiness level; demonstrate independence in gathering vocabulary knowledge when considering a word or phrase important to comprehension or expression.

ACTIVITY 3.14

PLAN
Materials: poster paper, Internet access; optional DVD/video player and video monitor
Suggested Pacing: 1 50-minute class period

TEACH
1 Review the Learning Targets and Preview with students to introduce the activity.

2 Have students read the Making Connections section. The text should help students see the relationship between editorial and opinion pieces and a literary text such as a satire.

3 Review vocabulary from the first half of the unit and preview additional vocabulary.

4 Read aloud the Essential Questions and have students think-pair-share their responses.

5 Next, read aloud the assignment in the Unpacking Embedded Assessment 2 box. To preview the skills and knowledge necessary for success on Embedded Assessment 2, students should locate the Assignment and Scoring Guide. Guide students through a **close reading** and unpacking of the prompts, steps, and scoring criteria. Use poster paper to create a **graphic organizer** listing the **skills** and knowledge they'll need.

6 Direct students' attention to the Planning Independent Reading box. Have students form small groups to identify authors and texts they know are satirical. Ask each group to add those authors and texts to a poster board that can remain visible to students throughout the unit.

7 Review the Literary Vocabulary box with students and see how familiar they are with the techniques of satire. Students should already be familiar with some of the terms. Then review the Introduction to Satire section. Have different volunteers read each characteristic aloud.

8 Form small groups and send students to the Internet to find examples of the terms and techniques related to satire.

9 Then have the students use poster paper to create visualizations of the techniques of satirical writing. Depending on the number of small groups, assign each group one or two techniques. Post these visuals for easy reference during the remainder of the unit.

10 **Vocabulary Development:** Discuss the Word Connections box with students. Ask them to think of other words that share the prefix *de-*. As an extension, have students complete the **Roots and Affixes Brainstorm** graphic organizer.

My Notes

VOCABULARY

LITERARY

Satire is a manner of writing that mixes a critical attitude with wit and humor in an effort to improve humankind and human institutions. Editorial cartoons are often rather satirical. You will learn more about satire in the second half of this unit.

Horatian satire pokes fun at human foibles and folly with a witty, gentle, and even indulgent tone.

Juvenalian satire denounces, sometimes harshly, human vice and error in dignified and solemn tones.

WORD CONNECTIONS

Roots and Affixes

Denounce begins with the Latin prefix *de-*, which means "remove from" or "do the opposite of." The root of *denounce* is from the Latin *nuntiare*, meaning "to report." Adding *de-* creates the meaning of reporting in a negative way. Determine the meaning of **derision** using the meaning of the Latin prefix *de-* and the Latin root *ride‾re*, meaning "to laugh."

🕐 Planning Independent Reading

In this unit, you will have the opportunity to further explore the entertaining genre of satire. Satire is a poplar genre for news outlets, television shows, and websites. Many famous works of literature utilize satire as well. Satire is an entertaining way for readers to critically analyze a topic, often in a humorous way.

Collaborate with peers to discuss satirical authors and texts. Include both modern and historical texts and authors. Based on this discussion, compile a list of works for independent reading based on your interests.

3. As you read the following text, use your metacognitive markers to indicate anything that provokes a question (?), anything about which you wish to comment or make a connection (*), and anything you find surprising (!). Be prepared to discuss your response.

Introduction to Satire

Satire is a literary genre that uses irony, wit, and sometimes sarcasm to expose humanity's vices and foibles, giving impetus to change or reform through ridicule. Types of direct satire include **Horatian satire** and **Juvenalian satire**, named after the Roman writers Horace and Juvenal, who made the genre famous. As you read satire, look for these characteristic techniques of satiric writing.

Irony: A mode of expression that uses words (verbal irony) or events (situational irony) to convey a reality different from and usually opposite to appearance or expectation. The surprise recognition by the audience often produces a comic effect. When a text intended to be ironic is not seen as such, the effect can be disastrous. To be an effective piece of sustained irony, there must be some sort of audience tip-off through style, tone, use of clear exaggeration, or other device.

Hyperbole: Deliberate exaggeration to achieve an effect; overstatement.

Litotes: A form of understatement that involves making an affirmative point by denying its opposite. Example: "The grave's a fine and private place, / But none, I think, do there embrace." (Andrew Marvell, "To His Coy Mistress")

Caricature: An exaggeration or other distortion of an individual's prominent features or characteristics to the point of making that individual appear ridiculous. The term is applied more often to graphic representations than to literary ones.

Wit: Most commonly understood as clever expression—whether aggressive or harmless, that is, with or without derogatory intent toward someone or something in particular. We also tend to think of wit as being characterized by a mocking or paradoxical quality, evoking laughter through apt phrasing.

Sarcasm: Intentional derision, generally directed at another person and intended to hurt. The term comes from a Greek word meaning "to tear flesh like dogs" and signifies a cutting remark. Sarcasm usually involves obvious verbal irony, achieving its effect by jeeringly stating the opposite of what is meant so as to heighten the insult.

Ridicule: Words intended to belittle a person or idea and arouse contemptuous laughter. The goal is to condemn or criticize by making the thing, idea, or person seem laughable and ridiculous.

Parody: An imitation of a work or of an author with the idea of ridiculing the author, ideas, or work. The parodist exploits the peculiarities of an author's expression: his or her propensity to use too many parentheses, certain favorite words, or other elements of the author's style.

Invective: Speech or writing that abuses, denounces, or attacks. It can be directed against a person, cause, idea, or system. It employs a heavy use of negative emotive language. Example: "I cannot but conclude the bulk of your natives to be the most pernicious race of little odious vermin that nature ever suffered to crawl upon the surface of the earth." (Jonathan Swift, *Gulliver's Travels*)

Characteristics of Satire Poster

Create a poster that includes text and visual elements to illustrate the different types of satire explained in the Introduction to Satire section. You may create your own examples or use examples from books, newspapers, or other print or online publications. Present your poster to the class.

My Notes

ASSESS

Use students' responses to the Characteristics of Satire Poster activity to assess their understanding of satirical elements.

ADAPT

If students have difficulty creating posters about satire, provide them with popular media representations of parody, satire, hyperbole, caricature, and so on, and have students work with partners or small groups to label each with sticky notes.

PLAN

Suggested Pacing: 1 50-minute class period

TEACH

1 Explain to students that while many writers use a serious tone to persuade their audiences, some use humor to entertain or to convey a serious message. Students will now examine how writers use humor to persuade and will practice doing so themselves.

2 Read the Learning Targets, Preview, As You Read, and About the Author sections with students. Help them understand the academic vocabulary they encounter.

3 FIRST READ: Conduct an **echo reading** of "Let's Hear It for the Cheerleaders." Use the Echo Reading to model Bouchier's tone to the class. The strength of his satire relies on his authorial persona's mild intellectual elitism.

 TEXT COMPLEXITY

Overall: Complex
Lexile: 1110L
Qualitative: Moderate Difficulty
Task: Challenging (Evaluate)

4 Pause after paragraph 1 and point out the hyperbole used.

LEVELED DIFFERENTIATED INSTRUCTION

Beginning If your class includes Spanish-speaking students who are at an early stage in their English language development, you may find it useful to have them look up the vocabulary terms from this activity using the Spanish/English glossary in the Resources section of the student edition.

5 As students are reading, monitor their progress. Be sure they are engaged with the text and annotating words, phrases, or sentences they find funny and instances of parody or caricature. Evaluate whether the selected reading mode is effective.

Learning Strategies

Diffusing
Marking the Text
Quickwrite

My Notes

Learning Targets

- Analyze the author's message embedded in the satire.
- Evaluate the author's use of satire to achieve a specific purpose.

Preview

In this activity, you will read a satirical article and analyze and explain the elements of satire in the article.

As You Read

- Highlight words, phrases, or sentences you find funny.
- Circle unknown words and phrases. Try to determine the meaning of the words by using context clues, word parts, or a dictionary.

About the Author

David Bouchier is a British writer who has lived in the United States since 1986. He has written fiction, nonfiction, commentaries, and humor columns for newspapers, literary journals, and magazines. He is also an award-winning essayist for National Public Radio.

Satire

Let's Hear It for the Cheerleaders

by **David Bouchier**

1 Strange things happen on college campuses in summer. I was nearly trampled to death the other day by a horde of very young women wearing very short red skirts and chanting something that sounded like "A fence! A fence!"

2 A fence might be a very good idea, perhaps with some razor wire and a warning sign saying "Danger: Cheerleaders Ahead." Long Island is host to more than a dozen cheerleader camps. For the educationally gifted, Hofstra and Adelphi Universities even offer cheerleading scholarships ("Give me an A! Give me an A!").

3 But I think there is some intellectual work to be done here. Cheerleading needs a history, a philosophy and, above all, a more sophisticated theory of communications.

4 The cheerleading phenomenon is almost unknown in the rest of the world. British soccer fans do their own cheerleading, with a medley of traditional songs, bricks and bottles. In less civilized parts of the world, fans express their enthusiasm by running onto the field and beating up the opposing

---

College and Career Readiness Standards

Focus Standards:

RI.11-12.1 Cite strong and thorough textual evidence to support analysis of what the text says explicitly as well as inferences drawn from the text, including determining where the text leaves matters uncertain.

RI.11-12.6 Determine an author's point of view or purpose in a text in which the rhetoric is particularly effective, analyzing how style and content contribute to the power, persuasiveness, or beauty of the text.

Additional Standards Addressed:
RI.11-12.4, RI.11-12.10

---

6 Pause after paragraph 6. Ask students how the author uses humor to point out what he feels is the uselessness of the skills cheerleaders learn.

team. Only in America do we have professional partisans to do the jumping and yelling for us.

My Notes

5 Strange as it may seem to foreigners, the cheerleading industry has many ardent supporters. It is said to build self-confidence, positive attitudes and a mysterious quality called spirit, which seems to involve smiling a lot. Cheerleading also teaches the value of teamwork, something that women have often despised in the past as a male excuse for mindless violence and idiotic loyalties. "Be 100 percent behind your team 100 percent of the time" is a slogan that would be heartily endorsed by Slobodan Milosevic, the Orange Order and the Irish Republican Army.

6 Young cheerleaders also acquire valuable practical skills: impossible balancing tricks, back flips and the brass lungs they will need for child raising or being heard at the departmental meeting. Above all, they learn to compete in hundreds of local and national events. Cheerleaders are clearly the corporate leaders and the political stars of the future.

7 Cheerleader culture is much broader and shallower than I had imagined. There are glossy magazines and webzines featuring the essential equipment: deodorants, contact lenses, Cheer Gear, makeup, party dresses and miracle diets. Novices can learn how to create a successful cheer routine with hot music, unique moves, fab formations, and multiple levels. They can also learn to make their own pom poms (called just "Poms"). There are international stars out there you've never heard of, and even a few anonymous muscular cheerleading males, whose job it is to support the base of the feminine pyramid.

8 Despite cheerleaders' obsession with pyramids, my research suggests that cheerleading began in ancient Greece, rather than in Egypt. The first cheerleaders were called Maenads, female attendants of the god Bacchus. Their task was to encourage the crowds to have a good time, with frenzied rites and extravagant gestures. The opposing squad, the Furies, were merciless goddesses of vengeance who would swing into violent action if their team was losing. The ancient Greeks must get the credit for being the first to give young women these important career opportunities.

9 So many teams were decimated by the Furies or led astray by the Maenads that cheerleading fell into disrepute for 2,000 years, until it was revived in a kinder, gentler form in the United States. But it's still a dangerous activity. In an average year, high school footballers lose 5.6 playing days to injuries, according to the January 1998 Harper's Index, a compilation of statistics. Cheerleaders lose 28.8 days. These accidents are blamed on excessive acrobatics and the passion for building taller and taller pyramids.

10 But all enthusiasm is dangerous, especially when it takes a physical form. If cheerleading is part of education, let's use it to educate by focusing on the message. Surely we can do better than waving our poms, doing somersaults and chanting:

novices: beginners
compilation: collection

Scaffolding the Text-Dependent Questions

1. In paragraph 1, what information does the reader understand that Bouchier's persona does not? What is the effect on the tone of the text? What are the cheerleaders actually saying when Bouchier hears "A fence"? How does this misunderstanding affect the readers? RI.11-12.1

2. In paragraph 5, what rhetorical devices does the author use to shape the readers' perception of cheerleading? What effects do these rhetorical devices have? What does the author say about spirit? What does the author say about teamwork? What is the purpose of the author using these rhetorical devices? RI.11-12.6

7 After reading the text for the first time, guide the class in a discussion by asking the Making Observations questions. Check students' general comprehension of the text based on their observations, asking follow-up questions if needed.

8 Pause after paragraph 11. Ask students how they feel about the author's revised words to the cheer.

 TEACHER TO TEACHER

This Horatian satire is only slightly concerned with changing behavior and is primarily for entertainment, as is Twain's "Advice to Youth" (Activity 3.19). In Activity 3.20, Twain's "The War Prayer" is Juvenalian satire; in it, a harsh, bitter tone prevails, and the aim is to change what Twain thinks is shameful behavior.

3.15

My Notes

Champs take it away

Now Play by Play

Move that ball

Win win win.

11 Let's face it, this is not exactly a stellar example of the sophisticated use of the English language. To reduce the risk of injury and make the sport more educational and less distracting for the fans, I propose to substitute verbal skills for physical high jinks. Routines should become more static, and chants should become more grammatical, more literary and more conducive to the kinder, gentler society we all hope for in the next century.

Why don't you fellows

Pick up that ball

And move it carefully

To the other end of the field?

12 If we really want to teach good social values, let's chant this famous verse from Grantland Rice:

For when the one great Scorer comes

To write against your name

He writes not that you won or lost

But how you played the game.

13 Now there's a catchy message for the millennium!

14 And why not bring that youthful spirit and those brilliant visuals out of the stadium and into the workplace? Cheerleaders should be in every office, with a chant for every corporate game. In a lawyer's office, for example, a spirited cry of "Rule of Law! Rule of Law! Sue! Sue! Sue!" accompanied by some eyepopping dance steps, would give courage and purpose to desk-bound drones. On Wall Street, a simple chant of "Go Greenspan! Low Interest! Never mind the Asians!" would create a positive environment for investment. And cheerleaders would share their boundless enthusiasm with the rest of us who, in the game of life, so often find ourselves on the losing team.

Making Observations

- Based on words or phrases you highlighted, which ones do you find funny?
- What new words do you find unfamiliar?

conducive: likely to bring about

Scaffolding the Text-Dependent Questions

3. What are two examples of Bouchier's use of diction to create a specific tone in paragraph 7? Is the author successful in creating the desired tone? What connotation does the word *shallower* have as it is used in this paragraph? What kind of tone does the usage of this word create? What about "fab formations"? What does it mean? What kind of tone does the use of the word *fab* create? RI.11-12.4

4. What does Bouchier parody in paragraph 11? For what purpose does the author include the parody? What does the author revise? How is his revision different than the original? What is he parodying by changing the lyrics? RI.11-12.6

Returning to the Text

- Return to the satire as you respond to the following questions. Use text evidence to support your responses.
- Write any additional questions you have about the text in your Reader/Writer Notebook.

1. In paragraph 1, what information does the reader understand that Bouchier's persona does not? What is the effect on the tone of the text?

   The cheerleaders chant "Offense! Offense!" rather than "A fence! A fence!" This

   misunderstanding establishes the persona as ignorant about the basics of competitive sports

   and cheerleading, which creates a humorous tone.

2. In paragraph 5, what rhetorical devices does the author use to shape the readers' perception of cheerleading? What effects do these rhetorical devices have?

   The author downplays what the supporters say are the positive attributes of cheerleading. He

   then uses hyperbole by saying the slogan would be endorsed by terrorist organizations and an

   evil world leader. This hyperbole adds a comedic element that mirrors the absurdity that the

   author perceives to be present in cheerleading.

3. What are two examples of Bouchier's use of diction to create a specific tone in paragraph 7? Is the author successful in creating the desired tone?

   Bouchier successfully uses diction to set up and undercut reader expectations with humorous

   effect. For example, the paragraph begins with a common phrase, "broader and ..." Readers

   expect that the next word will be something positive, such as *deeper*. However, the reader is

   surprised to encounter a negative word, *shallower,* instead. The second sentence introduces

   a list with the phrase "essential equipment," but then the reader encounters frivolous items

   such as "party dresses and miracle diets."

4. What does Bouchier parody in paragraph 11? For what purpose does the author include the parody?

   In paragraph 11, Bouchier parodies a cheer. Contrasted with the cheer in paragraph 10,

   Bouchier's cheer is grammatically and philosophically more sophisticated, stating the idea in

   a single sentence that players should be encouraged to move the ball down the field gently.

   The author's purpose is to use humor and irony to point out that the aggressive nature of the

   original cheer no longer aligns with the kinder, gentler goals of modern society.

Scaffolding the Text-Dependent Questions

5. For what purpose does the author write this satire about cheerleading? Is the author successful in achieving this purpose? What aspects of cheerleading does the author make fun of? Why do you think he chooses to make fun of those aspects? What does he seem to think is wrong with cheerleading? RI.11-12.6

ACTIVITY 3.15 continued

9 **RETURNING TO THE TEXT:** Guide students to return to the text to answer the text-dependent comprehension questions. Invite them to work in pairs to reread the text and answer the questions. If they have difficulty, scaffold the questions by rephrasing them or breaking them down into smaller parts. See the Scaffolding the Text-Dependent Questions boxes for suggestions.

LEVELED DIFFERENTIATED INSTRUCTION

In this activity, students might need support examining how authors use diction to create humor.

Developing Have small groups complete the **Word Choice Analyzer** graphic organizer to analyze Bouchier's use of diction to create humor in paragraph 7. Provide sentence frames: *The phrase* much broader and shallower *is unexpected because _____. The author's description of the items as* essential equipment *is humorous because _____.*

Expanding Have students complete the **Word Choice Analyzer** graphic organizer to analyze Bouchier's use of diction to create humor in paragraph 7. Reread the paragraph aloud and ask guiding questions as students complete the handout: *What unexpected phrases does the author use to describe cheerleader culture? When is the author not being fully serious in his diction?*

Bridging Provide students with the **Word Choice Analyzer** graphic organizer. As they reread paragraph 7 to find examples of humorous diction, explain that tongue in cheek means saying something without meaning it. Ask students to look for more tongue-in-cheek writing in the satire.

10 When students have completed the Returning to the Text questions, have them form small groups and direct them to the graphic organizer in the Working from the Text section. They should identify the satirical techniques and analyze and evaluate the purpose behind the usage of each technique. Encourage them to discuss the different examples.

11 Have groups select their most insightful analyses and share them with the class.

3.15

5. For what purpose does the author write this satire about cheerleading? Is the author successful in achieving this purpose?

The author writes the satire for the purpose of pointing out that cheerleading is not an

effective tool for preparing youth to become contributors in modern society. While the author

is somewhat successful in pointing out some of the dated practices of cheerleading, he

overlooks or ignores some of the positive attributes of the sport, including work ethic needed

for success and physical fitness benefits.

Working from the Text

6. Use the graphic organizer to identify the type of satire used in each quote. Then analyze and evaluate the purpose of each quote. An example has been provided to get you started.

Satirical Passage	Type of Satire	Purpose
"I was nearly trampled to death the other day by a horde of very young women…"	hyperbole	successfully builds humor and sets tone
"The opposing squad, the Furies, were merciless goddesses of vengeance who would swing into violent action if their team was losing."	caricature	successfully creates an exaggerated personification of cheerleaders
"…the brass lungs they will need for child raising or being heard at the departmental meeting.	wit	to take a humorous look at a potential benefit of all of the screaming and yelling cheerleaders do; successfully points out that there's not a real long-term benefit or career preparation
"Why don't you fellows Pick up that ball And move it carefully To the other end of the field?"	parody	Successfully uses humor to poke fun at the simplistic language that comprise the majority of cheers

☑ Check Your Understanding

Quickwrite: In your Reader/Writer Notebook, explain how Dave Bouchier's article fits the definition of satire. Support your answer with evidence from the text.

Determining the Meaning of Unknown Words

When you are reading a text and find a word you do not know, there are several ways to determine the word's meaning.

First of all, look for **context clues** and use the reading strategy of diffusing. What meanings and **connotations** do surrounding words and sentences provide?

> Example: What does the word *ardent* mean in the following text?

> The cheerleading industry has many **ardent** supporters. It is said to build self-confidence, positive attitudes, and a mysterious quality called spirit, which seems to involve smiling a lot. Cheerleading also teaches the value of teamwork, something that women have often despised in the past as a male excuse for mindless violence and idiotic loyalties. "Be 100 percent behind your team 100 percent of the time" is a slogan that would be heartily endorsed by Slobodan Milosevic, the Orange Order and the Irish Republican Army.

Here, *ardent* is clearly modifying *supporters*. The second sentence tells you that people believe many good things about cheerleading, so you can probably tell that *ardent* means "enthusiastic" or "passionate." But you need to analyze the connotation of the word to properly analyze the author's word choice. The paragraph goes on to shed a negative light on other people and organizations who had "ardent" supporters. Because of this, the imagery and connotations created here are of supporters who are frenzied and blindly support the cause.

☑ Check Your Understanding

Read the following text and use context clues to determine the meaning of *brass*.

> Young cheerleaders also acquire valuable practical skills: impossible balancing tricks, back flips and the **brass** lungs they will need for child raising or being heard at the departmental meeting.

First, jot notes based on context clues. Then look up the word in a good dictionary or dictionary of usage. What was the word's original, literal meaning? Is it still used that way? What connotations and imagery are created by the word's use in this context?

7. Based on your observations, place the text on the continuum. Be prepared to justify your answer.

```
1 —— 2 —— 3 —— 4 —— 5 —— 6 —— 7 —— 8 —— 9 —— 10
Horatian                                    Juvenalian
```

The left side of the diagram is characterized by subtle, playful, good-humored, and sympathetic satire. The right side is harsher, more pointed, and perhaps intolerant satire.

Students may point out Bouchier's playful nature and lean toward Horatian, or they might point out his overt/scathing criticisms and lean toward Juvenalian.

---

12 Review students' Quickwrites from the Check Your Understanding task. Ensure that students have provided supporting text evidence and commentary for each element in the definition of satire.

13 Review the Determining Meaning of Unknown Words section with students. They should be experienced with this skill, but this review is a good opportunity to assess them.

14 Give students time to complete the next Check Your Understanding task. Have students justify their answers to student step 7 with their groups.

ASSESS

Review students' responses to the Check Your Understanding tasks. Check to make sure they can clearly and accurately define *satire* and appropriately justify their responses to their assessment of the author's diction.

ADAPT

If students need additional help explaining how Bouchier's article fits the definition of satire, provide them with a **graphic organizer** with three labels: *speaker's adopted persona*, *conveys a particular perspective on a topic*, and *makes a point about the topic*. Have students work in pairs or small groups to gather evidence from the text for each element of satire.

Alternatively, have students revisit Schroth's editorial "Abolish High School Football!" in Activity 3.7. Ask students to create a graphic organizer (e.g., a **T-chart** or **Venn diagram**) comparing this editorial to Bouchier's essay. Students should consider how they could make Schroth's point by being satiric. Would it be as effective as a straightforward argument? Why or why not?

PLAN

Materials: various satirical cartoons (collect these ahead of time yourself or as a homework assignment instruct students to bring examples to class), Internet access (one excellent source for current political cartoons that often use satire is http://politicalhumor.about.com/od/politicalcartoons/ig/Political-Cartoons/)

Suggested Pacing: 1 50-minute class period

TEACH

1 Review the Learning Targets and Preview with students. Make sure they understand that they will be analyzing satirical cartoons in this activity.

2 Review the Setting a Purpose for Viewing section. Give students time to answer the questions individually and then discuss answers together as a class.

3 Revisit the difference between Horatian and Juvenalian satire. On the board, draw the continuum diagram from Activity 3.15 and ask students to explain where on the continuum they would place the cartoon. Be sure students successfully justify their answers.

Learning Strategies

Discussion Groups
Graphic Organizer
Think-Pair-Share

My Notes

Learning Targets

• Analyze cartoons for satirical content and techniques.
• Compare and contrast cartoons to determine purposes for satire.

Preview

In this activity, you will analyze cartoons for their satirical content and techniques.

Setting a Purpose for Viewing

1. You may want to review the satirical techniques you already know as you examine the cartoon. How does the visual content contribute to the cartoon's overall tone? As you examine the cartoon, consider the following questions and record your answers.

   • What elements of satire are present in the cartoon? _____

   • What is the implied message of the artist? _____

   • Is the cartoon effective in presenting the implied message? _____

   • Where does the cartoon fit in the Horatian to Juvenalian continuum? Justify your placement. _____

About the Author

Jen Sorensen (b. 1974) is an American cartoonist and illustrator. Her cartoons appear in alternative newsweeklies around the country, including her local paper, *The Austin Chronicle*. In 2014, she became the first woman to win the Herblock Prize, and in 2017 she was named a Pulitzer Prize finalist in Editorial Cartooning. The cartoon featured in this activity was part of the submission that made her a finalist. The cartoon was created in response to the public health disaster in Flint, Michigan, where 100,000 residents were exposed to toxic water.

College and Career Readiness Standards

Focus Standards:

RI.11-12.1 Cite strong and thorough textual evidence to support analysis of what the text says explicitly as well as inferences drawn from the text, including determining where the text leaves matters uncertain.

RI.11-12.6 Determine an author's point of view or purpose in a text in which the rhetoric is

particularly effective, analyzing how style and content contribute to the power, persuasiveness, or beauty of the text.

Additional Standards Addressed:

W.11-12.2a, W.11-12.2b, W.11-12.2d

3.16

Editorial Cartoon

Analyzing Cartoons as a Group

Your teacher will assign you an additional cartoon to analyze with your group. Use the same questions as before to guide your viewing. Record your answers in your Reader/Writer Notebook.

> **Writing Prompt: Informational**
>
> Review the sample cartoons and consider the artist's purpose for satire in each cartoon. Then, in an essay, explain how each cartoon seeks to affect the reader's perception of the subject. Be sure to:
>
> - Introduce the artist's purpose in a topic statement.
> - Include concrete details and examples from the cartoon to support your claim.
> - Use precise language, including metaphor, simile, or analogy, to explain your ideas.

WRITING PROMPT: INFORMATIONAL

The following standards are addressed in the writing prompt:
- W.11-12.2a
- W.11-12.2b
- W.11-12.2d

ACTIVITY 3.16 continued

4 For the Analyzing Cartoons as a Group task, begin by placing students in pairs.

5 Give each pair a political cartoon and have them answer the questions in the Setting a Purpose for Viewing section.

6 Have pairs join with one or two other pairs to form discussion groups of four to six students and compare their political cartoons. Direct groups to discuss where on the continuum they would place each of their cartoons. Make sure students can justify each placement. One member from each group should then share with the class which cartoon the group felt was most Juvenalian and the reasons for that choice.

7 Read the Writing Prompt with students and answer any questions. Give students time to write.

ASSESS

Use students' responses to the writing prompt to assess their ability to identify and analyze satire in a political cartoon. Make sure that students understand the connection between purpose and satirical technique, a skill they will need in preparing the satirical piece for the Embedded Assessment.

ADAPT

If students are struggling to apply the concepts of Horatian and Juvenalian satire to the sample cartoons, create a T-chart with *Horatian* on one side and *Juvenalian* on the other. As a class, **brainstorm** tone words, subjects, and contemporary examples that could be placed in each category. (For example, under *Horatian*, students might include *silly, playful, comedic, cell phone use, cheerleaders, Saturday Night Live*.) This activity checks students' understanding but also helps them begin the process of brainstorming topics for the original satire for Embedded Assessment 2.

ACTIVITY 3.17

PLAN

Suggested Pacing: 1 50-minute class period

TEACH

1 Ask students to respond to the following prompt in a **quickwrite:** Why might humor be a useful tool when trying to convey a serious message?

2 In sharing responses, ensure that students understand that humor allows writers to make a point obliquely and to ambush readers with a new truth as they are laughing.

3 Ask if students have ever resorted to CliffsNotes or another similar publication (e.g., SparkNotes). Why or why not? What were the benefits of using such a guide? The drawbacks?

4 Read the Learning Targets and Preview with students.

5 Read the As You Read and About the Author sections aloud. Ask students if they are familiar with *The Onion* and, if not, explain that it publishes satirical articles written in the style of news stories.

6 Direct students' attention to the Independent Reading Link, which gives students the opportunity to discuss the purposes of different satirical pieces.

Learning Strategies

Drafting
Graphic Organizer
Marking the Text

My Notes

Learning Targets

- Explore the impact of ridicule on the reader's perception of a writer's subject.
- Analyze and evaluate the author's use of satire to achieve a specific purpose.
- Evaluate how the author's diction contributes to the tone of the text.

Preview

In this activity, you will read and analyze an article from the satirical publication *The Onion*. Then you will write a literary analysis that reviews the satirical techniques used in the article.

As You Read

- Highlight words, phrases, or sentences you find funny.
- Circle unknown words and phrases. Try to determine the meaning of the words by using context clues, word parts, or a dictionary.
- Put a star next to text that shows the author is parodying the form of a news article.

About the Author

The Onion calls itself "America's Finest News Source," and its motto, *Tu stultus es*, is Latin for "You are a fool/idiot." Once a print publication available in select Midwest cities, *The Onion* moved online and is now solely available online. Its history is steeped in being a satirical "news" source. It rarely breaks character and presents its satirical articles as if they were serious news content. *The Onion*'s satire reaches the "About" section of its website, where it touts that it "enjoys a daily readership of 4.3 trillion." (At last count, the world population was only about 7.4 billion.) For the uninformed, *The Onion* often fools readers who do not realize that it is a satirical publication.

INDEPENDENT READING LINK

Read and Discuss

Discuss with a group what one of your independent reading texts is satirizing. Discuss the author's purpose and the primary mode of the satire.

College and Career Readiness Standards

Focus Standards:

RI.11-12.1 Cite strong and thorough textual evidence to support analysis of what the text says explicitly as well as inferences drawn from the text, including determining where the text leaves matters uncertain.

RI.11-12.4 Determine the meaning of words and phrases as they are used in a text, including figurative, connotative, and technical meanings; analyze how an author uses and refines the meaning of a key term or terms over the course of a text (e.g., how Madison defines faction in Federalist No. 10).

RI.11-12.6 Determine an author's point of view or purpose in a text in which the rhetoric is particularly effective, analyzing how style and content contribute to the power, persuasiveness, or beauty of the text.

Satire

Girl Moved to Tears by Of Mice and Men Cliffs Notes

*from **The Onion***

1 CHARLOTTESVILLE, VA—In what she described as "the most emotional moment" of her academic life, University of Virginia sophomore communications major Grace Weaver sobbed openly upon concluding Steinbeck's **seminal** work of American fiction *Of Mice And Men*'s Cliffs Notes early last week.

2 "This book has changed me in a way that only great literature summaries can," said Weaver, who was so shaken by the experience that she requested an extension on her English 229 essay. "The humanity displayed in the Character Flowchart really stirred something in me. And Lennie's childlike innocence was beautifully captured through the simple, ranch-hand slang words like 'mentally handicapped' and 'retarded.'"

3 Added Weaver: "I never wanted the synopsis to end."

4 Weaver, who formed an "instant connection" with Lennie's character-description paragraph, said she began to suspect the novel might end tragically after reading the fourth sentence which suggested the gentle giant's strength and fascination with soft things would "lead to his untimely **demise**."

5 "I was amazed at how attached to him I had become just from the critical **commentary**," said Weaver, still clutching the yellow-and-black-striped study guide. "When I got to the last sentence—'George shoots Lennie in the head'—it seemed so abrupt. But I found out later that the '**ephemeral** nature of life' is a major theme of the novel."

6 Weaver was assigned *Of Mice And Men*—a novel scholars have called "a masterpiece of **austere** prose" and "the most skillful example of American naturalism under 110 pages"—as part of her early twentieth-century fiction course, and purchased the Cliffs Notes from a cardboard rack at her local Barnes & Noble. John Whittier-Ferguson, her professor for the class, told reporters this was not the first time one of his students has expressed interest in the novel's plot summary.

7 "It's one of those universal American stories," said Ferguson after being informed of Weaver's choice to read the Cliffs Notes instead of the pocket-sized novel. "I look forward to skimming her essay on the importance of following your dreams and randomly assigning it a grade."

8 Though she completed the two-page brief synopsis in one sitting, Weaver said she felt strangely drawn into the plot overview and continued on, exploring the more fleshed-out chapter summaries.

GRAMMAR & USAGE

Dash

Writers use dashes to force readers to pay attention to a particular part of a sentence. A dash interrupts the flow of the sentence and signals for the reader to slow down and get ready for what he or she is going to read next. Dashes also tend to create more dramatic tension in a sentence than commas do.

Notice how the writer uses dashes effectively in this text to heighten the irony and humor. In paragraph 5, the writer sets the line *George shoots Lennie in the head* between dashes to emphasize the clash between what the student expects to read and what she is surprised to read.

Find another example in the text of a dash and practice saying the sentence aloud with a partner to note how the punctuation changes the pacing and emphasis of the sentence.

---

seminal: very original
demise: death
commentary: explanations
ephemeral: short-lived
austere: plain, simple

ACTIVITY 3.17 continued

7 **FIRST READ:** Conduct a read aloud of "Girl Moved to Tears by *Of Mice and Men* Cliffs Notes." Consider having the article read aloud using a newscaster's voice. This would help illustrate the humor. Pause after paragraph 1. Ask students what is ironic about someone being moved to tears by reading Cliffs Notes.

TEXT COMPLEXITY

Overall: Very Complex
Lexile: 1420L
Qualitative: High Difficulty
Task: Moderate (Analyze)

8 As students are reading, monitor their progress. Be sure they are engaged with and annotating the text. Evaluate whether the selected reading mode is effective.

9 Read aloud the Grammar & Usage sidebar about the dash. Help students scan the text to find the sentences that use dashes. Read aloud those sentences to emphasize the pauses the dashes create. Discuss with students these guidelines for using a dash in their writing because students may be tempted to use dashes when commas, periods, or colons are more appropriate.

- Use dashes deliberately and sparingly, only when the information between the dashes interrupts the sentence or is only loosely related.
- Dashes may be used to frame an ironic remark.
- Too many dashes will make the writing seem choppy and informal.

College and Career Readiness Standards

W.11-12.2b Develop the topic thoroughly by selecting the most significant and relevant facts, extended definitions, concrete details, quotations, or other information and examples appropriate to the audience's knowledge of the topic.

Additional Standards Addressed:
RI.11-12.10, W.11-12.2a, W.11-12.2f

10 After reading the text for the first time, guide the class in a discussion by asking the Making Observations questions. Check students' general comprehension of the text based on their observations, asking follow-up questions if needed.

3.17

My Notes

9 "There's something to be said for putting in that extra time with a good story," Weaver said. "You just get more out of it. I'm also going to try to find that book about rabbits that George was always reading to Lennie, so that I can really understand that important allusion."

10 Within an hour of completing the Cliffs Notes, Weaver was already telling friends and classmates that Steinbeck was her favorite author, as well as reciting select quotations from the "Important Quotations" section for their benefit.

11 "When I read those quotes, found out which characters they were attributed to, and inferred their context from the chapter outlines to piece together their significance, I was just blown away," said a teary-eyed Weaver. "And the way Steinbeck wove the theme of hands all the way through the section entitled 'Hands'—he definitely deserved to win that Nobel Prize."

12 Weaver's roommate, Giulia Crenshaw, has already borrowed the dog-eared, highlighted summary of the classic Depression-era saga, and is expecting to enjoy reading what Weaver described as "a really sad story about two brothers who love to farm."

13 "I loved this book so much, I'm going to read all of Steinbeck's Cliffs Notes," said Weaver. "But first I'm going to go to the library to check out the original version *Of Mice And Men* starring John Malkovich and Gary Sinise."

Making Observations
- What words, phrases, or sentences do you find funny?
- Based on the words you circled, which ones do you find confusing and have to look up?
- How does the headline set your expectations of the article's tone?

Scaffolding the Text-Dependent Questions

1. How does the author's diction in paragraph 2 help establish the tone of the article? How is the phrase "great literature summaries" ironic? What tone does this phrase establish? RI.11-12.6

2. In paragraph 7, how does the author's use of the term *pocket-sized* novel shape the reader's opinion about people who choose to read Cliffs Notes? What does *pocket-sized* novel say about the novel's length? What does this comment say about Weaver's work ethic? RI.11-12.4

3. In paragraph 12, what is ironic about Weaver's description of the story? What is the purpose of this irony? Is the author successful in this use of irony? Are Lennie and George brothers? Do they love to farm? How is Weaver's love of the story ironic? Why does the author use this irony? RI.11-12.6

Returning to the Text

- Return to the satire as you respond to the following questions. Use text evidence to support your responses.
- Write any additional questions you have about the text in your Reader/Writer Notebook.

1. How does the authors' diction in paragraph 2 help establish the tone of the article?

"This book has changed me in a way that only great literature summaries can" establishes a

satirical tone of ridicule. The paradox of "great literature summaries" helps set the tone that

the author will be ridiculing Weaver for her choice to read the Cliffs Notes rather than the

actual novel.

2. In paragraph 7, how does the author's use of the term *pocket-sized novel* shape the reader's opinion about people who choose to read Cliffs Notes?

The words *pocket-sized novel* inform the reader that the novel is actually very short. This

language helps shape readers' opinions that Weaver and people like her are too lazy to even

read a short novel.

3. In paragraph 12, what is ironic about Weaver's description of the story? What is the purpose of this irony? Is the author successful in this use of irony?

Weaver's description that Of *Mice and Men* is about "two brothers who love to farm" shows

that she doesn't comprehend the basic plot and characterization of the story. It is ironic

that she is so affected by something she doesn't understand. This use of irony is successful

because it humorously ridicules people who feel moved by a novel they did not actually read.

11 RETURNING TO THE TEXT: Guide students to return to the text to answer the text-dependent comprehension questions. Invite them to work as a whole class to reread the text and answer the questions. If they have difficulty, scaffold the questions by rephrasing them or breaking them down into smaller parts. See the Scaffolding the Text-Dependent Questions boxes for suggestions.

12 Have students work with a partner to complete the **graphic organizer** in the Working from the Text section.

13 Give students a few minutes to answer the Check Your Understanding question. Then complete the Writing Prompt activity as a group.

ASSESS

Review students' responses to the Check Your Understanding question. Ensure that students have included evidence from the text to support their claims of objectivity or subjectivity.

To assess students' ability to analyze satirical techniques, meet with groups or individuals and prompt each student to explain aspects of their group's response to the Writing Prompt.

ADAPT

To help students decide whether the tone of the piece is objective or subjective, have them take part in small **discussion groups** about the piece. Tell the group to consider the following questions:

- Is the author writing about an actual event or a made-up event? Explain.
- What point is the author trying to make?
- Is this point objective or subjective?

If students have difficulty analyzing the satirical techniques in the piece, have them use the graphic organizer to analyze at least four humorous passages in the text.

3.17

Working from the Text

4. Select three satirical words or phrases from the article. Identify the type of satire each quote uses and explain the purpose.

Satirical Passage	Type of Satire	Purpose
"great literature summaries"	wit	adds humor, establishes tone
"I look forward to skimming her essay on the importance of following your dreams and randomly assigning it a grade."	irony	adds a layer of humor by having the professor not actually read her essay
"When I read those quotes, found out which characters they were attributed to, and inferred their context from the chapter outlines to piece together their significance, I was just blown away"	irony	adds humor and pokes fun at the student's thought process behind going through this elaborate process to understand the context of the quote rather than just reading the novel

☑ Check Your Understanding

Is the tone of the piece objective or subjective?

✍ Writing Prompt: Rhetorical Analysis

As a group, review the satirical techniques in Activity 3.14. Then write a group analysis of the author's purpose for writing the satire "Girl Moved to Tears by *Of Mice and Men* Cliffs Notes." Evaluate whether the author achieved the purpose. Be sure to:

- State the purpose of the satire in a topic statement. What is the author criticizing?
- Select relevant examples of satire from the text. Analyze and evaluate the purpose of each.
- Evaluate how the author's use of diction contributed to tone and shaped the perception of readers.
- Include a conclusion that summarizes your analysis and evaluation.

✍ WRITING PROMPT: RHETORICAL ANALYSIS

The following standards are addressed in the writing prompt:

- W.11-12.2a
- W.11-12.2b
- W.11-12.9b
- W.11-12.2f

Writing a Parody

Learning Targets

- Examine and evaluate how an author uses parody to critique a subject.
- Plan, compose, and publish an original parody of a mass-media program.

Preview

In this activity, you will read a parody by Dave Barry and create one of your own about some aspect of television programming.

Learning Strategies

Drafting
Marking the Text
Oral Reading

Introducing Parody

Parody is a specific technique that imitates an author or a work for the purpose of humor. The parodist exploits the peculiarities of an author's expression or the characteristics of a typical format.

1. Based on your discussion of this definition, brainstorm a list of parodies you're familiar with. Think of popular music, television, movies, print sources, etc.

2. As you watch the news excerpt provided by your teacher, make a list of things in the show that might be ripe for parody. Think about the people you see, the show's style, the graphics used, the stories reported, etc., that are typical of this show and of news broadcasts in general.

As You Read

- Highlight words, phrases, or sentences you find particularly funny.
- Circle unknown words and phrases. Try to determine the meaning of the words by using context clues, word parts, or a dictionary.
- In the My Notes section, keep a running list of the different elements of television news shows Barry is parodying.

About the Author

Dave Barry (b. 1947) is a writer and journalist who made a career out of humorous writing. He wrote a weekly humor column for the *Miami Herald* for more than 20 years, but his work was syndicated around the country. Barry won a Pulitzer Prize for commentary in 1988 and is the only humor writer to win this prestigious award, given to him because of "his consistently effective use of humor as a device for presenting fresh insights into serious concerns."

My Notes

ACTIVITY 3.18

PLAN

Materials: recorded or online segment of a local evening news broadcast
Suggested Pacing: 1 50-minute class period

TEACH

1 Read aloud the Learning Targets and Preview. Make sure students understand that they will be creating their own parody in this activity.

2 Then read aloud the Introducing Parody section. Discuss the definition of parody.

3 Prompt students to share examples of parodies on television (for example, *Saturday Night Live*, *Family Guy*, *The Daily Show*, etc.).

4 Ask students to expand their list of examples to consider what else a parodist might mimic.

5 You will need to record (or have access to an online source that can stream) a segment of TV news for this step. After students watch the segment, ask them what elements they might mimic if they wanted to parody this show or genre. What are some genre conventions and stylistic features they might highlight in their parody? If students struggle to think of ideas, show them a clip of a classroom-appropriate news parody from your list of examples. Point out the elements of the parody for students.

6 Read the As You Read and About the Author sections with students. **Brainstorm** with students some of the strategies they can use for **annotating** the different elements of television news shows in the article.

College and Career Readiness Standards

Focus Standards:

RI.11-12.1 Cite strong and thorough textual evidence to support analysis of what the text says explicitly as well as inferences drawn from the text, including determining where the text leaves matters uncertain.

RI.11-12.5 Analyze and evaluate the effectiveness of the structure an author uses in his or her exposition or argument, including whether the structure makes points clear, convincing, and engaging.

RI.11-12.6 Determine an author's point of view or purpose in a text in which the rhetoric is particularly effective, analyzing how style and content contribute to the power, persuasiveness, or beauty of the text.

7 **FIRST READ:** Conduct a read aloud of "In Depth but Shallowly." Pause after paragraph 1. Ask students how the content of the first paragraph signals that this will be a parody.

 TEXT COMPLEXITY

Overall: Accessible
Lexile: 1000L
Qualitative: Moderate Difficulty
Task: Challenging (Create)

3.18

My Notes

Parody

In Depth, but Shallowly

by **Dave Barry**

1   If you want to take your mind off the troubles of the real world, you should watch local TV news shows. I know of no better way to escape reality, except perhaps heavy drinking.

2   Local TV news programs have given a whole new definition to the word *news*. To most people, *news* means *information* about events that affect a lot of people. On local TV news shows, news means anything that you can take a picture of, especially if a local TV News Personality can stand in front of it. This is why they are so fond of accidents, burning buildings, and crowds: these are good for standing in front of.

3   On the other hand, local TV news shows tend to avoid stories about things that local TV News Personalities cannot stand in front of, such as budgets and taxes and the economy. If you want to get a local TV news show to do a story on the budget, your best bet is to involve it in a car crash.

4   I travel around the country a lot, and as far as I can tell, virtually all local TV news shows follow the same format. First you hear some exciting music, the kind you hear in space movies, while the screen shows local TV News Personalities standing in front of various News Events. Then you hear the announcer:

5   ANNOUNCER: From the On-the-Spot Action Eyewitness News Studios, this is the On-The-Spot Action Eyewitness News, featuring Anchorman Wilson Westbrook, Co-Anchor-person Stella Snape, Minority-Group Member James Edwards, Genial Sports Personality Jim Johnson, Humorous Weatherperson Dr. Reed Stevens, and Norm Perkins on drums. And now, here's Wilson Westbrook.

6   WESTBROOK: Good evening. Tonight from the On-the-Spot Action Eyewitness News Studios we have actual color film of a burning building, actual color film of two cars after they ran into each other, actual color film of the front of a building in which one person shot another person, actual color film of another burning building, and special reports on roller-skating and child abuse. But for the big story tonight, we go to City Hall, where On-the-Spot Reporter Reese Kernel is standing live.

7   KERNEL: I am standing here live in front of City Hall being televised by the On-the-Spot Action Eyewitness News minicam with Mayor Bryce Hallbread.

College and Career Readiness Standards

W.11-12.4 Produce clear and coherent writing in which the development, organization, and style are appropriate to task, purpose, and audience.

W.11-12.5 Develop and strengthen writing as needed by planning, revising, editing, rewriting, or trying a new approach, focusing on addressing what is most significant for a specific purpose and audience.

Additional Standards Addressed:
RI.11-12.10

8 Pause after paragraph 16. Ask students to identify what is humorous about Westbrook's comments about the burning building and the car crash.

My Notes

8 MAYOR: That's "Hallwood."

9 KERNEL: What?

10 MAYOR: My name is "Hallwood." You said "Hallbread."

11 KERNEL: Look, Hallbread, do you want to be on the news or don't you?

12 MAYOR: Yes, of course, it's just that my name is—

13 KERNEL Listen, this is the top-rated news show in the three-county area, and if you think I have time to memorize every stupid detail, you'd better think again.

14 MAYOR: I'm sorry. "Hallbread" is just fine, really.

15 KERNEL: Thank you, Mayor Hallbread. And now back to Wilson Westbrook in the On-the-Spot Action Eyewitness News Studios.

16 WESTBROOK: Thank you, Reese; keep us posted if anything further develops on that important story. And now, as I promised earlier, we have actual color film of various objects that either burned or crashed, which we will project on the screen behind me while I talk about them. Here is a building on fire. Here is another building on fire. Here is a car crash. This film was shot years ago, but you can safely assume that objects just like these crashed or burned in the three-county area today. And now we go to my Co-Anchorperson, Stella Snape, for a Special Report on her exhaustive three-week investigation into the problem of child abuse in the three-county area. Well, Stella, what did you find?

17 SNAPE: Wilson, I found that child abuse is very sad. What happens is that people abuse children. It's just awful. Here you see some actual color film of me standing in front of a house. Most of your child abuse occurs in houses. Note that I am wearing subdued colors.

18 WESTBROOK (reading from a script): Are any efforts under way here in the three-county area to combat child abuse?

19 SNAPE: Yes.

20 WESTBROOK: Thank you, Stella, for that informative report. On the lighter side, On-the-Spot Action Eyewitness Reporter Terri Tompkins has prepared a three-part series on roller-skating in the three-county area.

21 TOMPKINS: Roller-skating has become a major craze in California and the three-county area, as you can see by this actual color film of me on roller skates outside the On-the-Spot Action Eyewitness News Studio. This certainly is a fun craze. Tomorrow, in Part Two of this series, we'll see actual color film of me falling down. On Wednesday we'll see me getting up.

Scaffolding the Text-Dependent Questions

3. In paragraph 5, what is the purpose behind the titles and names of the imagined news team during the announcer's introduction? Does the author's choice of names and titles achieve that purpose? How many men and how many women does Barry describe? What are their names and titles? What do those names and titles say about the stereotypes in TV news? RI.11-12.6

4. During the exchange between Snape and Westbrook in paragraphs 17–20, what is Barry parodying with Stella Snape's report on child abuse? How does his choice of language shape the perception readers have on the way local news reports handle this kind of story? Does Stella Snape's report say anything that you don't already know? When Westbrook asks about ways to combat child abuse, how does Snape respond? What does this exchange reveal about Barry's point of view on "serious" news stories? RI.11-12.6

9 Pause after paragraph 23. Ask students to identify what is humorous about the crowd's reaction.

10 After reading the text for the first time, guide the class in a discussion by asking the Making Observations questions. Check students' general comprehension of the text based on their observations, asking follow-up questions if needed.

⭐ **TEACHER TO TEACHER**

Consider performing the "script" portion of Barry's essay as a Reader's Theater. Encourage students to imitate the styles of the anchors and reporters in the segment they watched. You might give a group of volunteers (there are 10 parts, including the announcer) a chance to practice this.

3.18

My Notes

22 WESTBROOK: We'll look forward to those reports. Our next story is from Minority-Group Reporter James Edwards, who, as he has for the last 324 consecutive broadcasts, spent the day in the minority-group sector of the three-county area finding out what minorities think.

23 EDWARDS: Wilson, I'm standing in front of a crowd of minority-group members, and as you can see, their mood is troubled. (*The crowd smiles and waves at the camera.*)

24 WESTBROOK: Good report, James. Well, we certainly had a sunny day here in the three-county area, didn't we, Humorous Weatherperson Dr. Reed Stevens?

25 STEVENS: Ha ha. We sure did, though I'm certainly troubled by that very troubling report Stella did on child abuse. But we should see continued warm weather through Wednesday. Here are a bunch of charts showing the relative humidity and stuff like that. Ha ha.

26 WESTBROOK: Ha ha. Well, things weren't nearly as bright on the sports scene, were they Genial Sports Personality Jim Johnson?

27 JOHNSON: No, Wilson, they certainly weren't. The Three-County Community College Cutlasses lost their fourth consecutive game today. Here you see actual color footage of me watching the game from the sidelines. The disgust is evident on my face. I intended to have actual color film of me interviewing the coach after the game, but the team bus crashed and everyone was killed.

28 WESTBROOK: Thank you, Jim. And now, here is Basil Holp, the General Manager of KUSP-TV, to present an Editorial Viewpoint:

29 HOLP: The management of KUSP-TV firmly believes that something ought to be done about earthquakes. From time to time we read in the papers that an earthquake has hit some wretched little country and knocked houses down and killed people. This should not be allowed to continue. Maybe we should have a tax or something. What the heck, we can afford it. The management of KUSP-TV is rolling in money.

30 ANNOUNCER: The preceding was the opinion of the management of KUSP-TV. People with opposing points of view are probably in the vast majority.

31 WESTBROOK: Well, that wraps up tonight's version of the On-the-Spot Action Eyewitness News. Tune in tonight to see essentially the same stories.

Making Observations

- Based on the list you created, what familiar elements of a television news show does Barry parody?
- How does the parody make you feel?

Scaffolding the Text-Dependent Questions

5. In the exchange between Westbrook and Edwards in paragraphs 22–23, what evidence in Edwards's minority-group report reveals Barry's message regarding this type of report? Does the word *troubled* accurately describe the actions of the crowd? Does this disparity show that Edwards is doing a good job or a poor job reporting on this group? Why is this performance surprising based on Thompkins's introduction? How does the length of this report compare or contrast to others in the parody? RI.11-12.1

6. Near the end of the broadcast, how does Barry use hyperbole in Holp's editorial viewpoint to critique the practices of local TV news shows? What problem does Holp describe? How does he propose to fix it? From what source does Holp get his news? What is the relationship between news and profit as illustrated by these exaggerations? RI.11-12.6

3.18

Returning to the Text

- Return to the parody as you respond to the following questions. Use text evidence to support your responses.
- Write any additional questions you have about the text in your Reader/Writer Notebook.

3. In paragraph 5, what is the purpose behind the titles and names of the imagined news team during the announcer's introduction? Does the author's choice of names and titles achieve that purpose?

Each member of the news team represents a stereotype based on Barry's observations. This

choice of names and titles successfully helps the author parody a standard local news crew

that can be seen in most parts of the country.

4. During the exchange between Snape and Westbrook in paragraphs 17–20, what is Barry parodying with Stella Snape's report on child abuse? How does his choice of language shape the perception readers have on the way local news reports handle this kind of story?

The report on child abuse parodies a serious news story. Barry's parody argues that local TV

news spends a lot of time, in this case an "exhaustive three-week investigation," only to state

obvious information. His choice to include the sentence "Note that I am wearing subdued

colors" shapes the readers' perception that news crews are more worried about how their

appearance ties to the mood of the story then they are about the content of their reporting.

5. In the exchange between Westbrook and Edwards in paragraphs 22–23, what evidence in Edwards's minority-group report reveals Barry's message regarding this type of report?

Despite spending the day with minorities for "the last 324 consecutive broadcasts,"

Minority-Group Reporter Edwards describes them as "troubled" as they smile and wave.

This disparity suggests that local TV news reporting is out of touch with minority viewpoints

and with reality. Edwards's report is also extremely short, one line in the script, suggesting

that minority reporting doesn't get much time on local TV news broadcasts.

6. Near the end of the broadcast, how does Barry use hyperbole in Holp's editorial viewpoint to critique the practices of local TV news shows?

Holp, noting that he gets his news from newspapers and not from his own news station,

says that because the management of KUSP-TV is "rolling in money," it might be able to do

something to stop earthquakes. This hyperbole highlights the connection between news

and profit rather than news and truth-telling and the disconnect between the station's

management and reality.

Scaffolding the Text-Dependent Questions

7. Does the author's choice to structure the text as a transcript of a new broadcast help or hurt the author's purpose? Explain your answer. What did you enjoy about the format of the transcript? What did you dislike about the format of the transcript? Did this format help or hurt the author's purpose? RI.11-12.5

---

11 **RETURNING TO THE TEXT:** Guide students to return to the text to answer the text-dependent comprehension questions. Invite them to work independently to reread the text and answer the questions. If they have difficulty, scaffold the questions by rephrasing them or breaking them down into smaller parts. See the Scaffolding the Text-Dependent Questions boxes for suggestions.

12 Have students work with a partner to complete the graphic organizer in the Working from the Text section. When they have completed the graphic organizer, have students share their insights with another pair.

7. Does the author's choice to structure the text as a transcript of a new broadcast help or hurt the author's purpose? Explain your answer.

It helps his purpose because, while a parody, it fairly well represents what a local new

broadcast is like while including humor that allows the readers to critique the work of local

news broadcasts.

Working from the Text

8. Read the following lines of text from Barry's "In Depth, but Shallowly." Evaluate how each line of text informs or shapes the perception of readers.

Text	How Text Informs or Shapes Readers' Perception
KERNEL: Listen, this is the top-rated news show in the three-county area, and if you think I have time to memorize every stupid detail, you'd better think again.	This line shapes readers' perception by portraying reporters as people who do not do sufficient research or preparation in their reporting.
Here is a building on fire. Here is another building on fire. Here is a car crash. This film was shot years ago, but you can safely assume that objects just like these crashed or burned in the three-county area today.	This line shapes readers' perception by poking fun at how news broadcasts report similar stories that happen almost daily. The stories are so repetitive that most people would not realize if they just showed file footage of the fires or crashes. It also criticizes the news program's constant focus on tragedies, which they essentially use as props.
The Three-County Community College Cutlasses lost their fourth consecutive game today. Here you see actual color footage of me watching the game from the sidelines. The disgust is evident on my face.	This line shapes readers' perception by illustrating how the reporters are more interested in showing themselves than the actual footage of the game.

3.18

☑ Check Your Understanding

Rank Barry's satirical intent on the scale. Justify your ranking.

1 —— 2 —— 3 —— 4 —— 5 —— 6 —— 7 —— 8 —— 9 —— 10

Just plain silly
(Horatian)

Biting sarcasm/criticism
(Juvenalian)

✍ Writing Prompt: Literary

Write a parody of some aspect of TV programming. Choose a partner and a subject (a genre like soap operas, sports broadcasts, reality shows, children's television programs or a specific show). Next, write your parody using the format of a script. Be sure to:

- Plan the tone, purpose, and audience by brainstorming and discussing with your partner.
- Organize your script in a way that best suits the purpose of your parody.
- Compose your script using appropriate formatting and grammar.
- Publish your finished script for your classmates to read.

Use the following questions as a basis for planning your parody.

Details: What images should you include? What images should you avoid? Put your subject in the middle of a circle, and then brainstorm a list of conventions and features that might be good parody material. Think about what things in the show are just a little annoying.

Tone/purpose: How critical should you be? Is it time for brutal sarcasm or playful wit? Is the show an offense to good taste or just a silly waste of time? Are you out to destroy or merely to tease?

Audience: How familiar is your audience with the show? What is their attitude toward the show? How will these answers affect what you should and should not do in your script? How will the use of irony, overt sarcasm, or ridicule affect your audience's response to your parody? You will present your script to your classmates in a reader's theater, so keep that audience in mind.

Organization: Focusing on the formulas of your subject, how should you start, develop, and end your script?

Diction: What patterns of speech can you identify that would be easy to parody? How stupid or cliché do you want to make your characters/personalities appear?

Syntax: What about the pacing of the script? Where should it read the most quickly? Where should the reader hang on every word? How can you accomplish this?

✍ WRITING PROMPT: LITERARY

The following standards are addressed in the writing prompt:

- W.11-12.5
- W.11-12.3c
- W.11-12.4
- W.11-12.5

ACTIVITY 3.18 continued

13 Have partners complete the Check Your Understanding task. Then have them move on to the Writing Prompt activity. Be sure they understand the assignment.

ASSESS

Review students' rankings for the Check Your Understanding task. Ensure that students provide reasons and evidence to support their rankings. This parody does not contain much harsh or biting satire. Since Barry is primarily writing to entertain, he and his audience can laugh together at the "truth" about TV news reporting.

Use students' responses to the Writing Prompt to assess their ability to effectively use elements of parody in a written piece.

ADAPT

If students need additional help ranking Barry's piece, have them work in small groups to decide whether the piece is closer to a ranking of 1 or 10 and why. Once this decision is made, students can discuss nuances of the piece that might place it on the scale between 2 and 5 or 6 and 9.

If students have difficulty writing the script, have them use rehearsals to fine-tune the writing process. Tell pairs to write a rough draft of the script and then rehearse it. For the rehearsal, have pairs ask volunteers to play certain parts. During the rehearsal, pairs should analyze how effectively the skit meets the requirements of parody, including details, tone, audience, organization, diction, and syntax. Pairs should then use their notes to revise the script.

PLAN

Suggested Pacing: 1 50-minute class period

TEACH

1 Read the Learning Targets and Preview with students. Have students consider the following questions:

- What advice do adults typically give teenagers?
- Why do adults feel it is necessary to pass on this information?
- Is this advice typically helpful? Do you typically heed that advice? If not, why not?

2 Discuss the Knowledge Question. Have students work in small groups to discuss what makes satire effective.

3 Read the As You Read and the About the Author sections with students. Help them understand the instructions for annotation. Ask students if they are familiar with Twain's writings beyond *Tom Sawyer* and *The Adventures of Huckleberry Finn*. Provide students with some of Mark Twain's famous quotes to introduce them to Twain's more humorous and satirical side.

4 **FIRST READ:** Introduce students to Mark Twain's "Advice to Youth" and point out that Twain wrote it in 1882. Using your best "wise old mentor" voice, read aloud the first three paragraphs. Pause after paragraph 3 and allow students to give their opinions about the type of advice Twain is giving.

 TEXT COMPLEXITY

Overall: Accessible
Lexile: 1040L
Qualitative: Moderate Difficulty
Task: Moderate (Analyze)

Learning Strategies

Graphic Organizer
Marking the Text
RAFT

Learning Targets

- Infer the meaning of a satire and evaluate details to understand key ideas.
- Examine and analyze how satirical techniques and syntax are used for comedic effect.
- Write a satirical lecture of advice using syntax for comedic effect.
- Integrate ideas from multiple texts to build knowledge and vocabulary about the art of satire.

Preview

In this activity, you will read a satirical essay by Mark Twain called "Advice to Youth."

As You Read

- Put a star next to any places where the text takes a surprising departure from where it seems to be going.
- Put a question mark next to any parts that you can tell are supposed to be funny but you don't quite get the joke.
- Circle unknown words and phrases. Try to determine the meaning of the words by using context clues, word parts, or a dictionary.

About the Author

Samuel Clemens, whose pen name was Mark Twain, was born in 1835 in Missouri. His most famous novel, *The Adventures of Huckleberry Finn*, caused a revolution in American literature. During his life, he was also famous for his humorous lectures, essays, and sayings.

📎 KNOWLEDGE QUEST

Knowledge Question:
What makes satire effective?
Across Activities 3.19 and 3.20, you will read two pieces of satire by the author Mark Twain. While you read and build knowledge about the topic, think about your answer to the Knowledge Question.

didactic: that teaches moral values

Satire

Advice to Youth

by **Mark Twain**

1   Being told I would be expected to talk here, I inquired what sort of talk I ought to make. They said it should be something suitable to youth—something **didactic**, instructive, or something in the nature of good advice. Very well. I have a few things in my mind which I have often longed to say for the instruction of the young; for it is in one's tender early years that such things will best take root and be most enduring and most valuable. First, then. I will say to you my young friends—and I say it beseechingly, urgingly—

2   Always obey your parents, when they are present. This is the best policy in the long run, because if you don't, they will make you. Most parents think they know better than you do, and you can generally make more by humoring that superstition than you can by acting on your own better judgment.

College and Career Readiness Standards

Focus Standards:

RI.11-12.1 Cite strong and thorough textual evidence to support analysis of what the text says explicitly as well as inferences drawn from the text, including determining where the text leaves matters uncertain.

RI.11-12.4 Determine the meaning of words and phrases as they are used in a text, including figurative, connotative, and technical meanings;

analyze how an author uses and refines the meaning of a key term or terms over the course of a text (e.g., how Madison defines faction in Federalist No. 10).

RI.11-12.5 Analyze and evaluate the effectiveness of the structure an author uses in his or her exposition or argument, including whether the structure makes points clear, convincing, and engaging.

5 Continue reading the text aloud. Pause after paragraph 5. Ask students how they feel about Twain's advice on lying.

My Notes

3 Be respectful to your superiors, if you have any, also to strangers, and sometimes to others. If a person offends you, and you are in doubt as to whether it was intentional or not, do not resort to extreme measures; simply watch your chance and hit him with a brick. That will be sufficient. If you shall find that he had not intended any offense, come out frankly and confess yourself in the wrong when you struck him; acknowledge it like a man and say you didn't mean to. Yes, always avoid violence; in this age of charity and kindliness, the time has gone by for such things. Leave dynamite to the low and unrefined.

4 Go to bed early, get up early—this is wise. Some authorities say get up with the sun; some say get up with one thing, others with another. But a lark is really the best thing to get up with. It gives you a splendid reputation with everybody to know that you get up with the lark; and if you get the right kind of lark, and work at him right, you can easily train him to get up at half past nine, every time—it's no trick at all.

5 Now as to the matter of lying. You want to be very careful about lying; otherwise you are nearly sure to get caught. Once caught, you can never again be in the eyes of the good and the pure, what you were before. Many a young person has injured himself permanently through a single clumsy and ill finished lie, the result of carelessness born of incomplete training. Some authorities hold that the young ought not to lie at all. That of course, is putting it rather stronger than necessary; still while I cannot go quite so far as that, I do **maintain**, and I believe I am right, that the young ought to be temperate in the use of this great art until practice and experience shall give them that confidence, elegance, and precision which alone can make the accomplishment graceful and profitable. Patience, diligence, painstaking attention to detail—these are requirements; these in time, will make the student perfect; upon these, and upon these only, may he rely as the sure foundation for future **eminence**. Think what tedious years of study, thought, practice, experience, went to the equipment of that **peerless** old master who was able to impose upon the whole world the lofty and sounding maxim that "Truth is mighty and will prevail"—the most majestic compound fracture of fact which any of woman born has yet achieved. For the history of our race, and each individual's experience, are sewn thick with evidences that a truth is not hard to kill, and that a lie well told is immortal. There is in Boston a monument of the man who discovered anesthesia; many people are aware, in these latter days, that that man didn't discover it at all, but stole the discovery from another man. Is this truth mighty, and will it prevail? Ah no, my hearers, the monument is made of hardy material, but the lie it tells will outlast it a million years. An awkward, feeble, leaky lie is a thing which you ought to make it your unceasing study to avoid; such a lie as that has no more real permanence than an average truth. Why, you might as well tell the truth at once and be done with it. A feeble, stupid, **preposterous** lie will not live two years—except it be a **slander** upon somebody. It is indestructible, then, of course, but that is no merit of yours. A final word: begin your practice of this gracious and beautiful art early— begin now. If I had begun earlier, I could have learned how.

> **maintain:** declare strongly
> **eminence:** success
> **peerless:** without equal
> **preposterous:** silly
> **slander:** harmful statement about someone

College and Career Readiness Standards

RI.11-12.6 Determine an author's point of view or purpose in a text in which the rhetoric is particularly effective, analyzing how style and content contribute to the power, persuasiveness, or beauty of the text.

W.11-12.4 Produce clear and coherent writing in which the development, organization, and style are appropriate to task, purpose, and audience.

Additional Standards Addressed:
RI.11-12.10, W.11-12.2a

6 **Vocabulary Development:**
Discuss the Word Connections box
with students. Ask them how the
words are similar. Then ask students
to think of other words that share
the prefix *in*, the root *estim*, or the
suffix *-able*, as in *inestimable*. As an
extension, have students complete
the **Roots and Affixes Brainstorm**
graphic organizer.

7 Finish reading the text aloud.

 TEACHER TO TEACHER

Explain in more detail the
instruction about putting question
marks next to parts where students
"miss the joke." Tell students that
as they read they will realize that
Twain is writing a satire that makes
a series of points meant to be
humorous. However, some of these
points will not seem funny, even
though the author means them
to be. There are many reasons for
this disparity between intent and
effect. Twain might use words that
are unfamiliar, thereby killing the
joke. Also, at times, Twain's writing
style is lengthy and complex. At
such places, the student might lose
the author's train of thought and
miss the humor. Twain might also
reference something that students
are not familiar with. For example,
they might not realize that Twain is
the author of *Innocents Abroad*.

8 After reading the text for the first
time, guide the class in a discussion
by asking the Knowledge Quest
questions. Check students' general
comprehension of the text based on
their observations, asking follow-up
questions if needed.

3.19

WORD CONNECTIONS

Roots and Affixes
The word **inestimable** is formed
from the prefix *in-*, meaning
"not"; the root *estim*, meaning
"to value"; and the suffix
-able, meaning "able to be."
Thus, something *inestimable*
is impossible to put a value on.
The words *estimate* and *esteem*
also derive from the same
Latin root.

My Notes

_____

precepts: rules

6 Never handle firearms carelessly. The sorrow and suffering that have
been caused through the innocent but heedless handling of firearms by the
young! Only four days ago, right in the next farm house to the one where
I am spending the summer, a grandmother, old and gray and sweet, one
of the loveliest spirits in the land, was sitting at her work, when her young
grandson crept in and got down an old, battered, rusty gun which had not been
touched for many years and was supposed not to be loaded, and pointed it at
her, laughing and threatening to shoot. In her fright she ran screaming and
pleading toward the door on the other side of the room; but as she passed him
he placed the gun almost against her very breast and pulled the trigger! He had
supposed it was not loaded. And he was right—it wasn't. So there wasn't any
harm done. It is the only case of that kind I ever heard of. Therefore, just the
same, don't you meddle with old unloaded firearms; they are the most deadly
and unerring things that have ever been created by man. You don't have to
take any pains at all with them; you don't have to have a rest, you don't have to
have any sights on the gun, you don't have to take aim, even. No, you just pick
out a relative and bang away, and you are sure to get him. A youth who can't
hit a cathedral at thirty yards with a Gatling gun in three quarters of an hour,
can take up an old empty musket and bag his grandmother every time, at a
hundred. Think what Waterloo would have been if one of the armies had been
boys armed with old muskets supposed not to be loaded, and the other army
had been composed of their female relations. The very thought of it makes
one shudder.

7 There are many sorts of books; but good ones are the sort for the young
to read. Remember that. They are a great, an inestimable and unspeakable
means of improvement. Therefore be careful in your selection, my young
friends; be very careful; confine yourselves exclusively to Robertson's Sermons,
Baxter's Saint's Rest, The Innocents Abroad, and works of that kind.

8 But I have said enough. I hope you will treasure up the instructions
which I have given you, and make them a guide to your feet and a light to your
understanding. Build your character thoughtfully and painstakingly upon these
precepts, and by and by, when you have got it built, you will be surprised and
gratified to see how nicely and sharply it resembles everybody else's.

⊘ Knowledge Quest

- What lines do you find funny?
- What jokes do you not fully understand?
- Based on the stars you placed throughout the text, where does the text
  surprise you?

Scaffolding the Text-Dependent Questions

**1. In paragraph 1, what does the word *nature*
mean in context?** What effect does it have on
the tone? What might Twain be making fun of by
using it? RI.11-12.4

**2. How does Twain satirize typical advice about
obeying one's parents in paragraph 2? How
does this advice shape the reader's perception?
Use text evidence to support your answer.** For
what reasons are children typically taught to
obey their parents? Why does Twain tell children
to obey their parents? How does this advice
affect the reader? RI.11-12.6

**3. Does Twain successfully change the meaning
of *get up with the lark* in paragraph 4 to create
humor? Explain your answer.** What does the idiom
get up with the lark usually mean? How does
Twain first use it? What difference in meaning does
the last sentence reveal? RI.11-12.4

Returning to the Text

- Return to the satire as you respond to the following questions. Use text evidence to support your responses.
- Write any additional questions you have about the text in your Reader/Writer Notebook.

1. **KQ** In paragraph 1, what does the word *nature* mean in context? What effect does it have on the tone?

Twain uses the word *nature* to refer to something with specific characteristics—in this instance, the characteristics of good advice. The effect this word has on the tone is Twain setting up that this is going to be a work of satire—he will be mocking the "nature of good advice."

2. How does Twain satirize typical advice about obeying one's parents in paragraph 2? How does this advice shape the reader's perception? Use text evidence to support your answer.

Twain echoes typical advice about obeying parents and then undercuts it with unexpected reasons. Usually, youth are told to obey their parents out of respect for their support and wisdom. Twain tells youth to obey their parents for selfish reasons: "to make more by humoring" the superstition that the parents know more than the youth. This use of language shapes the perception of readers by making them think that the advice Twain is about to give is not ordinary advice.

3. Does Twain successfully change the meaning of *get up with the lark* in paragraph 4 to create humor? Explain your answer.

Yes, Twain adds great humor to the advice because if you follow his advice, you could sleep in and still say you get up with the lark, which people would interpret to mean that you get up early.

4. Which words and phrases in paragraph 5 express the likelihood of learning to tell the perfect "immortal" lie? What is Twain's real message?

Twain paints a picture of the difficulty of lying, first warning "you are nearly sure to get caught" if you are not "very careful." He says "the young ought to be temperate in the use" of lies until they can do it profitably. He describes "tedious years of study, thought, practice, experience" and "unceasing study" to avoid "feeble" lies, saying "why you might as well tell the truth." At the end of the paragraph, he reveals he cannot lie as he describes. Twain's message is that lying well is an impossible task.

9 RETURNING TO THE TEXT: Guide students to return to the text to answer the text-dependent comprehension questions. Invite them to work in pairs to reread the text and answer the questions. If they have difficulty, scaffold the questions by rephrasing them or breaking them down into smaller parts. See the Scaffolding the Text-Dependent Questions boxes for suggestions.

Scaffolding the Text-Dependent Questions

4. **Which words and phrases in paragraph 5 express the likelihood of learning to tell the perfect "immortal" lie? What is Twain's real message?** What is likely to happen if a liar is not "very careful"? What kind of study is required to tell a great lie? What is a "feeble" lie no better than? Is Twain himself able to do what he describes? RI.11-12.6

5. **What is the effect of the paradox Twain presents in the line "A feeble, stupid, preposterous lie will not live two years—except it be a slander upon somebody. It is indestructible, then"?** Why would a "feeble, stupid, preposterous lie" have a short life? (Is two years short?) What is slander? In what way can it be indestructible? RI.11-12.5

10 Give students time to complete the Working from the Text step and the Quickwrite in Check Your Understanding.

11 Ask students what makes this piece funny and then guide them to discuss how Twain structures sentences for comedic effect.

LEVELED DIFFERENTIATED INSTRUCTION

In this activity, students might need support understanding and writing cumulative sentences.

Expanding Display both example sentences on the board and work together to identify the main idea and detail phrases in each. Distribute the **Idea Connector** graphic organizer. Provide the following main ideas for "Sentence One" and have students use the organizer to complete the cumulative sentence patterns: *Something all young people should know is _____. Something all grown-ups should know is _____.*

Bridging Call on student volunteers to point out the main idea and phrasal details in the examples. Have students work collaboratively to complete the **Idea Connector** graphic organizer to combine ideas together in different ways for their "Advice to Youth" paragraphs.

Extend Explain that cumulative or loose sentences are a popular tool for humor and satire writers such as Mark Twain and Jonathan Swift. Have students explore this technique by researching it in Strunk and White's *The Elements of Style*. Have them present their findings and additional examples from literature to the class.

5. What is the effect of the paradox Twain presents in the line "A feeble, stupid, preposterous lie will not live two years—except it be a slander upon somebody. It is indestructible, then"?

The lines add humor to the text by pointing out that lies are often innocent—until they are not. He comically points out you could get sued for slander, which actually is one of the worst possible results of lying.

6. How does the last sentence suggest Twain's purpose for the satire?

Twain says if the youth follow his advice, their characters will "resemble everybody else's." Following his advice as stated would mean manipulating one's parents, hitting people who *might* have meant to offend, perfecting the "immortal" lie, and shooting relatives accidentally. Doing these things would not make one a good person, but they describe what "everybody [else]" does. Twain thus humorously advises youth to be *better* than everybody else.

7. **KQ** How is Twain's use of satire effective?

Twain's use of satire is effective because he takes a well-worn trope (advice to youth) and turns the audience's expectations of what it will be by using humor in order to point out certain truth. Because there is truth in what he says, it moves beyond just being funny for comedy's sake and instead becomes a pointed criticism.

Working from the Text

8. *Didactic* (Greek, *didaktikos*: "apt at teaching") is a term often used to describe a speaker's or writer's tone when that speaker or writer is attempting to educate or inform an audience. Provide an example of textual evidence for why Twain's piece could be described as didactic.

☑ Check Your Understanding

Quickwrite: Where does "Advice to Youth" fall on the Horatian to Juvenalian continuum? Identify textual support to justify your answer.

Scaffolding the Text-Dependent Questions

6. How does the last sentence suggest Twain's purpose for the satire? Whom will you resemble if you follow Twain's advice? On the surface, what does Twain advise people to do? Are you able to think of people who act as he describes? Does Twain really want youth to follow his advice? RI.11-12.6

7. How is Twain's use of satire effective? What is he making fun of? What in his satire is true? What would his audience expect to hear in a speech like this? RI.11-12.1

LANGUAGE & WRITER'S CRAFT: Cumulative or Loose Sentence Patterns

Cumulative (or **loose**) sentences are a type of diction in which sentences have a main idea that is followed by a series of phrases that supply further details about a person, place, event, or idea. Writers tend to use this style of diction to establish an informal or conversational tone to their writing. Consider this example in which the main idea or clause is in italics followed by a series of phrases.

"*We reached New York that morning* after a turbulent flight and some exciting experiences, tired but exhilarated, full of stories to tell our friends and neighbors."

In "Advice to Youth," Mark Twain uses cumulative sentences to establish a comedic tone. Notice how this works in the second sentence of his speech:

"*They said it should be something suitable to youth*—something didactic, instructive, or something in the nature of good advice."

By listing out the "suitable" qualities that "they" suggest, Twain seems to wink knowingly at the audience in a conversational way. This establishes his desired comedic tone.

PRACTICE In the graphic, identify at least three pieces of advice Twain renders to his audience. Write the main clause in the first column. Then write the main or modifying phrase or clause in the second column. Finally, in the third column, evaluate how the loose sentence pattern affects the tone.

Main Clause 1	Main Clause 2 or Modifying Phrase/Clause	Effect on Meaning
Always obey your parents ...	when they are present	Makes the advice conditional and therefore comic.
You want to be very careful about lying;	otherwise you are nearly sure to get caught.	Gives an unlikely reason to not lie, adds comedy because it is probably not good advice for why not to lie
A feeble, stupid, preposterous lie will not live two years	—except it be a slander upon somebody.	Adds a comedic yet serious twist to the advice by stating a potential serious outcome of lying

Writing Prompt: Literary

Write your own lecture of advice to a particular audience. Use a RAFT to select a role for you to play and an audience to whom to impart your great wisdom about your topic. Be sure to:

- Select a topic that is specific to your audience.
- Use an appropriate format in which to deliver your message to your audience (e.g., an editorial, a letter, etc.) and follow the format's conventions.
- Use loose sentence patterns to create a humorous effect.

WRITING PROMPT: LITERARY

The following standards are addressed in the writing prompt:
- W.11-12.3c
- W.11-12.4

---

12 Read the Language & Writer's Craft feature on cumulative or loose sentence patterns aloud with students. After the reading, have students work with a partner to complete the graphic organizer by identifying more examples of loose sentences in the text.

13 Direct students to the Writing Prompt, where they will use a **RAFT** to generate a role for themselves and an audience to whom they will write a short advice column. If you think they need help coming up with creative choices, guide them through this writing as a class. Have students share examples when they are finished.

ASSESS

Review students' quickwrites for the Check Your Understanding task. To reinforce this activity, have students rank each example of textual support on the Horatian to Juvenalian continuum from Activity 3.18.

Students' responses to the writing prompt should demonstrate an ability to use an appropriate format to convey a written satiric message and to follow the format's conventions.

ADAPT

If students have difficulty selecting an audience for their lecture, have them list three topics they want to treat in a satirical manner. Then have them choose at least one appropriate audience for each topic and provide reasons why the audience is appropriate. Have students select the best topic/audience for their lecture from these lists.

ACTIVITY 3.20

PLAN

Materials: poster paper
Suggested Pacing: 1 50-minute
class period

TEACH

1 Read the Learning Targets, Preview, and As You Read sections with students. Help them understand the instructions for annotation.

 TEACHER TO TEACHER

Twain is as well known for his biting Juvenalian satire as he is for his more comic Horatian satire. For example, "Advice to Youth" is a more Horatian, or lighthearted, commentary on adult expectations of and advice to young people. However, in the following text, "The War Prayer," Twain presents a much more Juvenalian, or pointed and biting, commentary on war. The last few satires in the unit are more Juvenalian in their technique and purpose. Be sure students understand the larger, more serious purposes of these satires and their bitter tones.

2 **Vocabulary Development:** Point out the Word Connections box. Discuss the word relationships of the word *invoke*. Then select a few compelling words from the text and ask students about the author's possible intent for using them. Elicit other words that the author could have used.

3 Review the Knowledge Question with students. Remind them to think about their answer to the Knowledge Question as they read and build knowledge about the topic.

4 **FIRST READ:** Conduct a read aloud of "The War Prayer." Pause after paragraph 1. Ask students if they have any questions or find any of the language confusing.

 TEXT COMPLEXITY

Overall: Very Complex
Lexile: 1240L
Qualitative: High Difficulty
Task: Challenging (Evaluate)

Learning Strategies

Graphic Organizer
Marking the Text
SOAPSTone

Learning Targets

- Compare and contrast two satirical texts and write responses that analyze the purpose of the satirical devices the authors use.
- Evaluate how an author's diction and syntax contribute to the tone.
- Integrate ideas from multiple texts to build knowledge and vocabulary about the art of satire.

Preview

In this activity, you will read another satirical piece by Mark Twain to analyze how the master of American humor used tone to appeal to an audience.

As You Read

- Highlight words, phrases, or sentences you find particularly funny.
- Identify and keep notes about the satirical techniques Twain uses.
- Circle unknown words and phrases. Try to determine the meaning of the words by using context clues, word parts, or a dictionary.

KNOWLEDGE QUEST

Knowledge Question:
What makes satire effective?

WORD CONNECTIONS

Word Relationships
The verb **invoke**, meaning "to ask for help," usually from a god, is derived from the Latin word *invocare*, meaning "to call." Other words based on *invocare* are *invoker*, *invocation*, and *invocatory*.

martial: military
sabers: heavy cavalry swords with curved blades
tumult: noise and confusion

Satire

The War Prayer

by **Mark Twain**

1 It was a time of great and exalting excitement. The country was up in arms, the war was on, in every breast burned the holy fire of patriotism; the drums were beating, the bands playing, the toy pistols popping, the bunched firecrackers hissing and spluttering; on every hand and far down the receding and fading spread of roofs and balconies a fluttering wilderness of flags flashed in the sun; daily the young volunteers marched down the wide avenue gay and fine in their new uniforms, the proud fathers and mothers and sisters and sweethearts cheering them with voices choked with happy emotion as they swung by; nightly the packed mass meetings listened, panting, to patriot oratory which stirred the deepest deeps of their hearts, and which they interrupted at briefest intervals with cyclones of applause, the tears running down their cheeks the while; in the churches the pastors preached devotion to flag and country, and invoked the God of Battles beseeching His aid in our good cause in outpourings of fervid eloquence which moved every listener. It was indeed a glad and gracious time, and the half dozen rash spirits that ventured to disapprove of the war and cast a doubt upon its righteousness straightway got such a stern and angry warning that for their personal safety's sake they quickly shrank out of sight and offended no more in that way.

2 Sunday morning came—next day the battalions would leave for the front; the church was filled; the volunteers were there, their young faces alight with **martial** dreams—visions of the stern advance, the gathering momentum, the rushing charge, the flashing **sabers**, the flight of the foe, the **tumult**, the

---

College and Career Readiness Standards

Focus Standards:

RI.11-12.1 Cite strong and thorough textual evidence to support analysis of what the text says explicitly as well as inferences drawn from the text, including determining where the text leaves matters uncertain.

RI.11-12.4 Determine the meaning of words and phrases as they are used in a text, including figurative, connotative, and technical meanings;

analyze how an author uses and refines the meaning of a key term or terms over the course of a text (e.g., how Madison defines faction in Federalist No. 10).

RI.11-12.6 Determine an author's point of view or purpose in a text in which the rhetoric is particularly effective, analyzing how style and content contribute to the power, persuasiveness, or beauty of the text.

My Notes

enveloping smoke, the fierce pursuit, the surrender! Then home from the war, bronzed heroes, welcomed, adored, submerged in golden seas of glory! With the volunteers sat their dear ones, proud, happy, and envied by the neighbors and friends who had no sons and brothers to send forth to the field of honor, there to win for the flag, or, failing, die the noblest of noble deaths. The service proceeded; a war chapter from the Old Testament was read; the first prayer was said; it was followed by an organ burst that shook the building, and with one impulse the house rose, with glowing eyes and beating hearts, and poured out that tremendous invocation—"God the all-terrible! Thou who ordainest! Thunder thy clarion and lightning thy sword!"

3 Then came the "long" prayer. None could remember the like of it for passionate pleading and moving and beautiful language. The burden of its **supplication** was, that an ever-merciful and benignant Father of us all would watch over our noble young soldiers, and aid, comfort, and encourage them in their patriotic work; bless them, shield them in the day of battle and the hour of peril, bear them in His mighty hand, make them strong and confident, invincible in the bloody onset; help them to crush the foe, grant to them and to their flag and country imperishable honor and glory—

4 An aged stranger entered and moved with slow and noiseless step up the main aisle, his eyes fixed upon the minister, his long body clothed in a robe that reached to his feet, his head bare, his white hair descending in a frothy **cataract** to his shoulders, his seamy face unnaturally pale, pale even to ghastliness. With all eyes following him and wondering, he made his silent way; without pausing, he ascended to the preacher's side and stood there waiting. With shut lids the preacher, unconscious of his presence, continued with his moving prayer, and at last finished it with the words, uttered in fervent appeal, "Bless our arms, grant us the victory, O Lord our God, Father and Protector of our land and flag!"

5 The stranger touched his arm, motioned him to step aside—which the startled minister did—and took his place. During some moments he surveyed the spellbound audience with solemn eyes, in which burned an uncanny light; then in a deep voice he said:

6 "I come from the Throne—bearing a message from Almighty God!" The words **smote** the house with a shock; if the stranger perceived it he gave no attention. "He has heard the prayer of His servant your shepherd, and will grant it if such shall be your desire after I, His messenger, shall have explained to you its import—that is to say, its full import. For it is like unto many of the prayers of men, in that it asks for more than he who utters it is aware of—except he pause and think.

7 "God's servant and yours has prayed his prayer. Has he paused and taken thought? Is it one prayer? No, it is two—one uttered, the other not. Both have reached the ear of Him Who heareth all supplications, the spoken and the unspoken. Ponder this—keep it in mind. If you would beseech a blessing upon yourself, beware! lest without intent you invoke a curse upon a neighbor at the same time. If you pray for the blessing of rain upon your crop which needs

supplication: plea
cataract: waterfall
smote: struck hard

Scaffolding the Text-Dependent Questions

1. In paragraph 1, what does the word *oratory* mean in context? What effect does it have on the tone? What connotation does the word have in the context of patriotism? RI.11-12.1

2. How do Twain's descriptions create a caricature in paragraph 1? What is the purpose of this paradox? How does Twain describe people, displays, events, and emotions in paragraph 1? What caricature do the descriptions create collectively? How are those who disapprove of war treated? What does this paradox show? RI.11-12.6

3. In paragraph 2, what are the townspeople's expectations for the war? What evidence supports this analysis? How do the young volunteers imagine the battle, its outcome, and their return? What do their families imagine will happen to the soldiers? RI.11-12.1

6 Pause after paragraph 8. Ask students to highlight the irony in the prayers of the people that the stranger brings to their attention.

7 After reading the text for the first time, guide the class in a discussion by asking the Knowledge Quest questions. Check students' general comprehension of the text based on their observations, asking follow-up questions if needed.

8 To provide students with more practice identifying how tone helps achieve a specific purpose, have them complete the Read and Respond in the Independent Reading Link.

3.20

My Notes

⬡ **INDEPENDENT READING LINK**

Read and Respond

Select an independent reading text. Explain how the author's tone helps achieve a specific purpose and support your analysis with evidence from the text.

commissioned: assigned the task

unavailing: useless

protract: prolong

beset: troubled

contrite: remorseful or apologetic

---

it, by that act you are possibly praying for a curse upon some neighbor's crop which may not need rain and can be injured by it.

8 "You have heard your servant's prayer—the uttered part of it. I am **commissioned** of God to put into words the other part of it—that part which the pastor—and also you in your hearts—fervently prayed silently. And ignorantly and unthinkingly? God grant that it was so! You heard these words: 'Grant us the victory, O Lord our God!' That is sufficient. The whole of the uttered prayer is compact into those pregnant words. Elaborations were not necessary. When you have prayed for victory you have prayed for many unmentioned results which follow victory—must follow it, cannot help but follow it. Upon the listening spirit of God fell also the unspoken part of the prayer. He commandeth me to put it into words. Listen!

9 "O Lord our Father, our young patriots, idols of our hearts, go forth to battle—be Thou near them! With them—in spirit—we also go forth from the sweet peace of our beloved firesides to smite the foe. O Lord our God, help us to tear their soldiers to bloody shreds with our shells; help us to cover their smiling fields with the pale forms of their patriot dead; help us to drown the thunder of the guns with the shrieks of their wounded, writhing in pain; help us to lay waste their humble homes with a hurricane of fire; help us to wring the hearts of their unoffending widows with **unavailing** grief; help us to turn them out roofless with little children to wander unfriended the wastes of their desolated land in rags and hunger and thirst, sports of the sun flames of summer and the icy winds of winter, broken in spirit, worn with travail, imploring Thee for the refuge of the grave and denied it—for our sakes who adore Thee, Lord, blast their hopes, blight their lives, **protract** their bitter pilgrimage, make heavy their steps, water their way with their tears, stain the white snow with the blood of their wounded feet! We ask it, in the spirit of love, of Him Who is the Source of Love, and Who is the ever-faithful refuge and friend of all that are sore **beset** and seek His aid with humble and **contrite** hearts. Amen.

(After a pause.)

10 "Ye have prayed it; if ye still desire it, speak! The messenger of the Most High waits!"

11 It was believed afterward that the man was a lunatic, because there was no sense in what he said.

⬡ **Knowledge Quest**

- What words, phrases, or sentences do you find particularly funny?
- What words do you find confusing?
- Based on the notes you took, what satirical techniques do you enjoy most?

Scaffolding the Text-Dependent Questions

4. In paragraph 4, how does the author's diction in the description of the messenger affect the mood of the story? Reread paragraph 4. How does the narrator describe the mysterious man? How does the man describe himself and his purpose? How do these descriptions change the mood? RI.11-12.4

5. Summarize the man's message to the townspeople as stated in his prayer in paragraph 9. How does this prayer affect the reader? Reread paragraph 9. If the people pray for their soldiers to defeat the enemy, what is the people's unstated prayer regarding the fate of the enemy? What should one always consider when praying or wishing for something? How is this idea meant to affect the reader? RI.11-12.1

Returning to the Text

- Return to the satire as you respond to the following questions. Use text evidence to support your responses.
- Write any additional questions you have about the text in your Reader/Writer Notebook.

1. **KQ** In paragraph 1, what does the word *oratory* mean in context? What effect does it have on the tone?

   Twain uses the word *oratory* to refer to a kind of speech—a patriotic speech in particular. The effect this word has on the tone is Twain satirizing the kinds of pomp and circumstance and ritual the country finds itself in during times of war, though through his satire he offers a critical view.

2. How do Twain's descriptions create a caricature in paragraph 1? What is the purpose of this paradox?

   Twain creates a caricature of a patriotic town by vividly describing people overcome by happy patriotic emotion. The mood is "glad and gracious." A few who "disapprove of the war" are run off. Paradoxically, the happy mood is at odds with the reality that soldiers are going to war and could die. Twain's purpose is to be critical of unquestioning patriotism.

3. In paragraph 2, what are the townspeople's expectations for the war? What evidence supports this analysis?

   The young volunteers imagine a grand battle ("the stern advance ... the flashing sabers"), an inevitable victory ("the flight of the foe ... the surrender!"), and a glorious return ("home from the war, bronzed heroes, welcomed, adored"). Their families also imagine they will "win for the flag" or perhaps "die the noblest of noble deaths."

4. In paragraph 4, how does the author's diction in the description of the messenger affect the mood of the story?

   The description, which includes the lines "An aged stranger entered and moved with slow and noiseless step" and "his seamy face unnaturally pale, pale even to ghastliness," creates an eerie mood because the messenger does not seem human.

9 RETURNING TO THE TEXT: Guide students to return to the text to answer the text-dependent comprehension questions. Invite them to work in small groups to reread the text and answer the questions. If they have difficulty, scaffold the questions by rephrasing them or breaking them down into smaller parts. See the Scaffolding the Text-Dependent Questions boxes for suggestions.

Scaffolding the Text-Dependent Questions

6. What can you infer about human nature from the town's reaction to the messenger in paragraph 11? Reread paragraphs 9–11. What awful consequences for the enemy does the messenger warn of in paragraph 9? From the townspeople's reaction, does it seem as if they will change their prayer? What does this reaction suggest about human nature? RI.11-12.1

7. How is Twain's use of satire effective? How is its satire different from "Advice to Youth"? What is he criticizing? What in his satire is true? How might readers recognize themselves in this story? RI.11-12.1

10 Guide students to return to the Knowledge Quest question they discussed before reading. Ask students how their response to this question has changed or been deepened after reading both pieces of satire.

11 Encourage students to continue building knowledge on this topic as suggested in the Independent Reading Link.

3.20

5. Summarize the man's message to the townspeople as stated in his prayer in paragraph 9. How does this prayer affect the reader?

The messenger says God hears the town's prayer but wants them to understand its full impact before granting it. A glorious victory for the town means horrible consequences for enemy soldiers and civilians. Twain warns readers that one should always consider the effects of one's prayers on others and not glorify war as something honorable and noble.

6. What can you infer about human nature from the town's reaction to the messenger in paragraph 11?

People tend to care only about themselves and their concerns. Even after hearing all the awful consequences of their prayer for victory, the townspeople dismiss God's messenger as a lunatic. Their unquestioning patriotism does not seem to change at all.

7. **KQ** How is Twain's use of satire effective? How is its satire different from "Advice to Youth"?

Twain's use of satire is effective because through the depictions in the story, he presents a deeper commentary on war. Far from just being a funny story, the satire here is more serious and serves a less lighthearted purpose than in "Advice to Youth."

 INDEPENDENT READING LINK

Read and Discuss

You can continue to build your knowledge about satire by reading these and other articles at ZINC Reading Labs. Search for keywords such as *satire*.

ZINC

 Knowledge Quest

With a partner, discuss how both of these satires are effective in making a point and how they represent different kinds of satire. Be sure to:

- Refer to evidence from both satires.
- Take turns speaking, responding, and asking one another follow-up questions.
- Ask clarifying questions.
- Write down notes and ideas about how satire can be effective and which kind of satire is most effective for different kinds of topics.

Working from the Text

8. Once you have finished reading the piece, conduct a comparative SOAPSTone, looking at the different ways in which Twain treats these drastically different topics. To help you organize your thoughts, complete the graphic organizer. Be prepared to discuss your responses.

	"Advice to Youth"	"The War Prayer"
Speaker	Twain himself	Twain via a fictitious narrator
Occasion	Twain is making a speech to youth.	Characters are gathering to celebrate and pray for people who are being sent off to war.
Audience	youth and adults	People who pray for things without thinking about the consequences of their prayers; also, people who believe war is glorious and heroic.
Purpose	to humorously satirize advice typically given to youth	to prompt people to think about typical ways of thinking about prayer, patriotism, and war
Subject	Advice to youth	Characters are gathering to celebrate and pray for people who are being sent off to war.
Tone	humorous	serious

9. As a follow-up to the comparative SOAPSTone activity, discuss the following questions:
   - How is the type of satire being used appropriate for the subject and purpose?
   - How do the terms *Horatian satire* and *Juvenalian satire* apply to the two satires by Twain?

10. Write a paragraph that compares an element of satire in both texts.

☑ Check Your Understanding

Transfer your answers to a poster and include a visual element that symbolizes the differences between the texts. Present your poster to the class.

12 After students finish the Returning to the Text questions, place them in groups of no more than four people. Direct them to the Working from the Text instructions on doing a **SOAPSTone** for both "The War Prayer" and "Advice to Youth," in which they look at the different ways Twain treats these drastically different topics. For example, the tone in "Advice to Youth" makes use of parody and is lighthearted and playful (Horatian). However, the tone in "The War Prayer" is solemn, disheartened, and indignant, reflecting Twain's distaste for the unthinking glorification of war as honorable and the jingoistic mentality that "God is on our side."

13 Allow time for students to complete the follow-up questions to the SOAPSTone activity.

14 For the Check Your Understanding task, instruct students to transfer their information from the SOAPSTone activity to poster paper and to include visual elements that symbolize and contrast the differences between the texts. Have students present their findings to the class. Then lead a class discussion in which students respond to the question: *How does a writer use tone to advance an opinion?* Evaluate information on posters as well as the content of students' discussions.

ASSESS

Review students' posters created for the Check Your Understanding task. To reinforce the activity, have students select phrases or sentences from each Twain piece and use them to support the visuals in the posters.

ADAPT

If students' posters do not reflect understanding of the task, have students look at examples of movie posters for various types of comedies. Have them use an **OPTIC chart** to analyze the posters. Then tell students to use some of these same elements in their own posters.

PLAN

Materials: optional: Internet access
Suggested Pacing: 2 50-minute class periods

TEACH

1 For the writing prompt at the end of this activity, students will need to **brainstorm** a list of controversial public issues. You may choose to conduct this brainstorming session before they read the articles or after.

2 Explain that writers often use satire to critique public policy but that the texts may vary dramatically in tone.

3 Read the Learning Targets, Preview, and As You Read sections with students. Help them understand the instructions for annotation.

4 **FIRST READ:** Conduct a read aloud of "Gambling in Schools." Pause after paragraph 2. Help students annotate sentences that have a satirical tone.

 TEXT COMPLEXITY

Overall: Complex
Lexile: 1210L
Qualitative: Moderate Difficulty
Task: Moderate (Analyze)

Learning Strategies

Brainstorming
Marking the Text

My Notes

minimal: basic

Learning Targets

- Analyze and evaluate how writers use diction and syntax to create a tone that helps achieve a specific purpose.
- Plan, organize, compose, revise, and edit a satirical narrative on a controversial topic.

Preview

In this activity, you will read two satirical pieces and use them as guides to begin work on your own.

As You Read

- Highlight words, phrases, or sentences you find particularly funny.
- Underline words, phrases, and sentences that contribute to the satiric tone and purpose of each essay.
- Circle unknown words and phrases. Try to determine the meaning of the words by using context clues, word parts, or a dictionary.

Satire

Gambling in Schools

by **Howard Mohr**

1 [When Minnesota jumped into legalized gambling, it was off the deep end without a lifeguard. First it was Canterbury Downs, a clean, well-lighted horse track that seemed more like a Lutheran church with betting windows. Then came Powerball, Daily Three, Gopher Five (named after the official state rodent), and Scratch-Offs. At the same time Native American casinos were springing up in the land of sky blue waters, raking it in with blackjack and slot machines and high-stakes bingo. What could possibly be next?]

2 Parents and teachers who have been worried sick about finding enough money just to maintain public schools at a **minimal** level, worry no more. The Minnesota Legislature last week approved the Education Gambling Bill. The bill allows Video Gaming Devices (VGDS) in K-12 classrooms. Only two machines per classroom will be permitted, unless the class size exceeds thirty, in which case one additional VGD machine will be permitted for each additional ten students. Class size, however, will not be a problem once the gambling revenue begins pouring in.

3 Students in math classes will be instructed in probability, statistics, and hot streaks. The VGDs in kindergarten classrooms will operate with nickels only. All students will be expected to do their assignments and homework before gambling, unless they're on a roll.

College and Career Readiness Standards

Focus Standards:

RL.11-12.4 Determine the meaning of words and phrases as they are used in the text, including figurative and connotative meanings; analyze the impact of specific word choices on meaning and tone, including words with multiple meanings or language that is particularly fresh, engaging, or beautiful.

W.11-12.5 Develop and strengthen writing as needed by planning, revising, editing, rewriting, or trying a new approach, focusing on addressing what is most significant for a specific purpose and audience.

Additional Standards Addressed:

RL.11-12.3, RL.11-12.5, RL.11-12.6, RL.11-12.10, W.11-12.3d, W.11-12.4

4   Powerball and Gopher Five tickets will be sold only in the lunchroom during the noon hour. But the attractive neon Minnesota lottery signs will be permitted at the main entrance of the school and near the scoreboard at games.

5   Pulltabs and Scratch-Offs are specifically outlawed in the bill because they make a big mess, according to the powerful Janitor's **Lobby**.

6   Off-track horse betting will be handled in the Principal's office, with a $2 and $5 window initially, but with the option of a $100 window after the first year. Race results will be available in convenient locations. The first half hour of the school day will be a "**handicapping** homeroom," but students will be encouraged to arrive early if they are psyched up and have the feeling that this is the day.

7   Each school system may publish and sell its own Tip Sheet or it can hire a professional tipster, such as "Gimp" Gordon or "Fast-Forward" Freddy, to be a counselor and role model.

8   Betting on high school sports will be forbidden, but the morning line for collegiate and professional sports will be broadcast on Channel One and posted in the principal's office near the sports betting window. As a safeguard, students will not be allowed to bet on sporting contests unless they have successfully passed Math II, "Point Spreads and Injuries."

9   Poker games will be operated as an extracurricular activity from the final bell until four a.m. The School will be the "house" and provide the dealers. There will be a 10 percent rakeoff for each pot up to a maximum of $10 per hand. Only Five-Card Draw, Stud, and Hold-Em will be permitted. Midnight Baseball, Spit in the Ocean, or Mission Impossible will not be permitted because they are silly games of chance and would send the wrong message to students.

10 Gambling will obviously bring new life and big money to the schools, but there are other advantages:

   1: Students will be prepared for jobs in the gambling industry after graduating.

   2: Part-time jobs will be created in the schools for change walkers, dealers, security officers, and so on.

   3: A wider variety of people will be attracted to the teaching profession.

   4: Discipline will be better because the hope of getting something for nothing is one of the oldest drives for excellence.

11 A bigger gambling issue faces the Legislature soon: Should gaming be permitted in hospitals and medical centers? And if so, how much and what kind? Would patients be able to bet the ponies from their beds? Could nurses deal blackjack in the sunroom? Could you go double or nothing with your physician?

My Notes

Making Observations

- What phrases or sentences make you laugh?
- How do you feel about gambling in schools?

> lobby: group that works to influence lawmakers
> handicapping: picking which horse will win a race

5   Pause after paragraph 10. Have students discuss what is satirical about the list in the paragraph.

6   After reading the text for the first time, guide the class in a discussion by asking the Making Observations questions. Check students' general comprehension of the text based on their observations, asking follow-up questions if needed.

Scaffolding the Text-Dependent Questions

1. What kind of tone does the phrase "off the deep end without a lifeguard" set for the text? Reread the first sentence. What does "off the deep end without a lifeguard" mean? What could happen to someone in that scenario? How does this contrast with the rest of the paragraph? RL.11-12.3

2. How is the last sentence in paragraph 9 ironic? How does this irony shape the reader's perception of the text? Read the last sentence in paragraph 9. How are these games different from poker games? What message might these games send to students? What message might poker games send to students? RL.11-12.6

7 RETURNING TO THE TEXT: Guide students to return to the text to answer the text-dependent comprehension questions. Invite them to work independently to reread the text and answer the questions. If they have difficulty, scaffold the questions by rephrasing them or breaking them down into smaller parts. See the Scaffolding the Text-Dependent Questions boxes for suggestions.

3.21

Returning to the Text

- Return to the satire as you respond to the following questions. Use text evidence to support your responses.
- Write any additional questions you have about the text in your Reader/Writer Notebook.

1. What kind of tone does the phrase "off the deep end without a lifeguard" set for the text?

The phrase indicates that the state of Minnesota has been reckless with its actions. It sets a tone that the text will be a biting criticism of those actions.

2. How is the last sentence in paragraph 9 ironic? How does this irony shape the reader's perception of the text?

It is ironic to condemn three specific types of poker as being "silly games of chance" when so many other games of chance, including other types of poker, are being allowed in school. The writer absurdly suggests that the legislature showed restraint by banning certain games. The author hopes that readers will apply his use of the words "send the wrong message" to the idea that gambling has been legalized in other places it should not be.

3. How does the shift to hospitals and medical centers in paragraph 11 convey Mohr's message on gambling as a means of financial support for public services?

By creating a scenario where gambling takes over schools, hospitals, and medical centers, Mohr shows his point of view that gambling should not be involved in public services in any way, even to support them financially. Taking money from the gambling industry may allow unwanted influences, as illustrated by the many negative ways gambling takes over schools in the satire.

Scaffolding the Text-Dependent Questions

3. **How does the shift to hospitals and medical centers in paragraph 11 convey Mohr's message on gambling as a means of financial support for public services?** How does Mohr imagine gambling could affect schools, hospitals, and medical centers in the satire? Are these effects largely positive or negative? RL.11-12.5

4. **What effect does Saukko's objective tone have in the sentence "we should generate as** much waste as possible from substances such as uranium-238, which has a half-life ... of one million years"? Reread the second sentence. How do the scientific facts in the sentence make you feel? Do they make the sentence seem objective or subjective? Does the tone match the content of the sentence? How does the tone grab readers' attention? RL.11-12.6

Satire

How to Poison the Earth

by **Linnea Saukko**

1   Poisoning the earth can be difficult because the earth is always trying to cleanse and renew itself. Keeping this in mind, we should generate as much waste as possible from substances such as uranium-238, which has a half-life (the time it takes for half of the substance to decay) of one million years, or plutonium, which has a half-life of only 0.5 million years but is so toxic that if distributed evenly, ten pounds of it could kill every person on the earth. Because the United States generates about eighteen tons of plutonium per year, it is about the best substance for long-term poisoning of the earth. It would help if we would build more nuclear power plants because each one generates only 500 pounds of plutonium each year. Of course, we must include persistent toxic chemicals such as polychlorinated biphenyl (PCB) and dichlorodiphenyltrichloroethane (DDT) to make sure we have enough toxins to poison the earth from the core to the outer atmosphere. First, we must develop many different ways of putting the waste from these nuclear and chemical substances in, on, and around the earth.

2   Putting these substances in the earth is a most important step in the poisoning process. With deep-well injection we can ensure that the earth is poisoned all the way to the core. Deep-well injection involves drilling a hole that is a few thousand feet deep and injecting toxic substances at extremely high pressures so they will penetrate deep into the earth. According to the Environmental Protection Agency (EPA), there are about 360 such deep injection wells in the United States. We cannot forget the groundwater aquifers that are closer to the surface. These must also be contaminated. This is easily done by shallow-well injection, which operates on the same principle as deep-well injection, only closer to the surface. The groundwater that has been injected with toxins will spread contamination beneath the earth. The EPA estimates that there are approximately 500,000 shallow injection wells in the United States.

3   Burying the toxins in the earth is the next best method. The toxins from landfills, dumps, and lagoons slowly seep into the earth, guaranteeing that contamination will last a long time. Because the EPA estimates there are only about 50,000 of these dumps in the United States, they should be located in areas where they will leak to the surrounding ground and surface water.

4   Applying pesticides and other poisons on the earth is another part of the poisoning process. This is good for coating the earth's surface so that the poisons will be absorbed by plants, will seep into the ground, and will run off into surface water.

GRAMMAR & USAGE

Verbal Phrases

A **gerund** is a verb ending with *-ing* and functioning as a noun. For example, the gerund of the verb *poison* is *poisoning*. A **gerund phrase** consists of a gerund, its object, and its modifiers. Notice the gerund phrase functioning as the subject in the first sentence of this text: "*Poisoning the earth can be difficult ...*"

A **participle** is a word formed from a verb that can also be used as an adjective. For example, the verb *rise* may be used as a past adjective (*the risen sun*) or a present adjective (*the rising sun*). A **participial phrase** consists of a participle and any modifiers. Notice this participial phrase from the text: "*Keeping this in mind*, we should generate ..."

Find two more examples of gerund phrases and participial phrases in the text.

ACTIVITY 3.21 continued

8   **FIRST READ:** Conduct a read aloud of "How to Poison the Earth." Pause after paragraph 1. Help students annotate sentences that have a satirical tone.

 TEXT COMPLEXITY

Overall: Complex
Lexile: 1290L
Qualitative: Moderate Difficulty
Task: Moderate (Analyze)

Scaffolding the Text-Dependent Questions

5. At the end of paragraph 1, the author says, "First, we must develop many different ways of putting the waste from these nuclear and chemical substances in, on, and around the earth." How does this language shape the reader's perception of the text? Do you agree with what the author is suggesting? Do you think this is the reaction the author intended readers to have? RL.11-12.4

6. How is the phrase "poisoned all the way to the core" in paragraph 2 an example of hyperbole? What effect does it have on the reader? How deep does Saukko say deep-well injection goes? How far is it to the center of Earth? How is "poisoned all the way to the core" an overstatement? How does this hyperbole affect the reader's response to Saukko's argument? RL.11-12.6

9 Pause after paragraph 5. Have students point out the satirical tone used to describe the importance of contaminating surface water.

10 After reading the text for the first time, guide the class in a discussion by asking the Making Observations questions. Check students' general comprehension of the text based on their observations, asking follow-up questions if needed.

11 Be sure students attend to the Grammar & Usage feature on verbal phrases. Invite students to work through paragraphs in pairs to find examples.

3.21

My Notes

5 Surface water is very important to contaminate because it will transport the poisons to places that cannot be contaminated directly. Lakes are good for long-term storage of pollutants while they release some of their contamination to rivers. The only trouble with rivers is that they act as a natural cleansing system for the earth. No matter how much poison is dumped into them, they will try to transport it away to reach the ocean eventually.

6 The ocean is very hard to contaminate because it has such a large volume and a natural buffering capacity that tends to neutralize some of the contamination. So in addition to the pollution from rivers, we must use the ocean as a dumping place for as many toxins as possible. The ocean currents will help transport the pollution to places that cannot otherwise be reached.

7 Now make sure that the air around the earth is very polluted. Combustion and evaporation are major mechanisms for doing this. We must continuously pollute because the wind will disperse the toxins while rain washes them from the air. But this is good because a few lakes are stripped of all living animals each year from acid rain. Because the lower atmosphere can cleanse itself fairly easily, we must explode nuclear tests bombs that shoot radioactive particles high into the upper atmosphere where they will circle the earth for years. Gravity must pull some of the particles to earth, so we must continue exploding these bombs.

8 So it is that easy. Just be sure to generate as many poisonous substances as possible and be sure they are distributed in, on, and around the entire earth at a greater rate than it can cleanse itself. By following these easy steps we can guarantee the poisoning of the earth.

Making Observations
- How does this text make you feel about pollution?
- What form of pollution mentioned in the text is a problem that you had not thought of before?

Scaffolding the Text-Dependent Questions

7. How does Saukko use irony throughout the text to convey her message? Review the definition of irony. Find a sentence with an example of irony in the text. What is the effect of that irony on the reader? How might that sentence be revised to *not* be ironic? What effect might that sentence then have on the reader? RL.11-12.6

Returning to the Text

- Return to the satire as you respond to the following questions. Use text evidence to support your responses.
- Write any additional questions you have about the text in your Reader/Writer Notebook.

4. What effect does Saukko's objective tone have in the sentence "we should generate as much waste as possible from substances such as uranium-238, which has a half-life ... of one million years"?

The author's lack of emotion has the effect of creating shock or horror in her readers because

she delivers horrifying information in such an emotionless tone. However, this ambivalent tone

mirrors the attitude most people have about pollutants such as these.

5. At the end of paragraph 1, the author says, "First, we must develop many different ways of putting the waste from these nuclear and chemical substances in, on, and around the earth." How does this language shape the reader's perception of the text?

Saukko ironically presents the ways of poisoning the earth in a methodical order. This is

meant to serve as a wake-up call to readers because people are methodically polluting the

earth in the ways she goes on to describe.

6. How is the phrase "poisoned all the way to the core" in paragraph 2 an example of hyperbole? What effect does it have on the reader?

The phrase "poisoned all the way to the core" is an overstatement of the depth of deep-

well injection. Saukko describes the wells as "a few thousand feet deep," whereas the

distance to the center of the earth is measured in thousands of miles. The prospect of Earth

being poisoned all the way through is frightening. However, recognizing the hyperbole also

undermines the fairly factual basis of other ironic statements.

7. How does Saukko use irony throughout the text to convey her message?

Saukko uses irony directly, saying the opposite of what she really thinks. By ironically

explaining, step-by-step, how to poison all areas of Earth, she clearly expresses her point of

view that people should be aware of the many different ways they are poisoning Earth and try

to avoid doing so.

ACTIVITY 3.21 continued

12 RETURNING TO THE TEXT: Guide students to return to the text to answer the text-dependent comprehension questions. Invite them to work in small groups to reread the text and answer the questions.

13 Move from group to group and listen in as students answer the text-dependent questions. If students have difficulty, scaffold the questions by rephrasing them or breaking them into smaller parts. See the Scaffolding the Text-Dependent Questions boxes for suggestions.

14 Have students complete the Working from the Text section. For student step 8, ask students to decide which essay makes its point more effectively and why. Invite students to share their responses.

15 Form two groups for student step 9. Assign the Mohr essay to one group and the Saukko essay to the other group. Give each group 10 minutes to build a case for the effectiveness of the assigned essay. After 10 minutes, ask two students from each group to come forward and **debate** the issue. Consider giving each student a minute and a half. Then bring two more students from each side forward to argue new evidence.

16 After the debate, lead the class in generating a list of criteria with which to evaluate the effectiveness of a satirical piece. This list will also be used in peer critiques to guide comments and revision.

Working from the Text

8. Which satire is more effective in making its point? Why?

_____
_____
_____
_____
_____
_____
_____
_____
_____
_____
_____

9. Meet with others who chose the same essay. Be prepared to debate with a member of the group who chose the other essay, using effective reasoning and evidence from the text to prove your claim. Be able to point to satirical techniques and purpose.

_____
_____
_____
_____
_____
_____
_____
_____
_____
_____
_____
_____
_____

Writing a Satire

The first task of writing a satire is to choose a topic you are informed and passionate about. Think of some of the topics written about in this unit: shallowness, football, war, gambling, and pollution.

Imagine that your school has a persistent problem with students being late to class. Evaluate how the steps that follow can get you started on a satirical piece of writing.

Step 1: Plan and Organize the Satire

Generate ideas by utilizing a planning strategy, such as brainstorming, journaling, reading, or discussing. Organize your satire in a way that is appropriate to the purpose, audience, topic, and context. See the sample satire planning that follows.

Identify the topic.
Students being late to class (tardiness)

State the problem in hyperbolic terms.
The staggering lack of students at the beginning of class leaves teachers paralyzed. (The diction overstates the severity of the problem: *paralyzed* and *staggering*.)

Propose an ironic solution.
If students are late, they must stand outside the door for 20 minutes. (This action does not solve the problem because students are still outside the classroom instead of being in class learning.)
1st offense: Students will carry around a 40-pound clock for the remainder of the day.
2nd offense: Students will receive jail time.
(The punishment does not fit the "crime.")

Step 2: Revise the Satire

Revise your satire to improve clarity, development, organization, style, diction, and sentence fluency, both within and between sentences. At this step, you can focus on revising sentences to include specific elements of satire that you may not have been able to work during your original draft.

Revise to add wit (wordplay, clever language, or rhetorical analogy).
Punishment will be doled out in a *timely* manner. (word play)
This problem is a *ticking time bomb*! (rhetorical analogy)

Revise to downplay the severity of the punishment using litotes.
Missing class and being ridiculed is a *small price to pay* to promote punctuality.

Step 3: Edit the Satire

Edit the satire to ensure that the spelling, grammar, and punctuation are all correct. Use a style guide as needed.

Step 4: Publish the Satire

Publish the finished satire for your intended audience to enjoy.

Sample paragraph using the preceding process:
It has come to my attention that students have been late to class at an alarming level. The staggering lack of students at the beginning of class leaves teachers paralyzed. To address this problem, we are adopting a new tardy policy. Following the first offense, students will carry around a 40-pound clock for the remainder of the day. Following the second offense, students will receive a night in jail, during which time they will be able to think about what they have done wrong. We promise to dole out this punishment in a timely manner because we have identified this issue as a ticking time bomb!

ACTIVITY 3.21 continued

17 Read through the Writing a Satire section as a class. Then have students complete the Check Your Understanding task.

 TEACHER TO TEACHER

The Check Your Understanding asks students to **brainstorm** a list of other school-related or societal issues that could serve as topics for the satirical pieces they will write in response to the Writing Prompt. If this brainstorming was conducted at the start of the activity, have students review their lists.

18 Have students complete the Writing Prompt by choosing a topic from the Check Your Understanding task. Encourage them to use the steps from the Writing a Satire section to guide their process in completing the Writing Prompt.

19 Have students complete the Independent Reading Checkpoint.

LEVELED DIFFERENTIATED INSTRUCTION

In this activity, students might need support prewriting, drafting, and editing a satirical narrative.

Developing Guide students to select a controversial topic already addressed in this unit, such as gambling or pollution, and to use the corresponding text as a writing model. Have small groups complete a **Conflict Map** graphic organizer to brainstorm about their topic. Have groups trade drafts and use the **Peer Editing** graphic organizer to help provide feedback. Then have students compose their final drafts.

Support Have students use the **Conflict Map** graphic organizer as prewriting support and the **Peer Editing** graphic organizer as a revision tool. During the revision stage, encourage students to focus on steps 4 and 5 from the Writing a Satire section, in which they revise their word choices to use techniques to make their point.

ASSESS

Students' responses to the Writing Prompt should show that they can effectively and humorously use hyperbole and ironic solutions.

ADAPT

If students have difficulty writing the satirical paragraph, have them view classroom-appropriate examples of satirical skits from programs such as *Saturday Night Live*. As they watch, tell them to note the topics being discussed and examples of hyperbole and irony.

3.21

☑ Check Your Understanding

Brainstorm a list of controversial public issues you could satirize.

✍ Writing Prompt: Literary

Choose one controversial topic from your brainstorm to develop. Compose a satirical narrative paragraph about the topic. Be sure to:

- Plan the setting, characters, problem, and narrative point of view of the satire.
- Organize the satire so that it states the problem in hyperbolic terms and proposes an ironic solution.
- Revise the satire to ensure that it includes fun, precise words; telling details; and sensory language to create vivid images.
- Publish the finished product.

📦 Independent Reading Checkpoint

Which independent reading text did you have the best personal connection to? Did you connect to the text because of the topic or purpose of the satire? Did you connect to the text because of the language and style of the satire? Write a paragraph telling which text and explaining why you had a personal connection to it.

WRITING PROMPT: LITERARY

The following standards are addressed in the writing prompt:

- W.11-12.5
- W.11-12.3c
- W.11-12.3d
- W.11-12.4, W.11-12.5

Writing a Satirical Piece

Suggested Pacing: 2 50-minute class periods

ASSIGNMENT

You have been studying how opinions are expressed and perceived in a democratic society through a variety of rhetorical formats including satire. Your assignment is to develop a satirical piece critiquing some aspect of our society.

Planning and Prewriting: Take time to create a plan for choosing a topic and audience.	▪ What has guided your choice of topics? Do you have the information to sustain a satiric treatment? ▪ Will your piece be more Horatian or Juvenalian? What techniques of satire apply well to that form (hyperbole, parody, irony, ridicule, etc.)? ▪ If you use parody, what typical conventions of the format do you plan to use as part of the satire? ▪ To whom will you address your satire and why? What is your satiric purpose—what effect do you hope to have on this audience?
Drafting: Decide how you will incorporate elements of satire.	▪ How will you demonstrate the flaws or foibles of your satire's subject? ▪ As you draft your essay, how will you stick to the conventions that you identified for your satire in your prewriting? ▪ What sort of tone is appropriate for the audience and purpose you identified?
Evaluating and Revising: Create opportunities to review and revise.	▪ How can you revise to add additional satirical language elements (loose and cumulative sentences, irony, hyperbole, and litotes)? ▪ What sort of strategies could you and a peer use to provide each other with feedback (e.g., evaluate with the Scoring Guide, use the SOAPSTone strategy)?
Checking and Editing for Publication: Be sure your work is the best it can be.	▪ How will you check for grammatical and technical accuracy? ▪ What sort of outside resources can help you to check your draft (e.g., a format guide, a dictionary, etc.)?

Reflection

After completing this Embedded Assessment, think about how you went about accomplishing this assignment, and respond to the following:

- Satire requires a sort of balancing act, mixing humor that draws in your audience with criticism that points out a particular flaw. How did you approach the challenge of balancing these two different elements?

1 Carefully review the assignment with students to be sure they understand their writing task.

2 **Planning and Prewriting:** Remind students to review the Scoring Guide criteria to ensure they understand the expectations for this assessment.

3 As students choose their topics, suggest that they use topics, ideas, and/or drafts from earlier activities as points of departure for this task. More advanced students might be prompted to identify a new topic.

4 **Drafting:** Encourage students to come up with two or three adjectives describing the tone they want to use. They should also decide on an organizational plan for the piece (e.g., lesser to greater foibles).

5 **Evaluating and Revising:** As part of revising, have students list existing satirical elements they have already used and identify places where they could make those more effective or where they could add others. Give students adequate opportunities to give and receive feedback.

6 **Checking and Editing for Publication:** Point out that they will lessen the effectiveness and "bite" of their satire if their essays include errors. When sneering at someone, one has to be careful not to give that person a reason to sneer back!

7 When students are ready to submit their work, consider using their pieces to create a satirical broadcast. Reserve a few class periods to record them reading or performing their satirical pieces. The shows *Saturday Night Live* and *A Prairie Home Companion* provide useful models for formatting the presentations.

8 **Reflection:** Students might benefit from a **think-pair-share** about satire and tone. Were any of the pieces "too" harsh? Does effective satire need to pull any punches? Why or why not?

College and Career Readiness Standards

Focus Standards:

W.11-12.1 Write arguments to support claims in an analysis of substantive topics or texts, using valid reasoning and relevant and sufficient evidence.

W.11-12.4 Produce clear and coherent writing in which the development, organization, and style are appropriate to task, purpose, and audience.

W.11-12.5 Develop and strengthen writing as needed by planning, revising, editing, rewriting, or trying a new approach, focusing on addressing what is most significant for a specific purpose and audience.

9 Portfolio: Be sure students address the Reflection question as a separate part of the Embedded Assessment assignment so they can include it separately. At this point, you may want to ask students to go to their portfolios and find previous unit Reflection questions so that they can get a sense of their growth as academic thinkers and producers.

All notes for and drafts of the piece should be collected and presented together to show the process students completed in successfully accomplishing the tasks.

SCORING GUIDE

When you score this Embedded Assessment, you may wish to download and print copies of the Scoring Guide from SpringBoard Digital to have a copy to mark up for each student's work.

SCORING GUIDE

Scoring Criteria	Exemplary	Proficient	Emerging	Incomplete
Ideas	The satire • offers insight into a topic that is relevant, current, and debatable • argues a convincingly persuasive position • skillfully demonstrates techniques of satire that are ideal for the topic.	The satire • presents a topic that is generally relevant, current, and debatable • argues a clear position • demonstrates techniques of satire that are suitable for the topic.	The satire • presents a topic that is not fully relevant, current, or debatable • argues a position • demonstrates techniques of satire that are somewhat suitable for the topic.	The satire • presents a topic that is irrelevant • includes a vague or unclear position • fails to demonstrate techniques of satire that are somewhat suitable for the topic.
Structure	The satire • presents ideas in an arrangement that is most conducive to the writer's position • is aptly organized using typical conventions of the format.	The satire • logically arranges ideas to support the writer's position • is organized appropriately using typical conventions of the format.	The satire • arranges ideas to somewhat support the writer's position • is mostly organized using typical conventions of the format.	The satire • arranges ideas in a way that detracts from the writer's position or may be irrelevant • is organized in a way that does not match the typical conventions of the format.
Use of Language	The satire • uses language elements (e.g., skillfully incorporating loose and cumulative sentences, irony, hyperbole, and litotes, etc.) extremely effectively • insightfully matches tone and satirical effect to the intended audience and purpose • contains almost no errors in standard writing conventions.	The satire • uses language elements (e.g., incorporating loose and cumulative sentences and satirical techniques) appropriately • applies appropriate tone and satirical effect for the intended audience and purpose • may contain minor errors in writing conventions that do not interfere with understanding.	The satire • uses language elements less effectively • struggles to match tone and satirical effect to the intended audience and purpose • includes some errors in conventions that interfere with the meaning.	The satire • does not use language elements • does not match tone and satirical effect to the intended audience and purpose • includes errors in writing conventions that seriously interfere with its meaning.

College and Career Readiness Standards

W.11-12.10 Write routinely over extended time frames (time for research, reflection, and revision) and shorter time frames (a single sitting or a day or two) for a range of tasks, purposes, and audiences.

L.11-12.6 Acquire and use accurately general academic and domain-specific words and phrases, sufficient for reading, writing, speaking, and listening at the college and career readiness level; demonstrate independence in gathering vocabulary knowledge when considering a word or phrase important to comprehension or expression.

Context

In this unit, students will analyze how multiple perspectives converge in a literary movement by conducting research and analyzing a variety of texts to create a collaborative presentation on the Harlem Renaissance. Their understanding of this cultural period in American History, famed for its creative outpouring of African American literature and arts, will prepare them to delve deeply into one work of fiction: Zora Neale Hurston's *Their Eyes Were Watching God*. They will apply their knowledge of the predominant philosophies, values, and beliefs of the Harlem Renaissance in order to analyze how Hurston's novel is both a reflection of and a departure from this literary movement.

Suggested Texts and Materials

You will need the following materials for this unit:

- Activity 4.2: Images and/or recordings from the Harlem Renaissance
- Activity 4.3: Artwork of the Harlem Renaissance, documentary film about the Harlem Renaissance, **OPTIC** graphic organizers
- Embedded Assessment 1: Technology for the multimedia presentations (e.g., a projector and speakers)
- Activity 4.8: Map of Florida showing Eatonville
- Activity 4.9: Audio recordings of different dialects (optional)
- Activities 4.10–4.17: A class set of *Their Eyes Were Watching God*, by Zora Neale Hurston

Instructional Sequence

In the first half of the unit, students will study the Harlem Renaissance by reading a mix of literature and informational texts and conducting research about the era. They will focus in on a particular aspect of this literary and artistic movement and create a presentation for Embedded Assessment 1.

Once they have established this context, students will examine several texts by Zora Neale Hurston and read the first nine chapters of *Their Eyes Were Watching* God as a class, building capacity for students to read Chapters 10–19 independently and exchange ideas in discussion groups. During reading, students will address elements of style and theme in preparation for Embedded Assessment 2: Writing an Analytical Essay.

AP® CONNECTIONS

In this unit, students will focus on refining these important skills and knowledge areas for AP/College Readiness:

- Researching and presenting the influence of American historical/philosophical eras on America's literary and social history (Activities 4.2–4.4)
- Analyzing the structure, style, and themes of a work of literary merit (Activities 4.10–4.16)
- Analyzing a writer's rich and complex writing style and using that analysis to refine their own writing style (Activity 4.8, 4.9)
- Employing strategies for active independent reading and sophisticated literary analysis (Activity 4.17)
- Focusing deliberate attention on the craft of sentence-level writing (Activities 4.3, 4.10, 4.11, 4.12)

SAT® CONNECTIONS

In this unit, students will practice many important skills that will help them succeed on the SAT and other college readiness exams, including:

- Recognizing and correcting grammatically incomplete sentences (LC 4.9)

Unpacked Embedded Assessments

Embedded Assessment 1: Presenting a Literary Movement	Embedded Assessment 2: Writing an Analytical Essay
Skills and Knowledge: • Collaborate to create an interactive multimedia presentation. • Generate research questions and gather relevant evidence. • Communicate an aspect of a literary movement in a clear thesis. • Organize a presentation to engage and inform an audience with an introduction, transitions, and a conclusion. • Integrate support from a variety of reliable sources. • Create an annotated bibliography. • Design and provide a note-taking tool for audience response. • Apply speaking and performing skills to an informative task.	**Skills and Knowledge:** • State a claim that connects an author's work to a literary movement. • Make a connection between elements of style and/or literary elements and theme. • Use relevant textual evidence from the novel to support a claim. • Incorporate details from other resources on the Harlem Renaissance. • Make effective stylistic choices in language, tone, and syntax. • Use the writing process to produce an organized and coherent essay.

Cognate Directory

Encouraging students to notice the connections between their primary language and English can help them develop academic vocabulary more quickly. If your class includes Spanish speakers, consider adding the following cognates to the classroom Word Wall. For English Language Learners whose primary language is not Spanish, consider using an online translator or dictionary to support comprehension of vocabulary terms.

Unit 4 Vocabulary Terms with Spanish Cognates

Academic Vocabulary		Literary Terms	
English	**Spanish**	**English**	**Spanish**
annotated bibliography	bibliografía anotada	dialect	dialecto
renaissance	renacimiento	indirect characterization	caracterización indirecta

Activity Features at a Glance

The activities in every ELA unit reflect the interconnected nature of reading, writing, listening, speaking, and thinking. The Activity Features at a Glance chart highlights the types of tasks or supports that students and teachers will encounter in each activity.

 Writing and Revision
 Grammar and Language
 Listening, Speaking, and Discussion
 Independent Reading
 Vocabulary Development
 ELL Support
 Knowledge Quest
Gaining Perspectives

ELA Activity	Activity Features
4.1	Listening, Independent Reading, ELL
4.2	Listening, Independent Reading, Vocabulary, ELL, Gaining Perspectives
4.3	Writing, Listening, Independent Reading, Vocabulary, ELL, Knowledge Quest
4.4	Listening
4.5	Listening, Vocabulary
4.6	Writing, Grammar, Listening, Independent Reading
4.7	Listening, Independent Reading
4.8	Writing, Grammar, Listening, Vocabulary, Knowledge Quest
4.9	Writing, Grammar, Listening, Vocabulary, ELL, Knowledge Quest

ELA Activity	Activity Features
LC 4.9	Writing, Grammar, Listening
4.10	Writing, Listening, Independent Reading, Vocabulary, ELL
4.11	Listening, ELL
4.12	Writing, Listening
4.13	Writing, Listening, Vocabulary, ELL
4.14	Listening, Independent Reading, ELL
4.15	Listening
4.16	Listening
4.17	Writing, Grammar, Listening, Independent Reading, Vocabulary

Unit Resources at a Glance

Formative Assessment Opportunities	Digital Assessments	Family Connections
Text-dependent questions Writing prompts Check Your Understanding tasks Focus on the Sentence tasks Language Checkpoint exercises Language & Writer's Craft practice	Activity Quizzes 4.2–4.17 Unit Assessment Part 1 Unit Assessment Part 2 **SBD**	Suggestions for Independent Reading Family Letters (English and Spanish) Student Reports **SBD**
English Language Development	**Foundational Skills**	**Independent Reading**
Leveled Differentiated Instruction Graphic Organizers ELD Strategies Language Workshop 4A Language Workshop 4B	Foundational Skills Screening Assessment Observational Look-fors Foundational Skills Workshop	My Independent Reading List Independent Reading Links Independent Reading Checkpoints Independent Reading Log Reader/Writer Notebook Suggestions for Independent Reading

Reading Plan for *Their Eyes Were Watching God*

Text Chunk	Corresponding Activity	Suggested Treatment of Text
Chapter 1	4.10 Janie's Return Home	Read **in class**
Chapter 2	4.11 Nanny's Story	Read **in class**
Chapters 3–4	4.12 Nanny, Janie, and Logan	Read as **homework prior to activity** Reread and analyze **in class**
Chapters 5–6	4.13 Janie's New Life	Read **in class**
Chapters 7–9	4.14 Janie's "Route of Tradition"	Read **in class**
Chapters 10–19	4.15 Discussion Groups	Read and discuss **in class** and as **homework**
Chapter 20	4.16 The End of a Long Journey	Read **in class**

ⓘ Suggestions for Independent Reading

This list, divided into the categories of **Literature** and **Nonfiction/Informational Text,** comprises titles related to the themes and content of the unit. For their independent reading, students can select from this wide array of titles, which have been chosen based on complexity and interest. Spanish-language titles are included for those students who can read with greater independence or at a higher grade level in Spanish than in English, since building on their first language literacy can bolster their acquisition of English. Titles on this list have been suggested by teachers and school librarians, but you should be sure to preview texts to assess their appropriateness for your specific students and setting. You can also encourage students to do their own research and select titles that intrigue them.

Unit 4: An American Journey

Literature		
Author	**Title**	**Lexile**
Bolden, Tonya	*Wake Up Our Souls*	1190L
Borges, Jorge Luis	*El Aleph*	940L
Brown, Daniel	*Boys in the Boat*	1000L
Chestnutt, Charles Waddell	*Stories of the Color Line*	N/A
Cofer, Judith Ortiz	*Una Isla como tú: Historias del barrio (An Island Like You: Stories of the Barrio)*	830L
Cullen, Countee	*Countee Cullen: Collected Poems*	N/A
Curtis, Christopher Paul	*The Watsons Go to Birmingham*	1000L
Denenberg, Barry	*The Journal of Ben Uchida*	850L
Fleischman, Paul	*Bull Run*	810L
Guy, Rosa	*The Friends*	730L
Hughes, Langston	*Weary Blues, The*	N/A
Hurston, Zora Neale	*Mules and Men*	960L
Hurston, Zora Neale	*Dust Tracks on a Road*	930L
Johnson, Helene	*This Waiting for Love: Helene Johnson, Poet of the Harlem Renaissance*	N/A
Johnson, James Weldon	*The Autobiography of an Ex-Colored Man*	1100L
Larson, Erik	*The Devil in White City*	1170L
Larson, Nella	*Quicksand*	N/A
Mackay, Claude	*Home to Harlem*	860L
Martinez, Victor	*Parrot in the Oven: Mi vida*	1000L
Mosely, Walter	*47*	860L
Rock, Peter	*My Abandonment*	N/A
Thurman, Wallace	*The Blacker the Berry...*	1070L
Toomer, Jean	*Cane*	HL660
Wright, Richard	*Native Son*	700L

Nonfiction/Informational Text		
Author	**Title**	**Lexile**
Avery, Laurence G. (editor)	*A Southern Life: Letters of Paul Green: 1916–1981*	1260L
Bernstein, Patricia	*The First Waco Horror: The Lynching of Jesse Washington and the Rise of the NAACP*	N/A
Bloom, Harold (editor)	*Black American Women Fiction Writers*	1290L
Close, Ellis	*The End of Anger: A New Generation's Take on Race and Rage*	N/A
Davis, Kenneth C.	*In the Shadow of Liberty: The Hidden History of Slavery, Four Presidents, and Five Black Lives*	1110L
Douglass, Frederick	*Narrative of the Life of Frederick Douglass: An American Slave*	920L
DuBois, W.E.B.	*The Souls of Black Folk*	1280L
Dwyer, Jim	*102 Minutes: The Unforgettable Story of the Fight to Survive Inside the Twin Towers*	N/A
Hauser, Brooke	*The New Kids: Big Dreams and Brave Journeys at A High School for Immigrant Teens*	1140L
Houston, Jeanne Wakatsuki and James D.	*Farewell to Manzanar*	1040L
Hughes, Langston	*The Big Sea: An Autobiography*	1090L
King, Martin Luther	*A Time to Break Silence: The Essential Works of Martin Luther King, Jr., for Students*	N/A
Kramer, Victor A.	*Harlem Renaissance Re-examined: A Revised and Expanded Edition*	1440L
McKissack, Lisa Beringer	*Women of the Harlem Renaissance*	960L
McPhee, John	*Assembling California*	N/A
Moody, Anne	*Coming of Age in Mississippi*	870L
Oppenheimer, Joanne	*Dear Miss Breed*	1040L
Philbrick, Nathaniel	*In the Heart of the Sea: The Tragedy of the Whaleship Essex*	1210L
Steinbeck, John	*Travels with Charley in Search of America*	1010L
Thorpe, Helen	*Just Like Us: The True Story of Four Mexican Girls Coming of Age in America*	1100L
Uchida, Yoshiko	*Desert Exile: The Uprooting of a Japanese-American Family*	1280L
Welch, Diana	*The Kids Are All Right*	N/A

Unit 4 Instructional Pathways

Instructional Pathways

Teachers can build customized pathways through this unit by making purposeful choices about which resources to use based on students' learning needs. The charts below outline a few possible pathways to show how teachers might integrate digital assessments, Language Workshops, Close Reading Workshops, and Writing Workshops into instruction. Additional planning resources—including detailed standards correlations—are available on SpringBoard Digital.

English Language Arts Unit 4: An American Journey		
Activity	**SBD Digital Assessments**	**Pacing**
Activity 4.1: Previewing the Unit	N/A	1
Activity 4.2: Developing Research Questions	Activity Quiz 4.2	2
Activity 4.3: The Historical Context of the Harlem Renaissance	Activity Quiz 4.3	2
Activity 4.4: Synthesizing Facts, Interpretations, and Media Formats	Activity Quiz 4.4	1
Activity 4.5: Documenting Your Sources	Activity Quiz 4.5	4
Activity 4.6: Finalizing Research and Organizing Your Presentation	Activity Quiz 4.6	1
Embedded Assessment 1: Presenting a Literary Movement: The Harlem Renaissance	**Unit Assessment Part 1**	3 · 1
Activity 4.7: Unpacking Embedded Assessment 2	Activity Quiz 4.7	1
Activity 4.8: "A Unity of Opposites"	Activity Quiz 4.8	2
Activity 4.9: The Tradition of Dialect	Activity Quiz 4.9	3
LC 4.9: Language Checkpoint: Punctuating Complete Sentences (optional)	Activity Quiz LC 4.9	1
Activity 4.10: Janie's Return Home	Activity Quiz 4.10	2
Activity 4.11: Nanny's Story	Activity Quiz 4.11	1
Activity 4.12: A Moral Dilemma	Activity Quiz 4.12	1
Activity 4.13: Janie's New Life	Activity Quiz 4.13	3
Activity 4.14: Janie's "Route of Tradition"	Activity Quiz 4.14	3
Activity 4.15: Discussion Groups	Activity Quiz 4.15	5
Activity 4.16: The End of a Long Journey	Activity Quiz 4.16	2
Activity 4.17: Reviewing the Reviews	Activity Quiz 4.17	1
Embedded Assessment 2: Writing an Analytical Essay	**Unit Assessment Part 2**	2 · 1

Total 50-minute Class Periods:	37–40

Language Development Pathway

Consider using some or all of the Language Workshop and Foundational Skills Workshop activities with English Language Learners or with any student who would benefit from extra support with academic English. More detailed guidance about the timing and purpose of each Language Workshop and Foundational Skills Workshop activity can be found in the Language Workshop teacher edition.

Language Workshop 4A and 4B		
Activity or Workshop		**Pacing**
Activity 4.1: Previewing the Unit		1
Language Workshop 4A.1: Genre Focus		1
Language Workshop 4A.2: Building Knowledge		1
Language Workshop 4A.3: Academic Vocabulary		1
Language Workshop 4A.4: Vocabulary Preview and Practice		1
Activity 4.2: Developing Research Questions	**OR** **Language Workshop 4A.5:** Close Reading of an Anchor Text*	2 / 1
	Language Workshop 4A.6: Academic Collaboration*	1
Language Workshop 4A.7: Language Checkpoint		1
Activity 4.3: The Historical Context of the Harlem Renaissance		2
Activity 4.4: Synthesizing Facts, Interpretations, and Media Formats		1
Activity 4.5: Documenting Your Sources		4
Activity 4.6: Finalizing Research and Organizing Your Presentation		1
Embedded Assessment 1: Presenting a Literary Movement: The Harlem Renaissance	**OR** **Collaborative Embedded Assessment: Researching and Presenting a Literary Movement**	3 / 7

Activity or Workshop		Pacing	
Language Workshop 4B.1: Genre Focus		1	
Activity 4.7: Unpacking Embedded Assessment 2		1	
Language Workshop 4B.2: Building Knowledge		1	
Activity 4.8: "A Unity of Opposites"		2	
Language Workshop 4B.3: Academic Vocabulary		1	
Language Workshop 4B.4: Vocabulary Preview and Practice		1	
Activity 4.9: The Tradition of Dialect	**Language Workshop 4B.5:** Close Reading of an Anchor Text*	3	1
	Language Workshop 4B.6: Academic Collaboration*		1
Language Workshop 4B.7: Language Checkpoint		1	
LC 4.9: Language Checkpoint: Punctuating Complete Sentences (optional)		1	
Activity 4.10: Janie's Return Home		2	
Activity 4.11: Nanny's Story		1	
Activity 4.12: A Moral Dilemma		1	
Activity 4.13: Janie's New Life		3	
Activity 4.14: Janie's "Route of Tradition"		3	
Activity 4.15: Discussion Groups		5	
Activity 4.16: The End of a Long Journey		2	
Activity 4.17: Reviewing the Reviews		1	
Embedded Assessment 2: Writing an Analytical Essay	**Collaborative Embedded Assessment:** Writing an Analytical Essay	2	4
	Total 50-minute Class Periods:	37–56	

(The "OR" label appears between Activity 4.9 and Language Workshops 4B.5/4B.6, and between the two Embedded Assessment options.)

* These activities are available in Spanish.

Foundational Skills Workshop

The Foundational Skills Workshop offers instructional and practice materials for providing small-group instruction to students who are still developing foundational reading skills.

Activity	Pacing
Activity 1: Practicing Letter-Sound Relationships	15 min.
Activity 2: Recognizing Words by Sight	10 min.
Activity 3: Words with Inconsistent but Common Spellings	
Activity 4: Irregularly Spelled Words	
Activity 5: Common Prefixes	
Activity 6: Common Suffixes	35–40 min. per activity
Activity 7: Using Roots and Affixes to Read Multisyllabic Words	
Activity 8: Reading Multisyllabic Words	
Activity 9: Reading Informational Text with Purpose and Understanding	
Activity 10: Reading Poetry with Fluency	

Flexible Pathways

Teachers may build a flexible pathway that focuses on developing students' close reading and writing skills with the Close Reading and Writing Workshops. Each workshop addresses a specific set of standards and includes multiple assessment opportunities to allow students to demonstrate the knowledge and skills that are the focus of that workshop.

Close Reading Workshops

Workshop	Genre Focus	Assessment Opportunities	Pacing
Close Reading Workshop 3: Poetry	Poetry Painting	Writing Prompt Debate/Discussion Multimedia Presentation	8

Writing Workshops

Workshop	Genre Focus	Assessment Opportunities	Pacing
Writing Workshop 5: Literary Analysis: Poetry	Literary Analysis Poetry	Writing as a Class Writing with a Peer Independent Writing	6
Writing Workshop 6: Research Writing	Research	Class Research Presentation Group Research Presentation Independent Research	8

Flexible Novel Unit

Activity	Pacing
Activity 1: Previewing Embedded Assessment 2: Writing an Analytical Essay	1
Activity 2: Asking and Answering Literal, Interpretive, and Universal Questions	1
Activity 3: Analyzing an Author's Diction	1.5
Activity 4: Analyzing Character	1
Activity 5: Understanding How an Author Establishes Setting	1
Activity 6: Analyzing How an Author Develops Plot and Character	1
Activity 7: Identifying Conflicts and Making Connections	2
Activity 8: Building Understanding of a Novel in Discussion Groups	5
Activity 9: Determining Theme	2
Activity 10: Reviewing the Reviews	1
Embedded Assessment: Writing an Analytical Essay	2
Total 50-minute Class Periods	**18.5**

UNIT 4

VISUAL PROMPT
Duke Ellington was a major presence in the Harlem Renaissance. He was famous for playing jazz, although he played other genres as well, such as classical, blues, and gospel. How does the music of an era influence writers?

AN AMERICAN JOURNEY

Like jars of ginger we are sealed
By nature's heritage.
But let us break the seal of years
With pungent thrusts of song,
For there is joy in long-dried tears
For whetted passions of a throng.

—from "To Usward" by Gwendolyn B. Bennett

Leveled Differentiated Instruction Directory

For guidance on differentiating tasks for English language learners at various levels of language proficiency, refer to the Leveled Differentiated Instruction suggestions in these activities:

4.1 Offer extra support for students at an early stage of English language development by exposing them to text in their home language.

4.2 Provide extra support for students at an early stage of English language development by exposing them to images or other visuals.

4.3 Support students in connecting figurative language to allusions through analysis and discussion.

4.9 Help students use the **Word Choice Analyzer** graphic organizer to analyze the author's use of dialogue in a text by doing a close reading of certain passages to understand the meaning of different phrases.

4.10 Use the **Character Map** graphic organizer to help students analyze a character.

UNIT 4

Read aloud the unit title, "An American Journey," and the quotation. Have students begin to think about cultural and literary movements by posing the unit's Essential Questions: How do cultural movements such as the Harlem Renaissance reflect and create people's attitudes and beliefs? (What is a cultural movement? What is the relationship between such a movement and social attitudes or beliefs?) How is one writer's work both a natural product of and a departure from the ideas of a specific literary movement in American literature? (Why might a writer consciously depart from a current social movement?) Share responses in partner, small-group, or whole-class discussion.

Have students look at the image and respond to the visual prompt. You may want to have students think-pair-share to write short responses or discuss their responses as a class.

CONTENTS

Have students skim/scan the activities and texts in this unit. Have them note any texts they have heard about but never read and any activities that sound particularly interesting.

GOALS

Have students read the goals for the unit and mark any words that are unfamiliar. Have students add these words to the classroom Word Wall along with definitions.

You may also want to post these goals in a visible place in the classroom for the duration of this unit, allowing you and your students to revisit the goals easily and gauge progress throughout the unit.

UNIT 4

VOCABULARY DEVELOPMENT

Adding to vocabulary knowledge is essential for reading fluency. Students will encounter new vocabulary in this course in multiple ways:

- Academic Vocabulary
- Literary Terms
- Vocabulary in Context (terms glossed in text selections)
- Word Connections
- Oral Discussions

Encourage students to use new vocabulary expressively in class discussions and in their writing. Have them keep a **Reader/Writer Notebook** in which they record new words, their meanings, and their pronunciations.

See the Resources section for examples of graphic organizers suitable for word study. Having students use word-study graphic organizers will greatly enhance their understanding of new words and their connection to unit concepts and to the broader use of advanced and discipline-based terms.

Have students review the list of academic and literary terms and sort them in a **QHT** chart. Revisit the chart periodically to see how students' understanding progresses throughout the unit.

LANGUAGE DEVELOPMENT

Several recurring SpringBoard features focus on building students' knowledge of grammar and usage concepts. Language and Writer's Craft features guide students to examine a writer's use of a language concept in context before incorporating the concept into their own writing. Grammar & Usage features briefly highlight and explain an interesting grammar or usage concept that appears in a text, both to improve students' reading comprehension and to increase their understanding of the concept. Periodic Language Checkpoints offer in-depth practice with standard English conventions and usage and ask students to revise sample sentences as well as their own work.

UNIT 4

An American Journey

GOALS

- To examine the literature of the Harlem Renaissance
- To analyze relationships among elements of a literary text
- To research how historical and social context shapes a work's literary elements
- To create and present a formal multimedia presentation

VOCABULARY

ACADEMIC
annotated bibliography
renaissance

LITERARY
book review
dialect
folktale
indirect characterization

CONTENTS

Leveled Differentiated Instruction Directory (continued)

4.11 Support students as they answer text-dependent questions by providing them with the **Key Idea and Details** graphic organizer.

4.13 Use the **Notes for Reading Independently** graphic organizer to support students' summaries of novel chapters.

4.14 Give students the **Conclusion Builder** graphic organizer as prewriting support.

CONTENTS

*Texts not included in these materials.

 My Independent Reading List

UNIT 4

INDEPENDENT READING

In this unit, students will have the opportunity to choose additional texts from the Harlem Renaissance to read independently. The Planning the Unit section of the Teacher Edition and the Resources section of the Student Edition contain guidance, Reading Logs, and Reading Lists to help students make reading selections. Independent Reading Links prompt students to actively respond to their reading and record responses in their Reader/Writer Notebooks or Reading Logs. Independent Reading Checkpoints allow for quick check-ins of independent reading prior to each Embedded Assessment.

KNOWLEDGE QUEST

Within the unit, students will engage in two Knowledge Quests. They will read collections of texts about what makes a community and self-awareness, building their understanding of the topics and related vocabulary. Each Knowledge Quest begins with a knowledge question and supporting questions that focus student learning. After students read the final text in a set, they will have the opportunity to return to the Knowledge Question and express their growing understanding of the topic by responding to a writing-to-sources prompt or engaging in an academic discussion.

➤ TEACHER TO TEACHER

The SpringBoard program is designed so that students interact with the texts in meaningful ways, such as note-taking and annotating, to facilitate comprehension and analysis. Have students use Reader/Writer Notebooks actively for vocabulary study, answers to text-dependent questions, predictions and questions about texts, reflections, responses to Independent Reading Links, and so on. The Reader/Writer Notebooks are not listed as part of the materials for each activity, but the expectation is that students will access them frequently.

ACTIVITY 4.1

PLAN

Materials: highlighters, chart paper or whiteboard
Suggested Pacing: 1 50-minute class period

TEACH

1 Ask a volunteer to read aloud the Learning Targets. Tell students that they will be examining a significant period in the development of American culture.

2 Read aloud the About the Unit section. Point out that the Harlem Renaissance represents a set of uniquely African American contributions to the American "marketplace of ideas" students examined in Unit 3. Ask students to jot down any questions they have about Unit 4.

3 Have students briefly write their answers to the two Essential Questions and then discuss their answers in pairs. Explain that they will revise their responses to these questions as their understanding of the Unit 4 content develops.

4 As a class, do a close reading of the assignment in Unpacking Embedded Assessment 1. Pause occasionally and ask questions to determine students' understanding of the assignment.

5 To help students complete the Unpacking Embedded Assessment 1 activity, create a web organizer on the board or on chart paper. Label the center circle *Citation Skills*. As a class, discuss the citation skills necessary to complete Embedded Assessment 1. Record student responses in the web, such as:

- knowledge of the Harlem Renaissance (e.g., historical context, philosophy and beliefs, art, daily life)
- knowledge of each medium and its conventions
- the ability to conduct print and online research

6 Students will independently read a literary work written during the Harlem Renaissance. Help students prepare their Independent Reading by allowing them to research independently or with a small group the literary works from the Harlem Renaissance movement. Encourage students to record

Learning Strategies

Marking the Text
Paraphrasing
Skimming/Scanning
Summarizing
Think-Pair-Share

My Notes

Learning Targets
- Preview the big ideas for the unit.
- Create a plan for independent reading.

Preview

In this activity, you will begin thinking about your first Embedded Assessment, a research project about the Harlem Renaissance.

About the Unit

Ever since the Pilgrims traveled to America, the concept of the "journey" has been part of the American experience. In this unit, you will take two journeys. First, you will experience a cultural journey by exploring the voices of the Harlem Renaissance. Your research will culminate in a multimedia research presentation. You will then study one voice of the Harlem Renaissance in depth by reading *Their Eyes Were Watching God* by Zora Neale Hurston. You will use your new knowledge of the predominant philosophies, values, and beliefs of the Harlem Renaissance to analyze how Hurston's novel is both a reflection of and a departure from this literary movement.

Essential Questions

Based on your current knowledge, respond to the following Essential Questions:

1. How do cultural movements such as the Harlem Renaissance reflect and create people's attitudes and beliefs?

2. How is one writer's work both a natural product of and a departure from the ideas of a specific literary movement in American literature?

Unpacking Embedded Assessment 1

Closely read the assignment for Embedded Assessment 1: Presenting a Literary Movement: The Harlem Renaissance.

Your assignment is to work in pairs or a small group to create an interactive multimedia research presentation about a topic related to the Harlem Renaissance. This presentation to your classmates should include a variety of media and must also include an annotated bibliography. Your presentation should focus on some aspect of the era that presents the values and ideas of the Harlem Renaissance, such as historical context, philosophy and beliefs, the arts, or daily life.

With your class, create a graphic organizer that details the knowledge and skills you must have to create an interactive, multimedia research presentation about a topic related to the Harlem Renaissance.

Independent Reading Plan

For your independent reading during this unit, select a novel, memoir, collection of short stories, or book of poetry from the Harlem Renaissance literary movement. Do some research to find a selection that interests you. Most bookshops and libraries have websites with reviews and comments, and some social media sites cater to book lovers.

College and Career Readiness Standards

Focus Standards:

RL.11-12.10 By the end of grade 11, read and comprehend literature, including stories, dramas, and poems, in the grades 11–CCR text complexity band proficiently, with scaffolding as needed at the high end of the range.

RI.11-12.10 By the end of grade 11, read and comprehend literary nonfiction in the grades 11–CCR text complexity band proficiently, with scaffolding as needed at the high end of the range.

RI.11-12.6 Determine an author's point of view or purpose in a text in which the rhetoric is particularly effective, analyzing how style and content contribute to the power, persuasiveness, or beauty of the text.

Additional Standards Addressed:

RL.11-12.1, RL.11-12.2

The Research Process

3. Embedded Assessment 1 requires you to complete a formal research project about a topic related to the Harlem Renaissance and then present the results of your research to your class. How familiar are you with the research process? Turn and talk to your partner about a research project you completed in the past. Take notes on your conversation in your Reader/Writer Notebook.

4. Read and paraphrase each step in the graphic organizer. Then try to think of any resources (Internet, librarian, your teacher, family or neighbors, historical societies or museums, books, documentaries, and so on) that you might use during each step.

Research Process Steps	Paraphrase	Resources You Might Use
1. Identify the topic to be researched.		
2. Prepare questions that will guide you toward the information you want to include in your presentation.		
3. Develop a plan for how and where you will conduct your research.		
4. Locate and evaluate sources for credibility and accuracy and to ensure that they are free from bias and faulty reasoning.		
5. Gather evidence; write additional questions to narrow or broaden research.		
6. Synthesize information from a variety of sources, making sure to include academic citations.		
7. Use an appropriate mode of delivery, whether written, oral, or multimodal, to present results.		

5. Throughout the next few activities, you will go through each step of the research process first as a class and then with your presentation groups. As you complete each step, you will critique the process to implement changes as needs occur and are identified. Before you begin, write down any questions that you may have and discuss them with a small group.

information about themes and topics they discover in their research. Then ask students to select two or three themes or topics that are of interest to them. Explain that they can use these themes and topics to guide their Independent Reading Plan.

LEVELED DIFFERENTIATED INSTRUCTION

In this activity, students may benefit from support when selecting independent reading titles.

Beginning Consider giving students who are at an early stage of English language development the option of reading a text in their home language. These students can build on native language literacy as they begin to develop academic English.

Extend Consider pairing more experienced readers with students who are in earlier stages of English language development.

7 Guide students to make a final choice and create their Independent Reading Plan.

8 Instruct students to complete student step 3 of The Research Process section. Then guide them as a class in the completion of the first two rows of the **Research Process Steps** graphic organizer. Then have students individually complete the chart.

9 Have students complete student step 5 of The Research Process section and discuss any questions they have with a small group.

ASSESS

Review students' Reader/Writer Notebooks for evidence of previewing and rating each considered text.

ADAPT

If students need additional help choosing a book, provide resources online or create a class library that may help them determine a suitable text. As the unit progresses, use your observations of students' skill levels to create groups and make reading assignments.

ACTIVITY 4.2

Learning Strategies

Close Reading
Discussion Groups
Marking the Text
Questioning the Text

Learning Targets

- Analyze the characteristics and structural elements of an informational text.
- Develop research questions about the Harlem Renaissance.

Preview

In this activity, you will read an informational text about the Harlem Renaissance and use it to generate potential research questions.

VOCABULARY

ACADEMIC

A renaissance is a rebirth or revival. The word is derived from the French *re*, meaning "again" and *naitre*, meaning "to be born." When spelled with a capital *R*, the word refers to a revival in art, literature, and learning of a historical period.

🎲 INDEPENDENT READING LINK

Read and Discuss
Use the definitions of the three types of questions that you reviewed for this activity to create questions for your independent reading selection. Read your questions to a small group. If anyone in the group disagrees with your designated question level, work together to reformulate the question.

What Do You Know About the Harlem Renaissance?

Asking questions to gain information is a useful practice before, during, and after reading a source. Asking before reading helps you determine the points you want to explore. Asking questions as you read and after you read you helps analyze the text and refine your research focus.

1. Your teacher will show you some images to help you recall what you already know about the Harlem Renaissance. Note your impressions of the images and the facts they bring to mind.

_____

_____

_____

_____

_____

_____

_____

_____

_____

_____

_____

_____

_____

2. Next, structure your notes into short, one-sentence statements and place your statements into the **K** column of the KWL chart that follows.

College and Career Readiness Standards

Focus Standards:

W.11-12.2 Write informative/explanatory texts to examine and convey complex ideas, concepts, and information clearly and accurately through the effective selection, organization, and analysis of content.

W.11-12.7 Conduct short as well as more sustained research projects to answer a question (including a self-generated question)

or solve a problem; narrow or broaden the inquiry when appropriate; synthesize multiple sources on the subject, demonstrating understanding of the subject under investigation.

SL.11-12.1b Work with peers to promote civil, democratic discussions and decision-making, set clear goals and deadlines, and establish individual roles as needed.

What I Know (K) About the Harlem Renaissance	What I Want to Know (W) About the Harlem Renaissance	What I Have Learned (L) About the Harlem Renaissance

3. Use what you have written in the **K** column as a basis for creating questions that will lead you to gain more information about the Harlem Renaissance. Write those questions in the KWL chart's **W** column. It may be helpful to review the levels of questions strategy before you begin writing your questions to make sure that you are asking level 2 questions.

Making Predictions Using Text Features

4. To increase your knowledge about the Harlem Renaissance, you are going to read an informational text titled "The Harlem Renaissance" by Kathleen Drowne and Patrick Huber. Writers of informational texts often use text features such as subtitles, section heads, and footnotes to help their readers know what is going to be discussed in the text. Before you begin reading, skim the text and note the text features used by the authors and use them to predict what you will learn about the Harlem Renaissance from the article. Write your predictions in your Reader/Writer Notebook.

College and Career Readiness Standards

SL.11-12.1c Propel conversations by posing and responding to questions that probe reasoning and evidence; ensure a hearing for a full range of positions on a topic or issue; clarify, verify, or challenge ideas and conclusions; and promote divergent and creative perspectives.

Additional Standards Addressed:
RI.11-12.1, RI.11-12.2, RI.11-12.3, RI.11-12.5, RI.11-12.6, W.11-12.2a, W.11-12.2b, W.11-12.2c, W.11-12.2d, W.11-12.2e, W.11-12.2f

ACTIVITY 4.2 continued

4 If necessary, pair students and ask them to work together to rewrite their notes into one-sentence statements and place them in the **K** column of the KWL chart as described in student step 3.

5 Before students complete student step 3 by writing their questions in the W column, consider introducing or reviewing **levels of questions**. You may wish to use the following example questions in relation to the Harlem Renaissance:

- Level 1 (literal, seeking a focused answer that can be found in the text or with further research): *Who was Ethel Waters?*
- Level 2 (interpretive, seeking an answer based on inferences from the text): *What were some similarities between Harlem Renaissance music and poetry?*
- Level 3 (universal, seeking a broader answer for a more inclusive topic): *Why is African American art important?*

6 Emphasize to students that they should construct Level 2 questions for the W column of their KWL charts.

7 Call students' attention to the Independent Reading Link. Direct them to create questions on all three levels for their independent reading selection and share their questions in small groups, working together to assess the level of each question and revise questions as needed. To assess their work, circulate among the groups pausing to make sure students have used all three types of questions appropriately.

8 Read aloud student step 4 in the Making Predictions Using Text Features section. Have volunteers locate and read aloud text features, such as section heads, footnotes, and vocabulary words they see in the informational text "The Harlem Renaissance."

9 Then have students individually write their predictions, based on the text features, of what they will learn from the article.

10 Ask volunteers to read aloud each bullet point in the As You Read section. Then call on students to paraphrase each bullet point to ensure that students understand how to annotate the text and where to write additional questions about the Harlem Renaissance.

11 Explain to students that they will practice annotating the About the Author section as a class. Have students read the About the Author section, circling unfamiliar words as they read. Model ways to determine the meanings of these words, whether through the use of word parts, context clues, or print or online references. Provide students with dictionaries as needed before they start to read the informational text.

12 **FIRST READ:** Conduct a shared reading of "The Harlem Renaissance." Pause after paragraph 1 to review why so many African Americans moved north and the problems they encountered when they relocated.

TEXT COMPLEXITY

Overall: Very Complex
Lexile: 1630L
Qualitative: High Difficulty
Task: Moderate (Analyze)

TEACHER TO TEACHER

Notice that the text is divided into four chunks. To support learning, you may choose to **jigsaw** this assignment by dividing the class into expert groups of four, with each person reading a different chunk. After students have read their assigned chunks, have readers of each chunk meet together to share information. Groups should chart the information they pull from each section of the text and work on the text-dependent questions together.

4.2

My Notes

As You Read

- Put an exclamation point next to any information you want to investigate further.
- Circle unknown words and phrases. Try to determine the meaning of the words by using context clues, word parts, or a dictionary.
- Write additional questions that occur to you about the information in the text in the **W** column of your KWL chart.

About the Authors

Kathleen Drowne and Patrick Huber teach English and U.S. history, respectively, at the Missouri University of Science and Technology. They are co-authors of *The 1920s* volume of the *American Popular Culture Through History* series. Drowne's other works include *Spirits of Defiance*, a study of Prohibition-era American literature. Huber is co-author of *A&R Pioneers: Architects of American Roots Music on Record*, a study of the origins of recorded music production in the United States.

Informational Text

The Harlem Renaissance

adapted from *The 1920s* by **Kathleen Drowne and Patrick Huber**

Historical Context
Chunk 1

1 Between 1915 and 1918, approximately half a million African Americans left the South for northern urban-industrial centers like Harlem, Chicago, St. Louis, and Detroit as part of the Great Migration. ... Most of these migrants moved north to find higher-paying jobs and to carve out better lives for themselves and their families. They also sought to escape segregation, sharecropping, and racial violence common in the South. The flood of African-American newcomers heightened competition with white workers for jobs, housing, and public facilities, and set off an unprecedented surge of race riots in northern and Midwestern cities.

2 For the most part, southern black migrants were disappointed by what they found in the North. Not only were well-paying jobs scarce for black workers in northern and Midwestern cities, but racist practices also forced these new arrivals to suffer the indignities of segregated schools, theaters, housing, and other facilities. Although the 1920s saw a tremendous flowering of African-American arts, particularly in Harlem and other northern cities,

Scaffolding the Text-Dependent Questions

5. What details in paragraph 1 help explain how social conditions of the time contributed to the development of the Harlem Renaissance? Reread paragraph 1. What drove African Americans from the South? What drew them to the North? What did they bring with them when they moved, and what resulted? RI.11-12.1

the decade overall was one of tense, turbulent, and sometimes violent relations between black and white Americans. (9–10)

3   Although the phrase "New Negro" dates to the late nineteenth century, it was not until the 1920s that this label gained currency as a description for middle-class African Americans who advocated a new sense of **militancy** and racial pride. Indeed, Alain Locke, an African-American philosopher, critic, and editor, titles his Harlem Renaissance literary anthology *The New Negro* (1925) in order to signal these powerful currents of black artistic consciousness, renewed civil rights advocacy, and racial **solidarity**. The National Association for the Advancement of Colored People (NAACP) and other organizations waged court battles in an attempt to secure African Americans' civil and political rights. Black writers, musicians, and artists, especially those who resided in Harlem, the so-called "Mecca[1] of the New Negro," used their work to celebrate African-American culture and challenge damaging racist stereotypes. Above all, "New Negroes" attempted to assert their own **agency** and participate fully in American culture, while resisting white America's attempts to cast them as a "problem" that somehow needed to be solved. Many critics, in hindsight, see the New Negro movement as overly optimistic and even naïve, but at the time this impulse toward self-expression, self-assertiveness, and self-determination was a driving force among some middle-class African Americans. (12–13)

Literature
Chunk 2

4   The Harlem Renaissance, sometimes called the Negro Renaissance or the New Negro Movement, describes the period roughly between the end of World War I and the onset of the Great Depression, during which African Americans produced a vast number of literary, musical, and artistic works. The artists associated with the Harlem Renaissance attempted to promote racial consciousness and black pride by creating new images of African Americans and by celebrating their blues and folklore traditions, in order ultimately to destroy old racist stereotypes. The works they created were, for the most part, confident, positive, and optimistic about the future of black America.

5   ... Thousands of black families crowded into Harlem, a large neighborhood in upper Manhattan loosely defined in the 1920s as the area between 110th and 155th Streets. This dramatic population shift transformed Harlem into the capital of African-American culture during the 1920s. ... Black people from the American South, the West Indies, and even Africa crowded into the neighborhood, competing for jobs and living space. Harlem became an important cultural crossroads, and talented writers such as Langston Hughes, Countee Cullen, Claude McKay, Jessie Fauset, and Zora Neale Hurston were only a few of the hundreds of young African Americans who flocked to Harlem to join the growing colony of black intellectuals fueling the Harlem Renaissance. (186–187)

---

[1] **Mecca:** a city in Saudi Arabia that is sacred to Islam; pilgrims travel there as part of their spiritual journey

WORD CONNECTIONS

Multiple-Meaning Words
The word currency has multiple meanings. Use a print or digital resource to clarify the correct meaning of the word *currency* in this context.

My Notes

militancy: aggressive behavior in support of a cause
solidarity: sense of togetherness
agency: ability to do things for oneself

13 While students read, monitor their progress. Be sure they are engaged with the text, placing exclamation points next to information they want to investigate further and circling unfamiliar words and phrases. Remind them to write questions that occur to them in the **W** column of the KWL chart.

14 Vocabulary Development: Pause after paragraph 3 to discuss the multiple-meaning word *currency*. Read the text in the Word Connections box and have students use a print or online resource to determine how the word is used in the first sentence of the paragraph.

⭐ TEACHER TO TEACHER

To support students' understanding of the term *Mecca*, show them a photo of the Muslim pilgrimage at Mecca, known as the Hajj. This **visual** will support students in developing background knowledge. Explain that vast numbers of people travel to Mecca each year and help students compare that movement of people to the one that happened in Harlem during the Harlem Renaissance.

15 Tell students to pause at the end of paragraph 4 to discuss why it is important for writers to create new images of African Americans in literature. Mention that as societies change, the ways in which they view themselves, their histories, and their people change. Students might support their observations on this subject with references to how African Americans and other minorities are represented in popular films and TV shows today.

Scaffolding the Text-Dependent Questions

6. Which sentence in paragraph 4 states the thesis of "The Harlem Renaissance"? Why was the thesis placed there and not at the beginning of the essay? Remember that an essay's thesis is a short summary of its main point. Which sentence in paragraph 4 summarizes the most information? What kind of information is contained in paragraphs 1–3? Why might that information precede the thesis? RI.11-12.5

7. What can you conclude about the authors' purpose, audience, and message from paragraphs 4 and 5 (Chunk 2) of "The Harlem Renaissance"? Reread the two paragraphs. What word describes what a reader gains from the content in these paragraphs? Within which group did the Harlem Renaissance arise? What observations do the writers make in paragraph 4? What viewpoint is supported by those observations? RI.11-12.6

ACTIVITY 4.2 continued

4.2

LEVELED DIFFERENTIATED INSTRUCTION

Consider using images or other visuals to support students in their English language development in comprehending the text of "The Harlem Renaissance."

Beginning Help students who are at the early stage in their English language development to develop background understanding of the era between the end of World War I and the onset of the Great Depression by sharing images of Harlem during the 1920s and asking them to say or write statements about what they observe.

Support Have student partners respond to the images by taking turns asking and answering questions about details within the images. Guide students to express how the images help them gain an understanding of life in Harlem between the end of World War I and the onset of the Great Depression.

⭐ TEACHER TO TEACHER

Most students spend time listening to and learning about current popular music and musicians. You may want to have students explore what they know about music from different time periods. Discuss thoughts about not only how music influences writers but also how it may help bring about social change.

16 Pause after paragraph 10. Highlight the Word Connections box and read aloud the information about the word *colloquialism*. Invite students to demonstrate their understanding of the term by giving examples of colloquialisms. You might get them started with these examples:

- 'Sup, bro?
- It's wicked cold out today.
- Ain't gonna happen.
- LOL

WORD CONNECTIONS

Content Connections
A colloquialism is a word or phrase used when speaking informally. One example of such a phrase is *the blues*, meaning a feeling of deep sadness. In music, this sadness is expressed by minor harmonies, slow rhythms, and melancholy lyrics.

My Notes

Music

Chunk 3

6   Although initially considered little more than a passing musical fad when it was first recorded in 1917, jazz became the most influential form of American popular music in the 1920s. Jazz combined elements of a wide range of music, including ragtime compositions, brass-band marches, minstrel numbers, and to a lesser degree, blues songs. ...

7   The enormous popularity of jazz provided new opportunities for African-American musicians to make records, occasionally perform on radio, and find work playing for live audiences. ...

8   With the advent of National Prohibition, Harlem nightclubs and cabarets, located above 125th Street in Manhattan, began to attract wealthy white partygoers and tourists who wanted to drink, dance, and hear "exotic" African-American music. In 1929, Variety listed 11 major nightclubs in Harlem that catered to predominately white crowds, including Small's Paradise, Connie's Inn, and the Cotton Club. These swanky nightclubs and cabarets employed hundreds of African-American jazz musicians during the late 1920s, including bandleader Edward "Duke" Ellington. ... (199–200)

The Duke Ellington Orchestra performs "Take the A Train" with singer Bette Roche in the film *Reveille with Beverly*, released in January 1943.

9   By far the greatest jazz musician of the 1920s was Louis Armstrong, a New Orleans born cornetist and trumpeter whose inventive solos and technical brilliance marked the pinnacle of hot jazz. ... (200)

10   Another influential form of African-American music that rose to prominence during the 1920s was the blues. Although it remains difficult to pinpoint an exact origin, the blues emerged sometime around the turn of the twentieth century and evolved from a variety of traditional black musical forms, including field hollers, work songs, ballads, and rags. ... Early folk blues reflected a variety of experiences of African-American life during segregation

Scaffolding the Text-Dependent Questions

8. How does the way the text is organized help the reader understand it? What textual evidence supports your answer? Examine how the text is organized. What purpose do the headers serve? How would you summarize the main idea of each section? How do the sections relate to one another? What does each section contribute to the overall text? Support your explanation with an example. RI.11-12.5

and often spoke of work, gambling, crime, alcohol, imprisonment, disasters, and hard times. Above all, the blues commented on the universal themes of troubled love relationships and sexual desires. ... (205)

11   One of the most influential vaudeville blues singers of the 1920s was Gertrude "Ma" Rainey, a flamboyant dresser who flaunted expensive beaded gowns, a necklace made of $20 gold pieces, and ostentatious diamond earrings and rings. ... Billed as "the Mother of the Blues," she recorded more than 100 songs over five years. ... Rainey's young protégé, Bessie Smith, emerged as an even greater vaudeville star. Smith's first record, "Gulf Coast Blues," coupled with "Downhearted Blues," made in 1923 for Columbia, sold 780,000 copies in its first six months. ... With her expressive, soulful phrasing, she remained the biggest blues star of the 1920s, and today she is unquestionably considered by music historians to be the greatest vaudeville blues singer of all times. (205–206)

Art
Chunk 4

12   One serious problem that plagued African-American artists during the 1920s was a lack of opportunity to study art and to show their work. Some museums refused to exhibit the work of black artists, and some art schools declined to consider black applicants for scholarships. In 1923, sculptor Augusta Savage brought this discrimination against black artists to the attention of the American public when, after being rejected for a summer school in France because of her race, she appealed to the press. After her story appeared in newspapers, many editorials and letters followed, and while she never did receive the scholarship, she did other black artists a great service by focusing public scrutiny on the problem. ...

13   Perhaps the best-known African-American painter of the Harlem Renaissance was Aaron Douglas. Douglas was a student of the German artist Winold Reiss, who painted African Americans neither as crude stereotypes nor as white people with dark complexions, but rather as dignified, unique individuals. Reiss encouraged Douglas to incorporate African imagery into his paintings, which he did with great success. His May 1927 cover for the Urban League's magazine *Opportunity*, for example, depicts the proud profile of a long-neck Magbetu woman with an elaborate African hairstyle. ... In 1928, Douglas became the first president of the Harlem Artists Guild, an organization that helped black artists secure federal funding from the Works Progress Administration during the Great Depression. (274)

My Notes

_____
_____
_____
_____
_____
_____
_____
_____
_____

Aaron Douglas painted "The Judgment Day" in 1939, more than a decade after creating the book illustration on which the painting is based. The illustration was one of seven created for a collection of poems titled *God's Trombones: Seven Negro Sermons in Verse* by James Weldon Johnson.

Making Observations
- What text features do you notice in this text?
- Were the predictions you made before reading the informational text correct?

Scaffolding the Text-Dependent Questions

9. What universal themes are reflected in blues music? How do they reflect the Harlem Renaissance? Cite text evidence in your response. What themes were prevalent in the music of the Harlem Renaissance? Whose life experiences are reflected in that music? What were those experiences? RI.11-12.3

10. Revisit the section on art in the text and explain the relationship among discrimination, racial stereotypes, and African American art during the Harlem Renaissance? What common racial stereotypes were represented in the art of that time? How easy was it for African American artists to exhibit their work? What was significant about the art of Aaron Douglas? How did his work confront racial stereotypes? RI.11-12.1

ACTIVITY 4.2 continued

17 Tell students to pause after paragraph 11. Tell students that *vaudeville* was the name for a type of popular entertainment during the early 20th century. Vaudeville combined comedy, song, and dance in energetic and upbeat ways. Have students skim Chunk 3 and name the forms of music that contributed to the Harlem Renaissance:
- ragtime
- brass-band
- minstrel
- jazz
- blues

18 Tell students to pause at the end of paragraph 12. Have students use context clues to determine the meaning of the word *scrutiny* in the paragraph's final sentence.

19 After reading the text for the first time, guide the class in a discussion by asking the Making Observations questions. Check students' general comprehension of the text based on their observations, asking follow-up questions if needed.

20 Tell students to review the predictions they made before reading "The Harlem Renaissance." Have volunteers share their predictions and determine their accuracy. Use their results in a brief discussion of how subtitles, section heads, and footnotes contribute to an informational text.

21 RETURNING TO THE TEXT:
Guide students to return to the text to respond to the text-dependent questions. Invite them to work in small groups to reread the text and answer the questions. Remind them to use text evidence in their responses.

22 Move from group to group and listen in as students answer the text-dependent questions. If they have difficulty, scaffold the questions by breaking them into smaller parts. See the Scaffolding the Text-Dependent Questions boxes for suggestions.

4.2

Returning to the Text

- Return to the informational text as you respond to the following questions. Use text evidence to support your responses.
- Write any additional questions you have about the text in your Reader/Writer Notebook.

5. What details in paragraph 1 help explain how social conditions of the time contributed to the development of the Harlem Renaissance?

Paragraph 1 states that African Americans relocated to the North in the early 1900s "to escape ... segregation, sharecropping, and racial violence" in the South. At the same time, they brought their heritage with them, hoping their voices would at last be heard.

6. Which sentence in paragraph 4 states the thesis of "The Harlem Renaissance"? Why was the thesis placed there and not at the beginning of the essay?

The thesis sentence is "The artists associated with the Harlem Renaissance attempted to promote racial consciousness and black pride by creating new images of African Americans and by celebrating their blues and folklore traditions, in order ultimately to destroy old racist stereotypes." The "Historical Context" is placed first to provide a context in which the thesis (and other sections) can be understood.

7. What can you conclude about the authors' purpose, audience, and message from paragraphs 4 and 5 (Chunk 2) of "The Harlem Renaissance"?

The amount of information presented shows that the authors' purpose is to inform. The final line of paragraph 4—"The works they created were, for the most part, confident, positive, and optimistic about the future of black America."—is one indication that the audience is those interested in African American history. The section conveys the message that the period's art was important and remarkable.

8. How does the way the text is organized help the reader understand it? What textual evidence supports your answer?

Arranging the text into sections helps readers build an overall picture of the Harlem Renaissance. A transition sentence in paragraph 4 moves the focus from historical context to specific topics: "The Harlem Renaissance ... describes the period ... during which African Americans produced ... literary, musical, and artistic works." The sections that follow each focus on a specific aspect of the main topic.

Scaffolding the Text-Dependent Questions

11. Why was Harlem called the "Mecca of the New Negro"? How does the author show this over the course of the text? Remember the significance of Mecca in Muslim culture. What does Mecca symbolize in a larger context? How might its significance be similar to that of Harlem for African Americans? From which parts of the world did African Americans come? What made Harlem important to African Americans' cultural development? What do the authors state about that importance? RI.11-12.2

23 Assist students in completing the Gaining Perspectives feature. Be sure to review ways students can use media to present their information.

9. What universal themes are reflected in blues music? How do they reflect the Harlem Renaissance? Cite text evidence in your response.

The blues reflects themes with which many people can relate, including that of people seeking

a better life and increased cultural expression. The music bridges the gap between African

Americans' new opportunities at the time and their heritage. Paragraph 10 points out that

blues music also expressed "African-American life during segregation" including "crime,

alcohol, imprisonment."

10. Revisit the section on art in the text and explain the relationship among discrimination, racial stereotypes, and African American art during the Harlem Renaissance?

Even as African American artists pursued their art, instances of discrimination were brought

to light. One sculptor in particular "brought this discrimination against black artists to the

attention of the American public" with the publication of her story. Paragraph 13 describes

how Aaron Douglas dispelled racial stereotypes with his art when he "painted African

Americans ... as dignified, unique individuals."

11. Why was Harlem called the "Mecca of the New Negro"? How does the author show this over the course of the text?

Black people from across the globe—"the American South, the West Indies, and even

Africa"—came to Harlem, much like Muslim pilgrims from all over the world travel to Mecca.

The author shows this by naming areas from which people migrated to Harlem and by

describing the strains of literature, music, and art that blended through a focused, vibrant

exchange.

 Gaining Perspectives

In the years between 1915 and 1918, Northern and Midwestern cities saw an influx of African American residents. People wanted a progressive life in a democracy—one where all people's rights were truly respected as well as protected by laws. With a partner, think about the social conditions that caused African Americans to move north. Then consider which cultural areas and communities began to flourish after the residential influx. Apply what you learn about the years between 1915 and 1918 as you research two other countries where signs of democratization helped communities flourish. Create a brief media presentation to share your findings with the class.

24 Read with the class student step 12 of the Working from the Text section. Make sure students understand what is expected of them by analyzing the first row of the graphic organizer. Point out that the entry *Literature* is a subhead in the informational text and that the names *Langston Hughes* and *Zora Neale Hurston* appear in the "Literature" subsection of the text, with the third name *James Weldon Johnson* having been obtained elsewhere.

25 Have students work independently to complete the graphic organizer. Remind them to model their responses on the example provided.

4.2

Working from the Text

12. Look back at the article "The Harlem Renaissance" and identify each area of artistic accomplishment addressed by the authors. Then write two or three descriptive sentences about each area, including two examples of Renaissance figures from the article and one from print or online sources. Maintain a formal register and informative tone in your writing and construct your sentences in an active voice.

Area of Accomplishment	Description and Examples
Literature	Harlem Renaissance writing was noteworthy for its confidence and optimism about the future of black America. Noted writers of the period include Langston Hughes, Zora Neale Hurston, and James Weldon Johnson.
Music	The Harlem Renaissance saw a flowering of jazz and blues music. Both combined elements of a wide range of music. Noted Harlem Renaissance musicians included Louis Armstrong, Gertrude Rainey, and Florence Mills.
Art	Visual art during the Harlem Renaissance often incorporated African imagery into contemporary American forms. Despite discrimination against black art and artists, some managed to achieve fame and success. Those included Augusta Savage, Aaron Douglas, and James Van Der Zee.

13. Return to the KWL chart at the start of the activity and complete the **L** column ("What I have Learned (**L**) About the Harlem Renaissance"). You may draw upon information you collected in the previous task along with any other evidence from the article that you find significant.

☑ Check Your Understanding

Turn back to "The Harlem Renaissance" and find one text feature the author used in the text. Why do you think the author chose to use this feature?

Participating Collaboratively

14. For the remainder of the activity, you will begin working in groups to prepare for your multimedia presentation. Before you and your group members review your KWL charts and the text you just read, review the following guidelines for effective collaboration.

Collaboration Guidelines
All group members should:
• Be prepared for collaborative discussions by reading your assigned sources and taking notes ahead of time.
• Be alert; use appropriate eye contact and engage with your group.
• Speak up so that the other group members can hear.
• Take turns speaking and listening; everyone should have the opportunity to share ideas.
• Agree upon criteria in which to evaluate the work of the group.
• Keep the goals of your collaboration in mind; stay on topic and watch the time.
• Ask relevant and insightful questions that build on other students' ideas and help the discussion.
• Offer ideas or judgments that are purposeful in moving the group toward your goals.
• Paraphrase comments from other group members to ensure understanding.
• Tolerate a range of positions and ambiguity in decision making.

15. Paraphrase the preceding points by writing the actions you will take in group collaborations as both a speaker and a listener.

As a speaker, I will ...	As a listener, I will ...

16. Now, practice participating collaboratively following the guidelines for collaboration you just reviewed. With your group members, you will choose a research topic and start generating research questions for your multimedia presentation on the Harlem Renaissance.

ACTIVITY 4.2 continued

26 With student step 12 completed, have students use the information in the graphic organizer and "The Harlem Renaissance" text to complete the **L** column of the KWL chart from earlier in this activity.

27 Give students time to respond to the Check Your Understanding task. Consider allowing students to work in pairs to locate and analyze a text feature.

28 Divide the class into groups of three or four students. Read aloud the introduction for the Participating Collaboratively section. Then have volunteers from the different groups take turns reading aloud and then paraphrasing the bulleted points in the Collaboration Guidelines box. Guide the activity, soliciting and answering questions and clarifying the guidelines as necessary.

29 Have students work independently to complete the graphic organizer in student step 15. Provide oral instructions while passing their completed organizers around their groups for review. Tell students to note any unclear text on the organizers for review when the organizer is returned to its writer.

30 Read student step 16 aloud as an introduction to the Choosing a Research Topic section.

ACTIVITY 4.2 continued

31 Have groups complete student step 17 in the Choosing a Research Topic section. They can begin by sharing the content of the **W** columns in their KWL charts from earlier in this activity, focusing on unanswered or recently revised questions. Have each group appoint a notetaker to track the topics that emerge from the brainstorming session. Groups should work together to identify one research topic. As students are working, walk around the classroom to make sure they are following the guidelines for collaboration.

32 Read aloud the Writing a Research Question section introduction. Then have volunteers read aloud the steps to write a good research question.

4.2

Choosing a Research Topic

17. Brainstorm possible research topics for your multimedia Harlem Renaissance presentation. Begin your brainstorming by considering the questions in the **W** column of your KWL chart ("What I **W**ant to Know About the Harlem Renaissance") that went unanswered or were refined after reading the text. Write down the topic ideas you have. Work with your group to choose one research topic, following the guidelines for collaboration.

Sample topics:

How African American music forms of the time influenced Harlem Renaissance poets

How jazz and blues changed popular music in the decades following the Harlem Renaissance

Why early 20th-century New York City was a fertile location for the rise of the Harlem Renaissance

Obstacles faced by "Harlem Renaissance men" like Paul Robeson in athletics and entertainment

The influence of Harlem Renaissance clothing on men's and women's fashion in the 1920s

How the NAACP and other activist groups arose from the racial unrest of the early 1900s

Writing a Research Question

A research question is a clear, focused, concise, and complex question that drives your research. Research questions help you focus your research by providing a path through the research process. Creating research questions will help you work toward supporting a clear thesis.

To write a research question:

```
Think about your general topic. What do you want to know?
                        ↓
Consider your audience. Keep your audience in mind when developing your
question. Would that particular audience be interested in this question?
                        ↓
Start asking questions. Ask open-ended "how" and "why" questions about
your general topic to help you think of different areas of your topic.
                        ↓
Evaluate your possible questions. Research questions should not be
answerable with a simple "yes" or "no" or by easily found facts. They should,
instead, require both research and analysis on the part of the researcher.
                        ↓
Hypothesize possible answers. After you have written your research question,
use what you already know to think of possible answers or explanations.
This will help guide your research.
```

18. Which of these questions can be considered effective research questions?

    Is watching television good for you? (bad research question)

    How do peers influence one's political opinions? (good research question)

    How many moons orbit the planets in our solar system? (bad research question)

    What connection is there between childhood eating habits and adult obesity? (good research question)

19. Practice writing research questions about the Harlem Renaissance. Write at least five possible questions. Then share your ideas with your group and use the flowchart to evaluate your questions.

    Research Topic:

    Research Questions:

20. With your group, come to a consensus about your major research question and record it. Then generate secondary questions to focus your research.

    Major Research Question: _____

    _____

    Secondary Research Questions: _____

    _____

    _____

    _____

    _____

☑ **Check Your Understanding**

Critique this part of the research process. Do you need to change your approach?

33 Have students examine the four potential research questions listed in student step 18. Help clarify as necessary what makes each question good or bad, comparing it to the step-by-step process presented previously.

34 Have groups examine their revised list of possible topics and choose the one they feel is best. Then have each student complete student step 19 by writing five possible research questions for the group's chosen topic.

35 Student groups should evaluate each possible research question from their members as directed in student step 19. Once a final research question is chosen, members of the group should independently generate secondary questions as directed in student step 20.

36 Have students complete the Check Your Understanding task to critique the process of developing research questions.

ASSESS

Review students' appraisals of the process of developing research questions. Their analyses should indicate an understanding of the process as presented in this activity. Suggestions for changes in approach should include a description as to how the change would improve the process.

ADAPT

If students need additional help writing research questions, model the skill through co-construction. You might do a **think-aloud** to demonstrate your process, using questions such as these:

• What more do I want to know from reading this text?

• What have I learned from this text?

• How does this text provide information that helps me understand aspects of the Harlem Renaissance?

My Notes

PLAN

Materials: artwork of the Harlem Renaissance, documentary film about the Harlem Renaissance, OPTIC graphic organizers, Internet access

Suggested Pacing: 2 50-minute class periods plus homework

TEACH

1 Read with students the Learning Targets and Preview. Tell students that they will be doing further work based upon the research questions they developed in the previous activity.

2 Read aloud the information in the Developing a Research Plan section. As you share the final sentence of the first paragraph, emphasize the parts of a research plan by writing them on the board and having students copy them into their Reader/Writer Notebooks:

- topic
- major research question
- secondary research questions
- sources
- timeline for reading/synthesizing sources (conducting research)

3 Read the Historical Context section as a class. Review the ways in which McCarthyism serves as the historical context for Arthur Miller's *The Crucible*.

4 Then place students in pairs. Give students time to read and respond to the prompt in the Independent Reading Link box.

5 Before presenting the documentary film segment to the class, read aloud Essential Question 1: How do cultural movements such as the Harlem Renaissance reflect and create people's attitudes and beliefs? Remind students to record details that connect to Essential Question 1 as they watch the documentary.

The Historical Context of the Harlem Renaissance

Learning Strategies

Discussion Groups
Marking the Text
OPTIC

INDEPENDENT READING LINK

Read and Respond

Think about how your independent reading text discusses the context of the Harlem Renaissance. What aspects of the Harlem Renaissance does your text deal with? How does it deal with them? Record your ideas using a graphic organizer similar to the one you will complete for this activity. Then share your graphic organizer with a peer.

My Notes

_____
_____
_____
_____
_____
_____
_____
_____
_____
_____
_____
_____
_____
_____
_____
_____
_____
_____

Learning Targets

- Work in groups to develop and revise a plan for researching the historical context of the Harlem Renaissance.
- Identify the philosophy, values, and beliefs of the Harlem Renaissance and write an informational text to articulate your understanding.
- Integrate ideas from multiple texts to build knowledge and vocabulary about communities.

Preview

In this activity, you will collaborate with a group to develop a research plan for Embedded Assessment 1.

Developing a Research Plan

A research plan is a road map that will help your group maximize your time researching your topic. For example, if you wanted to purchase a car, you wouldn't waste your time going to every dealership or looking through all the auto sale ads until you found the right one, would you? No, you would read reviews to find the car that has all the features you want at the right price, and then you would find out which dealership nearby had that car for sale. There are millions of sources in the library and on the Internet. If you do not take the time to plan your research, you could become overwhelmed by the excess of information available. A research plan includes your topic, major and secondary research questions, a list of sources that are likely to include the information that you need to answer those questions, and a timeline for reading and synthesizing those sources.

1. You already have your topic and major and secondary research questions. In this activity, you will begin to refine those aspects of your plan by conducting guided research about the Harlem Renaissance.

Historical Context

Understanding the historical context of a literary work can be essential to understanding the text. For example, understanding the historical context of McCarthyism in America provides essential background knowledge for the reader to fully comprehend Arthur Miller's social commentary in *The Crucible*. When researching a literary period like the Harlem Renaissance, it is important to draw information from both primary and secondary sources to support your understanding. As you study the works included in this activity, try to answer your research questions.

2. Your class will view a documentary film together. Then your teacher will assign your discussion group one set of additional sources to investigate. Mark the text for evidence that helps you infer information, and then take notes on the graphic organizer in the Working from the Text section.

3. Be sure to mark the vocabulary that is essential to understanding the text as you take notes. If needed, include definitions to clarify what you read.

SOURCE 1: DOCUMENTARY FILM

You will begin building understanding of the Harlem Renaissance by watching a segment of a film that your teacher will share with you. Your purpose for watching

---

College and Career Readiness Standards

Focus Standards:

W.11-12.2 Write informative/explanatory texts to examine and convey complex ideas, concepts, and information clearly and accurately through the effective selection, organization, and analysis of content.

W.11-12.7 Conduct short as well as more sustained research projects to answer a question (including a self-generated question) or solve a problem; narrow or broaden the inquiry when appropriate; synthesize multiple sources on the subject, demonstrating understanding of the subject under investigation.

SL.11-12.1b Work with peers to promote civil, democratic discussions and decision-making, set clear goals and deadlines, and establish individual roles as needed.

this film is to help you develop an answer to Essential Question 1: How do cultural movements such as the Harlem Renaissance reflect and create people's attitudes and beliefs? Take notes on this film and the rest of the research sources provided.

SOURCE 2: ART

Your group's research will focus on the art created during the Harlem Renaissance. Descriptions of primary artists follow, but you may also choose to add others to this list. Your cooperative group should share the artwork, noting textual evidence from the art and explaining what this information tells you about the Harlem Renaissance. For the reading of the visual texts, consider using the OPTIC strategy.

About the Artist: Augusta Savage

Augusta Savage (1892–1962)—artist, activist, and educator—was born in Green Cove Springs, Florida. An important African American artist, Savage began making art as a child using the natural clay found in her community. She liked to sculpt animals and other small figures. But her father, a Methodist minister, did not approve of this activity and did whatever he could to stop her. Savage once said that her father "almost whipped all the art out of me."

Art to Research: *Lift Every Voice and Sing*, sculpture by Augusta Savage

About the Artist: Lois Mailou Jones

In the 1930s, the art of Lois Mailou Jones (1905–1998) reflected the influences of African traditions. She designed African-style masks and in 1938 painted *Les Fétiches*[1], which depicts masks in five distinct ethnic styles. During a year in Paris, she produced landscapes and figure studies, but African influences reemerged in her art in the late 1960s and early 1970s, particularly after two tours of Africa.

Art to Research: *Les Fétiches* by Lois Mailou Jones

About the Artist: Aaron Douglas

Aaron Douglas (1899–1979) was an African American painter and graphic artist who played a leading role in the Harlem Renaissance of the 1920s and 1930s. His first major commission, to illustrate Alain Locke's book *The New Negro*, prompted requests for graphics from other Harlem Renaissance writers. By 1939, Douglas started teaching at Fisk University, where he remained for the next 27 years.

Art to Research: *Rise, Shine for Thy Light Has Come!* by Aaron Douglas

About the Artist: Palmer C. Hayden

Palmer C. Hayden (1890–1973) was born Peyton Hedgeman in Wide Water, Virginia. He took his artistic name from the corrupted pronunciation of Peyton Hedgeman by a commanding sergeant during World War I. Hayden was among the first African American artists to use African subjects and designs in his painting.

Art to Research: *Midsummer Night in Harlem* by Palmer Hayden

[1] **Les Fétiches:** related to the English word *fetish*, an object believed to have magical powers

My Notes

TEACHER TO TEACHER

Activity 4.3 requires students to view a documentary film about the Harlem Renaissance and to research art from the era. Consult the Source 1 and Source 2 sections in the student edition before class to ensure that the selected sources are appropriate for completing the activity. To find suitable resources for students, consider websites maintained by the Library of Congress; the National Museums of African-American Art and Culture, American Art, and American History; and public radio and television stations.

6 Prepare students to view the documentary by reading as a class the Working from the Text section near the end of the activity. Then show the documentary, ensuring students are **taking notes** in the first column of the graphic organizer.

7 Divide the class into eight small **discussion groups** to share their notes and discuss the documentary. Regroup for a whole-class discussion of the film.

8 Ask a student to read aloud the first paragraph of the Source 2: Art section.

9 Break students into four or more expert groups with three to five students in each group. Provide each group with computers and/or print sources for research and distribute **OPTIC** graphic organizers. Assign each group a Harlem Renaissance work of visual art to research. In their groups, have students use the graphic organizers to analyze the images.

College and Career Readiness Standards

SL.11-12.1c Propel conversations by posing and responding to questions that probe reasoning and evidence; ensure a hearing for a full range of positions on a topic or issue; clarify, verify, or challenge ideas and conclusions; and promote divergent and creative perspectives.

Additional Standards Addressed:

RL.11-12.2, RL.11-12.4, RL.11-12.5, RL.11-12.7, RI.11-12.1, RI.11-12.2, RI.11-12.3, RI.11-12.4, W.11-12.2a, W.11-12.2b, W.11-12.2c, W.11-12.2d, W.11-12.2e, W.11-12.2f, W.11-12.4, W.11-12.9, L.11-12.6

10 Return the class to a whole group. Prepare students to read Source 3 by reading the Word Connections box as a class. Discuss how the word *metamorphosis* might be connected to the title of the text.

11 Review the tasks for As You Read, emphasizing that students should underline words and phrases that indicate the author's feelings about the Harlem Renaissance.

12 Discuss the Knowledge Question. Have students work in small groups to talk about the makeup and features of a community, including communities where they live.

13 Have students read the About the Author section about Alain Leroy Locke. Discuss the two instances of quotation mark use in the section. Discuss the purpose served by the quotes.

14 **FIRST READ:** Conduct a shared reading within the assigned expert groups of "Introduction to *The New Negro*." Pause after paragraph 2. Point out that Locke considers the change from the American Negro to the "New Negro" to be so momentous that he describes it with the same word used to describe the transformation of a caterpillar to a butterfly. Discuss how the students' understanding of the connection between metamorphosis and the title has changed since reading the first two paragraphs. Ask students to consider why the author uses *metamorphosis* instead of *change*.

 TEXT COMPLEXITY

Overall: Complex
Lexile: 1250L
Qualitative: Moderate Difficulty
Task: Moderate (Analyze)

4.3

My Notes

_____
_____
_____
_____
_____
_____
_____
_____
_____
_____
_____
_____
_____
_____

✒ KNOWLEDGE QUEST

Knowledge Question:
What makes up a community?
Across Activity 4.3, you will read an informational text about the Harlem community, two poems about Harlem, and a literary criticism piece that analyzes a poem about community life in Harlem. While you read and build knowledge about the topic of communities, think about your answer to the Knowledge Question.

WORD CONNECTIONS

Content Connections
The word **metamorphosis** is often used in science to refer to a major change in animal life. In this informational text, it has a historical context but a similar meaning: a major change in the appearance or character of someone or something.

SOURCE 3: INFORMATIONAL TEXT

As You Read

- Refer to the chart in the Working from the Texts section to guide your notes.
- Underline words and phrases that indicate the author's feelings about the Harlem Renaissance.
- Circle unknown words and phrases. Try to determine the meaning of the words by using context clues, word parts, or a dictionary.

About the Author

Alain Leroy Locke (1885–1954) was an American writer, philosopher, educator, and patron of the arts. In *The Black 100*, Locke ranks as the 36th most influential African American ever, past or present. Distinguished as the first African American Rhodes Scholar in 1907, Locke was the philosophical architect—the acknowledged "Dean"—of the Harlem Renaissance, a period of growth connected with the "New Negro" movement from 1919 to 1934.

Informational Text

Introduction to *The New Negro*

by **Alain Locke, 1925**

1   In the last decade something beyond the watch and guard of statistics has happened in the life of the American Negro and the three *norns*[2] who have traditionally presided over the Negro problem have a changeling in their laps. The Sociologist, the Philanthropist, the Race-leader are not unaware of the New Negro, but they are at a loss to account for him. He simply cannot be swathed in their formulæ. For the younger generation is vibrant with a new psychology; the new spirit is awake in the masses, and under the very eyes of the professional observers is transforming what has been a perennial problem into the progressive phases of contemporary Negro life.

2   Could such a metamorphosis have taken place as suddenly as it has appeared to? The answer is no; not because the New Negro is not here, but because the Old Negro had long become more of a myth than a man. The Old Negro, we must remember, was a creature of moral debate and historical controversy. ...

---

[2] **norns:** three Norse goddesses of fate, comparable to the Greek Fates, who ensured that what was meant to happen to each person did happen

---

Scaffolding the Text-Dependent Questions

4. **What metaphor does Locke use in paragraph 4 to describe the movement that led to the Harlem Renaissance? How does the metaphor help explain the concept of a community at this time in history?** A metaphor states a similarity between two unlike things, using words to create a visual image. To what does the author compare the movement of people to the North? What similarity does he find between those two things? RI.11-12.4

5. **What additional elements of diversity does Locke note in the population of Harlem that were not mentioned in the text in Activity 4.2? How does his expanded description develop the main idea of this text?** How were the groups in Harlem classified and described in Activity 4.2? What is different about Locke's approach? What does this paragraph contribute to the text as a whole? RI.11-12.3

3   In the very process of being transplanted, the Negro is becoming transformed.

4   The tide of Negro migration, northward and city-ward, is not to be fully explained as a blind flood started by the demands of war industry coupled with the shutting off of foreign migration, or by the pressure of poor crops coupled with increased social terrorism in certain sections of the South and Southwest. Neither labor demand, the bollweevil, nor the Ku Klux Klan is a basic factor, however contributory any or all of them may have been. The wash and rush of this human tide on the beach line of the northern city centers is to be explained primarily in terms of a new vision of opportunity, of social and economic freedom, of a spirit to seize, even in the face of an **extortionate** and heavy toil, a chance for the improvement of conditions. With each successive wave of it, the movement of the Negro becomes more and more a mass movement toward the larger and the more democratic chance—in the Negro's case a deliberate flight not only from countryside to city, but from medieval America to modern.

5   Take Harlem as an instance of this. Here in Manhattan is not merely the largest Negro community in the world, but the first concentration in history of so many diverse elements of Negro life. It has attracted the African, the West Indian, the Negro American; has brought together the Negro of the North and the Negro of the South; the man from the city and the man from the town and village; the peasant, the student, the business man, the professional man, artist, poet, musician, adventurer and worker, preacher and criminal, exploiter and social outcast. Each group has come with its own separate motives and for its own special ends, but their greatest experience has been the finding of one another. **Proscription** and prejudice have thrown these dissimilar elements into a common area of contact and interaction. Within this area, race sympathy and unity have determined a further fusing of sentiment and experience. So what began in terms of segregation becomes more and more, as its elements mix and react, the laboratory of a great racewelding. Hitherto, it must be admitted that American Negroes have been a race more in name than in fact, or to be exact, more in sentiment than in experience. The chief bond between them has been that of a common condition rather than a common consciousness; a problem in common rather than a life in common. In Harlem, Negro life is seizing upon its first chances for group expression and self-determination. It is—or promises at least to be—a race capital. That is why our comparison is taken with those **nascent** centers of folk-expression and self-determination which are playing a creative part in the world today. Without pretense to their political significance, Harlem has the same role to play for the New Negro as Dublin has had for the New Ireland or Prague for the New Czechoslovakia.

My Notes

WORD CONNECTIONS

Multiple-Meaning Words
The meaning of the word **concentration** varies greatly depending on its use. In some uses, it means "mental focus." The word can also mean "many people or things in one place," as in this passage. In cooking or science, the *concentration* is the amount of an ingredient in a mixture.

extortionate: excessive or harsh
proscription: legal restraint
nascent: beginning

⊘ Knowledge Quest
- What facts in the text catch your attention?
- How is Harlem a community of people?

Scaffolding the Text-Dependent Questions

6. How does the author's definition of "race" in paragraph 5 contribute to a greater understanding of the larger context and movement of the Harlem Renaissance? How does the author describe race in paragraph 5? How literally does he take the concept of a Negro "race"? What historical events does he reference? How do those events relate to Locke's own concept of the Negro race? What is that concept? RI.11-12.4

15 As the class reads the remainder of the text, remind them to employ annotatations. Pause occasionally to give students time to fill out the graphic organizer near the end of Activity 4.3.

16 Pause after reading paragraph 4. Ask students to state what Locke thinks are the two forces driving African American migration. Which of these forces does Locke feel is the stronger of the two?

17 After reading the text for the first time, guide the class in a discussion by asking the Knowledge Quest questions. Check students' general comprehension of the text based on their observations, asking follow-up questions if needed.

18 **RETURNING TO THE TEXT:** Guide students to return to the text to respond to the text-dependent questions. Have students work in pairs or small groups to reread the text and answer the questions. Remind them to use text evidence in their responses.

19 Circulate as students work, listening to their responses. If they have difficulty, scaffold the questions by rephrasing them or breaking them into smaller parts. See the Scaffolding the Text-Dependent Questions boxes for suggestions.

4.3

Returning to the Text

- Return to the informational text as you respond to the following questions. Use text evidence to support your responses.
- Write any additional questions you have about the text in your Reader/Writer Notebook.

4. **KQ** What metaphor does Locke use in paragraph 4 to describe the movement that led to the Harlem Renaissance? How does the metaphor help explain the concept of a community at this time in history?

Locke describes African American migration to the North as "the wash and rush of this human tide on the beach line of the northern city centers." He adds that "with each successive wave ... the movement of the Negro becomes more and more a mass movement toward the larger and the more democratic chance." The imagery in the text describes how this "tide of people" is struggling to find their new place in a community.

5. What additional elements of diversity does Locke note in the population of Harlem that were not mentioned in the text in Activity 4.2? How does his expanded description develop the main idea of this text?

Locke describes the "New Negro" as an entity not easily defined or explained by sociology or circumstances. In paragraph 5, he lists various groups of people, setting them opposite each other to show the diversity: "the Negro of the North and the Negro of the South; the man from the city and the man from the town ..." He says the movement is a beginning to be further developed.

6. How does the author's definition of "race" in paragraph 5 contribute to a greater understanding of the larger context and movement of the Harlem Renaissance?

In paragraph 5, Locke says, "American Negroes have been a race more in name than in fact." He refers to the coming together of African Americans from diverse locations "into a common area of contact and interaction." Each group contributed something unique to the whole, forming a culture of "New Negroes" who find "a life in common," which will lead to a cohesive "race."

7. Review both "The Harlem Renaissance" in Activity 4.2 and Locke's piece. How does each piece explain the reasons for the Great Migration? How do these reasons support each piece's theme?

In "The Harlem Renaissance," the authors cite the reason for the Great Migration: "to carve out better lives for themselves and their families." This supports their theme that the Harlem Renaissance sprang from a desire for opportunity and cultural expression. Locke's theme is that a new life in common was a key goal of the Harlem Renaissance.

Scaffolding the Text-Dependent Questions

7. Review both "The Harlem Renaissance" in Activity 4.2 and Locke's piece. How does each author explain the reasons for the Great Migration? How do these reasons support each author's theme? What was the Great Migration? What reasons for it are cited in "The Harlem Renaissance"? How did those reasons support that piece's theme, and what is that theme? Find the sentence in paragraph 4 of Locke's piece where he explains the drive behind African American migration to Northern cities. What reason does give for that migration? How does it support the theme of that piece? RI.11-12.2

8. **KQ** Using a print or digital source, determine and list possible meanings of the word *concentration*. Which meaning is applicable to the word's use in the second sentence of paragraph 5? Explain.

Definitions of the word include "mental focus," "many people or things in one place," and "the

amount of a specific ingredient in a mixture." Its context in the sentence "Here in Manhattan

is not merely the largest Negro community in the world, but the first concentration in history

of so many diverse elements of Negro life" indicates that it means "many things (elements of

Negro life) in one place."

Scaffolding the Text-Dependent Questions

8. Using a print or digital source, determine and list possible meanings of the word *concentration*. Which meaning is applicable to the word's use in the second sentence of paragraph 5? Explain. Consult a print or online dictionary for possible meanings of the word. What are those meanings? Reread the sentence and examine the context of the word as it is used there. Compare its use to the possible definitions. Which definition is most applicable, and why? RI.11-12.4

ACTIVITY 4.3 continued

20 Read aloud the As You Read section. Ensure students understand the instructions for annotation. If necessary, review sound devices and rhyme scheme with students.

21 Then ask students to work in pairs to read the About the Author section, underlining the themes that are common in Bennett's works. Ask partners to infer why "To Usward" is significant to the Harlem Renaissance.

22 **FIRST READ:** Conduct a shared reading of "To Usward."

23 **Vocabulary Development:** Pause after line 9 to read aloud the material on the root *ent*. Apply the information in the Word Connections box to a brief analysis of the word *identity* in line 8 and the word *entity* in line 9.

24 As students are reading, monitor their progress. Be sure they are engaged with the text, highlighting and labeling sound devices, marking the poem's rhyme scheme, and consulting the chart in this activity's Working from the Text section as a guide to their note-taking.

4.3

My Notes

SOURCE 4: POETRY AND MUSIC

As You Read

- Highlight and label sound devices (such as assonance, consonance, alliteration, and rhyme) used by the writer.
- Mark references to the community.
- Refer to the chart in the Working from the Text section to guide your notes.

About the Author

Gwendolyn B. Bennett (1902–1981) was an African American writer who contributed to *Opportunity*, a magazine that chronicled cultural advancements in Harlem. Though often overlooked, she was an accomplished writer in poetry and prose. Her heritage is a main theme in her poetry, and her works reflect the shared themes and motifs of the Harlem Renaissance. Racial pride, rediscovery of Africa, recognition of African music, and dance are common themes in Bennett's works. Bennett read the following poem on March 21, 1924, at a gathering of writers. Some historians say that this night was the official beginning of the Harlem Renaissance.

Poetry

To Usward

by **Gwendolyn B. Bennett** (1924)

Let us be still

As ginger jars[3] are still

Upon a Chinese shelf.

And let us be contained

5   By entities of Self. ...

Not still with lethargy and sloth,

But quiet with the pushing of our growth.

Not self-contained with smug identity

But conscious of the strength in entity.

---

[3] **ginger jar:** a large porcelain container with a wide mouth, a spherical shape, and a domed lid

---

KNOWLEDGE QUEST

Knowledge Question:
What makes up a community?

WORD CONNECTIONS

Roots and Affixes
The root *ent* comes from Latin and means "being." The suffix *-ity* means "a quality or state." Words using this suffix with this root include *nonentity* and *identity*.

Scaffolding the Text-Dependent Questions

9. How do lines 7–9 of the poem support Alain Locke's descriptions in "Introduction to *The New Negro*" of a community's growth? How do the lines describe the community? How did Locke describe Harlem's community? RL.11-12.7

10. How does the poem reflect themes similar to those expressed in "The Harlem Renaissance"? Recall how the text of "The Harlem Renaissance" is arranged. In which of those sections would "To Usward" most neatly fit thematically? Why? RL.11-12.7

4.3

10 If any have a song to sing

That's different from the rest,

Oh let them sing

Before the urgency of Youth's **behest**!

For some of us have songs to sing

15 Of jungle heat and fires,

And some of us are solemn grown

With pitiful desires,

And there are those who feel the pull

Of seas beneath the skies,

20 And some there be who want to croon

Of Negro lullabies.

We claim no part with racial **dearth**;

We want to sing the songs of birth!

And so we stand like ginger jars

25 Like ginger jars bound round

With dust and age;

Like jars of ginger we are sealed

By nature's heritage.

But let us break the seal of years

30 With pungent thrusts of song,

For there is joy in long-dried tears

For whetted passions of a throng.

My Notes

⊘ Knowledge Quest

- Based on what you highlighted, what do you notice about the words of the poem?
- What references or imagery about the community stand out to you?
- What emotions does the poem suggest to you?

---

behest: desire or request
dearth: lack

Scaffolding the Text-Dependent Questions

11. Does Bennett use a single rhyme scheme or multiple rhyme schemes in her poem? Explain and describe the effect that choice creates. Analyze how rhyme is used in the poem. Begin by comparing the rhyme schemes of the first nine lines and second nine lines. What do you discover? Is the same pattern repeated as the poem continues? What "feel" is created by the way Bennett uses rhyme? RL.11-12.5

12. What sound device does Bennett use in line 10–14, and what is its effect? Examine the lines for the use of similar or identical words. Which two words appear most often? What do those words exemplify? How do the words themselves describe the effect they create? RL.11-12.4

ACTIVITY 4.3 continued

25 Ask students to pause after line 23. Ask students to explain the play on words that Bennett makes with the word she chooses to rhyme with *birth*. Prompt students to consider how that choice affects the impact of her statement on line 23.

26 After reading the text for the first time, guide the class in a discussion by asking the Knowledge Quest questions. Check students' general comprehension of the text based on their observations, asking follow-up questions if needed.

★ TEACHER TO TEACHER

Consider having a student look up the allusion to "ginger jars" to contextualize their use as centuries-old objects for display or as ceremonial gifts.

LEVELED DIFFERENTIATED INSTRUCTION

In this activity, students might need clarifications to link figurative language to an allusion.

Beginning Help students look through lines 14–21 of "To Usward" to find examples of figurative language. Ask students how they know the author is alluding to a topic. Guide students to understand that the author is focusing on stories of the past that an individual might tell.

Developing Ask partners to work together to find examples of figurative language throughout the poem "To Usward." Have them discuss the phrase *songs of birth* and how this is an allusion to the stories of the past that an individual might tell. Then have them think about the title of the poem and the literal meaning of the word *usward*. Guide students to understand that *usward* combines the words *us* and *onward*, alluding to the progression of the African American community during this time.

Support Explain that authors sometimes use figurative language as symbolism about a topic. Remind students of how to allude to a topic and then have partners brainstorm an allusion for a topic of their own.

Extend Encourage students to look at other literature throughout the activity to find similar language. Challenge students to make a T-chart that contains the example of figurative language on the left side and its literal meaning on the right side.

27 **RETURNING TO THE TEXT:** Guide students to return to the text to respond to the text-dependent questions. Invite them to work in their expert groups to reread the text and answer the questions. Remind them to use text evidence in their responses.

28 Move from expert group to expert group and listen in as students answer the text-dependent questions. If they have difficulty, scaffold the questions by rephrasing them or breaking them into smaller parts. See the Scaffolding the Text-Dependent Questions boxes for suggestions.

4.3

Returning to the Text
- Return to the poem as you respond to the following questions. Use text evidence to support your responses.
- Write any additional questions you have about the text in your Reader/Writer Notebook.

9. **KQ** How do lines 7–9 of the poem support Alain Locke's descriptions in "Introduction to *The New Negro*" of a community's growth?

Lines 7–9 of the poem describe a community pushing toward growth with strength in unity.

Similarly, Alain Locke describes the Harlem community's growth as a "fusing of sentiment and experience."

10. How does the poem reflect themes similar to those expressed in "The Harlem Renaissance"?

Both Bennett's poem and "The Harlem Renaissance" focus on artistic expression in Harlem.

The poem focuses on music, expanding on the variety and richness of this aspect of culture by relating it to the diverse backgrounds of the people in Harlem.

11. Does Bennett use a single rhyme scheme or multiple rhyme schemes in her poem? Explain and describe the effect that choice creates.

Bennett uses a variety of rhyme schemes throughout the poem. The rhyme scheme for the poem's first nine lines, for example, is a-a-b-c-b-d-d-e-e. The nine lines that follow have a rhyme scheme of a-b-a-b-a-c-d-c-e. These and the other non-repeating variations of the rhyme scheme create an improvisational effect similar to jazz music.

12. What sound device does Bennett use in lines 10–14, and what is its effect?

Bennett uses alliteration with the words *song* and *sing*. Its effect is to single out those words and their similarity to each other, creating a musical feel to the words themselves.

13. How does the author use the word *pungent* in line 30 to support the symbolism of a human experience?

The speaker in the poem uses the allusion of ginger jars on a shelf to symbolize individuals.

The speaker goes on to describe people breaking free with "pungent" thrusts of song, relating the strength and volume of singing to the strength of ginger's spice.

Scaffolding the Text-Dependent Questions

13. **How does the author use the word *pungent* in line 30 to support the symbolism of a human experience?** What allusion is being made? How does the speaker describe people? RL.11-12.4

As You Read

- Make mental images as you read the poem.
- Circle unknown words and phrases. Try to determine the meaning of the words by using context clues, word parts, or a dictionary.
- Refer to the chart in Working from the Texts to guide your note-taking.

About the Author

James Weldon Johnson (1871–1938) was an American author, lawyer, politician, and activist. He is remembered largely for his leadership within the NAACP, the oldest and largest civil rights organization in the United States. His writing included novels, poems, and collections of folklore. His poem "Lift Every Voice and Sing" was first performed publicly by 500 schoolchildren on Lincoln's birthday in 1900. It was later set to music by Johnson's brother and adopted by the NAACP as its official song. It is often referred to as "The Black National Anthem."

Poetry

Lift Every Voice and Sing

by **James Weldon Johnson**

Lift every voice and sing

Till earth and heaven ring,

Ring with the harmonies of Liberty;

Let our rejoicing rise

5 High as the listening skies,

Let it resound loud as the rolling sea.

Sing a song full of the faith that the dark past has taught us,

Sing a song full of the hope that the present has brought us,

Facing the rising sun of our new day begun

My Notes

KNOWLEDGE QUEST

Knowledge Question:
What makes up a community?

In 1939, Augusta Savage was commissioned to create a sculpture for the New York World's Fair. Titled "The Harp," the work was strongly influenced by Weldon's poem.

Scaffolding the Text-Dependent Questions

14. How does the poem support statements in this section's previous text and poem about the Harlem Renaissance? What sentiments about progression and hope does it echo from the other texts? RL.11-12.7

15. What poetic technique(s) does the poet use to add meaning and beauty to the poem?

How does this engage the reader? What technique is used in lines 7–8? Where else in the poem is the same or a similar technique used? How does the result of this technique help explain why the poem was later set to music? RL.11-12.5

29 Read the As You Read section with the group or groups to which "Lift Every Voice and Sing" is assigned. Help them understand the instructions for annotation.

30 Have students read the About the Author section about James Weldon Johnson. Ask them what they think is meant by "The Black National Anthem."

31 FIRST READ: Conduct a **Choral Reading** within the assigned group or groups of "Lift Every Voice and Sing." Choral reading provides an opportunity for students to grasp the musicality of the work. Pause after line 6 to note the rhyme scheme thus far and how conducive it is to being set to music.

32 As students are reading, monitor their progress. Be sure they are engaged with the text, circling and trying to define unknown words and consulting the chart in this activity's Working from the Text section as a guide for their note-taking. Remind them to evoke mental images as they read the poem.

33 Pause after line 12 to read aloud the text of the Word Connections box. Have a volunteer explain why the "chastening rod" is described as "bitter."

34 Tell students to pause after line 21. Ask volunteers to identify two words for the tone conveyed by the imagery in lines 17–21.

35 Pause after line 29 to discuss the nature of the fear the speaker expresses in lines 28–29. Ask students to include in their discussion the poet's use of the word *lest* in these lines. As needed, have students look up the meaning of *lest* in a print or online dictionary.

36 After reading the text for the first time, guide the class in a discussion by asking the Knowledge Quest questions. Check students' general comprehension of the text based on their observations, asking follow-up questions if needed.

TEACHER TO TEACHER

When student groups conduct discussions, be sure they note the connection between Johnson's poem and the Augusta Savage sculpture of the same name covered in Source 2.

WORD CONNECTIONS

Etymology
The word **chastening** originally meant "punishment" in old French. In Middle English this meaning changed to "correcting someone's behavior." The term *chastening rod* elicits images of punishments that enslaved people endured, so it still carries the idea of correction. *Chastening* may also mean "causing someone to feel sad or embarrassed."

My Notes

10 Let us march on till victory is won.

Stony the road we trod,

Bitter the chastening rod,

Felt in the days when hope unborn had died;

Yet with a steady beat,

15 Have not our weary feet

Come to the place for which our fathers sighed?

We have come over a way that with tears has been watered,

We have come, treading our path through the blood of the slaughtered,

Out from the gloomy past,

20 Till now we stand at last

Where the white gleam of our bright star is cast.

God of our weary years,

God of our silent tears,

Thou who has brought us thus far on the way;

25 Thou who has by Thy might

Led us into the light,

Keep us forever in the path, we pray.

Lest our feet stray from the places, our God, where we met Thee,

Lest, our hearts drunk with the wine of the world, we forget Thee;

30 Shadowed beneath Thy hand,

May we forever stand.

True to our God,

True to our native land.

Ⓥ Knowledge Quest
- What images catch your attention in the poem?
- What references or imagery about the community stands out to you?
- What words and phrases in the poem catch your attention?

Scaffolding the Text-Dependent Questions

16. How do the first six lines of the poem establish themes that are carried throughout the remainder of the poem? Reread the first six lines. What image is being evoked? Which words in those lines strongly evoke that image? How do those lines work together to create a single sentiment? What is that sentiment? Where and how is it reinforced later in the poem? RL.11-12.2

17. Explain the poet's use of the phrase *rising sun* as a metaphor in lines 9–10 of the poem. What message is being conveyed, and what is the tone of that message? Reread the two lines. What sentiment is connoted by each line's image? How do the two images work together? What mood does the author convey by combining them? What qualities is he calling for his audience to draw upon in themselves? RL.11-12.4

4.3

Returning to the Text

- Return to the lyrics as you respond to the following questions. Use text evidence to support your responses.
- Write any additional questions you have about the text in your Reader/Writer Notebook.

14. **KQ** How does the poem support statements in this section's previous text and poem about the Harlem Renaissance?

These sentiments echo the statements of progression and hope in the future in Locke's

informational text (which uses words like *progressive* and *metamorphosis*) and Bennett's

poem (which uses phrases like *pushing of our growth* and *break the seal of years*).

15. What poetic technique(s) does the poet use to add meaning and beauty to the poem? How does this engage the reader?

Johnson uses repetition to both stress particular ideas and add rhythm to the poem. The

repetition in lines 7–8, for example, reinforces the concepts of faith, hope, and optimism while

at the same time making the poem itself sound like a song: "Sing a song full of the faith that

the dark past has taught us, / Sing a song full of the hope that the present has brought us."

16. How do the first six lines of the poem establish themes that are carried throughout the remainder of the poem?

Words such as *voice, sing, ring,* and *harmonies* establish the theme of music. *Voice, ring,*

and *harmonies* also connect to the themes of democracy and liberty. The ideas of voice

and harmony are important to democracy and liberty because free people can use their

voices democratically to create a harmonious society. "[E]arth and heaven," "rejoicing," and

"listening skies" convey a religious theme

17. **KQ** Explain the poet's use of the phrase *rising sun* as a metaphor in lines 9–10 of the poem. What message is being conveyed, and what is the tone of that message?

Johnson uses the metaphor of a rising sun to convey a tone of freshness and optimism. While

he makes it clear that the victory of freedom has yet to be won, he also expresses confidence

that it will come about if African Americans and their supporters "march on," another

metaphor, that one being used to symbolize perseverance in the struggle for equality.

37 **RETURNING TO THE TEXT:** Guide students to return to the text to respond to the text-dependent questions. Invite them to work in their expert groups to reread the text and answer the questions. Remind them to use text evidence in their responses.

38 Move from expert group to expert group and listen in as students answer the text-dependent questions. If they have difficulty, scaffold the questions by rephrasing them or breaking them into smaller parts. See the Scaffolding the Text-Dependent Questions boxes for suggestions.

39 Read the As You Read section with the groups to which "Excerpt from 'On "From the Dark Tower"'" has been assigned. Help them understand the instructions for annotation.

40 Have students read the About the Author section about Eugenia W. Collier. Point out that they will be reading literary criticism as well as a poem. Ask them what they expect the tone of the text to be.

41 **FIRST READ:** Conduct a shared reading of "Excerpt from 'On "From the Dark Tower."'" Pause before beginning paragraph 1 to note the text feature beneath the title and that feature's purpose.

 TEXT COMPLEXITY

Overall: Complex
Lexile: 1170L
Qualitative: Moderate Difficulty
Task: Moderate (Analyze)

42 As students are reading, monitor their progress. Be sure they are engaged with the text, summarizing each paragraph as directed, circling and trying to define unknown words, and consulting the chart in this activity's Working from the Text section as a guide to their note-taking.

4.3

My Notes

⊘ KNOWLEDGE QUEST

Knowledge Question:
What makes up a community?

SOURCES 5: POETRY AND LITERARY CRITICISM

As You Read

- Summarize the main idea of each paragraph in the My Notes section.
- Circle unknown words and phrases. Try to determine the meaning of the words by using context clues, word parts, or a dictionary.
- Refer to the chart in the Working from the Text section to guide your notes.

About the Author

Eugenia W. Collier (b. 1928) is an African American writer and critic best known for her 1969 short story "Marigolds." She was born in Baltimore, Maryland. The former English Chair at Morgan State University, Collier has also taught at Coppin State College (now University), the University of Maryland, and Howard University. She graduated magna cum laude from Howard University in 1948 and was awarded an MA from Columbia University two years later. In 1976, she earned a PhD from the University of Maryland. Since retiring in 1996, Collier continues to live in Baltimore and occasionally visits classes to discuss writing and her stories.

Literary Criticism

Excerpt from "On 'From the Dark Tower'"

by **Eugenia W. Collier**

College Language Association Journal 11.1 (1967)

1 It seems to me that a poem which effectively expresses the spirit of Harlem Renaissance poetry is "From the Dark Tower," by Countee Cullen. It is a restrained, dignified, poignant work, influenced in form by Keats and Shelley rather than by the moderns.

2 Incidentally, The Dark Tower was actually a place on 136th Street in Harlem, where a number of the poets used to gather. Perhaps Cullen knew he was speaking for the others, too, when he wrote:

> We shall not always plant while others reap
> The golden increment of bursting fruit,
> Not always countenance, abject and mute
> That lesser men should hold their brothers cheap;
> Not everlastingly while others sleep
> Shall we beguile their limbs with mellow flute,
> Not always bend to some more subtle brute;
> We were not made eternally to weep.

Scaffolding the Text-Dependent Questions

18. In paragraph 1, what does the word *spirit* mean in context? How does this word connect to the idea of a community? What qualities does this spirit have? RI.11-12.4

19. How does Collier classify "From the Dark Tower"? What evidence does she give to support her classification? Examine the first paragraph, where Collier introduces the poem she is analyzing. Which sentence in that paragraph is an actual description of the poem? How do the lines she quotes in the following paragraph reinforce that description? What images does she highlight? How does each relate to what was happening at the time in the Harlem Renaissance? How does each relate to what happened to African Americans in the period before that? RI.11-12.1

The night whose sable breast relieves the stark
White stars is no less lovely being dark,
And there are buds that cannot bloom at all
In light, but crumple, piteous, and fall;
So in the dark we hide the heart that bleeds,
And wait, and tend our agonizing seeds.

My Notes

3 Let us examine the symbolism contained in the poem. Here we have the often-used symbol of planting seeds and reaping fruit. This symbol invariably refers to the natural sequence of things—the hope eventually realized, or the "just deserts" finally obtained. The sowing-reaping symbol here effectively expresses the frustration that inevitably falls to the individual or group of people caught in an unjust system. The image of a person planting the seeds of his labor, knowing even as he plants that "others" will pluck the fruit, is a picture of the frustration which is so often the Negro's lot. The image necessarily (and perhaps unconsciously) implies certain questions: What must be the feelings of the one who plants? How long will he continue to plant without reward? Will he not eventually stop planting, or perhaps begin seizing the fruit which is rightfully his? In what light does he see himself? How does he regard the "others" who "reap the golden increment of bursting fruit"? What physical and emotional damage results to the laborer from this arrangement to which obviously he never consented?

4 In his basic symbol then, Cullen expresses the crux of the protest poem which so flourished in the Harlem Renaissance. In poem after poem, articulate young Negroes answered these questions or asked them again, these questions and many more. And in the asking, and in the answering, they were speaking of the old, well-worn (though never quite realized) American ideals.

5 In the octave[4] of the poem, Cullen answers some of these questions. The grim promise "not always" tolls ominously like an iron bell through the first eight lines. "We shall not always plant while others reap," he promises. By degrees he probes deeper and deeper into the actual meaning of the image. In the next two lines he points out one of many strange paradoxes of social injustice: that the "abject and mute" victim must permit himself to be considered inferior by "lesser men"—that is, men who have lost a measure of their humanity because they have degraded their brothers. This image is a statement of a loss of human values—the "abject and mute" victim of an unjust social system, bereft of spirit, silently serving another who has himself suffered a different kind of loss in robbing his fellow man of his potential—that is, the fruit of his seed. Perhaps this destruction of the human spirit is the "more subtle brute" of which the poet speaks. The last line of the octave promises eventual change in the words, "We were not made eternally to weep." Yet it implies that relief is still a long way off. It is in the sestet[5] that the poem itself blossoms into full-blown dark beauty. With the skill of an impressionistic

---

[4] **octave:** an eight-line stanza or section of a sonnet characterized by a specific rhyme scheme and setting out the problem of the sonnet

[5] **sestet:** a six-line stanza or section of a sonnet with a specific rhyme scheme that usually answers the problem set out in the octave

43 Tell students to pause after paragraph 3 and note what Collier feels is the poem's most significant image. Prompt students to explain their choice based on the text of the poem.

Scaffolding the Text-Dependent Questions

20. What structure does the author use to discuss her interpretation of the poem? How does her choice affect the reader's understanding of the poem and its interpretation? How does the author organize her comments about the poem within the essay? Is her interpretation sequential, thematic, or compare and contrast, or does it take another approach? What image does she find particularly striking? How do Collier's comments help clarify the poem's many layers of meaning? RI.11-12.5

44 Tell students to pause after paragraph 6. Have them explain what the author means by the statement "The poet now splashes a shocking red onto his black and white canvas." Prompt students to find Collier's description of the effect of this "splashing."

45 After reading the text for the first time, guide the class in a discussion by asking the Knowledge Quest questions. Check students' general comprehension of the text based on their observations, asking follow-up questions if needed.

4.3

Countee Cullen was an American poet, novelist, children's writer, and playwright during the Harlem Renaissance.

My Notes

painter, the poet juxtaposes black and white into a canvas of brilliant contrasts. The night is pictured as being beautiful because It Is dark—a welcome relief from the stark whiteness of the stars. The image suggests the pride in Negritude which became important in the Harlem Renaissance—the pride in the physical beauty of black people, the Negro folk culture which has enriched America, the strength which the Negro has earned through suffering. Cullen describes the night as being not only a lovely thing, but also a sheltering thing. The image of the buds that cannot bloom in light suggests that the Negro's experience has created a unique place for him in American culture: there are songs that he alone can sing.

6 The final couplet combines the beautiful and sheltering concept of darkness with the basic symbol of futile planting. The poet now splashes a shocking red onto his black and white canvas. The dark becomes not only a shelter for developing buds, but also a place to conceal gaping wounds. These two lines are quiet but extremely disturbing:

"So in the dark we hide the heart that bleeds, / And wait, and tend our agonizing seeds." And the reader cannot help wondering, what sort of plant will grow from these "agonizing seeds"?

⊘ Knowledge Quest
- What questions does this literary criticism raise for you?
- What impression do you get of the poem being analyzed?
- How was the Dark Tower a community?

Scaffolding the Text-Dependent Questions

21. According to Collier, what does the dark night represent? How does the historical context support her interpretation? Examine paragraph 5 in particular. What does Collier say about the poet's use of the words *night* and *dark*? According to her, what does the poem's darkness symbolize: beauty or despair, danger or safety? How does she feel African American artists of the time earned the right to participate in American culture? RI.11-12.1

Returning to the Text

- Return to the literary criticism as you respond to the following questions. Use text evidence to support your responses.
- Write any additional questions you have about the text in your Reader/Writer Notebook.

18. **KQ** In paragraph 1, what does the word *spirit* mean in context? How does this word connect to the idea of a community?

The author uses the word *spirit* to refer to the qualities or elements of the Harlem

Renaissance. In this context, *spirit* describes the qualities that define the Harlem Renaissance

community.

19. How does Collier classify "From the Dark Tower"? What evidence does she give to support her classification?

In the first paragraph, Collier describes the poem as "a restrained, dignified, poignant work,

influenced in form by Keats and Shelley rather than by the moderns." She quotes several lines

of the poem to demonstrate her point; its structure is indeed more sonnet-like than modern.

She also calls the work a "protest poem," pointing out that it is thematically characteristic of

the poetry of its time and place.

20. What structure does the author use to discuss her interpretation of the poem? How does her choice affect the reader's understanding of the poem and its interpretation?

Collier discusses the poem in a linear fashion, addressing each stanza in sequence. She

also uses a thematic approach, introducing the theme in paragraph 3 and then referring to

it throughout the essay. She says the poet incorporates "the often-used symbol of planting

seeds and reaping fruit" and then analyzes that symbolism. This approach enables readers to

grasp the deeper meaning of the poem.

21. According to Collier, what does the dark night represent? How does the historical context support her interpretation?

Collier says the words *night* and *dark* in the poem represent "the pride in the physical beauty

of black people, ... the strength which the Negro has earned through suffering." She also

interprets the night as "a sheltering thing," saying, "the Negro's experience has created a

unique place for him in American culture." The unique heritage of African American artists

entitles their voices to be heard.

Scaffolding the Text-Dependent Questions

22. **What analysis does Collier apply to the imagery of planting seeds and reaping fruit, and how does she argue that it supports the central message of "From the Dark Tower"?** Revisit the references in Collier's text to *fruit, buds, seeds, blooms,* and the like in paragraph 3. Examine the context of each use. What human activities and situations are being described in this metaphoric language? What is actually being sown and reaped? Who is doing the sowing, and who is doing the reaping? RL.11-12.4

23. **How does the text help define what makes the Harlem Renaissance a community?** How did poetry play a part in the community? To what community does the title of the text refer? RI.11-12.3

ACTIVITY 4.3 continued

46 **RETURNING TO THE TEXT:** Guide students to return to the text to respond to the text-dependent questions. Invite them to work in their expert groups to reread the text and answer the questions. Remind them to use text evidence in their responses.

47 Move from expert group to expert group and listen in as students answer the text-dependent questions. If they have difficulty, scaffold the questions by rephrasing them or breaking them into smaller parts. See the Scaffolding the Text-Dependent Questions boxes for suggestions.

48 Introduce students to the Closing the Knowledge Quest box. Have them work with a partner to reflect on their understanding of the Harlem Renaissance community and what makes a community. Ask volunteers to share their responses with the class.

49 Encourage students to continue building knowledge on this topic as suggested in the Independent Reading link.

50 When students have completed their **graphic organizer**, reconfigure expert student **discussion groups** through the **jigsaw** approach, ensuring that each new jigsaw group contains one or two students from the expert group(s) for each of the primary sources. Students will then take turns presenting information on the primary sources to the group based on their annotations, Returning to the Text responses, and graphic organizer notations. Encourage students to complete their graphic organizers based on the new information and to engage in **note-taking** during the presentations.

22. What analysis does Collier apply to the imagery of planting seeds and reaping fruit, and how does she argue that it supports the central message of "From the Dark Tower"?

Collier interprets the imagery as an "often-used symbol" that invariably

refers to "the natural sequence of things." She argues that Cullen is using

the symbol to represent an unjust system, where African Americans sow

the seeds of labor only to have others reap the fruit that they did not plant

themselves.

23. **KQ** How does the text help define what makes the Harlem Renaissance a community?

The text helps define what makes the Harlem Renaissance a community

by aiming to show how the poetry written by the community expresses its

"spirit." Collier points out that the "Dark Tower" refers to a place in Harlem

where a community of poets gathered.

INDEPENDENT READING LINK

You can continue to build your knowledge about communities by reading other articles at ZINC Reading Labs. Search for keywords such as *unity* or *community*.

ZINC

Knowledge Quest

After reading these texts about communities, think about what makes up a community and why. With a partner, write an informative text about the makeup of a community. Respond to the following questions: *What is a community you know? Who is in this community? Is it big, small, or somewhere in between? How else can you describe your community? How do you feel about the ways in which you belong to this community?* Be sure to:

- Develop the topic with concrete details that give facts, not opinions, about your community.
- Use precise language to manage the complexity of your topic.

Working from the Text

24. As you examine the preceding sources, make notes about your understanding of these readings by completing the following graphic organizer or by creating your own graphic organizer in your Reader/Writer Notebook. Note each category in the graphic organizer and write notes as to what you can infer from the text about the literary and artistic movement known as the Harlem Renaissance. Be sure to cite textual evidence to support your understanding.

	Documentary Film	Art	Informational Text	Poetry
Historical Context		Sculpture was created as part of the 1939 New York World's Fair.	Locke defines the "New Negro" of Harlem. Collier identifies the poem as a celebration of "darkness," of the pride and hope for the future.	Poets give voice to the optimism of the time and place.
Values and Beliefs		Savage's sculpture of singing offers promises of hope. Pride in imagery of Harlem and of African heritage	Locke is an intellectual spokesperson. The poetry speaks to the sense of future the pride of the Harlem Renaissance will bring.	Reflects an expression of hope and the variety and multiple identities of African American voices.
Genres and Style		Art reflects the movement of pride, optimism, and solidarity.	Academic essays define new cultural awakening. Collier as a critic gives credibility and value to the poetic voices of the Harlem Renaissance.	Poetry that expresses the experience of African Americans—and their pride, celebration, and optimism—is a typical genre.
Significant Authors and Works		Flowering of sculpture and art by African American men and women Augusta Savage Palmer Hayden Aaron Douglas Lois Mailou Jones	Alain Locke Eugenia Collier	James Weldon Johnson Gwendolyn Bennett Countee Cullen

51 Invite students to use the information in their completed graphic organizer to complete the Focus on the Sentence exercise.

52 Give students time to respond to the Writing Prompt. Consider allowing them to consult with other members of their expert groups as they write their informational texts.

53 Read aloud the Revising Your Plan and Modifying Your Major Research Question section. Have students revisit the graphic organizer in student step 4 of Activity 4.1 and use student steps 1–5 as a guide to reconsidering their:

- topics
- major research questions
- secondary research questions
- source lists
- research timelines

Tell students to record updates to their research plans in their Reader/Writer Notebooks.

ASSESS

In reviewing students' informational texts, look for well-stated topic sentences, the effective use of transition words and phrases, and a smoothly flowing conclusion that connects to the paragraph's points and topic. After assessing their texts, you may wish to review ways to integrate quotations and other textual evidence into informational writing.

ADAPT

If students need additional help writing their informational texts, have them work with partners to complete a **Web Organizer** graphic organizer by writing the chosen aspect of the Harlem Renaissance in the center circle and then using the radiating circles to record evidence from the source materials. For each piece of evidence, students should state how it connects to the aspect listed in the center circle.

4.3

☑ Focus on the Sentence

Examine the observations and information you have placed in the graphic organizer. Write four different sentences that combine ideas from the sources you have analyzed using the sentence structures indicated.

Statement: Savage's sculpture and Harlem Renaissance poetry are similar in that both express hope and optimism.

Question: How does Alain Locke's analysis of the Harlem Renaissance compare with that of Eugenia Collier?

Exclamation: James Weldon Johnson is a poet, while Alain Locke is an intellectual!

Command: Compare information presented in the documentary film with that presented by Locke and Collier.

✍ Writing Prompt: Informational

Select one aspect of the Harlem Renaissance, such as its history, values and beliefs, authors and works, or genres and styles. Write an informational text that describes your understanding of that aspect. Use the information you have read in both primary and secondary sources for reference. Develop your text by using the most significant and relevant facts and details from these references. Be sure to:

- Begin your paragraph with a well-stated topic sentence.
- Provide lead-ins to cite textual evidence, using transition words and phrases to connect ideas and create a cohesive paragraph.
- End with a conclusion that follows logically from the points presented and refers to your topic.

Revising Your Plan and Modifying Your Major Research Question

25. Now that you have conducted research from a variety of sources, it's time to look again at your major research question. Does it need to be modified based on what you have learned? Do you have additional secondary research questions? Record updates to your research questions and plan in your Reader/Writer Notebook.

 ## WRITING PROMPT: INFORMATIONAL

The following standards are addressed in the Writing Prompt:

- W.11-12.2a
- W.11-12.2c
- W.11-12.2f

Synthesizing Facts, Interpretations, and Media Formats

Learning Targets
- Locate and select appropriate sources to answer research questions.
- Choose an appropriate delivery method for research results.

Preview
In this activity, you will locate relevant sources and consider the best media format for presenting your research.

Learning Strategies
Close Reading
Discussion Groups
Marking the Text
Questioning the Text

Locating Relevant Sources

Before continuing your group work with the creation of your multimedia informational presentation, your teacher will guide you through an exercise in locating relevant sources.

Remember that a relevant, or usable, source is:

- **accurate:** consists of truthful, verifiable information.
- **credible:** from a source known to be trustworthy.
- **free of bias:** factual and presented without an attempt to support an opinion.
- **free of faulty reasoning:** logically sound and free of fallacies like those you learned about in Unit 3.

1. For this exercise, your teacher and your class will locate a relevant source in response to the question *What was the role of visual artists during the Harlem Renaissance?* Create a research plan by:
    - listing the types of visual arts common during the time of the Harlem Renaissance (approximately 1918–1937). folk art, painting, illustration, sculpture, photography, printmaking, filmmaking
    - constructing online searches designed to locate informative sources about these Harlem Renaissance art types. "Harlem Renaissance folk art"; "Harlem Renaissance painting"; "Harlem Renaissance illustration"; etc.

2. Execute your research plan with the guidance of your teacher. Then, as a class, construct secondary online searches to help you find a relevant source. Once everyone has agreed on the choice of a relevant source, discuss whether the source is primary or secondary and how you know it is accurate, credible, and free of bias and faulty reasoning.

Presenting Your Results

For a multimedia presentation, you must begin to consider how you will present this information to your audience and what information you will share.

3. Consult this list of some possible media formats. When you meet with your group members, discuss which media formats will best provide the vehicles for your presentations. What other multimedia formats can you add? Add them to the list.

presentation slides	social media	chart, map, or diagram
music	blog	brochure
video	billboard	timeline
poster	photographs	board game
scene from a play	advertisement	newspaper article
letter	review of a performance	interview

My Notes

College and Career Readiness Standards

Focus Standards:

W.11-12.8 Gather relevant information from multiple authoritative print and digital sources, using advanced searches effectively; assess the strengths and limitations of each source in terms of the task, purpose, and audience; integrate information into the text selectively to maintain the flow of ideas, avoiding plagiarism and over-reliance on any one source and following a standard format for citation.

W.11-12.9 Draw evidence from literary or informational texts to support analysis, reflection, and research.

ACTIVITY 4.4

PLAN

Materials: Internet access
Suggested Pacing: 1 50-minute class period

TEACH

1 Read aloud the Learning Targets and Preview. Now that students have closely examined the process of developing and revising a research plan, analyzing sources. and writing informational text, they will need to practice locating relevant sources and choosing how best to present the information they find.

2 The two student steps in the Locating Relevant Sources section lay out a procedure for creating and executing a research plan and analyzing sources. Guide students in completing these steps as instructed. Have them examine and classify each possible relevant source by asking:

- *Is it accurate and credible?* Have students confirm that the source contains truthful, trustworthy information by checking whether the author's name and organizational affiliations are included, whether the date of the article is noted, whether the website has a .gov or .edu domain name or a good general reputation for credibility, whether the site seems well-designed and presented, and whether the information can be confirmed by other sites known to be reliable.
- *Is it free of bias?* Have students confirm that the source is bias-free. They should look for evidence of omitted facts and evidence, words with particularly positive or negative connotations, appeals to emotion rather than reason, overgeneralizations, and omission or ridicule of information that disagrees with that of the source.
- *Is it logical?* Have students confirm that the source is free of faulty reasoning by analyzing it for the logical fallacies they learned about in the previous unit.

Then have students determine whether the source is a primary or secondary one by analyzing it according to the definitions of:

- **primary source:** one that provides firsthand information about its subject (letters, diaries, portraits, recordings, photographs, newspaper accounts)
- **secondary source:** one that provides information from someone who did not have firsthand exposure to the topic (encyclopedia articles, textbooks, interpretive articles); secondary sources are often based on primary sources.

3 Ask students to work in their small groups to examine, the list of media formats in student step 3. Give groups time to **brainstorm** more possibilities and to determine which ones might be the best to enrich their media presentation and which ones group members feel confident about being able to create.

4 Guide students through the process of completing an example on the **Synthesizing Facts, Interpretations, and Media Formats** graphic organizer by doing the following:

- Chart a fact with a source and page number notation.
- Generate reflective questions to clarify meaning.
- Consider appropriate formats to represent information.
- Consider what information to include in the presentation.

4.4

Other possible media formats:

_____

_____

4. Listen as your teacher reads aloud the information in the first three rows of the table. Then work together as a class to complete the row for the class research question.

Synthesizing Facts, Interpretations, and Media Formats			
Research Facts	**Reflection**	**Possible Media Formats**	**Possible Commentary**
Record pertinent information from the source and include page numbers. Be sure to use quotation marks for a direct quotation.	_Include questions and comments on the facts presented._	_Consider possible media resources to convey the facts (i.e., the best media resource to share this information with my classmates)._	_Note ideas for content to include in the media resource (i.e., commentary that will support my understanding of the research information)._
Class Research Question: What was the role of visual artists during the Harlem Renaissance?			
"... the decade overall was one of tense, turbulent, and sometimes violent relations between black and white Americans."	Did or how did the artists escape the violence and tension?	Possibly pictures of artists, pictures from scenes at Cotton Club	Explain that a number of wealthy white people supported the artists financially.
Your Research Question:			
"Another influential form of African-American music that rose to prominence during the 1920s was the blues."	Who were some leading blues singers? What does "the blues" sound like?	Picture of performers Music/mp3 player	Show picture of the performers and provide some biographical information; during information sharing, have Bessie Smith's music in the background.
"Perhaps the best-known African American painter of the Harlem Renaissance was Aaron Douglas."	Why is he so well known?	Presentation slides showing a collection of Douglas's work Music/mp3 player	Research key information on each painting—when it was done, what influenced Douglas. Continue to play blues or jazz music as I present this artwork and give background information.
"In 1923, sculptor Augusta Savage brought this discrimination against black artists to the attention of the American public when, after being rejected for a summer school in France because of her race, she appealed to the press."	What were Savage's complaints? What points did she make? What were the results of her efforts?	Radio talk show interview with Savage (Student A is Savage; Student B is the radio talk host asking the questions.)	Research information on her charges. Possibly find newspaper accounts of them or a biographical sketch that explains her complaints. Use this information to devise questions and her responses.

College and Career Readiness Standards

W.11-12.6 Use technology, including the Internet, to produce, publish, and update individual or shared writing products in response to ongoing feedback, including new arguments or information.

Additional Standards Addressed:
W.11-12.5, W.11-12.2f

4.4

Your Turn

5. Locate at least two relevant sources—one print, one electronic—that you can share with your group as support for the major research question. Read the sources and examine them for credibility, bias, accuracy, and faulty reasoning. Then, for each source, complete the first column of the Synthesizing Facts, Interpretations, and Media Formats graphic organizer; you will complete the remaining columns later with your presentation group. Make enough copies of both sources for everyone in your presentation group.

☑ Check Your Understanding

Why do you think it is important to draw information from more than one source? What could happen if you use a source that is not credible? How does having more than one source help you check the validity of a document? Record your thoughts in your Reader/Writer Notebook and then discuss with a partner.

5 Give groups time to decide on their topics and research questions. Remind them that their focus questions might change as they build their knowledge about the Harlem Renaissance.

6 Each student is to find two sources that he or she thinks will help answer the group's research question.

7 Groups can work together to investigate possible sources by doing brief Internet or library searches of resources. Then they can divide up the work. Before meeting in groups again, students should read or study the sources and complete the first column of the graphic organizer. Suggest that students make copies of the chart for each group member so that all have copies for review during the next activity.

8 Allow students time to complete the Check Your Understanding task independently in their Reader/Writer notebooks. Then have students compare their thoughts with a partner and ask volunteers to share their discussion.

ASSESS

Use students' responses on their graphic organizers to assess their ability to locate and analyze appropriate sources.

ADAPT

If students need additional help finding and vetting sources they will need to do their research, provide a specific list of possible reference sources. (You might want to ask the school librarian to assist you with this list.) Then lead students to discuss the type of information each includes. Have students meet in their small groups to identify sources on the list that might be specific to their questions.

Materials: copies of sources that students make to share with their group members, MLA source books, Internet access

Suggested Pacing: 4 50-minute class periods

TEACH

1 Read the Learning Targets and Preview with students. Tell them that they will be learning about the importance of creating properly annotated bibliographies in research papers.

2 Have students begin by reading the instructions in the Sharing Research Information section. Remind them that they were introduced to the **Synthesizing Facts, Interpretations, and Media Formats** graphic organizer in Activity 4.4.

3 Read with students the Using Source Materials Ethically section. Stress the meanings of the words *ethically* and *plagiarism* and their relationship to each other.

4 **Vocabulary Development:** Review the meaning of the term *annotated bibliography* with students. Have them work in pairs to define the term in their own words.

5 Read aloud the Citing Sources section as a class. Then explain that these annotated bibliography entry models illustrate the most common types of sources students are likely to use in their research. If possible, provide MLA source books or direct students to an online source that models citations for sources not shown here.

▶ TEACHER TO TEACHER

Consider giving students options for using the graphic organizer. If they have personal methods of note-taking that they find work better for them, encourage them to practice this independence, but be sure they take notes.

Learning Strategies

Discussion Groups
Marking the Text
Note-taking

My Notes

Learning Targets

- Summarize and evaluate research sources in an annotated bibliography.
- Understand the use of academic citations and annotations as a means of avoiding plagiarism.

Preview

In this activity, you will consult print or online references as a guide to create an annotated bibliography for your multimedia informational presentation.

Sharing Research Information

1. You will now read and analyze the information that other members of your group have provided. Each of you should share copies of research information. For each source, take notes on a Synthesizing Facts, Interpretations, and Media Formats graphic organizer or another effective note-taking format.

Using Source Materials Ethically

To do something **ethically** means to do it in a way that does not violate principles of honesty or integrity. When writing, this means not only using the most relevant, accurate, and credible sources possible but also avoiding intentional or unintentional **plagiarism**, the uncredited use of someone else's words or ideas.

Plagiarism can be avoided by:

- paraphrasing, or rephrasing text into your own words.
- quoting, or copying a text word for word, placing it within quotation marks, and clearly stating the source of the quote.
- citing, or using established formatting guidelines to indicate the source and author of the material you are using.

Citing Sources

2. Consult a reference such as the *MLA Handbook* or another reference that your teacher specifies to find the proper methods of citation for your research. You may also search the web using a search term such as "MLA style sheet" to get information about citation methods.

3. After you decide on the sources that your writing group will use, prepare an **annotated bibliography** that you will include in your presentation. Remember that anything coming from an outside source must be cited, including paraphrased and quoted text. Note the following elements of annotated bibliographies:

   - After each documentation of source, a note explains the content of the source and its value.
   - It gives readers information on the sources and provides proof of the validity and reliability of the sources.
   - Notes are written in third-person objective academic voice.

VOCABULARY

ACADEMIC
An annotated bibliography cites complete information about sources, provides a critical review of each source, and provides notes about the informational value of each source.

College and Career Readiness Standards

Focus Standards:

W.11-12.8 Gather relevant information from multiple authoritative print and digital sources, using advanced searches effectively; assess the strengths and limitations of each source in terms of the task, purpose, and audience; integrate information into the text selectively to maintain the flow of ideas, avoiding plagiarism and over-reliance on any one source and following a standard format for citation.

W.11-12.9 Draw evidence from literary or informational texts to support analysis, reflection, and research.

Additional Standards Addressed:

W.11-12.7, W.11-12.9

The following are examples of entries from an annotated bibliography.

Bessie Smith, 31 March 2012. *www.redhotjazz.com/bessie.html*.

This informative website offers a summary of Bessie Smith's contribution to the development of jazz music and her relationships with other great jazz performers. It also provides an alphabetized listing of her recordings along with recording date, place of recording, and production company. Two other helpful sections are the names of the musicians who accompanied her recordings and a bibliography. For anyone exploring the musical aspect of the Harlem Renaissance, this is a helpful resource.

Drowne, Kathleen, and Patrick Huber. *The 1920s*. Ed. Ray B. Browne. Westport, CT: Greenwood Press, 2004.

The book is part of a series titled *American Popular Culture Through History*. It provides information to build background knowledge of the 1920s with such topics as "Everyday America," "Leisure Activities," "Food and Drink," and "Visual Arts." It is a helpful resource for understanding the philosophy, historical context, arts, and daily life of the 1920s.

Ford, Nick Aaron. "A Study in Race Relations—a Meeting with Zora Neale Hurston," *Zora Neale Hurston*. Ed. Harold Bloom. Philadelphia, PA: Chelsea House Publishers, 1986. 7–10.

Ford divides this essay into two parts. Part I relates a casual encounter between the writer and Zora Neale Hurston, who told him, "I have ceased to think in terms of race; I think only in terms of individuals." Part II provides readers an explanation of the traditional portrayal of to in literature up to the Harlem Renaissance. He then explains why Hurston's beliefs are in conflict with her contemporaries. This essay and others in this book outline the varying attitudes toward Hurston's writing, from her contemporaries to modern scholars.

Continuing Research

4. Continue to research so that you gather well-documented information that will support an accurate and detailed presentation. You might find that additional sources will lead to secondary questions that lead from the major question. As you gather information, complete a Synthesizing Facts, Interpretations, and Media Formats graphic organizer for sources that you consider supportive of your research question.

5. After your writing group has analyzed the sources, prepare an annotated bibliography entry for each source that you find most informative and supportive of your major research question. Ensure equal participation within your group by distributing the writing to each member of your group. Remember:

   • Use an appropriate bibliographic format.
   • Explain why the source supports your research question.
   • Use the appropriate point of view.

☑ Check Your Understanding

Describe the importance of proper citation in one sentence by using the following stem:

Using an annotated bibliography is a way to make certain that _____.

6 Essential to this research process is the consideration of multiple sources that present various perspectives on a topic. Begin this process by asking students to review their research questions. Then have them review the sources that group members have contributed for consideration.

7 Ask students to work in their **discussion groups** to complete a Synthesizing Facts, Interpretations, and Media Formats graphic organizer. This graphic organizer requires that students think about how they will present information in various media formats.

8 After all members of each group have agreed on the sources, they should discuss how this information answers their research question. Students should write possible answers to their research question based on their research. Require each member of the group to generate an annotated bibliography entry of at least one source.

9 Give students time to respond to the Check Your Understanding task. They should be able to complete the task independently.

ASSESS

Review students' graphic organizers and annotated bibliographies to assess their understanding of the research process. Ensure that the information is tied logically to the groups' research questions.

ADAPT

If students need additional help searching for information and deciding which information is relevant and important, consider providing a list of questions to guide their review of sources, which might include:

• How does this source answer my group's research question?
• What is the most important information that I should use for the presentation?
• Which aspect of the research topic does this source address: historical context, philosophy, the arts, or daily life?

ACTIVITY 4.6

PLAN

Materials: student-selected research sources, Internet access
Suggested Pacing: 1 50-minute class period

TEACH

1 Read the Learning Targets and Preview with the class. Tell students that this activity will provide them with instruction on organizing and presenting their research.

2 Lead a class discussion on the content of the Participating Collaboratively section in Activity 4.2. Briefly discuss each bullet point in the Collaboration Guidelines before continuing.

3 Divide students into groups and have them focus on the Synthesizing Your Research section. Remind them that "synthesizing" information means to combine smaller items of information into a cohesive whole.

4 Have groups review and revise their research plans as instructed in student step 1. Remind them that this includes consideration of their:

- topics
- major research questions
- minor research questions
- source lists
- research timelines

5 Have students complete student step 2 individually so each of them has a copy of their major and secondary research questions to guide them through student step 3.

6 Give individuals or pairs of group members time to analyze their assigned sources. Assist them as necessary in constructing and using their source chart. Consider projecting a copy of the chart or reproducing it on the board. Model organizing information in a manner that suits the topic, purpose, and audience.

ACTIVITY
4.6

Finalizing Research and Organizing Your Presentation

Learning Strategies

Drafting
Note-taking
Sharing and Responding

My Notes

Learning Targets

- Construct a thesis statement that answers a research question.
- Collaboratively plan and organize research to create an informational multimedia presentation.
- Practice giving a formal presentation and revising it as needed.

Preview

In this activity, you will synthesize your research, write a thesis, and organize your presentation.

Synthesizing Your Research

Collaborate with your group to complete the construction and polishing of your group's informational multimedia presentation. Review the procedures you established in the Participating Collaboratively task in Activity 4.2 before continuing. Then follow these steps to synthesize your research:

1. Conduct a group review and revision of your research plan.

2. Write your agreed-upon major research question and secondary research questions.

Major research question: _____

_____

Secondary research questions: _____

_____

3. Distribute your chosen sources among individuals or pairs of group members. Each person/pair should conduct a final examination of an assigned source to make certain it is relevant and adequately addresses your group's research questions. Collaborate to organize your pieces of information using a chart similar to the one that follows. Use separate writing paper or a flipchart, if available.

Source	Relevant Information in Source	Information's Location in Source

Keep your chart as a resource to consult as you organize your presentation. As you proceed, remember that your group's goal is to present your information in a way that suits your topic, audience, and purpose.

College and Career Readiness Standards

Focus Standards:

W.11-12.8 Gather relevant information from multiple authoritative print and digital sources, using advanced searches effectively; assess the strengths and limitations of each source in terms of the task, purpose, and audience; integrate information into the text selectively to maintain the flow of ideas, avoiding plagiarism and over-reliance on any one source and following a standard format for citation.

W.11-12.1b Work with peers to promote civil, democratic discussions and decision-making, set clear goals and deadlines, and establish individual roles as needed.

W.11-12.1c Propel conversations by posing and responding to questions that probe reasoning and evidence; ensure a hearing for a full range of positions on a topic or issue; clarify, verify, or challenge ideas and conclusions; and promote divergent and creative perspectives.

LANGUAGE & WRITER'S CRAFT: Writing a Thesis Statement

A thesis statement usually appears at the beginning of the introductory paragraph of an essay, and it offers a specific summary of the main point or claim of the essay. The thesis statement fulfills the following criteria:

- It answers the major research question.
- It reflects an opinion that can be argued with reasoning and evidence from your source.
- It provides the organization of ideas.

Study these sample research questions and the thesis statement that answers each question. Analyze how each statement meets the requirements of an effective thesis statement.

Research Question	Thesis Statement
How did Alain Locke contribute to the Harlem Renaissance movement?	Alain Locke, an influential leader of the Harlem Renaissance, instilled purpose and responsibility into the young writers of the time with his essays and leadership.
Why was jazz music such an influential art form during the Harlem Renaissance?	Reflecting the historical context and daily life of the Harlem Renaissance, jazz music gave musicians a new outlet of expression.
Major question: Why were Jessie Redmon Fauset's novels viewed with dismissive criticism during the Harlem Renaissance? Secondary question: Why is her work being revisited today?	Jessie Redmon Fauset, whose Harlem Renaissance novels were received with mixed reviews when they were first released, is now viewed as one of America's first black feminist writers for her portrayal of race relations and black women.

PRACTICE Now that you have collected sources that support your major research question, create a thesis statement for your presentation.

Organizing Your Presentation

4. Now that you have your thesis statement, you will need to organize your research so that it supports your thesis. Divide your topic into subtopics and sort your individual pieces of information into those subtopics. Since this is going to be a multimedia presentation, planning will also include making decisions about which type of media you will use to present each subtopic. Create a chart similar to the one that follows to sort your information into subtopics and organize the use of media in your presentation.

College and Career Readiness Standards

SL.11-12.2 Write informative/explanatory texts to examine and convey complex ideas, concepts, and information clearly and accurately through the effective selection, organization, and analysis of content.

SL.11-12.4 Present information, findings, and supporting evidence, conveying a clear and distinct perspective, such that listeners can follow the line of reasoning, alternative or opposing perspectives are addressed, and the organization, development, substance, and style are appropriate to purpose, audience, and a range of formal and informal tasks.

Additional Standards Addressed:
W.11-12.2a, W.11-12.2b, W.11-12.9

7 Draw students' attention to the Language & Writer's Craft box. Have a volunteer read the introductory text aloud. Then discuss how each of the three sample research questions (including the major/secondary paired questions) generates the thesis statement with which it is paired. Model the fact that other thesis statements could be easily generated from those same research questions. For example:

- Alternate answer to the first major research question: *Alain Locke, the first African American to win a Rhodes Scholarship, is a primary reason that the Harlem Renaissance is widely known today.*
- Alternate answer to the second major research question: *The widespread availability of recorded jazz music on phonograph disks spread its influence far and wide.*
- Alternate answer to the third (major and secondary) research question: *The novels of Jessie Redmon Fauset were criticized mostly by mainstream readers, while intellectuals of the era admired them for many of the same reasons feminists admire them today.*

8 Ask volunteers to identify the parts of each thesis that illustrate the three criteria for an effective thesis statement. Provide a model using the first thesis statement:

- **answers a question:** *Instilled purpose and responsibility into the young writers*
- **reflects an opinion:** *influential leader*
- **provides organization:** *with his essays and leadership*

9 Have students work individually to complete the Language & Writer's Craft's Practice activity. Choose students to read their research questions and thesis statements to the class.

10 Give groups time to work together in planing and executing student step 4 in the Organizing Your Presentation section. Remind them to work in accordance with the Collaboration Guidelines they learned in Activity 4.2 and reviewed earlier in this activity. They should study their research information and decide how they will arrange it to support their thesis statements by organizing their presentations into subtopics with the graphic organizer in this step.

11 Give groups time to respond to the Drafting the Embedded Assessment Writing Prompt as a way to draft scripts and choose media for their presentations. Group members can work individually or in pairs.

12 Before students begin **drafting** script sections for their presentations, remind them to use an appropriate academic voice when writing, even when creating media presentations. The prompt is intended to ensure that each student contributes.

4.6

Subtopic	Pieces of Information Contained in the Subtopic	Media to Be Used in Presentation of Subtopic

5. Next, distribute your subtopics among individuals or pairs. Each person/pair is to write a "script" according to the following Writing Prompt.

Drafting the Embedded Assessment

Each group member will select one subtopic from the information the group has gathered. Generate a draft of a script for that section of your presentation. As you draft your section, consider the media that you will use. Be sure to:

- Begin with a thesis statement that answers the major research question and clearly states your opinion.
- Include commentary that directly explains the connection between the research and the thesis statement. Provide in-text documentation of the research through the use of details and examples.
- Make effective use of rhetorical devices.
- Smoothly transition from one topic and media type to another.

6. Reassemble your group and have the author(s) of each script present it orally, reading aloud both the informational text and descriptions of how the chosen media will be used. Use a chart like the following to assess each script as it is read.

Name of Subtopic and Subtopic Presenter(s):

Does the subtopic presentation...	Observations, Examples, and Comments
... exhibit a logical structure?	
... exhibit smooth transitions?	
... contain clear, accurate evidence?	
... contain well-chosen details?	
... make good use of rhetorical devices?	

DRAFTING THE EMBEDDED ASSESSMENT

The following standards are addressed in the Writing Prompt:

- W.11-12.2a
- W.11-12.2b
- W.11-12.2b
- W.11-12.2c

7. Once every subtopic has been analyzed, collaborate on assembling the final draft for your presentation including writing an effective introduction that is engaging and informative and a conclusion that follows from the thesis and the ideas developed. Place notes in the text of your script with suggestions about the effective use of eye contact, pauses, enunciation, gestures, and other oratorical devices as appropriate.

8. Finally, give the script for your multimedia presentation one last review as a group.

Presenting Your Research

As your group presents your work to the class, your teacher will offer suggestions on effectively using eye contact, speaking style, gestures, and word choice to better communicate your group's ideas. Take notes on this feedback in your Reader/Writer notebook. Afterward, discuss with your group how to integrate your teacher's guidance and recommendations into your presentation. Revisit and repeat relevant portions of your presentation to practice the suggested improvements.

Providing for Audience Note-Taking

During your presentation, you will want your audience to take notes to capture your main idea and the evidence you present in support of that idea. As you think about ways to provide for note-taking, keep these questions in mind:

- What type of note-taking graphic organizer could you create for your classmates to use in taking effective notes on your presentation?
- What information do you need to provide on your graphic organizer?

☑ Check Your Understanding

Write a short reflection on the experience you have had conducting this research. What was it like to work in your group? What went well, and what was difficult?

🛈 Independent Reading Checkpoint

Review the independent reading you have completed so far. Review any notes you took about how the texts relate to the Harlem Renaissance. Look for information in the texts that you can use as source material for your multimedia presentation.

My Notes

ACTIVITY 4.6 continued

13 Regroup students to have them **share and respond** as they critique individual drafts. Based on peer responses, students should revise their portions of the group's presentation, clarifying ideas, correcting documentation, and providing additional sources.

14 Student groups should work together to create media scripts that combine individual drafts. Provide refresher mini-lessons on using transitions for coherence as well as writing effective introductions and reflective conclusions.

15 Attend to group script-readings as outlined in the Presenting Your Research section. Make sure students note your feedback in their Reader/Writer Notebooks.

16 Allow students to choose a **note-taking** graphic organizer.

17 Give students time to respond individually to the Check Your Understanding task. As necessary, help them analyze and appraise the collaboration and presentation they completed in this activity.

18 Make sure students attend to the Independent Reading Checkpoint. Direct them to review their notes for material to add to their presentations. To assess their independent reading, set a date to check the notes in students' notebooks.

ASSESS

Use students' drafts to assess their ability to write a thesis statement that answers a major research question, to explain the connection between the thesis statement and research, and to create smooth transitions between ideas and media.

ADAPT

Following peer feedback, conference with students who have similar revision needs. Conduct mini-lessons to guide students to improve their drafts.

Reinforce the importance of using a variety of types of sources. For example, if students have relied solely on electronic sources, encourage them to examine essays, books, visual texts, or recordings.

EMBEDDED ASSESSMENT 1

Materials: technology that students will need (LCD projector, screen, computer, speakers, etc.)
Suggested Pacing: 3 50-minute class periods

 TEACHER TO TEACHER

It might be helpful to have copies of the graphic organizers from Activities 4.3 and 4.4 available to students or be sure students return to their graphic organizers as resources to help them successfully complete the Embedded Assessment.

1 Planning: Remind students to review the Scoring Guide criteria for this assignment.

2 Consider giving students ideas for presenting using various media. For example, if a group focuses on the historical context of the Harlem Renaissance, one member might do an oral retelling of letters written by some of those who migrated north during the Great Migration, another might prepare a PowerPoint presentation that summarizes the life and/or philosophy of one of the leaders of the period, one might present a chart that displays the disparities in economic growth of groups of people living in Harlem, and another might prepare a timeline showing the beginning of the Harlem Renaissance and the development of ideas through the 1920s.

3 Drafting: It is important that students in a group plan for and draft scripts that include smooth and nondisruptive transitions between presenters.

4 Evaluating and Revising: Time for and attention to this crucial step must be built into the drafting and creation of the presentation.

5 Rehearsal and Presentation: Encourage students to record the rehearsals of their presentations to gather feedback for revision. Students should understand that you expect a formal, academic, and engaging presentation.

EMBEDDED ASSESSMENT 1

Presenting a Literary Movement: The Harlem Renaissance

 ASSIGNMENT

Your assignment is to work in pairs or a small group to create an interactive multimedia research presentation about a topic related to the Harlem Renaissance. This presentation to your classmates should include a variety of media and must also include an annotated bibliography. Your presentation should focus on some aspect of the era that represents the values and ideas of the Harlem Renaissance, such as historical context, philosophy and beliefs, the arts, or daily life.

Planning: Make a plan to conduct research to gather relevant and engaging resources.	■ Is the research that you have done sufficient for your presentation? What questions still need to be answered? ■ Have you sufficiently critiqued and revised your research plan? ■ Have you examined and modified your major research question as new information is introduced? ■ How will you collaborate on the tasks that remain? Consider both the preparation and the delivery of each section of your group's presentation. ■ What resource will you provide your audience so they can take notes that emphasize the main idea and the evidence of your presentation?
Drafting: Be sure you organize and showcase a variety of multimedia.	■ How will you ensure that your presentation has an engaging introduction and a reflective conclusion? ■ Are you making sufficient and appropriate use of rhetorical devices, details, examples, and commentary? ■ How can group members who are working on separate elements check in to make sure you avoid omission or repetition of ideas? ■ How can you structure your presentation to take advantage of the different media types you are using so that the content is engaging to the audience?
Evaluating and Revising: Create time to review, reflect upon, and revise drafts.	■ Do all of your details and commentary support your thesis? ■ Do you provide transitions that allow smooth shifts from one element to the next? ■ Are all sources correctly referenced and/or cited?
Rehearsal and Presentation: Take time to rehearse so the presentation moves smoothly and creates clear connections for the listeners.	■ How can you use the speaking and performing guidelines from Unit 2 as a resource? ■ How can group members provide each other with helpful and constructive feedback? ■ How can you use the Scoring Guide as a resource before the final presentation?

Reflection

After completing this Embedded Assessment, think about how you went about accomplishing this assignment and respond to the following:

This assessment required incorporating multiple media types into one coherent presentation. How was that task challenging, and what advantages did it bring over a presentation that uses one media type?

College and Career Readiness Standards

Focus Standards:

W.11-12.5 Develop and strengthen writing as needed by planning, revising, editing, rewriting, or trying a new approach, focusing on addressing what is most significant for a specific purpose and audience.

W.11-12.6 Use technology, including the Internet, to produce, publish, and update individual or shared writing products in response to ongoing feedback, including new arguments or information.

W.11-12.7 Conduct short as well as more sustained research projects to answer a question (including a self-generated question) or solve a problem; narrow or broaden the inquiry when appropriate; synthesize multiple sources on the subject, demonstrating understanding of the subject under investigation.

SCORING GUIDE

Scoring Criteria	Exemplary	Proficient	Emerging	Incomplete
Ideas	The presentation • provides an extensive, well-researched response to the topic • includes substantial support for the ideas presented about the subject • includes interaction by providing an appropriate note-taking tool for the audience.	The presentation • provides a researched response to the topic • provides adequate support for the ideas presented about the subject • includes interaction by providing a note-taking tool for the audience.	The presentation • attempts to respond to the topic with research but has a weak or uneven focus • provides partial support for the ideas presented about the subject • provides a note-taking tool for the audience but does not use it.	The presentation • does not address all aspects of the topic • provides inadequate support for the ideas presented about the subject • does not provide a note-taking tool for the audience.
Structure	The presentation • provides an engaging thesis and sophisticated context • uses appropriate and effective transitional devices to move from one point to the next • concludes with an in-depth reflection that brings closure • includes a complete annotated bibliography with correct citations, summaries, and source evaluations.	The presentation • introduces the topic, contains a thesis and sets the context • uses transitional devices to move the reader from one point to the next • concludes with an adequate reflection and brings closure • includes an annotated bibliography with citations, summaries, and source evaluations.	The presentation • introduces the topic, contains a thesis, and attempts to set the context • attempts to use transitional devices to move the reader with uneven results • concludes with some reflection and attempts to bring closure • includes an incomplete annotated bibliography.	The presentation • does not appropriately introduce the topic, contains an unclear thesis, and/or does not adequately explain the context • does not use transitions • does not provide sufficient reflection and/or bring closure • lacks an annotated bibliography with citations, summaries, and source evaluations.
Use of Language	The presentation • effectively addresses the intended audience • seamlessly integrates research • shows a command of grammar, punctuation, and conventions.	The presentation • accurately addresses the intended audience • clearly integrates research • shows an appropriate use of conventions; some minor errors are evident.	The presentation • does little to address the intended audience • attempts to integrate research • contains errors in conventions, many of which interfere with meaning.	The presentation • does not address the intended audience • contains very little integration of research • contains extensive errors in grammar, punctuation, and conventions.

6 Consider requiring students to submit copies of their research information and the drafts they wrote for Activity 4.6.

7 **Reflection:** Note that including this reflection in each student's body of reflective responses can prepare them for an end-of-the-year, in-depth self-evaluation of their learning over the course of the school year.

8 Once this assignment is turned in, give students time to clean out their working folder and organize and transfer material to the portfolios. In this case, much of the work they have done can be included in a final assembly of the presentation. It would be best if all the students in a presentation group could have a copy of the entire presentation.

9 To score this Embedded Assessment, you may wish to download and print copies of the **Scoring Guide** from SpringBoard Digital to have a copy to mark for each student's work.

College and Career Readiness Standards

W.11-12.8 Gather relevant information from multiple authoritative print and digital sources, using advanced searches effectively; assess the strengths and limitations of each source in terms of the task, purpose, and audience; integrate information into the text selectively to maintain the flow of ideas, avoiding plagiarism and overreliance on any one source and following a standard format for citation.

W.11-12.9 Draw evidence from literary or informational texts to support analysis, reflection, and research.

SL.11-12.5 Make strategic use of digital media (e.g., textual, graphical, audio, visual, and interactive elements) in presentations to enhance understanding of findings, reasoning, and evidence and to add interest.

ACTIVITY 4.7

PLAN

Materials: chart paper, markers
Suggested Pacing: 1 50-minute class period

TEACH

1 Read the Learning Targets, Preview, and Making Connections sections with students. Then draw a web on the board. Write *Zora Neale Hurston* in the center circle. Ask students to recall information about Hurston from the first half of the unit. Record their responses in the web.

2 Draw a second web on the board and write *Harlem Renaissance* in the center circle. Ask students to share what they recall about the era and what made it unique. Record their responses in the web.

3 Have volunteers read aloud the Essential Questions and then have students work with a partner to discuss their responses. As students work, write the Essential Questions on chart paper. Ask volunteers to share their answers and record their responses on chart paper. Keep responses displayed throughout the unit and consider as a class how students' answers to the Essential Questions have changed after reading each text.

4 Read the assignment as a class. Then read the paragraph under the assignment and give students time to create graphic organizers in their Reader/Writer notebook.

5 Review the Independent Reading Plan, reminding students to take notes and annotate their texts.

ASSESS

Review students' graphic organizers to assess their understanding of the skills needed for Embedded Assessment 2.

ADAPT

If students need additional help identifying skills they will need to write an analytical essay, work as a small group to discuss analysis and essay writing. Make a T-chart on the board. As a small group, list the skills necessary for writing an essay on one side of the chart and analysis skills on the other side. Have students make the chart in their Reader/Writer Notebooks.

Unpacking Embedded Assessment 2

Learning Strategies

Drafting
Marking the Text
Note-taking
Predicting
Think-Pair-Share

Learning Targets
- Preview the knowledge and skills needed to be successful on the EA.
- Create a plan for independent reading.

Preview

In this activity, you will begin preparing to write an essay about the writing of Zora Neale Hurston.

My Notes

Making Connections

One of the great literary discoveries after the Harlem Renaissance has been Zora Neale Hurston's novel *Their Eyes Were Watching God*. It was unappreciated by some of Hurston's male contemporaries in the literary and artistic movement. Upon its first publication in 1937, the novel slipped out of print until Alice Walker, the author of *The Color Purple*, brought it back to the public eye in the 1970s. Since then, Hurston's story of Janie Crawford, a woman on a journey of self-discovery, has received wide acclaim by diverse readers and has made its own journey into the canon of American literature.

Essential Questions

Respond to the Essential Questions based on your study of the first part of the unit:

1. How do cultural movements such as the Harlem Renaissance reflect and create people's attitudes and beliefs?

2. How is one writer's work both a natural product of and a departure from the ideas of a specific literary movement in American literature?

Unpacking Embedded Assessment 2

Read closely and mark the text for the skills and knowledge you will need to accomplish the assignment for Embedded Assessment 2: Writing an Analytical Essay.

Write an analytical essay in which you discuss how Zora Neale Hurston's writing is both a reflection of and a departure from the ideas of the Harlem Renaissance. Include aspects of the Harlem Renaissance that you see reflected in Hurston's writing as well as characteristics of Hurston's writing that are departures from selected aspects of the Harlem Renaissance.

As you unpack the Embedded Assessment, create a graphic organizer that details the skills and knowledge required to complete the assignment successfully.

Independent Reading Plan

For your independent reading during this part of the unit, continue reading novels, memoirs, short stories, or books of poetry from the Harlem Renaissance literary movement. Take notes or mark the text with sticky notes when you find information that directly relates to the Harlem Renaissance. Share your observations with a small group.

College and Career Readiness Standards

Focus Standards:

W.11-12.5 Develop and strengthen writing as needed by planning, revising, editing, rewriting, or trying a new approach, focusing on addressing what is most significant for a specific purpose and audience.

Additional Standards Addressed:

W.11-12.4, SL.11-12.1b, SL.11-12.1c

"A Unity of Opposites"

Learning Targets

- Understand the historical context of a text.
- Analyze how an author's diction and syntax contribute to the voice of a text.
- Make inferences by synthesizing and finding evidence in a primary and secondary source.
- Integrate ideas from multiple texts to build knowledge and vocabulary on different perspectives about self-awareness and the understanding of self.

Preview

American author Alice Walker once said of Zora Neale Hurston, "[She] became an orphan at nine, a runaway at fourteen, maid and manicurist before she was twenty, and with one dress and a dream—managed to become Zora Neale Hurston, author and anthropologist." In this activity, you will read an essay written by Hurston in 1928 to better understand the historical context of her work.

As You Read

- Underline words and phrases that the author uses to describe herself.
- While you read, jot down questions you have about the essay in the My Notes section.
- Circle unknown words and phrases. Try to determine the meaning of the words by using context clues, word parts, or a dictionary.

About the Author

Zora Neale Hurston (1891–1960) was a novelist, essayist, anthropologist, and vibrant part of the Harlem Renaissance. She grew up in the small town of Eatonville, Florida—the first incorporated black township. Hurston's idyllic childhood was interrupted by the death of her mother when Hurston was only 9. She struggled to finish high school, which she still had not accomplished by age 26. Despite her early struggles, Hurston went on to graduate from Barnard College in 1928. *Their Eyes Were Watching God* is considered her master work. "How It Feels to Be Colored Me," originally published in the May 1928 edition of *The World Tomorrow*, was a contentious essay. It obviously did not fit with the ideologies of racial segregation, but it also did not completely mesh with the flowering of black pride associated with the Harlem Renaissance.

Learning Strategies

Diffusing
Marking the Text
Quickwrite

My Notes

College and Career Readiness Standards

Focus Standards:

RL.11-12.1 Cite strong and thorough textual evidence to support analysis of what the text says explicitly as well as inferences drawn from the text, including determining where the text leaves matters uncertain.

RL.11-12.4 Determine the meaning of words and phrases as they are used in the text, including figurative and connotative meanings;

analyze the impact of specific word choices on meaning and tone, including words with multiple meanings or language that is particularly fresh, engaging, or beautiful. (Include Shakespeare as well as other authors.)

RL.11-12.9 Demonstrate knowledge of eighteenth-, nineteenth- and early-twentieth-century foundational works of American literature, including how two or more texts from the same period treat similar themes or topics.

ACTIVITY 4.8

PLAN

Suggested Pacing: 2 50-minute class periods

TEACH

1 Read the Learning Targets and Preview with students. Write the terms *historical context, diction, syntax, voice, primary source*, and *secondary source* on the board. For each term, ask students to provide definitions and examples and write their answers on the board. Guide students to make the connection between historical context, primary sources, and secondary sources.

2 Lead a discussion around the Alice Walker quote in the Preview, and ask students how this quote provides historical context for Zora Neale Hurston and how the quote informs their understanding of her as a writer. Discuss Walker's diction; her use of the words *runaway* and *managed* conveys a certain tone or attitude of wonder and appreciation.

3 Read aloud the As You Read section. Make sure students understand what they need to be annotating for as they read.

4 Have students read About the Author section independently. Encourage students to ask any questions they have about the author or the historical context. You may want to clarify what an anthropologist does as fieldwork and discuss how that work can contribute to being an author. If possible, show students where Eatonville, Florida, is on a map. Activate prior knowledge by asking students what they know about the ideologies of racial segregation from the Jim Crow era.

5 Discuss the Knowledge Question. Have students work in small groups to discuss different perspectives about self-awareness and their understanding of self

6 FIRST READ: Based on the complexity of the passage and your knowledge of your students, you may choose to conduct the first reading in a variety of ways:

- independent reading
- paired reading
- small-group reading
- read aloud

TEXT COMPLEXITY

Overall: Accessible
Lexile: 930L
Qualitative: Moderate Difficulty
Task: Moderate (Analyze)

7 As students are reading, monitor their progress. Be sure they are engaged with the text and annotating words and phrases that indicate the author's beliefs about herself; text that discusses the philosophy, arts, and daily life of the Harlem Renaissance; and unknown words or phrases. Evaluate whether the selected reading mode is effective.

8 Vocabulary Development: Discuss the Word Connections with students. Select a few compelling words from the text that share the same cognate, and ask students to describe how knowing what the cognate means can help them determine the rest of the word's meaning. Elicit other words that the author could have used.

TEACHER TO TEACHER

When you return to the text, ask students to circle all the verbs in paragraphs 3 and 4. Next, ask students what these verbs indicate about the author's attitude toward her life. Students may note that they're in the past tense, which indicates that the author is reflecting on an event from her past, and that they're colorful and lively, indicating positive, affectionate memories. The overall tone of this piece is self-affirming.

4.8

KNOWLEDGE QUEST

Knowledge Question:

How can a person's sense of self affect the outcome of a situation?

Across Activities 4.8 and 4.9, you will read an essay and a short story by Zora Neale Hurston. While you read and build knowledge about the topic, think about your answer to the Knowledge Question.

WORD CONNECTIONS

Cognates

The English word *proscenium* means "the part of a stage that is in front of the curtain." The Spanish word *proscenio* has the same root and also describes the part of the stage closest to the audience: the part of the stage that is between the curtain and the orchestra.

first-nighter: person who attends an opening performance
oleanders: evergreen shrubs with fragrant flowers

Essay

How It Feels to Be Colored Me

by **Zora Neale Hurston**

1 I am colored but I offer nothing in the way of extenuating circumstances except the fact that I am the only Negro in the United States whose grandfather on the mother's side was *not* an Indian chief.

2 I remember the very day that I became colored. Up to my thirteenth year I lived in the little Negro town of Eatonville, Florida. It is exclusively a colored town. The only white people I knew passed through the town going to or coming from Orlando. The native whites rode dusty horses; the Northern tourists chugged down the sandy village road in automobiles. The town knew the Southerners and never stopped cane chewing when they passed. But the Northerners were something else again. They were peered at cautiously from behind curtains by the timid. The more venturesome would come out on the porch to watch them go past and got just as much pleasure out of the tourists as the tourists got out of the village.

3 The front porch might seem a daring place for the rest of the town, but it was a gallery seat for me. My favorite place was atop the gatepost. Proscenium box for a born **first-nighter**. Not only did I enjoy the show, but I didn't mind the actors knowing that I liked it. I usually spoke to them in passing. I'd wave at them and when they returned my salute, I would say something like this: "Howdy-do-well-I-thank-you-where-you-goin'?" Usually the automobile or the horse paused at this, and after a queer exchange of compliments, I would probably "go a piece of the way" with them, as we say in farthest Florida. If one of my family happened to come to the front in time to see me, of course, negotiations would be rudely broken off. But even so, it is clear that I was the first "welcome-to-our-state" Floridian, and I hope the Miami Chamber of Commerce will please take notice.

4 During this period, white people differed from colored to me only in that they rode through town and never lived there. They liked to hear me "speak pieces" and sing and wanted to see me dance the parse-me-la, and gave me generously of their small silver for doing these things, which seemed strange to me, for I wanted to do them so much that I needed bribing to stop. Only they didn't know it. The colored people gave no dimes. They deplored any joyful tendencies in me, but I was their Zora nevertheless. I belonged to them, to the nearby hotels, to the county—everybody's Zora.

5 But changes came in the family when I was thirteen, and I was sent to school in Jacksonville. I left Eatonville, the town of the **oleanders**, as Zora. When I disembarked from the riverboat at Jacksonville, she was no more. It

---

College and Career Readiness Standards

RL.11-12.10 By the end of grade 11, read and comprehend literature, including stories, dramas, and poems, in the grades 11–CCR text complexity band proficiently, with scaffolding as needed at the high end of the range.

SL.11-12.1c Propel conversations by posing and responding to questions that probe

reasoning and evidence; ensure a hearing for a full range of positions on a topic or issue; clarify, verify, or challenge ideas and conclusions; and promote divergent and creative perspectives.

Additional Standards Addressed:

RL.11-12.2, L.11-12.4

seemed that I had suffered a sea change. I was not Zora of Orange County any more, I was now a little colored girl. I found it out in certain ways. In my heart as well as in the mirror, I became a fast brown—warranted not to rub nor run.

6   But I am not tragically colored. There is no great sorrow dammed up in my soul, nor lurking behind my eyes. I do not mind at all. I do not belong to the sobbing school of Negrohood who hold that nature somehow has given them a lowdown dirty deal and whose feelings are all hurt about it. Even in the helter-skelter skirmish that is my life, I have seen that the world is to the strong regardless of a little **pigmentation** more or less. No, I do not weep at the world—I am too busy sharpening my oyster knife.[1]

7   Someone is always at my elbow reminding me that I am the granddaughter of slaves. It fails to register depression with me. Slavery is sixty years in the past. The operation was successful and the patient is doing well, thank you. The terrible struggle that made me an American out of a potential slave said, "On the line!" The Reconstruction said, "Get set!" and the generation before said, "Go!" I am off to a flying start and I must not halt in the stretch to look behind and weep. Slavery is the price I paid for civilization, and the choice was not with me. It is a bully adventure and worth all that I have paid through my ancestors for it. No one on earth ever had a greater chance for glory. The world to be won and nothing to be lost. It is thrilling to think—to know that for any act of mine, I shall get twice as much praise or twice as much blame. It is quite exciting to hold the center of the national stage, with the spectators not knowing whether to laugh or to weep.

Zora Neale Hurston and friend at a recording site, Belle Glade, Florida. This photograph was taken by Alan Lomax in 1935 as part of the Library of Congress's effort to record the sights and sounds of the diverse cultures of Florida, including those of working-class black Americans, struggling with Jim Crow segregation and racial discrimination.

[1] **oyster knife:** a reference to the saying "The world is my oyster"

GRAMMAR & USAGE

Dashes

Writers use **dashes** to amplify a point or to further explain. Notice the author's use of a dash in this sentence to amplify her point: "I belonged to them, to the nearby hotels, to the country—everybody's Zora".

Commas, parentheses, or colons can provide a similar effect, but in this instance the dash slows the reader down enough to understand that the author is further emphasizing to whom she belongs.

Try revising another sentence from this essay by replacing a dash with a colon, a comma, or parentheses. How does your revision change the way you read the sentence?

My Notes

pigmentation: natural coloring

ACTIVITY 4.8 continued

9 Pause to point out the Grammar & Usage box and allow students time to revise one of the sentences in the essay. Have them compare their revision with a partner and discuss how the meaning is changed.

➡ TEACHER TO TEACHER

Consider leading a discussion of the metaphor Hurston employs in paragraph 7, beginning with "The terrible struggle that made me an American …" in which Hurston compares the post-slavery African American experience to a footrace.

Scaffolding the Text-Dependent Questions

1. What happened to change Hurston's perspective of herself and her race? Why was this significant given the time period in which she lived? Support your answer. What was happening in African American culture during Hurston's lifetime? During the first part of her life, how did Hurston view herself? How did her perspective change? What event contributed to this change? RI.11-12.1

2. How does the author's use of the word *fast* in paragraph 5 relate to her self-awareness? What are the multiple meanings of *fast*? Which meaning fits this context? What conflict does Hurston face between her internal sense of self and external definitions of her? L.11-12.4

My Notes

8 The position of my white neighbor is much more difficult. No brown specter pulls up a chair beside me when I sit down to eat. No dark ghost thrusts its leg against mine in bed. The game of keeping what one has is never so exciting as the game of getting.

9 I do not always feel colored. Even now I often achieve the unconscious Zora of Eatonville before the Hegira.[2] I feel most colored when I am thrown against a sharp white background.

10 For instance at Barnard.[3] "Beside the waters of the Hudson" I feel my race. Among the thousand white persons, I am a dark rock surged upon, and overswept, but through it all, I remain myself. When covered by the waters, I am; and the ebb but reveals me again.

11 Sometimes it is the other way around. A white person is set down in our midst, but the contrast is just as sharp for me. For instance, when I sit in the drafty basement that is The New World Cabaret with a white person, my color comes. We enter chatting about any little nothing that we have in common and are seated by the jazz waiters. In the abrupt way that jazz orchestras have, this one plunges into a number. It loses no time in **circumlocutions**, but gets right down to business. It constricts the thorax and splits the heart with its tempo and narcotic harmonies. This orchestra grows rambunctious, rears on its hind legs and attacks the tonal veil with primitive fury, rending it, clawing it until it breaks through the jungle beyond. I follow those heathen—follow them exultingly. I dance wildly inside myself; I yell within, I whoop; I shake my assegai[4] above my head, I hurl it true to the mark *yeeeeooww!* I am in the jungle and living in the jungle way. My face is painted red and yellow and my body is painted blue. My pulse is throbbing like a war drum. I want to slaughter something— give pain, give death to what, I do not know.

12 But the piece ends. The men of the orchestra wipe their lips and rest their fingers. I creep back slowly to the **veneer** we call civilization with the last tone and find the white friend sitting motionless in his seat, smoking calmly.

13 "Good music they have here," he remarks, drumming the table with his fingertips.

14 Music. The great blobs of purple and red emotion have not touched him. He has only heard what I felt. He is far away and I see him dimly across the ocean and the continent that have fallen between us. He is so pale with his whiteness then and I am *so* colored.

15 At certain times I have no race. I am *me*. When I set my hat at a certain angle and saunter down Seventh Avenue, Harlem City, feeling as snooty as the lions in front of the Forty-Second Street Library, for instance. So far as my feelings are concerned, Peggy Hopkins Joyce on the Boule Mich with

circumlocutions: the use of many words to say something that could be simplified

veneer: attractive but superficial appearance

---

[2] **Hegira:** Mohammed's flight from Mecca to Medina in AD 622; hence, any trip or journey, especially one made to escape a dangerous or undesirable situation

[3] **Barnard:** the college in New York City from which Hurston graduated in 1928

[4] **assegai** (*n.*): a slender spear or javelin with an iron tip, used in southern Africa

---

Scaffolding the Text-Dependent Questions

3. Why does Hurston choose to use the word *circumlocutions* in paragraph 11? How does this word contribute to the meaning of the text? What does the word *circumlocutions* mean? What event happens in this paragraph? What does the author contrast in her description of this event? RL.11-12.4

4. What role does the author's use of figurative language play in developing the theme? What evidence from the text supports your answer? What metaphors does the author use? What is the overall theme of the piece? How does each metaphor relate to the theme? RL.11-12.2

her gorgeous raiment, stately carriage, knees knocking together in a most aristocratic manner, has nothing on me. The cosmic Zora emerges. I belong to no race nor time. I am the eternal feminine with its string of beads.

My Notes

16 I have no separate feeling about being an American citizen and colored. I am merely a fragment of the great Soul that surges within the boundaries. My country, right or wrong.

17 Sometimes, I feel discriminated against, but it does not make me angry. It merely astonishes me. How can *any* deny themselves the pleasure of my company? It's beyond me.

18 But in the main, I feel like a brown bag of miscellany propped against a wall. Against a wall in company with other bags, white, red, and yellow. Pour out the contents, and there is discovered a jumble of small things priceless and worthless. A **first-water** diamond, an empty spool, bits of broken glass, lengths of string, a key to a door long since crumbled away, a rusty knife blade, old shoes saved for a road that never was and never will be, a nail bent under the weight of things too heavy for any nail, a dried flower or two still a little fragrant. In your hand is a brown bag. On the ground before you is the jumble it held—so much like the jumble in the bags, could they be emptied, that all might be dumped in a single heap and the bags refilled without altering the content of any greatly. A bit of colored glass more or less would not matter. Perhaps that is how the Great Stuffer of Bags filled them in the first place—who knows?

Ø Knowledge Quest
- What details about Hurston's experience stand out to you?
- What details tell you about Hurston's awareness of self?

first-water: of the best quality

Scaffolding the Text-Dependent Questions

5. How does the metaphor in the last paragraph relate to Hurston's statements earlier in the essay? How do the themes of the essay reflect those of the Harlem Renaissance? What metaphor is in the final paragraph? Which themes of the Harlem Renaissance are reflected in this essay? How does the author's writing support or deviate from those themes? RL.11-12.2

ACTIVITY 4.8 continued

10 Hurston uses an extended metaphor in paragraph 18 to share her perception of herself with the reader. During Returning to the Text, **read aloud** the last paragraph and ask students to **mark the words or phrases** that convey this metaphor. Ask students to respond to the following question using **think-pair-share**: *How does this metaphor define Hurston as a natural product of and a departure from the ideas of the Harlem Renaissance?*

11 You might consider having students create a visual response to Hurston's lines in paragraph 18: "In your hand is a brown bag. On the ground before you is the jumble it held …" What items might students see if they tipped out the contents of the metaphorical bag that is themselves? Students can sketch or describe the items.

★ TEACHER TO TEACHER

Paragraph 18 is a good place to review sentence types. Number the sentences in the paragraph and then identify the following kinds of sentences by their numbers:

Simple sentences: 1, 5, 7
Compound sentences: 3
Compound-complex sentences: 6, 8
Fragments: 2, 4
Commands: 3
Inverted word order: 3 (second clause), 5, 6

12 After reading the text for the first time, guide the class in a brief discussion by asking the Knowledge Quest questions. Ask students what they can recall and what details about Hurston's experience stood out to them and why as well as how they could tell Hurston changed after she left Eatonville.

13 Based on the observations you make during the first reading, you may want to adjust the reading mode. For example, you may decide for the second reading to read aloud certain complex passages, or you may group students differently.

14 RETURNING TO THE TEXT:
During the second reading, students will be returning to the text to answer the text-dependent comprehension questions. You may choose to have students reread and work on the questions in a variety of ways:

- independently
- in pairs
- in small groups
- together as a class

15 Have students answer the text-dependent questions. If they have difficulty, scaffold the questions by rephrasing them or breaking them into smaller parts. See the Scaffolding the Text-Dependent Questions boxes for suggestions.

4.8

Returning to the Text

- Return to the essay as you respond to the following questions. Use text evidence to support your responses.
- Write any additional questions you have about the text in your Reader/Writer Notebook.

1. **KQ** What happened to change Hurston's perspective of herself and her race? Why was this significant given the time period in which she lived? Support your answer.

   In paragraph 5, Hurston describes the effects of moving: "I was not Zora of Orange County any more, I was now a little colored girl." Her new circumstances and location showed her that other people viewed her differently from the way she viewed herself, which promoted a shift in perspective not realized in Hurston's life.

2. **KQ** How does the author's use of the word *fast* in paragraph 5 relate to her self-awareness?

   In this context, the word *fast* means "attached firmly." Therefore, Hurston means that she would remain true to herself, "in my heart as well as in the mirror." Hurston is saying that her color would not change even though she had left the exclusively African American town.

3. Why does Hurston choose to use the word *circumlocutions* in paragraph 11? How does this word contribute to the tone of the text?

   This word refers to the practice of using many words to say something that could be said more directly with fewer. In using this word, the author creates a stark contrast between the music and the emotion of its driving force and her companion's detached comment in paragraph 13, "Good music they have here."

4. What role does the author's use of figurative language play in developing the theme? What evidence from the text supports your answer?

   The author uses metaphors to develop theme. For example, in paragraph 6, "too busy sharpening my oyster knife" develops the theme of hard work leading to success. When people refer to the world as their oyster, they are saying that the world has treasures for the taking, just as one can easily take an oyster's valuable pearl.

5. How does the metaphor in the last paragraph relate to Hurston's statements earlier in the essay? How do the themes of the essay reflect those of the Harlem Renaissance?

The metaphor in the last paragraph conveys the theme of the effects of racism. Earlier in the

essay, Hurston asserts her individuality, "When covered by the waters, I am; and the ebb but

reveals me again." This theme relates to the Harlem Renaissance because artists of the time

sought to shatter society's ideas of what African Americans could do.

Appreciating the Author's Craft

Voice is an author's style, the quality that makes his or her writing unique and that conveys his or her attitude, personality, or character in a text. Authors deliberately use specific diction and syntax to create a unique voice in their writing. Return to the text and underline all the words and phrases that Hurston places in quotations or italicizes. Then answer the following question.

6. How do Hurston's diction and syntax contribute to the voice of the text? How would you describe her voice?

_____

_____

_____

_____

Secondary Source Reading

In his essay "Zora Neale Hurston: 'A Negro Way of Speaking,'" Henry Louis Gates Jr. says of Hurston:

> Virtually ignored after the early fifties, even by the Black Arts movement in the sixties, an otherwise noisy and intense spell of black image- and myth-making that rescued so many black writers from remaindered oblivion, Hurston embodied a more or less harmonious but nevertheless problematic unity of opposites. It is this complexity that refuses to lend itself to the glib categories of 'radical' or 'conservative,' 'black' or 'Negro,' 'revolutionary' or 'Uncle Tom'—categories of little use in literary criticism. It is this same complexity, embodied in her fiction, that, until Alice Walker published her important essay ("In Search of Zora Neale Hurston") in Ms. magazine in 1975, had made Hurston's place in black literary history an ambiguous one at best.

7. With a small group, discuss and analyze Gates's interpretation of Hurston's contribution to black literary history. Discuss what evidence he provides for his interpretation and its validity.

Gates highlights the notion that black literary history did not know how to categorize Hurston,

particularly during an era that that sought to define things as "radical" or "conservative."

Gates means that Hurston defied political labeling. Since Hurston was mainly interested in

investigating her experience as an African American woman through the writing of literature

rather than politics, Gates points out how difficult it was to analyze her through the lens of

anything other than literary criticism.

ACTIVITY 4.8 continued

16 Read aloud Appreciating the Author's Craft and ask a volunteer to paraphrase the difference between voice, diction, and syntax. Then have students work independently to complete student step 6. Ask volunteers to share their findings with the class and write similar answers on the board in a connected mind map.

17 Bring students' attention to the quotation from Henry Louis Gates Jr. and discuss why this activity is titled 'A Unity of Opposites.' Ask students to explain Gates's use of this phrase in his description of Hurston.

18 Guide students to form small groups to complete student step 7. Allow groups time to return to the quote and annotate it for evidence. Then guide them to debate and analyze the interpretation Gates presents in the quote. After groups have written down their answers, ask volunteers to share their responses for the class to discuss.

19 Have a volunteer read aloud the instructions for student step 8. Encourage them to return to their annotations from both texts in order to organize their ideas. As students complete the **double-entry journal**, have them keep in mind Gates's description of "a unity of opposites."

20 Consider using the first two entries in the two-column response for modeling the importance of two requirements:

- **making a statement of inference:** "an excitement for the future" and "welcoming the Northern visitors"
- **textual evidence:** "I am off to a flying start ..." and "They were peered at cautiously ... but it was a gallery seat for me."

21 Direct students to complete this graphic organizer either individually or in pairs with one student entering ideas in the left column and the partner completing the right column. This assessment can gauge students' ability to make inferences and support them with textual evidence.

22 Allow students time to complete student step 9 by using their chart to write a brief analysis. Ask volunteers to share and create a column on the board to keep track of students' ideas.

23 Have students complete Check Your Understanding independently. Be sure students are able to make a connection between the historical context of the Harlem Renaissance and Hurston's writing.

ASSESS

Review students' responses to the Check Your Understanding task. Ensure that students can articulate the defining characteristics of the Harlem Renaissance and connect them to the ideas and style of writers of the era, including for Hurston.

ADAPT

If students have not mastered evaluating primary sources, have them work with partners to list the insights and limitations of Hurston's essay in understanding her as a writer and the Harlem Renaissance.

To extend learning, have students read Locke's entire essay from the "Introduction to *The New Negro*." (It is easily found online.) Following the reading of Hurston's essay, ask students to prepare a comparison and contrast of Locke's essay to Hurston's. Advise them to consider "a unity of opposites."

4.8

Working from the Text

8. Review your notes about the ideas and values of Harlem Renaissance. Then review your responses to the text-dependent questions associated with Hurston's essay. Use this two-column note organizer to consider Hurston's philosophy and to identify why Gates described Hurston as a "unity of opposites." Enter inferences that you make from her text and cite textual evidence that supports your inferences.

What philosophies and beliefs did Hurston share with the Harlem Renaissance?	In what ways did Hurston follow her own path?
• an excitement for the future: "I am off to a flying start ..." • recognition of her genealogical past: "... reminding me that I am the granddaughter of slaves." • pride and excitement for the accomplishments of her race: "It is quite exciting to hold the center of the national stage ..." • an enjoyment of jazz as a new form of music: "Music. The great blobs of purple and red emotion have not touched him. He has only heard what I felt." • experiences racial differences: "I am a dark rock surged upon ... When I sit in the drafty basement that is The New World Cabaret with a white person, my color comes."	• welcoming the Northern visitors: "They were peered at cautiously ... but it was a gallery seat for me." • enjoyment of life: "'speak pieces' and sing and ... dance the parse-me-la ... The colored people gave no dimes." • sure of her place in the world: "regardless of a little pigmentation ... I am too busy sharpening my oyster knife." • attitude toward being colored: "I am not tragically colored ... I do not belong to the sobbing school of Negrohood ... I do not always feel colored." • attitude toward races: "that all might be dumped in a single heap and the bags refilled without altering the content of any greatly."

9. Use the evidence and inferences you made in the chart to write a brief analysis of the ways in which the Harlem Renaissance shaped Hurston's philosophy and the ways in which Hurston trod her own path.

☑ Check Your Understanding

Quickwrite: How did the historical context of the Harlem Renaissance shape and influence writers such as Hurston?

The Tradition of Dialect

Learning Targets

- Explore how writers use dialogue and dialect to bring their stories to life.
- Identify how Hurston's style distinguished her as a unique voice during the Harlem Renaissance.
- Integrate ideas from multiple texts to build knowledge and vocabulary on different perspectives about self-awareness and the understanding of self.

Preview

In this activity, you will examine the way in which an author uses dialogue and dialect to capture how characters speak.

An Introduction to Dialect

Hurston is noted for her gifted storytelling and for honoring oral tradition, including **dialect**. An author's use of dialect validates the oral traditions of a people, a time, and a place. It also contributes to the voice of a text, shaping the perceptions of the reader about the characters and setting. Through their choice of dialect, authors create a representation of the spoken language, which helps record the history of language as it evolves over generations. Your reading of "Sweat" introduces you to Hurston's entertaining use of the oral tradition.

1. Preview one of Hurston's most famous short stories, "Sweat," by scanning Chunk 1 and underlining unfamiliar words. Listen carefully as your teacher reads aloud the first section of "Sweat." You will hear that Hurston reproduces the actual speech of the characters.

2. Next, work with a small group to formulate some "pronunciation rules" for pronouncing the words. Use the following graphic organizer to guide your work. Some examples have been provided for you.

Dialect	Conventional English
dat, wid	that, with (*th* is often replaced by *d*)
skeer	scare (so *keer* must be *care*)
ah	I (so *mah* would be *my*)
fuh	for

3. Practice reading the dialogue in paragraphs 5–8 out loud in your group, taking turns to read each sentence in dialect. Take time to discuss how hearing the dialect spoken creates a particular voice and what perception it gives you about the characters and setting.

As You Read

- Highlight the story's details to create a mental image of the characters and setting.
- Underline words and phrases that are allusions to Christianity and the Bible.
- Circle unknown words and phrases. Try to determine the meaning of the words by using context clues, word parts, or a dictionary. and try rereading, using background knowledge, asking questions, or annotating to deepen your understanding.

Learning Strategies

Drafting
Marking the Text
Oral Interpretation
Skimming/Scanning
Think-Pair-Share

LITERARY

Dialect is the distinctive language, including the sounds, spelling, grammar, and diction, of a specific group or class of people at a certain time period and in a certain geographical region.

VOCABULARY

My Notes

College and Career Readiness Standards

Focus Standards:

RL.11-12.4 Determine the meaning of words and phrases as they are used in the text, including figurative and connotative meanings; analyze the impact of specific word choices on meaning and tone, including words with multiple meanings or language that is particularly fresh, engaging, or beautiful. (Include Shakespeare as well as other authors.)

RL11-12.7 Analyze multiple interpretations of a story, drama, or poem (e.g., recorded or live production of a play or recorded novel or poetry), evaluating how each version interprets the source text. (Include at least one play by Shakespeare and one play by an American dramatist.)

PLAN

Materials: highlighters or colored pencils; optional: audio clips of different dialects, e-book audio recording on SpringBoard Digital
Suggested Pacing: 3 50-minute class periods

TEACHER TO TEACHER

"Sweat" is a powerful introduction to Hurston's use of dialect and allusions as well as to some key issues and dominant patterns of literary composition, or motifs, present in *Their Eyes Were Watching God*: relationships between men and women; the community sitting in judgment; and a woman's search for herself, expressed in the way she speaks and thinks.

TEACH

1 Read aloud the Learning Targets and Preview.

2 Vocabulary Development: Write the words *dialogue* and *dialect* on the board and have students determine the meaning of each. If possible, play audio clips of different dialects from around the country.

3 Read the An Introduction to Dialect section with students. Lead a discussion asking students why an author might choose to incorporate dialect in their writing and the effect it has to read it. Ask them to scan the first chunk of "Sweat" and mark the text by circling unfamiliar words.

4 Rehearse and then read aloud paragraphs 1–6 or find an oral reading online. One oral interpretation can be found in the e-book on SpringBoard Digital. Advise students to pay close attention to the reading and continue to circle unfamiliar words. Point out that usage is a matter of convention, can change over time, and is sometimes contested.

5 Have students work in small discussion groups to complete the graphic organizer, using the annotations they make while previewing Chunk 1. Encourage students to use context clues and say any unfamiliar words or phrases aloud. If you anticipate students will have difficulty with the dialect in *Their Eyes Were Watching God*, have them make this glossary into a bookmark to use when they start reading the novel.

6 Read the As You Read section with students and elicit what it means to create a mental image while reading. Ask students what *allusion* means and what context clues they might find to help them spot allusions to Christianity and the Bible. Remind students to annotate the story by underlining these allusions.

7 Review the Knowledge Question with students. Remind them to think about their answer to the Knowledge Question as they read and build knowledge about the topic.

8 FIRST READ: Based on the complexity of the passage and your knowledge of your students, you may choose to conduct the first reading in a variety of ways:

- guided reading
- independent reading
- paired reading
- small-group reading
- read aloud

TEXT COMPLEXITY

Overall: Complex
Lexile: 910L
Qualitative: Moderate Difficulty
Task: Challenging (Evaluate)

9 If you select guided reading, have students stop after reading Chunk 1 independently. Check for understanding, making certain that students can identify and describe the main characters of the story: Delia, a long-suffering wife and washerwoman; and her cruel and brutal husband, Sykes.

10 Lead students in a guided reading of the third paragraph and facilitate a discussion regarding how Hurston might use the whip symbolically.

4.9

KNOWLEDGE QUEST

Knowledge Question:
How can a person's sense of self affect the outcome of a situation?

My Notes

_____

_____

_____

_____

_____

_____

_____

_____

_____

_____

galvanized: made of metal covered with zinc

Short Story

Sweat

by Zora Neale Hurston

Chunk 1

1 It was eleven o'clock of a Spring night in Florida. It was Sunday. Any other night, Delia Jones would have been in bed for two hours by this time. But she was a wash-woman, and Monday morning meant a great deal to her. So she collected the soiled clothes on Saturday when she returned the clean things. Sunday night after church, she sorted them and put the white things to soak. It saved her almost a half day's start. A great hamper in the bedroom held the clothes that she brought home. It was so much neater than a number of bundles lying around.

2 She squatted in the kitchen floor beside the great pile of clothes, sorting them into small heaps according to color, and humming a song in a mournful key, but wondering through it all where Sykes, her husband, had gone with her horse and buckboard.

3 Just then something long, round, limp and black fell upon her shoulders and slithered to the floor beside her. A great terror took hold of her. It softened her knees and dried her mouth so that it was a full minute before she could cry out or move. Then she saw that it was the big bull whip her husband liked to carry when he drove.

4 She lifted her eyes to the door and saw him standing there bent over with laughter at her fright. She screamed at him.

5 "Sykes, what you throw dat whip on me like dat? You know it would skeer me—looks just like a snake, an' you knows how skeered Ah is of snakes."

6 "Course Ah knowed it! That's how come Ah done it." He slapped his leg with his hand and almost rolled on the ground in his mirth. "If you such a big fool dat you got to have a fit over a earth worm or a string, Ah don't keer how bad Ah skeer you."

Chunk 2

7 "You aint got no business doing it. Gawd knows it's a sin. Some day Ah'mgointuh drop dead from some of yo' foolishness. 'Nother thing, where you been wid mah rig? Ah feeds dat pony. He aint fuh you to be drivin' wid no bull whip."

8 "You sho is one aggravatin' nigger woman!" he declared and stepped into the room. She resumed her work and did not answer him at once. "Ah done tole you time and again to keep them white folks' clothes outa dis house."

9 He picked up the whip and glared down at her. Delia went on with her work. She went out into the yard and returned with a **galvanized** tub and set

---

College and Career Readiness Standards

Additional Standards Addressed:
RL.11-12.1, RL.11-12.2, RL.11-12.3, RL.11-12.5, RL.11-12.6, RL.11-12.9, W.11-12.1, W.11-12.5, SL.11-12.1c, L.11-12.1, L.11-12.2, L.11-12.3a

it on the washbench. She saw that Sykes had kicked all of the clothes together again, and now stood in her way **truculently**, his whole manner hoping, *praying*, for an argument. But she walked calmly around him and commenced to re-sort the things.

10 "Next time, Ah'm gointer kick 'em outdoors," he threatened as he struck a match along the leg of his corduroy **breeches**.

11 Delia never looked up from her work, and her thin, stooped shoulders sagged further.

12 "Ah aint for no fuss t'night, Sykes. Ah just come from taking sacrament at the church house."

13 He snorted scornfully. "Yeah, you just come from de church house on a Sunday night, but heah you is gone to work on them clothes. You ain't nothing but a hypocrite. One of them amen-corner Christians—sing, whoop, and shout, then come home and wash white folks clothes on the Sabbath."

14 He stepped roughly upon the whitest pile of things, kicking them helter-skelter as he crossed the room. His wife gave a little scream of dismay, and quickly gathered them together again.

15 "Sykes, you quit grindin' dirt into these clothes! How can Ah git through by Sat'day if Ah don't start on Sunday?"

16 "Ah don't keer if you never git through. Anyhow, Ah done promised Gawd and a couple of other men, Ah aint gointer have it in mah house. Don't gimme no lip neither, else Ah'll throw 'em out and put mah fist up side yo' head to boot."

17 Delia's habitual meekness seemed to slip from her shoulders like a blown scarf. She was on her feet; her poor little body, her bare knuckly hands bravely defying the strapping hulk before her.

18 "Looka heah, Sykes, you done gone too fur. Ah been married to you fur fifteen years, and Ah been takin' in washin' for fifteen years. Sweat, sweat, sweat! Work and sweat, cry and sweat, pray and sweat!"

19 "What's that got to do with me?" he asked brutally.

20 "What's it got to do with you, Sykes? Mah tub of suds is filled yo' belly with vittles more times than yo' hands is filled it. *Mah* sweat is done paid for this house and Ah reckon Ah kin keep on sweatin' in it."

21 She seized the iron skillet from the stove and struck a defensive pose, which act surprised him greatly, coming from her. It cowed him and he did not strike her as he usually did.

22 "Naw you won't," she panted, "that ole snaggle-toothed black woman you runnin' with aint comin' heah to pile up on *mah* sweat and blood. You aint paid fur nothin' on this place, and Ah'm gointer stay right heah till Ah'm toted out foot foremost."

My Notes

truculently: angrily
breeches: short pants
vittles: food and drink
snaggle-toothed: with an irregular, broken, or projecting tooth

ACTIVITY 4.9 continued

TEACHER TO TEACHER

Students may need help identifying the many Biblical allusions in "Sweat." Have them work in pairs or groups to create lists of allusions they can refer to when they complete the chart in the Working from the Text section.

Note that paragraph 8 contains an offensive phrase. The word also appears again in paragraphs 42 and 88. In paragraph 8, the phrase is an important indication of Sykes's treatment of his wife. In other paragraphs, the word is used to denigrate Sykes.

11 Read Chunk 2 aloud while students mark the text for words and phrases that describe conflicts in the story. Allow students to compare, contrast, and discuss their annotations.

Scaffolding the Text-Dependent Questions

4. What role does dialect play in the development of the tone of the story? Describe the dialogue in this story. How might reading passages of it out loud help you understand the text? How does this technique prepare readers for what might happen in the story? RL.11-12.4

5. How do the words and actions of Sykes in paragraphs 4–6 foreshadow possible events in the story? Why might Sykes be "hoping, *praying*, for an argument" in paragraph 9? How does it shape your perception of him? Look back at paragraphs 4–6. What does Sykes say and do in paragraphs 4–6? What clue do his words in paragraph 9 give about his character? What does the reader learn about the relationship between Sykes and Delia in these opening paragraphs? RL.11-12.2, RL.11-12.3

12 You might consider having students pause after reading paragraph 24 to discuss the "new Delia" and Sykes's reaction. Review the information about the multiple meanings of the word *pass* (as a noun, the act of going past or the completion of a course). Then ask students what they think Hurston is saying about Sykes's relationship with Delia.

TEACHER TO TEACHER

It is important for students to understand that porch talkers play a significant role in Hurston's work, providing comic relief while passing judgment with impressive verbal dexterity.

13 For Chunk 3, if you are continuing with guided reading, have students demonstrate their oral interpretation skills by engaging in Reader's Theater to bring the characters to life. For this task, you will need readers for the eight characters (Jim Merchant, Joe Lindsay, Moss, Walter Thomas, Elijah Moseley, Joe Clarke, Old Man Anderson, and Sykes) and one or more students to read the part of the narrator. Students will be more successful with Reader's Theater if you allow them time to read Chunk 3 independently in preparation for reading in parts. Advise them to mark the text for their lines. The audience should mark the text to show the opinions that the men on the porch have of Delia, Sykes, and Bertha. Ensure that students give respectful performances of the characters.

4.9

WORD CONNECTIONS

Multiple-Meaning Words
The most common meaning of the word **pass** is "to move past." It can mean to cause something to move in a specified way or to give something to someone using the hands. Something that *passes* can happen, take place, end, or go away. The author uses the word in the context of an idiom, meaning a situation is very bad.

My Notes

matrimonial: relating to marriage
earthworks: a raised bank or wall made of soil

23 "Well, you better quit gittin' me riled up, else they'll be totin' you out sooner than you expect. Ah'm so tired of you Ah don't know whut to do. Gawd! how Ah hates skinny wimmen!"

24 A little awed by this new Delia, he sidled out of the door and slammed the back gate after him. He did not say where he had gone, but she knew too well. She knew very well that he would not return until nearly daybreak also. Her work over, she went on to bed but not to sleep at once. Things had come to a pretty pass!

25 She lay awake, gazing upon the debris that cluttered their **matrimonial** trail. Not an image left standing along the way. Anything like flowers had long ago been drowned in the salty stream that had been pressed from her heart. Her tears, her sweat, her blood. She had brought love to the union and he had brought a longing after the flesh. Two months after the wedding, he had given her the first brutal beating. She had the memory of his numerous trips to Orlando with all of his wages when he had returned to her penniless, even before the first year had passed. She was young and soft then, but now she thought of her knotty, muscled limbs, her harsh knuckly hands, and drew herself up into an unhappy little ball in the middle of the big feather bed. Too late now to hope for love, even if it were not Bertha it would be someone else. This case differed from the others only in that she was bolder than the others. Too late for everything except her little home.

26 She had built it for her old days, and planted one by one the trees and flowers there. It was lovely to her, lovely.

27 Somehow, before sleep came, she found herself saying aloud: "Oh well, whatever goes over the Devil's back, is got to come under his belly. Sometime or ruther, Sykes, like everybody else, is gointer reap his sowing." After that she was able to build a spiritual **earthworks** against her husband. His shells could no longer reach her. *Amen.* She went to sleep and slept until he announced his presence in bed by kicking her feet and rudely snatching the cover away.

28 "Gimme some kivah heah, an' git yo' damn foots over on yo' own side! Ah oughter mash you in yo' mouf fuh drawing dat skillet on me."

29 Delia went clear to the rail without answering him. A triumphant indifference to all that he was or did.

Chunk 3

30 The week was as full of work for Delia as all other weeks, and Saturday found her behind her little pony, collecting and delivering clothes.

31 It was a hot, hot day near the end of July. The village men on Joe Clarke's porch even chewed cane listlessly. They did not hurl the cane-knots as usual. They let them dribble over the edge of the porch. Even conversation had collapsed under the heat.

32 "Heah come Delia Jones," Jim Merchant said, as the shaggy pony came 'round the bend of the road toward them. The rusty buckboard was heaped with baskets of crisp, clean laundry.

Scaffolding the Text-Dependent Questions

6. How does the author describe Delia's character? Why is establishing this important to the story? Look at paragraph 11 and then at paragraph 17. What specific words and phrases does the author use to describe Delia's character? What glimpse does Hurston give readers that Delia's character will change? How do Delia's actions and attitudes affect the story? RL.11–12.3

7. How does the author choose to give exposition about the characters? How does this choice contribute to the meaning of the story? Look at paragraph 20 and then at paragraph 25. Which specific words or phrases does the author use to refer to things that have happened in the past? How does the author use metaphor or other figurative language to explain the characters' perceptions of the past and the present? How do the author's descriptions help readers understand the story? RL.11-12.3

33 "Yep," Joe Lindsay agreed. "Hot or col', rain or shine, jes ez reg'lar ez de weeks roll roun' Delia carries 'em an' fetches 'em on Sat'day."

34 "She better if she wanter eat," said Moss. "Sykes Jones aint wuth de shot an' powder hit would tek tuh kill 'em. Not to *huh* he aint."

35 "He sho' aint," Walter Thomas chimed in. "It's too bad, too, cause she wuz a right pritty li'l trick when he got huh. Ah'd uh mah'ied huh mahseff if he hadnter beat me to it."

36 Delia nodded briefly at the men as she drove past.

37 "Too much knockin' will ruin any 'oman. He done beat huh 'nough tuh kill three women, let 'lone change they looks," said Elijah Moseley. "How Sykes kin stommuck dat big black greasy Mogul he's layin' roun wid, gits me. Ah swear dat eight-rock couldn't kiss a sardine can Ah done throwed out de back do' 'way las' yeah."

38 "Aw, she's fat, thass how come. He's allus been crazy 'bout fat women," put in Merchant. "He'd a' been tied up wid one long time ago if he could a' found one tuh have him. Did Ah tell yuh 'bout him come sidlin' roun' *mah* wife—bringin' her a basket uh pee-cans outa his yard fuh a present? Yessir, mah wife! She tol' him tuh take 'em right straight back home, cause Delia works so hard ovah dat washtub she reckon everything on de place taste lak sweat an' soapsuds. Ah jus' wisht Ah'd a' caught 'im 'roun' dere! Ah'd a' made his hips ketch on fiah down dat shell road."

39 "Ah know he done it, too. Ah sees 'im grinnin' at every 'oman dat passes," Walter Thomas said. "But even so, he useter eat some mighty big hunks uh humble pie tuh git dat lil' 'oman he got. She wuz ez pritty ez a speckled pup! Dat wuz fifteen yeahs ago. He useter be so skeered uh losin' huh, she could make him do some parts of a husband's duty. Dey never wuz de same in de mind."

40 "There oughter be a law about him," said Lindsay. "He aint fit tuh carry guts tuh a bear."

41 Clarke spoke for the first time. "Taint no law on earth dat kin make a man be decent if it aint in 'im. There's plenty men dat takes a wife lak dey do a joint uh sugar-cane. It's round, juicy an' sweet when dey gits it. But dey squeeze an' grind, squeeze an' grind an' wring tell dey wring every drop uh pleasure dat's in 'em out. When dey's satisfied dat dey is wrung dry, dey treats 'em jes lak dey do a cane-chew. Dey throws 'em away. Dey knows whut dey is doin' while dey is at it, an' hates theirselves fuh it but they keeps on hangin' after huh tell she's empty. Den dey hates huh fuh bein' a cane-chew an' in de way."

42 "We oughter take Sykes an' dat stray 'oman uh his'n down in Lake Howell swamp an' lay on de rawhide till they cain't say 'Lawd a' mussy.' He allus wuz uh ovahbearin' niggah, but since dat white 'oman from up north done teached 'im how to run a automobile, he done got too biggety to live—an' we oughter kill 'im," Old Man Anderson advised.

43 A grunt of approval went around the porch. But the heat was melting their civic virtue and Elijah Moseley began to bait Joe Clarke.

My Notes

ACTIVITY 4.9 continued

LEVELED DIFFERENTIATED INSTRUCTION

In this activity, students might need support as they read dialogue about Delia's transformation from meek to strong.

Developing Help students find the place in paragraph 17 that sets off Delia's transformation from meek to strong. Then work with them to read the dialogue that follows. Ask students to explain how the dialogue in paragraph 18 illustrates a turning point for Delia. Ask: *Why might Delia have used a strong, defiant tone as she said these words? How is her speech different here than in paragraph 12?*

Expanding Have students reread paragraph 17 and ask them how this paragraph marks the beginning of Delia's transformation. Then have them find examples of dialogue between paragraph 11 and 20 that show Delia's character as both meek and strong.

Bridging Have students find the paragraph in the story that marks the beginning of Delia's transformation. Then have them find examples of dialogue between paragraph 11 and 29 that show Delia's character as both meek and strong. Have partners discuss the struggle between Delia and Sykes and how the dialogue between them changes throughout the story.

Scaffolding the Text-Dependent Questions

8. Why does Delia reflect in paragraph 25 that "debris … cluttered their matrimonial trail"? What is the significance of this in relation to the overall theme and to the story's placement as part of the Harlem Renaissance? What debris clutters their marriage? What effect has it had on the situation? How might this theme fit within the context of the Harlem Renaissance? RL.11-12.2

9. What role do Delia's memories have in creating a sense of self-awareness? How do these memories eventually cause her to change her character? Reread paragraphs 20 and 25. What memories does Delia express? How does her character change? Which specific aspects of the memories relate to things happening in the present time? RL.11-12.1

Support Before all students discuss the dialogue in "Sweat," write examples of words and phrases on the board or have students underline them in the text. Explain that the author uses specific words, spelling, and dialect to help the reader paint a more vivid picture in his or her mind.

Extend Ask partners to find additional examples of dialogue throughout the text that show Delia's growing strength. Then ask them to reread the dialogue in Chunk 3. Ask: *How does the dialogue between the men on the porch now paint an inaccurate picture of Delia? What does Delia know that the men do not? Why do you think the author chose to include this portion of the text?*

14 If some students feel comfortable with the dialect, guide volunteers to read aloud sections of Chunk 4 while the remaining students follow along silently. Have students mark the text to identify figurative language, including metaphors and similes. Use **think-pair-share** to give students an opportunity to discuss the effects of the figurative language and images.

My Notes

🔵 **INDEPENDENT READING LINK**

Read and Connect
Browse through your independent reading selection for this unit. Find examples of each level of diction that you studied in this activity. Mark the text by color-coding the examples.

subscribed: paid

44 "Come on, Joe, git a melon outa dere an' slice it up for yo' customers. We'se all sufferin' wid de heat. De bear's done got *me!*"

45 "Thass right, Joe, a watermelon is jes' whut Ah needs tuh cure de eppizudicks," Walter Thomas joined forces with Moseley. "Come on dere, Joe. We all is steady customers an' you aint set us up in a long time. Ah chooses dat long, bowlegged Floridy favorite."

46 "A god, an' be dough. You all gimme twenty cents and slice way," Clarke retorted. "Ah needs a col' slice m'self. Heah, everybody chip in. Ah'll lend y'll mah meat knife."

47 The money was quickly **subscribed** and the huge melon brought forth. At that moment, Sykes and Bertha arrived. A determined silence fell on the porch and the melon was put away again.

48 Merchant snapped down the blade of his jackknife and moved toward the store door.

49 "Come on in, Joe, an' gimme a slab uh sow belly an' uh pound uh coffee—almost fuhgot 'twas Sat'day. Got to git on home." Most of the men left also.

50 Just then Delia drove past on her way home, as Sykes was ordering magnificently for Bertha. It pleased him for Delia to see.

51 "Git whutsoever yo' heart desires, Honey. Wait a minute, Joe. Give huh two bottles uh strawberry soda-water, uh quart uh parched ground-peas, an' a block uh chewin' gum."

52 With all this they left the store, with Sykes reminding Bertha that this was his town and she could have it if she wanted it.

53 The men returned soon after they left, and held their watermelon feast.

54 "Where did Sykes Jones git da 'oman from nohow?" Lindsay asked.

55 "Ovah Apopka. Guess dey musta been cleanin' out de town when she lef'. She don't look lak a thing but a hunk uh liver wid hair on it."

56 "Well, she sho' kin squall," Dave Carter contributed. "When she gits ready tuh laff, she jes' opens huh mouf an' latches it back tuh de las' notch. No ole grandpa alligator down in Lake Bell ain't got nothin' on huh."

Chunk 4

57 Bertha had been in town three months now. Sykes was still paying her room rent at Della Lewis'—the only house in town that would have taken her in. Sykes took her frequently to Winter Park to "stomps." He still assured her that he was the swellest man in the state.

58 "Sho' you kin have dat lil' ole house soon's Ah kin git dat 'oman outa dere. Everything b'longs tuh me an' you sho' kin have it. Ah sho' 'bominates uh skinny 'oman. Lawdy, you sho' is got one portly shape on you! You kin git *anything* you wants. Dis is *mah* town an' you sho' kin have it."

Scaffolding the Text-Dependent Questions

10. Why are the neighborhood men against Sykes? How do their views contribute to a theme of the story? Reread paragraphs 34–41. What complaints do the neighborhood men voice against Sykes? What views and opinions do they express? What is the theme of the story? RL.11-12.2

11. What point of view does the author use to tell the story? How does her choice contribute to the effectiveness of the story? How would the story change if it were told from a different point of view? Which clues at the beginning of the story indicate the point of view? How does the point of view affect the reader? RL.11-12.6

My Notes

59 Delia's work-worn knees crawled over the earth in Gethsemane and up the rocks of Calvary many, many times during these months. She avoided the villagers and meeting places in her efforts to be blind and deaf. But Bertha **nullified** this to a degree, by coming to Delia's house to call Sykes out to her at the gate.

60 Delia and Sykes fought all the time now with no peaceful interludes. They slept and ate in silence. Two or three times Delia had attempted a timid friendliness, but she was repulsed each time. It was plain that the breaches must remain agape.

* * *

61 The sun had burned July to August. The heat streamed down like a million hot arrows, **smiting** all things living upon the earth. Grass withered, leaves browned, snakes went blind in shedding and men and dogs went mad. Dog days!

62 Delia came home one day and found Sykes there before her. She wondered, but started to go on into the house without speaking, even though he was standing in the kitchen door and she must either stoop under his arm or ask him to move. He made no room for her. She noticed a soap box beside the steps, but paid no particular attention to it, knowing that he must have brought it there. As she was stooping to pass under his outstretched arm, he suddenly pushed her backward, laughingly.

63 "Look in de box dere Delia, Ah done brung yuh somethin'!"

64 She nearly fell upon the box in her stumbling, and when she saw what it held, she all but fainted outright.

65 "Sykes! Sykes, mah Gawd! You take dat rattlesnake 'way from heah! You *gottuh*. Oh, Jesus, have mussy!"

66 "Ah aint gut tuh do nuthin' uh de kin'—fact is Ah aint got tuh do nothin' but die. Taint no use uh you puttin' on airs makin' out lak you skeered uh dat snake—he's goiner stay right heah tell he die. He wouldn't bite me cause Ah knows how tuh handle 'im. Nohow he wouldn't risk breakin' out his fangs 'gin yo' skinny laigs."

67 "Naw, now Sykes, don't keep dat thing 'roun' heah tuh skeer me tuh death. You knows Ah'm even feared uh earth worms. Thass de biggest snake Ah evah did see. Kill 'im Sykes, please."

68 "Doan ast me tuh do nothin' fuh yuh. Goin' roun' tryin' tuh be so damn astorperious. Naw, Ah aint gonna kill it. Ah think uh damn sight mo' uh him dan you! Dat's a nice snake an' anybody doan lak 'im kin jes' hit de grit."

69 The village soon heard that Sykes had the snake, and came to see and ask questions.

> nullified: made to have no effect
> smiting: hitting, afflicting

Scaffolding the Text-Dependent Questions

12. What figurative language does the author use to describe Delia's response to Bertha living in town? In what ways is this consistent or inconsistent with what the reader knows of Delia's character? What figurative language does the author use in paragraph 59? What is the literal and figurative meaning of specific words in the phrases? Why does the author use these specific words to refer to Delia? How does Hurston explain Delia's response to Bertha? RL.11-12.4

13. Why might the author use the word *pouring* to describe the snake's action in paragraph 91? What does the action suggest? What connotation does the word have? RL.11-12.4

15 Lead a reading of Chunk 5 and guide students to mark the text for words and phrases the characters use to describe each other. Prompt students to discuss the effects of these descriptions.

My Notes

70 "How de hen-fire did you ketch dat six-foot rattler, Sykes?" Thomas asked.

71 "He's full uh frogs so he caint hardly move, thass how Ah eased up on 'm. But Ah'm a snake charmer an' knows how tuh handle 'em. Shux, dat aint nothin'. Ah could ketch one eve'y day if Ah so wanted tuh."

72 "Whut he needs is a heavy hick'ry club leaned real heavy on his head. Dat's de bes' way tuh charm a rattlesnake."

73 "Naw, Walt, y'all jes' don't understand dese diamon' backs lak Ah do," said Sykes in a superior tone of voice.

Chunk 5

74 The village agreed with Walter, but the snake stayed on. His box remained by the kitchen door with its screen wire covering. Two or three days later it had digested its meal of frogs and literally came to life. It rattled at every movement in the kitchen or the yard. One day as Delia came down the kitchen steps she saw his chalky-white fangs curved like **scimitars** hung in the wire meshes. This time she did not run away with averted eyes as usual. She stood for a long time in the doorway in a red fury that grew bloodier for every second that she regarded the creature that was her torment.

75 That night she broached the subject as soon as Sykes sat down to the table.

76 "Sykes, Ah wants you tuh take dat snake 'way fum heah. You done starved me an' Ah put up widcher, you done beat me an Ah took dat, but you done kilt all mah insides bringin' dat varmint heah."

77 Sykes poured out a saucer full of coffee and drank it deliberately before he answered her.

78 "A whole lot Ah keer 'bout how you feels inside uh out. Dat snake aint goin' no damn wheah till Ah gits ready fuh 'im tuh go. So fur as beatin' is concerned, yuh aint took near all dat you gointer take ef yuh stay 'roun' *me*."

79 Delia pushed back her plate and got up from the table. "Ah hates you, Sykes," she said calmly. "Ah hates you tuh de same degree dat Ah useter love yuh. Ah done took an' took till mah belly is full up tuh mah neck. Dat's de reason Ah got mah letter fum de church an' moved mah membership tuh Woodbridge—so Ah don't haftuh take no sacrament wid yuh. Ah don't wantuh see yuh 'roun' me a-tall. Lay 'roun' wid dat 'oman all yuh wants tuh, but gwan 'way fum me an' mah house. Ah hates yuh lak uh suck-egg dog."

80 Sykes almost let the huge wad of corn bread and collard greens he was chewing fall out of his mouth in amazement. He had a hard time whipping himself up to the proper fury to try to answer Delia.

81 "Well, Ah'm glad you does hate me. Ah'm sho' tiahed uh you hangin' ontuh me. Ah don't want yuh. Look at yuh stringey ole neck! Yo' rawbony laigs an' arms is enough tuh cut uh man tuh death. You looks jes' lak de devvul's doll-baby tuh *me*. You cain't hate me no worse dan Ah hates you. Ah been hatin' *you* fuh years."

scimitars: swords with a curved blade

Scaffolding the Text-Dependent Questions

14. How is the story structured overall? How does this structure build meaning for the reader? What types of writing does the author include in the story: dialogue, description, action, flashback? How are the parts of the story arranged? How does the arrangement affect readers? RL.11-12.5

82 "Yo' ole black hide don't look lak nothin' tuh me, but uh **passle** uh wrinkled up rubber, wid yo' big ole yeahs flappin' on each side lak uh paih uh buzzard wings. Don't think Ah'm gointuh be run 'way fum mah house neither. Ah'm goin' tuh de white folks bout *you*, mah young man, de very nex' time you lay yo' han's on me. Mah cup is done run ovah." Delia said this with no signs of fear and Sykes departed from the house, threatening her, but made not the slightest move to carry out any of them.

Chunk 6

83 That night he did not return at all, and the next day being Sunday, Delia was glad she did not have to quarrel before she hitched up her pony and drove the four miles to Woodbridge.

84 She stayed to the night service—"love feast"—which was very warm and full of spirit. In the emotional winds her domestic trials were borne far and wide so that she sang as she drove homeward,

> Jurden water, black an' col'
>
> Chills de body, not de soul
>
> An' Ah wantah cross Jurden in uh calm time.

85 She came from the barn to the kitchen door and stopped.

86 "Whut's de mattah, ol' satan, you aint kickin' up yo' racket?" She addressed the snake's box. Complete silence. She went on into the house with a new hope in its birth struggles. Perhaps her threat to go to the white folks had frightened Sykes! Perhaps he was sorry! Fifteen years of misery and suppression had brought Delia to the place where she would hope *anything* that looked towards a way over or through her wall of inhibitions.

87 She felt in the match safe behind the stove at once for a match. There was only one there.

88 "Dat niggah wouldn't fetch nothin' heah tuh save his rotten neck, but he kin run thew whut Ah brings quick enough. Now he done toted off nigh on tuh haff uh box uh matches. He done had dat 'oman heah in mah house, too."

89 Nobody but a woman could tell how she knew this even before she struck the match. But she did and it put her into a new fury.

90 Presently she brought in the tubs to put the white things to soak. This time she decided she need not bring the hamper out of the bedroom; she would go in there and do the sorting. She picked up the pot-bellied lamp and went in. The room was small and the hamper stood hard by the foot of the white iron bed. She could sit and reach through the bedposts—resting as she worked.

My Notes

passle: large number

ACTIVITY 4.9 continued

16 Ask students to read Chunk 6 independently or with partners. Guide them to mark the text for references to the snake as they read: "Dat ol' scratch is woke up now!" (paragraph 98) is an allusion that connects the snake to the imagery of the devil.

GRAMMAR & USAGE

Language Change

Our world is vast, and throughout the world, dialect and speech have varied from place to place and over time. For this reason, authors sometimes use their own experiences to light up a story with language that may be considered complex. For example, phrases in "Sweat" may include nonconventional variations in spelling, grammar, punctuation, and meaning, such as:

- "... Mah *sweat is done paid for this house* ..." (paragraph 20)
- "... *jez ez reg' lar ez de weeks roll roun'* ..." (paragraph 33)
- "*Too much knockin'* ..." (paragraph 37)

These words give a more accurate account of the story as it plays out in the author's mind.

Find two examples in the text of phrases that include variations in dialect and work with a partner to discuss the literal meaning of the phrases.

As a group, evaluate why an author might choose to use a nonconventional word or phrase in a story.

91 "Ah wantah cross Jurden in uh calm time." She was singing again. The mood of the "love feast" had returned. She threw back the lid of the basket almost gaily. Then, moved by both horror and terror, she sprang back toward the door. *There lay the snake in the basket!* He moved sluggishly at first, but even as she turned round and round, jumped up and down in an insanity of fear, he began to stir vigorously. She saw him pouring his awful beauty from the basket upon the bed, then she seized the lamp and ran as fast as she could to the kitchen. The wind from the open door blew out the light and the darkness added to her terror. She sped to the darkness of the yard, slamming the door after her before she thought to set down the lamp. She did not feel safe even on the ground, so she climbed up in the hay barn.

92 There for an hour or more she lay sprawled upon the hay a gibbering wreck.

93 Finally, she grew quiet, and after that, coherent thought. With this, stalked through her a cold, bloody rage. Hours of this. A period of introspection, a space of retrospection, then a mixture of both. Out of this an awful calm.

94 "Well, Ah done de bes' Ah could. If things aint right, Gawd knows taint mah fault."

95 She went to sleep—a twitchy sleep—and woke up to a faint gray sky. There was a loud hollow sound below. She peered out. Sykes was at the wood-pile, demolishing a wire-covered box.

96 He hurried to the kitchen door, but hung outside there some minutes before he entered, and stood some minutes more inside before he closed it after him.

97 The gray in the sky was spreading. Delia descended without fear now, and crouched beneath the low bedroom window. The drawn shade shut out the dawn, shut in the night. But the thin walls held back no sound.

98 "Dat ol' scratch is woke up now!" She mused at the tremendous whirr inside, which every woodsman knows, is one of the sound illusions. The rattler is a ventriloquist. His whirr sounds to the right, to the left, straight ahead, behind, close under foot—everywhere but where it is. Woe to him who guesses wrong unless he is prepared to hold up his end of the argument! Sometimes he strikes without rattling at all.

99 Inside, Sykes heard nothing until he knocked a pot lid off the stove while trying to reach the match safe in the dark. He had emptied his pockets at Bertha's.

100 The snake seemed to wake up under the stove and Sykes made a quick leap into the bedroom. In spite of the gin he had had, his head was clearing now.

101 "Mah Gawd!" he chattered, "ef Ah could on'y strack uh light!"

102 The rattling ceased for a moment as he stood paralyzed. He waited. It seemed that the snake waited also.

103 "Oh, fuh de light! Ah thought he'd be too sick"—Sykes was muttering to himself when the whirr began again, closer, right underfoot this time. Long before this, Sykes' ability to think had been flattened down to primitive instinct and he leaped—onto the bed.

104 Outside Delia heard a cry that might have come from a maddened chimpanzee, a stricken gorilla. All the terror, all the horror, all the rage that man possibly could express, without a recognizable human sound.

105 A tremendous stir inside there, another series of animal screams, the intermittent whirr of the reptile. The shade torn violently down from the window, letting in the red dawn, a huge brown hand seizing the window stick, great dull blows upon the wooden floor punctuating the gibberish of sound long after the rattle of the snake had abruptly subsided. All this Delia could see and hear from her place beneath the window, and it made her ill. She crept over to the four-o'clocks and stretched herself on the cool earth to recover.

106 She lay there. "Delia, Delia!" She could hear Sykes calling in a most despairing tone as one who expected no answer. The sun crept on up, and he called. Delia could not move—her legs were gone flabby. She never moved, he called, and the sun kept rising.

107 "Mah Gawd!" She heard him moan, "Mah Gawd fum Heben!" She heard him stumbling about and got up from her flower-bed. The sun was growing warm. As she approached the door she heard him call out hopefully, "Delia, is dat you Ah heah?"

108 She saw him on his hands and knees as soon as she reached the door. He crept an inch or two toward her—all that he was able, and she saw his horribly swollen neck and his one open eye shining with hope. A surge of pity too strong to support bore her away from that eye that must, could not, fail to see the tubs. He would see the lamp. Orlando with its doctors was too far. She could scarcely reach the Chinaberry tree, where she waited in the growing heat while inside she knew the cold river was creeping up and up to extinguish that eye which must know by now that she knew.

⬿ Knowledge Quest
- Based on your highlights, how do you picture the story's setting?
- What language does the author use to write about Delia's self awareness?

GRAMMAR & USAGE

Sentence Fragments
In paragraph 105, Hurston uses three **sentence fragments**, or incomplete sentences, to describe what Delia sees and hears. The first two fragments focus on sound and lack the verbs necessary to make them complete sentences. The third focuses on movement. The fragments in this paragraph are deliberate snapshots of sounds, actions, and colors that work together to create a vivid scene. Write your own series of three fragment sentences in Hurston's style to describe a scene from your day.

four-o'clocks: a flower that opens in the cool of the evening

ACTIVITY 4.9 continued

17 Once the reading is complete, poll students to find out whether they think Sykes deserves his fate. Facilitate a discussion regarding Delia's culpability in Sykes's death. Then ask students to locate and explain text that foreshadows the story's end.

18 Be sure students attend to the Grammar & Usage features earlier in the activity. Allow students time to work with a partner to find examples of language changes in the text and discuss with a group.

19 After reading the text for the first time, guide students in a brief discussion by asking the Knowledge Quest questions. Revisit students' annotations and elicit information about the story's setting and characters.

Scaffolding the Text-Dependent Questions

15. How does the end of the story affect the reader? In what ways does the outcome reflect one or more of the themes in the story and its historical context? What happens at the end of the story? Why might readers expect or not expect this outcome? What happens that reflects other actions and outcomes of the time period during which Hurston wrote the story? RL.11-12.2

16. Which common themes of the times does the story reflect? In what ways does the story differ from those themes and ideals? What is Delia's main goal in the story? Look back at paragraphs 74 and 82. What were the goals of people in African American society at the time? RL.11-12.2

20 RETURNING TO THE TEXT:
During the second reading, students will be returning to the text to answer the text-dependent comprehension questions. You may choose to have students reread and work on the questions in a variety of ways:

- independently
- in pairs
- in small groups
- together as a class

21 Have students answer the text-dependent questions. If they have difficulty, scaffold the questions by rephrasing them or breaking them into smaller parts. See the Scaffolding the Text-Dependent Questions boxes for suggestions.

4.9

Returning to the Text

- Return to the short story as you respond to the following questions. Use text evidence to support your responses.
- Write any additional questions you have about the text in your Reader/Writer Notebook.

4. What role does dialect play in the development of the tone of the story?

Dialect is the common language spoken in a certain area. In this case, the dialect used in the story provides insight into the characters' backgrounds and attitudes. It portrays the setting and forces readers to hear the characters' voices as they read. The author uses this technique to convey a sense of oral storytelling that seems to drift along and then surprise the reader.

5. How do the words and actions of Sykes in paragraphs 46 foreshadow possible events in the story? Why might Sykes be "hoping, *praying*, for an argument" in paragraph 9? How does it shape your perception of him?

The author's descriptions of Syke's appearance and behavior shape the audience's perception of Sykes as manipulative and bullying. In paragraph 4, Sykes reacts to Delia's fear of the snake by "standing there bent over with laughter at her fright," which foreshadows that he will use Delia's fear against her again. It also foreshadows that snakes will play a role in the story.

6. How does the author describe Delia's character? Why is establishing this important to the story?

Readers need to understand Delia's character to grasp not only how she changes during the story but why this change is important. At first Delia is worn down and meek, as seen in paragraphs 11 and 17 [a] "her thin, stooped shoulders sagged further"—but then "Delia's habitual meekness seemed to slip from her shoulders like a blown scarf."

7. How does the author choose to give exposition about the characters? How does this choice contribute to the meaning of the story?

Delia reminds Sykes in paragraph 20: "Mah tub of suds is filled yo' belly with vittles more times than yo' hands is filled it." In paragraph 25, the metaphor "[a]nything like flowers had long ago been drowned in the salty stream that had been pressed from her heart" shows that if there had ever been romance in the marriage, her tears have washed it away. Knowing the role of the past leads to an understanding of why Delia changes.

8. Why does Delia reflect in paragraph 25 that "debris ... cluttered their matrimonial trail"? What is the significance of this in relation to the overall theme and to the story's placement as part of the Harlem Renaissance?

One of the themes of the time period was letting go of the pain of the past and reaching

toward the future. Delia does the same as the story progresses, and this scene lays the

foundation for her reaching toward the future and practicing self-determination.

9. **KQ** What role do Delia's memories have in creating a sense of self-awareness? How do these memories eventually cause her to change her character?

Delia's memories of a younger self remind her of the sharp contrast between then and now.

Delia is aware that she feels less beautiful and more weary. She realizes that these changes

have come from life's stressful circumstances, and little by little, she persists.

10. Why are the neighborhood men against Sykes? How do their views contribute to a theme of the story?

According to Moss in paragraph 34, "Sykes Jones aint wuth de shot an' powder hit would tek

tuh kill 'em." Clarke offers a summary opinion in paragraph 41: "Taint no law on earth dat kin

make a man be decent if it aint in 'im." He then expands on Elijah's comments about beating

and using women up, which reinforces the theme that women like Delia are individuals with a

right to life, emotion, and recognition.

11. What point of view does the author use to tell the story? How does her choice contribute to the effectiveness of the story? How would the story change if it were told from a different point of view?

The author tells the story in third-person point of view. An omniscient narrator tells Delia's

story with insight into her thoughts and emotions yet in a more detached way than if Delia told

the story in first person. The elements of omniscience and detachment emphasize the emotion

of the story more than if it had been recited in first-person point of view.

12. What figurative language does the author use to describe Delia's response to Bertha living in town? In what ways is this consistent or inconsistent with what the reader knows of Delia's character?

The metaphor in paragraph 59 reveals Delia's hardworking and religious character: "Delia's work-worn knees crawled over the earth in Gethsemane and up the rocks of Calvary many, many times during these months." The metaphor pictures Delia's self-sacrifice in "her efforts to be blind and deaf" along with a possible image of her prayers for strength to keep going. The fact that Delia keeps to herself and endures in silence is also alluded to with this metaphor.

13. **KQ** Why might the author use the word *pouring* to describe the snake's action in paragraph 91?

The author uses pouring as imagery for how the snake heaves itself out of Delia's laundry tub and onto the floor. By using the word pouring, the author is saying that the snake moves as fast as water, or that it looks quick, fluid, or oozing as it moves out of the tub.

14. How is the story structured overall? How does this structure build meaning for the reader?

In between sections of dialogue, the author intersperses paragraphs of description. This provides a breath, or pause, in the reader's interpretation of the diction Hurston employs. The descriptive paragraphs serve as transitions between scenes, creating a clarity that aids in understanding the story. Brief descriptive sentences within sections of dialogue also provide breaks for readers, allowing them to make sure they understand what is said.

15. How does the end of the story affect the reader? In what ways does the outcome reflect one or more of the themes in the story and its historical context?

The end surprises the reader, not in fact but in method. Delia survives through her self-determination and desire to rise above circumstances, as those who participated in the Harlem Renaissance envisioned.

16. Which common themes of the times does the story reflect? In what ways does the story differ from those themes and ideals?

Over the course of the story, Delia begins to stand up for herself, which echoes the Harlem Renaissance theme of African Americans standing up for their rights and to have their voices heard. But the main difference between this story and the larger movement is that Delia doesn't pursue a collective consciousness or unity with a group of like-minded people; her survival is an individual pursuit.

4.9

 Knowledge Quest

After reading Hurston's works, think about how Delia's self-awareness helped her to focus on a higher purpose. With a partner, discuss how self-awareness can create hope for a positive outcome out of a negative situation. Answer these questions: *What is self-awareness? How can a person's self-awareness help him or her make the right decisions? Why is it important to "check in" with your feelings about a subject?* After your discussion, write down your thoughts and opinions in the space. Be sure to:

- Respond thoughtfully to diverse perspectives.
- Determine any additional information needed to propel the discussion.
- Promote a civil, democratic discussion.

 INDEPENDENT READING LINK

You can continue to build your knowledge about this theme by reading related fiction at ZINC Reading Labs. Select the **fiction** filter and type keywords such as *self* or *perception* in the **Search all ZINC articles** field.

ZINC

Working from the Text

17. "Sweat" is steeped in Christian symbolism, a sign of the culture Hurston was raised in and was writing for. Work with a partner to find allusions to the Bible and Christian symbols in the story. Explain how the literary device of allusions creates meaning in the text.

Allusions	Effect on the Text
Some allusions include:	Traditional symbol of treacherous or wicked influence
Snake: Garden of Eden	
Delia calls the snake "ol' satan" and "ol' scratch"	Delia associates the snake (and perhaps by association Sykes) with the Devil.
"Delia's work-worn knees crawled over the earth in Gethsemane and up the rocks of Calvary ..."	Delia is compared to Jesus, suffering and sacrificing. This puts all the blame on Sykes.
"Mah cup is done run ovah"	Delia quotes the 23rd Psalm, but with a slightly different meaning.
Crossing the River Jordan to the Promised Land	

22 Return to the Knowledge Question presented to students. Have them work with a partner on the Closing the Knowledge Quest task to reflect on their understanding of self-awareness. Ask volunteers to share their responses with the class.

23 Encourage students to continue building knowledge on this topic by reading related fiction at ZINC Reading Labs in the Independent Reading Link.

24 Review with students what the term *Christian symbolism* might mean and ask volunteers to share examples they noticed in the story. Discuss what it means to use the literary device of allusion, its effect on a story, and the sense a reader makes of it. Have students complete the Working from the Text activity by filling out the graphic organizer in pairs and then compare their answers with another pair.

25 After time for group discussion, have students complete student step 17 independently and ask volunteers to share their answers.

26 Elicit from students the difference between diction and syntax as well as what the terms *mood, voice,* and *tone* mean. Guide students to read the Language & Writer's Craft feature on levels of diction. Then have them complete the Practice portion and share it with a partner.

LEVELED DIFFERENTIATED INSTRUCTION

In this activity, students might need support analyzing the author's use of different levels of diction in a text.

Developing Review the definitions of *neutral diction* and *dialect* and then read aloud examples from the story to highlight the differences between the two. Have small groups use the **Word Choice Analyzer** graphic organizer to examine both neutral diction and dialect in the story.

Expanding Review the definitions of *neutral diction* and *dialect*. Have partners review the story, using the **Word Choice Analyzer** graphic organizer to decipher the meaning of examples of each. Have them discuss ways in which neutral diction and dialect differ and then revise the phrases of neutral diction into dialect and vice versa.

Bridging Have partners use the **Word Choice Analyzer** graphic organizer to decipher the meaning of phrases from each of the four levels of diction in the story. Circulate to assist as needed, especially as partners revise these examples from one level to the next.

27 Read aloud the information in the Literary Analysis section. Elicit from students any previous experience they have writing a literary analysis and any tips or frustrations they encountered. Make sure students understand the difference between summary and analysis.

28 Have a volunteer read aloud the Writing Prompt and encourage students to ask any questions they might have about what it entails.

4.9

18. Look back over the chart you filled out in order to discuss and write a brief analysis of what specific purpose Huston's use of allusions achieves in the text.

LANGUAGE & WRITER'S CRAFT: Levels of Diction

An author can choose to use a variety of diction and syntax in order to shape the mood, voice, or tone of their writing. Huston is known for using different levels of diction, including dialect, in her writing. Review the levels of diction summarized and the following examples.

Formal or high diction usually contains words that make the tone sound educated. It uses complicated syntax and effective and impressive word choices. Unlike informal diction, formal diction avoids slang, contractions, and other informal expressions.

Example: *In Zora Neale Hurston's short story "Sweat," she alternates between a neutral narrative voice and the specific Floridian dialect of her characters in dialogue, revealing sociological context about the setting and the background cultural influences that shape their lives.*

Neutral diction uses ordinary words and syntax without complicated words. It can include some elements of informal diction, such as contractions.

Example: *In Zora Neale Hurston's short story "Sweat," she switches between a narrator's voice and the dialect of her characters in dialogue. The difference shows the setting and context of the characters' lives.*

Informal or low diction is the type of relaxed language people use in typical conversations. Contractions, slang, and idioms are some typical markers of this type of diction.

Example: *In "Sweat," Hurston flips between a narrator's voice and characters talking in dialect. It's hard to understand the dialect sometimes, but it shows where the characters are from.*

Dialect is regional language, which has its own syntax, words, and grammar. In literature, dialect often divides characters into different sectors of society.

Example: *Well, Ah done de bes' Ah could. If things aint right, Gawd knows taint mah fault.*

PRACTICE Find one example of each level that Hurston uses in "Sweat." Choose one sentence and revise it into a different level of diction. Compare your revision with a partner's and discuss how it changes the voice of text.

4.9

Literary Analysis

The purpose of a response-to-literature essay is to demonstrate thoughtful understanding of a literary passage. Writing a literary analysis begins with planning what aspects you will analyze through brainstorming, outlining, and finding textual evidence to support your analysis. With the information you've gathered, you can then craft an analysis of the text and the author's stylistic technique and support it with textual evidence to convey meaning to the reader. A literary analysis includes the following:

- a well-crafted thesis statement that demonstrates understanding of the literary element being analyzed
- body paragraphs that cite textual evidence to support the thesis
- effective transitions that connect ideas and move smoothly through the essay
- original commentary on the writer's response to the literature
- concluding statements that follow from the ideas introduced in the thesis and developed in the essay

Writing Prompt: Literary Analysis

Analyze the extent to which Hurston's story is a tribute to the lives of ordinary African American people. Choose a method of prewriting and then draft a response to this story. In your analysis, address the literary elements you have studied, including Hurston's use of diction, and explain how her use of diction and syntax shapes the mood, voice, and tone of the story. Your writing should be composed using only formal diction. Be sure to:

- Choose a writing structure that conveys your purpose, audience, topic, and context.
- Include a thesis statement that analyzes the author's use of diction and syntax.
- Cite textual evidence and give commentary to support your analysis.
- Provide a conclusion that restates your claim and supports the ideas developed in the argument.

Revising and Editing with Peer Review

After you have completed your draft, pair with a writing partner and read your partner's essay. You'll be reading each other's essays to help improve clarity, development of ideas, organization, style, word choices, and sentence structure. Provide peer response by giving the following feedback:

- Underline the thesis statement. Does the thesis give direction to the essay?
- Underline the topic sentence in each body paragraph.
- Put a wavy line under any sentence that feels unclear or out of place.
- Place a box around any language that doesn't seem formal or academic or where another word might be more appropriate.
- If you find textual evidence not followed by documentation, write a suggestion in the margin for either a lead-in or a parenthetical method of citing the source.
- Place a * on commentary sentences that precede or follow the textual evidence.
- If commentary is missing, make a note in the margin indicating the need to add it.
- Mark the explanation about Hurston's use of diction with a +.
- Highlight the sentences that clearly discuss how the literary elements add meaning to the text.
- Note any places where syntax is choppy or overly wordy or where standard English conventions are not being used properly.
- Circle the conclusion.

WRITING PROMPT: LITERARY ANALYSIS

The following standards are addressed in the Writing Prompt:
- W.11-12.4
- W.11-12.2a
- W.11-12.2b
- W.11-12.2f

ACTIVITY 4.9 continued

29 As students complete the Writing Prompt, you may want to provide a series of possible sentence starters for the thesis. For example: *While Zora Neale Hurston's story "Sweat" uses a specific dialect in order to _____.*

30 Suggest that students construct outlines or graphic organizers that are structured according to the literary elements they plan to discuss. Then allow students time to complete a **draft** of their literary analysis.

31 Have students pair up to read Revising and Editing with Peer Review. As a class, discuss the importance of getting feedback on writing and then role-play with a volunteer how to offer constructive feedback. If necessary, write sentence frames on the board to help guide positive and constructive conversations, such as: *I really enjoyed _____. Have you considered trying to _____ to make this part more _____?*

32 Remind students to complete the Independent Reading Link. Review levels of diction as needed.

ASSESS

Use students' responses to the Writing Prompt to assess their ability to write a coherent and insightful literary analysis. Students should demonstrate thoughtful analysis of Hurston's diction and its effect on mood, voice, and tone. Ask students to submit both a first draft and a revised draft with evidence of peer revision and editing.

ADAPT

If students have not mastered the elements of literary analysis writing, have them work in pairs to outline their ideas before they begin writing.

PLAN

Materials: highlighters, draft responses from Activity 4.9
Suggested Pacing: 1 50-minute class period

TEACH

1 Read aloud the Learning Targets and Preview with students. Clarify any definitions that students need to know for the lesson.

2 Introduce the topic of types of clauses by writing or projecting the following examples on the board:

- *The class listened.* (independent clause)
- *While the teacher spoke* (dependent clause)

3 Ask students which of the examples is a complete sentence. If they need guidance, point out the independent clause (*The class listened*) and ask them to identify the subject (*The class*) and verb (*listened*). Explain that this makes it a complete sentence. Elicit ideas from students about why the second sentence is incomplete. Help them notice that the word *while* makes it seem that something is missing.

4 Read aloud the first paragraph in the Analyzing Types of Clauses section.

5 Have students complete the task in student step 1. In addition to writing the number of independent clauses next to each sentence, students could also label the subject(s) and verb(s) that make up each independent clause. Review responses and clarify as needed.

6 Ask a student volunteer to read aloud the paragraph about dependent clauses. Label the marker word *while* in the example *While the teacher spoke* and explain to students that noticing words like this can help them identify dependent clauses.

7 In student step 2, students should highlight the marker words that they identify.

Learning Targets

- Understand how different types of clauses combine to form complete sentences.
- Analyze the use of sentence fragments for effect.
- Apply an understanding of sentence boundaries and punctuation when revising writing.

Preview

In this activity, you will analyze different types of clauses in order to create complete sentences as well as how sentence fragments can be used for literary effect.

Analyzing Types of Clauses

Knowing the difference between types of clauses can help writers identify complete and incomplete sentences when revising their work. For a sentence to be considered complete, it must contain at least one **independent clause**. At a minimum, an independent clause includes a subject and a verb, and it expresses a complete idea.

1. Look at these examples from "Sweat" by Zora Neale Hurston. How many independent clauses does each sentence contain?

   She peered out. 1

   The sun had burned July to August. 1

   Grass withered, leaves browned, snakes went blind in shedding, and men and dogs went mad. 4

   She picked up the pot-bellied lamp and went in. 1

In addition to at least one independent clause, a sentence may contain dependent clauses. Like an independent clause, a **dependent clause** contains a subject and a verb. However, a dependent clause cannot stand alone as a complete sentence because it does not express a complete idea. Dependent clauses often include a word such as *as, because, before, if, since, unless, when,* or *while,* which shows that the clause needs more information.

2. Read the following sentences from "Sweat." Mark any words that introduce a dependent clause. Then identify the independent and dependent clauses in each sentence.

   She wondered, but started to go on into the house without speaking, even though he was standing in the kitchen door and she must either stoop under his arm or ask him to move.

   As she was stooping to pass under his outstretched arm, he suddenly pushed her backward.

   That night she broached the subject as soon as Sykes sat down to the table.

College and Career Readiness Standards

Focus Standards:

W.11-12.5 Develop and strengthen writing as needed by planning, revising, editing, rewriting, or trying a new approach, focusing on addressing what is most significant for a specific purpose and audience.

L.11-12.2 Demonstrate command of the conventions of standard English capitalization, punctuation, and spelling when writing.

Additional Standards Addressed:

W.11-12.4

Using Sentence Fragments for Effect

If a group of words written as a sentence lacks at least one independent clause, it is a sentence fragment. In academic contexts, writers typically avoid sentence fragments because fragments can make writing seem informal or unclear. However, fragments are often used by literary writers—especially in works of fiction—to create effect.

> **3.** Read the excerpt from "Sweat" and mark any sentence fragments. Then discuss with a partner why the author might have chosen to use fragments in this passage.
>
> Finally, she grew quiet, and after that, coherent thought. With this, stalked through her a cold, bloody rage. Hours of this. A period of introspection, a space of retrospection, then a mixture of both. Out of this an awful calm.

Using Complete Sentences in Formal Writing

While writers sometimes make intentional choices to use sentence fragments for effect, it is important to be able to recognize and correct the unintentional use of incomplete or incorrectly punctuated sentences in your own writing. More often than not, following the conventions of academic writing will help you communicate clearly with your audience.

4. Read the descriptions of common sentence errors and the examples of each in the chart. Revise each example sentence into a complete, conventional sentence with conventional punctuation.

Common Sentence Errors	Example	Conventional Sentence
Sentence fragment: a group of words that lacks an independent clause	"All the terror, all the horror, all the rage that man possibly could express..."	Possible response: He made a sound that expressed all the terror, all the horror, and all the rage that man possibly could express.
Run-on sentence: two or more independent clauses joined by short connector words—such as *and, but, or*—without necessary punctuation (usually a comma or semicolon)	The author uses many allusions in the story but the snake is the most obvious symbol and it carries both literal and metaphorical significance.	Possible response: The author uses many allusions in the story, but the snake is the most obvious symbol to many readers. It carries both literal and metaphorical significance.

8 Read aloud the Using Sentence Fragments for Effect section. Explain that fragments are not always inappropriate in writing and that they can be used purposefully to create a specific effect, like creating tension or a unique tone.

9 Have students complete the first task in student step 3 and then ask them to **think-pair-share** their ideas about why the author would choose to write in fragments. Consider reading the excerpt aloud to emphasize the intended effect.

10 Have a student read aloud the Using Complete Sentences in Formal Writing section. Have them quickly brainstorm a few kinds of formal and informal writing (e.g., social media posts, text messages, fictional stories, class writing assignments, Embedded Assessments). As a whole group, discuss whether sentence fragments would be considered appropriate in each.

11 For student step 4, use a **jigsaw** by combining students in groups of four and assigning one type of error to each student in the group. Have students become "experts" on their assigned error by reading the example and then writing the conventional sentence. Then have students take turns explaining each error to their group members.

12 Ask volunteers to share their revised sentences so that different correction options can be reviewed as a class. Consider having the student volunteers write their revisions on the board for the entire class to see.

13 Have students mark the Revising text to show how they would change each sentence to eliminate errors. There are multiple ways to revise the paragraph, but the original text appears in blue in the teacher edition.

LC 4.9

Common Sentence Errors	Example	Conventional Sentence
Comma splice: two or more independent clauses joined with only a comma	Delia deserves respect, the neighborhood men think Sykes is worthless.	Possible response: Delia deserves respect, while the neighborhood men think Sykes is worthless.
Fused sentence: two or more independent clauses joined without punctuation or connector words	Delia looked over Sykes looked at the ground.	Possible response: Delia looked over; Sykes looked at the ground.

Revising

Read the following paragraph from an article about Zora Neale Hurston's hometown of Eatonville, Florida. Identify sentences that need to be revised in order to be considered complete sentences with correct punctuation. Annotate the paragraph to show how you would revise it.

[1] It may be small and hard to find but Eatonville is important for two reasons, it was the first all-black incorporated town in the United States, it was the childhood home of Zora Neale Hurston. [2] Much of Hurston's writing is set here, many of her characters are thinly disguised versions of actual residents. [3] Eatonville gave Hurston her best material and a few years ago the favor was returned. [4] The Hurston connection gave Eatonville an argument; to save itself from being paved over. [5] Hurston and Eatonville have always been closely linked. To understand one. You have to understand the other.

[1] It may be small and hard to find, but Eatonville is important for two reasons: it was the first all-black incorporated town in the United States, and it was the childhood home of Zora Neale Hurston. [2] Much of Hurston's writing is set here, and many of her characters are thinly disguised versions of actual residents. [3] Eatonville gave Hurston her best material, and a few years ago, the favor was returned. [4] The Hurston connection gave Eatonville an argument to save itself from being paved over. [5] Hurston and Eatonville have always been closely linked: to understand one, you have to understand the other.

Check Your Understanding

Looking at the paragraph you just revised, think about what questions you might ask the writer to help her revise sentences that are incomplete or that need different punctuation. Add these questions to your Editor's Checklist as a reminder to check your own work for complete, correctly punctuated sentences.

Questions may include: Do I have any run-on sentences that need a punctuation mark, such as a comma? Do I have dependent clauses that need to be connected to independent clauses in order to be a complete idea?

Practice

In Activity 4.9, you reviewed a peer's response to the Writing Prompt about the story "Sweat." Exchange your draft again—with the same peer or a different partner—and examine the writing specifically for correct use of complete sentences with correct punctuation. Put an exclamation point next to any incomplete or incorrectly punctuated sentences and work with your partner to revise them.

14 Allow students time to complete Check Your Understanding task. Remind them to use constructive, specific language when coming up with questions to ask the writer. Ask volunteers to share the questions they came up with.

15 Read aloud the instructions in the Practice section. Model for students how to identify and mark incomplete or incorrectly punctuated sentences by writing a few sentences on the board as examples. Then allow students time to complete the Practice section with a partner.

ASSESS

Student work should show that they are able to consistently make proper punctuation choices for sentences in their writing and recognize when they make unintentional errors or sentence fragmentation choices.

ADAPT

If students need additional practice, consider having them look for purposeful use of fragments as they continue to read *Their Eyes Were Watching God* throughout Unit 4. This will provide occasions for students to analyze sentence fragments and the use of punctuation to form complete sentences. Additionally, Hurston's shifts between dialect and narration provide clear opportunities to address how a writer uses sentence punctuation and fragmentation intentionally for effect.

ACTIVITY 4.10

PLAN

Materials: *Their Eyes Were Watching God*, Chapter 1; *Their Eyes Were Watching God*, film (2005), directed by Darnell Martin; double-entry journals

Suggested pacing: 2 50-minute class periods

TEACH

1 Read aloud the Learning Targets and Preview with students. Write the terms *explicit meaning, implicit meaning, direct characterization, indirect characterization,* and *foreshadowing* on the board. Elicit from students the differences between explicit meaning and implicit meaning as well as between direct characterization and indirect characterization. Write their answers on the board in T-chart columns and point students to examples in the text they just read if possible by first examining one of the characters in "Sweat" for direct and indirect characterization. In addition, ask students to define and provide examples of foreshadowing in books or movies.

2 Read aloud the information in The Double-Entry Journal for students, pausing to demonstrate or model on the board or projector. Then read aloud the first three paragraphs of *Their Eyes Were Watching God*. Have students help with a summary of the text and add the summary to the left side of a double-entry journal model you draw on the board. Elicit from students any questions, details, connections, predictions, or inferences about the first three paragraphs and add those to the right column of the model journal.

3 Explain to students the purpose of keeping the **double-entry journal**: to document their insights and keep a record of textual evidence that might support their thinking for Embedded Assessment 2.

4 Read aloud the Predicting Using Text Features section and have students discuss their prediction with a classmate. Ask volunteers to share their predictions and then write them on the board in a connected mind map you draw around the title of the novel.

Learning Strategies

Double-Entry Journal
Oral Interpretation
Quickwrite
Think-Pair-Share

My Notes

Learning Targets

- Discuss explicit and implicit meaning of a text.
- Identify and analyze direct and indirect characterization.
- Analyze how foreshadowing shapes the author's portrayal of the plot.

Preview

In this activity, you will begin reading the novel *Their Eyes Were Watching God* in order to make predictions, discuss meaning, analyze the author's use of characterization, and evaluate the use of foreshadowing.

The Double-Entry Journal

1. As you read *Their Eyes Were Watching God*, you will take notes in a double-entry journal. Copy or summarize passages from the book on the left side (textual evidence) and write your response to each passage on the right side (commentary). Draw a horizontal line under each entry. For reference, record the page number of each quote.

   Responses could include the following:

   - **questions** that will help you clarify what is happening in the novel
   - **details** about characters or plot events
   - **connections** you make to personal experiences, ideas in other texts, and society
   - **predictions** about how characters will react to events
   - **inferences** (logical conclusions) about why characters are saying or doing things and the evidence that supports your inference

2. Create a double-entry journal in your Reader/Writer Notebook to use as you read and discuss the first chapter together as a class. Try to use a variety of responses (questions, detail, connection, prediction, inference). As you read the novel independently, you will continue to use the double-entry journal to note the connection between the research that has been presented about the Harlem Renaissance and the events and ideas of the novel. In your notes, cite textual evidence. Include commentary that shows how Hurston's work is characteristic of the Harlem Renaissance as well as elements that illustrate Hurston's departure from the Harlem Renaissance and its philosophy/beliefs, historical context, relation to the arts, and daily life.

Predicting Using Text Features

3. Authors choose novel titles for many reasons. For example, the protagonist in the novel *Gone with the Wind* refers to her town being overtaken by the Yankees and wonders whether her home was "also gone with the wind which had swept through Georgia." Predict the meaning of the title *Their Eyes Were Watching God*.

College and Career Readiness Standards

Focus Standards:

RL.11-12.1 Cite strong and thorough textual evidence to support analysis of what the text says explicitly as well as inferences drawn from the text, including determining where the text leaves matters uncertain.

RL.11-12.2 Determine two or more themes or central ideas of a text and analyze their development over the course of the text,

including how they interact and build on one another to produce a complex account; provide an objective summary of the text.

RL.11-12.3 Analyze the impact of the author's choices regarding how to develop and relate elements of a story or drama (e.g., where a story is set, how the action is ordered, how the characters are introduced and developed).

Beginning the Novel: Men and Women

4. Read the first two paragraphs of Chapter 1. What distinction do the first two paragraphs make between men and women?

5. What questions do these paragraphs raise for you?

6. *Male students*: Interpret and analyze the first paragraph. Note your findings and be prepared to present them to the female students in your class.

   Female students: Interpret and analyze the second paragraph. Note your findings and be prepared to present them to the male students in your class.

7. **Collaborative Conversation:** As a class, discuss the first two paragraphs of Chapter 1 and compare your interpretations of them. Take turns pointing out sentences that contain explicit meaning and sentences that contain implicit meaning and discuss their differences and how each kind of sentence aids in helping you understand the meaning of these paragraphs. Record your notes from the conversation in your Reader/Writer Notebook.

Characterization in Chapter 1

The way an author portrays characters also influences the relationship between them and the themes, setting, and plot of a text. However, authors need to find ways to create a well-rounded depiction of their characters by both telling about them and showing their actions, thoughts, and relationships. An author uses **direct characterization** to tell the audience who and what the character is:

- *So the beginning of this was a woman and she had come back from burying the dead.*

Sentences like this help the reader create a visual picture of the character in their mind. Yet just as in real life, people also gather information and first impressions about others indirectly—the way a person treats other people or behaves. An author uses **indirect characterization** to show things that reveal the personality of a character.

Methods of indirect characterization include the following:

- **the character's appearance:** *The women took the faded shirt and muddy overalls and laid them away for remembrance.*
- **what the character says:** *"Ah' m tryin' to soak some uh de tiredness and de dirt outa muh feet."*
- **what the character thinks:** *Seeing the woman as she was made them remember the envy they had stored up from other times.*
- **what the character does:** *Her speech was pleasant enough, but she kept walking straight to her gate.*
- **what other characters say about a character:** *"Humph. Y' all let her yuh. If she ain' t got manners enough to stop and let folks know how she been makin' out, let her g' wan."*

My Notes

VOCABULARY

LITERARY

Indirect characterization is any method—except for direct characterization—that a writer uses to develop characters other than simply telling the reader what to think of the character.

College and Career Readiness Standards

RL.11-12.7 Analyze multiple interpretations of a story, drama, or poem (e.g., recorded or live production of a play or recorded novel or poetry), evaluating how each version interprets the source text. (Include at least one play by Shakespeare and one play by an American dramatist.)

RI.11-12.10 Cite strong and thorough textual evidence to support analysis of what the text says explicitly as well as inferences drawn from the text, including determining where the text leaves matters uncertain.

W.11-12.4 Produce clear and coherent writing in which the development, organization, and style are appropriate to task, purpose, and audience.

ACTIVITY 4.10 continued

TEACHER TO TEACHER

For students who struggle with the dialect, consider allowing them to listen to Ruby Dee's reading of the text in the film version of *Their Eyes Were Watching God*.

5 Lead a **shared reading** of the first two paragraphs of Chapter 1 and ask students to focus on the roles of men and women. Allow students time to respond to student steps 4 and 5. Next, ask students to discuss their responses in a **think-pair-share**.

6 Reread the opening passages of the novel; however, this time ask the male students to read and analyze the first paragraph and ask the female students to read and analyze the second paragraph. Guide students to understand how to identify whether a sentence contains explicit or implicit meaning. After students have analyzed and discussed their responses, lead students in a group discussion on the distinction Hurston is making between men and women.

7 **Vocabulary Development:** Review the meaning of the Literary Vocabulary *indirect characterization* with students. Have them work in pairs to define this term in their own words and compare it to *direct characterization*.

8 Read aloud the information in the Characterization in Chapter 1 section and refer students back to the earlier discussion and related board work around direct and indirect characterization. As you go through each example, elicit insight from students about what they can infer through Hurston's characterization. In reviewing characterization, ask students why Hurston chooses to have Janie introduced through others first.

9 Continue the reading of Chapter 1. Then have students work in pairs and reread the scene to explore what they know about the novel's protagonist, Janie, by filling out the chart in student step 8. If necessary, model filling out the first row of the chart for students by rereading the first three paragraphs, identifying the quote, making an inference, and deciding if it is direct or indirect. After pairs complete the chart, ask volunteers to share their observations and evidence.

10 Direct students to student step 9 and allow them time to create a few blank charts in their notebooks for the upcoming chapters.

LEVELED DIFFERENTIATED INSTRUCTION

In this activity, students might need support analyzing Janie.

Developing Prior to answering the text-dependent questions, have small groups use the **Character Map** graphic organizer to analyze Janie. Encourage them to focus on recording textual evidence that describes how she acts, what she says, and what the narrator and other characters say about her.

Expanding Have partners use the **Character Map** graphic organizer to analyze the character of Janie. Encourage them to focus on textual evidence describing how she acts and what the other characters think about her. Allow partners to share their answers with other groups to add to their notes.

Bridging Provide students with the **Character Map** graphic organizer to help them identify textual evidence from the novel about Janie's character to use when answering the higher-level characterization questions.

Extend Remind students that exposition is the beginning step of the plot mountain story structure. Have students create a plot diagram to fill in as they continue working with the novel and film in this unit. The details about Janie and the porch sitters will provide the "exposition" portion of the diagram.

4.10

8. Complete the following chart using evidence from Chapter 1.

Janie Mae Crawford		
Character Detail	How does the reader learn this?	Direct or Indirect?
She's come back after time away.	"So the beginning of this was a woman and she had come back from burying the dead."	Direct
Other people are envious of her.	"It was a weapon against her strength and if it turned out of no significance, still it was a hope that she might fall to their level some day."	Indirect
She looks different than she did when she left town—things are possibly worse for her now.	"What she doin coming back here in dem overhalls? Can't she find no dress to put on? Where's dat blue satin dress she left here in?"	Indirect
Her life while she's been gone has been a mystery to everyone.	"Well, nobody don't know if it's anything to tell or not. Me, Ah'm her best friend, and Ah don't know."	Indirect
She knows other people are judging her.	"Well, Ah see Mouth-Almighty is still sittin' in de same place. And Ah reckon they got me up in they mouth now."	Indirect

9. Continue using a chart like the one you just completed for Janie and the other characters you meet as you continue to read the novel.

College and Career Readiness Standards

SL.11-12.1c Propel conversations by posing and responding to questions that probe reasoning and evidence; ensure a hearing for a full range of positions on a topic or issue; clarify, verify, or challenge ideas and conclusions; and promote divergent and creative perspectives.

SL.11-12.1d Respond thoughtfully to diverse perspectives; synthesize comments, claims, and evidence made on all sides of an issue; resolve contradictions when possible; and determine what additional information or research is required to deepen the investigation or complete the task.

The Porch Sitters

In the novel, upon her return, Janie is greeted by the "porch sitters": townspeople sitting on porches and discussing their thoughts on ideas on where she's been and the kind of person she is. Huston uses the porch sitters as a kind of **chorus:** a group that serves to provide commentary about the action that is taking place. In ancient Greece, many playwrights used a chorus to serve as an extra narrative voice that would provide key information about everything that happened "offstage." In *Their Eyes Were Watching God*, the porch sitters fill in the blanks with conjecture about where Janie might have been and what happened before she left, helping provide the reader with context.

10. In paragraph 4, what does the author mean by saying of the porch sitters that "they sat in judgment"? What does this tell you about them and their relationship with Janie?

Huston portrays the porch sitters as judgmental of Janie's life, both before and after her return. Although they operate as a kind of chorus to fill in context and provide some indirect characterization about Janie, their view on Janie is not neutral and is possibly biased. Therefore, the reader must take their speculation of Janie with a grain of salt.

11. Revisit the role of the porch sitters in "Sweat" in Chunk 3. How do they compare to the porch sitters in Chapter 1 of *Their Eyes Were Watching God*?

The porch sitters in "Sweat" seem to serve a similar "chorus" purpose as the porch sitters in *Their Eyes Were Watching God*. They pass judgment on Delia in a similar way as the porch sitters do with Janie, particularly when it comes to how she looks and her relationship. However, they reserve the worst of their judgment for Sykes and his impact on Delia. All the same, they can't be bothered to do much more than gossip and make idle threats.

☑ Focus on the Sentence

After reading Chapter 1, reflect on how Janie is characterized. Write two sentences about how Hurston characterizes Janie starting with the subordinating conjunctions.

While Hurston uses some direct characterization in introducing Janie to the reader, she largely introduces her through the lens of how the entire town views her.

Although Janie seems to be proud and hold her head high upon her return home, Hurston shows that Janie is also aware that the town is judging her for her past.

My Notes

ACTIVITY 4.10 continued

11 Read aloud The Porch Sitters section. Elicit from students what their first impression of the porch sitters is and whether the sitters seem to be a subjective or objective "chorus."

12 You may want students to use their **oral interpretation** skills to create a Reader's Theater of the comments made by the porch sitters. If each reader stops at a dash, you could have 10 readers. Remind students that one method of indirect characterization allows readers to discover what others think of a character. Ask what these characters think of the woman returning home.

13 Have students work independently to complete student step 10 and ask them what evidence they have to support their answer.

14 Allow students time to return to "Sweat" in order to complete student step 11. Have students work with a partner to discuss the comparison between the porch sitters in both stories. Ask volunteers to share their answers. Discuss especially how the men and women talk about each other. The motif of the "porch," or "Mouth Almighty," has to do with passing judgment.

15 Have students complete the Focus on the Sentence section independently. Remind them about the difference between direct and indirect characterization and have them return the chart they completed previously to help with any ideas about how Janie is characterized.

16 Read aloud the Plot Development section with students. It might be helpful for visual learners to see on the board the difference between a linear plot (a line moving in one direction) and a nonlinear plot (a line that circles back or jumps ahead in time). Write the terms *flashback* and *foreshadowing* on the board and ask volunteers to describe the difference between them.

17 Have students work with a partner to complete student step 12. After students complete their graphic organizers, ask volunteers to share their observations and have the class vote on the result of what is being foreshadowed. Keep the predictions in a visible place so you can return to them later.

18 Read aloud student step 13 to remind students to keep track of any other instances of flashbacks and foreshadowing they come across.

19 After students have finished reading Chapter 1, model for them the recording of ideas in their double-entry journals, including page numbers and commentary. Remind students of the requirements for Embedded Assessment 2 and the elements of the Harlem Renaissance: philosophy/beliefs, historical context, the arts, and daily life. As students note evidence in their journals, they should make connections to these elements, which will serve as the basis for their analytical essays.

20 Direct students to the Comparing Different Mediums: Film section. Have students work together to compare the opening of the novel *Their Eyes Were Watching God* to the opening of the 2005 film directed by Darnell Martin. Ask: *How are the characters alike and different? How do these different mediums focus on the same aspects of the storyline but in different ways?*

21 Have students respond to the Independent Reading Link. Encourage students to conduct any additional research about references to the Harlem Renaissance in their independent reading and provide them with the time and resources to do so. Then have students compare their journal entries with a classmate.

ASSESS

In the porch sitters responses, check that students identify the conflict between Janie and the porch sitters.

ADAPT

Support students in documenting in their journals by chunking the text in Chapter 1.

To extend learning, consider adding a third column to the double-entry journal. Label this column *Harlem Renaissance*. Students can begin noting and processing how the text represents Hurston's work as a product of and a departure from the Harlem Renaissance.

4.10

🔵 INDEPENDENT READING LINK

Read and Respond

Choose a chunk of text from your independent reading selection. Following the procedure you learned in this activity, use a double-entry journal to note connections between the historical information you have learned about the Harlem Renaissance and the events and characters in your text.

Plot Development

When a writer presents the events of a story the way events happen in real life—in time order—it is called *linear plot development*. Sometimes, though, a writer needs to tell about an event from the past or hint about an event in the future. To share an event that happened at a point in time before the time of the story, a writer uses flashback. To hint at a future event, a writer uses foreshadowing. The use of such techniques is called *nonlinear plot development*.

12. Reread Janie's conversation with Pheoby in Chapter 1. Identify examples of foreshadowing and use them to make inferences. Write your evidence and inferences in the following graphic organizer.

Evidence of Foreshadowing in the Novel	Inference About What Is Being Foreshadowed

13. Continue to look for additional examples of flashbacks and foreshadowing as you read the novel and add them to your double-entry journal. Evaluate how these different literary elements shape the author's portrayal of the plot.

Comparing Different Mediums: Film

14. A novel and its accompanying film may or may not follow an identical storyline. As you watch the film *Their Eyes Were Watching God*, think about Janie Mae Crawford's character in the novel. Copy the following chart in your Reader/Writer Notebook to help you evaluate how the film interprets Janie Mae Crawford's internal traits in the novel.

Janie Mae Crawford		
Internal Trait		
How the Film Interprets This Trait		

Nanny's Story

Learning Targets

- Evaluate how Hurston's use of varying points of view shape the reader's understanding of the plot.
- Make comparisons about the message of a poem and a speech.
- Analyze how the historical, social, and economic contexts of the setting influence the plot, characterization, and theme.

Preview

In this activity, you will compare a poem by Langston Hughes and Chapter 2 of *Their Eyes Were Watching God*.

Point of View in Chapter 2

One of the hallmarks of Hurston's writing style is her use of narrative voice. She uses a variety of narrative points of view to tell the story, offer characterization, and convey a message. Authors usually choose to primarily use one point of view to tell their story:

First-person point of view comes directly from a character's perspective and uses the pronoun *I*.

Third-person omniscient point of view comes from a narrator who can see into every character's thoughts and observe their actions. It uses pronouns such as *he, she,* or *they*.

Third-person limited point of view also comes from a narrator with more distance, but he or she can only see into one character's thoughts.

Note all the points of view you find in Chapter 2. As you continue to read *Their Eyes Were Watching God*, pay attention to the way Hurston skillfully shifts between different narrative voices, or points of view.

1. In the following chart, identify the different points of view in the excerpts and describe the effect or purpose of each type.

Point of View	Example	Effect or Purpose
First-person	"And, Janie, maybe it wasn't much, but Ah done de best Ah kin by you. Ah raked and scraped and bought dis lil piece uh land so you wouldn't have to stay in de white folks' yard and tuck yo' head befo' other chillun at school."	Chapter 2 contains a long story by Nanny that is told in the first-person point of view. Its purpose is to show Nanny's experience through her own perspective rather than be told by another narrator. It has the effect of giving a different perspective than Janie's from a character who knows her well.

Learning Strategies

Double-Entry Journal
Marking the Text
Think-Pair-Share

My Notes

_____
_____
_____
_____
_____
_____
_____
_____
_____
_____
_____
_____
_____
_____
_____
_____
_____

College and Career Readiness Standards

Focus Standards:

RL.11-12.1 Cite strong and thorough textual evidence to support analysis of what the text says explicitly as well as inferences drawn from the text, including determining where the text leaves matters uncertain.

RL.11-12.2 Determine two or more themes or central ideas of a text and analyze their development over the course of the text, including how they interact and build on one another to produce a complex account; provide an objective summary of the text.

RL.11-12.3 Analyze the impact of the author's choices regarding how to develop and relate elements of a story or drama (e.g., where a story is set, how the action is ordered, how the characters are introduced and developed).

ACTIVITY 4.11

PLAN

Materials: *Their Eyes Were Watching God*, Chapter 2; double-entry journals; Key Ideas and Details graphic organizer; Evaluating Online Sources graphic organizer
Suggested Pacing: 1 50-minute class period

TEACH

1 Read aloud the Learning Targets and Preview and have a volunteer summarize what students will be doing in this activity. Lead a brief discussion asking students how historical, social, and economic contexts might influence the plot, characterization, and theme of a book or poem.

2 Remind students that Langston Hughes was a contemporary of Hurston's. Explain that the purpose of reading this poem now is to study two works with similar ideas.

3 Read aloud the Point of View in Chapter 2 section. Ask students why they think Hurston might have chosen to write from different points of view and what effects they have noticed about those points of view on the plot so far. Ask why the author begins the story with an omniscient point of view and what this point of view conveys to readers.

4 After students have read Chapter 2 or while they are reading, guide them to complete student step 1 by filling out the chart for the different points of view as they encounter them. Review the completed charts as a class to clarify each type of point of view and its effects or purpose.

5 Ask students to use the **double-entry journal** to keep track of the figurative language, especially metaphors that Nanny and Janie use to describe their lives. Notice that Nanny's images are diametrically opposed to Janie's images. **Think-pair-share** student examples of figurative language and discuss the effect of Hurston's use of figurative language to construct and reflect a character's identity.

6 Guide students to make the connection between point of view and the novel's theme of the search for self. Reread the paragraph mentioned in student step 3 so students can hear out loud how the point of view begins to change; then ask them what they noticed. Have students complete student steps 2 and 3 independently and ask volunteers to share their answers.

7 Ask a volunteer to read aloud the As You Read section. Have students explain how they know if a word relates to emotions; elicit a few examples to help the class make connections.

4.11

Point of View	Example	Effect or Purpose
Third-person omniscient	"The people all saw her come because it was sundown. The sun was gone, but he had left his footprints in the sky. It was the time for sitting on porches beside the road. It was the time to hear things and talk. These sitters had been tongueless, earless, eyeless conveniences all day long."	This point of view provides a broad perspective on the townspeople, portraying them as a group. The effect here is one that sets them apart from Janie, who is considered an outsider, and serves to demonstrate how they are similar and she is different.
Third-person omniscient	"It was a spring afternoon in West Florida. Janie had spent most of the day under a blossoming pear tree in the back-yard. She had been spending every minute that she could steal from her chores under that tree for the last three days. That was to say, ever since the first tiny bloom had opened. It had called her to come and gaze on a mystery."	The purpose of this point of view is to give a bird's-eye view of Janie in the setting she is in. It widens the context of her life and has the effect of condensing time "for the last three days." It doesn't allow the reader access to her first-person thoughts, and so the reader can only guess as to what she is thinking inside her mind.

2. **What theme does Hurston introduce with Janie's story about playing with the Washburn children?**

   As Janie looks at the picture, she does not recognize herself. With this comment, Hurston furthers the theme of search for self.

3. **At the paragraph that begins, "Pheoby's hungry listening helped Janie to tell her story," the narrative point of view begins to change. How does moving to this third-person narration affect your understanding of Janie?**

   The paragraph continues with, "So she went on thinking back to her young years ..." With this third-person limited point of view, Hurston allows us to see the workings of Janie's mind as she starts retelling her story. Continuing with the episode between Janie and Johnny Taylor, the reader gets a close look at Janie's desires and dreams. Very subtly, the third-person limited narrator becomes the omniscient narrator, for she also begins to tell us of Nanny's dream and the voices she heard, providing us with knowledge of Nanny's character.

As You Read

- Underline words that relate to emotions.
- Circle unknown words and phrases. Try to determine the meaning of the words by using context clues, word parts, or a dictionary.

College and Career Readiness Standards

RL.11-12.5 Analyze how an author's choices concerning how to structure specific parts of a text (e.g., the choice of where to begin or end a story, the choice to provide a comedic or tragic resolution) contribute to its overall structure and meaning as well as its aesthetic impact.

Additional Standards Addressed:
RL.11-12.4, RL.11-12.7, RL.11-12.9, W.11-12.4, W.11-12.8

Poetry

Mother to Son

by **Langston Hughes**

    Well, son, I'll tell you:

    Life for me ain't been no crystal stair.

    It's had tacks in it,

    And splinters,

5   And boards torn up,

    And places with no carpet on the floor—

    Bare.

    But all the time

    I'se been a-climbin' on,

10 And reachin' landin's,

    And turnin' corners,

    And sometimes goin' in the dark

    Where there ain't been no light.

    So, boy, don't you turn back.

15 Don't you set down on the steps.

    'Cause you finds it's kinder hard.

    Don't you fall now—

    For I'se still goin', honey,

    I'se still climbin',

20 And life for me ain't been no crystal stair.

My Notes

Making Observations

- What are you first thoughts about the poem?
- Based on the words you underlined, what emotions stand out to you in the poem?

ACTIVITY 4.11 continued

8 **FIRST READ:** Read the poem aloud or play the audio of the passage available on SpringBoard Digital. Ask students to read along and remind them to annotate as they listen to the poem for the first time.

9 After hearing the poem for the first time, guide the class in a discussion by asking the Making Observations questions. Revisit students' annotations to find any common words or emotions they underlined or noticed. If more than one student made the same annotation, point out the poet's effectiveness in getting the reader to feel a particular emotion.

★ TEACHER TO TEACHER

You may choose to blend reading techniques by having students read Hughes's poem "Mother to Son" independently as a scaffolding text for Chapter 2 of *Their Eyes Were Watching God*. Have students mark the text for metaphors. Next, reread the poem aloud and ask students to identify the words or phrases they have marked. Discuss Hughes's use of metaphors and what these images add to the text.

Scaffolding the Text-Dependent Questions

4. Who is the speaker in the poem? Who is the speaker speaking to? What is the situation? Is the speaker the mother or the son? Which clues help you identify the speaker? Does the speaker characterize life as easy or difficult? What is the speaker's outlook on life? RL.11-12.1

5. What is the mood created by the diction Hughes uses in the line "And reachin' landin's / And turnin' corners, / And sometimes goin' in the dark / Where there ain't been no light."? What repetitions of words does he use? What does that repetition emphasize? What feeling does it create in the reader? RL.11-12.4

10 RETURNING TO THE TEXT: Ask students to reread the poem in pairs before answering the text-dependent questions. Remind them to use text evidence as they respond to the questions.

If they have difficulty with the Returning to the Text questions, scaffold the questions by rephrasing them or breaking them into smaller parts. See the Scaffolding the Text-Dependent Questions boxes for suggestions.

LEVELED DIFFERENTIATED INSTRUCTION

In this activity, students might need support completing text-dependent questions.

Developing Prior to the second read, provide small groups with the **Key Idea and Details** graphic organizer. Guide students to the key idea that even though the mother's life has been difficult, she has not given up. Have groups complete the organizer during the second read and then collaborate to answer the questions.

Expanding Prior to the second read, provide partners with the **Key Idea and Details** graphic organizer. Have partners work together to answer text-dependent question 4. Then have them select either question 5 or 6 to answer using their responses to the organizer.

Bridging Allow students to work collaboratively to identify the key idea of the poem for the **Key Idea and Details** graphic organizer. Remind them that supporting details explain, clarify, and tell more about the key idea. As students perform their second read, encourage them to pay close attention to the lines that support the key idea.

4.11

Returning to the Text

- Return to the poem as you respond to the following questions. Use text evidence to support your responses.
- Write any additional questions you have about the text in your Reader/Writer Notebook.

4. Who is the speaker in the poem? Who is the speaker speaking to? What is the situation?

A concerned mother is speaking to her son. The mother is trying to explain to her son that even though her life has been difficult, she has not given up or lost hope. She still has hope for her son and encourages him to hold onto that hope.

5. What is the mood created by the diction Hughes uses in the line "And reachin' landin's, / And turnin' corners, / And sometimes goin' in the dark / Where there ain't been no light."?

By repeating *and* Hughes emphasizes the never-ending twists and turns of the mother's life: "And reachin' landin's, / And turnin' corners, / And sometimes goin' in the dark / Where there ain't been no light." The diction has the emotional effect of creating the feeling of striving and struggling with no place to stop and rest.

6. How does Hughes use the metaphor of the staircase? What purpose does it achieve? What message does the poem ultimately convey?

Hughes uses the metaphor of the staircase to allow the reader to help the reader visualize the struggle of climbing up a staircase while making the connection that life is like walking up stairs that can at times be difficult, "torn up," and "bare." The poem ultimately conveys the message that although the speaker's life may at times feel like a struggle to "climb," she keeps climbing, and so should the reader, even if the urge to sit down or turn back is overwhelming.

7. What is the effect of Hughes's use of repetition and line breaks in the poem?

Hughes repeats the word and at the beginning of a number of lines, and in conjunction with the use of line breaks, the repetition creates both a visual and spoken effect of struggling and weariness, as the reader is forced to "climb" to the next line much as the speaker must struggle to climb to a better station in life.

☑ Focus on the Sentence

Choose the correct placement for the commas in this sentence and underline the appositive.

Hughes's use of line breaks and repetition which mimics the struggle of climbing stairs is able to convey a message of continuing in the face of struggle.

Hughes's use of line breaks and repetition, which mimics the struggle of climbing stairs, is able to convey a message of continuing in the face of struggle.

Scaffolding the Text-Dependent Questions

6. How does Hughes use the metaphor of the staircase? What purpose does it achieve? What message does the poem ultimately convey? What does the metaphor allow the reader to visualize? What feelings does it conjure? How does the speaker feel about her life? How do her feelings change during the poem? RL.11-12.1

7. What is the effect of Hughes's use of repetition and line breaks in the poem? What words does he repeat? What is the visual effect of the line breaks in the poem? What does the reader "see"? How does it feel to speak the poem out loud? RL.11-12.5

Making Text-to-Text Comparisons

My Notes

8. As Nanny becomes the narrator of her story in Chapter 2, she says to Janie:

"Ah was born back due in slavery so it wasn't for me to fulfill my dreams of whut a woman oughta be and to do. Dat's one of de hold-backs of slavery. But nothing can't stop you from wishin'. Ah didn't want to be used for a work-ox and a brood-sow and Ah didn't want mah daughter used dat way neither. It sho wasn't mah will for things to happen lak they did. Ah even hated de way you was born. But, all de same Ah said thank god, Ah got another chance. Ah wanted to preach a great sermon about colored women sittin' on high, but they wasn't no pulpit for me. Freedom found me wid a baby daughter in mah arms, so Ah said Ah'd take a broom and a cook-pot and throw up a highway through de wilderness for her. She would expound what Ah felt. ...

"Ah wouldn't marry nobody, though. Ah could have uh heap uh times, cause Ah didn't want nobody mistreating mah baby. So Ah got with some good white people and come down here in West Florida to work and make de sun shine on both sides of de street for Leafy.

"Mah Madam help me wid her just lak she been doin' wid you. Ah put her in school when it got so it was a school to put her in. Ah was 'spectin to make a school teacher outa her."

Explain the differences in Janie's desires and Nanny's plans for her.

9. Make a text-to-text comparison between the voice and advice in "Mother to Son" and Nanny's voice and concerns in her speech to Janie.

Historical, Social, and Economic Context of Setting

The setting a writer uses in a text informs the context of the story, according to its time and place. A story that takes place in an impoverished New York City neighborhood in the 19th century will lend itself differently to a plot than a story that takes place in a medieval castle. Authors may even choose to incorporate historical events into a fictional text. But where characters live, when they live, and how they live will shape the story they are in as well as the ways in which they act.

Their Eyes Were Watching God takes place in the South, in an era in which African Americans had few rights and even less in the way of economic equality with whites. This context influences the decisions that the characters in the story make about where to live and how to live.

Support Have student partners complete the **Key Idea and Details** graphic organizer. Visit pairs as needed to guide them as they identify the key idea that even though the mother's life has been difficult, she has not given up on her child. Encourage them to work together to identify supporting details in the text. Have pairs exchange graphic organizers to review the details that support the key idea and ask and answer each other's questions about the details they chose.

11 Have students respond to the Focus on the Sentence task. Make sure students understand the role of an appositive before reading the sentence.

12 Read aloud student step 8 of the Making Text-to-Text Comparisons section with students. Ask volunteers to summarize what Nanny is saying in the passage along with what they notice about the difference between what Nanny and Janie want for Janie's life. Then have students complete student step 9 independently.

13 Guide students to understand that they will be making a text-to-text comparison between elements of the poem they read and *Their Eyes Were Watching God*. Have students work in pairs and encourage them to create a graphic organizer for each side of the comparison in order to identify the voice and advice in each text. Allow students time to complete student step 10 and ask volunteers to share their comparison with the class.

14 Read aloud the Historical, Social, and Economic Context of Setting section with students. Invite the class to think about the context of their own lives—where do they live? What era do they live in? What events have happened during their lifetime that may someday be considered historic? Guide students to recall what they already know about the context for *Their Eyes Were Watching God* and how it informs their understanding of the novel so far.

4.11

15 Organize students into small groups and guide them to understand that they will be researching more about the historical, social, and economic context of *Their Eyes Were Watching God*. Review with students the difference between and importance of primary and secondary sources. Then allow groups the time and resources to conduct their research and complete the graphic organizer in student step 10. Have groups provide a brief presentation to the class of the information they discovered and allow other groups to ask questions about it.

16 Have students reconvene in their groups to complete student step 11. Remind them to consider how the contexts of life for Nanny and Janie are similar and different and how their life contexts might have shaped each of them differently. Encourage students to return to previous annotations in order to complete their charts as well as return to Chapter 2 and then ask volunteers to share their findings. Write similar answers on the board in a connected mind map. As students name possible themes, write them on the board as well as in a place that can continue to be added to as they come up.

10. With a small group, research some facts about the historical, social, and economic context of *Their Eyes Were Watching God*. Aim to find a mix of facts from primary and secondary sources.

Historical Context	Social Context	Economic Context
Hurston published the novel near the end of a literary period called the Harlem Renaissance, during which African American authors focused on investigating and celebrating their cultural identities. However, the novel can arguably be read in the context of Southern literature as well as African American literature. Many scholars have debated and argued over which context the novel should be read through.	Hurston studied anthropology at Barnard College, and her research on rural black folklore informed the social and historical context of the novel. Hurston also grew up in Eatonville, Florida, which was the first all-black incorporated town in the United States. In many ways, the novel can also be read through the lens of feminist literature, as Hurston depicts Janie as an independent woman.	Hurston published the novel during an era in which the economy was crashing due to the Depression and during which political and class tensions were growing between whites and blacks. There was also a divide within the African American arts community as to how blackness should be represented by its creators, with many calling for work to be more political and confront injustices.

11. With your group, return to Chapter 2 of the text and reread Nanny's story. As you read, record details about how the context of her life affects Janie as well as how it influences the plot and theme of the novel.

Evidence from Nanny's Story	How It Affects Janie	How It Affects the Plot	How It Affects the Theme
"You know, honey, us colored folks is branches without roots and that makes things come round in queer ways. Ah was born back in slavery so it wasn't for me to fulfill my dreams of whut a woman oughta be and to do."	Nanny points out that because of being born into slavery, she never had the opportunities that Janie has, and that is why she is so concerned about the choices Janie makes and her future.	This context affects the plot of the book by showing the root of Nanny's concern and caring for Janie—that she has pinned many of her hopes and dreams onto Janie having a successful life.	Nanny's experience affects the themes of gender roles and independence because it shows the divide between her generation and Janie's and how she encourages Janie to strive for marriage in order to be taken care of.
"But then she kept on astin me how come mah baby look white. So Ah told her, 'Ah don't know nothin' but what Ah'm told tuh do, 'cause Ah ain't nothin' but uh nigger and uh slave."	Nanny's revelation affects Janie because it reveals that she was raped by her master, which also means that Janie is partly white. It also demonstrates how few choices Nanny had in her own life when it came to love.	This context affects the plot of the book by showing how the things that happened to Nanny affect Janie's life as well. Nanny sees Janie as having chance to have a different life because she has more freedom and choice.	Nanny's experience affects the theme of independence because it shows how she never had any agency over her own life as a slave and how the things that happened to her affected her family for generations.

4.11

Evidence from Nanny's Story	How It Affects Janie	How It Affects the Plot	How It Affects the Theme
"Ah raked and scraped and bought dis lil piece uh land so you wouldn't have to stay in de white folks' yard and tuck yo' head befo' other chillum at school."	Nanny's sacrifices affect Janie because they allow her some independence and freedom. At the same time, Nanny places many of her aspirations on Janie to fulfill.	Nanny's decisions affect the plot of the book because they show that even though she felt she had no agency in her life, she made sacrifices so that Janie would have more opportunities.	Nanny's experience affects the themes of gender roles, relations, and independence. Her ideas about gender roles and relations are different from Janie's, and therefore they clash on the point of marriage.

12. What connections can you make between the historical, social, and economic context that you researched about the novel and Nanny and Janie's experience? How might Hurston's experience have influenced the novel and its characters?

Making Connections to the Harlem Renaissance

13. As you revisit Chapter 2, use your double-entry journal to take notes. As you make your journal entries, keep in mind how the values, beliefs, history, arts, and concerns with daily life that characterize the Harlem Renaissance are embodied in Hurston's work.

ACTIVITY 4.11 continued

17 ● Have groups discuss the questions in student step 12 by referring to the chart they filled out. Have each group write a brief answer and have a representative from each group share the group's answer with the class. Note any similar answers.

18 ● Ask students to read student step 13 and remind them to revisit Chapter 2 and continue adding to their **double-entry journal**.

19 ● Have students keep all their reading responses in writing portfolios in preparation for the Embedded Assessment 2 essay.

ASSESS

Review students' responses to the text-to-text comparison task to assess their ability to make connections between two texts. Ensure that students have supported their claims with reasons and textual evidence.

Use students' responses to the research to assess their ability to make connections to the contexts of each text and accurately find information from a mix of primary and secondary sources. Their research should come from valid sources and demonstrate an understanding of the kinds of contexts they should be looking for.

ADAPT

If students need help making a text-to-text comparison, provide them with graphic organizer models that will help them break down each text's voice and advice.

If students need help conducting and organizing research into different contexts, provide them with a checklist for how to differentiate between primary and secondary sources as well as the **Evaluating Online Sources** graphic organizer to make sure their sources are reputable. Provide a list of resources or video clips that students can use to gather information.

ACTIVITY
4.12   A Moral Dilemma

PLAN

Materials: *Their Eyes Were Watching God,* Chapters 3 and 4; double-entry journals; timer
Suggested pacing: 1 50-minute class period

TEACH

1 Read aloud the Learning Targets and Preview with students. Create a T-chart on the board with columns labeled *Harlem Renaissance Themes* and Their Eyes Were Watching God *Themes.* Have students brainstorm ideas for themes to put in both columns and to note any overlap between themes.

2 Discuss with students what it means to have a moral dilemma. You may want to play a game by posing a moral question, such as: *If someone you knew was very sick or dying and needed medicine you couldn't afford, would you steal it?* Encourage students to examine the connection between motivation and a moral dilemma.

3 Read aloud the information in the section A Moral Dilemma: Chapters 3 and 4. Ask students to think of any examples from other books or films of characters who encountered moral dilemmas and how they solved them.

4 Point out student step 1 to students to guide their reading of Chapters 3 and 4. Allow students to read the chapters independently, with a partner, or in small reading groups while recording notes in the chart. After students are finished, come back together as a class to discuss students' findings. Then have students complete student step 2 independently and compare their answer with a classmate's.

ACTIVITY
4.12   A Moral Dilemma

Learning Strategies

Close Reading
Discussion Groups
Double-Entry Journal
Drafting
Predicting
Quickwrite

Learning Targets

- Analyze the behavior of characters in order to understand their underlying motivations and moral dilemmas.
- Make connections between the themes of the Harlem Renaissance and the text.

Preview

In this activity, you will analyze a character's behavior, motivations, and moral dilemmas and how they influence the plot.

My Notes

A Moral Dilemma: Chapters 3 and 4

What drives people to make decisions? Authors must consider this question when directing the actions of their characters, and underlying motivations often drive a person's behavior—whether they want something, are hiding something, or are torn between right and wrong. Underlying motivations can cause moral dilemmas that influence the plot and theme of a story. Consider the story of a person who covets an important object that doesn't belong to them—what actions might they take? How might it compromise their beliefs about themselves? What would they learn?

1. As you read Chapters 3 and 4, record notes about Janie's behaviors and underlying motivations. Then think about what moral dilemmas are created as a result and ultimately how Janie's choices about the moral dilemma influence the plot.

Janie's Behaviors and Motivations	What moral dilemmas occur as a result?	How do Janie's choices about the moral dilemma influence the plot?
Janie realizes she doesn't love Logan but wants to believe she will after they are married.	Janie marries Logan despite her lack of feeling love and only becomes more disillusioned and conflicted.	Janie's choice to marry Logan results in her dissatisfaction, which leads her to leave him for Joe.
Janie flirts with Joe after meeting him.	Janie's encounter with Joe leaves her with the dilemma of whether to stay with Logan.	Janie's choice to go with Joe leads her to leave her life behind for a new one.

2. Explain how Janie's moral dilemma influences the theme.

Janie's moral dilemma influences the theme of desire, love, and independence. Her beliefs about love lead her to realize she has made the wrong choice in marrying Logan and then to leave Logan for Joe, who she thinks can provide her with the love she desires. Her dilemma also displays her ultimate sense of independence in believing she should be the one to govern her own happiness despite the judgment she receives from others.

College and Career Readiness Standards

Focus Standards:

RL.11-12.1 Cite strong and thorough textual evidence to support analysis of what the text says explicitly as well as inferences drawn from the text, including determining where the text leaves matters uncertain.

RL.11-12.3 Analyze the impact of the author's choices regarding how to develop and relate elements of a story or drama (e.g., where a story is set, how the action is ordered, how the characters are introduced and developed).

Additional Standards Addressed:

W.11-12.1a, W.11-12.1e

✅ Focus on the Sentence

Use what you have observed about Janie's moral dilemma so far to complete the following sentences.

Janie faces a moral dilemma because of her conflicting feelings of being married to Logan.

Janie wants to believe she will love Logan after they are married, but she finds that isn't the case.

Joe is different than Logan, so Janie sees an opportunity for desire and independence at last.

Making Connections to the Harlem Renaissance

3. Discuss the questions that follow and take notes in your double-entry journal.

   • As Janie evaluates her marriage to Logan Killicks, Hurston presents the recurring image of the horizon: "The familiar people and things had failed her so she hung over the gate and looked up the road towards way off. She knew now that marriage did not make love. Janie's first dream was dead, so she became a woman." Discuss how Janie's frustration helps her growing self-awareness.

   Nanny accuses Janie of having a "mouf full uh foolishness" when Janie expresses her discontent in marriage. Even though Janie still desires "things sweet" from marriage, she realizes she will not get them from Logan. She finally stands up to him when he expects her to chop wood. Next, she refuses to help with the mules, making her more aware of her desires.

   • What other images add meaning to the text and define Hurston's style as a Harlem Renaissance writer?

   Joe Stark "did not represent sun-up and pollen and blooming trees, but he spoke of far horizons." (images of new beginnings)

✅ Check Your Understanding

What symbolic act does Janie perform when she leaves Logan? At the end of Chapter 4, examine the paragraph that begins, "The morning road air ..." How does Hurston's word choice echo the optimism of the Harlem Renaissance?

She throws away her apron. Janie looks forward to leaving with Joe. She experiences a "feeling of sudden newness and change," as reflected in the optimism of the Harlem Renaissance.

My Notes

ACTIVITY 4.12 continued

5 Guide students to complete the Focus on the Sentence task independently. Remind them of the fact that they are creating sentences that can follow modifiers such as *because, but,* and *so.*

6 Remind students that they should be making connections to the Harlem Renaissance as they read. Have students get into discussion groups to discuss the questions in student step 3. Guide them to return to the text and look for images that Hurston presents. After students finish discussing and writing, ask volunteers to share their answers.

▶ TEACHER TO TEACHER

Consider this plan for cooperative discussion: Assign one question to each group member. Give students time to review their double-entry journals for possible ideas and to review the text of Chapters 3 and 4. As students begin their discussion, set the timer so that each student has a minute or two minutes to lead the discussion.

7 Read aloud the Check Your Understanding task. If necessary, remind students what a "symbolic act" might mean in the context of the novel and discuss with them what "optimism" in the Harlem Renaissance looked like. Guide them to return to the text and reread the complete paragraph at the end of Chapter 4. Have students complete the Check Your Understanding task independently and share their response with a classmate.

8 Remind students that Embedded Assessment 2 requires that they compare and contrast Hurston's writing and ideals to the beliefs of the Harlem Renaissance. As practice in making these connections, the Writing Prompt includes an excerpt from literary criticism.

9 Read aloud the Writing Prompt and walk students through a possible annotation of the excerpt by noting how it helps inform an understanding of the novel. Encourage students to ask any clarifying questions and model on the board how they might outline an argumentative essay to include a thesis, reasons, evidence, and conclusion. Allow students time to outline and write their essay.

ASSESS

Responses to the Check Your Understanding task should show students' comprehension of how Hurston's word choices reflect the optimism of the Harlem Renaissance. Make sure that students discuss Janie's symbolic act as in illustration of this optimism.

Ensure that students have drawn a clear connection between the literary criticism and Hurston's novel and that they can articulate how Nanny's desires for Janie are a departure from the ideals of the Harlem Renaissance. Identify which students need more support in writing thesis sentences and citing textual evidence.

ADAPT

The "Be sure to" points of the Writing Prompt represent skills that students must demonstrate in Embedded Assessment 2. Support students by using mini-lessons to review these skills if necessary.

If students have not mastered making text-to-text connections, guide them in rereading Hemenway's criticism. Point out important statements that Hemenway makes about Nanny's character and how her character illustrates the ideas from which Hurston departs.

4.12

My Notes

✍ Writing Prompt: Argumentative

Scholar Robert E. Hemenway wrote *Zora Neal Hurston: A Literary Biography*. This excerpt from the biography explains that Nanny represents a belief from which Hurston departed in her writing. Read the excerpt and make a text-to-text connection to *Their Eyes Were Watching God*.

> People erred because they wanted to be above others, an impulse which eventually led to denying the humanity of those below. .... Janie's grandmother ... thinks that freedom is symbolized by achieving the position on high. Zora Hurston had always known, just as Janie discovers, that there was no air to breathe there. She had always identified with what she called 'the poor Negro, the real one in the furrows and the cane breaks.' She bitterly criticized black leaders who ignored this figure...

Review Chapters 2 and 3. Think about Nanny's desires for Janie to have a life far different from her own and Leafy's as well as Nanny's belief "that freedom is symbolized by achieving the position on high." Write a paragraph explaining how these ideas are contrary to Hurston's own ideas. Include information about how Nanny represents ideas held during the Harlem Renaissance and if and how Hurston departs from those. Be sure to:

- Include a thesis statement that defines your opinion and gives direction to your writing.
- Clarify the relationships among your thesis statement, reasons, and supporting evidence from the text.
- Write a strong conclusion that follows from your claim and supports the argument you presented.

✍ WRITING PROMPT: ARGUMENTATIVE

The following standards are addressed in the Writing Prompt:
- W.11-12.1a
- W.11-12.1a
- W.11-12.1e

Janie's New Life

Learning Targets

- Evaluate how an author's use of language informs and shapes the perception of readers.
- Defend or challenge an author's claims using relevant text evidence.

Preview

In this activity, you will identify characteristics of folktales that are evident in the novel and evaluate how they shape the perception of the reader.

Learning Strategies

Close Reading
Discussion Groups
Double-Entry Journal
Questioning the Text
Think-Pair-Share

Questioning the Text: Chapter 5

1. Read Chapter 5 and then write three questions for each of the following levels of questions to help you gain a deeper understanding of the text. Use the following examples as models.

Literal	Interpretive	Universal
What does Joe Starks say when the audience requests that Janie speak?	Based on Joe Starks's statements about women, what can the reader infer about Joe's attitude toward women?	How does society define male and female roles?

2. Share your questions with your classmates. With your class, choose three questions that best identify the central issues of Chapter 5. Write those questions here.

1. _____

   _____

2. _____

   _____

3. _____

   _____

College and Career Readiness Standards

Focus Standards:

RL.11-12.1 Cite strong and thorough textual evidence to support analysis of what the text says explicitly as well as inferences drawn from the text, including determining where the text leaves matters uncertain.

RL.11-12.2 Determine two or more themes or central ideas of a text and analyze their development over the course of the text, including how they interact and build on one another to produce a complex account; provide an objective summary of the text.

ACTIVITY 4.13

PLAN

Materials: *Their Eyes Were Watching God,* Chapters 5 and 6; double-entry journals; chart paper and markers; timer

Suggested pacing: 3 50-minute class periods:

TEACH

1 Ask a volunteer to read aloud the Learning Targets and Preview. Write the term *folktales* on the board and elicit from students the qualities that folktales have as a genre. Write their ideas on the board in a connected mind map. Then guide students to make connections between the elements they've identified in folktales and similar elements in the novel.

2 Allow students time to read Chapter 5 independently, with a partner, or in small groups. Remind them to continue taking notes in their double-entry journals.

3 Read aloud student step 1 in the section Questioning the Text: Chapter 5. **Questioning the text** through levels of questions is an important skill that good readers practice constantly, usually without realizing it. This activity will help students develop this skill. Review the levels of questions (literal, interpretive, and universal) with students and discuss the different kinds of responses that each type of question elicits. Ask volunteers for examples of each kind of question to write on the board. You might have students **think-pair-share** to write the three levels of questions in the chart.

4 After students complete their questions, conduct a whole-class sharing of the questions. Focus on interpretive questions and have the class choose the three or four questions that identify the central issues of this chapter, as noted in student step 2. Use the questions as the basis of a class discussion of Chapter 5.

5 Read aloud the information in the section Oral Tradition: Chapter 6 with students.

6 **Vocabulary Development:** Review the meaning of the Literary Vocabulary *folktale* with students. Have them work in pairs to define the term in their own words. Remind them of the earlier discussion in which they brainstormed different elements that folktales contain.

7 Have students read student step 3. Elicit from them what it means to be an anthropologist and how that line of work may have shaped Hurston's understanding and knowledge of folktale elements.

8 Clarify any of the stated characteristics before students begin reading Chapter 6. Divide students into groups. Assign each group one or more rows of the graphic organizer in student step 3 to complete as they read.

9 Distribute markers and pieces of chart paper to each group, one piece of paper for each row of the graphic organizer that groups are completing. Ask groups to nominate one member to record their responses on chart paper. Have the recorder write the element of the oral tradition at the top of each piece of paper.

10 Then have groups read the text together, pausing to add to their graphic organizers as necessary. Remind groups to also write their responses on their chart paper.

11 When groups have finished reading, post the chart paper around the room. Have students participate in a **gallery walk** by viewing each piece of chart paper in order to complete their graphic organizers.

4.13

VOCABULARY

LITERARY
A **folktale** is a story without a known author that has been preserved through oral retelling and is part of the oral tradition in literature.

Oral Tradition: Chapter 6

A **folktale** has many or all of the following characteristics.

- It is generally handed down to a group orally.
- It is characteristic of the time and place in which it is told.
- It speaks to universal and timeless themes.
- It tries to explain human life and how people deal with life or the origin of something.
- It often contains a story about about a common person.
- The characters struggle with natural events.
- The stories validate elements of a culture.
- It may entertain with exaggerated characters, conflicts, or dialogue.

3. As an anthropologist, Hurston collected stories, conversations, and other aspects of oral tradition that she then infused into her writing. In Chapter 6, Hurston presents two layers of the oral tradition: her omniscient narrator tells the readers a story of the porch sitters, and their conversations carry the stories of Matt's mule. As you read Chapter 6, track the elements of the oral tradition in the following graphic organizer and think about how these elements contribute to the effects on the reader.

Elements of the Oral Tradition and the Folktale	Example from the Chapter	Effects on the Perception of the Reader
Folktales, myths, fairy tales	"Us all knows he's mean. Ah seen 'im when he took after on ugh dem Roberts chillum ..."	Lige tells the story of the mule as he "soothed" his story. The word *soothed* implies a soft, drawn-out telling of a story.
Reflection of time and place in which they are told, especially the use of dialect	"Does feed de ornery varmint!"	Use of dialectal diction, *ornery varmint* recalls language of the rural South.
Exaggerated characters or situations for the sake of humor or glorification of deeds	"You mean tuh tell me you rode dat mule all de way from West Florida down heah?" "Sho he did, Lige. But he didn't mean thu. He suz satisfied up dere, but de mule muzn't ..."	Giving the mule human desires exaggerates the story and adds humor.

College and Career Readiness Standards

RL.11-12.4 Determine the meaning of words and phrases as they are used in the text, including figurative and connotative meanings; analyze the impact of specific word choices on meaning and tone, including words with multiple meanings or language that is particularly fresh, engaging, or beautiful. (Include Shakespeare as well as other authors.)

W.11-12.4 Produce clear and coherent writing in which the development, organization, and style are appropriate to task, purpose, and audience.

Additional Standards Addressed:
RI.11-12.10, W.11-12.1a, W.11-12.1c, W.11-12.5

12 After students have completed the gallery walk, come back together as a class to discuss students' findings and observations about how Hurston includes elements of oral traditions and folktales.

Elements of the Oral Tradition and the Folktale	Example from the Chapter	Effects on the Perception of the Reader
Humans coping with the world in which they live	"When the people sat around the porch for others to look at and see, it was nice. The fact that they thought pictures were always crayon enlargements of life made it even nicer to listen to."	Janie finds some comfort in listening to the exaggerated stories of the "mule talker."
Common people as characters	"Janie loved the conversation and sometimes she thought up good stories on the mule, but Joe had forbidden her to indulge. He didn't want her talking after such trashy people."	Joe looks upon the common people of the porch as "trashy." He elevates his status by looking down on them.
Characters struggle with nature	"Less ketch Matt's mule fuh 'im and have some fun." "Now, Lum, you know dat mule ain't aimin' tuh let hisself be caught. Less watch you do it."	This struggle is man-made, and the recounting of this struggle shows man's often-foolish attempts at conquering nature.
Validates aspects of a culture	"Out in the swamp they made great ceremony over the mule. They mocked everything human in death."	In an ironic validation, the "funeral" is a parody of a culture's traditions of celebrating life.
Universal and timeless themes	"Everybody enjoyed themselves to the highest and then finally the mule was left to the already impatient buzzards." "All they needed was to see Matt's long spare shape coming down the street and by the time he got to the porch they were ready for him."	Dominance of nature Unjust and brutal treatment of others for the sake of entertainment

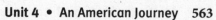

13 Reread Janie's assessment of Joe's setting the mule free as well as the response Hambo shares and then lead the class in a discussion of the effect Joe's treatment has on the mule. Ask students to consider why Joe buys and pampers the mule. Some critics have argued that Joe's overfeeding and special treatment lead to the mule's death, mirroring the gradual, cumulative effect of Joe's "special treatment" of Janie. Allow students to weigh in on this view and then have them answer the first bullet point in student step 4 independently.

14 Have students discuss the setting, describing Eatonville and its citizens and how this young town is affecting Joe, Janie, and their relationship. Guide students to make the connection between the setting and the historical and social contexts of the novel. Then have them answer the second bullet point in student step 4 independently.

15 Reread the part of Chapter 6 that begins, "She had an inside and an outside now and suddenly she knew how not to mix them." Guide students in an analytical discussion of what this line might mean and then have them answer the final bullet point in student step 4 independently.

LEVELED DIFFERENTIATED INSTRUCTION

In this activity, students might need support summarizing narrative elements in Chapters 5 and 6.

Beginning Assign small groups Chapter 5 or 6. Have groups complete the **Notes for Reading Independently** graphic organizer for their chapter. Facilitate a group discussion in which students share their findings and add to their notes. Allow groups to work collaboratively on the interpretive questions in student step 4.

4.13

My Notes

4. Think about the characters, setting, and conflicts in Chapters 5 and 6. Then write analytical responses to the interpretive questions that follow.

- How has Joe enslaved Janie? What comments does he make that illustrate his view of husbands and wives? Do you see any parallels between Joe's treatment of the mule and his treatment of Janie?

  He tells her how to dress ("She must look on herself as the bell-cow …"; "Whut make her keep her head tied up lak some ole 'oman round de store?"). He will not allow Janie to speak on the porch ("mah wife don't know nothin' 'bout no speech-makin'"). He criticizes her ("He gits on her ever now and then when she make little mistakes round de store.").

  Janie sees parallels between herself and the mule. Perhaps she expresses her own understanding and desire to be released from Jody's control when she tells him, "Freein' dat mule makes uh mighty big man outa you. Something like George Washington and Lincoln. Abraham Lincoln, he had de whole United States tuh rule so he freed de Negroes. You got uh town so you freed uh mule."

- Hurston often used Eatonville, her real-life childhood home, as a setting in her work. Describe Eatonville as it is presented in *Their Eyes Were Watching God*. What effect is the young town having on Joe, Janie, and their marriage?

  It is destroying their marriage; Joe feels he must rule, and Janie is the ruled.

- "She had an inside and an outside now and suddenly she knew how not to mix them." When have you seen evidence of the two sides of Janie in Chapters 5 and 6? What is the reason for this disparity?

  She desires to speak up, to have freedom; however, she remains submissive to Joe. She argues with Joe, yet she wishes for reconciliation. "She pressed her teeth together and learned to hush."

Making Text-to-Text Connections

In his essay "One of the New Realists" (Chelsea House Publishers, 1986), Benjamin Brawly describes Zora Neale Hurston:

> She would get together a group of men in a railroad or turpentine camp or in a phosphate mining village, talk informally until they were no longer self-conscious, and then see which could outdo the other with his yarn. ... Like some others who have dealt in folk-lore, Miss Hurston has not escaped criticism at the hands of those who frowned upon her broad humor and the lowly nature of her material. Her interest, however, is not in solving problems, the chief concern being with individuals. As for the untutored Negro, she presents him without apology, a character as good as other characters but different.

☑ Check Your Understanding

Briefly summarize Brawly's description of Hurston.

My Notes

✍ Writing Prompt: Argumentative

Review the characteristics of folktales and the portions of Chapter 6 that reflect folktale characteristics. Write a paragraph in which you agree or disagree with critics who "frowned upon [Hurston's] broad humor and the lowly nature of her material." Be sure to:

- Include a clear statement of your claim that either agrees or disagrees with the critic in the topic sentence.
- Demonstrate your understanding of the folktale elements of the mule story by including examples of the elements in your claim. Embed any quotations using correct conventions.
- Use varied syntax and edit your draft to demonstrate command of the conventions of Standard English.

✍ WRITING PROMPT: ARGUMENTATIVE

The following standards are addressed in the writing prompt:

- W.11-12.1a
- W.11-12.4
- W.11-12.1c

ACTIVITY 4.13 continued

Bridging Have partners collaborate on summarizing the characters, setting, and conflicts in Chapters 5 and 6 using the **Notes for Reading Independently** graphic organizer.

Extend Have students work collaboratively to complete the interpretive questions and write a brief paragraph that creates a text-to-text connection between Chapter 5 or 6 with the poem "Mother and Son" or the excerpt from Hemenway's literary criticism of Zora Neale Hurston.

16 Read aloud or have students read the critical excerpt in the Making Text-to-Text Connections section.

17 Before students respond to the Check Your Understanding task, have them mark the text for descriptions of Hurston.

18 Go over the Writing Prompt with students and review with them the work they've done on identifying characteristics of folktales in the novel. Give students time to draft their responses to the Writing Prompt.

ASSESS

Review students' summaries from the Check Your Understanding task to ensure that they have included all Brawly's main points and important details in their own words.

Use students' responses to the Writing Prompt to assess their understanding of folktale characteristics and their ability to evaluate the validity of a critical opinion and write an argument.

ADAPT

If students need additional help generating an analysis that agrees or disagrees with critical commentary, have them create a graphic organizer that lists points of agreement and disagreement with Hurston's critics. Help them determine which side has a stronger argument. Then have them work in pairs to draft a thesis statement and find evidence to support it.

PLAN

Materials: *Their Eyes Were Watching God*, Chapters 7–9; double-entry journals; sticky notes
Suggested pacing: 3 50-minute class periods

TEACH

1 Read aloud the Learning Targets and Preview with students, discussing what an emotional response looks like. Ask students to describe some of the characters' emotional responses in the novel.

2 Make a link between Chapters 6 and 7. In Chapter 6, the reader is told that Janie "pressed her teeth together and learned to hush." However, at the end of Chapter 6, Janie speaks up. Before reading Chapter 7, draw students' attention to the last three paragraphs of Chapter 6. Have students **think-pair-share** their ideas for student step 1.

3 Guide students to recall what rising action entails, perhaps by drawing a plot diagram on the board and asking volunteers to label the introduction, rising action, climax, falling action, and resolution. Remind students to pay close attention to the rising action in Chapters 7 and 8 as described in student step 2.

4 Conduct a **close reading** of the first two paragraphs of Chapter 7 to respond to student step 3. Have students write their answers independently. Ask volunteers to share their responses with the class.

5 Review the graphic organizer with students. Remind them to keep track of important plot developments and Janie's emotional responses. Allow them time to read Chapters 7 and 8.

6 As students complete the graphic organizer, consider modeling the use of precise adjectives by describing how Janie reacts to Joe insulting and abusing her.

7 Provide students with blank copies of the graphic organizer and allow them time to fill it out for the Independent Reading Link. Have each student complete a Venn diagram or short paragraph to compare Janie to the main character from his or her Independent Reading text.

Janie's "Route of Tradition"

Learning Strategies

Double-Entry Journal
Marking the Text
Predicting

INDEPENDENT READING LINK

Read and Connect
Choose a chunk of text from your independent reading selection. Complete a chart like the one you used for this activity. Show important plot developments and assign adjectives to describe the main character's emotional response to these developments. Then compare and contrast your main character's responses with Janie's responses.

Learning Targets

• Use textual evidence to track key actions and characters' emotional responses.
• Analyze how Hurston's writing reflects and departs from the ideas of the Harlem Renaissance.

Preview

In this activity, you will read Chapters 7, 8, and 9 and analyze how characters respond to developments in the plot.

Character Study: Chapters 7, 8, and 9

1. Review the ending of Chapter 6, beginning with "Janie did what she had never done before ..." Think about what this action means to Janie's character development. Turn to a partner and share your ideas.

2. As you read Chapters 7 and 8, give close attention to the rising actions and the conflicts that compound Janie's feelings of being "a rut in the road."

3. After reading the first two paragraphs of Chapter 7, describe how the author's use of imagery expresses Janie's sense of her marriage. How does her behavior at the beginning of this chapter compare with her actions at the end of Chapter 6?

"The years took the fight out of Janie's face." Beginning with Chapter 7, Janie has learned to "say nothing." She sometimes dreams of the future but settles into a controlled presence around Joe. At the end of Chapter 6, Janie has dared to speak up and give her opinion in the porch sitters' conversation.

4. As you read Chapters 7 and 8, use this graphic organizer to record characters' actions and emotional responses.

Important Plot Developments	Adjectives to Describe Janie's Emotional Response
Chapter 7 Answers should include: • Janie insults Joe publicly. • Joe strikes Janie in public.	**Chapter 7** • She is hurt and ashamed.

College and Career Readiness Standards

Focus Standards:

RL.11-12.1 Cite strong and thorough textual evidence to support analysis of what the text says explicitly as well as inferences drawn from the text, including determining where the text leaves matters uncertain.

RL.11-12.2 Determine two or more themes or central ideas of a text and analyze their development over the course of the text,

including how they interact and build on one another to produce a complex account; provide an objective summary of the text.

RL.11-12.3 Analyze the impact of the author's choices regarding how to develop and relate elements of a story or drama (e.g., where a story is set, how the action is ordered, how the characters are introduced and developed).

Important Plot Developments	Adjectives to Describe Janie's Emotional Response
Chapter 8	**Chapter 8**
Answers might include:	• She is puzzled and confused.
• Joe moves out of the bedroom.	• "She was worried about his not eating …"
• Joe begins to show physical symptoms of illness.	• "She was sorry about the root doctor …"
• Joe begins to listen to the advice of a faker and to suspect Janie of trying to poison him.	• She begins peacefully, "Ah ain't been such uh good wife …" and concludes with the angry accusation "… dat ain't whu Ah rushed off down the road tuh find out about you."
• Janie brings in a doctor who tells her that Joe's kidneys have stopped functioning.	• She is proud of the "handsome woman."
• Janie tells Joe how she feels, but he argues with her and then dies.	
• Janie takes stock of her physical appearance before informing the community of Joe's death.	

5. How are Hurston's beliefs in the power of the individual reflected in Janie's character?

   Note the descriptors in the right column: "She begins peacefully" and "She is proud."

6. How does Janie's character reflect and depart from the Harlem Renaissance? Again, note the words in the right-hand column.

7. Think about the critical commentaries that are provided in the graphic organizer that follows. Identify textual evidence from Chapters 7, 8, and 9 and complete the columns of the graphic organizer.

Aspects of the Harlem Renaissance	Examples from Chapters 7, 8, or 9	Is it a natural product of the ideas of a specific historical period in American literature?	Is it a departure from the ideas of a specific historical period in American literature?
Historical Context *"The conflict which Janie represents, between freedom or passion and restraint or reserve, has a special quality in black fiction. … The condition in slavery was the ultimate restriction in which freedom to be oneself is out of the question." —from "Their Eyes Were Watching God" by Roger Rosenblatt*	"People who never had known what it was to enter the gate of the Mayor's yard unless it were to do some menial job now paraded in and out as his confidants." (p. 79)	Hurston, in a critical manner, shows Joe as the slaveholder, ruling over his "plantation."	

8. At the end of Chapter 8, Joe has died. In a **close reading** of the last paragraph of the chapter, discuss the metaphor "starched and ironed her face" as symbolic of her relationship to the people of Eatonville (forming her face into just what people wanted to see). Allow students to discuss what this metaphor means and what it says about Janie and her relationships with others. Revisit the discussion of Janie's inner and outer selves from Chapters 5 and 6.

9. Instruct students to read Chapter 9 and continue to analyze Janie's character. Ask them to mark the text (using sticky notes) to identify passages that reveal the contrast between the inner and outer Janie. Lead students in a discussion about how long these two Janies have existed; ask them to predict whether both will continue to exist.

10. Have students work independently to answer student step 5 and 6 and remind them to cite textual evidence and refer to the organizer they've filled out about Janie's emotional responses.

11. In preparation for the analysis required for Embedded Assessment 2, guide students to recall the aspects of the Harlem Renaissance that they have studied previously. Have students work in small groups to discuss, compare notes, and complete the graphic organizer in student step 7. Have students identify textual evidence in Chapters 7, 8, and 9 that connects to each category on the graphic organizer. Ensure that students complete the third column by making the connection between the texts (the novel and the critical reviews) and the Essential Question.

12. After students complete the graphic organizer, go over each category as a class, sharing ideas and evidence.

College and Career Readiness Standards

RL.11-12.4 Determine the meaning of words and phrases as they are used in the text, including figurative and connotative meanings; analyze the impact of specific word choices on meaning and tone, including words with multiple meanings or language that is particularly fresh, engaging, or beautiful. (Include Shakespeare as well as other authors.)

RL.11-12.9 Demonstrate knowledge of eighteenth-, nineteenth- and early-twentieth-century foundational works of American literature, including how two or more texts from the same period treat similar themes or topics.

13 Allow students time to complete the Check Your Understanding task. Encourage students to create an outline to support their claim that uses textual evidence.

LEVELED DIFFERENTIATED INSTRUCTION

In this activity, students might need support writing a claim about Hurston and the Harlem Renaissance.

Developing Group students according to which aspect they wish to write about. Provide the **Conclusion Builder** graphic organizer as prewriting support.

Expanding Pair students according to which aspect they wish to write about. Have them use the **Conclusion Builder** graphic organizer to record evidence from multiple sources. Have them collaborate on writing a clear thesis statement.

Support Provide the **Conclusion Builder** graphic organizer as prewriting support for student responses. Pair students and have them record evidence for one side of the issue before collaborating on one response.

Extend If students are ready for an extra challenge, have them meet in small groups to develop a checklist for elements that should appear in the thesis, supporting details, and conclusion of their finished paragraph.

ASSESS

Review students' responses to the Check Your Understanding task to assess their ability to support a claim using evidence.

ADAPT

If students need additional help supporting a claim, have them work in pairs to review the graphic organizers they created for this activity. Tell them to select one aspect of the Harlem Renaissance. Then tell them complete a T-chart that lists ways Hurston's work reflects and departs from this aspect of the Harlem Renaissance.

4.14

Aspects of the Harlem Renaissance	Examples from Chapters 7, 8, or 9	Is it a natural product of the ideas of a specific historical period in American literature?	Is it a departure from the ideas of a specific historical period in American literature?
Philosophy/Beliefs *"Some believed that it was the duty of black artists to picture their race in the 'best' possible light, thereby implying that only middle-class blacks were worthy of being depicted in art. … [James Weldon] Johnson shows his acceptance of the lower social classes … as a source for literary materials."* —from "Zora Neale Hurston's America" by Theresa R. Love	"Uh woman by herself is uh pitiful thing." (p. 86)		It Reinforces Hurston's use of dialect to distinguish class. Rather than following the "duty of black artist," Hurston chose to "show acceptance of the lower social class."
The Arts *"Their Eyes Were Watching God, a novel of intense power, evidences the strength and power of African-American culture. … Here characters were outsiders in America because they were the inheritors of a culture different from that of others."* —from "The Outsider" by Addison Gayle Jr.	"He had always been scornful of root-doctors and all their kind, but now she saw a faker from over around Altamonte Springs hanging around the place most daily." (p. 78)	Hurston refers to the cultures of the islands … voodoo and medicine men, emphasizing the African American cultural heritage.	However, the irony is that Joe, who has bought into the middle-class white man's world, has resorted to the medicine man for help.
Daily Life *"In rebelling against the definition of black women and moving to assert her own individuality, Janie must travel the route of tradition."* from "The Outsider," by Addison Gayle, Jr.	"She got nothing from Jody except what money could buy, and she was giving away what she didn't value." (p. 72) "She knew that she was a much better cook than the old woman, and cleaner about the kitchen. So she bought a beef-bone and made him some soup. (p. 78)	Hurston portrays Janie as the traditional wife, accepting what she has, carrying out her duties as a wife. At this point, even after 20 years, she is traveling "the route of tradition" in her marriage.	

☑ Check Your Understanding

After you have completed the graphic organizer, choose one aspect of the Harlem Renaissance and write a paragraph to support the claim that Zora Neal Hurston's work is both a natural product of and a departure from the ideas of the Harlem Renaissance.

College and Career Readiness Standards

W.11-12.8 Gather relevant information from multiple authoritative print and digital sources, using advanced searches effectively; assess the strengths and limitations of each source in terms of the task, purpose, and audience; integrate information into the text selectively to maintain the flow of ideas, avoiding plagiarism and overreliance on any one source and following a standard format for citation.

Additional Standards Addressed:
RL.11-12.5, RI.11-12.10, SL.11-12.1b, SL.11-12.1c

Discussion Groups

Learning Targets

- Prepare for discussion though the use of levels of questions and collecting information from notes and other sources.
- Work collaboratively to synthesize information and develop an understanding of *Their Eyes Were Watching God*.

Preview

In this activity, you will read the remaining chapters of the novel in groups using collaborative group guidelines.

Learning Strategies

Discussion Groups
Double-Entry Journal
Note-taking
Questioning the Text

Novel Study: The Remaining Chapters

You have approached the first half of *Their Eyes Were Watching God* in a variety of ways, such as shared reading, oral reading, and guided reading. For the second half of the novel, you will move to greater independence, reading on your own and participating in student-led discussion groups.

The remaining chapters of the novel can be divided into these broad chunks:

- Chapters 10–13 (Janie and Tea Cake in Eatonville)
- Chapters 14–19 (Janie and Tea Cake on the Muck)

You will read Chapter 20 with your class in the next activity.

1. For each chapter from Chapter 10 to 19, you will write literal, interpretive, and universal questions to help guide your group discussions and deepen your understanding of the text.

2. You will meet with your discussion group to create a schedule for reading, making sure that your schedule reflects the timeline provided by your teacher. Make sure that each group member writes down the reading schedule in his or her calendar; it is imperative that each member of the group maintain the reading schedule in order for discussions to be effective.

3. A model of a note-taking guide is provided for you. You may copy this guide into your Reader/Writer Notebook or modify it to fit your discussions; just be sure to take good notes during each discussion. These notes will help you understand the novel and prepare for writing an analytical essay.

Discussion Group Reading

4. To guide your discussion group's reading, consider these aspects of the Harlem Renaissance to trace throughout the novel:

- historical context
- philosophy/beliefs
- the arts
- daily life

As you discover textual evidence that connects to each of these aspects, write your levels of questions. Be prepared to discuss these points by identifying how the text illustrates Hurston's reflections of the Harlem Renaissance and her departures from its common themes.

My Notes

College and Career Readiness Standards

Focus Standards:

RL.11-12.1 Cite strong and thorough textual evidence to support analysis of what the text says explicitly as well as inferences drawn from the text, including determining where the text leaves matters uncertain.

RL.11-12.2 Determine two or more themes or central ideas of a text and analyze their development over the course of the text,

including how they interact and build on one another to produce a complex account; provide an objective summary of the text.

RL.11-12.3 Analyze the impact of the author's choices regarding how to develop and relate elements of a story or drama (e.g., where a story is set, how the action is ordered, how the characters are introduced and developed).

ACTIVITY 4.15

PLAN

Materials: *Their Eyes Were Watching God*, Chapters 10–19; double-entry journals; student-created reading schedule and reading assignments based on graphic organizer; timer
Suggested pacing: 5 50-minute class periods

TEACH

1 Read aloud the Learning Targets and Preview with students and clarify any questions they might have about the information.

2 Now that students are familiar with Hurston's style, they will take responsibility as they read the second half of the book in **discussion groups**.

3 Go over the information in the Novel Study: The Remaining Chapters section and student step 1 with students. Review with students the differences between asking literal, interpretative, and universal questions by having students revisit the questions they came up with in the previous activity.

4 Reinforce the importance of creating a reading schedule as noted in student step 2. Remind students of the task for the Embedded Assessment 2 assignment. The goal of the discussion groups and the **note-taking** is to prepare each member of the group to write a successful analytical essay.

5 Discuss good note-taking skills as a class and ask students to share any tips and insights they have about taking memorable, useful notes.

6 Discuss guidelines for conducting effective group discussions such as equal participation, preparation, time management, and respect for members' ideas and contributions.

7 Read aloud the Discussion Group Reading section and allow students to ask clarifying questions. If students need hints about how to approach the different possible topics, refer them back to the graphic organizer in the previous activity. Have students create levels of questions to facilitate discussions of these topics.

8 Point out to students that they should continue to take notes in their journals about these topics as they are reading and discussing each chapter.

9 Introduce students to the note-taking guide in student step 5. Help them to understand that they should choose a note-taking method that works best for them.

10 Assign students to groups (or allow them to choose their own). Be sure to give the groups a deadline for finishing the novel.

11 Go over the information in the After-Reading Discussions section with students.

12 Be sure students attend to the Check Your Understanding task at the end of each discussion group meeting. Encourage students within groups to share their summaries and experiences with each other.

13 Allow students time to conduct these sessions. Circulate among groups during each session to ensure that students are keeping on track with their reading calendar, keeping notes and recording information, and conducting group discussion in a respectful, orderly fashion. Check students' graphic organizers while circulating to ensure they are making connections between the text and its contexts as well as asking engaged levels of questions.

TEACHER TO TEACHER

As students will be reusing these graphic organizers daily, consider having them create an online, shared document to allow for note-taking and collaboration.

ASSESS

Review the Check Your Understanding summaries and reflective comments as a way to monitor the effectiveness of group note-taking.

ADAPT

If students need additional help writing a summary, have them collaborate in their small groups to complete a Paraphrasing and Summarizing Map. Each group member should be required to contribute an individual idea to the organizer.

4.15

5. You might use the following note-taking guide as a model for your notes, continue your double-entry journal, or create something similar to capture your discussions. Complete your notes before meeting with your discussion group.

Today's date:	Reading assignment:
Interpretive questions based on the reading assignment	Universal questions based on the reading assignment

After-Reading Discussions

6. As you meet with your discussion group, share your questions and discuss potential answers. To maintain order and ensure that all group members participate cooperatively, appoint one member as the timer. The timer should limit each member's comments to one or two minutes. Proceed to rotate around the group and follow the time limit. Take notes from your group members' comments to collect information to help you with Embedded Assessment 2.

Use a graphic organizer like this or your Reader/Writer Notebook to take notes during the group's discussion.

Today's topics:	
Topic 1:	Topic 2:
Notes:	Notes:

☑ Check Your Understanding

At the end of each discussion group meeting, write a summary of what you have learned in the meeting and reflect on the group process.

College and Career Readiness Standards

SL.11-12.1b Work with peers to promote civil, democratic discussions and decision making, set clear goals and deadlines, and establish individual roles as needed.

SL.11-12.1c Propel conversations by posing and responding to questions that probe reasoning and evidence; ensure a hearing for a full range of positions on a topic or issue; clarify, verify, or challenge ideas and conclusions; and promote divergent and creative perspectives.

Additional Standards Addressed:
W.11-12.8, W.11-12.10

The End of a Long Journey

Learning Targets

- Identify and evaluate the images and motifs that create the plot structure and thematic design of the novel.
- Participate in a collaborative discussion that synthesizes insights and interpretations.

Preview

In this activity, you will read the last chapter of *Their Eyes Were Watching God* and evaluate how Hurston's use of literary elements such as plot, character, setting, and point of view develops the theme and supports the author's purpose.

Learning Strategies

Discussion Groups
Marking the Text
Note-taking

My Notes

Novel Study: Completing the Book

1. Chapter 20 provides the final "frame" of Janie's story. Hurston chose to organize this novel by having Chapters 1 and 20 frame Janie's telling of her story to Pheoby. By the end of the novel, if you return to the first scene, you have a much clearer understanding of Janie's perception of her life and her "grand journey."

   Your purposes for reading this last chapter include:

   - to evaluate the organizational structure of the frame story
   - to mark the text for evidence of images and motifs that you recognize as being repeated throughout the novel (use sticky notes)

2. Mark the text and make your final entries into your double-entry journal. Be prepared to share these entries with your discussion group.

Thematic Development

Writing a Thematic Statement: Now that you have read the novel and discussed it at length, think about the major themes presented. Write a thematic statement in which you synthesize your understanding of the novel's literary elements and how they informed your interpretation of the author's purpose.

Keep in mind the guidelines for writing the thematic statement:

- It is one sentence that states the text's universal meaning about life, its central insight into life.
- It avoids summarizing the story, stating a moral, or reducing the story to a cliché.
- It can be supported by the imagery, characters, and events in the story.

Sample response: Janie's story conveys a journey of self-discovery and growing beyond limits imposed by others.

College and Career Readiness Standards

Focus Standards:

RL.11-12.3 Analyze the impact of the author's choices regarding how to develop and relate elements of a story or drama (e.g., where a story is set, how the action is ordered, how the characters are introduced and developed).

SL.11-12.1a Initiate and participate effectively in a range of collaborative discussions (one-on-one, in groups, and teacher-led) with diverse partners on grades 11–12 topics, texts, and issues, building on others' ideas and expressing their own clearly and persuasively.

PLAN

Materials: *Their Eyes Were Watching God,* Chapter 20; double-entry journals; sticky notes
Suggested Pacing: 2 50-minute class periods

TEACH

1 Have a volunteer read aloud the Learning Targets and Preview. Review with students the motifs that recur throughout the story: the horizon, clothing, mules, the pear tree, the porch, woman's place, and journey.

2 Read aloud the information in the first paragraph of student step 1 of the section Novel Study: Completing the Book. Guide students to recall the way the novel began as a frame tale.

3 Lead a shared reading of the last chapter and guide students to annotate the text for evidence of images and motifs that they recognize.

4 Allow students time to complete student step 2 with any final entries in their double-entry journal.

5 Review the guidelines for a thematic statement and model writing one on the board with assistance from students.

6 Give students time to compose their own thematic statements in their **discussion groups** and then have the other members provide feedback.

7 Conduct a whole-class discussion and allow each group to share one thematic statement. Ask each group how the thematic statement connects to aspects of the Harlem Renaissance.

ASSESS

Students' thematic statements should assert the text's central insight; their writing should be supported by textual evidence.

ADAPT

If students need additional help writing a thematic statement, give them a model to analyze or provide sentence frames.

PLAN

Materials: double-entry journals
Suggested Pacing: 1 50-minute class period

TEACH

 TEACHER TO TEACHER

The critical reviews provided here present varied opinions about Zora Neale Hurston, her work, and her place in the panoply of Harlem Renaissance writers. Studying these reviews will give students more perspectives on Hurston and provide textual evidence for their work on Embedded Assessment 2.

1 Read the Learning Targets and Preview with students. Ask students to consider all the literary criticism they have read about the novel so far and with which insights they have agreed or disagreed.

2 You may have students read, annotate, and discuss the book reviews in small groups or in pairs before you conduct a **whole-class discussion.**

3 Annotating and posing questions are strategies that require students to respond critically to the opinions of the reviewers. Note that these reviews were all written at the time the novel was published. More recent critical reviews might have a very different tone and perspective.

4 Go over the information and directions in student step 1 of the Reading Reviews section with students. Direct students to the literary definition of a book review and ask them to comment on book reviews they've read or written themselves. Then allow students time to look over the reviews on the back cover of the book and discuss them with a classmate.

5 To help students complete student step 2, model how to annotate Book Review 1 by connecting its ideas to how Hurston was a product of and a departure from the ideas in the Harlem Renaissance. Students can refer to their thematic statement from the previous activity to help them connect the review to their understanding of the novel's themes.

Learning Strategies

Socratic Seminar

VOCABULARY

LITERARY
A book review is a formal assessment or examination of a book.

My Notes

Learning Targets

- Evaluate multiple critical reviews in light of the ideas of the Harlem Renaissance.
- Identify and evaluate multiple thematic interpretations of a novel.

Preview

In this activity, you will read and evaluate multiple critical reviews of the novel you just finished and choose one to defend or challenge.

Reading Reviews

1. Much has been written in response to *Their Eyes Were Watching God*. Henry Louis Gates explains, "The curious aspect of the widespread critical attention being shown to Hurston's texts is that so many critics embracing such a diversity of theoretic approaches seem to find something new at which to marvel in her texts." Look at the back cover of the novel. It most likely has quotes from people who have written reviews of the book. Read and discuss the quotes with a partner.

2. Read the book review excerpts that follow and annotate in the margins, comparing each one to your understanding of the themes of *Their Eyes Were Watching God*. Ask yourself, "How does this interpretation help me understand how Hurston is a product of and a departure from the ideas of the Harlem Renaissance?"

Book Review 1

"It is folklore fiction at its best, which we gratefully accept as an overdue replacement for so much faulty local color fiction about Negroes. But when will the Negro novelist of maturity, who knows how to tell a story convincingly—which is Miss Hurston's cradle gift, come to grips with motive fiction and social document fiction? Progressive southern fiction has already banished the legend of these entertaining pseudo-primitives whom the reading public still loves to laugh with, weep over and envy. Having gotten rid of condescension, let us now get over oversimplification!"
—Alain Locke, *Opportunity*, June 1, 1938

Book Review 2

"Miss Hurston can write; but her prose is cloaked in that facile sensuality that has dogged Negro expression since the days of Phyllis Wheatley. Her dialogue manages to catch the psychological movements of the Negro folk-mind in their pure simplicity, but that's as far as it goes. Miss Hurston *voluntarily* continues in her novel the tradition which was forced upon the Negro in the theater, that is, the minstrel technique that makes the 'white folks' laugh. Her characters eat and laugh and cry and work and kill; they swing like a pendulum eternally in that safe and narrow orbit in which America likes to see the Negro live: between laughter and tears. [...] The sensory sweep of her novel carries no theme, no message, no thought. In the main, her novel is not addressed to the

College and Career Readiness Standards

Focus Standards:

RL.11-12.7 Analyze multiple interpretations of a story, drama, or poem (e.g., recorded or live production of a play or recorded novel or poetry), evaluating how each version interprets the source text.

RI.11-12.5 Analyze and evaluate the effectiveness of the structure an author uses in his or her exposition or argument, including whether the structure makes points clear, convincing, and engaging.

Additional Standards Addressed:

RI.11-12.1, W.11-12.1a, W.11-12.1b, W.11-12.1d, W.11-12.1e, W.11-12.5, SL.11-12.1a, SL.11-12.1b, SL.11-12.1c, SL.11-12.1d, L.11-12.5

Negro, but to a white audience whose chauvinistic tastes she knows how to satisfy. She exploits the phase of Negro life which is 'quaint,' the phase which evokes a piteous smile on the lips of the 'superior' race."
—Richard Wright, "Between Laughter and Tears," *New Masses*, 5 October 1937, p. 25

Book Review 3

"In a rich prose (which has, at the same time, a sort of nervous sensibility) she tells the tale of a girl who 'wanted things sweet with mah marriage, lak when you sit under a pear tree and think.' Janie did not get sweetness when her Grandma married her to Mister Killicks with his sixty acres of West Florida land, and his sagging belly, and his toenails that looked like mules' foots; and she didn't get it when she ran off with Joe Starks and got to be the Mayor's wife, and sat on her own store porch. But when Tea Cake came along with his trampish clothes and his easy ways and his nice grin that made even a middle-aged woman like Janie sort of wishful the minute she sets eyes on him, he handed her the keys of the kingdom, and their life together (what there was of it) was rapture and fun and tenderness and understanding—the perfect relationship of man and woman, whether they be black or white."
—Sheila Hibben, *The New York Herald Tribune Weekly Book Review*, September 26, 1937

Book Review 4

"The story of Janie's life down on the muck of Florida Glades, bean picking, hunting and the men shooting dice in the evening and how the hurricane came up and drove the animals and the Indians and finally the black people and the white people before it, and how Tea Cake, in Janie's eyes the 'son of Evening Son,' and incidentally the best crap shooter in the place, made Janie sing and glitter all over at last, is a little epic all by itself. Indeed, from first to last this is a well nigh perfect story—a little **sententious** at the start, but the rest is simple and beautiful and shining with humor."
—Lucille Tompkins, *The New York Times Book Review*, September 26, 1937

Making Observations

- Which reviews do you immediately agree or disagree with?
- What questions do you have after reading each review?

GRAMMAR & USAGE

Quoted Text

Notice how Hurston's words are enclosed in single quotation marks in the first sentence of Book Review 3. When quoting a critic who is quoting a part of a text, you must use double quotation marks around the critic's words and single quotation marks around the words of the text to distinguish them.

In Book Review 2, the review leaves out a part of the quote and lets the reader know by using ellipses [...] to signify that some text has been omitted.

Try shortening a quote from either book review. Use the proper quotation marks and substitute ellipses for the parts you want to omit.

WORD CONNECTIONS

Etymology

The word **chauvinistic** first described someone who had an exaggerated patriotism that could be seen as more of a vice than a virtue. The term came from the last name of a soldier who served in Napoleon's army, who was known for his fanatical patriotism. Today the meaning is similar: believing, with disapproval or contempt for others, that your country or gender is superior.

---

sententious: self-righteous

---

6 • Vocabulary Development: After students read Book Review 2, have the class review the Word Connections box discussion about the etymology of the word *chauvinistic*. Ask students about to what or whom *chauvinistic* refers toward the end of Book Review 2 as well as why the author may have chosen to use this word.

7 Pause after students read each review to address the Making Observations question *What questions do you have after reading each review?* Allow students to ask their questions and discuss possible answers as a class.

8 Be sure students attend to the Grammar & Usage feature on quoted text. Practice double quotations with students as needed and allow students time to shorten a quote from one of the book reviews.

9 Students can use the **double-entry journal** to record quotations they may want to use in the essay they will write for the Embedded Assessment. At this point, emphasize that it is important for them to complete the double-entry journal. Their collection of textual evidence and notes will be invaluable as they begin Embedded Assessment 2.

10 After students finish reading and annotating, ask them the first Making Observations question: *Which reviews do you immediately agree or disagree with?* Allow students time to debate their thoughts on some of the reviews and encourage them to support their argument with evidence.

Scaffolding the Text-Dependent Questions

3. What is the main idea in Locke's review? What does he applaud or criticize about the novel and/or Hurston's writing? What evidence from the text supports your answer? Is he more negative or more positive? RI.11-12.1

4. How does the structure of Tompkins's review reflect her opinion? How might this also reflect the artistic voices of the Harlem Renaissance? How did artist voices seek to establish a cultural identity? RI.11-12.5

5. How does Wright's opinion of Hurston's novel compare to the "psychological movements of the Negro folk-mind" and the themes and goals of the Harlem Renaissance? What textual evidence supports your answer? What does Wright claim about Hurston's dialogue? Why doesn't he believe her novel improves society's perceptions of African Americans? RI.11-12.5

11 **RETURNING TO THE TEXT:** Have students answer the text-dependent questions. If they have difficulty, scaffold the questions by rephrasing them or breaking them into smaller parts. See the Scaffolding the Text-Dependent Questions boxes for suggestions.

4.17

Returning to the Text

- Return to the book reviews as you respond to the following questions. Use text evidence to support your responses.
- Write any additional questions you have about the book reviews in your Reader/Writer Notebook.

3. **What is the main idea in Locke's review? What does he applaud or criticize about the novel and/or Hurston's writing? What evidence from the text supports your answer?**

Locke praises Hurston's fiction, saying it is "folklore fiction at its best, ... an overdue replacement for so much faulty local color fiction about Negroes." However, he has more negative than positive to say about this particular work. Locke believes Hurston did not use her abilities to their fullest extent to promote her views and contributions to the Negro community. These views are expressed in his rhetorical question: "When will the Negro novelist of maturity ... come to grips with motive fiction and social document fiction?"

4. **How does the structure of Tompkins's review reflect her opinion? How might this also reflect the artistic voices of the Harlem Renaissance? Support your answer with evidence from the text.**

Tompkins's review begins with a run-on sentence that spans 6 lines, concluding, "The story of Janie's life ... is a little epic all by itself." The sentence structure and syntax provide a linguistic picture of the all-encompassing, epic nature of the story. She goes on to say that "from first to last this is a well nigh perfect story," one that is "simple and beautiful and shining with humor." Artists of the Harlem Renaissance carried their heritage and past with them and wove them into their present and hopes for the future as they sought to establish a cultural identity and purposeful voice. They wanted to show everyone that "from first to last," their story was indeed "simple and beautiful and shining with humor."

5. **How does Wright's opinion of Hurston's novel compare to the "psychological movements of the Negro folk-mind" and the themes and goals of the Harlem Renaissance? What textual evidence supports your answer?**

Wright claims that Hurston's dialogue supports the simplicity of the Negro folk-mind, which in itself carries critical tones of his perception of the movement. He accuses Hurston of choosing to continue the tradition of the "minstrel technique that makes the 'white folks' laugh" with the goal of playing to her audience. According to Wright, Hurston's novel does little or nothing to improve society's perception of African Americans, in contrast to the goals of the Harlem Renaissance.

Scaffolding the Text-Dependent Questions

6. **How does Tompkins's review expand on Hibben's ideas? Taken together, how do these reviews contribute to an understanding of Hurston's possible goals in writing the novel? What does Tompkins say the story is about? What do both authors agree on?** RI.11-12.5

6. How does Tompkins's review expand on Hibben's ideas? Taken together, how do these reviews contribute to an understanding of Hurston's possible goals in writing the novel?

Hibben provides little more than a brief overview of the progression of the novel, specifically

pertaining to Janie's search for happiness. Tompkins fills in the gaps, saying that the story

is about "Janie's life down on the muck of Florida Glades, bean picking, hunting ... " Both

reviews point to the role of Tea Cake as the fulfillment of Janie's dreams: in Hibben's words,

"he handed her the keys of the kingdom," and according to Tompkins, "in Janie's eyes [he

was] the 'son of Evening Son.'" Hurston may have set out to write an epic tale or a story of

evolving relationships between men and women. If so, according to these reviewers, she has

accomplished her purpose.

Socratic Seminar

7. Craft three or four interpretive and universal questions about each of the four critical reviews. Then use these questions in a Socratic Seminar to connect these reviews to your understanding the Harlem Renaissance.

☑ Check Your Understanding

Summarize a point made by one of your classmates.

📝 Writing Prompt: Argumentative

Once you have discussed the critical reviews, choose one and defend or challenge. Connect your understanding of the critical review to the values, historical context, arts, or daily life championed by the movement known as the Harlem Renaissance. Be sure to:

- Begin your argument with a thesis sentence that introduces a precise claim.
- Establish the significance of the claim, distinguishing it from opposing claims.
- Continue to develop the claim and counterclaim fairly and thoroughly.
- Supply relevant text evidence, including quotations and commentary from the review and novel, to support your thesis.
- Establish and maintain a formal style as you write.
- Provide a conclusion that supports your argument and thesis.

🕐 Independent Reading Checkpoint

Review your independent reading. Suppose you were going to write a critical review for it. Using the book reviews in this activity as a model, identify at least two thematic interpretations of the selection. Think about how you might use this information in a critical review. Share your ideas with a group.

WRITING PROMPT: ARGUMENTATIVE

The following standards are addressed in the Writing Prompt:

- W.11-12.1a
- W.11-12.1b
- W.11-12.1b
- W.11-12.1b
- W.11-12.1d
- W.11-12.1e

---

12 Guide students to complete student step 7 in the Socratic Seminar section independently. Remind them of the difference between interpretive and universal questions by writing a few on the board in a T-chart. Ask volunteers for examples to put in each column.

13 Allow students time to complete the **Socratic Seminar** after they write their questions. Have students orally share a summary point made by one of their classmates in answer to the Check Your Understanding prompt.

14 Go over the Writing Prompt with students and if necessary help them to recall the values, historical context, arts, and daily life of the Harlem Renaissance.

15 Have students complete the Independent Reading Checkpoint. Allow students time to discuss their ideas for a critical review with a group.

ASSESS

Review students' questions to ensure that they are interpretive or analytical in nature. Monitor the Socratic Seminar to ensure students contribute equally and productively and to assess students' ability to connect the critical reviews to Harlem Renaissance values.

Use students' responses to the Writing Prompt to gauge their understanding of how to defend, challenge, or qualify a critical review.

ADAPT

If students need additional help **questioning the text** of a critical review, review the levels of questions. Then model crafting one interpretive or universal question. Have students help you use the question to make connections.

If students have not mastered writing an argument, allow them to work in pairs to choose a critical review. They can work collaboratively to write a thesis statement, gather evidence, and review each other's drafts.

Materials: students' double-entry journal notes taken for Activities 4.8–4.17

Suggested Pacing: 2 50-minute class periods plus homework

1 Read aloud the text in the Assignment box and comment on each of the rows in the chart as a way to support students' thorough understanding of expectations of the assessment process.

2 Planning and Prewriting: Ensure that students understand the requirements of the Writing Prompt. Remind them to review all the works they have read by Hurston and the Scoring Guide criteria to ensure they understand the expectations for this assessment.

3 Alert students that they will need their double-entry journal, their notes for Activities 4.8–4.17 for reference, and their notes on the Harlem Renaissance (taken during the research project presentations) for reference resources.

4 Drafting: You might want to limit the number of sources that students can use in their essays. Be sure they draft a works cited page. Remind them to cite sources correctly.

5 Evaluating and Revising the Draft: Use this as an opportunity to have students share and respond to drafts in writing groups to get feedback about possible revisions.

6 Checking and Editing for Publication: Remind students to take the time to do more than simply spell-check their essays. Advise them to use their **Editor's/Writer's Checklists** as they revise their drafts. They should specifically check for the grammar topics covered in this unit, including correct end punctuation, run-ons and fragments, and unnecessary punctuation. Students should also ensure that their response employs appropriate diction.

Writing an Analytical Essay

 ASSIGNMENT

Write an analytical essay in which you discuss how Zora Neale Hurston's writing is both a reflection of and a departure from the ideas of the Harlem Renaissance. Include aspects of the Harlem Renaissance that you see reflected in Hurston's writing as well as characteristics of Hurston's writing that are departures from selected aspects of the Harlem Renaissance.

Planning and Prewriting: Take time to make a plan for your essay.	■ What resources on the Harlem Renaissance can you use to help you plan your work? ■ What writings by Zora Neale Hurston will you refer to? ■ What elements of the Harlem Renaissance do you recognize in Hurston's writing, and what elements of her writings seem to be departures from those aspects?
Drafting: Determine the structure and how you will incorporate your evidence.	■ How can you state your claim as a single thesis statement so that it captures your thinking? ■ What organizational pattern will best allow you to compare Hurston's work to aspects of the Harlem Renaissance? How will you use textual evidence from your sources to support your ideas? How will you use commentary to explain how this evidence relates to your thesis? ■ Is the evidence that you use cited in a way that will allow your audience to know which source is being used every time? Does your works cited page provide all the information necessary for your audience?
Evaluating and Revising the Draft: Make your work the best it can be.	■ How can you use transitions so that one idea moves smoothly to the next? ■ How will you use the Scoring Guide and peer responses to help guide your revision?
Checking and Editing for Publication: Confirm that your final draft is ready for publication.	■ How will you ensure that your essay maintains an academic, formal tone; that it seamlessly embeds quotations within the text; and that it uses varied syntax? ■ How will you check for grammatical and technical accuracy?

Reflection

After completing this Embedded Assessment, think about how you went about accomplishing this assignment and respond to the following question:

- How did the use of both primary and secondary sources help you examine how writers' works can be a product of both their time and their own personal perspective?

College and Career Readiness Standards

Focus Standards:

W.11-12.1 Write arguments to support claims in an analysis of substantive topics or texts, using valid reasoning and relevant and sufficient evidence.

W.11-12.2 Write informative/explanatory texts to examine and convey complex ideas, concepts, and information clearly and accurately through the effective selection, organization, and analysis of content.

W.11-12.4 Produce clear and coherent writing in which the development, organization, and style are appropriate to task, purpose, and audience.

W.11-12.5 Develop and strengthen writing as needed by planning, revising, editing, rewriting, or trying a new approach, focusing on addressing what is most significant for a specific purpose and audience.

SCORING GUIDE

Scoring Criteria	Exemplary	Proficient	Emerging	Incomplete
Ideas	The essay • presents a convincing, thorough, and perceptive understanding of Hurston's writings as well as aspects of the Harlem Renaissance • contains analysis that demonstrates an exceptional insight into Hurston's writings and the Harlem Renaissance • uses clear and effective specific and well-chosen examples that yield detailed support for the analysis.	The essay • demonstrates a solid understanding of Hurston's writing and the Harlem Renaissance and provides a convincing text • contains analysis that demonstrates a general insight into Hurston's writings and the Harlem Renaissance • uses appropriate examples to support the position.	The essay • demonstrates an uneven understanding of Hurston's writing and/or the Harlem Renaissance and does not create a convincing text • attempts to analyze Hurston's writings and the Harlem Renaissance, but the analysis may be simplistic or replaced by summary • uses evidence to support the position with a weak or unclear connection to the claim.	The essay • demonstrates a superficial understanding of Hurston's writings and the Harlem Renaissance and provides an underdeveloped text • lacks an analysis of Hurston's writings and the Harlem Renaissance • uses evidence to support the position that may be weak or provides too few examples.
Structure	The essay • is exceptionally well organized • moves smoothly and comfortably between ideas • uses clear and effective transitions to enhance the essay's coherence.	The essay • is clearly organized • sequences ideas in a way that is easy to follow • uses transitions to move between ideas.	The essay • is organized with some lapses in structure or coherence • sequences ideas in a way that may be confusing at times • inconsistently uses transitions.	The essay • is organized in a way that impedes the ideas presented • sequences ideas in a way that is difficult to follow • jumps too rapidly between ideas and lacks transitions.
Use of Language	The essay • employs stylistic choices in language that are exceptional • successfully weaves textual evidence from the novel into its own prose • demonstrates strong control and mastery of standard writing conventions.	The essay • employs stylistic choices in language that are clear and appropriate • weaves textual evidence from the novel into its own prose accurately • demonstrates control of standard writing conventions, and though some errors may appear, they do not seriously impede readability.	The essay • uses stylistic choices in language that are uneven • attempts to incorporate textual evidence from the novel into its own prose yet may do so awkwardly or inaccurately • contains errors in standard writing conventions that interfere with the meaning.	The essay • uses stylistic choices in language that are not appropriate for the topic • does not incorporate textual evidence from the novel • contains frequent errors in standard writing conventions that severely interfere with the meaning.

College and Career Readiness Standards

W.11-12.10 Write routinely over extended time frames (time for research, reflection, and revision) and shorter time frames (a single sitting or a day or two) for a range of tasks, purposes, and audiences.

L.11-12.1 Demonstrate command of the conventions of standard English grammar and usage when writing or speaking.

L.11-12.2 Demonstrate command of the conventions of standard English capitalization, punctuation, and spelling when writing.

EMBEDDED ASSESSMENT 2 continued

7 Reflection: Remind them that this is the final reflection of the year. Once students have completed this reflection and have added it to the others created during the year, ask them to review all their reflections and consider which one gives them the most information about themselves and their growth as readers, writers, presenters, speakers, and listeners.

8 Allow for a portfolio review. This is the time for students to conduct an end-of-year self-evaluation, using the work collected over the year as evidence of growth in learning.

9 The self-evaluation can be conducted in a variety of ways, but it should reflect a level of self-discovery about individual strengths and challenges faced during the academic year.

10 Students may choose to write a letter to next year's teacher or to create a final portfolio of samples of best work with a description of each work. They could even write a final reflection that synthesizes all the reflective thinking about learning over the year.

SCORING GUIDE

When you score this Embedded Assessment, you might consider downloading and printing copies of the Scoring Guide from SpringBoard Digital. Make copies for all students so that you have a copy to mark for each student's work.

Resources

Independent Reading

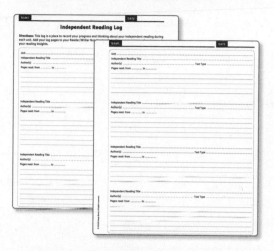

Learning Strategies

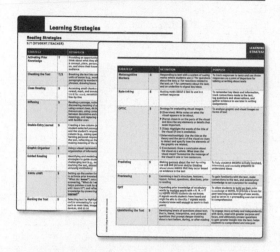

Graphic Organizers

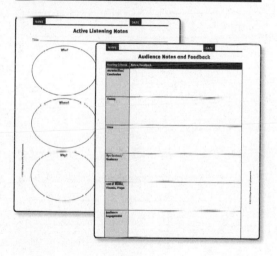

English-Spanish Glossary

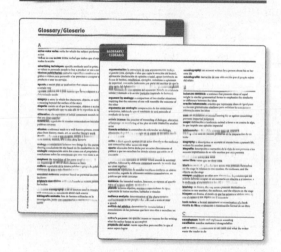

Index of Skills

Index of Authors and Titles

Independent Reading Log

Directions: This log is a place to record your progress and thinking about your independent reading during each unit. Add your log pages to your Reader/Writer Notebook or keep them as a separate place to record your reading insights.

Unit _____

Independent Reading Title _____

Author(s) _____ Text Type _____

Pages read: from _____ to _____

_____
_____
_____
_____
_____

Independent Reading Title _____

Author(s) _____ Text Type _____

Pages read: from _____ to _____

_____
_____
_____
_____
_____
_____

Independent Reading Title _____

Author(s) _____ Text Type _____

Pages read: from _____ to _____

_____
_____
_____
_____
_____
_____

Unit _____

Independent Reading Title _____

Author(s) _____ Text Type _____

Pages read: from _____ to _____

_____
_____
_____
_____
_____

Independent Reading Title _____

Author(s) _____ Text Type _____

Pages read: from _____ to _____

_____
_____
_____
_____
_____
_____

Independent Reading Title _____

Author(s) _____ Text Type _____

Pages read: from _____ to _____

_____
_____
_____
_____
_____

Independent Reading Title _____

Author(s) _____ Text Type _____

Pages read: from _____ to _____

_____
_____
_____
_____
_____

Learning Strategies

Reading Strategies

S/T (STUDENT/TEACHER)

STRATEGY		DEFINITION	PURPOSE
Activating Prior Knowledge	T	Providing an opportunity for students to think about what they already know about a concept, place, person, culture, and so on, and share their knowledge with a wider audience	To prepare students to encounter new concepts, places, persons, cultures, and so on, prior to reading a text; an Anticipation Guide and a Quickwrite can be used to activate and assess prior knowledge
Chunking the Text	T/S	Breaking the text into smaller, manageable units of sense (e.g., words, sentences, paragraphs) by numbering, separating phrases, drawing boxes	To reduce the intimidation factor when encountering long words, sentences, or whole texts; to increase comprehension of difficult or challenging text
Close Reading	S	Accessing small chunks of text to read, reread, mark, and annotate key passages, word-for-word, sentence-by-sentence, and line-by-line	To develop comprehensive understanding by engaging in one or more focused readings of a text
Diffusing	S	Reading a passage, noting unfamiliar words, discovering meaning of unfamiliar words using context clues, dictionaries, and/or thesauruses, using context to distinguish between denotative and connotative meanings, and replacing unfamiliar words with familiar ones	To facilitate a close reading of text, the use of resources, an understanding of synonyms, and increased comprehension of text
Double-Entry Journal	S	Creating a two-column journal with a student-selected passage in one column and the student's response in the second column (e.g., asking questions of the text, forming personal responses, interpreting the text, reflecting on the process of making meaning of the text)	To assist in note-taking and organizing key textual elements and responses noted during reading in order to generate textual support that can be incorporated into a piece of writing at a later time
Graphic Organizer	S	Using a visual representation for the organization of information from the text	To facilitate increased comprehension and discussion
Guided Reading	T	Identifying and modeling a series of strategies to guide students through challenging text (e.g., making predictions, marking the text, skimming the text, diffusing vocabulary)	To model for students the use of multiple strategies to make meaning of challenging texts and help them learn to apply the strategies independently
KWHL Chart	S	Setting up discussion that allows students to activate prior knowledge by answering, "What do I **know**?"; sets a purpose by answering, "What do I **want** to know?"; helps preview a task by answering, **"How** will I learn it?"; and reflects on new knowledge by answering, "What have I **learned**?"	To organize thinking, access prior knowledge, and reflect on learning to increase comprehension and engagement
Marking the Text	S	Selecting text by highlighting, underlining, and/or annotating for specific components, such as main idea, imagery, literary devices, and so on	To focus reading for specific purposes, such as author's craft, and to organize information from selections; to facilitate reexamination of a text

STRATEGY		DEFINITION	PURPOSE
Metacognitive Markers	S	Responding to text with a system of cueing marks where students use a ? for questions about the text; a ! for reactions related to the text; an * for comments about the text; and an underline to signal key ideas	To track responses to texts and use those responses as a point of departure for talking or writing about texts
Note-taking	S	Making notes about a text to use in a written response	To remember key ideas and information, track connections made to the text, log questions and observations, and gather evidence to use later in writing assignments
OPTIC	S	Strategy for evaluating visual images. **O** (Overview): Write notes on what the visual appears to be about. **P** (Parts): Zoom in on the parts of the visual and describe any elements or details that seem important. **T** (Title): Highlight the words of the title of the visual (if one is available). **I** (Interrelationships): Use the title as the theory and the parts of the visual as clues to detect and specify how the elements of the graphic are related. **C** (Conclusion): Draw a conclusion about the visual as a whole. What does the visual mean? Summarize the message of the visual in one or two sentences.	To analyze graphic and visual images as forms of text
Predicting	S	Making guesses about the text by using the title and pictures and/or thinking ahead about events that may occur based on evidence in the text	To help students become actively involved, interested, and mentally prepared to understand ideas
Previewing	S	Examining a text's structure, features, layout, format, questions, directions, prior to reading	To gain familiarity with the text, make connections to the text, and extend prior knowledge to set a purpose for reading
QHT	S	Expanding prior knowledge of vocabulary words by marking words with a **Q**, **H**, or **T** (Q signals words students do not know; H signals words students have heard and might be able to identify; T signals words students know well enough to teach to their peers)	To allow students to build on their prior knowledge of words, to provide a forum for peer teaching and learning of new words, and to serve as a prereading exercise to aid in comprehension
Questioning the Text	S	Developing levels of questions about text; that is, literal, interpretive, and universal questions that prompt deeper thinking about a text before, during, or after reading	To engage more actively and independently with texts, read with greater purpose and focus, and ultimately answer questions to gain greater insight into the text; helps students to comprehend and interpret

STRATEGY		DEFINITION	PURPOSE
Paraphrasing	S	Restating in one's own words the essential information expressed in a text, whether it be narration, dialogue, or informational text, while maintaining the original text's meaning	To encourage and facilitate comprehension of challenging text
RAFT	S	Primarily used to generate new text, this strategy can also be used to analyze a text by examining the role of the speaker (R), the intended audience (A), the format of the text (F), and the topic of the text (T)	To initiate reader response; to facilitate an analysis of a text to gain focus prior to creating a new text
Rereading	S	Encountering the same text with more than one reading	To identify additional details; to clarify meaning and/or reinforce comprehension of texts
SIFT	S	Analyzing a fictional text by examining stylistic elements, especially symbol, imagery, and figures of speech, in order to show how all work together to reveal tone and theme	To focus and facilitate an analysis of a fictional text by examining the title and text for symbolism, identifying images and sensory details, analyzing figurative language, and identifying how all these elements reveal tone and theme
Skimming/Scanning	S	Skimming by rapid or superficial reading of a text to form an overall impression or to obtain a general understanding of the material; scanning focuses on key words, phrases, or specific details and provides speedy recognition of information	To quickly form an overall impression prior to an in-depth study of a text; to answer specific questions or quickly locate targeted information or detail in a text
SMELL	S	Analyzing a persuasive speech or essay by asking five essential questions: • **S**ender-receiver relationship—What is the sender-receiver relationship? Who are the images and language meant to attract? Describe the speaker of the text. • **M**essage—What is the message? Summarize the statement made in the text. • **E**motional Strategies—What is the desired effect? • **L**ogical Strategies—What logic is operating? How does it (or its absence) affect the message? Consider the logic of the images as well as the words. • **L**anguage—What does the language of the text describe? How does it affect the meaning and effectiveness of the writing? Consider the language of the images as well as the words.	To analyze a persuasive speech or essay by focusing on five essential characteristics of the genre; analysis is related to rhetorical devices, logical fallacies, and how an author's use of language achieves specific purposes
SOAPSTone	S	Analyzing text by discussing and identifying **S**peaker, **O**ccasion, **A**udience, **P**urpose, **S**ubject, and **T**one	To facilitate the analysis of specific elements of nonfiction, literary, and informational texts, and show the relationship among the elements to an understanding of the whole

STRATEGY		DEFINITION	PURPOSE
Summarizing	S	Giving a brief statement of the main points or essential information expressed in a text, whether it be narration, dialogue, or informational text	To facilitate comprehension and recall of a text
Think Aloud	S/T	Talking through a difficult passage or task by using a form of metacognition whereby the reader expresses how he/she has made sense of the text	To reflect on how readers make meaning of challenging texts and to facilitate discussion
TP-CASTT	S	Analyzing a poetic text by identifying and discussing **T**itle, **P**araphrase, **C**onnotation, **A**ttitude, **S**hift, **T**heme, and **T**itle again	To facilitate the analysis of specific elements of a literary text, especially poetry. To show how the elements work together to create meaning
Visualizing	S	Forming a picture (mentally and/or literally) while reading a text to deepen understanding	To increase reading comprehension, deepen understanding, and promote active engagement with text
Word Maps	S	Using a clearly defined graphic organizer such as concept circles or word webs to identify and reinforce word meanings	To provide a visual tool for identifying and remembering multiple aspects of words and word meanings
Word Sort	T	Organizing and sorting words into categories designated by the teacher or selected by the student and providing a written or oral justification for the classifications	To solidify understanding of word meanings by considering the multiple uses, meanings, and relationships of word parts, words, and groups of words

Writing Strategies

S/T (STUDENT/TEACHER)

STRATEGY		DEFINITION	PURPOSE
Adding	S	Enhancing a text by finding areas to add facts, details, examples, and commentary; smoothing out transitions; and clarifying and strengthening ideas and assertions	To improve, refine, and clarify the writer's thoughts during drafting and/or revision
Brainstorming	S	Using a flexible but deliberate process of listing multiple ideas in a short period of time without excluding any idea from the preliminary list	To generate ideas, concepts, or key words that provide a focus and/or establish organization as part of the prewriting or revision process
Deleting	S	Enhancing a text by eliminating words, phrases, sentences, or ideas that inhibit clarity and cohesiveness	To improve, refine, and clarify the writer's thoughts during drafting and/or revision
Drafting	S	Composing a text in its initial form before developing it	To incorporate brainstormed or initial ideas into a written format
Freewriting	S	Writing freely without constraints in order to generate ideas and capture thinking	To generate ideas when planning a piece of writing, or to refine and clarify thoughts, spark new ideas, and/or generate content during drafting and/or revision
Generating Questions	S	Clarifying and developing ideas by asking questions of the draft. May be part of self-editing or peer editing	To clarify and develop ideas in a draft; used during drafting and as part of writer response
Graphic Organizer	S	Organizing ideas and information visually (e.g., Venn diagrams, flowcharts, cluster maps)	To provide a visual system for organizing multiple ideas, details, and/or textual support to be included in a piece of writing
Guided Writing	T	Modeling the writing that students are expected to produce by guiding students through the planning, generation of ideas, organization, drafting, revision, editing, and publication of texts before students are asked to perform the same process; co-constructing texts with students as part of guided writing	To demonstrate the writing process
Looping	S	Selecting one section of a draft to elaborate on by generating new ideas, and then repeating the process with the newly-written section	To generate new content during drafting and revision
Manipulatives	T	Providing tactile and kinesthetic experiences to engage students in the process of writing by physically maneuvering words, phrases, or sentences to reconstruct text in as many different ways as possible and note how meaning changes with each rearrangement	To appeal to kinesthetic learners and help students visualize the form and function of various parts of speech, stylistic concerns, sentence structure, and so on

STRATEGY		DEFINITION	PURPOSE
Mapping	S	Creating a graphic organizer that serves as a visual representation of the organizational plan for a written text	To plan the structure and organization of a text
Marking the Draft	S	Interacting with a draft by highlighting, underlining, color-coding, and annotating to indicate edits and suggestions for revision	To encourage focused, reflective thinking about revising and editing drafts
Note-taking	S	Making notes about a discussion to use in a written response	To record relevant evidence and information shared in discussion to use later in writing assignments
Outlining	S	Using a system of numerals and letters in order to identify topics and supporting details and ensure an appropriate balance of ideas	To plan the structure and organization of a text
Quickwrite	S	Writing for a short, specific amount of time in response to a prompt provided	To generate multiple ideas in a quick fashion that could be turned into longer pieces of writing at a later time
RAFT	S	Generating a new text and/or transforming a text by identifying and manipulating its Role, Audience, Format, and Topic	To generate a text by identifying the Role, Audience, Format, and/or Topic that will be most appropriate for the intended purpose
Rearranging	S	Selecting components of a text and moving them to another place within the text and/or modifying the order in which the author's ideas are presented	To refine and clarify the writer's thoughts during drafting and/or revision
Self-Editing/Peer Editing	S	Working individually or with a partner to examine a text closely in order to identify areas that might need to be corrected for grammar, punctuation, spelling	To provide a systematic process for editing a written text to ensure correctness of identified components such as conventions of standard English
Sharing and Responding	S	Communicating with another person or a small group of peers who respond to a piece of writing as focused readers (not necessarily as evaluators)	To make suggestions for improvement to the work of others and/or to receive appropriate and relevant feedback on the writer's own work, used during the drafting and revision process
Sketching	S	Drawing or sketching ideas or ordering of ideas (includes storyboarding, visualizing)	To generate and/or clarify ideas by visualizing them (may be part of prewriting)
Substituting/ Replacing	S	Replacing original words or phrases in a text with new words or phrases that achieve the desired effect	To refine and clarify the writer's thoughts during drafting and/or revision; to develop the writer's diction
TWIST	S	Arriving at a thesis statement that incorporates the following literary elements: **T**one, **W**ord choice (diction), **I**magery, **S**tyle, and **T**heme	To craft an interpretive thesis in response to a prompt about a text

STRATEGY		DEFINITION	PURPOSE
Visual/Auditory Prompts	T	Providing visual stimuli (e.g., a piece of art, film clip, visual media) or auditory stimuli (e.g., music, sound effects, radio broadcast, etc.) prior to writing	To encourage response to varied stimuli; to provide an opportunity for students of various learning styles to create a written text
Webbing	S	Developing a graphic organizer that consists of a series of circles connected with lines to indicate relationships among ideas	To generate ideas, concepts, or key words that provide a focus and/or establish organization prior to writing an initial draft and/or during the revision process
Writer's Checklist	T/S	Using a co-constructed checklist (that could be written on a bookmark and/or displayed on the wall) in order to look for specific features of a writing text and check for accuracy	To focus on key areas of the writing process so that the writer can effectively revise a draft and correct mistakes
Writing Groups	S	A type of discussion group devoted to sharing and responding to student work	To facilitate a collaborative approach to generating ideas for and revising writing

Speaking and Listening Strategies

S/T (STUDENT/TEACHER)

STRATEGY		DEFINITION	PURPOSE
Choral Reading	T/S	Reading text lines aloud in student groups and/or individually to present an interpretation	To develop fluency; differentiate between the reading of statements and questions; practice phrasing, pacing, and reading dialogue; show how a character's emotions are captured through vocal stress and intonation
Debate	T	Engaging in a structured argument to examine both sides of an issue	To provide students with an opportunity to collect and orally present evidence supporting the affirmative and negative arguments of a proposition or issue
Drama Games	T	Participating in creative dramatics (e.g., pantomime, tableau, role-playing) to reinforce an oral literacy skill or develop a deeper understanding of a concept	To engage students in the reading and presenting of text and to create meaning through a kinesthetic approach
Fishbowl (Inner/outer circles)	T	Discussing specific topics within groups; some students will form the inner circle and model appropriate discussion techniques while an outer circle of students listens to and evaluates the discussion process of the inner circle in order to respond effectively	To provide students with an opportunity to engage in a formal discussion and to experience roles both as participant and active listener; students also have the responsibility of supporting their opinions and responses using specific textual evidence
Note-taking	S	Creating a record of information while listening to a speaker or reading a text	To facilitate active listening or close reading; to record and organize ideas that assist in processing information
Oral Reading	S	Reading aloud one's own text or the texts of others (e.g., echo reading, choral reading, paired readings)	To share one's own work or the work of others; build fluency and increase confidence in presenting to a group
Rehearsal	T/S	Encouraging multiple practices of a piece of text prior to a performance	To provide students with an opportunity to clarify the meaning of a text prior to a performance as they refine the use of dramatic conventions (e.g., gestures, vocal interpretations, facial expressions)
Role-Playing	S	Assuming the role or persona of a character	To develop the voice, emotions, and mannerisms of a character to facilitate improved comprehension of a text
Socratic Seminar	T	Tying a focused discussion to an essential question, topic, or selected text in which students ask questions of each other; questions initiate a conversation that continues with a series of responses and additional questions	To help students formulate questions that address issues (in lieu of simply stating their opinions) to facilitate their own discussion and arrive at a new understanding; students also have the responsibility of supporting their opinions and responses using specific textual evidence

Collaborative Strategies

S/T (STUDENT/TEACHER)

STRATEGY		DEFINITION	PURPOSE
Discussion Groups	T/S	Engaging in an interactive, small-group discussion, often with an assigned role; to consider a topic, text, or question	To gain new understanding of or insight into a text from multiple perspectives
Jigsaw	T	In groups, students read different texts or passages from a single text, then share and exchange information from their reading with another group. They then return to their original groups to share their new knowledge.	To summarize and present information to others in a way that facilitates an understanding of a text (or multiple texts) without having each student read the text in its entirety
Literature Circles	T	Groups of students read the same text to participate in a mutual reading experience; based on the objective(s) of the lesson, students take on a variety of roles throughout the reading experience; texts may be selected based on individual preferences or on the demands of the text.	To provide opportunities for students to interact with one another as they read, respond to, and interpret a common text
Think-Pair-Share	T/S	Pairing with a peer to share ideas before sharing ideas and discussion with a larger group	To construct meaning about a topic or question; to test thinking in relation to the ideas of others; to prepare for a discussion with a larger group

English Language Development Strategies

S/T (STUDENT/TEACHER)

STRATEGY		DEFINITION	PURPOSE
Choral Reading	S/T	Reading a text or part of a text aloud in pairs, groups, or as a whole class	To build students' fluency, expression, and self-confidence when reading short texts and to provide a model for fluent reading as students follow along
Cloze Reading	T	Reading aloud a text in which certain key words—such as target vocabulary terms or words with strong context clues—have been omitted and replaced with blanks; when reading the text aloud, the teacher pauses to allow students to fill in the blanks, sometimes with the support of a word bank. Teachers may differentiate by omitting more words for students with higher language proficiency.	To support students in processing and constructing meaning from texts rather than just reading words without comprehension; cloze reading can be used to encourage struggling readers to consider context as they read a passage, and it can also be used with more proficient students as a way to study word choice, shades of meaning, and register (or formality) of words

STRATEGY		DEFINITION	PURPOSE
Cognate Bridge	S/T	Adding cognates to the class Word Wall to create a bridge between English vocabulary terms and their cognates; cognates are words in different languages that sound alike and have a similar meaning because they have a common origin. For example, the words *analogy* and *analogía* in English and Spanish both derive from the Greek word *analogos*.	To facilitate the development of academic language in English by leveraging students' native language resources; highlighting cognates can also help students build vocabulary by recognizing patterns in word roots, prefixes, and suffixes
Conferencing	S/T	Students collaborate with peers to eliminate gaps in understanding or confusion about a text or task. Students first work in pairs to generate questions. Then they join another pair to try to answer their questions. The class debriefs as needed.	To build learner autonomy by encouraging students to identify gaps in understanding and to fill those gaps through meaningful interaction with peers
Discourse Starters	S/T	Students use sentence starters with key academic language to engage in academic conversations. (See the **Discourse Starters** available in the Resources section of the student and teacher editions.)	To promote academic conversations by providing patterned expressions often used in academic discourse; this can alleviate some of the challenge of impromptu class discussions, allowing students to focus their thinking on ideas rather than on the formulation of a response
Echo Reading	S/T	Modeling the pronunciation and intonation of a word, phrase, sentence, paragraph, or other segment of text and then having students imitate, or echo, the teacher's reading	To model pronunciation, phrasing, and intonation of new or challenging language; to boost reading fluency and expression in struggling students
Four Corners	T	Labeling the four corners of the classroom with opinion statements (e.g., Strongly Agree, Agree, Disagree, Strongly Disagree) and having students move into the corner that corresponds to their opinion about a claim; students then discuss their reasoning with their corner group before reporting to the class. Four Corners can by modified in numerous ways. For example, corners can be labeled with words with shades of meaning (e.g., *capable, proficient, skillful, talented*) so that students can discuss the best word choice in a given context.	To provide students with a low-stakes opportunity to state an opinion and discuss ideas or reasoning before speaking in front of a larger group; to allow for additional processing time before asking students to share their ideas; to formatively assess students' ability to support ideas with reasoning and/or evidence

STRATEGY		DEFINITION	PURPOSE
Visual Response	S/T	Using visuals—like pictures, sketches, flow charts, pantomime, or graphic organizers—to demonstrate thinking, analysis, or interpretation of a text or other stimulus; for example, students could use sketches to depict the emotional or physical changes a character experiences over the course of a story.	To foster critical thinking and processing of information without depending on language as the primary medium for communicating one's thinking; to enable students to engage in the cognitive demands of a lesson even when they are still developing English language proficiency
Reading Roles	S/T	Students are divided into groups and assigned defined roles (see below) as they read and discuss a text. After reading a predetermined portion of the text, students pause to engage in a discussion as follows: • **Summarizer**: briefly restates the main points of the text selection • **Questioner**: poses questions about the text • **Clarifier**: tries to address the questions posed in the previous step • **Predictor**: offers a prediction of what will come next in the text	To support reading, analysis, and discussion of a text with a structured, student-centered protocol; roles can be assigned based on students' language proficiency (e.g., stronger students serve as clarifiers), and additional roles may be used for broader differentiation. For example: • **Cognate finder**: looks for any words that seem similar to words in another, known language • **Visualizer**: sketches visuals to accompany the passage
Visual Prompts	T	Using visuals to introduce new vocabulary, build background knowledge, clarify information, provide instructions, or otherwise support understanding with visual aids	To support comprehension and learning with nonlinguistic input
Round Table Writing	S/T	Students engage in the writing, editing, and revising process in a group by writing a brief response to a prompt, such as a quickwrite, and then shifting papers to the next person in the group. That person writes feedback before shifting papers again to the next group member. The process repeats until all members of the group have provided feedback. Students then discuss the feedback and revise their writing. Teachers have the option of instructing students to read for different elements at each rotation; for example, the first reader could check for spelling, the second for word choice, the third for ideas, and so on.	To scaffold the peer editing process and to provide a way for students to support each other's language development

Graphic Organizer Directory

Contents

Active Listening Feedback

Presenter's name: _____

Content

What is the presenter's purpose? _____

What is the presenter's main point? _____

Do you agree with the presenter? Why or why not? _____

_____

_____

Form

Did the presenter use a clear, loud voice? ☐ yes ☐ no

Did the presenter make eye contact? ☐ yes ☐ no

One thing I really liked about the presentation:

_____

_____

_____

One question I still have:

_____

_____

_____

Other comments or notes:

Active Listening Notes

Title: _____

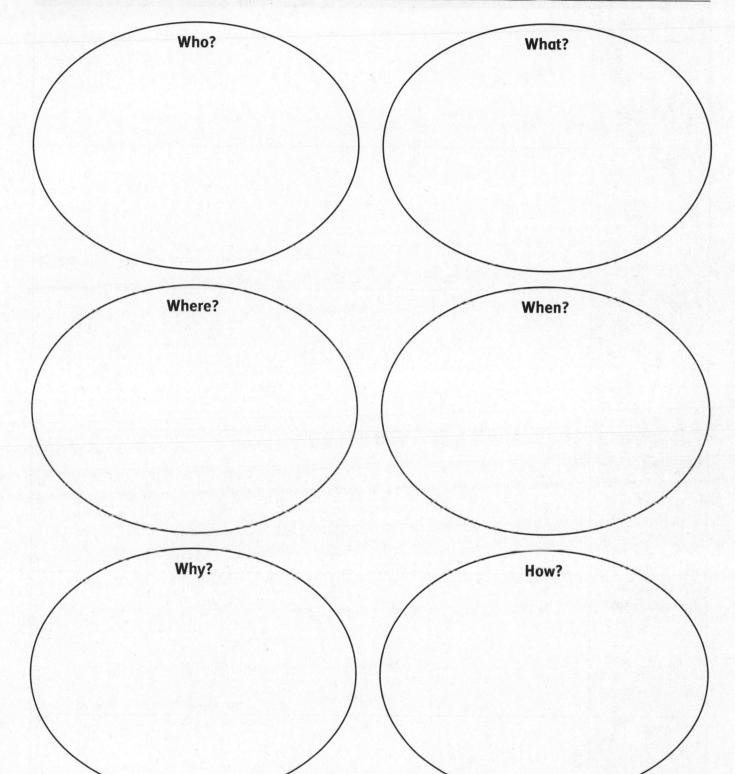

Who?

What?

Where?

When?

Why?

How?

Audience Notes and Feedback

Scoring Criteria	Notes/Feedback
Introduction/ Conclusion	
Timing	
Voice	
Eye Contact/ Gestures	
Use of Media, Visuals, Props	
Audience Engagement	

Cause and Effect

Title: _____

Cause: What happened?

→

Effect: An effect of this is

Cause: What happened?

→

Effect: An effect of this is

Cause: What happened?

→

Effect: An effect of this is

Cause: What happened?

→

Effect: An effect of this is

Character Map

Character name: _____

What does the character look like?

How does the character act and feel?

What do other characters say or think about the character?

Collaborative Dialogue

Topic: _____

Use the space below to record ideas.

"Wh-" Prompts
Who?   What?   Where?   When?   Why?

Speaker 1

Speaker 2

Conclusion Builder

Evidence

Evidence

Evidence

Based on this evidence, I can conclude

Conflict Map

Title: _____

What is the main conflict in this story?

What causes this conflict?

How is the conflict resolved?

What are some other ways the conflict could have been resolved?

Conversation for Quickwrite

1. Turn to a partner and restate the prompt in your own words.

2. Brainstorm key words to use in your quickwrite response.

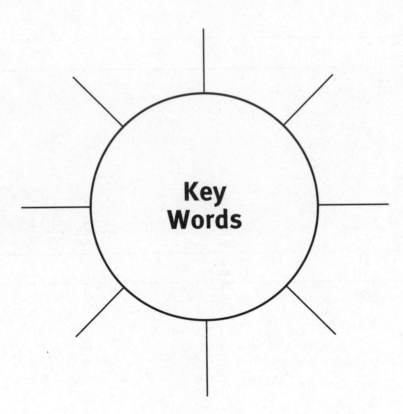

Key
Words

3. Take turns explaining your ideas to your partner. Try using some of the key words you brainstormed.

4. On your own, write a response to the quickwrite.

Definition and Reflection

Academic Vocabulary Word
Definition in own words
Illustration (literal or symbolic)

My experiences with this concept:

- I haven't really thought about this concept.

  _____

- I have only thought about this concept in English Language Arts class.

  _____

- I have applied this concept in other classes.

  _____

- I have applied this concept outside of school.

  _____

My level of understanding:

- I am still trying to understand this concept.

  _____

- I am familiar with this concept, but I am not comfortable applying it.

  _____

- I am very comfortable with this concept and I know how to apply it.

  _____

- I could teach this concept to another classmate.

  _____

Discourse Starters

Questioning and Discussing a Text

One question I have is _____.

Could this mean _____?

Why do you think the author _____?

I understand _____, but I wonder _____.

I notice that _____.

I think this (word/sentence/paragraph) means _____.

I think _____ because the text says _____.

In paragraph _____, the author says _____.

According to the text, _____.

One way to interpret _____ is _____.

Summarizing

The main events that take place are _____.

The major points of the text are _____.

The main idea of _____ is _____.

One central idea of this text is _____.

Another central idea is _____.

All in all, the message is _____.

The author's main purpose is to _____.

Basically, the author is saying that _____.

Comparing and Contrasting

_____ and _____ are similar because _____.

_____ and _____ are similar in that they both _____.

_____ is _____. Similarly, _____ is _____.

One thing _____ and _____ have in common is _____.

_____ and _____ are different because _____.

_____ and _____ are different in that _____.

_____ is _____. On the other hand, _____ is _____.

One difference between _____ and _____ is _____.

Clarifying

I'm not sure I understand the instructions.

Could you repeat that please?

I have a question about _____.

I am having trouble with _____.

Will you explain that again?

Could you clarify _____?

Would you mind helping me with _____?

Which (page/paragraph/section) are we reading?

How do you spell/pronounce _____?

Discourse Starters

Agreeing and Disagreeing

I agree with the idea that _____ because _____.

I share your point of view because _____.

You made a good point when you said _____.

I agree with (a person) that _____.

Although I agree that _____, I also think _____.

I understand where you're coming from, but _____.

I disagree with the idea that _____ because _____.

I see it a different way because _____.

You have a point, but the evidence suggests _____.

Arguing and Persuading with Evidence

I believe that _____ because _____.

It is clear that _____ because _____.

One reason I think _____ is _____.

Based on evidence in the text, I think _____.

Evidence such as _____ suggests that _____.

An example to support my position is _____.

This is evident because _____.

What evidence supports the idea that _____?

Can you explain why you think _____?

Evaluating

This is effective because _____.

The evidence _____ is strong because _____.

This is convincing because _____.

I see why the author _____, but I think _____.

This is not very effective because _____.

The evidence _____ is weak because _____.

This would have been better if _____.

What do you think about the writer's choice to _____?

Why do you think _____ (is/isn't) effective?

Giving Feedback and Suggesting

The part where you _____ is strong because _____.

What impressed me the most is how you _____.

This is a good start. Maybe you should add _____.

I like how you _____, but I would try _____.

You might consider changing _____.

I would suggest revising _____ so that _____.

One suggestion would be to _____.

Why did you choose _____?

A better choice might be _____.

This would be clearer if _____.

Editor's Checklist

Over the course of the year with SpringBoard, customize this Editor's Checklist as your knowledge of language conventions grows. The three examples below show you how to write a good checklist item.

	Are all the sentences complete?
	Do the subject and verb of each sentence agree?
	Do all the sentences have correct punctuation?

Writer's Checklist

Ideas

	Does your first paragraph hook the reader?
	Is the purpose of your writing clear (to inform, to make an argument, etc.)?
	Is the genre of writing appropriate for your purpose?
	Is your main idea clear and easy to summarize?
	Does your text contain details and information that support your main idea?
	Are the ideas in the text well organized?
	Do you connect your ideas by using transitions?
	Do you use parallel structure to keep your ideas clear?
	Does each paragraph have a conclusion that transitions to the next paragraph?
	Does your writing end with a strong conclusion that restates the original purpose of the text?

Language

	Do you keep a consistent point of view throughout?
	Do you use the present tense when writing about a text?
	Are any shifts in verb tense easy to follow and necessary?
	Have you removed unnecessary or confusing words?
	Do you use vivid verbs and descriptive adjectives when appropriate?
	Do you use different styles of language (like figurative or sensory) when appropriate?
	Do you use a variety of sentence types?
	Do you vary the way you begin your sentences?
	Did you split up run-on sentences?
	Are your pronoun references clear?

Evaluating Online Sources

The URL
• What is its domain?
    • .com = a for-profit organization
    • .gov, .mil, .us (or other country code) = a government site
    • .edu = affiliated with an educational institution
    • .org = a nonprofit organization
• Is this URL someone's personal page?
• Do you recognize who is publishing this page?	

Sponsor: • Does the website give information about the organization or group that sponsors it? • Does it have a link (often called "About Us") that leads you to that information? • What do you learn?	
Timeliness: • When was the page last updated (usually this is posted at the top or bottom of the page)? • Is the topic something that changes frequently, like current events or technology?	
Purpose: • What is the purpose of the page? • What is its target audience? • Does it present information, opinion, or both? • Is it primarily objective or subjective? • How do you know?	
Author: • What credentials does the author have? • Is this person or group considered an authority on the topic?	
Links • Does the page provide links? • Do they work? • Are they helpful? • Are they objective or subjective?	

Fallacies 101

Ad Baculum (Scare Tactics)	If you don't support the party's tax plan, you and your family will be reduced to poverty. Chairman of the Board: "All those opposed to my arguments for the opening of a new department, signify by saying, 'I resign.'"
Ad hoc	Person 1: I should have gotten an A on that test. Person 2: You didn't study for that test at all. Person 1: That class is useless!
Ad Hominem (Against the Man)/ Genetic Fallacy	"My opponent, a vicious and evil person, should absolutely never be elected to office." The Volkswagen Beetle is an evil car because it was originally designed by Hitler's army.
Ad Populum	You should turn to channel 6. It's the most watched channel this year. There is always a long line at that restaurant, so the food must be really good.
Appeal To Pity	"Jonathan couldn't have cheated! He's such a nice boy and he tries so hard."
Argument from Outrage	The airline cancelled my flight an hour before takeoff and wouldn't tell me why. This is an outrage! We should all boycott the company.
Circular Reasoning	Emotional support animals should be allowed on airplanes, so the airline should change its policy. The policy should be changed because emotional support animals should be allowed on planes!
Either/Or (False Dilemma)	We can either stop using cars or destroy Earth. We must drill now or we'll remain dependent on foreign oil suppliers.
Faulty Analogies	Buying into the stock market is the same as betting on a horse race.
Hasty Generalization	They hit two home runs in the first inning of the season. This team is going all the way to the World Series!
Non-sequitur	I always see her with a book in her hands. She must hate watching TV.
Post Hoc	I ate a turkey sandwich and now I feel tired, so the turkey must have made me tired.
Red Herring	The new dress code banning t-shirts isn't fair. Students have the right to free speech just like anyone else.
Slippery Slope Fallacy	"If I don't study for the test, then I'm going to get a bad grade. If I get a bad grade on the test, I'll get a bad grade in the class, and I won't get into a good college. Getting into a good college is the most important part of getting a good job; so if I don't study for the test, I won't get a good job!"
Straw Man	People say that Mark Twain was a good author, but I disagree. If he was such a good author, why didn't he write using his own name?

Idea and Argument Evaluator

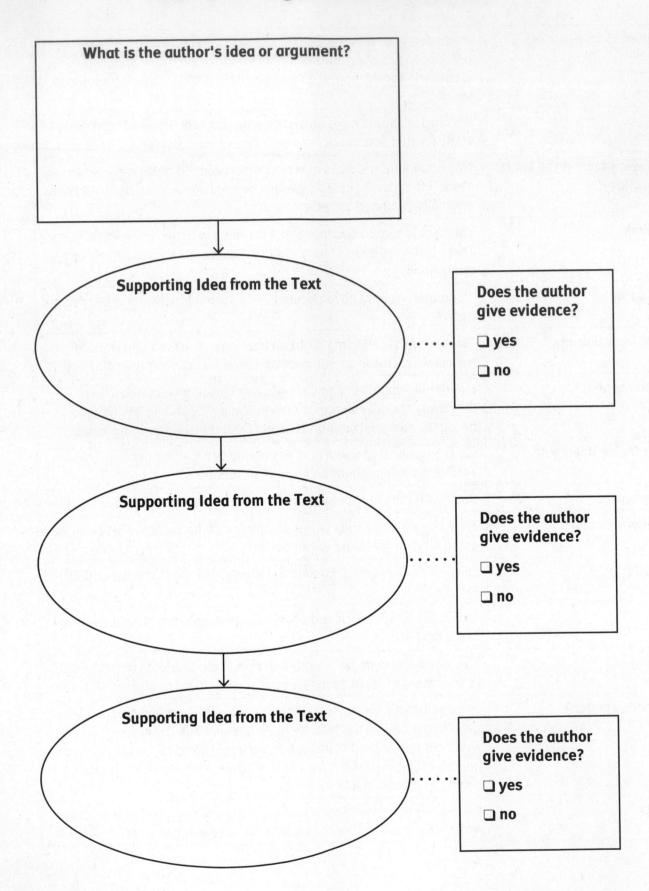

What is the author's idea or argument?

Supporting Idea from the Text

Does the author give evidence?

❏ yes

❏ no

Supporting Idea from the Text

Does the author give evidence?

❏ yes

❏ no

Supporting Idea from the Text

Does the author give evidence?

❏ yes

❏ no

Idea Connector

Directions: Write two simple sentences about the same topic. Next, write transition words around the Idea Connector. Then, choose an appropriate word to connect ideas in the two sentences. Write your combined sentence in the space below.

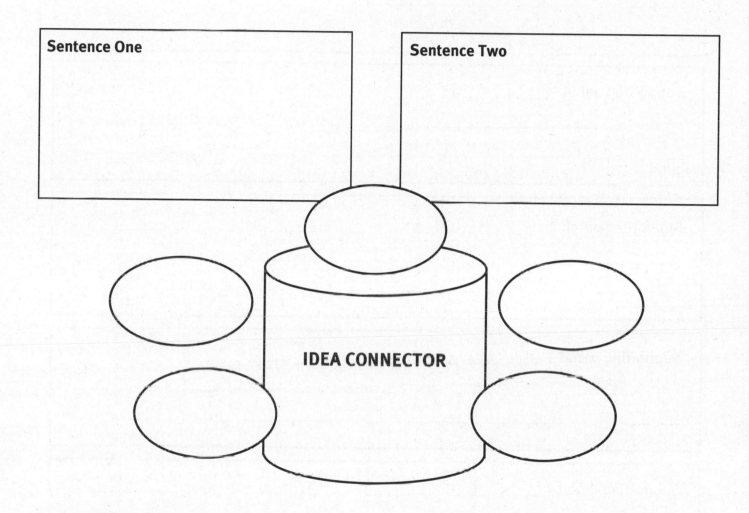

Sentence One

Sentence Two

IDEA CONNECTOR

Combined Sentence

Key Idea and Details Chart

Title/Topic _____

Key Idea _____

_____

_____

Supporting detail 1 _____

_____

_____

Supporting detail 2 _____

_____

_____

Supporting detail 3 _____

_____

_____

Supporting detail 4 _____

_____

_____

Restate topic sentence: _____

_____

Concluding sentence: _____

_____

_____

Narrative Analysis and Writing

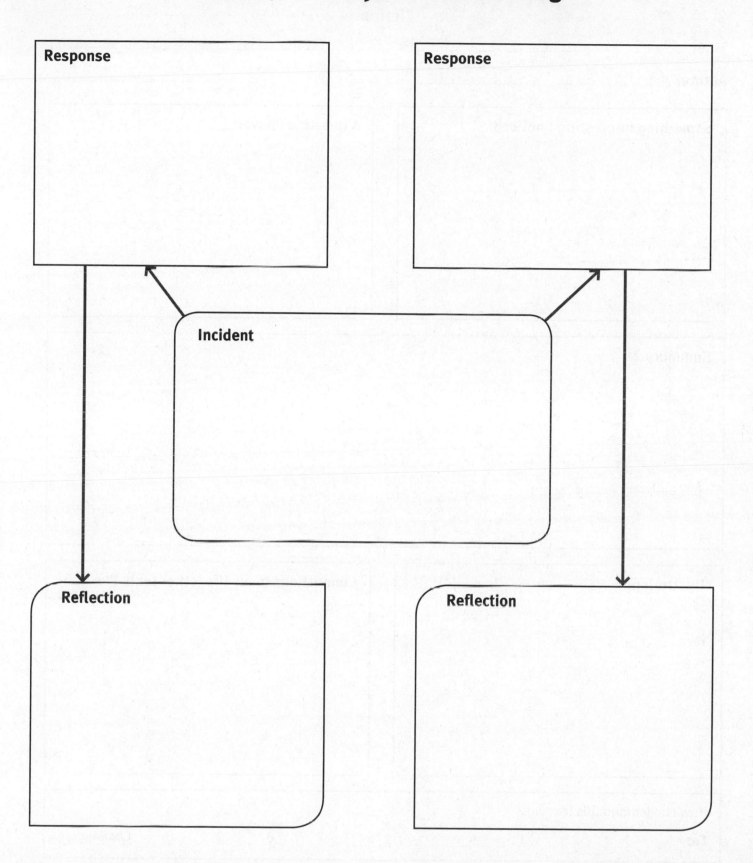

Response

Response

Incident

Reflection

Reflection

Notes for Reading Independently
Fiction

Title: _____

Author: _____

Something interesting I noticed:	A question I have:

Summary:

Illustration:

Connections to my life/other texts I've read:

How challenging this text was:

Easy   1   2   3   4   5   6   7   8   9   10   *Challenging*

Notes for Reading Independently
Nonfiction

Title: _____

Author: _____

Main idea:	Facts I learned:

Summary:

Questions I still have:	Connections to my life/other texts I've read:

How challenging this text was:

Easy   1   2   3   4   5   6   7   8   9   10   *Challenging*

Opinion Builder

Reason

Reason

Based on these reasons, my opinion is

Reason

Reason

OPTIC

Title of Piece: _____

Artist: _____   **Type of artwork:** _____

Overview	Look at the artwork for at least 10 seconds. Generate questions; e.g., What is the subject? What strikes you as interesting, odd, etc.? What is happening?
Parts	Look closely at the artwork, making note of important elements and details. Ask additional questions, such as: Who are the figures? What is the setting and time period? What symbols are present? What historical information would aid understanding of this piece?
Title	Consider what the title and any written elements of the text suggest about meaning. How does the title relate to what is portrayed?
Interrelationships	Look for connections between and among the title, caption, and the parts of the art. How are the different elements related?
Conclusion	Form a conclusion about the meaning/theme of the text. Remember the questions you asked when you first examined it. Be prepared to support your conclusions with evidence.

Paragraph Frame for Conclusions

Conclusion Words and Phrases

shows that

based on

suggests that

leads to

indicates that

influences

The _____ (story, poem, play, passage, etc.) shows that (helps us to conclude that) _____

_____

There are several reasons why. First, _____

_____

_____

_____

A second reason is _____

_____

_____

_____

Finally, _____

_____

_____

_____

In conclusion, _____

_____

_____

_____

Paragraph Frame for Sequencing

Sequence Words and Phrases

at the beginning

in the first place

as a result

later

eventually

in the end

lastly

In the _____ (story, poem, play, passage, etc.)

there are three important _____

(events, steps, directions, etc.)

First, _____

_____

_____

_____

Second, _____

_____

_____

_____

Third, _____

_____

_____

_____

Finally, _____

_____

_____

_____

_____

Paraphrasing and Summarizing Map

What does the text say?	How can I say it in my own words?

How can I use my own words to summarize the text?

Peer Editing

Writer's name: _____

Did the writer answer the prompt? ☐ yes ☐ no

Did the writer use appropriate details or evidence to develop their writing? ☐ yes ☐ no

Is the writing organized in a way that makes sense? ☐ yes ☐ no

Did the writer use a variety of sentence types to make the writing more interesting? ☐ yes ☐ no

Are there any spelling or punctuation mistakes? ☐ yes ☐ no

Are there any grammar errors? ☐ yes ☐ no

Two things I really liked about the writer's story:

1. _____
_____
_____

2. _____
_____
_____

One thing I think the writer could do to improve the writing:

1. _____
_____
_____

Other comments or notes:

Persuasive/Argument Writing Map

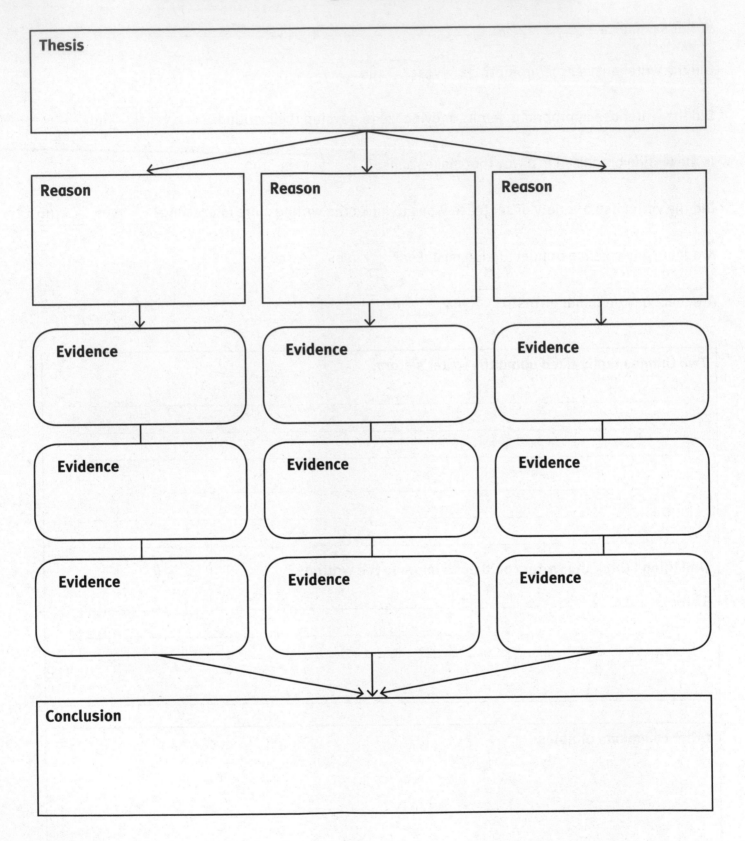

Thesis

Reason

Reason

Reason

Evidence

Evidence

Evidence

Evidence

Evidence

Evidence

Evidence

Evidence

Evidence

Conclusion

Presenting Scoring Guide

Scoring Criteria	Exemplary	Proficient	Emerging	Incomplete
Introduction / Conclusion	The presentation • provides a clear, engaging, and appropriate introduction to the topic or performance • provides a clear, engaging, and appropriate conclusion that closes, summarizes, draws connections to broader themes, or supports the ideas presented.	The presentation • provides a clear and appropriate introduction to the topic or performance • provides a clear and appropriate conclusion that closes, summarizes, draws connections to broader themes, or supports the ideas presented.	The presentation • provides an adequate introduction to the topic or performance • provides an adequate conclusion that closes, summarizes, draws connections to broader themes, or supports the ideas presented.	The presentation • does not provide an introduction to the topic or performance • does not provide a conclusion that closes, summarizes, draws connections to broader themes, or supports the ideas presented.
Timing	The presentation • thoroughly delivers its intended message within the allotted time • is thoughtfully and appropriately paced throughout.	The presentation • mostly delivers its intended message within the allotted time • is appropriately paced most of the time.	The presentation • delivers some of its intended message within the allotted time • is sometimes not paced appropriately.	The presentation • does not deliver its intended message within the allotted time • is not paced appropriately.
Voice (Volume, Enunciation, Rate)	The presentation • is delivered with adequate volume enabling audience members to fully comprehend what is said • is delivered with clear enunciation.	The presentation • is delivered with adequate volume enabling audience members to mostly comprehend what is said • is delivered with mostly clear enunciation.	The presentation • is delivered with somewhat adequate volume enabling audience members to comprehend some of what is said • is delivered with somewhat clear enunciation.	The presentation • is not delivered with adequate volume, so that audience members are unable to comprehend what is said • is delivered with unclear enunciation.
Eye Contact / Gestures	The presentation • is delivered with appropriate eye contact that helps engage audience members • makes use of natural gestures and/or body language to convey meaning.	The presentation • is delivered with some appropriate eye contact that helps engage audience members • makes use of gestures and/or body language to convey meaning.	The presentation • is delivered with occasional eye contact that sometimes engages audience members • makes some use of gestures and/or body language to convey meaning.	The presentation • is not delivered with eye contact to engage audience members • makes little or no use of gestures and/or body language to convey meaning.
Use of Media, Visuals, Props	The presentation • makes use of highly engaging visuals, multimedia, and/or props that enhance delivery.	The presentation • makes use of visuals, multimedia, and/or props that enhance delivery.	The presentation • makes use of some visuals, multimedia, and/or props that somewhat enhance delivery.	The presentation • makes use of few or no visuals, multimedia, and/or props that enhance delivery.
Audience Engagement	The presentation • includes thoughtful and appropriate interactions with and responses to audience members.	The presentation • includes appropriate interactions with and responses to audience members.	The presentation • includes a few interactions with and responses to audience members.	The presentation • does not include interactions with and responses to audience members.

RAFT

Role	Who or what are you as a writer?
Audience	As a writer, to whom are you writing?
Format	As a writer, what format would be appropriate for your audience (essay, letter, speech, poem, etc.)?
Topic	As a writer, what is the subject of your writing? What points do you want to make?

Roots and Affixes Brainstorm

Directions: Write the root or affix in the circle. Brainstorm or use a dictionary to find the meaning of the root or affix and add it to the circle. Then, find words that use that root or affix. Write one word in each box. Write a sentence for each word.

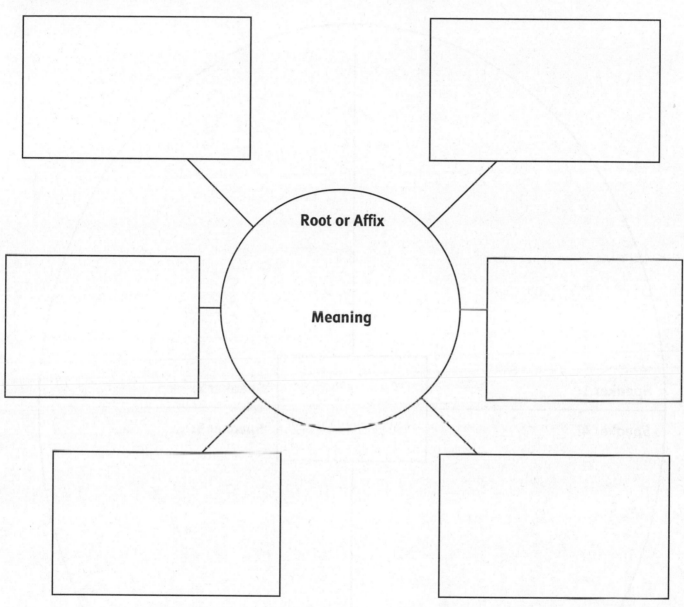

Root or Affix

Meaning

Round Table Discussion

Directions: Write the topic in the center box. One student begins by stating his or her ideas while the student to the left takes notes. Then the next student speaks while the student to his or her left takes notes, and so on.

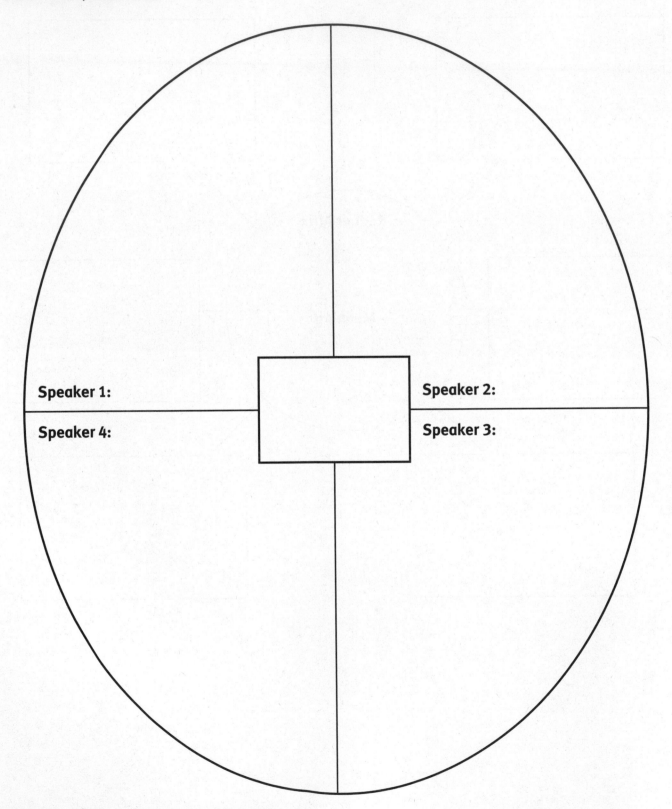

Speaker 1:

Speaker 2:

Speaker 4:

Speaker 3:

Sequence of Events Time Line

Title: _____

What happened first?

Next?

Beginning   Middle   End

Then?

Finally?

SMELL

Sender-Receiver Relationship—Who are the senders and receivers of the message, and what is their relationship (consider what different audiences the text may be addressing)?
Message—What is a literal summary of the content? What is the meaning/significance of this information?
Emotional Strategies—What emotional appeals (*pathos*) are included? What seems to be their desired effect?
Logical Strategies—What logical arguments/appeals (*logos*) are included? What is their effect?
Language—What specific language is used to support the message? How does it affect the text's effectiveness? Consider both images and actual words.

SOAPSTone

SOAPSTone	Analysis	Textual Support
Subject What does the reader know about the writer?		
Occasion What are the circumstances surrounding this text?		
Audience Who is the target audience?		
Purpose Why did the author write this text?		
Subject What is the topic?		
Tone What is the author's tone, or attitude?		

Text Structure Stairs

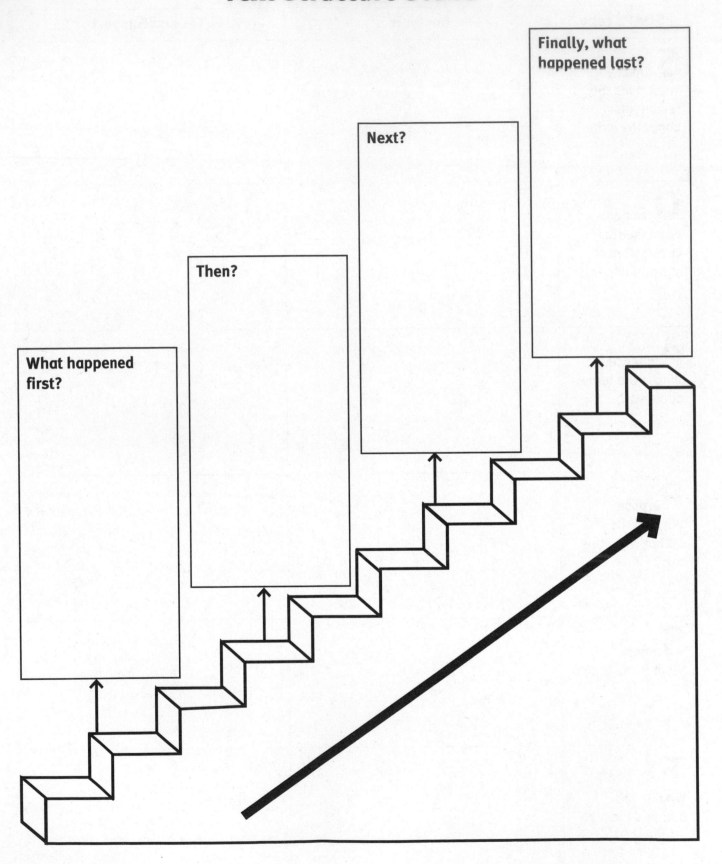

Finally, what happened last?

Next?

Then?

What happened first?

TP-CASTT Analysis

Poem Title:

Author:

Title: Make a Prediction. What do you think the title means before you read the poem?

Paraphrase: Translate the poem in your own words. What is the poem about? Rephrase difficult sections word for word.

Connotation: Look beyond the literal meaning of key words and images to their associations.

Attitude: What is the speaker's attitude? What is the author's attitude? How does the author feel about the speaker, about other characters, about the subject?

Shifts: Where do the shifts in tone, setting, voice, etc., occur? Look for time and place, keywords, punctuation, stanza divisions, changes in length or rhyme, and sentence structure. What is the purpose of each shift? How do they contribute to effect and meaning?

Title: Reexamine the title. What do you think it means now in the context of the poem?

Theme: Think of the literal and metaphorical layers of the poem. Then determine the overall theme. The theme must be written in a complete sentence.

TP-CASTT

Poem Title:

Author:

Title		
Paraphrase		
Connotation		
Attitude		
Shifts		
Title		
Theme		

Unknown Word Solver

Unknown Word

Can you find any context clues? List them.

Do you recognize any word parts?

Prefix:

Root Word:

Suffix:

Do you know another meaning of this word that does not make sense in this context?

Does it look or sound like a word in another language?

What is the dictionary definition?

How can you define the word in your own words?

Venn Diagram for Writing a Comparison

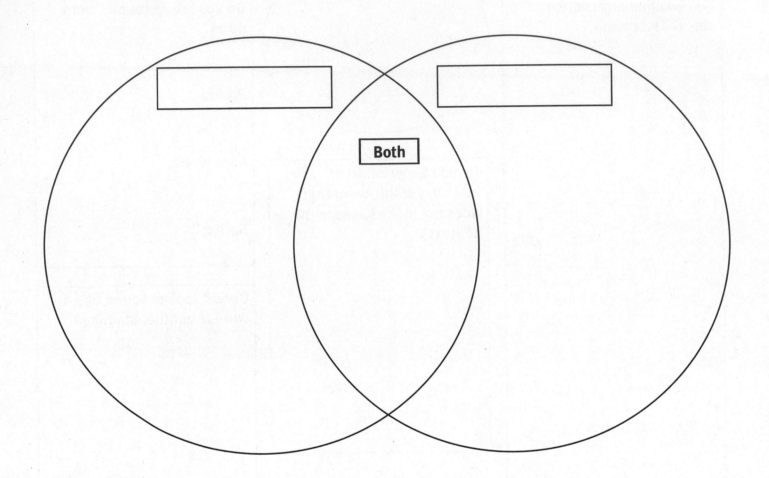

They are similar in that _____	They are different in that _____

Verbal & Visual Word Association

Definition in Your Own Words	Important Elements

Academic Vocabulary Word

Visual Representation	Personal Association

Web Organizer

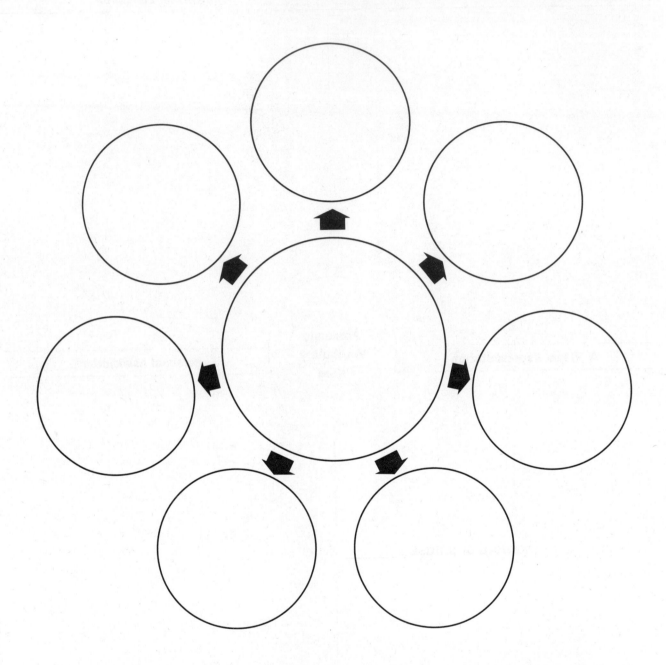

Word Choice Analyzer

Word or phrase from the text	Definition of word or phrase	How can I restate the definition in my own words?	What effect did the author produce by choosing these words?

Explain Your Analysis

The author uses the word or phrase _____ , which means

_____

Another way to say this is _____

_____

I think the author chose these words to _____

_____

_____

One way I can modify this sentence to add detail is to _____

_____

Word Map

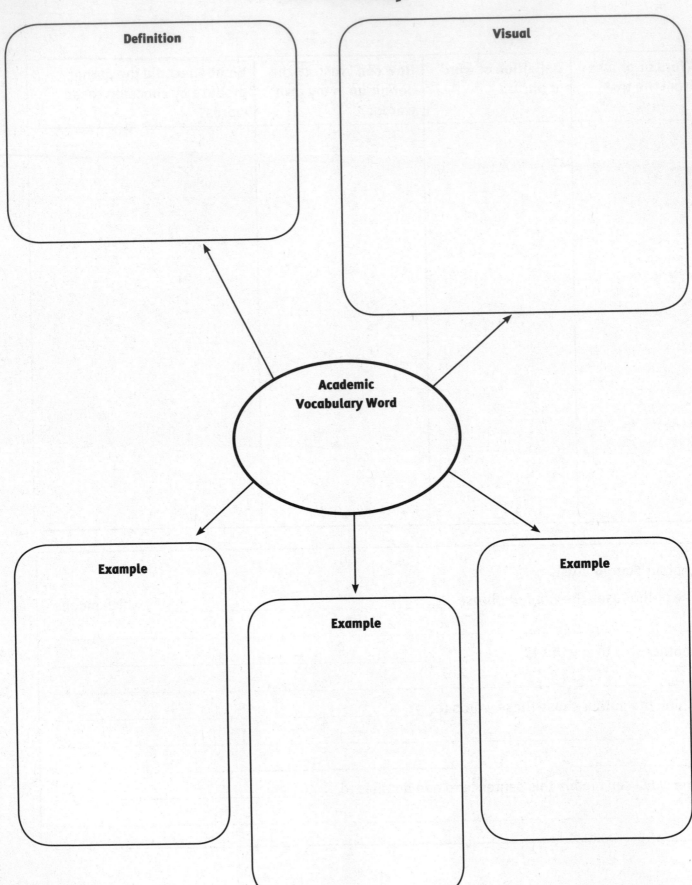

Definition

Visual

Academic Vocabulary Word

Example

Example

Example

Glossary/Glosario

A

active-voice verbs: verbs for which the subject performs the action

verbos en voz activa: forma verbal que indica que el sujeto realiza la acción

advertising techniques: specific methods used in print, graphics, or videos to persuade people to buy a product or use a service

técnicas publicitarias: métodos específicos usados en impresos, gráfica o videos para persuadir a las personas a comprar un producto o usar un servicio

agenda: a secret plan or motivation that causes someone to act in a certain way

agenda: motivación o plan secreto que lleva a alguien a actuar de determinado modo

allegory: a story in which the characters, objects, or actions have a meaning beyond the surface of the story

alegoría: cuento en el que los personajes, objetos o acciones tienen un significado que va más allá de la superficie de la historia

alliteration: the repetition of initial consonant sounds in words that are close together

aliteración: repetición de sonidos consonánticos iniciales en palabras cercanas

allusion: a reference made to a well-known person, event, or place from history, music, art, or another literary work

alusión: referencia a una persona, evento o lugar muy conocidos de la historia, música, arte u otra obra literaria

analogy: a comparison between two things for the purpose of drawing conclusions on one based on its similarities to the other

analogía: comparación entre dos cosas con el propósito de sacar conclusiones sobre las semejanzas que una cosa tiene a otra

anaphora: the repetition of the same word or group of words at the beginnings of two or more clauses or lines

anáfora: repetición de la misma palabra o grupo de palabras al comienzo de una o más cláusulas o versos

anecdotal evidence: evidence based on personal accounts of incidents

evidencia anecdótica: evidencia basada en relatos personales de los hechos

annotated bibliography: a list of sources used in research along with comments or summaries about each source

bibliografía anotada: lista de fuentes utilizadas en la investigación, junto con comentarios o resúmenes acerca de cada fuente

antagonist: the character who opposes or struggles against the main character

antagonista: personaje que se opone o lucha contra el personaje principal

aphorism: a short statement expressing an opinion or general truth

aforismo: afirmación corta que expresa una opinión o verdad general

appeals: the efforts to persuade an audience that a certain concept is true by directing statements toward reasoning or logic, character, or senses and emotions

llamados: serie de esfuerzos que alguien realiza con el fin de convencer a una audiencia de que determinado concepto es verdadero, persuadiéndola de ello mediante el uso del razonamiento o la lógica o bien apelando a su carácter, sentidos o emociones

Archetypal Criticism: criticism that deals with symbols and patterns that recur in the literature of widely diverse cultures

crítica de arquetipos: examinación de la literatura basada en símbolos y diseño

archetypes: universal symbols—images, characters, motifs, or patterns—that recur in the myths, dreams, oral traditions, songs, literature, and other texts of peoples widely separated by time and place

arquetipos: símbolos universales—imágenes, personajes, motivos o patrones—reiterativos en los mitos, el arte y la literatura alrededor del mundo

archival footage: film footage taken from another, previously recorded, source

cortometraje de archivo: fragmento de película tomada de otra fuente grabada previamente

argument: a form of writing that presents a particular claim or idea and supports it with evidence

argumento: forma de redacción que presenta una opinión o idea particular y la apoya con evidencia

argumentation: the act or process of arguing that includes the *hook* (quotation, example, or idea that catches readers' attention), *claim* (the opinion or thesis statement), *support* (evidence in the form of facts, statistics, examples, anecdotes, or expert opinions), *concession* (the writer's admission that the other side of the argument has a valid point), *refutation* (a well-reasoned denial of an opponent's point, based on solid evidence), and *call to action* (a request of readers)

argumentación: la estructura de una argumentación incluye el *gancho* (cita, ejemplo o idea que capta la atención del lector), *afirmación* (declaración de opinión o tesis), *apoyo* (evidencia en forma de hechos, estadísticas, ejemplos, anécdotas u opiniones de expertos), *concesión* (admisión por parte del escritor de que la otra parte del debate tiene un punto válido), *refutación* (negación bien razonada de una opinión del oponente, basada en evidencia sólida) y *llamado a la acción* (petición inspirada de lectores)

argument by analogy: a comparison of two similar situations, implying that the outcome of one will resemble the outcome of the other

argumento por analogía: comparación de dos situaciones semejantes, infiriendo que el resultado de será parecido al resultado de la otra

artistic license: the practice of rewording of dialogue, alteration of language, or reordering of the plot of a text created by another artist

licencia artística: la costumbre de reformular un diálogo, aliteración de palabras, o arreglo de la trama de un texto creado por otro artista

aside: a short speech spoken by an actor directly to the audience and unheard by other actors on stage

aparte: alocución breve dicha por un actor directamente al público y que no escuchan los demás actores que están en el escenario

assonance: the repetition of similar vowel sounds in accented syllables, followed by different consonant sounds, in words that are close together

asonancia: repetición de sonidos vocálicos similares en sílabas acentuadas, seguida de diferentes sonidos consonánticos, en palabras que están cercanas

audience: the intended readers, listeners, or viewers of specific types of written, spoken, or visual texts

público: lectores objetivo, oyentes o espectadores de tipos específicos de textos escritos, hablados o visuales

audience analysis: determination of the characteristics and knowledge of the people who will read a work or hear a speech

análisis del público: determinar las características y conocimiento de las personas que leen una obra o escuchan un discurso

author's purpose: the specific reason or reasons for the writing; what the author hopes to accomplish

propósito del autor: razón específica para escribir; lo que el autor espera lograr

autobiography: an account written by a person about his or her own life

autobiografía: narración de una vida escrita por el propio sujeto del relato

B

balanced sentence: a sentence that presents ideas of equal weight in similar grammatical forms to emphasize the similarity or difference between the ideas

oración balanceada: oración que representa ideas de igual peso en formas gramaticales similares para enfatizar la semejanza o diferencia entre las ideas

bias: an inclination or mental leaning for or against something; prevents impartial judgment

sesgo: inclinación o tendencia mental a favor o en contra de algo, lo que impide una opinión imparcial

bibliography: a list of the sources used for research

bibliografía: lista de fuentes primarias en la preparación de un texto

biography: a description or account of events from a person's life, written by another person

biografía: descripción o narración de la vida de una persona o los sucesos importantes de su vida escritos por otra persona

blank verse: unrhymed verse

verso libre: verso que no tiene rima

block: to create the plan for how actors will position themselves on the stage in relation to one another, the audience, and the objects on the stage

ensayar: establecer un plan para determinar la posición que los actores deberán ocupar en un escenario en relación a sí mismos, a la audiencia, al escenario y a los objetos del mismo

blocking: in drama, the way actors position themselves in relation to one another, the audience, and the objects on the stage

bloqueo: en drama, el modo en que los actores se sitúan entre sí, con el público y los objetos en el escenario

book review: a formal assessment or examination of a book

reseña de libro: evaluación o examinación formal de un libro

C

cacophonous: harsh and unpleasant sounding

cacofónico: sonidos molestos y desagradables

call to action: a restatement of the claim and what the writer wants the reader to do

llamado a la acción: repetición de la afirmación y lo que el escritor quiere que el lector responda

caricature: a visual or verbal representation in which characteristics or traits are exaggerated or distorted for emphasis

caricatura: representación visual o verbal en la que las características o rasgos se exageran o se distorsionan para dar énfasis

catalog poem: a poem that uses repetition and variation in the creation of a list, or catalog, of objects or desires, plans, or memories

lista en poema: poema que usa repetición y variación en la creación de una lista o catálogo, de objetos o deseos o planes o memorias

cause: an action, event, or situation that brings about a particular result

causa: acción, suceso o situación que produce un resultado particular

caveat: a cautionary detail to be thought through carefully when analyzing something

exhortación: advertencia o consejo a tener muy en cuenta a la hora de interpretar o analizar algo

censor: to examine materials for objectionable content
censurar: examinar materiales por contenido desagradable

censorship: the act of suppressing public speech or publication of materials deemed to be offensive by the censor
censura: acto de suprimir un discurso público o publicación de materiales considerados ofensivos por un censor

challenge: to oppose or refute a statement that has been made
poner en duda: oponerse a algo o refutar una declaración que alguien ha hecho

characterization: the methods a writer uses to develop characters
caracterización: métodos que usa un escritor para desarrollar personajes

characters: people, animals, or imaginary creatures that take part in the action of a story. A short story usually centers on a *main character* but may also contain one or more *minor characters*, who are not as complex, but whose thoughts, words, or actions move the plot along. A character who is *dynamic* changes in response to the events of the narrative; a character who is *static* remains the same throughout the narrative. A *round* character is fully developed—he or she shows a variety of traits; a *flat* character is one-dimensional, usually showing only one trait.

personajes: personas, animales o criaturas imaginarias que participan en la acción de un cuento. Un cuento corto normalmente se centra en un *personaje principal*, pero puede también contener uno o más *personajes secundarios*, que no son tan complejos, pero cuyos pensamientos, palabras o acciones hacen avanzar la trama. Un personaje que es *dinámico* cambia según los eventos del relato; un personaje que es *estático* permanece igual a lo largo del relato. Un personaje *complejo* está completamente desarrollado: muestra una diversidad de rasgos; un personaje *simple* es unidimensional, mostrando normalmente sólo un rasgo.

character foil: a character whose actions or thoughts are juxtaposed against those of a major character in order to highlight key attributes of the major character
antagonista: personaje cuyas acciones o pensamientos se yuxtaponen a los de un personaje principal con el fin de destacar atributos clave del personaje principal

character sketch: a brief description of a literary character
reseña del personaje: breve descripción de un personaje literario

chorus: in traditional or classic drama, a group of performers who speak as one and comment on the action of the play
coro: en el drama tradicional o clásico, grupo de actores que hablan al unísono y comentan la acción de la obra teatral

cinematic elements: the features of cinema—movies, film, video—that contribute to its form and structure: *angle* (the view from which the image is shot), *framing* (how a scene is structured), *lighting* (the type of lighting used to light a scene), *mise en scène* (the composition, setting, or staging of an image, or a scene in a film), and *sound* (the sound effects and music accompanying each scene)
elementos cinematográficos: las características del cine—películas, filmaciones, video—que contribuyen a darle forma y estructura: *angulación* (vista desde la cual se toma la imagen), *encuadre* (cómo se estructura una escena), iluminación (tipo de *iluminación* que se usa para una escena), y *montaje* (composición, ambiente o escenificación de una imagen o escena en una película), y *sonido* (efectos sonoros y música que acompañan cada escena)

cinematic techniques: the methods a director uses to communicate meaning and to evoke particular emotional responses from viewers
técnicas cinematográficas: métodos que emplea un director para comunicar un significado y evocar cierta respuesta emocional de los videntes

claim: a thesis statement describing the position the writer is taking on an issue
afirmación: declaración de opinión (o tesis) que asevera una idea o establece un debate hacia una posición específica

cliché: an overused expression or idea
cliché: expresión o idea que se usa en exceso

climax: the point at which the action reaches its peak; the point of greatest interest or suspense in a story; the turning point at which the outcome of a conflict is decided
clímax: punto en el que la acción alcanza su punto culminante; punto de mayor interés en un cuento; punto de inflexión en el que se decide el resultado del conflicto

coherence: the quality of unity or logical connection among ideas; the clear and orderly presentation of ideas in a paragraph or essay
coherencia: calidad de unidad o relación lógica entre las ideas; presentación clara y ordenada de las ideas en un párrafo o ensayo

commentary: the expression of opinions or explanations about an event or situation
comentario: expresión oral o escrita de opiniones o explicaciones sobre una situación, tema o suceso

commentary: explanations about the significance or importance of supporting details or examples in an analysis
comentario: explicaciones acerca de la importancia de los detalles que tienen apoyo o ejemplos en un análisis

complementary: combined in a way that enhances all elements combined
complementario: combinar dos o más elementos de una manera que mejora los dos

complex character: a character that has multiple or conflicting motivations
personaje complejo: personaje que tiene motivaciones multiples o conflictivas

complex sentence: a sentence containing one independent clause and one or more subordinate clauses
oración compleja: oración que contiene una cláusula independiente y una o más cláusulas subordinadas

complications: the events in a plot that develop a conflict; the complications move the plot forward in its rising action
complicaciones: sucesos de una trama que desarrollan el conflicto; las complicaciones hacen avanzar la trama en su acción ascendente

components: the parts or elements of a whole
componentes: partes o elementos que conforman un todo

compound sentence: a sentence containing two independent clauses
oración compuesta: oración que contiene dos cláusulas independientes

concession: an admission in an argument that the opposing side has valid points
concesión: admitir en un debate que el lado opositor tiene opiniones válidas

concluding statement: a statement that follows from and supports the claim made in an argument
declaración concluyente: declaración que sigue de la afirmación, o la apoya, en un argumento

conflict: a struggle or problem in a story. An *internal conflict* occurs when a character struggles between opposing needs or desires or emotions within his or her own mind. An *external conflict* occurs when a character struggles against an outside force. This force may be another character, a societal expectation, or something in the physical world.
conflicto: lucha o problema en un cuento. Un *conflicto interno* ocurre cuando un personaje lucha entre necesidades o deseos o emociones que se contraponen dentro de su mente. Un *conflicto externo* ocurre cuando un personaje lucha contra una fuerza externa. Esta fuerza puede ser otro personaje, una expectativa social o algo del mundo físico.

connotation: the associations and emotional overtones attached to a word beyond its literal definition, or denotation; a connotation may be positive, negative, or neutral
connotación: asociaciones y alusiones emocionales unidas a una palabra más allá de su definición literal o denotación; una connotación puede ser positiva, negativa, o neutra

consonance: the repetition of final consonant sounds in stressed syllables with different vowel sounds
consonancia: repetición de sonidos consonánticos finales en sílabas acentuadas con diferentes sonidos vocálicos

context: the circumstances or conditions in which something exists or takes place
contexto: circunstancias o condiciones en las que algo ocurre

conventions: standard features, practices, and forms associated with the way something is usually done
convenciones: prácticas y formas usuales asociadas con las costumbres de hacer algo

counterarguments: the arguments that can be made to oppose a viewpoint
contraargumentos: argumentos que se presentan para rebatir un punto de vista

counterclaim: a position taken by someone with an opposing viewpoint
contrarreclamación: posición que toma una persona con un punto de vista contrario

couplet: two consecutive lines of verse with end rhyme; a couplet usually expresses a complete unit of thought
copla: dos líneas de versos consecutivos con rima final; una copla normalmente expresa una unidad de pensamiento completa

credibility: the quality of being trusted or believed
credibilidad: calidad de ser confiable o creíble

critical lens: a particular identifiable perspective as in Reader Response Criticism, Cultural Criticism, etc., through which a text can be analyzed and interpreted
ojo crítico: punto de vista particular identificable como por ejemplo Teoría de la recepción, Crítica sociocultural, etc., por medio del que se puede analizar e interpretar un texto

cultural conflict: a struggle that occurs when people with different cultural expectations or attitudes interact
conflicto cultural: lucha que ocurre cuando interactúan personas con diferentes expectativas o actitudes culturales

Cultural Criticism: criticism that focuses on the elements of culture and how they affect one's perceptions and understanding of texts
crítica cultural: analizar un texto basándose en elementos culturales y como ellos afectan la percepción y lacomprensión de textos

culture: the shared set of arts, ideals, skills, institutions, customs, attitude, values, and achievements that characterize a group of people, and that are passed on or taught to succeeding generations
cultura: conjunto de artes, ideas, destrezas, instituciones, costumbres, actitud, valores y logros compartidos que caracterizan a un grupo de personas, y que se transfieren o enseñan a las generaciones siguientes

cumulative (or loose) sentence: a sentence in which the main clause comes first, followed by subordinate structures or clauses
oración acumulativa (o frases sueltas): oración cuya cláusula principal viene primero, seguida de estructuras o cláusulas subordinadas

D

deductive reasoning: a process of drawing a specific conclusion from general information
razonamiento deductivo: proceso en que se usa información general para sacar una conclusión específica

defend: to support a statement that has been made
defender: dar apoyo a una declaración que alguien ha hecho

denotation: the precise meaning of a word
denotación: significado literal de una palabra

detail: a specific fact, observation, or incident; any of the small pieces or parts that make up something else
detalle: hecho, observación o incidente específico; cualquiera de las pequeñas piezas o partes que constituyen otra cosa

dialect: the distinctive language—including the sounds, spelling, grammar, and diction—of a specific group or class of people
dialecto: lenguaje distintivo, incluyendo sonidos, ortografía, gramática y dicción, de un grupo o clase específico de personas

dialogue: the words spoken by characters in a narrative or film
diálogo: palabras que dicen los personajes en un relato o película

dialogue tags: the phrases that attribute a quotation to the speaker, for example, *she said* or *he bellowed*
marcas del diálogo: frases que atribuyen la cita de un hablante, por ejemplo, *dijo ella* o *bramó él.*

diction: a writer's word choices, which often convey voice and tone
dicción: selección de palabras por parte del escritor; elemento estilístico que ayuda a transmitir voz y tono

diegetic sound: any sound that can logically be heard by characters on screen
sonido diegético: sonidos lógicos que los personajes pueden oír en una escena en la pantalla

direct characterization: specific information about a character provided by the narrator or author
caracterización directa: información específica sobre un personaje creada por un narrador o autor

discourse: the language or speech used in a particular context or subject
discurso: lenguaje o habla usada en un contexto o tema en particular

documentary or nonfiction film: a genre of filmmaking that provides a visual record of actual events using photographs, video footage, and interviews
documental o película de no-ficción: género cinematográfico que realiza un registro visual de sucesos basados en hechos por medio del uso de fotografías, registro en videos y entrevistas

dominant group: a more powerful group that may perceive another group as marginalized or subordinate
grupo dominante: un grupo más poderoso que puede percibir a otro grupo como maginado o subordinado

drama: a play written for stage, radio, film, or television, usually about a serious topic or situation
drama: obra teatral escrita para representar en un escenario, radio, cine o televisión, normalmente sobre un tema o situación seria

dramatic irony: a form of irony in which the reader or audience knows more about the circumstances or future events than the characters within the scene
ironía dramática: una forma de la ironía en que los lectores o el público sabe más sobre las circunstancias o sucesos futuros que los personajes en la escena

dramaturge: a member of an acting company who helps the director and actors make informed decisions about the performance by researching information relevant to the play and its context
dramaturgo: socio de una compañía teatral que ayuda al director y a los actores tomar decisiones informadas sobre la interpretación investigando información relevante a la obra teatral y su contexto

dynamic (or round) character: a character who evolves and grows in the story and has a complex personality
personaje dinámico: personaje complejo que evoluciona a lo largo de la trama literaria

E

editorial: an article in a newspaper or magazine expressing the opinion of its editor or publisher
editorial: artículo de periódico o revista, que expresa la opinión de su editor

effect: the result or influence of using a specific literary or cinematic device; a result produced by a cause
efecto: resultado o influencia de usar un recurso literario o cinematográfico específico; resultado o producto de una causa

elaborate: to expand on or add information or detail about a point and thus to develop the point more fully
elaborar: extender o agregar información o detalles sobre un asunto, y asi desarrollar el asunto de manera más completa

empirical evidence: evidence based on experiences and direct observation through research
evidencia empírica: evidencia basada en experiencias y en la observación directa por medio de la investigación

emulate: to imitate an original work or person
emular: imitar una obra original

enfranchisement: having the rights of citizenship, such as the right to vote

emancipación: tener los derechos de la ciudananía, tales como el derecho al voto

epigram: a short, witty saying
epigrama: dicho corto e ingenioso

epigraph: a phrase, quotation, or poem that is set at the beginning of a document or component
epígrafe: frase, cita, o poema que aparece al comienzo de un documento o componente

epithet: a descriptive word or phrase used in place of or along with a name
epíteto: palabra o frase descriptiva usada en lugar de o junto con un nombre

ethos: (ethical appeal) a rhetorical appeal that focuses on the character or qualifications of the speaker
ethos: (recurso ético) recurso retórico centrado en la ética o en el carácter o capacidades del orador

euphonious: a harmonious or pleasing sound
eufónico: un sonido armonioso y agradable

evaluate: to make a judgment based on an analysis about the value or worth of the information, idea, or object
evaluar: dar una opinión basándose en un análisis sobre el valor o mérito de la información, idea, u objeto

evidence: the information that supports a position in an argument; forms of evidence include facts, statistics (numerical facts), expert opinions, examples, and anecdotes; *see also* anecdotal, empirical, and logical evidence
evidencia: información que apoya o prueba una idea o afirmación; formas de evidencia incluyen hechos, estadística (datos numéricos), opiniones de expertos, ejemplos y anécdotas; *ver también* evidencia anecdótica, empírica y lógica

exaggeration: a statement that represents something as larger, better, or worse than it really is
exageración: representar algo como más grande, mejor o peor que lo que realmente es

exemplification: the act of defining by example by showing specific, relevant examples that fit a writer's definition of a topic or concept
ejemplificación: definir por ejemplo mostrando ejempos específicos y relevantes que se ajustan a la definición de un tema o concepto del escritor

explanatory writing: a form of writing whose purpose is to explain, describe, or give information about a topic in order to inform a reader

escrito explicativo: forma de la escritura cuyo propósito es explicar, describir o dar información sobre un tema para informar al lector

explicit theme: a theme that is clearly stated by the writer
tema explícito: tema que está claramente establecido por el escritor

exposition: events that give a reader background information needed to understand a story (characters are introduced, the setting is described, and the conflict begins to unfold)
exposición: sucesos que dan al lector los antecedentes necesarios para comprender un cuento. Durante la exposición, se presentan los personajes, se describe el ambiente y se comienza a revelar el conflicto.

extended metaphor: a comparison between two unlike things that continues throughout a series of sentences in a paragraph or lines in a poem
metáfora extendida: metáfora que se extiende por varios versos o a través de un poema completo

external coherence: unity or logical connection between paragraphs with effective transitions and transitional devices
coherencia externa: unidad o conexión lógica entre párrafos con transiciones efectivas y recursos transitionales

eye rhymes: words that appear to rhyme because of identical spelling patterns but do not actually rhyme, for example, *cough* and *through*
falsas rimas: palabras, en inglés, que poseen una terminación idéntica y, por tanto, nos llevan erróneamente a pensar que riman, tales como *cough* y *through*

F

fallacy: a false or misleading argument
falacia: argumento o poema falso o engañoso

falling action: the events in a play, story, or novel that follow the climax, or moment of greatest suspense, and lead to the resolution
acción descendente: sucesos de una obra teatral, cuento o novela posteriores al clímax, o momento de mayor suspenso, y que conllevan a la resolución

faux pas: an embarrassing act or remark in a social situation (borrowed from French)
metedura de pata: comportamiento o comentario embarazoso en el marco de una situación social

Feminist Criticism: criticism that focuses on relationships between genders and examines a text based on the patterns of thought, behavior, values, enfranchisement, and power in relations between and within the sexes
crítica feminista: se enfoca en la relación entre los sexos y examina un texto basándose en el diseño de pensamiento, comportamiento, valores, emancipación, y poder en las relaciones entre los sexos

figurative: symbolic or emblematic; not literal
figurativo: simbólico o emblemático, no literal

figurative language: the use of words to describe one thing in terms of another
lenguaje figurativo: lenguaje imaginativo o figuras retóricas que no pretenden ser tomados literalmente; el lenguaje figurativo usa figuras literarias

film techniques: the methods a director uses to communicate meaning and to evoke particular emotional responses in viewers
técnicas cinematográficas: metodos que usa un director en la comunicación del significado y evocar una respuesta emocional específica en los videntes

fixed form: a form of poetry in which the length and pattern are determined by established usage of tradition, such as a sonnet
forma fija: forma de poesía en la que la longitud y el patrón están determinados por el uso de la tradición, como un soneto

flashback: an interruption or transition to a time before the current events in a narrative
flashback: interrupción en la secuencia de los sucesos para relatar sucesos ocurridos en el pasado

flat (or static) character: a character who is uncomplicated and stays the same without changing or growing during the story
personaje estático: personaje no complicado que permanence del mismo caracter y que no cambia a lo largo de una historia

folktale: a story without a known author that has been preserved through oral retellings
cuento folclórico: cuento sin autor conocido que se ha conservado por medio de relatos orales

footage: literally, a length of film; the expression is still used to refer to digital video clips
metraje: literalmente, la longitud de una película; la expresión aún se usa para referirse a video clips digitales

foreshadowing: the use of hints or clues in a narrative to suggest future action
presagio: uso de claves o pistas en un relato para sugerir una acción futura

form: the particular structure or organization of a work
forma: estructura o organización particular de una obra

found poem: a poem consisting of words, phrases, and/or lines that come directly from another text
poema encontrado: poema compuesto de palabras, frases o pasajes sacados directamente de otros textos

free verse: poetry without a fixed pattern of meter and rhyme
verso libre: poesía que no sigue ningún patrón, ritmo o rima regular

G

genre: a kind or style of literature or art, each with its own specific characteristics. For example, poetry, short story, and novel are literary genres. Painting and sculpture are artistic genres.
género: tipo o estilo de literatura o arte, cada uno con sus propias características específicas. Por ejemplo, la poesía, el cuento corto y la novela son géneros literarios. La pintura y la escultura son géneros artísticos.

genre conventions: the essential features and format that characterize a particular genre, or style of literature or art
convenciones genéricas: características básicas y el formato que caracterizan un género específico

graphic novel: a book-length narrative, or story, in the form of a comic strip rather than words
novela gráfica: narrativa o cuento del largo de un libro, en forma de tira cómica más que palabras

graphics: images or text used to provide information on screen
gráfica: imágenes o texto que se usa para dar información en pantalla

H

hamartia: a tragic hero's fatal flaw; an ingrained character trait that causes a hero to make decisions leading to his or her death or downfall
hamartia: error fatal de un héroe trágico; característica propia de un personaje que causa que un héroe tome decisiones que finalmente llevan a su muerte o caída

hero: the main character or protagonist of a play, with whom audiences become emotionally invested
héroe: personaje principal o protagonista de una obra teatral, con el que el público se involucra emocionalmente

historical context: the circumstances or conditions in which something takes place

contexto historico: circuntancias o condiciones en las cuales algo sucede o pasa

Historical Criticism: criticism used to uncover meaning in a literary text by examining the text in the context of the time period in which it was created
historicismo: método crítico que se usa para revelar el significado de un texto literario mediante el examen de dicho texto en el contexto de la época en que fue escrito

hook: an opening in an argument or a piece of writing that grabs the reader's attention
gancho: cita, anécdota o ejemplo interesante al comienzo de un escrito, que capta la atención del lector

Horatian satire: satire that pokes fun at human foibles and folly with a witty, gentle, even indulgent tone
sátira de Horacio: sátira en que se burla de las debilidades y locuras con un tono suave, ingenioso, hasta indulgente

humor: the quality of being amusing
humor: calidad de ser divertido

hyperbole: exaggeration used to suggest strong emotion or create a comic effect
hipérbole: exageración que se usa para sugerir una emoción fuerte o crear un efecto cómico

I

iamb: a metrical foot that consists of an unstressed syllable followed by a stressed syllable
yambo: pie métrico que consta de una sílaba átona seguida de una sílaba acentuada

iambic pentameter: a rhythmic pattern of five feet (or units), each consisting of one unstressed syllable followed by a stressed syllable
pentámetro yámbico: patrón rítmico de cinco pies (o unidades) de una sílaba átona seguida de una sílaba acentuada

image: a word or phrase that appeals to one of more of the five senses and creates a picture
imagen: palabra o frase que apela a uno o más de los cinco sentido y crea un cuadro

imagery: the verbal expression of sensory experience; descriptive or figurative language used to create word pictures; imagery is created by details that appeal to one or more of the five senses
imaginería: lenguaje descriptivo o figurativo utilizado para crear imágenes verbales; la imaginería es creada por detalles que apelan a uno o más de los cinco sentidos

imperialism: a policy of extending the rule or influence of a country over other countries or colonies; the political, military, or economic domination of one country by another
imperialismo: política de extender el dominio o la influencia de un país sobre otros países o colonias; dominio político; militar o económico de un país sobre otro(s)

implied theme: a theme that is understood through the writer's diction, language construction, and use of literary devices
tema implícito: tema que se entiende a través de la dicción del escritor, construcción lingüística y uso de recursos literarios

indirect characterization: a narrator's or author's development of a character through the character's interactions with others, thoughts about circumstances, or speaking his or her thoughts aloud
caracterización indirecta: el desarrollo de un personaje según un narrador o autor por las interacciones del personaje con otros, pensamientos sobre las circunstancias, o su habilidad de enunciar sus pensamientos en voz alta

inductive reasoning: a process of looking at individual facts to draw a general conclusion
razonamiento inductivo: proceso de observación de hechos individuales para sacar una conclusión general

inference: a conclusion about ideas or information not directly stated
inferencia: conclusion sobre las ideas o información no presentadas directamente

interior monologue: a literary device in which a character's internal emotions and thoughts are presented
monólogo interior: recurso literario en el que se presentan las emociones internas y pensamientos de un personaje

interpretation: the act of making meaning from something, such as a text
interpretación: acto de interpretar un significado de algo, tal como un texto

internal coherence: unity or logical connection within paragraphs
coherencia interna: unidad o conexión lógica entre párrafos

irony: a literary device that exploits readers' expectations; irony occurs when what happens turns out to be quite different from what was expected. *Dramatic irony* is a form of irony in which the reader or audience knows more about the circumstances or future events in a story than the characters within it; *verbal irony* occurs when a speaker or narrator says one thing while meaning the opposite; *situational irony* occurs when an event contradicts the expectations of the characters or the reader.

ironía: recurso literario que explota las expectativas de los lectores; la ironía ocurre cuando lo que se espera resulta ser bastante diferente de lo que realmente ocurre. La *ironía dramática* es una forma de ironía en la que el lector o la audiencia saben más acerca de las circunstancias o sucesos futuros de un cuento que los personajes del mismo; la *ironía verbal* ocurre cuando un orador o narrador dice una cosa queriendo decir lo contrario; la *ironía situacional* ocurre cuando un suceso contradice las expectativas de los personajes o del lector.

J

justice: the quality of being reasonable and fair in the administration of the law; the ideal of rightness or fairness
justicia: calidad de ser razonable e imparcial en la administración de la ley; ideal de rectitud o equidad

Juvenalian satire: satire that denounces, sometimes harshly, human vice and error in dignified and solemn tones
sátira de Juvenal: sátira de denuncia, a veces con aspereza, los vicios y errores humanos con tonos dignos y solemnes

juxtaposition: the arrangement of two or more things for the purpose of comparison
yuxtaposición: ordenamiento de dos o más cosas con el objeto de compararlas

L

lede: an alternative spelling of lead; the opening of a news article or a single sentence that describes the main point of the article
entradilla: comienzo de una información periodística que resume lo más importante de ella

lining out: the process of creating line breaks to add shape and meaning in free verse poetry
llamada y respuesta: proceso de crear rupturas de lineas para dar forma y significado en la poesía del verso libre

literal: explicitly stated in a text; exact
literal: algo expresado de modo explícito y exacto en un texto

literal language: the exact meanings, or denotations, of words
lenguaje literal: los signficados y denotaciones exactos de las palabras

Literary Criticism: the formal practice of interpreting, evaluating, and explaining the meaning and significance of literary works
crítica literaria: práctica formal de interpretar, evaluar y explicar el significado y el valor de obras literarias

literary theory: a systematic study of literature using various methods to analyze texts

teoría literaria: intento de establecer principios para interpretar y evaluar textos literarios

logical evidence: evidence based on facts and a clear rationale
evidencia lógica: evidencia basada en hechos y una clara fundamentación

logical fallacy: a statement that is false because it is based on an error in reasoning
argumento falaz: afirmación de carácter falso por el hecho de estar basada en un error de razonamiento

logos: (logical appeal) a rhetorical appeal to reason or logic
logos: (apelación lógica) apelación retórica que usa la evidencia factual y la lógica para apelar al sentido de la razón

M

main idea: a statement (often one sentence) that summarizes the key details of a text
idea principal: declaración (con frecuencia una oración) que resume los detalles claves de un texto

marginalize: to relegate or confine a person to a lower or outer limit
marginar: relegar o confinar a una persona a un límite bajo o ajeno

Marxist Criticism: criticism that asserts that economics provides the foundation for all social, political, and ideological reality
crítica marxista: ver un texto a través de la perspectiva en que la economía proporciona la fundación de toda realidad social, política, e ideológica

media: collectively refers to the organizations that communicate information to the public
medios de comunicación: colectivamente refiere a las organizaciones que comunican información al público

media channel: a method an organization uses to communicate, such as radio, television, website, newspaper, or magazine
canales mediaticos: método que usa una organización en la comunicación como radio, televisión, sitios de web, periódico, o revista

metacognition: the ability to know and be aware of one's own thought processes; self-reflection
metacognición: capacidad de conocer y estar consciente de los propios procesos del pensamiento; introspección

metaphor: a comparison between two unlike things in which one thing is spoken of as if it were another, for example, the moon was a crisp white cracker

metáfora: comparación entre dos cosas diferentes en la que se habla de una cosa como si fuera otra, por ejemplo, la luna era una galletita blanca crujiente

meter: a pattern of stressed and unstressed syllables in poetry
métrica: patrón de sílabas acentuadas y átonas en poesía

mise en scène: the composition, or setting, of a stage
puesta en escena: la composición o el lugar de un escenario

monologue: a dramatic speech delivered by a single character in a play
monólogo: discurso dramático que hace un solo personaje en una obra teatral

montage: a composite picture that is created by bringing together a number of images and arranging them to create a connected whole
montaje: cuadro compuesto que se crea al reunir un número de imágenes y que al organizarlas se crea un todo relacionado

mood: the atmosphere or predominant emotion in a literary work, the effect of the words on the audience
carácter: atmósfera o sentimiento general en una obra literaria

motif: a recurrent image, symbol, theme, character type, subject, or narrative detail that becomes a unifying element in an artistic work or text
motivo: imagen, símbolo, tema, tipo de personaje, tema o detalle narrativo recurrente que se convierte en un elemento unificador en una obra artística

motive: a character's reason for behaving in a certain way
motivación: razón esgrimida por un personaje para obrar de determinado modo

musical (or sound) device: the use of sound to convey and reinforce the meaning or experience of poetry
aparatos musicales: uso del sonido para transmitir y reforzar el significado o experiencia de la poesía

myth: a traditional story that explains the actions of gods or heroes or the origins of the elements of nature
mito: cuento tradicional que explica las acciones de dioses o héroes, o los orígenes de los elementos de la naturaleza

N

narration: the act of telling a story
narración: acto de contar un cuento

narrative: a story about a series of events that includes character development, plot structure, and theme; can be a work of fiction or nonfiction

narrativa: narración sobre una serie de sucesos que incluye el desarrollo de personajes, estructora del argumento, y el tema; puede ser una obra de ficción o no ficción

narrative arc: the story line of a text, including a beginning (*exposition*), a middle (the *rising action*), a high point (*climax*), and an end (the *falling action* and *resolution*)

arco narrativo: línea argumental de un texto, que consta de un comienzo (*exposición*), una parte media (*acción creciente*), un punto culminante (*clímax*) y un final (*acción decreciente y resolución*)

narrative pacing: the speed at which a narrative moves

compás de la narrativa: la rapidez en que una narrativa pasa

narrator: the person telling the story

narrador: persona que cuenta una historia

non-diegetic sound: sound that cannot logically be heard by the characters on screen; examples include mood music and voice-overs

sonido no diegético: voces y comentarios superpuestos; sonidos que no provienen de la acción en pantalla.

nut graf: an abbreviation of the expression *nutshell paragraph*; a statement that tells readers of a news article why they should care about what happened

epítome: texto introductorio que hace entender a los lectores por qué debería importarles la noticia que se relata a continuación

O

objective: based on factual information

objetivo: basado en información de hechos

objective tone: a tone that is more clinical and that is not influenced by emotion

tono objetivo: tono que es mas aséptico y que no se deja influir por la emoción

objectivity: the representation of facts or ideas without injecting personal feelings or biases

objetividad: representación de los hechos o ideas sin agregar sentimientos o prejuicios personales

ode: a lyric poem expressing feelings or thoughts of a speaker, often celebrating a person, event, or thing

oda: poema lírico que expresa sentimientos o pensamientos de un orador, que frecuentemente celebra a una persona, suceso o cosa

omniscient narrator: a narrator who knows all and tells a story from the perspective of multiple characters

narrador omnisciente: narrador que conoce todo lo sucedido sobre un determinado acontecimiento y relata la historia desde la perspectiva de varios personajes

onomatopoeia: the occurrence of a word whose sound suggests its meaning

onomatopeya: palabras cuyo sonido sugiere su significado

oral interpretation: a planned oral reading that expresses the meaning of a written text

interpretación oral: lectura oral planeada que interpreta el signficado de un text escrito

oral tradition: the passing down of stories, tales, proverbs, and other culturally important ideas through oral retellings

tradición oral: traspaso de historias, cuentos, proverbios y otras historias de importancia cultural por medio de relatos orales

oxymoron: words that appear to contradict each other; for example, cold fire

oxímoron: palabras que parecen contradecirse mutuamente; por ejemplo, fuego frío

P

paradox: a statement that contains two seemingly incompatible points

paradoja: declaración que contiene dos asuntos aparentemente incompatibles

parallel structure (parallelism): refers to a grammatical or structural similarity between sentences or parts of a sentence, so that elements of equal importance are equally developed and similarly phrased for emphasis

estructura paralela (paralelismo): se refiere a una similitud gramatical o estructural entre oraciones o partes de una oración, de modo que los elementos de igual importancia se desarrollen por igual y se expresen de manera similar para dar énfasis

paraphrase: to briefly restate ideas from another source in one's own words

parafrasear: volver a presentar las ideas de otra fuente en nuestras propias palabras

parenthetical citations: used for citing sources directly in an essay

citas parentéticas: usadas en citas de fuentes primarias en un ensayo

parody: a literary or artistic work that imitates the characteristic style of an author or a work for comic effect or ridicule

parodia: obra literaria o artística que imita el estilo característico de un autor o una obra para dar un efecto cómico o ridículo

passive-voice verbs: verb form in which the subject receives the action; the passive voice consists of a form of the verb *be* plus a past participle of the verb

verbos en voz pasiva: forma verbal en la que el sujeto recibe la acción; la voz pasiva se forma con el verbo *ser* más el participio pasado de un verbo

pathos: (emotional appeal) a rhetorical appeal to the reader's or listener's senses or emotions
pathos: (apelación emocional) apelación retórica a los sentidos o emociones de los lectores u oyentes

patriarchal: having the male as head of the household and with authority over women and children
patriarcal: sociedad en que el varón es jefe del hogar en el cual mantiene autoridad sobre las mujeres y niños

perception: one person's interpretation of sensory or conceptual information
percepción: interpretación de una persona en cuanto a información sensorial o conceptual

periodic sentence: a sentence that makes sense only when the end of the sentence is reached, that is, when the main clause comes last
oración periódica: oración que tiene sentido sólo cuando se llega al final de la oración, es decir, cuando la cláusula principal viene al final

persona: the voice assumed by a writer to express ideas or beliefs that may not be his or her own
personaje: voz que asume un escritor para expresar ideas o creencias que pueden no ser las propias

personification: a figure of speech that gives human qualities to an animal, object, or idea
personificación: figura literaria que da características humanas a un animal, objeto o idea

perspective: a way of looking at the world or a mental concept about things or events, one that judges relationships within or among things or events
perspectiva: manera de visualizar el mundo o concepto mental de las cosas o sucesos, que juzga las relaciones dentro o entre cosas o sucesos

persuasive argument: an argument that convinces readers to accept or believe a writer's perspective on a topic
argumento persuasivo: argumento que convence a los lectores a aceptar o creer en la perspectiva de un escritor acerca de un tema

photo essay: a collection of photographic images that reveal the author's perspective on a subject
ensayo fotográfico: recolección de imágenes fotográficas que revelan la perspectiva del autor acerca de un tema

plagiarism: the unattributed use of another writer's words or ideas
plagio: usar como propias las palabras o ideas de otro escritor

plot: the sequence of related events that make up a story
trama: secuencia de sucesos relacionados que conforman un cuento o novela

poetic structure: the organization of words, lines, and images as well as ideas
estructura poética: organización de las palabras, versos e imágenes, así como también de las ideas

poetry: language written in lines and stanzas
poesía: género literario que se concreta en un poema y está sujeto a medida o cadencia

point of view: the perspective from which a narrative is told, that is, first person, third-person limited, or third-person omniscient
punto de vista: perspectiva desde la cual se cuenta un relato, es decir, primera persona, tercera persona limitada o tercera persona omnisciente

precept: a rule, instruction, or principle that guides a person's actions and/or moral behavior
precepto: regla, instrucción o principio que guía las acciones de una persona y/o conducta moral de alguien

primary footage: film footage shot by the filmmaker for the text at hand
metraje principal: filmación hecha por el cineasta para el texto que tiene a mano

primary source: an original document or image created by someone who experiences an event first hand
fuente primaria: documento original que contiene información de primera mano acerca de un tema

prologue: the introduction or preface to a literary work
prólogo: introducción o prefacio de una obra literaria

prose: ordinary written or spoken language, using sentences and paragraphs, without deliberate or regular meter or rhyme; not poetry or song
prosa: forma común del lenguaje escrito o hablado, usando oraciones y párrafos, sin métrica o rima deliberada o regular; ni poesía ni canción

prosody: the pattern and rhythm of sounds in poetry, including stress and intonation
prosodia: rasgos fónicos de la métrica de la poesía, incluidos el énfasis y la entonación

protagonist: the central character in a work of literature, the one who is involved in the main conflict in the plot
protagonista: personaje central de una obra literaria, el que participa en el conflicto principal de la trama

proverb: a short saying about a general truth
proverbio: dicho corto sobre una verdad general

Q

qualify: to consider to what extent a statement is true or untrue (to what extent you agree or disagree)
calificar: consider hasta qué punto una declaración es verdadera o falsa

quatrain: a four-line stanza in a poem
cuarteta: en un poema, estrofa de cuatro versos

R

rationale: an explanation for a belief, statement, or behavior
fundamento: cimientos o bases en los que se apoya una creencia, afirmación o comportamiento

Reader Response Criticism: criticism that focuses on a reader's active engagement with a piece of print or nonprint text; shaped by the reader's own experiences, social ethics, moral values, and general views of the world
crítica de reacción del lector: análisis de un texto basado en las experiencias, ética social, valores, y percepciones generales del mundo

reasoning: the thinking or logic used to make a claim in an argument
razonamiento: pensamiento o lógica que se usa para hacer una afirmación en un argumento

rebuttal: a reason why a counterargument is wrong
refutación: razón por la cual un contraargumento es erróneo

refrain: a regularly repeated line or group of lines in a poem or song, usually at the end of a stanza
estribillo: verso o grupo de versos que se repiten con regularidad en un poema o canción, normalmente al final de una estrofa

refutation: the reasoning used to disprove an opposing point
refutación: razonamiento que se usa para rechazar una opinión contraria

reliability: the extent to which a source provides quality and trustworthy information
confiabilidad: grado en el que una fuente da información confiable y de buena calidad

renaissance: a rebirth or revival
renacimiento: un volver a nacer o una reanimación

repetition: the use of any element of language—a sound, a word, a phrase, a line, or a stanza—more than once
repetición: uso de cualquier elemento del lenguaje—un sonido, una palabra, una frase, un verso o una estrofa—más de una vez

resolution (denouement): the end of a text, in which the main conflict is finally resolved

resolución (desenlace): final de una obra teatral, cuento o novela, en el que el conflicto principal finalmente se resuelve

résumé: a document that outlines a person's skills, education, and work history
currículum vitae: documento que resume las destrezas, educación y experiencia laboral de una persona

retrospective: looking back to analyze the events in one's past
retrospectiva: mirar atrás en el tiempo para analizar los acontecimientos del pasado de una persona

revise: to rework or reorganize a piece of writing to improve its logic and flow after completing a first draft
revisar: rehacer o reorganizar un escrito para mejorar su lógica y fluidez tras haber terminado un primer borrador

rhetoric: the art of using words to persuade in writing or speaking
retórica: arte de usar las palabras para persuadir por escrito o de manera hablada

rhetorical appeals: emotional, ethical, and logical arguments used to persuade an audience to agree with the writer or speaker
recursos retóricos: uso de argumentos emocionales, éticos y lógicos para persuadir por escrito o de manera hablada

rhetorical context: the subject, purpose, audience, occasion, or situation in which writing or speaking occurs
contexto retórico: sujeto, propósito, audiencia, ocasión o situación en que ocurre el escrito

rhetorical devices: specific techniques used in writing or speaking to create a literary effect or enhance effectiveness
dispositivos retóricos: técnicas específicas que se usan al escribir o al hablar para crear un efecto literario o mejorar la efectividad

rhetorical question: a question that is asked for effect or one for which the answer is obvious
pregunta retórica: pregunta hecha para producir un efecto o cuya respuesta es obvia

rhetorical slanters: rhetorical devices used to present a subject in a biased way
sesgos retóricos: recursos retóricos que se usan para presentar un determinado asunto de un modo tendencioso

rhyme: the repetition of sounds at the ends of words
rima: repetición de sonidos al final de las palabras

rhyme scheme: a consistent pattern of rhyme throughout a poem
esquema de la rima: patrón consistente de una rima a lo largo de un poema

rhythm: the pattern of stressed and unstressed syllables in spoken or written language, especially in poetry

ritmo: patrón de sílabas acentuadas y no acentuadas en lenguaje hablado o escrito, especialmente en poesía

rising action: the movement of a plot toward a climax or moment of greatest excitement; the rising action is fueled by the characters' responses to the conflict
acción ascendente: movimiento de una trama hacia el clímax o momento de mayor emoción; la acción ascendente es impulsada por las reacciones de los personajes ante el conflicto

dynamic (or round) character: a character who evolves and grows in the story and has a complex personality
personaje dinámico: personaje que evoluciona y crece en la historia y que tiene una personalidad compleja

S

sarcasm: deliberate, often ironic ridicule
sarcasmo: burla deliberada, de carácter generalmente irónico

satire: a manner of writing that mocks social conventions, actions, or attitudes with wit and humor
sátira: manera de escribir en que se burla de convenciones sociales, acciones, o actitudes con ingenio y humor

scenario: an outline, a brief account, a script, or a synopsis of a proposed series of events
escenario: bosquejo, relato breve, libreto o sinopsis de una serie de sucesos propuestos

secondary audience: a group that may receive a message intended for a target audience
audiencia secundaria: grupo que puede recibir un mensaje orientado a una audiencia específica

secondary source: a discussion about or commentary on a primary source; the key feature of a secondary source is that it offers an interpretation of information gathered from primary sources
fuente secundaria: discusión o comentario acerca de una fuente primaria; la característica clave de una fuente secundaria es que ofrece una interpretación de la información recopilada en las fuentes primarias

sensory details: details that appeal to or evoke one or more of the five senses—sight, sound, smell, taste, and touch
detalles sensoriales: detalles que apelan o evocan uno o más de los cinco sentidos—vista, oído, gusto, olfato, y tacto

sensory images: images that appeal to the reader's senses—sight, sound, smell, taste, and touch
imágenes sensoriales: imágenes que apelan a los sentidos del lector—vista, oído, olfato, gusto, y tacto

sequence of events: the order in which things happen in a story

secuencia de eventos: orden en que los sucesos de una historia pasan:

setting: the time and place in which a story happens
ambiente: tiempo y lugar en el que ocurre un relato

simile: a comparison of two different things or ideas using the words *like* or *as*, for example, the moon was as white as milk
símil: comparación entre dos o más cosas o ideas diferentes usando las palabras *como* o *tan*, por ejemplo, la luna estaba tan blanca como la leche

situational irony: a form of irony that occurs when an event contradicts the expectations of the characters or the reader
ironía situacional: ocurre cuando un evento contradice las espectativas de los personajes o el lector

slanters: rhetorical devices used to present the subject in a biased way
soslayo: recursos retóricos para presentar el tema de modo sesgado

slogan: a short, catchy phrase used for advertising by a business, club, or political party
eslogan: frase corta y tendenciosa que usa como publicidad para un negocio, club o partido político

social commentary: an expression of an opinion with the goal of promoting change by appealing to a sense of justice
comentario social: expresión de una opinión con el objeto de promover el cambio al apelar a un sentido de justicia

soliloquy: a long speech delivered by an actor alone on the stage; represents the character's internal thoughts
soliloquio: discurso largo realizado por un actor sobre el escenario que representa sus pensamientos internos

sonnet: a 14-line lyric poem, usually written in iambic pentameter and following a strict pattern of rhyme
soneto: poema lírico de catorce versos, normalmente escrito en un pentámetro yámbico y que sigue un patrón de rima estricto

sound bite: a short excerpt from the recording of a speech or piece of music which captures the essence of the longer recording
cuña: corto fragmento de una grabación o de una pieza musical que capta la esencia de la grabación completa

speaker: the imaginary voice or persona of the writer or author
orador: voz o persona imaginaria del escritor o autor

stage directions: instructions written into the script of a play that indicate stage actions, movements of performers, or production requirements
direcciones escénicas: instrucciones escritas en un guión o drama que indican acción, movimiento de actors, o requisitos de la producción

stakeholder: a person motivated or affected by a course of action

participante: persona motivada o afectada por el curso de una acción

stanza: a group of lines, usually similar in length and pattern, that form a unit within a poem

estrofa: grupo de versos, normalmente similares en longitud y patrón, que forman una unidad dentro de un poema

static (or flat) character: a character who is uncomplicated and remains the same without changing or growing throughout a narrative

personaje estático: personaje que no cambia a lo largo de una narrativa

stereotype: an oversimplified, generalized conception, opinion, and/or image about particular groups of people

estereotipo: concepto generalizado, opinión y/o imagen demasiado simplificada acerca de grupos específicos de personas

stichomythia: in drama, the delivery of dialogue in a rapid, fast-paced manner, with actors speaking emotionally and leaving very little time between speakers

esticomitia: en el drama, es la rendición del diálogo de una manera rápida con actores que hablan con emoción, dejando espacio muy breve entre los hablantes

storyboard: a tool to show images and sequencing for the purpose of visualizing a film or a story

guión gráfico: método de mostrar imágenes y secuencias con el propósito de visualizar una película o historia

strategize: to plan the actions one will take to complete a task

estrategizar: planear las acciones de uno para cumplir una tarea

structure: the way a literary work is organized; the arrangement of the parts in a literary work

estructura: manera en que la obra literaria está organizada; disposición de las partes en una obra literaria

style: the distinctive way a writer uses language, characterized by elements of diction, syntax, imagery, organization, and so on

estilo: manera distintiva en que un escritor usa el lenguaje, caracterizada por elementos de dicción, sintaxis, lenguaje figurado, etc.

subculture: a smaller subsection of a culture, for example, within the culture of a high school may be many subcultures

subcultura: subsección más pequeña de una cultura, por ejemplo, dentro de la cultura de una escuela secundaria puede haber muchas subculturas

subjective: based on a person's point of view, opinions, values, or emotions

subjetivo: basado en el punto de vista, las opiniones, los valores o las emociones de alguien

subjective tone: a tone that is obviously influenced by the author's feelings or emotions

tono subjetivo: tono obviamente influído por los sentimientos o emociones del autor

subjectivity: judgment based on one's personal point of view, opinion, or values

subjetividad: en base en nuestro punto de vista, opinión o valores personales

subordinate: a person or group that is perceived as having a lower social or economic status

subordinado: persona o grupo percibido de ser de rango social o estado económico bajo

subplot: a secondary or side story that develops from and supports the main plot and usually involves minor characters

argumento secundario: una historia secundaria o periférica que apoya el argumento principal y que suele involucrar a personajes secundarios o menores

subtext: the underlying or implicit meaning in dialogue or the implied relationship between characters in a book, movie, play, or film; the subtext of a work is not explicitly stated

subtexto: significado subyacente o implícito en el diálogo o la relación implícita entre los personajes de un libro, película, u obra teatral. El subtexto de una obra no se establece de manera explícita.

survey: a method of collecting data from a group of people; it can be written, such as a print or online questionnaire, or oral, such as an in-person interview

encuesta: método para recolectar datos de un grupo de personas; puede ser escrita, como un impreso o cuestionario en línea, u oral, como en una entrevista personal

symbol: anything (object, animal, event, person, or place) that represents itself but also stands for something else on a figurative level

símbolo: cualquier cosa (objeto, animal, evento, persona o lugar) que se representa a sí misma, pero también representa otra cosa a nivel figurativo

symbolic: serving as a symbol; involving the use of symbols or symbolism

simbólico: que sirve como símbolo; que implica el uso de símbolos o simbolismo

synecdoche: a figure of speech in which a part is used to represent the whole or vice versa

sinécdoque: figura retórica en que una parte se usa para representar el todo, o vice-versa

syntax: the arrangement of words and the order of grammatical elements in a sentence; the way in which words are put together to make meaningful elements, such as phrases, clauses, and sentences

sintaxis: disposición de las palabras y orden de los elementos gramaticales en una oración; manera en que las palabras se juntan para formar elementos significativos como frases, cláusulas y oraciones

synthesis: the act of combining ideas from different sources to create, express, or support a new idea

síntesis: acto de combinar ideas de diferentes fuentes para crear, expresar o apoyar una nueva idea

synthesize: to combine ideas from different sources to create, express, or support a new idea or claim

sintetizar: combinar ideas procedentes de distintas fuentes para crear, expresar o sustentar una nueva idea o afirmación

T

target audience: the intended group for which a work is designed to appeal or reach

público objetivo: grupo al que se pretende apelar o llegar con una obra

tenor: the intent, tone, or attitude conveyed by the words in a text

tenor: intención, tono o actitud transmitida por las palabras de un texto

textual evidence: the details, quotations, and examples from a text that support the analysis or argument presented

evidencia textual: detalles, citas, y ejemplos de un texto que apoyan el análisis o la argumentación presentada

theatrical elements: elements used by dramatists and directors to tell a story on stage. Elements include *costumes* (the clothing worn by actors to express their characters), *makeup* (cosmetics used to change actors' appearances and express their characters), *props* (objects used to help set the scene, advance a plot, and make a story realistic), *set* (the place where the action takes place, as suggested by objects, such as furniture, placed on a stage), and *acting choices* (gestures, movements, staging, and vocal techniques actors use to convey their characters and tell a story).

elementos teatrales: elementos utilizados por los dramaturgos y directores para contar una historia en el escenario. Los elementos incluyen *vestuario* (ropa que usan los actores para expresar sus personajes), *maquillaje* (cosméticos que se usan para cambiar la apariencia de los actores y expresar sus personajes), *elementos* (objetos que se usan para ayudar a montar la escena, avanzar la trama y crear una historia realista), *plató* (lugar donde tiene lugar la acción, según lo sugieren los objetos, como muebles, colocados sobre un escenario), y *opciones de actuación* (gestos, movimientos, representación y técnicas vocales que se usan para transmitir sus personajes y narrar una historia).

thematic statement: an interpretive statement articulating the central meaning or message of a text

oración temática: afirmación interpretativa que articula el significado o mensaje central de un texto

theme: a writer's central idea or main message; *see also* explicit theme, implied theme

tema: idea central o mensaje principal acerca de la vida de un escritor; *véase también* tema explícito, tema implícito

thesis: the main idea or point of an essay or article; in an argumentative essay the thesis is the writer's position on an issue

tesis: idea o punto principal de un ensayo o artículo; en un ensayo argumentativo, la tesis es la opinión del autor acerca de un tema

thumbnail sketch: a small drawing made to plan the composition of a more detailed or finished image that will be created later

boceto en miniatura: pequeño dibujo realizado para planificar la composición de una imagen más amplia o detallada que será posteriormente creada

tone: a writer's (or speaker's) attitude toward a subject, character, or audience

tono: actitud de un escritor u orador acerca de un tema

topic sentence: a sentence that states the main idea of a paragraph; in an essay, the topic sentence also makes a point that supports the thesis statement

oración principal: oración que establece la idea principal de un párrafo; en un ensayo, la oración principal también establece una proposición que apoya el enunciado de la tesis

tragedy: a dramatic play that tells the story of a character, usually of a noble class, who meets an untimely and unhappy death or downfall, often because of a specific character flaw or twist of fate

tragedia: obra teatral dramática que cuenta la historia de un personaje, normalmente de origen noble, que encuentra una muerte o caída imprevista o infeliz, con frecuencia debido a un defecto específico del personaje o una vuelta del destino

tragic hero: an archetypal hero based on the Greek concept of tragedy; the tragic hero has a flaw that makes him or her vulnerable to downfall or death

héroe trágico: héroe arquetípico basado en el concepto griego de la tragedia; el héroe trágico tiene un defecto que lo hace vulnerable a la caída o a la muerte

transcript: a written copy or record of a conversation that takes place between two or more people

transcripción: copia escrita de una conversación que sucede entre dos o más personas

U

unconventional: eccentric; unusual; original

no convencional: excéntrico; inusual; original

understatement: the representation of something as smaller or less significant than it really is; the opposite of exaggeration or hyperbole

subestimación: representación de algo como más pequeño o menos importante de lo que realmente es; lo opuesto a la exageración o hipérbole

V

valid: believable or truthful

válido: creíble o verídico

validity: the quality of truth or accuracy in a source

validez: calidad de verdad o precisión en una fuente

verbal irony: a form of irony that occurs when a speaker or narrator says one thing while meaning the opposite

ironía verbal: ocurre cuando un hablante o narrador dice una cosa mientras quiere decir lo opuesto

verbatim: in the exact words of a source

textualmente: palabras citadas exactamente como fueron expresadas

verify: to prove or confirm that something is true

verificar: probar o confirmar que algo es verdadero

vignette: a picture or visual or a brief descriptive literary piece

viñeta: ilustración o representación visual o pieza literaria descriptiva breve

visual delivery: the way a performer on stage interprets plot, character, and conflict through movement, gestures, and facial expressions

presentación visual: manera en que un actor en un escenario interpreta trama, carácter, y conflicto a través de movimiento, gestos, y expresiones de la cara

visual rhetoric: an argument or points made by visuals such as photographs or by other visual features of a text

retórica visual: argumentos o asuntos representados en visuales como fotos u otros rasgos visuales de un texto

visualize: to form a mental picture of something

visualizar: formarse una imagen mental de algo

vocal delivery: the way a performer on stage expresses the meaning of a text through volume, pitch, rate or speed of speech, pauses, pronunciation, and articulation

presentación vocal: manera en que se expresan las palabras en el escenario, por medio del volumen, tono, rapidez o velocidad del discurso, pausas, pronunciación y articulación

voice: a writer's (or speaker's) distinctive use of language to express ideas as well as his or her persona

voz: manera en que el escritor u orador usa las palabras y el tono para expresar ideas, así como también su personaje o personalidad

Index of Skills

Literary Skills

Ad baculum (scare tactics), 412
Ad hominem (genetic fallacy), 235, 412
Ad misericodism (appeal to pity), 412
Ad populum (bandwagon), 235, 411
Alliteration, 310
Allusion, 41, 275, 279, 291, 293, 302, 359, 360, 361, 419, 525, 539, 540
Analogy, 172, 275, 302, 310, 373, 401–402, 410, 433
Analytical essay, 308, 576
Anaphora, 271, 302, 310
Anecdote, 41, 172, 410
Annotated bibliography, 472, 508–509, 514
Appeal to pity (ad misericodism), 412
Arguable thesis, 104, 348, 350
Argument
  audience of, 117, 332, 379
  author's, 257
  clear and organized, 393
  compelling, 391, 399, 400, 410
  deductive, 357
  developing, 257, 308, 333, 338, 392, 400
  elements and characteristics of, 104, 111, 275, 280, 310–311, 354
  fallacy's effect on, 319
  focus of essay, 101, 118, 175, 257, 370
  inductive, 357
  key terms for, 392
  logical, 243, 379
  objective tone, 224, 331, 333, 393, 400
  refuting, 104, 111, 121, 172, 176, 351, 354, 355, 356, 357, 393, 403
  ridicule and sarcasm's effect on, 378
  structure of, 103–104, 111, 117, 118, 119, 121, 175, 275, 280, 286, 312, 332, 333, 354, 357
  subjective tone, 331
  supporting, 101, 104, 111, 113, 119, 170, 172, 175, 185, 244, 275, 279, 287, 313, 314, 328, 330, 348, 357, 381, 389–390, 393, 399, 400, 401–402, 403, 421
  tone of, 118, 268, 270, 331
Argument from outrage, 412
  argumentative text. See also Editorial
Assonance, 492
Attitude (*See also* Tone (attitude))
  of author/speaker, 13, 14, 84, 89, 91, 141, 142, 143, 152, 154, 161, 165, 243, 255, 273, 274, 523

of characters, 213, 561
of narrator, 25, 26
of readers/listeners, 509
Audience, 50, 59, 81, 92, 104, 111, 117, 160, 169, 173, 176, 205, 239, 272, 273, 299, 332, 379, 391, 392, 403, 414, 445, 457, 465, 467, 468, 480, 541
Author's craft, 26, 118, 523
Author's purpose, 49, 50–51, 57, 58, 66, 89, 90, 91, 92, 109, 118, 119, 126, 159, 186, 205, 208, 218, 253, 263, 282, 291, 408, 429–430, 433, 434, 438, 450, 480, 571, 575
Autobiographies, 6
Bandwagon (ad populum), 235, 411
Bias
  of authors, 331, 381
  defined, 363
  by headlines, 364, 366
  identifying, 365–366, 371, 372, 375, 381
  by photos, captions, and camera angles, 364, 366, 389
  of rhetoric, 373–375
  by source control, 365, 366
  through placement, 364, 365, 381
  through selection and omission, 364, 365, 381, 389
  through statistics and crowd count, 364–365, 366, 401
  types of, 363, 365–366
Big ideas, 5, 33
Biographies, 6
Book reviews, 572–573, 574–575
Call to action, 104, 111, 122, 127, 265, 271, 275, 280, 285, 287, 313, 314, 332
Camera angles, bias by, 364, 366
Captions, bias by, 364, 366, 389
Caricature, 424, 455
Case studies, 410
Causal relationships, 401, 412
Cause-and-effect text structure, 31, 91
Central conflict, 237
Central idea, 25, 90, 225, 255, 279, 370
Central image, 74
Central message, 165, 502
Characterization, 135, 149, 150, 208, 211–213, 238, 536, 547–549, 551
Characters, 6, 27, 75, 145, 263, 466, 525, 537–538, 547–548, 550, 556–557, 562, 563, 564, 571

actions of, 211, 213, 217, 218, 220, 223, 224, 226, 237, 536, 547, 558, 566
analyzing, 210, 211, 212, 213, 217, 224, 229, 232, 236, 238, 258, 537
changes of, 139, 141, 142, 217, 218, 537
choices of, 238, 558
descriptions of, 211
development of, 226, 227, 228, 237, 281, 566
direct characterization, 547, 548
dramatic elements of, 145, 217
dramatic presentations, 145
emotional responses of, 260, 566–567
foil, 213, 258
historical context of, 182
hysteria, 260
indirect characterization, 226, 547, 548
mental images of, 525
moral dilemmas of, 217, 220, 232–233, 558, 559
motivation of, 211, 212, 213, 217, 218, 223, 224, 558
note taking chart, 211, 212, 213, 217
study of, 566–568
tone affecting, 13
uniqueness of, 75
voice developing, 225, 226
Character study, 566–568
Chiasmus, 303, 310
Chorus, 549
Chronological text structure, 31, 91, 158
Claim, 45, 83, 104, 111, 117, 119, 120, 121, 160, 165, 170, 173, 176, 185, 257, 265, 275, 280, 281, 282, 287, 313, 338, 349, 350, 351, 355, 356, 358, 389–390, 393, 400, 401–402, 410, 420, 464, 511, 541, 565, 568, 575, 576
Classification definition strategy, 41, 42, 43, 45, 70
Climax, 145, 227, 228, 238
Colloquialisms, 169
Commentary, 567
Compare-contrast text structure, 31, 91
Comparisons, 58, 69, 132, 138, 159, 170, 266, 307, 310, 373, 401, 408, 547
Concessions, 104, 111, 118, 287, 332, 349, 351, 356, 357
Conclusion, 53, 54, 58, 70, 104, 118, 165, 186, 281, 286, 332, 357, 408
Conflict, 218, 223, 224, 226, 227, 228, 237, 261, 262, 263, 562, 564, 566

Reading Skills

Writing Skills

rhetorical analysis, 45, 257, 307, 391, 438

satirical narrative paragraph, 466

scripts, 222, 226, 237, 260, 445, 512–513

Writing with partners, 32, 50, 51, 64, 65, 287, 393, 445, 502

Media Skills

Art, as historical sources, 472, 479, 481, 482, 487, 495, 502, 503

Camera angles, bias by, 364, 366

Captions, bias of, 364, 366, 389

Create a poster, 213, 302, 457

Crowd counts, bias through, 364–365, 366

Documentary films, as historical sources, 486–487

Evaluating sources, 97, 175, 372, 515

Examining cartoons, 381, 432–433

Graphics, 382, 388, 389, 419

Headlines, bias of, 364, 366

Illustrations, 8, 193
analyzing, 193

Images, analyzing, 48, 53–54, 96, 207, 379

Interactive multimedia presentation (*See* Multimedia presentation)

Media formats, 341, 382, 403, 415, 421, 445, 451, 505–506, 511, 512, 514

MLA style sheet, 175, 508

Multimedia presentation, 472, 481, 509–515
generating research questions, 473, 474, 475, 483, 484–485, 506, 509, 510
organizing, 511, 514
presenting, 505–507
topic selection, 472, 473, 483, 484

Murals, analyzing, 10, 11

News sources, 319, 340
accuracy and trustworthiness of, 340, 363
analyzing bias of, 371, 375
bias of, 319, 363–364, 371, 372
characteristics of, 341, 342
credibility and accuracy of, 363, 371, 372
digital, 341
multimodal, 341, 342
print features, 382, 388, 417, 419
secondary audience, 341
target audience, 341, 342, 343, 379

Omission, bias through, 364, 365, 381

Online resources, 13, 68, 97, 320, 323, 330, 341, 342, 356, 379, 473, 482, 491, 505

Photographs, analyzing, 9, 96

Photos, bias by, 364, 366

Placement, bias through, 364, 365, 381

Political cartoons, analyzing, 8

Presenting poster, 457

Print and graphic features, analyzing, 382, 419

Publishing, 393

Puff pieces, 365

Reading and creating editorial cartoon, 415–419

Researching images, 97, 98

Satirical cartoons, analyzing, 432–433

Sculptures, analyzing, 487, 495

Selection, bias through, 364, 365, 381, 389

Setting purpose for viewing, 96, 432, 486–487

Source control, bias by, 365, 366

Special formatting, 382

Statistics, bias through, 364, 366, 401

Text divisions, 382

Video footage, analyzing, 302

Visual presentations, 12, 98

Visual prompt, 1, 177, 315, 469

Visual text
analyzing, 7–12, 487
creating, 12

Speaking and Listening Skills

Audience, 59, 173, 186, 216, 239, 260, 263, 266, 267, 272, 273, 274, 285, 286, 287, 291, 293, 299, 303, 313, 414, 451, 484, 510, 513, 514, 515

Blocking (movement), 215, 216, 229, 230

Class discussion, 5, 14, 51, 211, 219, 546, 561

Collaboration guidelines, 58, 261, 263, 266, 333, 421, 456, 483, 484

Collaborative conversations, 547

Collaborative Discussion, 5, 12, 13, 44, 51, 92, 171, 174, 181, 272, 333, 371, 424, 483

Communicating effectively, 221, 266–267, 275, 281, 375, 513

Consensus, 174

Debate, 311, 464

Delivery, 145, 181, 263, 288, 290, 310, 473, 513, 514

Developing speaking skills, 266–267

Dialogue, 227, 229, 237, 260, 263, 525

Director, 216

Discussion groups, 6, 136, 172–174, 197, 198, 206, 219, 261, 266, 272, 280, 282, 302, 371, 375, 402, 432, 433, 438, 569–570, 571, 575

Drama Game, 209–210

Dramatic presentations
elements of scripts, 145, 218
interpreting relationships, 214, 215, 217, 223, 229, 230, 233, 239
performing, 209, 216, 237, 260, 261, 266
preparing for, 209, 261–262
scene, 145, 181, 261–262–264

Enunciation, 266, 267, 288, 293, 310, 513

Eye contact, 266, 267, 293, 310, 483, 513

Facial expressions, 215, 216, 217, 229, 230, 303

Fallacy Face-Off, 414

Feedback, 96, 216, 260, 267, 313, 375, 513, 514

Gestures, 215, 216, 217, 229, 230, 266, 293, 303, 310, 313, 314, 513

Graphic organizer, 5, 50, 59, 101, 265, 272–273, 286, 472, 473, 486, 506, 507, 508, 509, 510, 511–512, 513, 525, 570

Group discussion, 6, 136, 172–174, 197, 198, 206, 219, 261, 266, 272, 280, 282, 302, 371, 375, 402, 432, 433, 438, 569–570, 571, 575

Inflection, 274, 303, 314

Interactive multimedia presentation (*See* Multimedia presentation)

Lecture of advice, 451

Mock Constitutional Convention, 51

Mock debate, 414

Monologues, 145, 260

Movement, 215, 216, 217, 229, 310

Multimedia components, 266, 267

Multimedia presentation, 481, 509–515
generating research questions, 473, 474, 475, 483, 484–485, 506, 509, 510
organizing, 511, 514
presenting, 505–507
topic selection, 472, 473, 483, 484

Note-taking, 173, 211, 219, 260, 261, 265, 310, 356, 456, 473, 486, 487, 513, 514, 515, 547, 569

Language Skills

Vocabulary Skills

Index of Authors and Titles

Credits

From "The Two Clashing Meanings of 'Free Speech'" by Teresa M. Bejan, *The Atlantic*, December 2, 2017.

"America and I" by Anzia Yezierska from *The Open Cage: An Anzia Yezierska Collection.* Copyright © 1979 by Louise Levitas Henniksen. Persea Books, Inc. New York.

"I, Too, Sing America" from *The Collected Poems of Langston Hughes* by Langston Hughes, edited by Arnold Rampersad with David Roessel, Associate Editor, copyright © 1994 by the Estate of Langston Hughes.

Used by permission of Alfred A. Knopf, a division of Random House, Inc.

"I, Too Sing América" by Julia Alvarez from *Writers on America*, edited by George Clack.

"Growing Up Asian in America" from *Making Waves: An Anthology of Writings by and About Asian Women* by Kesaya E. Noda. Copyright © 1989 by Kesaya E. Noda. Beacon Press.

"Is the American Dream Still Possible?" by David Wallechinsky from *Parade* (April 23, 2006). Copyright © 2006 Parade Publications.

"Let America Be America Again" from *The Collected Poems of Langston Hughes* by Langston Hughes, edited by Arnold Rampersad with David Roessel, Associate Editor, copyright © 1994 by the Estate of Langston Hughes. Used by permission of Alfred A. Knopf, a division of Random House, Inc.

"Ellis Island" by Joseph Bruchac from *The Remembered Earth*, © 1979, Red Earth Press, Albuquerque, NM.

David Ignatow, "Europe and America" from *Against the Evidence: Selected Poems, 1934–1994* copyright © 1993 by David Ignatow and reprinted by permission of Wesleyan University Press.

"My Uncle's Favorite Coffee Shop" from *Fuel* by Naomi Shibab Nye, copyright © 1998 by Naomi Shibab Nye. Used by the permission of BOA Editions Ltd.

"Sonnet: Ladies' Home Journal" from *Emily's Bread: Poems* by Sandra Gilbert, copyright © 1984 by Sandra M. Gilbert.

From *A Raisin in the Sun* by Lorraine Hansberry, copyright © 1958 by Robert Nemiroff, as an unpublished work. Copyright © 1959, 1966, 1984 by Robert Nemiroff. Copyright renewed 1986, 1987 by Robert Nemiroff. Used by permission of Random House, Inc.

"Who Burns for the Perfection of Paper" from *City of Coughing and Dead Radiators* by Martin Espada. Copyright © 1993 by Martin Espada. Used by permission of W.W. Norton & Company, Inc.

"Roberto Acuna Talks About Farm Workers" from *Working* by Studs Terkel. Copyright © 1997 Studs Terkel. Reprinted by permission of Donadio & Olson, Inc.

Keynote Address to the 2004 Democratic National Convention from *Words That Changed a Nation: The Most Celebrated Speeches of Barack Obama.* Copyright © 2009 by Pacific Publishing Studio.

"The Right to Fail" from *The Lunacy Boom* by William Zinsser. Copyright © 1969, 1970 by William K. Zinsser. Reproduced by permission of the author.

"The Lessons of Salem" from *Newsweek*, Aug. 31, 1992, © 1992 Newsweek, Inc. All rights reserved. Used by permission and protected by the Copyright Laws of the United States. The printing, copying, redistribution, or retransmission of the Material without express written permission is prohibited. http://www.newsweek.com

"Why I Wrote *The Crucible*: An Artist's Answer to Politics" by Arthur Miller, originally published in *The New Yorker*. Copyright © 1996 by Arthur Miller, reprinted with permission of The Wylie Agency LLC.

"The Role of Media in Democracy" by George A. Krimsky from *Democracy*, USIA Electronic Journal, Vol. 2, No. 1, February 1997.

"How the Rise of the Daily Me Threatens Democracy" by Cass Sunstein as appeared in the *Financial Times*, Jan. 11, 2008. Reprinted by permission of Cass Sunstein.

"The Newspaper Is Dying—Hooray for Democracy" by Andrew Potter as appeared in *McClean's Magazine*, April 7, 2008. Used by permission of the author.

"Facebook Photos Sting Minnesota High School Students," *The Associated Press*, January 11, 2008. Used by permission of The Associated Press copyright © 2009. All rights reserved.

"Abolish High School Football!" by Raymond Schroth. Used by permission of the author.

"Separate and Unequal: Indian Schools, a Nation's Neglect" by the Star Tribune Editorial Board, the *Star Tribune*, April 2, 2015. Reprinted with permission.

"Time to Raise the Bar in High Schools" by Jack O'Connell from *Ventura County Star*, June 13, 2004. Used by permission.

"New Michigan Graduation Requirements Shortchange Many Students" by Nick Thomas from *Online Newshour Extra* (posted Sept. 14, 2006). © 2006 MacNeil-Lehrer Productions. Reprinted with permission.

"The NYC Subway Is Not 'Beyond Repair'" from *The Atlantic*, June 13, 2018.

"An Inside Look at Editorial Cartoons" by Bill Brennen, *The Grand Island Independent*, March 27, 2001. Courtesy of The Grand Island Independent.

"Let's Hear It for the Cheerleaders" by David Bouchier, from *The New York Times*, August 2, 1998. Copyright © 1998 The New York Times. All rights reserved. Used by permission and protected by the Copyright Laws of the United States. The print, copying, redistribution, or retransmission of the Material without express written permission is prohibited. HYPERLINK "http://www.nytimes.com" http://www.nytimes.com

"Girl Moved to Tears by *Of Mice and Men* Cliffs Notes" from *The Onion*, August 18, 2008. Copyright © 2009, by Onion, Inc.

Reprinted with permission of The Onion. HYPERLINK "http://www.theonion.com" http://www. theonion.com

"In Depth, but Shallowly" from *Bad Habits: A 100% Fact Free Book* by Dave Barry, humorist. Used by permission.

"Gambling in Schools" by Howard Mohr, from *Mirth of a Nation: The Best Contemporary Humor* compiled by Michael J. Rosen, Harper Paperbacks, 2000. Used by permission.

"How to Poison the Earth" by Linnea Saukko from *Student Writers at Work and in the Company of Other Writers*. Copyright © 1984 by Bedford/St. Martin's and used with permission of the publisher.

"The Harlem Renaissance" adapted from *The 1920s* by Kathleen Drowne and Patrick Huber. Copyright © 2004 by Kathleen Drowne and Patrick Huber. *American Popular Culture Through History Series*, Greenwood.

From *The New Negro* by Alain Locke. Copyright © 1925 by Albert and Charles Boni. Touchstone.

"To Usward" by Gwendolyn B. Bennett from *Shadow Dreams: Women's Poetry of the Harlem Renaissance*, edited by Maureen Honey. Copyright © 1989 by Rutgers University Press.

"From 'On a Dark Tower'" by Eugenia W. Collier, *College Language Association Journal* 11.1 (1967).

"Sweat" by Zora Neale Hurston, from *The Complete Stores of Zora Neale Hurston*, edited by Henry Louis Gates, Jr., and Sieglinda Lemke. Introduction copyright © 1995 by Henry Louis Gates, Jr. and Sieglinde Lemke. HarperCollins Publishers. Compilation copyright © 1995 by Vivian Bowden, Lois J. Hurston Gaston, Clifford Hurston, Lucy Ann Hurston, Winifred Hurston Clark, Zora Mack Goins, Edgar Huroton, Sr., and Barbara Hurston Lewis.

"Mother to Son" from *The Collected Poems of Langston Hughes* by Langston Hughes, edited by Arnold Rampersad with David Roessel, Associate Editor, copyright © 1994 by the Estate of Langston Hughes. Used by permission of Alfred A. Knopf, a division of Random House, Inc.

Image Credits

n/a mariakraynova / iStock; 1 Photo courtesy of Ellen Moses; 8 PRO-IMMIGRATION CARTOON 'Welcome to All!' An 1880 American cartoon by Joseph Keppler in favor of unrestricted immigration. / Granger / Bridgeman Images; 9 World's Highest Standard of Living...', 1937 (litho), Bourke-White, Margaret (1904-71) / Private Collection / Peter Newark American Pictures / Bridgeman Images; 10 Stepping into the American Dream (acrylic on canvas), Cortada, Xavier / Private Collection / Bridgeman Images; 15 Pictorial Press Ltd / Alamy Stock Photo; 24 Library of Congress/Prints and Photographs Division; 34 © Teresa M. Bejan; 35 Steven Senne/ASSOCIATED PRESS; 48 The Signing of the Constitution of the United States in 1787, 1940 (oil on canvas), Christy, Howard Chandler (1873-1952) / Hall of Representatives, Washington D.C., USA / Bridgeman Images; 53 Everett Collection, Inc / Alamy Stock Photo; 55 Granger Historical Picture Archive / Alamy Stock Photo; 56 Andrew_Howe/iStock; 65 By [Daderot] [Public domain], via Wikimedia Commons; 66 Colonial farmer, 2002 (w/c on paper), Frey, Matthew (b.1974) / Private Collection / Wood Ronsaville Harlin, Inc. USA / Bridgeman Images; 73 Stocktrek Images, Inc./ Alamy Stock Photo; Pilotenschlaeger by Franz Koeck, 1933-1945 (b/w photo) / © SZ Photo / Bridgeman Images; 76 Everett Collection; 77 Harlem Jig, 2001 (oil on board), Bootman, Colin / Private Collection / Bridgeman Images; 77 Ramon Espinosa/ AP Photo; 78 Ka_Li/Shutterstock; 84 © Kesaya E. Noda; 96 Joe Rosenthal/Library of Congress; 108 World History Archive / Alamy Stock Photo; 113 Ann Johansson/Corbis Entertainment/ Getty Images; 124 Builders #1, 1972 (w/c, gouache & graphite), Lawrence, Jacob (1917-2000) / Saint Louis Art Museum, Missouri, USA / Eliza McMillan Trust / Bridgeman Images; 128 Joseph Bruchac (b/w photo) / © Chris Felver / Bridgeman Images; 129 Postcard of the Immigration receiving station, Ellis Island, New York City, 1940 (colour litho), American School, (20th century) / Private Collection / Peter Newark American Pictures / Bridgeman Images; 131 Photograph by LaVerne Harrell Clark 02/17/1971, courtesy of The University of Arizona Poetry Center. Photograph copyright © 2011 Arizona Board of Regents.; 133 © 2017 Shevaun Williams; 133 Fiona Osbaldstone © 2018 College Board; 146 David Attie/Getty Images; 148 Image by Kevin Berne; 152 © Bryce Richter; 154 Raoul Benavides/Getty Images; 155 The Granger Collection; 157 Ted Streshinsky/Corbis/Getty Images; 161 Official portrait of President-elect Barack Obama/Pete Souza/ Library of Congress/Prints and Photographs Division; 164 Jim Rogash/WireImage/Getty Images; 177 Sarin Images/The Granger Collection; 184 North Wind Picture Archives / Alamy Stock Photo; 187 GRANGER / GRANGER — All rights reserved.; 188 By Peter Pelham [Public domain], via Wikimedia Commons; 190 Witches of Salem - a girl bewitched at a trial in 1692 (colour litho), American School / Private Collection / Peter Newark American Pictures / Bridgeman Images; 193 Charles Walker Collection / Alamy Stock Photo; 195 Courtesy of the "SalemWitch

Trials Documentary Archive" <salem.lib.virginia.edu>; 201 Courtesy of the "SalemWitch Trials Documentary Archive" <salem.lib.virginia.edu>; 203 Everett Collection Inc / Alamy Stock Photo; 207 Salem Witch Trials (litho), English School, (20th century) / Private Collection / © Look and Learn / Bridgeman Images; 208 Alfred Eisenstaedt/The LIFE Picture Collection/ Getty Images; 216 Geraint Lewis / Alamy Stock Photo; 222 Xinhua / Alamy Stock Photo; 231 Geraint Lewis / Alamy Stock Photo; 240 Margaret Chase Smith/Library of Congress/Prints and Photographs Division; 246 Everett Collection Inc / Alamy Stock Photo; "I have here in my hand--" / Herblock/Library of Congress/ Prints and Photographs Division; 268 ClassicStock / Alamy Stock Photo; 269 Abraham Lincoln delivering his second inaugural address as President of the United States, Washington, D.C./Library of Congress/ Prints and Photographs Division; 276 North Wind Picture Archives / Alamy Stock Photo; 278 By http://www.patrickhenrylibrary.org/islandora/object/ islandora%3A308] [Public domain], via Wikimedia Commons; 284 Universal History Archive / UIG / Bridgeman Images; 290 Everett Collection Inc / Alamy Stock Photo; 295 Associated Press; 315 Solstock / iStock; 323 Jessica Hill/AP Photo; 346 Jamie McCarthy/Getty Images; 351 © Andrew Potter; 368 Johannes Berg/Bloomberg/Getty Images; 377 TerryJ/iStockphoto; 382 © The Star Tribune; 395 Sam Edwards/Caiaimage/OJO+/Getty Images; 397 Monkeybusinessimages/iStockphoto; 407 Kristina Blokhin / Alamy Stock Photo; 426 Courtesy of David Bouchier; 427 XonkArts/DigitalVision Vectors/Getty Images; 432 © Jen Sorensen; 433 © Jen Sorensen; 439 WENN Rights Ltd / Alamy Stock Photo; 441 Tetiana Yurchenko/Shutterstock; 446 Hulton Archive/Getty Images; 461 CSA Images/Getty Images; 469 © Mario Burger; 478 Bettmann/Getty Images; 479 B Christopher / Alamy Stock Photo; 488 Portrait of Portrait of Alain LeRoy Locke as a young man(photo) / Private Collection / Prismatic Pictures / Bridgeman Images; 493 Ginger jar and cover, Kangxi Period, 1661-1722 (porcelain), Chinese School, Qing Dynasty (1644-1912) / Private Collection / Photo © Christie's Images / Bridgeman Images; 495 James Weldon Johnson, half-length portrait at desk with telephone/Library of Congress/ Prints and Photographs Division; 495 Manuscripts and Archives Division, The New York Public Library. "Art - Sculpture - Harp (Augusta Savage) - Harp" The New York Public Library Digital Collections. 1935 - 1945. http://digitalcollections.nypl.org/items/5e66b3e9- 03a1-d471-e040-e00a180654d7; 500 Portrait of Countee Cullen (1903–46) (photo) / Private Collection / Prismatic Pictures / Bridgeman Images; 517 Everett Collection Historical / Alamy Stock Photo; 519 Zora Neale Hurston and an unidentified man probably at a recording site, Belle Glade, Florida/Library of Congress/ Prints and Photographs Division; 521 African American children outdoors, Eatonville, Florida; Zora Neale Hurston and three boys in Eatonville, Florida; Children playing singing game and dancing outdoors, Eatonville, Florida/Library of Congress/ Prints and Photographs Division; 526 Woman hanging laundry on the line, Eatonville, Fla., taken during the Lomax, Hurston, Barnicle 1935 expedition to Georgia, Florida and the Bahamas/Library of Congress/ Prints and Photographs Division; 535 Chinaberry tree in yard of Joseph LaBlanc, Crowley, Louisiana. These trees grow quickly and produce ample shade in two years/Library of Congress/ Prints and Photographs Division; 553 Mother and son in Harlem / Mario De Biasi per Mondadori Portfolio / Bridgeman Images